D1309094

UNDERSTANDING AMERICAN GOVERNMENT

FIFTH EDITION

UNDERSTANDING AMERICAN GOVERNMENT

SUSAN WELCH

THE PENNSYLVANIA STATE UNIVERSITY

JOHN GRUHL

UNIVERSITY OF NEBRASKA–LINCOLN

JOHN COMER

UNIVERSITY OF NEBRASKA–LINCOLN

SUSAN M. RIGDON

UNIVERSITY OF ILLINOIS AT URBANA–CHAMPAIGN

JAN VERMEER

NEBRASKA WESLEYAN UNIVERSITY

WEST/WADSWORTH

I(T)P® AN INTERNATIONAL THOMPSON PUBLISHING COMPANY

Belmont, CA · Albany, NY · Bonn · Boston · Cincinnati · Detroit
Johannesburg · London · Los Angeles · Madrid · Melbourne
Mexico City · Minneapolis/St. Paul · New York · Paris
San Francisco · Singapore · Tokyo · Toronto · Washington

Political Science Editor:
Clark Baxter

Senior Development Editor:
Sharon Adams-Poore

Editorial Assistant:
Melissa Gleason

Marketing Manager:
Jay Hu

Print Buyer:
Barbara Britton

Permissions Editor:
Susan Walters

Production:
Hal Lockwood, Penmarin Books

Cover Designer:
Rosa + Wesley

Interior Design:
Seventeenth Street Studios

Artwork:
Randy Miyake and Seventeenth Street Studios

Copy Editor:
Pat Lewis

Cover Image:
Michael Waine/The Stock Market

Compositor:
Carlisle Communications

Printer:
Von Hoffman Press

Printed in the United States of America
1 2 3 4 5 6 7 8 9 10

For more information, contact Wadsworth Publishing Company, 10 Davis Drive, Belmont, CA 94002, or electronically at http://www.wadsworth.com

International Thomson Publishing Europe
Berkshire House
168-173 High Holborn
London, WC1V 7AA, United Kingdom

Nelson ITP Australia
102 Dodds Street
South Melbourne
Victoria 3205 Australia

Nelson Canada
1120 Birchmount Road
Scarborough, Ontario
Canada M1K 5G4

International Thomson Publishing South Africa
Building 18, Constantia Park
138 Sixteenth Road, P.O. Box 2459
Halfway House, 1685 South Africa

International Thomson Editores
Seneca, 53
Col. Polanco
11560 México D.F. México

International Thomson Publishing Asia
60 Albert Street
#15-01 Albert Complex
Singapore 189969

International Thomson Publishing Japan
Hirakawa-cho Kyowa Building, 3F
2-2-1 Hirakawa-cho Chiyoda-ku
Tokyo 102 Japan

ISBN 0-534-55359-1

BRIEF CONTENTS

Part One / The American System

Part Two / Links between People and Government

Part Three / Institutions

Part Four / Civil Liberties and Rights

CONTENTS

PREFACE

Popular esteem for American political institutions appears to be at a new low. The public alternates between curiosity about, and revulsion toward, politics and politicians. Yet beneath the scandals, and the attempts of elected officials to gain political advantage or minimize political disadvantage from these scandals, the role of government in our lives remains crucial. The fifth edition of our text, *Understanding American Government*, tries, as did the previous editions, to demonstrate to students why government is important, and to interest students in learning about the exciting, important, and controversial issues in American public life. We believe an introductory course succeeds if most students develop an understanding of major ideas, an interest in learning more about American government, and an ability to begin to understand and evaluate the news they hear about American political issues. Although a firm grounding in the essential "nuts and bolts" of American government is crucial, other approaches are helpful in motivating students' interest in government.

We offer the essential "nuts and bolts" of American government, but we also want the student to understand why (and sometimes how) these important features have evolved, their impact on government and individuals, and why they are controversial (if they are) and worth learning. For example, we prefer students to leave the course remembering why campaign finance laws were created and why they have the impact they do than to memorize specific dollar limitations on giving for different types of candidates from different types of organizations. The latter will change or will soon be forgotten, but understanding the "whys" will help the student understand the campaign finance issue long after the course is over.

We have also tried to interest students by describing and discussing the impact of various features of government. For example, students who do not understand why learning about voter registration laws is important may "see the light" when they understand the link between such laws and low voter turnout. Therefore, a particular emphasis throughout the book is on the *impact* of government: how individual features of government affect its responsiveness to different groups (in Lasswell's terms, "Who gets what and why?"). We realize that nothing in American politics is simple; rarely does one feature of government produce, by itself, a clear outcome. Nevertheless, we think that students will be more willing to learn about government if they see some relationships between how government operates and the impact it has on them as citizens of America.

CHANGES IN THE FIFTH EDITION

We have revised substantially this edition. We have added two new features to reflect the current political climate. The first, Into the 21st Century, describes changes we are seeing in American politics as we end this century and speculates on developments as we enter the next. Most of these changes are linked to technology, which is reshaping many political practices and institutions and posing new public policy issues. These features include such diverse topics as teledemocracy (Chapter 4), the increasing use of technology in lobbying (Chapter 5), the permanent political campaign (Chapter 7), privacy in the information age (Chapter 14), and regulating cyberporn (Chapter 14).

A second feature attempts to confront students' overwhelming cynicism about government by providing examples of What Government Does Right. In an age when government bashing is the accepted norm, and in a book in which we are critical of many practices of government institutions and politicians, we thought it useful to give students some examples of successful governmental activities. After all, our government is entering its third century, and it would not be doing so unless at least some of its activities were successful. Examples include effective disaster relief (Chapter 3), the impact of the Voting Rights Act on the expansion of suffrage (Chapter 7), and the work ethic of justices (Chapter 13).

Writing the fifth edition gave us an opportunity to rethink several parts of the book as well as to update throughout. Chapter 1 has been thoroughly reorganized and revised, with a new focus on the American people and American culture. In Chapter 5, we have reorganized some of the material on interest group typologies, and in Chapter 6, Political Parties, we have a new discussion of party weaknesses and strengths and the contemporary party system. In Chapter 8, our treatment of the media explores why the media focus on scandal, and the changes brought about by the emergence of around-the-clock news channels. Both Chapters 7 and 11, on campaign finance and the presidency, cover the political impact of the emergence of the Lewinsky scandal from the Whitewater and Jones investigations. Although the book was written before the outcome of the impeachment efforts is known, students will have an understanding of the events leading up to these efforts. More generally, the chapter on the presidency has been substantially revised and reorganized, and includes a new section on the political role of First Ladies.

As always, we have updated the judiciary, civil liberties, and civil rights chapters to incorporate new Supreme Court decisions. Chapter 15, Civil Rights, includes a new treatment of the women's movement, a new section on sexual harassment and another on discrimination against men, a new discussion on the contemporary status of African Americans, and a revised treatment of affirmative action.

We are delighted to have the opportunity to write a fifth edition and to improve the text further in ways suggested by our students and readers. We have been extremely pleased by the reaction of instructors and students to our first four editions.

SPECIAL FEATURES

Student interest and analytic abilities grow when confronted with a clash of views about important issues. Today there is much discussion about how to stimulate the critical thinking abilities of students. Beginning with the first edition, our text has provided features especially designed to do this by involving students in the controversies—and excitement—of American politics.

YOU ARE THERE. Each chapter opens with a scenario called You Are There. In a page or two the student reads about a real-life political dilemma faced by a public official or a private citizen involved in a controversial issue. Students are asked to put themselves in that individual's shoes, to weigh the pros and cons, and to decide what should be done. The instructor may want to poll the entire class and use the You Are There as a basis for class discussion. In the Epilogue at the end of the chapter, we reveal the actual decision and discuss it in light of the ideas presented in the chapter.

More than one-third of the You Are There features in this edition are new. They focus on such timely topics as the question of whether the president can be sued while in office, the power of the tobacco lobby in fighting government action against them, the awkward dilemma facing Vice President Gore as the scandals surrounding President Clinton unfold, and the domestic political issues facing President Clinton as he planned his 1998 trip to China.

AMERICAN DIVERSITY. In many chapters, American Diversity boxes illustrate the impact of the social diversity of the American population on political life. The boxes help students understand how a diversity of backgrounds and attitudes shapes views of politics and positions on issues.

INTO THE 21ST CENTURY. Found in many chapters, these boxes focus on a key issue or political development related to a political institution or process. They are designed to help students hone their analytic abilities by showing them how developments outside of politics, often in the realm of technology, have important political implications.

WHAT GOVERNMENT DOES RIGHT. These boxes illustrate some of the successes of government. We believe this is a timely feature, given the antigovernment sentiment currently so pervasive. Far from being the ennobling activity as envisioned by the ancients, government now appears to be seen largely as corrupt and ineffective. Given this image, students might wonder why we have government at all. This feature gives students an opportunity to read about some concrete examples of government successes and think about the reasons for the existence of government.

SYMBOLIC SOLUTIONS FOR COMPLEX PROBLEMS? This feature helps students evaluate whether commonly discussed solutions to complex public problems might work, or whether some might be only symbolic or actually might make the problem worse.

BOXES. In each chapter, several boxes highlighting interesting aspects of American politics draw the students into the material. Many illustrate how government and politics really work in a particular situation—how a corporation lobbies for government benefits, how a seemingly powerless group is able to organize for political action, how interest groups solicit money by mail, and how political polls are done—while others highlight features of government that may be of particular interest to students—what standard of risk should government use in regulating acne medication, how ethnicity shapes voting behavior, and the impact of federal programs on students.

Several other features help students organize their study.

OUTLINE. Each chapter begins with an outline of its contents.

KEY TERMS. Key terms are boldfaced within the text and listed at the end of each chapter and the glossary.

FURTHER READING. A brief, annotated list of further readings contains works that might be useful to a student doing research or looking for further reading.

ELECTRONIC RESOURCES. Each chapter lists addresses of particularly interesting or useful sites on the Internet that relate directly to the topics covered in the chapter.

GLOSSARY. A glossary at the end of the book defines terms that may be unfamiliar to students.

THE ORGANIZATION AND CONTENTS OF THE BOOK

While the basic organization of American government books is fairly standard, our text has a unique chapter on money and politics and a half chapter on environmental politics. Other features include a civil rights chapter that integrates a thorough treatment of constitutional issues concerning minorities and women, a discussion of the civil rights and women's rights movements, and contemporary research on the political status of these groups. We include in this chapter the special legal problems of Hispanics and Native Americans.

The organization of the book is straightforward. After material on democracy, the Constitution, and federalism, the book covers linkages, including money and politics, then institutions, and finally policy. Civil liberties and rights are treated after the chapter on the judiciary. But the book is flexible enough that instructors can modify the order of the chapters. Some instructors will prefer to cover institutions before process. Others may prefer to discuss civil liberties and rights when discussing the Constitution.

SUPPLEMENTARY MATERIALS

The supplementary materials complement the book.

INFOTRAC COLLEGE EDITION. An online university library that lets students explore and use full-length articles from more than 700 periodicals for four months. When students log on with their personal ID, they will see immediately how easy it is to search. Students can print out the articles, which date back as far as three years. Includes readings from *U.S. News and World Report*, *National Review*, and *Washington Monthly* magazines.

INSTRUCTOR'S MANUAL. Prepared by Pamela Imperato, University of North Dakota. Each chapter contains chapter outlines, suggested assignments, recommended Internet sites, and, particularly valuable, an extensive section correlating each chapter's content to the other components (see below) of the complete ancillary package. This Other Resources section makes full use of the multimedia products available with this text by suggesting relevant InfoTrac articles, transparencies, Power Point slides, clips from the Political Science Video Library, especially *CNN American Government Today*, and portions of the CD-ROM *America at Odds*.

TESTBANK. Also prepared by Pamela Imperato, University of North Dakota. Contains multiple-choice questions, fill-in-the-blanks, and long and short essay questions.

WORLD CLASS TOOLS TESTING. This is a fully integrated collection of test creation, delivery, and classroom management tools, including all the test questions from the printed test bank. The package comprises World Class Test, Test Online, and World Class Manager software.

TRANSPARENCY ACETATES PACKAGE. Includes seventy-five four-color acetates featuring diagrams, charts, tables, and figures from the text and from other sources.

POWERPOINT PACKAGE. Includes all the images from the acetate package.

CD-ROM *AMERICA AT ODDS*. This interactive CD-ROM was developed for the Introductory American Government course to engage students and enable them to research issues, discuss ideas, formulate opinions, and interpret data in an interactive format. The *America at Odds* CD-ROM will engage students in the study of American government through twenty interactive modules covering enduring and multidimensional issues in American politics. These issues are presented in a rich mix of media, including digital video and audio, photos, graphics, text, and Internet technology.

POLITICAL SCIENCE VIDEO LIBRARY. Includes CNN videos and Grade Improvement: Taking Charge of Your Learning.

STUDY GUIDE. Each chapter contains a prose summary, an outline, key terms, concepts, events, and people, multiple-choice questions, essay topics, and critical thinking exercises. There is one version of the study guide that will accompany both versions of the text.

COMPUTERIZED STUDY GUIDE. An interactive study guide that lets students know why they answered incorrectly and guides them to the correct answer.

THINKING GLOBALLY, ACTING LOCALLY. This is a new supplement designed to help students get involved and become active citizens, authored by John Soares. Topics include tips to writing letters to the editor, volunteering, how to change laws, and registering to vote.

AMERICAN GOVERNMENT INTERNET ACTIVITIES. Prepared by Karen Casto, it contains activities for all major topics in the text. Students are asked to surf the 'net to obtain answers to interesting questions.

THE HANDBOOK OF SELECTED CASES. Includes over thirty Supreme Court cases.

THE HANDBOOK OF SELECTED LEGISLATION. Includes twelve excerpts of legislation passed by the U.S. Congress that has a great impact on American politics.

READINGS IN AMERICAN GOVERNMENT. Includes interesting, timely, and thought-provoking articles that relate to material covered in the text. Articles cover dynamic topics ranging from "Passion at Yale" (coed dorms) to "President Clinton's Way with Women."

AN INTRODUCTION TO CRITICAL THINKING AND WRITING IN AMERICAN POLITICS. Introduces students to a number of critical thinking rules and guidelines to writing a successful research paper.

THE COLLEGE SURVIVAL GUIDE. Hints and references to aid college students by Bruce M. Rowe.

YOUR RESEARCH: DATA ANALYSIS FOR AMERICAN GOVERNMENT. Prepared by Eric Plutzer, Pennsylvania State University, this consists of graphics-oriented statistics software, a workbook, and data sets (IBM platform).

WESTLAW. Free WestLaw hours to qualified adopters.

THE WADSWORTH POLITICAL SCIENCE RESOURCE CENTER. HTTP://POLITICALSCIENCE.WADSWORTH.COM This site includes information on all of Wadsworth/West's political science texts in American Government, Comparative Politics, International Politics, Constitutional Law, and Texas politics. The Resource Center contains information on surfing the Web, links to general political sites, a career center, election updates, and a discussion forum. Each major text has a companion Web site that includes self-quizzes, chapter links to various related Web sites, discussion topics, and more. The America at Odds section of the site corresponds with the interactive CD-ROM of the same name, which is intended for the introductory American Government course. Visit the Welch home page for quizzes and more.

ACKNOWLEDGMENTS

We would like to thank the many people who have aided and sustained us during the lengthy course of this project. We first acknowledge the work of Margery Ambrosius, the coauthor of Chapter 12, for her intellectual contribution to this book. Our current and former University of Nebraska and Penn State colleagues have been most tolerant and helpful. We thank them all. In particular, we appreciate the assistance of John Hibbing, Philip Dyer, Robert Miewald, Beth Theiss-Morse, Louis Picard, John Peters, David Rapkin, Peter Maslowski, David Forsythe, W. Randy Newell, and Steven Daniels who provided us with data, bibliographic information, and other insights that we have used here. We are especially grateful to Philip Dyer, Alan Booth, Louis Picard, Robert Miewald, and John Hibbing who read one or more chapters and saved us from a variety of errors.

We are also grateful to the many other readers of our draft manuscript, as listed on page xix. Without their assistance the book would have been less accurate, less complete, and less lively.

We are also grateful to those instructors who have used the book and relayed their comments and suggestions to us. Our students at the University of Nebraska have also provided invaluable reactions to the previous editions.

Others too have been of great assistance to us. Jeff Walz, Staci Beavers, and Michael Moore provided essential service and help in producing the ancillary materials for the book.

Several people at Wadsworth Publishing also deserve our thanks. Clark Baxter has been a continual source of encouragement and optimism from the beginning of the first edition through the last decision on the fifth. We are greatly in debt to Randall Goodall, who designed this edition of the book, and to Hal Humphrey and Hal Lockwood, who produced it.

REVIEWERS

REVIEWERS OF THE NEW EDITION

Peter G. Howse
American River College
David W. Hunt
Triton College
Pamela Imperato
University of North Dakota
Donald C. Williams
Western New England College

REVIEWERS OF PREVIOUS EDITIONS

Alan Abramowitz
State University of New York at Stony Brook
Larry Adams
Baruch College—City University of New York
Danny M. Adkison
Oklahoma State University
James Alt
Harvard University
Margery Marzahn Ambrosius
Kansas State University
Kevin Bailey
North Harris Community College
Kennette M. Benedict
Northwestern University
Timothy Bledsoe
Wayne State University
Jon Bond
Texas A&M University
Paul R. Brace
New York University
Joseph V. Brogan
La Salle University
James R. Brown, Jr.
Central Washington University
Chalmers Brumbaugh
Elon College
Richard G. Buckner, Jr.
Santa Fe Community College
Ronald Busch
Cleveland State University
Carl D. Cavalli
Memphis State University
Richard A. Champagne
University of Wisconsin, Madison
Michael Connelly
Southwestern Oklahoma State University
Gary Copeland
University of Oklahoma
George H. Cox, Jr.
Georgia Southern College
Paige Cubbison
Miami-Dade University
Landon Curry
Southwest Texas State University
Jack DeSario
Case Western Reserve University
Robert E. DiClerico
West Virginia University
Ernest A. Dover, Jr.
Midwestern State University
Georgia Duerst-Lahti
Beloit College
Ann H. Elder
Illinois State University
Ghassan E. El-Eid
Butler University
C. Lawrence Evans
College of William and Mary
Murray Fischel
Kent State University
Bobbe Fitzhugh
Eastern Wyoming College
Marianne Fraser
University of Utah
Jarvis Gamble
Owens Community College
David Garrison
Collin County Community College
Phillip L. Gianos
California State University—Fullerton
Doris A. Graber
University of Illinois—Chicago
Ruth M. Grubel
University of Wisconsin—Whitewater
Stefan D. Haag
Austin Community College
Larry M. Hall
Belmont University
Edward Harpham
University of Texas—Dallas
Peter O. Haslund
Santa Barbara City College
Richard P. Heil
Fort Hays State University

Peggy Heilig
University of Illinois at Urbana
Craig Hendricks
Long Beach City College
Marjorie Hershey
Indiana University
Samuel B. Hoff
Delaware State College
Robert D. Holsworth
Virginia Commonwealth University
Jesse C. Horton
San Antonio College
Gerald Houseman
Indiana University
Jerald Johnson
University of Vermont
Loch Johnson
University of Georgia
Evan M. Jones
St. Cloud State University
Henry C. Kenski
University of Arizona
Matt Kerbel
Villanova University
Marshall R. King
Maryville College
Orma Lindford
Kansas State University
Peter J. Longo
University of Nebraska—Kearney
Roger C. Lowery
University of North Carolina—Wilmington
H. R. Mahood
Memphis State University
Jarol B. Manheim
The George Washington University
A. Nick Minton
University of Massachusetts—Lowell
Matthew Moen
University of Maine
Michael Nelson
Vanderbilt University
Bruce Nesmith
Coe College
Walter Noelke
Angelo State University
Thomas Payette
Henry Ford Community College
Theodore B. Pedeliski
University of North Dakota
Jerry Perkins
Texas Tech University
Toni Phillips
University of Arkansas
C. Herman Pritchett
University of California—Santa Barbara
Charles Prysby
University of North Carolina—Greensboro
Sandra L. Quinn-Musgrove
Our Lady of the Lake University
Donald R. Ranish
Antelope Valley Community College
Linda Richter
Kansas State University
Jerry Sandvick
North Hennepin Community College
James Richard Sauder
University of New Mexico
Eleanor A. Schwab
South Dakota State University
Earl Sheridan
University of North Carolina—Wilmington
Edward Sidlow
Northwestern University
Cynthia Slaughter
Angelo State University
John Squibb
Lincolnland Community College
M. H. Tajalli-Tehrani
Southwest Texas State University
Kristine A. Thompson
Moorehead State University
R. Mark Tiller
Austin Community College
Gordon J. Tolle
South Dakota State University
Susan Tolleson-Rinehart
Texas Tech University
Bernadyne Weatherford
Rowan College of New Jersey
Richard Unruh
Fresno Pacific College
Jay Van Bruggen
Clarion University of Pennsylvania
Kenny Whitby
University of South Carolina
Clifford J. Wirth
University of New Hampshire
Ann Wynia
North Hennepin Community College
Mary D. Young
Southwestern Michigan College

ABOUT THE AUTHORS

SUSAN WELCH received her A.B. and Ph.D. degrees from the University of Illinois at Urbana-Champaign. She is currently Dean of the College of the Liberal Arts and Professor of Political Science at The Pennsylvania State University. Her teaching and research areas include legislatures, state and urban politics, and women and minorities in politics. She has edited the *American Politics Quarterly*.

JOHN GRUHL, a Professor of Political Science, received his A.B. from DePauw University in Greencastle, Indiana, and his Ph.D. from the University of California at Santa Barbara. Since joining the University of Nebraska faculty in 1976, he has taught and done research in the areas of judicial process, criminal justice, and civil rights and liberties. He won University of Nebraska campus-wide distinguished teaching awards in 1979 and 1986 for excellence in undergraduate teaching, and became a charter member of the University's Academy of Distinguished Teachers in 1995.

JOHN COMER is a Professor of Political Science at the University of Nebraska. He received his A.B. in political science from Miami University of Ohio in 1965 and his Ph.D. from the Ohio State University in 1971. His teaching and research focus on interest groups, public opinion, voting behavior, and political parties.

SUSAN RIGDON received A.B. and Ph.D. degrees in political science from the University of Illinois in 1966 and 1971. She has taught American Government at several institutions in the U.S. and China, and has other teaching and research interests in foreign policy, comparative government, and political development. She is a Research Associate in Anthropology at the University of Illinois at Urbana-Champaign.

JAN VERMEER is Professor of Political Science at Nebraska Wesleyan University. He received his B.A. from the University of California at Santa Barbara and his A.M. and Ph.D. from Princeton University. He has won two campus-wide teaching awards, most recently in 1996. His research has centered on media and politics and on congressional elections.

UNDERSTANDING AMERICAN GOVERNMENT

Italian immigrants arrive at Ellis Island, New York, in 1910 (right). Elementary students in Brentwood, California, where the multicultural present looks like America's future (below).

Joseph Kossuth Dixon, courtesy Library of Congress

Schapiro, Liaison International

PART ONE THE AMERICAN SYSTEM

America is more a melting pot than ever, with increasing population diversity and increasing rates of intermarriage among different racial and ethnic groups. This computer-generated matrix from Time *magazine reflects the changing face of America. Move across from the left and down from the top to see resulting progeny.*

Photographs: Ted Thai/*Time* magazine, computer morphing: Kin Wah Lam, design: Walter Bernard and Milton Glaser.

1 AMERICAN DEMOCRACY

OUTLINE

- **The American People**
  - Cultural Diversity
  - Immigration and Political Cleavage
  - Economic and Geographic Diversity
- **Diversity and Politics**
- **Political Culture**
- **American Democracy: The Core Values**
  - Individual Liberty
  - Political Equality
  - Majority Rule
  - Minority Rights
  - Economic Rights
- **American Democracy in Practice**
  - Classical Democracy
  - Pluralism
  - Pluralism Reconsidered
- **Conclusion: Is Government Responsive?**

YOU ARE THERE

Is Politics Futile?

In this section of following chapters, you will be asked to step into the shoes of decision-makers and analyze how and why they made certain key decisions. But here you are asked to be, well—*you.*

You are sitting there reading your American government text but wondering how much you are really interested in government or politics. You know that every two years there is a national election, every other one to elect a president, and that, on or between these dates, there are a host of state and local elections for governors, mayors, city councils, and school, library, and county board members. Perhaps in the next election you will be a first-time voter, or maybe you already have several campaigns under your belt. Yet each time an election approaches, you ask yourself whether it is worth the effort. Maybe you are one of those people who shares Groucho Marx's observation that "politics is the art of finding trouble everywhere, diagnosing it incorrectly, and applying the wrong remedy."

If you are going to vote, you will have to make decisions on dozens of candidates. Do you have the time to get to know something about each of them and to read up on the issues? Maybe you should vote only for those candidates whose positions you know and only in those elections you think will have a significant impact on your life. And what about the campaigns leading up to election day? Should you become active in a political party, write letters in support of an issue, make campaign contributions, attend rallies, or campaign for candidates? And what about all the other efforts to influence policy outcomes that do not involve electoral politics? Should you join one or more of the many interest groups that lobby unelected officials such as bureaucrats, political appointees, and federal judges?

You are a busy person, so why bother to get involved in politics? Surely, if you vote, you will have done your civic duty. You look at the news and see dog-eat-dog, negative campaigning, character attacks, investigations into the most intimate aspects of the lives of public figures, gridlock caused by party conflict in Congress and state legislatures, and huge campaign donations buying access to candidates or officials. You know that interest groups and legislators spend years debating issues, such as government's role in health care, yet all they appear to achieve is a standoff. Who needs it? After all, government works: your mail comes, your grandparents' Social Security checks arrive on time, your state issued you a driver's license, the roads are paved, the bridges and dams hold up, the schools are open, and we have a large military establishment, local law enforcement, a great-looking capital city, and a massive infrastructure. America has social stability and a well-functioning economy. Government is doing the basics. Why should you get involved in politics?

One obvious argument that you are well aware of is that if you do not, others will, and they may not agree with your idea of what government should be doing to solve the country's problems and prepare for the future. This is a huge country—it is economically, ethnically, and religiously diverse, and becoming more so every year. There will always be divergent views and therefore competing interests trying to shape government policy. You know that if you opt out, and candidates are elected and policies made that you disagree with, quite frankly, you will not have much basis for complaint. Furthermore, you know that participation is integral to the concept on which our form of government is founded. Americans have fought for generations to expand rights to the point where virtually every citizen eighteen or older has full rights of participation. What did they do it for?

What will you do? Are you going to vote in some, all, or none of the upcoming local, state, and federal elections? Do you believe the major parties and candidates differ sufficiently on the issues or philosophically to make your vote worth casting? If your candidates are elected, do you think they will be able to move government in the direction you want it to go? Do you care enough about some issues that you might be willing to invest time and effort, beyond voting, to influence policy? Do you think that if you do get involved, you as an ordinary citizen will have any chance of reaching policymakers with your views? What would it take to get you involved in government and the political process?

There may be conflict in our political life, but Americans are members of one community. We are parties to a single legal contract, the Constitution, and are all equally subject to the protections and obligations of a common set of laws. We also share an economic system, and although the Constitution has little to say about its nature, our government is deeply implicated in its successes and failures. In fact, government's role in managing the economy is sufficient to link the level of confidence we have in government to how well the economy is doing, or at minimum to how well we are doing. Our economic well-being also affects how much we participate and how much access we have to policymakers.

If government is the instrument for forging one interest out of many in order to legislate and to speak for the country as a whole in matters of national interest, then **politics** is a means through which individual and group interests compete to shape government's impact on society's problems and goals. Interests compete through political parties and many other extragovernmental organizations. The institutions of government were also created to represent competing interests as well as to mediate among them. So politics is also the art of governing.

Inconsistencies dominate American political life. Americans cherish the symbols of democracy, but deplore its realities.[1] We visit Washington to marvel at the Washington Monument, the Jefferson and Lincoln Memorials, the Capitol, and the White House. We show these symbols of our democracy to our children, hoping they will revere them. We cherish the Declaration of Independence and the Constitution.

But at the same time that we prize these symbols of democracy, we condemn the reality of democracy. We refer to debates over issues as quarrels or "bickering"; we call compromises "selling out"; we label conflict as mere self-interest; we tag interest groups and political parties as "special interests." We have little tolerance for the slow pace at which government deals with the nation's problems. In other words, we love the concept of democracy, but hate the rough and tumble, the give and take, and the conflict of democracy in action.[2]

How do people, politics, government, and the economy come together to form the "American system"? How might these relationships change as we head into the twenty-first century? This chapter provides short answers to these questions by profiling the American people, identifying the political values we share, and describing how they are expressed in our form of government. It also briefly describes how democracy, when practiced by people who are ethnically, economically, and religiously diverse and scattered across a vast and varied landscape, is destined to be characterized as much by competition and conflict as by cooperation and community. All of these topics will be developed in greater detail in later chapters.

THE AMERICAN PEOPLE

When the poet Walt Whitman wrote, "Here is not merely a nation but a teeming Nation of nations," he said a lot about our country and its politics.[3] It is a cliché, yet true, that the United States is a land of immigrants, peopled by individuals from all over the world. Americans are a conglomeration of religions, races, ethnicities, cultural traditions, and socioeconomic groups, or what one historian calls "a collision of histories."[4]

Cultural Diversity

From its beginnings the American population has been characterized by diversity. The original inhabitants settled North America probably after crossing a land bridge from Asia thousands of years ago. Although sometimes characterized by a single term such as Indians or Native Americans, they went on to found many different civilizations, both agricultural and

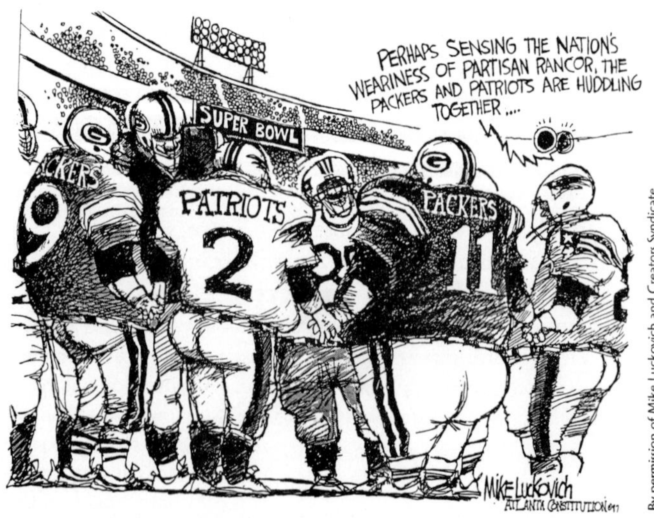

By permission of Mike Luckovich and Creators Syndicate

Immigrants crowd a New York City neighborhood in 1900.

UPI/Corbis-Bettmann

hunting/gathering. Their nations were competitive and at times at war, and their differences substantial enough to doom eighteenth-century efforts to form pan-Indian alliances against European colonization.[5] Today the Census Bureau recognizes 554 different tribes, many fewer than 200 years ago, but still suggestive of the wide array of cultures that predated European settlement.

The umbrella term *European* is itself somewhat deceptive in that European settlers emigrated from countries that not only differed linguistically, religiously, and politically, but also had often been at war with one another. Migrants carried some of these conflicts with them to America. Because the colonies were ruled from England and its language and culture were dominant, we tend to think of early Americans as Anglos and Protestants. But the earliest European settlers of the southeastern and southwestern territories were more likely to be Roman Catholics from France and Spain than Anglo-Protestants. And over time, Germany, a distinctly non-Anglo country and one evenly split between Catholics and Protestants, provided more immigrants to America than England. By preference, or to avoid discrimination by earlier-arriving or more dominant settlers, immigrants often self-segregated into territories (Quakers to Pennsylvania, Catholics to Maryland), which later became states. At the time the Constitution was adopted, six of the thirteen original states had established religions.[6] These different beliefs and traditions contributed to the rise of distinctive local cultures and to the varying character of state governments and politics.

Like European settlers, Africans too came from a huge continent that encompassed many languages and cultures. Even though the European slave trade was concentrated in coastal areas of Africa, the men and women forcibly removed to the Americas did not share a common tradition. Their experience in the American colonies, however, united them in a common condition as noncitizens lacking all political and economic rights.

The ethnic, racial, and religious composition of the American population broadened further in the mid to late nineteenth century as new waves of settlers came from southern and eastern Europe, China, and Japan, as well as Ireland and Germany (Figure 1). They included large numbers of Roman Catholics, Eastern and Russian

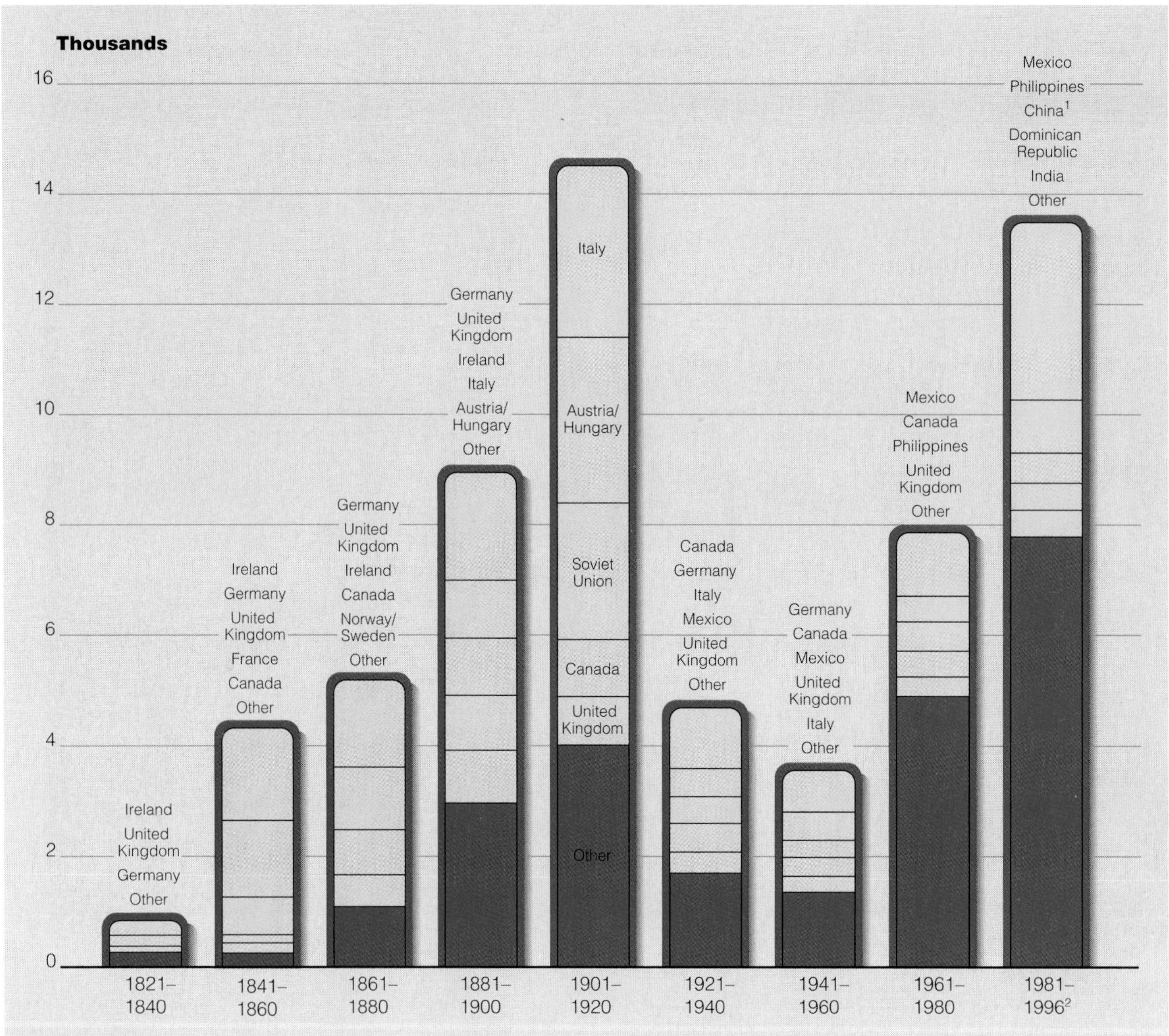

FIGURE 1

Immigrants Admitted to the United States from the Top Five Countries of Last Residence: 1821 to 1996

1. Includes People's Republic of China and Taiwan.
2. Sixteen-year period.

SOURCE: 1996 *Statistical Yearbook of the Immigration and Naturalization Service,* p. 14.

Orthodox, Jews, and some Buddhists. Immigration continued at high levels into the twentieth century before peaking in the decade 1905–1914, when more than 10 million immigrants entered the country.

Not all immigrants who came, stayed. In addition to deportations, almost 30% of arrivals in the early 1900s returned voluntarily to their home countries each year (compared to about 20% of today's arrivals). For a few years during the Great Depression of the 1930s, more people left the United States than entered.[7] Then, following the peak years of the second decade until the end of World War II, there was a deliberate effort to slow the rate of new arrivals. It was not until the decade 1987–1996 that immigration reached its peak level to date (1991).

By 1998, 10% of all residents of the United States were foreign-born, less than the 15% in the peak year 1910, but of greater political and economic impact than the numbers suggest. Almost two-thirds of all immigrants settle in only six states (New York, California, Illinois, New Jersey, Texas, and Florida). In 1992 when California had 330,000 new arrivals, Wyoming had 281.[8] Still the 14% of Chicago's population that was foreign-born in 1996

Sebastiao Slagado/Contact Press Images

Russian emigrants wait at Moscow Airport for their flight to America.

compares to about half in 1910; and the 20% of foreign-born among New York City's residents compares to 40% in 1910, when another 40% had foreign-born parents.[9]

Of the more than 10 million who arrived between 1987 and 1996, the majority came from Asia, Latin America, and eastern Europe. Of those entering in 1996, more were born in Mexico than any other country (18%), while 34% were from Asia.[10] This shift in national origin of immigrants was due in part to significant changes in immigration law in the 1960s (see the box "Immigration: The Law, the Ideal"). If current trends continue, the three-quarters population share held by white non-Hispanics in 1995 will fall to a bare majority by the middle of the next century.

Americans' religious profile is also changing. Although a large majority still identify themselves as Christians (87%), Americans now claim affiliation with 1,600 different religions and denominations and include 5.5 million Jews; 750,000–1,000,000 Buddhists and about the same number of Hindus; and as many Muslims as Presbyterians (3.5 million).[11]

Immigration and Political Cleavage

Much is made of racial and ethnic conflict in American history. But some of the most intense political cleavages have arisen between older and new immigrants. There have always been some native-born Americans who fear economic competition from newcomers or perceive non-English-speaking people or anyone with different traditions and religious practices as a cultural threat. So throughout our history there has been antiforeign, or nativist, sentiment, even by first-generation immigrants,

IMMIGRATION: THE LAW, THE IDEAL

"Give me your tired, your poor, your huddled masses yearning to breathe free. . . ." These words from Emma Lazarus's poem—engraved on the Statue of Liberty—capture the ideal of the United States as a refuge for the world's outcasts: political and religious dissidents and the economically downtrodden. Despite the high-flown rhetoric, U.S. law has not always reflected the ideals in Lazarus's poem. Not all newcomers have been made welcome on arrival, and some were not even invited to apply. Yet the ideal remains that America's doors are open to those fleeing persecution and to industrious people looking for new opportunities. But since these categories potentially encompass hundreds of millions of people, only a small fraction of refugees and opportunity seekers can settle in the United States. Thus, rules must be established to determine who qualifies for an immigration visa, who is entitled to refugee status, and how many people will be allowed to take up residency in the United States each year.

Few people would argue with the proposition that every country has the right to control its borders, but there are many disagreements over the standards used to regulate immigration. For most of its history, the United States has used immigration law to populate the country, stimulate the economy, give refuge to political and religious dissidents, and, until fairly recent times, regulate the ethnic and racial composition of the population. It has not always been able to pursue these goals simultaneously.

Regulation of immigration began in 1798 when Congress gave the president power to deport people he deemed "dangerous to the peace and safety" of the country. An 1807 law, implementing a provision in the new constitution, prohibited the "importation" of Africans for purposes of slavery. Then, for almost 70 years, there was no new federal regulation, but some state governments, especially those in the underpopulated interior, did pass laws encouraging immigration. During this period tens of thousands of laborers were brought into the country to build railroads, canals, and other large infrastructure projects, settle the West, and work in the new factories.

State laws became invalid in 1876 when the Supreme Court ruled that regulating immigration was the provenance of Congress. About this time Congress began passing laws restricting immigration by category of person, putting criminals and prostitutes first on the list. In 1882, the prohibition was extended to the mentally ill and incompetent and all who were unable to support themselves. Laws passed up through the end of World War II added new categories of people prohibited entry: anarchists and revolutionaries, members of Communist parties or affiliated groups, polygamists, alcoholics, vagrants, stowaways, and those with contagious diseases or convicted of "moral depravity."

As immigration law evolved during these decades, it also had the clear purpose of maintaining the ethnic balance of the country: immigration was largely restricted to the countries already represented in the American population. For example, in the Exclusion Act of 1882, Congress suspended immigration of Chinese laborers, many of whom had come in the mid-nineteenth century to mine gold and to help build the railroads. It barred reentry to those who had gone back to China to visit their families and citizenship to those who were here. (It was not until 1943 that Congress allotted entry quotas to Chinese, who at the time were our World War II allies.) Restrictive policies never worked exactly as intended, however, because too few people in the preferred countries of Europe had motive to emigrate. This led to periods of labor shortfalls and an influx of eastern and southern Europeans, as well as large numbers of non-Europeans, such as Japanese (many of whom entered indirectly through Hawaii, then a U.S. territory) and Mexican agricultural laborers.

Ethnic and racial restrictions were not eliminated until the Immigration and Naturalization Act of 1965 replaced them with a preference system that targets family reunification and specific job skills. During the past thirty years, this system has undergone considerable tinkering, including an amnesty that gave permanent residency to 2.6 million illegal residents between 1989 and 1992, but the priority system

---

but the political impact of antiforeign sentiment is typically greatest when immigration levels are high. Hence strong nativist sentiments influenced the politics of the mid-1800s, the 1920s, and the 1990s.

The "Know-Nothings" won popularity in the 1840s by spreading fear of a Catholic takeover. Patriotic fervor during World War I produced hostility toward Americans of German birth or descent. In 1918, Iowa's governor required all groups of two or more people to speak only English, even when using the telephone.[12] From 1924 to 1965, federal law limited immigration from most areas outside western Europe.

In 1991, Republican presidential candidate Patrick Buchanan complained that immigration is about to "submerge" our "predominantly Caucasian Western society" and warned about a "dilution" of our European heritage.[13] A newspaper criticized immigrants who "bring with them their non-Christian Third World cultures, poverty-mindedness and a tendency toward crime."[14]

Although each generation of immigrants has faced resentment from preceding generations, each has contributed to the building of America. Early European immigrants settled the eastern seaboard and pushed remains in place. A 1990 law set a flexible cap of 675,000 on annual admissions. Almost 500,000 of these slots are reserved each year for family-sponsored immigrants (close relatives who are *not* members of the immediate family), and 140,000 are reserved for those with in-demand job skills.

To ensure that people from all parts of the world have a chance to apply, the Immigration and Naturalization Service (INS) divides the world into regions and assigns quotas to countries within each region, which it adjusts annually. There is also a "diversity" quota, which sets aside 55,000 slots per year for people in countries where a low number of visa requests had been granted in the previous five years.

Despite the ceiling placed on annual admissions, the actual number of legal entries fluctuates substantially because, even after the numerical cap is reached, an unlimited number of additional persons can qualify for residency if they fall into one of the off-quota categories: asylees and refugees, for example, and immediate family members of U.S. citizens. Thus, the actual number of legal immigrants who entered in 1996 was 915,900. During much of the Cold War, anyone fleeing a Communist country was pretty much guaranteed refugee or asylee status. In this way several million Cubans, Russians, eastern Europeans, Vietnamese, Cambodians, and Laotians emigrated, and thousands of Chinese were granted permanent residency under an amnesty following the Tiananmen Square massacre.

The *immediate* family members of citizens are another large source of off-quota admissions. This should remain the case in coming years as permanent residents, especially those from Asia, Europe, and Africa, are choosing to become citizens in much higher percentages than previously. When they do, all immediate members of their families living outside the United States automatically qualify for residency visas.

Other off-quota sources of immigration are the foreign students numbering close to half a million who enter the country annually on nonimmigration visas. Many look for work here after graduation and convert to permanent residency status. Some people on tourist or work visas simply overstay their allotted time, and many more enter with no papers at all. No one knows exactly how many people are living illegally in the United States, but guestimates set illegal entries at about 275,000 each year and the total illegal population at roughly 20% of the foreign-born population. If that estimate is correct, close to 2% of all residents of the United States are here illegally. California, a border state, and New York City, a port of entry, have illegal alien populations estimated in the hundreds of thousands.

The INS does deport thousands of illegal aliens each year (including 37,000 with criminal records in 1996), but given the off-quota provisions of the law and the porousness of our borders, the INS has generally not been effective in controlling the actual number of people who take up residency each year.

Overall, immigration law is an example of how laws passed by Congress reflect principle, as well as competition and compromise. To the extent that the post-1965 laws eliminated racial and ethnic barriers to immigration, they allow for a fuller realization of the sentiments in Lazarus's poem. But the current emphasis on family reunification, priority job skills, and diversity also reflects the realignment of interest group power in the political process and illustrates how Congress responds to the demands of business, new voters, and the growing power of race- and ethnic-based interest groups.

SOURCES: *1996 Statistical Yearbook of the Immigration and Naturalization Service;* Immigration and Nationality Act, Title II (available at the INS Web site: http://www.ins.usdoj.gov/); Dick Kirschten, "American Dreamers," *National Journal*, July 5, 1997, pp. 1364–1369; Leon Bouvier and Robert W. Gardner, "Immigration to the U.S.: The Unfinished Story," *Population Bulletin* 41:4 (November 1986), pp. 3–51; "Congress Clears Overhaul of Immigration Law," *Congressional Quarterly* (October 18, 1986), pp. 2595–2598); Eric Schmitt, "4 Lawmakers Hope to End Immigration Service," *New York Times*, February 2, 1998, p. A16.

west to open the frontier. Africans helped build the South's economy with slave labor. Germans helped develop the Midwest into an agricultural heartland, while Irish, Italian, Polish, and Russian newcomers provided labor for America's industrial revolution and turned many cities into huge metropolises.

Chinese immigrants helped build the transcontinental railroad linking East and West, and Japanese and Hispanics helped California become our top food producer. All immigrant groups have gone on from their initial roles to play a fuller part in American life. Yet today the debate continues about whether immigrants are an asset or a problem for our society.

Economic and Geographic Diversity

Diversity involves more than just differences in national and cultural origins. Where people settle once they arrive, what they do for a living, and how much they earn are all potential bases for political difference, and over time are probably much more important than country of origin. Although racial and ethnic cleavages have garnered much of the attention throughout our history, economic diversity is at least as important.

Though we think of America as a land of opportunity, most people who are born poor in the United

CENSUS AND SENSIBILITY

Every ten years the U.S. government takes a census of the American population. This should be a fairly straightforward statistical procedure, but it has often been a contentious political issue. This is largely because the census does much more than establish the size and geographic distribution of the population; its findings have important political and economic consequences. Of special significance are the figures that establish the racial and ethnic breakdown of the population. These data have become essential for implementation of the Voting Rights Act and court rulings stemming from the modern civil rights movement, as well as for "a smorgasbord of set-asides and entitlements and affirmative-action programs."[1]

Unlike in the past, today the collection of information on the racial heritage of Americans has greater significance for inclusion than for exclusion. Racial categories have been used since the first census was taken in 1790, when Americans were identified as white males, white females, other (free blacks, and Indians living off reservations, for example), and slaves (obviously not a racial category, but since only people of African descent were enslaved, "slave" became synonymous with "black"). Some states classified as "black" people with as little as 1/32 African ancestry, consigning them to political and economic exclusion. Over the years, as immigration broadened the population's ethnic and racial base, the census became more sensitive to gradations of racial difference so that by 1890 there were eight categories: white, black, mulatto, quadroon (1/4 black), octoroon (1/8 black), Chinese, Japanese, and Indian.

While Canada has long since stopped categorizing citizens by race in its census, the United States has switched to broader categories. Each person counted in the 1990 census was asked to self-identify with one of four racial groups: black; white; American Indian or Native Alaskan; Asian or Pacific Islander; and, where applicable, also to claim a Hispanic/Latino ethnic heritage. (A large percentage of Hispanic Americans are of mixed race ancestry: European, Native American, African, or Asian.) Complaints about this classificatory scheme have intensified as immigration and interracial marriage have steadily increased the number of

"We've thought and thought, but we're at a loss about what to call ourselves. Any ideas?"

States stay poor. Opportunities knock harder and more often for those who are born into the upper and middle classes. And, although our society is not as class conscious as many others, our personal economic situations play an important part in shaping our views toward politics and our role in it. Most people who are poor, for example, do not vote, but those who do tend to vote Democratic. Most well-off Americans do vote, and they vote in larger numbers for Republicans than Democrats.

Regional and residential differences can also be important, especially since they often intertwine with economic interests. Farmers in California and the Midwest, for example, are more likely to be supportive of farm subsidy legislation than city-dwellers are. City-dwellers may be far more enthusiastic about federal laws creating national parks or wilderness areas than the western ranchers who use the land to graze their livestock. Affluent suburbanites and residents of decaying urban areas may have quite different views of tax increases to improve public schools. The classic and most costly example of regional conflict in our history was the division between South and North over the right of southern states to secede from the Union in order to maintain a regional economic system rooted in slavery. Although in that case economic and political disparities led to bloody conflict, diversity usually leads to no more than political difference. At the same time cultural diversity adds greatly to the richness of our common tradition.

DIVERSITY AND POLITICS

There is nothing new or strange about organizing around difference. Up to a point, it is common sense. How we are situated in the world in terms of power, money, geography, race, ethnicity, and religion, for example, affects our perceptions of the world. As a result, people tend to define society's problems differently and have conflicting multiracial Americans, many of whom object to characterizing their heritage in a single census category. The archetypal representative of this dilemma is golf pro Tiger Woods, who describes himself as a "Cablinasian," a person of white, African, American Indian, and Asian ancestry. Why, Woods asks, should he be asked to identify himself with only one part of his ancestry, and how would he decide which one to choose?[2]

In response to these considerations, the census for the year 2000 will offer five racial categories (Native Hawaiians and Pacific Islanders will be split off from Asians), while retaining the Hispanic ethnic designation. A "multiracial" category was rejected in favor of letting each person check more than one box—even if, as in the case of Tiger Woods, that turns out to be four boxes. This may allow more Americans to identify their ancestry accurately, but it could create a host of problems for census analysts. In determining what percentage of Americans belongs to each category, will a data analyzer count Tiger Woods and others who check multiple boxes more than once, divide them into fractions, or just assign them to a single category? This may seem ridiculous, but it is a very real problem to the Census Bureau. Laws guaranteeing equal access and representation have meant, in practice, that the racial or ethnic composition of the population affects who is admitted to universities, how the boundaries of legislative districts are drawn, whether school districts need to submit desegregation plans, and whether minorities are adequately represented among workers hired on federally funded projects and among business owners receiving federal contracts.

The new categories are therefore of great concern to interest groups representing American minorities. The National Association for the Advancement of Colored People (NAACP), for example, does not want the political clout and greater opportunities it has worked decades to win diminished just because people who were classified as black for purposes of exclusion under the old "one-drop-of-blood" standard now are counted as white or Asian because they self-identify as multiracial. One NAACP official said, "Let those mixed race people check all the boxes they want—but COUNT them as black."[3] One Hispanic American organization has asked that "Hispanic" be categorized as a race rather than an ethnicity, and the Arab American Institute wants a special protected category to be created for people of Middle Eastern ancestry. An official of an Asian American interest group said she opposed the multiple-choice approach because racial and ethnic data are collected for a reason and, "If you can't tabulate it, you've undermined the ability of the federal government to provide information that will help set policy and help ensure that the civil rights laws are effectively enforced. That is the bottom line."[4] Or, as it was more bluntly put by a member of the House committee that oversees the Census Bureau, "The numbers drive the dollars."[5]

1. Lawrence Wright, "One Drop of Blood," *The New Yorker*, July 25, 1994, p. 47.
2. Rochelle L. Stanfield, "Multiple Choice," *National Journal*, November 22, 1997, pp. 2352–2355.
3. Stanfield, p. 2355.
4. Ibid.
5. Representative Thomas C. Sawyer (D.-Ohio) quoted in Wright, p. 47.

OTHER SOURCES: Jack E. White, "I'm Just Who I Am," *Time*, May 5, 1997, pp. 30–36.

views about what government should do about them. Reconciling these is what the political process is for.

Why, when the American population has always been so heterogeneous, does diversity seem to have so much more meaning in contemporary political life? The reason in part is that, while society was diverse in the early decades of the republic, the political spectrum was narrow. The majority were excluded from participation. Those granted full rights of participation varied from state to state, but two groups—women and African American men, with the exception of a small number of free black men living in the North—were comprehensively shut out after the ratification of the Constitution, as were some unpropertied white men.

Diversity's scope for expression has been greatly broadened through the slow expansion of the electorate and the general opening up of the political system. This process (discussed in Chapter 7) included the extension of voting rights to African American men and, almost 50 years later, to women. About the same time citizenship was granted to American Indians and to residents of Puerto Rico, whose country had been incorporated as a U.S. territory after the Spanish-American War. Although full black suffrage was not effectively achieved until the 1960s, the voting and politically active public has been becoming gradually more heterogeneous since the 1920s.

Two later developments, the adoption—beginning in the Nixon administration—of race, gender, and ethnic preference programs by the federal government, and the wave of immigration from Asia and Latin America in the 1980s and 1990s, have increased the importance of diversity in American politics.

As government adopted affirmative action policies to compensate for historical discrimination (Chapter 15), an individual's race, gender, or ethnicity took on added political importance. Their use as factors influencing the division of public resources has given rise to what one cultural historian calls "identitarianism,"[15] or what many others call **identity politics.** This is the practice of organizing on the basis of one's sex, ethnic

Illegal immigrants wait to cross the border to California.

© Don Barletti, *Los Angeles Times*

or racial identity, or sexual orientation to compete for public resources and to influence public policy.

Paradoxically, identity politics has intensified during a period in which racial and ethnic boundaries are beginning to erode. There is evidence that America is a melting pot for millions. Among white ethnic groups, so much intermarriage has occurred that many people cannot identify their ancestry. In the 1990 census, 100 million Americans could name no specific ancestry or reported multiple ancestries.[16]

Despite the discrimination still faced by many Americans whose ancestry is not European, distinctions are beginning to erode. For example, one government study showed that 6% of people considering themselves black, one-third who considered themselves Asian, and 70% of those who considered themselves American Indian were thought to be white by survey researchers. A study of infant deaths showed that many infants were classified by a different race at death than on their birth certificates. A quarter of those who identified themselves as American Indian on the census did not claim American Indian ancestry. Interracial marriages and interracial children are becoming increasingly common. More than half the births to an American Indian parent and one-third of the births to an Asian American parent had one parent of a different race. One-fourth of the children born to a Hispanic parent had a non-Hispanic other parent.[17]

All of these examples indicate that once seemingly clear notions of "race" as either black or white are becoming confused as we become an increasingly multiracial society. One survey showed that one-third of African Americans believe that blacks are not a single race, and almost half of both black and white respondents believed that government should not collect information on race at all (see box "Census and Sensibility").[18]

POLITICAL CULTURE

In recent years diversity has become a political catchword and has been raised to the level of a civic virtue. Yet our motto is "E Pluribus Unum"—"One Out of Many"—referring to a union of many states and one people out of many traditions. There is a popular saying that Americans are people of many cultures united by a single idea. But what is that single idea and is it, however fundamental, sufficient to form a political culture? A **po-**

Alon Reininger/Contact Press Images

Kentucky Fried Chicken follows a Korean American parade in Los Angeles.

litical culture is a shared body of values and beliefs that shapes perception and attitudes toward politics and government and, in turn, influences political behavior.

Governments rely for their stability and vitality on the positive affect of citizens: their identity with the country and its method of governing, and their adoption of political values and behavior necessary to sustain the system. The only alternatives are for government to be ineffective or to gain compliance through force or other punitive measures. So it is essential for Americans to share a basic belief in the founding principles and institutions of government, including the individual's relationship to government and role in the political process.

In a democracy, sharing a political culture does not mean that citizens must agree on specific issues or even generally on what government's role should be in dealing with the country's problems. Democracy embraces conflict and competition just as it requires cooperation and a sense of community. A basic function of government is to establish the rules under which interests can compete. So the essence of political culture is not agreement on issues, but the acceptance of the rights and obligations of citizenship and of the rules for participating in the political process. These shared values reduce the strains produced by our differences and allow us to compete intensely on some issues while cooperating on others.

The significance of political culture—even its definition—has long been a topic of debate. Some argue that every country in the world, regardless of its level of development, is composed of "competing political cultures, not a single political culture."[19] While American society has often been characterized as a melting pot, it has been a slow melt. It is easy to forget that not long ago an identity as a Virginian or Pennsylvanian was much more important than being an American. And it was not until the Civil War, under the influence of Lincoln's powerful reference at Gettysburg to the "unfinished work" of preserving the Union, that Americans began referring to the United States with the singular "is" rather than the plural "are."[20] Our "nation of nations" is crosscut with cultural, political, and economic cleavages, but despite our sometimes overwhelming diversity, most Americans do share some basic goals and values.

AMERICAN DEMOCRACY: THE CORE VALUES

The words Americans use to characterize their form of government are less likely to come from the Constitution than from the second paragraph of the Declaration of Independence: "We hold these Truths to be self-evident, that all Men are created equal, that they are endowed by the Creator with certain unalienable Rights, that among these are Life, Liberty, and the Pursuit of Happiness. . . ."

These words suggest the basic assumptions, or core beliefs, on which the American system was founded: universal truths that can be known and acted upon; equality before the law; belief in a higher power that transcends human law; and rights that are entitlements at birth and therefore can be neither granted nor taken away by government. The fundamental concept is liberty, especially the freedom to pursue one's livelihood and other personal goals that lead to a "happy" life.

The Declaration was primarily a political argument for separation from Great Britain and, as such, was concerned with the basic principles and philosophy of government.[21] Guaranteeing the rights of individuals, the Declaration postulated, was the primary reason for government to exist. The Constitution reinforced the Declaration's emphasis on equality, while specifying other core principles of American democracy: majority rule exercised through elected representatives, and minority rights (a reference to political or religious minorities, not to racial or ethnic minorities). But unlike the Declaration, the Constitution had to deal with the practical problems of governing and of creating institutions that would protect the rights and pursuits of the individual while balancing them against the public interest. Thus, while the Declaration is all principle, the Constitution, of necessity, is founded on political compromise.

In this section we look briefly at each of the core principles of American democracy. A more detailed description of their legal expression in the Constitution is provided in Chapter 2.

Individual Liberty

Our belief in individual liberty has roots in the Judeo-Christian belief that every individual is equal and has worth before God. It has also been shaped by the works of the English philosophers Thomas Hobbes and John Locke. Briefly, they wrote that individuals give some of their rights to government so it can protect them from each other. Individuals then use their remaining liberties to pursue their individually defined visions of the good life. These ideas are part of social contract theory, which we discuss in Chapter 2.

Influenced by these ideas, early Americans emphasized individual liberty over other goals of government. James Madison, for example, justified the Constitution by writing that government's job is to protect the "diversity" of interests and abilities that exists among individuals. Liberty is also reflected in our long tradition of rights, deriving from Great Britain's. Usually, these rights are framed as powers *denied* to government—for example, government shall not deny freedom of assembly nor engage in unreasonable searches and seizures. Essentially, this means the overall right to be left alone by the government. Such individualistic values have molded popular expectations. Immigrants often came and still come to America to be their own bosses. The other side of this coin is that we are also at liberty to fail and accept the consequences. Although the opportunities for many individuals to get ahead in America are limited by prejudice and poverty, living in a society with an explicit commitment to individual liberty can be exciting and liberating.

Political Equality

Although the Judeo-Christian belief that all people are equal in the eyes of God reflects one type of equality, it led logically to other types, such as political equality. The ancient Greek emphasis on the opportunity and responsibility of all citizens to participate in ruling their city-states also contributed to our notion of political equality. Thus, the Declaration of Independence proclaimed that "all Men are created equal." This did not mean that all people are born with equal talents or abilities. It meant that all citizens are born with equal standing before government and are entitled to equal rights.

In the early years of our country, however, as in the ancient Greek city-states, full rights of citizenship were conferred only on those thought to have the intellectual and moral judgment to act in the public interest. This wisdom could be acquired from experience in the public arena, such as through one's work, not just by formal education. In both Greece and the United States, such thinking denied political rights to slaves, who were believed incapable of independent judgment, and women, whose knowledge was seen as limited to the private or domestic sphere. This left a deep tension between the value of the individual conferred by religious belief and the secular Greek concepts of political rights rooted in circumstances of birth or acquired experience. Over time, this conflict was resolved in favor of the inherent worth of every individual and hence the political equality of all.

Americans have long considered themselves relatively equal politically and socially if not economically. Or, at minimum, they believe they are inherently equal, even when that condition cannot be realized in the political arena. Alexis de Tocqueville, a perceptive Frenchman who traveled through the United States in the 1830s, observed that Americans felt more equal than Europeans did. De Tocqueville attributed this feeling to the absence of a hereditary monarchy and aristocracy in this country. There was no tradition in America of looking up to kings and queens and aristocrats as one's "betters."

A belief in political equality leads to **popular sovereignty,** or rule by the people. Abraham Lincoln ex-

"We can't come to an agreement about how to fix your car, Mr. Simons. Sometimes that's the way things happen in a democracy."

pressed this concept when he spoke of "government of the people, by the people and for the people." If individuals are equal, no one person or small group has the right to rule others. Instead, the people collectively rule themselves. And so we arrive at our form of government, a **democracy.** The word *democracy*, derived from the Greek, means "authority of the people." If all political authority resides in the people, then the people have the right to govern themselves.

Majority Rule

If political authority rests in the people collectively, and if all people are equal, then the majority should rule. That is, when there are disagreements over policies, majorities rather than minorities should decide. If individuals are equal, then policies should be determined according to the desires of the greater number. Otherwise, some individuals would be bestowed with more authority than others.

Majority rule helps provide the support necessary to control the governed. Those in the minority go along because they accept this principle and expect to be in the majority on other issues. At a minimum, the minority expects those in the majority to respect their basic rights. If these expectations are not fulfilled, the minority is less likely to accept majority rule and tolerate majority decisions. Thus, majority rule necessarily entails minority rights.

Minority Rights

While majority rule is important, it sometimes conflicts with minority rights. Majorities make decisions *for* "the people" but in doing so do not *become* "the people." "The people" includes members of the majority *and* members of the minority. As a result, majorities that harm minority rights diminish everyone's rights. Sadly, as James Madison and other writers of the Constitution feared, majorities in the United States have sometimes forgotten this principle, the most egregious example being the enslavement of African Americans. At various times in our history, ethnic, political, and religious minorities have been denied basic rights. The idea that everyone loses when minority rights are trampled is a lesson that does not stay learned.

Thus, democratic principles sometimes contradict each other. These principles are goals more than reality. Americans have struggled for two centuries to reconcile practice with democratic aims and to perfect a system of government that was revolutionary for its time.

Economic Rights

The centrality of private property rights in the Founders' thinking about government is a subject we leave to Chapter 2. Here we call attention to the relationship between the political principles briefly described above and economic rights. Everyone is familiar with the idea that the American Revolution was triggered by what the colonists saw as unfair taxation and other economic burdens placed on them by the British Parliament. To a certain extent, Americans fought the Revolution to be left alone to pursue their livelihoods and to ensure that they would not have to give up any part of their wealth without their consent.

Economic freedom, specifically the right to own property, is an adjunct to our concepts of individual liberty and the "pursuit of happiness." But just as tension exists between majority and minority rights and between individual liberty and the good of all, so also there is potential conflict between the political equality the Declaration avows and the property rights it protects. Inevitably, some people, through inheritance, luck, or initiative, amass more wealth and power than others and come to exercise more influence over government. The ancient Greeks feared that democracy could not tolerate extremes of wealth and poverty. They thought a wealthy minority, out of smugness, and an impoverished minority, out of desperation, would try to act independently of the rest of the people and consequently would disregard the public interest. Early Americans worried less about this. They thought they could create a government that would protect individual diversity, including economic disparity, and still survive. But the pursuit of the goal of political equality in a real world of great economic inequities has led government to a much greater role in regulating economic activity than the Founders anticipated.

AMERICAN DEMOCRACY IN PRACTICE

Democratic principles come alive only when people participate in government. But the principle of rule by the people can be implemented in various forms. In a large and complex society, as ours already was in 1789, direct democracy is not practical.

A **direct democracy** permits citizens to vote on most issues. The best example of a direct democracy is the town meeting, which has been the traditional government of many New England towns for over 350 years. Although town meetings today are often attended by relatively small numbers of citizens, they still offer one of the few opportunities people have to govern themselves directly. Citizens attending town meetings make their own decisions (e.g., whether to put parking meters on the main street) and elect officers to enforce them (such as the police chief and city clerk).

Our national government is an **indirect democracy,** or a **republic.** Citizens have an indirect impact on government because they select policymakers to make decisions for them. Members of Congress, not rank-and-file citizens, vote bills into law. But these officials are not rulers; they are the representatives of the people and draw their authority from law sanctioned by the people.

Classical Democracy

The Greek philosopher Aristotle's definition of democracy emphasized the importance of citizen participation in government through debating, voting, and holding office. We call this vision **classical democracy.** In a classical democracy, citizens are committed to learning about and participating in government. They are well informed, discuss public affairs regularly, tell public officials what they think, and vote. Some political theorists think that, compared to individuals who do not take their roles as democratic citizens seriously, those who do are more likely to see the complexities in issues and, while disagreeing with each other, still share common goals and work together to accomplish them.[22]

Political scientists initially accepted the classical democratic view as a fairly accurate picture of American politics. By the 1940s, however, as they used information from surveys and voter turnout records, they discovered that many fewer citizens take advantage of their democratic rights than classical democratic theory predicts. For example, voting is a routine political activity. It is the easiest way to participate in politics and the least costly in terms of time and energy. Yet only one-half of Americans vote in presidential elections and only one-third have voted in recent congressional elections. Even fewer vote in local elections. Instead of being motivated to participate in politics as in a classical democracy, most citizens are little involved. In fact, one-fifth of the electorate does nothing at all political, not even discussing politics.[23]

Only about one-tenth of the population takes full advantage of opportunities to participate. These activists give money to candidates, make phone calls, distribute leaflets, write letters to legislators, attend meetings, or join neighbors to work for a common end (such as neighborhood preservation).

Why does the reality of political participation fall short of classical democratic expectations? One recent analysis argues that many Americans do not participate because they are turned off by, among other things, long political campaigns in which sound bites and negative campaigning replace meaningful dialogue about issues.[24] Another and more enduring explanation is that political participation is class based: people who participate tend to have more money and education. The working class and America's poorest, unlike their counterparts in many European countries, lack strong trade unions and political parties to represent them. American trade unions involve mostly the middle and better-off workers. American political parties appeal more to middle-class than working-class interests too. Thus, the poor do not have strong organizations to promote their political participation.

The poor also tend to belong to fewer organizations of any kind (civic groups, labor unions, or issue-oriented groups) than do the middle or upper classes. As a result, they have fewer opportunities to be drawn into political action through such associations.

INTO THE 21ST CENTURY

SOMETIMES A CLOUDY CRYSTAL BALL

Studying politics is not just looking at what happened in the past or what is happening in the present. It also involves analyzing how processes and trends of today are likely to affect the future. We make judgments about the future in our analyses throughout this book. But we have also developed a special feature that you will find in most chapters, *Into the 21st Century.* In those features we look at some ways political institutions and processes are likely to develop as we move into the next century and next millennium. Many of these boxes will focus on the impact of technology and the changing American population.

In this introductory box, though, we will admit that our prognostications, and those of other analysts, may be far off-track. Although we try to compile the best information possible and subject it to the most intelligent analysis we are capable of, in 20 years a reader picking up this text might have occasion to laugh. This point was brought home to us by a feature in *Newsweek* summarizing a variety of predictions made over the past several decades by eminent scientists, business leaders, and entertainment moguls. These predictions should serve to remind us that any prediction is limited by factors we cannot now foresee.

- "Computers in the future may . . . perhaps only weigh 1.5 tons." (1949, *Popular Mechanics,* in its forecast about computer technology)
- "Airplanes are interesting toys but of no military value." (1911, Marshal Ferdinand Foch, future World War I commander)
- "The horse is here to stay but the automobile is only a novelty—a fad." (1903, a bank president advising Henry Ford's lawyer not to invest in the Ford Motor Company)
- "There is no reason for any individual to have a computer in their home." (1977, Kenneth Olsen, founder of Digital Equipment Corporation)
- "[Television] won't be able to hold on to any market it captures after the first six months. People will soon get tired of staring at a plywood box every night." (1946, Darryl F. Zanuck, head of 20th Century Fox)
- "Everything that can be invented has been invented." (1899, U.S. commissioner of patents Charles Duell)
- "I have no political ambitions for myself or my children." (1936, Joseph P. Kennedy, father of John F., Robert, and Edward Kennedy)

SOURCE: *Newsweek,* January 27, 1997, p. 86.

In addition, political participation requires both time and money. Many poor adults are single heads of families with little spare time for political activity or resources for transportation and babysitters.

Race and ethnicity explain political participation too, but not as well. Blacks and Hispanics participate less than others, but this is due primarily to their average lower education and income levels. At each education and income level, blacks and Hispanics participate at about the same rates as whites.

Age also explains participation in politics. Young people participate much less than their elders. The middle-aged—the highest participators—are more apt to be established in a career and family life and have more time and money to devote to political activities. They are also less apt to be infirm than older people.

Thus, American government is not a classical democracy. Only a small minority of citizens fully participate in politics. Majorities cannot rule when most people do not take advantage of their rights by voting or trying to influence government or each other.[25] Furthermore, those who do participate are not representative of the whole population in class and other social characteristics. This can have an important impact on the kind of public policy we have. Elected officials chosen by people with more money and education are unlikely to have the same perspectives as those chosen by people with less money and education.

Pluralism

In the 1950s, many political scientists thought they knew how American democracy operated. In a theory called **pluralism,** they sought to reconcile democratic principles with the evidence that most people do not participate actively in politics.

Pluralists maintain that government is responsive to groups of citizens working together to promote their common interests.[26] Individuals join others with like beliefs to influence government.

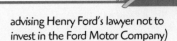

The pluralist view maintains that enough people belong to interest groups to ensure that government ultimately hears everyone. Group leaders and paid staff represent rank-and-file members to decision-makers. According to pluralist theory, this process produces a kind of balance in which no group loses so often that it stops competing. As a result, no group or small number of groups can dominate government. This encourages people to continue to "play the game" by finding ways to compromise with each other. It also leads government to avoid major policy changes to maintain the balance and the popular support that comes with it.

Pluralist theory is attractive because it says democracy can "work" without everyone participating in politics. There is some validity to this theory. Thousands of interest groups in Washington employ experts to represent them in congressional corridors, bureaucratic agencies, and courtrooms.

As Chapter 5 shows, however, many people and issues fall through the cracks of interest group representation. The poor are especially unlikely to be organized and to have many resources to fight political battles. Groups do not represent them well or at all. In addition, intense competitions between well-organized groups on some issues—such as abortion—sometimes make compromise difficult.

Groups may not always even represent the interests of their members. In 1915, Robert Michels formulated the "iron law of oligarchy."[27] This "law" says that effective power in a group, no matter what its size, usually goes to a few, an oligarchy or an elite. In fact, groups create elites by electing officers and hiring staffs. As they spend more time on group affairs and develop ties to public officials, group leaders may come to see group interests differently than do many members.

Pluralism Reconsidered

The failure of pluralist theory to acknowledge the limited power of citizens with average or below-average incomes has led some political scientists to argue that American democracy is much less democratic than pluralists believed. Some theorists maintain that the holders of a few top jobs in key parts of the society dominate governmental decision making. These leaders include the chief officials of major corporations, universities, foundations, and media outlets, as well as the heads of important agencies of government, such as the Defense Department.

One political scientist identified 7,314 key jobs in major organizations such as these.[28] Some especially important jobs led to memberships on the boards of directors of other organizations. In addition, he found that about 4,300 elite business leaders controlled well over 50% of America's corporate wealth and that almost 40% of them had once held a government post. If this is right, relatively few people share the most powerful jobs and make some of the most important decisions in America.

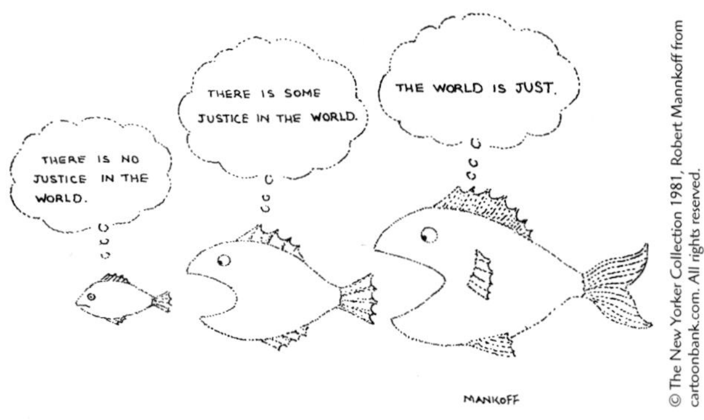

The argument that government is run by the few rather than the many has found credibility with the public. A 1990 survey reported that 77% of a large sample believed that government is run by "a few big interests."[29]

It is often hard to know what is *really* going on in Washington and easy to be frustrated when the process yields outcomes we do not like. It is misleading, however, to think that a few powerful people determine everything. America's diversity produces too many different interests and opinions to permit this. Nevertheless, such explanations are useful because they remind us that tremendous inequalities of resources exist, enabling some parts of society to influence government more than others.

Gradually, most political scientists have come to agree that interest groups do not represent everyone, especially the poor, the working class, and the apathetic. Yet a handful of people in powerful positions do not decide everything either. Sometimes policy reveals a mix of influences.

Current perspectives on how government works stress the "veto" many interest groups have in issues affecting them. Some political scientists have labeled this **hyperpluralism,** suggesting a pluralist system run wild. With so many interests, it is difficult to find common ground to work out solutions to problems. The close ties of many interests to congressional committees and subcommittees considering legislation allow them to stop policy ideas they dislike. And modern technology heightens their impact. A witness to congressional hearings on tax reform reported that lobbyists used cellular phones to produce floods of protest by phone or fax the instant anyone "even *thought*" about something they opposed.[30] There are so many powerful groups with clout that attempts to alter the status quo or change national priorities are extremely difficult. Presidents Carter, Reagan, and Clinton found this out when they tried to make major changes in energy, budget, and health care policy, respectively. The Clinton White House tried to work with over 1,100 interest groups on health care reform, to no avail.[31] Efforts to bring about major changes in national domestic priorities are extremely difficult. It is telling that one of the most sweeping changes in entrenched policy was the overhaul of the welfare system, a reform whose impact will be felt primarily by the poorest and least politically active Americans.

The difficulties created by interest group vetoes often contribute to gridlock and what one observer calls the "blame game."[32] Gridlock occurs when policies are not enacted or administered effectively because the president and Congress cannot agree on what to do. Politicians representing different interests often blame each other for this inaction, or play the "blame game," when they see that gridlock is likely to keep them from getting what they want. The blame game encourages elected officials to distrust each other and furthers public cynicism about government's responsiveness and effectiveness.

Given the presence of many strong groups and their veto opportunities, passing a law means fashioning compromises out of competing group views.[33] In addition to being slow, the process often leads to vaguely worded laws giving actual policymaking authority to bureaucrats who work less visibly with interest group help. In effect, agencies and interest groups, not Congress, often legislate. Thus, chemical industry lobbyists help write regulations on hazardous waste, and military contractors help the Pentagon write weapons contracts.

The growth of bureaucratic policymaking makes our democracy more indirect than the writers of the Constitution intended. Most citizens cannot monitor and influence the actions of a president, 535 members of Congress organized into over 300 committees and subcommittees, *and* bureaucratic agencies. The leaders of major interest groups can, and this gives them considerable power. The possibility that these leaders may be relatively independent of their rank-and-file memberships makes them even more important.

These views challenge the pluralist explanation by concluding that government responds to many but not all groups. This suggests a hybrid explanation of American government stressing the clout of more powerful groups, whose leaders may belong to a larger, more diversified elite.

CONCLUSION: IS GOVERNMENT RESPONSIVE?

America has a split political personality. Most people have a low opinion of Congress, yet we reelect most of its members. We love the idea that the average person has a say in government, yet half of us do not vote, even in presidential elections.

"Remember when people had only themselves to blame?"

We criticize big government while complaining that it does not do very much. As one newspaper columnist put it: "All the evidence suggests that when Americans look at Washington they see a conniving bunch of hustlers playing an insider's game at the expense of the nation."[34] Most people feel that government is out of their control and unrepresentative of their interests.

Why do we act as if we dislike democracy in action? Has government failed? Are the laws it enacts not what the people want? Is it the fault of the media, emphasizing mostly the negative side of government? Are average citizens actually shut out of the process? Or is the problem really the fault of citizens, and not government at all?

American government is characterized by conflict and compromise because Americans do not agree on either the nature of the problems that confront us or their solutions. If we all agreed, there would be no need for debate, bargaining, compromise, or delays.

Although we are not equally well situated to influence policymakers, there are more avenues for political participation now than ever before.

In contemporary America, the number of organized interests and their effectiveness in making their views known have multiplied so dramatically that government officials are besieged by a cacophony of views. And this has happened in an era when the workings of government are increasingly in public view.

We have argued that much of this is a necessary component of a democratic system in a large and diverse nation. Nonetheless, to say we must live with debate, compromise, and slowness in our system does not mean we cannot improve and speed the workings of government. In coming chapters, we will carefully examine the major institutions and processes of our democracy to see if we can shed light on how they contribute to public dissatisfaction and how they might be improved.

EPILOGUE

What Will You Do?

This is the only epilogue where the authors cannot provide the outcome of the decision-making process. But we can speculate. Based on present evidence, there is only one chance in two that you will cast your vote in the presidential election in 2000—that chance is even less if you are under 25 years of age. The chance that you voted in the 1998 off-year election is only 40%; that you will vote in any local elections, from 10% to 20%; and that you will become politically active beyond voting, only 20%. Where did you fit into this pattern?

One sociologist has pointed to the paradox of Americans praising economic entrepreneurialism at the same time they refuse to accept the responsibilities of national citizenship. Collectively, we have been accused of practicing "couch potato politics."[35] Most of us, even those highly dissatisfied with the way government works, do not want a king, a dictator, or an emperor to make decisions for us. Indeed, democracy assumes that majorities control government and indirect democracy assumes that citizens control their representatives. This means that people need to get up off their couches and participate.

More than 2,000 years ago Aristotle wrote that politics is the most noble endeavor in which people can engage, partly because it helps them know themselves and partly because it forces them to relate to others. Through political participation individuals pursue their own needs and interests, but not without consideration for the needs of other citizens. In other words, it is through politics that we learn to balance our own needs and interests against the good of the political community as a whole.

Today Americans are less inclined to share Aristotle's conception of politics than the cynical view of novelist Gore Vidal that "who collects what money from whom in order to spend on what is all there is to politics."[36] About their unwillingness to get involved in issue debates or the electoral process, Americans often say, "It's all politics." Of course, issue debates and elections are political because the competition to determine what policy will be is essential to government. Politics is inescapable because divergence of interest is unavoidable.

For all their anger with government over the years, many Americans are not well informed about it, nor do most participate in it. This includes college-age voters. A recent survey found that only 14% of those entering college in 1997 said they "discuss politics" often; only 27% called "keeping up with political affairs" important.[37] That many Americans are not well informed about government helps to explain the public's attraction to quick fixes and seemingly easy solutions. Thus, many Americans continue to demand tax cuts, but oppose spending cuts that affect them (half of all households receive some sort of federal financial payment).[38] They want democracy but no arguments or compromises.

Quick fixes look good to those who are poorly informed about government and who resent the debating, compromises, and slowness of democracy. But quick fixes and free lunches are a lot alike: there is no such thing.

Politics is necessary to govern a democratic society. Ignoring politics and the institutions we have to represent ourselves, such as political parties and interest groups, will not eliminate politics. Rather, it would eliminate the most effective ways yet developed for the public to influence government's decisions.

KEY TERMS

politics
identity politics
political culture
popular sovereignty
democracy
direct democracy
indirect democracy
republic
classical democracy
pluralism
hyperpluralism

FURTHER READING

John E. Chubb and Paul E. Peterson, *Can the Government Govern?* (Washington, D.C.: Brookings Institution, 1989). A collection of case studies showing how the public interest often suffers when elected officials and bureaucrats avoid hard policy choices by playing the blame game with each other and "special interests."

Edward Countryman, *Americans: A Collision of Histories* (New York: Hill & Wang, 1996). A historian traces the history of the dominant ethnic groups in America from 1600 to 1900. He argues that the very different experiences of Native, African, and European Americans mean that there is no unified American history and no one "type" who can be identified as American.

William Greider, *Who Will Tell the People: The Betrayal of American Democracy* (New York: Simon & Schuster, 1992). A populist perspective that views Washington politics as a "grand bazaar" where wealthy interest groups exchange favors with public officials who want to maintain their power.

John R. Hibbing and Beth Theiss-Morse, *Congress as Public Enemy: Public Attitudes toward American Political Institutions* (Cambridge: Cambridge University Press, 1995). The authors argue that the public is fed up with Congress because Congress is where the internal workings of democracy—the debates, appeals to self, partisan, and group interest, compromises, and inefficiencies—are most obvious.

Harold Lasswell, *Politics: Who Gets What, When, How* (New York: New World Publishing, 1958). A classic treatment of some very practical political problems.

Pauline Maier, *American Scripture: The Making of the Declaration of Independence* (New York: Alfred Knopf, 1997). A historian offers a revisionist view of the importance of the Declaration by arguing that its language was not original but rather was almost identical in content to that of 90 other declarations written in the colonies at the same time. Given the widespread agreement on language and principles in all these documents, she judges the Declaration "an expression of the American mind."

Michael Pertschuk, *Giant Killers* (New York: W. W. Norton, 1986). A public interest lobbyist describes several major congressional battles in the 1980s showing that the side with money and status does not always win.

Michael J. Sandel, *Democracy's Discontent: America in Search of a Public Philosophy* (Cambridge, Mass.: Harvard University Press, Belknap Press, 1996): A political theorist argues that American politics is "ill-equipped to allay discontent" over the unraveling moral fabric of the country and suggests that one reason is the supremacy of individual rights over community interests.

Hedrick Smith, *The Power Game: How Washington Works* (New York: Random House, 1988). A Pulitzer Prize–winning journalist's account of the colorful personalities and complex alliances that shape national policymaking. Loaded with good anecdotes.

ELECTRONIC RESOURCES

In each chapter we will provide a few addresses to the Internet for particularly useful or interesting sites relevant to the chapter. Today, you can access information, including statistics and information about public officials, that was formerly accessible only in libraries. Unlike library call numbers, however, Internet addresses sometimes change.

http://www.toqueville.org/

This site allows you to follow the eighteenth-century French writer Alexis de Tocqueville on his travels through the United States. His comments about the American character are still widely cited today, as you will see in your textbook.

http://www.fedstats.gov/index20.html

This site of the Immigration and Naturalization Service leads you to official statistics on immigration flows to the United States. http://www.fedstats.gov is a central link to all federal statistics.

http://www.whitehouse.gov/WH/html/handbook.html

This is a central federal government site providing links to all branches of government, federal agencies and commissions, and important policy areas.

INFOTRAC CITATIONS

"More to Come Costs of Immigration"
"No Justice for Immigrants"
"Bad Choices for Big Jobs"
"Confessions of a Recovering Bigot"

NOTES

1. See John Hibbing and Beth Theiss-Morse, *Congress as Public Enemy: Public Attitudes toward American Political Institutions* (Cambridge: Cambridge University Press, 1995); Hibbing and Theiss-Morse, "Civics Is Not Enough; Teaching Barbarics in K-12," forthcoming in *PS*; Gabriel A. Almond and Sidney Verba, *The Civic Culture* (Boston: Little, Brown, 1965), p. 64.

2. Hibbing and Theiss-Morse, *Congress*.

3. Walt Whitman, *Leaves of Grass and Selected Prose*, ed. Lawrence Buell (New York: Random House, 1981), p. 449.

4. Edward Countryman, *Americans: A Collision of Histories* (New York: Hill & Wang, 1996), pp. 3–22.

5. John Sugden, *Tecumseh: A Life* (New York: Henry Holt & Co., A John Macrae Book, 1998).

6. Michael J. Sandel, *Democracy's Discontent: America in Search of a Public Philosophy* (Cambridge, Mass.: Harvard University Press, Belknap Press, 1997). Sandel points out that the Constitution prohibited only the federal government, not the states, from establishing an official religion.

7. Dick Kirschten, "American Dreamer," *National Journal*, July 5, 1997, p. 1364; Susan Welch and Timothy Bledsoe, *Urban Reform and Its Consequences* (Chicago: University of Chicago Press, 1988), p. 2.

8. *Statistical Abstract of the United States*, 1994. Table 10.

9. *1996 Statistical Abstract of the Immigration and Naturalization Service*, p. 11.

10. Kirschten, p. 1364.

11. "Belief by the Numbers," *New York Times Magazine*, December 7, 1997, pp. 60–61; Gustav Niebur, "Makeup of American Religion Is Looking More like Mosaic, Data Say," *New York Times*, April 12, 1998, p. 12.

12. Robert Reinhold, "Resentment against New Immigrants," *New York Times*, October 26, 1986, p. 6E.

13. George F. Will, "Buchanan Takes Aim," *Washington Post National Weekly Edition*, December 16–22, 1991, p. 28.

14. The *Christian American*, quoted in Dick Kirschten, "Building Blocs," *National Journal*, September 26, 1993, p. 2173.

15. Walter Benn Michaels, *Our America: Nativism, Modernism, and Pluralism* (Durham, N.C.: Duke University Press, 1997).

16. Bureau of the Census, *General Social and Economy Characteristics: U.S. Summary* (Washington, D.C.: U.S. Government Printing Office, 1990), Part 1, Table 12.

17. Antonio McDaniel, "The Dynamic Racial Composition of the United States," *Daedalus* (Winter 1995), pp. 179–198; Lawrence Wright, "One Drop of Blood," *New Yorker*, July 25, 1994, pp. 46–55.

18. Reported in Tom Morganthau, "What Color Is Black?" *Newsweek*, February 13, 1995, p. 64. Data on black-white intermarriage are found in Susan Kalish "Interracial Baby Boomlet in Progress?" *Population Today* 20 (December 1992), pp. 1–2.

19. Michael Thompson, Richard Ellis, and Aaron Wildavsky, *Cultural Theory* (Boulder, Colo.: Westview Press, 1990), p. 216.

20. Garry Wills, *Lincoln at Gettysburg: The Words That Remade America* (New York: Simon & Schuster, 1992), p. 145.

21. For a discussion of the Declaration of Independence's origins in pragmatism versus the political philosophy of the Founders see Pauline Maier, *American Scripture: Making the Declaration of Independence* (New York: Alfred Knopf, 1997).

22. For a discussion of this see Mark Warren, "Democratic Theory and Self-Transformation," *American Political Science Review* 86 (March, 1992), pp. 8–23.

23. This discussion draws on Sidney Verba and Norman Nie, *Participation in America* (New York: Harper & Row, 1972); and Stephen Earl Bennett and Linda L. M. Bennett, "Political Participation," in Samuel Long, ed., *Annual Review of Political Science* (Norwood, N.J.: Ablex Publishing Group, 1986).

24. E. J. Dionne, Jr., *Why Americans Hate Politics* (New York: Simon & Schuster, 1991).

25. Robert A. Dahl, *A Preface to Democratic Theory* (Chicago: University of Chicago Press, 1956), p. 142.

26. See Arthur F. Bentley, *The Process of Government* (Chicago: University of Chicago Press, 1908); and David Truman, *The Governmental Process* (New York: A. A. Knopf, 1951).

27. Robert Michels, *Political Parties* (New York: Collier Books, 1915).

28. Thomas R. Dye, *Who's Running America? The Bush Era* (Englewood Cliffs, N.J.: Prentice-Hall, 1990), p. 12.

29. Cited in Allen D. Hertzke, *Echoes of Discontent: Jesse Jackson, Pat Robertson, and the Resurgence of Populism* (Washington, DC: CQ Press, 1993) p. 235.

30. Reported in Robert Wright, "Hyper Democracy," *Time*, January 23, 1995, p. 18.

31. David S. Broder, "Can We Govern?" *Washington Post National Weekly Edition*, January 31–February 6, 1994, p. 23.

32. Hedrick Smith, *The Power Game: How Washington Works* (New York: Random House, 1988), chapter 17.

33. For example, see Theodore J. Lowi, *The End of Liberalism*, 2d ed. (New York: W. W. Norton, 1979).

34. *New York Times* columnist Russell Baker, reprinted in the *Champaign-Urbana News-Gazette*, August 29, 1997, p. A4.

35. This was the headline on an op-ed piece by the sociologist Alan Wolfe in the *New York Times*, March 15, 1998, section 4, p. 17. He was summarizing the results of a survey of middle-class opinion he published in *One Nation, After All* (New York: Viking, 1997).

36. Gore Vidal, "Coached by Camelot," *The New Yorker*, December 1, 1997, p. 88.

37. "Politics Losing Its Appeal to College Frosh," *Champaign-Urbana News-Gazette*, January 12, 1998, p. D1. The 1997 responses are from a poll of college students the American Council on Education has been conducting annually since 1966.

38. Michael Wines, "Taxpayers Are Angry. They're Expensive, Too," *New York Times*, November 20, 1994, p. E5.

Courtesy of Winterthur Museum

2 THE CONSTITUTION

OUTLINE

YOU ARE THERE

The Case of the Confidential Tapes

In June 1972, a security guard for the Watergate building in Washington, D.C., noticed that tape had been placed across the latch of a door to keep it from locking. The guard peeled off the tape. When he made his rounds later, he noticed that more tape had been placed across the latch. He called the police.

The police encountered five burglars in the headquarters of the Democratic National Committee. Wearing surgical gloves and carrying tear gas guns, photographic equipment, and electronic gear, they had been installing wiretaps on the Democratic Party's phones.

No one expected this break-in to lead to the White House. The *Washington Post* assigned two young reporters who usually covered local matters to the story. But the unlikely pair of Bob Woodward, a Yale graduate, and Carl Bernstein, a college dropout, were ambitious, and they uncovered a series of bizarre connections. The burglars had links to President Richard Nixon's Committee to Reelect the President (CREEP).

The administration dismissed the break-in as the work of overzealous underlings. Even the press called it a "caper." Indeed, it was hard to imagine that high officials in the administration could be responsible. In public opinion polls, Nixon enjoyed an enormous lead, almost 20%, over the various Democrats vying for their party's nomination to challenge him in the fall election. Risky tactics seemed unnecessary.

But Woodward and Bernstein discovered that White House staff members had engaged in other criminal and unethical actions to sabotage the Democrats' campaign. They had forged letters accusing some of the Democrats' candidates of homosexual acts. Later they had obtained and publicized psychiatric records, causing the Democrats' vice presidential nominee to resign.

Nixon won reelection handily, but the revelations forced his two top aides to resign and prompted the Senate to establish a special committee to investigate what was being called the **Watergate scandal.** When investigators happened to ask a lower-level aide to the president if there was a taping device in the Oval Office, he said, "I was hoping you fellows wouldn't ask me about that." Then he revealed what only a handful of aides had known—that Nixon had secretly tape-recorded conversations in nine locations in the White House, the Executive Office Building across the street, and Camp David in Maryland. Nixon had intended to create a comprehensive record of his presidency to demonstrate his greatness.[1]

The tapes could confirm or refute charges of White House complicity in the break-in and cover-up, but Nixon refused to release them. Special Prosecutor Archibald Cox filed suit to force Nixon to do so, and federal trial court Judge John Sirica ordered him to do so. After the federal appeals court affirmed the trial court's decision, Nixon demanded that his attorney general fire Cox. The attorney general and deputy attorney general both refused and resigned in protest. Then the third-ranking official in the Justice Department, Robert Bork, fired the special prosecutor. (Bork later would be nominated to the Supreme Court by President Reagan.)

The public furor over this "Saturday Night Massacre" was so intense that Nixon finally did release some tapes. But one crucial tape contained a mysterious 18-minute gap that a presidential aide speculated was caused by "some sinister force."

To mollify critics, Nixon appointed a new special prosecutor, Leon Jaworski. After his investigation, Jaworski presented evidence to a grand jury that indicted seven of the president's aides for the cover-up, specifically for obstruction of justice, and even named the president as an "unindicted coconspirator."

The House Judiciary Committee considered impeaching the president, and Jaworski subpoenaed more tapes. Nixon issued edited transcripts of the conversations but not the tapes themselves. As a compromise he proposed that one person listen to the tapes—a senator who was 72 years old and hard of hearing. Frustrated, Jaworski went to court, where Judge Sirica ordered Nixon to release the tapes. When Nixon refused, Jaworski appealed directly to the Supreme Court.

Washington Post *reporters Carl Bernstein (left) and Bob Woodward uncovered the Watergate scandal.*

You are Chief Justice Warren Burger, appointed to the Court by President Nixon in 1969 partly because of your calls for more law and order. Three of your brethren also were appointed by Nixon. In the case of *United States v. Nixon,* you are faced with a question that could lead to a grave constitutional showdown with the president. Special Prosecutor Jaworski claims he needs the tapes because they contain evidence pertaining to the upcoming trial of the president's aides indicted for the cover-up. Without all relevant evidence, which possibly could vindicate the aides, the trial court might not convict them.

President Nixon claims he has **executive privilege**—authority to withhold information from the courts and Congress. Although the Constitution does not mention such a privilege, Nixon claims the privilege is inherent in the powers of the presidency. Without it presidents could not guarantee confidentiality in conversations with other officials or even foreign leaders. This could make it difficult for them to govern.

There are few precedents to guide you. Many past presidents exercised executive privilege when pressed for information by Congress. In these instances, Congress ordinarily acquiesced rather than sued for the information, so the courts did not rule on the existence of the privilege. Once, in 1953, the Eisenhower administration invoked the privilege, and the Supreme Court upheld the claim. However, that case involved national security.[2]

In addition to considering the merits of the opposing sides, you also need to consider the extent of the Court's power. The Court lacks strong means to enforce its rulings. It has to rely on its authority as the highest interpreter of the law in the country. Therefore, if the Court orders Nixon to relinquish the tapes and Nixon refuses, there would be little the Court could do. The refusal would show future officials they could disregard your orders with impunity.

In this high-stakes contest, do you and your brethren on the Court order Nixon to turn over the tapes, or do you accept his claim of executive privilege?

Early settlers came to America for many reasons. Some came to escape religious persecution, others to establish their own religious orthodoxy. Some came to get rich, others to avoid debtors' prison. Some came to enrich their families or companies in the Old World, others to flee the closed society of that world. Some came as free persons, others as indentured servants or slaves. Few came to practice self-government. Yet the desire for self-government was evident from the beginning.[3] The settlers who arrived in Jamestown in 1607 established the first representative assembly in America. The pilgrims who reached Plymouth in 1620 drew up the Mayflower Compact in which they vowed to "solemnly & mutually in the presence of God, and one of another, covenant and combine our selves together into a civill body politick." They pledged to establish laws for "the generall good of the colonie" and in return promised "all due submission and obedience."[4]

During the next century and a half, the colonies adopted constitutions and elected representative assemblies. Of course, the colonies lived under British rule; they had to accept the appointment of royal governors and the presence of British troops. But a vast ocean separated the two continents. At such a distance, Britain could not wield the control it might at closer reach. Consequently, it granted the colonies a measure of autonomy, with which they practiced a degree of self-government.

These early efforts toward self-government led to conflict with the mother government. In 1774 the colonies established the Continental Congress to coordinate their action. Within months the conflict reached flashpoint, and the Congress urged the colonies to form their own governments. In 1776 the Congress adopted the Declaration of Independence.

After six years of war, the Americans accepted the British surrender. At the time it seemed they had met their biggest test. Yet they would find fomenting a revolution easier than fashioning a government, and drafting a declaration of independence easier than crafting a constitution.

THE ARTICLES OF CONFEDERATION

Even before the war ended, the Continental Congress passed a constitution, and in 1781 the states ratified it. This first constitution, the **Articles of Confederation,** formed a "league of friendship" among the states. As a confederation, it allowed each state to retain its "sovereignty" and "independence." That is, it made the states supreme over the national government.

Under the Articles, however, Americans would face problems with both their national and state governments.

National Government Problems

The Articles established a Congress, with one house in which each state had one vote. But the Articles strictly limited the powers that Congress could exercise, and they provided no executive or judicial branch.

The Articles reflected the colonial experience under the British government. The leaders feared a powerful central government with a powerful executive like a king. They thought such a government would be too strong and too distant to guarantee individual liberty. Additionally, the Articles reflected a lack of national identity among the people. Most did not view themselves as Americans yet. As Edmund Randolph remarked, "I am not really an American, I am a Virginian."[5] Consequently, the leaders established a very decentralized government that left most authority to the states.

The Articles satisfied many people. Most people were small farmers, and although many of them sank into debt during the depression that followed the war, they felt they could influence the state governments to help them. They realized they could not influence a distant central government as readily.

But the Articles frustrated bankers, merchants, manufacturers, and others in the upper classes. They envisioned a great commercial empire replacing the agricultural society that existed in the late eighteenth century. More than local trade, they wanted national and even international trade. For this they needed uniform laws, stable money, sound credit, and enforceable debt collection. They needed a strong central government that could protect them against debtors and against state governments sympathetic to debtors. The Articles provided neither the foreign security nor the domestic climate necessary to nourish these requisites of a commercial empire.

After the war the army disbanded, leaving the country vulnerable to hostile forces surrounding it. Britain maintained outposts with troops in the Northwest Territory (now the Midwest), in violation of the peace treaty, and an army in Canada. Spain, which had occupied Florida and California for a long time and had claimed the Mississippi River valley as a result of a treaty before the war, posed a threat. Barbary pirates from North Africa seized American ships and sailors.

Congress could not raise an army, because it could not draft individuals directly, or finance an army, because it could not tax individuals directly. Instead, it had to ask the states for soldiers and money. The states, however, were not always sympathetic to the problems of the distant government. And although Congress could make treaties with foreign countries, the states made, or broke, treaties independently of Congress. Without the ability to establish a credible army or negotiate a binding treaty, the government could not get the British troops out of the country. Neither could it get the British government to ease restrictions on shipping or the Spanish government to permit navigation on the Mississippi River.

In addition to an inability to confront foreign threats, the Articles demonstrated an inability to cope with domestic crises. The country bore a heavy war debt that brought the government close to bankruptcy. Since Congress could not tax individuals directly, it could not shore up the shaky government.

The states competed with each other for commercial advantage. As independent governments, they imposed tariffs on goods from other states. The tariffs slowed the growth of businesses.

In short, the government under the Articles seemed too decentralized to ensure either peace or prosperity. The Articles, one leader concluded, gave Congress the privilege of asking for everything, while reserving to each state the prerogative of granting nothing.[6] A similar situation exists today in the United Nations, which must rely on member countries to furnish troops for its peacekeeping forces and dues for its operating expenses.

State Government Problems

There were other conflicts closer to home. State constitutions adopted during the Revolution made the state legislatures more representative than the colonial legislatures had been. And most state legislatures began to hold elections every year. The result was heightened interest among candidates and turnover among legislators. In the eyes of national leaders, there was much pandering to voters and horsetrading by politicians as various factions vied for control. The process seemed up for grabs. According to the Vermont Council of

Censors, laws were "altered—realtered—made better—made worse; and kept in such a fluctuating position that persons in civil commission scarce know what is law."[7] In short, state governments were experiencing more democracy than any other governments in the world at the time. National leaders, stunned by the changes in the few years since the Revolution, considered this development an "excess of democracy."

Moreover, state constitutions made the legislative branch the most powerful. Some state legislatures began to dominate the other branches, and national leaders called them "tyrannical."

The national leaders, most of whom were wealthy and many of whom were creditors, pointed to the laws passed in some states that relieved debtors of some of their obligations. The farmers who were in debt pressed the legislatures for relief that would slow or shrink the payments owed to their creditors. Some legislatures granted such relief.

While these laws worried the leaders, **Shays's Rebellion** in western Massachusetts in 1786 and 1787 scared them. Boston merchants who had loaned Massachusetts money during the war insisted on being repaid in full so they could trade with foreign merchants. The state levied steep taxes that many farmers could not pay during the hard times. The law authorized foreclosure—sale of the farmers' property for the taxes—and jail for the debtors. The law essentially transferred wealth from the farmers to the merchants. The farmers protested the legislature's refusal to grant any relief from the law. Bands of farmers blocked entrances to courthouses where judges were scheduled to hear cases calling for foreclosure and jail. Led by Daniel Shays, some marched to the Springfield arsenal to seize weapons. Although they were defeated by the militia, their sympathizers were victorious in the next election, and the legislature did provide some relief from the law.

Both the revolt and the legislature's change in policy frightened the wealthy. To them it raised the specter of "mob rule." Nathaniel Gorham, the president of the Continental Congress and a prominent merchant, wrote Prince Henry of Prussia, announcing "the failure of our free institutions" and asking if the prince would agree to become king of America (the prince declined).[8] Just months after the uprising, Congress approved a convention for "the sole and express purpose of revising the Articles of Confederation."

To a significant extent, then, the debate at the time reflected a conflict between two competing visions of the future American political economy—agricultural or commercial.[9] Most leaders espoused the latter, and the combination of national problems and state problems prompted them to push for a new government.

THE CONSTITUTION

The Constitutional Convention

THE SETTING

The **Constitutional Convention** convened in Philadelphia, then the country's largest city, in 1787. That year the Industrial Revolution was continuing to sweep Europe and beginning to reach this continent. The first American cotton mill opened in Massachusetts and the first American steamboat plied the Delaware River.[10]

State legislatures chose 74 delegates to the convention; 55 attended. They met at the Pennsylvania State House—now Independence Hall—in the same room where some of them had signed the Declaration of Independence 11 years before.

Delegates came from every state except Rhode Island. That state was controlled by farmers and debtors who feared that the convention would weaken states' powers to relieve debtors of their debts.

The delegates were distinguished by their education, experience, and enlightenment. Benjamin Franklin, of Pennsylvania, was the best-known American in the world. He had been a printer, scientist, and diplomat. At 81 he was the oldest delegate. George Washington, of Virginia, was the most respected American in the country. As the commander of the revolutionary army, he was a national hero. He was chosen to preside over the convention. The presence of men like Franklin and Washington gave the convention legitimacy.

The delegates quickly determined that the Articles were hopeless. Rather than revise them, as instructed by Congress, the delegates decided to start over and draft a new constitution.[11] But what would they substitute for the Articles?

THE PREDICAMENT

The delegates came to the convention because they suffered under a government that was too weak. Yet previously Americans had fought a revolution because they chafed under a government that was too strong. "The nation lived in a nearly constant alternation of fears that it would cease being a nation altogether or become too much of one."[12] People feared both anarchy and tyranny.

This predicament was made clear by the diversity of opinions among the leaders. At one extreme was Patrick Henry, of Virginia, who had been a firebrand of the Revolution. He felt the government would become too strong, perhaps even become a monarchy, in reaction to the current problems with the Articles. He said

AMERICAN DIVERSITY

FOUNDING MOTHERS

Charles Francis Adams, a grandson of President John Adams and Abigail Adams, declared in 1840, "The heroism of the females of the Revolution has gone from memory with the generation that witnessed it, and nothing, absolutely nothing remains upon the ear of the young of the present day."[1] That statement is still true today; in the volumes written about the revolutionary and Constitution-making eras, much is said of the "founding fathers" and very little about the "founding mothers." Although no women were at the Constitutional Convention, in many other ways women contributed significantly to the political ferment of the time. The political role of women during the Constitution-making era was probably greater than it would be again for a century.

Before the Revolutionary War, women were active in encouraging opposition to the British. Groups of women, some called the "daughters of liberty," led boycotts of British goods as part of the protest campaign against taxation without representation. A few women were political pamphleteers, helping to increase public sentiment for independence. One of those pamphlet writers, Mercy Otis Warren, of Massachusetts, was thought to be the first person to urge the Massachusetts delegates to the Continental Congress to vote for separation from Britain.[2] Throughout the period before and after the Revolution, Warren shared her political ideas in personal correspondence with leading statesmen of the time, such as John Adams and Thomas Jefferson. Later she wrote a three-volume history of the American Revolution.

Many women were part of the American army during the battles for independence. Most filled traditional women's roles as cooks, seamstresses, and nurses, but some disguised themselves as men (this was before a military bureaucracy mandated preenlistment physical exams) and fought in battle. One such woman, wounded in action in 1776, is the only Revolutionary War veteran buried at West Point. Still other women fought to defend their homes using hatchets, farm implements, and pots of boiling lye in addition to muskets.

Following independence, some women continued an active political role. Mercy Warren, for example, campaigned against the proposed Constitution because she felt it was not democratic enough.

Independence did not bring any improvement in the political rights of women. In fact, after the Constitution was adopted, some rights that women had held before were gradually lost, such as the right of some women to vote. It was to be another century before the rights of women became a full-fledged part of our national political agenda.

1. Quoted in Linda Grant DePauw and Conover Hunt, *Remember the Ladies* (New York: Viking Press, 1976), p. 9.
2. Alice Felt Tyler, *Freedom's Ferment* (New York: Harper & Row, 1962).

The Metropolitan Museum of Art, Bequest of Charles Allen Munn, 1924 (24-90-35)

This English political cartoon satirizes a gathering of leading women in North Carolina who drew up a resolution to boycott taxed English goods and tea.

he "smelt a rat" and did not attend the convention. At the other extreme was Alexander Hamilton, of New York, who had been an aide to General Washington during the war and had seen the government's inability to supply and pay its own troops. Since then he had called for a stronger national government. He wanted one that could veto the laws of the state governments. And he wanted one person to serve as chief executive for life and others to serve as senators for life. He did attend the convention but, finding little agreement with his proposals, participated infrequently.

In between were those like James Madison, of Virginia. Small and frail, timid and self-conscious as a speaker, he was nonetheless intelligent and savvy as a politician. He had operated behind the scenes to convene the convention and to secure George Washington's attendance. (He publicized that Washington would attend without asking Washington first. Washington, who was in retirement, did not plan to attend and only reluctantly agreed to do so because of the expectation that he would.)[13] Madison had secretly drafted a plan for a new government, one that was a total departure from the government under the Articles, and this plan set the agenda for the convention. During the convention and the ratification process, Madison was "up to his ears in politics, advising, persuading, softening the harsh word, playing down this difficulty and exaggerating that, engaging in debate, harsh controversy, polemics, and sly maneuver."[14] In the end, his views, more than anyone else's, would prevail, and he would be called the Father of the Constitution.

CONSENSUS

Despite disagreements, the delegates did see eye to eye on the most fundamental issues. They agreed that the government should be a republic—an indirect democracy—in which people could vote for at least some of the officials who would represent them. This was the only form of government they seriously considered. They also agreed that the national government should be supreme over the state governments. At the same time, they thought the government should be limited, with checks to prevent it from exercising too much power.

They agreed that the national government should have three separate branches—legislative, executive, and judicial—to exercise separate powers. They thought both the legislative and executive branches should be strong.

CONFLICT

Although there was considerable agreement over the fundamental principles and elemental structure of the new government, the delegates quarreled about the specific provisions concerning representation, slavery, and trade.

REPRESENTATION There was sharp conflict between delegates from large states and those from small states over representations. Large states sought a strong central government that they could control; small states feared a government that would control them.

When the convention began, Edmund Randolph introduced the Virginia Plan drafted by Madison. According to this plan, the central government would be strong. The legislature would have more power than under the Articles, and a national executive and national judiciary also would have considerable power. The legislature would be divided into two houses, with representation based on population in each.

But delegates from the small states calculated that the three largest states—Pennsylvania, Virginia, and Massachusetts—would have a majority of the representatives and could control the legislature. These delegates countered with the New Jersey Plan, introduced by William Paterson. According to this plan, the central government would be relatively strong, although not as strong as under the Virginia Plan. But the primary difference was that the legislature would be one house, with representation by states, which would have one vote each. This was exactly the same as the structure of Congress under the Articles, also designed to prevent the large states from controlling the legislature.

The convention deadlocked. George Washington wrote that he almost despaired of reaching agreement. To ease tensions Benjamin Franklin suggested that the delegates begin each day with a prayer, but they could not agree on this either; Alexander Hamilton insisted they did not need "foreign aid."

Faced with the possibility that the convention would disband without a constitution, the delegates compromised. Delegates from Connecticut and other states proposed a plan in which the legislature would have two houses. In one, representation would be based on population, and members would be elected by voters. In the other, representation would be by states, and members would be selected by state legislatures. Presumably, the large states would dominate the former, the small states the latter. The delegates narrowly approved this **Great Compromise,** or Connecticut Compromise. Delegates from the large states still objected, but those from the small states made it clear that such a compromise was necessary for their agreement and, in turn, their states' ratification. The large states, though, did extract a concession that all taxing and spending bills must originate in the house in which representation was based on population. This provision would allow the large states to take the initiative on these important measures.

The compromise was "great" in that it not only resolved this critical issue but paved the way for resolution of other issues.

SLAVERY In addition to conflict between large states and small states over representation, there was conflict

Historical Society of Pennsylvania

This plan of a slave ship shows the overcrowding that led to inhumane conditions, rampant disease, and high mortality.

between northern states and southern states over slavery, trade, and taxation.

With representation in one house based on population, the delegates had to decide how to apportion the seats. They agreed that Indians would not count as part of the population but differed about slaves. Delegates from the South, where slaves were one-third of the population, wanted slaves to count fully in order to boost the number of their representatives. They argued that their use of slaves produced wealth that benefited the entire nation. Delegates from the North, where most states had outlawed slavery or at least the slave trade after the Revolution, did not want slaves to count at all. Gouverneur Morris, of Pennsylvania, said the southerners' position "comes to this: that the inhabitant of Georgia and South Carolina who goes to the coast of Africa, and in defiance of the most sacred laws of humanity tears away his fellow creatures from their dearest connections and damns them to the most cruel bondages, shall have more votes in a government instituted for the protection of the rights of mankind than the citizen of Pennsylvania or New Jersey who views with a laudable horror so nefarious a practice."[15] Others pointed out that slaves were not considered persons when it came to rights such as voting. Nevertheless, southerners asserted that they would not support a constitution if slaves were not counted at least partially. In the **Three-fifths Compromise,** the delegates agreed that three-fifths of the slaves would be counted in apportioning the seats.

As a result, the votes of southern whites would be worth more than those of northerners in electing members to the House of Representatives and presidents (because the Electoral College would be based on membership in Congress). Between 1788 and 1860, 9 of the 15 presidents, including all five who served two terms, were slaveowners.[16]

Although northerners had to accept this compromise in order to win southerners' support for the Constitution, northerners apparently did not contest two other provisions addressing slavery. Southerners pushed through one provision forbidding Congress to ban the importation of slaves before 1808 and another requiring free states to return any escaped slaves to their owners in slave states. In these provisions southerners won most of what they wanted; even the provision permitting Congress to ban the slave trade in 1808 was hardly a limitation because by then planters would have enough slaves to fulfill their needs by natural population increases rather than importation. In return, northerners, representing most shippers, got authority for Congress to regulate commerce by a simple majority rather than a two-thirds majority. Thus, northerners conceded two provisions reinforcing slavery in order to benefit shippers.[17]

Yet the framers were embarrassed by the hypocrisy of claiming to have been enslaved by the British while allowing enslavement of blacks. The framers' embarrassment is reflected in their language. The three provisions reinforcing slavery never mention "slavery" or "slaves"; one gingerly refers to "free persons" and "other persons."

The unwillingness to tackle the slavery issue more directly has been called the "Greatest Compromise" by one political scientist.[18] But an attempt to abolish slavery would have caused the five southern states to refuse to ratify the Constitution.

TRADE AND TAXATION Slavery also underlay a compromise on trade and taxation. With a manufacturing economy, northerners sought protection for their businesses. In particular, they wanted a tax on manufactured goods imported from Britain. Without a tax, these goods would be cheaper than northern goods; but with a tax, northern goods would be more competitive—and prices for southern consumers more expensive. With an agricultural economy, southerners sought free trade for their plantations.

THE FOUNDERS AND THE PEOPLE

Democracy is "the worst of all political evils."
—Elbridge Gerry

"[T]he people have ever been and ever will be unfit to retain the exercise of power in their own hands."
—William Livingston

"[T]he people [should] have as little to do as may be about the government."
—Roger Sherman

"Notwithstanding the oppression and injustice experienced among us from democracy, the genius of the people is in favor of it, and the genius of the people must be consulted."
—George Mason

"It seems indispensable that the mass of citizens should not be without a voice in making the laws which they are to obey, in choosing the magistrates who are to administer them."
—James Madison

In part these statements reflect the Founders' support for republicanism and opposition to democracy, as they defined the terms. But in a more general sense, these statements reflect the Founders' ambivalence about "the people." Rationally, they believed in popular sovereignty, but emotionally they feared it. Perhaps no statement illustrates this ambivalence more than the one by New England clergyman Jeremy Belknap: "Let it stand as a principle that government originates from the people; but let the people be taught . . . that they are not able to govern themselves."

SOURCE: Richard Hofstadter, *The American Political Tradition and the Men Who Made It* (New York: Vintage, 1948), pp. 3–17.

They wanted a guarantee that there would be no tax on agricultural products exported to Britain. Such a tax would make their products less competitive abroad and, they worried, amount to an indirect tax on slavery—the labor responsible for the products. The delegates compromised by allowing Congress to tax imported goods but not exported ones. Tariffs on imported goods would become a point of controversy between the North and South in the years leading up to the Civil War.

With all issues resolved, a committee was appointed to write the final draft. Gouverneur Morris was the member of the committee most responsible for the polished style of the document. He was also largely responsible for the stirring preamble. In earlier drafts the preamble had not referred to "the people" but had listed the states. Morris's change signaled a shift in emphasis from the states to the people directly.

After 17 weeks of debate, the Constitution was ready. On September 17, 1787, 39 of the original 55 delegates signed it. Some delegates had left when they saw the direction the convention was taking, and 3 others refused to sign, feeling that the Constitution gave too much authority to the national government. Most of the rest were not entirely happy with the result—even Madison, who was most responsible for the content of the document, was despondent that his plan for a national legislature was compromised by having one house with representation by states—but they thought it was the best they could do. Benjamin Franklin had some qualms, but he was more optimistic. Referring to the sun painted on the back of George Washington's chair, he remarked that throughout the proceedings he had wondered whether it was a rising or a setting sun. "But now . . . I have the happiness to know that it is a rising and not a setting sun."

Features of the Constitution

William Gladstone, a British prime minister in the nineteenth century, said the American Constitution was "the most wonderful work ever struck off at a given time by the brain and purpose of man."[19] To see why it was unique, it is necessary to examine its major features.

A WRITTEN CONSTITUTION

The Founders established the idea of a written constitution, first in the Articles of Confederation and then more prominently in the Constitution itself. Other Western countries had constitutions that served as their supreme law, but these constitutions were not written or, if written, not as a single document. For example, the British constitution, which consisted of various customs, declarations, acts of Parliament, and precedents of courts, was partly unwritten and partly written. To Americans this was no constitution at all. They felt that a constitution should be a fundamental law above all other laws—not a mixture of customs and laws.

This belief is reflected in Americans' use of social contract theory. A **social contract,** not a literal contract like a business contract, is an implied agreement between the people and their government. The people give up part of their liberty to the government, which in exchange protects the remainder of their liberty. The Mayflower Compact was a very general form of social contract, whereas the written Constitution, stipulating the powers and limits of government, was a more specific form of social contract.

A REPUBLIC

The Founders distinguished between a democracy and a republic. For them a "democracy" meant a **direct democracy,** which permits citizens to vote on most issues; and a "republic" meant an **indirect democracy,** which allows citizens to vote for their representatives who make governmental policies.

The Founders opposed a direct democracy for the whole country. Many individual towns in New England had a direct democracy (and some still do), but these communities were small and manageable. Some city-states of ancient Greece and medieval Europe had a direct democracy, but they could not sustain it. The Founders thought a large country would have even less ability to do so because people could not be brought together in one place in order to act. The Founders also believed human nature was such that people could not withstand the passions of the moment and would be swayed by a demagogue to take unwise action. Eventually, democracy would collapse into tyranny. "Remember," John Adams wrote, "democracy never lasts long. It soon wastes, exhausts, and murders itself. There never was a democracy yet that did not commit suicide."[20]

The Founders favored an indirect democracy—a republic—because they firmly believed the people should have some voice in government for it to be based on the consent of the governed. So the Founders provided that the people could elect representatives to the House and that the state legislators, themselves elected by the people, could select senators and members of the Electoral College, who would choose the president. In this way the people would have a voice but one filtered through their presumably wiser representatives.

The Founders considered a democracy radical and a republic only slightly less radical. Because they believed the country could not maintain a democracy, they worried that it might not be able to maintain a republic either. When the Constitutional Convention closed, Benjamin Franklin was approached by a woman who asked, "Well, Doctor, what have we got, a republic or a monarchy?" Franklin responded, "A republic, madam, if you can keep it."

FRAGMENTATION OF POWER

Other countries assumed that government must have a concentration of power to be strong enough to govern. However, when the Founders made our national government more powerful than it had been under the Articles, they feared they also had made it more capable of oppression, and therefore they fragmented its power.

The Founders believed people were selfish, coveting more and more property, and that leaders lusted after more and more power. They assumed such human nature was unchangeable. Madison speculated, "If men were angels, no government would be necessary." But, alas, Madison said, men are not angels. Therefore, "In framing a government which is to be administered by men over men, the great difficulty lies in this: you must first enable the government to control the governed; and in the next place oblige it to control itself."[21] The Founders decided the way to oblige government to control itself was to structure it to prevent any one leader, group of leaders, or factions of people from exercising power over more than a small part of it. Thus, the Founders fragmented government's power. This is reflected in three concepts they built into the structure of government—federalism, separation of powers, and checks and balances.

FEDERALISM The first division of power was between the national government and the state governments. This division of power is called **federalism.** Foreign governments had been "unitary"; that is, the central government wielded all authority. At the other extreme, the U.S. government under the Articles had been "confederal," which meant that although there was some division of power, the state governments wielded almost all authority. The Founders wanted a strong national government, but they also wanted, or at least realized they would have to accept, reasonably strong state governments as well. They invented a federal system as a compromise between the unitary and confederal systems. (Chapter 3 explains these types of government further.)

Branch:	Legislative Congress		Executive Presidency	Judicial Federal Courts
	House	Senate	President	Judges
Officials chosen by:	People	People, (originally, state legislatures)	Electoral College, whose members are chosen by the people (originally, by state legislatures)	President, with advice and consent of Senate
For term of:	2 years	6 years	4 years	Life
To represent primarily:	Common people Large states	Wealthy people Small states	All people	Constitution

FIGURE 1

Separation of Powers

Separation of powers, as envisioned by the Founders, means not only that government functions are to be performed by different branches, but also that officials of these branches are to be chosen by different people, for different terms, and to represent different constituencies.

SEPARATION OF POWERS The second division of power was within the national government. The power to make, administer, and judge the laws was split into three branches—legislative, executive, and judicial (see Figure 1). In the legislative branch, the power was split further into two houses. This **separation of powers** contrasts with the British parliamentary system in which the legislature, Parliament, is supreme. Both executive and judicial officials are drawn from it and responsible to it. Madison expressed the American view of such an arrangement when he said that "the accumulation of all powers, legislative, executive, and judiciary, in the same hands . . . may justly be pronounced the very definition of tyranny."[22]

To reinforce the separation of powers, officials of the three branches were chosen by different means. Representatives were elected by the people (at that time mostly white men who owned property), senators were selected by the state legislatures, and the president was selected by the Electoral College, whose members were selected by the states. Only federal judges were chosen by officials in the other branches. They were nominated by the president and confirmed by the Senate. Once appointed, however, they were allowed to serve for "good behavior"—essentially life—so they had much independence. (Since the Constitution was written, the Seventeenth Amendment has provided for election of senators by the people, and the state legislatures have provided for election of members of the Electoral College by the people.)

Officials of the branches were also chosen at different times. Representatives were given a two-year term, senators a six-year term (with one-third of them up for reelection every two years), and the president a four-year term. These staggered terms would make it less likely that temporary passions in society would bring about a massive switch of officials or policies.

The Senate was designed to act as a conservative brake on the House, due to senators' selection by state legislatures and their longer terms. After returning from France, Thomas Jefferson met with George Washington over breakfast. Jefferson protested the establishment of a legislature with two houses. Washington supposedly asked, "Why did you pour that coffee into your saucer?" "To cool it," Jefferson replied. Similarly, Washington explained, "We pour legislation into the senatorial saucer to cool it."[23]

CHECKS AND BALANCES To guarantee separation of powers, the Founders built in overlapping powers called **checks and balances** (see Figure 2). Madison suggested that "the great security against a gradual concentration of the several powers in the same department consists in giving those who administer each department the necessary constitutional means and personal motives to resist encroachments by the others. . . . *Ambition must be made to counteract ambition*."[24] To that end, each branch was given some authority over the others. If one branch abused its power, the others could use their checks to thwart it.

Thus, rather than a simple system of separation of powers, ours is a complex, even contradictory, system of both separation of powers and checks and balances. The principle of separation of powers gives each branch its own sphere of authority, but the system of checks and balances allows each

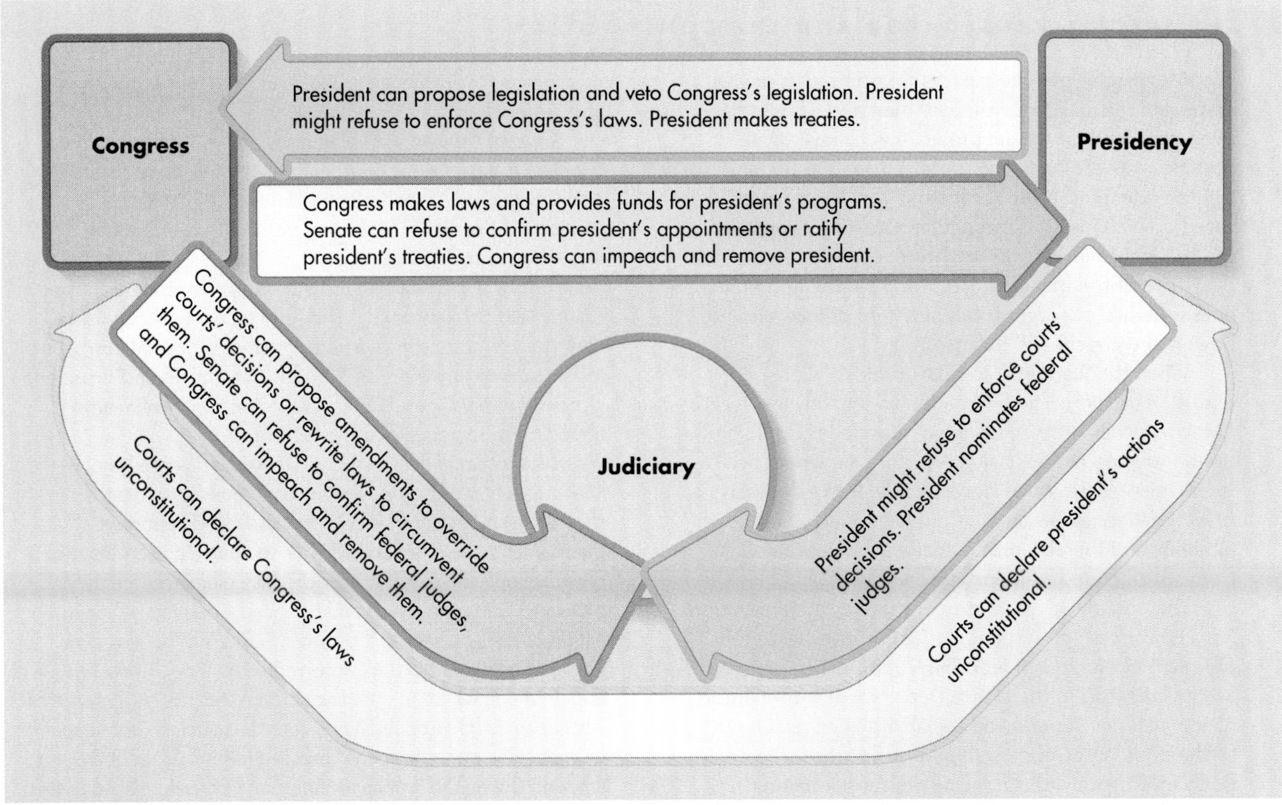

FIGURE 2

Checks and Balances

Most of the major checks and balances between the three branches are explicit in the Constitution, though some are not. For example, the courts' power to declare congressional laws or presidential actions unconstitutional—their power of "judicial review"—is not mentioned. And the president's power to refuse to enforce congressional laws or judicial decisions is not mentioned or even implied. In fact, it contradicts the Constitution, but sometimes it is asserted by the president nonetheless.

branch to intrude into the other branches' spheres. For example, because of separation of powers, Congress makes the laws, but due to checks and balances, the president can veto them and the courts can rule them unconstitutional. In these ways all three branches are involved in legislating. One political scientist calls ours "a government of separated institutions sharing powers."[25]

With federalism, separation of powers, and checks and balances, the Founders expected conflict. They invited the parts of government to struggle against each other in order to limit each other's ability to dominate all. At the same time, the Founders hoped for "balanced government." The national and state governments would represent different interests, and the branches within the national government would represent different interests. The House would represent the "common" people and the large states; the Senate, the wealthy people and the small states; the president, all the people; and the Supreme Court, the Constitution. The parts of government would have to compromise to get anything accomplished. Although each part would struggle for more power, it could not accumulate enough to dominate the others. Eventually, its leaders would have to compromise and adopt policies in the interest of all of the parts and their constituencies. Paradoxically, then, the Founders expected narrow conflict to produce broader harmony.

Motives of the Founders

To understand the Constitution better, it is useful to consider the motives of the Founders. Were they selfless patriots, sharing their wisdom and experience? Or were they selfish property owners, protecting their interests? To answer these questions it is necessary to look at the philosophical ideas, political experience, and economic interests that influenced these men.

PHILOSOPHICAL IDEAS

The Founders were exceptionally well educated intellectuals who incorporated philosophical ideas into the Constitution. At a time when the average

THE SPECIAL PROSECUTOR AND THE CONSTITUTION

The first **special prosecutor** was appointed during the Watergate scandal. Since then 20 men and women have been appointed as special prosecutors to investigate possible wrongdoing in the Carter, Reagan, Bush, and Clinton administrations.[1] Seven of them have investigated officials in the Clinton administration, including the president himself and the First Lady as well. How did the office of the special prosecutor develop, and how does it fit into our constitutional system of separation of powers and checks and balances?

When the Watergate scandal unfolded, Congress distrusted the Nixon administration to properly investigate its own officials. Instead, Congress pressured the administration to appoint a special prosecutor who would be independent of the White House and the Justice Department. After the Watergate scandal, Congress passed a law to establish, and thereby institutionalize, this position. (Later, Congress amended and renewed the law.)

The underlying assumption is that any administration has a conflict of interest if it is asked to investigate the president or his close aides or high appointees, because any investigators in the Justice Department would report to the attorney general and the attorney general reports to the president. Congress sought prosecutors who could freely investigate without facing pressure or fearing retribution from the administration.

The law locates the office of the special prosecutor, now officially called the **independent counsel,** outside the executive branch, and the law grants the office much independence, not only from the executive branch but also from the legislative and judicial branches. As a result, this unusual law fits awkwardly into our constitutional system. In some ways it defies both separation of powers and checks and balances.

When sufficient evidence of wrongdoing is presented to the attorney general, she is required to call for an independent counsel.[2] Then a panel of three judges, appointed by the chief justice of the Supreme Court, appoints a lawyer to serve as the independent counsel. Then the counsel, with a large budget to hire other lawyers and staffers, conducts an investigation of the official(s) suspected of wrongdoing. The counsel can be removed only by the attorney general and only for "good cause," which includes such things as corruption, misconduct, or physical or mental impairment.

The first investigations under this new law focused on minor matters—for example, whether Carter's chief of staff used cocaine at a New York disco—and although they uncovered some evidence of crimes, most did not lead to indictments for crimes. However, the investigation of the Iran-contra affair (covered in Chapter 11) spotlighted major accusations—whether Reagan's aides violated congressional policies and undermined Congress's role in our government—and did result in numerous charges and convictions.

One of Reagan's officials under investigation claimed that the independent counsel law violated the constitutional principle of separation of powers by shifting a traditional executive function—prosecution—from the executive branch to the special prosecutor, who is independent of the executive branch. However, the Supreme Court held the law valid.[3] The justices, while recognizing that the law was a departure from the traditional concept of separation of powers, emphasized that it reflected sufficient checks and balances.[4] Only Justice Antonin Scalia, who advocates a strong executive, dissented.

Now other justices might wish they had dissented also. In the 1990s, special prosecutors have become more aggressive than in the 1980s, and recent investigations have raised important questions: Do these prosecutors have too much power? Do they take too long and spend too much? And, ultimately, are they subject to adequate checks and balances? Consider the investigation of Henry Cisneros, the former secretary of housing and urban development in the Clinton administration. Before his appointment, when he was mayor of San Antonio, he had an affair while married. He stopped it and confessed publicly. But he sent his ex-mistress "support payments" and lied to his wife about the amount. During the routine investigation of presidential nominees for administrative positions, he stupidly cited the same figure to the FBI. When the FBI detected the discrepancy, the agency was furious and demanded a special prosecutor. The attorney general felt obligated, under the law, to call for one. As of mid-1998, the investigation had lasted more than four years and cost taxpayers about $4 million, and Cisneros, who left government for a higher-paying job to finance his defense, had been indicted for perjury.

The **Whitewater investigation** of the Clintons and some of their former associates has also raised questions about the power of the special prosecutor. The investigation was supposed to focus on a land deal that lost money in Arkansas 15 years earlier. Although the investigation netted some convictions—against a former governor of Arkansas, a former law partner of Hillary Clinton, and two former investment partners of Bill and Hillary Clinton—it did not yield serious charges against the Clintons themselves. But when a secretary turned over her surreptitious tape recordings of telephone conversations with a White House intern whom the secretary had befriended, the examination of the Clintons' property investments broadened to scrutiny of the president's sex life.[5]

The independent counsel, Kenneth Starr, has pursued the Clintons, in the eyes of one observer, "with a ferocity rarely seen outside the Discovery Channel."[6] Starr subpoenaed women who were rumored to have had affairs with the president, as well as underlings in the White House, such as stewards and valets, who might have seen the president and some woman. Starr put tremendous pressure on the intern, Monica Lewinsky, detaining her without a lawyer and threatening her with prosecution for perjury. Starr even subpoenaed Lewinsky's mother, requiring her to testify before a grand jury about her daughter's sex life and Lewinsky's book-buying records from Washington bookstores. When criticism of his office appeared in the media, he subpoenaed a White House communications aide, demanding that the aide reveal his contacts in the media. Although Starr, who has extensive ties to the right wing of the Republican Party, was within his authority under the law when he broadened the investigation and employed at least most, and perhaps all, of these high-pressure tactics, his conduct has prompted people to wonder whether he is simply "a conscientious prosecutor or a political hit man."[7]

Although Starr's motives might be above reproach, his actions show how powerful his office has become. Not only do prosecutors have much independence, but they have considerable discretion to broaden their investigation, and they have nearly unlimited time and unlimited budgets. The Whitewater investigation, as of late 1998, had lasted over five years and cost $35 million—a sum greater than the entire budget for the police force of the District of Columbia in a year.[8] (Part of the delay has been due to stalling by the White House.) An investigation of Samuel Pierce, the secretary of housing and urban development in the Reagan administration, began in 1988 and was still continuing in 1998. The investigation of the Iran-contra affair cost $48 million by the time it concluded.

With the expectations that surround special prosecutors, and with the power and resources granted them, they no doubt feel that they have to do enough to justify all the time and money spent. They may well feel pressure to pin charges on their targets, even if the wrongdoing is so minor that most local prosecutors would dismiss such cases rather than push them through the criminal justice system.

So should the office of the independent counsel still be considered constitutional? Remember, the Founders believed that ambitious officials would seek excessive power and could be controlled only by the system of separation of powers and checks and balances. Should we applaud the development of the independent counsel, because the office serves as a check and balance against the executive branch? Or should we abhor it, because the office gives tremendous power to one individual who operates largely outside the three branches and is subject to relatively few restraints by the three branches?[9]

The Independent Counsel Act expires in 1999. It could be renewed, amended, or allowed to die. Members of Congress will decide after weighing their partisan feelings and their principled conclusions about the law. So far both parties have been more partisan than principled in this debate. In the 1980s Republicans objected to the power of the office when special prosecutors were investigating officials in the Reagan and Bush administrations, but Republicans were a minority in Congress then. In the 1990s Democrats have objected to the power of the office, but they are a minority in Congress now. In these two decades, the dominant party in Congress has been willing to overlook the power—and even the occasional abuses—of some special prosecutors because the investigations have embarrassed the other party's officials in the executive branch.

If the law is allowed to die, the attorney general could still appoint a special prosecutor, as attorney generals did during Watergate and once in the early 1990s when the law had lapsed. The attorney general would face pressure to appoint a special prosecutor whenever Congress considered the alleged wrongdoing serious enough. Yet the attorney general would not be required to call for one every time there was evidence of wrongdoing. Without the law, then, there would be fewer special prosecutors.

1. "Special Prosecutor Investigations," *National Journal,* February 1, 1997, p. 218. For a review and an assessment of the early investigations, see Katy J. Harriger, *Independent Justice* (Lawrence, Kan.: University Press of Kansas, 1992).

2. The attorney general has some limited discretion to decide whether the evidence is "specific" and "credible" and to determine the scope of the investigation. But our criminal laws are so broad that it is very difficult to limit the scope of the investigation.

3. *Morrison v. Olson,* 487 U.S. 654 (1988).

4. The Court also observed that the law did not reflect an effort by Congress to grab executive power for itself.

5. Initially, the prosecutor justified linking these two disparate strands by saying the president might have told the women facts pertaining to the land deal. Later, he justified his examination by saying that Vernon Jordan, a presidential confidante, might have "bought" the silence of the former law partner of Hillary Clinton (by steering clients to his law practice), and that Jordan might also have "bought" the silence of the intern (by trying to find her a job). It would be illegal if Jordan made such efforts in exchange for their silence.

6. Richard Cohen, cited on the *Washington Post* Web site, February 26, 1998.

7. Richard Lacayo and Adam Cohen, "Inside Starr and His Operation," *Time,* February 9, 1998, p. 43. For a summary of his ties, see Jane Mayer, "How Independent Is the Counsel?" *The New Yorker,* April 22, 1996, p. 56.

8. "Numbers," *Time,* February 2, 1998, p. 17.

9. There are some checks on paper, but so far these have not been significant in practice. Congress appropriates money for the investigation, and it can exercise oversight of the investigation, as it can over the operations of other agencies. The judges who appointed the counsel conduct audits to determine if the money has been spent properly, and they officially terminate the investigation when they conclude that it is completed.

"Sorry we're late, but Kenneth Starr subpoenaed our regular babysitter."

person did not dream of going to college, a majority of the Founders graduated from college. As learned men, they shared a common library of writers and philosophers.

The framers of the Constitution reflected the ideals of the Enlightenment, a pattern of thought emphasizing the use of reason, rather than tradition or religion, to solve problems; they studied past governments to determine why they had failed in the hope they could apply these lessons to the present.

From all accounts the framers engaged in a level of debate at the convention that was rare in politics, citing philosophers ranging from the ancient Greeks to the modern British and French. Even when they did not mention them explicitly, their comments seemed to reflect the writings of particular philosophers.

The views of John Locke, a seventeenth-century English philosopher, underlay many of the ideas of the Founders. In fact, his views permeate the Declaration of Independence and Constitution more than those of any other single person.

Locke, like some previous philosophers, believed people had **natural rights.** These rights were inherent; they existed from the moment people were born. And they were inalienable; they were given by God so they could not be taken away. One of the most important was the right to property. When people worked the land, clearing it and planting it, they mixed their labor with it. This act, according to Locke, made the land their property. Some people, due to more work or better luck, would accumulate more property than others. Thus, the right to property would result in inequality of wealth. Yet he thought it would lead to greater productivity for society. This view of property appealed to Americans who saw an abundance of land in the new country.

Locke wrote that people came together to form government through a social contract that established a **limited government,** strong enough to protect their rights but not too strong to threaten these rights. This government should not act without the consent of the governed. To make its decisions, this government should follow majority rule. (Locke never resolved the conflict between majority rule and natural rights—that is, between majority rule and minority rights for those who disagree with the majority.)

The views of Charles de Montesquieu, an eighteenth-century French philosopher, also influenced the debate at the convention and the provisions of the Constitution itself. Others had suggested separation of powers before, but Montesquieu refined the concept and added that of checks and balances. The Founders, referring to him as "the celebrated Montesquieu," cited him more than any other thinker.[26] (Presumably, they cited him more than Locke because by this time Locke's views had so permeated American society that the Founders considered them just "common sense.")[27]

The principles of the system of mechanics formulated by Isaac Newton, a British mathematician of the late seventeenth and early eighteenth century, also pervaded the provisions of the Constitution. As Newton viewed nature as a machine, so the Founders saw the constitutional structure as a machine, with different parts having different functions and balancing each other. Newton's principle of action and reaction is manifested in the Founders' system of checks and balances. Both the natural environment and the constitutional structure were viewed as self-regulating systems.[28]

POLITICAL EXPERIENCE

Although the Founders were intellectuals, they were also practical politicians. According to one interpretation, they were "first and foremost superb democratic politicians" and the convention was "a nationalist reform caucus which had to operate with great delicacy and skill in a political cosmos full of enemies."[29]

The Founders brought extensive political experience to the convention: 8 had signed the Declaration of Independence; 39 had served in Congress; 7 had been governors; many had held other state offices; some had helped write their state constitutions. The framers drew upon this experience. For example, while they cited Montesquieu in discussing separation of powers, they also referred to the experience of colonial and state governments that already had some separation of powers.

As practical politicians, "no matter what their private dreams might be, they had to take home an acceptable package and defend it—and their own political futures—against predictable attack."[30] So they compromised the difficult issues and ducked the stickiest ones. Ultimately, they pieced together a Constitution that allowed each delegate to go home and announce that his state had won something.

ECONOMIC INTERESTS

Historian Charles Beard sparked a lively debate when he published *An Economic Interpretation of the Constitution* in 1913.[31] Beard argued that those with money and investments in manufacturing and shipping dominated the Constitutional Convention and state ratification conventions and that they produced a document that would increase their wealth. (After Beard published his conclusions, an Ohio newspaper proclaimed, "Scavengers, hyena-like, desecrate the graves of the dead patriots we revere.")[32] Later scholars questioned Beard's facts and interpretations, pointing out that support for the Constitution was not based strictly on wealth.[33]

Although some of Beard's specific points do not hold up, his underlying position that the Founders represented an elite that sought to protect its property from the masses seems more valid. The delegates to the Constitutional Convention were an elite. They included prosperous planters, manufacturers, shippers, and lawyers. About one-third were slaveowners. Most came from families of prominence and married into other families of prominence. Not all were wealthy, but most were at least well-to-do. Only one, a delegate from Georgia, was a yeoman farmer like most men in the country. In short, "this was a convention of the well-bred, the well-fed, the well-read, and the well-wed."[34]

The Founders supported the right to property. The promise of land and perhaps riches enticed most immigrants to come to America.[35] A desire for freedom from arbitrary taxes and trade restrictions spurred some colonists to fight in the Revolution.[36] And the inability of the government under the Articles to provide a healthy economy prompted the Founders to convene the Constitutional Convention. They probably agreed with Madison that "the first object of government" is to protect property.[37]

The Founders' emphasis on property was not as elitist as it might seem, however. Land was plentiful

CONSTITUTIONAL PROVISIONS PROTECTING PROPERTY

Numerous constitutional provisions, some obvious and others not, were designed to protect property:

"The Times, Places and Manner of holding Elections for Senators and Representatives, shall be prescribed in each State by the Legislature thereof."	Allows state to set property qualifications to vote.
"The Congress shall have Power . . . To coin Money."	Centralizes currency.
"No State shall . . . emit bills of credit."	Prevents states from printing paper money.
"Congress shall have Power . . . To establish uniform Laws on the subject of Bankruptcies."	Allows Congress to prevent states from relieving debtors of obligation to pay.
"No State shall . . . pass any . . . Law impairing the Obligation of Contracts."	Prevents states from relieving debtors of obligation to pay.
"The United States shall guarantee to every State [protection] against domestic Violence."	Protects states from debtor uprisings.
"Congress shall have Power . . . To provide for calling forth the Militia to execute the Laws of the Union, suppress insurrections."	Protects creditors from debtor uprisings.

AMERICAN DIVERSITY

DID THE IROQUOIS INFLUENCE THE FOUNDERS?

For many years popular writers portrayed Native Americans as simple savages. To some they were "bloodthirsty savages." To others they were "noble savages." But to almost all writers, Indians were so preoccupied by surviving that they had little time for anything but hunting and fighting. Yet these Native Americans had far more sophisticated societies than most writers, until recently, gave them credit for.

Although most Americans are aware that the colonists adopted the tactics of Indian warfare—the forerunner of modern guerrilla warfare—to defeat the British in the Revolutionary War, few Americans realize that the colonists mirrored several other Indian practices in founding the country. In fact, the colonists used some concepts similar to those of the Iroquois in the Declaration of Independence, Articles of Confederation, and Constitution.

The Iroquois, who inhabited what is now New York State, included the Cayugas, Mohawks, Oneidas, Onondagas, and Senecas. (After the early 1700s they also included the Tuscaroras, who migrated from the Carolinas.) After generations of bloody warfare, the "Five Nations" formed the **Iroquois Confederacy** sometime between 1000 and 1450, according to various estimates.[1]

IROQUOIS GOVERNMENT

The Confederacy adopted a constitution called the "Great Law of Peace." Although some provisions were not written, others were recorded on "wampum belts," constructed of shells sewn in intricate patterns on hides. Few white Americans realized that the Iroquois constitution was partly written until it was transcribed into English in the late nineteenth century.

The Great Law provided for a union with federalism, checks and balances, restrictions on the power of the leaders, opportunities for participation by the people, and some natural rights and equality for the people.

Federalism was most apparent. Each of the Five Nations was essentially a state within a state. Each was allowed to govern its internal affairs. (Even non-Iroquois nations conquered by the Iroquois were allowed to keep their form of government as long as they did not make war on other nations.)

Checks and balances were incorporated in several ways. The Confederacy established a system of clans that overlapped the boundaries of the nations. Members of clans were considered relatives despite living in different nations. Thus, the system of clans was designed to operate like the system of checks and balances in the U.S. Constitution: Where checks and balances were intended to prevent the dominance of one branch of government, or one faction that got control of a branch of government, clans were intended to prevent the dominance of one nation in the Confederacy.

The Confederacy used governing procedures that also entailed checks and balances. The "older brothers — Mohawks and Senecas—were on "one side of the house." The "younger brothers"—Cayugas and Oneidas—were on the "opposite side of the house." The "firekeepers"—Onondagas—would break the tie if the two sides disagreed. If the two sides agreed, the "firekeepers" could veto the measure, but then the two sides could override the veto. Thus, the governing council was analogous to a two-house legislature and an executive with a limited veto.

The Great Law had elaborate provisions for the selection and obligations of the chiefs who sat on the governing council. Most chiefs were selected by women from extended families that had hereditary power. Thus, these women were permitted to participate in making these important political decisions, although they themselves were not permitted to serve on the council.

The chiefs were obligated to communicate with the people—send messages to them and consider requests from them. The chiefs were expected to tolerate anger and criticism by the people and to reflect "endless patience" and "calm deliberation." The chiefs were to be the people's servants rather than their masters. As such, they were not supposed to accumulate more wealth than the people. (In fact, there was some pressure to give away their material possessions, so they would be poorer than the people.) If the chiefs failed to follow these rules, they could be recalled or impeached.

and, with westward expansion, even more would be available. Already most men were middle-class farmers who owned some property. Many who owned no property could foresee the day when they would, so most Americans wanted to protect property.

The Founders diverged from the farmers in their desire to protect other property in addition to land, such as wealth and credit. Of the 55 delegates, 40 were owners of government bonds that had depreciated under the Articles, and 24 were moneylenders.[38] So the delegates included provisions to protect commerce, including imports and exports, contracts, and debts, and provisions to regulate currency, bankruptcy, and taxes (see the box, "Constitutional Provisions Protecting Property").

Political scientists and historians disagree about which of these three influences on the Founders—philosophical, political, or economic—was most important. Actually, the influences are difficult to separate because they reinforce each other; the framers' ideas point to the same sort of constitution

The Great Law also provided for some natural rights and equality. There was significant separation of church and state. There was no state religion, and the duties of the civil chiefs were distinct from those of the religious leaders. The Great Law upheld freedom of expression in religious and political matters, and it reflected tolerance of different races and national origins. For example, its adoption rules included no restrictions on the basis of race or national origin. Even some Anglo-Americans received full citizenship in the Confederacy.

Thus, in various ways the Iroquois government, unlike the Indian civilizations in Central and South America, reflected characteristics we consider democratic.[2] As one historian concluded, "all these things were part of the American way of life before Columbus landed."[3]

IROQUOIS INFLUENCE ON AMERICAN GOVERNMENT?

In colonial times the Iroquois occupied land between the English on the Atlantic coast and the French in what is now southern Canada. The Iroquois controlled the only level mountain pass and the best communication and trade route between the English and the French. The Iroquois were the balance of power between these settlers, whose nations were at war with each other.

Britain tried to forge an alliance with the Iroquois. Colonial envoys and Indian chiefs held treaty councils to establish the alliance. As early as 1744 one chief, Canassatego, advised the colonies to unite, as the Iroquois had, for the colonists' protection (and for the Indians' convenience—to reduce the confusion of dealing with separate colonies). Benjamin Franklin, who served as an envoy and as the printer of the proceedings of the councils, was fascinated by the Iroquois and seemed influenced by Canassatego's advice. He too urged the colonies to unite, and he proposed a plan very similar to the Iroquois Confederacy. But the plan was not adopted by the colonies, which fretted that it would deny their individual independence. It was not accepted by the Crown either, which feared that it would establish the colonies' joint independence from the mother country. The colonies would not unite until the Crown imposed the Stamp Act and other measures two decades later.

Many colonists were intrigued by Iroquois ways. Franklin found a market eager for his accounts of the treaty councils. He printed accounts of 13 councils in 26 years. An official in New York's colonial government published a systematic description of Iroquois government in 1727 and expanded it in 1747. Other officials asked the Iroquois for information about their confederacy's structure.

Over the years there was much intermingling between European and Native American cultures. (At least one colonial official was adopted by the Mohawks, and another was allowed to serve on their councils and even lead their war parties at times.) And some Founders admired certain Indian practices and ideas. Besides Franklin, Thomas Jefferson and Thomas Paine, for example, were attracted to the Iroquois' emphasis on natural rights and their restrictions on their leaders' power and wealth. Thus, "the American frontier became a laboratory for democracy precisely at a time when colonial leaders were searching for alternatives to what they regarded as European tyranny and class stratification."[4]

Historians debate whether the Iroquois actually influenced the Founders. The parallels between the Iroquois government and our Declaration of Independence, Articles of Confederation, and Constitution could be coincidental. Political ideas can take root in more than one society simultaneously. But the parallels are striking and the possibilities are intriguing. The roots of our political ideas might be more numerous and complex than we have assumed.[5]

SOURCE: Bruce E. Johansen, *Forgotten Founders* (Ipswich, Mass.: Gambit, 1982). Additional sources are cited, especially in Chapter 1.

1. Johansen, p. 22.
2. Johansen, pp. 17–18.
3. Felix Cohen, quoted in Johansen, p. 13.
4. Johansen, p. xv.
5. At least fragments of evidence suggest that Native Americans influenced European philosophers, such as Locke, Montesquieu, and Rousseau, who in turn influenced the colonists. Some Iroquois chiefs had been to Europe, and the Europeans were as intrigued by their ways as the colonists were. Johansen, pp. 14, 52.

that their political experience and economic interests do.[39]

Ratification of the Constitution

The Constitution specified that ratification would occur through conventions in the states and that the document would take effect with approval of conventions in 9 of the 13 states. The framers purposely did not provide for approval by the state legislatures because they feared that some legislatures would reject the Constitution because it reduced their power. Too, the framers wanted the broader base of support for the new government that ratification conventions would provide.

Technically, the procedures for ratification were illegal. According to the Articles of Confederation, which were still in effect, any changes had to be approved by all 13 states. However, the framers suspected that they would not find support in all states.

Indeed, ratification was uncertain. Many people opposed the Constitution, and there was a lively campaign against it in newspapers, pamphlets, and mass meetings. And although the procedures required ratification by only nine states, the framers realized they needed support from all of the largest states and much of the public to lend legitimacy to the new government.

Knowing opponents would charge them with setting up a national government to dominate the state governments, those who supported the Constitution ingeniously adopted the name **Federalists** to emphasize a real division of power between the national and state governments. They dubbed their opponents **Antifederalists** to imply that they did not want a division of power between the governments.

The Antifederalists faulted the Constitution for lacking a bill of rights. The Constitution did contain some protection for individual rights, such as the provision that the writ of habeas corpus, which protects against arbitrary arrest and detention, cannot be suspended except during rebellion or invasion, and the provision that a criminal defendant has a right to a jury trial. But the framers made no effort to include most of the rights people believed they had, because most states already had a bill of rights in their own constitutions. The framers also thought that by fragmenting power no branch could become strong enough to deny individual rights. Yet critics demanded provisions protecting various rights of criminal defendants and freedom of the press. In response, the Federalists promised to propose amendments guaranteeing these rights as soon as the government began.

The Antifederalists also criticized the Constitution for other reasons. Localists at heart, they were wary of entrusting power to officials far away; they correctly claimed that republics historically worked only in small geographical areas where the population was more homogeneous and the officials were closer to the people. They worried that the central government, to function effectively, would accumulate too much power and the presidency would become a monarchy or Congress an aristocracy. One delegate to the Massachusetts convention blasted the Federalists:

These lawyers, and men of learning and moneyed men, that talk so finely, and gloss over matters so smoothly, to make us poor illiterate people swallow down the pill, expect to get into Congress themselves; they expect to . . . get all the power and all the money into their own hands, and then they will swallow up all us little folks . . . just as the whale swallowed up Jonah![40]

But the Antifederalists had no alternative plan. They were divided; some wanted to amend the Articles, while others wanted to reject both the Articles and the Constitution in favor of some yet undetermined form of government. Their lack of unity on an alternative was instrumental in their inability to win support.[41]

"Religious freedom is my immediate goal, but my long range plan is to go into real estate."

Ratification was quick in some states, a bitter struggle in others. Within three months after the Constitutional Convention, Delaware became the first state to ratify, and six months later New Hampshire became the necessary ninth. The Constitution took effect and the new government began in 1788, with George Washington becoming president. Within one year, North Carolina and Rhode Island, both of which initially rejected the Constitution, became the last states to approve it.

Changing the Constitution

The framers expected their document to last; Madison wrote, "We have framed a constitution that will probably be still around when there are 196 million people."[42] Yet because the framers realized it would need some changes, they drafted a Constitution that can be changed either formally by constitutional amendment or informally by judicial interpretation or political practice. In doing so, they left a legacy for later governments. "The example of changing a Constitution, by assembling the wise men of the state, instead of assembling armies," Jefferson noted, "will be worth as much to the world as the former examples we had given them."[43]

THE FEDERALIST PAPERS

Out of the great debate over ratification came a series of essays considered the premier example of American political philosophy. Titled the ***Federalist Papers,*** these essays were written by Alexander Hamilton, James Madison, and John Jay. At the urging of Hamilton,[1] the authors wrote 85 essays that appeared in New York newspapers during the ratification debates there. The authors tried to convince delegates to the convention to vote for ratification.

In the fashion of the time, the papers were published anonymously—by "Publius" (Latin for "Public Man"). They were so unified in approach that few of the authors' contemporaries could discern their pens at work. Given the arguments and compromises at the Constitutional Convention, one political scientist speculated that the framers who read the essays "must have discovered with some surprise what a coherent and well-thought-out document they had prepared."[2]

Despite the unity of the papers, political scientists have identified the authors of individual ones. Hamilton wrote most of those describing the defects of the Articles, Madison most of those explaining the structure of the new government, including the famous #10 and #51 (reprinted at the back of this book). Before he became sick, Jay, who was secretary of foreign affairs, wrote a few concerning foreign policy.

Actually, there is little evidence that the essays swayed any of the delegates. Yet they have endured because readers see them as an original source of political thinking and as one of the best guides to the intentions of the framers. Judges rely upon them when they interpret various provisions of the Constitution.

1. Although Hamilton worried that the Constitution would not establish a strong enough government, he thought it was preferable to the Articles, which he despised.
2. John P. Roche, ed., *Origins of American Political Thought* (New York: Harper & Row, 1967), p. 163.

BY CONSTITUTIONAL AMENDMENT

That the Articles of Confederation could be amended only by a unanimous vote of the states posed an almost insurmountable barrier to any amendment at all. The framers of the Constitution made sure this experience would not repeat itself. Yet they did not make amendment easy; the procedures do not require unanimity, but they do require widespread agreement.

PROCEDURES The procedures for amendment entail action by both the national government and the state governments. Amendments can be proposed in either of two ways—by a two-thirds vote of both houses of Congress or by a national convention called by Congress at the request of two-thirds of the state legislatures. Congress then specifies which way amendments must be ratified—either by three-fourths of the state legislatures or by ratifying conventions in three-fourths of the states. Among these avenues, the usual route has been proposal by Congress and ratification by state legislatures (see Figure 3).

AMENDMENTS In the first Congress under the Constitution, the Federalists fulfilled their promise to support a bill of rights. Madison drafted the amendments, Congress proposed them, and the states ratified 10 of them in 1791. This **Bill of Rights** includes freedom of expression—speech, press, assembly, and religion (First Amendment). It also includes numerous rights for those accused of crimes—protection against unreasonable searches and seizures (Fourth), protection against compulsory self-incrimination (Fifth), guarantee of due process of law (Fifth), the right to counsel and a jury trial in criminal cases (Sixth), and protection against excessive bail and fines, and cruel and unusual punishment (Eighth). It also includes a jury trial in civil cases (Seventh).

In addition to these major rights, the Bill of Rights includes two amendments that grew out of the colonial experience with Great Britain—the right to bear arms for a militia (Second) and the right not to have soldiers quartered in homes during peacetime (Third). The Bill of Rights also includes two general amendments—a statement that the listing of these rights does not mean these are the only ones people have (Ninth) and a statement that the powers not given to the national government are reserved to the states (Tenth).

Among the other 17 amendments to the Constitution, the strongest theme is the expansion of citizenship rights:

- Abolition of slavery (Thirteenth, 1865)
- Equal protection, due process of law (Fourteenth, 1868)
- Right to vote for black men (Fifteenth, 1870)
- Direct election of senators (Seventeenth, 1913)
- Right to vote for women (Nineteenth, 1920)
- Right to vote in presidential elections for District of Columbia residents (Twenty-third, 1960)
- Abolition of poll tax in federal elections (Twenty-fourth, 1964)
- Right to vote for persons 18 and older (Twenty-sixth, 1971)

Another theme is the increase of federal power. Many amendments, notably those regarding voting, take authority away from the states and authorize Congress to enforce these rights by "appropriate legislation."

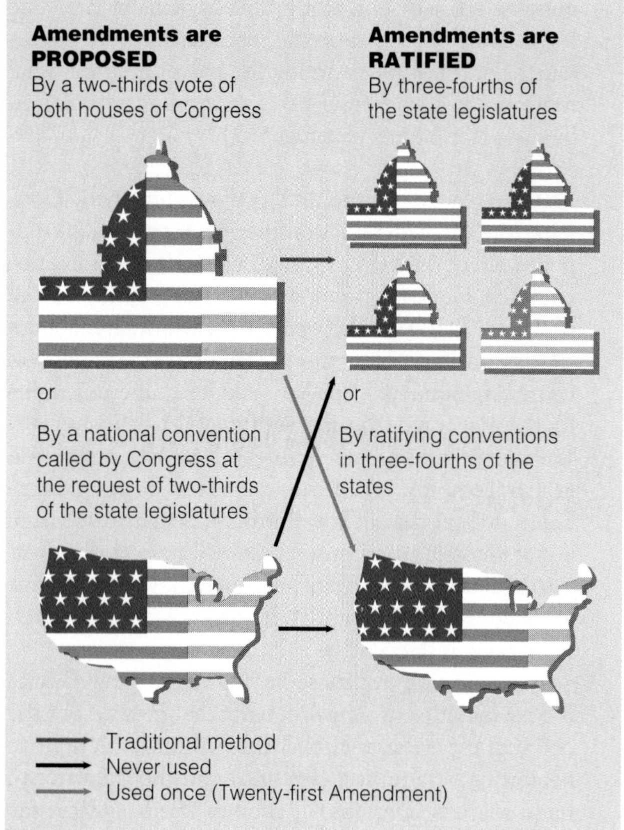
Amendments are PROPOSED
By a two-thirds vote of both houses of Congress
Amendments are RATIFIED
By three-fourths of the state legislatures
or
By a national convention called by Congress at the request of two-thirds of the state legislatures
or
By ratifying conventions in three-fourths of the states
Traditional method
Never used
Used once (Twenty-first Amendment)

FIGURE 3
Avenues for Constitutional Amendment

Most amendments proposed by Congress were ratified by the states, although some were not. Recently, two proposed amendments were not ratified. One would have provided equal rights for women (this amendment will be discussed in Chapter 15), and the other would have given congressional representation to the District of Columbia, as though it were a state.

These and other recent amendments have had time limits for ratification—usually seven years—set by Congress. But an amendment preventing members of Congress from giving themselves a midterm pay raise, written by Madison and passed by Congress in 1789, had no time limit. Once Michigan ratified it in 1992, it reached the three-fourths mark and became the Twenty-seventh Amendment.

Although the Constitution expressly provides for change by amendment, its ambiguity about some subjects and silence about others virtually guarantee change by interpretation and practice as well.

BY JUDICIAL INTERPRETATION

If there is disagreement about what the Constitution means, who is to interpret it? Although the Constitution does not say, the judicial branch has taken on this role. To decide disputes before them, the courts must determine what the relevant provisions of the Constitution mean. By saying the provisions mean one thing rather than another, the courts can, in effect, change the Constitution. Woodrow Wilson called the Supreme Court "a constitutional convention in continuous session." The Court has interpreted the Constitution in ways that to bring about the same results as new amendments. (Chapters 13, 14, and 15 provide many examples.)

BY POLITICAL PRACTICE

Political practice has accounted for some very important changes. These include the rise of political parties and the demise of the Electoral College as an independent body. They also include the development of the cabinet to advise the president and the development of the committee system to operate the two houses of Congress. (Chapters 6, 7, and 10 explain these changes.)

The Founders would be surprised to learn that only 17 amendments, aside from the Bill of Rights, have been adopted in about 200 years. In part this is due to their wisdom, but in part it is due to changes in judicial interpretation and political practice, which have combined to create a "living Constitution."

CONCLUSION: DOES THE CONSTITUTION ALLOW GOVERNMENT TO BE RESPONSIVE?

Soon after ratification, the Constitution became accepted by the people. It took on the aura of a secular Bible. People embraced it, consulted it for guidance, cited it for support, and debated the meaning of its provisions.

The Constitution has proved so popular that many countries have copied parts of it. Almost all of the nations in the world today have a constitution written as a single document. Many have provisions similar to those in our Constitution. The Kenyan constitution speaks of "freedom of expression," the Costa Rican gives the "right to petition," and the German says that "all persons shall be equal before the law." And officials and groups in eastern European countries, emerging from Communist governments, and South Africa, transforming its apartheid regime, considered provisions in our Constitution as they changed theirs.[44]

But the brevity of our Constitution remains unique; with just 89 sentences, it is far shorter than those of other nations. Because it is short, it is necessarily general; because it is general, it is necessarily ambiguous; because it is ambiguous, it is necessarily open to interpretation. This provides succeeding generations the opportunity to adapt the Constitution to changing times. The longer, more detailed, and less flexible constitutions of other nations become outdated and periodically need complete revision.

In 1987, our Constitution celebrated its bicentennial as the oldest written constitution in the world. During the same 200 years, France, for example, had 10 distinct constitutional orders, including five republics, two empires, one monarchy, one plebiscitary dictatorship, and one puppet dictatorship during World War II. During the past 66 years, Thailand has had 17 constitutions.[45]

Although our Constitution, and the institutions it established, have been responsive enough to survive, are they responsive enough to allow us to solve our problems? Can a constitution written by a small circle of men whose fastest mode of travel was horseback continue to serve masses of diverse people, some of whom have traveled by spaceship?

Intended to construct a government responsive to the masses of people to a limited extent, the Constitution set up a republic, which allowed the people to elect some representatives who would make their laws. This gave the people more say in government than people in other countries enjoyed at the time.

But the Constitution was intended to construct a government unresponsive to the masses of people to a large extent. It was expected to filter the public's passions and purify their selfish desires. Consequently, the Founders limited participation in government, allowing people to vote only for members of the House of Representatives—not for members of the Senate or the president.

Moreover, the Founders fragmented the power of government. Federalism, separation of powers, and checks and balances combine to make it difficult for any one group to capture all of government. Instead, one faction might control one branch, another faction another branch, and so on, with the result a standoff. Then the factions must compromise to accomplish anything.

Since the time of the founding, changes in the Constitution, whether by amendment, interpretation, or practice, have expanded opportunities for participation in government. But the changes have done little to modify the fragmentation of power, which remains the primary legacy of the Founders.

This structure has prevented many abuses of power, though it has not always worked. During the Vietnam War, for example, one branch—the presidency—exercised vast power while the others acquiesced. This structure also has provided the opportunity for one branch to pick up the slack when the others became sluggish. The overlapping of powers ensured by checks and balances allows every branch to act on virtually every issue it chooses to. In the 1950s, President Eisenhower and Congress were reluctant to push for civil rights for blacks, but the Supreme Court did so by declaring segregation unconstitutional in a series of cases.

But the system's very advantage has become its primary disadvantage. In their efforts to fragment power so that no branch could accumulate too much, the Founders divided power to the point where the branches sometimes cannot wield enough. In their efforts to build a government that requires a national majority to act, they built one that allows a small minority to block action. This problem has become increasingly acute as society has become increasingly complex. Like a mechanical device that operates only when all of its parts function in harmony, the system moves only when there is consensus or compromise. Consensus is rare in a large heterogeneous society; compromise is common, but it requires a long time as well as the realization by competing interests that they cannot achieve much of what they want without compromise. Even then, compromise often results in only a partial solution.

At best the system moves inefficiently and incrementally. At worst it moves hardly at all; the Constitution has established a government that is slow to respond to change. One political scientist characterizes it as a "negative, do-nothing system."[46] Although other political scientists consider this characterization an exaggeration, virtually all agree that the system is structured to preserve the status quo and to respond to the groups that want to maintain it.

Yet some political scientists believe the American people actually prefer this arrangement. Because the people are suspicious of government, they may be reluctant to let one party dominate it and use it to advance that party's policies. In surveys many people—a quarter to a third of those polled—say they think it is good for one party to control the presidency and the other to control Congress.[47] In presidential and congressional elections, more than a quarter of the voters split their ticket between the two major parties.[48] As a result, between 1968 and 1998 opposing parties controlled the executive and legislative branches for all but six years.

Although voters elected a Democratic president, Bill Clinton, and a Democratic Congress in 1992, they elected Republican majorities for both houses of Congress in the congressional elections in 1994, and they reelected the Democratic president and retained the Republican majorities for both houses of Congress in 1996. For this campaign both parties assumed that a bloc of swing voters preferred divided government. Clinton ran against the Republican Congress, especially against Speaker of the House Newt Gingrich (R-Ga.). Republican congressional candidates ran against the president, urging voters to reelect them so they could keep an eye on him. Both parties' strategies

SYMBOLIC SOLUTIONS FOR COMPLEX PROBLEMS?

MAKING ENGLISH THE OFFICIAL NATIONAL LANGUAGE

Some chapters have a box examining what we consider largely a symbolic solution for what is actually a complex problem. The proposal is symbolic in that it appears to address the problem, but because of the complexity of the problem, the solution is not likely to solve the problem or, possibly, even ameliorate it.

The symbolic solution tends to be a simple solution—we could title these boxes "Simple Solutions for Complex Problems?"—and a simple solution is not likely to solve a complex problem. (There might, of course, be exceptions, as there are to other generalizations.)

People tell pollsters they favor many of these ideas. But we want students to recognize that these ideas, so appealing at first glance, are more symbolic than substantive. We want students to recognize that politicians, political parties, and interest groups might urge adoption of these ideas because they are trying to rally people to their side for other reasons. They might see these ideas as ways to gain support in an election campaign or in a policy fight. At a time when national problems seem intractable, it is tempting for politicians to claim they can solve them, even if they cannot. And it is tempting for politicians to claim they can solve them quickly, as most of these proposals imply, even when they cannot. Or proponents might see these as ways to advance some hidden agenda. For example, before the 1994 elections many Republicans called for term limits for members of Congress partly because they saw term limits as a way to oust entrenched Democrats from Congress.

We believe that citizens should demand real solutions for real problems and should not allow themselves to be manipulated or appeased by proposals that merely pretend to address the problems. Symbolic actions can be useful, especially as protests in the early stages of controversies, but they must give way to substantive efforts if problems are to be resolved.

We do need to emphasize, however, that reasonable people can disagree and some readers might want to adopt these proposals even if they are largely symbolic. Other readers might want them for other reasons. We will elaborate in individual boxes.

In this chapter we focus on the proposal for a constitutional amendment making English the official national language. This proposal is a reaction to the influx of immigrants in recent decades. Their sheer numbers and their heavy concentration in a few areas of the country concern residents there. This proposal is also a reaction to bilingual education, in which students with a native language other than English are taught some material in their native language. (Bilingual education is covered in Chapter 15.). These developments, as well as provocative remarks by some leaders of ethnic groups, contribute to the perception of native-born Americans that many immigrants do not want to assimilate—to shed their foreign ways and adopt our "American ways." In their support for a constitutional amendment, some native-born Americans are sincerely worried, while others are simply annoyed by the inability of many immigrants to speak English.

Of course, the United States has had waves of immigrants before. However, most waves have not been as large and have not included as diverse a group of people as now. In the past, most immigrants were Europeans. Now, many are Latin Americans, many are Asians, and some are Middle Easterners as well. Los Angeles offers election ballots in Spanish, Chinese, Japanese, Vietnamese, Korean, and Tagalog. Its county courts provide interpreters for about 80 languages. (Even so, confusion occurs. A police officer testified that he had read a suspect his Miranda rights in the Taishan dialect of Chinese, but the judge discovered that the man understood only the Cantonese dialect, so he had to disregard the confession.)[1]

Groups like *U.S. English* and *English First* have sounded the alarm: "If this continues, the next American president could well be elected by people who can't read or speak English!" Almost half of the states have passed laws making English their official language, and some members of Congress have proposed a constitutional amendment for the entire country.

It is not clear what effect the amendment would have. Election ballots and other materials, such as Social Security applications, income tax forms, and Park Service pamphlets, now printed in various languages probably would be printed only in English, and bilingual education programs in public schools probably would be scaled back. The amendment would not restrict private, religious, or ceremonial use of foreign languages.

But no doubt there would be different interpretations of the amendment by different branches of the government in different parts of the country. When California made English its official language in the 1980s, one city council fired librarians for buying foreign language books and subscribing to foreign language magazines. In some cities teachers forbade students to speak foreign languages among themselves, and hospitals prohibited employees from speaking any

---

seemed to work, and the voters got divided government again.

Perhaps Americans, despite their demands for "change," actually are fearful of change. When the Democratic president and Congress called for significant reforms after the 1992 elections, citizens objected. Then, when the Republican congressional leaders called for significant reforms in the opposite direction after the 1994 elections, again citizens balked. Both times the parties assumed the people language but English. One official reprimanded a worker who spoke Spanish to a co-worker in the hallway, and another fired workers who spoke Filipino to patients who spoke that language.[2]

Despite uncertainty about the interpretation of an amendment, might one nonetheless prompt people who do not speak English to learn the language?

The underlying assumption is that immigrants are taking longer to learn English than in the past and that some are refusing to learn it at all. It is true that some immigrant communities are so large that people can survive without learning English. Some Mexican immigrants in parts of the Southwest and some Cuban immigrants in parts of Florida speak Spanish alone. Contrary to some perceptions, however, most immigrants feel pressure to learn English. It helps them land jobs and function in the broader society. Their children, who grow up and attend schools in this society, learn English, which puts more pressure on their parents.

A survey of Hispanics in 40 cities found that more than 90% thought U.S. citizens and residents should learn English.[3] A survey of Hispanics in south Florida found that 98% thought it was important for their children to read and write "perfect English."[4] And their children apparently agree. More than four-fifths of immigrant children in south Florida and more than two thirds of those in San Diego prefer English to their familial language.[5]

Another study of immigrants underscored the value they put on succeeding in school. These families are more likely to have rules about doing homework and maintaining grades (including rules limiting television) than they are to have requirements about performing household chores or part-time jobs.[6] Their efforts to succeed in school as a way to make it in society reflect similar efforts by past immigrants.

It should not be surprising, then, that current immigrants are mastering English. Of 17.3 million Spanish speakers in the United States, less than 10% do not speak English.[7] Cuban Americans are learning it as fast or faster than any previous group in history.[8] Mexican Americans are learning it as they stay longer in the United States. Although most of those who come for work and plan to return to Mexico do not speak English or do not speak it well, most of those who plan to remain in the United States learn to speak more English, and almost all of their children learn to speak fluent English.[9] Thus, the process takes time, but it does work.

Consequently, a constitutional amendment making English the official national language would be little more than a symbolic solution. Immigrants already are learning English.

Some advocates of an amendment acknowledge that it would be a symbol—a symbol of national unity at a time when there is more diversity than ever before. Thus, the debate is not just about prodding immigrants to learn English; it is also about persuading them to assimilate. Yet it is hard to see what an amendment would accomplish beyond what learning English and adapting to society already are accomplishing.

If the concern is that substantial immigration is not desirable, changing immigration laws would be a more direct solution. If the problem is that bilingual education is not successful, changing bilingual programs would be a more direct solution.

In fact, an amendment might be counterproductive. It could encourage more xenophobia—fear of foreigners—and more intolerance of diversity. It could result in more discrimination against even legal immigrants. Abolition of bilingual ballots might disfranchise some, and abolition of bilingual forms might make it difficult for some to receive government services for which they are eligible. An amendment could also restrict freedom of speech if it is interpreted to forbid government employees from speaking foreign languages in certain situations. Thus, Arizona's law was struck down as a violation of the First Amendment.

1. Otto Friedrich, "The Changing Face of America," *Time*, July 8, 1985, p. 29.
2. Eloise Salholz, "Say It in English," *Newsweek*, February 20, 1989, p. 23; Margaret Carlson, "Only English Spoken Here," *Time*, December 5, 1988, p. 29; Elaine Elinson, "On the Job, English Only Rules Are on the Rise," *Civil Liberties* (Fall 1990), p. 5.
3. Lynne Duke, "English Spoken Here," *Washington Post National Weekly Edition*, December 21–27, 1992, p. 37.
4. Salholz, "Say It in English," p. 23.
5. Joel Kotkin, "Can the Melting Pot Be Reheated?" *Washington Post National Weekly Edition*, July 11–17, 1994, p. 23.
6. Nathan Caplan, Marcella H. Choy, and John K. Whitmore, *Children of the Boat People: A Study of Educational Success* (Ann Arbor: University of Michigan Press, 1992).
7. 1990 Census of the Population, Social and Economic Characteristics, Part I, Table 13; Less than 5% of Asian-language speakers and less than 2% of other language speakers do not speak English.
8. Thomas Boswell and James Curtis, *The Cuban American Experience* (Totowa, N.J.: Rowman & Allanheld, 1983), p. 191.
9. Kevin F. McCarthy and R. Burciaga Valdez, *Current and Future Effects of Mexican Immigration in California—Executive Summary* (Santa Monica: Rand Corporation, 1985), p. 27.

wanted change—until it looked like the people would get it.

Although the voters might be more satisfied with the status quo than they admit to pollsters, the parties definitely are not satisfied with it. They are frustrated with many years of divided government and their inability to dislodge the other party from the other branch. As a result, they have fought for control of the third branch—the judiciary—by engaging in more fractious battles over presidential nominations to the Supreme Court and lower federal courts. Also, they have tried to tarnish their opponents by focusing more on scandals and conducting congressional investigations and criminal prosecutions—a process two political scientists have called "Revelation, Investigation, Prosecution" (R.I.P.).[49] Thus, a culture of scandal now supplements the usual cycle of elections in American politics.

EPILOGUE

The President Complies

Chief Justice Warren Burger announced the unanimous decision in the case of *United States v. Nixon:* The president must turn over the tapes.[50] The Court acknowledged the existence of executive privilege in general but rejected it in this situation because another court needed the information for an upcoming trial and because the information did not relate to national security.

The Court emphasized that courts would determine the legitimacy of claims of executive privilege, not presidents, as Nixon wanted. Because of separation of powers, Nixon argued, neither the judicial nor legislative branch should involve itself in this executive decision. However, this president, who as a high school student in Whittier, California, had won a prize from the Kiwanis Club for the best oration on the Constitution, ignored the system of checks and balances, which limits separation of powers. In this case, checks and balances authorized the courts to conduct criminal trials of the president's aides and Congress to conduct impeachment proceedings against the president. To do so, the courts and Congress needed the information on the tapes.

Within days of the Court's decision, the House Judiciary Committee passed three articles of impeachment. These charged Nixon with obstruction of justice, by covering up a crime; defiance of the committee's subpoenas for the tapes; and abuse of power. Nevertheless, some Republicans maintained there was no "smoking gun"—that is, no clear evidence of crimes. They said the impeachment effort was strictly political.

Regardless, Nixon's support in Congress dwindled, and he found himself caught between a rock and a hard spot: releasing the tapes would furnish more evidence for impeachment, but not releasing them would spur impeachment. He reportedly considered disregarding the decision but, after 12 days of weighing his options, complied with the order.

Releasing the tapes did reveal a smoking gun. Although the tapes did not show that Nixon participated in planning the break-in, they did show that he participated in covering it up. When the burglars blackmailed the administration, Nixon approved paying them hush money. He ordered the head of his reelection committee to "stonewall it" and "cover up." He and an aide formulated a plan to have the CIA thwart the FBI in its investigation of the scandal. When his top aides were subpoenaed to appear before the grand jury, he encouraged them to lie.

In addition to this evidence of crimes, the tapes revealed much vulgarity and profanity in Nixon's conversations. Such language undercut the public's positive image of Nixon.

The tapes, printed as a book that became an instant best-seller, repelled the public. When it became clear that public opinion would force the House to impeach him and the Senate to remove him, Nixon decided to resign. On August 9, 1974, he became the first American president to do so. Vice President Gerald Ford became the new president.

Although the smoking gun had been found, some people still thought the crimes relatively minor and the punishment excessively harsh. But Nixon was not driven from office solely or even primarily because of the break-in. Rather, he lost the public's trust because of the cover-up. He had campaigned for president on a "law and order" platform and had sworn an oath of office "to take care that the laws be faithfully executed." During the cover-up, he had repeatedly proclaimed that he was innocent of any wrongdoing. As the evidence came to light, the hypocrisy and lying became too much for the public to stomach. Ultimately, Nixon could not lead the public he had misled for so long.

Despite depression and cynicism about the scandal, many people saw that the system had worked as it was supposed to. The Founders had divided power to make it difficult for any one branch to amass too much power. In the face of the president's efforts to exercise vast power, the courts, with their orders to turn over the tapes, and Congress, with its Senate Watergate Committee hearings and House Judiciary Committee impeachment proceedings, checked the president's abuse of power. In addition, the media, with its extensive publicity, first prompted and then reinforced the actions of the courts and Congress.

However, although the system worked, it worked slowly. More than two years elapsed between the break-in and the resignation. For more than half the length of a presidential term, the president and many of his aides were so preoccupied with Watergate they could not devote sufficient attention to other problems facing the country.

When the affair was over, 21 of the president's men were convicted and sentenced to prison for their Watergate crimes. Except for one, a burglar who was most uncooperative and who served 52 months (G. Gordon Liddy, who now hosts a radio talk show), the men served from 4 to 12 months. Nixon, who could have and probably would have been prosecuted after leaving office, received a pardon from President Ford before any prosecution could begin.

Nine years after the resignation, the security guard who discovered the break-in was convicted for shoplifting in Augusta, Georgia. Unemployed, he had stolen a pair of shoes for his son. Unlike the president's men, he received the maximum sentence—12 months for the $12 shoes.

Congress passed a law mandating that other, unreleased tapes and documents be turned over to the National Archives, which was to make public any that related to Watergate or had "general historic significance." The Archives has slowly released these materials. On one tape, Nixon is heard remarking to his chief of

President Nixon at a press conference.

staff, "I always wondered about that taping equipment, but I'm damn glad we have it, aren't you?"[51]

Not only does Nixon's voice remain, but the effects of Watergate linger. The public has become less trustful of government officials, and the media have become more suspicious of them. The parties have become more aware of the benefits of a scandal involving their opponents. In the wake of Watergate, the Democrats captured the White House and gained many seats in Congress. These results have prompted both parties to point accusing fingers and to launch congressional investigations—though only against members of the other party—even when the alleged transgressions have been far less serious than those in Watergate. Thus, Watergate also contributed to the culture of scandal that afflicts American politics today.

KEY TERMS

Watergate scandal
executive privilege
Articles of Confederation
Shays's Rebellion
Constitutional Convention
Great Compromise
Three-fifths Compromise
social contract
direct democracy
indirect democracy
federalism
separation of powers
checks and balances
Whitewater investigation
special prosecutor/independent counsel
natural rights
limited government
Iroquois Confederacy
Federalists
Antifederalists
Federalist Papers
Bill of Rights

FURTHER READING

Leonard W. Levy, ed., *Essays on the Making of the Constitution* (New York: Oxford University Press, 1969). These essays address the question, Was the Constitution an undemocratic document framed and ratified by an undemocratic minority for an undemocratic society?

Clinton Rossiter, 1787: *The Grand Convention* (New York: Macmillan, 1966). A lively account of the Constitutional Convention and the ratification campaign.

Theodore H. White, *Breach of Faith* (New York: Atheneum, 1975). A chronicle of the Watergate scandal as a Greek tragedy in which actors on both sides behaved in such ways as to fulfill their destinies.

Bob Woodward and Carl Bernstein, *All the President's Men* (New York: Simon & Schuster, 1974). A riveting account of journalistic sleuthing by the two reporters who broke the Watergate story.

ELECTRONIC RESOURCES

http://lcweb.loc.gov/exhibits/declara/declaral.html
At this site, you can learn more about how the Declaration of Independence was written and see a special Library of Congress exhibit on the Declaration.

http://etext.virginia.edu/jefferson/quotations/jeffsite.html
This home page, sponsored by the University of Virginia, links to a variety of sites where you can access Jefferson's writings, autobiography, and other related Jeffersonia.

http://www.yahoo.com/Arts/Humanities/History/U_S__History/20th_Century/1970s/Watergate/Watergate_25th_Anniversary/
Links to documents concerning the Watergate affair, compiled 25 years later.

http://www.nwbuildnet.com/nwbn/usconstitutionsearch.html
Even the Constitution has a home page. Here it is, with links to other historical documents and to PBS Project Democracy. Another Constitution page with interesting links is http://www.usconstitution.net/, a site originally set up by a political science student as a class project.

INFOTRAC CITATIONS

"The Legacy of Slavery Lingers"
"Keep Your Amendments Off My Constitution"
"English as the Official American Language"

NOTES

1. Nixon thought he might be considered an American Disraeli. (Benjamin Disraeli, a British prime minister in the nineteenth century, was a Tory who had progressive ideas.) Nixon praised Robert Blake's biography of Disraeli, and one cabinet secretary remarked, in 1971, "The similarities are great, Mr. President, but what a pity that Blake could not quote Disraeli's conversations." Nixon did not destroy the tapes, even after they became a liability, apparently for this reason. Sidney Blumenthal, "The Longest Campaign," *The New Yorker*, August 8, 1994, p. 37.

2. *United States v. Reynolds*, 345 U.S. 1 (1953).

3. The Indians, of course, had their own governments, and the Spanish may have established St. Augustine, Florida, or Santa Fe, New Mexico, before the English established Jamestown. These Spanish settlements were extensions of Spanish colonization of Mexico and were governed by Spanish officials in Mexico City.

4. This is not to suggest that the Pilgrims believed in democracy. Apparently, they were motivated to draft the compact by threats from some on the *Mayflower* that when the ship landed they would "use their owne libertie; for none had power to command them." Thus, the compact was designed to bind them to the laws of the colony. Richard Shenkman, "*I Love Paul Revere, Whether He Rode or Not*" (New York: HarperCollins, 1991), pp. 141–142.

5. David Hawke, *A Transaction of Free Men* (New York: Scribner's, 1964), p. 209.

6. Louis Fisher, *President and Congress* (New York: Free Press, 1972), p. 14.

7. Gordon S. Wood, "The Origins of the Constitution," *This Constitution: A Bicentennial Chronicle* (Summer 1987), pp. 10–11.

8. Eric Black, *Our Constitution* (Boulder, Colo.: Westview Press, 1988), p. 6. Shays, eventually pardoned by Massachusetts, settled in New York and became a staunch Federalist (Black, p. 8).

9. For development of this idea, see Kenneth M. Dolbeare and Linda J. Medcalf, "The Political Economy of the Constitution," *This Constitution: A Bicentennial Chronicle* (Spring 1987), pp. 4–10.

10. Black, *Our Constitution*, p. 59.

11. The Constitution, however, would reflect numerous aspects of the Articles. See Donald S. Lutz, "The Articles of Confederation as the Background to the Federal Republic," *Publius* 20 (Winter 1990), pp. 55–70.

12. Robert McCloskey, *The American Supreme Court* (Chicago: University of Chicago Press, 1960), p. 29.

13. Fred Barbash, "James Madison: A Man for the '80s," *Washington Post National Weekly Edition*, March 30, 1987, p. 23.

14. Robert A. Dahl, *A Preface to Democratic Theory* (Chicago: University of Chicago Press, 1956), p. 5. Yet, according to a poll in 1987, the bicentennial of the Constitution, only 1% of the public identified Madison as the one who played the biggest role in creating the Constitution. Most—31%—said Thomas Jefferson, who was a diplomat in France during the convention. Black, *Our Constitution*, p. 15.

15. Paul Finkelman, "Slavery at the Philadelphia Convention," *This Constitution: A Bicentennial Chronicle* (1987), pp. 25–30.

16. Finkelman, "Slavery at the Philadelphia Convention," p. 29.

17. Finkelman, "Slavery at the Philadelphia Convention."

18. Theodore J. Lowi, *American Government* (Hinsdale, Ill.: Dryden Press, 1976), p. 97.

19. C. Herman Pritchett, *Constitutional Law of the Federal System* (Englewood Cliffs, N.J.: Prentice-Hall, 1984), p. xi.

20. Richard Hofstadter, *The American Political Tradition and the Men Who Made It* (New York: Random House, 1948), p. 13.

21. *Federalist Paper* #51.

22. *Federalist Paper* #47.

23. Max Farrand, *The Framing of the Constitution of the United States* (New Haven: Yale University Press, 1913).

24. *Federalist Paper* #51.

25. Richard E. Neustadt, *Presidential Power and the Modern Presidents* (New York: Macmillan, 1990), p. 29.

26. Donald S. Lutz, "The Relative Influence of European Writers on Later Eighteenth-Century American Political Thought," *American Political Science Review* 78 (March 1984), pp. 139–197.

27. Alpheus T. Mason and Richard H. Leach, *In Quest of Freedom: American Political Thought and Practice*, 2d ed. (Englewood Cliffs, N.J.: Prentice-Hall, 1973), p. 51.

28. For development of this idea, see Martin Landau, "A Self-Correcting System: The Constitution of the United States," *This Constitution: A Bicentennial Chronicle* (Summer 1986), pp. 4–10.

29. John P. Roche, "The Founding Fathers: A Reform Caucus in Action," *American Political Science Review* 56 (March 1962), pp. 799–816.

30. Ibid.

31. Charles Beard, *An Economic Interpretation of the Constitution* (New York: Macmillan, 1913).

32. Ellen Nore, "Charles A. Beard's Economic Interpretation of the Origins of the Constitution," *This Constitution* (Winter 1987), p. 39.

33. R. E. Brown, *Charles Beard and the Constitution* (Princeton: Princeton University Press, 1956); Forrest MacDonald, *We the People* (Chicago: University of Chicago Press, 1976).

34. James MacGregor Burns, *The Vineyard of Liberty* (New York: Alfred Knopf, 1982), p. 33.

35. Bernard Bailyn, *Voyagers to the West* (New York: Alfred Knopf, 1986), p. 20.

36. The Boston Tea Party, contrary to myth, was not prompted by higher taxes on British tea. Parliament lowered the taxes to give the British East India Company, facing bankruptcy, an advantage in the colonial market. This threatened American shippers who smuggled tea from Holland and controlled about three-fourths of the market. The shippers resented Parliament's attempt to manipulate the economy from thousands of miles away. Shenkman, "*I Love Paul Revere, Whether He Rode or Not*," p. 155.

37. *Federalist Paper* #10.

38. Black, *Our Constitution*, p. 21.

39. Calvin C. Jillson and Cecil L. Eubanks, "The Political Structure of Constitution Making," *American Journal of Political Science* 29 (August 1984), pp. 435–458.

40. Jonathan Elliot, *The Debates in the Several State Conventions on the Adoption of the Federal Constitution as Recommended by the General Convention at Philadelphia, in 1787*, 2d ed., 5 vols. (Philadelphia, 1896), vol. 2, p. 102; as quoted in Cecilia M. Kenyon, "Men of Little Faith," in John P. Roche, ed., *Origins of American Political Thought* (New York: Harper & Row, 1967), pp. 197–198.

41. For Antifederalist thinking, see W. B. Allen and Gordon Lloyd, eds., *The Essential Antifederalist* (Lanham, Md.: University Press of America, 1985); John F. Manley and Kenneth M. Dolbeare, *The Case against the Constitution* (Armonk, N.Y.: M. E. Sharpe, 1987).

42. "A Fundamental Contentment," *This Constitution: A Bicentennial Chronicle* (Fall 1984), p. 44.

43. Charles Warren, *The Making of the Constitution* (Boston: Little, Brown, 1928), p. xiv. Jefferson made this observation from afar, as he was ambassador to France during the Constitutional Convention.

44. "South Africa Looks at U.S. Constitution," *Lincoln Sunday Journal-Star (New York Times)*, October 7, 1990; David Remnick, " 'We, the People,' from the Russian," *Washington Post National Weekly Edition*, September 10–16, 1990, p. 11.

45. Since Thailand became a constitutional monarchy in 1932. Anthony DePalma, "Constitutions Are the New Writers' Market," *New York Times*, November 30, 1997, Week in Review, p. 3.

46. Harold J. Spaeth, *Supreme Court Policy Making* (San Francisco: W. H. Freeman, 1979), p. 13.

47. Richard Morin, "Happy Days Are Here Again," *Washington Post National Weekly Edition*, August 25, 1997, p. 35.

48. About 25% split their ticket between candidates for president and representative. In addition, others split their vote between candidates for president and senator or between candidates for representative and senator. For an examination of the research about divided government, see Morris Fiorina, *Divided Government*, 2d ed. (Boston: Allyn & Bacon, 1996), p. 153.

49. Benjamin Ginsberg and Martin Shefter, *Politics by Other Means: The Declining Importance of Elections in America* (New York: Basic Books, 1990).

50. 418 U.S. 683 (1974).

51. "Tapes Confirm Nixon Approved Hush Money," *Lincoln Journal* (AP), June 5, 1991.

After efforts of residents of Quincy, Missouri, failed to prevent a flood, the federal government worked with state and local governments to provide disaster relief.

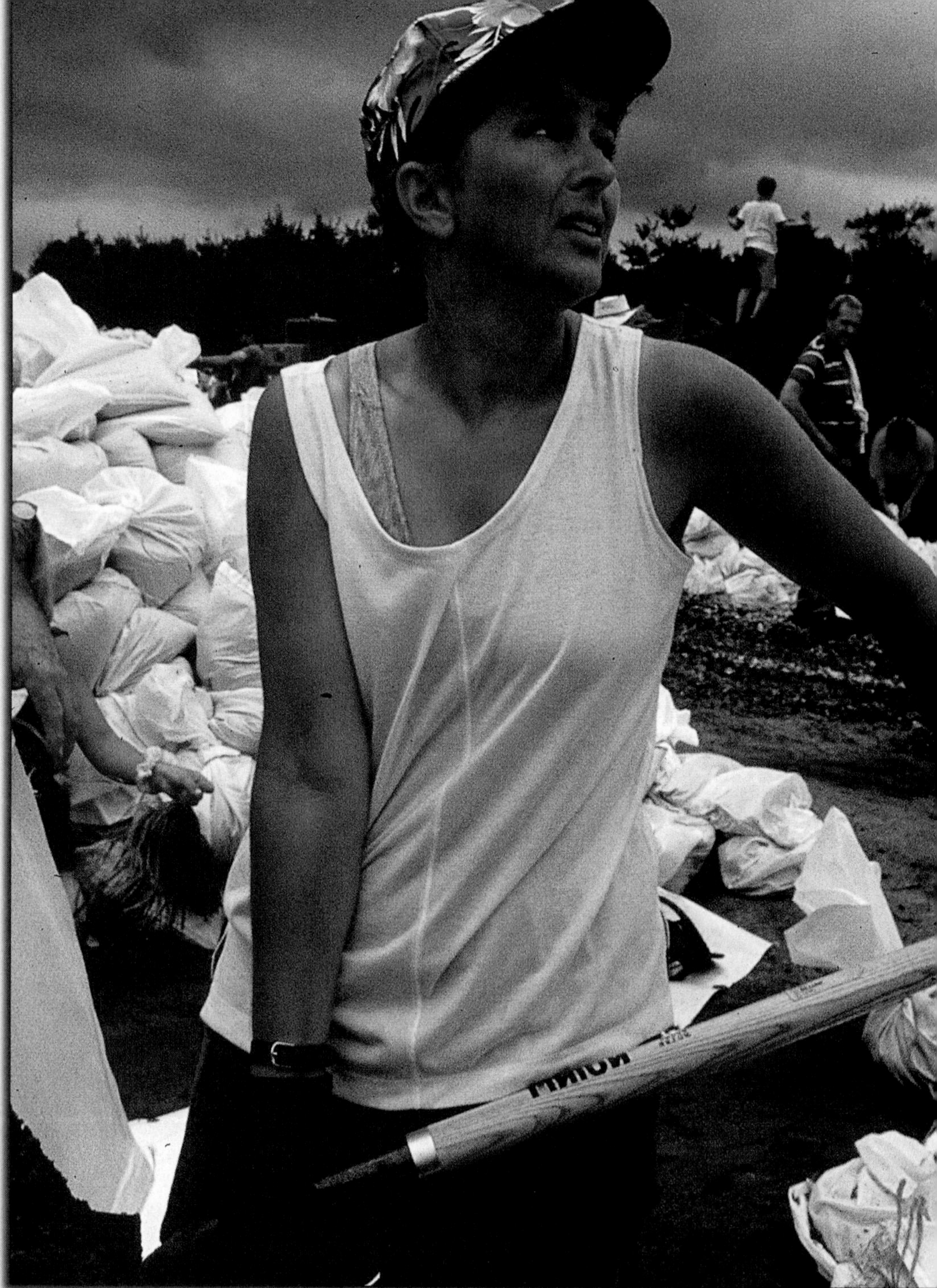

Ron Haviv/SABA

3 FEDERALISM AND THE GROWTH OF GOVERNMENT

YOU ARE THERE

Should the President Expand Federal Lands?

You are Bill Clinton, president of the United States, running for reelection to a second term in office. When you were first elected in 1992, you received less than a majority of the popular vote, because of the presence of a third candidate, H. Ross Perot. You would like nothing better than to win another term with over 50% of the votes cast; however, this is not a sure thing, because Perot is again on the ballot. Although it seems likely that you will rather handily beat the Republican nominee, former Kansas senator Bob Dole, winning the election with 45% or so of the popular vote will hardly be a resounding popular endorsement. In our federal system, presidents are elected on a state-by-state basis, with larger states being worth more "electoral votes" (see Chapter 7 on the Electoral College), so you want to make sure you get more votes than your opponents in large, competitive states such as California.

And so you are considering some dramatic actions, including declaring a large portion of southern Utah a national monument, effectively preserving it in its current undeveloped state. The area, known as the Grand Staircase–Escalante area, is marked by beautiful deserts, remarkable geological formations, and remote streams and rivers. On one side, the area borders Bryce National Park; on the other, it borders Capitol Reef National Park and the Glen Canyon National Recreation Area. With one stroke of your presidential pen, you can protect this region for future generations to enjoy as it is now.

There are some good reasons to declare the area a national monument. For one, it is one of the last large sections of the country free from nearby pollution sources, such as big cities and large industries. For another, the beauty of the area is truly remarkable. Utah tourism officials have long promoted it as a destination for people who want to get away from it all (and we do mean all). Politically, making this declaration would solidify the support of environmentalists, outdoor enthusiasts, and conservationists, who are crucial to winning California and perhaps some other western states, too.[1] Although your environmental record in your first term has not been bad, you can point to very few specific actions that would endear you to ecology-minded voters. Winning their support is one of your campaign goals.

Many residents of southern Utah will resent your action, however. From their perspective, the Grand Staircase–Escalante area should continue to be used for cattle ranching and logging and should be further developed by mining. One coal mining concern is ready to proceed with mining, and officials predict that the development could pump up to $3 billion into the state's economy. Declaring the area a national monument and protecting it as a wilderness area, however, would put an end to the mining plans. Besides local residents do not think of the area as a wilderness in any case. Pointing to some existing roads, suitable chiefly for four-wheel drive vehicles, they say that a wilderness is by definition not accessible by automobile.

More importantly, Utahans would see your action as another example of the federal government using its power to impose its will on the states. The federal government owns millions of acres of land in the West. Indeed, in several western states (Alaska, Idaho, Oregon, Utah), the federal government owns over 50% of the land.[2] In Nevada, it owns 87%.

State and local governments have little control over how federal land is used. Through the Bureau of Land Management and the Forest Service, the federal government places restrictions on the use of federal land. It limits the number of cattle that can graze the land, the amount of timber that can be cut from forested lands, and, in some areas, the kind of vehicles that can drive on the land. Although the federal government tries to balance the interests of farmers and ranchers with environmental concerns, any regulation arouses angry protests. As one irate state legislator noted, "The federal government has a stranglehold on the rural West."[3]

The antagonism of many westerners to the federal regulations is growing. To aid their cause, they have enlisted the machinery of local governments; at least 35 (and perhaps as many as 300) counties in the West have said that federally owned lands in the county fall under their jurisdiction.[4] Such disputes strike at the heart of federal authority and our federalist structure. What are the limits of national and state powers?

You are uncertain how much to worry about what Utahans think. You have little chance of carrying the state in the election; you came in third there in 1992, and polls indicate Dole will beat you there this year. But you worry that you will be accused of political opportunism. Even if there are good reasons for declaring the area a national monument, opponents are likely to criticize your motives. If people believe that you acted to win the election rather than to protect this wilderness area, you will again appear to be "Slick Willy," a name your opponents have called you in the past. But you sincerely think this area deserves to be designated a national monument; this may simply be a time when political motives coincide with genuine policy concerns. You know that kind of convergence of motives occurs much more frequently than cynics would admit.

On the other hand, you recall that when you were governor of Arkansas, you would have deeply resented a president shutting you out of a decision so important to your state. A middle ground might be to ask Congress to preserve the Grand Staircase area by passing appropriate legislation. Although this would still be a federal action, at least Utah's representatives and senators, as well as those of other states, could help make the decision. But if you make the declaration alone, as permitted by a broad reading of the Antiquities Act, Congress, the states, and the public are effectively kept out of the decision-making process.

It is now late September, and the time seems right to make a decision. What do you do? Do you declare the Grand Staircase a national monument, or do you wait and pass up this opportunity to court the political support of environmentalists in the western states?

Most Americans claim to believe that state governments are more responsive to them than the federal government (Table 1), but over the past 60 years they have asked the federal government to get involved in almost every policy issue imaginable. Many Americans decry the growth of big government, and yet few realize that over the past 25 years, the size of state governments has doubled while the federal government has grown hardly at all. Most Americans want small government, but they also want a government powerful enough to keep the peace abroad and responsive to their needs at home.

These issues of the size and scope of the federal government relative to the states are not new. They are the same issues that the Founders debated at the Constitutional Convention in 1787. The issue of whether the states or the national government should have the final say in political decisions was the central conflict in the Civil War (1861–1865), which ultimately determined that the national government, not the states, was supreme.

Because of this outcome, and because of the tasks we ask government to do, we live in a nation with a strong central government. Yet we vigorously disagree about just how strong that government should be. Critics accuse the national government and its programs of being too large, too expensive, and too intrusive on the rights of the states and the people. Yet when members of Congress suggest cutting programs severely or transferring responsibilities back to the states, the public outcry is vociferous. And even though our system of powers at both the national and state levels contributes to the messiness of democracy that the public dislikes, there is little support for streamlining or centralizing powers at the national level.

TABLE 1

The Public Trusts the States More

	STATE	FEDERAL
Which government do you trust to:		
do a better job running things?	70%	27%
establish rules about who can receive welfare?	70	25
set rules for workplace safety?	55	42
set Medicare and Medicaid regulations?	52	43
set environmental rules for clean air?		
and clean water?	51	47
protect civil rights?	35	61

SOURCE: Washington Post–ABC Poll, reported in Richard Morin, "Power to the States," *Washington Post National Weekly Edition,* March 27–April 2, 1995, p. 37.

These contradictions are perhaps endemic to a federal system. In this chapter we will examine the nature of American federalism and how it has changed as government has grown.

FEDERAL AND OTHER SYSTEMS

Federal Systems

The term **federalism** describes a system in which power is constitutionally divided between a central government and subnational or local governments (in

Corbis-Bettmann

Federalism is the only domestic issue in the United States over which several million Americans fought and 500,000 combatants died. This photograph shows the remains of Richmond, Virginia, after a Civil War battle.

the United States the subnational governments are the states). Both levels of government receive their grants of power from a higher authority—the will of the people as expressed in a constitution, for example. Each level can deal directly with individuals to tax, regulate, or provide benefits.

Power granted to each level is not necessarily exclusive. In fact, in the United States only one power is left solely to the states, and that is the power to determine whether they shall exist. States cannot be abolished or altered without their own consent. That power is an essential element in federalism.

Nearly 90% of all nations have unitary systems, but several large nations have federal systems—for example, Germany, Canada, India, and Brazil. Federal systems vary greatly in their basic economic and political characteristics; they are similar only in that each has a written constitution allocating some powers to the national and some to the subnational governments.

Unitary Systems

In contrast to the federal system, in a **unitary system** the national government creates subnational governments and gives them what power it wishes. Thus, the national government is supreme. In Britain, for example, the national government can give or take away any power of the subnational governments or can even abolish them, as it did with some counties several years ago. And, in unitary Sweden, the national parliament abolished 90% of its local governments from 1952 to 1975.

In the United States, the 50 states are each unitary with respect to their local governments; cities, counties, and school districts can be altered or even eliminated by state governments.

The distinction between unitary and federal is not at all related to the distinction between democracy and authoritarianism. Some unitary systems are among the most democratic in the world (Britain and Sweden); others are authoritarian (Egypt and Ghana). Nor are only federal systems decentralized. All modern governments have to decentralize power because a central government, even in a unitary system, cannot run every local service or deal with every local problem.

Confederal Systems

The third arrangement between central and subnational governments is confederal. In a **confederal system,** the central government has only those powers given to it by the subnational governments; it cannot act directly on citizens. Two examples of confederal systems are the United States under the Articles of Confederation and the United Nations. The lack of central authority in such systems makes them basically unworkable in modern nations.

THE POLITICAL BASES OF FEDERALISM

Why do some nations choose a federal form of government while others do not? The Founders of the United States chose federalism as one means of limiting governmental power. Federalism also allowed the Founders to incorporate the states into the new government; no one thought seriously about abolishing the states. Another reason for choosing federalism was that it could help deal with national diversity. Federal systems are often, though not always, ethnically, linguistically, religiously, or racially diverse. We in the United States are not as diverse as the peoples of India, for example, but we are a nation of many ethnic groups, races, religions, and political traditions.

Our nation remains diverse, and our states reflect that diversity. Despite our national media networks, franchises and chains bringing the same products to all parts of the country, and transportation systems that carry us across the nation in only a few hours, there are still significant differences among us, and not just whether we prefer Texas chili or New England clam chowder. Different states and regions have developed somewhat different political styles and attitudes. Most governors of Pennsylvania, for example, could never be elected in Idaho, and vice versa. Ways of looking at politics, partisan preferences, ideology, appropriate ways of organizing for political action, and other political features vary greatly across our nation.

In Chapter 1, we defined political culture as a shared body of values and beliefs that shapes perceptions and attitudes toward politics and government and, in turn, influences behavior. In the United States, three cultures predominate, each with distinctive ways of looking at and participating in politics.[5] In a *moralistic* political culture, found in New England and the upper Midwest, politics is viewed as a way of improving life, and people have a strong sense that they should participate. In an *individualistic* political culture, typical of the industrial Midwest and the East, the ultimate objective of politics is not so much to create a better life but to get benefits for yourself and your group. In a *traditionalistic* political culture, still present in parts of the South, politics is left to a small elite and is seen not as a way to further the public good but as a way to maintain the status quo.

In addition to cultural differences, marked ethnic and other demographic disparities also differentiate the states. In New Mexico, for instance, almost 40% of the population is of Hispanic origin, while in Maine non-Hispanic whites make up over 98% of the population, and in Mississippi African Americans make up over 30%.[6] In Florida, almost as many people are over age 65 (18% of the population) as are under 17 (22%), but in Utah, young people outnumber senior citizens by more than four to one. And in New Jersey, the median family income is 80% higher than in West Virginia ($44,000 versus $25,000).

These disparities make for different politics in the states. The priorities of older people (health care, for instance) are different than those of younger people (education, for example). In states with larger numbers of Latinos and black Americans, civil rights issues are more salient than in states with more homogeneous populations. And states whose citizens are poorer face greater demands for services and have correspondingly fewer resources to provide them.

States also vary in how liberal their policies are. One way to measure this is to determine how much the states spend on various activities such as education and health care and how restrictive or lenient their policies are toward gambling and crime.[7] The map in Figure 1 illustrates the results of one such analysis. The differences among the states can be explained by how "liberal" (see Chapter 4) each state's citizens are and by the kind of political culture the state has. State policies reflect the different views and social and economic circumstances of their citizens.

Thus, state boundaries mean something beyond identifying the government to which state taxes are paid. In policy areas as diverse as economic development, welfare, and regulation of personal morality (such as gambling and prostitution), states vary widely. Federalism, even with a strong national government, does provide some autonomy for states to adopt and maintain policies consistent with their own political cultures.

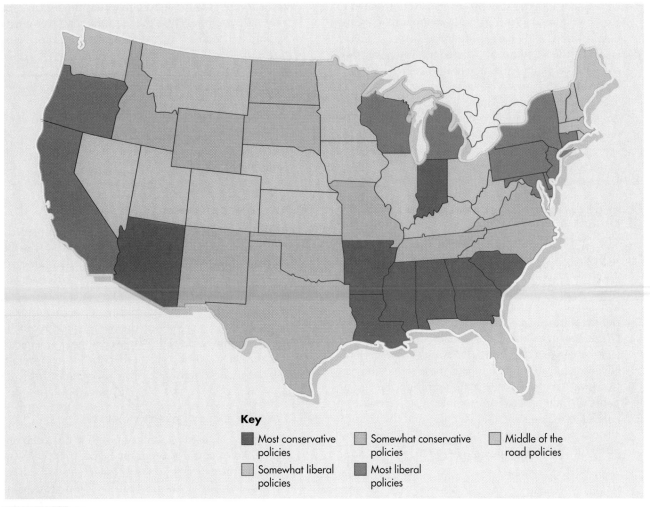

Key
Most conservative policies
Somewhat conservative policies
Middle of the road policies
Somewhat liberal policies
Most liberal policies

FIGURE 1

States Vary in How Liberal or Conservative Their Policies Are

SOURCE: Robert S. Erikson, Gerald C. Wright, and John P. McIver, *Statehouse Democracy: Public Opinion and Policy in the American States* (New York: Cambridge University Press, 1993), Table 4.2, p. 77.

THE CONSTITUTIONAL BASES OF FEDERALISM

Major Features of the System

As we saw in Chapter 2, the Founders were unsure how to solve the problem of national versus state powers. All wanted limited government. Although they saw federalism as one way to limit government power by dividing it, there was little debate over the concept of federalism, and the main outlines emerged only as the Founders dealt with other issues. The major features of nation-state relationships outlined by the Constitution include a strong national government, prohibition of certain powers to the states, and some limitations on national powers.

STRONG NATIONAL GOVERNMENT

Although the Founders did not all agree on how strong the national government should be, all did agree that they wanted a national government stronger than that of the Articles of Confederation. They wanted a national government able to tax without the permission of the states and one able to carry out foreign and domestic policies without the states' consent. Thus, the Constitution grants many specific powers to Congress, including taxation and regulation of commerce, which gives tremendous power to the national government and allows it to be independent of the will of the state governments. The clause granting Congress the power to make all laws **"necessary and proper"** for carrying out its specific powers—sometimes called the **implied powers clause**—also strengthened the national government. This grant of power soon was interpreted to mean that Congress could legislate in almost any area it wished.

In addition, the **supremacy clause** contributed to a strong national government. It says that treaties, the Constitution, and "laws made in pursuance thereof" are to be the supreme law of the land whenever they come into conflict with state laws or state actions.

Although it was a compromise decision, a president independent of Congress and the state legislatures also strengthened the national government. The president's power to be commander in chief and to execute the laws of the United States further enlarged national powers.

PROHIBITION OF CERTAIN POWERS TO THE STATES

The Constitution forbids states to undertake actions that might conflict with the power of the national government; they cannot enter into treaties, keep troops or navies, make war, print or coin money, or levy import or export taxes on goods. These prohibitions reaffirmed that the national government was to be supreme in making foreign policy and regulating interstate commerce. Under the Articles, the national government was limited in both these areas. The new Constitution also forbade states to infringe on certain rights of individuals. For example, a state could not pass a law making an action a crime and then punish citizens who committed the "crime" before it was made illegal (called an *ex post facto* law).

SOME LIMITATIONS ON NATIONAL POWERS

The Constitution prohibits the creation of new states within existing states, the combination of two states, or the change of existing state boundaries without the approval of the legislatures of the affected states.

The Tenth Amendment granted to the states and to the people those powers not granted by the Constitution to the national government. At the time, this was considered a significant limit on national powers. Since then, the broad construction of Congress's "necessary and proper" powers has made the Tenth Amendment inconsequential. Recently, there have been attempts to breathe life into this amendment, but thus far they have had only limited success.[8]

These three features—a strong national government, prohibition of certain powers to the states, and some limitations on national powers—ensured a strong national government as well as a significant role for the states. The Founders believed that this arrangement would limit the ability of any one government to tyrannize its citizens and that the diversity of interests in the system would prevent the formation of a national majority that could trample minority rights. Similarly, a central government would ensure that states could protect the rights of their citizens against arbitrary local majorities. Many believed that the primary virtue of a federal system was that the authority of government was limited because it was divided between two levels.

Interpretations of Federalism

The Founders left the exact details of the nation-state relationship vague because they could not agree on specifics. It is not surprising that different views of federalism emerged.[9]

NATION-CENTERED FEDERALISM

In the *Federalist Papers*, Alexander Hamilton clearly articulated the view that national power was to be supreme. This nation-centered view of federalism rests on the assumption that the Constitution is a document ratified by the people. The states have many powers, but the national government has the ultimate responsibility for preserving the nation and the viability of the states as well. Nation-centered federalism was the view used by northerners to justify a war to prevent the southern states from seceding in 1861.

STATE-CENTERED FEDERALISM

Another view, used by southerners to justify their defiance of the central government before the Civil War, held that the Constitution is a product of state action. In this view, the states created the union. State-centered federalists argue that the grant of powers to Congress is limited to those items specifically mentioned in Article I. Madison said, "The powers delegated . . . to the federal government are few and defined. Those which are to remain in the state governments are numerous and indefinite."[10] In this view, any attempt by Congress to go beyond these explicitly listed powers violates state authority.

DUAL FEDERALISM

Dual federalism is the idea that the Constitution created a system in which the national government and the states each have separate grants of power, with each supreme in its own sphere. In this view, the two levels of government are essentially equal. Their differences derive from their different jurisdictions, not from any inequality.

COOPERATIVE FEDERALISM

The term **cooperative federalism** refers to the continuing cooperation among federal, state, and local officials in carrying out the business of government. The term encompasses the relationship of federal

FEDERALISM AND THE "MISCHIEFS OF FACTION"

Probably the most influential work of American political theory was written by James Madison in *Federalist Paper* #10 (reprinted in the appendix to this book). This work helps explain the attraction of a federalist system for Madison and many of the other Founders.

In *Federalist* #10, Madison asserted that it is inevitable that factions—groups of citizens seeking some goal contrary to the rights of other citizens or to the well-being of the whole country—will threaten the stability of nations. To cure the "**mischiefs of faction**" Madison said government had either to remove the causes of faction or to control its effects.

Madison believed the government could never remove the causes of faction because this would require changing selfish human nature, which he thought impossible. It also would require taking away freedom by outlawing opinions and strictly regulating behavior. People would inevitably have different ideas and beliefs, and government, he thought, should not try to prevent this.

Because one could not remove the causes of faction without too greatly inhibiting freedom, Madison recommended that a properly constructed government should control its effects. If a faction were less than a majority, Madison believed it could be controlled through majority rule, the majority defeating the minority faction. If the faction were a majority, however, then a greater problem arose, but one for which Madison had an answer.

To control a majority faction, one had only to limit the ability of a majority to carry out its wishes. Madison believed this was impossible in a small democracy, where there is little check on a majority determined to do something. But in a large federalist system, there are many checks on a majority faction—more interests competing with each other and large distances to separate those who might scheme to deprive others of liberty. As Madison noted, "The influence of factious leaders may kindle a flame within their particular States, but will be unable to spread a general conflagration through the other States." Having many states and having them spread over a large territory were, in Madison's view, major checks against majority tyranny.

and state officials when distributing payments to farmers, providing welfare services, planning highways, organizing centers for the elderly, and carrying out all the functions that the national and state governments jointly fund and organize. It also refers to informal cooperation in locating criminals, tracking down mysterious diseases, and many other activities. A person speaking of cooperative federalism is not evaluating the legalistic relationship of national and state governments but rather referring to day-to-day joint activities.

FEDERALISM AND THE GROWTH OF GOVERNMENT

In 200 years, our national government has grown from a few hundred people with relatively limited impact on the residents of 13 small states to a government employing millions, affecting the daily lives of most of the population of more than 260 million people. This transformation is closely related to the changing way in which Americans understand the federal system.

Over the years, the dominant interpretations of federalism have shifted among the nation-centered, state-centered, and dual views. Changing interpretations have reflected court opinions, pressing economic needs, the philosophies of those in the executive and legislative branches, and changing public demands. The most general trend has been away from state-centered and toward nation-centered federalism, but there have been significant shorter-term trends in the opposite direction. Moreover, the term *cooperative federalism* has come into use since World War II to describe everyday relations between national and state officials.

Early Nationalist Period

Very soon after the Constitution was ratified, the federal courts became the arbiters of the Constitution. (Note that we are using "federal" to mean "national," a confusing but common usage. "Federal government" normally means "national government.") John Marshall, chief justice of the United States from 1801 to 1835, was a firm nationalist, and the decisions of his Court emphasized the need for a strong national government. The Marshall-led Supreme Court not only held that decisions of the state courts could be overturned by the federal courts, it also, in the case of *McCulloch v. Maryland*, gave approval to the broad interpretation of Congress's implied powers in the Constitution.

MCCULLOCH V. MARYLAND

The broad interpretation of the clause giving Congress the right to make all laws "necessary and proper" to carry out the powers that the Constitution gives it, grew out of a case involving the establishment of a national bank. Because the Constitution does not explicitly grant Congress the authority to charter banks, many people thought Congress may have been infringing on rights the Constitution left to the states. Ironically, it was John Calhoun, later to become the leading states' rights advocate, who introduced a bill to charter a Bank of the United States.

U.S. Department of Agriculture

In a spirit of optimism amidst the turmoil of the Civil War, Congress in 1862 established federal support for the land grant colleges, a striking example of intergovernmental cooperation in the nineteenth century. Today many of these institutions are among our finest universities. Here, students plow on the campus of The Pennsylvania State University, one of the first land grant colleges.

Once established, the bank was immediately unpopular because it competed with smaller banks operating under state laws and because some of its branches engaged in reckless and even fraudulent practices. When the government of Maryland levied a tax on the notes—what we would now call currency—issued by the Baltimore branch of the bank, the constitutionality of the bank was called into question and a case was brought to the Supreme Court.

In **McCulloch v. Maryland,** John Marshall wrote one of his most influential decisions.[11] Pronouncing the tax unconstitutional, Marshall wrote that "the power to tax involves the power to destroy." The states should not have the power to destroy the bank, he stated, because the bank was "necessary and proper" to carry out Congress's powers to collect taxes, borrow money, regulate commerce, and raise an army. Marshall argued that if the goal of the legislation is legitimate and constitutional, "all means which are appropriate, which are plainly adapted to that end, which are not prohibited, but consistent with the letter and spirit of the Constitution, are constitutional."

Thus, Marshall interpreted "necessary" quite loosely. The bank was probably not necessary, but it was "useful." This interpretation of the implied powers clause allowed Congress, and thus the national government, to wield much more authority than the Constitution gave it explicitly.

Although there was some negative reaction—"a deadly blow has been struck at the sovereignty of the states," cried one Baltimore newspaper—the Court maintained its strongly nationalistic position as long as Marshall was chief justice.

EARLY GROWTH OF GOVERNMENT

At the same time the courts were interpreting national powers broadly, the national government was exercising its powers on a rather small scale. The federal government had only 1,000 employees in the administration of George Washington, and this number had increased to 33,000 during the presidency of James Buchanan 70 years later. The national government also raised relatively little revenue. But state governments were also small and had limited functions. There were only a few federal-state cooperative activities. For example, the federal government gave land to the states to support education and participated in joint federal-state-private ventures, such as canal-building projects initiated by the states.

Thus, the early nationalist period was characterized by the growth of nation-centered federalism in legal doctrine, by small-scale state and national government, and by a few intergovernmental cooperative activities responding to the needs of an expanding nation.

Pre–Civil War Period

In 1836, the Court began to interpret the Tenth Amendment as a strict limitation on federal powers, holding that powers to provide for public health, safety, and order were *exclusively* powers of the state governments, not of the national government. This dual federalism interpretation eroded some of the nation-centered federal interpretations of the Marshall Court while continuing to uphold the rights of the federal courts to interpret the Constitution.

At the same time, champions of the state-centered view of federalism were gaining ascendance in the South. Southern leaders feared that the federal government, dominated by the increasingly populous North, would regulate or even abolish slavery. John Calhoun, one of the leading proponents for the state-centered view, even went so far as to say that a state could nullify laws of Congress (the doctrine of nullification). According to Calhoun, a state could withdraw from the Union if it wished. When the South did secede from the Union in 1861, it called itself the Confederate States of America, emphasizing the supremacy of the states embedded in a confederal system. After the Civil War, the vision of state-centered federalism largely lost its credibility.

The Civil War to the New Deal

After the Civil War, vast urbanization and industrialization took place throughout the United States. Living and working conditions for many city-dwellers were appalling. Adults as well as children who moved into the cities often took jobs in sweatshops—factories where they worked long hours in unsafe conditions for low pay.

Spurred by revelations of these unsafe and degrading conditions, states and sometimes Congress tried to regulate working conditions, working hours, and pay through such means as child labor and industrial safety laws. Beginning in the 1880s, a conservative Supreme Court used the dual federalism doctrine to rule unconstitutional many of these attempts. It often decided that Congress and the states had overstepped their powers. From 1874 to 1937, the Supreme Court found 50 federal and 400 state laws unconstitutional.[12] Before the Civil War, in contrast, the Court overturned only 2 congressional and 60 state laws.

At the same time that the Court was limiting both state and national action in regulating business and industry, both levels of government were slowly expanding. The revenues of both grew—the United States through an income tax finally ratified in 1913, the states and localities through gasoline and cigarette taxes, higher property taxes, and some state income taxes. Federal support for state programs also grew through land and case grants given by the federal government to the states.[13] By the late 1920s, however, most governmental functions still rested primarily in state and local hands. The states were clearly the dominant partner in providing most services, from health and sanitation to police and fire protection. The federal government provided few direct services to individuals, nor did it regulate their behavior. The Great Depression signaled a dramatic shift in this arrangement.

The New Deal

To grasp the scope of the changes that have taken place in our federal structure between 1930 and today, consider the report of a sociologist who studied community life in Muncie, Indiana.[14] In 1924 the federal government in Muncie was symbolized by little more than the post office and the American flag. Today, two-thirds of the households in Muncie depend in part on federal funds—federal employment, Social Security, welfare payments, food stamps, veterans benefits, student scholarships and loans, Medicare and Medicaid, and many other smaller programs.

In large part, the Great Depression brought about these changes. During the stock market crash of 1929, wealthy people became poor overnight. In the depths of the Depression one-fourth of the workforce was unemployed, and banks failed daily.

Unlike today, there was no systematic national program of relief for the unemployed then—no unemployment compensation, no food stamps, no welfare, nothing to help put food on the table and pay the rent. Millions were hungry, homeless, and hopeless. States and localities, which had the responsibility for providing relief to the poor, were overwhelmed; they did not have the funds or organizational resources to cope with the millions needing help. And private charities did not have enough resources to even begin to assume the burden.

The magnitude of the economic crisis led to the election of a Democrat, Franklin Delano Roosevelt, in 1932. He formulated, and Congress passed, a program called the **New Deal.** Its purpose was to stimulate economic recovery and aid the victims of the depression who were unemployed, hungry, and often in ill health. New Deal legislation regulated many activities of business

AP/Wide World Photos

President Roosevelt's confidence, along with the hopes people had in his New Deal programs, led to public support for the expansion of the role of the federal government.

and labor, set up a welfare system for the first time, and began large-scale federal-state cooperation in funding and administering programs through federal **grants-in-aid.** These grants-in-aid provided federal money to states (and occasionally to local governments) to set up programs to help people—for example, the aged poor or the unemployed.

These measures had strong political support, although they were opposed by many business and conservative groups and initially by the Supreme Court, which was still following the dual federalism doctrine. But after the reelection of Roosevelt in 1936, the Court became more favorable toward New Deal legislation, and later resignations of two conservative judges ensured that the Court would be sympathetic to the New Deal (see Chapter 13 for more on the Court and the New Deal.)

The Court decisions approving New Deal legislation were, in a sense, a return to the nation-centered federalism of John Marshall's day. But although the Supreme Court ratified much of the New Deal, it also approved more sweeping *state* regulations of business and labor than had the more conservative pre–New Deal Court. Thus, the change in Court philosophy did not enlarge the federal role at the expense of the powers of the states. *It enlarged the powers of both state and federal government.* In doing so, the Court responded to preferences on the part of taxpayers for a more active government to cope with the tragedy of the Depression. The limited government desired by the Founders became less limited as both state and national government grew.

Changes in patterns of taxing and spending soon reflected the green light given to federal involvement with the states and localities. As Figure 2 indicates, the federal share of spending for domestic needs (omitting spending for the military) nearly tripled from 17% in 1929, before the New Deal, to 47% in 1939, a decade later. The state share stayed constant while the local share dropped dramatically. Local governments did not spend less, but the state and federal governments spent more. Likewise state spending increased, but not as much as federal spending. The federal government raised more revenue and in turn gave much of it to the states and localities in the form of grants-in-aid to carry out programs such as unemployment compensation, free school lunches, emergency welfare relief, farm surpluses to the needy, and other programs.

The New Deal brought a dramatic change in the relationship of the national government to its citizens. Before this, when the national government directly touched the lives of citizens, it usually was to give or sell them something, such as land for settlers or subsidies for businesses helping develop the frontier.[15] With New Deal programs the federal government directly affected the lives of its citizens through its regulations (of banks and working conditions, for example) and its redistributive policies designed to protect the poor (such as Social Security and Aid to Dependent Children).

From the New Deal to the Great Society

During the years that followed the initiation of the New Deal, federal aid to states increased steadily but not dramatically. But federal support to the states carried conditions. For example, local administrators of Aid to Dependent Children programs had to be hired through a merit system, not because of political or personal connections. Construction funds for highways could be spent only on highways whose designs met professional standards. Thus, federal "strings" accompanied federal money.

By the 1950s, some public officials became uneasy about the growing size of the federal government and its involvement in so many state and local programs. Yet under President Dwight D. Eisenhower, a Republican concerned about the growth of federal involvement, many new federal grants-in-aid to the states were added, ranging from the massively expensive interstate highway program to collegiate programs in science, engineering, and languages. Federal grants-in-aid spending nearly tripled during his administration (1952–1960).

The 1960s witnessed an explosion in federal programs. Mostly a consequence of President Lyndon Johnson's Great Society, new programs of federal aid mushroomed both in number and in cost. Federal support for state and local activities extended to almost every area imaginable, including former state and local preserves such as local law enforcement, urban mass transit, and public education.

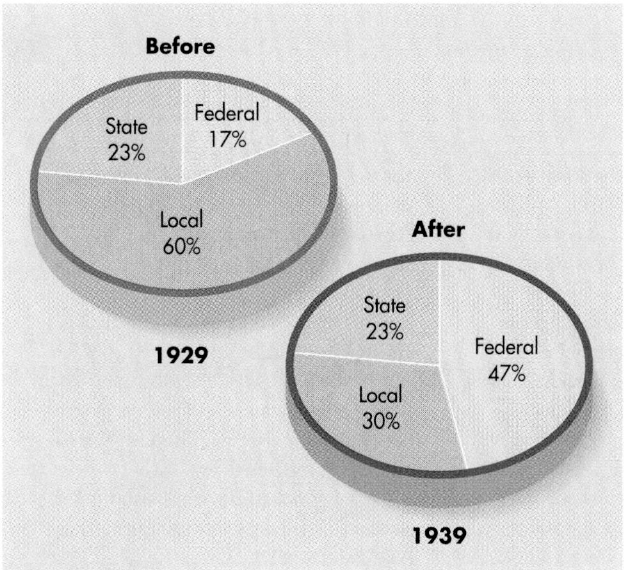

FIGURE 2

The New Deal Increased Federal and State Spending

Share of nonmilitary spending by each level of government, before and after New Deal legislation.

SOURCE: "Significant Features of Fiscal Federalism," *Advisory Commission on Intergovernmental Relations* (Washington, D.C.: U.S. Government Printing Office, 1979), p. 7.

A new feature of the Great Society era was an increasing number of grants going directly to localities. Because they believed the state legislatures were unresponsive to their interests, urban and other local governments now demanded, and got, direct federal support that bypassed states.

The vast increase in programs and the multiplying requirements and conditions of the grants made federal aid ever more complex. State and local officials felt hamstrung by the increasingly burdensome regulations.

New Federalism

The continuing expansion of the federal government during the 1950s and its explosive growth in the 1960s led to a reaction in the 1970s. Alarmed at the growth of the national government, elected officials of both parties called for reevaluation of the scope of federal activity. Republican leaders were especially vocal in their belief that the national government was becoming too large and that many federal activities could be better handled by the states.

Both President Richard Nixon (1968–1974) and President Ronald Reagan (1980–1988) advocated a **new federalism.** Their definitions were quite different.

President Nixon proposed two important innovations: **general revenue sharing** and **block grants.** General revenue sharing gave states and cities money to spend as they saw fit, subject to only a few conditions (for example, the money could not be used to support activities that discriminated on the basis of race, age, or sex). This program was in place from 1972 through 1987. Block grants gave states and localities some leeway on spending federal funds for designated purposes, such as community development. Because the limitations that accompany block grants are less rigid than those on grants-in-aid, states welcomed them. But block grants still enable Congress and the president to set priorities for spending by designating the purposes for which the funds can be used. In 1996 Congress turned welfare over to the states by making it a block grant, giving states some discretion in running its aid programs.

Although Jimmy Carter began to decrease federal spending on grants to states and localities, Ronald Reagan made curbing the growth of the federal government a main theme of his administration. Using a dual federalist rhetoric, Reagan articulated a vision of a smaller federal government and more powerful states.[16] However, Reagan's major impact on nation-state relationships was through his budget priorities. By massively increasing military spending and running huge deficits requiring ever larger interest payments, the amount of money available for domestic spending shrank. Money spent on federal grants-in-aid declined substantially relative to overall spending during the 1980s.

Thus, whereas the centerpiece of Nixon's "new federalism" was to provide *more* unrestricted or minimally restricted federal funds to states and localities, Reagan's "new federalism" was directed toward dramatically *reducing* federal support for the states. States and localities were told to support new programs with their own resources.

During the 1970s and 1980s, many states modernized and expanded their tax systems and were then able to take advantage of the economic boom in the 1980s. With these resources, the states enacted hundreds of new programs in many areas, especially education, child care and child protection, and economic development. Moreover, as the federal government backed away from increased regulations, state regulation increased in areas as diverse as the insurance industry, environmental protection, and consumer affairs.

Today, however, cuts in federal aid to states threaten their ability to maintain services such as education, housing, and Medicaid. During the federal budget deadlock in 1995–1996, many states found it difficult to budget, because they could not predict how much grant money and other federal funds they could count on. This demonstrates how much states depend on federal money to meet their needs. The prosperity of the last six years, however, has filled state tax coffers, so the impact of reduced federal aid has been

WHAT GOVERNMENT DOES RIGHT

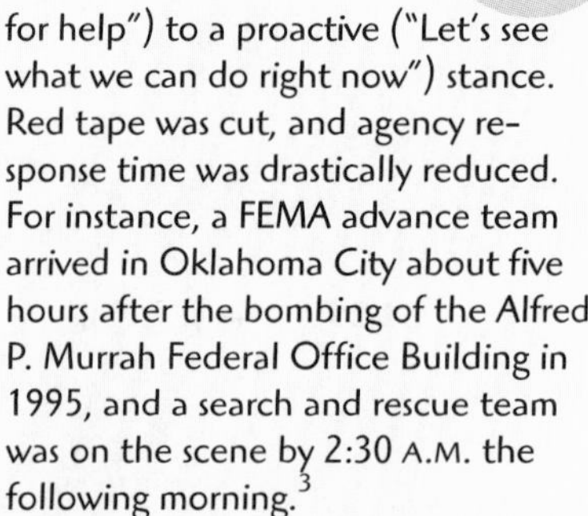

RESPONDING TO DISASTERS

Problems get all the publicity, or so it seems. When public officials accept favors from industries they are supposed to regulate or when government buys hammers at outrageous prices, we hear about it, largely through the media. When we hear such stories often and hear little about when government does its job well, we naturally become cynical about government, whatever the level. And we have become most cynical about the federal government because its officials and activities are most closely monitored by the media.

Nevertheless, our government does work. And it does some things exceedingly well. Tom Hanks's HBO miniseries, "From the Earth to the Moon," dramatized a spectacularly successful 1960s project—putting a man on the moon. Less spectacularly, government every day performs thousands of tasks and performs them responsibly and effectively. Despite the popular saying "Good enough for government work," government's standards are as high, if not higher, than those in the private sector. In this and succeeding chapters, we will highlight some examples where government indeed works well.

DISASTER RELIEF AND FEDERALISM

One of the roles of the national government is to undertake tasks that the states cannot handle themselves. Providing "for the common defence," in the words of the Preamble to the Constitution, is the classic example. Only the national government can effectively protect the nation from foreign enemies.

Assisting states in times of natural disaster is another example. The destruction caused by a hurricane, flood, tornado, or earthquake may be so severe and widespread that the resources of the affected states and localities are overwhelmed. And if the damage is not quickly repaired, the local economy slows, people lose jobs, and recovery is difficult. Paradoxically, just when the need for state and local government action is the greatest, their resources are stretched to the breaking point. When they need to spend money to rebuild roads, bridges, buildings, and houses, their tax revenues dip significantly. When people can't work, no income taxes are withheld; when people can't shop, because stores are destroyed, sales taxes are not collected. No state can deal with a natural disaster that causes millions of dollars of damage.

However, the national government can respond, even when the affected state can't. The national government helps out in disaster situations through the Federal Emergency Management Agency (FEMA). Originally set up in 1979 to cope with the effects of a nuclear attack,[1] the agency has in recent years been called to assist in areas struck by natural disasters. When the president declares a state or locality a federal disaster area, FEMA provides financial help, temporary shelters, and a host of other aid.

Until recently, the agency's performance got low marks. It was especially criticized for an inadequate response to Hurricane Andrew in south Florida in 1992. It took three days for the agency to begin distributing emergency food and water, and medical help was delayed, too. Senator Ernest Hollings (D-S.C.) once described FEMA as "the sorriest bunch of bureaucratic jackasses I've ever known."[2] The agency's response to Hurricane Andrew reinforced that image.

The widespread criticism FEMA received from both Republicans and Democrats led to some major changes. New appointees now had significant disaster relief experience. And FEMA changed its approach, from a reactive ("Let's see if they ask for help") to a proactive ("Let's see what we can do right now") stance. Red tape was cut, and agency response time was drastically reduced. For instance, a FEMA advance team arrived in Oklahoma City about five hours after the bombing of the Alfred P. Murrah Federal Office Building in 1995, and a search and rescue team was on the scene by 2:30 A.M. the following morning.[3]

The agency responded with similar success to the devastating floods in the Midwest in 1993. When the Des Moines (Iowa) Water Works was on the verge of collapse, FEMA set up water distribution centers and water purification systems within a day. FEMA provided clean water to Des Moines residents for over two weeks.

The rejuvenated Federal Emergency Management Agency stands as a clear example of federalism in action. No matter how much independent autonomy we want states to have, states cannot always respond adequately to disasters of catastrophic proportions. But the national government can. When the national government rolls up its sleeves to help out, it underlines that we are all part of the same nation, sharing its benefits and helping to carry each other's burdens. An earthquake in California, a tornado in Alabama, or a blizzard in Minnesota affects us all indirectly, no matter where we live. And our federal system offers a mechanism for alleviating local distress without undermining the independence of the states that comprise our Union.

1. Ted Gup, "How FEMA Learned to Stop Worrying about Civilians and Love the Bomb," *Mother Jones*, January/February 1994, p. 28.
2. Quoted in Daniel Franklin, "The FEMA Phoenix," *The Washington Monthly*, July/August 1995, p. 38.
3. Franklin, "The FEMA Phoenix," p. 32.

NEW DEAL LEGISLATION PASSED DURING ROOSEVELT'S FIRST TERM

March 9, 1933	Emergency Banking Act
March 31, 1933	Civilian Conservation Corps created
May 12, 1933	Agricultural Adjustment Act
May 12, 1933	Federal Emergency Relief Act
May 18, 1933	Tennessee Valley Authority created
June 5, 1933	Nation taken off gold standard
June 13, 1933	Home Owners Loan Corporation created
June 16, 1933	Federal Deposit Insurance Corporation created
June 16, 1933	Farm Credit Administration created
June 16, 1933	National Industrial Recovery Act
January 30, 1934	Dollar devalued
June 6, 1934	Securities and Exchange Commission authorized
June 12, 1934	Reciprocal Tariff Act
June 19, 1934	Federal Communications Commission created
June 27, 1934	Railroad Retirement Act
June 28, 1934	Federal Housing Administration authorized
April 8, 1935	Works Progress Administration created
July 5, 1935	National Labor Relations Act
August 14, 1935	Social Security Act
August 26, 1935	Federal Power Commission created
August 30, 1935	National Bituminous Coal Conservation Act
February 19, 1936	Soil Conservation and Domestic Allotment Act

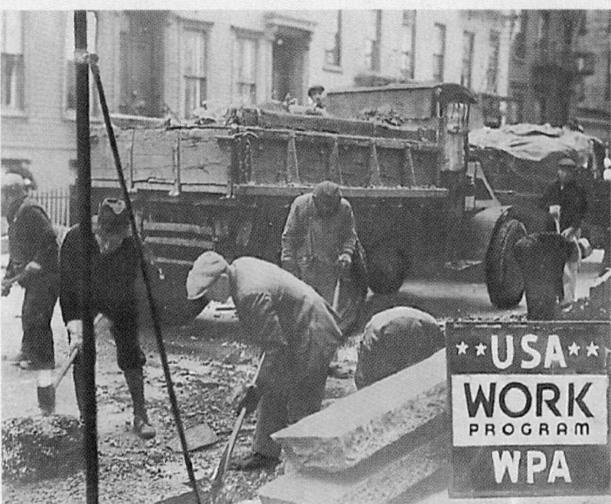

Franklin Roosevelt took office on March 4, 1933. He immediately sent to Congress a group of legislative proposals, many of which Congress passed within 100 days. Roosevelt's program, known as the New Deal, enlarged the role of the federal government. Shown in the photo are civilians employed in the Works Progress Administration (WPA), a New Deal agency that built schools, roads, airports, and post offices in many towns in the late 1930s. Though the term boondoggle *was coined in reference to some WPA projects, the agency was successful in putting millions to work and improving the nation's public buildings, roads, and bridges.*

SOURCE: List compiled by Lee Epstein and Thomas Walker, *Constitutional Law for a Changing America: Institutional Powers and Constraints* (Washington, DC: CQ Press, 1992), p. 283.

masked. When another economic downturn occurs, the states may have difficulty providing citizens with services at the current level.

In the last several years, the new Republican majority in Congress has taken other steps to return power to the states. Welfare has now been returned to the states and is funded with a federal block grant for most but not all the costs. Congress also passed legislation allowing states once again to set speed limits on interstate and other federal highways. States were quick to respond, with western states, especially, raising the speed limit to 70 or 75 miles per hour.

CONTEMPORARY FEDERALISM

Today's federalism is a mixture of cooperation and conflict. One expert calls it "competitive federalism," because states and the federal government are competing for leadership of the nation's domestic policy.[17] In this section, we will review some of the major features of today's federalism and then return to some of the areas of conflict and contention that are the subject of current debate.

ARE STATES REALLY CLOSER TO THE PEOPLE?

Much current rhetoric suggests that many federal government programs, such as health care, welfare, education, and environmental protection, for example, should be turned over to the states because the states are "closer to the people." But what does that mean?

Those who argue that states are closer to the people point to the relative smallness of states. The United States has nearly 260 million residents. Although 7 states have over 10 million people, and California has over 30 million, most (32) states have fewer than 5 million residents. Thus, it should be possible for individuals to have more say in state government than national. Moreover, on the whole, states are more homogeneous in their cultures than the nation, and these state cultures lead to different policy preferences: Residents of traditionalistic states, on average, have different views of desirable government action than residents of individualistic or moralistic states. Thus, state public policy can be more sensitive to the preferences of state communities. Being closer to the people may also mean that state governments can respond more quickly to changes in the public mood; state legislators are closer to the grassroots than national legislators. Finally, smaller government should be more efficient.

However, reality is not always as simple as a slogan. Except in a few very small states, where town meetings still prevail, it is difficult for individuals to have much say in their state government as well as their national government. States are not small entities, even if they are a lot smaller than the federal government. In fact, states have more employees than the federal government and are growing faster (see figure). Moreover, most people know a lot more about what is going on in Washington than they do about what is going on in Lincoln, Springfield, Sacramento, or Harrisburg, to name a few state capitals, and in that sense have more tools to make the federal government responsive than they do the state government. (How many talk shows or CNN clones focus on what is going on in the statehouse?) There is also evidence that being "closer to the people" also means being more susceptible to the pressures of big money, and the relative homogeneity of state populations may make it easier to steamroller the rights of small groups. Finally, there is no evidence that state governments are less corrupt or more efficient than the federal government.[1] Indeed, federal pressure has been a major influence on professionalizing of state bureaucracies.

These problems with state governments do not mean that turning some federal programs back to the states is necessarily a bad idea. The problems do suggest, though, that we need to look beyond slogans to the reality of politics, national and state.

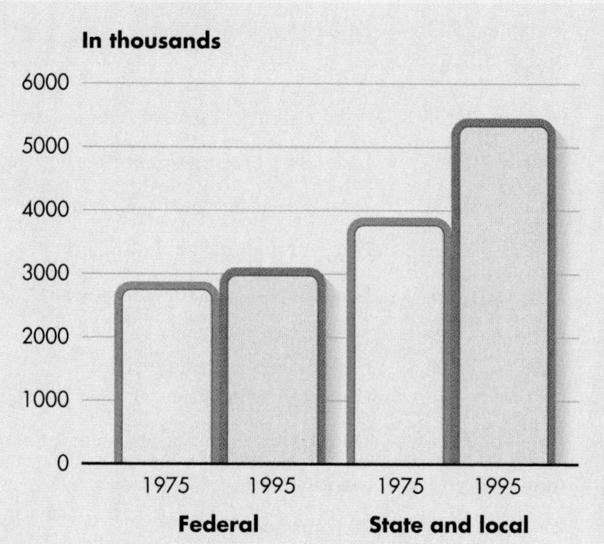

Number of Employees in the Federal and State Governments, 1975–1995

SOURCE: *Statistical Abstract of the United States*, 1995, Tables 540 and 508.

1. See for recent discussions, Richard Cohen, "States Aren't Saints Either," *Washington Post National Weekly Edition*, April 3–9, 1995, p. 28; R. W. Apple, "You Say You Want a Devolution," *New York Times*, January 29, 1995, Section 4, p. 1.

Federal-State Relations

COOPERATION

Much federal-state activity is cooperative. Given the large number of governments in the United States (Table 2), it is essential that they cooperate. And they do. States and the federal government work together in a myriad of activities in almost every area of policy. One example of informal but intensive cooperation is the National Disease Control Center, which helps state and local governments with health emergencies. National and state police and other crime-fighting agencies share data on crimes and criminals. Another area of cooperation is joint regulatory activity. The federal government and the states jointly regulate some businesses and industry. The federal government sets standards, and each state decides whether to enforce the standard itself or let the federal government do it. Joint activity is found in several areas, including occupational safety and environmental regulation.

TABLE 2

Number of Government Units in the United States

Part of the reason that intergovernmental relations in the United States are so complex is that there are so many governments. Though the number of school districts has decreased dramatically in the last 40 years, and the number of townships has declined slowly, the number of "special districts"—created for a single purpose, such as parks, airports, or flood control management—continues to grow.

	STATES	COUNTIES	MUNICIPALITIES	TOWNSHIPS AND TOWNS	SCHOOL DISTRICTS	SPECIAL DISTRICTS
1942	48	3,050	16,220	18,919	108,579	8,299
1992	50	3,043	19,279	16,656	19,422	31,555

SOURCE: *Statistical Abstract of the United States, 1997* (Washington, D.C.: U.S. Government Printing Office, 1997), Table 474.

Another important area of federal-state cooperation is federal grants to states (Figure 3). The federal government gives funds to states to cope with problems that do not stop at state borders. Federal grant-in-aid programs represent a compromise between those who want a nationally administered program and those who want to keep a program at the state or local level. Unemployment compensation, administered by the states under federal regulation and funding, is a good example. Moreover, despite some examples of inefficiency, major federal programs have succeeded in helping state and local governments meet real needs, and along the way, they have increased the professionalism of state and local bureaucrats.

Federal programs often serve the interests of state and local officials, who would rather have programs paid for by federal taxes than state and local taxes. And the system greatly benefits many different kinds of interest groups that demand national action when they are spurned by the states. Groups of all ideological stripes pragmatically seek federal aid. For example, both conservatives and liberals supported a federal grant program helping states collect child support money from nonpaying divorced or unmarried fathers.

STATES AND LOCALITIES AS LOBBYISTS

A crucial part of the relationship of the states to the federal government concerns lobbying. The importance of federal money to states and localities and the need for coordination between federal and state bureaucracies have stimulated the organization of groups of state and local officials, such as the National Conference of State Legislatures, the National League of Cities, and the American Public Welfare Association. These groups lobby for favorable legislation for states and localities and work with federal agencies to ensure that new regulations are implemented in a way acceptable to the states. Most of these organizations have multimillion-dollar budgets and employ a sizable staff of lobbyists and researchers. Many individual states and cities have their own Washington lobbyists, and these lobbyists appear to have some positive effect on increasing federal aid.[18]

But why should states lobby when they all have members of the House and of the Senate in Congress? For one thing, lobbying organizations can help coordinate legislators' efforts by contacting large numbers of members at the same time. Moreover, the members of Congress may not always agree with the state leaders. They may represent different parties, for instance, or urban interests may be stronger in the state while the members of Congress disproportionately represent rural and suburban areas. Finally, these lobbying organizations can present a national perspective on how a problem affects various localities.

CONFLICT

Current federal-state relations are also characterized by conflict. One of the sharpest clashes concerns so-called **unfunded mandates.** When Congress passes laws requiring states to do something, usually to regulate, it often transfers money to the states to cover part of the cost of the activity, but not always. When federal funding is not provided or is not enough to cover the expenses, the states have to come up with the necessary money. Critics call these unfunded mandates. For example, the federal government requires the states to deduct child support from the wages of parents who fall behind on payments. The state is also to deduct payments automatically from paychecks of fathers of children whose mothers are on welfare.[19] States that fail to carry out these mandates risk losing the federal contributions to their welfare funds.

Environmental regulations are, overall, the most expensive federal mandates. Meeting federal standards for clean air and water is projected to cost billions. Other recent federal regulations include a mandate that states and localities provide for the education of illegal immigrants and one that requires, among other things, public buildings, sidewalks, and transportation to be accessible to the handicapped.

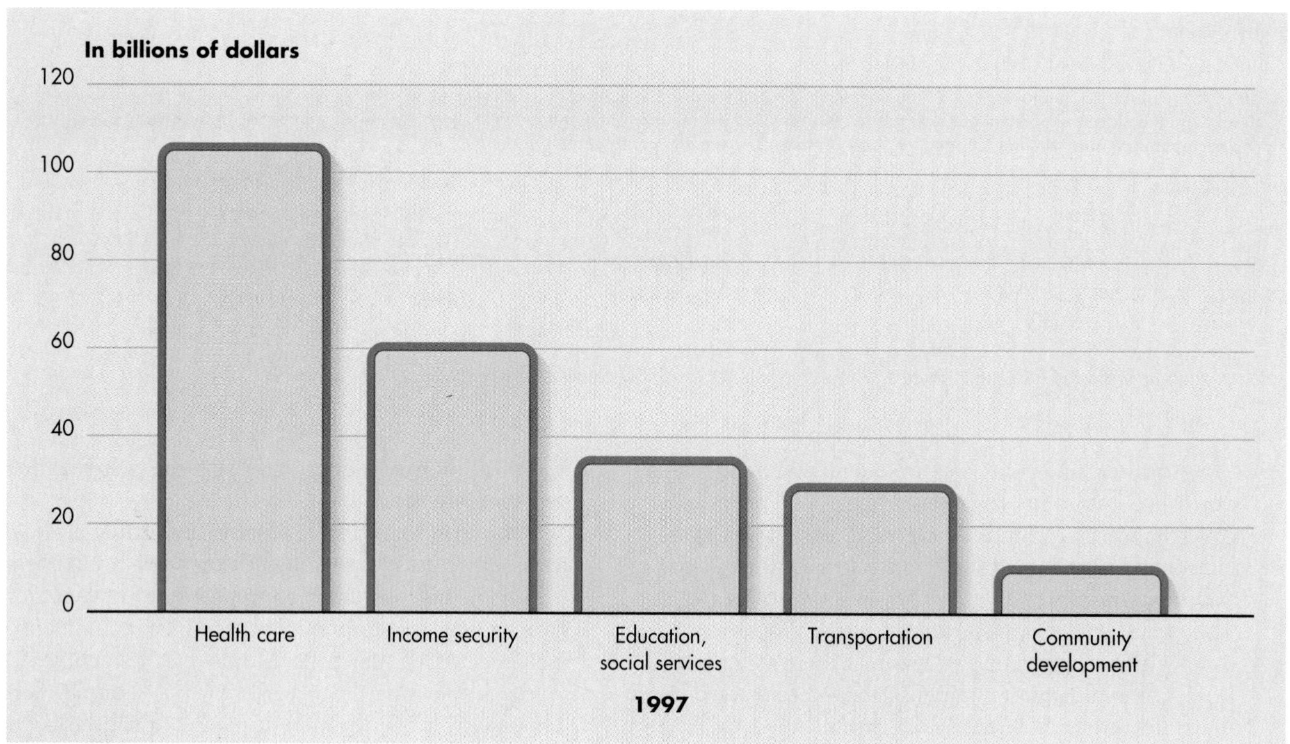

FIGURE 3

What Does the Federal Government Give the States Money to Do?

Most of the $245 billion the federal government gave to the states went for programs in these areas.

SOURCE: *Statistical Abstract of the United States*, Washington, D.C.: U.S. Government Printing Office, 1997, Table 482.

The burdens of these and other mandates led to a plank in the Republicans' 1994 "Contract with America" calling for legislation to reduce such mandates. Some conservatives would like to abolish unfunded mandates completely. Others believe that unfunded mandates are sometimes beneficial, but that their costs should be made more public at the time legislation is passed. Still others believe the attack on unfunded mandates is really an attack on all regulatory action by the federal government. This group believes that expecting states to enact significant regulations in some areas is impracticable.

Another area of conflict is more basic. Some favor a radical shift in federal-state responsibilities, with a return to some form of dual federalism. States would handle many more programs than they do now, and the federal government would shrink in size, scope, and cost.

Proponents of this view do not all have the same assumptions. Some believe that government has a role to play in solving societal problems and that the states are capable of handling that role. Others believe that government has no role and that turning programs over to the states will kill them.

Even though most people agree there are some areas that the federal government should leave to the states, the problem is that there is little consensus on what those areas are. For example, some argue that the federal government should leave health care to the states but centralize welfare programs at the federal level. Others believe exactly the opposite.

A little-known example of federal-state-local cooperation is fire-fighting in wilderness areas. In 1988, more than 15,000 firefighters converged to fight summer fires in Yellowstone and surrounding areas. Led by members of the U.S. Forest Service and other federal agencies, the firefighters were sent by state and local governments of every state.

Interstate Relations

CONSTITUTIONAL REQUIREMENTS

The Constitution established rules governing states' relationships with each other. One important provision is the **full faith and credit clause,** which requires states to recognize contracts. If you marry in Ohio, Pennsylvania must recognize your marriage. The Constitution also provides that if a fugitive from justice flees from one state to another, he or she is supposed to be extradited, that is, sent back to the state with jurisdiction.

VOLUNTARY COOPERATION

Most state-to-state interaction is informal and voluntary, with state officials consulting with officials in other states about common problems and states borrowing ideas from one another. Sometimes states enter into formal agreements, called interstate compacts, to deal with a common problem—operating a port or allocating water from a river basin, for example.

INTERSTATE COMPETITION

Changing economic patterns and an overall loss of economic competitiveness by the United States in the world market have stimulated vigorous competition among the states to attract new businesses and jobs. They advertise the advantages of their states to prospective new businesses: low taxes, good climate, a skilled workforce, low wages, and little government regulation. This growing competition prompts states to give tax advantages and other financial incentives to businesses willing to relocate there.

Critics believe that these offers serve mostly to erode a state's tax base and have little impact on most business relocation decisions. Evidence indicates that low taxes are not the primary reason for business relocation.[20] Nevertheless, without some special break for businesses, states now feel at a competitive disadvantage in recruiting them. Business interests pressure states to adopt legislation more favorable to business.

State-Local Relations

Another important feature of contemporary federalism is the relationship of states to their localities—counties, cities, and special districts. These relationships are defined by state constitutions; they are not dealt with in the federal constitution. States differ in the autonomy they grant to their localities. In some states, **home rule** charters give local governments considerable autonomy in such matters as setting tax rates, regulating land use, and choosing their form of local government. In many states, cities of different sizes have different degrees of autonomy. Although localities are creatures of their states, whereas states exist independently of the national government, some of the same problems that affect national-state relations also affect state-local relations. City and county officials often wish for more authority and fewer mandates from the state.

WHO, ME? STUDENTS AS RECIPIENTS OF FEDERAL AID

All college students are direct or indirect recipients of federal grant dollars. Your college or university was probably built in part by federal funds, some of your faculty were supported by federal funds during their training, and the federal government helps hundreds of thousands of college students each year through grants and low-interest loans. If you are less than 60 years old, it is likely that part of your elementary or secondary education (including your school lunches) also was paid for by federal money, even if you went to a private school.

If you live in a city with a municipal bus or subway system, your bus fare is lowered by as much as half because it is partially supported by federal dollars. Even if you do not ride a bus or subway, the federal government has paid for part of your transportation—whatever it is—by contributing to the funding of many streets and roads. If you drive to another city during your school holidays, you drive over highways for which Uncle Sam has paid up to 90% of the cost. If you fly, you fly into airports that are partially paid for by the federal government.

If you or your parents have been unemployed, your unemployment compensation is paid in part by the federal government through a grant program. If one of your parents died while you were a youngster, you probably received Social Security benefits, and if you have lived in poverty, you may have received AFDC (Aid to Families with Dependent Children).

If you feel that you have been affected by none of these grants, here is a final example. If you have a flush toilet, it is probably connected to a sewer paid for by, you guessed it, Uncle Sam, who has spent hundreds of millions of dollars in grants to local communities for sewer construction.

CONCLUSION: IS FEDERALISM RESPONSIVE?

Across the United States, our beliefs in democracy, freedom, and equality bind us together. In many ways we are becoming more alike, as rapid transportation, television and other forms of instant communication, fast-food

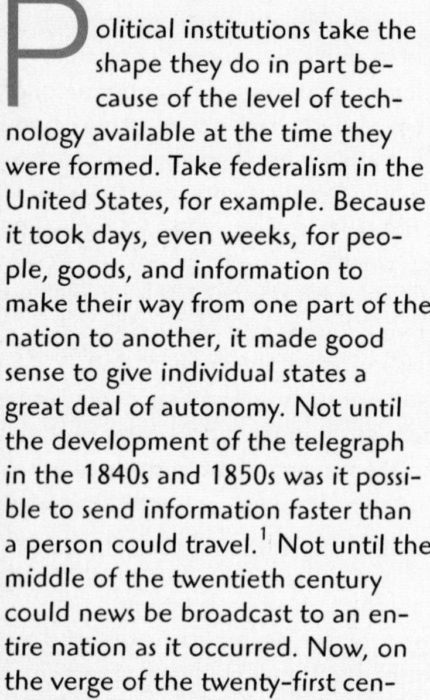

INTO THE 21ST CENTURY

FEDERALISM IN THE NEXT CENTURY: SURFING THE WEB

Political institutions take the shape they do in part because of the level of technology available at the time they were formed. Take federalism in the United States, for example. Because it took days, even weeks, for people, goods, and information to make their way from one part of the nation to another, it made good sense to give individual states a great deal of autonomy. Not until the development of the telegraph in the 1840s and 1850s was it possible to send information faster than a person could travel.[1] Not until the middle of the twentieth century could news be broadcast to an entire nation as it occurred. Now, on the verge of the twenty-first century, a new revolution in obtaining, providing, and sharing information is occurring.

The Internet and the World Wide Web now make it possible for governmental agencies at all levels to provide access to tremendous amounts of information. Texts of legislative bills, election results, policy analyses, and statistics of all sorts can readily be found. Interest groups and academic organizations are also beginning to use the www to publicize their perspectives and insights. At the same time, anyone with a computer and an Internet service provider can get access to virtually all of this information almost instantaneously. Right now the only limitations seem to be the speed of the user's modem and the bandwidth of the connection at the computer holding the information (the wider the bandwidth, the more users can access the information and the faster it can be provided).

Like most other institutions, federalism will be affected by this information revolution. When information could travel only slowly, it made sense to have most decisions made at the state and local level, where the information was available. When information flowed more freely, it made sense to have decisions made where the information was centrally collected, which was frequently Washington, D.C. Now that information is becoming available cheaply and easily all over the nation, the political landscape is being affected.

One way is through increasing cooperation and coordination among states. The Internet is not going to decrease competition among states for industry or for river water, but the widespread availability of information is going to make it possible for policymakers in one state to know what their colleagues in other states are doing. There is no need to telephone people who may not be available or who may not have the needed information at their fingertips, and there is no need to explain or justify the information request. Just access the right Web pages. With more information of this sort, policymakers can more readily learn from each other and can adjust their proposals to avoid conflicts.

But another effect will be negative, at least in the short run. Decision-makers will inevitably encounter such a glut of information that it will be almost impossible to deal with it all. As more states and the national government put more and more documents and data on their Web sites, policymakers will be hard-pressed to keep up with the flow. But disregarding information that could be quickly found entails political risk. "If they had only looked at this document," someone could charge, "drastic mistakes could have been avoided." In the near term, officials who excel in gathering and using information may have a great advantage over those who may have more substantive experience but who barely know a modem from a CD-ROM.

States seem currently to be in a better position to exploit the Internet and the Web than the federal government. State governments lagged behind Washington in computerizing their operations, but now that they have taken advantage of the latest technology, the machines on their officials' desks tend to be newer and more capable of fast Internet access. One federal staffer complained that "My computer is older than I am."[2] Moreover, in their dealings with the federal government in the past, states have been at an information disadvantage. The desire to redress the information balance gives state and local officials a greater motivation to exploit Internet resources than their federal colleagues. And it does not take much money: San Carlos, California, spends about $50 a month to rent computer space for its Web site.[3]

Although states will continue to rely on federal funds, states that make judicious use of the WWW will be able to reduce their dependence on federal officials for information the states need. While the twenty-first century will continue to see a nation-centered federalism, it may be one with greater autonomy for states than they experienced for most of the twentieth century.

1. James W. Carey, "Technology and Ideology: The Case of the Telegraph," in *Fourth Annual Communication Research Symposium: Proceedings*, ed. Joseph P. McKerns (Knoxville, Tenn.: University of Tennessee, 1981).
2. Quoted in Steven Greenhouse, "The State Department: A Snail in Age of E-Mail," *New York Times*, March 6, 1995, p. A6.
3. "A Guide to Desktop Technology in Government," *Governing*, vol. 10, no. 1, October 1996, p. 90.

franchises, hotel chains, and other nationwide businesses bring about an increasing similarity in what we think about, our tastes in culture and food, and even political activities. But to say that Alabama is more like New York than it used to be is certainly not to say they are alike. Our federal system helps us accommodate this diversity by allowing both state and federal governments a role in making policy.

Our Founders probably did not foresee a federal system like the one we have now; the federal government has surpassed the states in power and scope of action. Yet one of the paradoxes of our system is that as the national government has gained extraordinary power, so have the states and localities. All levels of government are stronger than in the eighteenth century. Federal power *and* state power have grown hand in hand.

It is probably foolish to pretend to know how the Founders might deal with our complex federal system. However, many of them were quite astute politicians who would undoubtedly recognize that our system evolved because various groups over time demanded national action. Yet we continue to believe in local control and grassroots government. Our system is a logical outcome of our contradictory impulses for national solutions and local control.

Is such a complex system responsive? It is very responsive in that groups and individuals making a demand that is rejected at one level of government can go to another level. The federal system creates multiple points of access, each with power to satisfy political demands. Yet the system is less responsive in that the same multiple levels and points of access also block demands. Civil rights groups, for example, were able to win voting rights for blacks in most states before the 1960s. But they were still blocked in several states until the national government acted. Thus, federalism creates opportunities for influence, but it also creates possibilities for roadblocks to achieving national political action. This, of course, is what Madison foresaw.

Does this complex federal system contribute toward the anger many Americans feel toward their government? Although hard evidence is not available, it certainly seems that the multiple points of access, and the ability to stop action at many levels, contributes to Americans' sense that their government is out of the control of the people.

EPILOGUE

Clinton Creates a New National Monument

On September 18, 1996, standing on the South Rim of the Grand Canyon, Bill Clinton declared the Grand Staircase–Escalante area a national monument to protect it from exploitation and development. He called the area a "great pillar in our bridge to tomorrow."[21] His decision was hailed by environmentalists. "This is a gutsy move," said one environmental leader.[22] Its effect on the November vote is unclear, although Clinton won a large vote in California and lost Utah, both as expected.

Many people in Utah, especially those living in or near the new national monument, expressed disgust and displeasure with Clinton's action. One county

Bill Boyle/*San Juan Record*

Deputies remove a protester who blocked county road crews from "improving" a road near the new Grand Staircase–Escalante National Monument.

commissioner estimated that his area lost as many as 900 jobs because the proposed coal mine cannot be built. "The most powerful politician in the world just kicked me in the teeth," he said.[23] Utah senator Orrin Hatch (R) was equally irritated, referring to Clinton's declaration as "the mother of all land-grabs."[24]

Utahans did not sit still. It turns out that wilderness designation is only available for areas that do not have mechanically maintained roads running through them. As a result, counties—and individuals—have been using road graders to "brighten up" vehicle tracks running through the area.[25] Both sides expect the courts will be asked at some point to decide exactly what can—and what cannot—be done in the newly protected wilderness area.

Much of the dispute has now moved behind the scenes, as national and local officials negotiate with each other to devise a management plan delineating what can and should be allowed in and around the new national monument. That, too, is how federalism works. Despite sometimes strong disagreements, each level of government needs the other to attain jointly desired ends; working together is the best way to try to accomplish their goals.

KEY TERMS

federalism
unitary system
confederal system
"necessary and proper"
implied powers clause
supremacy clause
dual federalism
cooperative federalism
"mischiefs of faction"
McCulloch v. Maryland
New Deal
grants-in-aid
new federalism
general revenue sharing
block grants
unfunded mandates
full faith and credit clause
home rule

FURTHER READING

Daniel Elazar, *American Federalism: A View from the States*, 3d ed. (New York: Harper & Row, 1984). Explores the development of intergovernmental relations and examines American political cultures.

Paul Peterson, Barry Rabe, and Kenneth Wong, *When Federalism Works* (Washington, D.C.: Brookings Institute, 1986). Challenges prevailing wisdom to argue that most federal grant programs work.

Jeffrey Pressman and Aaron Wildavsky, *Implementation* (Berkeley, Calif.: University of California Press, 1973). A classic look at the difficulties of translating federal laws into working programs when dealing with a multiplicity of state and local governments.

Alice Rivlin, *Reviving the American Dream: The Economy, the States, and the Federal Government* (Washington, D.C.: Brookings Institute, 1992). An analysis of the fiscal relations between the federal government and the states by Clinton's budget director.

John Steinbeck, *The Grapes of Wrath* (New York: Viking, 1939). A novel portraying the conditions facing the country that set the stage for the New Deal.

David Walker, *The Rebirth of Federalism* (Chatham, N.J.: Chatham House, 1995). A recent look at contemporary trends.

ELECTRONIC RESOURCES

http://csgcomm.csg.org/

The home page of the Council of State Governments, a cooperative organization that seeks to promote the interchange of ideas among states and also lobbies Congress for legislation helpful to the states. Its home page contains links to individual state home pages and provides updates on national issues of importance to the states.

http://www.ncsl.org/public/guide.htm#policy

The home page of the National Council of State Legislatures. The council promotes reform and increased efficiency in state legislatures, helps facilitate interstate cooperation, and lobbies for state issues. Its home page also provides information about current issues of relevance to states.

http://www.geocities.com/Athens/4545/

This site connects to many other sites with information on the New Deal and President Franklin Roosevelt. One of the links is http://www.ipl.org/ref/POTUS/fdroosevelt.html, which connects to biographies of, and information about, all U.S. presidents.

INFOTRAC CITATIONS

"A Monumental Challenge"
"Earthquake Victims Hit the Jackpot"
"Mandate Watch"

NOTES

1. Daniel Glick and Sharon Begley, "Monument in the Red Rock," *Newsweek*, September 30, 1996, p. 61.
2. *Statistical Abstract of the United States, 1994* (Washington, D.C.: U.S. Government Printing Office, 1994), Table 354.
3. Christopher John Farley, "The West Is Wild Again," *Time*, March 20, 1995, p. 46.
4. Erik Larson, "Unrest in the West," *Time*, October 23, 1995, p. 54.
5. These ideas come from Daniel Elazar, *American Federalism: A View from the States*, 3d ed. (New York: Harper & Row, 1984).
6. The figures in this paragraph come from George E. Hall and Deirdre A. Gagnin, eds., *1997 County and City Extra: Annual Metro, City, and County Data Book* (Lanham, Md.: Bernan Press, 1997).
7. Robert S. Erikson, Gerald C. Wright, and John P. McIver, *Statehouse Democracy: Public Opinion and Policy in the American States* (New York: Cambridge University Press, 1993).
8. A 1976 Supreme Court decision used the Tenth Amendment as a reason to forbid the federal government to extend minimum wage and hour laws to state and local government employees. See

National League of Cities v. Usery, 426 U.S. 833 (1976). This decision was partially overruled in 1985. See *Garcia v. San Antonio Metropolitan Transit Authority*, 469 U.S. 528 (1985).

9. The following discussion is drawn from Richard Leach, *American Federalism* (New York: W. W. Norton, 1970), chapter 1. See also Christopher Hamilton and Donald Wells, *Federalism, Power and Political Economy: A New Theory of Federalism's Impact on American Life* (Englewood Cliffs, N.J.: Prentice Hall, 1990).

10. *Federalist Paper* #45.

11. *McCulloch v. Maryland*, 4 Wheat. 316 (1819).

12. Alfred Kelly and Winfred Harbeson, *The American Constitution: Its Origins and Development* (New York: W. W. Norton, 1976).

13. Daniel Elazar, *The American Partnership* (Chicago: University of Chicago Press, 1962).

14. Perhaps because he is a sociologist (!), Theodore Caplan did not fully appreciate the extent of federal involvement in Muncie, even in 1924—the support of veterans, schools, roads, and hospitals by federal land grants. Nevertheless, his major point is valid: The federal presence there was nothing compared to now. Caplan is quoted in Daniel Walker, *Toward a Functioning Federalism* (Cambridge, Mass.: Winthrop, 1981), pp. 3–4.

15. Theodore Lowi, *The Personal President* (Ithaca, N.Y.: Cornell University Press, 1985).

16. Paul Peterson, Barry Rabe, and Kenneth Wong, *When Federalism Works* (Washington, D.C.: Brookings Institute, 1986). See also John Schwartz, *America's Hidden Success*, 2d ed. (New York: W. W. Norton, 1988); David Walker, *The Rebirth of Federalism: Slouching toward Washington* (Chatham, N.J.: Chatham House, 1995).

17. Alice Rivlin, *Reviving the American Dream: The Economy, the States and the Federal Government* (Washington, D.C.: Brookings Institute, 1992).

18. Neil Berch, "Why Do Some States Play the Federal Aid Game Better than Others?" *American Politics Quarterly* 20 (July, 1992), pp. 366–377.

19. See Mary Ann Glendon, *Abortion and Divorce in Western Law* (Cambridge, Mass.: Harvard University Press, 1987), pp. 87–88; see also Susan Welch, Sue Thomas, and Margery Ambrosius, "Family Policy," in Virginia Gray and Herbert Jacob, *State Politics and Policy*, 5th ed. (Boston: Little, Brown, 1995).

20. Enid F. Beaumont and Harold Hovey, "State, Local and Federal Development Policies: New Federalism Patterns, Chaos, or What?" *Public Administration Review* 45 (March/April 1985), pp. 327–332; Barry Rubin and C. Kurt Zorn, "Sensible State and Local Development," *Public Administration Review* 45 (March/April 1985), pp. 333–339.

21. Michael Satchell, "Clinton's 'Mother of All Land-grabs,'" *U.S. News and World Report*, January 20, 1997, p. 44.

22. Quoted in Glick and Begley, "Monument in the Red Rock."

23. Glick and Begley, "Monument in the Red Rock."

24. Satchell, "Clinton's 'Mother of All Land-grabs.'"

25. Tom Kenworthy, "Ah, Wilderness!—but Not Right Here," *The Washington Post National Weekly Edition*, December 9–15, 1996, p. 31.

Teddy Roosevelt called the presidency a "bully pulpit" at which he could speak, through the press, to the people to persuade them to support his programs (top). Journalists fill the Los Angeles Coliseum for the 1984 Olympics (below).

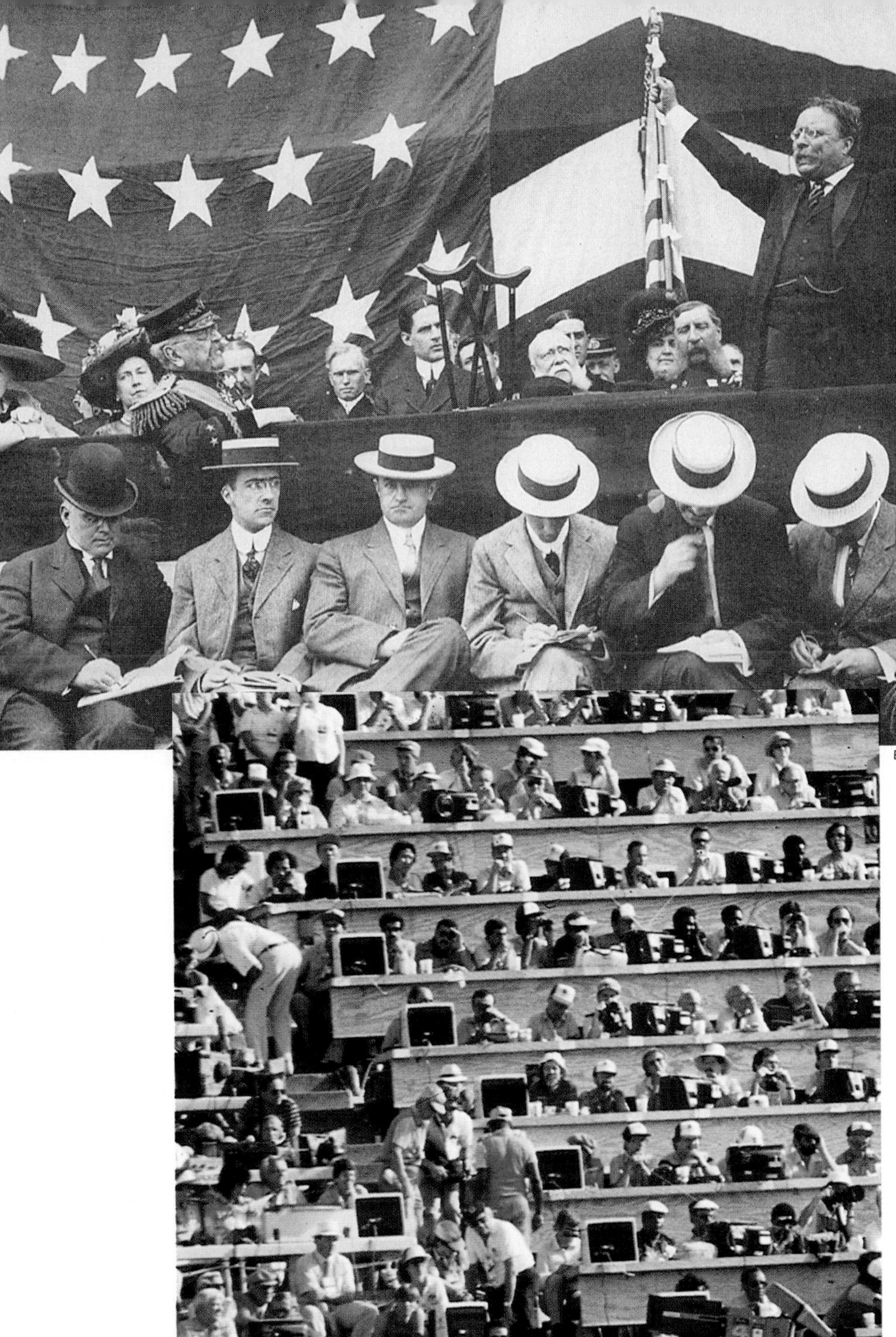

Brown Brothers

Woodfin Camp and Associates

PART TWO LINKS BETWEEN PEOPLE AND GOVERNMENT

Robb Kendrik Photography

4 PUBLIC OPINION

OUTLINE

YOU ARE THERE

Should a Pollster Make Public Details of His Polls?

It is 1996 and you are Frank Luntz, leading pollster, consultant, and strategist for the Republican Party.[1] After receiving your doctorate in political science at Oxford University, you started Luntz Research Companies in Arlington, Virginia. In the short time you have been in the business, you have become something of a personality, appearing regularly on a number of television shows such as *Nightline, Crossfire, The NewsHour, Good Morning America,* and others. *Time* magazine recently named you one of America's most promising leaders under 40. *USA Today* describes you as one of the most influential minds in the Republican Party. You won the *Washington Post* "Crystal Ball" award for being the most accurate pundit. You were the first pollster to predict Republican success in winning control of Congress in 1994.

Your research was the basis for the Republican Contract with America, 10 proposals that the party promised to consider if it won control of Congress in 1994. Your polls showed that each element of the Contract was supported by 60% or more of the American people. Majority support for proposals such as a balanced budget, welfare reform, and a middle-class tax cut were important in getting Republican candidates for the House to sign the Contract and agree to bring the proposals up for consideration should the party win a majority.

The Contract became the centerpiece of the 1994 campaign. You and others pushed it on the talk show circuit and evening news. You also discussed the poll results that suggested the Contract was a sure winner. When the election results were finally in, you looked like a political genius. For the first time since 1954, the Republicans won control of both the Senate and the House.

Your rising star quality was only partially diminished by a complaint registered with the Committee on Standards of the American Association for Public Opinion Research (AAPOR) concerning the polls you did on the Contract. The AAPOR, an organization of 1,400 research professionals in government agencies, universities, and commercial polling firms, monitors polls, at least those that are made public, to ensure that pollsters follow accepted procedures and practices in conducting and reporting polls. Although the organization has no legal authority, it can censure or publicly reprimand pollsters who violate professional standards. The organization cannot stop anyone from polling, but censure can hurt a pollster's professional reputation.

In response to the complaint, the AAPOR asked you to report the questions and other details of your Contract polls. When pollsters make their results public, most comply with AAPOR standards and provide information on how their polls are conducted. It is a way for other pollsters, the press, government officials, and the public to evaluate the reliability of a poll. To report a poll publicly but withhold information on how the poll was conducted, in the words of the AAPOR, "undermines the credibility of all polls." It also undermines the public agenda because poll results influence which issues get attention. The public can be misled into thinking that some issues are more important than they really are.

How do you respond to the AAPOR? Do you satisfy the organization and others in the polling community by releasing the information? Doing so is likely to maintain your professional standing, perhaps even enhance it as you demonstrate that you abide by the professional and ethical standards of the profession. Although the Republican Party technically owns the poll, the Contract received a great deal of attention in the campaign. You and others have been discussing the poll results for more than two years. Other than the information requested by the AAPOR, little regarding the polls is still private. Moreover, if the items in the Contract are as popular as you say, the information may spur added interest in the Contract and help influence Congress to pass it.

Or do you withhold the information? You are not a member of the AAPOR. Censure is unlikely to damage your reputation a great deal. In time, everyone may simply forget the whole thing. Moreover, you know that, in fact, your questions were loaded to get the results you wanted, exactly the kind of polling methods the AAPOR finds unprofessional. For example, to show that the majority of Americans favored legal reform, you reported responses to the statement "We should stop excessive legal claims, frivolous lawsuits and overzealous lawyers." It would be hard for anyone to disagree with this statement. Revealing these sorts of questions would be embarrassing even though the polls have served the purposes you wanted. What do you do and why?

Feelings about public opinion are contradictory. In a democracy we want leaders to be responsive to public opinion. Yet often we complain that elected officials do not lead but simply follow the latest trends in public opinion polls. And the polls are contradictory, too. Many Americans are angry with government. They do not trust it; they think it is too big and spends too much money. At the same time, they like the services government provides them, and very few Americans are willing to cut spending so drastically as to eliminate their favorite service or program.

In this chapter we will explore public opinion to better understand these contradictions. We will describe how public opinion is formed and measured, discuss the pattern of public opinion on some important issues, and assess the extent to which government is responsive to public opinion. Because political science is primarily interested in opinions that affect government, the focus of this chapter is public opinion about political issues, personalities, institutions, and events.

NATURE OF PUBLIC OPINION

We can define **public opinion** as the collection of individual opinions toward issues or objects of general interest, that is, those that concern a significant number of people. Public opinion can be described in terms of direction, intensity, and stability. Direction refers to whether public opinion is positive or negative. Generally, it is mixed: Some individuals have a positive opinion, others negative. Intensity refers to the strength of opinion. Intense opinions often give rise to behavior. Pro-life and pro-choice advocates, for example, are likely to act on their opinions and vote against members of Congress opposed to their positions.

Most public issues are not of interest to most people. Individuals may feel intensely about one or two issues that directly affect them, but not everyone, or even a majority, is intense about the same issues. The relative absence of severe economic and social divisions in the United States explains the lack of intense opinions. With the possible exception of the racial and states' rights issues that almost destroyed the nation in the 1860s, there has been nothing like the long-standing, divisive class and religious conflicts of many European nations.

Opinions also differ in stability. An opinion is more likely to change when an individual lacks intensity or information about an issue. The opinions of citizens toward abortion are more stable than their opinions toward candidates running for president, especially at the beginning of the campaign. A good example is opinion polls following the party nominating conventions in 1992. They showed Bill Clinton's margins over George Bush seesawing back and forth from day to day (Figure 1). At this stage of the campaign, many voters were undecided. Some opposed Bush but did not know enough about Clinton to support him firmly. They would see something on television or read something in the press favorable to Clinton and report a preference for him, and then see something unfavorable and shift to Bush.[2]

FORMATION OF PUBLIC OPINION

People have opinions about issues and objects because they learn them in a process called **political socialization.**

As with other types of learning, individuals learn about politics by being exposed to new information from parents, peers, schools, the media, political leaders, and the community. These sources are referred to as **agents of political socialization.** Individuals also can learn about politics through direct personal experience.

Political learning begins at an early age and continues through life. Reasoning capacity as well as the demands placed upon an individual influences what is learned.[3] Very young children are unable to distinguish the political from the nonpolitical world. If fact, young children have difficulty separating political figures from cartoon characters. Some confuse the political with the religious. Twenty-five percent of a sample of five- and six-year-olds reported that the president takes his orders directly from God.[4] By first grade, however, children begin to see government as distinct and unique.[5]

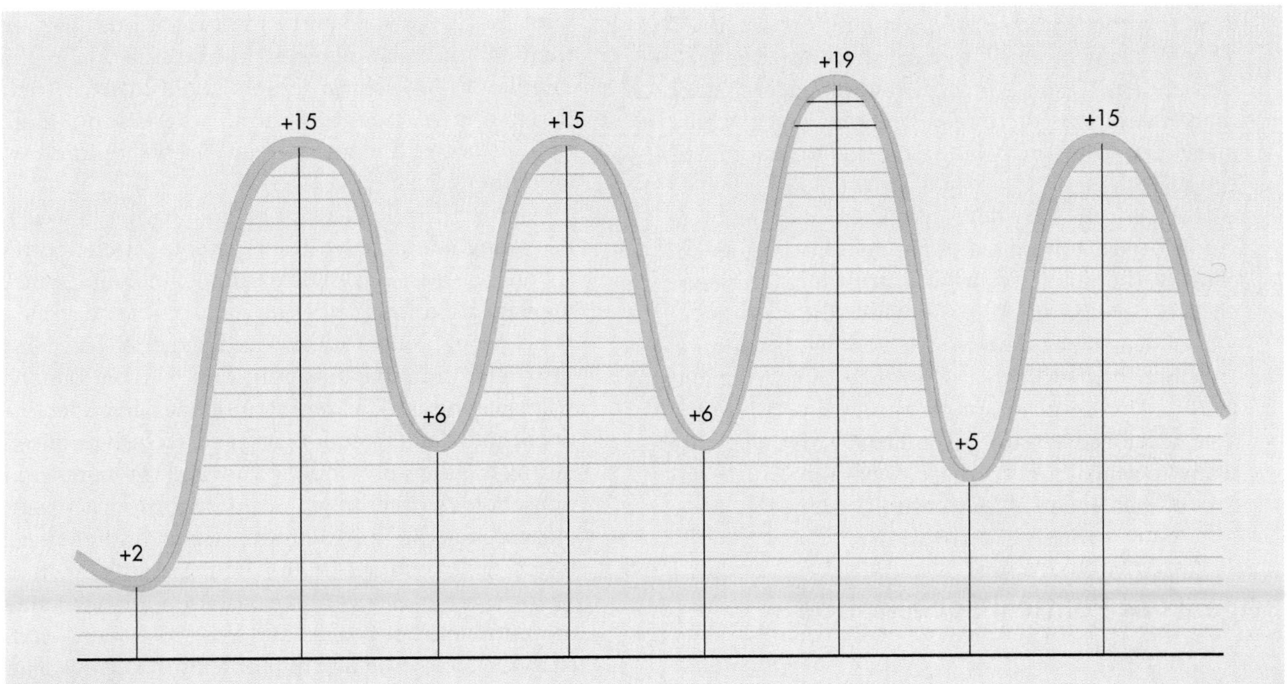

FIGURE 1

The Presidential "Poller Coaster"

Clinton's margins over Bush rose and fell dramatically early in the 1992 campaign.

SOURCE: *USA Today,* October 3, 1992. Polls taken August 20 to September 2, 1992. The term "poller coaster" was coined by Richard Morin, "The Ups and Downs of Political Poll-Taking," *Washington Post National Weekly Edition,* October 5, 1992, p. 37.

The inability to understand abstract concepts or complex institutions means the child's conception of government is limited. Most identify government with the president.[6] Children can recognize the president—they see him on television—and understand that he is a leader of the nation much as the parent is a leader of the family. In general, experiences with parents and other adult figures provide children with a basis for understanding remote authority figures such as the president.[7] Positive feelings toward parents are also responsible for positive feelings toward the president. Children describe the president as good and helpful[8] and view him as more powerful than he really is.[9]

With age, children are introduced to political ideas and institutions by parents, teachers, peers, and the media. Their conception of government broadens to include Congress and such things as voting, freedom, and democracy. The idealization of the president gives way to a more complex and realistic image. The process can be accelerated by events and parental and community reaction to them. Children were much less positive toward the president and government in the 1970s than in the 1960s. The 1970s were a period when support for government among adults was declining. The Watergate scandal in 1973 lowered both adults' and children's evaluations of the president.[10] We might expect that Clinton's sexual scandals and the impeachment proceedings of 1998 might also lower such evaluations.

The effects of Watergate did not last. Although children socialized in the late 1960s and early 1970s were more cynical toward government than others, as they matured their opinions changed and became less cynical.[11]

In adolescence, political understanding expands still further. Children discuss politics with family and friends. Political activity, however limited, begins. By their middle teens, individuals begin to develop positions on issues.[12] Some fifteen- and sixteen-year-olds have political opinions similar to many adults'. They begin to recognize faults in the system but still believe the United States is better than other countries. They rate the country low in limiting violence and fostering political morality, but they rate it high in providing educational opportunities, a good standard of living, and science and technology.[13] For most, the positive feelings toward American government learned earlier are reinforced.

In adulthood, opinions toward specific policies and personalities develop, and political activity becomes more serious. Most Americans do not develop a critical perspective toward government, and few are asked or pushed to criticism, other than in superficial ways, by the schools, press, or political leaders.[14] Though many are disillusioned, their negative feelings are passive and directed toward leaders rather than institutions or toward symbolic issues, which make Americans angry but rarely lead to major institutional changes. One study in the 1990s showed that Americans have developed surprisingly ambivalent attitudes toward major national institutions. In general, the public seems to distrust most those aspects of our institutions that involve the overt workings of democracy. They dislike conflict, bargaining, and lobbying. Still, in the absence of a major upheaval, depression, or war, for most, the positive feelings developed toward government early in life are likely to remain and perhaps even cushion the impact of such events if they occur.[15]

Agents of Political Socialization

FAMILY

Children are not born little Republicans and Democrats. Most learn these allegiances from the family. Individuals are influenced by the family throughout life. Families are particularly important in shaping the opinions of children, however, because of the strong emotional ties among members and because of parents' near exclusive control of their children's early lives.

The family influences opinions in several ways. First, parents share their opinions directly with children, who may adopt them.

Second, parents say or do things that children imitate. They may overhear parents' comments about the Republican or Democratic Party, for example, and repeat what they hear. Many initially learn a party identification in this way.

Third, children may transfer or generalize opinions from parents to other objects. When children are less positive toward parents, they are also less positive toward the president and other authority figures.[16]

Fourth, the family shapes the personality of the child. This may affect the child's political opinions. For example, the family contributes to self-esteem, and self-esteem is related to having political opinions and a willingness to express them.

Fifth, the family places children in a network of social and economic relationships that influences how they view the world and how the world views them. Children who live in a middle-class suburb view themselves and the world around them differently than children who live in poor inner city areas.

The influence of the family is strongest when children clearly perceive what the parents' opinion is and that the matter is important to the parents. In the case of party identification, cues are frequent and unambiguous. In one study, 72% of a sample of high school seniors could identify their parents' party identification, whereas no more than 36% could identify their parents' opinion on any other issue.[17]

Parental influence is not immutable, however. As young adults leave their parents' circle, correspondence between their opinions, including party identification, and those of their parents declines. New people, institutions, and experiences come into play in shaping opinions.[18] Even among younger children, parental influence may decline over time. Parents no longer have exclusive control during a child's preschool years, and the number of households with both parents working or with a single parent who works means that children have fewer daily contact hours with parents. Consequently, other agents of socialization are becoming more influential. For example, we turn more often to the schools to deal with problems the family dealt with in the past.

Black Star

This boy, at a white supremacist rally, likely was socialized in these views by his parents.

SCHOOL

A child of our acquaintance who came to the United States at the age of five could not speak English and did not know the name of his new country. After a few months of kindergarten, he knew that George Washington and Abraham Lincoln were good presidents, he was able to recount stories of the Pilgrims, he could draw the flag, and he felt strongly that the United States was the best country in the world. This child illustrates the importance of the school in political socialization and how values and symbols of government are explicitly taught in American schools, as they are in schools in all nations.[19]

Schools promote patriotic rituals, such as beginning each day with the Pledge of Allegiance, and include patriotic songs and programs in many activities. In the lower grades, children celebrate national holidays such as Presidents' Day and Thanksgiving and learn the history and symbols associated with them. Such exercises foster awe and respect for government.

In the upper grades, mock conventions, elections, Girls' and Boys' State, and student government introduce students to the operation of government. School clubs often operate with democratic procedures and reinforce the concepts of voting and majority rule. The state of Illinois even let the state's elementary school children vote to select the official state animal, fish, and tree, conveying the message that voting is the way things are decided.

Textbooks often foster commitment to government and the status quo. Those used in elementary grades emphasize compliance with authority and the need to be a "good" citizen. They are less likely to emphasize the need for citizens to participate in politics and uphold democratic values. Even textbooks in advanced grades present idealized versions of the way government works and exaggerate the role of citizens in holding public officials accountable and in shaping public policy. They do not help students understand that conflicts and differences of opinion are inevitable in a large and diverse nation.

Nor do civic courses or teachers make much of a difference in fostering participation and support for democratic values.[20] Only a minority of a sample of 17-year-olds could list four or more ways to influence politics. Sixty percent of a sample of high school seniors favored allowing the police and other groups to censor books and movies.[21]

The failure of the schools to foster political participation and commitment to democratic values is attributed by some to the "hidden curriculum."[22] They point out that schools are not democratic institutions where students are encouraged to participate in a meaningful way. In such an environment, the values of participation and democracy are unlikely to develop.

Education—the skills that it provides and experiences it represents—does make a difference, however. People who have more years of formal education are generally more interested in and knowledgeable about politics.[23] They are also more likely to participate in politics and to be politically tolerant. But educated Americans are no more likely than others to appreciate that democratic politics and government involves disagreements, arguments, bargaining, and compromise—in other words, to understand the reality of politics in a democratic society.

The major impact of schooling (kindergarten through high school) is that it helps create "good" citizens. Citizens are taught to accept political authority and the institutions of government and to channel political activity in legitimate and supportive ways. Thus, the schools provide a valuable service to the government, its leaders, and institutions.

Studies show that a college education alters one's outlook and opinions. Many go to college to get a job that pays a high salary. Some attend to expand their knowledge and understanding of the world. Others enroll because their parents want them to or simply because everyone else does. No one goes to develop more liberal opinions, but this is often the result.[24]

College students are more liberal than the population as a whole, and the longer they are in college, the more liberal they become. Seniors are more liberal than freshmen, and graduate students are more liberal than undergraduates.

Some argue that college professors indoctrinate students. A Carnegie Commission survey showed that 64% of the social science faculty in the nation's colleges identified themselves as liberal and only 20% regarded themselves as conservative. Faculty in other disciplines are much less likely to be liberal, however. For example, 30% of the business and 55% of the natural science faculty identified themselves as liberal. Although the potential for influence exists, and college professors, no doubt, affect some students, their impact is probably not great. Indeed, it is college that provides students with the self-confidence and independence that enable them to resist indoctrination.

Students' attitudes vary over time. During the height of the Vietnam War (1968–1971), students were more likely to identify themselves as liberal in outlook than students before and after the war. (Liberal attitudes are discussed in more detail later in the chapter.) During the same period, college faculty changed very little. Thus, students are not simply a reflection of their college classroom teachers. At large universities, where the largest percentage of students attend college, the environment is sufficiently diverse to reinforce all points of view.

It is possible that college students are liberal in outlook because college attracts those who are more

TABLE 1

Opinions of College Freshman, 1997

	PERCENTAGE WHO AGREE
Federal government is not doing enough to control pollution.	81
Federal government needs to do more to control sale of handguns.	81
National health care is needed to cover everyone's medical costs.	72
Affirmative action in college admissions should be abolished.	50
Abortion should be abolished.	54
Courts show too much concern for rights of criminals.	39
The death penalty should be abolished.	24
Racial discrimination is no longer a problem.	20

SOURCE: Linda Sax et al., *The American Freshman: National Norms for Fall 1997* (Los Angeles: Higher Education Research Institute, Graduate School of Education and Information Studies, 1997).

liberal in the first place. Although this may have been true in the early 1970s when 38% of college freshmen identified themselves as liberal compared to 26% for the nation as a whole, today 24% of college freshmen identify themselves as liberal compared to 25% of the nation.[25] At the same time, there has been only a slight increase in the percentage of conservatives among freshmen. The biggest shift has been from liberal to middle of the road. Whereas 45% of college freshmen in 1970 were moderate, this figure increased to 60% in the 1980s, before falling to 55% in 1997.[26]

On issues, college freshmen look much like the population as a whole, liberal on some issues but conservative on others. They are liberal in wanting the government to do more to control pollution and the sale of handguns and provide national health care to cover everyone's medical costs. They are conservative in wishing to retain the death penalty, believing that the courts show too much concern for the rights of criminals, and asserting that racial discrimination is no longer a problem. They are divided on abortion and affirmative action in college admissions (Table 1).

The most distinctive characteristic of college freshmen in 1997 was their lack of interest in politics. Only 14% said that they had discussed politics in the past year, and only 27% considered it very important to keep up to date with politics. These figures, which have been declining since the 1960s, represent an all-time low.[27] In many respects, the political apathy that has gripped adults is also reflected in college freshmen. College freshmen are likely to become more politically active as they age, but the low levels of activism at which they begin college set an upper limit on how active they are likely to become.

PEERS

In many instances, peers simply reinforce the opinions of the family or school. When there is a conflict between peer and parental socialization, peers sometimes win but only on issues of special relevance to youth. For example, peer influence is more important than family influence on the issue of whether 18-year-olds should be allowed to vote, but parental influence appears to be more significant with respect to partisanship and vote choice.[28] Peers have the most influence when the peer group is attractive to the individual and when the individual spends more time with the group. The influence of peer groups on young teenagers and young adults may be increasing as many, particularly in the nation's inner cities, have joined gangs to satisfy needs traditionally provided for in the family. Friends and associates, of course, take on greater importance for adults.

MASS MEDIA

The primary effect of the media on children is to increase their level of information about politics. For adults the media primarily influence what people think about, that is, the issues, events, and personalities they pay attention to,[29] but the media also influence opinions about issues and individuals. Research shows that changes in public opinion tend to follow sentiments expressed by television news commentators.[30] We will examine the impact of the media in more detail in Chapter 8.

ADULT SOCIALIZATION

Not all political socialization occurs in childhood. It is a lifelong process; opinions change as we have new experiences.

Citizens' encounters with government have the potential to change their opinions about politics. Many Americans who were particularly hard hit by the Great Depression, for example, became active in the political process for the first time. Most of these new voters voted Democratic in 1932, and many have voted Democratic ever since. The war in Vietnam was another event that influenced masses of people. Some took to the streets to protest the war; others rejected their country and traveled to Canada to avoid the draft. Watergate was yet another event that affected the opinions of millions of Americans. In contrast, even though the political scandals surrounding President Clinton attracted much attention, there is no evidence that they have deeply affected opinions.

OPINIONS ON ABORTION

Issues that involve moral questions have the greatest potential to be divisive. Slavery was a moral issue that almost destroyed the nation. In the first decades of this century, prohibition—banning the sale of alcoholic beverages—was a divisive moral issue. In 1992, whether gays should be permitted to serve in the military emerged as a moral issue. Abortion is another.

Abortion emerged as a moral issue in the 1970s. There are two dimensions to public opinion on this issue. One involves the health and safety of the mother or child. The vast majority of Americans endorse legal abortion when the mother's health may be endangered, the child is likely to have a serious defect, or the pregnancy is the result of rape or incest. This pattern of opinion has been reasonably stable over the past decade.

The other dimension relates to the personal preferences of the mother. Americans are divided on whether a legal abortion is acceptable when the family has a low income and does not want any more children or when the mother is unmarried and does not want to marry the father.

Although the accompanying graphs do not reveal intensity, the patterns in boxes a, b, and c show agreement, or consensus, whereas boxes d, e, and f reveal disagreement, or conflict.

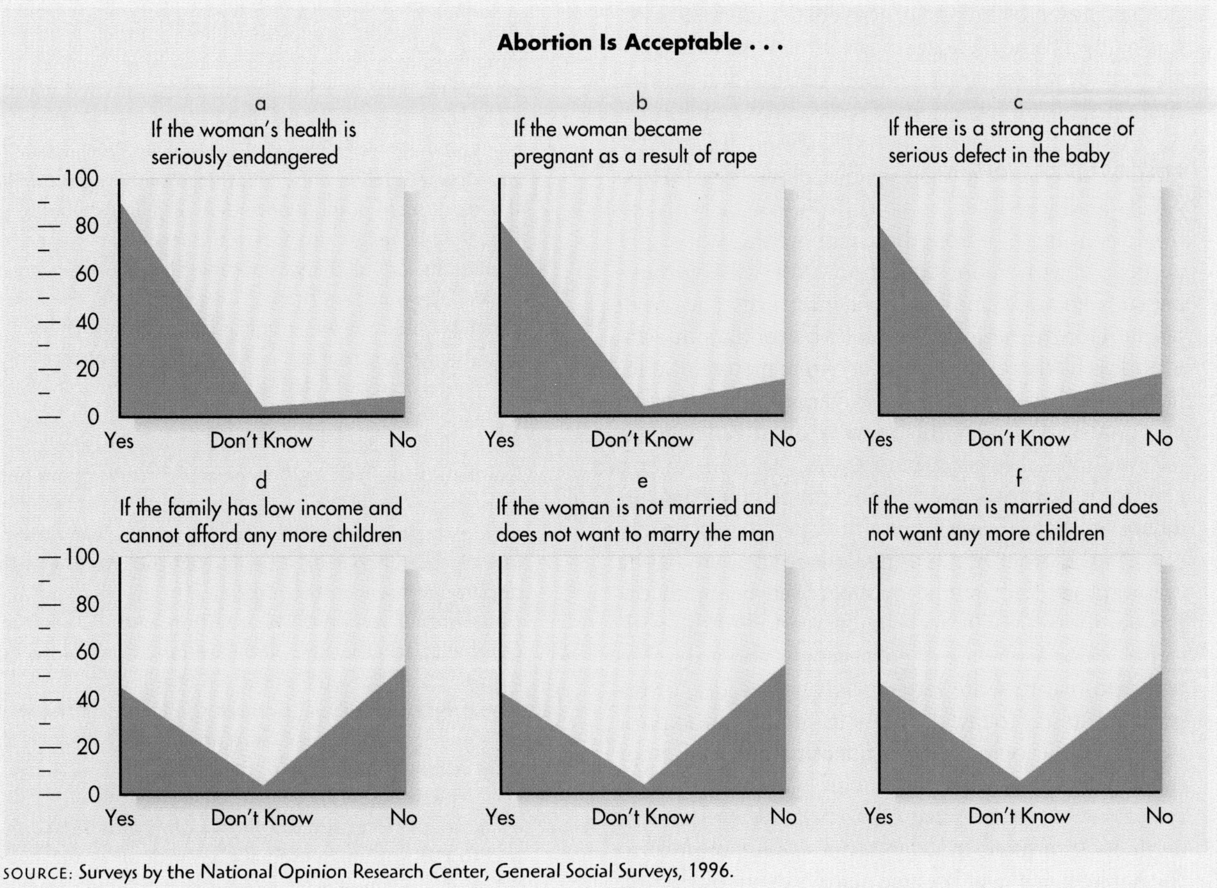

SOURCE: Surveys by the National Opinion Research Center, General Social Surveys, 1996.

Opinions also change with changed personal situations. Marriage, divorce, unemployment, or a move to a new location can all affect political opinions.[31]

Impact of Political Socialization

Each new generation of Americans is socialized to a large extent by the preceding generations. In many ways each new generation will look and act much like the one that came before. In this sense, political socialization is biased against change. Typically, it leads to support for and compliance with government and the social order. Although many disagree with particular government policies, few question the basic structure of government.

Yet the impact of political socialization is not the same for all groups of people. The socialization experiences of poor rural children are different from those of rich suburban ones. Children from low-income families are more cynical about government; black children feel less able to influence government and are less inclined to trust it.[32] These sentiments are likely to persist into adulthood.

MEASURING PUBLIC OPINION

Public opinion is typically measured by asking individuals to answer questions in a survey or poll. Before polls began to be used, other techniques were employed; these still persist and are now used alongside polls. Elected officials listen to opinions of people who write or talk to them; journalists gauge public opinion by talking selectively to individuals; letters written to newspaper editors or newspaper editorials partially reflect public opinion. Protests and demonstrations also are reflections of some public opinion.

All of these techniques provide an incomplete picture, however. Letters to public officials and newspapers are more likely to come from people with extreme opinions[33] or from those with writing skills, that is, people with more education. Nor will opinions culled from a few conversations match the pattern of opinion for the nation as a whole. Editorial opinion is even less likely to provide an accurate picture of public opinion because most newspaper publishers tend to be conservative, and this view is often reflected in their editorials. In most presidential elections in this century, newspapers have favored the Republican candidate by about three to one.[34]

On the other hand, using polls to measure public opinion may shift public opinion from being an expression of the public to being a creation of the pollsters.[35] Prior to the use of polls, people who wanted to be heard had to write letters, deliver speeches, or organize protests. Today, the pollsters initiate the expression of public opinion by conducting a poll. Rather than focusing on what the public is exercised about, polls concentrate on what pollsters and their sponsors are most interested in. Many issues of importance to the public may never become matters of public debate.

In spite of these concerns, polling is the only accurate way to assess what the nation as a whole thinks about political issues and personalities. In this sense, polls are the best measure of public opinion.

Early Polling Efforts

The first attempts to measure popular sentiments on a large scale were the **straw polls** (or unscientific polls) developed by newspapers in the nineteenth century.[36] In 1824, the *Harrisburg Pennsylvanian*, in perhaps the first poll assessing candidate preferences, sent reporters to check on support for the four presidential contenders that year. In July, the paper reported that Andrew Jackson was the popular choice over John Quincy Adams, Henry Clay, and William H. Crawford. Jackson also received the most votes in the election, but

WORDS DO MAKE A DIFFERENCE

A major problem for public opinion pollsters is designing questions that accurately measure what the public believes about issues. "It's not the case that a few words don't make a lot of difference in a poll question." What? Get the picture? Poorly worded questions, such as those with double negatives, can confuse the public and lead pollsters to draw the wrong conclusions.

This was illustrated recently in a poll sponsored by the American Jewish Committee to find out the proportion of Americans who doubt that the Holocaust (the mass murder of millions of Jews by the Nazis in World War II) happened. The survey asked the following question: "As you know, the term Holocaust usually refers to the killing of millions of Jews in Nazi death camps during World War II. Does it seem possible or does it seem impossible to you that the Nazi extermination of the Jews never happened?" The results: 22% said it was possible that the Holocaust never happened: another 12% were not sure. The conclusion: About one-third of the country either doubted the truth of the Holocaust or was uncertain.

Since no reputable historian or anyone with the slightest knowledge of world affairs denies that the Holocaust happened, this "finding" was shocking. Commentators reflected on how the public could be so ignorant of one of the major events, not just of twentieth-century history, but of all recorded history. On further investigation, however, it seems that the wording of the question influenced the responses.

Another version of the question asked "Does it seem possible to you that the Nazi extermination of Jews never happened, or do you feel certain that it happened?" This time only 1% said it was possible the Holocaust never happened. Eight percent were unsure, and 90% said they were certain the Holocaust happened.

Why the difference? A study of 13 polls with estimates of Holocaust doubters from 1% to 46% found that studies with high estimates used double-negative wording. For example, to express that the Holocaust happened, one had to respond "impossible" that it "never happened." Such wording often results in a response that is exactly the opposite of what is intended.

What do Americans really know about the Holocaust? Nine of 10 have heard of the Holocaust; however, only two-thirds are able to identify the Holocaust correctly. In 1992, knowledge of the Holocaust increased with publicity surrounding the opening of the Holocaust Museum in Washington and the release of the Academy Award–winning movie *Schindler's List.*

SOURCE: Richard Morin, "From Confusing Questions, Confusing Answers," *Washington Post National Weekly Edition*, July 18–24, 1994, p. 37.

John Quincy Adams was elected president after the contest was decided in the House of Representatives. Toward the end of the nineteenth century, the *New York Herald* regularly tried to forecast election outcomes in local, state, and national races. During presidential election years, the paper collected estimates from reporters and political leaders across the country and predicted the Electoral College vote by state.

Straw polls are still employed today. Some newspapers have interviewers who ask adults at shopping malls and other locations their voting preferences. Some have readers return coupons printed in the papers. Television and radio stations often ask questions and provide two telephone numbers for listeners to call—one for yes, one for no. The votes then are electronically recorded.

The major problem with straw polls is that there is no way to ensure that the sample of individuals giving opinions is representative of the larger population. Generally speaking, they are not.

The famed *Literary Digest* poll is a good example. This magazine conducted polls of presidential preferences between 1916 and 1936. As many as 18 million ballots were mailed out to persons drawn from telephone directories and automobile registration lists. Although the purpose was less to measure public opinion than to boost subscriptions, the *Digest* did have a pretty good record. It predicted the winners in 1924, 1928, and 1932. In 1936, however, the magazine predicted Alfred Landon would win, but Franklin Delano Roosevelt won by a landslide. The erroneous prediction ended the magazine's polling, and in 1938 the *Digest* went out of business.

A bias in the *Digest*'s polling procedure that the editors failed to consider led to erroneous results. At the time, owners of telephones and automobiles were disproportionately middle- and high-income individuals who could afford a telephone or car in the depths of the Great Depression; these people were much more likely to vote for Landon (a Republican) than were lower-income people.[37] Since the survey was drawn from telephone directories and auto registrations, lower-income people were disproportionately excluded from the poll.

Emergence of Scientific Polling

Scientific polling began after World War I, inspired by the new field of business known as marketing research. After the war, demand for consumer goods rose, and American business, no longer engaged in the production of war materials, turned to satisfying consumer demand. Businesses used marketing research to identify what consumers wanted and, perhaps more important, how products should be packaged so consumers would buy them. For example, the American Tobacco Company changed from a green to a white package during World War II because it found that a white package was more attractive to women smokers.[38]

The application of mathematical principles of probability was also important to the development of scientific polling. To check the rates of defects in manufactured products, random or spot inspections of a few items, called a sample, were made. From these, projections of defects among the entire group of items could be made. From this use of sampling, it was a small step to conclude that sampling a small number of individuals could provide information about a larger population.

In the early 1930s, George Gallup and several others, using probability-based sampling techniques, began polling opinions on a wide scale. In 1936, Gallup predicted that the *Literary Digest* would be wrong and that Roosevelt would be reelected with 55.7% of the vote. Though Gallup underestimated Roosevelt's actual vote (he won 62.5%), his correct prediction of a landslide lent credibility to probability-based polls.

Increasingly, polls were used by government. In 1940, Roosevelt became the first president to use polls on a regular basis, employing a social scientist to measure trends in public opinion about the war in Europe. Most major American universities have a unit that does survey research, and there are hundreds of commercial marketing research firms, private pollsters, and newspaper polls.

Polls and Politics

For politicians, polls have become what the oracle of Delphi was to the ancient Greeks and Merlin was to King Arthur: a divine source of wisdom. During the budget debate between President Clinton and congressional Republicans, Republicans used polls that told them that promising to "put the government on a diet" would be popular in the upcoming 1996 election. Polls directed Clinton to counter by accusing the Republicans of trying to cut Medicare. When the media wanted to make sense out of the debate, they conducted still more polls.[39]

John Kennedy commissioned 16 polls during his three years as president. Richard Nixon conducted 233 over six years in the White House. Bill Clinton spent $4.5 million on polls in his first two and a half years in office, enough to buy 150 polls.[40] In addition, members of Congress, state officeholders, political parties, political candidates, and media poll. The number of polls is staggering.

Pollsters can conduct a poll at a moment's notice and have the results within a few hours. But can polls be taken at face value?

On clearly defined issues that the public has thought about carefully and on which they hold strong views, such as how they will vote in tomorrow's election, a well-designed poll can accurately reflect the winner. For example, all eight of the election eve polls in the 1996 presidential election predicted the winner. One got it exactly right, finding Clinton with a 9% advantage over Dole. The president's actual margin of victory was 8.4%. All but one poll predicted each candidate's total within a few percentage points.[41] The fact that seven out of eight of these polls overstated the president's total and understated Dole's led some to charge that polls conducted by the news media have a Democratic bias. Analysis of the results suggested that the slight pro-Democratic bias may be due to the differential willingness of different kinds of people to respond on the phone to an interviewer.

On issues that the public has not thought much about and where choices are less clearly defined, polls rarely provide a meaningful guide to what the public thinks. Poll results on the appeal of Steve Forbes jumped up and down when he was seeking the Republican nomination in early 1996, because voters did not know much about him.

Even when issues are well defined and opinions are fairly stable, it is increasingly difficult to obtain a sample that provides a representative picture of public opinion. Many respondents refuse to be interviewed,[42] some because they do not want to be bothered, others because they fear they will be asked to buy something or contribute money. Nonrespondents, those who refuse or cannot be reached, number from one-half to two-thirds of those called, and these people are more likely to be better educated, more affluent, and live in suburbs rather than cities and rural areas.[43] Many of these nonrespondents are more likely to vote Republican. Thus, a poll can result in a distorted picture.

"One final question: Do you now own or have you ever owned a fur coat?"

Another problem for pollsters is the tendency of some respondents to express an opinion when they do not have one. No one wants to appear ignorant. Some respondents volunteer an answer even though they know little or nothing about a subject. The problem is getting worse as pollsters increasingly probe topics on which the public has no opinion and on which there is little reason to believe it should. For example, pollsters have asked whether the public thought President Reagan's colon cancer was serious and whether the bloody glove originally fit O. J. Simpson.[44]

Although polls can be biased because of these problems, some pollsters and politicians consciously distort poll results. Today, many pollsters come from political consulting backgrounds and poll exclusively for members of one political party. Rather than provide accurate information about public opinion, their goal is to present their client in the most favorable light.[45]

An example of misuse is the "push poll." A pollster asks whether the person called is for John Jones, Mary Smith, or undecided in the upcoming congressional election. If the answer is Smith or undecided, the person is asked: "If you were told that Smith's hobby is driving a high-powered sports car at dangerous speeds through residential neighborhoods to see how many children and pets she can run over, would that make a difference in your vote?" You are asked your preference again. The idea is to see if certain "information" can "push" voters away from a candidate or a neutral opinion toward the candidate favored by those doing the poll.[46] Learning the weaknesses of the opposition has always been a part of politics, but push polls seek to manipulate opinion, rarely focus on a candidate's issue positions, and often distort a candidate's record and the facts.

An even more vicious tactic is to pump thousands of calls into a district or state under the guise of conducting a poll but with the intent of spreading false information about a candidate.[47] Steve Forbes accused the Dole campaign of spreading false information under the guise of a poll when both were campaigning for the Republican presidential nomination in 1996. Both the push poll and the phony poll are corruptions of the political process as well as violations of polling ethics.

From the Collections of the St. Louis Mercantile Library

Harry Truman exults in incorrect headlines, based on poll results and early returns, the morning after the 1948 election.

SLOP SURVEYS ARE SLOPPY SURVEYS

SLOP is an acronym for self-selected listener opinion polls. SLOP surveys are telephone call-in polls, which are being used increasingly by radio and television stations and even by newspapers. Why attach such a negative label to call-in polls? The answer is simple: the results are meaningless because those who call in do not reflect the views of the general public.

An example was CBS's survey to gauge public reaction to President Bush's 1992 State of the Union address. The program allowed viewers to dial and then respond to a series of recorded questions by pushing buttons on their telephone. CBS recorded the views of more than 300,000 respondents. In an effort to measure representativeness, at the same time, CBS also conducted a survey of 1,241 adults. A comparison of the two polls revealed that the results differed by 10% or more on seven of the nine questions. One question asked whether respondents were better off or worse off than four years ago. In the call-in poll, 54% said they were worse off, compared to 32% in the scientific survey. Viewers who felt they were worse off called in greater proportions than viewers who felt they were better off. In other words, viewers who are angrier or more concerned may be more likely to use their telephones to express their opinions.

Another problem with call-in polls is that people can call in more than once. *Parade* magazine conducted a call-in poll on abortion and received more than 300,000 responses. It later acknowledged that 21% of the callers may have voiced their opinion more than once. Obviously, if the views of some people are counted two or more times, the results will not be representative of the general public.

Despite these problems, SLOP surveys are likely to continue. As one pollster put it, ". . . it's a good show. And who's going to give up a good show just for the truth?"

SOURCES: Richard Morin, "Another Contribution to SLOPpy Journalism," *Washington Post National Weekly Edition,* February 10, 1992, p. 38. Richard Morin, "Numbers from Nowhere: The Hoax of the Call-in 'Polls,' " *Washington Post,* February 9, 1992, p. B3.

In spite of problems and abuses, polls still provide a valuable service to the nation. If direct democracy like the New England town meeting is the ideal, the use of public opinion polls is about as close as the modern state is likely to get to it. Polls help interpret the meaning of elections. When voters cast their ballots for one candidate over another, all anyone knows for sure is that a majority preferred one candidate. Polls can help reveal what elections mean in terms of policy preferences, and thus help make the government more responsive to voters. For example, the Republicans claimed their victory in the 1994 congressional elections was an indication that voters supported the party's "Contract with America." However, polls showed that most Americans had never heard of it (see You Are There, Chapter 6).

Polls, however, have a down side. Poor standing in the polls may discourage otherwise viable candidates from entering a race, leaving the field to others who have less chance of winning or who lack the skills necessary to govern effectively. George Bush's standing in the polls in January 1991, at the start of the Gulf War, made him appear a sure winner in the 1992 presidential election. Several prominent Democrats chose not to seek the presidency in 1992, leaving the field to others and limiting voters' choice.

Polls also have a negative effect on political campaigns. Prior to polling, the purpose of campaigns was to reveal the candidates' views on the issues and their solutions to the pressing problems of the day. Instead, polls focus attention on the electorate and what they think. Polls find out what the voters want, and the candidates develop images to suit the market.

The ease of polling also means that judgment and leadership often give way to the sentiments expressed in public opinion polls. Politicians rarely make a decision without one. Rather than educate the public regarding the merits of particular policies, politicians seem to follow the polls blindly.

INTO THE 21ST CENTURY

TELEDEMOCRACY: IF POLITICIANS CAN'T DO THE JOB, CAN WE?

Although Americans are not as sour about government and politicians as they were a few years ago, many still feel Washington is out of touch with the concerns of average men and women. Unemployment is down and personal income is up, yet Americans are still concerned about their jobs and providing for their families.[1] Official Washington, on the other hand, seems preoccupied with scandals and is engaged in partisan bickering over issues of little importance to average citizens. Some say that if politicians are not doing the job, perhaps we should do it ourselves.

"Teledemocracy" is a twenty-first-century version of the New England town meeting. It assumes that citizens would be better off if they bypassed political leaders and made government decisions themselves. Indeed, as one commentator argues, "nostalgia is growing for a high-tech update of Athenian democracy or of . . . townspeople gathered around a cast-iron stove in rural Vermont."[2]

Town meetings have indeed been a tradition of many New England towns for 350 years. They are an exercise in direct democracy: Citizens in a local community come together to discuss public issues and make local laws.

During the 1992 presidential election campaign, Ross Perot talked about the possibility of an electronic town meeting in which everyone in the nation could be part of a discussion and preference vote on some policy. His idea was to link Americans electronically. During the campaign, he had a satellite broadcast that linked rallies in six different states. Participants could hear one another cheer as Perot spoke to them from Florida. President Clinton employed a similar format when he participated in a televised question-and-answer session with citizens in four cities. Citizens in television studios in Atlanta, Miami, and Seattle could interact directly with the president in a Detroit studio.

"Teledemocracy" would go a long way toward transforming our representative democracy into a direct democracy. The president, or perhaps the leadership of Congress or the political parties, would identify an issue such as the flat tax or reform of Social Security. Then the president, the cabinet secretaries, members of Congress, policy experts, or even ordinary citizens would lay out the arguments, pro and con, and ask Americans to register their preferences by pushing a button. Although the preferences would not be binding, elected politicians would probably feel tremendous pressure to follow them as though they were.

If the technology existed to do it—which it does not yet—would teledemocracy be a good idea? Perot—and Newt Gingrich too—envisions it as a cure for government gridlock and the influence of special interests. The idea that citizens might bypass the machinery of representative democracy and directly influence government decisions has a gut-level appeal, especially if government is not responding quickly to problems facing the country. Teledemocracy appeals to those Americans who are displeased by the processes of modern democracy, including lobbying and compromise. However, most issues that cause gridlock do so because they are difficult and complex and have no easy solutions. There are not

For example, when Rodney King, a black man who was stopped for speeding, was beaten by four white police officers in Los Angeles in 1992, the incident created a furor, and when the officers' first trial resulted in a verdict of not guilty, it led to a riot. President Bush was in a quandary about what to do. His aides were divided. Some said he should give speeches emphasizing the need for racial harmony, and some said he should propose programs providing urban renewal for big cities. But others said he should do neither. So he tried to follow the polls. At first, he defended the police and called their chief "an American hero." After the first trial he declared, "The system has worked." But in a couple of days, he said he was "stunned" and felt "a deep sense of personal frustration and anguish" about the verdict. As the public changed their responses in the polls, he changed his messages to the public. Ultimately, analysis of the polls showed no clear mandate, so Bush did not do anything except approve some emergency aid to cope with the destruction from the riots.[48]

As the number of polls, both good and bad, increases, their importance for the public and perhaps politicians may decline. The sheer number of polls may lead everyone to take them less seriously. Moreover, if politicians allow themselves to be driven by poll results, no one will gain an advantage from the information the polls provide.[49] Still, it is unlikely that ambitious politicians bent on winning at all cost will abandon something that may help them win.

HOW INFORMED IS PUBLIC OPINION?

Many Americans are uninformed or misinformed concerning government and politics. Only one-fourth can name their two senators,[50] and only one-third can name their just two options, for example, to reforming the tax system. There are dozens. How could these be explained in a short television program? Legislative bills are often hundreds of pages long with many complex provisions.

The Founders' fear of a tyrannical majority moved by passion led them to create a representative democracy with checks and balances to ensure that decisions would be filtered and made deliberately rather than hastily. Checks and balances guard against popular whims and demagoguery while protecting minority rights. A long process of writing, rewriting, and amending legislation contributes, in many cases, to better legislation that takes into account the complex interests of society. Bills passed without taking account of minority viewpoints or complex issues can be very bad bills. As one political scientist notes, "Look at history. The reality of human experience is that emotional responses have turned to utter tragedy time and time again." It was Hitler, after all, who pioneered the electronic referendum, using radio broadcasts to drum up votes to support his rise to power.

Proponents like Perot and Gingrich believe that teledemocracy would increase participation. It could stimulate interest and get people to think about alternatives and trade-offs involved in choosing one policy rather than another.

Yet rates of participation were low in an early experiment with electronic democracy at the local level. It is likely that the same interested, educated people who participate in politics now would be the major participants in teledemocracy. And of course, not everyone has a computer to participate in teledemocracy. There is now about one computer for every 10 adults,[3] a figure likely to grow substantially. Still, the poor are clearly at a disadvantage in this sort of voting system.

This vision of an electronic national referendum is perhaps extreme. In other respects, however, direct democracy is already here. Citizens are wired to Washington through public opinion polls, talk radio, faxes, phones, and e-mail. From C-SPAN's studios just off Capitol Hill, lawmakers chat with callers live—including those who have been monitoring lawmakers' activities via the C-SPAN cameras. More messages pass through the Beltway barrier than ever before, and politicians pay attention to them.

Judging from what we already have, more direct democracy may not satisfy the public. It may make things worse. Intensely held opinions unfiltered by the political process lead to dubious laws that do not address real issues. For example, "three strikes and you're out," or life imprisonment for a third conviction of a serious crime, was created by talk radio and won support in the White House and Congress through telephone polls, talk shows, and faxes. "Three strikes" laws are unlikely to affect crime, but they are likely to increase citizens' frustration with government when they find that in spite of the laws crime is still a major problem.

1. "Why Are We So Angry," *U.S. News and World Report,* November 7, 1994, p. 31.
2. Kevin Phillips, "Virtual Washington," *Time,* Spring 1995, p. 60.
3. Ibid., p. 65.

U.S. representative.[51] More than one-third do not know the party of their representative,[52] and 40% do not know which party controls Congress.[53]

Many Americans are unable to identify prominent political personalities (see Table 2). Six years after he was elected vice president, 24% could not identify George Bush. More people can identify the judge on the television show *The People's Court* than can identify the chief justice of the United States.[54] In spite of increases in education, levels of knowledge regarding politics have not changed much since the 1940s.[55]

Although Americans revere the Constitution and see it as a blueprint for democracy, many don't know what is in it. One-third think it established English as the country's official language, and one in six thinks it established America as a Christian nation. One-fourth cannot name a single First Amendment right and only 6% can name all four.[56]

Only a small percentage of Americans can identify a single piece of legislation passed by Congress.[57] Nearly 60% were ignorant of a plan passed by the House of Representatives in 1995 to balance the federal budget.[58]

Misperception regarding government policies is widespread. While polls show Americans in favor of reducing the size of the federal government, more than 70% are unaware that the number of federal employees has decreased in recent years.[59] Seven out of ten feel that the country spends too much on foreign aid, and two out of three say the country should cut spending on foreign aid. However, one-half estimate foreign aid to be about 15 times greater than it is. Asked what an appropriate spending level would be, the average answer is 8 times more than the country actually spends. Thus, 70% think the country spends too much on foreign aid but many would support an amount substantially higher.[60]

Another example of Americans not knowing what they think they know is that 24% agreed and

FOCUS GROUPS: MEASURING OR MANIPULATING PUBLIC OPINION?

Ever wonder where the ideas for political ads come from? Many come from people like you, meeting in focus groups. A focus group is a dozen or so ordinary people who are brought together to share their opinions on everything from grocery products to television sitcoms. They are also used by political candidates to examine voters' attitudes. Focus group leaders ask questions such as, "If Bill Clinton came to your house for dinner, what would you talk about?" or "If the candidate were a color, what would he be?" Sessions are taped and consultants spend hours poring over every word and gesture in an effort to find out what is on voters' minds.

Unlike in public opinion polls, the samples are not drawn scientifically, nor is a great deal of time spent ensuring that questions used to measure opinions are fair and unbiased. The only requirement is that participants feel comfortable enough with each other to share their thoughts. It is considered risky to mix people of different social characteristics, for example, blue- with white-collar workers, blacks with whites, even men with women.

The objective in using focus groups is to identify feelings that lurk below the surface, rarely being voiced publicly but nevertheless affecting votes. Yes–no–I don't know answers in public opinion polls reveal the substance but not the texture of public opinion. Feelings censored from public comments often rise to the surface in focus groups. These feelings are likely to come into play when people vote.

The 1992 presidential campaigns illustrate the growing reliance on focus groups. Every ad was tested with a focus group. The Clinton campaign began holding focus groups in New Hampshire even before the candidate announced. Personal responsibility and welfare reform, centrist themes from Clinton's earlier days, bombed when tested in focus groups. With high unemployment and depressed real estate values, New Hampshire residents did not want to hear about personal responsibility. And instead of viewing welfare recipients as freeloaders, they recognized them as people who had lost their jobs to the recession and could no longer make it—people very much like themselves. In response to this information, Clinton abandoned his message and developed a new one, tailored to New Hampshire.

Between New Hampshire and the convention, the Clinton campaign convened focus groups at every major crisis. And focus groups were behind the idea to profile Clinton's humble beginnings at the Democratic National Convention. His Georgetown, Yale, and Oxford education had given many voters the impression that he was a Bush-style blue blood.

On the Republican side, focus groups pushed the campaign to capitalize on voters' image of Clinton as a "slick politician." Focus groups revealed Barbara Bush as one of Bush's positives, so she was profiled during the Republican National Convention.

Focus group participants invariably come away with a sense of empowerment, a feeling that someone is genuinely interested in their opinions. Most forget what they suspected at the beginning, that they are being used for the $50 fee. To be sure, politicians are interested in their opinions, but not to make the system more responsive to them. Rather, politicians use their opinions to produce a potent message that will influence their vote. As a former Perot pollster put it, "They're the guinea pigs allowing us to exploit the electorate."

SOURCE: Elizabeth Kolbert, "Test-Marketing a President," *The New York Times Magazine*, August 30, 1992, p. 18.

19% disagreed that the Public Affairs Act of 1975 should be repealed. The problem is that they offered an opinion on something that does not exist.[61] The question was a ploy to see how many would volunteer an answer when they have no opinion.

Most Americans do not think much about politics. Their major concerns are family and work. Lack of concern for government means that politicians can sometimes ignore what the public wants and what it needs. That is, politicians can be less responsive to the public.

Although the public may not pay much attention to politics and is uninformed on many things, some political scientists argue that average citizens know what they need to know to make sound political judgments.[62] Most do take an active interest in politics when their personal stake is affected. Eighty percent know that Congress passed a law requiring employers to provide family leave following the birth of a child or a family emergency. Family leave touches people directly.

Although many can no doubt make sound political judgments, others are unable to do so. Polls show that those who are less politically knowledgeable find it difficult to sort through the claims and counterclaims of politicians. Some support candidates and policies that work against their self-interest.[63]

Adding to the problem are public officials who fail to educate the public on issues. Politicians often do not like to discuss issues, especially controversial ones. When they do, public awareness increases. After President Reagan made an issue of American support for the Nicaraguan contras, for example, awareness of the issue and the side the United States was supporting jumped from 25% to 59%.[64]

PUBLIC OPINION

Public opinion polls cover virtually every aspect of American life. Polls have reported the number of California drivers with paraphernalia hanging from their rearview mirrors and Iowans

TABLE 2

Political Ignorance of the Public

	PERCENTAGE UNABLE TO IDENTIFY
Who is in Washington:	
Vice president	40
Speaker of the House	46
Their Senate representatives	54
Majority leader in Senate	66
Their House representative	67
What goes on in Washington:	
That the number of federal employees decreased in past three years	72
That the government spends more on Medicare than on foreign aid	73
That the House passed a plan to balance the budget	75
That the Senate passed a plan to balance the budget	78

SOURCE: Richard Morin, "Tuned Out, Turned Off," *Washington Post National Weekly Edition*, February 5–11, 1996, pp. 6–8.

with ornaments on their lawns. Political polls examine opinions about political issues and political candidates, whether the American people are liberal or conservative, and whether this influences their positions on issues and preferences for political candidates. Although it is important to know how Americans stand on current issues and how they feel about political candidates, it is also important to know what they think about government: its founding principles, political institutions, and political leaders. This is especially true when large numbers of Americans see government and politics as unimportant or even feel hostile toward them.

We begin by discussing ideology, what it is, what the labels liberal and conservative mean, and whether Americans identify themselves as liberal or conservative. We then look at how ideology relates to opinions on specific issues such as social welfare, social issues, and race. We also explore how ideology is related to political tolerance, whether Americans are willing to extend rights and liberties to individuals who do not share their opinions. Finally, we look at trust in government: Do Americans trust their government to do the right thing, and are liberals more trusting than conservatives?

Ideology

The term **ideology** refers to a highly organized and coherent set of opinions. In the extreme, one who is ideological takes a position on all issues consistent with his or her ideology. *Liberalism* and *conservatism* are terms used to describe the current major ideologies in American politics. Liberals are sometimes identified by the label "left" or "left wing" and conservatives by the label "right" or "right wing." These terms date from the postrevolutionary French National Assembly where conservatives occupied the right side of the chamber and liberals occupied the left side.

A **liberal** is someone who believes in a national government that plays an active role in domestic policies, providing help to individuals and communities in areas such as health, education, and welfare. In the New Deal era of Roosevelt, liberalism was seen as a way to use government authority to expand opportunities and improve the quality of life for all. With this as their platform, the Democrats came to power in the 1930s and dominated American politics through the 1960s. Since the 1960s, liberalism has been identified with some less popular policies, particularly the civil rights policies of the Democrats. These policies threatened the white-dominated social order in the South and white ethnic communities in the North. Blacks increased their support for the Democratic Party, and many whites, especially in the South, increased their support for the Republican Party. The term was also linked to the anti-Vietnam War protests and to Supreme Court decisions that expanded the rights of persons accused of crimes, legalized abortion, and barred mandatory prayers in public schools.

A **conservative** is someone who believes that the domestic role of government should be minimized and that individuals are responsible for their own well-being. However, conservatives often support increases in military spending, and recently, the label has also been attached to those, often affiliated with fundamentalist religions, who favor government action banning abortions and approving mandatory school prayers.

To what extent are Americans ideological? Do the ideological labels liberal and conservative describe the opinions of the American people? One way to find out whether a person is liberal or conservative is to ask. The greatest percentage of Americans opt for the middle, identifying themselves as moderate or centrist. Comparing the percentage of liberals to conservatives reveals conservatives to be slightly more numerous. These distributions have changed very little in the past 15 years.

Public opinion remains more complex than just a liberal and conservative dichotomy. Many people agree with the liberal position on some issues and the conservative position on others. Sometimes these individuals are labeled "moderates." This label suggests middle-of-the-road opinions, a designation that fits some people, but other moderates are really just inconsistent, not always choosing the liberal or conservative side of an issue.

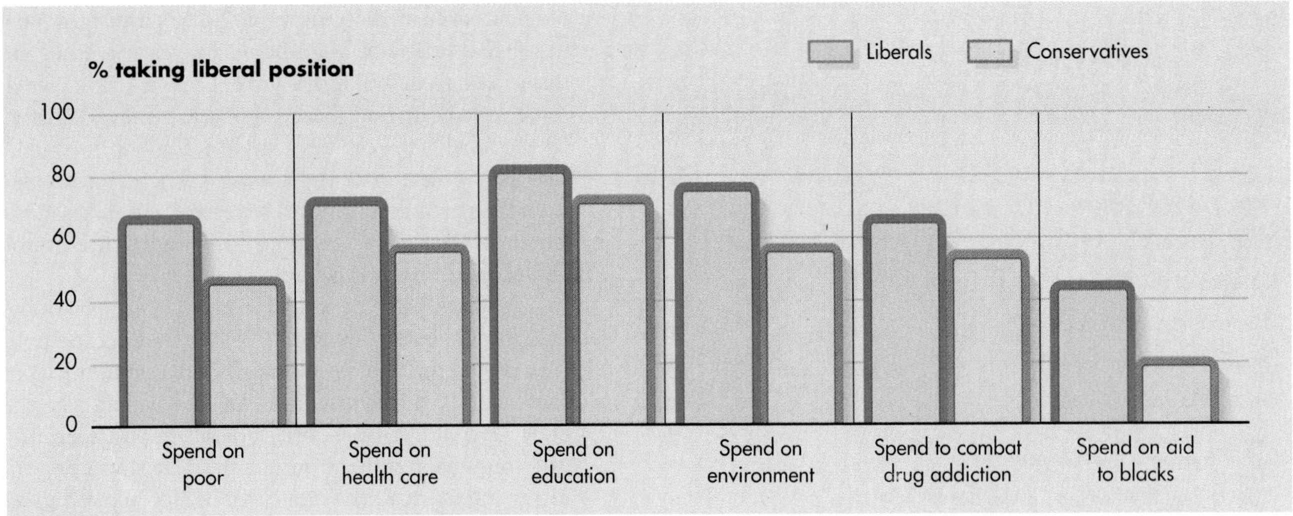

FIGURE 2

Self-Identified Liberals and Conservatives Differ Modestly on Spending for Social Services

SOURCE: 1993 General Social Survey.

Self-identifications are helpful, but one cannot be sure that individuals actually know what the label means or that they support the positions identified with the label. Although liberals and conservatives do take different positions on a number of issues, on most issues a majority of liberals and conservatives take the same position. On social welfare issues, for example, most liberals and conservatives endorse increased spending for health care, education, and the environment and to combat drugs. Majorities of liberals and conservatives have similar feelings on issues of race and are supportive of civil liberties for all Americans whatever their views. Both tend to agree on the failings of the government. All of this means that most Americans are not very ideological. While many call themselves liberals and conservatives, these groups do not represent cohesive blocs of citizens with opposing issue positions seeking to control the government to enact their position into law.

Why aren't Americans more ideological? First, we are not very interested in politics. Much of what we find important in life falls outside politics. We are concerned about our families and jobs, which for the most part are not directly and immediately affected by government. Lack of interest leads to lack of intensity. Even where majorities of liberals and conservatives disagree—as, for example, on abortion and prayer in school—the feelings of most are not very intense, perhaps because most are not touched by these issues.

Second, political candidates and parties do not usually mobilize their followings with ideological or issue appeals. Both candidates and parties try to be all things to all people, for reasons we will discuss more fully in Chapter 6, and often blunt the ideological or issue content of their message in order to attract support from both the right and the left.

Nonetheless, political leaders of both parties are more ideological than the rank and file. Obviously, political leaders are more interested in politics, and this contributes to the intensity of their feelings. And whereas a few years ago scholars talked of "the end of ideology," today they remark on its increase in American political debates.

Social Welfare and the Proper Role of Government

Government programs to help individuals deal with economic hardship started during the Great Depression in the 1930s. These included programs to provide aid for the elderly (Social Security), unemployed, and poor (Aid to Families with Dependent Children). Most Americans supported government assistance of this kind in the 1930s and support it today (see Figure 2).

Still, Americans have mixed feelings about social welfare spending. Support is high for Social Security and for helping the poor. About half feel that the nation is spending too little to assist the poor and poor children, and slightly fewer think we spend too little on Social Security.[65] Nearly 85% favored provisions of the Clinton health care plan that would have subsidized medical costs for low-income families and the unemployed.

On the other hand, support for "welfare," especially Aid to Families with Dependent Children, is much lower. Polls show most (60% to 80%) supported the reforms that require persons on welfare to work and get off welfare after two years. Over 50% feel, however, that it is unfair for the government to cut off payments after two years if there is no other source of income. Most Americans (75%) believe the answer to welfare is job training and are willing to pay more in the short term to provide it. Americans appear to favor helping the poor, but they do not like "welfare," which for decades has been the target of both government officials and the media. They believe that requiring work and training for jobs are the keys to welfare reform.

Americans approve increased spending for education, health care, the environment, drug rehabilitation, and crime and law enforcement. For example, two-thirds favor increased spending for improving and protecting the nation's health. About a third favor increases in spending for the nation's highways and bridges, mass transportation, and parks; less than 10% oppose additional funding in these areas.

In spite of these sentiments, Americans think their taxes are too high. Seventy-six percent favor a middle-class tax cut. Forty-one percent would prefer to have fewer services and reduced taxes, while only 20% say the government should provide more services and increase taxes.

Consistent with Republican goals to devolve functions of government from the national to state levels, 75% want the states to take over many of the responsibilities performed by the national government.[66] Only 12% say that the national government does the best job of spending tax dollars in an efficient and constructive manner. Thirty-two percent say that state governments do the best job.

The preference for state over national government is linked to lack of confidence in the national government. Complaints include that the government wastes money, spends too much on the wrong things, takes too long to solve problems, and offers ineffective solutions to problems. It is possible (indeed likely) that the greater visibility of the national government compared to state governments in turn leads to this relative lack of confidence. If our state legislatures were covered by television to the extent that Congress is, the evaluations by the public would probably be quite different.

Americans have not, however, given up on the national government. They want it managed better and want to see better performance from government employees. Few want to see the government made smaller by cutting spending and programs.

Social Issues

Beginning in the 1960s, so-called social issues, those relating to family, school, and church, became topics of political debate. Examples of social issues include abortion, prayer in public schools, restrictions on pornography, tolerance of homosexuals, crime, and the role of women in society.

Social issues represent a clash of values between those seeking to preserve traditional moral standards and those seeking to establish new ones. Many Americans feel that government policy has encouraged the decline in moral standards and increased permissiveness. Spurred by a rising crime rate in the 1960s and 1970s, Americans felt increasingly that the courts were not severe enough with criminals. Forty-eight percent responded that the courts were not harsh enough with criminals in 1965; 84% felt this way in 1996.[67] Increasing numbers of Americans, 77% in 1996, were also willing to endorse the death penalty for murder.[68]

The position of liberals and conservatives on social issues is opposite of what it is on social welfare. On social welfare issues, liberals are likely to support government action, but on social issues they reject government involvement. Liberals generally prefer to leave questions of religious belief and sexual morality to individuals to decide for themselves, while conservatives are more willing to call upon government to enforce particular standards of behavior.

Conservatives, for example, are more likely to favor a ban on abortion and to require prayer in public schools (see Figure 3). They are more willing to support capital punishment. Conservatives are considerably more likely than liberals to respond that homosexual relations are always wrong and somewhat more likely to subscribe to traditional roles for women. For example, conservatives are slightly more likely to feel that women should take care of the home and leave running the country to men. The vast majority of both liberals and conservatives, however, are open to men and women running the country and would support a woman for president.

Race

Public opinion has influenced as well as responded to the progress of the black struggle for equality. Although the historical record extends to colonial times, the polling record begins in the 1940s. It shows white America increasingly opposed to discrimination and segregation, at least in principle.[69] In fact, the change might be characterized as revolutionary. For example, whereas only one-third of whites accepted the idea of black and white children going to the same schools in 1942, in the 1980s more than 90% approved. Today nearly everyone (98%) agrees. Over 80% respond that they have no objection to sending their children to schools where more than half of the students are black. Nearly two-thirds would not object to schools where most of the students are black. The percentage believing that whites have a right to keep blacks out of their neighborhood has been cut in half since 1963, and a 1996 survey found that two-thirds

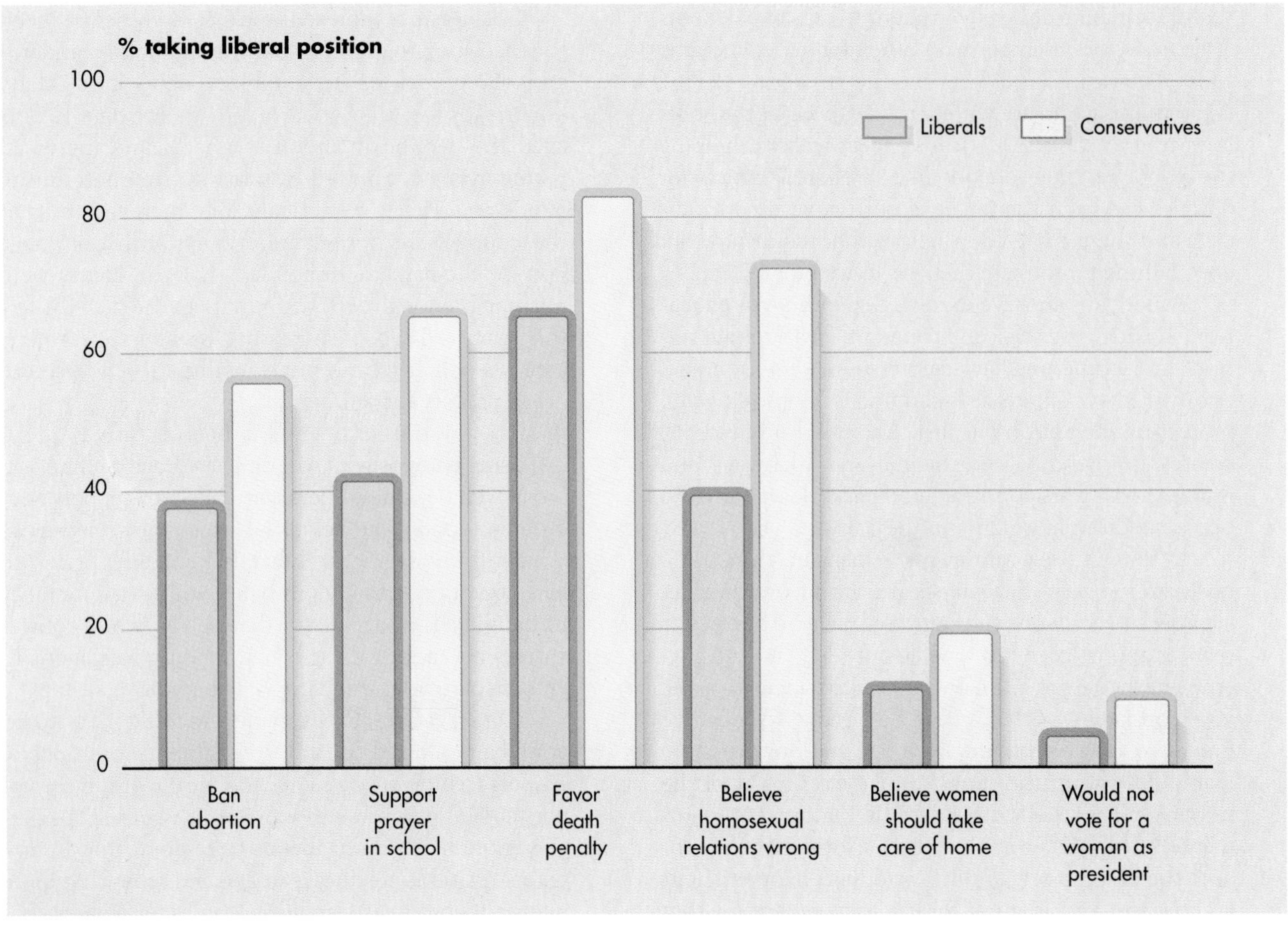

FIGURE 3

Self-Identified Liberals and Conservatives Differ on Many Social Issues

SOURCE: 1996 General Social Survey.

of white Americans live in integrated neighborhoods and that two-thirds claim they have a fairly close friend who is black (80% of blacks claim they have a fairly close white friend).[70] Thirty-eight percent of whites were against laws forbidding intermarriage in 1963; 87% were opposed in 1996.[71]

Only 37% expressed a willingness to vote for a black candidate for president in 1958; in 1996, 92% expressed such willingness. These findings suggest that white America is becoming much more tolerant of racial diversity (see Figure 4). Although the North continues to be more supportive of black rights than the South, whites in both regions show increased acceptance of blacks.

Public opinion can change because individuals change or because older individuals with one set of opinions are replaced by a new generation with a different set. Changes in whites' racial opinions through 1960 occurred for both reasons. In the 1970s, most changes occurred because of replacement. Differences in socialization between those born in the 1920s and 1930s and those born in the 1950s and 1960s have led to much greater support for racial integration.

There is, however, another side to the issue. White America has been much slower to accept government initiatives to achieve racial equality. For example, 38% approved the federal government's ensuring fair treatment for blacks in jobs in 1964; only 28% endorsed the idea in 1996. Busing to achieve racial balance in schools has never had much appeal to whites. Thirteen percent endorsed the idea in 1972, and 33% did so in 1996.

Unwillingness to endorse government initiatives to end segregation often reflects racist sentiments.[72] Such racism is not necessarily based on the previously widespread perception that blacks are biologically inferior, but instead is grounded in the belief that blacks lack the moral character to improve themselves.[73] For example, most whites believe that blacks are more likely than whites to lack motivation and to prefer living on welfare to working. Many whites believe that if blacks tried, they could overcome prejudice on their own without special favors.[74] Of course, some oppose government help for blacks on principle. They object to being told what to do by government or feel government assistance for blacks is discrimination against whites. For some, government help violates their sense that individuals have a responsibility to provide for themselves.

Another reason that white Americans are reluctant to accept government intervention is that many have closed their eyes to the racial prejudice that still exists. Less than one-fourth of whites see the discrimination in education and housing. Only a small majority of whites are aware of discrimination in hiring and promotion, and they overwhelmingly reject racial preferences (even without quotas) to redress discrimination.[75] Three out of four Americans oppose affirmative action programs that give preference to minorities and women to make up for past and current discrimination. A majority of whites believe affirmative action hurts white men.[76] It is not only Republicans and conservatives who oppose racial preferences, but Democrats and liberals as well.[77] (We will explore affirmative action in more detail in Chapter 15.)

Blacks see things quite differently. About a third believe that there is discrimination in education, about half believe discrimination exists in housing and getting an unskilled job, and about two-thirds see discrimination in getting a skilled job or managerial position.[78]

What do blacks believe should be done about race discrimination? Although the polling record for blacks does not extend as far back as it does for whites, blacks have overwhelmingly endorsed integration. Nearly all blacks have responded consistently that blacks and whites should go to the same schools and that blacks have a right to live anywhere they want to. Intermarriage is approved by three out of four blacks.

Like whites, blacks have become somewhat less supportive of government initiatives. In 1964, 92% thought the national government should ensure blacks fair treatment in jobs; by 1996, only 64% did. Support for government assistance in school integration has also declined, from 82% in 1964 to 57% in 1994. Some blacks fear that government initiatives will only antagonize whites. Others believe government aid hurts blacks by making them too dependent. Still others believe government is ineffective in bringing about an end to discrimination.

Self-identified liberals and conservatives also differ on race issues. Liberals are somewhat more likely to oppose laws that ban racial intermarriage, to disagree that whites have a right to keep blacks out of their neighborhood, and to be willing to send their children to a school where most are a different race. However, differences are fairly small (5 to 9 percentage points), and majorities of both liberals and conservatives take the pro-equality position on each issue. Nevertheless, because there are gaps between abstractions about equality and concrete issues such as affirmative action and between survey questions and real-life dilemmas, issues of race remain the most vexing in our society.

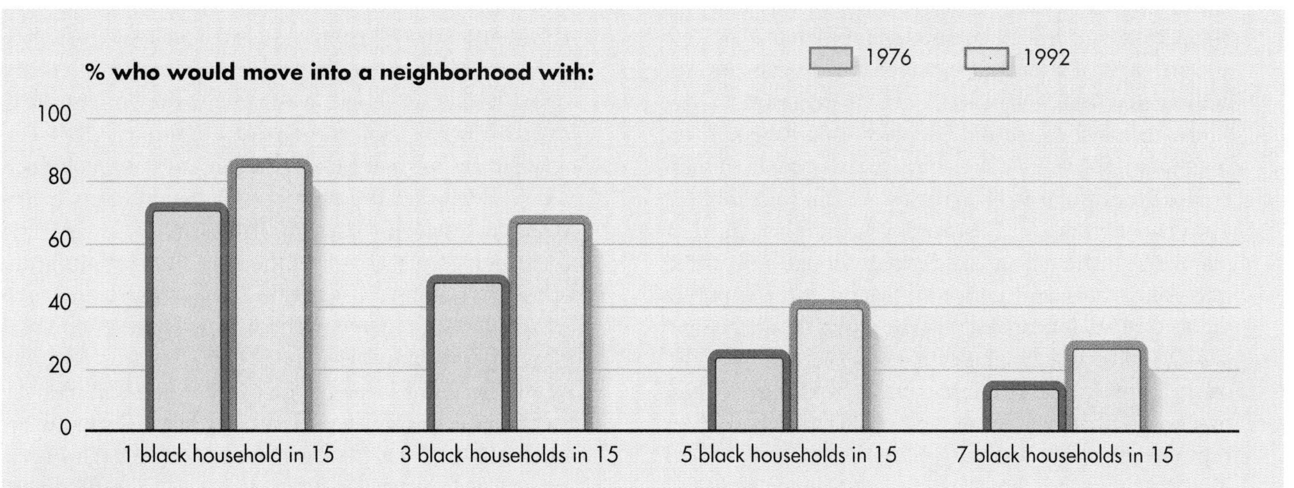

FIGURE 4

Whites Have Grown More Accepting of Neighborhood Integration

Residential segregation is the linchpin of racial separation in America. Such segregation influences the quality and nature of schools, employment opportunities, and the amenities of daily life. In the past 20 years, American cities have become somewhat less segregated, stimulated in part by whites' changing attitudes about residential segregation.

SOURCE: Douglas Massey and Nancy Denton, *American Apartheid* (Cambridge: Harvard University Press, 1993).

Political Tolerance

Political tolerance is the willingness of individuals to extend procedural rights and liberties to people with whom they disagree. Tolerance is important because it embodies many elements essential to democratic government, such as freedom of speech and assembly.

J. William Fulbright, the former senator from Arkansas, once said, "Americans believe in the right to free speech until someone tries to exercise it." In other words, people are tolerant in the abstract but not when called upon to support speakers they disagree with. More than 85% of Americans claim to believe in free speech for all,[79] yet a 1954 nationwide survey found that only 37% of the respondents would allow a person opposed to churches and religion to speak in their communities.[80] Even fewer would permit an admitted communist to speak. More highly educated people were more tolerant than those with less education, and political elites were more tolerant than the general public.

The finding that elites were more tolerant than the general public was reassuring. After all, many elites are in a position to deprive people of rights, and elites help shape public opinion. Later studies have revealed, however, that elites are more tolerant than the general public largely because they are better educated.[81] Elites, however, do influence the opinions of the general public on civil liberties. When elites agree among themselves, the general public is more likely to reflect this consensus.[82]

More recent studies suggest that Americans have become substantially more tolerant of communists, socialists, and atheists.[83] However, overall levels of tolerance may not have increased that much.

In the 1950s, people perceived communists and socialists as a major threat. As the perception of the threat diminished, so did people's fears. Research on tolerance, therefore, has first asked people which groups they dislike and then assessed their tolerance toward those groups.[84] Two-thirds or more thought that members of their least-liked group should be banned from being president and from teaching in the public schools. Many responded that the group should be outlawed, indicating a high degree of intolerance. On the other hand, in the 1970s, the public was more willing to allow their least-liked group to speak and teach than they were to allow communists to do so in 1954.[85] This suggests that tolerance may have increased. Thus, although intolerance remains, it seems that the public has grown more tolerant since the 1950s.

While increased levels of political tolerance since the 1950s are a reason to be positive, economic insecurity in the 1980s and early 1990s helped promote negative feelings toward minorities and immigrants and others outside the mainstream. A majority of whites, for example, agree that equal rights for racial minorities have gone too far. Eighty-two percent agree that people coming to live in the United States should be restricted and controlled more than they are now.[86] Such sentiments are not likely to lead to a loss of civil liberties unless political elites direct citizens' fears in an attempt to gain political advantage.

In general, liberals tend to be more tolerant than conservatives, at least toward communists, atheists, racists, and those who would support a military government. For example, in 1996, 74% of those who identified themselves as liberals in a national survey indicated a willingness to allow a communist to speak in their community; 64% of the conservatives took this position.[87] The difference, however, may reflect that conservatives view communists as a bigger threat than liberals do. Liberals may be equally intolerant toward groups they perceive as threatening. In general, intolerance is not caused by ideology, but by personality, the tendency to see the world as a dangerous place, specific beliefs about individuals and groups, and lack of support for the principles of democracy.[88]

Trust in Government

An important dimension of public opinion is the trust or support citizens have for their government, its institutions and officials, and for their fellow citizens. With high levels of trust, citizens might do everything government demands. They would pay their taxes and, if called upon to do so, defend the government. They might also gullibly accept anything officials tell them. At low levels of trust, citizens would be more skeptical; they might even disobey the law. At the lowest levels, they might try to overthrow the government or commit violent acts against it, as with the Oklahoma City bombing. Thus, democratic government "depends on a fine balance between trust and distrust."[89]

Public trust of government has declined significantly in the last 30 years. In the early 1960s, Americans were supportive of the government. A comparison of five nations—the United States, Britain, West Germany, Italy, and Mexico—found Americans to be the most positive about the responsiveness and performance of government; 95% of the Americans sampled pointed to the government when asked what aspects of the nation they were proud of.[90] The picture that emerged was one of trust and confidence.

The pattern, however, changed sometime in the mid-1960s. Trust in government declined after 1964 and continued to decline through 1980 (see Figure 5).

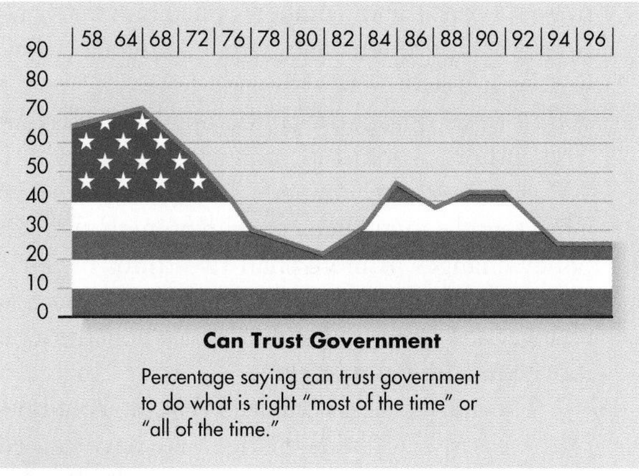

FIGURE 5

Trust in Government Declined During the 1960s and 1970s

SOURCE: National Election Studies, the Center for Political Studies.

The pattern was characteristic not only of opinions toward government but of opinions toward all major institutions in society, including the medical profession, business, and the press. Government responsiveness also was rated less positively during the 1960s and 1970s.

Why did levels of trust and confidence in government decline? One answer is the performance of government itself. In the mid to late 1960s, the nation was divided over a number of issues, including what to do about the war in Vietnam and the civil rights demands of blacks. Many people wanted the government to do everything possible to win the war in Vietnam, whereas others wanted an immediate withdrawal of U.S. forces; the Johnson and Nixon policies of limited and prolonged war were unresponsive to both sides.

The civil rights struggle also divided the nation. Some wanted government to do more to speed the progress of blacks and other minorities, whereas others thought government was moving too fast. Once more, government chose a middle course fully responsive to neither side.[91]

Following on the heels of these seemingly intractable problems, the early 1970s brought news of Watergate and corruption in government, and after 1973 the nation experienced economic problems, inflation, high interest rates, and unemployment. The government was little more successful in dealing with these than it was with the problems of the 1960s. Levels of trust again declined.

Between 1980 and 1984, levels of trust and confidence in government increased modestly. People seemed to respond to what appeared to be an improved economy and a few foreign policy successes. President Reagan's personal popularity seemed to inspire confidence on the part of the American people.

Reagan's involvement in the Iran-contra scandal, a sense that his administration lacked compassion, and popular dissatisfaction with domestic and foreign policy diminished his appeal, however, and no doubt contributed to a decline in trust between 1984 and 1986.[92] In the 1990s, trust has remained low.[93] Following the 1994 election, President Clinton and the Republican majority deadlocked over health care reform, welfare, and the budget deficit. Resolution of the welfare debate and a balanced budget agreement raised public assessments of both the president and Congress prior to the 1998 election, but trust remained low compared to the 1960s.

As we have suggested, one explanation for declining trust is policy failure. Citizens have become increasingly oriented to government in terms of the services (jobs and high standard of living) they expect government to provide. When performance falls short of expectations, trust in government falls.[94] One study documents the link between confidence in government and the state of the economy. Between 1966 and 1980, every percentage increase in unemployment lowered confidence in government by almost 3%.[95]

Expressions of trust in government may involve more than evaluations of government performance, however. Societal problems may also cause declining trust. Recent studies have found that trust in government is tied to public concern about declining morality and values, something over which government has limited control.[96] Declining levels of trust may have less to do with failed government performance than with the public's sense that the nation is doing badly on a number of fronts. If this is so, an improving economy is unlikely to make a big difference in levels of trust.

Another theory for declining trust focuses on process.[97] Declining trust is highly correlated with the increasing visibility of government. As Americans see more of their federal government on a day-to-day basis, through C-SPAN and newscasts, they like and trust it less. Talk radio and television interpret what are normal parts of the democratic process—lobbying, bargaining, negotiating, and compromise—as cynical acts done only for the self-interest of an individual, interest group, or political party. Of course, there is plenty of self-interest in politics, as in any other form of human endeavor, but compromise and negotiation are a necessary part of a democratic process. Since most Americans seem neither to understand nor like that part of the process, the more exposure the process gets, the less the public likes it.

Both policy and process have contributed to declining trust in government. Moreover, the two reinforce each other. Policy deadlock contributes to negative reactions to process, but even when the process yields significant policies, the public visibility of the mechanics of the policy process, with its negotiations and deals, still contributes to cynicism and mistrust.

Levels of trust among liberals and conservatives are frequently influenced by the party that occupies the White House. During Republican administrations, liberals tend to be less trusting; when Democrats hold office, liberals are more trusting.[98]

Negative feelings toward government and society in general are not unique to the United States.[99] Seventy percent of Canadians responded in a recent survey that their country was moving in the wrong direction. Forty-four percent in Japan responded the same way, and given that country's recent economic woes, this number is probably higher today.

In the United States, a prosperous economy and expanded job opportunities in recent years have increased citizen confidence. Nevertheless, competition and technological change continue, and government at the present seems unwilling or unable to cushion the impact on working men and women. An economic downturn is likely to undermine the recent rise in public confidence.

Companies can move operations and individuals can transfer capital across national boundaries at will. While this creates economic opportunity, it also creates anxiety. Individuals are unclear what they need or should do to protect themselves and their families.

At the same time, however, Americans as well as citizens in other industrialized countries report that they are content with the lives they lead. Citizens' negative response to government and their concern for the future may result from what they read and see in the news and the political rhetoric of politicians as much as it does from their personal situation.[100] Thus, citizens' negativism may be due to the expanding scope of the media in developed countries.

CONCLUSION: IS GOVERNMENT RESPONSIVE TO PUBLIC OPINION?

Our interest in public opinion stems in part from the belief that in a democracy government should be responsive to the wishes of the people. But is it? Political scientists have had only limited success answering this question because of the difficulty in measuring influence.

The most direct way to assess whether public policy is responsive to public opinion is to compare changes in policy with changes in opinion. The largest study of this type examined several hundred public opinion surveys done between 1935 and 1979. From these surveys, the researchers culled hundreds of questions, each of which dealt with a particular policy and had been asked more than one time. On more than 300 of these questions, public opinion had changed. The authors of the study compared changes in these 300 opinions with changes, if any, in public policy. They found congruence between opinion changes and policy changes in more than two-thirds of the opinions. Congruence was most likely when the opinion change was large and stable and when the opinion moved in a liberal direction.

The authors acknowledged that in about one-half of the cases, the policy change may have caused the opinion change, but in the other half the opinion change probably caused the policy change or they both affected each other. Although in many instances policy was not congruent with public opinion, on important issues, when changes in public opinion were clear-cut, policy usually became consistent with opinion.[101]

Although policy usually changes with changes in opinions, sometimes it does not. One reason is that reelection does not rest with the entire public but with the voting public, and those who vote often differ in their policy preferences from those who do not.[102] To the extent that elected public officials are responsive to voters, and voters differ from nonvoters, public policy will not reflect public opinion.

Then, too, elected public officials must pay attention not only to the direction of public opinion but also to its intensity. It may be advantageous for an elected official to vote in support of a minority opinion that is intensely held. A minority with intense feelings is more likely to vote against a candidate who does not support its position than is a group with weak preferences. When elected officials are confronted with an intense minority, public policy may not reflect public opinion.

Moreover, public opinion is not the only influence on public policy, nor is it necessarily the most important. Interest groups, political parties, other institutions of government, and public officials' own preferences also influence policy, and they may or may not agree with public opinion. Where the preferences of the various influences do not agree, policy generally will reflect a compromise among them.

Finally, there is nothing sacred about public opinion. Even when a majority of the public favors a course of action, one should not assume that this is the most desirable course; the public can be wrong. This possibility led the Founders to establish a government that was partially insulated from the influence of public opinion. In other words, we do not have complete and immediate correspondence between opinion and policy because the Founders did not want instant government responsiveness. They built a federal system with separation of powers and many checks and balances to ensure that the majority could not steamroll the minority. Thus, one should not expect public policy to reflect public opinion perfectly. The fact that policy usually comes to reflect large and stable majorities does indicate, however, that government is eventually responsive on important issues. Indeed, some observers think politicians pay too much attention to public opinion, to the point that leaders are fearful of leading or of offending the competing groups pulling in opposite directions. The result is more gridlock.

EPILOGUE

Luntz Eventually Reveals Loaded Questions

Initially, Luntz ignored the AAPOR's request. After a year, he provided some information, including sample sizes, interviewing dates, and how respondents were selected, but would not provide question wording or results of questions he said measured popular support for the Contract. He argued that such information was the property of the Republican Party and implied that while he would like to supply the information, he would not betray a client's trust. Although the AAPOR rarely issues a public reprimand against nonmembers, because of Luntz's continued refusal to provide information and because his polls had received so much publicity, the AAPOR voted to censure him.

Luntz later admitted that his polls were flawed. The results were based on loaded questions, designed by him to ensure support for the Contract. Luntz's polling was designed to manipulate the public rather than to find out what the public thought.

Luntz remains a highly sought-after consultant and strategist. In spite of his playing fast and loose with his Contract polls, he continues to advise Republicans on how to win elections. His most recent activity includes a 222-page manifesto advising Republicans on language they can use to win votes. His advice to the party on family issues is to refer to values, morality, spirituality, and faith in God. On deregulation, he advises repeating the phrase "Deregulation should lead to lower prices for all consumers." He offers slogans to attract the votes of women, minorities, and other groups that the party has had difficulty winning over in the past. He says the American people think that Clinton feels their pain, while they think the Republican Party feels nothing. Linguistically, he argues, the party is out of touch. Luntz's *Language for the 21st Century,* as he calls it, is a how-to marketing strategy for Republican politicians.

KEY TERMS

public opinion
political socialization
agents of political socialization
straw polls
ideology
liberal
conservative
political tolerance

FURTHER READING

Herbert Asher, *Polling and the Public: What Every Citizen Should Know* (Washington, D.C.: CQ Press, 1998). An introduction to polling methodology and the influence of polls on American politics as well as advice to citizens on how to evaluate polls.

Paul Brace and Barbara Hinckley, *Follow the Leader: Opinion Polls and the Modern President* (New York: Basic Books, 1992). A survey of how recent presidents have allowed the results of public opinion polls to influence their position on issues.

Susan Herbst, *Numbered Voices: How Opinion Polling Has Shaped American Politics* (Chicago: University of Chicago Press, 1993). A historical review of the way public opinion has been measured and the way the evolution of measurement techniques has affected the definition of public opinion.

Celinda Lake, *Public Opinion Polling: A Handbook for Public Interest and Citizen Advocacy Groups* (Washington, D.C.: Island Press, 1987). A step-by-step treatment for lay audiences on how to conduct a public opinion poll.

Thomas E. Mann and Gary R. Orren, eds., *Media Polls and American Politics* (Washington, D.C.: Brookings, 1992). Several essays focusing on the influence of media-conducted polls on American political institutions and elections.

Benjamin I. Page and Robert Y. Shapiro, *The Rational Public: Fifty Years of Trends in American's Policy Preferences* (Chicago: University of Chicago Press, 1992). An examination of the influence of public opinion on public policy using public opinion polling information generated over the past 50 years.

ELECTRONIC RESOURCES

Many polling firms have homepages. Below is a sampling of some of the more reputable ones.

http://www.ropercenter.uconn.edu
The Roper Center webpage contains information on the current and past presidents' job performance and a listing of current Roper surveys.

http://www.irss.unc.edu/data_ archive/pollsearch.html
The Louis Harris Center archive webpage links to current and past Harris surveys. Frequencies are available for all questions and information can be downloaded and analyzed.

http://www.icpsr.umich.edu.gss/home.htm
The General Social Survey provides data on a variety of political and social issues gathered in surveys from 1972 to 1996. Data from one or more years can be analyzed online.

http://www.gallup.com
The Gallup Center does weekly national surveys on political and social issues. The webpage links to past Gallup newsletters, special reports and trends in public opinion including the public support for the president and Congress and the public mood.

http://www.umich.edu/~nes/
The National Election Studies of the University of Michigan webpage provides access to the most recent national election study. This information can be analyzed online.

http://www.usatoday.com/elect/eg/equidex.htm
The webpage links to surveys carried in USA Today.

http://www.people-press.org./
The Pew Center webpage provides recent polling information.

INFOTRAC CITATIONS

"Moderate Attitudes of 'Generation 2001'"
"Preparing for Trial: An Uncommon Approach"
"Despite Tough Talk, States Avoid Workforce"
"America's Civic Condition"

NOTES

1. Richard Morin, "A Pollster's Peers Cry Foul," *Washington Post National Weekly Edition*, April 28, 1997, p. 13; American Association for Public Opinion Research, "Major Opinion Research Association Finds Pollster Frank Luntz Violated Ethics Code," news release, April 23, 1997; Ceci Connolly, "For the Republicans, a Campaign Primer," *Washington Post National Weekly Edition*, September 15, 1997, p. 13.

2. Richard Morin, "The Ups and Downs of Political Poll-Taking," *Washington Post National Weekly Edition*, October 5, 1992, p. 37.

3. T. E. Cook, "The Bear Market in Political Socialization and the Costs of Misunderstood Psychological Theories," *American Political Science Review* 79 (December 1985), pp. 1079–1093.

4. S. W. Moore et al., "The Civic Awareness of Five- and Six-Year-Olds," *Western Political Quarterly* 29 (August 1976), p. 418.

5. R. W. Connell, *The Child's Construction of Politics* (Carlton, Victoria: Melbourne University Press, 1971).

6. F. I. Greenstein, *Children and Politics* (New Haven, Conn.: Yale University Press, 1965), p. 122; see also F. I. Greenstein, "The Benevolent Leader Revisited: Children's Images of Political Leaders in Three Democracies," *American Political Science Review* 69 (December 1975), pp. 1317–1398; R. D. Hess and J. V. Torney, *The Development of Attitudes in Children* (Chicago: Aldine, 1967).

7. Hess and Torney, *Development of Attitudes in Children;* Connell, *Child's Construction of Politics*.

8. Greenstein, *Children and Politics;* Greenstein, "The Benevolent Leader"; and Hess and Torney, *Development of Attitudes in Children*.

9. Connell, *Child's Construction of Politics*.

10. F. C. Arterton, "The Impact of Watergate on Children's Attitudes toward the President," *Political Science Quarterly* 89 (June 1974), pp. 269–288; also F. Haratwig and C. Tidmarch, "Children and Political Reality: Changing Images of the President," paper presented at the 1974 Annual Meeting of the Southern Political Science Association; J. Dennis and C. Webster, "Children's Images of the President and Government in 1962 and 1974," *American Politics Quarterly* 4 (October 1975), pp. 386–405; R. P. Hawkins, S. Pingree, and D. Roberts, "Watergate and Political Socialization," *American Politics Quarterly* 4 (October 1975), pp. 406–436.

11. M. A. Delli Carpini, *Stability and Change in American Politics: The Coming of Age of the Generation of the 1960s* (New York: New York University Press, 1986), pp. 86–89.

12. R. Merelman, *Political Socialization and Educational Climates* (New York: Holt, Rinehart & Winston, 1971), p. 54.

13. R. Sigel and M. Hoskin, *The Political Involvement of Adolescents* (New Brunswick, N.J.: Rutgers University Press, 1981).

14. J. Citrin, "Comment: The Political Relevance of Trust in Government," *American Political Science Review* 68 (September 1974), pp. 973–1001; J. Citrin and D. P. Green, "Presidential Leadership and the Resurgence of Trust in Government," *British Journal of Political Science* 16 (1986), pp. 431–453.

15. John Hibbing and Elizabeth Theiss-Morse, *Congress as Public Enemy: Public Attitudes toward American Political Institutions* (Cambridge: Cambridge University Press, 1995). It is plausible to assume that the content of early political socialization influences what is learned later, but the assumption has not been adequately tested. Thus, we might expect the positive opinions toward government and politics developed early in childhood to condition the impact of traumatic events later in life. D. Easton and J. Dennis, *Children and the Political System: Origins of Regime Legitimacy* (New York: McGraw-Hill, 1969); R. Weissberg, *Political Learning, Political Choice and Democratic Citizenship* (Englewood Cliffs, N.J.: Prentice-Hall, 1974). See also D. D. Searing, J. J. Schwartz, and A. E. Line, "The Structuring Principle: Political Socialization and Belief System," *American Political Science Review* 67 (June 1973), pp. 414–432.

16. D. Jaros, H. Hirsch, and F. Fleron, Jr., "The Malevolent Leader: Political Socialization in an American Subculture," *American Political Science Review* 62 (June 1968), pp. 564–575.

17. K. Tedin, "The Influence of Parents on the Political Attitudes of Adolescents," *American Political Science Review* 68 (December 1974), pp. 1579–1592.

18. M. Kent Jennings, *Generations and Politics* (Princeton: Princeton University Press, 1981).

19. On the impact of the public schools and teachers on political socialization, particularly in the area of loyalty and patriotism, see Hess and Torney, *Development of Attitudes in Children*.

20. K. Langton and M. K. Jennings, "Political Socialization and the High School Civics Curriculum," *American Political Science Review* 62 (September 1968), pp. 852–877; D. Goldenson, "An Alternative View about the Role of the Secondary School in Political Socialization: A Field Experimental Study of the Development of Civil Liberties Attitudes," *Theory and Research in Social Education* 6 (March 1978), pp. 44–72.

21. The study of 17-year-olds is reported by E. Shantz, "Sideline Citizens," in Byron Massiales, ed., *Political Youth, Traditional Schools* (Englewood Cliffs, N.J.: Prentice-Hall, 1972), pp. 69–70; the study of high school seniors is reported by H. H. Remmers and R. D. Franklin, "Sweet Land of Liberty," in H. H. Remmers, ed., *Anti-Democratic Attitudes in American Schools* (Evanston, Ill.: Northwestern University Press, 1963), p. 62.

22. R. Merelman, "Democratic Politics and the Culture of American Education," *American Political Science Review* 74 (June 1980), pp. 319–332.

23. G. Almond and S. Verba, *Civic Culture* (Boston: Little, Brown, 1965); John R. Hibbing and Elizabeth Theiss-Morse, "Civics Is Not Enough: Teaching Barbarics in K-12," *P.S* (March 1992), p. 12.

24. Material for this section is drawn from E. C. Ladd and S. M. Lipset, *The Divided Academy* (New York: McGraw-Hill, 1975); C. Kesler, "The Movement of Student Opinion," *The National Review* (November 23) 1979, p. 29; E. L. Boyer, *College: The Undergraduate Experience in America* (New York: Harper & Row, 1986); "Fact File: Attitudes and Characteristics of This Year's Freshman," *The Chronicle of Higher Education* (January 11, 1989) pp. A33–A34; General Social Survey, National Opinion Research Center, 1984, p. 87.

25. Alexander W. Astin et al., *The American Freshman: Thirty Year Trends* (Los Angeles: Higher Education Research Institute, Graduate School of Education and Information Studies, 1997).

26. Linda Sax et al., *The American Freshman: National Norms for Fall 1997* (Los Angeles: Higher Education Research Institute, Graduate School of Education and Information Studies, 1997).

27. Ibid.

28. M. K. Jennings and R. G. Niemi, *The Political Character of Adolescence* (Princeton: Princeton University Press, 1974), p. 243.

29. M. McCombs and D. Shaw, "The Agenda Setting Function of the Media," *Public Opinion Quarterly* 36 (Summer 1972), pp. 176–187.

30. B. I. Page, R. Shapiro, and G. R. Dempsey, "What Moves Public Opinion?" *American Political Science Review* 81 (March 1987), pp. 23–44.

31. H. Weissberg, "Marital Differences in Voting," *Public Opinion Quarterly* 51 (1987), pp. 335–343.

32. P. R. Abramson, *Political Attitudes in America* (San Francisco: Freeman, 1983), pp. 150, 213; see also Paul R. Abramson, *The Political Socialization of Black Americans* (New York: Free Press, 1977).

33. P. E. Converse, A. R. Clausen, and W. Miller, "Electoral Myth and Reality," *American Political Science Review* 59 (1965), pp. 321–326.

34. J. P. Robinson, "The Press as Kingmaker: What Surveys Show from the Last Five Campaigns," *Journalism Quarterly* 49 (Summer 1974), p. 592.

35. Susan Herbst, *Numbered Voices: How Opinion Polling Has Shaped American Politics* (Chicago: University of Chicago Press, 1993); Benjamin Ginsberg, "How Polling Changes Public Opinion" in *Manipulating Public Opinion*, ed., Michael Margolis and Gary Mauser (Pacific Grove, Calif.: Brooks/Cole, 1989).

36. For a review of the history of polling, see Bernard Hennessy, *Public Opinion*, 4th ed. (Monterey, Calif.: Brooks/Cole, 1983), pp. 42–44, 46–50. See also C. Roll and A. Cantril, *Polls: Their Use and Misuse in Politics* (New York: Basic Books, 1972), pp. 3–16.

37. P. Squire, "The 1936 Literary Digest Poll, " *Public Opinion Quarterly* 52 (1988), pp. 125–133; see also Don Cahalan, "The Digest Poll Rides Again," *Public Opinion Quarterly* 53 (1989), pp. 107–113.

38. Hennessy, *Public Opinion*, p. 46.

39. "Consulting the Oracle," *U.S. News and World Report*, December 4, 1995, pp. 52–55.

40. Ibid.

41. Richard Morin, "The Election Post-Mortem," *Washington Post National Weekly Edition*, January 13, 1997, p. 34; Richard Morin, "Standing on the Record," *Washington Post National Weekly Edition*, September 30, 1996, p. 37.

42. "All Things Considered," National Public Radio, October 30, 1992.

43. "Consulting the Oracle," p. 53.

44. Ibid.

45. R. Morin, "Surveying the Surveyors," *Washington Post National Weekly Edition*, March 2, 1992, p. 37.

46. David Broder, "Push Polls Plunge Politics to a New Low," *Lincoln Star*, October 9, 1994, p. 5E.

47. Ibid.

48. Ann Devroy, "George Bush's Identity Crisis," *Washington Post National Weekly Edition*, August 24–30, 1992, pp. 6–7.

49. Richard Morin, "When the Method Becomes the Message," *Washington Post National Weekly Edition*, December 19–25, 1994, p. 33.

50. Richard Morin, "Tuned Out, Turned Off," *Washington Post National Weekly Edition*, February 5–11, 1996, pp. 6–8.

51. Ibid.

52. Ibid.

53. Richard Morin, "They Know Only What They Don't Like," *Washington Post National Weekly Edition*, October 3–9, 1994, p. 37.

54. 1986 National Election Study, Center for Political Studies, University of Michigan; "Wapner Top Judge in Recognition Poll," *Lincoln Star*, June 23, 1989, p. 1 (*Washington Post* syndication).

55. Michael X. Delli Carpini and Scott Keeter, "U.S. Public Knowledge of Politics," *Public Opinion Quarterly* (Winter, 1991), pp. 583–612.

56. Richard Morin, "We Love It—What We Know of It," *Washington Post National Weekly Edition*, September 22, 1997, p. 35.

57. Morin, "They Know Only What They Don't Like."

58. Morin, "Tuned Out, Turned Off."

59. Ibid.

60. Richard Morin, "Foreign Aid: Mired in Misunderstanding," *Washington Post National Weekly Edition*, March 20–26, 1995, p. 37.

61. Richard Morin, "What Informed Public Opinion?" *Washington Post National Weekly Edition*, April 10–16, 1995, p. 36.

62. V. O. Key, *The Responsible Electorate* (Cambridge, Mass.: Harvard University Press, 1966); N. Nie, S. Verba, and J. R. Petrocik, *The Changing American Voter* (Cambridge, Mass.: Harvard University Press, 1976), chapter 18.

63. Morin, "Tuned Out, Turned Off."

64. B. Sussman, "When Politicians Talk about Issues People Listen," *Washington Post National Weekly Edition*, August 18, 1986, p. 37.

65. Data in this section are summarized in *The Public Perspective* 6, no. 2 (February/March, 1995), pp. 39–46.

66. Data here are from Peter Hart Research Associates Survey for the Council for Excellence in Government, March 16–18, 1995.

67. General Social Survey, 1996.

68. Ibid.

69. This section draws heavily on H. Schuman, C. Steeh, and L. Bobo, *Racial Attitudes in America* (Cambridge, Mass.: Harvard University Press, 1985); data summaries are drawn from the General Social Surveys of the National Opinion Research Center, University of Chicago, and National Elections Studies of CPS, University of Michigan; see also L. Sigelman and S. Welch, *Black Americans' Views of Racial Inequality* (Cambridge, Mass.: Cambridge University Press, 1991).

70. General Social Survey, 1996; *Washington Post National Weekly Edition*, October 30, 1989, p. 37.

71. General Social Surveys, 1996; "Whites Retain Negative Views of Minorities, a Survey Finds," *New York Times*, January 10, 1991, p. C19; M. Jackman, "General and Applied Tolerance: Does Education Increase Commitment to Racial Inequality?" *American*

Journal of Political Science 22 (1978), pp. 302–324; M. Jackman, "Education and Policy Commitment to Racial Equality," *American Journal of Political Science* 25 (1981), pp. 256–269; D. Kinder and D. Sears, "Prejudice and Politics," *Journal of Personality and Social Psychology* 40 (1981), pp. 414–431.

72. "Whites Retain Negative Views."

73. Donald Kinder and Lynn Saunders, *Divided by Color: Racial Politics and Democratic Ideals* (Chicago: University of Chicago Press, 1996); H. Schuman and L. Bobo, "Survey-Based Experiments on White Attitudes toward Residential Integration," *American Journal of Sociology* 94 (1988), pp. 272–294; W. R. Merriman and E. Carmines, "The Limits of Liberal Tolerance: The Case of Racial Politics," *Polity* 20 (1988), pp. 519–526; see also Schuman, Steeh, and Bobo, *Racial Attitudes*.

74. Kinder and Saunders, *Divided by Color;* L. Sigelman and S. Welch, "A Dream Deferred: Black Attitudes toward Race and Inequality," unpublished manuscript, 1989.

75. Kinder and Saunders, *Divided by Color;* ABC/*Washington Post* Poll, 1981.

76. Richard Morin, "No Place for Calm and Quiet Opinions," *Washington Post National Weekly Edition*, April 24–30, 1994, p. 34.

77. Martin Gilens and Paul Sniderman, "Affirmative Action and the Politics of Realignment." Paper presented at the Midwest Political Science Association Meeting, Chicago, Ill., 1995; Paul Sniderman and Thomas Piazza, *The Scar of Race* (Cambridge, Mass: Harvard University Press, 1993).

78. ABC/*Washington Post* Poll, 1981 and 1986.

79. J. Sullivan, G. Marcus, S. Feldman, and J. Pierson, "Sources of Political Tolerance: A Multivariate Analysis," *American Political Science Review* 75 (March 1981), pp. 92–106.

80. S. Stouffer, *Communism, Conformity, and Civil Liberties* (New York: John Wiley & Sons, 1954).

81. R. W. Jackman, "Political Elites, Mass Publics, and Support for Democratic Principles," *Journal of Politics* 34 (August 1972), p. 753.

82. H. McClosky and J. Zaller, *The American Ethos: Public Attitudes toward Capitalism and Democracy* (Cambridge, Mass.: Harvard University Press, 1986).

83. C. Z. Nunn, H. H. Crockett, Jr., and J. A. Williams, *Tolerance for Nonconformity* (San Francisco: Jossey-Bass, 1976).

84. J. Sullivan, J. Pierson, and G. Marcus, "An Alternative Conceptualization of Tolerance: Illusory Increases 1950s–1970s," *American Political Science Review* 73 (September 1979), pp. 781–794. For a critique of this study, see P. M. Sniderman, P. E. Tetlock, J. M. Glaser, D. P. Gress, and M. Hout, "Principled Tolerance and the American Mass Public," *British Journal of Political Science* 19 (January 1989), pp. 25–46.

85. P. Abramson, "Comments on Sullivan, Pierson, and Marcus," *American Political Science Review* 74 (June 1980): pp. 780–81.

86. "Polls Find Americans Angry, Anxious, Less Altruistic," *Lincoln Journal* (September 21, 1994), p. 9.

87. General Social Survey, 1996.

88. George Marcus et al., *With Malice toward Some: How People Make Civil Liberties Judgments* (Cambridge: Cambridge University Press, 1995).

89. Judith Shklar, quoted in Paul Taylor, "In Watergate's Wake: The Good, the Bad, and the Ugly," *Washington Post National Weekly Edition*, June 22, 1992, p. 25.

90. Almond and Verba, *Civic Culture*, pp. 64–68.

91. A. Miller, "Political Issues and Trust in Government, 1964–1970," *American Political Science Review* 68 (September 1974), pp. 951–972.

92. A. Miller and S. Borrelli, "Confidence in Government during the 1980s," *American Politics Quarterly* 19 (April 1991), pp. 147–173.

93. "Clinton's High Victory Rate Conceals Disappointments," *Congressional Quarterly Weekly Reports* (December 31, 1994), pp. 3619–3623.

94. T. J. Lowi, *The Personal President* (Ithaca, N.Y.: Cornell University Press, 1995).

95. S. M. Lipset and W. Schneider, *The Confidence Gap* (New York: Free Press, 1983).

96. Richard Morin, "Less Than Meets the Eye," *Washington Post National Weekly Edition*, March 16, 1998, p. 35.

97. Hibbing and Theiss-Morse, *Congress as Public Enemy*.

98. General Social Survey, 1990.

99. Richard Morin, "I'm OK; My Government's Not," *Washington Post National Weekly Edition*, July 26–August 1, 1993, p. 37.

100. Ibid.

101. Benjamin Page and Robert Shapiro, "Effects of Public Opinion on Policy," *American Political Science Review* 77 (March 1983), pp. 175–190.

102. Sidney Verba and Norman H. Nie, *Participation in America: Political Democracy and Social Equality* (New York: Harper & Row, 1972), chapter 15.

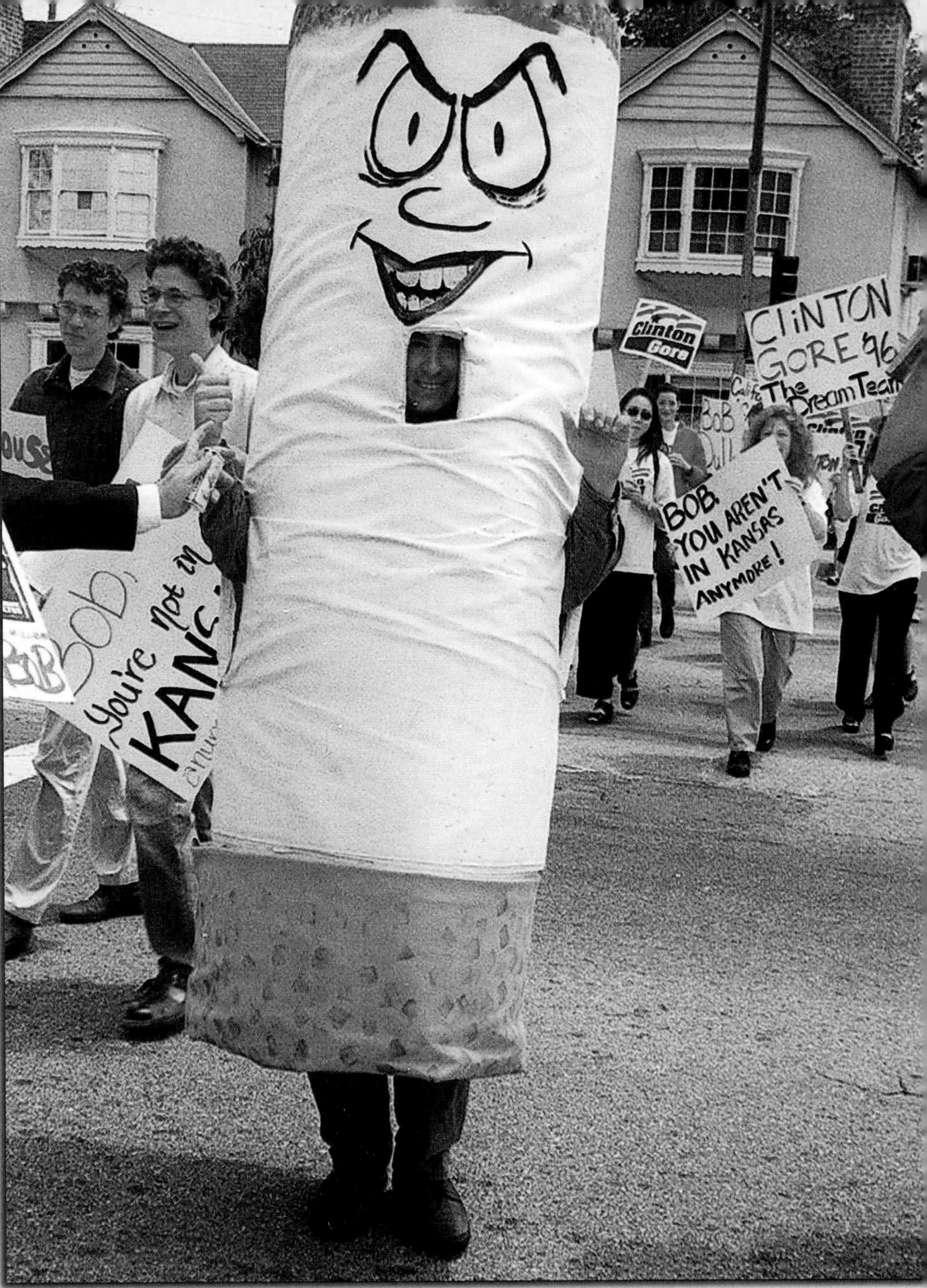

Damian Dovarganes, AP/Wide World Photos

5 INTEREST GROUPS

OUTLINE

- **Group Formation**
  - Why Interest Groups Form
  - Why People Join
  - Who Joins?
  - Have Americans Stopped Joining?
- **Types of Interest Groups**
  - Private Interest Groups
  - Public Interest Groups
- **Tactics of Interest Groups**
  - Direct Lobbying Techniques
  - Indirect Lobbying Techniques
  - Protest and Civil Disobedience
- **Success of Interest Groups**
  - Resources
  - Competition and Goals
- **Conclusion: Do Interest Groups Help Make Government Responsive?**

YOU ARE THERE

Do You Make More Concessions or Do You Fight?

You are Steven Goldstone, the CEO of RJR Nabisco. Your company owns RJ Reynolds, the nation's second largest tobacco company. It is June 1998, and you and the tobacco industry, historically one of the strongest and most powerful interests in Washington, are faced with paying billions of dollars in damages, strict regulation of tobacco advertising, regulation of nicotine as a drug, and heavy fines if youth smoking does not decrease over the next 10 years. In the past, you might have been able to stave off such threats, but today you are willing to accept higher taxes and government restrictions, if they are coupled with protection from unending lawsuits with the potential to bankrupt the industry. But you are not in a position to make demands.

Public opinion has turned against you, and you have lost major allies in Congress. Recent polls show that more than 70% of Americans, many of them smokers, mistrust tobacco companies and believe they are run by greedy executives who make a profit from marketing cigarettes to children and teens. Indeed, one news article labeled the tobacco industry "the Libya of American commerce."[1] This view is supported by research that shows that Joe Camel, an RJ Reynolds' creation, is as recognizable to six-year-olds as Mickey Mouse. Your industry's image has also been tarnished because you knew of the dangers of smoking long before warnings appeared on cigarettes. But the companies suppressed the evidence of health risks and publicly denied that there were any. Many Americans recall you and your fellow CEOs swearing before a congressional committee that cigarettes are not addictive. Recent disclosure of internal company documents confirms that your industry did indeed target teenagers with ads—and with some success. Three thousand teens and preteens begin smoking every day, a statistic the president has labeled "a national tragedy."

Republicans in Congress, once your staunch supporters, are also turning away. House Speaker Newt Gingrich recently told you and other CEOs that the party would not protect you against lawsuits. Gingrich, whose father and grandfather died of lung cancer, is fearful that protection for tobacco companies will lead to other industries descending on Washington seeking protection and that Clinton and the Democrats will use the issue against the Republicans in the 1998 elections.

Your opponents have also gained strength. There is no doubt that smoking causes cancer and exacerbates heart and lung diseases. Smoking is the leading cause of preventable death in the United States, claiming more than 400,000 lives a year and $100 billion in medical costs. Public health organizations have spread the word about tobacco's dangers through their own advertising campaign.

Furthermore, you and the industry are feeling pressure to strike a deal. A jury recently ruled for the first time that a tobacco company was liable for the death of a lung cancer victim. The jurors awarded the victim's family $750,000. More suits are already in litigation and even more are likely to follow. President Clinton has granted the Food and Drug Administration authority to regulate tobacco as a drug. Four states have successfully settled lawsuits recouping billions of dollars in claims against the tobacco industry for the costs entailed in treating sick smokers. More state suits are pending.

A year ago you were a key figure in an agreement that was worked out between the industry and a number of state leaders. In it, industry leaders agreed to pay $370 billion over 25 years and restrict the marketing and advertising of cigarettes. In return, state leaders agreed to limit the liability that tobacco companies face in lawsuits. Though by no means a good deal for tobacco, the agreement will enable the industry to survive. By supporting it, the industry may avoid more severe restrictions or even an outright ban on tobacco. Your task now is to get Congress to accept the package.

While your position is weakened, you still have some bargaining power. The number of teens who begin smoking each day is likely to decrease only if the industry raises the price of cigarettes and restricts

The tobacco industry has been fighting desperately to avoid restrictions. Here a tobacco company lawyer argues in court.

advertising, and you will not agree to these measures without legal protection. You are prepared to argue in court that the First Amendment allows you to advertise your product. There are also 50 million Americans who smoke and can be mobilized to oppose any increase in the cost of cigarettes. Cigarettes also provide tax revenue to the states and national government and 700,000 jobs.

Legislators from tobacco-growing states, such as Kentucky and North Carolina, are also supportive of your industry. On the other side, many groups opposed to tobacco, including the Campaign for Tobacco Free Kids, the American Medical Association, and the American Cancer Society, endorsed the agreement as a way to immediately curb youth smoking. State leaders who negotiated it are lobbying Congress to accept it.

But some in Congress have their own ideas and have introduced bills that differ from the agreement. The bill with the most support would cost the industry $526 billion over 25 years, impose restrictions on tobacco ads, set goals for reducing teenage smoking, and regulate tobacco as a drug. It would not, however, include the protection against lawsuits that you think is necessary for the industry to survive.

What do you do? In addition to the concessions you have already made, you can make one more. You can abandon your demand for protection against lawsuits, a concession you believe will kill the industry. Or you can fight the bill by mobilizing what few friends you have on Capitol Hill and among the grassroots public. It will be an uphill fight with little chance of success. Which will you choose, and why?

In the United States everything from fruits to nuts is organized. From apple growers to filbert producers, every interest has an organization to represent it. These organizations touch every aspect of our lives; members of the American College of Obstetrics and Gynecology bring us into the world, and members of the National Funeral Directors Association usher us out.

Organizations that try to achieve at least some of their goals with government assistance are called **interest groups.** Fruit and nut growers want government subsidies and protection from imported products; doctors and funeral directors want to be free of government controls. The efforts of interest groups to influence government are called **lobbying.** Lobbying may involve direct contact between a lobbyist, or consultant or lawyer, as they prefer to be called, and a government official; or it may involve indirect action, such as attempts to sway public opinion, which will in turn influence officials.

People organize and lobby because these are ways for them to enhance their influence. As one Washington lobbyist put it, "Democracy is not a spectator sport. If you want to have a hand in shaping the nation, you must get into it with more than your one vote on the Tuesday after the first Monday in November."[2] Or as another put it, somewhat more forcefully, "The modern government is huge, pervasive, intrusive into everybody's life. If you just let things take their course and don't get involved in the game, you get trampled on."[3]

The Founders feared the harmful effects of interest groups. Madison was intent on "curing the mischiefs of faction" through separation of powers, checks and balances, and federalism. Today, many people bemoan the "mischiefs of faction" or "special interests" because they seem to block government actions favoring the larger interests of society.[4] Sometimes it seems that everyone is represented in Washington but the people.

Do interest groups undermine the people's interests? Or do they make government more responsive by giving people greater representation in the political process? These are the difficult questions we explore in this chapter.

GROUP FORMATION

Throughout most of its history, America has been a nation of joiners. As early as the 1830s, the Frenchman Alexis de Tocqueville, who traveled in America, noted the tendency of Americans to join groups: "In no country in the world has the principle of association been more successfully used or applied to a greater multitude of objects than in America."[5] Even now Americans are more likely than citizens in other countries to belong to groups.[6]

The United States is especially fertile for the growth of groups. Compared to most other countries, it is racially, religiously, and ethnically diverse. These differences give rise to different interests and views on public issues and often lead to the formation of groups that express those views.[7]

Groups can organize because of the freedom to speak, assemble, and petition government, guaranteed in the First Amendment to the Constitution. Without such freedom, only groups favored by the government—or groups whose members are willing to be punished for their actions—could exist.

The federal structure also encourages the proliferation of groups. It is not enough to have a national organization. Because state and local governments have significant power, groups also must be organized at those levels to protect their interests.

In 1773 a group of colonists organized to protest British taxes on tea by throwing tea into Boston Harbor. In 1989 groups organized to protest a congressional pay increase by sending teabags to their representatives in Washington.

Why Interest Groups Form

The formation of interest groups occurs in waves.[8] In some periods formation is rapid and extensive, whereas at other times there is very little activity.

Social and economic stress often account for these surges.[9] The stress of the Revolutionary War period activated groups for and against independence. The slavery controversy in the decades before the Civil War energized groups on both sides of the issue. After the war, rapid industrialization led to the formation of trade unions and business associations. Economic problems in agricultural areas spurred the development of farm groups.

The greatest surge in group formation occurred between 1900 and 1920. Stimulated by the shocks of industrialization, urbanization, immigration, and the government's response to them, groups such as the United States Chamber of Commerce, American Medical Association, American Farm Bureau Federation, National Association for the Advancement of Colored People (NAACP), Socialist and Communist Parties, and countless others formed.[10]

The 1960s and 1970s witnessed another interest group explosion, directed primarily toward Washington. As the national government expanded in power and influence in the post–World War II period, it increasingly became the center of interest group efforts to satisfy demands for favorable public policy. Spurred by the success of civil rights and war protest movements in the 1960s, other groups representing racial minorities, women, consumers, the poor, the elderly, and the environment organized. Business lobbying surged in the late 1970s as a response to the success of consumer and environmental groups in prompting government to increase the regulation of occupational safety and environmental standards.[11]

Technological changes also accelerate group formation. A national network of railroads and the telegraph contributed to the surge in the early 1900s. Computer-generated direct mail appeals, to solicit funds and mobilize members to action, as well as WATS lines (wide-area telephone service), increased the ability of groups to form and mobilize in the 1960s and 1970s. The number of groups increased by 60% between 1960 and 1980, and the number sending representatives to Washington doubled.[12] In the 1990s, the spread of personal computers and the growing system of computer networks known as the Internet has facilitated communication between people with an endless variety of narrow interests. PCs and the Internet are particularly useful for those who wish to organize citizens but who lack financial resources for more sophisticated approaches.[13] For example, members and sympathizers of militia groups are able to use the Internet to keep each other informed about group activities.

Group organizers also play a role in group formation.[14] These entrepreneurs often come from established groups. They gain experience and then strike out on their own. Many civil rights activists of the 1950s and early 1960s founded organizations in the late 1960s. Some used their skills to organize groups against the war in Vietnam and later to organize groups for women's rights and environmental causes.[15] Thus the formation of one group often opens the door to the formation of others.

The government is also important to group formation. Government attempts to deal with perceived problems often generate organized opposition groups, such as the increase in business lobbying in response to environmental lobbying. In addition, government provides direct financial assistance to some groups,

FOR RIGHT TO UNDRESS, NUDISTS FLEX RIGHT TO REDRESS

For those of you who get the urge to go skinny-dipping in the public pool or tan in the nude at the neighborhood park, the 17,000-member Naturalist Society, the nation's most politically active organization of nudists, is out to help.

Although the National Park Service allows nude beaches in remote areas, conflicts occur at more accessible beaches. Members argue that they "are tired of always moving farther down the beach." To protect their right to clothing-optional recreation, as members call it, the organization retained a Washington lobbyist to make its case to Congress.

The first task of their newly hired lobbyist is to make the issue less attention grabbing. The strategy is to become just another pestering group in Washington. When the smirks fade from the faces of official Washington, the group believes it will be taken more seriously.

Politically, nudists are divided into conservative and liberal camps. Conservatives tend to join the Florida-based Sunbathing Association, which claims 36,000 members. They prefer to be left alone and gravitate toward private clubs. Liberals are more likely to join the Naturalist Society and use public beaches.

Besides beach access, nudists are addressing other issues as well, including child custody and jobs. Many have lost children and jobs because of their penchant for nude recreation.

SOURCE: "The Right to Undress," *Common Cause Magazine* (January/February 1991), pp. 6–7.

particularly nonprofit organizations. Groups as diverse as the American Council of Education, the National Governors Association, and the National Council of Senior Citizens obtain a large percentage of their budgets through federal grants and contracts.[16]

Why People Join

Most people join groups voluntarily because of the benefits groups provide.[17] Some are attracted to groups for political or ideological reasons. Members of Common Cause join because they support the group's goals of campaign finance reform and ethics in government. The benefits are the psychological satisfaction of being identified with the cause and the prospect that the group will succeed. Some groups offer monetary benefits to members such as discounted prices for goods and services. The large nonfarm membership of the Farm Bureau often is attributed to the cut-rate insurance policies offered through the organization.[18] The American Association of Retired Persons (AARP) provides health, home, and auto insurance; a motor club; a travel service; investment counseling; discount drugs and medicines; and a magazine. These services attract members and generate millions of dollars for the organization. Two-thirds of the AARP's revenue comes from business activities that provide discount services to members. Groups also provide social benefits. Some people join groups to make friends.

Because most groups seek to expand their membership and people join for different reasons, most groups provide a mix of benefits. The National Rifle Association (NRA) lobbies against gun regulation and control. Some people join for this reason. Others join to secure other NRA services: *The American Rifleman* (a monthly magazine), a hunter's information service, low-cost firearm insurance, membership in local gun clubs, and shooting competitions.[19] Still others join because they enjoy associating with fellow gun enthusiasts.

Some people join groups because they are coerced. For example, in many states lawyers must join the state bar association to practice law.

Who Joins?

Not all people are equally likely to join groups.[20] Those with higher incomes and education are more likely to belong. They can afford membership dues, have the leisure necessary to take part, and have the social and intellectual skills that facilitate group participation. They also appear more attractive to many groups and therefore are more apt to be recruited. Whites more often belong to groups than blacks, but mostly because of their higher average income and education.[21]

Have Americans Stopped Joining?

Americans still join organized groups but at a lower rate than previously.[22] Church membership and church-related activities have declined over the past 20 years. Membership in labor unions, once the most common organizational affiliation among American workers, has been declining for nearly four decades. Membership in the PTA has decreased during the past generation. In general, fewer people are joining and volunteering for a variety of civic and fraternal organizations. The declining impulse to join with others in common pursuits may even have influenced recreational activity. Although more Americans than ever bowl, league bowling is down by more than 40%. If the decline represented just a loss of revenue from the pizza and beer consumed by leagues, only bowling proprietors would care. However, the decline also means the loss of close personal relationships that foster discussion of public issues and trust among citizens, which are important to the success of government.

Some argue that the decline in membership in organized groups is not a serious problem, because informal social ties provide the same opportunity.[23] Yet people today claim that they are busier than ever before and that, between their work life and their family life, they have little time for other pursuits. Women's lives, in particular, have changed over the past generation, with most women now in the paid workforce. Women used to be the backbone of most local civic, religious, political, and educational groups, but working women now have less time to devote to such volunteer activity.

Others point to the increasing membership of mass organizations.[24] Many of these organizations are what are called "checkbook organizations," where members' only link to the organization is the occasional check they send to support it.

Other organizations are more than that, but most of the mass-membership organizations, like the National Organization of Women (NOW) and the American Association of Retired Persons (AARP), do not link members socially. Members do not know each other. They pay dues and are on a mailing list. Their ties are to common symbols, leaders, and ideals, but not to one another. In terms of connecting citizens to one another, such organizations fall short.

TYPES OF INTEREST GROUPS

Interest groups come in all sizes. Some have large memberships, such as the American Federation of Labor–Congress of Industrial Organizations (AFL-CIO) with 13 million members. Others have small memberships, such as the Mushroom Growers Association with 14. Some have no members at all.

Corporations have no members at all but act as interest groups when they lobby government.[25] Some groups lobby on behalf of specific interests and are funded by the government, private foundations, other

JOINING WITH OTHERS IS NOT ALWAYS GOOD FOR THE BODY POLITIC

Although groups can be important to the success of democratic government by fostering trust and commitment to the broader social community, not all groups and forms of social interaction are beneficial to democracy. For example, many militia groups are bent on destroying government. When the leaders of the Viper militia were arrested in Arizona, the group had been planning a massive bombing of government buildings using ammonium nitrate bombs, similar to the one used to destroy the federal building in Oklahoma City. A Montana group calling itself the "Freemen" declared their independence from the United States, labeling the government a "de facto corporate prostitute." The Freemen reject government authority, refuse to pay taxes, and question the validity of U.S. currency. They held off FBI agents for several months before being arrested.

Although these groups fit Tocqueville's description of a classic American association, a small group of like-minded neighbors gathering together for a common purpose, they live in a world of paranoia, hate, and fear. They believe that government has betrayed the people, subverted the Constitution, and sold out to a mysterious "New World Order," a one-world government. They believe that "the nation is already under siege by troops hovering in black helicopters who have embedded interstate road signs with directional codes that only they can read." Some groups also believe that Jews, blacks, or immigrants are trying to take over the government. And some even believe that bar codes in grocery stores are secret codes ordered by a foreign government, that bar codes on dollars allow government agents to drive by houses and determine how much money the occupants have, and that the government has installed electronic devices in car ignitions to stall autos on the day the "New World Order" takes over.[1]

Militias collect weapons and cache food; they train in the woods and await an invasion from a United Nations force. Although their rage is, theoretically, directed against the forces of the "New World Order," in practice it is aimed at federal agents and policies. Members have a particular hatred for gun control laws, believing that such laws are part of a plot by foreign agents to disarm America and take over.

Of course, not all members of militias believe these conspiracy theories. Nor did most start out believing in conspiracies, but they were drawn in as their personal situations made them susceptible. Years of drought threatened the Freemen with loss of everything. Rather than give up, they attacked government for not responding to their concerns.

Experts have tracked 800 militia groups, many of them formed in the past few years. Active members are estimated at no more than 100,000 nationwide. Tocqueville would probably not be surprised to learn that America leads the world in militia groups.

1. "Inside the World of the Paranoid," *New York Times*, April 30, 1995, section 4, p. 1.

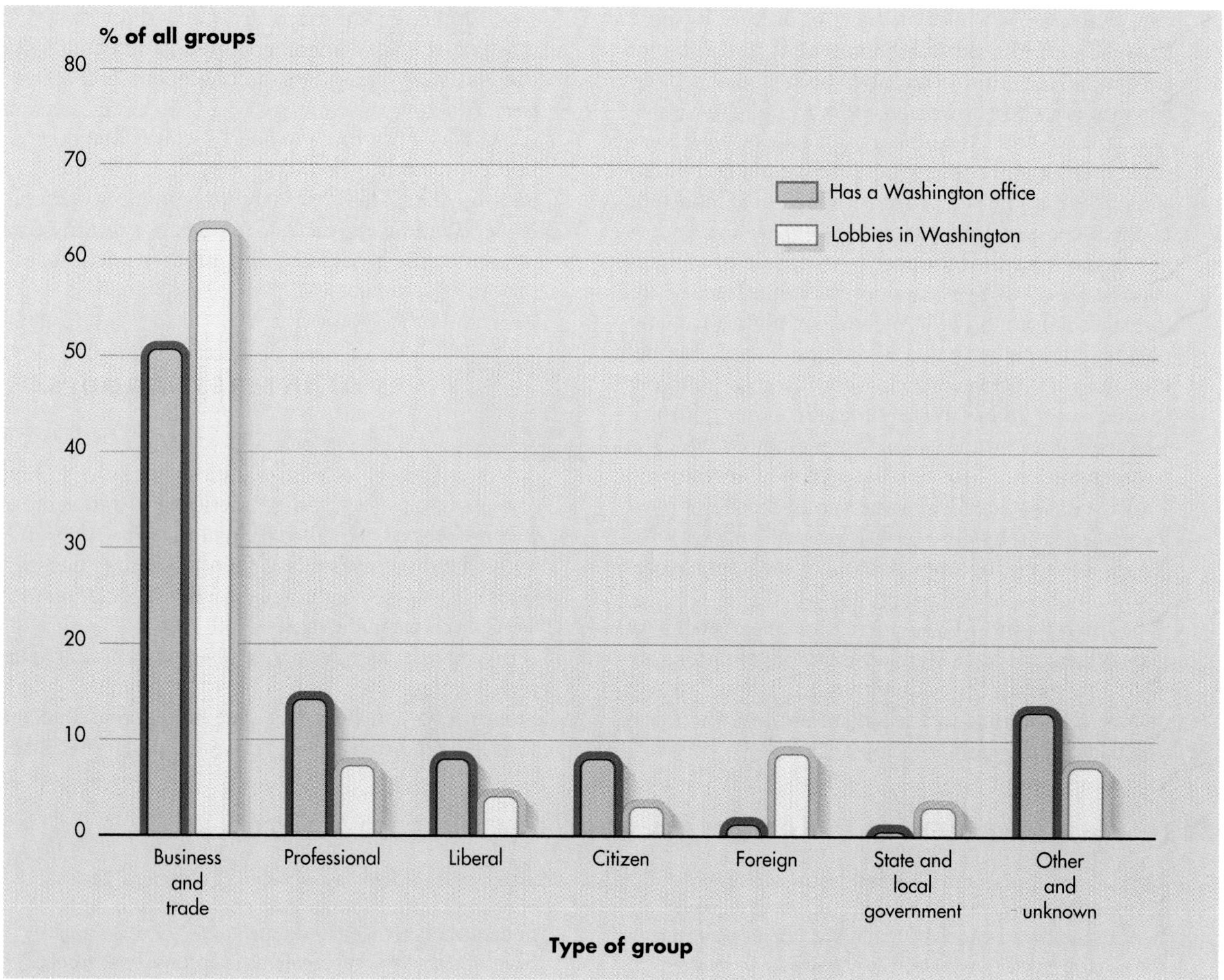

FIGURE 1

Business Interests Dominate the Contemporary Interest Group System

Note: Groups with a Washington office number 2,810, and 6,601 groups lobby there. "Liberal" groups are those representing women, minorities, the poor, labor, and the elderly. "Citizen" includes public interest groups such as Common Cause.

SOURCE: K. L. Schlozman and J. T. Tierney, *Organized Interests and American Democracy* (New York: Harper & Row, 1986), p. 67.

groups, or fees but have no members. The Children's Defense Fund (CDF) is one example. Founded in 1973, its staff of 90, funded entirely from private funds, lobbies on behalf of children.[26]

Some groups have only "checkbook" members. Their main link to the organization is the occasional check they send to support it. They may receive a newsletter and requests to write their senator or representative, but they do not interact with other members or participate in decision making. Many **political action committees (PACs)** operate this way. They raise money through direct mail and channel it to political candidates. How the money is spent is determined solely by the organization's leaders.

Some interest groups are formally organized, with appointed or elected leaders, regular meetings, and dues-paying members. Some are large corporations whose leaders are the corporate officers hired by boards of directors. Others have no leaders and few prescribed rules.

Thus, interest groups can be distinguished according to their membership and organizational structure. They also can be distinguished by their goals. Though groups can be categorized by their goals in different ways, we will look at groups that have private interests and groups that have public interests.

Private Interest Groups

Private interest groups pursue chiefly economic interests that benefit their members. Three important examples are groups representing business, labor, and agriculture.

BUSINESS

Business organizations are the most numerous and most powerful interest groups (see Figure 1). Some have argued that the major cleavage in American politics is between business groups on the one hand and government and not-for-profit institutions on the other.[27] E. E. Schattschneider notes that "the struggle for power is largely a confrontation of two major power systems, government and business."[28]

Today, however, there is little confrontation. Government is highly supportive of business. Organized labor, traditionally a balance to business, is seeing its membership shrink every year. Republicans traditionally favor business, and recently Democrats have come to also.[29] This shift reflects business's financial contribution to Democrats, the decline of labor's clout, and the consequent election of more moderate and conservative Democrats sympathetic to business. With Clinton in the White House, business won major international trade agreements. It was able to secure "most favored nation" trade privileges for China in spite of human rights violations by that country. Despite courting by the Clinton administration, business lobbies defeated the administration's economic stimulus package and health care reform proposal, which would have required employers to provide employee health insurance. They also stymied labor's goal of prohibiting permanent replacement of striking workers.

If the Republicans continue to control Congress, and organized labor continues to decline in size and influence, business groups can expect even more success in winning favors from government.[30] To make sure this happens, business outspends labor by about seven to one, almost all of it going to Republican candidates since the 1994 elections when Republicans won a majority in Congress.

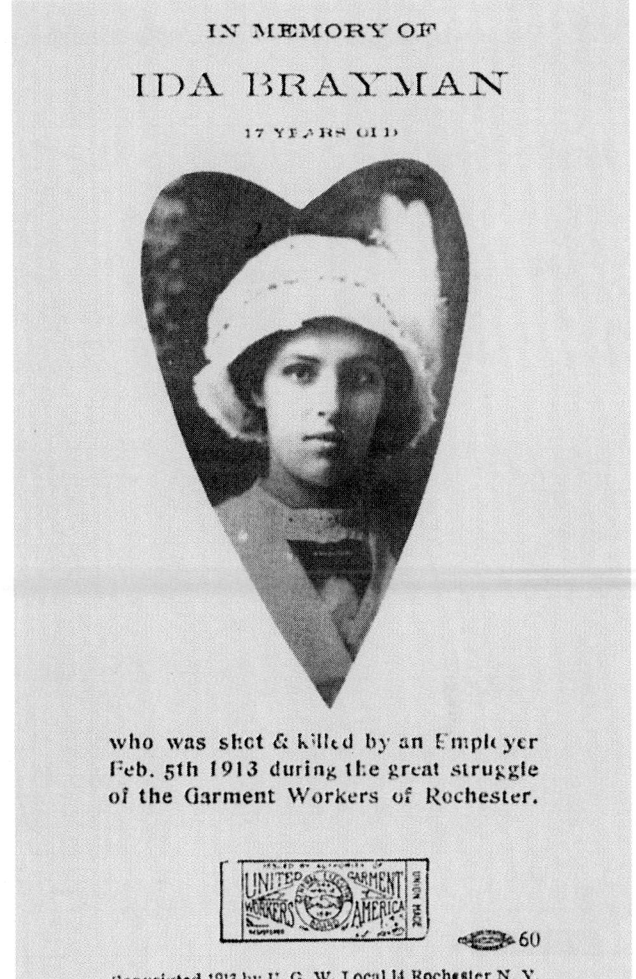

IN MEMORY OF
IDA BRAYMAN
17 YEARS OLD
who was shot & killed by an Employer
Feb. 5th 1913 during the great struggle
of the Garment Workers of Rochester.
UNITED GARMENT WORKERS OF AMERICA
60
Copyrighted 1913 by U. G. W. Local 14 Rochester N. Y.

Gotham Book Mart, New York

This postcard commemorates the death of a 17-year-old woman striking for recognition of her union, an eight-hour day, and extra pay for overtime and holidays.

LABOR

Although there are more than 100 labor unions in the United States, the AFL-CIO is probably the most important politically. It is a confederation of 88 trade and industrial unions with 13 million members. It has a staff of 500 and includes some of the most skillful lobbyists in Washington. Through its Committee on Political Education (COPE), it provides substantial sums of money as well as a pool of campaign workers to candidates for public office, typically Democratic candidates. In recent years labor has lobbied hard but unsuccessfully to eliminate the right of employers to hire replacement workers for striking employees; to defeat the North American Free Trade Agreement between the United States, Mexico, and Canada, which may mean a loss of American jobs; and to adopt national health care reform.

Clearly, the political influence of labor unions has waned since the 1960s. The primary reason is that membership has declined. Only 14% of the nonagricultural workforce belongs to unions (see Figure 2). Declining membership reflects changes in the economy. In the 1970s and 1980s, millions from the "baby boom" generation entered the job market but could not find jobs. The oversupply of workers, along with a fear of inflation and presidents hostile to unions, created pressures to keep wages low.

Although the economy has boomed in the 1990s,[31] union membership continues to decline. Many of the new jobs are being created in the service industry, including information technology and the financial world, where there is no tradition of unions. With the exception of teachers and government employees, until recently unions have shown little interest in organizing those in clerical and other service occupations.

Labor's political influence has also declined because its membership is located primarily in the Northeast and Midwest, which are declining in population and losing representation in Congress. In the

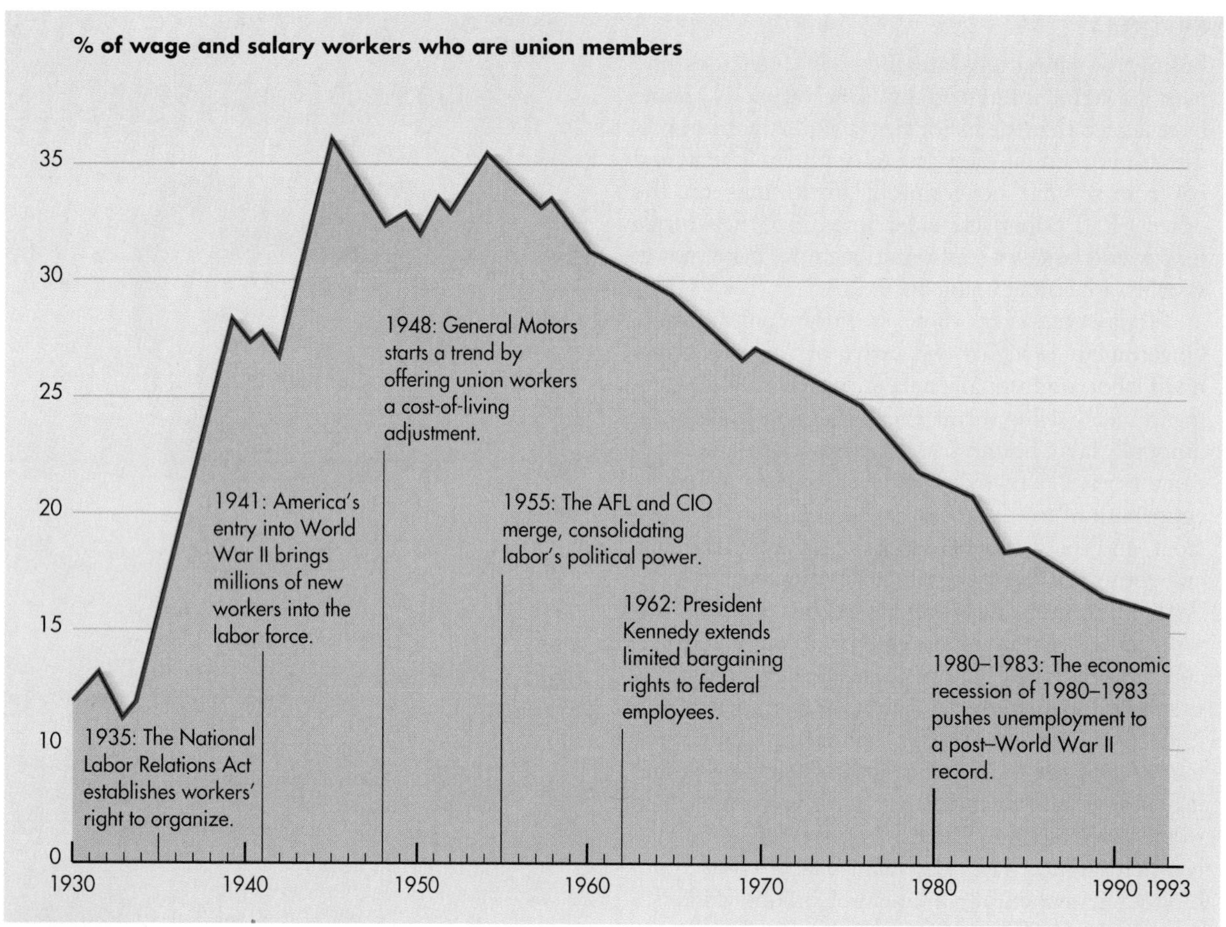
% of wage and salary workers who are union members
35
30
25
20
15
10
0
1930
1940
1950
1960
1970
1980
1990 1993
1935: The National Labor Relations Act establishes workers' right to organize.
1941: America's entry into World War II brings millions of new workers into the labor force.
1948: General Motors starts a trend by offering union workers a cost-of-living adjustment.
1955: The AFL and CIO merge, consolidating labor's political power.
1962: President Kennedy extends limited bargaining rights to federal employees.
1980–1983: The economic recession of 1980–1983 pushes unemployment to a post–World War II record.

FIGURE 2

Union Membership Has Decreased

SOURCES: Christoph Blumrich, *Newsweek*, September 5, 1983, p. 51; *Statistical Abstract of the United States, 1990; Lincoln Journal,* March 1993.

South and Southwest, where population is increasing, opposition to unions is strong and only a small percentage of the workforce is unionized.

Global competition also threatens unions. Such competition robs labor of its most powerful weapon—the strike. Fearful that they will be replaced or that their employers will suffer in the competitive marketplace, employees are unwilling to strike. In testimony in the early 1990s, the AFL-CIO signaled its willingness to curb the right to strike if Congress would restrict the right of business to use replacement workers during a strike.[32]

Some businesses have also frustrated union efforts to organize workers by opting for a "progressive management" approach to keep workers satisfied. Others have threatened to fire pro-union employees or predicted dire consequences from unionization; both tactics are illegal.

Energized by the Republican takeover of Congress in 1994 and the election of new leadership, the AFL-CIO sent out 1,000 organizers during 1996 to campaign for labor's friends and against its enemies. The union also funneled millions of dollars to Democratic candidates in an effort to win back a congressional majority that would be more sympathetic to labor. The effort met with mixed success. The Republicans' majority shrank only slightly and only in the House, as they remained in control after the 1996 elections. Nevertheless, union successes in some well-publicized strikes, such as that against UPS in 1997, did give labor some new energy.

Nevertheless, union membership continues to decline, in spite of an economy generating millions of new jobs each year.[33] Labor will continue its efforts to win new members—its political influence depends on it and it has no alternative—but success is likely to be limited. Business and the press have convinced many Americans that unions are something that working men and women do not need.[34]

AGRICULTURE

Agricultural interests are represented by a variety of general and specialized groups. The American Farm Bureau Federation, the largest of the general agriculture interest groups, began when the federal government established the agricultural extension service with agents in rural locations to help farmers. To encourage cooperation with agents, the government offered grants to states that organized county farm bureaus. By 1919 a national organization was formed.

Despite its roots, the Farm Bureau today is staunchly opposed to government intervention in the economy, including subsidies to farmers. This reflects the conservative ideology of the large and wealthy farm interests that dominate the organization. Despite opposition to government subsidies, many members benefit from them.

The National Farmers' Union, which is considerably smaller than the Farm Bureau, represents small farming interests. It strongly supports government subsidies to farmers. The American Agriculture Movement (AAM), which began as a protest movement by farmers who were badly hurt by falling prices in the mid-1970s, also speaks out primarily on issues that benefit small farmers and ranchers.[35]

Along with the general interest groups, hundreds of commodity organizations promote specific products and operate much like business trade associations. Examples include cattle, cotton, milk, tobacco, and wool producers. Large agribusiness firms such as Cargill also have powerful lobbies in Washington.

As we enter the twenty-first century, American agriculture is dominated by agribusiness and corporate farms. The individual small farmer is playing a smaller role and has relatively little political clout.

Public Interest Groups

Public interest groups, which number more than 2,500 with 40 million members,[36] lobby for benefits that cannot be limited or restricted to their members. The National Taxpayers Union lobbies for reduced taxes not only for its members but for everyone who pays taxes. Amnesty International lobbies for the rights of political prisoners around the world even though none of its members are prisoners. Although nearly all groups think of themselves as pursuing the public interest, the label applies only to those working for other than personal or corporate interests. "Public interest" does not mean that a majority of the public necessarily favors the goals of these groups.

Public interest groups are not new, but they increased dramatically in number and size during the late 1960s and early 1970s. Several factors account for this surge. Americans were becoming increasingly distrustful of government, which appeared to favor special interests over more general interests. The need for a balance between the two led many to join public interest groups. Many middle-class Americans also had the financial means to support public interest groups. The new technology mentioned earlier also made it possible to reach and mobilize large numbers of them.[37]

While many of the public interest groups that were established during the 1960s and 1970s were "shoestring" operations staffed by idealistic social reformers with few professional skills, the public interest organizations of today have larger budgets and memberships and a cadre of professionals—attorneys, management consultants, direct-mail fund-raisers, and communications directors—handling day-to-day operations and seeking to influence government with a variety of strategies and tactics.[38]

MULTIPLE-ISSUE GROUPS

Some public interest groups are multiple-issue groups, involved with a broad range of issues. Others have a narrower focus and are often referred to as single-issue groups. In this section, we provide some examples of well-known multiple-issue groups.

WOMEN'S GROUPS Groups advocating women's equality have mushroomed in the past two decades and range from large, mass-based organizations with a broad agenda, such as the National Organization for Women (NOW), to much smaller groups with very specific interests such as electing women to public office.

NOW is the largest women's group with 250,000 total members and chapters in all 50 states.[39] With a national board made up of regional representatives and national salaried officers, NOW is well organized. It has field representatives and organizers, researchers, lobbyists, and specialists in various policy areas such as reproductive freedom and economic rights.

NOW is funded largely from membership dues but has actively solicited funds by mail. It also receives income from subscriptions and selling such things as T-shirts and posters. Private foundations interested in promoting women's rights also provide significant funding.

Although NOW began as a protest movement, today its focus is on lobbying at the national, state, and local levels. It provides leadership training and education for local and state groups and works with a shifting coalition of other women's rights groups.

In 1996, NOW sponsored a "Fight the Right" march in San Francisco and was joined by groups representing labor, minorities, immigrants, gays and lesbians, and religious and civil rights organizations. Activists marched to defend affirmative action, reproductive rights, and gay and lesbian rights and against racism, immigrant bashing, policies that attack the poor, and violence toward women. Gloria Steinem, a feminist leader, energized the crowd by charging that the Republican Party is controlled by an "extremist ultra-right wing.

Corbis-Bettmann

The first wave of women's organizations campaigned for women's right to vote. Here, some of 20,000 marchers parade for women's rights in New York City in 1917.

They are racist, sexist, and homophobic. They are for everything we are against."[40]

In recent years the women's movement has divided between groups pushing an ideological agenda, like NOW, which continues to see abortion as a major concern, and more pragmatic groups such as the National Women's Political Caucus, which sees its task as electing women to public office regardless of their stands on the issues.

EMILY—short for "Early Money Is Like Yeast" (it makes the dough rise)—is an organization that recruits, trains, and endorses pro-choice Democratic women candidates and then works to fund and elect them to public office. The organization holds seminars for candidates, campaign managers, and press secretaries. It has helped elect five women to the Senate and 34 to the House. In 1994, it contributed over $8 million to Democratic candidates, the largest contributor to the party. In 1996 it spent $10 million to get out the vote.[41]

RELIGIOUS GROUPS Religious groups often lobby on political issues. The National Council of Churches, representing liberal Protestant denominations, has spoken out on civil rights, human rights, and other social issues. Catholic groups have been active in both antiabortion and antinuclear movements. Jewish groups have been involved in lobbying for liberal issues, such as the rights of workers and minorities.

Jewish groups have been particularly active in lobbying for Israel. Since its beginning in 1951, the pro-Israel lobby has lost on only three key decisions, all involving the sale of U.S. arms to Egypt and Saudi Arabia. The success of Jewish groups in lobbying for Israel reflects their commitment, organization, and political skill, and an opposition Arab lobby that is weak by comparison.[42]

Conservative Christian groups, sometimes called fundamentalists, have had an especially big impact on American politics in recent years. Identified by a "born again" experience, a desire to win converts to Jesus Christ, and a literal interpretation of the Bible, and spurred by what they saw as a decline in traditional values, members of the Christian right became active in politics in the 1970s.[43] The National Association of Evangelicals, representing conservative Protestant denominations, gained in visibility and prestige as the membership in conservative churches increased while membership in mainline churches declined.[44]

Opposed to abortion, divorce, homosexuality, and women's rights, conservative Christians were the major force behind the effort of television evangelist Pat Robertson to win the Republican presidential nomination in 1988. Following his loss of the nomination, Robertson converted a mailing list of two million names into the Christian Coalition under the leadership of Ralph Reed. Unlike the religious right groups of the 1980s, which were primarily concerned with spreading their message through television and radio, the Coalition runs training seminars at which participants are taught how to win control of the Republican Party from the ground up. Operating quietly in the early 1990s, Reed cautioned his followers never to mention the Christian Coalition among Republicans. By 1992, the organization had gained dominance or leverage in twenty state parties.[45]

The Coalition had over a million members, half of whom paid $15 annual dues. The Coalition emerged as a political powerhouse that included schools, newspapers, magazines, radio and television stations, and thousands of politically mobilized churches. The organization is seen by religious right leaders as a counterweight to a "liberal establishment" controlled by "secular humanists who are exerting every effort to debase and eliminate Bible-based Christianity from our society."[46]

The network involved itself heavily in political campaigns in the 1990s. The Coalition raised money, registered voters, ran phone banks, and graded legislators.[47] In the 1996 elections, the group distributed 45 million voter guides, many through churches on the Sunday before the election, which compared Republicans and Democrats on several "key" issues.

Still the most powerful organization in the Republican Party, the Coalition has suffered from a change in leadership, the emergence of competing Christian organizations, and a middle-of-the-road Clinton administration that has left conservative Christians without something to rally against.[48] Reed, who raised a record $26 million in 1996, left the organization. Without an issue like gays in the military or distributing condoms in the public schools, the Coalition has a more difficult time mobilizing its members.

In spite of these problems, the Coalition hopes to broaden its appeal. This will not be easy, however. If it moves to the left, it may lose the enthusiasm and support of its supporters on the right. Already some supporters have become agitated by efforts to merge family and social issues with the traditional economic concerns of the Republican Party.[49]

'94 Christian Coalition

VOTER GUIDE

WASHINGTON
Congressional
District 5

Tom Foley (D)	ISSUES	George Nethercutt (R)
Opposes	Term Limits for Congress	Supports
Opposes	Balanced Budget Amendment	Supports
Supports	Taxpayer Funding of Abortion	Opposes
Opposes	Parental Choice in Education (Vouchers)	Supports
No Response*	Voluntary Prayer in Public Schools	Supports
No Response*	Homosexuals in the Military	Opposes
Supports	Banning Ownership of Legal Firearms	Opposes
No Response*	Capital Punishment for Murder	Supports
Supports	Federal Government Control of Health Care	Opposes
Supports	Raising Federal Income Taxes	Opposes

*Each candidate was sent a 1994 Federal Issues Survey by certified mail or facsimile machine. When possible, positions of candidates on issues were verified or determined using voting records and/or public statements.

Paid for and authorized by the Christian Coalition; Post Office Box 1990; Chesapeake, Virginia 23327-1990. The Christian Coalition is a pro-family citizen action organization. This voter guide is provided for educational purposes only and is not to be construed as an endorsement of any candidate or political party.

★ Vote on November 8 ★

Courtesy of Christian Coalition

Voter guides were distributed to churches on the Sunday before the election in 1994. Similar guides were distributed in 1996.

The Interfaith Alliance began in 1994 to counter the message and political activity of the Christian Coalition and other conservative religious groups. Comprised of mainstream and minority religious and secular groups, it has chapters in 17 states and represents hundreds of churches, faith, and civic organizations. The group holds rallies and public forums dealing with family values, poverty, and discrimination. It opposes prayer in schools but takes no position on abortion. Like the Coalition, it produces voter guides and campaign literature. The organization elected members to local school boards and was active in a number of presidential primaries in 1996.[50]

GAYS AND LESBIANS Gay rights organizations have a shorter history than most other major political groups. The first groups formed after World War II in an era when gays were labeled as deviates on the rare occasions when they came to public attention. For example, in 1954, after a raid of a bar where gay men congregated, a Miami newspaper headline read "Perverts Seized in Bar Raids." Early gay and lesbian groups focused largely on sharing information about how to survive and how to fight police repression.[51]

In the middle 1960s, a few gays followed the example of the civil rights movement and organized small public demonstrations. Other gays argued that such demonstrations undermined the safety and well-being of the homosexual subculture, which then existed underground in many large cities. Nonetheless, during the 1960s the gay rights movement became more radical and visible. Like Vietnam War protesters, women's rights advocates, and civil rights activists, many gays embarked upon active protests to challenge the status quo. News of a violent confrontation between gays and the police after a 1969 police raid of a gay bar in New York City helped fuel this new "gay liberation" movement. Street protests became common in large cities. Gays formed clubs on campuses. In 1972, the issue of civil rights for gays was discussed in the presidential campaign, and in 1973 the American Psychiatric Association removed homosexuality from its lists of mental disorders.

Discrimination against gays and lesbians has lessened but still exists. Gays and lesbians can be dismissed from the military if their sexual orientation becomes known. Being gay often means losing a job, being evicted, or losing custody of a child, if divorced.

The AIDS epidemic, which began in 1981, opened a new chapter in the fight for rights of gays and lesbians. The media attention on AIDS and its impact on the gay community led to new discussions about discrimination against gays. It also revealed that many entertainers and other celebrities were gay.

Today, gays and lesbians want to be free of discrimination and to be able to enjoy the same rights as other citizens, including access to spousal health and death benefits provided to employees. This desire for economic equality is the basis of the call to legitimize same-sex marriage (although the economic issues could, in part, be resolved without legitimizing same-sex marriage, which is probably the most controversial and emotional gay issue).

Not surprisingly, different gay rights groups use different tactics. Some groups work comfortably within the mainstream, raising money for political candidates, for example. Others focus on specific issues, such as supporting those with AIDS. Groups like Queer Nation are oriented toward dramatic political action. Though most gays and lesbians probably vote Democratic, the Log Cabin Federation is a group of gay Republicans.

Evidence is accumulating that lobbying by gay and lesbian groups is paying off. In a recent poll, 70% agreed that gays should have equal rights in hiring and firing; 78% favored increasing efforts for AIDS research, prevention, and care; and 57% supported a bill to ban workplace discrimination against gays.[52] However, the public is much less supportive of lifestyle issues such as legalizing gay marriages.

TABLE 1

The AARP Is a Big Business

ACTIVITY	AARP'S 1994 REVENUE, IN MILLIONS OF DOLLARS
Health insurance	$120.0
Visa/MasterCard	8.7
Auto/home insurance	35.0
Car rental	4.5
Mutual funds	7.6
Pharmacy	4.3
Motor club	1.9

ELDERLY While the population of the nation as a whole has tripled since 1900, the number of elderly has increased eightfold. Today, persons over 65 constitute more than 12% of the population. Several groups, sometimes called the "gray lobby," represent their interests.

Founded in 1958 to provide insurance to the elderly, the American Association of Retired Persons (AARP), with 33 million members, is the nation's largest and one of its most powerful interest groups. Recruited by direct mail and word of mouth, the AARP attracts 8,000 new members a day. For $8, anyone over 50 can join and use the numerous benefits provided by the organization[53] (see Table 1).

With 1,800 employees and 18 lobbyists, the AARP has become a potent political force. The AARP's lobbying efforts are directed primarily at preserving and expanding government benefits to the elderly, which total about $14 billion each month.[54] The Reagan administration quickly dropped the idea of cutting cost-of-living increases in Social Security to reduce the nation's deficit when the AARP and others protested. Reagan's budget director lamented, "These are people who have plenty of time on their hands, who are well organized, who vote regularly, and they are a massive political force."[55] Although programs for the elderly represent one-third of the budget, politicians are reluctant to touch them. Those who have suggested doing so have earned themselves the AARP label "granny-basher." Mindful of their political influence, Clinton got the AARP to support his effort to reform health care by including long-term nursing home care.

Influence is exercised primarily by a flood of correspondence to members of Congress from AARP

Seniors demonstrate against Medicare cuts.

members. There is no congressional district where the AARP is not 50,000 strong.[56]

To counterbalance the power of the gray lobby, a number of groups such as Americans for Generational Equity and the Children's Defense Fund have formed, but they are small by comparison.

ENVIRONMENTAL GROUPS Environmental groups are another example of multiple-issue groups. Earth Day 1970 marked the beginning of the environmental movement in the United States. Spurred by an oil spill in California, what was to be a "teach-in" on college campuses mushroomed into a day of national environmental awareness with an estimated 20 million Americans taking part. A minority movement in the 1970s, the environmental lobby today is large and active and its values are supported by most Americans.[57]

Some environmental groups, such as the National Audubon Society, Sierra Club, and the Natural Resources Defense Council, have permanent offices in Washington with highly skilled professionals who carry out a full range of lobbying activities. All experienced substantial growth in membership and finances during the 1980s, when the Reagan administration threatened to undo the environmental gains of the 1970s.[58]

The so-called Greens are environmental groups that shun conventional lobbying approaches and are more confrontational. Groups like Greenpeace, Earth First!, and the Sea Shepherds seek a "green cultural revolution." Local citizen groups have also organized in support of local environmental concerns such as the location of toxic or nuclear waste dumps. Citizens, skeptical of government and corporate claims that such facilities are safe, want them located elsewhere.[59]

SINGLE-ISSUE GROUPS

Single-issue groups pursue public interest goals but are distinguished by their intense concern for a single issue and their reluctance to compromise. Members of the National Rifle Association (NRA) passionately oppose most forms of government control of firearms. For years, although a majority of Americans support gun control, the NRA has successfully lobbied Congress to prevent significant gun control. The group has members in every congressional district and is well organized to mobilize them. It spent a great deal of money in a losing battle to defeat the Brady Act, which requires a five-day waiting period in order to purchase a gun. It also failed to prevent a ban on sales of assault weapons.

Although the NRA remains a major political force, antigun sentiment is growing as more and more Americans respond to increasing gun violence that touches cities, suburbs, and small towns. The result is an increase in the political influence of antigun groups such as Handgun Control and politicians more willing to take on the NRA.

The NRA's image was tarnished when a fundraising letter at the time of the bombing of the federal building in Oklahoma City referred to federal law enforcement officers as "jackbooted government thugs, wearing black, armed to the teeth, who break down a door, open fire with an automatic

Art Streiber/Creative Photographers inc.

Charlton Heston strikes a tough-guy pose as president of the NRA.

weapon and kill or maim law-abiding citizens." The jackboot reference, which is associated with Nazi stormtroopers, led former president George Bush (a longtime NRA member and supporter) to resign his membership. The organization lost more than 300,000 members in 1995.

The abortion controversy has generated a number of single-issue groups. The National Right to Life Committee seeks a constitutional amendment banning all abortions. The committee works to elect candidates who favor such an amendment and defeat those who do not. After the 1989 and 1992 Supreme Court decisions allowing more state regulation of abortion, pro-life groups turned their attention to state legislators. They pushed for laws requiring informed consent, waiting periods, and parental consent for minors. In 1996, the organization activated its 8 million members and contributed heavily on behalf of Republican candidates.

Operation Rescue is a confrontational antiabortion group whose strategy has been to deny access to abortion clinics to women seeking abortions, as well as to disrupt abortion clinic operations and harass physicians who do abortions. Many "rescuers" have been jailed for their activities. The organization's direct action approach was dealt a blow when Congress passed the Freedom of Access to Clinic Entrances Act in 1994. The law made it a federal crime to hinder abortions by using threats, force, or obstruction. Although peaceful demonstrations that do not block clinic entrances are still legal, the law has discouraged some protesters as demonstrations at clinics have declined.

Historically, abortion has played a significant role in the Republican Party's presidential nomination process; it is a very important issue for social conservatives who typically back a strong pro-life candidate but less important for moderate Republicans who are primarily interested in economic issues and government spending. The conflict often surfaces in the party's platform as it did in 1996. Social conservatives prevented a pro-choice plank but avoided a major conflict by permitting pro-choice Republicans to register their opinion in an appendix to the platform.

Members of the national Abortion Rights Action League and Planned Parenthood are fervently committed to protecting women's right to abortion. Planned Parenthood is the oldest, largest, and best-financed advocate of reproductive freedom for women.

Since 1988, the organization has mounted a major effort to win policymakers to the pro-choice point of view. Using the theme that Americans want abortion to be safe and legal, ads were placed in national newspapers. Testimony was provided by physicians who treated botched abortions in the days when abortion was illegal, by clergy involved in counseling, and by women who underwent illegal abortion because they had no choice. Three months before the 1989 Supreme Court decision allowing state regulation of abortion (for more on this see Chapter 14), 300,000 pro-choice activists staged a march in Washington. Calling the event the "March for Women's Lives," the goal was to recast the issue in terms of freedom and choice rather

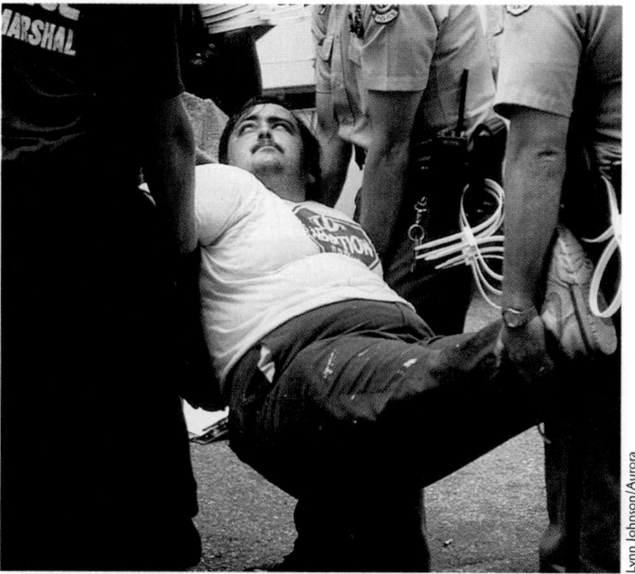

Lynn Johnson/Aurora

The right-to-life movement is considered a single-issue group.

than abortion. The three-day event received substantial publicity and demonstrated to members of Congress that the movement could mobilize a large number of supporters.[60]

Single-issue groups have increased in number since the mid-1960s. Some view this trend with alarm, because when groups clash over a highly emotional issue and are unwilling to compromise, government cannot resolve the issue.[61] The issue commands excessive time and energy of policymakers at the expense of broader issues that may be more important.

On the other hand, single-issue groups have always been part of politics.[62] These groups may even be beneficial because they represent interests that may not be well represented in Congress. Fears about single-issue groups may result from the groups' own exaggerated claims of influence, their heavy media coverage, and, in the case of some antiabortion groups, their confrontational tactics.

TACTICS OF INTEREST GROUPS

Interest groups engage in a variety of tactics to secure their goals. Some try to influence policymakers directly, whereas others seek to mold public opinion and influence policymakers indirectly. Sometimes interest groups form broad coalitions or engage in protest activity, both of which involve direct and indirect techniques.

Direct Lobbying Techniques

Direct lobbying techniques involve personal encounters between lobbyists and public officials. Some lobbyists are volunteers; others are permanent, salaried employees of the groups they represent; and others are contract lobbyists, "hired guns" who represent any individual or group willing to pay for the service. Contract lobbyists include the numerous Washington lawyers affiliated with the city's most prestigious law firms. Many have worked for government, so they can boast of contacts in government and access to policymakers to plead their clients' cases. Most firms recruit from the ranks of both Republicans and Democrats to assure access regardless of which party controls government.

MAKING PERSONAL CONTACTS

Making personal contacts, in an office or in a more informal setting, is the most effective lobbying technique. Compared to other forms of lobbying, direct personal contact is relatively inexpensive, and it minimizes problems of misinterpretation by allowing questions to be answered on the spot.

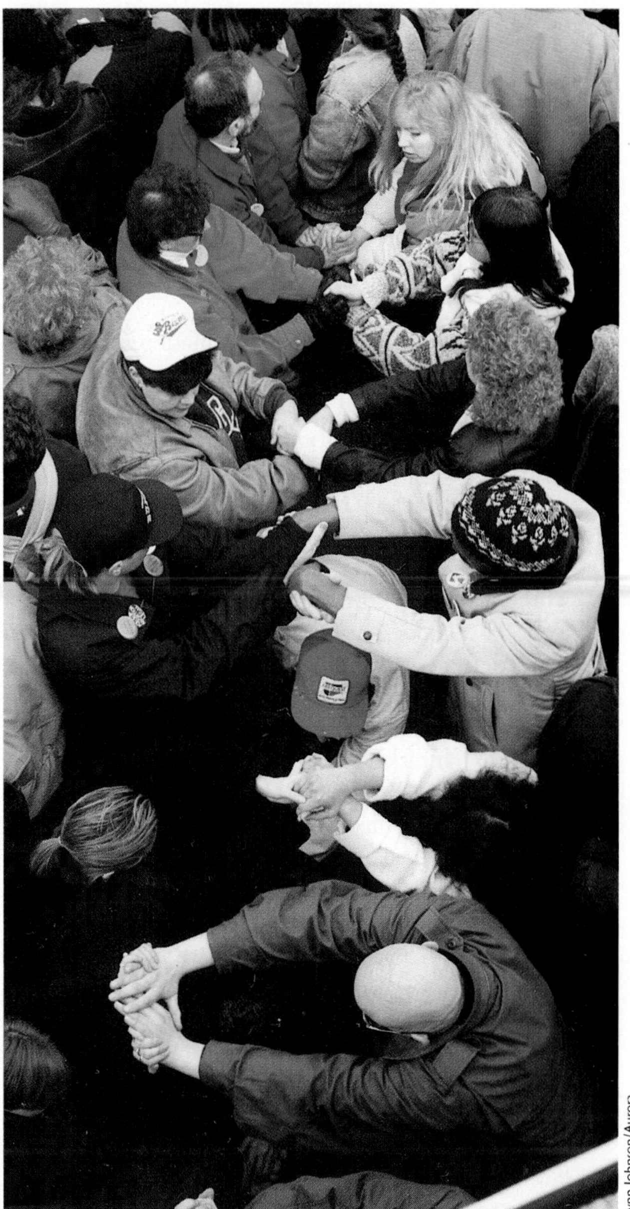
Lynn Johnson/Aurora

Pro-choice advocates form a human corridor to protect patients and workers entering a clinic in Buffalo.

Lobbyists know that whereas contacting every legislator is unnecessary, contacting key legislators, those who sit on the committees having jurisdiction over matters of interest to the lobbyists, and staff serving those committees, is critical.[63] Conventional wisdom also suggests that only those legislators who support a group's position or who are known to be undecided should be contacted directly.[64] Putting undue pressure on known opponents may jeopardize prospects for working together in the future on other issues.

To a large extent, lobbying is building relationships based on friendship. As a former chair of the House Budget Committee put it, "The most effective lobbyists here are the ones you don't think of as lobbyists." Referring to one prominent Washington lobbyist, he said, "I don't think of him as a lobbyist. He's almost a constituent, or a friend." Barbara Boxer, then a Democratic representative from California, referring to the same gentleman, described him as "a lovely, wonderful guy. In the whole time I've known him, he's never asked me to vote for anything." At a gathering she joked, he's almost "a member of the family."[65]

PROVIDING EXPERTISE

Although all groups provide information to public officials, some are known for providing information based on accurate and reliable research. Ralph Nader's organization, Public Citizen, which says that it lobbies for the average citizen, has such a reputation. In recent years, Public Citizen has lobbied against the erosion of government regulations dealing with clean air and water, safe drugs, food, and the workplace. It has also worked to limit corporate gifts, such as fancy vacations, to members of Congress and for campaign finance reform (see Chapter 9).

Lobbyists often have a great deal of knowledge and expertise that is useful in drafting legislation. A legislator may ask a lobbyist to draft a bill, or both may work together in drafting legislation. Sometimes interest groups themselves draft legislation and ask a sympathetic legislator to introduce it. General Electric drafted a tax reform measure that saved it millions in taxes. There is nothing illegal about this.

TESTIFYING AT HEARINGS

Testifying at congressional hearings is designed to establish a group's credentials as a "player" in the policy area as well as to convince its own constituents that it is doing its job. A member of a prominent Washington law firm with responsibility at his firm for prepping witnesses to testify identified the Boy Scout motto, "Be Prepared," as the most important principle to follow in getting ready for a hearing. Beyond that, he offers a few other tips: Keep it short. Time is at a premium in Washington. No one has an hour to listen to you. Don't read your statement. Good salespeople don't have prepared statements. They know the product and can talk to you about it. Don't be arrogant. Some witnesses are short with members because they believe committee members don't understand their business. Too bad. Most members of Congress don't care about your business; they are going to make a decision based on what they hear. Don't guess. If you don't know the answer to a question, say so and promise to supply the answer later. Don't be hokey, but illustrate whenever possible. It is easier to focus on a wrecked fender in a hearing room than to visualize a set of statistics.[66]

Another advantage of testifying is that it provides free publicity. Staging sometimes occurs. A lobbyist might ask a sympathetic legislator to raise certain questions that the lobbyist is prepared to answer or to indicate in advance what questions will be asked. Sometimes celebrities are invited to testify. In a not unprecedented but certainly rare move, Hillary Rodham Clinton, the principal player in developing the president's health care reform, testified before several congressional committees. This White House effort prompted a former Reagan aid to quip, they (the Clinton White House) "do PR the way (former chair of the Joint Chiefs) Colin Powell does war: maximum use of force."[67]

"Mr. Speaker, will the gentleman from Small Firearms yield the floor to the gentleman from Big Tobacco?"

GIVING MONEY

Lobbyists try to ensure access to legislators, and giving money is one way to guarantee this. A longtime financial backer of Ronald Reagan once said that having a dialogue with a politician is fine, "but with a little money they hear you better."[68] One Democrat commented in a similar vein, "Who do members of Congress see? They'll certainly see the one who gives the money. It's hard to say no to someone who gives you $5,000."[69]

The primary way groups channel money to legislators is through campaign contributions. Groups, including businesses and unions, may set up political action committees (PACs) to give money to campaigns of political candidates.

The number of PACs has grown dramatically since the mid-1970s as has the amount of money they have contributed. (We discuss PACs more fully in Chapter 9.)

LOBBYING THE BUREAUCRACY

For lobbyists, the battle is not over when a bill is passed. Lobbyists also must influence bureaucrats who implement policy. For example, regulations outlawing sex discrimination in educational institutions were drafted largely in the Department of Education with only broad guidelines from Congress. Although the legislation was passed in 1972, both women's rights groups and interests opposing them continue to lobby over the interpretation of the regulations (particularly with regard to equity in women's athletics).

In influencing bureaucrats, interest groups use most of the tactics already described. They also try to influence who gets appointed to bureaucratic positions. Someone opposed by the major agricultural interest groups is not likely to be appointed secretary of agriculture. Nor is someone unsympathetic to labor apt to be appointed head of the Labor Department. The auto industry vetoed a number of Clinton's nominees to head the National Highway Traffic Safety Administration. While consumer groups want someone interested in promoting automobile safety, the industry is looking for someone more sympathetic to their interests and concerns. Of course, groups do not always succeed in their opposition. President Reagan appointed as heads of several agencies persons strongly opposed by interest groups sympathetic to the agency's activities. He appointed a secretary of the interior opposed to many governmental efforts to protect public land and an Environmental Protection Agency head who opposed most government efforts to protect the environment.

The influence of groups in the appointment process is especially crucial in the case of appointments to regulatory agencies such as the Food and Drug Administration. By influencing appointments to an agency, the regulated industry can improve its prospects of favorable treatment.

THE TEN COMMANDMENTS OF LOBBYING

I Thou shalt speak only the truth, and speak it clearly and succinctly; on two pages and in 15-second sound bites.

II Thou shalt translate the rustle of thy grassroots into letters, phone calls, and personal visits.

III Thou shalt not underestimate thy opponent, for he surely packeth a rabbit punch.

IV Help thy friends with reelection; but in victory, dwelleth not on the power of thy PAC.

V Thou shalt know thy issue and believe in it, but be ready to compromise; half a loaf will feed some of thy people.

VI Runneth not out of patience. If thou can not harvest this year, the next session may be bountiful.

VII Love thy neighbor; thou wilst need him for a coalition.

VIII Study arithmetic, that thou may count noses. If thou can count 51, rejoice. Thou shalt win in the Senate.

IX Honor the hard-working staff, for they prepare the position papers for the members.

X Be humble in victory, for thy bill may yet be vetoed.

SOURCE: Ernest Wittenberg and Elisabeth Wittenberg, *How to Win in Washington* (Cambridge, Mass.: Blackwell, 1989), p. 16.

LOBBYING THE COURTS

Like bureaucrats, judges also make policy. Some interest groups try to achieve their goals by getting involved in cases and persuading courts to rule in their favor. Although most groups do not initiate litigation, some use it as their primary tactic. Litigation has been employed extensively by civil liberties organizations, particularly the American Civil Liberties Union (ACLU), civil rights organizations such as the NAACP, environmental groups such as the Sierra Club, and public interest groups such as Common Cause. Litigation often is used by groups that lack influence in Congress and the bureaucracy.

Groups can file civil suits, represent defendants in criminal cases, or file friend of the court briefs, which are written arguments asking the court to decide a case a particular way.[70]

Some groups use the courts to make their opponents negotiate with them. Environmental groups frequently challenge developers who threaten the environment in order to force them to bear the costs of defending themselves and to delay the project. The next time, developers may be more willing to make concessions beforehand to avoid lengthy and costly litigation.

Groups try to influence the courts indirectly by lobbying the Senate to support or oppose judicial nominees.

Indirect Lobbying Techniques

Traditionally, lobbyists employed tactics of direct persuasion almost exclusively—providing information, advice, and occasionally pressure. More recently, interest groups are going public, that is, mobilizing their activists and molding and activating public opinion. A recent study of 175 lobbying groups found that most were doing more of all kinds of lobbying activity, but

INTO THE 21ST CENTURY

LOBBYING GOES HIGH TECH

The so-called information superhighway is changing the way lobbyists, public officials, and the public communicate. As personal contact with members of Congress or their staffs becomes increasingly difficult, more lobbyists are turning to electronic mail to communicate with members of Congress. Although e-mail is not a substitute for a personal visit, only veteran lobbyists with strong personal relationships developed over the years are likely to be consistently able to gain personal access. For those new to the profession or those who lack personal relationships, e-mail may be the only alternative. Moreover, it is quick and cheap.

The information superhighway is aiding lobbyists in other ways too. Web pages allow lobbyists (and the public) opportunities to find out easily the status of bills, schedules of hearings, and other relevant information (some of these sites are listed in the note). One site, *incongress,* is described as a "one stop shop of all the information that's floating around town." For a fee, lobbyists and interest groups can post issue-related information on the site. The information can be read by anyone who has access to the Internet.

Grassroots lobbying is also easier with the Internet. Interest groups have sites that not only provide information about an issue but also invite browsers to send e-mail messages to public officials. For example, *www.globalwarmingcost.org* concerns the United Nations' treaty to combat global warming. Sponsored by Western Fuels, an energy producer, the site encourages browsers to take a negative stand against the treaty and to register that negative opinion with the president and their member of Congress.

The site begins with "A United Nations Treaty regarding global warming will cost you! This website provides you with the free means to tell Washington to reject the UN treaty. Your views are important. An easily sent, free, E-mail message can help make a difference." The page asks readers to "learn" how global warming costs them by clicking on various icons for business, families, seniors, workers, and farmers. When the reader clicks on an icon, the next page provides information on how much families, for example, will pay. Readers can type in their own monthly energy costs for gasoline, electricity, and heating costs and be told how much the treaty will cost them in additional charges for energy (as calculated by this antitreaty group). After readers indicate who they are and where they live, a letter is composed and sent to representatives in Congress, the president, and the vice president.

By using this technique, the group avoids the time and expense of recruiting citizens to write letters or following up to ensure that letters have been written. Moreover, because the letters come from constituents, members of Congress and their staff will pay at least some attention to them. Of course, these mass e-mail campaigns, with each message the same, may win some attention now because of their novelty, but we can expect that eventually they will be viewed as no more persuasive than mass postcard campaigns.

NOTE: The Web sites mentioned in the text are good places to start. Try **http://www.incongress.com/** and **www.globalwarmingcost.org.** Another useful site is **http://congress.org/main.html,** which will help you locate and send an e-mail to your member of Congress.

SOURCE: Ed Henry, "It's the '90s': Old Dogs, New Tricks," *Roll Call Monthly* (November 1997), p. 1.

the largest increases were in going public.[71] Talking with the media increased the most, and mobilizing the grassroots to send letters and telegrams and make telephone calls was second.

MOBILIZING THE GRASS ROOTS

The constituency of an interest group—the group's members or those whom the group serves—can help communicate the group's position to public officials. The National Rifle Association is effective in mobilizing its members. The NRA can generate thousands of letters within a few days. As one senator remarked, "I'd rather be a deer in hunting season than run afoul of the NRA crowd."[72]

Conservative Christian minister Jerry Falwell activated his "gospel grapevine" to flood the White House and Congress in opposition to the president's plan to lift the ban on homosexuals in the military. Warning of a new radical homosexual rights agenda, he urged viewers of his "Old Time Gospel Hour" to call and register their opinions.

Grassroots lobbying was the hallmark of the effort to derail or modify Clinton's health care reform proposal. Industries affected by the proposed change lined up their own supporters. Cigarette companies rallied tobacco growers to oppose increases in the cigarette taxes. The Pharmaceutical Manufacturers Association had the presidents of 26 drug companies write letters to 600,000 workers asking them to write Congress warning of dangers in price controls. Insurance agents provided their clients with a booklet called "A Citizen's Guide to Health Care Reform" and urged them to contact their representatives. The American Medical Association (AMA) sent 660,000 physicians and 48,000 medical students a questionnaire marked "For Patients" with 10 questions on Clinton's health care proposal. The chief lobbyist for the National Federation of Independent Business, which also opposed the Clinton plan, says "You use the people back home to sensitize members of Congress and staff. I get listened to on the Hill because they know I have 600,000 small businessmen behind me back home. The grass roots gives me standing."[73]

Appeals to write or phone policymakers often exaggerate the severity of the problem and the strength of the opposition. Only the threat of imminent failure or a monstrous adversary with superior resources is sufficient to move most members. Because of the difficulty in mobilizing members and the cost in time and money, grassroots efforts are typically a last resort. Besides, as one lobbyist put it, members of Congress "hate it when you call in the dogs."[74]

To be successful, mass letter writing and phone calls must look sincere and spontaneous. Groups often send members sample letters to help them know what to write, but letters that appear unique are most effective. Campaigns producing thousands of postcards generally are not effective unless representatives do not hear from the other side.

Sometimes grassroots lobbying involves more than phoning or writing letters. A lobbyist for the nation's hospitals opposed to the Clinton plan for health care reform encouraged hospital administrators across the nation to get acquainted with their representative, work with the member to organize town meetings to discuss issues, and guide the member on a tour of the local hospital to point out how many people are employed and what the hospital means to the local community. "If done well, the member summoned to the Oval Office can turn to the president and say 'I can't go with you on this, Mr. President, because I promised the people in my district.' "[75]

MOLDING PUBLIC AND ELITE OPINION

Groups use public relations techniques to shape public opinion as well as the opinions of policymakers. Ads in newspapers and magazines and on radio and television supply information, foster an image, promote a particular policy, or some combination of these. Tobacco interests spent millions in mobilizing public opinion to oppose tobacco legislation. Lockheed Martin, a defense contractor, tried to persuade Congress to purchase the company's F-22 fighter jet with an ad appearing in several publications widely read by members. The ad featured a postcard on a black background. On the card, which is dated June 18, 2007, a wife and mother writes home telling her husband and son not to worry because "those F-22s upstairs" are "ruling the sky." Across the bottom of the ad is the caption: "One day in the future, someone you love may be depending on the F-22. . . ." According to the company, the ad was an attempt to give a human dimension to an issue that often is shrouded in Pentagon jargon and mind-numbing statistics. But Senator Dale Bumpers (D-Ark.) accused the firm of pandering to the emotions of lawmakers.[76]

Of course, by themselves ads are unlikely to move policymakers to action or shift public opinion dramatically in the short run. They are most effective in combination with other tactics.

Groups may stage events such as rallies or pickets to attract media coverage to their cause. For example, those opposing racial segregation in South Africa have won considerable attention picketing and protesting outside the South African embassy in Washington, D.C. They were especially effective because they enlisted members of Congress, community leaders, and other celebrities in their protests. Arrests of members of Congress and other celebrities for trespassing kept the issue in the limelight for months.

Framing the terms of the debate is crucial in winning public support. Those arguing in favor of tort reform (limiting damages courts will award to those injured in auto accidents, air disasters, unsuccessful surgeries, or other mishaps) focus on the few outrageously huge settlements for seemingly innocuous injuries. Those arguing against such changes focus on the poor widows left penniless after being permanently incapacitated by the rapacious behavior of a wealthy corporation.[77]

A tactic increasingly used by interest groups to influence public opinion is rating members of Congress. Groups may choose a number of votes crucial to their concerns such as abortion, conservation, or consumer affairs. Or they may select many votes reflecting a liberal or conservative outlook. They then publicize the votes to their members with the ultimate objective of trying to defeat candidates who vote against their positions. The impact of these ratings is probably minimal unless they are used in a concerted effort to target certain members for defeat.

COALITION BUILDING

Coalitions, networks of groups with similar concerns, help individual groups press their demands. Coalitions can be large and focused on many issues or small and very specific. For example, 7-Eleven stores, Kingsford charcoal, amusement parks, and lawn and garden centers joined the Daylight Saving Time Coalition to lobby Congress to extend daylight saving time. All wanted additional daylight hours to snack, grill, play, or till the soil, which would mean more money in their pockets.

Coalitions formed around the health care reform issue in 1995. The AFL-CIO, American Airlines,

CAPS OFF TO THE BEER LOBBY

Do you like to have a beer now and then? If so, perhaps membership in the Beer Drinkers of America is for you. But then again maybe it is not. While an organization for beer drinkers may seem slightly odd, an organization for beer producers and sellers seems quite likely.

A "fact sheet" put out by the organization says that the group has a membership of 700,000 beer drinkers. Their mission is to mobilize members to fight things such as taxes on beer, restrictions on advertising, and deposit laws, ostensibly on behalf of beer drinkers.

How did the group get started? One version is that a few fellow beer drinkers decided to oppose a proposed tax on beer on the ballot in New Mexico. (We can visualize a couple of mad-as-hell couch potatoes sitting in a mobile home in the desert flinging empties at the TV and clamoring that they weren't going to take it any more.) A more plausible version is that the group was the brainchild of a lobbyist trying to help a client beat back the beer tax. The lobbyist and a friend persuaded one beer company to put up some seed money and many beer retailers to spread the word. In less than a year, 4,000 signed on. Today, money comes from two beer companies and from beer wholesalers who pressure their employees to join. Of the 700,000, only 150,000, most of whom are employed by the beer industry, actually pay dues; the rest support the group by signing petitions and writing letters.

Unfortunately for all the real beer drinkers in the country, the organization is a tool of the industry. Why all the deception? The industry hopes to use the group to scare members of Congress. Members might vote against the industry but they don't want to go back to their districts having voted against "Joe Six Pack." Increasingly, groups try to couch their real intent behind a name that they know will conjure up positive images on the part of the public and maybe policymakers.

SOURCE: Sean Holton, "Beer Biz Leaves 1 Drinker Foaming," *Orlando Sentinel*, September 12, 1993, pp. 1A, 7A.

Chrysler Corporation, the American College of Physicians and the League of Women Voters supported health care reform, and the American Conservative Union, United Seniors Union, Citizens for a Sound Economy, and National Taxpayers joined a coalition of Citizens Against Health Rationing. Similarly, more than 2,700 companies and trade associations were members of USA*NAFTA, a coalition supporting the trade agreement.[78]

Coalitions demonstrate broad support for an issue and also take advantage of the different strengths of groups. One group may be adept at grassroots lobbying, another at public relations. One may have lots of money, another lots of members.

The growth of coalitions in recent years reflects a number of changes in the policy process.[79] Issues have become increasingly complex. Legislation often affects a variety of interests, which makes it easier to form coalitions among groups representing the interests. In addition, changes in technology make it easier for groups to communicate with each other and with constituents. And the number of interest groups is larger than it used to be, especially the number of public interest groups. Many such groups have limited resources, and coalitions help them stretch their lobbying efforts. Some "black hat" business groups, with image problems, seek to associate themselves with "white hat" organizations ranging from labor unions to consumer groups.[80] The decentralization of Congress and the weakness of political parties also have led to coalition building to win needed majorities at the various stages of the policy process.

Coalitions vary in their duration—some are short term, whereas others are permanent. Coalitions involved with the health care issue remained only until the issue was resolved. Coalitions supporting and opposing NAFTA ceased to exist when Congress approved the measure.

On the other hand, the Leadership Conference on Civil Rights is a permanent coalition of 185 civil rights, ethnic, religious and other groups (Elks, Actors Equity, YMCA, and the National Funeral Directors and Morticians Association). Unlike short-term coalitions, permanent ones need to be sensitive to how today's actions will affect future cooperation. Some issues may be avoided even though a majority of coalition members want to deal with them. When a coalition is unified, however, it can be formidable.

In elections, coordination among PACs in channeling money to political candidates is widespread. Business PACs, for example, take their lead from the Business-Industry Political Action Committee (BIPAC). Information is shared on candidates' issue positions, likelihood of winning, and need for funding.

Protest and Civil Disobedience

Groups that lack access or hold unpopular positions can protest. They can target policymakers directly or indirectly through public opinion. In recent years, issues as diverse as abortion, American support for the Contras in Nicaragua, busing to promote school integration, nuclear weapons, and the poor farm economy in the Midwest have generated protest marches and rallies.

Peaceful but illegal protest activity, where those involved allow themselves to be arrested and punished, is called civil disobedience. Greenpeace is an environmental and peace group that practices civil disobedience. It started in 1971 when a group of environmen-

Greenpeace attempts to influence public opinion with dramatic events. Here, Greenpeace protests dumping of nuclear waste at sea, while dumpers prepare to drop a barrel of waste on the Greenpeace protesters.

talists and peace activists sent two boats to Amchitka Island near Alaska to protest a U.S. underground nuclear weapon test. The boats were named *Greenpeace*, linking the environment and peace. Although the boats failed to reach the island, the publicity generated by the affair led Washington to cancel the test.

Throughout the 1970s and 1980s, Greenpeace staged a number of such protests. To protest dumping of toxic wastes and sewage in the ocean, 13 Greenpeace activists lowered themselves from a New York bridge and hung there for eight hours, preventing any sewage barges from carrying wastes out to sea. All were arrested. To protect endangered whales, members placed themselves in the path of a harpoon, narrowly missing being struck. Others parachuted over coal-powered power plants to protest acid rain. Their goal was to generate publicity and dramatic photographs that would activate the general population.

Greenpeace and several other protest organizations have moved away from the confrontational, "in your face" style of politics in recent years.[81] As they have found a sympathetic ear, that is, someone in government willing to listen, they have opted for an inside strategy, working with those in power rather than against them. Protest groups often drop the "yelling and screaming" for more conventional lobbying techniques once they have access to policymakers. It has also become increasingly difficult to draw media coverage to another story of a group of protesters willing to risk life and limb in the interest of preserving or preventing something, and it is publicity that makes such activities politically effective. The first time, these stories are front-page news. The second time, they are buried inside, if they get covered at all.

Protest can generate awareness of an issue, but to be successful, it must influence mass or elite opinion. Often it is the first step in a long struggle that takes years to resolve. Sometimes the first result is hostility toward the group using it. Antiwar protest by college students in the 1960s and 1970s angered not only government officials, who targeted the leaders for harassment, but also many citizens. In the early years of the women's movement, the media labeled many female protesters "bra burners" even though it is not clear that any woman ever burned a bra.

Extended protests are difficult because they demand more skill by the leaders and sacrifices from the participants. Continued participation, essential to success, robs participants of a normal life. It can mean jail, physical harm, or even death and requires discipline to refrain from violence, even when violence is used against the protesters.

The civil rights movement provides the best example of the successful use of extended protest and civil disobedience in twentieth-century America. By peacefully demonstrating against legalized segregation in the South, black and some white protesters drew the nation's attention to the discrepancy between the American values of equality and democracy and the southern laws that separated blacks from whites in every aspect of life. Protesters used tactics such as sit-ins, marches, and boycotts. Confrontations with authorities often won protesters national attention and public support, which eventually led to change.

All tactics can be effective, but some lend themselves better to some groups than others. For example, business groups with great financial resources can pay for skillful lobbyists and donate to political candidates. Labor unions have many members and can help candidates canvass and get out the vote. Public interest groups rely on activating public opinion and, where members are intensely committed to a cause, protest.

SUCCESS OF INTEREST GROUPS

Although no interest group gets everything it wants from government, some are more successful than others. Politics is not a game of chance, where only luck determines winners and losers. Knowing what to do and how to do it—strategy and tactics—are important, as are resources, competition, and goals.

Resources

Although large size does not guarantee success, large groups have advantages. They can get the attention of public officials by claiming to speak for more people or by threatening to mobilize members against them.

The geographical distribution of members of a group is also important. Because organized labor is concentrated in the Northeast, it has less influence in other parts of the country, particularly in lobbying Congress. The Chamber of Commerce, on the other hand, has members and influence throughout the country.

Other things being equal, a group with well-educated members has an advantage because highly educated people are more likely than others to communicate with public officials and contribute to lobbying efforts.

Group cohesion and intensity are also advantages. Public officials are unlikely to respond to a group if it cannot agree on what it wants or if it does not appear to feel very strongly about its position. For example, in recent years the NAACP has suffered from deep splits within its leadership. Some of these divisions are over tactics: Should the organization be more confrontational and aggressive or work cooperatively and passively within the system to achieve its goals? Some splits are over allies: Should the NAACP work with groups like Louis Farrakhan's Nation of Islam or restrict itself to more moderate and mainstream civil rights organizations? Such splits diminish the clout of a group.

A large **market share,** the number of members in a group compared to its potential membership, is another advantage. For years the AMA enrolled a large percentage (70% or more) of the nation's doctors as members. As its membership (as a percentage of the total number of doctors) declined, so did its influence.

The more money a group has, the more successful it probably will be. Not only does money buy skilled lobbyists and access to elected officials, it is also necessary for indirect lobbying efforts.

Knowledge is a major resource too. If leaders of a group are experts in a policy area, they are more apt to get the attention of public officials. Knowledge of how things get done in Washington is also helpful, which is why many groups employ former members of Congress and the executive branch as lobbyists.

When Bob Dole resigned from the Senate in 1995 to run for president, he indicated that if he lost the presidency, he would have no place to go but back to his hometown of Russell, Kansas. If he had done that, he would have been quite unusual. Few members of Congress return to their roots once their political careers are over. Most move into high-paying positions with the dozens of law firms in Washington that lobby government. Indeed, Dole went to work for one that includes former senator and treasury secretary Lloyd Bentsen and former Senate majority leader George Mitchell. The firm refers to Dole and the others as our "rock stars." Dole's job is to "make rain," which means recruiting clients who will bring in millions of dollars for his firm's 168 other lawyers and lobbyists. Dole's motto is "a client a day."[82]

Finally, public image is important. A negative public image often troubles new, change-oriented groups, such as the animal rights movement. Many of the country's traditional interest groups, big business and organized labor, also suffer from a poor image, being viewed as too powerful and self-serving.

Few groups are blessed with all resources, but the more resources a group has, the better its chances of getting what it wants from government.

ORGANIZING PROTEST: THE MONTGOMERY BUS BOYCOTT

AP/Wide World Photos

Rosa Parks being fingerprinted after her arrest.

The 1955 Montgomery, Alabama, bus boycott was the first successful civil rights protest, and it brought its 26-year-old leader, Dr. Martin Luther King, Jr., to national prominence. Montgomery, like most southern cities, required blacks to sit in the back of public buses while whites sat in the front. The dividing line between the two was a "no man's land" where blacks could sit if there were no whites. If whites needed the seats, blacks had to give them up and move to the back.

One afternoon, Rosa Parks, a seamstress at a local department store and a leader in the local chapter of the National Association for the Advancement of Colored People (NAACP), boarded the bus to go home. The bus was filled and when a white man boarded, the driver called on the four blacks behind the whites to move to the back. Three got up and moved, but Mrs. Parks, tired from a long day and of the injustice of always having to move for white people, said she did not have to move because she was in "no man's land." Under a law that gave him the authority to enforce segregation, the bus driver arrested her.

That evening a group of black women professors at the black state college in Montgomery, led by Jo Ann Robinson, drafted a letter of protest. They called on blacks to stay off the buses on Monday to protest the arrest. They worked through the night making 35,000 copies of their letter to distribute to Montgomery's black residents. Fearful for their jobs and concerned that the state would cut funds to the black college if it became known they had used state facilities to produce the letter, they worked quickly and quietly.

The following day black leaders met and agreed to the boycott. More leaflets were drafted calling on blacks to stay off the buses on Monday. On Sunday, black ministers encouraged their members to support the boycott, and on Monday 90% of the blacks walked to work, rode in black-owned taxis, or shared rides in private cars.

The boycott inspired confidence and pride in the black community and signaled a subtle change in the opinions of blacks toward race relations. This was obvious when, as nervous white police looked on, hundreds of blacks jammed the courthouse to see that Rosa Parks was safely released after her formal conviction. And it was obvious later that evening at a mass rally when Martin Luther King cried out, "There comes a time when people get tired of being trampled over by the iron feet of oppression. There comes a time when people get tired of being pushed out of the glittering sunlight of life's July, and left standing amidst the piercing chill of an Alpine November." After noting that the glory of American democracy is the right to protest, King appealed to the strong religious faith of the crowd, "If we are wrong, God Almighty is wrong. . . . If we are wrong, Jesus of Nazareth was merely a utopian dreamer. . . . If we are wrong, justice is a lie." These words and this speech established King as a charismatic leader for the civil rights movement.

Each day of the boycott was a trial for blacks and their leaders. Thousands had to find a way to get to work and leaders struggled to keep a massive carpool going. However, each evening's rally built up morale for the next day's boycott. Later the rallies became prayer services, as the black community prayed for strength to keep on walking, for courage to remain nonviolent, and for guidance to those who oppressed them.

The city bus line was losing money. City leaders urged more whites to ride the bus to make up lost revenue, but few did. Recognizing that the boycott could not go on forever, black leaders agreed to end it if the rules regarding the seating of blacks in "no man's land" were relaxed. Thinking they were on the verge of breaking the boycott, the city leaders refused. Police began to harass carpoolers and issue bogus tickets for trumped-up violations. Then the city leaders issued an ultimatum: Settle or face arrest. A white grand jury indicted more than 100 boycott leaders for the alleged crime of organizing the protest. In the spirit of nonviolence, the black leaders, including King, surrendered.

The decision to arrest the leaders proved to be the turning point of the boycott. The editor of the local white paper said it was "the dumbest act that has ever been done in Montgomery."[1] With the mass arrests, the boycott finally received national attention. Reporters from all over the world streamed into Montgomery to cover the story. The publicity brought public and financial support. The arrests caused the boycott to become a national event and its leader, Martin Luther King, a national figure. A year later, the U.S. Supreme Court declared Alabama's local and state laws requiring segregation in buses unconstitutional, and when the city complied with the Court's order, the boycott ended.

Rosa Parks became a hero of the civil rights movement. She has been honored many times since then, and millions saw her appearance at the 1988 Democratic National Convention.

1. Taylor Branch, *Parting the Waters, America in the King Years* (New York: Simon & Schuster, 1988), p. 83.

SOURCES: Taylor Branch, *Parting the Waters,* chapters 4 and 5; and Juan Williams, *Eyes on the Prize* (New York: Viking Press, 1987).

Competition and Goals

Success also depends on group competition and goals. Many groups are successful because they face weak opponents. Supporters of gun control have public opinion on their side, but their main lobbying group, the National Council to Control Handguns, has a membership of only 400,000 and a budget of $7.5 million, a fraction of the NRA's. Used-car dealers successfully lobbied against "the lemon law," which would have required them to tell customers of any defects in cars. Few lobbyists represented the other side. These mismatches between groups occur frequently on highly technical issues where one side has more expertise, the public has little interest, or both.

When a group competes with other groups of nearly equal resources, the outcome is often a compromise or a stalemate. The Clean Air Act was not rewritten for years because the auto industry, which wanted a weaker law, and the environmental lobby, which wanted a tougher one, were about equal in strength. The increased clout of the environmental forces finally led to a strengthening of the law in 1990.

Groups that work to preserve the status quo are generally more successful than groups promoting change; it is usually easier to prevent government action than to bring it about. Separation of powers among the Congress, executive branch, and the courts; checks and balances within each branch; and division of authority between the states and national government provide interest groups with numerous points in the political process to exercise influence. Groups wishing to change policy have to persuade officials throughout the political process to go along; groups opposed to change only have to persuade officials at one point in the process. Groups promoting change must win over the House, Senate, White House, bureaucracy, and courts; groups against change need convince only one of them.

Groups are more likely to be successful in securing very narrow and specific benefits than they are in promoting broad policy changes. For example, corporations are concerned with broad policy issues, but they are more likely to be successful in obtaining exemptions from major policy initiatives than they are in winning or losing on the policy itself. The tax code is riddled with exemptions for corporations; the beneficiaries are rarely identified by name. The 1986 changes in the tax code contained an exemption for Phillips Petroleum, identified in the bill as a "corporation incorporated on June 13, 1917, which has its principal place of business in Bartlesville, Oklahoma."[83] Phillips was not concerned about the basic tax changes because it was not affected by them. Such exemptions are unlikely to receive media attention or become controversial. In this way, politicians are able to satisfy a major interest group without risking a hostile public reaction.

CONCLUSION: DO INTEREST GROUPS HELP MAKE GOVERNMENT RESPONSIVE?

Interest groups provide representation that helps make government more responsive. Although elected officials are representatives, they cannot adequately represent all interests in our diverse society. Interest groups pick up some of the slack by representing the views and opinions of their members and constituents and communicating these to political decision makers. This does not mean that all members agree with everything group leaders say or do, or that group leaders are accountable to their members. Group leaders often develop perspectives somewhat different from those of their members. In most instances, however, groups do represent and speak for at least some of the interests of their members. In voluntary organizations particularly, leaders are likely to reflect the interests of their members. If they do not, members can simply exercise their option to leave. Even "checkbook" members can withhold their support if they disagree with group leaders.

Interest groups do not represent, however, all interests or all interests equally. In 1960, E. E. Schattschneider described the pressure system as small in terms of members and biased toward business and the wealthy. At that time no more than 1,500 groups were included, and more than 50% represented either corporations or trade and business associations.[84] Few groups represented consumers, taxpayers, the environment, women, and minorities.

The pressure system has changed since Schattschneider wrote, but its bias remains. The number of interest groups exploded in the 1960s and 1970s, with many of the new groups representing consumers, environmentalists, minorities, and other nonbusiness interests, but these were more than offset by an increase in the number of corporations in the pressure system.

Business interests still dominate, as we saw earlier. Indeed, business had a greater presence in Washington in the 1990s than it did in the 1960s. Nearly two-thirds of the groups in Washington at last count represented either corporations or trade associations. Groups representing minorities, women, the poor, and elderly are less than 10% of all groups with an office in Washington and only 5% of all groups that lobby.

This bias in the pressure system is a big advantage for business and wealthy interests, and it may be increasing. Over the past three decades, business groups have gained in numbers and influence relative to other groups. Labor unions and the Democratic Party, strong supporters of legislation to improve the welfare of the working class, often in opposition to business and wealthy interests, have declined or shifted their focus. As one political analyst put it, "The nature of representative government in the

U.S. has changed, so that more and more of the weight of influence in Washington comes from interest groups, not voters."[85] And interest groups are predominantly looking out for the interests of business. This is not to say that working- and middle-class Americans, or at least some of them, do not benefit from policies favoring the interests of business. But a system where business interests must compete on a more equal basis with the interests of labor and other groups is likely to be more sensitive to the needs of average men and women.

How can we preserve the constitutional rights of interest groups to form and petition government and still keep government responsive to the needs of all its citizens? Recognizing and correcting imbalances in group strength is not simple or easy. Groups currently enjoying an advantage will fight to keep it.

EPILOGUE

The Tobacco Industry Fights Back

With the survival of the industry at stake, not to mention high-paying jobs, Steven Goldstone and the other tobacco CEOs decided to fight by changing public opinion. Although Congress will ultimately decide the issue of liability from lawsuits, the public can push Congress one way or the other, particularly in an election year.

The tobacco industry decided to try to change the terms of the debate. The industry launched a massive advertising campaign portraying government efforts to regulate tobacco as just another attempt by "big government" to spend the "hard earned dollars of the American taxpayer" on a venture that will create another "government bureaucracy" and still not solve the problem. The industry cast itself as a victim targeted by government. Goldstone commented, "I am very confident that the American people are more willing to listen than the people in Washington are."[86]

The industry's Republican allies were also more comfortable when the debate was about taxes rather than teen smoking. Indeed, some, including Speaker Gingrich, who had backed away from tobacco in the fear that Clinton would use the issue against the Republicans, joined with the industry in its efforts to portray tobacco legislation as a back-door attempt to raise taxes and expand government regulation. Another central idea of the campaign was to convince Americans that a violent black market in cigarettes might develop if the legislation passed.[87] The campaign, costing $40 million, included a national radio, television, and newspaper ad campaign, along with one directed at members of Congress and opinion elites; an 800 number for citizens to call for more information, company spokespeople available to make the industry's case to the media and community and civics groups; a direct-mail campaign enlisting potential allies such as tobacco employees, shareholders, distributors, and retailers; and a Web site.

Lawmakers' offices were suddenly deluged with calls and postcards from people opposing the bill. Even though the legislation's proponents responded with an ad campaign of their own, the newly created public opposition[88] provided some in Congress with a way to vote against what was initially a popular bill. As a result, the tobacco legislation, which seemed assured of passage in May 1998, died in June. Republicans wishing to avoid the appearance of knuckling under to an industry that contributes heavily to their party vowed to pass a leaner, less costly bill directed at curbing teen smoking.[89]

Tobacco executives are sworn in to testify before Congress.

Jessica Persson/Agence France-Presse/Corbis-Bettmann

KEY TERMS

interest groups
lobbying
political action committees (PACs)
private interest groups
public interest groups
single-issue groups
coalitions
market share

FURTHER READING

Jeffrey M. Berry, *The Interest Group Society*, 2d ed. (Boston: Little, Brown, 1989). *A general survey of interest groups in American politics. It covers political action committees, lobbyists and lobbying, the internal dynamics of groups, and the problems that interest groups present to society.*

Jeffrey Birnbaum, *The Lobbyists: How Influence Peddlers Get Their Way in Washington* (New York: Times Books, 1993). *A study of lobbyists' activities surrounding major issues considered by Congress in the 1989–1990 session.*

Michael Pertschuk, *Giant Killers* (New York: W. W. Norton, 1986). *How low-budget lobbies can sometimes defeat the big guys by superior organization, tactics, and luck.*

E. E. Schattschneider, *The Semi-Sovereign People* (New York: Henry Holt & Company, 1975). *A classical statement on how interest group politics benefit business and corporate interests by limiting the involvement of citizens in the political process.*

Ernest Wittenberg and Elisabeth Wittenberg, *How to Win in Washington: Very Practical Advice about Lobbying, the Grassroots and the Media* (Cambridge, Mass.: Basil Blackwell, 1989). *A "how to" book for average citizens.*

ELECTRONIC RESOURCES

Most of the organizations discussed in the chapter have their own home pages. Here is a sampling:

http://www.aflcio.org/home.htm
The home page of the largest union in America, the AFL-CIO. It contains official union documents and press releases, news on issues important to the labor movement, a link to information on high corporate executive salaries in the United States, and links to other labor-related groups.

http://www.nam.org/
The National Association of Manufacturers' Web page. It contains material similar to that on the AFL-CIO page but from a business perspective. It also contains suggestions for getting out the vote.

http://www.bcer.org/orgs/
The home page of the Business Coalition for Educational Reform. It provides links to a variety of national business lobbying organizations.

http://www.fb.com/
The Farm Bureau's Web page. It contains similar information from the perspective of the more prosperous and conservative sector of agriculture, along with updates on the weather and on commodity prices.

http://www.nfu.org/
The National Farmers' Union Web page. It provides information from the perspective of smaller, less prosperous farmers.

http://www.aarp.org/
The AARP's excellent Web page. It allows you to register to vote, join the AARP, learn about the AARP's position and congressional testimony on issues affecting the elderly, find out about classes on computers for senior citizens, and much more.

http://www.apsanet.org/
The American Political Science Association's home page. Use it to find out about the organization to which your professor belongs.

http://www.house.gov/commerce/TobaccoDocs/documents.html
This site allows you to read internal tobacco industry documents released by Congress.

http://www.tobacco-litigation.com/toblinks.html-ssi
An antitobacco page, but it provides links to documents as well as opinions on the tobacco regulation controversy.

INFOTRAC CITATIONS

"Congress Snuffs Out the Tobacco Bill"
"Mainstreaming the Militia"
"Who Really Speaks for the Elderly?"
"Loggers vs. Greenpeace"

NOTES

1. Jeffrey Goldberg, "Big Tobacco's Endgame," *New York Times Magazine*, June 21, 1998, p. 36. Information on Gingrich's father is also from this source. Other sources include Ceci Connolly and John Mintz, "How Big Tobacco Got Smoked," *Washington Post National Weekly Edition*, April 6, 1998, pp. 6–7; Ceci Connolly and John Mintz, "The Mississippi Connection," *Washington Post National Weekly Edition*, April 6, 1998, pp. 8–9; Saundra Tory and John Schwartz, "Making Nice to Make a Deal," *Washington Post National Weekly Edition*, March 9, 1998, p. 29; James Carney, "McCain's Big Deal," *Time*, April 13, 1998, pp. 62–64; John Bresnahan, "Tobacco Lobbyists Prepare for Fight," *Roll Call*, May 1998, pp. 1 and 13; Alan Greenblatt, "Tobacco Debate Rages on, Keeping Bill Alive, if Unwieldy," *Congressional Quarterly Weekly Report* (June 13, 1998), pp. 1605–1607.

2. Ernest Wittenberg and Elisabeth Wittenberg, *How to Win in Washington* (Cambridge, Mass.: Blackwell, 1989), p. 24.

3. Jeffrey Birnbaum, *The Lobbyists* (New York: Times Books, 1992), p. 32.

4. M. A. Peterson and J. L. Walker, "Interest Group Responses to Partisan Change: The Impact of the Reagan Administration upon the National Interest Group System," in A. J. Cigler and B. A. Loomis, eds., *Interest Group Politics*, 2d ed. (Washington, D.C.: CQ Press, 1987), p. 162.

5. A. de Tocqueville, *Democracy in America* (New York: Knopf, 1945), p. 191.

6. G. Almond and S. Verba, *Civil Culture* (Boston: Little, Brown, 1965), pp. 266–306.

7. D. Truman, *The Governmental Process* (New York: Knopf, 1964), pp. 25–26.

8. Ibid., p. 59.

9. Ibid., pp. 26–33.

10. J. Q. Wilson, *Political Organization* (New York: Basic Books, 1973), p. 198.

11. G. K. Wilson, *Interest Groups in America* (Oxford: Oxford University Press, 1981), chapter 5; see also G. K. Wilson, "American Business and Politics," in Cigler and Loomis, *Interest Group Politics*, pp. 221–235.

12. K. L. Schlozman and J. T. Tierney, "More of the Same: Washington Pressure Group Activity in a Decade of Change," *Journal of Politics* 45 (May 1983), pp. 335–356.

13. Christopher H. Foreman, Jr., "Grassroots Victim Organizations: Mobilizing for Personal and Public Health," in A. J. Cigler and B. A. Loomis, eds., *Interest Group Politics*, 4th ed. (Washington, D.C.: CQ Press, 1994), pp. 33–53.

14. R. H. Salisbury, "An Exchange Theory of Interest Groups," *Midwest Journal of Political Science* 13 (February 1969), pp. 1–32.

15. J. M. Berry, *The Interest Group Society* (Boston: Little Brown, 1984), pp. 26–28.

16. J. L. Walker, "The Origins and Maintenance of Interest Groups in America," *American Political Science Review* 77 (June 1983), pp. 398–400; see also *National Journal* (August 1981), p. 1376.

17. Wilson, *Political Organization*, chapter 3.

18. C. Brown, "Explanations of Interest Group Membership over Time," *American Politics Quarterly* 17 (January 1989), pp. 32–53.

19. C. Brown, "Explanations of Interest Group Membership." The National Rifle Association. Annual Meeting of Midwest P.S. Association, 1987.

20. National Opinion Research Center, General Social Surveys, 1987.

21. N. Babchuk and R. Thompson, "The Voluntary Associations of Negroes," *American Sociological Review* 27 (October 1962), pp. 662–665; see also P. Klobus-Edwards, J. Edwards, and D. Klemmach, "Differences in Social Participation of Blacks and Whites," *Social Forces* 56 (1978), pp. 1035–1052.

22. Robert D. Putnam, "Bowling Alone: America's Declining Social Capital," *Journal of Democracy* (January 1995), pp. 65–78; see also Robert J. Samuelson, "Join the Club," *Washington Post National Weekly Edition*, April 15–21, 1996, p. 5.

23. Samuelson, "Join the Club."

24. Richard Stengel, "Bowling Together," *Time*, July 22, 1996, p. 35.

25. M. T. Hayes, "The New Group Universe" in Cigler and Loomis, *Interest Group Politics*, 2d ed., pp. 133–145.

26. C. Tomkins, "A Sense of Urgency," *New Yorker*, March 27, 1989, pp. 48–74.

27. Walker, "The Origins and Maintenance of Interest Groups in America."

28. E. E. Schattschneider, *Semi-Sovereign People* (New York: Holt, Rinehart, & Winston, 1960), p. 118.

29. David Broder and Michael Weisskopf, "Finding New Friends on the Hill," *Washington Post National Weekly Edition*, October 3–9, 1994, p. 11.

30. Peter Behr, "The Corporate Winning Streak," *Washington Post National Weekly Edition*, January 30–February 5, 1995, p. 24.

31. P. E. Johnson, "Organized Labor in an Era of Blue Collar Decline," in A. J. Cigler and B. A. Loomis, eds., *Interest Group Politics*, 3d ed. (Washington, D.C.: CQ Press, 1991), pp. 33–62.

32. F. Swoboda, "Striking Out as a Weapon against Management," *Washington Post National Weekly Edition*, July 13, 1992, p. 20.

33. Frank Swoboda, "Leadership Labor in the Vineyards," *Washington Post National Weekly Edition*, November 6–12, 1995, p. 20; Jeffrey Birnbaum and Eric Pooley, "New Party Bosses," *Time*, April 8, 1996, pp. 28–32.

34. Steven Greenhouse, "Union Membership Slides despite Increased Organizing," *New York Times*, March 22, 1998, p. 8a.

35. A. J. Cigler and J. M. Hansen, "Group Formation through Protest: The American Agriculture Movement," in A. J. Cigler and B. A. Loomis, eds., *Interest Group Politics*, 1st ed. (Washington, D.C.: CQ Press, 1983), chapter 4; A. J. Cigler, "Organizational Maintenance and Political Activity on the Cheap: The American Agriculture Movement," in Cigler and Loomis, *Interest Group Politics*, 1st ed., pp. 81–108.

36. A. S. McFarland, *Common Cause* (Chatham, N.J.: Chatham House, 1984); see also A. S. McFarland, *Public Interest Lobbies: Decision Making on Energy* (Washington, D.C.: American Enterprise Institute, 1976).

37. R. G. Shaiko, "More Bang for the Buck: The New Era of Full Service Public Interest Groups," in Cigler and Loomis, *Interest Group Politics*, 3d ed., p. 109.

38. Ibid., p. 120.

39. For a discussion of the evolution of NOW and its success in lobbying Congress, see A. N. Costain and W. D. Costain, "The Women's Lobby: Impact of a Movement on Congress," in Cigler and Loomis, *Interest Group Politics*, 1st ed.

40. Melinda Shelton, "A Rainbow March to Fight the 'Ultra' Right," at www.now.org/nnt/05-96/march.html.

41. Birnbaum and Pooley, "New Party Bosses."

42. E. M. Uslaner, "A Tower of Babel on Foreign Policy," in Cigler and Loomis, *Interest Group Politics*, 3d ed., p. 309.

43. K. Wald, *Religion and Politics* (New York: St. Martin's Press, 1985), pp. 182–212.

44. James L. Guth, John C. Green, Lyman A. Jellstedt, and Corwin E. Wmidt, "Onward Christian Soldiers: Religious Activist Groups in American Politics," in Cigler and Loomis, *Interest Group Politics*, 3d ed., p. 57.

45. Sidney Blumental, "Christian Soldiers," *New Yorker*, July 18, 1994, p. 36.

46. Ibid., p. 37.

47. David Von Drehle and Thomas B. Edsall, "The Religious Right Returns," *Washington Post National Weekly Edition*, August 29–September 4, 1994, p. 6; "Prodding Voters to the Right," *Time*, November 21, 1994, p. 62.

48. Ceci Connolly and Dan Balz, "The Christian Coalition, Born Again," *Washington Post National Weekly Edition*, January 5, 1998, p. 15.

49. "Religious Right Returns," p. 6.

50. Charles Levendosky, "Alternative Religious Voice Finally Being Raised," *Lincoln Journal-Star* (March 3, 1996), p. 7b.

51. The source for most of the next paragraphs is Eric Marcus, *Making History: The Struggle for Gay and Lesbian Equal Rights 1945–1990* (New York: Harper-Collins, 1992). Also see Jeffrey Schmalz, "Gay Politics Goes Mainstream," *New York Times Magazine*, October 11, 1992, pp. 18ff.

52. Gabriel Rotello, "94 Was a Good Year for Gay Rights," *Lincoln Journal-Star*, January 7, 1995, p. 10.

53. J. Tierney, "Old Money, New Power," *New York Times Magazine*, October 23, 1988, p. 69.

54. "Grays on the Go," *Time*, February 22, 1988, p. 69.

55. "Gray Power," *Time*, January 4, 1988, p. 36.

56. "Our Footloose Correspondents," *New Yorker*, August 8, 1988, p. 70.

57. C. J. Bosso, "Adaption and Change in the Environmental Movement" in Cigler and Loomis, *Interest Group Politics*, 3d ed., pp. 155–156.

58. Ibid., p. 162.

59. Ibid., p. 169.

60. A. Rubin, "Interest Groups and Abortion Politics in the Post-Webster Era," in Cigler and Loomis, *Interest Group Politics*, 3d ed., pp. 249–251; *Congressional Quarterly Weekly Report* (March 27, 1993), pp. 755–757.

61. D. Broder, "Let 100 Single-Issue Groups Bloom," *Washington Post*, January 7, 1979, pp. C1–C2; see also D. Broder, *The Party's Over: The Failure of Politics in America* (New York: Harper & Row, 1972).

62.. Wilson, *Interest Groups*, chapter 4.

63. P. M. Evans, "Lobbying the Committee: Interest Groups and the House Public Works and Transportation Committee, in the Post-Webster Era," in Cigler and Loomis, *Interest Group Politics*, 3d ed., pp. 257–276.

64. Berry, *Interest Group Society*, p. 188.

65. Jeffrey Birnbaum, *The Lobbyists* (New York: Times Books, 1992), p. 40.

66. Wittenberg and Wittenberg, *How to Win in Washington*, p. 24.

67. David Broder and Spencer Rich, "The Health Care Battle Begins," *Washington Post National Weekly Edition*, September 27–October 3, 1993, p. 6.

68. E. Drew, *Politics and Money: The New Road to Corruption* (New York: Macmillan, 1983), p. 78.

69. Ibid.

70. For an article dealing with the success of interest group litigation at the district court level see L. Epstein and C. K. Rowland, "Debunking the Myth of Interest Group Invincibility in the Courts," *American Political Science Review* 85 (March 1991), pp. 205–220.

71. S. Kernell, *Going Public* (Washington, D.C.: CQ Press, 1986), p. 34.

72. R. Harris, "If You Love Your Grass," *New Yorker*, April 20, 1968, p. 57.

73. Michael Weisskopf, "Letting No Grass Roots Grow under Their Feet," *Washington Post National Weekly Edition*, October 18–24, 1993, pp. 20–21.

74. Evans, "Lobbying the Committee," p. 269.

75. Sandra Boodman, "Health Care's Power Player," *Washington Post National Weekly Edition*, February 14–20, 1994, pp. 6–7.

76. Michael Towle, "Ad for Fighter Plane Aimed at Congress," *Lincoln Journal-Star*, May 2, 1997, p. 7a.

77. Birnbaum, *The Lobbyists*, p. 40.

78. Dan Balz and David Broder, "Take Two Lobbyists and Call Me in the Morning," *Washington Post National Weekly Edition*, October 18–24, 1993, pp. 10–11.

79. Much of the information in this section is taken from B. A. Loomis, "Coalitions of Interests: Building Bridges in the Balkanized State," in Cigler and Loomis, *Interest Group Politics*, 2d ed., pp. 258–274.

80. Birnbaum, *The Lobbyists*, p. 83.

81. Cary Goldberg, "How Political Theater Lost Its Audience," *New York Times*, September 21, 1997, p. 6.

82. David Segal, "Bob Dole Leads the Cast of Rainmakers," *Washington Post National Weekly Edition*, September 22, 1997, p. 20.

83. Dan Clawson, Alan Neustadtl, and Denise Scott, *Money Talks* (New York: Basic Books, 1992), p. 91.

84. Schattschneider, *Semi-Sovereign People*, chapter 2.

85. Kevin Phillips, "Fat City," *Time*, September 26, 1995, p. 51.

86. Goldberg, "Big Tobacco's Endgame," p. 67.

87. Ibid.

88. Saundra Torry, "One for the Record," *Washington Post National Weekly Edition*, May 25, 1998, p. 10.

89. "Confidential Tobacco PR Memo," at www.citizen.org/tobacco/premo.htm.

The Republican Party has tried to pull blue-collar workers away from their traditional home in the Democratic Party. Former President Ronald Reagan was especially effective in luring these voters.

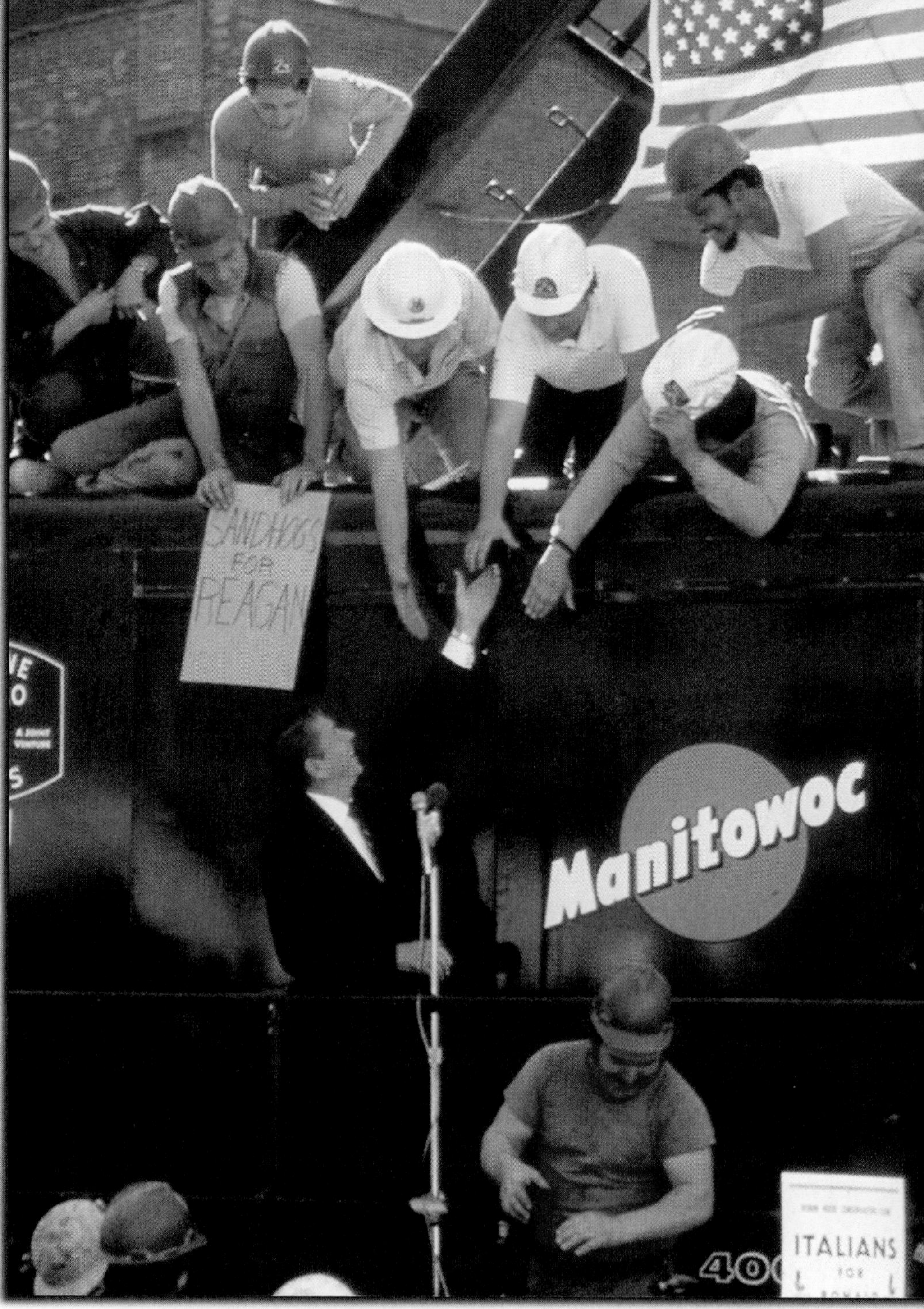

Andy Levin

6 POLITICAL PARTIES

OUTLINE

- **What Are Political Parties?**
- **Development and Change in the Party System**
  - Preparty Politics: The Founders' Views of Political Parties
  - First Party System: Development of Parties
  - Second Party System: Rise of the Democrats
  - Third Party System: Rise of the Republicans
  - Fourth Party System: Republican Dominance
  - Fifth Party System: Democratic Dominance
  - Has the Fifth Party System Realigned?
- **The Parties Today**
- **Characteristics of the Party System**
  - Two Parties
  - Fragmentation
  - Moderation
  - Minor Parties in American Politics
- **Party in the Electorate**
  - Party Identification
  - Characteristics of Democrats and Republicans
- **Party in Government**
- **Party Organization**
  - National Party Organization
  - State and Local Party Organizations
  - Big-City Party Organizations
- **The Nominating Process**
  - Caucuses
  - Conventions
  - Primaries
- **Conclusion: Do Political Parties Make Government More Responsive?**

YOU ARE THERE

Should the Republicans Offer the Voters a "Contract"?

You are Newt Gingrich, a Republican member of the House of Representatives from Georgia. Although it is early 1994, you sense that your party has a good chance to gain many congressional seats in the November elections, and an outside chance to become the majority party. Voter anger, coupled with the redistricting that changed many district lines in 1992, led a record number of House incumbents (48) to retire. Four other incumbents were defeated in primary elections, leaving 52 seats open. This offers a large opportunity for Republicans to take control of the House. If they do, you will likely become the Speaker of the House, the most powerful office in the House of Representatives.

You have been a key member of the Republican congressional party almost from your first day in Washington. You were one of the first to discover the potential of C-SPAN to get your messages to the public. Your political action committee, GOPAC, raises money from conservative business leaders and uses it to recruit and train Republican candidates who believe in your conservative message.[1] You even provide a list of words tested in focus groups that Republican candidates should use in the campaign: Democrats are to be associated with decay, sickness, stagnation, corruption and waste, and Republicans with change, truth, morality, courage, and family, for example. In the last election, 21 of 47 newly elected Republicans were GOPAC recruits.

Now you are focusing on the strategies and tactics that will ensure a successful 1994 congressional campaign. At a meeting with fellow Republican members of the House, Richard Armey (Texas), Bill Paxon (New York), Tom DeLay (Texas), and others, you discuss the possibility of offering voters a specific platform of actions that your party would take if elected.[2]

Such a possibility is unheard of in off-year (non–presidential election) congressional elections. During presidential election years, parties offer platforms of promises. Though often vague, these platforms distinguish the two major parties, and the winning presidential candidate usually will try to follow through on at least some of the more specific ideas. But congressional elections are generally much less focused on national party goals. These elections tend to be highly individual, with incumbents having great advantages, and both incumbents and challengers tend to focus on local and state issues.

In recent campaigns, candidates have waged highly negative campaigns, both responding to and fueling voter anger at politics and politicians. And during this election year, voters are even more angry than in 1992, when they spurned George Bush's bid for a second term. Fueled by radio and television talk show hosts, Americans said they were fed up with politics as usual: with politicians attuned more to special interest groups than voters, members of Congress who had been in Washington so long they had forgotten the people back home, and elected officials who were unwilling to balance the federal budget. Americans were dubious about their economic futures, terrified of crime, and furious at the breakdown in morality. They blamed government for these problems, or at least for not doing something about them. They especially blamed Democrats, who had controlled Congress for 40 years. Most of all, the public seemed to believe that government was no longer accountable to the people.

You think, however, that playing on the voters' negative feelings may not be quite enough to win the majority that you want. Negativism will win some votes, but you believe that the voters want something more positive. Providing a "platform" for this midyear election might be unique enough to draw voters' attention and give a focus to the campaign rhetoric of Republican candidates throughout the nation.

However, there are potential drawbacks to this idea. Exactly what should be part of such a platform? Like the Democrats, your party has significant divisions among its members, especially over issues of morality, such as abortion rights and school prayer, and over budget issues too. Political parties in the United States are not tightly disciplined

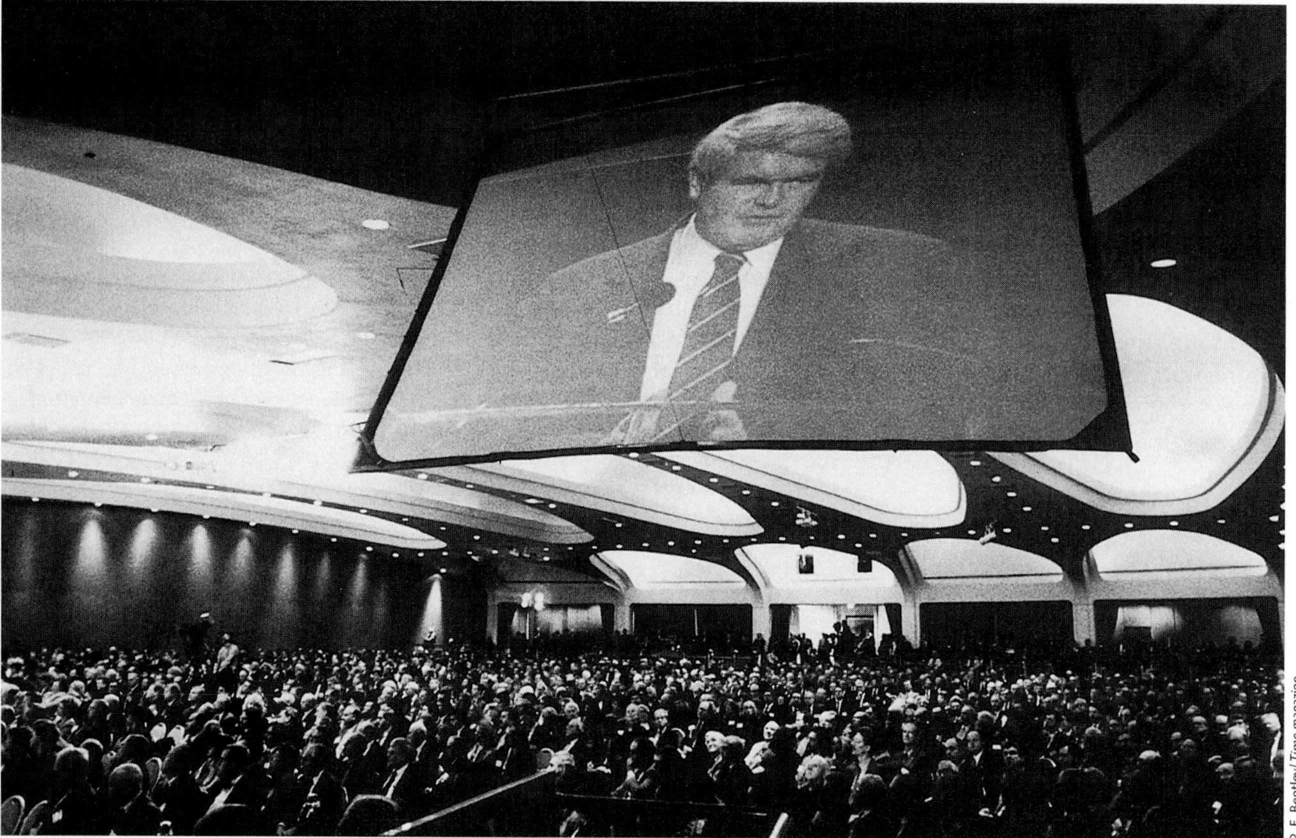

Newt Gingrich

organizations characterized by shared values on all major issues. Drawing up a platform that everyone could agree on would not be an easy task, and a public fight among members over the terms of such a platform would negate any benefits of having one at all.

Moreover, if such a platform could be constructed, there would be a danger that Republicans would be labeled a failure if they could not carry out that platform. Being specific about what the party wanted to do might make it easier for Democrats and other skeptics to point to all the platform promises that were not accomplished. And the more specific the platform, the easier it would be to spot and criticize these failures.

There is also the prospect that you will misread public opinion and the whole thing will backfire. Abstract positions such as reducing the size of government have more appeal than targeting specific government programs for elimination.

What do you decide? Do you go ahead with a Republican platform, risking party division and possible failure to deliver on your promises? Or do you follow a more traditional approach, focusing almost entirely on what is wrong with the Clinton presidency and the Democratic Congress?

George Washington warned against the "baneful" effects of parties and described them as the people's worst enemies. But, more recently, a respected political scientist, E. E. Schattschneider, argued that "political parties created democracy and that democracy was impossible without them."[3] The public echoes these contradictory views. Many believe that parties create conflict where none exists, yet most identify with one of our two major parties.[4]

These same feelings exist among candidates for office. They often avoid political parties by establishing their own personal campaign organizations and raising their own funds. If elected, they often do not follow the party line. At the same time, candidates for national and state offices are nominated in the name of political parties, they rely on parties for assistance, and they have little chance of winning unless they are Democrats or Republicans.

In this chapter, we examine American political parties to see why they are important and why many observers believe that if they become less important and effective, our system of government may not work as well as it does.

WHAT ARE POLITICAL PARTIES?

Political parties are a major link between people and government. They provide a way for the public to have some say about who serves in government and what policies are chosen. Political parties generally are defined as organizations that seek to control government by recruiting, nominating, and electing their members to public office. They consist of three interrelated components: the **party in the electorate,** those who identify with the party; the **party in government,** those who are appointed or elected to office as members of a political party; and the formal **party organization,** the party "professionals" who run the party at the national, state, and local levels (see Figure 1).[5]

In linking the public and government policymakers, parties serve several purposes. They help select public officials by recruiting and screening candidates and then providing campaign resources. They help empower citizens by activating and interesting them in politics. Individually, citizens have little power, but collectively, through parties, they can influence government.

Many voters feel an attachment to a political party, an affiliation they acquire early in life that aids them in deciding among competing candidates. Some voters simply vote their party identification, with little or no knowledge of candidates or issues. But a party vote is, in part, an issue vote. Political parties do have relatively consistent stances on issues, and this is clear to most voters. Since the 1930s, the Democratic Party has favored an expanded role for the national government in dealing with the country's social and economic problems, while the Republican Party has favored minimizing the role of the national government in the economy but expanding it in morality issues.

Most voters recognize this difference. Knowing a candidate belongs to a party is a clue to the candidate's general preference regarding the role of the national government in such issues as health care, transportation, communication, energy, and the environment. Voters therefore do not need to study each candidate's position on such issues in great detail, a difficult and

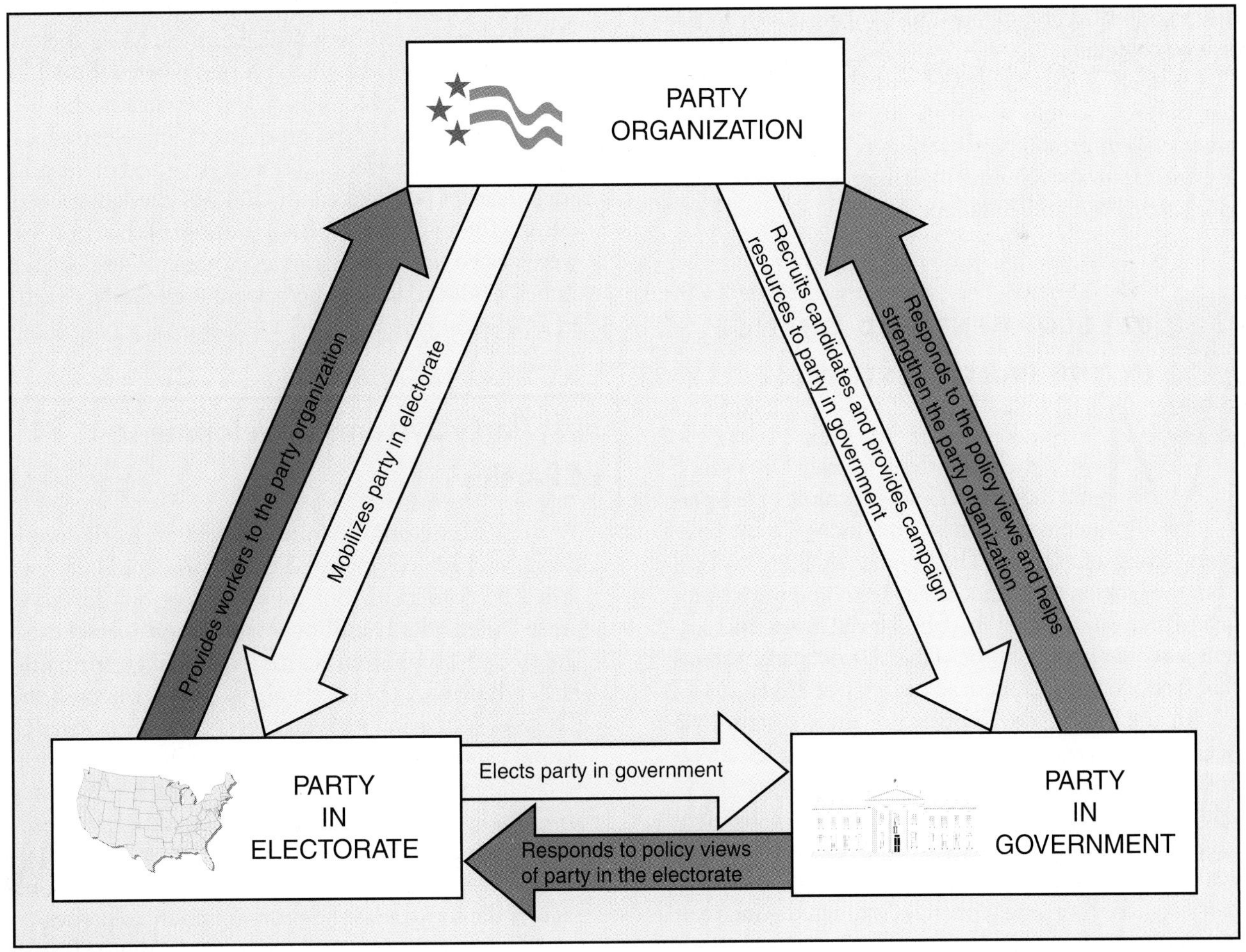

FIGURE 1

The Three Components of Political Parties

time-consuming task. The party label provides a general understanding of where the candidate stands. This is one reason why Schattschneider believed democracy was impossible without political parties. When citizens select a party, they have a clearer understanding of what their selection means in terms of the policy direction of the nation. Without the party label, citizens have no idea of how their vote for an individual candidate translates into public policy.

The party in government plays an important role in organizing and operating government; it formulates policy options and ultimately decides which to support or oppose. When political parties represent individuals from widely different backgrounds and interests, parties aid society by aggregating and mediating conflicts and contributing to political and social stability.

It is not fashionable to argue in favor of political parties and point to their contributions to democracy. Most Americans see parties as part of the "mess in Washington." Many believe that parties are responsible for the government's inability to act in dealing with the nation's problems and that partisan debates are meaningless squabbles. Many feel that parties create differences where none exist, rather than reflect and represent real differences in how to solve the nation's problems.

In fact, without political parties, it is likely that our political system would be more fragmented and media and interest groups even more powerful. Parties are organizations that bind together people from all regions, religions, and economic groups.

DEVELOPMENT AND CHANGE IN THE PARTY SYSTEM

Most Americans think of the Democratic and Republican Parties as more or less permanent fixtures, and indeed they have been around a long time. The Democratic Party evolved from the Jacksonian Democrats in 1832, and the Republican Party was founded in 1854. Nevertheless, the current party system is only one of five distinct party systems that have existed in American history (see Figure 2).

In tracing the development of these systems, we need to keep two things in mind. First, parties developed after the nation's founding, grew to be very powerful in the late nineteenth century, and have declined in influence since then.

Second, there have been periods of stability in the party system when one party has dominated American politics and won most elections. There have also been periods of transition and instability when neither party has dominated, and control of government has been divided between the parties or has shifted back and forth. In transition periods, issues emerge that are difficult to resolve, and voters establish new party loyalties based on them. The transition from one stable party system to another is called a **realignment.**

Preparty Politics: The Founders' Views of Political Parties

Most of the Founders viewed political parties as dangerous to stable government. This antiparty feeling was rooted in three basic beliefs. First, the Founders thought parties created and exploited conflicts that undermined consensus on public policy. Second, they thought parties were instruments by which a small and narrow interest could impose its will on society. And third, they believed parties stifled independent thought and behavior. [6]

Madison feared political parties as much as interest groups because he felt both pursued selfish interests at the expense of the common good. He referred to both as "factions" in *Federalist* #10. John Adams dreaded what he considered the greatest political evil, the formation of rival political parties.

Therefore, it is not surprising that the Constitution does not mention political parties. Nevertheless, it created a system in which parties, or something like them, were inevitable. When the Founders established popular elections as the mechanism for selecting political leaders, an agency for organizing and mobilizing supporters of political candidates was needed. Indeed, despite their antiparty feelings, several of the Founders were active in the first parties. Thomas Jefferson and James Madison, for example, were the founders of the first political party.

First Party System: Development of Parties

With Washington's unanimous election to the presidency in 1788, it appeared the nation could be governed by consensus. But differences of opinion soon arose. Alexander Hamilton, Washington's secretary of the treasury, supported a strong national government. His following, the Federalists, were opposed by Thomas Jefferson, secretary of state, who feared a strong central government. The conflict led Jefferson to challenge Federalist John Adams for the presidency in 1796. Jefferson lost, but he then recruited able leaders in each state, founded newspapers, established political clubs, and in 1800 ran again and won. Jefferson's victory demonstrated the utility of political parties.

By Jefferson's second term, more than 90% of members of Congress were either Federalists or Jeffersonians (later called Jeffersonian Republicans) and consistently voted in support of their party.[7]

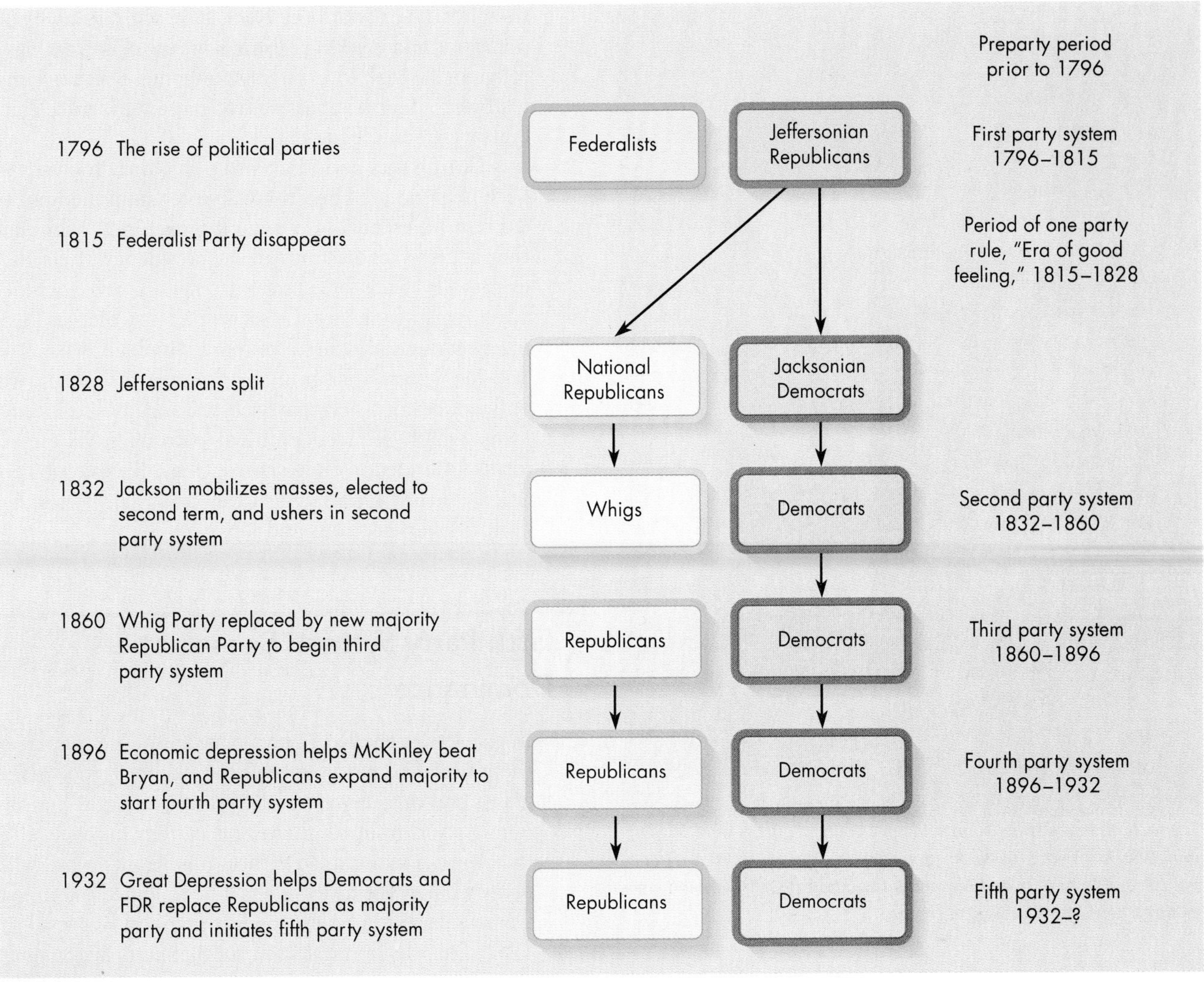
Preparty period
prior to 1796
1796 The rise of political parties
Federalists
Jeffersonian Republicans
First party system
1796–1815
1815 Federalist Party disappears
Period of one party rule, "Era of good feeling," 1815–1828
1828 Jeffersonians split
National Republicans
Jacksonian Democrats
1832 Jackson mobilizes masses, elected to second term, and ushers in second party system
Whigs
Democrats
Second party system
1832–1860
1860 Whig Party replaced by new majority Republican Party to begin third party system
Republicans
Democrats
Third party system
1860–1896
1896 Economic depression helps McKinley beat Bryan, and Republicans expand majority to start fourth party system
Republicans
Democrats
Fourth party system
1896–1932
1932 Great Depression helps Democrats and FDR replace Republicans as majority party and initiates fifth party system
Republicans
Democrats
Fifth party system
1932–?

FIGURE 2

The Five American Party Systems

Second Party System: Rise of the Democrats

The Jeffersonian Republicans split into factions. One of these developed into the Democratic Party, led by Andrew Jackson, who won the presidency in 1828.

The Jacksonian Democrats emphasized the common person and encouraged popular participation. As a result of their efforts, the vote was expanded to all white adult males. Presidential electors were selected in popular elections rather than by state legislatures, and the party convention became the instrument used to nominate presidential and other party candidates. No longer did members of the party in Congress select the party's presidential nominee. Instead, conventions opened up decisions to local as well as national party elites.

Many political leaders deplored Jackson's efforts to mobilize the masses. John Quincy Adams called Jackson a "barbarian." An Adams supporter referred to Jackson's victory as "the howl of raving Democracy."[8]

Jackson's popular appeal and the organizational effort of his party brought large numbers to the polls for the first time. By 1828, more than a million votes were cast for president. Building on the efforts of Jefferson, Jackson introduced a uniquely American idea, a mass-population-based party organization.

Third Party System: Rise of the Republicans

The conflict over slavery brought a new party alignment. Abolitionists and proslavery factions split the Whig Party, which had been the primary opposition to the Democrats. By 1860, the Whigs disappeared and a new party, the Republicans (not related to the Jeffersonian or National Republicans), emerged. The Republicans (also known as the GOP—Grand Old Party), reflecting

The Granger Collection, New York

The factions that developed into the first political parties were already vying with each other in Washington's administration. Thomas Jefferson (second from left) and Alexander Hamilton (fourth from left) are pictured here with Washington (right).

abolitionist sentiment, nominated Abraham Lincoln for president. Northern Democrats who opposed slavery joined Republicans to form a new majority party.

After the Civil War, the Republicans usually won the presidency and controlled Congress. After 1876, however, elections were close and the parties evenly matched in Congress.

Parties were strong during this period. They controlled nominations for office and mobilized voters through extensive local organizations. Big-city political machines provided employment and other help for many new immigrants in exchange for their allegiance. Corruption—vote buying and political payoffs—linked poor immigrants, big business, and party leaders in strong party machines.

Fourth Party System: Republican Dominance

The election of 1896 ushered in another party alignment. Democrat William Jennings Bryan appealed to southerners and farmers of the plains. He played to their hostility toward the Northeast, with its large corporations and growing ethnic working class. His was a religious appeal too, pitting fundamentalists against Catholics. But his appeal was too narrow and the Democrats were soundly defeated.

During this period a third party, the Progressives, became popular. The Progressives championed political reform, especially of big-city machines. Although the Progressives did not win the presidency, their ideas eventually were enacted into law. These included voter registration and the secret ballot, which reduced election fraud; the direct primary, which allowed rank-and-file voters to nominate their party's candidates and reduce control by party bosses; and civil service reform, which reduced political patronage. These reforms, intended to check corruption, all weakened political parties. They gave parties, and their bosses, less control over elections and jobs.

Fifth Party System: Democratic Dominance

In the 1920s, the Republicans began to lose support in the cities. The party ignored the plight of poor immigrants and in Congress pushed through quotas limiting immigration from southern and eastern Europe. After the Depression hit in 1929, these immigrants, along with many women voting for the first time, joined traditional Democrats in the South to elect Franklin Roosevelt in 1932. This election reflected another party alignment.

The **New Deal coalition,** composed of city dwellers, blue-collar workers, Catholic and Jewish immigrants, blacks, and southerners, elected Roosevelt to an unprecedented four terms. The coalition was an odd alliance of northern liberals and southern conservatives. It stuck together in the 1930s and 1940s because of Roosevelt's personality and skill and because northerners did not seriously challenge southern racial policies.

But the coalition came unglued after Roosevelt's death. The Republicans, by nominating a popular war hero, General Dwight D. Eisenhower, won the presidency in 1952 and 1956. Although the Democrats regained the White House in 1960, the civil rights movement and the Vietnam War divided them sharply, and they lost again in 1968 and 1972.[9] They won in 1976 by nominating a southerner—Jimmy Carter—and because the Republicans suffered from the Watergate scandal. Even though the Democrats dominated Congress until 1994, they had much less success in winning the presidency. Democrats have won the White House only three times since 1964, suggesting that the fifth party system may have ended.

The Granger Collection, New York

In 1828, opponents of Andrew Jackson called him a jackass (left). Political cartoonists and journalists began to use the donkey to symbolize Jackson and the Democratic Party. In the 1870s, Thomas Nast popularized the donkey as a symbol of the party in his cartoons and originated the elephant as a symbol of the Republican Party. His 1874 cartoon (right) showed the Democratic donkey dressed as a lion frightening the other animals of the jungle, including the Republican elephant.

Has the Fifth Party System Realigned?

The fifth party system has changed, but has a major realignment occurred? Many of the signs that preceded major realignments of the party system have been present for some time. Even though **ticket splitting,** voting for a member of one party for one office but a member of another party for a different one, has declined during the 1990s, it is twice as common as it was in the 1950s (see Figure 3).[10] At the national level, the Republicans have occupied the White House and the Democrats have controlled Congress most of the time since 1968 (Figure 3).

Realigning periods also are characterized by compelling issues that fracture the unity of the major parties.[11] In the years before 1860, slavery was such an issue. It divided the Democrats and destroyed the Whigs. In 1932, economic issues led many Republicans away from their party to the Democrats. As memories of the Depression and influence of Depression-era economic issues fade, the potential exists for new issues to mobilize and realign voters.

The dominant Democratic coalition is less cohesive than in the heyday of the fifth party system. Blue-collar ethnics and Catholics have found the Democrats much less attractive.[12] As New Deal policies succeeded, blue-collar workers became much less concerned with economic security and turned their attention to other issues. Many were upset with the party's promotion of civil rights. Divisions in the party over the Vietnam War pushed many who were in favor of the war, particularly blue-collar union members, to the Republicans. Some objected to the Democratic Party's positions on social issues such as opposition to capital punishment, prayer in schools, and support for abortion and the rights of criminal defendants.

In the 1980s, economic concerns returned. Blue-collar workers found their standard of living eroding and felt left behind.[13] This did not move them back to their Democratic roots, however. They resented what they believed to be the Democrats' favoritism toward minorities and policies that seemed to free citizens from personal responsibility for their actions (for example, crime policies that some saw as "coddling criminals"). The big-city machines that once mobilized workers to vote Democratic are gone, and the labor unions, which did the same, are dramatically weakened.

On the other hand, some changes drove some voters to the Democratic Party. Northern white Protestants and white-collar workers are somewhat less Republican than they used to be. Many of them are employed by government and more sympathetic to government's role in solving societal problems. The Democrats also increasingly appeal to better-educated voters, who support Democratic initiatives such as health care reform, commitment to the environment, and abortion rights.[14]

In general, then, there has been some evidence of realignment focused on issues of government size and scope, with parties becoming more homogeneous.[15]

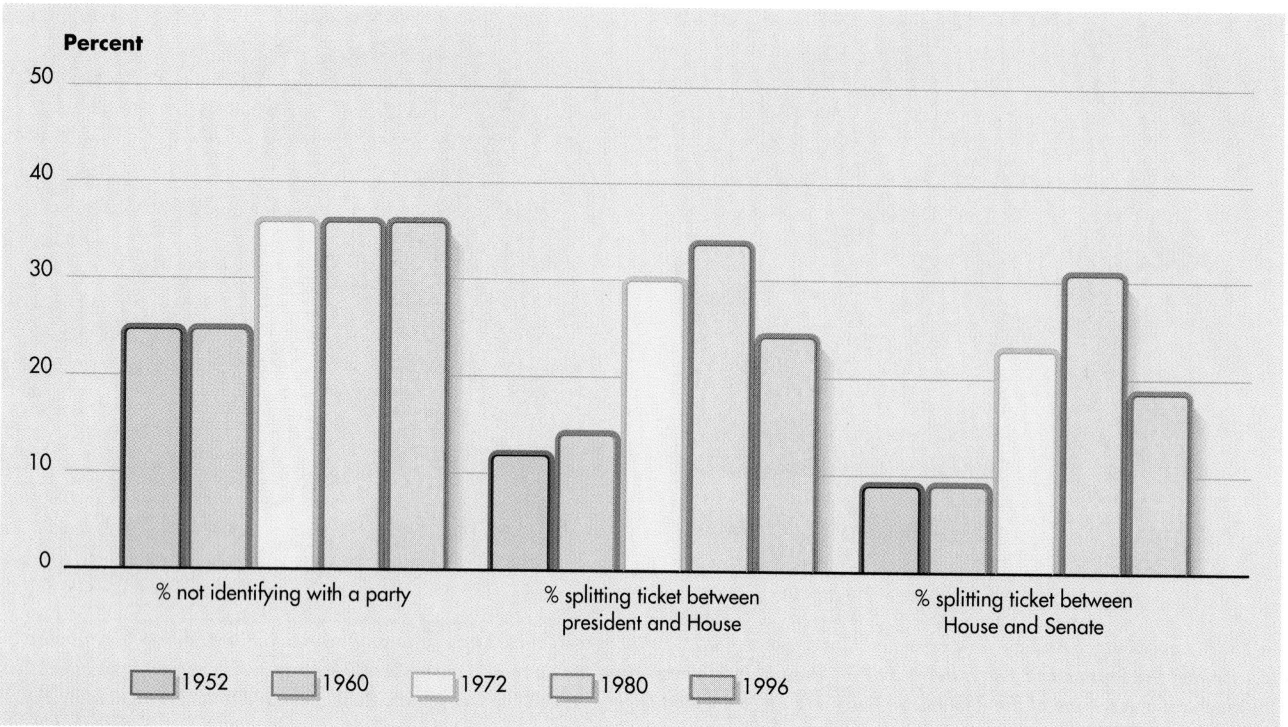

FIGURE 3

Is Partisanship Reemerging?

SOURCE: CPS National Election Studies.

Although only a modest realignment has occurred nationally, a regional one, confined to the South, has certainly occurred. Long a bastion of Democratic Party strength, the South began to drift away in the 1950s and showed major signs of change in 1964. For the first time in a century, the Republicans carried several southern states in the presidential election. Upset with the civil rights policies of the national Democratic Party, many white southerners voted for Barry Goldwater, the Republican nominee.

Since 1968 Republicans have carried the South in all presidential elections, except for Jimmy Carter's election in 1976. Even then, a majority of white southerners voted for Ford. Carter won the region on the strength of the black vote. Clinton carried his home state, Arkansas, and that of his running mate, Tennessee. He also picked up Louisiana and Georgia but, like Carter, lost the majority of white Southerners.

White southerners increasingly vote for Republicans in congressional races too. In 1994, 1996, and 1998, they cast the majority of their votes for Republicans. The shift has led a few Democratic members of Congress to change their party in an effort to take advantage of the changing loyalties of white southerners. For the first time since Reconstruction, a majority of governors, U.S. house members, and senators from the 11 southern states are Republican.[16]

The change in party identification among white southerners is the main reason that polls have shown a decline in Democratic loyalties nationwide. The shift of white southerners to the Republican Party not only makes the South more Republican, but it also makes the Republicans more conservative. The change also gives the party system a somewhat more ideological look. The southern Democrats who changed tend to be conservatives and are more ideologically compatible with policies of the Republican Party.

The race issue, which spurred this realignment, continues to play a role. Where white southerners in the 1950s and 1960s claimed "betrayal" by the national Democratic Party for its policies urging equality for blacks, they now say they object to its policies accepting affirmative action for minorities. The polarization between the races has sharpened the realignment. Defection of white southerners from the Democratic Party has left a southern Republican Party that is largely white and a Democratic Party that is largely black. Southern whites who are asked their party affiliation sometimes retort, "I'm white, aren't I?" meaning "I'm Republican."[17]

There also has been some **dealignment.**[18] More individuals have opted for independence as parties become less and less relevant. About one-third of all citizens do not choose to identify with a political party. Many voters who became eligible to vote for the first time during the 1980s and 1990s have not been attracted to either party, and some older voters lack firm attachments to their party. Many say that there is nothing that they like or dislike about parties. Similarly, the number who have something positive to say about one party and something negative to say about the other has declined; these trends suggest that parties are not as important to citizens as they were in the 1950s and 1960s.[19]

Candidates and the issues they choose to focus on have become more important. Citizen indifference to political parties and their decline in importance make it difficult for parties to link citizens to government and to enhance citizens' influence over government actions.

Dealignment also makes realignment less likely. Citizens who think parties are not important are unlikely to switch when their party fails to deal with the nation's problems. Nor are independents likely to be drawn to a political party in search of answers to national problems. Though some believe that the country is in the midst of a "rolling realignment," a movement of the nation to the right and the Republican Party in fits and starts since the early 1970s, the Democratic Party continues to be the party of choice for a plurality of Americans—a fact that is inconsistent with the idea of a rolling realignment.

THE PARTIES TODAY

Generally, each party is more ideologically homogenous than it used to be, with most Republicans considering themselves conservative. In fact, the Republican Party represents an uneasy coalition of traditional conservatives, motivated primarily by a desire to minimize government intervention in the economy, and new conservatives, motivated primarily by a desire to institutionalize their religious and moral values. Called the religious right, the new conservatives want to increase government intervention in such areas as abortion, prayers in school, and pornography. In many states, the religious right controls the Republican Party. Since the 1992 Republican National Convention, the right has avoided open confrontations with moderate Republicans, and national party leaders have stressed issues such as lower taxes and smaller government, on which both agree. With white born-again Christians 17% of the electorate, winning elections may depend on keeping more divisive issues such as abortion in the background.

Class differences are also apparent among conservatives. Many traditional conservatives are upper-middle and upper class, while many new conservatives are lower-middle class. The two factions were united in their hate for communism and their support for Reagan. But the disintegration of the Soviet Union and the Communist bloc and the departure of Reagan leave them with less in common.[20]

In spite of these differences, Republicans won control of Congress in 1994 for the first time in 40 years. They increased their strength in the states, controlling 26 state legislatures and electing 30 state governors. Some herald this as a long-awaited Republican realignment.

The Democrats are also divided. Some want to return to their liberal roots by appealing to working men and women and denouncing Republican support for big business and wealthy taxpayers. Others want the party to appeal to moderates who want lower taxes, less government, and more local control. A Clinton adviser says, "We can't define ourselves as the party of government."[21] The party is unlikely, however, to win back control of Congress unless it can appeal to both its liberal base and the moderate middle. The key is to offer solutions to or, at least, assistance in dealing with problems and real concerns of voters, namely stagnant incomes, job security, and family care. Even if the party runs on these issues, it may lose to a Republican Party that has raised more money, registered more voters, and recruited good candidates to challenge Democratic incumbents. In parts of the South, Democrats have been unable to recruit candidates to run under the party's label.

PAC contributions shifted sharply in favor of Republicans following the 1994 election. When the Democrats controlled Congress, nearly all PACs contributed more to Democrats than Republicans. Now PACs give more to Republicans.

Polls continue to show a slight advantage for the Democrats in the number of voters who identify with the party, but this support is strong only among older voters and minorities. Older voters have been shaped by the New Deal. A Democratic pollster quipped that "there are a lot of Democrats, the bad news is they will be dead by the next election."[22] Although the passage of the "motor voter" bill, which allows citizens to register to vote when they renew their driver's license, was expected to help Democrats, early analyses suggest it had little partisan effect.

The Democrats' strategy in 1996 was to convince voters that the Republican majority was out of step with mainstream Americans. At the presidential level, President Clinton defeated Robert Dole by co-opting traditional Republican positions that were popular, such as balancing the budget, and attacking Republican positions that were unpopular, such as rolling back environmental regulations.[23] Clinton rallied traditional Democrats and won solid support from independents. He was helped considerably by a very strong economy and a Dole campaign that failed to ignite much interest on the part of voters. However, Republicans retained control of Congress. Thus, the voters sent a status quo message.

In 1998, Republicans clung to their slim majority in Congress owing to incumbent advantage, superiority in raising campaign funds, and a reasonably satisfied electorate. However, even if they also capture the presidency, this would not necessarily signal a realignment and permanent Republican majority. It would be a reflection of continued volatility among voters as they respond to economic conditions and specific issues.

CHARACTERISTICS OF THE PARTY SYSTEM

The American party system is characterized by some intriguing and even unique qualities.

Two Parties

First, the American party system is a **two-party system.** Only two parties win seats in Congress, and only two parties compete effectively for the presidency. The development and perpetuation of two parties is rare among the nations of the world.

In western Europe, for example, **multiparty systems** are the rule. Italy has 9 national parties and several regional parties; Germany has 5. Great Britain, although predominantly a two-party system, now has at least 3 significant minor parties. Multiparty systems also are found in Canada, which has 3 parties, and Israel, which has more than 20.

Why do we have a two-party system? The most common explanation is the nature of our election system.[24] Public officials are elected from **single-member districts** under a **winner-take-all** arrangement. This means only one individual is elected from a district or state—the individual who receives the most votes. This contrasts with **proportional representation** where public officials are elected from multimember districts and the number of seats awarded to each party within each district is roughly equal to the percentage of the vote the party receives in the district. Thus, representation in the national legislature is approximately proportional to the popular vote each party receives nationwide.

In single-member district, winner-take-all systems, only the major parties have much chance of winning legislative seats. With little chance of winning office, minor parties tend to die or merge with one of the major parties. However, where seats are awarded in proportion to the vote, even a modest showing in the election—15% or less—may win a seat or two in the national assembly and provide a foundation upon which to build. Under such a scheme, a party, regardless of its electoral strength, has a presence in the legislature and someone to speak in support of its policy positions and issues.

While the election system influences the party system, the party system also influences the election system. Where only two parties exist, it is to their advantage to maintain an election system that undermines the development and growth of minor parties. For example, legislatures, controlled by the two parties, have tried to make it as difficult as possible for third parties to get on the ballot (though the courts have struck down many of these laws). Where several parties exist, it is to their advantage to establish an election system that benefits many parties.[25]

Fragmentation

The federal system, with its fragmentation of power between state and national levels, leads to fragmentation within parties. State and local parties have their own resources and power bases separate from those of the national parties.

Power also is fragmented at each level. At the national level, power is shared among the president and members of Congress. No one controls the party. Presidents often have a difficult time winning support for their policies among their party members in Congress. As parties have weakened, this problem has become more apparent. During the last year of President Bush's term, House Republicans supported him only 71% of the time, Senate Republicans 73%. In 1997 House Democrats supported President Clinton 71% of the time, Senate Democrats 85%. On a few major issues early in Clinton's term, congressional Democrats broke with him. For the North American Free Trade Agreement (NAFTA), two of the top three majority leaders in the House actually led the opposition and two of the top three majority leaders in the Senate joined the opposition. Three Democratic committee chairs and 17 subcommittee chairs in both the House and Senate joined with Republicans in defeating a Democratic-sponsored crime bill. To their dismay, these leaders later learned that the party's failure to pass legislation dealing with crime and other issues contributed to voters' disgust with the party and the Republican takeover in the 1994 elections.

These defections illustrate members' independence from their party. To be reelected, they need to satisfy only a plurality of the voters in their district or state, not the president. When Clinton considered a gas tax increase to reduce the deficit, Democratic Senator Herbert Kohl (Wisconsin) told him the increase would be no more than 4.3 cents per gallon. Clinton had to accept this figure because the bill's outcome was in doubt and the senator's vote was crucial. Kohl, a multimillionaire, paid for his initial election campaign

INTO THE 21ST CENTURY

THIRD PARTIES AND INDEPENDENT CANDIDATES

Will the twenty-first century see the development of a multiparty system in the United States?[1] During the twentieth century, only candidates of the major parties have won the presidency, even though candidates of minor parties contest every election. But recent evidence suggests that third-party candidates may have a better chance to win the presidency. Few Americans had heard of Ross Perot prior to his presidential run in 1992, yet he was able to get his name on the ballot in every state and to win a remarkable 19% of the popular vote. His willingness to use his personal fortune to fund his campaign, including buying large blocks of expensive television time, made him a highly visible alternative to his major party opposition.

Opportunities for independent and minor party candidates are better than in the past. Many Americans would like to see an alternative to the major parties. Over half of those polled in 1994 indicated that the United States needs a third major party,[2] and this proportion stayed constant even after Republicans took control of Congress in 1995.

Americans are less attached to the major parties than they used to be. Their antiparty feelings are unlikely to be as strong toward minority parties as toward the major ones. Those who claim to be above partisan politics, as did Perot, are attractive to many voters.

The current system also allows wealthy candidates to spend as much as they want on getting themselves elected, again opening the door to minor party and independent candidates. Perot would not have made much of an impact if he had not been able to buy hours of television time and other campaign support with his own money. Most Americans learned about Perot from his appearances on television or from viewing his "info-mercials," aired on time purchased with his own funds. In the twenty-first century, wealthy candidates who are willing to invest in their own campaigns are increasingly likely to surface.

But there are significant barriers to the emergence of new parties. Public support for the idea of a minor party is fickle. Interest in a new party declined in 1996, probably in response to satisfaction with a booming economy, a near balanced budget, other policy successes, and the perceived deficiencies of Perot as a candidate.

But even when times seem right for a new party, there are other barriers. Some are structural, such as state laws that make it difficult for minor party and independent candidates to get on the ballot and federal laws that make it difficult to secure public funding for campaigning.

There are also psychological barriers. Many voters are reluctant to cast a vote for a third-party or independent candidate, believing that there is little chance such a candidate can win. Nearly one-third of those who expressed a first preference for Ross Perot in 1992 voted for one of the major party candidates.[3] Many did so because they felt Perot could not win. Often the major parties will use the "wasted vote" argument against a third-party or independent candidate, as they did in 1992 and 1996. And even though partisanship has weakened, minor party and independent candidates face the long-standing major party loyalties of most Americans.

There are also practical barriers to third-party and independent candidates winning public office in the United States. First, it is difficult to raise money. Voters are reluctant to vote for a candidate who cannot win, and they are also reluctant to contribute money to one. Second, third parties and independent candidates are rarely taken seriously by the media and thus receive less coverage than the major party candidates. This fuels a perception that they are less legitimate and less worthy of voter and financial support. Third, it is difficult for third parties to recruit qualified and experienced candidates. Most elected politicians are either Republicans or Democrats and recognize that they are most likely to succeed in winning national office if they run as a major party candidate. Fourth, should a third-party or independent candidate have a marketable idea, one that is attractive to voters, the major parties will soon co-opt it and present it as their own, eliminating the need for an alternative to the major parties. Perot's strong position on the need to eliminate the budget deficit in the 1992 campaign was at least partially responsible for the major parties' renewed efforts to deal with the problem in the 1996 campaign. Finally, third parties and independent candidates have done well only in elections when the nation has faced significant social and economic problems, and the major parties failed to respond.

Despite these barriers, as we enter the twenty-first century, the antiparty public sentiment and a campaign finance system that allows candidates to spend unlimited amounts of their own money provide significant opportunities for the emergence of minor parties. Whether the right candidate will come along at the right time to capitalize on these opportunities is something beyond our powers of prediction.

1. The problems faced by third parties is discussed in Steven Rosenstone, Roy Behr, and Edward Lazarus, *Third Parties in America* (Princeton, N.J.: Princeton University Press, 1984).

2. Times Mirror Center for the People and the Press, as reprinted in the *New York Times* (September 21, 1994): A21.

3. Paul Abramson et al., "Third Party and Independent Candidates in American Politics: Wallace, Anderson, and Perot," *Political Science Quarterly* 110, 3 (Fall, 1995).

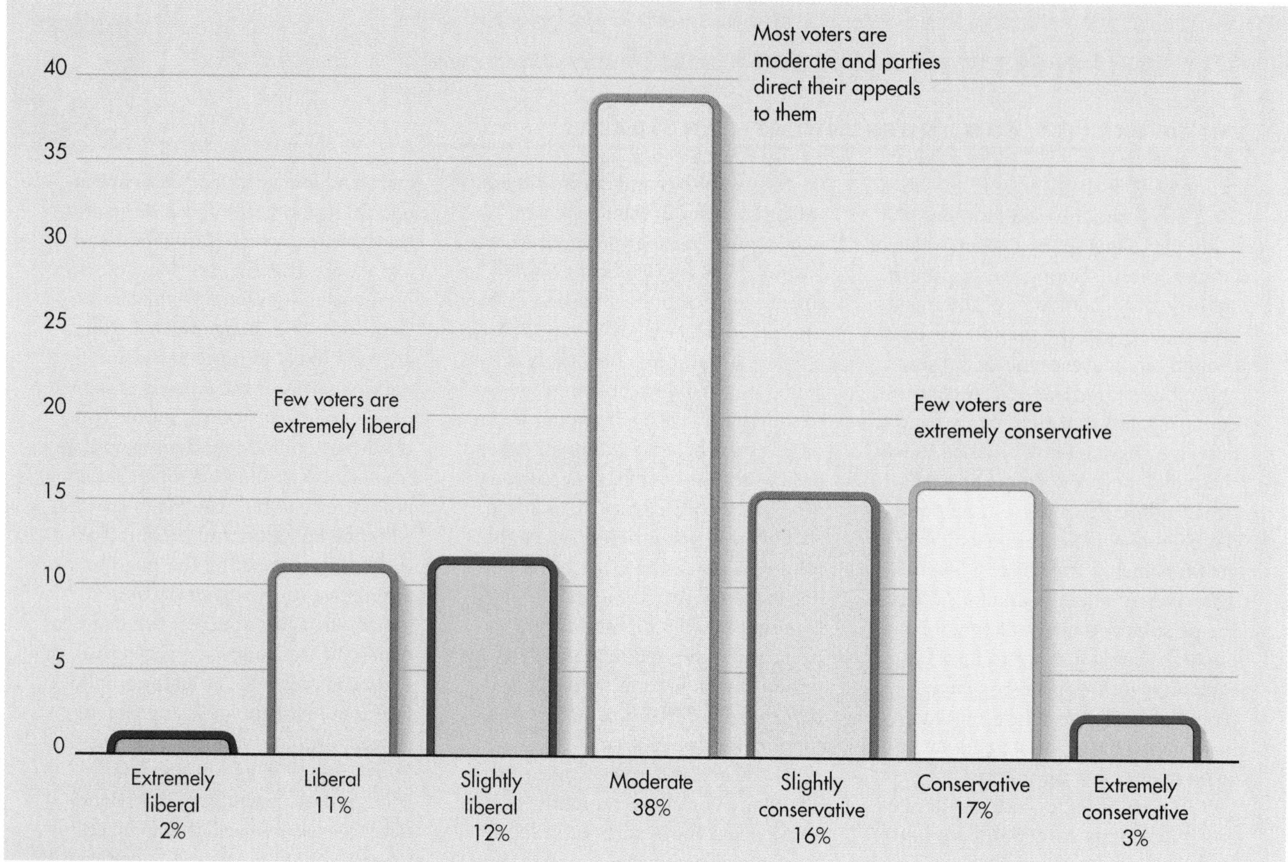

FIGURE 4

Parties Aim Their Campaigns to the Middle, Where the Voters Are

SOURCE: Data from 1996 General Social Survey, National Opinion Research Center. The labels (such as "liberal") were self-descriptions.

and could pay for a reelection bid, so he felt no obligation to his party. Such independence makes it difficult to forge a unified party.

Moderation

American political parties are moderate; there are no extremely liberal or extremely conservative major parties. One reason for this is that the people themselves are moderate (see Figure 4). To attract the most voters, the parties try to appear moderate.

Because parties try to attract many voters, both have liberals as well as conservatives, though the Democratic Party has more liberals and fewer conservatives than the Republican Party. This combination prompts parties to moderate their appeals and nominate moderate candidates. When liberal or conservative candidates do get nominated, they usually move toward the middle on some issues or at least portray themselves as moderate. Reagan, when running for reelection, embraced a conciliatory stance toward the Soviet Union in contrast to his earlier "evil empire" posture. Bill Clinton became a "new kind" of Democrat. The implication is that, unlike those in the past who catered to minorities and special interests, he would deal with the problems of middle America.

Minor Parties in American Politics

Sometimes called "third parties," minor parties are as varied as the causes they represent. Some are one-issue parties, like the American Know-Nothing Party (1856), which ran on a platform opposing immigrants and Catholics, and the Prohibition Party (1869 to the present), which campaigns to ban the sale of liquor.

Other parties advocate radical change in the American political system. Economic protest parties, such as the Populist Party of 1892, sometimes appear when economic conditions are especially bad and disappear when times improve. Since the 1920s, the Communist Party has espoused the adoption of a communist system.

Some parties are simply candidates who failed to receive their party's nomination and decided to go it alone. In 1968, Alabama Governor George Wallace split from the Democratic Party to run for president as the candidate of the conservative American Independent Party. Failing to get the Republican nomination, John Anderson launched a third-party campaign in 1980. Though both Wallace and Anderson had significant public support, neither won a large number of votes nor had much influence on the election outcome.

Ross Perot's third-party candidacy in 1992 had no association with either party. He simply decided to run. Although he polled 19% of the vote, his candidacy did not influence the election's outcome.

Minor parties face many obstacles in trying to establish themselves. Because a sizable portion of the electorate is firmly attached to the existing parties, minor party candidates find it difficult to attract voter support and money and to develop lasting state and local organizations. Even voters who favor the ideas or minor party candidates will not vote for them because in a close race between the major party candidates, a vote for a minor party is seen as a "wasted" vote. Such a vote may even be counterproductive, taking away votes from a voter's second choice and perhaps contributing to, the least preferred candidate winning the election. Most third-party movements die after their candidate's defeat. Perot was able to overcome some of these problems by drawing on his personal fortune. His "United We Stand America" movement from his campaign in 1992 became the Reform Party in 1996 and served as the organizational base for his run for the presidency in 1996. However, he won only 7% of the vote.

PARTY IN THE ELECTORATE

Earlier we identified three distinct but interrelated aspects of political parties: the party in the electorate, the party in government, and the party organization (Figure 1, p. 137). We can now examine each.

The party in the electorate—those individuals who identify with a political party—are a party's grassroots supporters. **Party identification** is a psychological link between individuals and a party; no formal or organization membership is necessary. In contrast, European parties do have members; members pay dues and sign a pledge that they accept the basic principles of the party. The percentage of voters who are members ranges from 1 or 2% in some countries to over 40% in others.

Party Identification

A majority of Americans identify with a political party (see Table 1). In 1996, 39% said they were Democrats, 28% Republicans, and 34% independent.

TABLE 1

Party Identification, 1960–1996

AFFILIATION	1960	1972	1980	1996
Strong Democrat	21	15	18	19
Weak Democrat	25	25	23	20
Independent Democrat*	8	11	11	14
Independent	8	13	13	9
Independent Republican*	7	11	10	11
Weak Republican	13	13	14	15
Strong Republican	14	10	9	13
Apolitical, do not know	4	2	2	1

*Independents who lean toward the Democrats or Republicans.

SOURCE: University of Michigan Survey Research Center CPS/NES.

In Chapter 4, we discussed how political socialization leads to party identification early in childhood. While this is true, party identification can change and often does as a person's life situation changes, such as moving to a new job or community, or in response to changes in issue positions that conflict with one's party. As we have seen, for example, the national Democratic Party's increased support for civil rights and other liberal policies caused many white southerners to leave the party.

Characteristics of Democrats and Republicans

Although people from all walks of life are found in each party, there are differences in the social composition of the parties. Republicans are somewhat younger than Democrats and those calling themselves independent (see Table 2). Republicans are somewhat better educated than Democrats, but independents have the highest percentage of college graduates. Women are better represented among the ranks of Democrats as are blacks. While the media typically point out the activities of religious fundamentalists in the Republican Party, an equal percentage of Democrats and Republicans claim to be fundamentalists. Religious fundamentalists are an even larger proportion of independents.

There is little difference in the occupational breakdown of the party followings. Again the biggest difference is between partisans and independents. Republicans have a larger percentage than Democrats of those earning over $50,000 or more, and fewer of those earning $20,000 or less. Independents fall in between

THE ELECTORATE OF THE 1990s

We have discussed the divisions within each of the two major parties. One survey organization has tried to describe these divisions more specifically by focusing on what different subgroups of the voting population really want. Though these sketches are necessarily to some extent superficial and time-bound, they do capture some of the complexity of the voting public.

Largely Republican

- *Enterprisers:* 12% of registered voters, 74% Republican. Antigovernment, antiwelfare, probusiness. Largely male, white, middle-aged, affluent, and college-educated. Key issue: Opposed to health care reform. Heroes: Ronald Reagan, Colin Powell, and Rush Limbaugh. Villains: Bill and Hillary Clinton, Ted Kennedy, and gay rights activists.
- *Moralists:* 20% of registered voters, 65% Republican. Antigovernment, antiwelfare, and anti–big business. Religious and socially intolerant. White, middle-aged, average income and education. Key issues: Support for prayer in school and harsher sentences for criminals. Heroes: Ronald Reagan and Colin Powell. Villains: Gay rights activists.
- *Libertarians:* 4% of registered voters, 54% Republican. Antigovernment, anti–social welfare, and probusiness. Tolerant but not religious. Male, white, highly educated, and affluent. Key issues: Cutting taxes and welfare. Hero: Colin Powell. Villains: Ted Kennedy, Louis Farrakhan, Jerry Falwell.

Largely Independent

- *New Economy Independents:* 19% of registered voters, 52% independent (27% Democrat). Strong environmentalists, but oppose government regulation. Pro–social welfare, but not sympathetic to blacks. Female, young and middle-aged, white-collar professionals and service workers, average income; 40% are working women. Key issues: Support for health care reform, stricter gun control, government spending for job training, and gay rights. No heroes. Villain: Jerry Falwell.
- *Bystanders:* None of the registered voters, but 8% of the population, 52% independent. Environmentalist. Young, female, less education and income. Key issues: none. Heroes: none. Villains: Tobacco companies.
- *Embittered:* 7% of registered voters, 39% independent, 36% Democrat; 25% African American. Antigovernment, antipolitician, and antibusiness. Religious and socially intolerant. Believe discrimination is barrier to black progress. Low skill, low income. Support school prayer and oppose government-funded abortions. Hero: John Kennedy. Villains: Insurance companies, MTV, Rush Limbaugh.

Largely Democrat

- *Seculars:* 10% of registered voters, 46% Democrat (31% independent who lean Democrat). Somewhat progovernment. Anticorporations. Strong commitment to environment. Tolerant. White, relatively young, highly educated, and affluent. Favor government funding for abortion, gun control, and gay rights. Oppose school prayer. Hero: Hillary Clinton. Villains: Rush Limbaugh, Jerry Falwell, Oliver North, Louis Farrakhan, tobacco companies.
- *New Democrats:* 8% registered voters, 62% Democrat, but most voted for Bush in 1988. Progovernment, proenvironment, more probusiness than other Democratic groups. Religious but not intolerant. Female, average income and education, high proportion of minorities, employed in social service and educational occupations. Key issues: Support for health care reform and job training. Heroes: Hillary Clinton and Colin Powell. Villain: Rush Limbaugh.
- *New Dealers:* 8% registered voters, 82% Democrat. Faith in government, but distrust politicians and big business. Conservative on race and social welfare programs. Strongly religious, moderately tolerant. Oldest group: one-third over 65. Labor unions, low income, no college. Oppose government-funded abortions and support prayer in schools, health care reform, and use of military force. Heroes: Franklin Roosevelt, John Kennedy, Jimmy Carter, Al Gore. Villain: Jerry Falwell.
- *Partisan Poor:* 8% registered voters, 89% Democrat. Progovernment, anti–big business; 41% nonwhite, blue collar, very poor. Favor government spending to help poor, job training, health care reform, and school prayer. Heroes: John Kennedy, Jimmy Carter, Bill and Hillary Clinton. Villain: Rush Limbaugh.

SOURCE: *The New Political Landscape.* Times Mirror Center for the People and the Press, October 1994.

the two, with less income than Democrats but more than Republicans. Conservatives clearly dominate in the Republican Party, with liberals most numerous in the Democratic Party. Here also, independents fall between the two party groups, having more liberals than the Republican Party but less than the Democrats, and more conservatives than the Democrats but fewer than the Republicans.

PARTY IN GOVERNMENT

Nationally, the party in government is the party's elected members of Congress and, for the party that occupies the White House, the president. The party in government links the party in the electorate to their government. The job of the

TABLE 2

Characteristics of Republicans, Democrats, and Independents

	REPUBLICAN	DEMOCRAT	INDEPENDENT
TOTAL	28%	42%	30%
Age 18–25	12	7	7
26–50	56	51	52
51–65	17	20	21
Over 65	15	22	20
Less than high school education	18	20	9
High school graduate	36	42	35
Some college education	13	11	11
College graduate	34	27	46
Men	49	38	51
Women	51	62	49
White	86	77	96
Black	12	21	2
Native American	1	1	1
Asian	1	1	1
Protestant fundamentalist	35	34	47
Protestant mainstream	30	29	28
Catholic	30	32	24
Jewish	3	3	1
Other	1	2	0
Professional and business	39	42	48
Other white collar	15	13	20
Blue collar	46	44	32
Under $20,000	42	55	47
$20,000 to $50,000	39	36	39
Over $50,000	19	8	14
Conservative	77	22	39
Moderate	18	32	40
Liberal	5	47	22

SOURCE: CPS/NES 1996.

party in government is to enact policies that party voters favor. This seems like a simple idea, but political scientists have waged great debates over how close the link between the party in government and the party in the electorate should be.

Proponents of **responsible party government** believe that political parties should take clear and contrasting positions on political issues and require their elected members to support the party's positions. "Responsible" party government is responsible in that

- voters have a choice among parties advocating different positions;
- elected members of the party support and vote for their party's position; and
- the party with a majority in the legislature enacts its position into law.

Given these conditions, voting for one party rather than another has definite policy consequences. It increases the prospects for popular control of government because a voter knows exactly what a vote for one party means for public policy. For example, in a responsible party system, if the Republican Party's position is pro-life and the Democratic Party's position is pro-choice, a vote for a Republican candidate will mean a pro-life position. Should the Republicans win a majority, a pro-life position would be enacted into law.

Great Britain is an example of responsible party government. Political parties are heavily involved in developing, articulating, and implementing public policy. If elected party members defect too often from the party's position, party leaders can deny them the right to stand for reelection as the party's candidates.

American political parties are not as responsible in this way. They do not always offer clear and contrasting policy positions. When they do, party leaders have only limited authority to force their elected members to accept the party's position.

Although the United States is not a responsible party government, it has some elements of party responsibility. The party links presidents with the members of their party in Congress. Members of the president's party in Congress support his policies substantially more often than members of the opposition. Parties also have important organizational and leadership functions in Congress.

Party influence is also visible in congressional voting[26] and increased dramatically during the 1980s. This reflects the realignment of the South. In the days before blacks were allowed to vote and before the Republicans offered real challenges in most southern districts, the vast majority of southern members of Congress were white conservative Democrats who voted with the Republicans almost as often as with their own party.[27] As white conservatives have moved into the Republican Party, districts with conservative white majorities are much more likely to elect Republicans rather than conservative Democrats. Districts with large numbers of black voters are more likely than before to elect blacks or moderate or liberal white Democrats. Thus, voting patterns of representatives from the South now divide along party lines as they do in the North.[28]

Republican control of both houses of Congress has increased the level of party unity. A number of conservative Republicans, committed to a very conservative agenda, were elected in 1994. Eager to

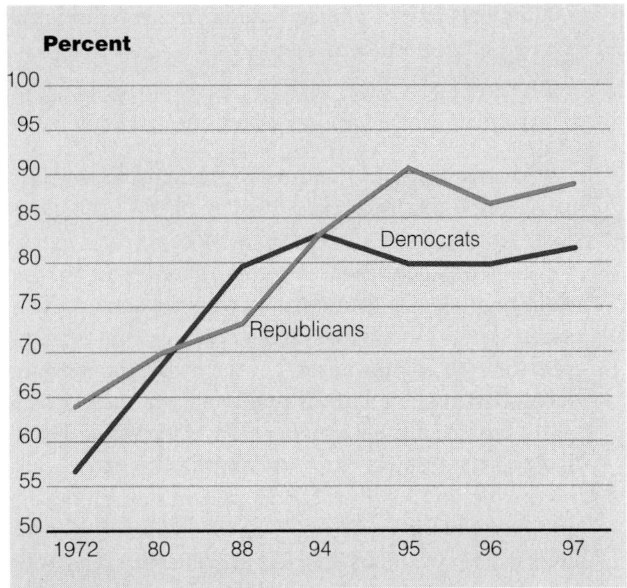

FIGURE 5

Party Unity Increased in the 1980s and Has Remained High

The average percentage of times that Democrats and Republicans in Congress voted with their party on votes where a majority of Democrats opposed a majority of Republicans

SOURCE: *Congressional Quarterly Weekly Report.*

retain control of Congress, moderate incumbent Republicans supported the program to show voters that the party could enact legislation and govern effectively.[29] Moderate Democrats, on the other hand, did not support the GOP's agenda so division between the parties reached record highs. On 69% of the votes in the Senate and 73% of the votes in the House, a majority of Republicans opposed a majority of Democrats. On these votes, both Republicans and Democrats supported their own party, on average, 80 to 90% of the time (see Figure 5). Party voting rivaled the British Parliament, our example of responsible party government.

Party unity remained high in 1996 and 1997 and is likely to continue to be high through the presidential election in 2000 and beyond. Each party has a distinct vision of the best public policies and believes it can win public support for those policies.

To achieve higher levels of party unity in the United States would require major changes in government. Party leaders would have to be given more power to maintain party discipline in Congress. The president and congressional majority would have to have common party ties. This could be accomplished on a continuing basis only through a constitutional change providing for a parliamentary system similar to Britain's, in which Congress would elect the president. Such a change is highly unlikely.

PARTY ORGANIZATION

The party organization is the third component of the political party. The major levels of party organization—national, state, and local—coincide with political units responsible for administering elections. Within the local parties there are further subdivisions. The smallest unit is usually the precinct-level organization. Several precincts comprise a ward or district; several wards comprise the city or county organization.

Although party organization seems hierarchical (organized from the top down), it is not. Party organization is a layered structure with each layer linked to, but independent of, the others. Higher levels cannot dictate to or impose penalties on lower levels to ensure compliance.

Party organization is only loosely connected with the party in government. This contrasts with the British system, in which the party leaders in Parliament try to maintain a tight grip on the party organization.

National Party Organization

The **national party chair** heads the national party organization, called the national committee (discussed below). The president appoints the chair of his party; for the party not occupying the White House, the national committee selects the chair. The national chairs are not very visible to the public. They do not receive much media attention, and their names are unknown to most. Haley Barbour, chair of the Republican National Committee from 1993 to 1998, was an exception. He was a frequent guest on TV talk shows and, before 1994, was the party's leading spokesman and constant critic of Bill Clinton. Barbour was also responsible for GOP-TV, the Republican National Committee's television network. This network, available via satellite, cable systems, the Internet, and TV stations nationwide, provides information on party activities, issues, and personalities. Barbour was also an effective fundraiser, wiping out the party's $4 million debt and raising $158 million with the aid of state parties in 1996.[30] Following his resignation in 1998, Barbour was implicated in a campaign funding scandal when information surfaced that he sought and accepted illegal contributions from foreign interests to fund a tax-exempt think tank used to develop Republican positions on issues. Barbour's counterpart in the Democratic Party, Donald Fowler, who shared the position with Senator Chris Dodd of Connecticut, was much less visible, as is often the case with the president's party. Like Barbour, Fowler was impli-

© 1983 The Washington Post Co
AUTH © SZEP
BECAUSE WE'VE ALWAYS REGISTERED REPUBLICAN, THAT'S WHY !
6/4

cated in campaign funding scandals in 1996 and resigned his position in 1998.

While the **national committees** are the primary governing institutions of the Democratic and Republican Parties, they seldom meet, and it is the national chair and the permanent staff who are the de facto national party organization. The national committees do choose the site of their party's national convention and establish the formula for determining how many delegates each state receives.

National committee members are selected from each state using a variety of methods established by each state party. While states are represented equally on the Republican National Committee (RNC), the Democratic National Committee (DNC) awards states additional seats based on population and support for Democratic candidates in elections. The DNC also includes the party's leaders in Congress, the leaders of several state and local Democratic organizations, and representatives from elements of the party that are often underrepresented on the committee including blacks, Hispanics, and youth.

Both major parties also have **House and Senate campaign committees,** which have grown in influence owing to their ability to raise and distribute campaign funds to their party's candidates for Congress.[31] The National Republican Senatorial Committee raised $25 million in 1997, the National Republican Congressional Committee $20 million. The Democratic Senatorial and Congressional Campaign Committees raised $12 million and $10 million, respectively. Most of the money was used to fund House and Senate candidates in the 1998 elections.

Described as hollow shells in the 1950s and 1960s, the national party organizations are stronger today than they have been since the early twentieth century. Behind their success is a steady flow of cash from large contributors that is used to assist candidates running for office and strengthen state and local party organizations. As we will see in Chapter 9, the parties can accept huge contributions from corporations, interest groups, and unions that individual candidates and campaigns cannot accept. The Republican Party has led the way in fundraising, but Democrats are not far behind. Both parties actively recruit candidates to run for office, train them in various campaign technologies, and provide funds to mount an effective campaign. The RNC recently launched its Nuts and Bolts seminars that are held throughout the country to provide training in fundraising, developing a campaign strategy, using media, speech writing, polling, and getting out the vote. The party also has an array of how-to manuals for candidates and state and local party organizers. Both parties have facilities to produce their own radio and television ads.

The increasing capacity of the national party organizations to offer candidates assistance in their campaigns may contribute to the rising level of party voting in Congress. Members of Congress no doubt do feel beholden to the national party and perhaps a commitment to support party positions. At the same time, members are less beholden to state and local parties. Thus, national party organizations are growing in influence at the expense of state and local parties.[32] Today, the close link between the national party organizations and the parties in Congress moves us closer to the responsible party government model.

State and Local Party Organizations

Each state and local party has a chair and committee to direct the activities of their party activists. In some communities, parties may be so weak and unimportant that there is little party organization. Because of this, someone who wants to become active in the party organization only has to show up at party meetings and be willing to work.

Big-City Party Organizations

Unlike most local party organizations today, the **political machine,** which flourished in some of the nation's largest cities in the late nineteenth and early twentieth centuries, was strong and powerful. At the head of the machine was a boss, who often served as mayor and directed operations in such a way as to maintain control over the city and the organization.

The machine relied on the votes of the poor and working class, many of whom had only recently immigrated from Europe. Most accounts of machine politics are negative, dwelling on graft and corruption.

A DAY IN THE LIFE OF A MACHINE POLITICIAN

George Washington Plunkitt was a ward leader in the infamous Tammany Hall machine, the Democratic Party organization that governed New York City for seven decades in the late nineteenth and early twentieth centuries. Although Plunkitt was on the city payroll, he did not have a free ride. The demands of his job were exhausting. Yet by providing needed services to his constituents he had many opportunities to build support for the party. Now government provides many of these services, thus making parties less vital. Entries from Plunkitt's diary illustrate the pervasive role of the party:

Newsweek/Wally McNamee

George Washington Plunkit holds forth in his unofficial office, a bootblack stand at the New York County Court House.

2:00 A.M. Aroused from sleep by a bartender who asked me to go to the police station and bail out a saloon keeper who had been arrested for violating the excise law. Furnished bail and returned to bed at three o'clock.

6:00 A.M. Awakened by fire engines. Hastened to the scene of the fire . . . found several tenants who had been burned out, took them to a hotel, supplied them with clothes, fed them, and arranged temporary quarters for them.

8:30 A.M. Went to the police court to secure the discharge of six "drunks," my constituents, by a timely word to the judge. Paid the fines of two.

9:00 A.M. Appeared in the municipal district court to direct one of my district captains to act as counsel for a widow about to be dispossessed. . . . Paid the rent of a poor family and gave them a dollar for food.

11:00 A.M. At home again. "Fixed" the troubles of four men waiting for me: one discharged by the Metropolitan Railway for neglect of duty; another wanted a job on the road; the third on the subway; and the fourth was looking for work with a gas company.

3:00 P.M. Attended the funeral of an Italian. Hurried back for the funeral of a Hebrew constituent. Went conspicuously to the front both in the Catholic church and the synagogue.

7:00 P.M. Went to district headquarters to preside over a meeting of election district captains, submitted lists of all the voters in their districts and told who were in need, who were in trouble, who might be won over [to Tammany] and how.

8:00 P.M. Went to a church fair. Took chances on everything, bought ice cream for the young girls and the children, kissed the little ones, flattered their mothers, and took the fathers out for something down at the corner.

9:00 P.M. At the clubhouse again. Spent $10 for a church excursion. Bought tickets for a baseball game. Listened to the complaints of a dozen pushcart peddlers who said they were being persecuted by the police. Promised to go to police headquarters in the morning and see about it.

10:30 P.M. Attended a Hebrew wedding reception and dance. Had previously sent a handsome wedding present to the bride.

12:00 P.M. In bed.

SOURCE: Alistair Cooke, *Alistair Cooke's America* (New York: Alfred A. Knopf, 1973), pp. 290–291; adapted from William L. Riordon, *Plunkitt of Tammany Hall* (New York: E. P. Dutton, 1963), pp. 91–93.

However, the machine provided a number of valuable services. In a period when there were no welfare agencies, the machine provided jobs, food, and fuel for the thousands of immigrants who had no place else to turn. In return, party leaders expected individuals to vote for machine candidates.

Business also benefited from machines. The machine provided (for a fee) permits for business expansion, licenses, new roads, utilities, and police and fire protection.

The key to the machine's success was **patronage,** that is, giving jobs to party loyalists when the party controlled local government. An army of city employees, whose jobs depended on the political success of the machine, would dutifully bring family and friends to the polls on election day. One of the last of the big-city bosses, Mayor Richard Daley, head of the Chicago machine during the 1960s and 1970s, controlled 35,000 public jobs and, indirectly through public contracts, 10,000 private ones.[33]

Reformers disturbed by corruption and by lower-class control of city politics eventually passed laws making it difficult for machines to operate. Merit examinations for city jobs, nonpartisan elections, secret ballots, and voter registration undercut the means that machines had to secure voter loyalty. Political machines were dealt another blow when the federal government assumed responsibility for welfare needs in the 1930s; individuals no longer had to rely on the machine. And with a more educated population and greater employment opportunities, patronage jobs were no longer as desirable.

THE NOMINATING PROCESS

The major function of political parties is to nominate and elect candidates to office. Often many candidates of one party want to run for the same office. Parties have devised three ways—caucuses, conventions, and primaries—to choose among these contenders.

Caucuses

A **caucus** is a meeting. In the early eighteenth century, party candidates were nominated by a small number of party leaders and officeholders in a caucus. It was criticized by many because so few people actually participated.

Conventions

By 1830, the increased number of voters in elections and the desire of parties to win their continued support led to new procedures to involve more voters in nominations. Caucuses of local residents selected delegates to attend county, state, and national conventions. These conventions then nominated candidates for public office.

Party conventions usually were controlled by party leaders who decided what happened and who was nominated. The leaders often made decisions behind the scenes in "smoke-filled rooms."

Primaries

In the early 1900s Progressive reformers argued that nominating conventions ignored the rank-and-file voter. Because they believed that party leaders in their "smoke-filled rooms" were corrupt and not to be trusted, reformers established the **direct primary** to increase citizen participation and check the influence of party bosses in nominations. The primary allows the voters in an election to choose the party's candidates. Today all states use primary elections, sometimes in conjunction with caucuses and conventions, to nominate candidates.

Primaries vary from state to state according to who is eligible to vote in them. A **closed primary** limits participation to those who are registered with a party or declare a preference for a party. Thus, only Democrats can vote in the Democratic Party's primary. An **open primary** imposes no such limits; regardless of party registration, one may vote in either party's primary.

Party leaders and others favoring strong parties oppose open primaries. They argue that only voters who are party supporters should be permitted to vote in the party's primary. They fear that independents and opposition partisans will vote for candidates who are less sympathetic to the party's position on issues or who are less likely to win.

A minority of states use runoff primaries, which pit the two highest vote-getters in the primary against each other for the party's nomination. Over the years, the inability of the Republican Party to compete effectively for office in the South meant that the winner of the Democratic Party's primary was virtually assured of winning the general election. Due to the large number of Democratic candidates, sometimes the winner of the primary did not have a majority of the vote. In those cases, some southern states used a runoff election between the two highest vote-getters in the primary.

Although primaries have increased citizen participation in nominations, turnout in primaries is quite low and unrepresentative. Turnout in presidential primaries averages at best 10%. While it is higher for primaries held early in the year, such as New Hampshire's, which is always first, for those that come later turnout is very low. Voters in primaries are unrepresentative of the public at large. Primary voters tend to have higher incomes and education and to be older, more interested in politics, and more partisan.[34]

Primaries also hurt the party organization and undermine the party in government. Candidates can bypass party leaders and appeal directly to voters. Candidates who oppose the party's issue positions can run and win the party's nomination, especially in elections in which voters do not know much about the candidates.

CONCLUSION: DO POLITICAL PARTIES MAKE GOVERNMENT MORE RESPONSIVE?

Although the Founders initially opposed the idea of political parties, some later turned to parties when they began to have serious differences of opinion about public policies. They recognized that their ideas could prevail if they aligned with others who agreed with them and together elected a majority in government. Then, as now, parties were a vehicle to organize a stable majority. For Jefferson and Madison, the important issue was the scope and power of national government. Jefferson's views prevailed, but only with the aid of the party he created.

While organizing a political party was a way for Jefferson, one of America's most influential leaders, to shape government, parties are also a way for average Americans to make government more responsive to them. Making government more accountable is the major contribution of political parties to democratic government. Democracy without political parties is difficult, and probably impossible, because there is no viable alternative to parties as a means of organizing a

WHY NOT RETURN TO THE "SMOKE-FILLED ROOMS"?

In addition to attracting a small and unrepresentative group of voters to the ballot box, primaries have other flaws. In some ways, the primary process is less responsive to voters than party conventions, where candidates were once selected by a small group of party leaders meeting in smoke-filled hotel rooms.

Primaries do not necessarily provide voters with much choice. Many primaries are uncontested. Often the presence of an incumbent deters challengers, or at least strong challengers. In either case, incumbents are generally renominated.

Primaries also may make the general election less competitive. The minority party (that is, the party less likely to win the general election) often has no strong candidate who can mount an effective campaign in the general election. In preprimary days, party leaders generally made sure there were some candidates running in the general election regardless of election prospects.

Another problem with primaries is that the electorate may nominate a candidate known by his or her party peers to be incompetent, difficult to work with, or lacking in character and integrity. Although the convention system does not guarantee that such candidates will be avoided, party leaders are more likely to know the real strengths and weaknesses of potential candidates than are voters, who must rely on the media for information. Indeed, voters have so little information about primary candidates that success often turns on name recognition.

Primaries hurt the most, however, by freeing candidates from supporting the party's program. It is nearly impossible for party leaders to withhold nominations from candidates who are party members in name only or who often vote with the other party. Thus, the party bonds are weakened and members can feel free to vote and act however they want.

This might seem desirable. But when candidates vote completely independent of their party, it is more difficult for voters to cast an informed vote. When parties offer a clear choice, voters know what they are voting for and can reward or punish the parties for what they do or plan to do in office. Thus, party voting can make government more responsive to the voters.

Some commentators have advocated returning to convention nominations. If we did so, the abuses that we associate with the smoke-filled rooms of a century ago would be less likely to occur today because of the greater likelihood of exposure by the media and hostile voter reaction. In states and localities where the parties are competitive, it is likely that conventions would produce strong candidates. This would give voters a real choice in the general election. However, in locales dominated by one party, the convention system would not necessarily produce stronger candidates than a primary. At the presidential level, smoke-filled rooms produced the likes of Franklin Roosevelt and John Kennedy. Perhaps the greatest argument for smoke-filled rooms is Harry Truman. Although a product of machine politics, Truman was honest and incorruptible. Tapped to be FDR's vice president in 1944 by party bosses who knew Roosevelt would not live out his term, Truman became an excellent president.

Why haven't we returned to the convention system? Primaries are widely accepted. They *seem* more democratic because more people are involved than in conventions, where only party activists participate. But the sheer number of people involved is only one aspect of democracy and probably not the most important. Democracy also implies that those making the nominations are representative of the public; primary electorates are not. Moreover, a democratic process must offer some choice, and primaries adversely affect competition.

Although it is unlikely that we will abolish primaries and return to conventions, in recent years party leaders have asserted more control in some states through preprimary endorsements. Parties endorse candidates for nomination. The endorsed candidates are listed first on the primary ballot or are simply publicized as the "official" party candidate. Although on occasion the preferred candidate is defeated, the voters usually go along with the party's choice. Such arrangements promote party strength and ultimately responsiveness to voters.

stable governing majority and making it accountable to the people.

Although in practice parties do not live up to this idea (what human institution does?), and there are certainly changes we might consider to make parties more responsible and responsive, Americans should be interested in strengthening parties. Without political parties that link candidates and voters on issues, voters are confronted with a hopelessly confusing array of candidates and have little idea of how a vote for any one of them will affect government. Without parties, the media, campaign consultants, lobbying groups, big donors, and self-financed wealthy candidates would play an even larger role in politics than they do now.

There is no doubt that parties are weaker than they were a century ago. But in the 1990s, parties are experiencing a resurgence in several key ways. In terms of the party in the electorate, the erosion of party strength has stopped. The proportion of voters disclaiming partisan allegiance has shrunk slightly after steady growth since the 1960s. Split-ticket voting has decreased rather dramatically in the last decade (see Figure 3).

The party in government is also stronger, at least in part. Party cohesion in Congress has increased. With the demise of the southern Democratic conservatives, the Democratic Party is much more homogeneous. Many members of both parties are more dependent on the national party committees for campaign support than they were a decade ago. Both these trends have contributed to the increase in party voting and support for the president by his own party.[35]

Finally, as we have seen, national party organizations have become much more powerful. Their activities are fueled by their ability to raise and spend essentially unlimited amounts of money due to loopholes in campaign finance laws (for more on this, see Chapter 9). While parties still compete for influence with interest groups, pollsters, campaign consultants, and the media, it is often funds raised by the national parties that buy the polling, campaign consultation, and media time. Both presidential and congressional candidates need the national party organizations because of the parties' revenue-raising ability.

Each component of our political parties—party in the electorate, party in government, and party organization—has shown significant signs of revitalization. Where parties have made few recent gains, however, is in their lack of control over the nomination process. Political parties have little influence over who can run for party office. In spite of name recognition, endorsements, and a cache of money to throw at the 1996 nomination, the Republican Party could not prevent Steve Forbes, a multimillionaire magazine publisher, and Pat Buchanan, a television personality—neither of whom had ever been elected to anything—and a host of others from entering the race and challenging the party's choice, Robert Dole. These candidates were taken seriously. They got airtime, coverage by national newspapers and magazines, and into presidential debates. They attacked Dole, undermining his chance of winning the presidency, and there was nothing much he or the party could do about it. Today, anyone can claim to belong to a party and run for the party's nomination for president or any other office. In the past, the party organization could discourage candidates with little chance of winning an election, by withholding its support, or threatening sanctions if necessary.

Today, there are many indications of a resurgence in party strength. Yet, split-ticket voting and the divided government it produces make it unclear how one's vote will affect what government does. Citizens elect a president of one party and a majority in Congress of another and wonder why there is gridlock in Washington. Voters see parties as instruments of delay and deadlock, not realizing that it is often lack of party discipline, and not the reverse, that causes the deadlock. Citizens have a greater prospect of influencing the direction of government if they elect those who are loyal and committed to a party. This factor is what led E. E. Schattschneider to reflect on the inevitability and necessity of parties in our American democracy.

EPILOGUE

The Republicans Adopt a Contract

Newt Gingrich and his fellow Republican leaders did introduce a "Contract with America" as a Republican "platform" for the 1994 election. The "Contract" was a 10-point platform, based on results of focus groups, consultation with business groups and other interests, and questionnaires sent to Republican candidates. The "Contract" promised that bills reflecting its provisions would be brought to a vote in the first 100 days of the new Congress. Republican leaders announced the "Contract" in September and published it as an ad in *TV Guide* in late October, only two weeks before the election.

The "Contract" proposed:

1. An amendment requiring a balanced federal budget by 2002, a constitutional amendment mandating a balanced budget amendment, and a line-item presidential veto.

2. An anticrime bill requiring mandatory prison sentences for crimes committed with a gun, limiting appeals in death penalty cases, giving police more leeway in seizing evidence, and building new prisons.

3. Welfare reform, involving prohibitions on mothers under 18 getting welfare, time limits for those receiving welfare, and cuts in overall welfare spending.

4. A family reinforcement act, including stricter enforcement of child support laws, stronger child pornography laws, and tax breaks for adoption and care of the elderly.

5. A middle-class tax cut.

6. A bill forbidding U.S. troops to serve under United Nations command and increasing spending on the military.

7. A bill raising the Social Security benefits limit (currently, Social Security recipients pay income tax—at the same rate as other Americans—on most of their Social Security benefits if they have a total income over a set amount).

8. A tax cut on capital gains (capital gains are profits from sale of property and other capital such as stocks and bonds), and a bill making government regulation of business more difficult.

9. A legal reform bill requiring losers in lawsuits to pay their opponents' legal fees and limiting juries from ordering corporations and doctors to pay a set amount to individuals harmed by defective products or medical malpractice.

10. A constitutional amendment setting term limits of 6 years in the House of Representatives and 12 years in the Senate.

The "Contract" avoided abortion and other moral issues on which the party was divided. It also avoided reform in campaign finance, also a subject over which Republicans differ.

Did the "Contract" win votes for the Republicans? Voters did defeat some incumbent Democrats and elect many new Republicans, but polls showed that most Americans never heard of the "Contract," or did not know what it said.[36] Nonetheless, it may have influenced some voters, especially more informed ones.

In other ways, the "Contract" was useful for the Republicans. It not only gave them a positive program to run on in the last weeks of the campaign, but it gave them a set of priorities for the new Congress.

The "Contract" also energized the Democrats after the election because it gave them a target to aim at. They said the "Contract" was economically unrealistic in calling for a balanced budget and at the same time income tax cuts (including those based on Social Security benefits), capital gains tax cuts, and increased military spending. They also said that the "Contract" benefited the rich more than others. The Democrats' message apparently got across. Near the close of the first 100 days, a majority of Americans told pollsters that the primary danger in Congress was that the Republicans would go too far in helping the rich and cutting needed services for ordinary people.[37]

The Republicans did have more trouble implementing the "Contract" than they expected in the postelection euphoria. Although they only promised to bring the provisions to a vote, citizens who supported the "Contract" likely expected them to get the provisions adopted. In the first 100 days, the Republicans passed, and President Clinton signed, some measures. Yet Republicans in the House failed to pass the term limits amendment, and the Republican majority in the Senate failed to pass the balanced budget amendment—the two most visible planks in the platform. The Republicans also came up short on some other measures. Those in the House, led by Gingrich, passed most provisions, but those in the Senate, who tend to be more moderate, weakened or blocked numerous provisions. And, of course, the Democrats voted against most provisions.

Regardless of whether the provisions of the "Contract" were passed or defeated, and regardless of whether the Republicans were helped or hurt, the "Contract" was a healthy step toward more responsible party government. Attentive voters saw that one party made explicit promises before an election and made real efforts to deliver them after the election. Voters can evaluate the party's effectiveness and, to the extent adopted, the effectiveness of the "Contract." This provides, according to one political scientist, "democratic accountability at its best."[38]

KEY TERMS

party in the electorate
party in government
party organization
realignment
New Deal coalition
ticket splitting
dealignment
two-party system
multiparty systems
single-member districts
winner-take-all
proportional representation
party identification
responsible party government
national party chair
national committees
House and Senate campaign committees
political machine
patronage
caucus
direct primary
closed primary
open primary
divided government

FURTHER READING

David Brooks, ed., *Backward and Upward: The New Conservative Writing* (New York: Vintage Books, 1996). This is a collection of combative, often funny essays from the political right. The authors hold nothing sacred, and their lampooning of various liberal beliefs shows that conservatism is as much about personality as ideology.

James Carville, *We're Right, They're Wrong: A Handbook for Spirited Progressives* (New York: Random House, 1996). In this book, President Clinton's chief campaign adviser and one of Washington's most prominent Democratic strategists responds to the Republicans' platform during the 1994 and 1996 elections. Carville includes such features as the Republicans' "Biggest Lies" and "Most Expensive Boondoggles."

Congressional Quarterly, *National Party Conventions: 1831–1996* (Washington, D.C.: Congressional Quarterly Press, 1997). All you ever wanted to know about each party's national nominating convention, including lists of keynote speakers, platforms, delegate selection rules, nominees, and more.

David J. Gillespie, *Politics at the Periphery: Third Parties in Two-Party America*. (Columbia, S.C.: University of South Carolina Press, 1993). This work provides both a historical review of the roles played by third parties in American politics and a look at the impact of recent third parties on election outcomes.

Stanley B. Greenberg, *Middle Class Dreams: The Politics and Power of the New American Majority* (New York: Times Books, 1995). President Clinton's adviser looks at the radical shape of American politics today and contends that both political parties have betrayed the middle class.

Edwin O'Connor, *The Last Hurrah* (New York: Bantam Books, 1957). A warm, intimate novel set in Boston in the 1950s that contrasts the old-style party election campaigns with new media-oriented ones.

William L. Riordon, *Plunkitt of Tammany Hall* (New York: Dutton, 1963). A series of witty talks by a ward boss of New York City's Democratic Party machine. A slice of Americana, this book discusses "honest graft" and other aspects of "practical politics" and in the process demonstrates why political machines flourished.

Mike Royko, *Boss: Richard J. Daley of Chicago* (New York: New American Library, 1971). An intriguing account of how the Chicago political machine operated under the late mayor Richard J. Daley.

Larry Sabato, *The Party's Just Begun* (Glenview, Ill.: Scott, Foresman, 1988). An overview of the American party system: why we need it, what it does, and how we can make it work better.

ELECTRONIC RESOURCES

http://www.rnc.org/

The home page of the Republican National Committee. It provides many links to government institutions, important Republican officeholders, the national committee headquarters, and issue positions. See GOP-TV through the Web.

http://democrats.org/party/convention/

The home page of the Democratic National Committee. It provides similar links from a Democratic perspective, as well as links to information about Democratic Party history and past Democratic conventions.

http://www.reformparty.org/convention 1998/

The home page of Ross Perot's Reform Party, with information on plans for 1998 and beyond.

http://www.politicalindex.com/sect8.htm

This site gives you a flavor of many of the minor parties involved in U.S. politics. Check out the links to the Green Party, the U.S. Taxpayers Party, the Communists, the Libertarians, and many others.

INFOTRAC CITATIONS

"The Year the GOP Went South"
"Rebels Return to Haunt Blair"
"Political Consultants and the Extension of Party Goals"

NOTES

1. Thomas B. Rosenstiel, "Gingrich Created Army," *Lincoln Star*, December 20, 1994, p. 1ff.

2. Dan Balz, "10 Hard Acts to Follow Up," *Washington Post National Weekly Edition*, November 28–December 4, 1994, p. 6.

3. E. E. Schattschneider, *Party Government* (New York: Holt, Rinehart & Winston, 1960), p. 1.

4. Jack Dennis, "Trends in Public Support for the American Party System," in *Parties and Elections in an Anti-Party Age*, ed. Jeff Fishel (Bloomington: Indiana University Press, 1978).

5. Frank Sorauf, *Political Parties in the American System*, 4th ed. (Boston: Little, Brown, 1980).

6. Richard Hofstadter, *The Idea of Party System: The Rise of Legitimate Opposition in the United States, 1780–1840* (Berkeley: University of California Press, 1969).

7. Theodore J. Lowi, *The Personal President: Power Invested, Promise Unfulfilled* (Ithaca, N.Y.: Cornell University Press, 1985).

8. James MacGregor Burns, *The Vineyard of Liberty* (New York: Knopf, 1982).

9. Kevin Phillips, *The Emerging Republican Majority* (New York: Doubleday, 1969).

10. Everett Carll Ladd, *Where Have All the Voters Gone?* (New York: W. W. Norton, 1982), p. 78; 1984 and 1988 data are from the 1984 and 1988 CPS National Election Study.

11. James L. Sundquist, *Dynamics of the Party System: Alignment and Realignment of Political Parties in the United States* (Washington, D.C.: Brookings Institution, 1973).

12. J. R. Petrocik and F. T. Steeper, "The Political Landscape in 1988," *Public Opinion Magazine* (September/October 1987), pp. 41–44; H. Norpoth, "Party Realignment in the 1980s," *Public Opinion Quarterly* 51 (Fall 1987), pp. 376–390.

13. Thomas Edsall, "The Democrats' Class and Gender Gap," *Washington Post National Weekly Edition*, June 6, 1994, p. 12.

14. Thomas Edsall, "The Fissure Running through the Democratic Party," *Washington Post National Weekly Edition*, June 6–12, 1994, p. 11.

15. Ibid.

16. Katharine Q. Seelye, "Democrats across U.S. Continue to Flee Party," *Lincoln Journal-Star*, October 7, 1995, p. 1A.

17. John Petrocik, "Realignment," *Journal of Politics* 49 (May 1987), pp. 347–375; George Rabinowitz, Paul-Henri Gurian, and Stuart MacDonald, "The Structure of Presidential Elections and the Process of Realignment," *American Journal of Political Science* 28 (November 1984), pp. 611–635; D. Broder, "The GOP Plays Dixie," *Washington Post National Weekly Edition*, September 12–18, 1988, p. 4; T. B. Edsall, "A Serious Case of White Flight," *Washington Post National Weekly Edition*, September 10–16, 1990, p. 13.

18. Walter Dean Burnham, *Critical Elections and the Mainstream of American Politics* (New York: W. W. Norton, 1970); Helmut Norpoth and Jerrold Rusk, "Partisan Dealignment in the American Electorate," *American Political Science Review* 76 (September 1982), pp. 522–537; David W. Rhode, "The Fall Elections: Realignment and Dealignment," *Chronicle of Higher Education* (December 14, 1994), pp. B1–B2.

19. Martin P. Wallenberg, *The Rise of Candidate-Centered Politics* (Cambridge, Mass.: Harvard University Press, 1991).

20. D. Sarasohn, "Wall Falls on Reagan Coalition," *Lincoln Sunday Journal Star*, February 18, 1990, p. 1C.

21. Steven Roberts, "Near Death Experience," *U.S. News and World Report*, November 6, 1996, p. 28.

22. Ibid.

23. Ann Devroy, "More to the Right, Mr. President—Now Grab the GOP Agenda," *Washington Post National Weekly Edition*, October 16–22, 1996, p. 13.

24. Maurice Duverger, *Political Parties* (New York: John Wiley & Sons, 1963). See also Edward R. Tune, "The Relationship between Seats and Votes in Two-Party Systems," *American Political Science Review* 67 (1973), pp. 540–554.

25. See also Lowi, *Personal President*. He makes the point that two parties survived in the United States despite the use of multimember districts in elections for Congress in the nineteenth century.

26. William R. Shaffer, *Party and Ideology in the United States Congress* (Lanham, Md.: University Press of America, 1980).

27. Bruce I. Oppenheimer, "The Importance of Elections in a Strong Congressional Era," in Benjamin Ginsberg and Alan Stone, eds., *Do Elections Matter?* (Armonck, N.Y.: M. E. Sharpe, 1996), pp. 120–138.

28. David Broder, "Polarization Growing Force for Political Parties," *Lincoln Journal-Star,* January 22, 1995, p. 4B.

29. Dan Carney, "As Hostilities Rage on the Hill, Partisan-Vote Rate Soars," *Congressional Quarterly Weekly Report,* January 27, 1996, pp. 199–200.

30. Lloyd Grove, "A Good Ol' Boy Going in for the Kill," *Washington Post National Weekly Edition,* August 22–28, 1994, pp. 13–14, 32.

31. Frank J. Sorauf, *Money in American Elections* (Glenview, Ill.: Scott, Foresman, 1988), pp. 121–153; Paul Herrnson, *Party Campaigning in the 1980s* (Cambridge, Mass.: Harvard University Press, 1988).

32. Xandra Kayden, "The Nationalization of the Party System," in Michael Malbin, ed., *Parties, Interest Groups, and Campaign Finance Laws* (Washington, D.C.: American Enterprise Institute, 1980).

33. Milton L. Rakove, *Don't Make No Waves, Don't Back No Losers* (Bloomington, Ind.: Indiana University Press, 1975).

34. Austin Ranney, *Participation in American Presidential Nominations, 1976* (Washington, D.C.: American Enterprise Institute, 1977). See also Austin Ranney, "Parties in State Politics," in Herbert Jacob and Kenneth Vines, eds., *Politics in the American States,* 3d ed. (Boston: Little, Brown, 1980), pp. 61–99.

35. Oppenheimer, "The Importance of Elections."

36. Richard Morin, "Myths and Messages in the Election Tea Leaves," *Washington Post National Weekly Edition,* November 21–27, 1994, p. 37.

37. Kevin Phillips, "GOP's Big-Bang Revolution Turns into a Wet Firecracker," *Lincoln Journal (Los Angeles Times),* April 4, 1995, p. 3.

38. Thomas Mann, quoted in John F. Starks, "100 Days of Attitude," *Time,* April 10, 1995, p. 32.

Few Americans see candidates in person anymore. Most see candidates only on TV. Here a studio audience is linked by satellite to Bill Clinton.

Dan Lamant/Matrix

7 ELECTIONS

- **The American Electorate**
  - Early Limits on Voting Rights
  - Blacks and the Right to Vote
  - The Voting Rights Act and the Redistricting Controversy
  - Women and the Right to Vote
  - Other Expansions of the Electorate
- **Voter Turnout**
  - Political Activism in the Nineteenth Century
  - Progressive Reforms
  - Recent Turnout
  - Who Does Not Vote?
  - Why Turnout Is Low
- **Other Campaign Participation**
- **Presidential Nominating Campaigns**
  - Who Runs for President and Why?
  - How a Candidate Wins the Nomination
  - Presidential Caucuses and Conventions
  - Presidential Primaries
  - Reforming the Nomination Process
  - The National Conventions
  - Independent and Third-Party Nominees
- **The General Election Campaign**
  - Campaign Organization
  - Images and Issues
  - The Electoral College
  - Campaign Strategies
  - The Media Campaign
  - Campaign Funding
- **Voting**
  - Party Loyalties
  - Candidate Evaluations
  - Issues
  - Parties, Candidates, and Issues
- **Conclusion: Do Elections Make Government Responsive?**

To Package or Not?

You are Bill Clinton. It is May 1992 and you are sure you will win the Democratic nomination for president, but unsure whether you can win the election. Your road to the nomination has been rocky; many people, including loyal Democrats, think you are a weak candidate. They fear you will drag the Democrats down to their fourth straight presidential election defeat. Now your campaign staff presents you with a plan that they think will lead to victory in November. But from your perspective the plan has significant problems.

You are one of six declared Democratic presidential candidates. None of you is well known; Paul Tsongas is a former U.S. senator from Massachusetts who dropped out of the Senate a decade earlier to battle cancer; Jerry Brown, a former governor of California; Tom Harkin, a U.S. senator from Iowa; Bob Kerrey, a U.S. senator and former governor of Nebraska; and Douglas Wilder, governor of Virginia, the first black ever to be elected governor. You and the others struggled for name recognition and votes in the snows of New Hampshire. Tsongas was predicted to win, since he had the advantage of being from neighboring Massachusetts. Your candidacy started strong, but soon floundered. Stories of your alleged womanizing flooded the media. The press gave extensive coverage to one woman, Gennifer Flowers, who claimed she had had a twelve-year affair with you. Fearing that your campaign would end soon after it began, you and your wife, Hillary, agreed to be on the television program *60 Minutes* to talk about these accusations and about your marriage. The show, which aired right after the Super Bowl, captured a huge audience. You denied having an affair with Flowers, admitted your marriage had had some hard times, but said you and Hillary had stuck together through good times and bad. The interview evoked sympathy for you. Polls showed that the scandal over Gennifer Flowers swayed only 11% of the voters, and 82% thought that enough had been said about your personal life.[1]

Just when you thought that crisis was over, the *Wall Street Journal* published a story on your draft record. Although many men your age had been drafted for the Vietnam War, many others avoided the draft, and you were one of them. The former ROTC head at the University of Arkansas claimed you had promised to join, but then changed your mind when you were no longer threatened by the draft. Your letter to the head, thanking him for "saving me from the draft," was a follow-up story that made the media rounds. A week before the New Hampshire primary, support for you in the polls dropped 17 points in 48 hours.[2] Polls indicated you could finish third behind both Tsongas and Kerrey.

Facing disaster, you spent the last week appearing on television night and day and meeting as many people as you could in malls and fast-food restaurants. New Hampshire had only 125,000 voters, and you must have met most of them. You finished second to Paul Tsongas, and promptly labeled yourself the winner—"the comeback kid."

After New Hampshire, you became the front runner when Tsongas's campaign sputtered and died. Yet throughout the primary season, voters were never really very enthusiastic about you.[3] Before the primary season was over, your campaign team assembled focus groups of voters and then prepared a report. It concluded that most voters did not really know much about you, but many did not like you anyway. You are viewed unfavorably by a large minority of Democratic voters and by about 40% of all general election voters. The report states that voters have a general impression that "[Clinton] will say what is necessary and that he does not 'talk straight.' " Moreover, you are in large part responsible for this image, your consultants inform you. They say that voters believe you are the ultimate politician: evasive, never gives a straight answer, always has handy lists and instant analysis. Moreover, voters say, "He's not real, he's privileged like the Kennedys, he can't stand up to special interests." The report concluded that people are discounting your messages because of their impression of you. And they do not like Hillary much either, perceiving her as unaffectionate and not interested in her family.[4] Indeed, many voters do not even know you and Hillary have a daughter, because Hillary has tried to shield her from the media.

Your consultants outline a comprehensive strategy to try to remake your image, to "reposition" you, to reflect your human qualities, and to show that you can stand up to special interests. They call for creating an image of an "honest, plain-folks idealist and his warm and loving wife."[5] To create this image, the plan suggests specific tactics, such as your appearances on television talk shows, playing your saxophone, making fun of yourself, and saying unpopular things to powerful groups in order to prove your independence. It also suggests ideas for making your family more prominent. It calls for "events where Bill and Hillary can go on dates with the American people." Finally, it suggests broad strategies, such as a populist message that would appeal to the middle class, calling for change and pointing out failures of government to bring about a secure economic future.

Your advisers believe that these messages work. In focus groups, people become much more favorable about you when they are given information about your coming from a small town, surviving your childhood with an alcoholic stepfather, working your way through Yale, and now asking for change in American society.

It angers you that voters do not know much about you. At a staff meeting, you give vent to these feelings: "So far as I'm concerned, we're at zero. . . . We don't exist in the national consciousness. . . . I don't think you can minimize how horrible I feel, having worked all my life to stand for things, having busted my butt for seven months and the American people don't know crap about it."[6] You want to inform people about your real background and beliefs, and you see that this is a well-thought-out plan to do that.

Yet you realize there's a risk to this strategy. One risk is that it will seem too much like a strategy. People already think you are a slick politician, and this plan seems so programmed, so, well, political. Voters may believe that any new image is just that: an image, not reality. Moreover, there is a risk that some of the activities suggested will not seem very presidential: appearances on TV talk shows, playing your sax, and "dates with the American people." Perhaps these kinds of activities will make you seem less presidential than Bush.

What do you decide? Adopt the plan or not?

Americans have fought and died in wars to preserve the rights of citizens to choose their leaders through democratic elections. Some have even died here at home, trying to exercise these rights. Despite this, most Americans take these important rights for granted; about half do not bother to vote even in presidential elections, and fewer still participate in other ways.

Moreover, the process by which we choose our leaders, especially the president, has been sharply criticized in recent years. Critics charge that election campaigns are meaningless and offer little information to the voters, that candidates pander to the most ill-informed and mean-spirited citizens, and that public relations and campaign spending, not positions on issues or strength of character, determine the winners.

In this chapter, we analyze why voting is important to a democracy and why, despite its importance, so few do it. We then examine political campaigns and elections to see how they affect the kinds of leaders and policies we have. We will see that the lack of participation by many reinforces the government's responsiveness to those who do participate, especially those who are well organized.

THE AMERICAN ELECTORATE

During the more than two centuries since the Constitution was written, two important developments have altered the right to vote, termed **suffrage.** First, suffrage gradually has been extended to include almost all citizens aged 18 or over. Second, deciding who may vote now lies largely in the hands of the federal government. The electorate has been widened mostly through constitutional amendments, congressional acts, and Supreme Court decisions.

Early Limits on Voting Rights

Although the Declaration of Independence stated that "all men are created equal," at the time of the Constitution and shortly thereafter, the central political right of voting was denied to most Americans. States decided who would be granted suffrage. In some only an estimated 10% of the white males could vote, whereas in others 80% could.[7]

Controversial property qualifications for voting existed in many states. Some argued that only those with an economic stake in society should have a say in political life. But critics of the property requirement repeated a story of Tom Paine's:

You require that a man shall have $60 worth of property, or he shall not vote. Very well . . . here is a man who today owns a jackass, and the jackass is worth $60. Today the man is a voter and he goes to the polls and deposits his vote. Tomorrow the jackass dies. The next day the man comes to vote without his jackass and he cannot vote at all. Now tell me, which was the voter, the man or the jackass?[8]

Because the Constitution gave states the power to regulate suffrage, the elimination of property requirements was a gradual process. By the 1820s, most were gone, although some lingered to mid-century.

In some states, religious tests also were applied. A voter had to be a member of the "established" church or could not be a member of certain religions (such as Roman Catholic or Jewish). However, religious tests disappeared even more quickly than property qualifications.

By the time of the Civil War, state action had expanded the rights of white men. However, neither slaves, Indians, nor southern free blacks could vote, although northern blacks could in a few states.[9] Women's voting rights were confined to local elections in a few states.[10]

Blacks and the Right to Vote

The Civil War began the long, slow, and often violent process of expanding the rights of blacks to full citizenship. Between 1865 and 1870, three amendments were passed to give political rights to former slaves and other blacks. One, the Fifteenth Amendment, prohibited the denial of voting rights on the basis of race and thus gave the right to vote to black men.

For a short time following the ratification of this amendment, a northern military presence in the South and close monitoring of southern politics enabled blacks to vote and hold office in the South, where 90% of all blacks lived. During this **Reconstruction** period, two southern blacks were elected to the Senate and 14 were elected to the House between 1869 and 1876.

Although blacks did not dominate politics or even receive a proportional share of offices, whites saw blacks' political activities as a threat to their own dominance. White southerners began to prevent blacks from voting through intimidation that ranged from mob violence and lynchings to economic sanctions against blacks who attempted to vote.

These methods, both violent and nonviolent, were tolerated by the North, where the public and political leaders had lost interest in the fate of blacks or had simply grown tired of the struggle. And in 1876, a compromise ended Reconstruction. In the wake of the disputed 1876 presidential election, southern Democrats agreed to support Republican Rutherford B. Hayes for president in return for an end to the northern military presence in the South and a hands-off policy toward activities there.

By the end of the nineteenth century, blacks were effectively disfranchised in all of the South. The last black southern member of Congress served to 1901. Another would not be elected until 1972.

The loss of black voting rights was legitimized in southern constitutions and laws. **Literacy tests** were often required, supposedly to make sure voters could read and write and thus evaluate political information. Most blacks, who had been denied education, were illiterate. Many whites also were illiterate, but fewer were barred from voting. Local election registrars exercised nearly complete discretion in deciding who had to take the test and how to administer and evaluate it. Educated blacks often were asked for legal interpretations of obscure constitutional provisions, which few could provide.

Library of Congress

Four of the men shown in this 1870 poster with Frederick Douglass (center) served in Congress: Hiram Revels in the Senate and Benjamin Turner, Josiah T. Walls, and Joseph Rainey in the House. Also pictured are writer William Wells Brown and Bishop Richard Allen, founder of the African Methodist Episcopal Church.

Some laws had exemptions that whites were allowed to take advantage of. An "understanding clause" exempted those who could not read and write but who could explain sections of the federal or state constitution to the satisfaction of the examiner, and a "good moral character clause" exempted those with such character. Again, local election registrars exercised discretion in deciding who understood the Constitution and who had good character. Finally, the **grandfather clause** exempted those whose grandfathers had the right to vote before 1867, that is, before blacks could legally vote in the South.

The **poll tax** also deprived blacks of voting rights. The tax, though only a couple of dollars, was often a sizable proportion of one's monthly income. In some states individuals had to pay not only for the present

AMERICAN DIVERSITY

BLACKS AND HISPANICS IN OFFICE

Before the Voting Rights Act, few African Americans held major public office. Only a handful were members of Congress, and few were state legislators, mayors of major cities, or other important political officers. Following the Voting Rights Act, southern blacks began to have the political clout to elect members of their own race to office for the first time. Progress, slow to be sure, has occurred; in 1968, there were only 23 black legislators in southern legislatures, but by 1993, there were over 300, including 42 in Mississippi. Virginia, the heart of the Confederacy, elected the nation's first black governor, Douglas Wilder. And 16 black members of Congress represent southern constituencies.

The number of northern black officeholders also has increased, reflecting heightened black political activity there too. Richard Hatcher, who became mayor of Gary, Indiana, in 1968, was the first black mayor of a major U.S. city. By 1993 there were 38 black mayors in northern and southern cities of 50,000 or more. This includes not only cities where blacks are a majority, such as New Orleans, Detroit, Baltimore, and Birmingham, but also cities where blacks are a minority, such as Seattle and Denver.

Nationally, the number of black officeholders has increased from an estimated 1,200 in 1969 to over 8,000 in 1993. Although this is far from proportional representation, it is a dramatic increase.

Hispanics too have improved their representation in political office. From a total of little more than 3,000 Hispanic public officials in 1985, their numbers have grown to nearly 5,500.

In sum, though progress seems slow, blacks and Hispanics, like other ethnic groups, are beginning to achieve political clout through elections.

SOURCES: *Statistical Abstract of the U.S., 1997* (Washington, D.C.: Government Printing Office, 1997), Tables 458 and 459. Joint Center for Political Studies, *National Roster of Black Elected Officials* (Washington, D.C., 1993).

election but for every past election in which they were eligible to vote but did not.

In the **white primary,** blacks were barred from voting in primary elections, where party nominees were chosen. Because the Democrats always won the general elections, the real contests were in the Democratic primaries. The states justified excluding blacks on the grounds that political parties were private, rather than governmental, organizations and thus could discriminate just as private clubs or individuals could.

Less formal means also were used to exclude blacks from voting. Registrars often closed their offices when blacks tried to register, or whites threatened blacks with the loss of jobs or housing if they tried to vote. Polling places were sometimes located far from black neighborhoods or were moved at the last minute without notifying potential voters. If these means failed, whites threatened or practiced violence. In one election in Mobile, whites wheeled a cannon to a polling place and aimed it at about 1,000 blacks lined up to vote.

The treatment of blacks by the southern establishment was summarized on the floor of the Senate by South Carolina Senator Benjamin ("Pitchfork Ben") Tillman, who served from 1895 to 1918. As he put it, "We took the government away. We stuffed ballot boxes. We shot them. We are not ashamed of it."

Over time, the Supreme Court and Congress outlawed the "legal" barriers to black voting in the South. The Court invalidated the grandfather clause in 1915 and the white primary in 1944. Through the Twenty-fourth Amendment, Congress abolished the poll tax for federal elections in 1964, and the Court invalidated the tax for state elections in 1966.[11] But threats of physical violence and economic reprisals still kept most southern blacks from voting. Although many blacks in the urban areas of the rim South (such as Florida, North Carolina, Tennessee, and Texas) could and did vote, those in the rural South and most in the Deep South could not; in 1960, black registration ranged from 5% to 40% in southern states.[12]

The Voting Rights Act and the Redistricting Controversy

The Voting Rights Act (VRA) dramatically changed the face of the electorate in the South and then later in other parts of the nation (see What Government Does Right). Given the success of the VRA and faced with an expanded black electorate, some white officials in areas of large black populations used new means to diminish the political clout of African Americans. Their technique was *gerrymandering* (see box "Racial Gerrymandering"). Through devices that political scientists call **"cracking, stacking, and packing,"** districts were drawn to minimize black representation depending on the size and configuration of the black and white populations. Cracking divides significant, concentrated black populations into two or more

WHAT GOVERNMENT DOES RIGHT

THE VOTING RIGHTS ACT ENFRANCHISES MILLIONS

Despite our shameful history of depriving African Americans of the right to vote, today black voting rates approach those of whites. In the deep South, much of this dramatic change was brought about by the passage of the **Voting Rights Act (VRA)** in 1965, which made it illegal to interfere with anyone's right to vote. The act suspended the use of literacy tests, and, most important, it sent federal voter registrars into counties where less than 50% of the voting age population (black and white) was registered. The premise of this requirement was that if so few had registered, there must be serious barriers to registration. All of Alabama, Mississippi, South Carolina, and Louisiana, substantial parts of North Carolina, and scattered counties in five northern states were included in the area covered by registrars.

Any changes in election procedures had to be approved by the Department of Justice or the U.S. District Court for the District of Columbia. States or counties had to show a clean record of not discriminating for 10 years before they could escape this supervision. Those who sought to deter blacks from voting through intimidation now had to face the force of the federal government.

Though black registration had been increasing in the rim South due to voter registration and education projects, the impact of the VRA in the Deep South was dramatic.[1] Within a year after federal registrars were sent, hundreds of thousands of southern blacks were registered, radically changing the nature of southern politics. In the most extreme case, Mississippi registration of blacks zoomed from 7% to 41%. In Alabama the black electorate doubled in four years.

Due to these increases, not only have dozens of blacks been elected, but white politicians must now court black voters to get elected. Even the late George Wallace, the segregationist Alabama governor who had opposed the civil rights movement in the 1960s, eagerly sought black votes in the 1970s and 1980s.

The VRA was renewed and expanded in 1970, 1975, and 1982. It now covers more states and other minorities, such as Hispanics, Asians, Native Americans, and Eskimos, and thus serves as a basic protection for minority voting rights. For example, states must provide bilingual ballots in counties in which 5% or more of the population does not speak English.

1. Richard Limpne, "Mass Mobilization or Government Intervention? The Growth of Black Registration in the South," *Journal of Politics* 57 (May 1995), pp. 425–442.

UPI/Corbis-Bettmann

Blacks line up to vote in Peachtree, Alabama, after enactment of the Voting Rights Act of 1965.

districts so that neither will be majority black; stacking combines a large black population with an even greater white population; and packing puts a huge black population into one district rather than two, where blacks might approach a majority in each.

Initially, the Supreme Court was reluctant to find these practices illegal without specific proof that their intent was to discriminate against black voters.[13] But in 1982, congressional revision of the VRA required states with large minority populations to draw boundaries in

RACIAL GERRYMANDERING

This North Carolina district (12), shown on the maps, was drawn after the 1990 census to create a black majority district. It consists of parts of 10 counties along the I-85 interstate and includes the predominantly black sections of Durham, Greensboro, Winston-Salem, and Charlotte. As one reporter noted, "In most electoral contests, candidates try to focus on finding out what the voters want. But in the 12th, the candidates face a challenge just *finding out who the voters are.*"[1]

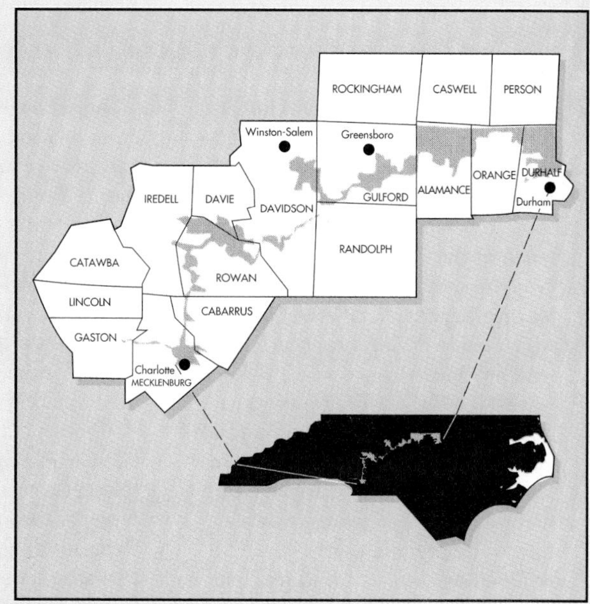

The practice of drawing strangely shaped districts to fulfill political objectives, called "gerrymandering," is hardly new in American politics. The name originated in 1812 when the Massachusetts legislature carved out a district that historian John Fiske said had a "dragonlike contour." When painter Gilbert Stuart saw the misshapen district, he drew in a head, wings, and claws and exclaimed, "That will do for a salamander!" Editor Benjamin Russell replied, "Better say Gerrymander," after Elbridge Gerry, then governor of Massachusetts.[2] Since then gerrymandering has been widely used by politicians to benefit their own political parties.

Supporters of racial gerrymandering believe it is the best way to increase minority representation. It provides a favorable setting for members of a minority racial group to elect members of their own race. But others argue that low numbers of racial and ethnic minorities in Congress cannot appropriately be changed by the use of deliberate gerrymanders. Some also object to the creation of majority-minority districts because they see the dangers of thereby creating other districts with fewer minorities. These other districts will be more white than before, with representatives who are less sensitive to the interests of minorities.

One possible reform that meets the objectives of both groups is **cumulative voting.** Under that system, members of Congress would not be elected from single-member districts, but from at-large districts in which several members of Congress would be elected at the same time. Voters would each have a number of votes equal to the number of seats in the district. They could apportion their votes among the candidates in any way that they preferred.

Members of any group, including racial, ethnic, religious, political, or economic groups, could target their votes on the candidates most likely to represent the group's interests. This election procedure could produce greater racial and ethnic diversity in representative bodies such as Congress without creating new districts on the basis of race or ethnicity.

This procedure is not totally new to the United States; it was used for many years in Illinois to elect members of their state's House of Representatives. Still, acceptance of cumulative voting for congressional districts seems remote.

1. Charles Mahtesian, "Blacks' Political Hopes Boosted by Newly Redrawn Districts," *Congressional Quarterly Weekly Report* (April 25, 1992), p. 1087.
2. *Guide to Congress,* 2d ed. (Washington, D.C.: Congressional Quarterly, Inc., 1976), p. 563; *Congressional Quarterly, The Race to Capitol Hill* (February 29, 1992), pp. 103–105.

OTHER SOURCES: Bruce E. Cain, "Voting Rights and Democratic Theory toward a Color-Blind Society?" *The Brookings Review,* Winter 1992, pp. 46–50; Carol M. Swain, "The Voting Rights Act: Some Unintended Consequences," *The Brookings Review,* Winter 1992, p. 51; Douglas Amy, *Real Choices/New Voices: The Case for Proportional Representation Elections in the United States* (New York: Columbia University Press, 1993).

ways to increase the probabilities that minorities will win seats. The focus of the voting rights legislation, then, turned from protecting the right of suffrage to trying to ensure that voting rights result in the election of African American and other minority officeholders. With this new statute as an indication of congressional intent, the Court then did strike down districting in North Carolina as inappropriately diluting black voting power.[14]

After the 1990 census, eleven new **majority-minority** congressional districts were created for blacks and six for Hispanics. All but one were actually won by blacks and Hispanics in the 1992 election. Partly as a result of this redistricting, blacks were elected to Congress for the first time since Reconstruction in Alabama, Florida, North Carolina, South Carolina, and Virginia. Hispanics were elected for the first time ever in Illinois and New Jersey. In all, 39 blacks and 19 Hispanics were elected to Congress, a dramatic increase from the 25 blacks and 10 Hispanics serving before the 1992 election.[15]

Women's contributions to the war effort during World War I helped lead to the ratification of the women's suffrage amendment in 1920. Here Broadway chorus women train as Home Guards during the war.

However, after this 1990 redistricting, which used extensive gerrymandering to create the majority-minority districts, some white voters challenged their legality. In a series of cases, the Supreme Court then ruled that racial gerrymandering, the drawing of district lines specifically to concentrate racial minorities to try to ensure the election of minority representatives, is as constitutionally suspect as the drawing of district lines to diffuse minority electoral strength.[16] To the surprise of many, despite the consequent redrawing of several majority-minority districts after the 1994 election, the African American incumbents were still able to win reelection in 1996.

Women and the Right to Vote

When property ownership defined the right to vote, women property owners could vote in some places. When property requirements were removed, suffrage came to be seen as a male right only. Women's right to vote was reintroduced in the 1820s in Tennessee school board elections.[17] From that time on, women had the vote in some places, usually only at the local level or for particular kinds of elections.

The national movement for women's suffrage did not gain momentum until after the Civil War. Before and during that war, many women helped lead the campaign to abolish slavery and establish full political rights for blacks. When black men got the vote after the Civil War, some women saw the paradox in their working to enfranchise these men when they themselves lacked the right to vote. Led by Susan B. Anthony, Elizabeth Cady Stanton, and others, they lobbied Congress and the state legislatures for voting rights for women.

The first suffrage bill was introduced in Congress in 1868 and each year thereafter until 1893. Most members were strong in their condemnation of women as potential voters. One senator claimed that if women could hold political views different from their husbands it would make "every home a hell on earth."

When Wyoming applied to join the union in 1889, it already had granted women the right to vote. Congress initially tried to bar Wyoming for that reason but then relented when the Wyoming territorial legislature declared, "We will remain out of the Union 100 years rather than come in without the women." Still, by 1910 women had complete suffrage rights in only four states.

AMERICAN DIVERSITY

WOMEN IN OFFICE

Even before women were given the right to vote nationally, they held political office. Women officeholders in colonial America were rare but not unknown. In 1715, for example, the Pennsylvania Assembly appointed a woman as tax collector.[1]

Elizabeth Cady Stanton, probably the first woman candidate for Congress, received 24 votes when she ran in 1866.[2] It was not until 1916 that the first woman member of Congress, Jeannette Rankin (R-Mont.), was actually elected. In 1872, Victoria Claflin Woodhull ran for president on the Equal Rights Party ticket teamed with abolitionist Frederick Douglass for vice president.

More than 100,000 women now hold elective office, but many of these offices are minor. Inroads by women into major national offices have been slow. Geraldine Ferraro's 1984 vice presidential candidacy was historic but not victorious. In recent years, women have only gradually increased their membership in Congress. But in the 1992 elections, women candidates won striking increases in national legislative office. Women nearly doubled their numbers in the House of Representatives and tripled their numbers in the Senate. Women have continued to gain seats, and by 1998 numbered 9 in the Senate and 53 in the House.

Real progress has been made in state and local governments. Women hold 26% of all statewide elective offices, although only three women, Christine Whitman (R-N.J.), Jane Dee Hull (R-Ariz.), and Jeanne Shaheen (D-N.H.), are governors. In 1969, only 4% of the state legislators were women; today 22% are. However, this progress has slowed in the late 1990s. In seven states, women hold more than 30% of state legislative seats, though in Alabama and Kentucky, they hold less than 10%.[3]

More than 20% of the city council seats in medium and large cities are now occupied by women, and about the same proportion are mayors of cities of 30,000 and larger. Women are twice as likely to be found on school boards, however, where they make up 40% of the members.

Does it make a difference in terms of policy to have women officeholders rather than men? Studies of the behavior of women members of Congress and other legislative bodies indicate that they are, on the whole, more liberal than men.[4] Women tend to give issues relating to women, children, and the family higher priority than male legislators do.[5] Women are also less likely to be involved in corrupt activities.

More and more women are getting graduate and professional education and working outside the home. These changes, coupled with increased public support for women taking an active role in politics, suggest that the trend toward more women in public office will continue.

AP/Wide World Photos

Barbara Boxer and Dianne Feinstein celebrate their 1992 election as U.S. senators from California. This was the first time any state has elected two women senators. Boxer received 57% of the women's vote but only 44% of the men's.

1. Joseph J. Kelley, *Pennsylvania: The Colonial Years* (Garden City, N.Y.: Doubleday, 1980), p. 143.
2. Elisabeth Griffin, *In Her Own Right* (New York: Oxford University Press, 1983).
3. Data are from Center for the American Woman and Politics, National Information Bank on Women in Public Office, Rutgers University. http://www.rci.rutgers.edu/~cawp/ and *Statistical Abstract 1997*, Tables 456–457.
4. Susan Welch, "Are Women More Liberal Than Men in the U.S. Congress?" *Legislative Studies Quarterly* 10 (February 1985), pp. 125–134.
5. Sue Thomas and Susan Welch, "The Impact of Gender on the Priorities and Activities of State Legislators," *Western Political Quarterly* (1991).

Powerful interests opposed suffrage for women. Liquor interests feared that women voters would press for prohibition because many women had been active in the temperance (antiliquor) movement. Other businesses feared that suffrage would lead to reforms to improve working conditions for women and children. Southern whites feared that it would lead to voting by black women and then by black men. Political bosses feared that women would favor political reform. The Catholic church opposed it as contrary to the proper role of women. According to some people, suffrage was a revolt against nature. Pregnant women might lose their babies, nursing mothers their milk, and women might grow beards or be raped at the polls (then frequently located in saloons or barber shops).[18] Others argued less hysterically that women should be protected from the unsavory practices of politics and should confine themselves to their traditional duties.

About 1910, however, the women's suffrage movement was reenergized, in part by ideas and tactics borrowed from the British women's suffrage movement. A new generation of leaders, including Alice Paul and Carrie Chapman Catt, began to lobby more vigorously, reach out to the working class, and engage in protest marches and picketing, new features of American politics. In 1917, when the National Women's party organized around-the-clock picketing of the White House, their arrest and forced feeding during jail hunger strikes embarrassed the administration and won the movement some support. These incidents, plus contributions by women to the war effort during World War I, led to adoption of the Nineteenth Amendment guaranteeing women the vote in 1920. Although only 37% of eligible women voted in the 1920 presidential election, as the habit of voting spread, women's rates of voting equaled those of men.

Other Expansions of the Electorate

Federal constitutional and legislative changes extended the franchise to young adults. Before 1971, almost all states required a voting age of 19 or more. The service of 18-year-olds in the Vietnam War brought protests that if these men were old enough to die for their country, they were old enough to vote. Yielding to these arguments and to the general recognition that young people were better educated than in the past, Congress adopted and the states ratified the Twenty-sixth Amendment giving 18-year-olds the right to vote.

Only convicted felons, the mentally incapable, noncitizens, and those not meeting minimal residence requirements are unable to vote now. Voting has come to be an essential right of citizenship rather than a privilege just for those qualified by birth or property. Paradoxically, however, as the *right* to vote has expanded, the proportion of eligible citizens *actually* voting has contracted.

VOTER TURNOUT

Political Activism in the Nineteenth Century

In 1896, an estimated 750,000 people—5% of all voters—took train excursions to visit presidential candidate William McKinley at his Ohio home during the campaign.[19] This amazing figure is but one indication of the high level of intense political interest and activity in the late nineteenth century.

In those days, politics was an active, not a spectator, sport. People voted at high rates, as much as 80% in the 1840 presidential election,[20] and they were very partisan. They thought independents were corrupt and ready to sell their votes to the highest bidder. Elaborate and well-organized parties printed and distributed the ballots. Voters, after being coached by party leaders, simply dropped their party's ballot into the box. Split-ticket voting and secrecy in making one's choice were impossible.

Progressive Reforms

The **Progressive reforms** of the early twentieth century brought radical changes to election politics. Progressive reformers, largely professional and upper middle class, sought to eliminate corruption from politics and voting. But they also meant to eliminate the influence of the lower classes, many of them recent immigrants. These two goals went hand in hand, because the lower classes were seen as the cause of corruption in politics.

The Progressive movement was responsible for several reforms: primary elections, voter registration laws, secret ballots, nonpartisan ballots (without party labels), and the denial of voting rights for aliens, which removed a major constituency of the urban party machines. The movement also introduced the merit system for public employment to reduce favoritism and payoffs in hiring.

The reforms, adopted by some states at the beginning of the century, and by others much later, were largely effective in cleaning up politics. But the reformers also achieved, to a very large extent, their goal of eliminating the lower classes from politics. Taking away most of the reason for the existence of the political parties—choosing candidates and printing and distributing ballots—caused the party organization to decline, which in turn produced a decline in political interest and activity on the part of the electorate. Without strong parties to mobilize voters, only the most interested and motivated participated. The new restrictions on voting meant that voters had to invest more time, energy, and thought in voting. They had to think about the election months in advance and travel to city hall to register.

As a consequence, politics began to be a spectator activity. Voter turnout declined sharply after the turn of the century.

Turnout figures from the nineteenth century are not entirely reliable and not exactly comparable with today's. In the days before voter registration, many aliens could vote and some people voted twice. In some instances, more people voted in a state election than lived there! Nevertheless, it is generally agreed that turnout was very high in the nineteenth century and that it has diminished substantially; it dropped from more than 77% from 1840 to 1896 to 54% in the 1920–1932 era, when the Progressive reforms were largely in place. During the New Deal era, when the Democratic Party mobilized new groups of voters, turnout rose again, but it has never achieved anything close to the levels of the nineteenth century.

Recent Turnout

Between 1964 and 1988, turnout in presidential elections slowly declined, from 62% to 50%. In 1992, turnout increased slightly, to 54%, but in 1996, it resumed its downward trend, to 49%. That is, of all citizens who could have registered and voted, less than half voted. This means that only one-fourth of the potential voters actually vote for the winning candidate.

The turnout for off-year congressional elections is even lower. It has not exceeded 45% since World War II, and in 1998 it was 36%. Turnout in primary elections is even lower. In 1986, it was an astoundingly low 10%.

Although nations count their turnouts differently, it is clear that Americans vote in much lower proportions than citizens of other Western democracies (Figure 1). Only Switzerland, which relatively recently gave women the right to vote, approximates our low turnout levels.

Within the United States, turnout varies greatly among the states. In the 1996 presidential election, for example, 65% of Maine's citizens voted, but only 39% of Nevada's did. Turnout tends to be lower in the South and higher in the northern Plains and Mountain states.[21]

These differences suggest that not only are there certain kinds of people who are unwilling to vote, but there are also certain kinds of laws and political traditions that depress voting turnout.

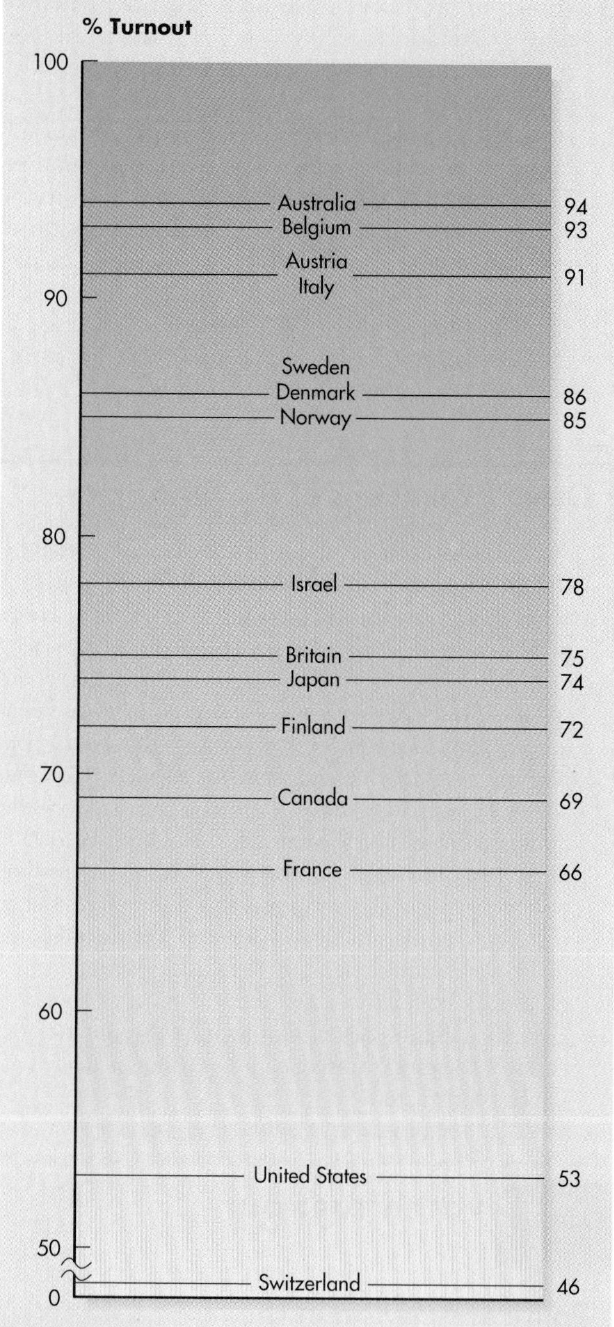

FIGURE 1

Turnout in the United States Is Lower Than in Most Other Democracies

SOURCES: Data are from national elections between 1986 and 1989. Richard Flickinger and Donley Studlar, "The Disappearing Voter?" *West European Politics* 15 (April 1992), pp. 1–16.

Who Does Not Vote?

Before we can explain why some people do not vote, we need to see who the nonvoters are. The most important thing to remember is that voting is related to education, income, and occupation, that is, to socioeconomic class. For example, if you are a college graduate, the chances are about 80% that you will vote; if you have less than a high school education, the chances are only about half that.[22] Differences between higher- and lower-income people are also quite large. Two out of three nonvoters have incomes below the average.[23] This class gap in turnout is widening. Although voting among all groups of Americans has declined in the past 30 years, the proportion of college-educated persons who participated fell by less than 10% while that of high school–educated persons dropped by nearly 20%.

Though many people take it for granted that those in the working class vote at lower rates than those in the middle and upper classes, in the United States these differences are far wider than in other nations[24] and far wider than in nineteenth-century America. So there appears to be something unique about the contemporary American political system that inhibits voting participation of all citizens, but particularly those whose income and educational level are below the average.

YOUNG PEOPLE VOTE LESS

Ratification of the Twenty-sixth Amendment to the U.S. Constitution in 1971 gave 18- to 20-year-olds the right to vote. Political observers expected that the campus activism of the Vietnam and civil rights era would be reflected in high voting turnouts among young people.

But in 1972, their first presidential election, less than half of young voters turned out, and even that small turnout has declined precipitously since. As the figure indicates, only 31% of 18- to 20-year-olds voted in 1996, compared with over 50% of their elders.

Why the low vote? One might expect that young people are more alienated from politics than their elders, but this does not seem to be true. Young voters are more trusting and less cynical. Others attribute low voting turnout to the high degree of mobility of young adults; they change their residences frequently and perhaps do not have time or do not take time to figure out how and where to register. Many young people are preoccupied with major life changes—going to college, leaving home, starting their first full-time job, getting married, starting a family. Then too, young people do not have the habit of voting.

In 1996, "Rock the Vote," a group organized to increase turnout among young adults, used a Web site to help those aged 18 to 24 register to vote. The group also set up registration tables at rock concerts and surfing championships. Despite these efforts, voting by young adults decreased.

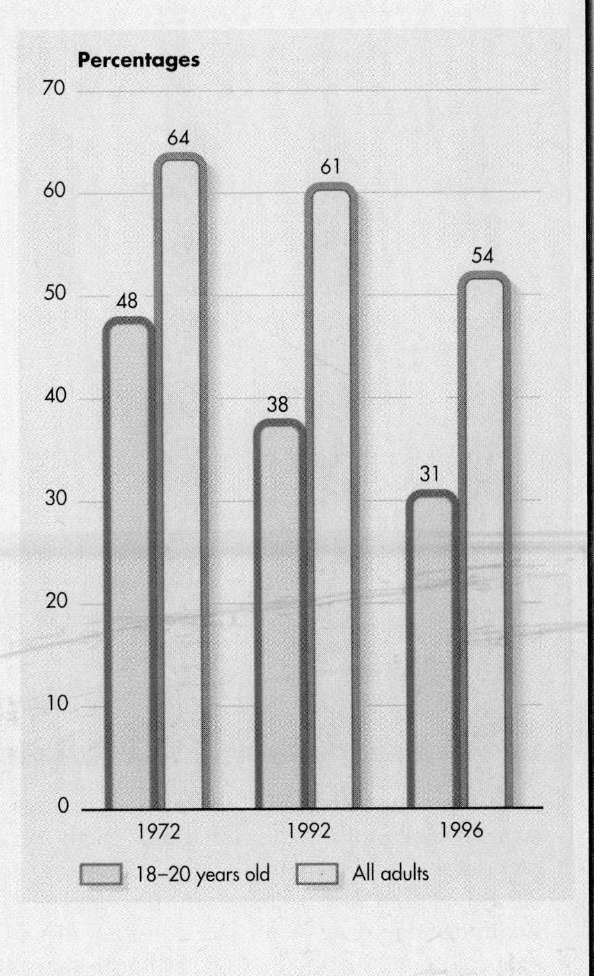

SOURCES: Current Population Reports, "Voting and Registration in the Election (various editions)," U.S. Census, series P20.

Voting is also much more common among older than younger people. The popular impression that young people often participate in politics was reinforced during the Vietnam years, when college campuses exploded with antiwar dissent. In fact, however, young people vote much less frequently than their elders. Those in their 40s and older have established their careers and families, and they have more time and money to devote to voting and other political activities.

Why Turnout Is Low

There are a number of possible reasons more Americans, especially low-income and young Americans, do not vote.

SATISFACTION AMONG VOTERS

One reason sometimes given for low rates of voter turnout is that nonvoters are satisfied; failing to vote is a passive form of consent to what government is doing.[25] This argument falls flat on two counts. First, voter turnout has decreased in an era when public trust in government has decreased, not increased. Levels of trust and voting turnout both started declining after 1964. And second, voter turnout is lower precisely among those groups of citizens who have least reason to be content, not those who have most reason to be so. If staying at home on election day was an indication of satisfaction, one would expect turnout to be lower among the well-off, not among the working class and the poor.

VOTERS ARE "TURNED OFF" BY POLITICAL CAMPAIGNS

About one-third of a group of nonvoters in the 1990 election, when asked why they did not vote, gave reasons suggesting they were disgusted with politics.[26] In explaining the low turnout in the 1988 campaign, one analyst commented, "The media

Some Account of some of the Bloody Deeds of

GEN. JACKSON.

Jacob Webb. David Morrow. John Harris. Henry Lewis. David Hunt. Edward Lindsey.

In this chapter there are eight photos, each marked with a blue band along the top, that illustrate American campaign tactics throughout the years. In this photo from the 1828 campaign, Andrew Jackson's opponents accused him of executing soldiers he commanded (as symbolized by the coffins). Jackson won anyway.

consultants, media and politicians gave this nation an awful election, and the public responded with appropriately awful turnouts."[27] The analyst was condemning the lack of real issues in the campaign, the negative advertising, and the constant attention paid by television to the polls telling people how they were going to vote (in 1988, there were 140 campaign polls, according to one count, and there were at least as many in 1992 and 1996).[28] These analyses surely contain some grains of truth, but how many? After all, people who are most likely to pay attention to the media, watch the ads, hear about the polls, and follow the campaigns are the most likely to vote, not the least. It is possible that the increasingly media-oriented campaigns have decreased overall turnout during the past generation (and we will have more to say about these campaigns later in the chapter). In fact, turnout is inversely related to media spending; the more the candidates spend, the lower the turnout. Moreover, voters who watch negative political ads are less likely to vote or to feel their vote counts.[29] The increase in negative advertising, then, helps explain declining turnout. However, negative advertising and other media attention cannot explain the class bias in nonvoting.

In addition to the *quality* of the campaigns, some people think turnout has declined because our elections are so frequent, campaigns last so long, and so many offices are contested that the public becomes bored, confused, or cynical.[30] At the presidential level, the sheer quantity of coverage, much of it focused repetitively on "who's winning," may simply bore people. Moreover, the continual public opinion polling and the widely publicized results may lead some to believe they don't need to vote.

At the local level voters elect so many officeholders, all the way down to weed and mosquito control commissioners, that many have no idea for whom or what they are voting. This proliferation of elective offices, thought by some to promote democracy and popular control, may promote only voter confusion and alienation. The problem is compounded because elections for different offices are held at different times. For example, most states have decided to hold elections for governor in nonpresidential election years. This decision probably reduces presidential election turnout by 7% and may reduce by one-third the number of those who vote for governor in those states.[31]

Primary elections are another problem. One estimate is that holding primary campaigns diminishes the general election turnout by 5%.[32]

By contrast, in Britain the time between calling an election (by the current government) and the actual election is only a month. In mid-March 1997, Prime Minister John Major called the election; on May 1, it was held. All campaigning was done during that time. There are no primaries. Moreover, as in most other parliamentary democracies, British citizens vote only for their representative in parliament and (at one other

SYMBOLIC SOLUTIONS FOR COMPLEX PROBLEMS?

SAME-DAY VOTER REGISTRATION

Voting turnout in the United States is second from lowest among the nations of the industrialized world. There are a number of possible remedies to this problem. One popular proposal is to allow voters to register when they go to the polling place on election day. This would reduce the costs of voting by reducing the time spent in finding and going to the registration office and the foresight necessary to remember to do so weeks or months in advance of the election. Moreover, by allowing same-day registration, states would put less premium on permanence of residence. Since Americans are a mobile population, this would increase the number of citizens eligible to vote.

But is same-day voter registration just a symbolic solution, making us feel that we are increasing citizen participation but really not? Or is same-day registration a real solution that might allow us to increase voter turnout? And if it is such a solution, are its benefits greater than the drawbacks of such a registration system?

States that make registration difficult (closing registration long before the election, not allowing absentee registration, not having regular office hours at the registrar's office, and so forth) have voter turnout about 9% less than states that make registration easier.[1] Since same-day registration is another way of making registration easier, we would expect it to improve turnout.

Three states (Maine, Minnesota, and Wisconsin) adopted same-day registration beginning in the 1970s, and that allows us to compare turnout between them and the other states. Since those three states have adopted same-day registration, their turnout in presidential elections has increased over 3%. The turnout rates in the other states, on average, have decreased almost 2% during that same time.[2] In other words, with everything else staying the same, same-day registration appears to improve voting turnout by about 5%. Other indicators of turnout change also suggest that same-day registration does lead to increased turnout.

Does the increase in turnout outweigh possible negative effects of this change? Opponents of the reform believe that it might lead to increased voter fraud; it might be easier for voters to vote multiple times, for example, if they do not have to register before the election. However, the existing system does not protect very well against voter fraud for someone determined to vote more than once, either. With the expansion of sophisticated computer tools, we might expect that the means to combat voter fraud are increasingly at hand, same-day voting or not.

Ultimately, though, we have to decide whether the expansion of the electorate by 5%, or, in another estimate, 8 million voters, is worth the additional risks that slightly more multiple voting might take place. And, whether or not we adopt same-day voting, we need to consider other means of increasing voter turnout too.

1. Steven Rosenstone and Ray Wolfinger, "The Effect of Registration Laws on Voter Turnout," *American Political Science Review* 72 (March 1978), pp. 22–45; G. Mitchell and C. Wlezien, "Voter Registration Laws and Turnout, 1972–1982," paper presented at the annual meeting of the Midwest Political Science Association, 1989.
2. Mark J. Fenster, "The Impact of Allowing Day of Registration Voting on Turnout in U.S. Elections from 1960 to 1992," *American Politics Quarterly* 22 (January 1994), pp. 74–87.

time) for the local representative. Voters are not faced with choices for a myriad of offices they barely recognize.

BARRIERS TO REGISTRATION

The necessity of registering has been a major impediment to voting. About one-quarter of nonvoters surveyed in 1990 indicated they did not vote because it was too difficult. As one commentator put it, "The United States is the only major democracy where government assumes no responsibility for helping citizens cope with voter registration procedures."[33] In many other nations, voter registrars go door to door to register voters, or voters are registered automatically when they pay taxes or receive public services. Difficult registration procedures have a special impact on low-income Americans, who were 17% less likely to vote in states with difficult registration procedures than in other states.[34]

Some states make it more convenient to register by having registration periods lasting up to election day (most states require registration at least 25 days before the election), registration in precincts or neighborhoods instead of one county office, registration by mail, registration offices open in the evenings and Saturday, and a policy of not purging voters who fail to vote from the registration lists. In other jurisdictions, voter registrars not only do not provide these options but actually try to hinder groups working to increase registration. They may refuse to allow volunteers to register voters outside the registration office.[35] One estimate is that voting turnout would be 9% higher if all states' procedures were similar to those of states that try to facilitate voter registration.[36]

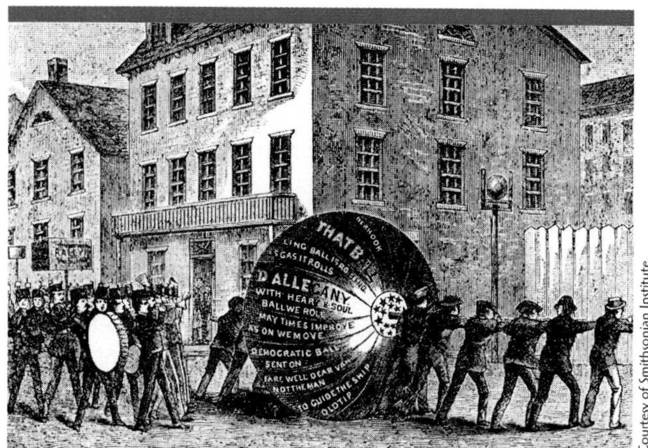
Courtesy of Smithsonian Institute.

From this 1840 Whig campaign gimmick came the phrase "keep the ball rolling."

To try to increase registration, Congress passed a law allowing people to register at public offices such as welfare offices and drivers' license bureaus (for this reason it is called the **"motor voter" law**).[37] Similar plans have increased registration in the 30 or so states that had these policies before the federal government did.[38] The law led to the greatest expansion of voter registration in American history; five million new voters registered. However, in the 1996 election, fewer voted than in 1992, indicating that the law did not have the desired effect of increasing turnout.

A related proposal suggests that change of address cards filed with the post office be accompanied by cards that go to the voting registration offices in the voter's former residence and new residence. Registration in the new residence would be automatic. One estimate is that the mobility of our society reduces voting by as much as 9%. The proposal also would reduce election fraud by removing names of residents who move from voting rosters.[39]

FAILURES OF PARTIES TO MOBILIZE VOTERS

Traditionally, political parties mobilized voters to turn out. As parties have declined in importance, they have become less effective in this role. The lack of effectiveness on the part of political parties in mobilizing millions of nonvoters, most of them working class or poor, is another reason for low voter turnout. Because of their low income, most of these nonvoters are Democrats. If mobilized, they would probably vote for Democrats, although in some elections the preferences of nonvoters have simply reflected the preferences of voters.[40]

Republicans are most fearful of this potential electorate. One conservative analyst wrote that a national registration plan, by tapping the voting power of the poor, "has the potential for altering the American party system."[41]

Even some Democrats are wary. The party has embraced social and economic reforms that attracted many middle-class and some business groups. The goals of these groups sometimes conflict with those of the poor, and the party's leaders do not want to threaten these constituencies. Moreover, in recent years the party has muted its appeals to the working class. This further reduces the incentives of working-class people to vote, and in turn decreases the incentive of Democrats to appeal to working-class voters.[42] However, increasing voter turnout has now become a partisan issue with most Democrats backing attempts to increase turnout (as they did with the motor voter plan), and most Republicans opposing them.

VOTING AS A RATIONAL CALCULATION OF COSTS AND BENEFITS

Nonvoting also may be the result of a rational calculation of the costs and benefits of voting. Economist Anthony Downs argues that people vote when they believe the perceived benefits of voting are greater than the costs.[43] If a voter sees a difference between the parties or candidates, and favors one party's position over the other, that voter has a reason to vote and can expect some benefit from doing so. For that reason, people who are highly partisan vote more than those less attached to a party, and people with a strong sense of political efficacy, the belief they can influence government, vote more than others.

Voters who see no difference between the candidates or parties, however, may believe that voting is not worth the effort it takes and that it is more rational to abstain. And in fact, 40% of nonvoters in 1990 gave only the excuse that they were "too busy," suggesting a large degree of apathy.[44] Nevertheless, some people will vote even if they think there is no difference between the candidates because they have a sense of civic duty, a belief that their responsibilities as citizens include voting. Most voters feel gratified that they have done their duties as citizens. In fact, more voters give this as an explanation for voting than any other reason, including the opportunity to influence policy.[45]

Downs assumes that the costs of voting are minimal, but, in reality, for many people the time, expense, and possible embarrassment of trying to register are greater than the perceived benefits of voting. This is especially true for lower-income people who perceive that neither party is attentive to their interests. Moreover, it is possible that the frequency, length, and media orientation of campaigns lower the perceived benefits of voting for people of all incomes by trivializing the election and emphasizing the negative.

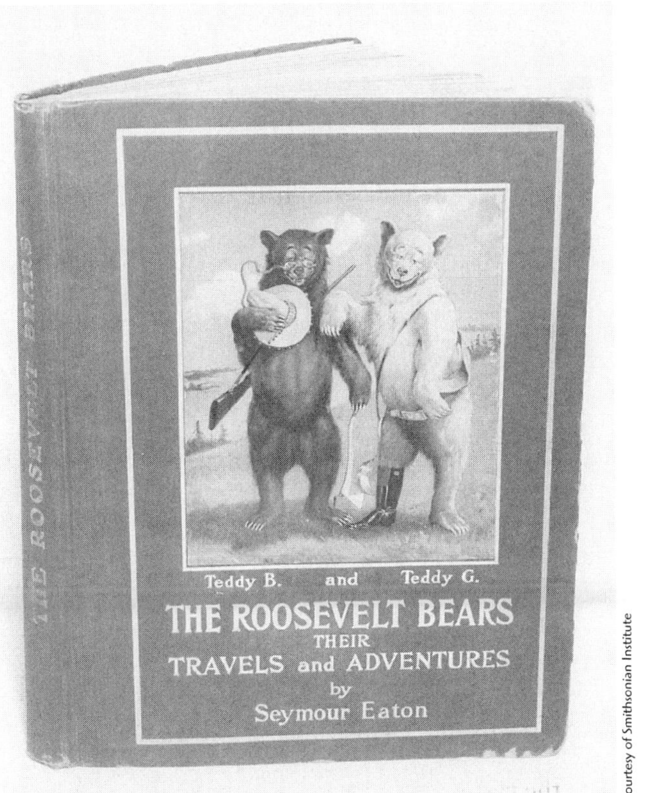

Courtesy of Smithsonian Institute

Voter turnout was higher in the days when campaigns were more fun and involved more people. Songs were often written about the candidates, and, here, a book about teddy bears reflects Theodore (Teddy) Roosevelt's popularity.

OTHER CAMPAIGN PARTICIPATION

We have seen that only about half of all Americans vote in presidential elections, and even fewer vote in off-year congressional races. Still fewer participate actively in political campaigns. For example, in a recent year, about one-quarter of the population said that they worked for a party or candidate. About an equal proportion claimed that they contributed money to a party or candidate. Smaller proportions attended political meetings or actually belonged to a political club.

Unlike voting, rates of participation in campaigns have not declined over the past 20 years. This suggests that people are not less political than they used to be, but that something about elections themselves has decreased voter turnout. Indeed, more people give money to candidates and parties than they used to, probably because, unlike 20 years ago, candidates and parties now use mass mailing techniques to solicit funds from supporters.[46] Hundreds of thousands of potential donors can be reached in a very short time.

Just as there is a strong class basis to voting, there is also a strong class basis to participation in campaign activities. Those with more education and income are more likely to participate. Those with only eight grades of education or less participate, on average, in only one of 12 types of political participation aside from voting, whereas those with college education participate in 3 or 4. Those with some college education actually increased their participation over the past 20 years, whereas those with less than a high school education decreased theirs. Thus, the class bias in participation, as in voting alone, has increased over time.[47]

Gender, race, age, and regional differences in participation also appear. Even taking education into account, men usually participate slightly more than women, whites somewhat more than blacks, older people more than younger people, and southerners more than northerners. But these differences change over time. Young people participated more than their elders, and blacks more than whites, during the late 1960s and early 1970s.[48] These were times of heightened interest in politics generally, and the anti-Vietnam War and civil rights movements drew many young and black people into political activity.

PRESIDENTIAL NOMINATING CAMPAIGNS

Many Americans believe in the Horatio Alger myth, that with hard work anyone can achieve great success. This myth has its parallel in politics, where it is sometimes said that any child can grow up to be president. In fact, only a few run for that office and even fewer are elected.

Who Runs for President and Why?

In deciding whether to run for president, individuals consider such things as the costs and risks of running and the probabilities of winning.[49] Most people have little chance of being president: They are unknown to the public, they do not have the financial resources or contacts to raise the money needed for a national campaign, they have jobs they could not leave to run a serious campaign, and their friends would probably ridicule them for even thinking of such a thing.

GAY POWER

In recent years, homosexuals have become more politically active. Spurred by the crisis of AIDS among the gay community and the initially slow response of the federal government to the disease, gays have begun to organize to exercise political clout.

How much clout can gays have? Even the number of gays in the United States is a politically sensitive question. Many gay activists argue that 10% of the population is gay. Various recent surveys of sexual activity indicate the number may be considerably lower, perhaps as low as 1%. Sexual orientation is not a question asked in standard national surveys, and if it were, it might not elicit truthful answers, so it is difficult to know the accuracy of the estimates. Whatever the numbers, homosexuals have been "coming out of the closet" in significant numbers in recent years.

Gay issues are now being openly considered in political campaigns. "Gay rights" includes a number of different things. Most discussed have been ending the ban on homosexuals in the military and giving homosexuals equal rights to jobs and housing. Some gay activists want legal recognition of same-sex marriages and a general acknowledgment of homosexuality as an acceptable lifestyle. The public overwhelmingly supports nondiscrimination in jobs and in the military but is not supportive of homosexual lifestyles and same-sex marriages.

Homosexual rights became a sort of closet issue in the 1992 elections. All the Democratic candidates courted the gay vote and all sought financial support from the gay community. These candidates, and Ross Perot, supported ending the ban on homosexuals in the military, for example. Clinton received strong support from the gay community; in some areas gays are a significant political force. In California, for example, perhaps as many as 10% of all voters are gay.

Most Republicans are less supportive of homosexual rights. Such rights are anathema to many fundamentalist Christians, who consider homosexuality a sin and thus a totally unacceptable lifestyle. These fundamentalists, and other conservatives, are an important part of the Republican constituency. At the 1992 Republican convention, some speakers overtly attacked gays and gay rights. However, as one conservative political analyst remarked, "The gay-bashing turned people off."

Tracey Litt/Impact Visuals

Barney Frank (D-Mass.), one of three openly gay members of Congress, at a fund-raiser.

President Bush, who had at least a dozen aides and officials who were gay, personally did not engage in direct gay-bashing. He and other top Republicans used more subtle attacks on gays and gay lifestyles, for example by calling for a return to "family values," a term that can mean almost anything but was intended to be a code word for traditional family values.

Several openly gay candidates have been elected recently, including three members of Congress and state legislators in several states. These successes are coming at a time when the gay community is being weakened through the AIDS epidemic, which has already caused about 150,000 deaths, two-thirds of them gay men. But AIDS has been important in encouraging gays to come out of the closet, and possibly has been important in encouraging broader tolerance of gays. Twice as many people now say they know someone who is a homosexual than did so in the mid-1980s. Even though there is no consensus on homosexual issues, it seems clear that gays are gaining legitimacy in the political process.

SOURCES: Jeffrey Schmalz, "Gay Politics Goes Mainstream," *New York Times Magazine*, October 11, 1992, p. 18ff. Much of this box is drawn from the Schmalz article; Bill McAllister and Michael Weisskopf, "Breaking through the 'Lavender Ceiling,' " *Washington Post National Weekly Edition*, November 14–20, 1994, p. 14.

But a few people are in a different position. Take, for instance, a hypothetical U.S. senator from Texas or a governor of California. By their vote-gathering ability in a large state, they have demonstrated some possibility that they could win. Their decision to run might hinge on such considerations as whether they think they could raise the money necessary to run a campaign, whether they are willing to sacrifice a good part of their private life and their privacy for a few years, and whether they would lose the office they currently hold if they run and lose.

These calculations are real. Most candidates for president are, in fact, senators or governors.[50] Vice presidents also frequently run, but until George Bush's victory, they had not been successful in this century.

Why do candidates run? An obvious reason is to gain the power and prestige of the presidency. But they may have other goals as well, such as to gain support for a particular policy or set of ideas.

Corbis-Bettmann

In the nineteenth century, politics involved most people, and political parades and festivities were common. Here a torchlight parade honors Grover Cleveland in Buffalo in the late 1880s.

Ronald Reagan, for example, clearly wanted to be president in part to spread his conservative ideology. Jesse Jackson wants to be president in part to help those at the bottom of the social ladder. Eugene McCarthy ran in 1968 to challenge Lyndon Johnson's Vietnam policy.

Sometimes candidates run to gain name recognition and publicity for the next election. Most successful candidates in recent years have run before. George Bush lost the nomination in 1980 before being elected in 1988; Ronald Reagan lost in 1976 before his victory in 1980; Richard Nixon lost in 1960 before winning in 1968.

Sometimes candidates run for the presidency to be considered for the vice presidency, probably viewing it as an eventual stepping-stone to the presidency. But only occasionally, such as when Reagan chose Bush in 1980 or Kennedy chose Johnson in 1960, do presidential candidates choose one of their defeated opponents to run as a vice presidential candidate. In 1988 and 1992, nominees passed over their defeated rivals in choosing vice presidential running mates.

How a Candidate Wins the Nomination

Presidential candidates try to win a majority of delegates at their party's national nominating convention in the summer preceding the November election. Delegates to those conventions are elected in state caucuses, conventions, and primaries. Candidates must campaign to win the support of those who attend caucuses and conventions and of primary voters.

Normally, candidates formally announce their candidacies in the year preceding the presidential election year. Then their aim is to persist and survive the long primary and caucus season that begins in February of election year and continues until only one candidate is left. Candidates use a number of methods to try to maximize their chances of survival. They carefully choose the primaries they will enter and to which they will devote their resources. Candidates must enter enough primaries so they are seen as national, not regional, candidates, but they cannot possibly devote time and resources to every primary or caucus. Especially important are the early events—the Iowa caucus and the New Hampshire primary—and the larger state primaries.

Candidates also try to survive by establishing themselves as *the* candidate for a particular policy or other constituency. In 1988, Pat Robertson hoped to win the loyalties of the new Christian Right within the Republican Party, but he was unsuccessful in enlisting enough of these voters to offset his unpopularity with other Republicans.

To compete successfully, candidates also need considerable media coverage. They must convince reporters that they are serious candidates with a real chance of winning. Journalists and candidates establish expectations for how well each candidate should do based on the results of polls, the quality of a candidate's campaign organization, the amount of money and time spent in the campaign, and the political complexion of the state. If a candidate performs below expectations, even though garnering the most votes, it may be interpreted by the press as a weakness and hurt the campaign. On the other hand, a strong showing when expectations are low can mean a boost to a candidate's campaign.

AMERICAN DIVERSITY

CAN AN AFRICAN AMERICAN BE ELECTED PRESIDENT?

The Jesse Jackson campaigns of 1984 and 1988 and that of Douglas Wilder in 1992 raise the question of whether a black person can be elected president. Or, more generally, will the American presidency continue to be held only by white, non-Jewish males?

These questions sound familiar. In 1960, some doubted that a Catholic could ever be elected president. At that time, only 71% of all voters said they would vote for a Catholic for president.[1] The only previous major-party Catholic candidate, Alfred Smith, had been soundly defeated by Herbert Hoover in 1928. But then John F. Kennedy was elected. Since then, two Catholics, Geraldine Ferraro and Sargent Shriver, have run as vice presidential nominees without much attention paid to their religion.

But race has been a more pronounced cleavage in American society than religion. Racism persists, and race influences all kinds of political debates, from welfare reform to the all-volunteer military. The party realignment that has occurred in the South is shaped by racial as well as class issues. A majority of white southerners, resentful of the Democratic Party's support of the civil rights struggle, has turned to the Republican Party.

Race was important in the 1988 campaign. It surfaced when the Republicans succeeded in tying Dukakis to Willie Horton, an African American convict who raped a woman while on furlough from prison. It also came up when Jesse Jackson's prominence in the Democratic Party was highlighted and made to seem somehow illegitimate and frightening. A campaign letter from the California Republican Party asked, "Why is it so urgent you decide now? . . . Here are two [reasons]." Below were two photos, one of Bush and Reagan, the other of Jackson and Dukakis. "If [Dukakis] is elected to the White House," it continued, "Jesse Jackson is sure to be swept into power on his coattails."[2]

This is not to say that all of those who voted against Jackson in the primaries or against the Democrats in the general election were racists. Jackson had no experience holding office and is identified with the most liberal wing of the Democratic Party.

Race seemed less important in 1996 when Colin Powell, an African American former chairman of the Joint Chiefs of Staff (the nation's highest military post), was considered a strong presidential candidate. Many from both parties were quite disappointed when he chose not to run.

As the figure shows, 8% to 9% of the public say they would not vote for a black or a woman who was their party's nominee, and a slightly lower proportion say they would not vote for a Jew. Although 8% to 9% is enough to make a difference in a close race, many more people today say they would vote for a black, Jew, or woman than said they would vote for a Catholic in 1960. John Kennedy's victory suggests that 8% or 9% is not an insurmountable barrier.

1. Barry Sussman, "A Black or Woman Does Better Today Than a Catholic in '60," *Washington Post National Weekly Edition,* November 21, 1983, p. 42.

2. "Though This Be Meanness, Yet There is a Method in It," *Washington Post National Weekly Edition,* October 10–16, 1988, p. 26.

Declining Numbers Oppose Blacks, Women, and Jews for President

SOURCE: Gallup Polls. The question asked was, "If your party nominated a generally well-qualified man for president and he happened to be a black [Jew], would you vote for him?" or, "If your party nominated a woman for president, would you vote for her if she were qualified for the job?" No questions were asked about blacks until 1958. The "1961" data for blacks are from 1963. The 1994 data are from the NORC's General Social Surveys.

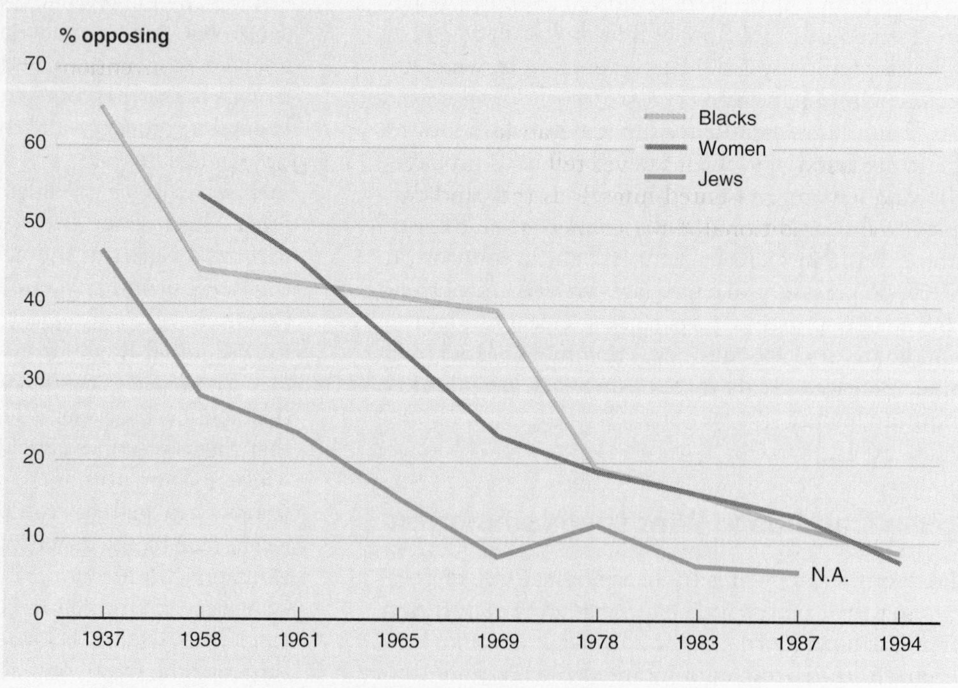

Consequently, candidates try to lower media expectations. It is not enough to win a primary; you have to win by at least as much as the media claims you should, or you will be seen as a loser. In the Republican race in 1988, Pat Robertson's organizers tried to counter media predictions for the Iowa caucuses by urging supporters to tell pollsters that they were not going to attend the caucuses. Because pollsters do not count people who do not plan to vote, this tactic could result in an artificially low prediction—and then a surprisingly high vote.[51]

Sometimes even losers are portrayed as winners if they do better than expected. For example, in 1968 in the New Hampshire primary, antiwar candidate Senator Eugene McCarthy won 40% of the vote against President Johnson, who had become increasingly unpopular because of the Vietnam War. Although McCarthy did not win, he did much better than expected, and the press interpreted the vote as a repudiation of Johnson's leadership.

In sum, then, the primary season is a game among the media, the candidates, and the voters, with the candidates trying to raise voter enthusiasm and lower media expectations simultaneously.

The common wisdom about presidential primaries is that the key ingredient is "momentum." That is, a candidate needs to win early, or at least do better than expected, to gain momentum, then keep winning to maintain momentum. Jimmy Carter's 1976 victory in the Iowa caucuses, which attracted tremendous media attention, which in turn led to further primary wins, is an illustration.

Early in the primary season, candidates try to find the position, slogan, or idea that will appeal to the most voters. To take advantage of what appeared to be America's distrust of Washington, D.C., Jimmy Carter tried to create an image of an honest person who would never tell a lie. In 1984, Ronald Reagan presented himself as the candidate embodying traditional America. As one of his staff aides wrote in a campaign memo, "Paint RR as the personification of all that is right with, or heroized by, America."[52]

Candidates must avoid making a big mistake or, worse yet, being caught covering up a mistake or untruth. Edmund Muskie's front-running candidacy ground to a halt in 1972 when he cried at a public appearance while denouncing a newspaper attack on his wife. Gary Hart's 1988 candidacy collapsed when the media discovered that his marriage did not prevent him from having affairs with other women. He compounded the damage by lying. The Muskie incident was taken by the media and public to indicate that he could not handle the stress of a campaign or, by inference, the presidency. The Hart incident raised questions about his character and honesty.

Courtesy of Smithsonian Institute

Soliciting votes by giving speeches and making appearances was once considered beneath the dignity of the presidential office. William Jennings Bryan was the first presidential candidate to break this tradition. In 1896 he traveled more than 18,000 miles and made more than 600 speeches in an effort to win voters. Although Bryan lost the election to William McKinley, his approach to campaigning became the standard. This photo illustrates how the term "stump speech" to refer to candidates' boilerplate campaign speeches may have developed.

Incumbent presidents seeking renomination do not have the same problems as their challengers. No incumbent who sought renomination has been denied it in this century.

In addition to these general strategies, candidates must deal specifically with the particular demands of caucuses, conventions, and primaries.

Presidential Caucuses and Conventions

Some states employ caucuses and conventions to select delegates to attend presidential nominating conventions. In 1992, one or both parties in 16 states selected delegates in caucuses.

The Iowa caucuses, except for their timing and newsworthiness, are similar to those in other states. Normally, the campaign in Iowa starts months before the caucuses are actually held. In 1988, presidential candidates spent a total of 999 days campaigning in Iowa. Campaigning is, in large part, personal. Democrat Bruce Babbitt reported that one caucus attender, a tropical fish hobbyist, said he would deliver his vote to Babbitt if he could tell him the "pH and sediment density of the Congo River at its mouth." Babbitt assigned a staffer to look into the question.[53]

In early February, the caucuses are held in private homes, schools, and churches, and all who consider themselves party members can attend. They debate

Wendell Willkie, Republican presidential candidate in 1940, rides into Elmwood, Indiana. In the days before television, motorcades allowed large numbers of people to see the candidates and were a way for the candidates to generate enthusiasm among the voters.

and vote on the candidates. The candidates receiving the most votes win delegates to later county and state conventions. The number of delegates is proportional to the vote that the candidate received at the caucuses (assuming the candidate got at least 15%).

Iowa, as the first state to hold its caucuses, normally gets the most attention. In 1988, 3,000 representatives of the media covered these caucuses. Although only a handful of delegates to the national convention are at stake, a win with the nation's political pros watching can establish a candidate as a serious contender and attract further media attention and financial donations important to continuing the campaign.

Presidential Primaries

Delegates to presidential nominating conventions are also selected in direct primaries, sometimes called **presidential preference primaries.** In these elections, governed by state laws and national party rules, voters indicate a preference for a presidential candidate, delegates committed to a candidate, or both. Some states have preference primaries, but delegates are actually selected in conventions. These primaries are often called "beauty contests" because they are meaningless in terms of winning delegates, though they can be important in showing popular support. Like other primaries, presidential primaries can be open or closed.

Until 1968, presidential preference primaries usually played an insignificant role in presidential nominations. Only a handful of states employed primaries to select delegates. The conventional wisdom was that primary victories could not guarantee nomination but a loss would spell sure defeat.

The insignificance of most primaries was illustrated in 1968 by Vice President Hubert Humphrey's ability to win the party's nomination without winning a single primary. Humphrey was able to win the nomination because a majority of the delegates to the convention in 1968 were selected through party caucuses and conventions, where party leaders supportive of Humphrey had considerable influence.

Humphrey's nomination severely divided the Democratic Party. Many constituencies within the party, particularly those opposed to the Vietnam War, were hostile to Humphrey and believed that the nomination was controlled by party elites out of step with the preferences of rank-and-file Democrats.

DELEGATE SELECTION REFORM

The response of the Democratic Party to these complaints was to change delegate selection procedures in order to make delegates more representative of

Corbis-Bettmann

The train "whistlestop" campaign was a staple of many presidential races. Here President Harry Truman gives a speech from the back of a train in 1948.

Democratic voters. One change established quotas for blacks, women, and young people to reflect the groups' percentages in each state's population. These reforms significantly increased minority and female representation in the 1972 convention and, quite unexpectedly, made the primary the preferred method of nomination. Criteria of openness and representativeness could be more easily satisfied through primary selection. In recent years, more than 70% of the Democratic delegates were chosen in primaries.

The Democrats have replaced quotas for minorities with guidelines urging minority involvement in party affairs. However, the quota remains that half the delegates must be women.

The Democratic Party reforms diminished the participation of party and elected officials. Critics felt that this weakened the party and increased the probability of nominating a candidate who could not work with party leaders. Since 1984, 15% to 20% of the delegates have been "superdelegates" appointed from among members of Congress and other party and public officials. The change was to help ensure that the party's nominee would be someone who could work with other elected officials within the party.

The Republican Party has not felt as much pressure to reform its delegate selection procedures. Republicans have tried to eliminate discrimination and increase participation in the selection process.

Reforming the Nomination Process

Each election year political observers discuss changing the presidential nomination process. They correctly complain that primaries tend to weaken political parties and have very low, unrepresentative turnouts. Moreover, the current system gives disproportionate influence to two small states, Iowa and New Hampshire, that come first in the process. Voters in most other states do not get to see most candidates; they have already been weeded out by the time the April, May, and June primaries occur. Moreover, some charge that the current system is influenced too much by the media, which exaggerates the victories of the winners and makes the losers seem weaker than they actually are.

Until recently, we could defend the primary system by pointing out two advantages of giving disproportionate influence to small states that select their delegates early. Only in these first small states do candidates come in contact with voters on a very personal basis. In large states, the primaries are strictly media events. Moreover, when small states came first, the candidates could test their popularity without spending millions of dollars. Those who were successful could then attract funds for the larger, more expensive races. This system gave little-known candidates a better chance than most alternative arrangements would have.

But by 1996, large states such as California, New York, Texas, Florida, and Illinois moved their primaries earlier into the primary season in order to increase their influence on the nominating process. And, on **Super Tuesday,** most Southern states hold their primaries simultaneously. Now candidates can no longer bank on doing well in the early small-state primary elections and then having some momentum to help in raising large sums of money. The demands for fund-raising have grown, because candidates must have money in hand long before the first primary in order to book and run the massive television campaigns needed to reach primary voters in these large states and in the South. As a result, little-known candidates have a tougher battle now than in previous election years.

Some observers are glad that we no longer have the "smoke-filled rooms" where party bosses chose nominees. Nevertheless, the primary system has weakened political parties, and the small primary electorate is unrepresentative of the general public. Indeed, these voters might be less representative of the public than the party bosses who met in smoke-filled rooms. And they know less about the nominees than did the party bosses. But the days when party leaders could anoint the nominees are probably gone forever.

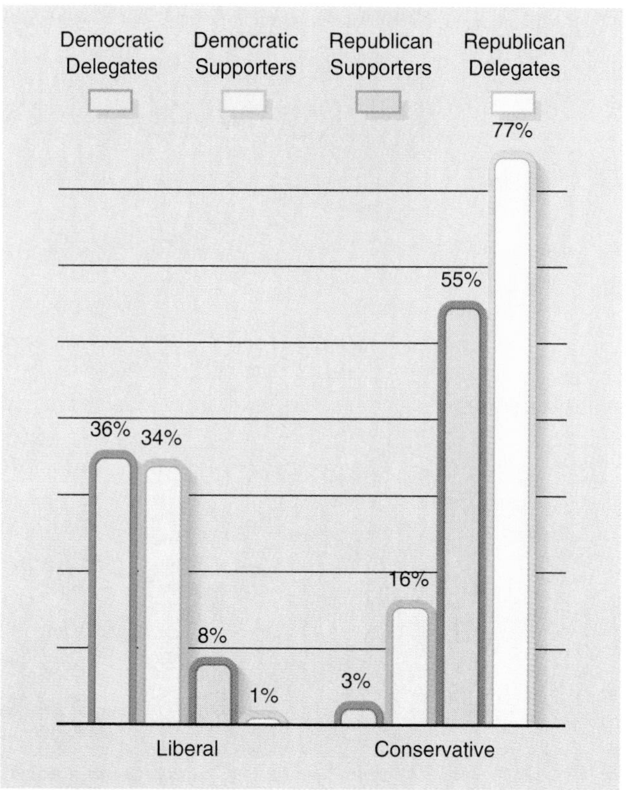

FIGURE 2

National Convention Delegates Are More Ideologically Extreme Than Rank-and-File Members

SOURCES: Data are from delegate and public surveys reported in *Washington Post National Weekly Edition,* August 26–September 1, 1996, p. A4 and August 12–18, 1996, p. A.

The National Conventions

Once selected, delegates attend their party's national nominating convention in the summer before the November election. Changes in party rules have reduced the convention's role from an arena where powerful party leaders came together and determined the party's nominee to a body that ratifies a choice based on the outcome of the primaries and caucuses.

In the "old" days, often many ballots were necessary before a winner emerged. In 1924, it took the Democrats 103 ballots to nominate John W. Davis. Now nominees are selected on the first ballot. In most election years, some experts predict a close nomination race, which would force the decision to be made at the convention. But in fact, the recent national party conventions served the purposes they have served for nearly 40 years—to endorse the nominee and his choice for vice president, to construct a party platform, to whip up enthusiasm for the ticket among party loyalists, and to present the party favorably to the national viewing audience. Thus, even without the nomination job, national conventions give meaning to the notion of a national party.

Before 1972, delegates were predominantly white and male. After 1972, the percentage of delegates who were black, women, and under 30 increased substantially. In 1992, 52% of the Democratic and 45% of the Republican delegates were women; 17% of the Democratic and 4% of the Republican delegates were black. The latter figures are fairly close to the percentage of blacks among each party's supporters.

Convention delegates are still unrepresentative in terms of education and income. Compared to the population, delegates to national party conventions are well educated and well-off financially. To spend a week at a convention requires more money and free time than the average American has.

Delegates also tend to be more ideologically extreme than each party's rank and file. Democratic delegates are generally more liberal and Republican delegates more conservative than their party's supporters (see Figure 2).

THE ACTIVITIES OF THE CONVENTION

National party conventions are full of color and excitement. They are a montage of balloons, placards, and demonstrations. Candidates and their lieutenants scurry in search of uncommitted delegates. Behind-the-scenes negotiators try to work out differences among factions of the party. Journalists are everywhere covering everything from the trivial to the momentous. The keynote address reviews the party's glorious past and speaks to a promising future. Each candidate is placed in nomination by a party notable who reviews the candidate's background and experience. The roll call of the states ratifies the party's choice, and on the last night delegates cheer the acceptance speeches of the presidential and vice presidential nominees. Those who contested the nomination often join the nominees on the platform at the end in a display of party unity.

Aside from these very visible aspects, each convention has three important committees. The credentials committee reviews any challenges that may arise to the right of specific delegates to participate. The rules committee formulates convention and party rules, such as those governing delegate selection. The platform committee drafts the party's platform. The contents of the platform can generate conflict. For example, in 1968 the Democrats fought bitterly over a platform provision calling for an end to the Vietnam War. The failure of the party's nominee, Humphrey, to support the provision led many antiwar Democrats to sit out the election. After supporting the Equal Rights Amendment for years, the Republicans split over it and did not endorse it in their 1980s' platforms.

Apart from being important symbols of the direction the party wants to take, do platforms mean anything? Surprisingly, amidst the platitudes, more than half of the most recent platforms contained pledges regarding proposed future actions, and most of those pledges were fulfilled.[54] Platforms do provide observant voters with information about what the party will do if elected.

In the 1950s, at the dawn of the television age, Democratic Party leaders instruct their delegates how to behave on camera.

Courtesy of Smithsonian Institute

THE MEDIA AND THE CONVENTION

Before 1932, nominees did not attend the convention. Acceptance of the nomination took place sometime afterward in a special ceremony. In 1932, Franklin Roosevelt broke with tradition and presented his acceptance speech to the convention and to a nationwide radio audience; he did not want to lose an opportunity to deliver his message to the American people. The Republicans did not follow his example until 1944. Since then, both parties' conventions have closed with the acceptance speeches of the presidential and vice presidential nominees.

With the beginning of radio coverage in 1924 and television coverage in 1940, the conventions have become media events. The parties try to put on a show they hope will attract voters to their candidates. Polls usually show the party's candidate doing better during and after the party's convention, called the "convention bounce," though the effect does not last long.[55]

Major addresses, such as the acceptance speech, are planned for peak viewing hours. Potentially disruptive credentials and platform proceedings often are scheduled for the early morning hours. Conventions have become tightly organized and highly orchestrated affairs where little is left to chance. The stakes are too high.

Control, however, has its limits. If there are deep cleavages in the party, it may be impossible to prevent them from surfacing at the convention during prime time. The 1968 Democratic Convention was filled with conflict—conflict inside the convention between the supporters of Hubert Humphrey and opponents of the Johnson policies on the Vietnam War and conflict outside the convention on the streets of Chicago between antiwar demonstrators and the Chicago police. Television covered both events, associating the division in the convention with the turmoil outside, and dimmed Humphrey's chances of winning the election.

In recent years, with the nomination settled well in advance of the convention and few vociferous floor fights over platforms, the conventions have been less dramatic and suspenseful. Consequently, the major networks are no longer showing them "gavel to gavel,"

Steve Leonard/Black Star

As a vice presidential candidate, Geraldine Ferraro drew large crowds and especially ignited the enthusiasm of many women.

leaving that coverage to specialty cable networks like CNN and C-SPAN. Party leaders' control over the conventions backfired in terms of attracting and retaining a mass audience throughout.

SELECTING A VICE PRESIDENTIAL NOMINEE

Selection of a vice presidential candidate normally is done by the party's presidential nominee, then merely ratified at the convention, although in 1956, Democratic nominee Adlai Stevenson broke with tradition and left the decision to the convention.

Presidential candidates usually select a vice presidential nominee who can "balance" the ticket in terms of region (Kennedy from Massachusetts chose Johnson of Texas in 1960), ideology (the more liberal Dukakis picked the more conservative Bentsen), Washington experience (in 1980, Washington outsider Reagan chose Washington insider Bush), and other characteristics. Gender traditionally has not been part of a ticket balancing effort, but since Walter Mondale's historic choice of Geraldine Ferraro in 1984, women are sometimes among those given consideration.

Bush's 1988 selection of Indiana senator Dan Quayle, however, did not illustrate any of the usual strategic considerations except that Quayle was from a different part of the country than Bush. Quayle, a conservative senator from Indiana, was youthful and charming but had little experience and was considered a lightweight. Though most of Bush's advisers seemed to think Quayle was a reasonably safe choice,[56] the media found that Quayle, though a hawk on the Vietnam issue, had spent his Vietnam years safely as a member of the Indiana National Guard. Debate raged over whether his family influence (his wealthy parents owned Indiana's largest newspapers) got him out of active service and into the guard. During the campaign, Bush's advisers would not let Quayle appear on network news shows or get close to metropolitan areas with major media markets.

Most observers believe Clinton's choice of Senator Albert Gore, Jr., was more astute. Though Gore did not, at first glance, fit the traditional image of a candidate chosen to balance the presidential candidate's characteristics (he was about the same age, of the same Baptist religion, from the same region, and of the same moderate Democratic ideology), or to bring with him a state with a large number of electoral college votes (Tennessee), he in fact did balance some of Clinton's weaknesses. Gore was a war veteran, while Clinton avoided service in Vietnam, and Gore's credentials as a family man had never been challenged. Gore had foreign policy expertise while Clinton did not. Perhaps more important, Gore's own moderate political philosophy strengthened Clinton's image as a moderate; Gore's youth strengthened Clinton's credibility as a candidate for change; and Gore's reputation as an environmentalist played well to many voters.

Do vice presidential choices affect the election outcome? In most cases probably not. As a cynical observer commented, "Pick anyone . . . if Quayle can't sink a ticket, nobody can."[57]

Independent and Third-Party Nominees

Independent and third-party candidates are part of every presidential campaign. Most of these candidates are invisible to all but the most avid political devotee. But sometimes strong independent candidates emerge, such as George Wallace in 1968, John Anderson in 1980, and Ross Perot in 1992 and 1996. The Perot candidacies were visible both because he had money to finance his campaign and because voters in recent years identify less strongly with parties and express more dissatisfaction with politics as usual. A strong independent candidate could influence the outcome of the election. Though many people thought Perot might have such an effect, his support was not strong enough.

It is not easy for independent candidates to get on the ballot. State laws control access to the ballot, and Democratic and Republican legislators and governors make those laws. Thus, the candidates of the Democratic and Republican Parties are automatically placed on the ballot in all 50 states, but independent candidates must demonstrate significant support to get on the ballot through petitions signed by voters.

THE GENERAL ELECTION CAMPAIGN

We take it for granted that the election campaign is what determines who wins. But consider this: Only once since 1952 has the candidate who was ahead in the polls in July, before the national conventions, lost. That year was 1988. Dukakis led in the preconvention period by 6 to 10 points.[58] This suggests that although campaigns can make a difference, a lot of other factors determine who is elected.

Campaign Organization

Staffing the campaign organization is crucial, not only to get talented people but also to get those with considerable national campaign experience and a variety of perspectives. In 1988, most of the Bush team were old hands in national campaigns, having had significant roles in Reagan's. Dukakis's staff members were much less experienced and, perhaps even more damaging, did not always appreciate that campaigns are run differently in California, Texas, or Illinois than in Massachusetts, Dukakis's home state. In 1992, the situation was different. Bush's team lacked the confidence and experience of Clinton's.

The candidate's own personal organization is only one part of the overall campaign organization. The national party organization and state parties also have some responsibilities, especially in registering potential party voters, getting them to the polls, and trying to make sure that the presidential candidate's local appearances will help the party's congressional and state candidates.

Images and Issues

Largely through the media, candidates try to create a favorable image and portray the opponent in an unfavorable way. The Bush campaign was remarkably successful at creating a negative image for Dukakis in 1988; Dukakis was unsuccessful in creating either a positive image for himself or reinforcing Bush's negative image.

In 1992, the Bush campaign struggled to create both a positive image for the president and a negative image for Clinton. But Bush could not find a focus for redefining himself, and his efforts to define a negative image for Clinton had limited success. Clinton was not Dukakis, who seemed not to grasp the damage the Bush campaign was doing to him. The Clinton team learned from the Dukakis debacle. They answered every attack Bush made, but at the same time they stayed focused on their own campaign message.

Issues also can be the basis for an appeal to voters. As they did in 1992, Democrats traditionally have used the "pocketbook" issues, arguing that economic times are better when Democrats are in the White House. In 1984, however, Reagan was successful in focusing on economic issues and taking credit for a strong economic recovery.

Issue appeals are usually general, and often candidates do not offer a clear-cut choice even on the most important controversies of the time. For example, the 1968 presidential election offered voters little choice on Vietnam policy, because the positions of candidates Nixon and Humphrey appeared very similar.[59] Voters who wanted to end the war by withdrawing and others who wanted to escalate the war had no real choice of candidates.

Ideally, the major campaign themes and strategies have been put into place by the end of the summer, but these themes and strategies are revised and updated on a daily, sometimes hourly, basis as the campaign progresses. Decisions are made not just by the candidate and the campaign manager but by a staff of key advisers who include media experts and pollsters. Sophisticated polling techniques are used to produce almost daily reports on shifts in public opinion across the nation and in particular regions. Thus, media ads can be added and deleted as polls reflect their impact. Campaign trips are modified or scratched as the candidate's organization sees new opportunities. And media events can be planned to complement the paid advertising the candidate runs.

The Electoral College

All planning for the campaign has to take into account the peculiar American institution of the **Electoral College.** In the United States we do not have a direct election of the president, although this may surprise those who thought they voted for Clinton or Bush. In fact, they voted for Clinton's or Bush's electors who formed part of the Electoral College.

Electors are party notables who gather in each state capitol in December after the presidential election to cast their votes for president and vice president. Each state has as many electors as its total representation in Congress (House plus Senate) (see Figure 3). The smallest states (and the District of Columbia) have 3, whereas the largest state—California—has 54.

With the exception of Maine and Nebraska, which divide some of their Electoral College votes

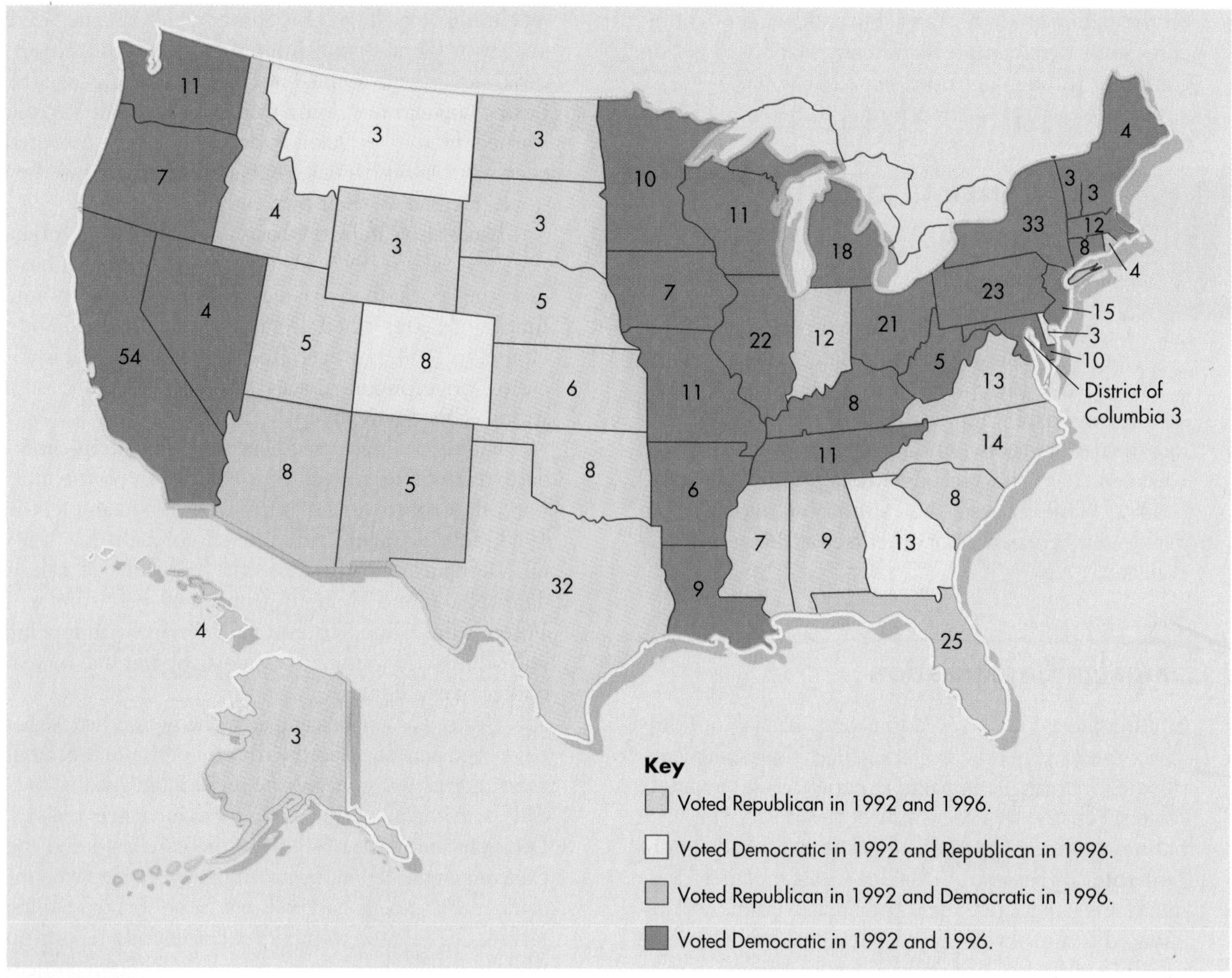

FIGURE 3

Clinton Wins 1996 Electoral Votes in the Industrial Heartland, Northeast, and Pacific Coast

The numbers inside the states indicate the electoral votes, out of a total of 538.

SOURCES: Richard Scammon and Alice McGilliaray, *American Votes 19* (Washington, D.C.: Congressional Quarterly, 1991), pp. 9–13; *Congressional Quarterly Reports,* November 7, 1992, p. 3549.

according to who wins in each congressional district, all of each state's electoral votes go to the candidate winning the most votes in that state. If one candidate wins a majority of the electors voting across the United States, that candidate wins. If no candidate wins a majority, the election is decided in the House of Representatives, where each state has one vote and a majority is necessary to win. This has not happened since 1824, when John Quincy Adams was chosen. If voting in the Electoral College for the vice president does not yield a majority, the Senate chooses the vice president, with each senator having one vote.

The Founders assumed that the Electoral College would have considerable power, with each elector exercising independent judgment and choosing from among a large number of candidates. They did not foresee the development of political parties. As state parties developed, the electors became part of the party process, pledged to party candidates. Thus, electors usually rubber stamp the choice of voters in each state rather than exercise their own judgment.

Because of the winner-take-all feature of the Electoral College, the system gives an advantage to large states and their urban populations. The 11 largest states have a majority (270) of the 538 votes. Candidates concentrate their efforts on these states.

The Electoral College is based on states, so it encourages campaigns designed to win "states." In this sense, it reinforces the federal system.

Campaign Strategies

Developing a strategy is an important element of a presidential campaign. But every strategy is surrounded by uncertainty, and even political pros cannot always predict the impact of a particular strategy.

THE ROLE OF THE ELECTORAL COLLEGE

Critics frequently suggest that the Electoral College, a complex and sometimes puzzling institution, should be reformed or abolished. One reform would keep the overall system but eliminate electors as individuals; electoral votes would automatically be cast according to a state's popular vote.

Abolishing the Electoral College in favor of a direct popular election is another reform idea that has some support. Votes would be counted nationwide; state totals would not matter. This proposal has been offered as a constitutional amendment in Congress several times but has never won approval. Even if passed in Congress, it probably would fail to obtain ratification by the necessary three-fourths of the state legislatures because many from both large and small states oppose it.

One reason that some argue for abolishing the Electoral College is that there are some undemocratic aspects to it, just as the Founders intended. The Electoral College makes it possible for the candidate with the most popular votes to lose the election. This has occurred three times: John Quincy Adams (1824), Rutherford B. Hayes (1876), and Benjamin Harrison (1888).

Critics of the Electoral College argue that these historical anomalies should not happen; in a democratic system, the person with the most votes should win. Further, the Electoral College often converts candidates with a plurality but not a majority of the popular vote into majority winners in the Electoral College. This may give a greater legitimacy to the winners. In 1960, John F. Kennedy won only 49.7% of the popular vote but a substantial 56% of the Electoral College vote. Significant margins of popular votes can be turned into the appearance of consensus too. For example, in 1984 President Reagan won 59% of the popular vote, but because he won in 49 states, he won 97% of the Electoral College vote.

Another undemocratic feature of the current system is the **faithless elector,** an elector who decides to cast a vote for a personal choice, not for that of his or her state's voters. Occasionally, electors do stray from their pledge—in 1988 a West Virginia elector voted for Lloyd Bentsen for president and later said she wished she had voted for Kitty Dukakis. Even though the intent of the Founders was to allow electors to cast their votes any way they desired, many people believe that in our more democratic era electors should be bound by the wishes of the voters. However, no faithless elector has ever made a difference in the outcome of an election.

Some people favor abolishing the College because direct election is a more understandable system. However, there is a need to formulate rules to deal with situations where no candidate gets a majority, and that makes the popular vote alternative more complicated than at first glance.

The major reason we retain the Electoral College system, though, is that in the current system, voters in large states receive more attention from candidates. Though small states are overrepresented in proportion to their populations, a 1-vote margin in Pennsylvania yields the candidate 23 electoral votes, a 1-vote margin in North Dakota only 3 electoral votes. So it is more important to get that extra vote in Pennsylvania than in North Dakota. Rational candidates and parties will direct their resources and perhaps tailor their policy views accordingly.

Although political scientists have debated the actual extent of the large-state bias in the current system, most believe it does exist and is significant.[1] Urbanites, especially central city residents, have more clout in the Electoral College system than they would have under a direct election system. Minority groups benefit too, because they are disproportionately located in urban areas. (However, one should not overstate this clout. The more liberal candidates, presumably those favored by the more urban interests, have lost most presidential elections since 1968.)

Supporters of the system argue that this urban bias is fair when viewed in the context of our other political institutions. The Senate, for example, overrepresents the interests of smaller, rural states because each state, regardless of population, has two votes. Many of the institutions of Congress, too, work in a way that gives an advantage to more conservative interests, often identified with rural America. The complex committee system and diffused power structure make dramatic changes in the status quo difficult.

Defenders of the Electoral College argue that to abolish it would remove a balance that exists in American politics: the conservative, rural bias of Congress on the one hand and the liberal, urban bias of the Electoral College on the other.

1. Lawrence Longley and James Dana, Jr., "New Empirical Estimates of the Biases of the Electoral College for the 1980s," *Western Political Quarterly* 37 (March 1984), pp. 157–175.

Candidates seek to do three things: mobilize those who are already loyal to them and their party; persuade independent voters that they are the best candidate; and try to convert the opposition. Most candidates emphasize mobilizing their own voters. Democrats have to work harder at this than Republicans because Democratic voters often do not vote and are more likely to vote for the other party than are Republicans.

Both parties must try to persuade independent voters because independents are the swing voters; their votes determine the outcome. In 1964, when Johnson trounced Republican Goldwater, 80% of Republicans voted for Goldwater. And in 1988, when Dukakis was soundly beaten by Bush, 75% of Democrats voted for Dukakis. It was the independent voters who determined the outcomes.

The crucial strategic question is where to allocate resources of time and money: where to campaign, where to buy media time and how much to buy, and where to spend money helping local organizations. Candidates must always remember that they have to win a majority of the Electoral College vote. The most populous states, with the largest number of electoral votes, are vital. Prime targets are those large states that could go to either party, such as Illinois, Texas, California, and New York.

Candidates also have to expand their existing bases of support. Most of the western states have been solidly Republican in their presidential loyalties. Republicans have been able to build on their solid western base and their strength in the South. They only have to carry a few of the large industrial states to win.

Democrats have a strategic problem given the western Republican bloc. Between the end of Reconstruction and 1948, the South was solidly Democratic, but there have been no solidly Democratic states in presidential elections since then (although Washington, D.C., has been solidly Democratic). Since 1976, the Democrats have consistently lost the South. During the 1980s, some strategists believed the Democrats should try to win back the South by choosing more conservative candidates. Others argued for a strategy to win without the South, aiming for the industrial states of the East and Midwest along with California and a few other states of the West. This has been Clinton's strategy (see Figure 3), though he won his own home state and Gore's (Arkansas and Tennessee) and picked up Louisiana and, in 1992, Georgia too. The nonsouthern strategy was used successfully by the Republicans between the 1870s and the 1920s, when they were able to capture the White House regularly without ever winning a southern state.

The Media Campaign

The media campaign consists of paid advertising, personal appearances on talk shows, debates, and coverage on news broadcasts and in print media. Candidates have the most control over paid advertising and the least over news coverage; but even there, campaigns spend hundreds of hours devising strategies to show their candidates to best advantage.

Campaigns are expensive because they rely so heavily on the media to get the candidate's message to the voters. As one observer argued, "Today's presidential campaign is essentially a mass media campaign. It is not that the mass media entirely determine what happens. . . . But it is no exaggeration to say that, for the large majority of voters, the campaign has little reality apart from the media version.[60]

IMPACT OF THE MEDIA

The media, through news coverage, personal appearances by candidates, and paid advertisements, help shape voters' opinions and choices in three ways. They inform, they help set the campaign agenda, and they help persuade voters.[61] In Chapter 8, we will discuss these effects.

USE OF THE MEDIA

MEDIA EVENTS Candidates try to use the media to their advantage by staging media events that allow them to be photographed doing and saying noncontroversial things in front of enthusiastic crowds and patriotic symbols. As Bush campaign strategist Roger Ailes proclaimed 20 years ago, "This is the beginning of a whole new concept. This is the way they'll be elected forevermore. The next guys will have to be performers."[62]

Candidates and their advisers try to design settings that will encourage television reporters to focus their stories on the candidate and put his or her policies in the best light.[63] In 1988, George Bush almost literally wrapped himself in the flag, frequently "pledging allegiance," until negative media reaction led his advisers to decide that they were overdoing it.

Candidates spend most of their time going from media market to media market, hoping to get both national and local coverage.[64] Some candidates are much better than others at using the media. Gerald Ford was plagued by media coverage that seemed to emphasize his bumbling.

ADVERTISING Paid advertisements allow candidates to focus on points most favorable to their case or to portray their opponents in the most negative light. Most political ads are quite short, 30 or 60 seconds in length. Television ads were first used in the 1952 campaign. One, linking the Democratic Truman administration to the unpopular Korean War, showed two soldiers in combat talking about the futility of war. Then one of the soldiers is hit and dies. The other one deliberately exposes himself to the enemy and is also killed. The announcer's voice says, "Vote Republican."[65] Today's ads are perhaps less melodramatic but still appeal to viewers' emotions. One classic set of ads that evoked a strong emotional response was the 1984 Reagan ads, depicting his policies as putting the country on the road to greatness again ("It's morning in America").[66]

Some ads are issue oriented. In 1988, for example, one Dukakis ad focused on the Democrat's plans for helping families pay for college education for their children.

Negative ads have become increasingly prominent. Sometimes these ads have more impact on public opinion than do positive ads. Candidates believe their media consultants who tell them, "People won't

NEGATIVE CAMPAIGNING

Almost all observers agree that negative campaigning was a successful strategy in the George Bush–Michael Dukakis 1988 presidential election. Over 60% of the public thought that Bush's campaign was dirty, but he won handily anyway. (Forty percent thought Dukakis's campaign was dirty.)[1] Bush successfully painted a picture of Dukakis as "not a patriot, no believer in law and order, no manly man, no lover of family . . . one of those loose lovers of 'them' and 'their' ways."[2] He did this in part by hitting Dukakis hard for vetoing a bill that would have made the Pledge of Allegiance mandatory in Massachusetts schools each day. Though Dukakis did this because he felt the bill was unconstitutional, Bush's campaign used the veto to challenge Dukakis's patriotism. And the Bush campaign linked Dukakis to Willie Horton, a black convict who was furloughed from the Massachusetts prison system while Dukakis was governor. Horton, while on furlough, raped a woman and terrorized her and her fiancé. Though 40 other states and the federal government had furlough programs, the Bush campaign used the Horton incident to portray Dukakis as soft on crime. The ad also appealed to those voters who were predisposed to be negative toward blacks. The impact of this ad is illustrated by the fact that three years later, focus groups of voters remembered little about the 1988 election except the Horton ads.[3]

Election analysts feared that the success of negative advertising in 1988 would set the stage for even more in 1992. But, much to the surprise of many, negative campaigning did not work so well in 1992. By October, the Bush campaign, failing to find its own focus, was reduced simply to portraying Clinton as a taxer and spender, a liar and a coward, and even a possible Soviet sympathizer. In a truly desperate moment, Bush claimed, "My dog Millie knows more about foreign affairs than these two bozos!" (the bozos were Clinton and Gore).

Why was this negative strategy less successful in 1992 and 1996 than in 1988? One possibility is that Clinton was a better candidate than Dukakis. Indeed, recalling the fate of the Dukakis campaign, Clinton's team was ready to respond to any negative the Bush campaign could offer. For example, when the Clinton campaign caught wind of upcoming Bush television ads, they prepared counterattacks to launch immediately. When the Bush campaign aired its "Night of the Living Dead" ad, which depicted Arkansas as a barren state populated by a lonely buzzard, Clinton's response was broadcast only 24 hours later.[4]

But the major difference between 1988 and 1992 may be that the voters were less receptive to negative campaigning because they were more concerned about real issues. A poor economy tends to focus voters' concerns. In 1992, the economy was sour and so were the voters. Early in the primary season, polls showed that voters were tired of hearing about Clinton's alleged womanizing. During the second presidential debate, the one with audience participation, both the moderator and a participant from the audience indicated they were annoyed with personal attacks and wanted to hear about the issues.

Edward Rollins, Ronald Reagan's 1984 campaign manager, summed up the 1992 campaign by noting, "It is not that negative campaigning does not work, it is that the voters this year did not want it. And George Bush talked about the draft about 200 times and his economic agenda about three times."[5] The lesson of the campaign may be, then, not that dirty campaigns do not work at all, but rather that there are some circumstances under which they will not work.

1. Richard Morin, "Relieved Rather than Elated," *Washington Post National Weekly Edition,* November 7–13, 1988, p. 42.
2. Gus Tyler, "After the Brawl Was Over," *New Leader,* November 28, 1988, p. 7.
3. Deborah Tannen, "Lies, Damned Lies, and Political Ads," *Washington Post National Weekly Edition,* September 21–27, 1992.
4. Howard Kurtz, "In Advertising Give and Take, Clinton Camp Took and Responded," *Washington Post,* November 6, 1992, p. A10.
5. Ann Devroy, "The Low Road That Went Nowhere," *Washington Post National Weekly Edition,* November 9–15, 1992, p. 7.

pay any attention [to positive ads]. Better to knock your opponent's head off."[67] And they see it reflected in the polls, where negative ads can sometimes have a dramatic short-term effect on a candidate's standing.

Although the 1988 campaign probably set a modern record for negative campaigning, the phenomenon is as American as apple pie. When Thomas Jefferson faced John Adams in 1796, a Federalist editorial called Jefferson "mean spirited, low-lived . . . the son of a half-breed Indian squaw" and prophesized that if he were elected, "Murder, robbery, rape, adultery and incest will be openly taught and practiced."[68] When Andrew Jackson ran for president in 1832, his mother was called a prostitute, his father a mulatto (someone of mixed races, black and white), his wife a profligate woman, and himself a bigamist.[69] A British observer of American elections in 1888 described them as a "tempest of invective and calumny . . . imagine all the accusations brought against all the candidates for the 670 seats in the English Parliament concentrated on one man, and read . . . daily for three months.[70]

But why does negative advertising sometimes work when most people say they do not like it? People may say they like to hear about issues, but their actions belie their words. Politics is just not that important to most people, and indeed many are woefully ignorant about specific issues. If one out of seven Americans cannot find the United States on a world map, how interested are they going to be in a discussion of foreign policy?[71] Most people have a pretty good general picture of where the parties stand on a whole variety of general issues, but they are not particularly attuned to listening to debates on specifics, and the candidates realize this.

Negative ads have both virtues and drawbacks. On the positive side, such ads provide some helpful information about issues.[72] During a campaign, a candidate might produce ten or fifteen 30-second ads, each providing new information, including information on issues. This material, though biased, is a valuable supplement to media news coverage, which focuses heavily on personalities, conflicts, and the "horse-race" aspect of campaigns.

Negative ads tend to reinforce previous inclinations. Thus, negative ads are more believable than positive ones at least to Republicans and independents, who are more cynical about politics and government to begin with. Some have found that negative ads decrease voter turnout by about 5%, chiefly among independents and moderates. However, a systematic analysis of all the studies of negative ads concluded that many negative effects have been exaggerated. There is little evidence, for example, that negative ads increase voter cynicism significantly.

There are checks on negative campaigns.[73] One check is the press, which could point out errors of fact. In recent campaigns, many in the press have tried to do this, but often end up simply giving more attention to the negative messages. The voters, who might become outraged, are another check. The third check is the candidate under attack, who in most cases will hit back. Clinton was aggressive in countering negative ads in both 1992 and 1996.

TELEVISED DEBATES Candidates also use televised debates as part of their media campaigns. In 1960 Kennedy challenged Nixon to debate during their presidential campaign. Nixon did not want to debate because as vice president he was already known and ahead in the polls. He remembered his first election to the House of Representatives when he challenged the incumbent to debate and, on the basis of his performance, won the election. Afterward he said the incumbent was a "damn fool" to debate. Nevertheless, Nixon did agree to debate, and when the two contenders squared off, presidential debates were televised to millions of homes across the country for the first time.

Nixon dutifully answered reporters' questions and rebutted Kennedy's assertions. But Kennedy came to project an image. He sought to demonstrate his vigor, to compensate for his youth and inexperience. He also sought to contrast his attractive appearance and personality with Nixon's. So he quickly answered reporters' specific questions and then directly addressed viewers about his general goals.

Kennedy's strategy worked. He appealed to people and convinced them that his youth and inexperience would not pose problems. While Kennedy remained calm, Nixon became very nervous. He smiled at inappropriate moments, his eyes darted back and forth, he had a five-o'clock shadow that gave him a somewhat sinister look, and beads of sweat rolled down his face.

According to public opinion polls, people who saw the debates thought that Kennedy performed better in three of the four. (The only debate in which they thought Nixon performed better was the one in which the candidates were not in the same studio side by side. They were in separate cities, and with this arrangement Nixon was less nervous.) Yet people who heard the debates on radio did not think Kennedy performed as well. They were not influenced by the visual contrast between the candidates. Clearly, television made the difference.

There were no more presidential debates for 16 years. The candidates who were ahead did not want to risk their lead. But in 1976 President Ford decided to debate Carter, and in 1980 President Carter decided to debate Reagan. Both incumbents were in trouble, and they thought they needed to debate to win. Although President Reagan was far ahead in 1984, he decided to debate Mondale because he did not want to seem afraid. By agreeing to debate, he solidified the precedent begun anew in 1976. Similarly, in 1992 Bush agreed to debate Clinton after a person dressed as a chicken began appearing at Bush rallies to emphasize that Bush was dodging the debates. It will not be easy for future presidential candidates to refuse to debate.

Because candidates have different strengths, each campaign wants the other to agree to a debate format that builds on its candidate's strengths. The "debate about debates" is a typical campaign issue that frequently overshadows other, more important issues. It has become as predictable a part of campaigns as the debates themselves.

Campaign Funding

Success in raising money is one of the keys to a successful political campaign. Although some of the money for presidential campaigns comes from public funds, much is raised privately. In Chapter 9 we will discuss campaign funding and its impact on politics.

VOTING

For 50 years political scientists have argued about how voters make their choices. Are parties most important? Issues? Personalities? Political scientist Stanley Kelley has argued that voters go through a simple process in deciding how to vote. They add up the things they like about each candidate and party and they

UPI/Corbis-Bettmann

Families all across the country gathered in front of their TV to watch the first televised presidential debates in 1960, featuring Senator John F. Kennedy (D-Mass.) and Vice President Richard Nixon (R-Calif.).

vote for the candidate with the highest number of "likes." If there is a tie, they vote on the basis of their party identification, if they have one. If they do not, they abstain. On the basis of this simple idea, Kelley explains more than 85% of the variation in voting choice.[74]

In making these calculations, then, voters consider three things:

- The party of the candidate, which has a great effect on how the voter views everything else about him or her.
- The candidate's personality, style, and appearance.
- The issue stands of the candidates and parties.

Despite considerable disagreement as to exactly how each of these is weighted in the voter's mind, political scientists can offer some general conclusions.

Party Loyalties

One's party loyalty, called party identification, is probably the most important factor influencing a person's vote: Democrats tend to vote for Democrats and Republicans for Republicans. This is most true for lower-level contests such as state legislative elections, but it is also true for presidential races because party preference influences how a voter perceives a candidate's personality and issue stance. For some people, party identification is their only source of information about candidates, and they vote on the basis of it alone.

However, since the turn of the century, and even since the 1950s, party has become less important to voters. There are more independents and more people who vote contrary to their partisan loyalties. Party loyalties seem to be in flux, and parties themselves have been weakened by competition from the media and interest groups. Nevertheless, if you are guessing how a person will vote, the best single bit of information to have is the person's party identification.[75] In 1996, for example, among those who went to the polls, 84% of all Democrats voted for Clinton and 80% of all Republicans voted for Dole.

How do people get to be Republicans and Democrats? Socioeconomic class is a very important predictor of the vote: the lower the income, the more likely to vote Democrat. But this general rule is cross-cut with distinctive ethnic and religious patterns (we use ethnic here to refer to differences of national origin and race).

For example, Jews are much more likely to vote Democratic than other whites of similar income. On the whole, they have a higher-than-average income, yet in 1996 about three-fourths of Jewish voters voted Democratic. As a group, they were exceeded in their Democratic allegiance only by blacks.[76]

"This year I'm not getting involved in any complicated issues. I'm just voting my straight ethnic prejudices."

Catholics used to be predominantly Democratic. They still are, but not as consistently. Though a majority of Catholics voted for Reagan in 1980 and 1984, they have returned to the Democratic fold in the 1990s. They favored Clinton by a margin of about 8% in 1992 and double that in 1996.

Blacks are probably the most distinctive group politically. About 90% usually vote Democratic, though "only" 85% did so in 1996.

Hispanics who, like blacks, also have lower-than-average incomes, are not as universally Democratic as blacks and have voted Republican in significant numbers. Nevertheless, almost three-quarters voted Democratic in recent congressional elections and for Clinton in 1996. Among Hispanics, Cuban Americans are much more likely to be Republican than either Mexican Americans or Puerto Ricans. Many are refugees or descendants of refugees from Castro's Cuba and are intensely anti-Communist.

The voting behavior of Asian Americans has been much less thoroughly studied than that of other groups (because until recently they were quite a small group). In 1996, their voting patterns resembled those of whites with a small plurality in favor of Dole, similar to whites' votes.

White Protestants generally give a majority of their vote to the Republicans and have done so for decades. However, as for other groups, income differences are important in determining the vote of Protestants.

Ethnicity and religion are important in determining the vote because they are shorthand terms for many other factors influencing political behavior—class, historical treatment within the society, and basic culture and values. Jews are predominantly Democratic, for example, because as a persecuted minority throughout much of their history, they have learned to identify with the underdog, even when their own economic circumstances move them into the middle or upper class. Catholics were sometimes discriminated against too; this discrimination plus their working-class status propelled them to the party of Roosevelt. As Catholics have moved into the middle class and as tolerance toward Catholics has grown, Catholics, like Protestants, have tended to vote their income. Moreover, evangelical Protestants (such as Southern Baptist and Assembly of God) are much more likely to vote for Republicans than are mainline Protestants (such as Episcopalians or Presbyterians).

Candidate Evaluations

Candidates' personalities and styles have had more impact as party influence has declined and as television has become voters' major source of information about elections. Reagan's popularity in 1984 is an example of the influence of a candidate and his personality. The perceived competence and integrity of candidates are other facets of candidate evaluation. Voters are less likely to support candidates who do not seem capable of handling the job, regardless of their issue positions. Jimmy Carter suffered in 1980 because of voter evaluations of his competence and leadership.

Issues

Issues are a third factor influencing the vote. Although Americans are probably more likely to vote on issues now than they were in the 1950s, issues only influence some voters some of the time. In 1984 and 1988, for example, voters' issue positions overall were closer to the positions of Mondale and Dukakis than to Reagan or Bush. And, in the 1996 election, 11% of those voters who considered themselves liberal voted for Bob Dole, and 20% of those who considered themselves conservative voted for Bill Clinton.

Still, although other factors also influence voters, many do cast issue votes. To cast an issue vote, voters have to be informed about issues and have opinions. In recent elections, more than 80% of the public could take a position on issues such as government spending, military spending, women's rights, and relations with Russia.[77] Knowledge about these issues may have been vague, but individuals were able to understand the issues enough to define their own general positions.

Also, for voters to cast issue votes, candidates must have detectable policy differences. A substantial minority of voters are able to detect some differences among presidential candidates. In recent elections, the percentages able to identify correctly

ANGRY WHITE MALES

If 1992 was the year of the woman in politics, 1994 was the year of the "angry white male." Feeling "left behind and left out," white men turned in large numbers to the Republicans in that off-year election.[1] Sixty-two percent of white male voters voted for Republican House candidates, compared to only 55% of women, the largest gender gap ever reported.[2] In some key races, the split was even greater. In California, for example, 59% of white male voters supported the conservative Republican nominee compared to 41% of white women.[3]

The term "angry white male" is not very precise. Obviously, not all white males are angry. Moreover, middle- and upper-class white males have traditionally voted Republican, so no special explanations are needed for their 1994 vote. But consider the lower- and working-class white males, who traditionally have been loyal to the Democratic Party. Why did they move toward the Republicans in 1994?

Some analysts argued that the issues of the 1994 campaign, such as taxes, spending, crime, and gun control, were issues of particular importance to men and to Republicans. Others argue that the shift of white men to the Republican Party was based on much broader issues of social and economic change. During the 1980s, the economic status of those with only high school educations declined. Although the economy was strong in the year before the 1994 election, many people face layoffs as American corporations "downsize" and jobs go elsewhere or nowhere. Men with high school educations can no longer expect to hold high-paying jobs or have jobs that pay more than their fathers earned.

Partly as a consequence, the world of the one-earner, male-centered family has also declined. Most families need two earners to even aspire to a middle-class existence. Most women are increasingly in the workforce and have an increasing amount of power within families.

Even though the economic declines in the fortunes of those with high school educations occurred mostly during the 1980s, under a Republican administration, many white males blame the Democrats. Partly this is because of the cultural changes. Many white men feel pushed aside by the demands of minority groups and women pursuing their agendas of equality. Although white men receive higher wages than any other group and control most businesses, educational institutions, legislative bodies, and other centers of power in America, working-class men do not share in this power. They are sliding downhill in their own economic power, and they believe that others are moving ahead. They see gains made by women and minorities in getting better jobs and access to higher education.

As one survey of white working-class Detroiters found, "These white Democratic defectors express a profound distaste for blacks. . . . Blacks constitute the explanation for [the whites'] vulnerability and for almost everything that has gone wrong in their lives."[4]

Some white males are also angry with women, especially their increasing economic and political power. In 1994, white males who voted Republican were twice as likely as other white men to think it unimportant that women be elected to office, for example.[5]

Working-class white males believe that public policies, especially affirmative action, are working to move women and minorities ahead, but not them. They overestimate how effective these policies are. They are angry with the Democrats since it is the party that has most strongly supported civil rights laws since the 1960s.

Angry white males, then, seem caught between two forces. Predominantly working class, their economic fortunes are not rosy. The rich are getting richer, but the working class is not. Because they are white males, no government policies seem to be directed toward helping them. Indeed, many minorities and women view them as oppressors or, at the least, beneficiaries of the existing system, not people who also need help. The resentment generated by these forces, then, propelled many "angry white males" to pull the Republican lever in the 1994 election.

1. Thomas B. Edsall, "The Democrats' Gender and Class Gap," *Washington Post National Weekly Edition,* June 6, 1994, p. 12.
2. Richard Morin and Barbara Vobejda, "It Was the Year of the Angry (White) Man," *Washington Post National Weekly Edition,* November 11–20, 1994, p. 37; "Portrait of the Electorate: Who Voted for Whom in the House," *New York Times,* November 13, 1994, p. 24.
3. Ibid.
4. Herbert Hill, "Black Workers, Organized Labor, and Title VII of the 1964 Civil Rights Act," in Herbert Hill and James Jones, eds., *Race in America* (Madison: University of Wisconsin Press, 1993), p. 329.
5. Richard Morin, "And How Did the Voters Judge the Media?" *Washington Post National Weekly Edition,* December 5–11, 1994, p. 37.

INTO THE 21ST CENTURY

THE PERMANENT CAMPAIGN

As we enter the twenty-first century, we appear to be entering an era of the **permanent campaign.** During each election cycle, the time between the completion of one election and the beginning of the next gets shorter and shorter. By spring 1997, only a few months after Clinton's reelection, candidates of both parties were already busy visiting New Hampshire and other early primary states, assembling field operations, hiring consultants and fund-raisers, and commissioning polls. No longer does the election campaign start in the election year; now it is nearly a four-year process.

Several factors are responsible for this change, some political and some technological. The political process has changed a great deal during the past 20 years. In particular, primaries have become the chief means by which candidates get nominated, and parties have shrunk in importance in the nominating process. The necessity to win primaries in different regions of the nation means that potential candidates must start early to become known to key political figures, and ultimately to the voting public, in these states. In the "old days," candidates only had to woo party leaders, a process, which, though not easy, was much less public and much less expensive than campaigning for primary victories.

Technology has also contributed to the permanent campaign. Certainly, in comparison to the turn of the twentieth century, transportation and communication technology have revolutionized campaigns. Then, of course, travel was by rail, ship, or horse, and candidates could not simply dart about the country spending the morning in New York and the afternoon in Seattle. Telephone communication was primitive, and there were no radios or televisions. The idea of potential candidates spending four years publicly campaigning for office under these conditions would have been ludicrous.

But even in comparison with only 30 years ago, the media and information technology have revolutionized campaigning and thus have contributed to the permanent campaign. Modern computer and telephone technology enable the media and private organizations to take the pulse of the public through opinion polls almost continually. As polls have become more common, they have become a source of fascination by the media (and as pollsters have discovered that the media appetite for polls is nearly insatiable, polls have proliferated). Whereas in the 1950s polls were rarely done and poll results were rarely discussed in media coverage of elections, by the 1980s hundreds of stories about each election campaign focus on poll results. Indeed, much of the media coverage of the campaign focuses on exactly that (see Chapter 8 for more on this). Thus, candidates must pay attention to how well they do in the polls, which means they must begin campaigning early to earn name recognition by the public.

And, more generally, the fact that campaigns have become media events means that candidates must begin early to establish themselves as worthy of media attention. Until candidates have organizations, fund-raisers, and pollsters, they are not taken seriously by the media. Nor would it be very rational to do otherwise, because a modern campaign cannot succeed without these things.

All of these factors, then—the decline of the party organizations and the increased importance of primaries, the growth of polling, and the overwhelming role the media now play in campaigns—have contributed to the perpetual motion that modern elections have become. As we enter the twenty-first century, these trends seem irreversible. Only the rolling back of the primary system would seem to make much difference, and that change is highly unlikely.

general differences between the major party candidates varied between 36 and 62%.[78]

In every election since 1972, more than 70% of those who could correctly identify the positions of the candidates as well as their own position on an important issue cast a vote consistent with their own position.[79] We call this issue voting. Issues with the highest proportion of issue voting were those that typically divided Republicans and Democrats, such as government spending, military spending, and government aid to the unemployed and minorities. However, because only one-third to two-thirds of the electorate was able to define both their own and the candidates' positions on each issue, the proportion of the total electorate that can be said to cast an "issue vote" is usually less than 40%, and for some issues it is much less.[80]

Some scholars have suggested that issue voting is really more of an evaluation of the current incumbents. If voters like the way incumbents, or the incumbent's party, have handled the job in general or in certain areas—the economy or foreign policy, for example—they will vote accordingly, even without much knowledge about the specifics of the issues.

Voting on the basis of past performance is called **retrospective voting.** There is good evidence that many people do this, especially according to economic conditions.[81] Voters support incumbents if national income is growing in the months preceding the election. Since World War II, the incumbent party has won a presidential election only once when the growth rate was less than 3% (Eisenhower in 1956) and lost only once when it was more than 3% (Ford in 1976). Unemployment and inflation seem to have less consistent effects on voting, and economic conditions two or three years before the election have little impact on voting.[82] The recession in the early Reagan years hurt Republicans in the congressional elections of 1982, but the recovery helped Reagan get reelected in 1984 and helped put Bush in the White House in 1988. The strong economy propelled Clinton's reelection too.

Parties, Candidates, and Issues

All three factors—parties, candidates, and issues—clearly matter. Party loyalties are especially important because they help shape our views about issues and candidates. However, if issues and candidates did not matter, the Democrats would have won every presidential election since the New Deal. Republican victories suggest that they often have had more attractive candidates (as in 1952, 1956, 1980, and 1984) or issue positions (in 1972 and in some respects in 1980). However, the Democrats' partisan advantage shrank throughout the 1980s. Though there are still more Democrats than Republicans, the margin is modest and the number of independents is growing.

Party loyalties have been even more important in congressional voting. The Democrats controlled the House continuously between 1954 and 1994 and controlled the Senate most of those years. However, the Democratic lock on the House was broken in the 1994 election, which found the Republicans winning control in a sweeping victory. Clearly, issues overcame traditional partisan habits in that election. Exactly which issues, however, were less than clear.

CONCLUSION: DO ELECTIONS MAKE GOVERNMENT RESPONSIVE?

Although election campaigns are far less successful in mobilizing voters and ensuring a high turnout today than they were in the past century, in a democracy, we expect elections to allow us to control government. Through them we can "throw the rascals out" and bring in new faces with better ideas, or so we think. But other than to change the party that controls government, do elections make a difference?

In the popular press, we hear a lot about "mandates." A president with a **mandate** is one who is clearly directed by the voters to take some particular course of action—reduce taxes or begin arms control talks, for example. George Bush had a substantial majority in his 1988 victory. But did he have a mandate? If so, what for? The campaign hardly talked about the budget deficit even though the election-day polls showed that this was the issue of concern to the largest group of voters. They, in turn, gave an overwhelming majority of *their* votes to Dukakis. On other issues, such as protecting the environment, Bush portrayed himself as a liberal. On many issues, ranging from abortion to day care to defense policy, the two candidates clearly differed. But did Bush's victory mean that he was to limit abortions, leave it to the states to fund day care, or continue the Reagan defense policy? Did he have a mandate on any of these issues?

Like most things in politics, the answer is not simple. Sometimes elections have an effect on policy, but often their effects are not clear-cut. In 1992, some voters chose a candidate on the basis of the economy, others the budget deficit issue, others on health care, and so on. Only one issue (the economy) was the primary concern of even a quarter of the voters.

In the surprising 1994 election, specific policy issues appeared to have little impact. Instead, voters appeared to be expressing their negative views about government generally. Though Republicans presented a "Contract with America," it is not clear which, if any, of the points of that contract, including a balanced budget amendment, term limits, cutting back welfare, spending cuts, and increasing military spending, have majority support.

Typically, even presidents are given a very vague mandate. Reagan's huge election victory in 1984 did not mean that the public agreed more with him than with Mondale on the issues, but mainly that they liked him and approved of the upturn in the economy. Still, over time a rough agreement develops between public attitudes and policies.[83]

It is primarily political parties that translate the mix of various issues into government action because voters' issue positions influence their party loyalties and their evaluations of candidates. A vote for the candidate of one's own party is usually a reflection of agreement on at least some important issues.[84] Once in office, the party in government helps sort out the issues for which there is a broad public mandate from those for which there is not.

Elections that appear to be mandates can become "mandates for disaster." More than one observer has pointed out that every twentieth-century president who has won election by 60% or more of the popular vote soon encountered serious political trouble. After his landslide in 1920, Warren Harding had his Teapot Dome scandal involving government corruption. Emboldened by his 1936 triumph, Franklin Roosevelt tried to pack the Supreme Court and was resoundingly defeated on that issue. Lyndon Johnson won by a landslide in 1964 and was soon mired in Vietnam. Richard Nixon smashed George

McGovern in 1972 but then had to resign because of Watergate. Ronald Reagan's resounding victory in 1984 (a shade less than 60%) was followed by the blunders of the Iran-contra affair. Of these presidents, only Roosevelt was able to recover fully from his political misfortune. Reagan regained his personal popularity but seemed to have little influence on policy after Iran-contra. One recent observer has argued that these disasters come because "the euphoria induced by overwhelming support at the polls evidently loosens the president's grip on reality."[85]

Elections can point out new directions for government and allow citizens to make it responsive to their needs, but the fact that many individuals do not vote means that the new directions may not reflect either the needs or wishes of the public. If election turnout falls too far, the legitimacy of elections may be threatened. People may come to believe that election results do not reflect the wishes of the majority. For this reason, this slow and steady decline of turnout should concern all of us. If elections promote government responsiveness to those who participate in them, higher turnouts help increase responsiveness.

EPILOGUE

The Package Works

Clinton decided to follow the blueprint laid out in his campaign team's report. Between the end of the primaries and the convention, Clinton worked hard getting free media coverage and beginning the process of redefining his image. Avid TV viewers saw him on the "Today" show, "MTV," "Good Morning America," "Larry King Live," and "Arsenio Hall," where he put on his sunglasses and played "Heartbreak Hotel" on his sax. The print press quickly picked up on the new themes. *U.S. News and World Report* discussed "The Bill Clinton Nobody Knows," while readers of *People* magazine were treated to a cover story, "At Home with the Clinton Family."

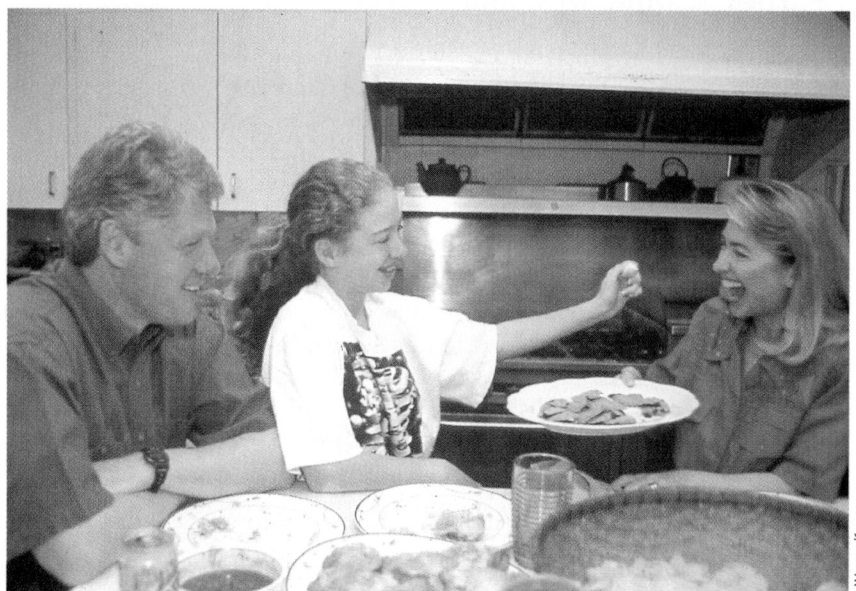
Ira Wyman/Sygma

The Clinton family became more prominent in Clinton's campaign after his campaign team discovered the public knew little about them.

From dead last in the three-way race in April, he began to gain strength in the polls. In a tie with his opponents before the Democratic convention, by the end of the convention, he was 24 points ahead.[86]

And after the convention, instead of lowering his profile as candidates often do between the convention and Labor Day, the traditional beginning of the fall campaign, Clinton and Gore took to the heartland in a bus caravan. Clinton's team recalled the fate of Michael Dukakis in 1988. Dukakis had a lead over George Bush in midsummer and stayed out of the public eye until Labor Day. His lead evaporated. The Clinton and Gore bus tour, on the other hand, kept the campaign in the public eye, offered numerous photo opportunities of Bill and Hillary practically every day, got Clinton and Gore on local media throughout the Midwest, and helped solidify the image of Clinton as an average, likable guy.

It is probably true that Republican focus groups and surveys identified Clinton's weaknesses just as accurately as did Clinton's own surveys. Indeed, a major part of President Bush's message was attacks on Clinton's family values, integrity, and trustworthiness. Bush and some of his campaign aides clearly thought this strategy would work in 1992, as it did in 1988 against Michael Dukakis. Though voters and analysts decried this negative strategy, it was successful in 1988. Because of the draft avoidance and womanizing charges, Clinton seemed to be an even better target than Dukakis.

But the Bush strategy failed for several reasons. Voters were more concerned about the fate of the economy than about alleged character flaws. Indeed, in the second presidential debate, which included audience participation, one woman complained that "the amount of time the candidates have spent in this campaign trashing their opponents' character and their programs is depressingly large."[87] Second, the Clinton team learned from the Dukakis debacle. They answered every attack Bush made, but at the same time they stayed focused on their own campaign message. And third, the image modification brought about by the Clinton team had changed the basic impressions that the public had of Clinton, making him more impervious to attack. As one journalist reported, "By the time Mr. Clinton and Mr. Gore took to the highways on bus trips with their wives—double dates with the American people—the old Clinton image was so faded it hardly remained."[88]

KEY TERMS

suffrage
Reconstruction
literacy tests
grandfather clause
poll tax
white primary
Voting Rights Act (VRA)
cracking, stacking, and packing
majority-minority districts
cumulative voting
Progressive reforms
motor voter law
presidential preference primaries
Super Tuesday
Electoral College
faithless elector
permanent campaign
retrospective voting
mandate

FURTHER READING

Stephen Ansolabehere and Shanto Iyengar, *Going Negative* (New York: Free Press, 1996). Two political scientists report the results of their research on the impact of negative television ads on voters and voting.

Dan Balz and Ronald Brownstein, *Storming the Gates* (Boston: Little, Brown, 1996). Two reporters examine the politics of the Republican takeover of Congress in 1994 and its impact on policy.

Taylor Branch, *Parting the Waters: America in the King Years* (New York: Simon & Schuster, 1988). *An excellent, readable account that illustrates the impact of political protest in changing America's race laws and to a considerable extent its attitudes about race.*

Robert Darcy, Susan Welch, and Janet Clark, *Women, Elections, and Representation* (Lincoln, Neb.: University of Nebraska Press, 1994). *An examination of the potential barriers faced by women candidates.*

Kathleen Hall Jamieson, *Packaging the Presidency* (New York: Oxford University Press, 1984). *The history and impact of presidential campaign advertising.*

Allan Lichtman and Ken De Cell, *The Thirteen Keys to the Presidency*. (Madison Books, 1990). *Focusing on 13 factors—"Keys"—that help explain presidential election outcomes, these authors correctly predict every election since 1860.*

Frances Fox Piven and Richard Cloward, *Why Americans Don't Vote* (New York: Pantheon, 1988). *The authors attribute nonvoting to restrictive registration laws and the disinterest of parties in mobilizing the working class.*

Theodore H. White, *The Making of the President*, 4 vols. (New York: Atheneum Publishers, 1961, 1965, 1969, 1973). *Journalistic accounts of presidential elections from 1960 to 1972. White was the first journalist to travel with the candidates and give an inside view of campaign strategy.*

ELECTRONIC RESOURCES

http://democrats.org/party/ and http://www.rnc.org
Links to the Democratic National Committee and the Republican National Committee. Each of these pages contains information about the campaign organizations of the two national parties.

http://www.spe.sony.com/classics/living/misc/rockvote.html
The Rock the Vote Web page mentioned in the text. Designed to get young voters out to vote.

http://odwin.ucsd.edu/idata/icpsr.html
This site, sponsored by the University of California at San Diego, provides access to information from national election studies done by political scientists since 1952. You can find out what voters thought on a broad variety of issues asked in each national election (presidential and most congressional) study.

INFOTRAC CITATIONS

"Racial Gerrymandering: How Is It Changing?"
"Easy Voting: Calling Jimmy Carter"
"March Madness: How the Primary Schedule Favors the Rich"

NOTES

1. "The Specter of Scandal," *Newsweek*, November/December 1992, p. 34.
2. *Newsweek*, July 20, 1992, p. 25.
3. Michael Kelly, "The Making of a First Family: A Blueprint," *New York Times*, November 14, 1992, p. lff.
4. Ibid. See also " 'Manhattan Project,' 1992," *Newsweek*, November 16, 1992, pp. 36–39.
5. Kelly, "The Making of a First Family."
6. "Manhattan Project," p. 38.
7. William Flanigan and Nancy H. Zingale, *Political Behavior of the American Electorate* (Boston: Allyn & Bacon, 1972), p. 13. See also Chilton Williamson, *American Suffrage from Property to Democracy* (Princeton, N.J.: Princeton University Press, 1960).
8. James MacGregor Burns, *Vineyard of Liberty* (New York: Knopf, 1982), p. 363.
9. August Meier and Elliot Rudwick, *From Plantation to Ghetto* (New York: Hill & Wang, 1966), p. 69.
10. Robert Darcy, Susan Welch, and Janet Clark, *Women, Elections, and Representation* (Lincoln: University of Nebraska Press, 1995).
11. Grandfather clause: *Guinn v. United States*, 238 U.S. 347, (1915); white primary: *Smith v. Allwright*, 321 U.S. 649, (1944).
12. Data on black and white voter registration in the southern states are from the *Statistical Abstract of the United States* (Washington, D.C.: U.S. Bureau of the Census, various years).
13. *City of Mobile v. Bolden*, 446 U.S. 55 (1980).
14. *Thornburg v. Gingles*, 478 U.S. 301 (1986).
15. Bob Benenson, "Arduous Ritual of Redistricting Ensures More Racial Diversity," *Congressional Quarterly Weekly Report* (October 24, 1992), p. 3385. For a very thorough review of the legal and behavioral impact of the Voting Rights Act, see Joseph P. Viteritti, "Unapportioned Justice: Local Elections Social Science and the Evolution of the Voting Rights Act," *Cornell Journal of Law and Public Policy* (Fall 1994), pp. 210–270.
16. *Shaw v. Reno* 125 L.Ed.2d 511, 113 S.Ct. 2816 (1993); *Miller v. Johnson*, 132 L.Ed.2d 762, 115 S.Ct. 2475 (1995); *Bush v. Vera*, 135 L.Ed.2d 248, 116 S.Ct. 1941 (1996).

17. Darcy, Welch, and Clark, *Women, Elections and Representation*.

18. The discussion in this paragraph is drawn largely from Lois Banner, *Women in Modern America* (New York: Harcourt Brace Jovanovich, 1974), pp. 88–90; Glenn Firebaugh and Kevin Chen, "Vote Turnout of Nineteenth Amendment Women," *American Journal of Sociology* 100 (January 1995), pp. 972–996.

19. Richard Jensen, "American Election Campaigns: A Theoretical and Historical Typology," paper delivered at the 1968 Midwest Political Science Association Meeting, quoted in Walter Dean Burnham, *Critical Elections and the Mainsprings of American Politics* (New York: W. W. Norton, 1970), p. 73.

20. Frances Fox Piven and Richard A. Cloward, *Why Americans Don't Vote* (New York: Pantheon, 1988), p. 30.

21. Daniel Elazar, *American Federalism: A View from the States* (New York: Thomas Y. Crowell, 1972); *Statistical Abstract, 1997, Table 465*.

22. Piven and Cloward, *Why Americans Don't Vote*, p. 162. See also G. Bingham Powell, Jr., "American Voter Turnout in Comparative Perspective," *American Political Science Review* 80 (March 1986), pp. 17–44.

23. Piven and Cloward, *Why Americans Don't Vote*, pp. 17–18. Data are from 1980.

24. Powell, "American Voter Turnout," p. 30; Piven and Cloward, *Why Americans Don't Vote*, p. 119.

25. George Will, "In Defense of Nonvoting," *Newsweek*, October 10, 1983, p. 96.

26. Richard Morin, "The Dog Ate My Forms, and, Well, I Couldn't Find a Pen," *Washington Post National Weekly Edition*, November 5–11, 1990, p. 38.

27. Curtis Gans, quoted in Jack Germond and Jules Witcover, "Listen to the Voters—and Nonvoters," *Minneapolis Star Tribune*, November 26, 1988. This effect was foreshadowed by Michael J. Robinson, "American Political Legitimacy in an Era of Electronic Journalism," in *Television as a Social Force*, ed. Douglass Cater and Richard Adler (New York: Praeger, 1975).

28. Gans, quoted in Germond and Witcover, "Listen to the Voters."

29. Priscilla Southwell, "Voter Turnout in the 1986 Congressional Elections," *American Politics Quarterly* 19 (January 1991), pp. 96–108; Stephen Ansolabehere, Shanto Iyengar, Adam Simon, and Nicholas Valentino, "Does Attack Advertising Demobilize the Electorate," *American Political Science Review* 88 (December 1994), pp. 829–838.

30. Curtis B. Gans, "The Empty Ballot Box," *Public Opinion* 1 (September/October 1978), pp. 54–57. See also Austin Ranney, *Channels of Power* (New York: Basic Books, 1983); and Richard Boyd, "The Effect of Election Calendars on Voter Turnout," paper presented at the Annual Meeting of the Midwest Political Science Association, April 1987, Chicago, Illinois.

31. Boyd, "The Effect of Election Calendars."

32. Ibid.

33. Piven and Cloward, *Why Americans Don't Vote*, p. 17.

34. Benjamin Ginsberg, *The Consequences of Consent: Elections, Citizen Control and Popular Acquiescence* (Reading, Mass.: Addison-Wesley, 1982), p. 37.

35. See Piven and Cloward, *Why Americans Don't Vote*, pp. 196–197 for illustrations of these kinds of informal barriers.

36. Raymond Wolfinger and Steven Rosenstone, *Who Votes?* (New Haven: Yale University Press, 1980), table 6.1.

37. James A. Barnes, "In Person: Marsha Nye Adler," *National Journal*, February 18, 1989, p. 420.

38. Piven and Cloward, *Why Americans Don't Vote*, pp. 230–231.

39. Peverill Squire, Raymond Wolfinger, and David Glass, "Residential Mobility and Voter Turnout," *American Political Science Review* 81 (March 1987), pp. 45–66. See also Samuel C. Patterson and Gregory A. Caldeira, "Mailing in the Vote: Correlates and Consequences of Absentee Voting," *American Journal of Political Science* 29 (November 1985), pp. 766–788.

40. For a review of this literature, see John Petrocik, "Voter Turnout and Electoral Preference," in Kay Schlozman, ed., *Elections in America* (Boston: Allen & Unwin, 1987).

41. Kevin Phillips and Paul Blackman, *Electoral Reform and Voter Participation* (Stanford, Calif.: American Enterprise System, 1975).

42. Kim Quaile Hill, Jan Leighley, and Angela Hinton-Anderson, "Lower-Class Mobilization and Policy Linkage in the U.S. States," *American Journal of Political Science* 39 (February 1995), pp. 75–86.

43. Anthony Downs, *An Economic Theory of Democracy* (New York: Harper & Row, 1957).

44. Morin, "The Dog Ate My Forms."

45. Kay Lehman Schlozman, Sidney Verba, and Henry Brady, "Participation's Not a Paradox: The View from American Activists," *British Journal of Political Science* 25 (January 1995), pp. 1–36.

46. Norman H. Nie, Sidney Verba, Henry Brady, Kay Lehman Schlozman, and Jane Junn, "Participation in America: Continuity and Change," paper presented at the Annual Meeting of the Midwest Political Science Association, Chicago, Illinois, April 1988. The standard work on American political participation is Sidney Verba and Norman Nie, *Participation in America* (New York: Harper & Row, 1972).

47. Nie et al., "Participation in America." Verba and Nie, *Participation in America*.

48. Paul Allen Beck and M. Kent Jennings, "Political Periods and Political Participation," *American Political Science Review* 73 (1979), pp. 737–750; Nie et al., "Participation in America."

49. The following discussion draws heavily upon John Aldrich, *Before the Convention* (Chicago: University of Chicago Press, 1980).

50. Ibid. See also David Rohde, "Risk Bearing and Progressive Ambition: The Case of Members of the United States House of Representatives," *American Journal of Political Science* 23 (February 1979), pp. 1–26.

51. "Political Grapevine," *Time*, February 8, 1988, p. 30.

52. "The Fall Campaign," *Newsweek*, Election Extra (November/December 1984), p. 88.

53. Bruce Babbitt, "Bruce Babbitt's View from the Wayside," *Washington Post National Weekly Edition*, February 24–March 6, 1988, p. 24. The 999 days figure is from the *Congressional Quarterly Weekly Report*, February 1, 1992, p. 257.

54. Gerald Pomper and Susan Lederman, *Elections in America* (New York: Longman, 1980), chapter 7.

55. Michael J. Robinson, "Where's the Beef?," in Austin Ranney, ed., *The American Election of 1984* (Durham, N.C.: Duke University Press, 1985).

56. "Squall in New Orleans," *Newsweek*, November 21, 1988, p. 103.

57. "Conventional Wisdom Watch," *Newsweek*, November 21, 1988, p. 18.

58. See *Congressional Quarterly*, July 23, 1988, p. 2015; Thomas Holbrook, "Campaigns, National Conventions and U.S. Presidential Elections," *American Journal of Political Science* 38 (November 1994), pp. 973–998.

59. Benjamin Page and Richard Brody, "Policy Voting and the Electoral Process," *American Political Review* 66 (1972), pp. 979–995.

60. Thomas F. Patterson, *Mass Media Elections* (New York: Praeger, 1980), p. 3.

61. The discussion of the functions of the media relies heavily on the excellent summary found in Stephen Ansolabehere, Roy Behr, and Shanto Iyengar, "Mass Media and Elections," *American Politics Quarterly* 19 (January 1991), pp. 109–139.

62. *Congressional Quarterly Weekly Reports*, July 30, 1971, p. 1622, quoted in Ansolabehere, Behr, and Iyengar, "Mass Media and Elections," p. 109.

63. Martin Schram, *The Great American Video Game: Presidential Politics in the Television Age* (New York: William Morrow, 1987).

64. Patterson, *Mass Media Election*, p. 4.

65. Robert McNeil, *The Influence of Television on American Politics* (New York: Harper & Row, 1968), p. 182.

66. Elisabeth Bumiller, "Selling Soup, Wine and Reagan," *Washington Post National Weekly Edition*, November 5, 1984, pp. 6–8.

67. Paul Taylor, "Pigsty Politics," *Washington Post National Weekly Edition*, February 13–19, 1989, p. 6.

68. Eileen Shields West, "Give 'em Hell These Days Is a Figure of Speech," *Smithsonian* (October 1988), pp. 149–151. The editorial was from the *Connecticut Courant*.

69. Charles Paul Freund, "But Then, Truth Has Never Been Important," *Washington Post National Weekly Edition*, November 7–13, 1988, p. 29.

70. Quoted in Freund, "But Then, Truth Has Never Been Important," p. 29.

71. Freund, "But Then, the Truth Has Never Been Important," p. 29.

72. Stephen Ansolabehere and Shanto Iyengar, *Going Negative* (New York: Free Press, 1996).

73. The study of negative advertising research was done by Richard Lau, Lee Sigelman, Caroline Heldman, and Paul Babbitt, "The Effects of Negative Political Advertisements," paper delivered at the Annual Meeting of the American Political Science Association, August 1997. Washington, D.C. Research on turnout is found in Ansolabehere and Iyengar, *Going Negative*. In her book, *Packaging the Presidency* (New York: Oxford University Press, 1984), Kathleen Jamieson also argued that there are checks on misleading advertising, but later ("Is the Truth Now Irrelevant in Presidential Campaigns?") she argued that these checks did not work well in 1988. See Jamieson, *Dirty Politics: Deception, Distraction and Democracy* (New York: Oxford University Press, 1992).

74. Stanley Kelley, Jr., *Interpreting Elections* (Princeton, N.J.: Princeton University Press, 1983); Stanley Kelley, Jr., Richard Ayres, and William G. Bower, "Registration and Voting: Putting First Things First," *American Political Science Review* 61 (June 1967), pp. 359–379.

75. J. Merrill Shanks and Warren E. Miller, "Partisanship, Policy and Performance: The Reagan Legacy in the 1988 Election," *British Journal of Political Science* 21 (April 1991), pp. 129–197; Eugene DeClerq, Thomas Hurley, and Norman Luttbeg, "Voting in American Presidential Elections," *American Political Quarterly* 3 (July 1975), updated and reported in David B. Hill and Norman Luttbeg, *Trends in American Electoral Behavior*, 2d ed. (Itasca, Ill.: F. E. Peacock, 1983), p. 50.

76. These data are from "Portrait of an Electorate," *New York Times*, November 10, 1996, p. 28. Lee Sigelman, "If You Prick Us, Do We Not Bleed? If You Tickle Us, Do We Not Laugh? Jews and Pocketbook Voting," paper prepared for presentation at the 1990 American Political Science Meeting: Susan Welch and Lee Sigelman, "The Politics of Hispanic Americans," *Social Science Quarterly*, 1991; *New York Times*, November 5, 1992, p. B9.

77. Paul Abramson, John H. Aldrich, and David Rohde, *Change and Continuity in the 1992 Elections*, revised ed. (Washington, D.C.: CQ Press, 1995), p. 181.

78. Ibid., p. 186.

79. Ibid.

80. Ibid.

81. Morris Fiorina, *Retrospective Voting in American National Elections* (New Haven: Yale University Press, 1981).

82. Edward Tufte, *Political Control of the Economy* (Princeton, N.J.: Princeton University Press, 1978); Douglas Hibbs, "The Mass Public and Macroeconomic Performance," *American Journal of Political Science* 23 (November 1979), pp. 705–731; John Hibbing and John Alford, "The Electoral Impact of Economic Conditions: Who Is Held Responsible," *American Journal of Political Science* 25 (1981), pp. 423–439.

83. Benjamin I. Page and Robert Shapiro, "Effects of Public Opinion on Policy," *American Political Science Review* 77 (March 1983), pp. 175–190.

84. Abramson, Aldrich, and Rohde, *Change and Continuity*. See also Benjamin Page and Calvin C. Jones, "Reciprocal Effects of Party Preferences, Party Loyalties and the Vote," in Richard Niemi and Herbert Weisberg, *Controversies in Voting Behavior*, 2d ed. (Washington, D.C.: CQ Press, 1984).

85. Arthur Schlesinger, Jr., *Wall Street Journal*, December 5, 1986.

86. This was the biggest convention bounce since polling began.

87. Maureen Dowd, "A No-Nonsense Sort of Talk Show," *New York Times* (October 16, 1992), p. 1.

88. Kelly, "The Making of a First Family." For scholarly works on the 1992 elections, see Robert Loevy, *The Flawed Path to the Presidency, 1992* (Albany: State University of New York Press, 1995); Robert Steed, Laurence Moreland, and Tod A. Baker, eds., *The 1992 Presidential Election in the South* (Westport, Conn.: Praeger, 1994); Abramson, Aldrich, and Rhode, *Change and Continuity*.

Photographers crush Monica Lewinsky, her father, and her step-mother.

Mylan Ryba/Globe Photos 1998

8 NEWS MEDIA

OUTLINE

YOU ARE THERE

Should You Pull Him Out of "the Closet"?

You are Michelangelo Signorile, a homosexual activist and a writer for *OutWeek*, a homosexual magazine. It is 1991 and you have to decide whether to publicize the fact that a high-ranking official in the Department of Defense is gay. You think that publication would be newsworthy given the department's stance against homosexuality in the military service. But you also are concerned about the ethical issues involved in publicizing this aspect of the person's private life.

Your own background in the media and in the movement have led you to hold these conflicting views. After college you worked for a public relations firm with clients in the entertainment business. When your clients sought publicity for their latest projects, you fed tidbits of information about them to the writers of gossip columns in newspapers. In this way, you planted their names in these columns. When the AIDS epidemic spread in the 1980s, you joined ACT UP (AIDS Coalition To Unleash Power), a group that used protest to gain publicity for its demands that the government invest more resources in the fight against the epidemic.

You know from your public relations work that gossip columnists prattle on about anything in a celebrity's private life except a celebrity's homosexuality. That is taboo. Columnists talk about a straight actor's affairs but not a gay actor's relationships. Sometimes they even pretend that a gay actor is straight by writing that he or she is "dating" someone of the opposite sex. The result, you feel, is to send a message that homosexuality is "so utterly grotesque that it should never be discussed."[1]

This message, you believe, reflects an unconscious conspiracy to keep homosexuals locked in "the closet"—that is, to keep them from revealing their sexual identity, sometimes even to their closest friends and relatives. You think this conspiracy is perpetuated by the government, the media, and the entertainment industry—even including some powerful homosexuals in these institutions who go along out of fear that their power, prestige, and income would plummet if the truth were revealed.

In recent years some gays have tried to reveal the homosexuality of other gays, but the mainstream media normally have not reported the revelations. In 1990 activists held a press conference on the steps of the Capitol and identified three members of the Senate and five members of the House of Representatives as gay. Activists also altered a billboard of an incumbent senator running for reelection—"Closeted Gay. Living a Lie. Voting to Oppress"—and demonstrated outside the homes of some members. But most media did not report these efforts.[2]

You were sympathetic with these efforts, and, still disgusted by the gossip columnists' practice of hiding the homosexuality of entertainers, you criticized their practice and implied that two columnists themselves were homosexuals. Your exposé prompted another writer to compare you to Senator Joseph McCarthy (R-Wis.), who shrilly and often falsely accused government employees of being communists in the 1950s.

Other journalists see no sinister motives behind the silence on homosexuality. They deny the existence of any conspiracy to keep homosexuals locked in "the closet." They say they do not publicize a person's homosexuality because of the likely consequences of the public's prejudices.

Now you have information that an assistant secretary of defense in the Bush administration is gay. You have no doubt about the accuracy of the information. Should you report it in *OutWeek*?

The official has a high position and considerable visibility. During the recent Persian Gulf War, he was the primary spokesman for the department.

Since the war the department's policy of discharging gay and lesbian military personnel has come under heavy fire. In the past decade the Pentagon has discharged perhaps 13,000 soldiers, sailors, airmen and women, and marines for homosexuality.[3] This policy rankles you and others in the gay and lesbian community. But you do not know whether the assistant secretary has any influence over the policy or whether he might be working on the inside to overturn it. Do these factors matter?

Although the policy does not apply to civilian officials, such as the assistant secretary, does the situation—being a gay spokesman for a department that discharges gay and lesbian personnel—reflect hypocrisy? If so, is the hypocrisy sufficient for you to reveal his homosexuality?

Or should a concern for privacy override your distaste of hypocrisy? There is no legal right to privacy for one's sexuality, but should there be an ethical right? Many gays think there should be. One called privacy "the central protection" for gays. Forsaking it would cause anguish for people and would ignore the complexities of their lives. Perhaps there are good reasons to allow some to remain in "the closet."[4]

Or do the media routinely disregard privacy to such an extent that it is irrelevant to consider? Reporters already cover out-of-wedlock births, abortions, affairs, and divorces of public figures. Is it pointless to try drawing the line at homosexuality?

Or are the media generally so invasive of people's private lives that their current practices should not serve as a guide for covering homosexuality? Reporting of people's "scandalous" conduct used to focus on their malfeasance or incompetence in public office. Now it has extended to their private behavior, including instances that occurred before they became public officials. Sometimes it has extended to their aides, who were not elected and do not hold public office. In the past decade, officials or candidates have been exposed for having a "shotgun" wedding, having affairs while married, smoking marijuana while in college, attending parties where others used cocaine, telling racist or sexist jokes, and a variety of other things.[5] Should people be defined publicly according to the way they lead their private lives or solely according to the way they perform their jobs? If some aspects of their private lives are relevant, is their sexual identity as heterosexual or homosexual relevant?

Jodi Buren/Time magazine

Michelangelo Signorile.

In this debate, it is not clear whether privacy helps or hurts the lives of gays. Keeping homosexuality secret certainly props up the walls of "the closet." This practice might make life more difficult for gay teenagers, who see few gay adults and who feel isolated. But challenging this practice might complicate the already difficult lives of gay adults still in "the closet."

So what do you do with the information?

A "medium" transmits something. The mass media—which include newspapers, magazines, books, radio, television, movies, and records—transmit communications to masses of people.

Although the media do not constitute a branch of government or even an organization established to influence government, such as a political party or interest group, they have an impact on government. In addition to providing entertainment, the media provide information about government and politics. This chapter focuses on the news media—the part of the media that delivers the news about government and politics.

THE MEDIA STATE

The media have developed and flourished to an extent the Founders could not have envisioned. As one political scientist noted, the media have become "pervasive . . . and atmospheric, an element of the air we breathe."[6] Without exaggeration, another observer concluded, "Ancient Sparta was a military state. John Calvin's Geneva was a religious state. Mid-nineteenth century England was Europe's first industrial state, and the contemporary United States is the world's first media state."[7]

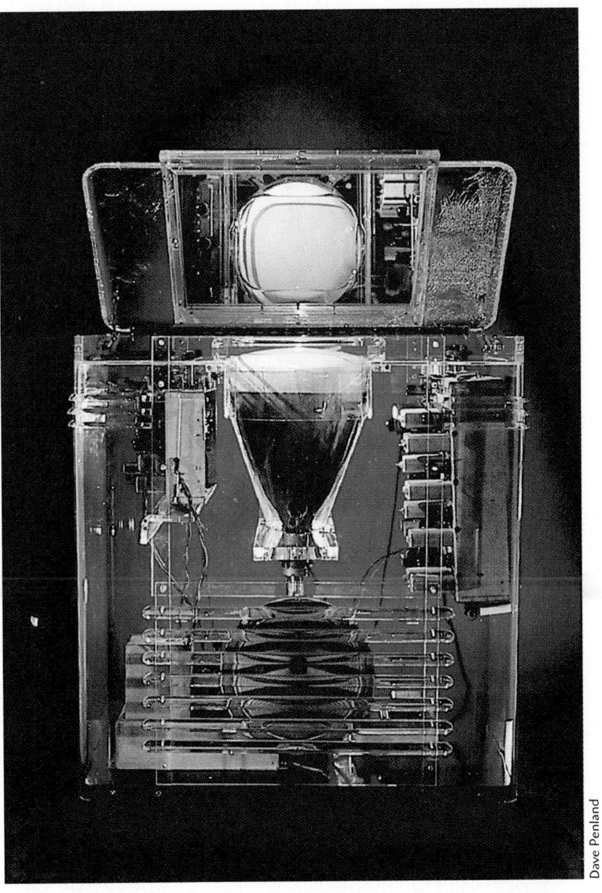
Dave Penland

Corbis-Bettmann

This television (left) made its debut in the Hall of Television at the New York World's Fair in 1939. President Franklin Roosevelt opened the fair by appearing on the tiny screen. Television coverage and programming was limited for years because the equipment, such as this camera, was so bulky (above).

Americans spend more time being exposed to the media than doing anything else. In a year, according to one calculation, the average full-time worker puts in 1,824 hours on the job, 2,737 hours in bed, and 3,256 hours exposed to the media (almost 9 hours a day).[8] Seventy-seven percent of adults read newspapers; the average person does so for three-and-a-half hours a week. The average person also reads two magazines for one-and-a-half hours a week.[9] Ninety-eight percent of American homes have a radio, and the same percent have a television. More homes have a television than have a toilet.[10] The average adult watches television three hours a day and the average child four. By the time the average child graduates from high school, he or she has spent more time in front of the tube than in class.[11] By the time the average American dies, he or she has spent one-and-a-half years just watching television commercials.[12]

Roles of the Media

American newspapers, which originated in colonial times, were the only regular media in the country for almost two centuries. Although they flourished and political magazines appeared in the 1800s, there were no "mass media" until the advent of the broadcast media. Radio, which became popular in the 1920s, and television, which became popular in the 1950s, reached people who could not or would not read.

People bought television sets to watch entertainment programs, but they also began to watch newscasts. At first the newscasts, lasting only 15 minutes and consisting solely of an anchor and a few correspondents talking, were not compelling. In 1963 the networks expanded the time to 30 minutes and altered the format to emphasize visual interest. That year, for the first time, people said they got more political information from television than from any other source.

As television grew in popularity, newspapers waned. People did not need them for the headlines anymore. Although newspapers began to provide in-depth analysis of news, which television did not, they struggled for readers and advertisers, and some folded.

These trends continued. Since 1970 the number of adults and the number of households in the country have increased significantly, but the circulation of daily newspapers has remained stagnant.[13] And the percentage of regular readers has declined (from 78% of adults in 1970 to 64% in 1995).[14] The percentage of young adults who are regular readers has declined the most.

Consequently, television has become the most important of the media for politics. According to surveys, people pay more attention to it and put more faith in it than in other media. This makes positive coverage on television essential for politicians.

Nevertheless, television has not fully eclipsed newspapers. Most people who say they get the bulk of their political information from television admit they do not watch the news daily, whereas more people who get the bulk of their political information from newspapers read the news sections daily. Because newspapers require more effort or provide more depth, they leave a longer-lasting impression; people remember what they read in newspapers better than what they watch on television.[15]

Moreover, national newspapers such as the *New York Times* and *Washington Post,* which blanket the country with in-depth international and national news, influence opinion leaders who, in turn, influence other persons.

Concentration of the Media

Journalism has always been a business, with media organizations seeking a profit, but in the middle and late twentieth century, it has become a bigger business. Small media organizations owned by local families or local companies have been taken over by chains or conglomerates. These large corporations have come to dominate the business and to constitute a national media.[16]

Although there are many media in the United States—approximately 1,700 daily newspapers, 10,800 radio stations, and 1,600 television stations[17]—these numbers are misleading. Chains and conglomerates own the newspapers and magazines with most of the readers, the radio stations with most of the listeners, and the television stations with most of the viewers (see Figure 1).[18]

In addition, other large corporations—the telecommunications companies, such as AT&T and its competitors, and computer companies, such as Microsoft—are establishing partnerships and alliances with the media conglomerates to control the information markets of the future. One analyst foresees "a multi-industry cartel."[19]

This trend toward concentration of the media is likely to continue. Already the media industry is the nation's ninth largest, just below aerospace and just above electronics equipment.[20] It is expected to become even larger in the future.

This trend toward concentration of the media raises serious questions: Will journalists remain free to express themselves? Will the media slant their coverage? (Will ABC air criticism of its owner Disney? Will NBC launch an investigation of its partner Microsoft?) Will the news become too homogenized?

Pressures toward homogenization are apparent. Already just one wire service—AP—supplies the international and national news for most newspapers. Only four radio networks—ABC, CBS, NBC, and Mutual—furnish the news for most radio stations, and only four television networks—ABC, CBS, NBC, and CNN—furnish the news for most television stations. Further, the huge conglomerates expect sizable profits, so they must attract a mass audience. It is likely that all will aim for the same audience—the most common denominator—and will provide very similar coverage.[21] Even if some other individuals want to start new media companies, which might be more creative and more appealing to a small segment of the audience, it is possible that they will be discouraged, perhaps crushed, by the conglomerates' power.

Regardless of the actual outcomes of these potential implications, another consequence of this trend toward concentration of the media seems inescapable: the power to provide information—essentially, to define reality for people—will lie in the hands of very few individuals.

Atomization of the Media

Despite the growing concentration of the media during the twentieth century, a contrary trend—an atomization of the media—has also developed in recent years. Whereas concentration has led to a national media, atomization has fragmented the influence of this national media. The major newspapers and broadcast networks have lost their dominance, while other media, some not even considered news organizations, have started to play a significant role in politics.

This trend is partly the result of technological changes. As explained, newspapers lost readers to television. Then the networks' national newscasts lost viewers to local stations' newscasts. Technological innovations enabled local stations to offer local and national news by joining a consortium of other stations around the country, linked by satellite, to share coverage of events of national interest.

Then the traditional stations lost viewers to cable television. With its multiplicity of channels, cable can offer competing newscasts and more specialized programs. Although much of cable's menu duplicates the networks' (and reflects Bruce Springsteen's complaint, "57 Channels, and Nothin' On"), its offerings are becoming more focused—"narrowcasting" to appeal to small segments of the audience in contrast to the networks' broadcasting to appeal to the overall audience. For example, C-SPAN covers Congress on three channels and, unlike the networks, lingers on members' speeches and committees' hearings. Even MTV, the music channel, covers presidential campaigns in formats that attract young viewers.

INTO THE 21ST CENTURY

FROM THE AIRWAVES TO CYBERSPACE

In an alliance between two contemporary communications giants, General Electric, which owns NBC, and Microsoft, which dominates the computer software business, formed a partnership in 1995 to establish another 24-hour cable news channel and an interactive online news service. The cable news channel is designed to compete around the world with CNN, while the online news service is intended to leap to the next level of news delivery. The service will allow people with computers to retrieve more information, data, and pictures about the events covered on the news channel. The cable news channel, MSNBC, has been launched, while the online service is being developed.

Network officials have long been frustrated by time constraints imposed by their fixed-time, half-hour slot. The schedule of the newscasts is not convenient for many people, and the brevity of the newscasts does not allow as much coverage as producers would like to provide. To cover a major event adequately, they need to assign numerous cameras, and perhaps a helicopter, and multiple correspondents, and perhaps an anchor. But often they obtain more footage and have more comments than they have time to include. By offering around-the-clock newscasts and on-demand interactive news as well, the network avoids this frustration. "We're moving to a world," an NBC official said, "where there are no time constraints." Microsoft, which already has conquered the computer software industry, wants to expand its reach and power. By allying with NBC, Microsoft can become a major actor in the news delivery business. The world will still have financial constraints, however. The market for 24-hour newscasts might not be big enough for another channel, much less the five that are in operation or in development (CNN, MSNBC, Fox, ABC, and CBS). Indeed, a news channel, even around the clock, might represent a view from the past; news on demand might represent the vision of the future. Either way, the GE/NBC-Microsoft partnership is positioned to take advantage of the market. One reason the media conglomerates are allying with other communications corporations is that technology is changing so fast that officials are uncertain what services will be sought and what will be left behind.

SOURCE: Ken Auletta, "The News Rush," *New Yorker*, March 18, 1996, pp. 42–45.

Other national cable networks cater to blacks and to Hispanics. A cable system in Los Angeles and New York caters to Jews. A cable channel in California broadcasts in Chinese, one in Hawaii broadcasts in Japanese, and one in Connecticut and Massachusetts broadcasts in Portuguese. Stations in New York also provide programs in Greek, Hindi, Korean, and Russian.

Cable has led to 24-hour news. CNN, created as a 24-hour news network, has a large audience. Now it is being challenged by Fox and by new cable stations of the three original networks.

The Internet has led to additional news sites. Major newspapers post their stories on their Web sites before the newspapers themselves are delivered. Self-styled "journalists" can post their "news" as well. Matt Drudge offers political gossip on his own Web site, the Drudge Report, from his one-bedroom apartment in Hollywood.[22]

With such proliferation of newscasts, the audience for the traditional nightly news has sunk to its lowest level since 1961[23]—two years before the networks attracted a mass audience by expanding the newscast from 15 to 30 minutes and emphasizing visual interest in the stories.

The trend toward atomization of the media is also partly the result of the populist backlash against government officials and established journalists, perceived as "Washington insiders," that has characterized American politics in the 1980s and 1990s. This is reflected most clearly in the popularity of radio and television talk shows. Many radio stations have some talk shows, and about 10% of the stations have an all-talk format, the fastest growing format in the business.[24] According to one 1993 survey, 17% percent of the public say they listen to these shows regularly; 25% more say they listen sometimes. (Eleven percent have tried to call in; 6% have gotten on the air.)[25] According to another 1993 survey, 44% of the public said these shows are their primary source of political information.[26] With millions of people listening, talk radio is a force in politics. It attracts a middle-class audience that serves as a national jury on governmental controversies.

When Congress voted itself a substantial pay raise in 1988, several talk show hosts decided to coordinate an attack. They contacted other stations, and the hosts all urged listeners to phone or fax their representatives. The deluge caused Congress to postpone and scale back the raise.

When *USA Today* reported congressional check kiting in 1992, talk shows turned to the issue. Most people ignored the newspapers' explanation that members who overdrew their checking accounts at the

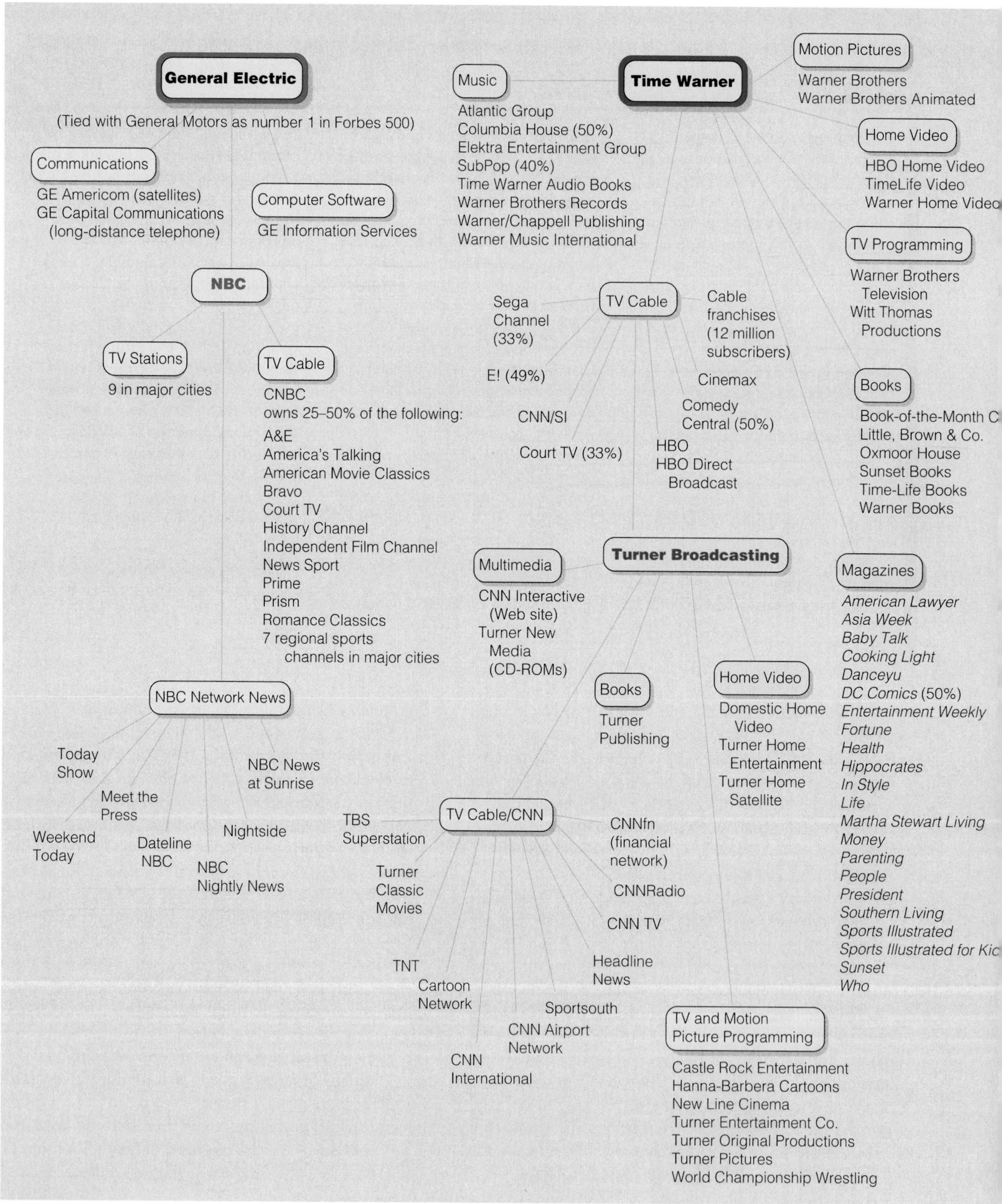

FIGURE 1

Media Conglomerates Dominate

The four huge conglomerates that own the major television networks also own many other media organizations. In addition, two of the four—General Electric and Westinghouse—are major defense contractors. Thus, our news comes from some of the most powerful companies in the country.

SOURCE: Mark Crispin Miller, "Free the Media," *The Nation*, June 3, 1996, p. 9.

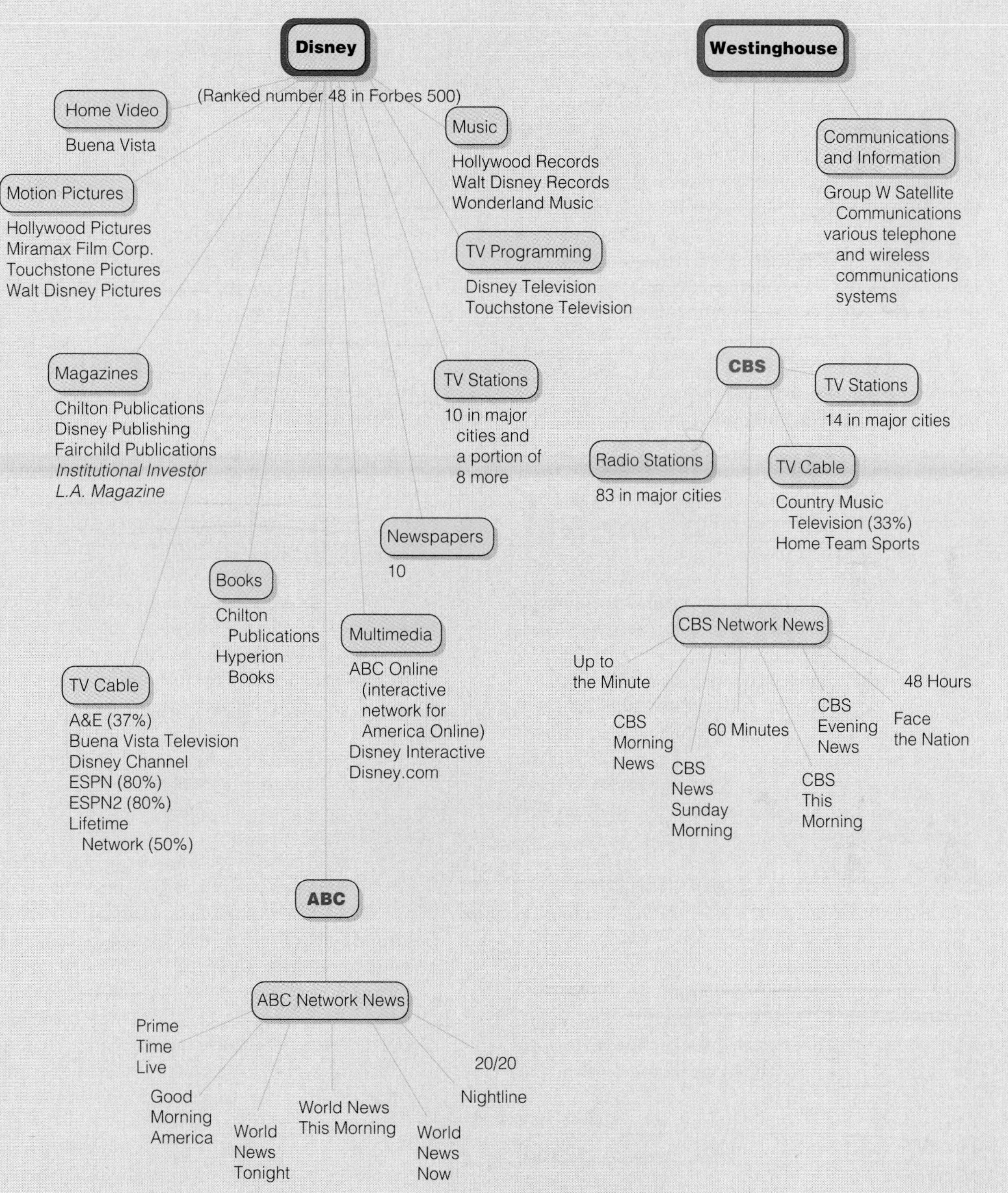

Disney
(Ranked number 48 in Forbes 500)
Home Video
Buena Vista
Motion Pictures
Hollywood Pictures
Miramax Film Corp.
Touchstone Pictures
Walt Disney Pictures
Music
Hollywood Records
Walt Disney Records
Wonderland Music
TV Programming
Disney Television
Touchstone Television
Magazines
Chilton Publications
Disney Publishing
Fairchild Publications
Institutional Investor
L.A. Magazine
TV Stations
10 in major cities and a portion of 8 more
Newspapers
10
Books
Chilton Publications
Hyperion Books
Multimedia
ABC Online (interactive network for America Online)
Disney Interactive
Disney.com
TV Cable
A&E (37%)
Buena Vista Television
Disney Channel
ESPN (80%)
ESPN2 (80%)
Lifetime Network (50%)
ABC
ABC Network News
Prime Time Live
Good Morning America
World News Tonight
World News This Morning
World News Now
Nightline
20/20
Westinghouse
Communications and Information
Group W Satellite Communications
various telephone and wireless communications systems
CBS
TV Stations
14 in major cities
Radio Stations
83 in major cities
TV Cable
Country Music Television (33%)
Home Team Sports
CBS Network News
Up to the Minute
CBS Morning News
CBS News Sunday Morning
60 Minutes
CBS This Morning
CBS Evening News
Face the Nation
48 Hours

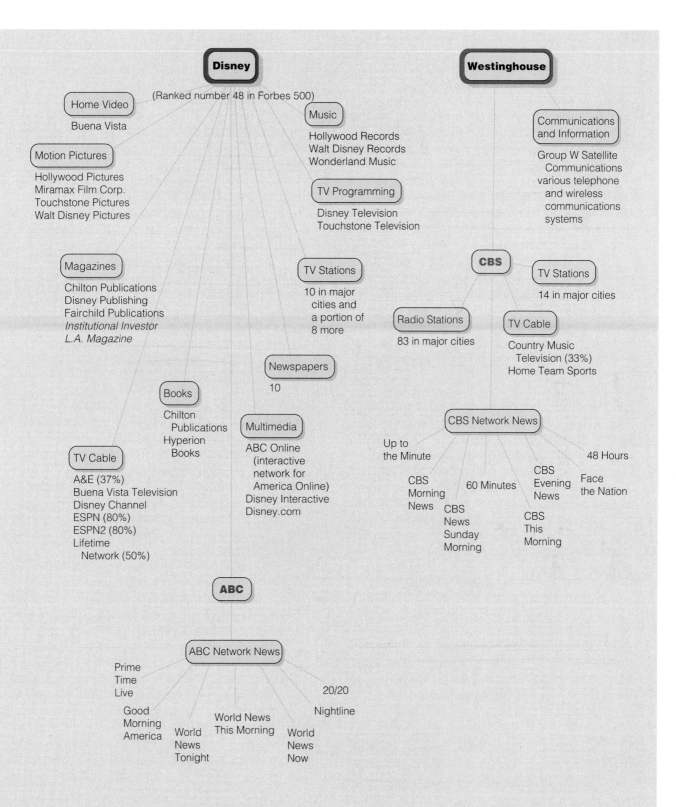

House of Representatives "bank" essentially had borrowed money from each other rather than taken any from the taxpayers. Cued by talk show hosts, people considered these overdrafts from the House "bank" equivalent to overdrafts from their own checking accounts. The vitriol prompted the retirement of some members and the reelection defeat of others.

When it came out that President Clinton's first choice for attorney general—Zoe Baird, a $500,000 a year corporate lawyer—and her husband had hired illegal aliens to provide day care for their children, listeners contacted their senators. As calls mounted, it became clear that she could not be confirmed, and her nomination was withdrawn.

For all three incidents, citizens' anger was fueled by talk shows reflecting middle-class indignation that officials were making too much money, getting too many benefits, and not playing by the rules other people had to play by. Although the major media initially had not considered these incidents important and had not covered them prominently, listeners of the talk shows had a different opinion.

The populist backlash is also reflected in the increasing attention paid to fringe media by the public and, in turn, by politicians trying to reach the public. In the 1992 presidential campaign, *The Star,* a supermarket tabloid, published allegations by Gennifer Flowers, a former nightclub singer, that she had had a 12-year affair with Bill Clinton while he was governor of Arkansas. The major media hesitated to repeat the *Star's* story—they had nothing but scorn for the tabloids, which, they insisted, did not practice true journalism—but within days most gave in, under the pretense of debating the propriety of reporting personal matters. The Clintons appeared on *60 Minutes* to refute the allegations (while sidestepping the question whether he had ever committed adultery). Whereupon Flowers appeared on *A Current Affair,* a syndicated television show, rated Clinton as a lover on a scale from 1 to 10, and sang "Stand By Your Man." Thus, Flowers did not need to take her story to the major media; she got the tabloid media to tell it and pay her for it ($150,000 from the *Star* and $25,000 from *A Current Affair*).[27] The continuing coverage precipitated a drop in Clinton's standing during the presidential primaries.

Then Ross Perot announced his candidacy for president on CNN's *Larry King Live,* a talk show, rather than through a press conference with the networks. Other candidates followed on various talk shows. Clinton fielded questions on the *Phil Donahue Show* and on MTV, and played the saxophone on the *Arsenio Hall Show.* President Bush, who initially called these appearances "weird," eventually courted sports fans on ESPN and country music fans on the Nashville Network.

Candidates use these shows to reach people who do not follow the major media and to communicate their messages without having them "filtered"—that is, condensed, simplified, distorted, or challenged—by professional reporters. But when prominent politicians appear on fringe shows, they help legitimize these shows and at the same time perhaps discredit their own ideas, which usually are not treated seriously. When Senator Bill Bradley (D-N.J.) appeared at a Houston radio station, ranked number one among men in the metropolitan area, with 400,000 listeners, he expected to discuss his new book. Instead, the disc jockeys had two women disrobe from the waist up to see his reaction.[28]

Candidates also buy television time for "electronic town meetings," shows in which they take questions from voters in several cities without any journalists or hosts present.

Because of the expanding role of fringe media, mainstream journalists envision a shrinking role for themselves. They no longer monopolize the market of political information; they no longer control the gates through which such information must pass.

In fact, according to one journalism professor, many citizens see no purpose in having journalists intervene in politics. "Max in Seattle feels as well represented by Julie's question from Houston as he would be by Sam Donaldson's inquiry from New York." (Actually, Max might prefer Julie's to Sam Donaldson's. Many citizens are annoyed by the "cult of toughness" among journalists that leads them to challenge public figures with "a level of shamelessness and aggression that ordinary people cannot manage.")[29]

This trend toward atomization of the media has significant implications beyond its impact on the national media and established journalists. Although this trend makes news more accessible to more people, it makes the news less analytical and less factual.

With such proliferation of news outlets and of newscasts around the clock, the competition among them is intense. They have more capacity than news to fill it, unless they repeat what others have already reported. So they feel tremendous pressure to locate new stories or identify new angles of old stories. In the process, less emphasis is placed on determining the accuracy of this information. Instead, there is a "commingling of fact, rumor, and opinion."[30] The line between traditional journalism and tabloid journalism is blurring.

This problem is aggravated by the fact that some fringe media are careless about the accuracy of the information they disseminate. In their quest for an audience, some pay for stories, possibly encouraging people to lie for the money; many sensationalize stories, possibly distorting the truth. Of course, the mainstream media also are commercial enterprises subject to the pressures of the marketplace (as will be addressed later in the chapter). At the same time, however, these established media are subject to the pressures of tradition. Reporters at major newspapers and broadcast networks often speak of their responsibility to follow certain journalistic norms, while members of the fringe media sometimes reflect the views of a radio talk show host who asserts, "The news isn't sacred to me. It's entertainment . . . designed to revel in the agony of others."[31]

This blurring of fact and rumor is particularly evident on the Internet, where there are no editors and where any person with a computer and a phone line can deliver any "fact," however erroneous, to the whole world. In 1997 Pierre Salinger, the respected press secretary to President Kennedy and then correspondent for ABC, announced in a speech to an airline association that the TWA flight that crashed off the coast of Long Island had been accidentally shot down by a navy missile and that this fact was being covered up by the U.S. government. The cause of the crash had been listed as "unknown," so Salinger's speech was reported prominently worldwide. When doubters asked how he learned this, Salinger replied that he received the information from a top intelligence agent in France. Salinger was hoodwinked. The information originated in the fertile imagination of a retired pilot in Florida who hypothesized this scenario and posted it on the Internet, where it eventually reached the intelligence agent in France.[32]

Interest groups eager to exploit the competitiveness that exists now add to the problem. When Vince Foster, deputy counsel for President Clinton, apparently committed suicide in a park, a right-wing group sent a fax to news organizations linking the suicide to the Whitewater land deal. The group passed the rumor that Foster died at an administration "safe house" and later was moved to the park. Talk show host Rush Limbaugh reported the rumor. Other talk show hosts repeated it, while some added the rumor that Foster was murdered. A few financial speculators spread the rumors as a way to manipulate the stock market, and the next day newspaper business sections repeated the rumors in articles about their effect on the stock market. Thus, through announcement and repetition by the media, the rumors came to seem true to many people—yet they remained just rumors[33] (and false ones, according to two independent counsels).

A similar pattern occurred when a conservative magazine, *Insight*, charged that the Clinton administration was "selling" burial plots in Arlington National Cemetery to "dozens of big-time political donors or friends of the Clintons." Because the cemetery is reserved for military veterans, anonymous officials were quoted as saying this was "corruption of the worst kind." The charge was repeated on talk radio, then aired in Congress when some members demanded an investigation. Within 48 hours it was reported by the mainstream media. Yet apparently there was no truth to it.[34]

The mainstream media have been uncertain how to act in such situations. They are reluctant to report rumors they are unable to verify. But they fear they will lose their audience if they fail to report stories that other media report. Usually, they decide to report the stories but in a different context—under the guise of addressing the political ramifications of the accusation or the journalistic ethics of publicizing it. Nevertheless, the effect is nearly the same—the accusation winds up in the mainstream media, and the public believes it. As a result, unscrupulous groups realize they can use the fringe media to manipulate the mainstream media into publicizing bogus charges. Thus, they can drag the mainstream media down to their level. (President Clinton's lawyer says it reminds him of when he lived with a bunch of guys in college: four were neat and one was a slob; by the end of the year, they were all slobs.)[35]

Meanwhile, the public is lost in this factual free-for-all. Most citizens are not well versed in the issues or very knowledgeable about the politicians. Without the help of professional journalists, many are not able to separate the blarney from the gospel truth when candidates and officials speak.

RELATIONSHIP BETWEEN THE MEDIA AND POLITICIANS

"Politicians live—and sometimes die—by the press. The press lives by politicians," according to a former presidential aide. "This relationship is at the center of our national life."36

Politicians and journalists need each other. Politicians need journalists in order to reach the public and to receive feedback from the public. They scan the major newspapers in the morning and the network newscasts in the evening. President Lyndon Johnson watched three network newscasts on three televisions simultaneously. Journalists need politicians in order to cover government. They seek a steady stream of fresh information to fill their news columns and newscasts. Just two days after the election of Bill Clinton, a chorus of reporters complained of a "news blackout" by the incoming administration.[37] A week later the chorus forced the president-elect to call a press conference to pacify the press corps, though he had no news yet and hardly any voice after the long campaign.[38]

The close relationship between the media and politicians is both a **symbiotic relationship,** meaning they use each other for their mutual advantage, and an **adversarial relationship,** meaning they fight each other.

Symbiotic Relationship

President Lyndon Johnson told individual reporters, "You help me and I'll help make you a big man in your profession." He gave exclusive interviews, told outrageous tales, and invited reporters to bunk overnight at his Texas ranch.[39] In return he expected favorable coverage.

Reporters get information from politicians in various ways. Some reporters are assigned to monitor beats. Washington beats include the White House, Congress, Supreme Court, State Department, Defense Department, and some other departments and agencies. Other reporters are assigned to cover specialized subjects, such as economics, energy issues, and environmental problems, which are addressed by several branches, departments, or agencies.

The government has press secretaries and public information officers who provide reporters with ideas and information for stories. The number of these officials is significant; one year the Defense Department employed almost 1,500 people just to handle press relations.[40]

The government supplies reporters with a variety of news sources, including copies of speeches, summaries of committee meetings, news releases, and news briefings about current events. Officials also grant interviews, hold press conferences, and stage "media events." The vast majority of reporters rely on these sources rather than engage in more difficult and time-consuming investigative reporting.

Interviews show the symbiotic nature of the relationship between reporters and politicians. During the early months of the Reagan presidency, *Washington Post* writer William Greider had a series of 18 off-the-record meetings with budget director David Stockman. Greider recounted:

> *Stockman and I were participating in a fairly routine transaction of Washington, a form of submerged communication which takes place regularly between selected members of the press and the highest officials of government. Our mutual motivation, despite our different interests, was crassly self-serving. It did not need to be spelled out between us. I would use him and he would use me. . . . I had established a valuable peephole on the inner policy debates of the new administration. And the young budget director had established a valuable connection with an important newspaper. I would get a jump on the unfolding strategies and decisions. He would be able to prod and influence the focus of our coverage, to communicate his views and positions under the cover of our "off the record" arrangement, to make known harsh assessments that a public official would not dare to voice in the more formal setting of a press conference, speech, or "on the record" interview.*[41]

Interviews can result in **leaks**—disclosures of information some officials want to keep secret. Other officials in the administration, Congress, or bureaucracy use leaks for many reasons. Officials in the administration might leak information about a proposed policy to test the water for it, without committing themselves or their offices to it, in case intense opposition surfaces. Or they might leak to warn their president or fellow officials about the foolishness of a pending policy. Or, engaged in infighting with other officials, they might leak to make the competitors or their policies look bad. Or officials who feel slighted might leak to call attention to their ideas or to force public debates rather than closed-door decisions on issues.

Most presidents get enraged by leaks. Reagan said he was "up to my keister" in leaks, and Nixon established a "plumbers" unit to wiretap aides and reporters and plug the leaks once they learned who was leaking. Nevertheless, despite accusations that leaks are from low-level employees in the opposite party, most are from high-ranking officials in the same party. "The ship of state," one experienced reporter noted, "is the only kind of ship that leaks mainly from the top."[42] During the Vietnam War, President Lyndon Johnson himself ordered an aide to leak the charge that steel companies were "profiteering" from the war. After an executive complained, Johnson assured him that the statement was inappropriate and that "if I find out some damn fool aide did it, I'll fire the sonuvabitch!"[43]

When George Bush was pondering his choice for a running mate for the 1988 election, his campaign manager, James Baker, leaked the fact that Senator Dan Quayle was one of the finalists. Baker saw this as a way to discourage Bush from choosing Quayle; he thought there would be so much opposition that Bush would have to select someone else. (Baker's ploy failed because the press did not take the idea seriously enough to criticize it.)[44]

After President Bush nominated Clarence Thomas to the Supreme Court, a Republican leaked the fact that Thomas had experimented with marijuana in college. The purpose was to innoculate Thomas from the greater controversy that might arise if the press discovered and revealed this fact closer to the vote on confirmation.[45] Then someone, presumably a Democrat, leaked the FBI report on Anita Hill's charges that Thomas had sexually harassed her. The report had been secret and Hill had refused to go public before. Once the information came to light, Hill felt forced to go public, and the Senate nearly denied confirmation.

Dan Adams/George Eastman House

Cynthia Johnson/Liaison

The pervasiveness of the media has increased tremendously. Andrew Jackson was the first president to have his photograph taken. Modern presidents must expect to have their photograph taken almost anywhere at almost any time.

When reporters get information before other reporters, they can **scoop** them. In 1980 NBC correspondent Chris Wallace scooped his colleagues in reporting that Reagan would choose Bush as his running mate. Although Wallace was first by just seconds, this helped him win a promotion to NBC White House correspondent.[46]

The tendency for officials to leak and for reporters to seek scoops creates a climate in which rumors, ostensibly facts, can be passed to reporters and hastily disseminated to the public without first being confirmed. Thus, the public was informed that Paula Jones knew about "distinguishing characteristics" of President Clinton's genitals. Only after this story was aired by many of the media and believed by much of the public was it reported to be apparently false.[47]

The interdependence between reporters and politicians, as reflected in the use of interviews, leaks, and scoops, usually results in more news for the public, but it can result in less. Before the Iran-contra affair came to light, some reporters relied on Lt. Col. Oliver North for information. Although many reporters suspected that North was involved in supplying the contras with arms despite congressional restrictions on such aid, North had been a valuable source and, as one reporter remarked, "his romantic derring-do and colorful antics made him more fun to talk to than other bureaucrats."[48] Reporters did not investigate North's involvement until the story broke in an obscure Lebanese magazine. If they had been willing to sacrifice their access to him, they could have publicized the affair far sooner.

Press conferences also show the symbiotic nature of the media-politician relationship. Theodore Roosevelt, the first president who cultivated close ties to correspondents, started the **presidential press conference.**[49] He held irregular and informal sessions while being shaved. Later presidents, uncomfortable with the "cross-examination," offered few sessions and demanded questions in advance.[50] But Franklin Roosevelt realized that the press conference could help him reach the public. Newspaper publishers detested him and criticized him in editorials, but by holding frequent sessions and permitting questions on the spot, he provided a steady stream of news, which editors felt obligated to publish. This news publicized his policies and his efforts to implement them.

John Kennedy saw that press conferences could help him reach the public more directly if he allowed the networks to televise them live.[51] Then editors could not filter his remarks.

Televising a press conference seems inherently contradictory. If a president wants to answer reporters, he can do so in private. If he wants to communicate with the public, he can do so in a formal speech, without risking an embarrassing question. So why would a president opt for a televised press conference? He might perform better in the less formal setting of a press conference. Or, like the youthful Kennedy, he might feel a need to demonstrate his competence to the watchful public.[52] With his intellect and wit, Kennedy expected to excel at the press conference, and he did.

As a result, presidents and their aides transformed the conference into a carefully orchestrated media show. Now an administration schedules a conference when it wants to convey a particular message. It might even limit questions to that topic. Aides identify potential questions, and the president rehearses appropriate answers. (Former press secretaries admit that they predicted at least 90% of the questions asked and often the exact reporters who asked them.)[53] Aides prepare a seating chart, and during the conference the president calls on the reporters he wants. Although he cannot ignore those from the major media, he can call disproportionately on those he knows will lob soft questions. Consequently, the conference usually helps the president.

Beaming the conference to the nation results in less news than having a casual exchange around the president's desk, which used to reveal his thinking on programs and decisions. Appearing in millions of homes, the president cannot be as open, cannot commit himself to a policy prematurely, and cannot allow himself to make a gaffe in front of the huge audience.

Televising the conference does not even provide much accountability, because one is scheduled when the administration wants and nearly every aspect is scripted or predicted in advance. For the most part, the conference offers an illusion of accountability.

The transformation of the conference frustrates reporters and prompts them to act as prosecutors. As one press secretary observed, they play a game of "I gotcha."[54] After Clinton's first conference, one reporter criticized him because "he didn't say a single thing he didn't mean to."[55] The reporter considered the conference a game in which the press tries to beat the president, and this time the press had lost because it could not trick him into saying something imprudent.

Still, reporters value the conference. Editors consider the president's remarks news, so the conference helps reporters do their job. It also gives them a chance to bask in the limelight.

According to a former press secretary, it gives them "fame, power in the eyes of their peers, recognition by their families, ego gratification, and lecture fees from the Storm Door and Sash Associations of the world."[56] (Business and professional associations pay well-known journalists handsome fees to speak at their annual meetings.)

Media events also show the symbiotic nature of the media-politician relationship. Staged for television, these events usually pair a photo opportunity and a speech to convey a particular impression of a politician's position on an issue.

The "photo op" frames the politician against a backdrop of things that symbolize clear values—for example, children or flags. Photo ops for economic issues often use factories, whether bustling to represent a success or abandoned to represent a failure. The backdrop is designed to be visually interesting to attract the cameras. The strategy is the same as that for advertisements of merchandise: Combine the product (the politician) with the symbols in the hope that the potential buyers

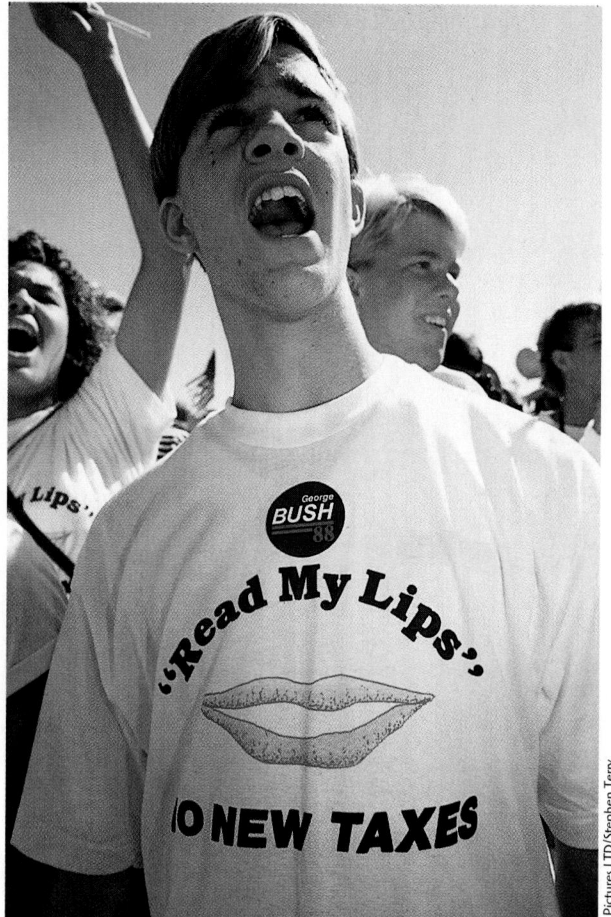

Sound bite journalism leads to sound bite politics.

(voters) will link the two.[57] In the 1992 campaign, President Bush peered into the Grand Canyon to demonstrate his credentials as an environmentalist, despite his limited record; Governor Clinton appeared at a bowling alley to demonstrate his credentials as an average "Joe," despite his Yale and Oxford education.

The speech in a media event is not a classical oration or even a cogent address with a beginning, middle, and end. It is an informal talk that emphasizes a few key words or phrases or sentences—almost slogans, because television editors allot time only for a short **sound bite.** And the amount of time is less and less. In 1968 the average sound bite of a presidential contender on the evening news was 42.3 seconds, but in 1988 it was just 9.8 seconds and in 1992 only 7.3 seconds.[58]

Speech writers plan accordingly. "A lot of writers figure out how they are going to get the part they want onto television," a former presidential aide explained. "They think of a news lead and write around it. And if the television lights don't go on as the speaker is approaching that news lead, he skips a few paragraphs and waits until they are lit to read the key part."[59] This does not produce coherent speeches, but the people watching on television will not know, and the few watching in person do not matter because they are just props. More significantly, such writing does not provide either group of people with an adequate explanation.

It is tempting to use media events to convey desirable but inaccurate impressions. When polls showed that the public thought Reagan slighted education because he cut federal money for student loans and schools, he traveled across the country to meet with teachers and students in a series of media events. Then, according to an aide, "The polls absolutely flip-flopped. He went from a negative rating to a positive rating [on education] overnight."[60] Yet he did not change his policies at all. Bush unveiled his anticrime package at a police academy, but later it was noticed that his budget proposed cutting funds for this academy.[61]

Perhaps more than any other source of news, media events illustrate the reliance of politicians on television, and of television on politicians. The head of CBS News said, "I'd like just once to have the courage to go on the air and say that such and such a candidate went to six cities today to stage six media events, none of which had anything to do with governing America."[62] Yet television fosters these events, and despite occasional swipes by correspondents, networks continue to show them.

Adversarial Relationship

Although the relationship between the media and politicians is symbiotic in some ways, it is adversarial in others. Since George Washington's administration, when conflicts developed between Federalists and Jeffersonians, the media have attacked politicians and politicians have attacked the media. In John Adams's administration, Federalists passed the Sedition Act of 1798, which prohibited much criticism of the government. Federalists used the act to imprison Jeffersonian editors. Not long after, President Andrew Jackson proposed a law to allow the government to shut down "incendiary" newspapers. Even now, a former press secretary commented, "There are very few politicians who do not cherish privately the notion that there should be some regulation of the news."[63]

The conflict stems from a fundamental difference in perspectives. Politicians want the media to help them accomplish their goals, so they hope the media will pass along their messages to the public exactly as they deliver them. But journalists see themselves as servants not of the government but of the public. They question officials until the public knows enough about a matter to hold the officials accountable. According to correspondent Sam Donaldson, "My job is not to say here's the church social with the apple pie, isn't it beautiful?"[64] But some go beyond skepticism to cynicism. In the eyes of Clinton aide George Stephanopoulos, they walk in the door "assuming that something is wrong and asking, 'What are you hiding?' "[65]

In contemporary society, information is power. The media and the government, especially the president, with the huge bureaucracy at his disposal, are the two primary sources of information. To the extent that the administration controls the flow of information, it can achieve its policy goals. To the extent that the media disseminate contradictory information, they can ensure that the administration's policy goals will be subject to public debate.

Inevitably, politicians fall short of their goals, and many blame the media for their failures. They confuse the message and the messenger, like Czar Peter the Great, who, when notified that the Russian army had lost a battle in 1700, promptly ordered the messenger strangled.

When President Kennedy became upset by the *New York Times* coverage of Vietnam, he asked the paper to transfer the correspondent out of Vietnam. (The paper refused.) When President Nixon became angry with major newspapers and networks, he had Vice President Agnew lash out at them. He also ordered the Department of Justice to investigate some for possible antitrust violations and the Internal Revenue Service to audit some for possible income tax violations.

However, it would be incorrect to think that the relationship between the media and politicians is usually adversarial. Normally, it is symbiotic. Although journalists like to think of themselves and try to portray themselves as adversaries who stand up to politicians, most rely upon politicians most of the time.[66]

Yet the relationship has become more adversarial since the Vietnam War and the Watergate scandal fueled cynicism about government's performance and officials' honesty. After Watergate Congress became more willing to launch investigations of administration officials, and reporters became more aggressive in reporting possible scandals.[67] "[M]any young reporters, without a sense of history, context, or proportion, saw scandal where none existed or at least treated any mistake, no matter how minor, as worthy of being called a 'gate.' "[68] From the Clinton administration alone, we have heard reporters speak of "Travelgate," "Filegate," "Koreagate," "Paulagate," and "Monicagate," as well as "Whitewatergate."

At the same time, politicians have become more persistent and sophisticated in their efforts to "spin" the media—to portray themselves and their programs in the most favorable light, regardless of the facts, and to shade the truth where necessary. In response, reporters have become more cynical. They "don't explicitly argue or analyze what they dislike in a political program but instead sound sneering and supercilious about the whole idea of politics." Then, when politicians become more cunning in their efforts to spin the media or to circumvent the reporters, "the press becomes even more determined to point out how insincere the politicians are."[69] And so the cycle continues.

In this climate, according to a network correspondent, "the most embarrassing, humiliating thing" for a

"Wait, those weren't lies. That was spin!"

journalist is not to have accused someone falsely, but to have been perceived as being taken, being "spun," by someone.[70] During the 1992 presidential campaign, Bush aides complimented a *New York Times* reporter for a fair article. "He looked at us like we had the plague. . . . The next thing we heard, a bunch of other reporters were grousing about [him] and accusing him of being a shill for Bush, of being 'in the tank.' By paying him a compliment we had compromised him."[71]

The increasing adversariness is also due to other factors mentioned earlier. There are so many media, with so much space to fill, that they have a voracious appetite for news and a steely incentive to compete against each other. They all look for something "new." As a result, they often magnify the trivial or distort the important.[72] And because the fringe media play a more prominent role, and because their stories usually appear in the mainstream media, most media pay more attention to politicians' personal shortcomings with sex, drugs, and alcohol and raise more questions about politicians' "character" than they ever used to.[73]

Yet the apparent toughness usually is "a toughness of demeanor," rather than a toughness of substantive journalism.[74] Reporters exhibit tough attitudes rather than conduct thorough investigations and careful analyses. In fact, few engage in investigative journalism. An examination of 224 incidents of criminal or unethical behavior by Reagan administration appointees found that only 13% were uncovered by reporters. Most were discovered through investigations by executive agencies or congressional committees, which then released the information to the press. Only incidents reflecting personal peccadillos of government officials, such as sexual offenses, were exposed first by reporters.[75]

Relationship between the Media and Recent Administrations

Franklin Roosevelt created the model that most contemporary presidents follow when interacting with the media. Newspaper publishers had no use for Roosevelt and his policies. In fact, a former correspondent recalls, "The publishers didn't just disagree with the New Deal. They hated it. And the reporters, who liked it, had to write as though they hated it, too."[76] Roosevelt saw he was not going to get favorable coverage, but he still wanted to reach the public. He used press conferences to provide a steady stream of news. This tactic enabled him to circumvent the publishers but gain access to their readers. He also used radio, giving a series of **fireside chats,** to advocate his policies and reassure his listeners in the throes of the Great Depression. He had a fine voice and a superb ability to speak informally—he commented about his family, even his dog, in a way to appeal to average people. (He drew so many listeners that he was granted as much airtime as he wanted, but he was shrewd enough to realize that too much would result in overexposure.) This tactic enabled him to avoid the filters of reporters and editors and take his case directly to the people.

REAGAN ADMINISTRATION

As a young man, Reagan idolized FDR and developed an imitation of him that included an appropriate accent and even a cigarette holder.[77] As president, Reagan duplicated Roosevelt's success in using the media, which dubbed him the "Great Communicator" for his uncanny ability to convey his broad themes.

The Reagan administration approached its relationship with the media as "political jujitsu."[78] A jujitsu fighter tries to use the adversary's force to his or her own advantage through a clever maneuver. The administration knew the media would cover the president extensively to fill their news columns and newscasts. An aide explained the strategy: "The media, while they won't admit it, are not in the news business; they're in entertainment. We tried to create the most entertaining, visually attractive scene to fill that box, so that the networks would have to use it."[79]

Aides sent advance agents days or weeks ahead of the president to prepare the "stage" for media events—the specific location, backdrops, lighting, and sound equipment. A trip to Korea was designed to show "the commander in chief on the front line against communism." The advance man went to the demilitarized zone separating North and South Korea and negotiated with the army and the Secret Service for the most photogenic setting. He demanded that the president be able to use the most exposed bunker, which meant that the army

Corbis-Bettmann

President Reagan, staged to reflect "American strength and resolve" in Korea.

had to erect telephone poles and string 30,000 yards of camouflage netting from them to hide Reagan from North Korean sharpshooters. The advance man also demanded that the army build camera platforms on a hill that remained exposed but offered the most dramatic angle to film Reagan surrounded by sandbags. Although the Secret Service wanted sandbags up to Reagan's neck, the advance man insisted that they be no more than four inches above his navel so viewers would get a clear picture of the president wearing his flak jacket and demonstrating "American strength and resolve."[80]

On a day-to-day basis, the administration planned its operations around its relationship with the media. In the morning aides met to plan public relations strategy for the day. They determined what "the line of the day"—the message—would be. They considered what questions the president would be asked and what answers he should give, and then they briefed him. Later in the day, after all his appearances, aides called each network to learn what stories about the president or his policies it was going to use on its evening newscast. If aides were not satisfied, they tried to convince the network to change its lineup. At night aides met to evaluate the success of their strategy and often called each network to praise or criticize its coverage.[81]

To set the agenda, and to prevent the media from setting it, the administration tried to control the president's appearances and restrict his comments. Aides especially worried that off-the-cuff comments would reveal Reagan's limited command of the facts and details behind his policies or would result in a blooper, such as the time he said that trees cause most air pollution. To keep such comments from damaging his image or at least overshadowing his message of the day, aides provided few opportunities for reporters to ask questions. When reporters asked questions inside a building, aides frequently demanded that the television lights be shut off so any answers could not be televised; outside they often ordered the helicopter's engines revved up so the questions would be drowned out. Aides scheduled few press conferences. Although conferences normally benefit presidents, they are subject to less control than media events and were considered too risky.

Paradoxically, Reagan was highly visible but not very accessible. By alternately using and avoiding the media, his administration succeeded in managing the news more than any other administration.

BUSH ADMINISTRATION

Bush rejected some of Reagan's efforts to manipulate the media, and, anyway, he lacked most of Reagan's appeal on television. So his administration deemphasized television appearances in favor of frequent press conferences and get-togethers with reporters. Occasionally, he telephoned reporters to talk or asked them to jog with him. In these settings his grasp of issues came across. He tried to impress reporters and, like Roosevelt, charm them, in the hope that he would receive favorable coverage. Journalists did consider Bush more accessible and open than Reagan.

For the invasion of Panama in 1989 and war with Iraq in 1991, however, the Bush administration insisted on strict control and censorship rather than accessibility and openness. When the United States invaded Panama to force General Manuel Noriega from office, reporters were delayed in arriving in Panama and then prevented from seeing most battles out of fear that they would witness civilian casualties.[82] When the United States fought Iraq, small pools of reporters were escorted to locations where American troops were living or fighting. Reporters were permitted to interview soldiers only when supervised by their officers, and they were allowed to send dispatches back to the United States only after they were cleared by military censors. The administration worried that pictures of American casualties or information about civilian casualties and property destruction would weaken support for the war.[83]

As a result of the administration's management of the news in the war against Iraq, television showed film of one precise bombing attack after another. Commentators lauded the "smart" bombs that were so accurate it was like having them "delivered by Federal Express." Yet after the war one official said only 7% of the bombs were "smart" bombs, and another said only 25% of the other bombs hit their targets. This means that at least 61,000 tons of bombs landed where they were not supposed to.[84]

Polls showed that most Americans approved the military's control of the news, and a majority even thought the military should have more control of the news. Only 19% thought the military was "hiding bad news from the public."[85]

CLINTON ADMINISTRATION

In his use of the media, Clinton emulates Roosevelt and Reagan. Like Roosevelt he tries to leapfrog reporters to reach citizens directly.[86] Like Reagan, he tries to focus on an issue and highlight a message of the day or week to influence public opinion on that issue.

Clinton is exceptionally knowledgeable about issues and policies and very articulate when speaking or even improvising. As one television critic observed, "We now have a president capable of speaking in complete sentences, each one with a subject, a verb and its various clauses arranged in grammatical order. Not only that, but each sentence . . . progresses logically to the next."[87]

Unlike Roosevelt and Reagan, however, Clinton is not enthralling. He lacks discipline and, as a result, talks too long and gives too many details for most listeners. He strays from his message of the day or week and thus blurs this message. Consequently, he does not effectively communicate his proposals, and many people do not really know what he stands for.

Clinton is impressive one on one, however, because of his knowledge and his charm. According to a network correspondent, not a staunch supporter, "He is the most charming man I have ever met."[88]

But reporters distrust him. During the campaign, they doubted some of his statements about his actions. Since he has been in office, they have doubted some of his answers to their questions. Many reporters think he does not tell the truth or at least does not leave an accurate impression. They consider him "a master of lawyerly evasion."[89]

Various slights have aggravated the relations. Upon taking office, Clinton insulted the major media by giving his first interview not to a national reporter, but to the political correspondent from MTV. Then the administration closed a White House passageway between the staff offices and the press room where reporters hung out to buttonhole aides. The administration revamped the White House travel office, which makes plane and hotel arrangements for reporters covering the president on trips, and scaled back its VIP treatment. Then reporters complained that they received cold food instead of hot food and cheap domestic champagne instead of the usual expensive imported champagne.

As a result of Clinton's dissembling and reporters' overreacting, the president has received much negative coverage throughout his time in office.[90] Especially damaging has been the general charge that Clinton reneged on his commitments. Although Clinton kept many promises—like most presidents, he kept more than he broke—the media focused on the ones he did not keep and the ones he was not able to keep.[91] The media, showing little recognition that bargaining and ultimately compromising are necessary for any president, characterized Clinton as a "waffler" and a "compromiser." (Serious observers did criticize Clinton for giving in too quickly in some disputes, but journalists went beyond questions about tactics.) Thus, the media have reinforced the naive belief of some citizens that politicians need not and should not bargain and compromise.

Some reporters observed that their colleagues felt "they had blown it" in covering the Reagan and Bush administrations and were determined not to be conned by this administration. Thus, they looked for manipulation or hypocrisy behind every act.[92] Some political scientists speculated that the media compensated for favoring Clinton over Bush in the election by being harsher on Clinton in office—perhaps, subconsciously, as a way to prove their critics wrong.[93]

Eventually, the investigations into the Whitewater land deal, revelations about the president's personal life, and concerns about his party's fund-raising raised ethical questions that swirled around his administration. They dominated the news and hindered his efforts to convey his messages and accomplish his goals. The Clintons became bitter toward the media, while reporters became more cynical toward the administration. The level of trust sank so low that during the 1996 campaign, after the president's opponent, Bob Dole, released his medical records because of concerns about his age, reporters asked why Clinton would not release his also. One asked the president's press secretary, "Does he have a sexually transmitted disease?"

Relationship between the Media and Congress

Members of Congress also use the media but have much less impact. Since 1970 nearly all have hired their own full-time press secretary who churns out press releases, distributes television tapes, and arranges interviews with reporters.[94] The Senate and House of Representatives have established recording studios for members, allowed television cameras into committee rooms, and supported creation of C-SPAN. Yet members still have trouble attracting the eye of the media. One president can be the subject of the media's focus, whereas 535 members of Congress cannot. Only a handful of powerful (or, occasionally, colorful) members receive much notice from the national media. Other members get attention from their home state or district media, but those from large urban areas with numerous representatives get little publicity or scrutiny even there.[95]

Since the congressional elections of 1994, Speaker of the House Newt Gingrich (R-Ga.) has gotten extraordinary coverage, even for a leader of Congress, because he was the point man for the Republican takeover of Congress and has been the leader of the Republican agenda in Congress.

Congressional committees also try to use the media to influence public opinion. After Arizona and California voters supported initiatives on their state ballots in 1996 to allow sick people to use marijuana, the Senate Judiciary Committee held a hearing to discredit the initiatives and discourage people in other states from following their lead. The hearing, titled "A Prescription for Addiction? The Arizona and California Medical Drug Use Initiatives," included five opponents and just one proponent of marijuana use for sick people. The chair, Senator Orrin Hatch (R-Utah), opened the hearing by stating that the voters were fooled by millions of dollars spent on "stealth campaigns designed to conceal their real objective: the legalization of drugs." Hatch also asserted that marijuana has no medical value. One witness, representing the Federal Drug Enforcement Administration, charged that proponents of the initiatives "cynically used the suffering and illness of vulnerable people to further their own agenda." Witnesses predicted that allowing sick people to use marijuana would result in other people using the drug and then trying harder drugs as well. All the charges are debatable—for example, a federal judge concluded that medical evidence shows that smoking marijuana can ease the symptoms of some patients with AIDS, cancer, or glaucoma—but the committee was not trying to investigate the facts; it was trying to sway public opinion.[96]

BIAS OF THE MEDIA

Every night Walter Cronkite, former anchor for CBS Evening News, signed off, "And that's the way it is." His statement implied that the network reported the news exactly the way it happened, that the network held a huge mirror to the world and reflected an image of the world to the viewers—without any distortion. Yet the media do not hold a mirror. They hold a searchlight that seeks and illuminates some things instead of others.[97]

For the congressional elections of 1992, Republicans campaigned against Democrats by linking them to President Clinton and by linking him to former President Carter. Both presidents, they charged, were failures. Time *magazine reinforced the Republicans' theme by running this series of computer-generated images showing Clinton becoming Carter.*

From all the events that occur in the world every day, the media can report only a handful as the news of the day. Even the fat *New York Times*, whose motto is "All the News That's Fit to Print," cannot include all the news. The media must decide what events are newsworthy. When the Wright brothers invited reporters to Kitty Hawk, North Carolina, to observe the first plane flight in 1903, none considered it newsworthy enough to cover. After the historic flight, only seven American newspapers reported it, and only two reported it on the front page.[98]

After the media decide what events to report, they must decide where to report them—on the front page or top of the newscast, or in a less prominent position. Then they must decide how to report them. Except for magazines, most media attempt to be "objective"; that is, they try to present facts rather than their opinions. Where the facts are in dispute, they try to present the positions of both sides. They are reluctant to evaluate these positions, although sometimes they do explain or interpret them.

In making these decisions, it would be natural for journalists' attitudes to affect their coverage. As one acknowledged, a reporter writes "from what he hears and sees and how he filters it through the lens of his own experience. No reporter is a robot."[99]

Political Bias

Historically, the press was politically biased. The first papers, which were established by political parties, parroted the party line. Even the independent papers, which succeeded them, advocated one side or the other. The attitudes of publishers, editors, and reporters seeped—sometimes flooded—into their prose. But papers gradually abandoned their ardor for editorializing and adopted the practice of objectivity to retain as many of their readers as possible.

Yet the public thinks the press is still biased. According to one survey, 41% think the press is "out to get" the groups they identify with: Executives believe the press is out to get businesses, and laborers believe it is out to get unions. Liberals believe it is biased against liberals, and conservatives believe it is biased against conservatives.[100]

Indeed, the public seems more critical today, when most media at least attempt to be objective, than in the past, when they did not even pretend to be. Then, citizens could subscribe to whichever local paper reflected their own biases (without ever recognizing that the paper reflected any biases). Now, as local newspapers have given way to national

broadcast networks, and as independently owned media have shrunk and chains and conglomerates have expanded to dominate the business, the public has fewer choices and is more sensitive to perceptions of bias.

BIAS FOR ESTABLISHED INSTITUTIONS AND VALUES

The media generally do reflect a bias for established institutions and values. This should not come as a surprise. Because the media are major businesses owned by large corporations, and because they need to retain their readers and viewers to make a profit, they consciously or unconsciously mirror the mainstream.

The media have a long history of bias against other ideologies, such as communism or even democratic socialism. The failures of noncapitalist economic systems are played up, the successes played down. In foreign policy matters, the U.S. government line usually is adopted. During the Cold War, this meant harsh attacks on the Soviet Union and leftist Latin American countries.[101]

During the Persian Gulf War, this meant embracing the administration's goals and questioning little of its propaganda.[102] Although this was partly due to the administration's manipulation of the news, it was also partly due to the media's own bias. Even when journalists obtained contradictory information, news organizations hesitated reporting it until later.[103] The result was "a frenzy of jingoism" during the fighting.[104]

Correlated with the media's support for established institutions and values is their reliance upon government officials for their news. A study of front-page stories from the *New York Times* and *Washington Post* over two decades found that 74% were based on statements by U.S. government officials.[105] This is striking considering that these papers have far more staffers and resources to do investigative journalism than other papers. Such heavy reliance upon government officials means that the stories are likely to bear their strong imprint. Similarly, a study of ABC's *Nightline*, which features news and interviews, found that 80% of the Americans interviewed on the program were from the government or corporate establishment (and 90% of these were white males). The watchdog group Fairness & Accuracy In Reporting (FAIR) found that representatives from peace, environmental, consumer, or labor groups were "hardly visible."[106]

Reporters turn to officials for news because it is easy and because, ironically, they want to avoid charges of bias. Reporters believe their peers, superiors, and the public all consider officials newsworthy. Ignoring them or downplaying them might be interpreted as showing bias against them.[107]

"On a personal note, my wife, Ann, and I have agreed to separate, as I've fallen in love with the sound of my own voice."

BIAS FOR PARTICULAR CANDIDATES AND POLICIES

Most debate about media bias revolves around charges that the media exhibit a preference for particular candidates and policies over others. Conservative groups, in particular, claim that the media are biased toward liberal candidates and policies, and they have gone so far as to mount an effort to buy CBS in order to change its newscasts.

In studying media bias, social scientists have examined the characteristics and behavior of journalists. They have found that journalists are not very representative of the public. They are disproportionately college-educated white males from the upper middle class. Further, they are disproportionately urban and secular, rather than rural and religious. They are disproportionately Democrats or independents leaning to the Democrats, rather than Republicans or independents leaning to the Republicans. Likewise, they identify themselves disproportionately as liberals rather than conservatives.[108]

But journalists do differ among themselves. Those who work for the prominent, influential organizations—large newspapers, wire services, news magazines, and radio and television networks—are more likely to be Democrats and liberals than those who work for nonprominent organizations—small newspapers and radio and television stations.[109]

Journalists in prominent organizations are more likely than the public to support the liberal position on issues. Large majorities support homosexuals' right to teach in public schools and affirmative action. They are also suspicious of big business, believing it is the sector of society that exerts the most influence but should exert much less.[110] At the same time, they support capitalism. Large majorities think businesses should be owned privately rather than publicly; businesses should be regulated less than they are; and businesses are fair to their workers. According to one study, 73% do not think that our institutions "need overhaul."[111] Thus, although these journalists are likely to be liberals, they are hardly extreme liberals or radicals.

These findings might seem to support the charge that the media are biased against conservatives, but this assumes that journalists' attitudes necessarily color what they report. Several factors mitigate the effect of journalists' attitudes. For one thing, journalists do not seem to have intense opinions. Most did not become journalists because of a commitment to political ideology but because of the opportunity to rub elbows with powerful people and be close to exciting events. "Each day brings new stories, new dramas in which journalists participate vicariously."[112] As a result, most "care more about the politics of an issue than about the issue itself,"[113] which makes them less likely to voice their views about the issue.

In addition, media organizations pressure journalists to muffle their views, partly out of a conviction that it is more professional to do so and partly out of a desire to avoid the headaches that could arise otherwise—debates among their staffers; complaints from their local radio and television affiliates; complaints from their audience; perhaps even complaints from the White House, Congress, or the Federal Communications Commission (FCC), which licenses them.

Sometimes media executives or editors pressure reporters because they have contrary views. Reporters learn not to explore certain subjects, not to ask certain questions. Reporters who pursue the stories regardless might find their copy edited, with the most critical portions deleted. The *New York Times*, despite its liberal reputation, altered reporters' stories on foreign affairs to hew more closely to administrations' conservative policies.[114] CBS toned down correspondents' stories about Reagan's economic policies.[115] Reporters who pursue the stories might find themselves transfered to another beat. One who covered El Salvador for the *New York Times* wrote a series of reports about the government's massacre of nearly a thousand peasants. The reports contradicted Reagan's assertions that the nation was making great strides in human rights. Under pressure, the *Times* pulled the reporter off this beat.[116] Ultimately, reporters who pursue the stories could find themselves fired.[117]

For all of these reasons, the media do not exhibit nearly as much **political bias** as would be expected from their journalists' attitudes. Although they do show a bias for established institutions and values, they do not show much bias for particular candidates in elections.

To measure bias, researchers use a technique called "content analysis." They scrutinize newspaper and television stories to determine whether there was an unequal amount of coverage, unequal use of favorable or unfavorable statements, or unequal use of a positive or negative tone. They consider insinuating verbs ("he conceded" rather than "he said") and pejorative adjectives ("her weak response" rather than "her response"), and for television stories they evaluate the announcers' nonverbal communication—voice inflection, eye movement, and body language.

Studies of coverage of several presidential campaigns found relatively little bias. The media typically gave the two major candidates equal attention and rarely made a favorable or unfavorable statement about them or used a positive or negative tone discussing them.[118] The studies did find some bias against incumbents, front-runners, and emerging challengers.[119] For these candidates, the media apparently took their watchdog role seriously.

Overall, then, there is less bias than the public believes or the candidates feel. When candidates complain, they usually are objecting to bad news or trying to manipulate the media. The strategy is to put reporters on the defensive so they will go easier on the candidate or harder on the opponent in the future. In the 1996 election Dole learned that reporters were considering publishing a story that he had an extramarital affair in 1968. Although the story did not appear in the major media, Dole criticized them for being biased. Later his aide told a reporter the criticism was "a preemptive strike."[120]

Yet the way in which the media cover campaigns can have different implications for different candidates. The media report the facts and all the details that contribute to the facts: that one candidate is leading while the other is trailing, that one campaign is surging while the other is slipping. This coverage has positive implications for the former—swaying undecided voters, galvanizing campaign workers, and attracting financial contributions—and negative implications for the latter. Such coverage does not benefit one party over the other party in election after election, but it can benefit one party's candidate over the other party's candidate in a particular election. It helped the Democrat Carter in 1976 but hurt him in 1980. It helped the Republican Bush in 1988 but hurt him in 1992.[121] Some people, especially supporters of the losers, consider such reporting biased. Journalists, however, consider it a reflection of reality.

There were numerous accusations of bias—for Clinton and against Bush—during the 1992 election, but the media's continuing coverage of the success of Clinton's campaign and the failure of Bush's campaign accounts for most (though not all) of the tilt.[122] During the primaries, Clinton faced much negative news, but during the general election, he received more positive coverage. As he climbed in the polls, his characterization by the press changed from "Slick Willie" to a dogged survivor. Meanwhile, Bush presided over a slow economy and ran a hesitant campaign, and he fell in the polls. There were also some accusations of bias in the 1996 election. Dole ran an unfocused campaign that never jelled, so the coverage appeared to favor Clinton.

There are two exceptions to the generalization that overt political bias in elections is minimal. First, the media usually give short shrift to third-party candidates. However, the media did pay much attention to Ross Perot's presidential bid in 1992 (though not in 1996) because he said he would spend $100 million on his campaign and because polls showed he could compete with Bush and Clinton.

Second, newspapers traditionally print editorials and columns that express opinions. In editorials before elections, papers often endorse candidates. Most owners are Republican, and this is one time many seek to influence the content of their papers. Since the first survey in 1932, more papers have endorsed the Republican presidential candidate, except in the election between Democratic President Lyndon Johnson and Republican Senator Barry Goldwater in 1964 and in the election between Clinton and Bush in 1992.[123]

The relative lack of bias in coverage of elections does not necessarily mean there is a lack of bias in coverage of other events. Because elections are highly visible and candidates are very sensitive about the coverage, the media might take more care to be neutral here than elsewhere. Researchers have not examined coverage of other events as much. A study of coverage of nuclear energy found an evolution from slightly pro- to strongly antinuclear power during the 1970s,[124] while one of school busing found a tilt for busing during the same decade,[125] and one of abortion found a tilt toward choice in the late 1980s.[126] Yet an analysis of news about the Iranian hostage seizure and the Soviet invasion of Afghanistan, both in 1980, revealed a slight conservative bias.[127]

An examination of coverage of the debate over the North American Free Trade Agreement (NAFTA) in 1996, drafted to ease trade between American and Canadian and Mexican companies, showed more emphasis on the benefits of free trade than on the loss of jobs that might result from the treaty. Thus, the media reflected the views of business more than those of workers. Analysts now suggest that the most significant bias is not liberal or conservative, but upper middle class over working class.[128] Such bias would usually favor the liberal positions on social issues and the conservative, or business, positions on economic issues. These views would closely match not only the social class of most journalists, but also their urban background and college education.

This chapter has focused on the news media, not the entertainment media. Popular television programs, movies, and records often promote ideas or trends that sometimes are characterized as liberal, such as diversity, multiculturalism, acceptance of racial minorities, acceptance of casual sex, and disparagement of traditional religion. (But these media also glorify violence and portray as routine the possession and use of guns. This emphasis certainly does not reflect liberal values.) Such entertainment might have as much or even more effect on individuals' views than the news does. But consideration of this aspect of the media is beyond the scope of this text.

BIAS AGAINST ALL CANDIDATES AND OFFICIALS

Some critics charge that there is a general bias against all candidates and officials—a negative undercurrent in reporting about government, regardless of who or what is covered. President Nixon's first vice president, Spiro Agnew, called journalists "nattering nabobs of negativism." Critics think this bias increased after the Watergate scandal made reporters more cynical.

There seems to be considerable validity to this charge. Analyses of newspapers, magazines, and television networks show that the overwhelming majority of the stories about government are neutral.[129] However, the rest of the stories are more often negative than positive.[130] Moreover, the number of stories that are negative is increasing (see Figure 2).

As a result, the media often convey the impression that the candidates are neither worthy of the office they seek nor the officials of the office they hold. They ultimately convey the impression that the political process itself is contemptible.[131]

Despite a tendency toward negativism, the tone appears to vary among the media. The national media, whose reporters are better educated and more experienced in national affairs, are far more critical than the local media. Television is more critical than newspapers and magazines.[132]

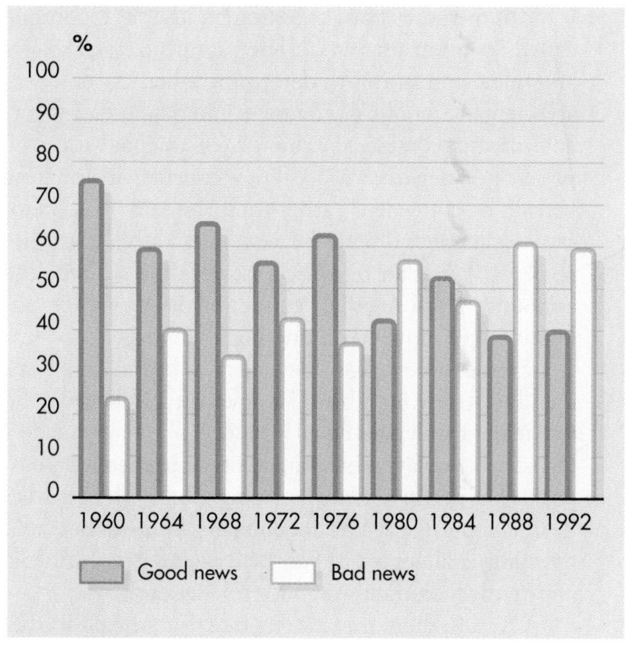

FIGURE 2

Bad News about Presidential Candidates Increases

In presidential campaigns in the 1960s and 1970s, candidates received primarily positive coverage. In the 1980s and 1990s, however, they have faced more negative coverage, according to an analysis of articles in Newsweek *and* Time.

Note: Analysis is based on paragraphs that can be categorized one way or the other. It does not include statements about "the horse race."

SOURCE: Thomas E. Patterson, *Out of Order* (New York: Vintage, 1994), p. 20.

Commercial Bias

Except for public radio and television networks and stations, American media are private businesses run for a profit. They must attract readers and listeners and viewers. With an audience, they can sell advertising. The larger the audience, the higher the price they can charge. A change of 1% in the ratings of a television news program in New York City, for example, can mean a difference of $5 million in advertising for a station in a year.[133] The opportunity to make a profit is so enormous that CBS's *60 Minutes*, the most watched program during some years, made more money in its first decade on the air than the entire Chrysler Corporation in the same decade.[134]

With chains and conglomerates taking over most media, the pressure to make a sizable profit has escalated. Where family owners used to be satisfied if their newspaper or radio station or television station made money, corporate executives now expect their media, like other big businesses on the stock market, to make the prevailing rate. They worry that financial analysts will rank them lower or that mutual fund managers will unload their stock if their earnings fall below those available "from investments anywhere else in the financial universe, from a shirt factory in Thailand to the latest Internet start-up."[135]

The pressure to make a profit and the need to attract an audience shape the media's presentation of the news and lead to a **commercial bias.** Sometimes this means that the media deliberately print or broadcast what advertisers want. At the request of the gas company sponsoring the drama *Judgment at Nuremberg*, one network bleeped the words "gas ovens" from descriptions of the Nazis' war crimes.[136] Other times the media censor themselves. When the auto industry was pressuring Congress to repeal seat belt and air bag regulations in the 1970s, the *New York Times* publisher urged the editors to present the industry position because it "would affect the advertising."[137] In articles on

WE'RE OUTSIDE THE HOME OF SOME PEOPLE WHO'VE JUST EXPERIENCED A GRAVE PERSONAL TRAGEDY TO BADGER AND HARASS THEM FOR THE SAKE OF A FEW RATINGS POINTS. LET'S WATCH.....
PIRARO.
© CHRONICLE FEATURES 1987
10-7

health, numerous magazines avoided references to the dangers of smoking for fear of losing advertising from tobacco companies. *Ms.* magazine, generally attentive to women's health, even avoided references to the increased dangers of smoking during pregnancy (at a time when it still accepted advertising).[138]

Usually, though, commercial bias means that the media must print or broadcast what the public wants, and this means that the media must entertain the public. This creates a "conflict between being an honest reporter and being a member of show business," network correspondent Roger Mudd confessed, "and that conflict is with me every day."[139]

The dilemma is most marked for television. Many people who watch television news are not interested in politics; a majority, in fact, say it covers too much politics.[140] Some watch the news because they were watching another program before the news and left the television on, others because they were going to watch another program after the news and turned the television on early. Networks feel pressure "to hook them and keep them."[141]

Therefore, networks try to make the everyday world of news seem as exciting as the make-believe world they depict in their other programs. One network instructed its staff: "Every news story should, without any sacrifice of probity or responsibility, display the attributes of fiction, of drama. It should have structure and conflict, problem and denouement, rising action and falling action, a beginning, a middle and an end."[142] As one executive says, television news is "info-tainment."[143]

So television anchors and newscasters, hired for their appearance and personality as well as their experience and ability, become show business stars. To enhance their appeal, networks and stations shape their image, ordering them to change their hairstyle and even, with tinted contact lenses, their eye color. They set up clothes calendars so newscasters will rotate their outfits.

Although appearance is important for both men and women newscasters, it is crucial for women. While viewers accept men aging on the screen, they do not seem to accept women aging. As one woman anchor commented, "The guys have got white hair, and the girls look like cheerleaders."[144] Indeed, according to one calculation, although a third of local anchors are women, only 3% are past 40; of the men 50% are past 40 and 16% are past 50.[145]

The commercial bias of the media has a number of consequences. One is emphasis on human interest stories. In 1980 UPI and CBS carried seven times more stories about President Jimmy Carter's beer-drinking brother, Billy, than about the Strategic Arms Limitation Talks (SALT) between the United States and the Soviet Union.[146] By 1990, the networks had mentioned President Bush's dog, Millie, in more stories than they mentioned three cabinet secretaries.[147]

The emphasis on human interest includes an emphasis on sex. In the past two decades, the media have examined the sexual affairs of numerous politicians. But this coverage pales in comparison with the treatment of the sexual escapades of President Clinton. When the allegations involving Monica Lewinsky became public, the pope was making a historic visit to Cuba. The networks, which had considered this visit so important that they had sent their anchors to broadcast from Havana, ordered them back to Washington to cover the racy allegations. At the same time, renewed violence in Northern Ireland threatened to scuttle the peace talks between Catholics and Protestants. Continued refusal from Iraq to cooperate with United Nations biological and chemical weapons inspectors threatened to escalate to military conflict. Yet reporters focused on what the president did with the former White House intern. The *Los Angeles Times* assigned 26 reporters to examine Lewinsky's life, interviewing baby-sitters and kindergarten classmates.[148] *Time* magazine e-mailed college classmates for personal information. The networks interviewed one person whose claim to fame was that he had lunch with her three years before. All along, one columnist laments, "We have . . . leapt to conclusions, purveyed rumor as fact, offered banalities with the breathless excitement of discovery, and sheltered vile slanderers all in the name of the public's right to know."[149]

The emphasis on human interest also includes an emphasis on crime. Although the national media give crime extensive coverage—who could ignore the O. J.

Simpson case?—this emphasis is most apparent for the local media, where television news is a combination of mayhem and happy talk (or, in Ralph Nader's words, "something that jerks your head up every 10 seconds, whether that is shootings, robberies, sports showdowns, or dramatic weather forecasts".)[150] The saying, "If it bleeds, it leads," expresses, tongue in cheek, the programming philosophy of some stations. Studies show that crime coverage fills about a third of the local news in many cities.[151]

The emphasis on human interest leads to another consequence of commercial bias—a **game orientation** in political reporting.[152] The underlying assumption is that politics is a game and politicians, whether candidates campaigning for election or officials performing in office, are the players. The corollary to the assumption is that the players are self-centered and self-interested. They are seeking victory for themselves and defeat for their opponents and are not concerned about the consequences of their proposals or the government's policies. Thus, through this game filter, politicians' strategies and tactics are highlighted, and new developments are presented according to how they help some players and hinder others. The substance and impact of the proposals and policies are slighted.

The game orientation appeals to journalists because it generates human interest. It offers new story lines as new information comes to light, much like a board game where "chance" cards inject unexpected scenarios and alter the players' moves and the game's outcomes. This orientation also appeals to journalists because it is easy and relatively free from charges of partisan or ideological bias. (Stories highlight which contestants are winning, not which ones should win or what consequences might result.) Analyzing policy lacks all of these advantages for journalists.

The game orientation attracts an audience, but it creates more public cynicism. The assumption that politics is a game and the corollary that the players are concerned solely with their own interests leads to the conclusion that their strategies and tactics are based mostly on manipulation and deception. Journalists, casting their wary eyes on politicians, look for manipulation and deception and interpret even sincere action in those ways.

For elections, the game orientation results in what is called "horse-race coverage," with "front-runners," "dark horses," and "also-rans." This coverage accounts for much of the total coverage of campaigns.[153] For example, in 1988 one-third of all network television stories about the presidential primaries referred to candidates' poll standings.[154] This is remarkable so early in the campaign, when most citizens know little about most candidates. It is likely that many viewers knew where the candidates were running in the race but not where they stood on the issues.

Horse-race coverage is not new and is not confined to television. An examination of presidential election coverage by metropolitan newspapers from 1888 through 1988 shows that the race was a staple of journalism long before the advent of broadcast media.[155] Yet other research suggests that the proportion of coverage focusing on the race has been increasing in recent decades (see Figure 3).

The quintessential reflection of horse-race coverage, reporting of candidates' poll standings, has increased greatly. Not only have the media reported more results of polls taken by commercial organizations, such as Gallup and Harris, but they have conducted more polls themselves. From 1976 to 1988, newspapers sponsored twice as many polls as before, and television stations sponsored three times as many. Since then, they have sponsored even more.[156] Now coverage of polls takes more space than coverage of candidates' speeches, and it usually appears as the lead or next-to-lead story.[157]

The emphasis upon human interest stories and horse-race aspects of an election led one observer to summarize the 1976 presidential campaign as follows:

> *I saw President Ford bump his head leaving an airplane. . . . I saw Carter playing softball in Plains, Georgia. I saw Carter kissing [daughter] Amy, I saw Carter hugging [mother] Lillian. I saw Carter, in dungarees, walking hand in hand through the peanut farm with [wife] Rosalyn. I saw Carter going to church, coming out of church. . . . I saw Ford misstate the problems of Eastern Europe—and a week of people commenting about his misstatement. I saw Ford bump his head again. I saw Ford in Ohio say how glad he was to be back in Iowa. I saw marching bands and hecklers, and I learned about the size of crowds and the significance of the size of crowds. . . .*
>
> *But in all the hours of high anxiety that I spent watching the network news, never did I hear what the candidates had to say about the campaign issues. That was not news.*[158]

Even after elections, the game orientation continues. During Reagan's first term, social programs were cut, income taxes were cut significantly, and military spending was increased sharply, but the main theme of media coverage was whether Reagan was "winning" or "losing" his battles with Congress and the bureaucracy. Similarly, when Clinton proposed a plan to overhaul the welfare system, all major newspapers focused on the political implications for his reelection; few even explained the plan, let alone its substantive implications. When he proposed more money for law enforcement, as a way to put "more cops on the beat," the media pointed out how this would sound in campaign ads but ignored where the extra officers would be, how much they would cost, and whether they would have any effect on crime.[159]

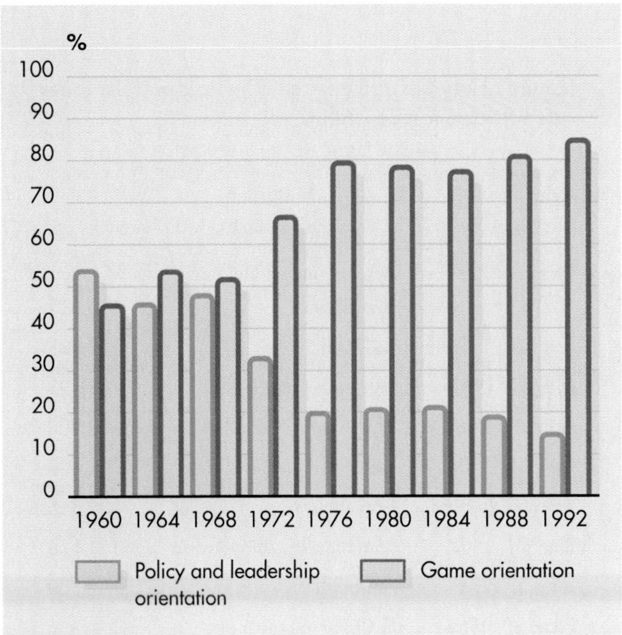

FIGURE 3

Game Orientation in Presidential Campaigns Increases

In presidential campaigns in the 1960s, policy and leadership issues received approximately equal coverage with the strategies and tactics and the successes and failures that reflect the game orientation. In the 1970s, 1980s, and 1990s, however, policy and leadership issues have received a much smaller proportion of the coverage, according to an analysis of articles on the front page of the New York Times.

Note: Analysis is based on articles that can be categorized one way or the other. It does not include other orientations, which received about 15% of the coverage.

SOURCE: Thomas E. Patterson, *Out of Order* (New York: Vintage, 1994), p. 74.

The emphasis on human interest leads to another consequence of commercial bias—an emphasis on controversy rather than agreement. Stories about conflict provide drama. Reporters, one admits, are "fight promoters" rather than consensus builders.[160] Reporters frame disputes as struggles between opposite camps. They depict attack and counterattack, using dueling sound bites from politicians and interjecting metaphors from wars. They talk about politicians who are "targets," who are "under fire," who receive "shots across their bow." They talk about politicians who engage in "search-and-destroy missions" and who "hold back no ammunition." Occasionally, they refer to a "cease-fire," but eventually they return to a "war of attrition" with "do-or-die" battles. Ultimately, they lament the politicians who "crashed in flames."[161]

So Representative Barney Frank (D-Mass.) realized: "I am now enjoying the best press of my life. And it's because I am attacking people and being negative. I get much more attention for three wisecracks and a point of order than I get for a full compromise to a difficult legislative solution."[162]

A researcher studying the coverage of the debate over health care reform in 1994 sat with reporters listening to Hillary Clinton present the administration's plan. For two hours she discussed the plan, including its substance and the arguments raised against it. The reporters "found it completely uninteresting. They were talking to each other, passing notes around. But as soon as she made a brief attack on the Republicans, there was a physiological reaction, this surge of adrenaline, all around me. The pens moved. The reporters arched forward. They wrote everything down rapidly. As soon as this part was over, they clearly weren't paying attention any more."[163] Not surprisingly, an experimental study later found that people who read 15 newspaper articles on the health care debate knew no more about the proposals than people who read just one article.[164]

All this emphasis on human interest, including the attention to sex and crime, to the game, and to controversy, helps explain why the media spotlight scandals. Since Watergate, which riveted the public, the media have played up other, lesser scandals. As one journalist himself has observed, "When a scandal is breaking, talk show figures wring their hands about the 'agony' of Watergate or Iran-Contra; but the truth is that journalists are happier at such moments than at any other time. The country's attention is turned toward Washington. People hang on disclosures of the latest 'inside' news. Life is energizing and sweet for Washington journalists, even if the scandal of the moment is a big wheel-spinning exercise for the country as a whole."[165]

But the scandal must seem interesting to receive extensive coverage. When members of Congress bounced checks at the House bank, one recalled, there was a "massive scramble to get the list of who bounced checks. . . . It was ya-hoo! . . . Reporters were lusting after it." But few were paying any attention to the "$400 billion worth of hot checks being written by the federal government."[166] The media considered the deficit too uninteresting and difficult to explain, until Perot made it a campaign issue.

When the savings and loan (S&L) scandal loomed in the 1980s, business reporters addressed it, but political reporters and editors ignored it for years. A banking reporter said, "You would relay this to your editors, but because it involved banking regulations, their eyes would glaze over."[167] The crisis was too complicated and too dull until it could be personalized and sensationalized. Finally, Charles Keating—the chair of a failed S&L and a highflier with three private jets, one with gold-plated bathroom fixtures—was linked to the scandal. Then "looted Rembrandts and party girls on yachts" were discovered, and the media and the public took notice.[168] But by this time the industry needed a

WHAT SELLS?

The most popular and least popular issues of *Time* magazine, measured by newsstand sales, show what kinds of news people are interested in. The most popular issues feature celebrities and disasters. The least popular issues often feature foreign affairs.

Hits

ISSUE DATE	COVER SUBJECT	COPIES SOLD
Sept. 15, 1997	Princess Diana "Commemorative"	1,183,758
Sept. 8, 1997	Death of Princess Diana	802,838
Aug. 19, 1974	President Ford/ Nixon's resignation	564,723
Dec. 22, 1980	Death of John Lennon	531,340
Mar. 19, 1984	Michael Jackson	500,290
Aug. 2, 1982	Herpes	468,021
Feb. 10, 1986	*Challenger* Explosion	462,492
Jan. 28, 1991	War in the Gulf	433,625
Aug. 15, 1983	Babies: "What Do They Know?"	423,156
June 2, 1980	Mount St. Helens	412,909

Misses

ISSUE DATE	COVER SUBJECT	COPIES SOLD
Oct. 10, 1994	Black Cultural Renaissance	100,827
Aug. 22, 1994	Baseball Strike	101,125
May 17, 1993	"Anguish Over Bosnia"	102,193
April 4, 1996	Nuclear Safety	108,900
June 10, 1996	Benjamin Netanyahu	109,300
March 29, 1993	Boris Yeltsin	109,365
Dec. 21, 1992	Somalia: Restoring Hope	111,176
June 3, 1996	Advocates for Children	111,700
Nov. 20, 1996	G.O.P. Front Runner Bob Dole	112,310
Oct. 24, 1994	America's Economy	113,041

SOURCE: *Time*, March 9, 1998, p. 177.

$500 billion bailout from the taxpayers to prevent more insolvent S&Ls from collapsing (and taking depositors' savings with them).

The commercial bias of the media leads to certain consequences for television specifically. One is emphasis on events, or those parts of events, that have visual interest. The networks have people whose job is to evaluate all film for visual appeal. Producers seek the events that promise the most action; camera operators shoot the parts of the events with the most action; and editors select the portions of the film with the most action.[169] Television thus focuses on disasters, crimes, and protests far more than they actually occur, and when it covers other events, it focuses on the most exciting aspects of them. Sometimes it distorts reality in order to hold the viewers' attention. In the summer of 1988, fires raged through Yellowstone National Park. Television showed a wall of flame night after night and called the park "a moonscape." As one lifeless scene followed another on the screen, NBC's Tom Brokaw intoned, "This is what's left of Yellowstone tonight." Yet three-fourths of the park, including its famed geysers and waterfalls, was nearly unscathed.[170]

The emphasis on visual interest often results in coverage of the interesting surface of events rather than the underlying substance—the protest but not the cause. When Iranians seized the American embassy and employees in 1980, the demonstrators discovered television's appetite for visual interest and teased it almost every night for more than a year. As the cameras arrived, they erupted with wild chants and threats, hung Jimmy Carter effigies, and shredded American flags. Yet the reasons for the seizure, rooted in Iranian problems, American policies, and superpower conflicts, were only briefly mentioned.[171]

Another consequence of commercial bias for television is that it covers the news very briefly. In a half-hour newscast, there are only 21 minutes without commercials. In that time, the networks broadcast only about one-third as many words as the *New York Times* prints on its front page alone. Although television conveys visual impressions as well, the contrast in the amount of information these media transmit is striking.

The stories are short—about one minute each—because the time is short and because the networks think viewers' attention spans are short. Indeed, a survey found that a majority of 18- to 34-year-olds who have remote controls typically watch more than one show at once.[172] Thus, networks do not allow leaders or experts to explain their thoughts about particular events or policies. Instead, networks take sound bites to illustrate what was said. Their correspondents usually do not have enough time to explain the events or policies or to provide background information about them.

A network correspondent was asked what went through his mind when he signed off each night. "Good night, dear viewer," he said. "I only hope you read the *New York Times* in the morning."[173]

When the chairman of the board of one network, in conversation with Reagan aide Michael Deaver, asked what the networks could do to provide more responsible reporting, Deaver answered, "Easy, . . . just eliminate ratings for news. You claim that news is not the same as entertainment. So why do you need ratings?" The chairman sighed, "Well, that's our big money-maker, the news."[174]

The same is true for individual stations. One financial analyst estimated that 40–50% of their profits come from news programs.[175]

Overall, commercial bias of the media results in no coverage or superficial coverage of many important stories. This, more than any political bias, makes it difficult for citizens, particularly those who rely on television, to become well informed.

IMPACT OF THE MEDIA ON POLITICS

It is difficult to measure the impact of the media on politics. Because the many media provide varied though similar coverage and reach different though overlapping audiences, it is exceedingly difficult to isolate the impact of particular media on particular groups of people. Other factors also influence people's knowledge, attitudes, and behavior toward politics. But there is considerable agreement that the media have a substantial impact on the public agenda, political parties and elections, and public opinion.

Impact on the Public Agenda

The most important impact of the media is **setting the agenda**—influencing the process by which problems are considered important and alternative policies are proposed and debated.[176] The media publicize an issue, and people exposed to the media talk about the issue with their fellow citizens. Eventually, enough consider it important and expect officials to try to resolve it.[177]

The media's impact is most noticeable for dramatic events that occur suddenly, such as the dismantling of the Berlin Wall. The impact is less noticeable for issues that evolve gradually. Watergate required months of coverage before making it on the public agenda, and AIDS required the death of actor Rock Hudson before making it.[178]

Even for issues that evolve gradually, however, cumulative coverage by the media can have an impact. After some years people told pollsters that drug use was the "most important problem" facing the country, and then they told pollsters that crime was. Studies comparing people's views with the media coverage of these problems and with the actual rates of these activities in the 1980s and 1990s show that people's views fluctuate more according to the media coverage than to the actual rates. When the media coverage increased, people considered the problems more serious, even when the actual rates of crime or drug use remained steady or decreased.[179]

The impact usually is greatest for stories that appear on the front page of the newspaper or top of the newscast rather than those buried in the back or at the end.[180] Many people who do not follow the news fully check the beginning of the newspaper or newscast for the "important" stories. Without being aware of it, they are accepting the media's role in identifying these stories as the important ones.

And the media's impact usually is greatest on people who are most interested in politics, because they are most likely to follow the news and discuss it with others.[181] Yet the impact varies according to the personal experiences of the audience. For instance, people with recent unemployment in their family will be more sensitive to news about unemployment than other people.

In shaping the agenda, the most prominent print organizations normally are the most powerful. The *New York Times* is preeminent for international politics, the *Washington Post* for domestic politics, and the specialized *Wall Street Journal* for economic matters. The AP wire service is influential, and *Newsweek* and *Time* magazines are also. Other media take their cues from these organizations. Even the television networks get most of their stories from these print media.[182]

In recent years, however, radio and television call-in shows set the agenda for some issues. In the 1992 presidential campaign, tabloid newspapers and nonnews television programs set the agenda for Clinton's sexual affairs.

For years the major media "controlled the gates through which news passed. If they didn't report it, by and large the rest of us didn't hear about it."[183] But now the mainstream media have no monopoly; the fringe media also can open the gates for some issues.

The media's power to influence the agenda has important implications. The media play a key role in deciding which problems government addresses and which it ignores. They also play a key role in increasing or decreasing politicians' ability to govern and to get reelected. By publicizing some issues, the media create a golden opportunity for politicians with the authority

© TSM, John Maher, 1994

The second half of the twentieth century might go down in history as "the age of television."

and ability to resolve these issues. At the same time, the media create a pitfall for those who lack the power to resolve these issues. Thus, the Iranian seizure of the American embassy and hostages became the prominent issue in the country in 1980. Every night CBS's Walter Cronkite signed off, "And that's the way it is, the _____ day of American hostages in captivity," as if anyone needed reminding. President Carter's lack of success in persuading Iranian officials to release the hostages or in directing an American invasion to rescue them cost him dearly in his reelection bid that year.

Yet the role of the media in shaping the agenda should not be overstated. Individuals' knowledge and experience lead them to consider some things unimportant even when the media do cover them. And, of course, individuals' interests prompt the media to cover some things in the first place.[184]

Moreover, politicians play an important role in shaping the agenda. For much legislation Congress initiates action and then the media publicize it.[185] For many issues the president initiates action. In 1995 President Clinton launched a campaign to reduce smoking by teenagers. The media printed and broadcast many stories about this problem. They could have done so years before or after, of course, but they followed the president's lead. For elections candidates usually establish the agenda of policy issues. By emphasizing issues they think will resonate with the public and reflect favorably on themselves, candidates pressure the media to cover these rather than other issues. But the media usually establish the agenda of nonpolicy issues, involving the candidates' personality and behavior.[186] The media are able to set the agenda for nonpolicy issues because these are more likely to catch the public's fancy.

Impact on Political Parties and Elections

The media have had an important impact on political parties and elections. In particular they have furthered the decline of parties, encouraged new types of candidates, and influenced campaigns.

POLITICAL PARTIES

Political parties have declined in power on the national level in large part because of the influence of the media. In the young republic, political parties created and controlled most newspapers. Naturally, the papers echoed the parties' views and the journalists bowed to the parties' leaders. The editor of one Democratic Party paper made sure a pail of fresh milk was left on the White House doorstep for President Andrew Jackson every morning, even if the editor had to deliver it himself.[187] People received much of their political information, however biased, from these papers.

When independent newspapers arose as profit-making businesses, the party papers declined and then disappeared. Eventually, people came to receive most of their political information from independent newspapers, magazines, radio stations, and television stations. Thus, people are no longer dependent upon parties for their political information.

In other ways as well, the media, especially television, have contributed to the decline of parties. In place of selection by party bosses, television allows candidates to appeal directly to the people. If candidates succeed in the primaries, parties have little choice but to nominate them. In place of campaign management by party bosses, television requires new expertise, so candidates assemble their own campaign organization. Television advertising requires substantial amounts of money, so party funds are inadequate and candidates approach other donors. Television also gives voters information so they can make up their own minds about how to vote, rather than rely on the party organization to tell them. Thus, the media have supplanted parties as the principal link between people and their leaders.

TYPES OF CANDIDATES

Television has encouraged new types of candidates for national offices. No longer must candidates be experienced politicians who worked their way up over many years. Celebrities from other fields with name recognition can move into prominent positions even without political experience. It is not coincidental that in recent years the House has had an actor (Fred Grandy, R-Iowa—"Gopher" on "Love Boat"), a rock singer (Sonny Bono, R-Cal.), a professional baseball pitcher (Jim Bunning, R-Ky.), a professional football quarterback (Jack Kemp, R-N.Y.), and a professional basketball player (Tom McMillen, D-Md.) and the Senate has had a professional basketball player (Bill Bradley, D-N.J.) and two astronauts (John Glenn, D-Ohio, and Harrison Schmitt, R-N.M.).[188] Nor is it coincidental that the Senate has had a television commentator (Jesse Helms, R-N.C.) and a businessman who appeared in his company's commercials (Rudy Boschwitz, R-Minn.). Alternatively, unknowns with talent can achieve rapid name recognition and move into prominent positions. Jimmy Carter, who had served one term as governor of Georgia, was relatively unknown elsewhere in the country when he ran for the Democratic nomination for president in 1976. People kept asking "Jimmy who?" But through effective use of television, he won enough primaries so the party had to nominate him, even though the leaders were uncomfortable with him.

At the same time that television has allowed newcomers to run, it also has imposed new requirements on candidates for national office. They must demonstrate an appealing appearance and performance on camera; they must be telegenic. President Franklin Roosevelt's body, crippled from polio and usually in a wheelchair, would not be impressive on television. President Harry Truman's style—"Give 'em hell"—would not be impressive on television either. Although effective in whistlestop speeches, it would be too "hot," too intense, to come into people's homes every day. A "cool," low-key style is more effective.

President Reagan was the quintessential politician for the television age. He was tall and trim with a handsome face and a smooth, reassuring voice. As a former actor, he could project his personality and convictions and deliver his lines and jokes better than any other politician. It is not an exaggeration to conclude, as one political scientist did, "Without a chance to display his infectious smile, his grandfatherly demeanor, and his 'nice guy' qualities to millions of Americans, Ronald Reagan, burdened by his image as a superannuated, intellectually lightweight movie actor with right-wing friends and ultraconservative leanings, might never have reached the presidency."[189]

Courtesy Franklin D. Roosevelt Library 73-113:61

Franklin Roosevelt spent much of his life in a wheelchair, but journalists did not photograph him in it. A friend snapped this rare picture.

Television has not created the public desire for politicians with an appealing personality. "When candidates shook hands firmly, kissed babies, and handed out cigars, the thrust was not on issues."[190] Yet television has exacerbated this emphasis on the right image.

CAMPAIGNS

The media affect nomination and election campaigns through their news and commentary and candidates' advertisements. They help set the campaign agenda, as already explained. They also inform and persuade.

The media provide information about the candidates and the issues, and they also interpret this information.[191] The public learns about the candidates and the issues,[192] but in the process the public is influenced in making its choices.

Information about the candidates can have a major impact especially at the nomination stage. In presidential elections, a party without an incumbent president running for reelection might field a dozen candidates. The media cannot cover all adequately, so they narrow the field by considering some "serious" and giving them more coverage. Once the primaries begin, they label some "winners" and others "losers," and they give the "winners" more coverage. In the Democratic race in

WASHINGTON, JEFFERSON, AND LINCOLN IN THE MEDIA AGE

How would three of America's greatest presidents have fared in the media age? George Washington cut an impressive figure, but he had a speech impediment.

Thomas Jefferson was tall—six feet, two inches, when the average American man was about five feet, five inches—but he was shy, even awkward, with people. And apparently he never made a political speech.

Abraham Lincoln was also tall, but he was gangly. According to contemporaries, he was homely in different ways at different times. One newspaper called him "the ugliest man in the Union."[1] He had a "ploughed" face and a "doughnut" complexion, protruding ears, and "spider" legs.[2] He also had a high-pitched voice.

A modern observer speculated how television would cover the Gettysburg Address, which, though brief, would not be brief enough: The cameras would focus on the network correspondent describing the scene and recalling the battle, while in the background Lincoln would be speaking. Finally, the cameras would focus on Lincoln concluding, "government of the people, by the people, for the people, shall not perish from the earth."[3]

Are there contemporary Washingtons, Jeffersons, and Lincolns who might make effective leaders but who would not qualify because they are ineffective on television?

1. Thomas E. Patterson, *Out of Order* (New York: Vintage, 1994), p. 9.
2. Marcus Cunliffe, "What Did Abraham Lincoln Look Like?" *Washington Post National Weekly Edition*, February 27, 1984, p. 35.
3. Thomas Griffith, "Always Articulate on Sunday," *Time*, June 6, 1983, p. 55.

1976, Carter finished second to "uncommitted" in the Iowa caucuses. This was enough to give him 23 times more coverage in *Time* and *Newsweek*, and 5 times more coverage on network television, than any of his rivals. Finishing first by just 4% in the New Hampshire primary landed him on the covers of *Time* and *Newsweek* and brought him 25 times more coverage on network television than the runner-up.[193] In the Democratic race in 1992, even before a single primary, the press proclaimed Clinton the front-runner, and several magazines put his picture on their cover, although half of the public did not know who he was.[194]

By making these judgments, the media strongly influence the election process at this stage.[195] Because few people have formed opinions about the candidates this early, they are open to impressions from the media. Therefore, when the media declare some candidates winners, they help create a bandwagon effect.[196] When they declare others losers, they make it hard for these candidates to attract contributors and volunteers and eventually supporters in the next primaries.

The media also can persuade voters directly. This can be seen in several ways.

Televised debates do not sway most viewers because people tend to engage in **selective perception,** which is a tendency to screen out information that contradicts their beliefs. Consequently, most people conclude that their candidate performed better.[197] However, the debates do sway some viewers, usually those who have moderate education and some interest in politics but who are not decided or, if decided, not strongly committed to one candidate. In 1960 the debates might have caused enough voters to cast their ballots for Kennedy that he won the election.[198]

Media commentary about the debates also sways some viewers. In 1976 Ford erroneously said there was "no Soviet domination of Eastern Europe." People surveyed within 12 hours after the debate said they thought Ford won. But the media zeroed in on this slip, and people surveyed later said they thought Carter won (see Table 1). In the first debate in 1984, Reagan appeared tired and confused. By a modest margin, people polled immediately after the debate said Mondale won. But the media focused on Reagan's age and abilities, and by increasingly large margins, people polled in the days after the debate said Mondale won. Perhaps viewers did not catch Ford's statement or, due to selective perception, notice Reagan's doddering, but the media called attention to them, which prompted many viewers to reconsider and reverse their verdict.

Newspaper endorsements of candidates also sway some readers, especially those with a ninth- through twelfth-grade education. People with less education are less likely to read editorials, while those with more education have more sources of information and more defined ideologies to guide their decisions.[199] Even if endorsements sway only a small percentage of voters, they could determine the outcome of tight races.[200] Endorsements are thought to have little effect on well-publicized races, although one study of the 1964 presidential election concluded that endorsements of President Johnson by monopoly newspapers in 223 counties across the North added about 5% to the vote he would have received in these counties otherwise.[201] Endorsements probably have more effect on relatively unpublicized races, such as for state legislator or local tax assessor, because voters have little other information to guide them.

Talk radio also influences listeners. People who listen to Rush Limbaugh are more likely to turn out to vote, to talk about politics, and to participate in campaigns. The same effect has been found with other talk shows too.[202]

TABLE 1

Media Commentary Influenced Perceptions of 1976 Debates

CANDIDATE VIEWERS FELT WON DEBATE	VIEWERS INTERVIEWED WITHIN 12 HOURS AFTER DEBATE	VIEWERS INTERVIEWED FROM 12 HOURS TO 48 HOURS AFTER DEBATE
Ford	53%	29%
Carter	35	58
Undecided	12	13

According to a study of people in Erie, Pennsylvania, and Los Angeles, media commentary on Ford's gaffe caused many to change their minds about which candidate won the debate. A majority of those interviewed before the commentary sunk in thought Ford won, whereas a majority of these interviewed later thought Carter won.

SOURCE: Thomas E. Patterson, *The Mass Media Election* (New York: Praeger, 1980), p. 123.

Impact on Public Opinion

Social scientists long thought that the media influenced the things people thought about but not the opinions they held about these things. Some contemporary research, however, demonstrates that the media do have a substantial impact on public opinion. A comparison of the networks' newscasts with the public's policy preferences in a wide variety of foreign and domestic issues for 15 years during the 1970s and 1980s shows that the media influence opinion about issues.[203] Other research shows that the media influence opinion about particular presidents.[204] They affect opinion indirectly, by providing the news and transmitting the views of various opinion leaders, as well as directly, through editorials and commentaries intended to sway opinion.

There is much speculation that the media have contributed to the public's cynicism toward government in recent decades. The media have undermined the public's perception of the integrity of government and officials not just by reporting real shortcomings of programs and administrators, but by engaging in several practices already addressed in this chapter. The negative bias in coverage of all candidates and officials directly undermines them, while the game orientation in coverage of them more subtly undermines them. The emphasis on conflict leads to a focus on politicians' most extreme statements, which alienates the public and, at the same time, polarizes it. The practice of objectivity—reporting what he said versus what she said without evaluating the truth of either—passes along some false statements and some misleading ones and confuses the public.[205] Many people complain, "You can't believe any of them."

Some researchers have concluded that the result of these practices is to foster **media malaise** among the public.[206] This is a feeling of cynicism and distrust, perhaps even despair, toward government and officials. Indeed, according to a 1995 survey, the public is even more cynical than journalists themselves. Seventy-seven percent of the public gave government officials a low rating for honesty and ethics, while only 40% of the journalists did so.[207] Most of the public believed that politicians could "never" be trusted to do the right thing. Yet the journalists saw the American political process as "a flawed but basically decent means of reconciling different points of view and solving collective problems."[208] They apparently report in a more cynical fashion than they actually feel because of the conventions of contemporary journalism. But the public, while deploring these practices, evidently sees them as reflections of reality. So cynical coverage by the press leads to even more cynical attitudes in the citizenry.[209]

The cynical attitudes have important implications for politics. They probably reduce satisfaction with candidates and officials and reduce turnout in elections. At the same time, they probably increase votes for "outsiders" who present themselves as "nonpoliticians."

CONCLUSION: ARE THE MEDIA RESPONSIVE?

The media have to be responsive to the people to make a profit. They present the news they think the people want. Because they believe the majority desire entertainment, or at least diversion, rather than education, they structure the news toward this end. According to a number of studies, they correctly assess their consumers.[210] For the majority who want entertainment, network television provides it. For the minority who want education, the better newspapers and magazines provide it. Public radio, with its hour-and-a-half nightly newscast, and public television, with its hour nightly newscast, also provide quality coverage. The media offer something for everyone.

When officials or citizens get upset with the media, they pointedly ask, "Who elected you?" Journalists

reply that the people—their readers or listeners or viewers—"elected them" by paying attention to their news columns or newscasts. At the same time, however, the people criticize the media. Almost three-fourths tell pollsters that the media get in the way of society's efforts to solve its problems. Only one-fourth say that the media help to solve the problems.[211]

To say the media are responsive, however, is not to say they perform well. Giving the people what they want most is not necessarily serving the country best. As one reporter lamented, "People seem to 'know' everything now—hearing the same news bulletins repeated around the clock—but they seem to understand precious little of what's really going on."[212] The media personalize and dramatize the news. The result is to simplify the news. Superficial coverage of complex events leaves the public unable to understand these events and, ultimately, unable to force the government to be responsive.

The media give us the big hype—"Hey, listen to this! Here's something new you can't miss!" They reflect a *crisis du jour* mentality in which everything is important but ultimately nothing is important. Almost any political development is important for a day or a week or occasionally a month. But almost no political development is important for long. So the media lurch from a supposed crisis to a real crisis, and back again. In the Clinton years, for example, the media have flitted from the caning of a teenager in Singapore to the making of nuclear weapons in North Korea; from a civil war in the former Yugoslavia to the appropriate commemoration for the fiftieth anniversary of the end of World War II with Japan; from the president's haircut in an airplane, which cost $200, to his first budget bill, which reduced the deficit; from the Clintons' possible corruption in the Whitewater land deal to the effort by a friend of the Clintons to get a White House job in the "Travelgate scandal"; from the secrecy of the health care task force to the substance of health care reform; from the denial of a presidential appointment for Zoe Baird because she hired illegal aliens to the denial of a presidential appointment for Kimba Wood because—well, somebody must remember; it was considered important. The headlines and the stories clamoring for attention go by in such a blur that after a while they all become a jumble for many people. They leave no sense of what's actually a crisis, what's just a problem, what's merely an irritant, and what's truly trivial.[213]

Thus, most news coverage is episodic, presenting an event as a single, idiosyncratic occurrence, rather than thematic, presenting the event as an example or reflection of a larger pattern. For instance, a story might focus on one hungry person or group of persons rather than on malnutrition as a national problem. Episodic coverage is more common because it is more entertaining—dramatic, with human interest—than thematic coverage. But episodic coverage makes it hard for people to see the connection between problems in society and the actions of government and its officials. Then people do not hold their leaders accountable for addressing or resolving the problems.[214]

The media's shortcomings are aggravated by a declining interest in politics and a decreasing number of people who read newspapers or watch newscasts. Although the public is better educated now than in the 1960s, it is less likely to follow the news and less able to answer questions about the government.[215] People under 35 especially reflect these trends. To keep these vanishing readers, many newspapers have revamped their formats. While some have improved their quality, more have emulated *USA Today* and reduced their substance to hold the attention spans of younger readers weaned on television. This has disturbing implications. Citizens who are not aware of the news or who do not understand it cannot fulfill their role in a democracy.

These trends come at a time when the media, despite their shortcomings, provide more news than ever and—with journalists better educated and better able to address complex topics—more effective news than ever. Because the media are somewhat responsive and effective, they have become powerful enough to serve as a check on government in many situations. This was evident during the major crises of recent decades. During the war in Vietnam, the media stood up to two presidents when Congress and the courts were relatively passive. During the Watergate scandal, the media led Congress and the courts in standing up to a president. The media serve as a check on the government in countless other situations. As a former government official noted, "Think how much chicanery dies on the drawing board when someone says, 'We'd better not do that; what if the press finds out?' "[216]

EPILOGUE

Signorile Revealed Official's Homosexuality

Michelangelo Signorile decided to publish information revealing that the assistant secretary of defense, Pete Williams, was homosexual.[217] Initially, the mainstream media refused to report the story. Most reporters on the Pentagon beat did not ask questions about the revelation or write articles about it. Most editors spiked the articles that reporters did write. Eventually, one reporter asked Williams directly. He refused to answer: "As a government spokesman, I stand here and I talk about government policy. I am not paid to discuss my personal opinions about that policy or talk about my personal life, and I don't intend to."[218] In subsequent weeks some mainstream newspapers and magazines decided to cover the story and name the official after all.

The brouhaha put the military's policy of discharging homosexuals on the agenda for the 1992 election. Candidate Bill Clinton criticized the hypocrisy of the situation and promised to change the policy. After Clinton's election, Williams, a political appointee of the Bush administration, left government for the private sector.

"Outing," as the practice of identifying gays and lesbians who remain in "the closet" came to be called, spread. While some activists engaged in outing through their writing, others sent faxes across the country, nailed posters to telephone poles, and confronted persons in public. Supermarket tabloids, always alert for sensational stories, engaged in outing of actors. Unlike the gay activists, these papers were motivated by the desire to boost circulation and increase profits.

Many homosexuals felt threatened by the spread of outing. Signorile remembers, "I was called every name in the book and fended off angry people everywhere I went."[219] Many heterosexuals who felt that the media already were too intrusive into private lives also criticized the practice. One political scientist called it "a despicable new movement."[220]

Signorile acknowledges the media might be too intrusive, but he says if the media cover the private lives of heterosexuals, they legitimately can cover the private lives of homosexuals. "Journalists," he adds, "are not in the business of providing comfort or making people feel better. They're in the business of telling the truth, whatever it is, whenever it is pertinent to a story."[221]

But when is a person's homosexuality "pertinent to a story"? Signorile would limit outing to public figures—famous persons who make lots of money from the public or wield considerable power over the public—and to situations that reflect hypocrisy, such as persons in government or the media who act contrary to the interests of homosexuals. Signorile admits these criteria are fuzzy and decisions need to be made on a case-by-case basis.

And he admits he is uneasy about some of what has happened. "I can't say I felt great about all this. It wasn't the outing I had a problem with, but the fact that I was using it as a bludgeoning and blackmailing tool. That wasn't what I originally had in mind. But as has been true in every revolution, there is always a person or group who kicks things off by doing something brutal. . . . We were under siege at the time, and I was operating with a siege mentality."[222]

His goal in outing is "to give courage to millions of gay people who stay in the closet out of fear and shame."[223] He especially wants to show gay teenagers, who are left "feeling alone, like freaks" and who experience more depression and suicide than straight teenagers, that there are gay adults who have made it—as Eddie Murphy and Oprah Winfrey show black kids that blacks can make it.[224]

With these words, Signorile indicates that he might be more an activist than a journalist. But in these times, when anyone with a fax machine or an Internet account can be a "journalist," the ethics of reporting have become more blurred.

KEY TERMS

symbiotic relationship
adversarial relationship
leaks
scoop
presidential press conference
media events
sound bite
fireside chats
political bias
commercial bias
game orientation
setting the agenda
selective perception
media malaise

FURTHER READING

The print media themselves are the primary sources for further reading. A good metropolitan newspaper or a weekly newsmagazine is essential. For political junkies, the *Washington Post National Weekly Edition*, a compilation of the newspaper's best articles and cartoons about politics during the week, is wonderful.

Timothy Crouse, *The Boys on the Bus* (New York: Random House, 1972). An irreverent account of press coverage of elections by a writer who reported on the reporters rather than on the candidates along the presidential campaign trail in 1972.

Kathleen Hall Jamieson and David S. Birdsell, *Presidential Debates* (New York: Oxford University Press, 1988). A history of presidential debates and a set of proposals for their reform.

John R. MacArthur, *Second Front: Censorship and Propaganda in the Gulf War* (New York: Hill & Wang, 1992). A searing critique of media coverage of the war.

Joe McGinniss, *The Selling of the President 1968* (New York: Simon & Schuster, 1969). An account of the often-comical efforts by Richard Nixon's advisers to transform him into a media candidate.

Nan Robertson, *The Girls in the Balcony: Women, Men, and the New York Times* (New York: Random House, 1992). A history of chauvinism at the country's most famous newspaper.

Tom Rosenstiel, *Strange Bedfellows: How Television and the Presidential Candidates Changed American Politics, 1992* (New York: Hyperion, 1993). A critical examination of media coverage of the 1992 campaign.

ELECTRONIC RESOURCES

http://www.pbs.org/wgbh/pages/frontline/shows/press
"Why Americans Hate the Press."

http://www.nytimes.com/

http://www.washingtonpost.com/

http://www.usatoday.com
The addresses for the New York Times, Washington Post, *and* USA Today, *respectively. Most major newspapers, and many local ones, have their own Web pages. These pages do not contain the full text of the printed papers, but they do include late-breaking news not included in the daily paper.*

INFOTRAC CITATIONS

"Nets Expand to Fill News Hole"

"Drudge Begrudged"

"The Edit Suite: Cockpit of Political Spot Post-Production"

"The Television Leaders' Debate in Britain: From Talking Heads to Headless Chickens"

NOTES

1. Michelangelo Signorile, *Queer in America: Sex, the Media, and the Closets of Power* (New York: Random House, 1993), p. 78.
2. Larry J. Sabato, *Feeding Frenzy: How Attack Journalism Has Transformed American Politics* (New York: Free Press, 1991), pp. 192–93.
3. Signorile, *Queer in America*, p. 138.
4. Ibid., p. 148.
5. Sabato, *Feeding Frenzy*, pp. 1, 8–22.
6. James David Barber, *The Pulse of Politics* (New York: W. W. Norton, 1980), p. 9.
7. Kevin Phillips, "A Matter of Privilege," *Harpers*, January 1977, pp. 95–97.
8. Richard Harwood, "So Many Media, So Little Time," *Washington Post National Weekly Edition*, September 7–13, 1992, p. 28.
9. Thomas R. Dye and L. Hannon Zeigler, *American Politics in the Media Age* (Monterey, Calif.: Brooks/Cole, 1983), pp. 123–124.
10. Edwin Diamond, *The Tin Kazoo* (Cambridge, Mass.: MIT Press, 1975), p. 13.
11. Doris A. Graber, *Mass Media and American Politics* (Washington, D.C.: Congressional Quarterly, 1980), p. 2.
12. William Lutz, *Doublespeak* (New York: Harper & Row, 1989), pp. 73–74.
13. Richard Harwood, "Nobody Reads Anymore," *Washington Post National Weekly Edition*, December 26, 1988–January 1, 1989, p. 29.
14. Elizabeth Gleick, "Read All about It," *Time*, October 21, 1998, p. 66.
15. Thomas E. Patterson, *The Mass Media Election* (New York: Praeger, 1980), pp. 58–60, 62–63.
16. J. Fred MacDonald, *One Nation under Television: The Rise and Decline of Network TV* (New York: Pantheon, 1991); S. Robert Lichter, Stanley Rothman, and Linda S. Lichter, *The Media Elite* (Bethesda, Md.: Adler & Adler, 1986), pp. 5–7.
17. Otto Friedrich, "Edging the Government out of TV," *Time*, August 17, 1987, p. 58; Edmund L. Andrews, "A New Tune for Radio: Hard Times," *New York Times*, March 1992.
18. Benjamin M. Compaine, *Who Owns the Media?* (White Plains, N.Y.: Knowledge Industry Publications, 1979) pp. 11, 76–77; Michael Parenti, *Inventing Reality* (New York: St. Martin's, 1986), p. 27; Paul Farhi, "You Can't Tell a Book by Its Cover," *Washington Post National Weekly Edition*, December 5–11, 1988, p. 21; Andrews, "A New Tune for Radio."
19. Ken Auletta, "American Keiretsu," *New Yorker*, October 20 and 27, 1997, p. 225.
20. Harwood, "So Many Media, So Little Time."
21. Robert Entman, *Democracy without Citizens: Media and the Decay of American Politics* (New York: Oxford University Press, 1989), pp. 91–101.
22. Howard Kurtz, "Welcome to Spin City," *Washington Post National Weekly Edition*, March 16, 1998, p. 6.
23. Elizabeth Kolbert, "For Talk Shows, Less News Is Good News," *New York Times*, June 28, 1992, p. E-2.
24. Howard Fineman, "The Power of Talk," *Time*, February 8, 1993, p. 25.
25. "The Vocal Minority in American Politics," Times Mirror Center for the People and the Press, Washington, D.C., July 1993.
26. Richard Corliss, "Look Who's Talking," *Time*, January 23, 1995, p. 23.
27. In addition, she received $50,000 for a book elaborating upon her story, $250,000 for posing nude for *Penthouse* magazine, and about $20,000 for appearing on German and Spanish television shows. "Flowers Says She Made Half Million from Story," *Lincoln Journal-Star* (AP), March 21, 1998.
28. Ernest Tollerson, "Politicians Try to Balance Risk against Rewards of Reaching Talk-Radio Audiences," *New York Times*, March 31, 1996, p. 12.
29. Richard Harwood, "The Growing Irrelevance of Journalists," *Washington Post National Weekly Edition*, November 2–8, 1992, p. 29.
30. Dan Balz, "A '90s Kind of Scandal," *Washington Post National Weekly Edition*, February 2, 1998, p. 8.
31. Corliss, "Look Who's Talking," p. 25.
32. Kurt Anderson, "The Age of Unreason," *New Yorker*, February 3, 1997, p. 42.
33. Tom Rosenstiel, *The Beat Goes On: President Clinton's First Year with the Media* (New York: Twentieth Century Fund, 1994), p. 35.
34. Howard Kurtz, "The Story That Wouldn't Stay Buried," *Washington Post National Weekly Edition*, December 1, 1997, p. 12.
35. Kurtz, "Welcome to Spin City."

36. Dom Bonafede, "Press Paying More Heed to Substance in Covering 1984 Presidential Election," *National Journal*, October 13, 1984, p. 1923.

37. "All Things Considered," National Public Radio, November 5, 1992.

38. "Comment: Take Five," *New Yorker*, November 23, 1992, p. 4.

39. Thomas M. DeFrank, "Playing the Media Game," *Newsweek*, April 17, 1989, p. 21.

40. Charles Peters, *How Washington Really Works* (Redding, Mass.: Addison-Wesley Publishing, 1980), p. 18.

41. William Greider, "Reporters and Their Sources," *Washington Monthly*, October 1982, pp. 13–15.

42. Daniel Schorr, "A Fact of Political Life," *Washington Post National Weekly Edition*, October 28–November 3, 1991, p. 32.

43. Howard Kurtz, "How Sources and Reporters Play the Game of Leaks," *Washington Post National Weekly Edition*, March 15–21, 1993, p. 25.

44. Elizabeth Drew, "Letter from Washington," *New Yorker*, September 12, 1988, p. 92.

45. Ann Devroy, "The Republicans, It Turns Out, Are a Veritable Fount of Leaks," *Washington Post National Weekly Edition*, November 18–24, 1991, p. 23.

46. William A. Henry III, "Scrounging for Good Air," *Time*, September 3, 1984, p. 7.

47. Adam Cohen, "The Press and the Dress," February 16, 1998, *Times*, pp. 51–54.

48. Jonathan Alter, "When Sources Get Immunity," *Newsweek*, January 19, 1987, p. 54.

49. Samuel Kernell, *Going Public: New Strategies of Presidential Leadership* (Washington, D.C.: Congressional Quarterly, 1986), p. 59.

50. Woodrow Wilson also tried to cultivate correspondents and host frequent sessions, but he did not have the knack for this activity and he scaled back the sessions. Kernell, *Going Public*, pp. 60–61. He did perceive that "[s]ome men of brilliant ability were in the group, but I soon discovered that the interest of the majority was in the personal and the trivial rather than in principles and policies." James Bennet, "The Flack Pack," *Washington Monthly*, November 1991, p. 27.

51. Dwight Eisenhower was actually the first president to let the networks televise his press conferences, but he did not do so to reach the public. When he wanted to reach the public, he made a formal speech. The networks found his conferences so untelegenic that they stopped covering the entire session each time. Kernell, *Going Public*, p. 68.

52. Kernell, *Going Public*, p. 104.

53. Bennet, "The Flack Pack," p. 19.

54. Dom Bonafede, " 'Mr. President,' " *National Journal*, October 29, 1988, p. 2756.

55. Garry Wills, ". . . But Don't Treat It as a Game," *Lincoln Journal* (Universal Press Syndicate), March 26, 1993.

56. James Fallows, *Breaking the News: How the Media Undermine American Democracy* (New York: Pantheon, 1996), p. 196.

57. Charles Hagen, "The Photo Op: Making Icons or Playing Politics?" *New York Times*, February 9, 1992, p. H28.

58. Kiku Adatto, cited in Howard Kurtz, "Networks Adapt to Changed Campaign Role," *Washington Post*, June 21, 1992, p. A19.

59. Lance Morrow, "Time Essay," *Time*, August 18, 1980, p. 78.

60. Steven R. Weisman, "The President and the Press," *New York Times Magazine*, October 14, 1984, p. 71.

61. Ronald H. Brown, "Republican Baloney About Crime," *Washington Post National Weekly Edition*, April 30–May 6, 1990, p. 29.

62. David Halberstam, "How Television Failed the American Voter," *Parade*, January 11, 1981, p. 8.

63. George E. Reedy, *The Twilight of the Presidency* (New York: New American Library, 1970), p. 112.

64. Thomas Griffith, "Winging It on Television," *Time*, March 14, 1983, p. 71.

65. "Talking about the Media Circus," *New York Times Magazines*, June 26, 1994, p. 63.

66. W. Lance Bennett, *News: The Politics of Illusion*, 2d ed. (New York: Longman, 1988).

67. Sabato, *Feeding Frenzy*.

68. Robert J. Bennett, "We Should Scuttle the Partisanship," *Washington Post National Weekly Edition*, March 24, 1997, p. 21.

69. Fallows, *Breaking the News*, pp. 62–63.

70. Joseph N. Cappella and Kathleen Hall Jamieson, *Spiral of Cynicism* (New York: Oxford University Press, 1997), p. 31.

71. Mary Matalin and James Carville, *All's Fair* (New York: Random House, 1994), pp. 184–185.

72. Sabato, *Feeding Frenzy*, p. 53.

73. See Sabato, *Feeding Frenzy*, for additional reasons for this increase.

74. Fallows, *Breaking the News*, p. 196.

75. John David Rausch, Jr., "The Pathology of Politics: Government, Press, and Scandal," *Extensions* (University of Oklahoma), Fall 1990, pp. 11–12.

76. William Rivers, "The Correspondents after 25 Years," *Columbia Journalism Review* 1 (Spring 1962), p. 5.

77. James David Barber, *Presidential Character* (Englewood Cliffs, N.J.: Prentice Hall, 1992), p. 238.

78. Hedrick Smith, *The Power Game* (New York: Random House, 1988), p. 403.

79. Timothy J. Russert, "For '92, the Networks Have to Do Better," *New York Times*, March 4, 1990.

80. Smith, *Power Game*, p. 420.

81. Weisman, "The President and the Press," pp. 71–72; Dick Kirschten, "Communications Reshuffling Intended to Help Reagan Do What He Does Best," *National Journal*, January 28, 1984, p. 154.

82. When Reagan ordered the invasion of Grenada in 1983, the administration excluded reporters. For two days the only news that reached the public came from the administration, and it was uniformly positive about both the need for and the success of the invasion. However, in response to criticism from the media, the Pentagon established a pool system for future wars. Representative groups of reporters would be allowed to cover the action and share their information with other media. The military could transport and protect a few pools more easily than a huge number of individual reporters. But what the Pentagon did not admit was that the military, while appearing to cooperate, could control reporters' access to battles, individuals, and other sources of information more easily as well.

83. Howard Kurtz, "The Press Pool's Chilling Effect on Covering the War," *Washington Post National Weekly Edition*, February 18–24, 1991, p. 12; "Keeping It All Pretty Quiet on the Mideastern Front," *Washington Post National Weekly Edition*, February 4–10, 1991, pp. 34–35.

84. Calculated from David Sarasohn, "Not So Smart," *Lincoln Journal* (Newhouse News Service), April 2, 1991.

85. Richard Morin, "The New War Cry: Stop the Press," *Washington Post National Weekly Edition*, February 11–17, 1991, p. 38.

86. Sidney Blumenthal, "The Syndicated Presidency," *New Yorker*, April 5, 1993, p. 45.

87. Robert P. Laurence, "Mr. President Proves He Has a Way with Words," *San Diego Union-Tribune*, March 24, 1993.

88. Brit Hume (NBC News).

89. Howard Kurtz, "Assessing—and Controlling—the Damage to the Presidency," *Washington Post National Weekly Edition*, February 2, 1998, p. 21.

90. For examination of coverage during Clinton's early time in office, see William Glaberson, "The Capitol Press vs. the President: Fair Coverage or Unreined Adversity?" *New York Times*, June 17, 1993, p. A11; Christopher Georges, "Bad News Bearers," *Washington Monthly*, July/August 1993, pp. 28–34.

91. Thomas E. Patterson, *Out of Order* (New York: Vintage, 1994), pp. 14, 244.

92. Howard Kurtz, "Rolling with the Punches from the Press Corps," *Washington Post National Weekly Edition*, January 24–30, 1994, p. 10; James Fallows, "The Media's Rush to Judgment," *Washington Monthly*, January/February 1994, pp. 10–11.

93. Mark P. Petracca, "Letters," *Washington Monthly*, September 1993, p. 2; Larry J. Sabato, cited in Howard Kurtz, "Is It Splitsville for Clinton and the Media?" *Washington Post National Weekly Edition*, February 8–14, 1993, p. 14.

94. Stephen Hess, *Live from Capitol Hill!* (Washington, D.C.: Brookings Institution, 1991), p. 62; Timothy E. Cook, *Making Laws & Making News: Media Strategies in the U.S. House of Representatives* (Washington, D.C.: Brookings Institution, 1989), p. 2.

95. Hess, *Live from Capitol Hill!*, p. 102.

96. Hendrik Hertzberg, "Comment: The Pot Perplex," *New Yorker*, January 6, 1997, pp. 4–5.

97. Edward Jay Epstein, *News from Nowhere* (New York: Random House, 1973), p. 13.

98. Graber, *Mass Media and American Politics*, p. 62.

99. Milton Coleman, "When the Candidate Is Black like Me," *Washington Post National Weekly Edition*, April 23, 1984, p. 9.

100. Roper Organization, "A Big Concern about the Media: Intruding on Grieving Families," *Washington Post National Weekly Edition*, June 6, 1984. Also, see Cappella and Jamieson, *Spiral of Cynicism*, p. 210.

101. Parenti, *Inventing Reality*, chapters 7–11; Charles E. Lindblom, *Politics and Markets* (New York: Basic Books, 1977); MacDonald, *One Nation under Television;* Dan Nimmo and James E. Combs, *Mediated Political Realities* (New York: Longman, 1983), p. 135.

102. John R. MacArthur, *Second Front: Censorship and Propaganda in the Gulf War* (New York: Hill & Wang, 1992); James Bennet, "How They Missed That Story," *Washington Monthly*, December 1990, pp. 8–16.

103. E.g., a videotape of Iraqis being killed reached two networks, but they refused to show it. Barber, *Presidential Character*, pp. 481–482.

104. Christopher Dickey, "Not Their Finest Hour," *Newsweek*, June 8, 1992, p. 66.

105. Leon V. Sigal, *Reporters and Officials* (Lexington, Mass.: D. C. Heath, 1973), pp. 120–121.

106. Lucy Howard, "Slanted 'Line'?" *Newsweek*, February 13, 1989, p. 6. See also Stephen Hess, *Live from Capitol Hill!*, p. 50. This tendency is less typical of local news. Trivia buffs might ask who has been the subject of the most cover articles in *Time* magazine—Richard Nixon (55). "Numbers," *Time*, March 9, 1998, p. 189.

107. Cook, *Making Laws & Making News*, p. 8.

108. Lichter et al., *The Media Elite*, pp. 21–25. See also Hess, *Live from Capitol Hill!*, Appendix A, pp. 110–130.

109. John Johnstone, Edward Slawski, and William Bowman, *The Newspeople* (Urbana, Ill.: University of Illinois Press, 1976), pp. 225–226.

110. Stanley Rothman and S. Robert Lichter, "Media and Business Elites: Two Classes in Conflict?" *The Public Interest* 69 (1982), pp. 111–125.

111. S. Robert Lichter and Stanley Rothman, "Media and Business Elites," *Public Opinion* (October/November 1981), p. 44.

112. Stephen Hess, *The Washington Reporters* (Washington, D.C.: Brookings Institution, 1981), p. 89; Lichter et al., *The Media Elite*, pp. 127–128.

113. James Fallows, "The Stoning of Donald Regan," *Washington Monthly*, June 1984, p. 57. Most individual reporters also probably care more about their career than ideology, but this could lead to bias. In 1976 one media analyst ran into an old friend, an NBC correspondent. When the analyst asked how she was doing, she answered, "Not so great. My candidate lost." That is, the candidate she had covered during the presidential primaries lost his bid for the nomination. Because reporters often follow "their" presidential candidate into office, she lost her chance to become NBC's White House correspondent. Graeme Browning, "Too Close for Comfort?" *National Journal*, October 3, 1992, p. 2243.

114. Parenti, *Inventing Reality*, pp. 38, 56–57.

115. Mark Hertsgaard, "How Ronald Reagan Turned News Hounds into Lap Dogs," *Washington Post National Weekly Edition*, August 29–September 4, 1988, p. 25.

116. Joel Millman, "How the Press Distorts the News from Central America," *Progressive* (October 1984), p. 20.

117. Epstein, *News from Nowhere*, pp. 206–207. This, however, is less of a problem than it used to be. Hess, *Washington Reporters*.

118. C. Richard Hofstetter, *Bias in the News* (Columbus, Ohio: Ohio State University Press, 1976); Graber, *Mass Media and Politics*, pp. 167–168; Michael J. Robinson, "Just How Liberal Is the News?" *Public Opinion* (February/March 1983), pp. 55–60; Maura Clancy and Michael J. Robinson, "General Election Coverage: Part I," *Public Opinion* 7 (December/January 1985), pp. 49–54, 59; Michael J. Robinson, "The Media Campaign, '84; Part II," *Public Opinion* 8 (February/March 1985), pp. 43–48.

119. Clancy and Robinson, "General Election Coverage"; Robinson, "The Media Campaign '84"; Michael J. Robinson, "Where's the Beef? Media and Media Elites in 1984," in Austin Ranney, ed., *The American Elections of 1984* (Durham, N.C.: Duke University Press, 1985), p. 184; Michael J. Robinson, "News Media Myths and Realities: What Network News Did and Didn't Do in the 1984 General Campaign," in Kay Lehman Schlozman, ed., *Elections in America* (Boston: Allen & Unwin, 1987), pp. 143–170.

120. Ken Auletta, "Inside Story," *New Yorker*, November 18, 1996, p. 55. Most journalists—89%, according to one poll—voted for Clinton over Bush, but after the election the media gave Clinton more negative coverage than they had given Bush in his first 18 months. "Dealing with Bias in the Press," *Civilization*, February/March 1997, pp. 24–27.

121. Patterson, *Out of Order*, p. 131.

122. Ibid., pp. 100–107.

123. "Clinton Gains More Support from Big Papers," *Lincoln Journal-Star* (*New York Times*), October 25, 1992.

124. Stanley Rothman and S. Robert Lichter, "The Nuclear Energy Debate," *Public Opinion* 5 (August/September 1982), pp. 47–48; Stanley Rothman and S. Robert Lichter, "Elite Ideology and Risk

Perception in Nuclear Energy Policy," *American Political Science Review* 81 (June 1987), pp. 383–404.

125. Lichter et al., *The Media Elite*, chapter 7.

126. Sabato, *Feeding Frenzy*, p. 87, and sources cited therein.

127. Robinson, "Just How Liberal Is the News?" p. 59.

128. Bruce Nussbaum, "The Myth of the Liberal Media," *Business Week*, November 11, 1996; Paul Starobin, "Bias Basics," *National Review*, October 28, 1996; Fallows, *Breaking the News*, p. 49.

129. Hofstetter, *Bias in the News;* Hess, *Live from Capitol Hill!*, pp. 12–13.

130. Robinson, "Just How Liberal Is the News?" p. 58; Arthur H. Miller, Edie N. Goldenberg, and Lutz Erbring, "Type-Set Politics," *American Political Science Review* 73 (1979), p. 69; Patterson, *Out of Order*, p. 6; Charles M. Tidmarch and John J. Pitney, Jr., "Covering Congress," *Polity* 17 (Spring 1985), pp. 463–483.

131. Patterson, *Out of Order*, pp. 25, 245.

132. Michael Baruch Grossman and Martha Joynt Kumar, *Portraying the President* (Baltimore: Johns Hopkins University Press, 1981).

133. "Anchorwoman Verdict Raises Mixed Opinions," *New York Times*, August 9, 1983.

134. Theodore H. White, *America in Search of Itself* (New York: Harper & Row, 1982), p. 186.

135. James Fallows, "On That Chart," *Nation*, June 3, 1996, p. 15.

136. George F. Will, "Prisoners of TV," *Newsweek*, January 10, 1977, p. 76.

137. Parenti, *Inventing Reality*, p. 48.

138. David Owen, "The Cigarette Companies: How They Get Away with Murder, Part II," *Washington Monthly*, March 1985, pp. 48–54. Also see Daniel Hellinger and Dennis R. Judd, *The Democratic Facade*, 2d ed. (Belmont, Calif.: Wadsworth, 1994), p. 59. Through the 1920s newspapers refrained from pointing out that popular "patent medicines" were usually useless and occasionally dangerous, because the purveyors bought more advertising than any other business. Mark Crispin Miller, "Free the Media," *Nation*, June 3, 1996, p. 10.

139. Martin A. Linsky, ed., *Television and the Presidential Elections* (Lexington, Mass.: D. C. Heath, 1983).

140. Barry Sussman, "News on TV: Mixed Reviews," *Washington Post National Weekly Edition*, September 3, 1984, p. 37.

141. Bill Carter, "Networks Fight Public's Shrinking Attention Span," *Lincoln Sunday Journal-Star* (New York Times), September 30, 1990.

142. Epstein, *News from Nowhere*, p. 4.

143. William A. Henry III, "Requiem for TV's Gender Gap," *Time*, August 22, 1983, p. 57.

144. Tom Jory, "TV Anchorwoman's Suit Exposes Subtle Bias in Hiring," *Lincoln Journal*, July 31, 1983, p. 1A.

145. Marlene Sanders and Marcia Rock, *Waiting for Prime Time: The Women of Television News* (Urbana, Ill., University of Illinois Press, 1988), pp. 147–148, cited in Hess, *Live from Capitol Hill!*, p. 120.

146. Robinson, "Just How Liberal Is the News?" p. 60.

147. "Tidbits and Outrages," *Washington Monthly*, February 1990, p. 44.

148. Eric Pooley, "Monica's World," *Time*, March 2, 1998, p. 40.

149. Donald Kaul, "The Bad Guys Are Still Winning," *Lincoln Journal Star*, April 4, 1998.

150. Fallows, *Breaking the News*, p. 201.

151. Lawrie Mifflin, "Crime Falls, but Not on TV," *New York Times*, July 6, 1997, p. E3. According to one researcher, crime coverage is also "the easiest, cheapest, laziest news to cover" because stations just listen to the police radio and then send a camera crew to shoot the story.

152. Patterson, *Out of Order*, pp. 53–59 and generally.

153. For 1976 presidential campaign: Thomas E. Patterson, *The Mass Media Election* (New York: Praeger, 1980), p. 24. For 1984 presidential campaign: Henry E. Brady and Richard Johnson, "What's the Primary Message: Horse Race or Issue Journalism?," in Gary R. Orren and Nelson W. Polsby, ed., *Media and Momentum* (Chatham, N.J.: Chatham House, 1987), pp. 127–186. For 1988 presidential campaign: Stephen Ansolabehere, Roy Behr, and Shanto Iyengar, "Mass Media and Elections: An Overview," *American Politics Quarterly* 19 (January 1991), p. 119. For 1992 presidential campaign and in general: Patterson, *Out of Order*. For 1992 congressional campaigns: Charles M. Tidmarch, Lisa J. Hyman, and Jill E. Sorkin, "Press Issue Agendas in the 1982 Congressional and Gubernatorial Election Campaigns," *Journal of Politics* 46 (November 1984), p. 1231.

154. S. Robert Lichter, Daniel Amundson, and Richard Noyes, "The Video Campaign: Network Coverage of the 1988 Primaries" (Washington, D.C.: American Enterprise Institute for Public Policy Research, 1988), p. 65.

155. Lee Sigelman and David Bullock, "Candidates, Issues, Horse Races, and Hoopla: Presidential Campaign Coverage, 1888–1988," *American Politics Quarterly* 19 (January 1991), pp. 5–32. So was emphasis upon human interest. In 1846 the *New York Tribune* described the culinary habits of Representative William "Sausage" Sawyer (D-Oh.), who ate a sausage on the floor of the House every afternoon: "What little grease is left on his hands he wipes on his almost bald head which saves any outlay for Pomatum. His mouth sometimes serves as a finger glass, his shirt-sleeves and pantaloons being called into requisition as a napkin. He uses a jackknife for a toothpick, and then he goes on the floor again to abuse the Whigs as the British party." Cook, *Making Law & Making News*, pp. 18–19.

156. Richard Morin, "Toward the Millenium, by the Numbers," *Washington Post National Weekly Edition*, July 7, 1997, p. 35.

157. Patterson, *Out of Order*, pp. 81–82.

158. Parenti, *Inventing Reality*, p. 15, quoting Malcolm MacDougall, "The Barkers of Snake Oil Politics," *Politics Today* (January/February 1980), p. 35.

159. Fallows, *Breaking the News*, pp. 162, 27.

160. David S. Broder, "Can We Govern?" *Washington Post National Weekly Edition*, January 31–February 6, 1994, p. 23.

161. Kathleen Hall Jamieson, *Dirty Politics: Deception, Distraction, Democracy* (New York: Oxford University Press, 1992), pp. 184–185.

162. Cappella and Jamieson, *Spiral of Cynicism*, p. 30.

163. Kathleen Hall Jamieson, quoted in Fallows, *Breaking the News*, p. 224.

164. Cappella and Jamieson, *Spiral of Cynicism*.

165. Fallows, *Breaking the News*, p. 133.

166. Stanley W. Cloud and Nancy Traver, "Mr. Smith Leaves Washington," *Time*, June 8, 1992, p. 65.

167. Howard Kurtz, "Asleep at the Switch," *Washington Post National Weekly Edition*, December 21–27, 1992, p. 6.

168. Larry Martz, "For the Media, a Pyrrhic Victory," *Newsweek*, June 22, 1992, p. 32. See also Hobart Rowen, "Uncle Sam's Underwriter," *Washington Post National Weekly Edition*, May 15–21, 1989, p. 5.

169. Epstein, *News from Nowhere*, pp. 179, 195.

170. T. R. Reid, "Media Wrong about Yellowstone," *Lincoln Journal* (Washington Post), July 24, 1989.

171. David L. Altheide, "Format and Symbol in Television Coverage of Terrorism in the United States and Great Britain," *International Studies Quarterly* 31 (1987), pp. 161–176.

172. John Horn, "Campaign Coverage Avoids Issues," *Lincoln Sunday Journal-Star,* September 25, 1988.

173. John Eisendrath, "An Eyewitness Account of Local TV News," *Washington Monthly,* September 1986, p. 21.

174. Michael Deaver, "Sound-Bite Campaigning: TV Made Us Do It," *Washington Post National Weekly Edition,* November 7–13, 1988, p. 34.

175. Hess, *Live from Capitol Hill!*, p. 34.

176. Donald L. Shaw and Maxwell E. McCombs, *The Emergence of American Political Issues: The Agenda-Setting Function of the Press* (St. Paul, Minn.: West, 1977). For a review of agenda-setting research, see Everett M. Rogers and James W. Dearing, "Agenda-Setting Research: Where Has It Been, Where Is It Going?" *Communication Yearbook* 11 (Newberry Park, Calif.: Sage, 1988), pp. 555–594.

177. Lutz Erbring, Edie N. Goldenberg, and Arthur H. Miller, "Front-Page News and Real-World Clues: A New Look at Agenda-Setting by the Media," *American Journal of Political Science* 24 (February 1980), pp. 16–49.

178. Michael Bruce MacKuen and Steven Lane Coombs, *More Than News* (Beverly Hills: Sage, 1981), p. 140; Rogers and Dearing, "Agenda-Setting Research," pp. 572–576; G. E. Lang and K. Lang, *The Battle for Public Opinion* (New York: Columbia University Press, 1983), pp. 58–59.

179. Richard Morin, "Public Enemy No. 1: Crime," *Washington Post National Weekly Edition,* January 24–30, 1994, p. 37; Molly Ivins, "Hard Questions, Easy Answers," *Lincoln Journal* (Creators Syndicate), July 7, 1994; Richard Morin, "A Public Paradox on the Drug War," *Washington Post National Weekly Edition,* March 23, 1998, p. 35.

180. Shanto Iyengar and Donald R. Kinder, *News That Matters* (Chicago: University of Chicago Press, 1987), pp. 42–45.

181. Erbring et al., "Front-Page News," p. 38; MacKuen and Coombs, *More Than News,* pp. 128–137.

182. Lichter et al., *The Media Elite,* p. 11.

183. Carl Sessions Stepp, "Establishment Media Have Lost Control of Campaign News Flow," *Lincoln Journal* (Hartford Courant), November 4, 1992.

184. Rogers and Dearing, "Agenda-Setting Research," p. 569; MacKuen and Coombs, *More Than News,* p. 101; Erbring et al., "Front-Page News," p. 38.

185. Rogers and Dearing, "Agenda-Setting Research," p. 577, citing Jack L. Walker, "Setting the Agenda in the U.S. Senate," *British Journal of Political Science* 7 (October 1977), pp. 423–445. See also Cook, *Making Laws & Making News,* pp. 116, 130–131.

186. Michael J. Robinson and Margaret A. Sheehan, *Over the Wire and on TV* (New York: Russell Sage Foundation and Basic Books, 1983); Robinson, "The Media Campaign, '84," pp. 45–47.

187. Thomas Griffith, "Leave Off the Label," *Time,* September 19, 1984, p. 63.

188. After one term, however, Schmitt was defeated by an opponent whose slogan was, "What on Earth has he ever done?"

189. Doris A. Graber, "Kind Pictures and Harsh Words: How Television Presents the Candidates," in Kay Lehman Schlozman, ed., *Elections in America* (Boston: Allen & Unwin, 1987), p. 141.

190. Ibid., p. 116.

191. The discussion of the functions of the media relies heavily on the excellent summary found in Stephen Ansolabehere, Roy Behr, and Shanto Iyengar, "Mass Media and Elections," *American Politics Quarterly* 19 (January 1991), pp. 109–139.

192. Bruce Buchanan, *Electing a President: The Markle Commission Report on Campaign '88* (Austin, Tex.: University of Texas Press, 1990); Montague Kean, *30-Second Politics* (New York: Praeger, 1989). Marion Just, Lori Wallach, and Ann Crigler, "Thirty Seconds or Thirty Minutes: Political Learning in an Election," paper presented at the Midwest Political Science Association Meeting, April 1987, Chicago, Illinois.

193. David Paletz and Robert Entrum, *Media—Power—Politics* (New York: Macmillan, 1981), pp. 35ff.

194. Patterson, *Out of Order,* p. 44.

195. Ansolabehere et al., "Mass Media and Elections," pp. 128–129; Christine F. Ridout, "The Role of Media Coverage of Iowa and New Hampshire in the 1988 Democratic Nomination," *American Politics Quarterly* 19 (January 1991), pp. 45–46, 53–54; Marc Howard Ross, "Television News and Candidate Fortunes in Presidential Nomination Campaigns," *American Politics Quarterly* 20 (January 1992), pp. 69–98.

196. Henry Brady, "Chances, Utilities, and Voting in Presidential Primaries," paper delivered at the Annual Meeting of the Public Choice Society, Phoenix, Arizona, cited in Ansolabehere et al., "Mass Media and Elections"; Bartels, *Presidential Primaries and the Dynamics of Public Choice* (Princeton: Princeton University Press, 1988).

197. Lee Sigelman and Carol K. Sigelman, "Judgments of the Carter-Reagan Debate," *Public Opinion Quarterly* 48 (1984), pp. 624–628.

198. Theodore H. White, *The Making of the President 1960* (New York: Atheneum House, 1961), p. 333.

199. MacKuen and Coombs, *More Than News,* p. 222.

200. For a review, see MacKuen and Coombs, *More Than News,* pp. 147–161.

201. Robert S. Erickson, "The Influence of Newspaper Endorsements in Presidential Elections," *American Journal of Political Science* 20 (May 1976), pp. 207–233.

202. David Barker, "The Talk Radio Community," *Social Science Quarterly* 79 (June 1998), pp. 261–272; C. Richard Hofstetter, "Political Talk Radio, Situational Involvement, and Political Mobilization," *Social Science Quarterly* 79 (June 1998), pp. 273–286.

203. Benjamin I. Page, Robert Y. Shapiro, and Glenn R. Dempsey, "What Moves Public Opinion?" *American Political Science Review* 81 (March 1987), pp. 23–43. Critical news and commentaries about presidents seem to lower their popularity. Darrell M. West, "Television and Presidential Popularity in America," *British Journal of Political Science* 21 (April 1991), pp. 199–214. Even television's "framing" of events, as isolated incidents or parts of patterns, affects viewers' opinions about these events. Shanto Iyengar, *Is Anyone Responsible? How Television Frames Political Issues* (Chicago: University of Chicago Press, 1991).

204. Iyengar, *Is Anyone Responsible?* Chs. 6, 8.

205. Kathleen Hall Jamieson, quoted in Howard Kurtz, "Tuning Out the News," *Washington Post National Weekly Edition,* May 29–June 4, 1995, p. 6; William Raspberry, "Blow-by-Blow Coverage," *Washington Post National Weekly Edition,* November 6–12, 1995, p. 29.

206. Michael J. Robinson, "Public Affairs Television and the Growth of Political Malaise," *American Political Science Review* 70 (1976), pp. 409–432; Miller, Goldenberg, and Erbring, "Type-Set Politics."

207. "Study: Public More Cynical Than Media," *Champaign-Urbana News Gazette (New York Times),* May 22, 1995.

208. Fallows, *Breaking the News,* pp. 202–203.

209. Also, see Cappella and Jamieson, *Spiral of Cynicism*.

210. Graber, *Mass Media*, p. 244; Doris Graber, *Processing News: How People Tame the Information Tide* (New York: Longman, 1984). A 1993 survey concluded that almost half of Americans over 16 have such limited reading and math skills that they are unfit for most jobs. One task the survey included was to paraphrase a newspaper story. Many people could scan the story but not paraphrase it when they finished it. Paul Gray, "Adding Up the Under-Skilled," *Time*, September 20, 1993, p. 75.

211. "The New Political Landscape," *Times Mirror Center for the People & the Press*, October 1994, p. 4.

212. Greider, "Reporters and Their Sources," p. 19.

213. Idea for this paragraph from James Fallows, "Did You Have a Good Week?" *Atlantic Monthly*, December 1994, pp. 32, 34.

214. Iyengar, *Is Anyone Responsible?*

215. Stephen Earl Bennett, "Trends in Americans' Political Information," *American Politics Quarterly* 17 (October 1989), pp. 422–435; Richard Zoglin, "The Tuned-Out Generation," *Time*, July 9, 1990, p. 64.

216. Peters, *How Washington Really Works*, p. 32.

217. Signorile wrote the article for *Outweek*, but before publication that magazine folded and the article was included in *The Advocate*, another homosexual magazine.

218. Signorile, *Queer in America*, p. 145.

219. Ibid., p. 92.

220. Sabato, *Feeding Frenzy*, p. 192.

221. Signorile, *Queer in America*, p. 149.

222. Ibid., pp. 303–304.

223. Ibid., p. ix.

224. Ibid., p. 81.

Working the crowd at a $5000-a-plate fund-raiser.

Ron Haviv, SABA

9 MONEY AND POLITICS

OUTLINE

YOU ARE THERE

Quid Pro Quo? Or No?

You are U.S. Senator Dennis DeConcini.[1] A moderate Democrat, you have represented Arizona since 1976. It is now 1987, and you are facing a decision whether to pressure federal savings and loan (S&L) regulators to go easy on Lincoln Savings and Loan, owned by Charles Keating, your constituent, acquaintance, and campaign donor.

You have known Keating for over a decade. He is a millionaire real estate developer who has, over the years, made generous campaign donations to local, Arizona, and national officeholders. He and his associates gave over $100,000 to campaign funds of Phoenix city council members around 1980, after which they made zoning decisions in his favor. Although Keating is a Republican, he joined your campaign finance committee and raised more than $33,000 for your 1982 campaign. He raised another $48,000 for you between 1985 and 1987 in preparation for your 1988 campaign. You returned the favors. You tried to get President Reagan to appoint Keating ambassador to the Bahamas. Your efforts were rebuffed, probably because Keating earlier had been in trouble with the Securities and Exchange Commission over an alleged bank fraud. And you have called on the president's chief of staff many times to lobby on behalf of a Keating associate for a spot on the Federal Home Loan Bank Board. Now Keating wants you to help him in his fight with the Federal Home Loan Bank Board and its regulators. The board wants to limit the investment activities of Keating's Lincoln Savings and Loan, owned by Keating's Arizona corporation.

Considering this problem, you think about the S & L industry. Before 1980, it was a boring business, investing only in houses. It operated according to the 3-6-3 principle: Offer 3% on savings, loan at 6% for home mortgages, and hit the golf course at 3 P.M.[2] But in the 1970s, inflation cut heavily into the industry's profits; other financial institutions offered much higher interest rates on savings, while charging far more on loans. To help the industry, and at the urging of both Presidents Carter and Reagan, Congress stepped in to deregulate. Deregulation allowed S&L institutions to pay higher interest, and to enable them to raise funds to pay that higher interest, Congress allowed them to invest in anything—from junk bonds to real estate. Then, it allowed S&L depositors to have an unlimited number of accounts, each insured up to $100,000. These moves were expected to make S&Ls more attractive to investors and more lucrative for owners. As President Reagan said in signing some S&L deregulation legislation, "I think we've hit the jackpot."[3]

After the deregulation legislation, the Reagan administration was lax in enforcing the new laws. The S&L regulatory agency, the Federal Home Loan Bank Board, lost half its veteran staff due to budget cuts and poor morale. Those who remained were told by their boss to let S&Ls pretend to be solvent even when they were not, in the hope that they would become stronger eventually.[4]

But two years after deregulation, a new chair of the board feared that insolvent S&Ls were undermining the stability of the whole banking system. The board voted to tighten investment regulations, especially concerning real estate, declaring that only a small proportion of any S&L's investments could be in real estate (most were supposed to be invested in low-risk outlets). This new regulation threatened the stability of S&Ls like Keating's, which had gone overboard in high-risk real estate investments. The board began investigating Keating's S&L, demanding documents and evidence concerning the value of real estate and other investments it had made. By 1987, Keating was complaining that the regulators were harassing his Lincoln S&L.

Keating asks you, along with several other senators, to help him get the regulators off his back. You have mixed feelings about this, though you are basically sympathetic. Helping constituents is part of your job. Keating is not just an average constituent, he is a big fund-raiser and donor to your campaigns. As far as you know, he is an honest businessman. In fact, a managing partner of the prestigious national accounting firm of Arthur Young & Company has written a letter to a fellow senator, John McCain (R-Ariz.), vouching for the Lincoln S&L and charging that it is being harassed by regulators. A respected accountant, Alan Greenspan (later to become chair of the Federal Reserve Bank), has written a letter to several senators also attesting to the S&L's financial health.

On the other hand, there are some warning signals. Your banking aide, an Arizonan whose family is in the S&L business, warns you that Keating takes too many risks. She recommends avoiding him. Others are suspicious too. Senator Jake Garn (R-Utah), for example, has said he will have nothing to do with Keating. Moreover, you are mindful of Senate ethics rules requiring senators to refrain not only from wrongdoing but from conduct giving "the appearance of wrongdoing."[5] While doing favors for constituents is a key element of your job, putting pressure on regulators on behalf of a large campaign contributor could certainly give "the appearance of wrongdoing."

What do you do? Do you help your constituent and campaign donor by trying to get federal regulators to go easy on the Lincoln S&L? That is, do you follow the practice of quid pro quo (tit for tat)? Or do you let the regulatory process work, perhaps closing down the S&L and the parent company in Arizona and angering a rich donor and fund-raiser?

Former Speaker of the House of Representatives Tip O'Neill once said, "There are four parts to any campaign. The candidate, the issues . . ., the campaign organization, and the money. Without money you can forget the other three."[6] Thus, conventional wisdom holds that "money is the mother's milk of politics." But we are not sure if that milk is tainted or pure. On the one hand, without money, candidates or people with new political ideas could never become known in our massive and complex society. Television spreads names and ideas almost instantaneously, so having money to buy television time means your ideas will be heard. In that sense, money contributes to open political debate.

On the other hand, money can be a corrupting influence on politics. At the least, it can buy access to those making decisions. At the worst, it can buy decisions. Money allows some points of view to be trumpeted while others are forced to whisper. Some candidates or groups can afford to spend hundreds of thousands of dollars for each prime-time minute of national television or for prestigious Washington law firms to lobby; others can afford only mimeographs and letters. Money increases inequities in political life.

Money, then, leads to a dilemma in politics. In our largely capitalist society, we expect substantial differences in wealth and income. In most cases, we see nothing wrong when those with great income buy goods and services that others cannot afford. But in politics, many people feel uneasy when those with great wealth are able to buy political favors. We feel so uneasy that we have outlawed certain kinds of buying of political favors, such as politicians paying voters for their votes or interest groups paying politicians and bureaucrats for their support.

But we are uneasy about other ways of limiting the influence of money. Many people feel that individuals or groups should be allowed to contribute as much money to candidates as they want, and that candidates should be permitted to buy as much media time to get their point of view across as they want and can afford. This view holds that contributing money and buying media time are forms of constitutionally guaranteed freedom of speech. The opposite view says that these practices distort the democratic process.

In this chapter, we first focus on the development of laws that regulate how money can influence politics, then we turn to the role and impact of money in elections, and finally we briefly examine conflict of interest on the part of decision makers in Congress and the executive branch.

THE DEVELOPMENT OF LAWS TO REGULATE MONEY AND POLITICS

Concern about the illegitimate influence of money on politics is as old as the Republic. In his campaign for the Virginia House of Burgesses in 1757, George Washington was accused of vote buying. He had given out 28 gallons of rum, 50 gallons of rum punch, 34 gallons of wine, 46 gallons of beer, and 2 gallons of cider.[7] Because there were only 391 voters in his district, he had provided more than a quart and a half of beverages per voter![8]

Obviously, George Washington survived these charges, and his constituents probably survived the effects of the rum and cider. But most discussions of the impact of money on politics were more sober. In his well-known analysis of controlling factions, James Madison, in *Federalist* #10, recognized that "the most common and durable source of factions has been the various and unequal distribution of property." Madison went on to say that although ideally no one should be allowed to make decisions affecting his or her own self-interest, almost any subject of legislation—taxes, tariffs, debts—involves self-interest. For those making laws, "every shilling with which

This Puck cartoon mocks President U.S. Grant's involvement in various corrupt activities. Grant (dressed in the flag suit) is shown supporting various political bosses and profiteers.

The Granger Collection, New York

they overburden the inferior number is a shilling saved to their own pockets."[9]

Madison hoped that the design of the new nation, with the power of the government divided among the branches of government and between the nation and the states, would mean that no one interest or faction would overwhelm the others. The interest of one person or group would check the interest of another.

This view of counterbalancing interests is an optimistic one and has not always worked. Over the decades, Americans have found it necessary to make additional rules to restrict the ways that those with money can try to influence policymakers.

Money in Nineteenth-Century American Politics

The influence of money on politics has shaped several epochs of American history. For example, from the earliest westward expansion of the nation, charges of graft and corruption surrounded the government's sale and giveaway of land. Indeed, the West was developed by giving land to speculators and railroads, sometimes after bribes. When Congress was debating whether to give federal land to the railroads, the lobbyists "camped in brigades around the Capitol building."[10]

The impact of money on political life was probably at its peak in the late nineteenth century. The United States grew from a small agrarian society to a large industrialized one. Oil exploration and refining, the growth of the steel industry, the railroad companies that were spanning the nation, and other large corporations produced many millionaires. This was the era of "robber barons," when the owners of giant corporations (called "trusts") openly bought political favors.

Business contributions to campaigns and to politicians were routine. One railroad president justified bribery of political officials by noting, "If you have to pay money to have the right thing done, it is only just and fair to do so."[11] Mark Hanna, a Republican fundraiser in the presidential election of 1896, assessed banks at a fixed percentage of their capital and also collected substantial sums from most insurance companies and large corporations.[12] However, Cornelius Vanderbilt, one of the wealthiest men of his time, refused to contribute to election campaigns, believing that it was cheaper to buy legislators after they were elected!

Not only did lobbyists bribe politicians, but politicians bribed reporters. In the 1872 presidential campaign, the Republican Party gave money to about 300 reporters in return for favorable coverage.[13]

Early Reforms

Around the turn of the century, the Progressive reformers and their allies in the press, called the **Muckrakers,** began to attack this overt corruption. They wanted to break the financial link between business and politicians. In 1907, a law prohibited corporations and banks from making contributions to political campaigns, and a few years later Congress mandated public reporting of campaign expenditures and set limits on campaign donations. Prohibitions against corporate giving to political campaigns were broadened over time to forbid utilities and labor unions from giving as well.

The **Teapot Dome scandal** of 1921 stimulated further attempts to limit the influence of money on electoral politics. The secretary of the interior in the Harding administration received almost $400,000 from two corporations that then were allowed to lease oil reserves in California and Wyoming (one of them was called the "Teapot Dome"). This led to the Federal Corrupt Practices Act (1925), which required the reporting of campaign contributions and expenditures.

At the turn of the century, rich New Yorkers, wearing vine leaves on their heads, enjoy their wealth.

The Byron Collection, Museum of the City of New York

Because none of these laws was enforced, each had only a momentary effect. Nevertheless, the reforms did seem to make open graft and bribery less acceptable and less common. Instead of outright bribes, political interests now sought to influence politicians through campaign contributions.

Labor unions, for example, set up **political action committees (PACs)** funded from dues. These committees then raised "voluntary" money from members to support candidates for elections. Then many businesses did the same.

THE ROLE OF MONEY IN ELECTION CAMPAIGNS

In 1971, changed conditions caused new laws to be passed.

Campaign Finance Laws

Prompted by the increasing use of television in campaigns, and the increasing cost of buying television time, in 1971 Congress passed a law regulating spending on advertising. The law limited the amount that candidates could donate to their own campaigns and required candidates to disclose the names and addresses of donors of more than $100.

In the course of the Watergate investigations, it became clear that corporations were not abiding by these restrictions. Several corporations secretly funded President Nixon's reelection campaign. For example, Nixon's Justice Department negotiated a settlement favorable to the ITT Corporation in a pending legal dispute soon after an ITT subsidiary gave the Republican National Committee $400,000.[14] Altogether, 21 individuals and 14 corporations were indicted for illegal campaign contributions, mostly but not entirely to the Nixon reelection campaign.

In response to these scandals, Congress again attempted to regulate campaign financing by passing the **Federal Election Campaign Act** in 1974. The following are key provisions of that law, the basics of which, along with individual state laws, regulate campaign finance today:

- Public financing of presidential campaigns. Each candidate is given tax dollars for his or her campaign, as we will see in more detail later.
- Limits on contributions of individuals and committees to campaigns for federal office.
- Limits on overall expenditures by candidates' organizations in presidential campaigns.
- Limits on overall expenditures by national party committees.
- Limits on expenditures by PACs.
- Limits on individual donations to PACs and to individual candidates.

"HONEST GRAFT"

The influence of money on local politics reached a high point in the late nineteenth century. Urban machines used money to cement a complex network of businesses, voters, and political party organizations. Business payoffs to government and party officials for licenses and contracts, and party payoffs to voters for their support, were the norm. Graft was tolerated and even expected.

As we saw in Chapter 6, George Washington Plunkitt was a famous leader of the New York City machine, Tammany Hall. Plunkitt, born in 1842, began life as a butcher's helper and ended up a millionaire through deals made in his role as a party leader and public official. He held a number of state and local public offices; at one point, he held four at the same time. He drew a salary for three of them simultaneously.

Plunkitt's view of graft illustrates the casual attitude about the influence of money on politics common among many of his time:

There's all the difference in the world between [honest graft and dishonest graft]. There's an honest graft, and I'm an example of how it works. I might sum up the whole thing by sayin': "I seen my opportunities and I took 'em."

Just let me explain. . . . My party's in power in the city, and it's goin' to undertake a lot of public improvements. Well, I'm tipped off, say, that they're going to lay out a new park at a certain place. I see my opportunity and take it. I go to that place and I buy up all the land I can in the neighborhood. Then the board of this or that makes its plan public, and there is a rush to get my land, which nobody cared particular for before. Ain't it perfectly honest to charge a good price and make a profit on my investment and foresight? Of course, it is. Well, that's honest graft.

Tammany was beat in 1901 because the people were deceived into believin' that it worked dishonest graft. . . . [They supposed] Tammany men were robbin' the city treasury or levyin' blackmail on disorderly houses, or workin' in with the gamblers and lawbreakers. . . . Why should the Tammany leaders go into such dirty business when there is so much honest graft lyin' around?

. . . I don't own a dishonest dollar. If my worst enemy was given the job of writin' my epitaph . . . he couldn't do more than write: George W. Plunkitt. He Seen His Opportunities, and He Took 'Em.

SOURCE: William L. Riordon, *Plunkitt of Tammany Hall* (New York: E. P. Dutton, 1963).

- Prohibitions on cash contributions of more than $100.
- The establishment of a bipartisan Federal Election Commission to enforce the law.

The 1974 act also imposed limits on spending by candidates' organizations in congressional races and limits on so-called **independent spending,** spending by groups not under the control of candidates. These limits were ruled unconstitutional and no longer obtain, however, a decision that has led to many of the problems with today's campaign finance system.

Because of the importance of money in campaigns, both elected officials and those who want something from the officials have found ways to get around the campaign finance laws.

Loopholes in the Reforms

The objectives of the 1974 law were to make the campaign finance system more open, to limit spending, and to force candidates to be less reliant on a few big donors. The law has not worked as it was intended, however. In 1976, the Supreme Court knocked a hole in it when it ruled that some portions of the act were unconstitutional.[15] In a case brought by an alliance of civil libertarians and conservatives, the Court struck down several spending limits for campaigns that were not publicly funded (in this case congressional campaigns). The Court argued that spending restrictions violated individuals' rights of free speech because spending in a campaign enables candidates to get their message out. Giving money is a form of expression protected by the Constitution.

In addition to the holes knocked into the law by the Supreme Court, it became clear that there were other loopholes in the law. (*Loophole* is a common term for aspects of a law that intentionally or unintentionally limit its effectiveness or restrict its coverage.) One important loophole was created by a little-noticed portion of the law reaffirming the right of unions and corporations to establish PACs using voluntary contributions. Now that there were limitations on the amount of money individuals could give to campaigns, PACs became the vehicle by which individuals could channel more money to their favorite candidates. Individuals could give a limited amount directly to candidates and then give $5,000 to each of several PACs, which in turn could give it to candidates.[16]

PACs quickly sprang up. Business and trade PACs multiplied especially quickly, from around 100 in 1974 to more than 4,700 today. Labor had dominated the PAC game before 1974; now, with fewer than 400 PACs, it finds itself completely outnumbered.

Several other loopholes also have been exploited by candidates, parties, and PACs. Individuals and PACs can avoid most rules and limitations by independent spending. In 1985, the Supreme Court ruled that PACs can spend unlimited amounts working on behalf of issues or candidates, publicly funded or not, as long as they do not give funds directly to parties or candidates.[17]

The Court assumed this spending would be meaningfully independent. However, "independent spending" often is done by organized groups with indirect links to the candidate. Today, interest groups and political parties themselves also can spend as much as they want as long as they are not actually campaigning for a candidate. Instead, they can engage in "issues advocacy" even if it only helps candidates of one party. In 1996, for instance, the AFL-CIO spent as much as $35 million on an advertising campaign urging support for many of President Clinton's priorities. The union targeted its television ads at congressional districts with Republican incumbents.[18] Because contributions to groups engaged in "issues advocacy" are not limited by law, large donors can provide a great deal of indirect support to candidates for office without violating laws limiting campaign contributions.

In addition to the independent spending loophole, there is also the **soft money** loophole. Donors who want to give more than their legal federal maximum can give to national party committees, which channel to state parties, which spend under less stringent state regulations. Soft money need not be reported to the federal government nor, sometimes, to the states.

Soft money is used for such things as voter registration drives, direct mailings, polling, and advertisements for nonfederal party candidates. Soft money, including union dues and corporate funds, also can be used at the federal level by national party committees for capital improvements such as new buildings and computers and for political advertising. Private donors and corporations also pay a large proportion of the costs of each party's national convention.

The soft money loophole allows people with money to spend as much as they want on their favorite presidential candidate or party. For 1996, the Democrats received $120 million in soft money from special interests, the Republicans $140 million. Sometimes the parties resort to questionable tactics to raise money. In late 1995, Republican National Committee chairman Haley Barbour sent letters to lobbyists offering incentives for contributing to the party. A contributor could be photographed with the GOP presidential candidates or have drinks in a private skybox at the Republican convention, depending on the size of the contribution. Dinner with President Clinton and Vice President Gore or visits to the White House were among the carrots the Democratic National Committee dangled in front of potential donors. As one observer commented, "Soft money is where rich people can play again."[19]

Yet another loophole is sometimes called "back pocket PACS." Members of Congress organize their own PACS and register them only at the state level. Since many states have lax campaign finance laws, this allows these state-registered PACs to receive contributions that are illegal under federal law, for example, from corporations and labor unions. Charles Keating's corporation gave $200,000 to a back pocket PAC run by John Glenn (D-Ohio).[20]

A final problem with the campaign finance laws is that inflation has changed the real value of the contribution and spending limits. The amount each candidate can spend does increase with inflation, but no other part of the system is indexed to inflation. The maximum $1,000 contribution is now worth only $340 in 1974 dollars. Thus, the contribution limits are unrealistically low.

How the System Works

PRESIDENTIAL ELECTIONS

Presidential candidates who accept public financing, as most do, may not spend more than $33 million to get the nomination (the money comes from a voluntary checkoff of $3 on individuals' tax returns; the spending limit increases each year to take inflation into account). Candidates who do not accept public funding, such as Ross Perot, can spend as much as they can raise. Once candidates receive their parties' nominations, public funding pays them each about $61 million for the general election campaign (also adjusted each election for inflation), and they can accept several million more from their party's national committee. At this point, fund-raising is supposed to be officially over for the candidates.

In fact, the 1996 election demonstrated that the federal election laws no longer have any practical effect. The soft money loophole and the independent spending loophole mean, in the words of one observer, that "The system we created in the 1970s has essentially collapsed. . . . It's the Wild West out there. It's anything goes."[21]

Because of the soft money loophole, national party organizations can collect as much money as they want from donors who can give as much as they want. The party organizations then spend the money largely for national television advertisements. The Democrats launched a huge advertising campaign using this device, and the Republicans responded with their own, eventually outspending the Democrats.[22] Advertisements funded with soft money are technically supposed to focus on issues, not the candidates, and are not to mention a specific election. This restriction is truly a fig leaf. As a spokesperson for the National Rifle Association commented, "It is foolish to believe there is any practical difference between issue advocacy and advocacy of a political candidate. What separates [them] is a line in the sand drawn on a windy day."

The Democrats' ads prominently featured Clinton. And the Republican National Committee made a 60-second advertisement for the Dole campaign; 56 seconds dealt with Dole's life, 4 seconds with issues. The ad was not challenged. And as Dole explained, "It never says

SELLING ACCESS TO THE WHITE HOUSE

Following the 1996 elections, the Lincoln Bedroom in the White House became a staple of editorial writers and late-night comedians. To raise soft money for the Democratic National Committee and thus for his campaign, President Clinton had invited big donors to the White House to have coffee with him and, in some cases, to stay overnight. Vice President Gore made phone calls from the White House soliciting funds. These and other revelations about fund-raising practices prompted new calls for campaign finance reform and for an independent investigation of Democratic fund-raising practices.

But as any student of campaign finance knows, these examples are only variants of practices that are endemic. Soft money is an ever growing loophole that has made campaign finance laws irrelevant. And selling access appears to be routine in both hard money and soft money fund-raising.

Republicans were the first to formally reward large soft money donations when, in 1975, they established the Republican Eagles. In exchange for a gift of $10,000 or more, members were invited to presidential functions at the White House. Donors of $2,500 or more could meet the Reagans and "wander through the entire second floor of the White House."[1] By 1988, the Republicans, reflecting increased costs of campaigns, had created "Team 100," with a gift of $100,000 the minimum for entrance. Eight members were made ambassadors when Bush was elected to office. A study showed that companies of Team 100 givers enjoyed "a clear pattern of favorable government treatment" including action on criminal charges and awarding of federal grants.[2] The Democrats responded with their own $100,000 group during the 1988 campaign but, of course, had no federal largesse to dispense, having lost the election.

Given the clear Republican success in fund-raising (Republicans have outspent Democrats in every modern presidential election including 1996), and with the Democrats' failure to raise money from smaller givers in 1992 (a direct-mail campaign raised $9 million from middle- and working-class donors but cost $8 million), President Clinton believed Democrats must radically improve their fund-raising capacity to win the 1996 election. He apparently agreed with his experts that enticements such as personal access to the White House and to him were necessary.

One journalist-expert on campaign finance arranged recent campaign finance activities into five categories. Though partly tongue-in-cheek, these categories illustrate just how confusing and probably non-commonsensical current finance laws are.[3] *"Tacky but Legal."* Sleepovers at the White House, as long as no solicitations for contributions took place, are legal. However, the degradation of a national shrine into a national joke is an unhappy side effect of these activities.

"Offensive and Questionable." White House coffees with President Clinton meeting donors are ethically offensive and legally questionable, even if the idea is not new. They seem particularly offensive if the donors had specific policy interests for which they are lobbying the government. And they are legally questionable because campaign donations that result in "any benefit" for the giver from the recipient are illegal.

"Possibly Illegal but No Big Deal." President Clinton and Vice President Gore made phone calls from the White House soliciting donors. Conceivably, this is illegal, because there is to be no fund-raising on federal property. For example, members of Congress cannot solicit funds from their offices. (At least one drives around the Capitol in his car using his cell phone.) However, the Justice Department in the 1970s declared the president's part of the White House "private," and this may stretch to cover the vice president too (though the vice president lives elsewhere). As the noted late-night political analyst (!) Jay Leno has joked, "Where do you expect the president to make fund-raising phone calls from—the local 7-11?"

"Seriously Troubling." There is nothing *illegal* about the president or vice president dialing for dollars. However, many people believe that it is clearly *inappropriate* for them to do this. Yet members of Congress routinely do this too.

"Over the Line." One of the most troubling aspects of the Democratic fund-raising activities in 1996 was the number of donors with unsavory backgrounds who bought access. One was a convicted felon, another an arms dealer. Individuals with specific policy interests were admitted to the White House repeatedly. One such individual, who paid $300,000 to the Democratic National Committee and was promoting a plan to build an oil pipeline in Central Asia, later told congressional investigators: "Sure I bought my way in. What of it?"[4] He then proceeded to reveal that, though he was invited to six functions at the White House, he did not get a private meeting with Clinton nor support for his pipeline. But would he donate again? Yes, because other oil company executives were there and "Now they know [I was] also there so they can't bluff me."

Even if all that is being bought and sold is access, access is worth something. If access did not influence policy, most people would not be trying to buy it.

Even if no favors were exchanged for money and nothing illegal transpired, most Americans probably believe that these activities are unethical and unbecoming a president. Indeed, the most troubling activities are the ones that are apparently legal. If the public believes such activities should be cleaned up, voters must elect members of Congress who agree. Otherwise, campaign finance activities will continue to provide material for cartoonists and comedians and embarrassment for public officials.

1. Quoted in Jane Mayer, "Inside the Money Machine," *New Yorker*, February 3, 1997, p. 34.
2. Ibid., p. 35.
3. The following paragraphs are drawn from Elizabeth Drew, "Washington's Scandal Scale," *Washington Post National Weekly Edition*, March 31, 1997, pp. 21–22. The categories are hers.
4. Clarence Page, "The Real Scandal in Campaign Finance Probe Is What's Still Legal," *Lincoln Journal-Star* (Chicago Tribune syndication), September 27, 1997.

that I'm running for President. I hope that it's fairly obvious since I'm the only one in the picture."[23]

Raising soft money for the campaign became a nearly full-time job for Clinton in 1996. Indeed he complained "I can't do anything but go to fund-raisers and shake hands. . . . I can't focus on a thing but the next fund-raiser."[24]

The other means by which the 1974 campaign finance law has been shredded is through independent spending. Major lobbying groups can raise and spend millions of dollars, using the money for advertisements on behalf of a specific candidate. In the 1996 election, organized labor spent $35 million, the majority on radio and TV advertisements. Interest groups, together, spent $135 million.[25]

Unfortunately, we have come full circle back to the conditions that led to the campaign finance reforms. As one observer indicated, "The fat cats have returned."[26]

CONGRESSIONAL ELECTIONS

Candidates for Congress rely on three sources of funding: PAC contributions, individual donations, and donations from their political parties. PAC contributions make up about half the funds for House seats and a quarter for Senate seats (Figure 1). Over time, PAC funds have grown in importance to candidates.

PACS There are vast differences in the funding activity of PACs. Although there are 4,700 PACs, about one-third do not contribute to any candidates, while about 400 give over $100,000 in total (Figure 2). Less than 10% of the PACs account for three-fourths of all PAC donations. Thus, the number of key PACs is relatively small. Some of the biggest spenders include well-known groups such as the National Rifle Association, the Teamsters, and the American Medical Association. But they also include less well-known groups such as the Association of Trial Lawyers, the American Federal-State-County-and-Municipal Employees, and the American Institute of CPAs.[27]

PACs differ in the targets of their donations, but some patterns are clear. PACs show a distinct preference for Republicans in the presidential races and for incumbents—Republicans or Democrats—in congressional races. PACs usually want to give to the can-

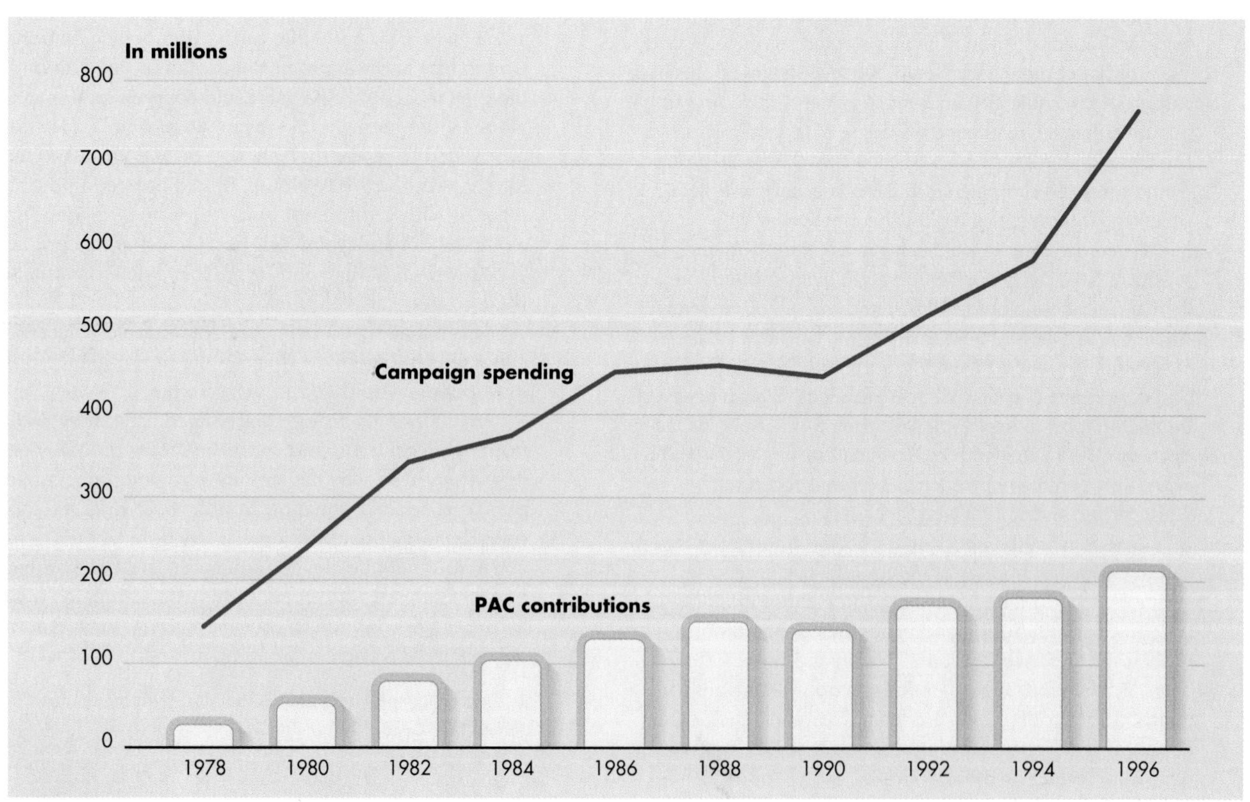

FIGURE 1

The Dough Rises: Congressional Campaign Spending

Congressional campaign spending rose sharply in the 1990s after slow growth in the 1980s. It came close to $1 billion in 1996.

Note: These data include only "hard money" reported to the Federal Election Commission.

SOURCES: We borrowed the title from EMILY's List Newsletter (May 1988). Data are from the Federal Election Commission (www.fec.gov/press/releases.htm).

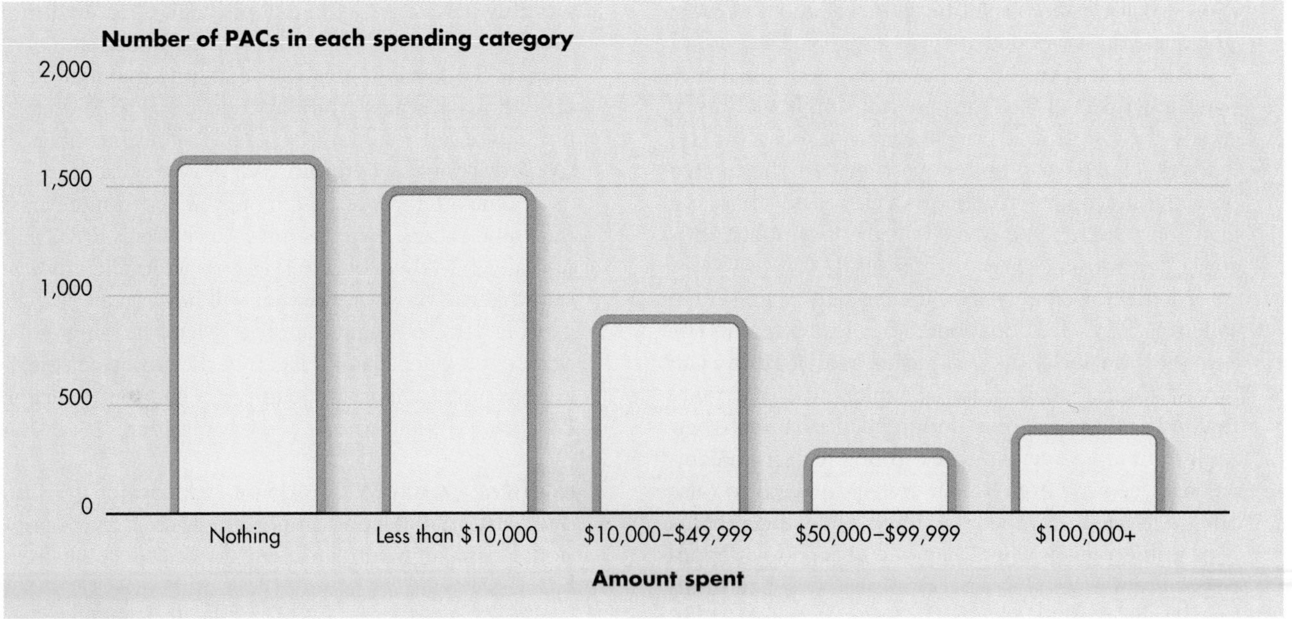

FIGURE 2

PAC Spending Levels Vary Greatly

SOURCE: Larry Makinson and Joshua Goldstein, *Open Secrets: The Encyclopedia of Congressional Money and Politics* (Washington, D.C.: Congressional Quarterly, Inc., 1994).

didate they believe will win so they will have access to a policymaker.

If they guess wrong, PACs often give to the winner *after* the election, a practice called "catching the late train." After the surprise Republican victories in the 1994 congressional elections, PACs raced to help winning Republicans pay their campaign debts (Figure 3). As one noted, "We gave to Democrats because they were in control, and we're likely to do the same for Republicans. The balance of power has shifted, and those who affect our company and our customers are in another party."[28] After the election, health care lobbyists paid $1,000 each to attend a breakfast for Republican Senate winner Fred Thompson (Tenn.) although many had contributed to Thompson's opponent before the election. During the election campaign, Newt Gingrich (R-Ga.) warned PACs that if the Republicans took power, those not on board would "suffer the two coldest years in Washington."

Although the majority of PACs are business related and are ideologically much more sympathetic to the Republicans, before 1994 PACs gave predominantly to the Democrats because they were the majority party. Now that the Republicans control both houses of Congress, PAC money is split even more lopsidedly in favor of the Republicans. For the majority of PACs, conservative ideological sentiment and the practical politics of supporting incumbents both point to the Republicans.[29]

What other criteria aside from incumbency guide PAC donations?[30] Most PACs give money to members in districts where the PACs have a substantial interest, such as a large number of union members for a union PAC or a large factory for a corporate PAC.

PACs also target contributions to members of key congressional committees. For example, PACs organized by defense contractors give disproportionately to members who serve on the Armed Services Committees, which have a big role in deciding what weapons to purchase. Unions and shipping companies involved in the maritime industry give large sums to those on the House Merchant Marine and Fisheries Committee and its Senate counterpart, Commerce, Science, and Transportation.[31] Members of congressional committees that specialize in tax law (Ways and Means, and Finance) and business regulations (Commerce) receive generous contributions from business PACs.

Women's PACs, including EMILY's List, one of 1992's biggest spending PACs, are unusual in focusing most of their money on nonincumbents. Their goal is to get more women elected, which means supporting nonincumbents with strong chances of winning.

SPECIAL INTERESTS AS VICTIMS? PAC contributions to congressional campaigns are products of mutual need. PACs need access to and votes of members of Congress, and members of Congress need (or think they need) large sums of money to win elections. Thus,

PAC donations are useful to members and to PACs. The question is whether they are useful to the public.

Although PACs try to buy access and sometimes votes, members of Congress are not simply victims of greedy PACs. Indeed, as one recent observer remarked, "There may be no question that the money flowing into campaign coffers is a crime. But there is a question whether the crime is bribery of public officials or extortion of private interests."[32]

Members themselves are increasingly aggressive in soliciting PACs for donations. They fear defeat in the next election and think that raising a lot of money can protect them. Senators, for example, must raise more than $18,000 each week during all six years of their term to fund an average-cost winning reelection campaign. A senator from a high-cost state needs to raise $60,000 a week. On the other hand, many incumbents raise millions even when they face little-known opponents. Phil Gramm (R-Tex.) continued to solicit funds from lobbyists even after he had raised more than $6 million and his opponent had only $20,000.

Thirty years ago most fund-raising by members of Congress was done in their home districts. Members did not want their constituents to think they were influenced by Washington lobbyists. Today, half of the PAC funds raised are raised in Washington.[33] Members of Congress continually hold fund-raisers to which dozens of lobbyists for PACs are invited. Well-known lobbyists get hundreds of invitations to congressional fund-raisers every year.[34] Indeed, the number of these events is so large that a private company sells a special monthly newsletter listing all of them. One Washington insider says of being asked by incumbents to give money, "Unless you give your max [the maximum the law allows], unless you lay out your $5,000 at a fundraiser, you don't have access. . . . They [members of Congress] don't ever return your phone calls."[35]

Some attempts to raise money are even more crass than fund-raisers. Some members keep lists of PACs that have given to them on their desks as an implicit indication that it is those groups that will have access. Others play one PAC off against another. Members might tell a representative of a bank PAC that they received contributions from savings and loan PACs and that the bank PAC should contribute or possibly miss out.[36]

NON-PAC SOURCES OF FUNDS Donations from individuals are a second important source of congressional campaign funds. Large donations come from business executives, entertainers, and lawyers.

Party organizations, such as the Democratic Congressional Campaign Committee and its Republican counterpart and the Republican Senate Campaign Committee and its Democratic counterpart, are the third source of funds. These party groups together gave almost $600 million in hard money in the 1996 campaign.

There is no question that the nature of raising money for campaigns has changed. Whatever the problems with the current system, however, we should be careful not to contrast it with an idealized version of the past. After all, almost 100 years ago Mark Twain observed: "It could probably be shown by facts and fig-

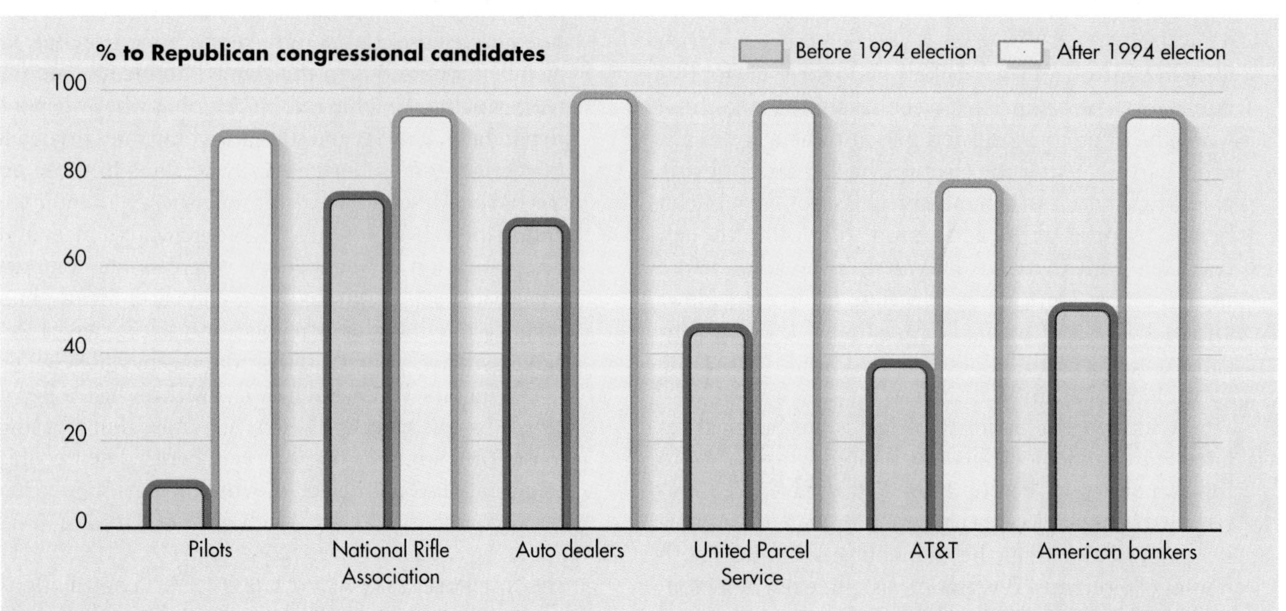

FIGURE 3

PACs Give Postelection Donations to Winners

SOURCE: Jonathan Salant and David Cloud, "To the '94 Election Victors Go the Fund Raising Spoils," *Congressional Quarterly*, April 15, 1995, p. 1056.

ures that there is no distinctly native American criminal class except Congress." Big interests always have had influence and access in Washington. The ways in which they exercise that influence are different now. In some ways, this influence is more open because the campaign finance reforms have made public the organizations working for special interests and the money they spend doing it. Thirty years ago we would not have known how much each member of Congress received from each lobbying group; today we do.

THE IMPACT OF CAMPAIGN MONEY

We have discussed several aspects of money in elections: how much there is, who contributes it, and how they do so. Now we turn to the question of what difference campaign money makes. An obvious question is whether money influences the outcomes of elections. But we also will focus on three other kinds of potential effects of money and the way it is raised: the recruitment of good candidates, the policy decisions of elected leaders, and the cynicism of the public.

Does the Campaign Finance System Deter Good Candidates?

When John Glenn, an unsuccessful Democratic candidate in 1984, was asked whether running for president had been worth it despite his defeat, Glenn replied: "My family was humiliated. I got myself whipped. I gained 16 pounds. And I'm more than $2.5 million in debt. Except for that, it was wonderful."[37] In 1998, nearing the end of his career, Glenn remarked in a similar vein: "I'd rather wrestle a gorilla than ask anyone for another 50 cents."[38]

Other presidential candidates have lamented the difficulties and humiliations of having to raise money; Jack Kemp, Richard Cheney, and Dan Quayle, all potential 1996 presidential candidates, bowed out early in 1995 indicating that the magnitude of necessary fund-raising was one reason.

The necessity of raising a lot of money deters congressional candidates too. As one leading congressional scholar noted, "Raising money is, by consensus, the most unpleasant part of a campaign. Many candidates find it demeaning to ask people for money and are uncomfortable with the implications of accepting it."[39] Senator Brock Adams (D-Wash.), who had served in the House until 1976 and then ran a decade later for the Senate, was shocked at the changes in fund-raising. "I never imagined how much of my personal time would be spent on fund raising. . . . I do not think a candidate for the U.S. Senate should have to sit in a motel room in Goldendale, Washington, at 6 in the morning and spend three hours on the phone talking to political action committees."[40] And, once elected, many new members of Congress are surprised and chagrined to find that they must begin raising funds for their next campaign almost before they are sworn into office.

Does Money Win Elections?

Money helps win elections, but other factors also determine the outcomes. The evidence is mixed as to the impact of money on winning presidential primaries. Some candidates are never considered serious because they do not have sufficient money to mount a large campaign. In that sense, money is crucial. But money alone cannot win. Sometimes the biggest spenders get nowhere. Beyond some point, money might not matter as much. Some analyses have shown that spending by the major Democratic and Republican presidential primary candidates in each state bears little relationship to whether or not they won that state.[41]

By the time presidential candidates are nominated, they already have spent a great deal. The name recognition achieved during the primaries and at the national conventions carries into the general election campaign. Presidential candidates receive extensive free media coverage in news stories. The amount that they spend after the convention is less likely to be as crucial. This is just as well for the health of the two-party system, because if money determined elections, the Republicans would have won every presidential election since World War II. However, of the presidential elections lost by the Democrats during that time, probably only the election of 1968 between Richard Nixon and Hubert Humphrey was close enough that it might have turned out differently had the Democrats been able to spend more.[42] When the elections are close, as in 1968, the Republicans definitely have the advantage by having more money.[43]

In congressional races, incumbents usually start with a huge advantage. Their name is recognized by many of their constituents. Challengers must buy media to achieve similar recognition. Thus, the ability of the challenger to raise and spend money is crucial. As Figure 4 shows, challengers to incumbents have a very low probability of winning unless they raise $500,000 or more. Every $10,000 spent by a House challenger increases his or her vote total by more than 2%. The amount of money incumbents spend seems unrelated to whether they win or not. As challengers spend more, so do incumbents.[44]

Recent elections offer contrasting lessons about the impact of money on elections. The two biggest spenders in the 1994 Senate races, Michael Huffington (R-Cal.) and Oliver North (R-Va.), both lost, as did four of the top six House spenders.[45]

But in 1992, supposedly an anti-incumbent year, 26 of 27 Senate incumbents outspent their challengers, and 23 were reelected. In 1994, another anti-incumbent year, over 90% of House incumbents were reelected, and most had a substantial funding advantage. Nonetheless, 34 Democratic incumbents lost in part because the Republican challengers were much better funded than most previous challengers.

Indeed, the fact that most challengers cannot raise the amounts of money that incumbents have readily available is probably an important reason most House incumbents get reelected. In 1990, for example, only 35 House incumbents faced opponents who raised as much as half the amount the incumbent did.

Does Money Buy Favorable Policies?

Donors are not a random cross section of the public. Even including donors who gave as little as $200 to a candidate, donors are considerably older, more likely to be white males, and have much higher incomes than most Americans. Indeed, over 80% had incomes over $100,000, and 20% had incomes over $500,000.

FIGURE 4

A Challenger's Success Is Related to Spending

SOURCE: Larry Makinson and Joshua Goldstein, *Open Secrets: The Encyclopedia of Congressional Money and Politics* (Washington, D.C.: Congressional Quarterly, Inc., 1994).

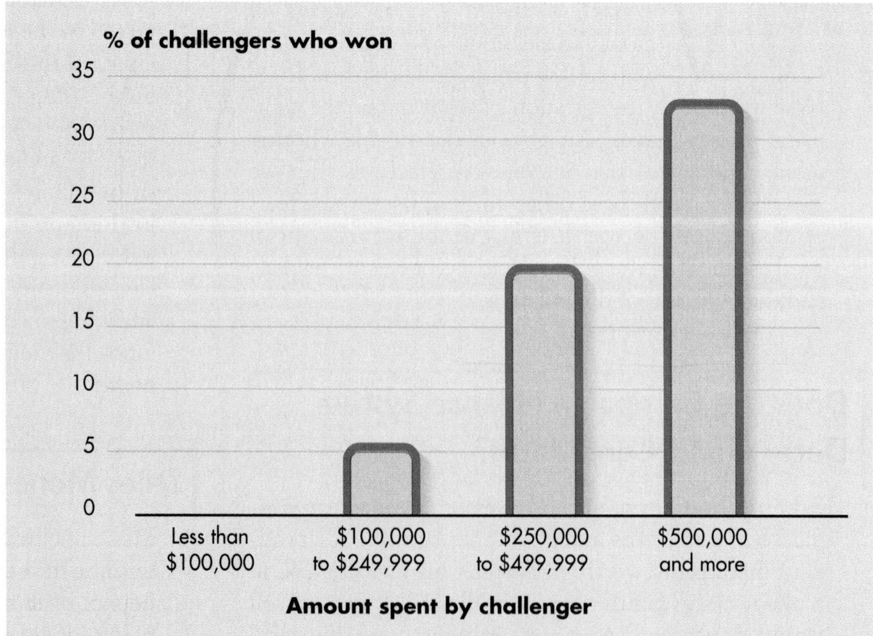

"I appreciate your offer, but I'm afraid I'm already bought and paid for."

More than half had recently talked to their congressional representative.

So money seems to buy access, and that access is by the wealthiest segment of the population, whose views on public issues are not necessarily representative of the larger population.

If money buys access, does it also buy votes? Both anecdotal and systematic evidence suggest that money does buy votes, although only under some conditions.

Money is not likely to buy votes on issues that are highly publicized, because legislators' constituents usually have strong views on these issues and legislators feel pressured to follow them.[46] For the same reason, money is less likely to buy roll-call votes on the floor of each house than votes in committees. The former are public and recorded; the latter are not as visible to the public. Compared to their activity on the floor, in committees, legislators with PAC support are more active in speaking and negotiating on behalf of the PAC's positions and offering amendments that reflect these positions.[47]

Money is also not likely to buy votes on moral issues, because legislators themselves often have firm views on these issues. These sorts of issues (abortion and school prayer, for example) also tend to be publicized.

But most matters that come to a vote are neither highly publicized nor moral issues. Most are relatively technical matters that constituents and legislators do not care as strongly about as do PACs. For these, members are susceptible. "You can't buy a Congressman for $50,000. But you can buy his vote," a member admitted. "It's done on a regular basis."[48]

One survey of members found that about one-fifth admit that political contributions have affected their votes on occasion, and another one-third are not sure.[49] Analysis of voting has revealed that contributions from the AFL-CIO affected voting on the minimum wage legislation, and contributions from the trucking interests led senators to vote against deregulation of trucking. Those senators facing reelection the year in which the vote was taken were most susceptible.[50] Voting is also related to donations in such disparate areas as minimum wage legislation, gun control, and regulation.[51]

One classic example concerns used-car legislation. Auto dealers spent $675,000 in the 1980 congressional elections. This investment seemed to pay off in 1982 when Congress voted against a rule requiring dealers to inform prospective buyers of any known defects in used cars. The senators who opposed the measure received twice as much money from the auto dealers' PAC as those who voted for it. In the House, those who opposed the measure received on average five times as much money as those who voted for it. Almost 85% of the representatives opposing the legislation had received PAC money.[52]

The relationship between PAC money and votes still existed even when the party and ideology of the members were taken into account. For conservatives, who might have voted against requiring auto dealers to list defects anyway, PAC contributions made only a marginal difference in their voting; but for liberals, PAC money substantially raised the probability that

MAILING FOR DOLLARS

The Environmental Defense Fund once sent out a mass fund-raising mailing promising new members a copy of the book *50 Simple Things You Can Do to Save the Earth.* The book's number-one suggestion: stop junk mail. Ironically, environmental groups, like others, fill mailboxes with junk mail, which eventually amounts to 3% of the volume in our landfills.

PACs and political parties soliciting members and funds send out hundreds of millions of letters annually. For example, the National Rifle Association sends 12 million letters monthly, and the American Association of Retired People sends 50 million a year just prospecting for new members.[1]

Most people look forward to mail more than other daily activities such as television, eating, and hobbies.[2] Mail solicitations for money by PACs and other political groups provide an interesting diversion. Many read the letters, are convinced by the arguments, and write checks.

Getting a good response from mail solicitations appears to be both an art and a science. Here are some of the tricks of the trade used by successful PACs.

The *mailing list* is one key to success. Letters are not sent out randomly. Mailing lists of potential contributors are shared among like-minded groups, so you are likely to receive such mailings if you have already contributed to a candidate or cause or even if you buy goods from mail-order catalogs. One estimate is that average Americans in professional occupations spend eight months of their lives simply opening and sorting political and business junk mail.

The *envelope* should be personalized, with real stamps, not metered ones. Often the words URGENT or REPLY REQUIRED stimulate a better response. One PAC sent out a mailing with the words FEDERAL TAX REDUCTION INFORMATION ENCLOSED prominently displayed on the envelope (the PAC letter dealt with the activities of a PAC working to reduce taxes).

The *letter* often is written on expensive-looking paper. The text is written in short paragraphs at the sixth- to eighth-grade level to capture the reader's attention. On the other hand, the letter is often fairly long. Four pages is typical, but many are longer.

The *opening paragraph* is usually an attention grabber such as, "I need your advice," or "This is the most urgent letter I have ever written."[3]

The *language* is usually emotional, overblown, and very negative. One 1995 Democratic fund-raising letter called Newt Gingrich a terrorist (the authors later apologized). The National Rifle Association's labeling of government agents as "jackbooted thugs" caused former President Bush to resign his membership. One NCPAC letter from Jesse Helms warned, "Your tax dollars are being used to pay for grade school courses that teach our children that cannibalism, wife swapping, and the murder of infants and the elderly are acceptable." Campaigning against PACs, an independent action PAC IAPAC warned that "money doesn't just talk, it leads many elected officials around on a leash."

Mailers use a personal approach, and their letters are sprinkled with "you"s. A mailing from the National Taxpayers Union offered instructions as to how "you can save America from Washington." Well-heeled PACs sometimes use computers to intersperse your name throughout the letter.

Enclosures are common. Solicitors often promise you something for your membership or send along a small gift, such as a signed picture, stickers, or a pin. "While trying to appeal to you with flattery for your intelligence and compassion, direct mail packages are designed on the assumption you are a self-indulgent idiot," commented one observer of the direct-mail scene.

A *donor card* is crucial. Cards are enclosed to make it easy for recipients to give. This card can be pretty emotional, too. For example, one conservative PAC offered recipients two choices on the donor card. If they contributed to the PAC, they could stick a stars and stripes flag on the card. If they refused to contribute, they should stick on the white flag of surrender!

1. Jill Smolowe, "Read This!!!!!!!!" *Time,* November 26, 1990, p. 63.
2. Larry Sabato, "Mailing for Dollars," *Psychology Today* 18 (October 1984), pp. 38–43. This box draws heavily on the Sabato article.
3. Sabato, "Mailing for Dollars." The remainder of the quotations are from this article, unless otherwise noted.

they would vote with the used-car dealers.[53] " 'Of course it was money,' one House member said. . . . 'Why else would they vote for used-car dealers?' "[54]

The relationship between PAC contributions and voting should not be exaggerated, however.[55] Even on these low visibility votes, a member's party and ideology are important. The constituency interests of members are also key factors explaining votes. For example, members with many union workers in their districts are going to vote for those interests regardless of how much or little they get in PAC contributions.[56] Members without these constituents, though, may be more swayed by PAC contributions.

Money not only can help buy votes and access, it can buy congressional influence with federal regulators. This type of influence is well illustrated by the relationship of Charles Keating and Senator DeConcini outlined earlier in this chapter. While this was an extreme case of favor giving, as long as members feel dependent on big donors for campaign funds, these "favors" are likely to remain common.

Although research on the impact of PAC contributions on the behavior of members of Congress is plentiful, we know less about how contributions affect the policies of presidential candidates. Large donations to presidential campaigns may be given in the hopes of buying access, but using money to win influence over presidential candidates is probably less successful than it is with other officials. Presidential candidates tend to have widely publicized views, and their actions as president are subject to intense scrutiny and publicity. Once in office presidents need donors less than donors need them, thus making the leverage of a campaign donation uncertain. Contributors sometimes find, as did one contributor to the campaign of Teddy Roosevelt, "We bought the son of a bitch but he did not stay bought."[57]

Still, analyses of large donors to, and fund-raisers for, the Bush campaign reveal that many were given special favors or benefits from the federal government. The Department of Labor reduced a proposed fine by nearly 90% against a large sugar farmer who gave \$200,000 to the campaign.[58] The president proposed incentives for using corn-based ethanol in auto fuels, a proposal that would cost consumers three-tenths of a cent per gallon of gas purchased and yield Archer-Daniels-Midland, which gave the Republican campaign more than \$1 million, a profit of \$30 to \$75 million.

While it is impossible to prove a cause-and-effect relationship in these cases, clearly large donors who expect favorable treatment have plenty of precedents to lead them to that conclusion. Thus, the leader of a watchdog group said, "The point is, we're not just electing politicians. . . . We're also electing their patrons and their priorities."[59]

The influence of big money in presidential campaigns probably makes both parties more conservative.

Dan Foote/Pen Tip

The biggest contributors to the Republicans in the last few presidential elections have been some of the most conservative people within that party. The big money contributors to the Democrats are, on the whole, less liberal than the mainstream of the party.

Some Democratic House leaders were surprised when members said they could not vote against a capital gains tax cut (which would benefit the wealthy) because it would anger their business contributors. "I get elected by voters. I get financed by contributors. Voters don't care about this, contributors do."[60]

Large contributions to presidential campaigns often lead to appointments to public office, especially ambassadorships. The "spoils system," as it is called, has been with us since at least the time of Andrew Jackson, so it cannot be blamed on modern PACs and soft money.

Campaign Money and Public Cynicism

We have seen repeatedly that public confidence and trust in government have diminished greatly over time. Some of the reasons for this declining trust have nothing to do with money. But public trust was certainly affected by the Watergate scandal, and it is likely that revelations about big money lobbying activity since then have not improved the public's view of the honesty of public officials.

The current system appears to play a part in alienating voters and reducing voting turnouts. Even if we believe that no votes are actually bought, the appearance of conflicts of interest that permeates the existing system and clearly disturbs the public should give pause to those interested in the health of our political system.

Walter Lippman, a famous American journalist, once said that American communities govern themselves "by fits and starts of unsuspecting complacency and violent suspicion." We think nothing is wrong, and

INTO THE 21ST CENTURY

CAMPAIGN FINANCE REFORM

Whether to regulate or ban large donations to political candidates is an issue that has been debated throughout the twentieth century. The intensity of the debate has risen to new levels at the end of the twentieth century and will likely continue into the twenty-first.

The concentration of fund-raising efforts on Washington lobbyists increasingly gives the appearance, and perhaps the reality, of simply buying elections and then votes. The conservative *Wall Street Journal* colorfully described the system in Washington as "the mutants' saloon in 'Star Wars'—a place where politicians, PACs, lawyers, and lobbyists for unions, business, or you-name-it shake each other down full time for political money and political support."[1]

Some observers believe that campaign finance should be deregulated. They believe that the best strategy is to allow individuals, PACs, corporations, and unions to give as much as they want to whom they want, but require each candidate to disclose, for each gift, who donated and how much they gave. By having full disclosure, members of the public would be informed about whom the candidate might be beholden to, and cast votes accordingly. Supporters of this approach argue for daily electronic filings of contributions and expenditures that would be posted on the Web by the Federal Election Commission (FEC). One political scientist likens this approach to the stock market: "Politicians, like public companies, should be required to reveal relevant data about their finances, and voters, like stock traders, would have what they needed to look out for themselves."[2]

Another approach to deregulation is that of Speaker Gingrich who argues that "since we cannot effectively stifle . . . special interest voices, let us submerge them in appeals from the parties. Strong parties could insulate legislators from pressures contributors might exert on them."[3]

The argument behind deregulation is that the existing system has not worked. In each election campaign, candidates and their supporters find new loopholes. Laws that seek to plug the loopholes will not work any better, supporters of deregulation believe. As a director of a successful conservative PAC once said, "Whatever changes they make in the law, we'll turn them to our advantage."[4]

Others believe that to deregulate campaign gifts would create a worse situation than we have now. Said one, "the last thing we need is a new system where politicians are owned by a very few powerful corporations or individuals or interests who lay down millions of dollars."[5] Opponents of deregulation fear that a wealthy individual, family, or interest group—a Ross Perot, for example—could gain political control over entire blocks of seats and that political offices would essentially be controlled by the highest bidder. Moreover, they argue that the public does not have the same knowledge about politics as stock market traders do about the economy.

Supporters of political reform also favor electronic filing and more "teeth" for the Federal Election Commission, but disagree with deregulators in most other respects. However, supporters of reform do not agree among themselves on other approaches. Some favor public funding of congressional races. Yet, as we have seen, public funding of the presidential election has not stopped PACs, unions, and corporations from giving millions. Others favor banning "soft money," requiring parties and interest groups involved in election advertising to raise and spend only funds subjected to campaign limits. Still others urge voluntary spending limits, limits on fund-raising by candidates outside their home states, or limits on media spending.

One proposal that had reasonably widespread support in Congress was sponsored by John McCain (R-Ariz.) and Russell Feingold (D-Wis.). Their approach combined voluntary spending limits and increases in the overall amount that individuals can give with the requirement that parties and candidates raise and spend only hard money, not soft money unregulated by law. The McCain-Feingold bill also mandated prompt electronic reporting and gave the FEC greater enforcement powers.

The McCain-Feingold bill had wide support from the Democrats and some support from Republicans, but it was killed in 1998 by the Republican leadership. Though this proposal or others are likely to continue to be on the agenda, it is clear that elected officials are more afraid of being without campaign donations than they are that voters will punish them for not supporting campaign reform.

And while it was the Republican leadership that killed the campaign finance bill in 1998, the commitment

then we think everything is wrong. So it is with our views of campaign money. For several years after the 1974 reforms, we thought things were going along pretty well. More recently, many have become convinced that the nation is in terrible jeopardy because of the influence of money. Whether we are overreacting or not, the issue of campaign finance reform is again alive.

CONFLICTS OF INTEREST

In addition to money's influence on political campaigns, it also leads to **conflicts of interest.** This term refers to officials making decisions that directly affect their own personal livelihoods or interests. The camof Democrats is also questionable. Ideologically, Democrats are more sympathetic to limiting the influence of big money, but practically, Democratic incumbents are heavily dependent upon their PAC "fixes." When a Republican president was in office, Democratic members of Congress could vote their ideological inclinations for campaign finance reform, resting assured that the president would veto any serious reforms. When Clinton took office and indicated his support for reform, Democrats found innumerable ways to avoid passing a serious bill. Now that Republicans control Congress, Democrats rue their failure. Business interests, ideologically more in tune with Republicans, have begun to fund them generously. Democrats are finding their sources of funding drying up.

Nevertheless, as we move to the twenty-first century, it is not clear that either party has much incentive to support campaign finance reform. What does seem to be true is that the public is repelled by the existing system (as the accompanying figure shows, support for change is overwhelming). Unfortunately, from the perspective of those who want to change it, the public reaction seems to be to turn away from politics and stay away from the polls rather than to vote against members opposing reform.

1. "Cleaning Up Reform," *Wall Street Journal,* November 10, 1983, p. 26.
2. Larry Sabato, quoted in David E. Rosenbaum, "Fixing Politics, More or Less," *New York Times,* December 22, 1996, p. E1.
3. David Broder, "Gingrich the Heretic," *Washington Post National Weekly Edition,* November 20–26, 1995, p. 4.
4. Larry Sabato, *PAC Power* (New York: W. W. Norton, 1984), p. 172.
5. Russell D. Feingold (D-Wis.) quoted in Sabato, *PAC Power.*

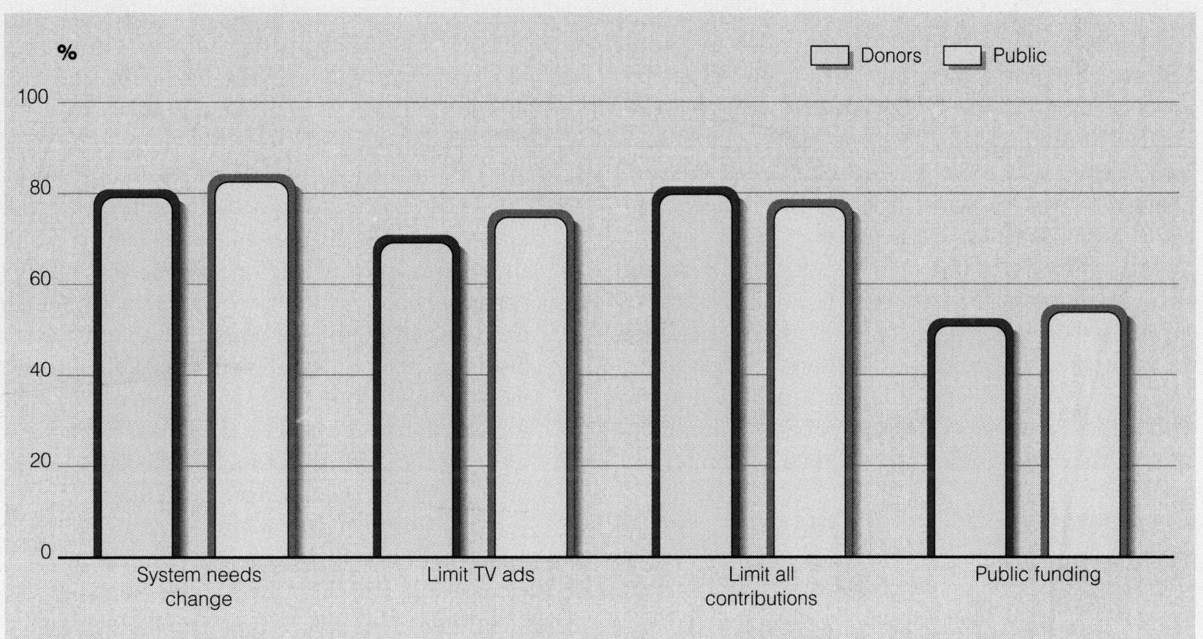

The Public and Donors Agree That the Campaign Finance System Needs to Be Fixed

SOURCE: *Washington Post* national survey, reported in Ruth Marcus and Charles Babcock, "Feeding the Election Machine," *Washington Post National Weekly Edition,* February 17, 1997, p. 10.

paign contribution system we have just described is certainly a huge conflict of interest. Presidents and members of Congress make decisions about policies affecting those who give them campaign money. But conflicts of interest are not confined to decisions involving sources of campaign money. As Madison noted, almost every decision involves potential conflicts of interest. Decisions made by presidents, bureaucrats, and members of Congress can affect their personal financial interests (including stocks, bonds, or other investments).

Despite periodic attempts to limit conflicts of interest, violations of ethics codes still occur in Congress

WHAT GOVERNMENT DOES RIGHT

ELIMINATING CONFLICT OF INTEREST IN THE JUDICIARY

Though it is difficult to find a widely agreed upon example of what government does right in the area of money and politics, the treatment of conflict of interest in the federal judiciary is such a case.

Because federal judges are appointed, not elected, the issue of campaign donations and how to regulate them does not occur. Though politics is certainly involved in the appointment of federal judges, there are no public campaigns and thus no need for television advertising and opinion polls (Chapter 13 describes the process of appointing federal judges).

Members of Congress routinely vote on issues that have a significant impact on their own financial holdings, whether they be in agriculture, information technology, or tobacco. Both members of Congress and the president often make decisions that have a big impact on their campaign donors.

But the situation for judges is different. They must withdraw from cases (called recusing) in which they have any financial interest in the outcome. [They] must also withdraw from cases when they have close ties to others with financial interests in the outcome.

Though no institution is perfect, and though federal judges are often attacked for their decisions, the federal judiciary is remarkably free from charges of conflict of financial interest. We almost take this for granted, yet the most cursory look at conflict of interest in the other two branches suggests that we should value this aspect of our independent judiciary.

and in the executive branch. In 1981, six House members and one senator were convicted in an FBI undercover operation known as Abscam. Five were even videotaped accepting cash. Incidents of blatant bribery such as this are rare, but conflicts of interests are more common. They are harder to deal with, however, because the issues are less clear-cut.

It is difficult to untangle the effects of personal financial interests, constituency interests, and party loyalties. For example, people on the Agriculture Committee with agribusiness interests, as most have, often represent districts with large agricultural interests. If those members vote in favor of agricultural interests, they are voting both for their own interests and for their constituents' interests. And they are likely to think that they are advancing the national interest at the same time. It appears that the impact of these personal interests on voting is fairly small once constituency interests are taken into account.[61]

UPI/Corbis-Bettmann

This secretly filmed picture shows the acceptance of money in the Abscam episode. As one of the implicated members said: "I'm gonna tell you something real simple and short. In this business, money talks and b _ _ _ s _ _ _ walks."

In the executive branch, decision-makers operate under much less direct public and media scrutiny. Yet they too may be acting on matters that affect their personal economic position. Since the Carter administration, all high-level administrative officials have been required to file public financial disclosure statements to allow the public to see when they are making decisions that benefit their own financial interests. But the rules do not require officials to step aside on matters that would affect them financially.

It is also a conflict of interest to use one's government position to line up a job following a public service career. The Ethics in Government Act of 1978 tries to regulate this. The act bars former public servants from lobbying their former agencies for a year and on matters in which they "personally and substantially" participated as public officials, for life. Current employees also are prohibited from participating in decisions affecting interests with which they are negotiating about future employment. But the act is not very stringently enforced. Because many companies that regularly deal with government think experience in government, especially in the agency that regulates the company's activities, is an asset, many officials take well-paying jobs in the industry they came to know while in government. Critics call this the "revolving door," referring to the movement of people from government service to the private sector and, sometimes, back again.

WHAT ABOUT WHITEWATER?

Since 1992, the topic of Whitewater has popped into the news every few weeks. It is an alleged scandal that involves President Clinton, his wife Hillary Rodham Clinton, an obscure savings and loan in Arkansas, and a suicide in Washington, D.C. The story of Whitewater has persisted since 1992, and most people long ago have forgotten, if they ever knew, what the supposed "scandal" is all about. Yet surfers on the Internet, as well as listeners on conservative talk radio, can read and hear about murders, suicide, and other plots that some people allege are connected to Whitewater.

The facts seem a lot less interesting or exciting than the lurid rumors. The facts appear to be that in the late 1970s, Bill and Hillary Clinton entered into a venture, called the Whitewater Development Company, whose purpose was to sell vacation lots in the Ozarks. The Clintons were a 50% partner in this deal, along with James McDougal, a political supporter of then-Governor Clinton. With an investment of $230,000, the Clintons lost somewhere between $45,000 and $68,000 in this venture, eventually selling their shares to McDougal.

Later, McDougal (but not the Clintons) purchased a savings and loan company, the Madison Guaranty, which, after a time, federal regulators declared to be insolvent. Meanwhile, Hillary Clinton, as a lawyer representing Madison Guaranty, petitioned the new state securities commissioner (who herself had formerly worked for a law firm that represented Madison), to permit the savings and loan to borrow money and remain in operation. But the appeal failed and the savings and loan was finally declared insolvent. It was taken over by the federal government in 1989, as part of the nationwide program to get the savings and loan industry back to financial solvency (see Chapter 18 for more on regulation of savings and loans).

All of this happened long before Bill Clinton was in the White House; and thus it has nothing to do with use or misuse of presidential power. Investigations by special prosecutors and Congress have revealed a kind of cronyism that especially affects politics in small towns and small states and that leads to conflicts of interest. There have been charges that funds were siphoned from Madison to Clinton's gubernatorial campaign, but these have not been proved.

The plot thickened, however, when Vincent Foster, another close Arkansas friend of the Clintons, a member of the Clinton White House staff, and the lawyer who had handled the Clinton's sale of their Whitewater holdings to McDougal, committed suicide in a Washington park in 1993.

Immediately, rumors spread that Foster had been murdered or committed suicide because of Whitewater. The motive for a political killing is obscure at best, as is the Whitewater link. Foster was beset by many political problems and despaired of his perceived lack of success in his Washington role. However, White House Counsel Bernard Nussbaum did remove Foster's Whitewater files before the police reached Foster's office, thus adding fuel to the flame. Clinton later fired Nussbaum.

In 1994, Attorney General Janet Reno appointed an independent counsel to investigate the entire Whitewater affair. Republicans in the Congress soon launched an investigation of their own. Four years later, several findings have been made that the Clintons did nothing wrong in the Whitewater matter, but congressional inquiries continue to fuel rumors. McDougal and his wife were imprisoned, though McDougal died and his wife was released for health reasons (she was jailed for refusing to testify and therefore was in contempt of court). While new revelations might throw entirely new light on the Clintons, for now it seems that sloppy financial record keeping, misdeeds by associates, cronyism, and a lack of candor about their complicated deals are their major failings. Most of the public seem bored with the continuing story, or nonstory, which seems to have taken on a life of its own in the fringes of the news media. However, in a move that certainly aroused public interest, the special prosecutor in 1998 enlarged the investigation to include Clinton's relationship with Monica Lewinsky and his truthfulness under oath about that relationship. At the time of this writing in 1998, that investigation has led to the president's admission that he lied about this relationship. This, in turn, has led to an impeachment inquiry.

Using a government job to line up lucrative private employment also can involve **influence peddling,** using one's access to powerful people to make money. Former high government officials can and do use their access to former colleagues to win jobs representing clients in business or labor. A well-publicized case of influence peddling was that of Michael Deaver, the deputy chief of staff and one of President Reagan's closest advisers during his first term. Deaver left government, immediately set up a public relations and lobbying firm, and began soliciting clients largely on the basis of his close relationship with the president.[62]

Conflicts of interest and influence peddling are bipartisan phenomena. Such accusations swirl around the Clinton White House, although no high official has yet been convicted of illegal acts in office. But President Clinton and Hillary Clinton have been accused of conflicts of interest in the long-running investigation of the "Whitewater affair" (see the box "What About Whitewater?"). A number of Clinton administration members, including a cabinet secretary, Mike Espy, have left office under ethical clouds relating to conflicts of interest and interest peddling. Some of the allegations of improper behavior (such as Whitewater) took place before the accused persons

ARE THERE DEMOCRATIC AND REPUBLICAN KINDS OF CORRUPTION?

Some observers have pointed out that while both Democrats and Republicans have ethical lapses, the kinds of ethics problems they have are quite different. Corrupt Democrats steal. They accept bribes and improper campaign donations, divert public funds to their own pockets, and, in general, engage in personal financial aggrandizement. This style of corruption is reminiscent of the "honest graft" of the big city political machines (see the box on Boss Plunkitt and "honest graft" earlier in the chapter). While some Republicans also steal, for example, former Vice President Spiro Agnew, who pleaded no contest to charges of kickbacks, bribery, and extortion, and former Representative Joseph McDade (R-Pa.), who has been indicted for bribery and racketeering (but not yet convicted), most of these sorts of scandals involved Democrats. Examples include most of those involved in Abscam, four of the Keating 5, four Democratic members of Congress convicted of graft in the last five years, and most recently Daniel Rostenkowski (D-Ill.), former chair of the Ways and Means Committee, convicted of corrupt acts involving mail fraud.

Republican ethical failings tend to be related to the use of government for improper means. President Nixon's Watergate scandal involved trying to use the powers of government to punish his personal enemies, and then lying about it. He also ordered Cambodia to be bombed and tried to keep it a secret. President Reagan tried to subvert the constitutional powers of Congress by secretly selling arms to Iran and supplying weapons to rebels in Nicaragua, both expressly against the law. While Democratic presidents have also been guilty of misuse of government power (for example, President Johnson lying about alleged attacks by the North Vietnamese on an American ship in order to justify getting the United States more deeply involved in the Vietnamese war and President Kennedy ordering the FBI to wiretap Reverend Martin Luther King), subverting government seems more a Republican style of corruption.

Why do these differences exist? They could be coincidental, of course. But one Democrat argued that these differences were tied to the class basis of the parties: "The lower classes steal, the upper classes defraud." A prominent Republican had a different view: "Most Republicans are contemptuous of government; few Democrats are." Whatever the reason, these examples suggest that partisanship extends to more than presidential preferences.

assumed their current roles in the federal government. The large number of such instances led some commentators to point out that the ethical standards in the executive office are a good deal higher than in Congress or in some states, like Arkansas.

Conflicts of interest can never be completely eradicated from government, but presidents can make their expectations clear. Presidents Bush and Clinton have shown more concern about ethical issues than their predecessors, though conflicts of interest have been regularly reported. Ironically, when such conflicts are made public instead of being ignored, public perceptions of lower ethical standards in government than elsewhere in society may be reinforced. There is little reason to think, however, that people in government are less ethical than those in business, labor, or other parts of the private sector.

CONCLUSION: DOES THE INFLUENCE OF MONEY MAKE GOVERNMENT LESS RESPONSIVE?

The influence of money in American politics is a perennial source of concern to those who want to live up to the democratic ideals of political equality and popular sovereignty. Our democratic values tell us that government should represent all, the poor as well as the rich, and that everyone should have an equal chance to influence government. We know that in the real world things do not work this way. We tolerate much inequality in access because that seems to be the way the world works in the private as well as in the public sphere, because everyone is not equally interested in influencing government, and because for most people the effort of changing this pattern would be greater than the benefits gained.

Nevertheless, our reaction to the influence of money seems to be cyclical. We tolerate it; then when stories of inside deals, influence peddling, and buying access and even votes become too frequent, we act to do something about it. We then slip back into apathy until the next cycle comes along.[63]

In recent history, the low point of the use of money to buy access was probably during the Watergate scandals associated with the 1972 election. We then reacted strongly to those scandals by passing new laws and in general cleaning up our campaign finance system. But as the years went by, we found ways to get around the laws until now large parts are nearly meaningless. Now it appears we are in another era of growing concern over ethical standards in government.

We should not think of our times as the low point in government morality. In political campaigns, big money is certainly less influential than it was a century ago. Campaign funding regulations have cleaned up some of the unethical practices of the Watergate era, although the growing soft money loopholes are returning us to that era. Disclosure laws have opened for public scrutiny the sources of campaign funds for candidates for federal offices. It is the disclosure laws that, at least in part, make us so aware of the sources of private money seeking to influence the political system.

Some commentators believe the standards of public conduct decreased during the 1980s and have remained low. But although conflicts of interest and influence peddling in government may shock some, they reflect the ethical standards of the larger society. Making money in any way possible seems to be the hallmark of modern times, the age of "pin-striped outlaws." Though several public officials during the 1980s and 1990s have resigned after embarrassing revelations of conflicts of interests and sometimes illegal activities, many leaders of the business world have also seemed intent on making their fast buck, regardless of the ethics or legality of their actions. Numerous Wall Street bankers bought and sold illegal insider tips, savings and loan officers looted their institutions of millions of dollars, military contractors cheated government, and many other executives made millions in shady deals that were just this side of legality. One businessman lamented, "We are all embarrassed by events that make the *Wall Street Journal* read more like the *Police Gazette*."[64]

We should not exaggerate the amount of money involved in politics. Corporations spend much more to attract consumers than politicians spend to attract voters. For example, Procter and Gamble spent nearly $2.7 billion on advertising in 1994, more than four times the cost of all congressional campaigns combined that year.[65] It is not the amount of money in politics as much as its possible effects that concern us.

But the effects of money are hard to pin down. It is difficult to measure exactly the influence of money on political outcomes. Money sometimes influences votes and policies. Campaign contributions have some impact on voting in Congress. But at other times money appears to have little impact.

We do not know exactly how presidential candidates might be influenced by huge campaign donations or whether bureaucrats are using promises of future jobs as trade-offs for current favors. We think that good candidates are hindered or deterred from running by a shortage of money or even just by the knowledge that they need to raise big money, but it is difficult to measure exactly how many. Even though money is very tangible, its influence sometimes is quite intangible.

To the extent that money has an impact, it limits the responsiveness of government to the average citizen. It causes some policymakers to be more responsive to the big interests than to the average person. This does not mean, though, that those with the most money always win. Organization and a sense of the public interest can sometimes defeat even big money.

In designing laws to regulate the use of money in political life, perhaps the best that reformers can reasonably hope for is a system in which public officials who want to be honest will not feel under pressure to be influenced by money. Certainly, there will always be a few "bad apples," and no political system can protect us completely from them. It should be enough to design rules and structures that ensure that people of average honesty who serve in public office are rewarded for putting the public interest, rather than their private interests, first. Our current laws, especially our congressional campaign finance laws, do not always do that. The penalties we suffer are less in politicians stealing from the public till (the money does not amount to much). They are more in the loss of public trust, an increasing alienation from government, and an anger at politicians who seem to be putting their interests before the public interest. Perhaps, then, even a largely symbolic effort by our legislators to limit the influence of money on the political process is important, because it sends the signal that they are aware of and accountable to, public concerns.

EPILOGUE

DeConcini Intervenes

DeConcini decided to help Keating. Though he insists he did not arrange a meeting with the Federal Home Loan Bank Board chair, Edward Gray, DeConcini attended such a meeting and took the lead in presenting Lincoln S&L's case. Participants included four other U.S. senators, Alan Cranston (D-Cal.), John McCain (R-Ariz.), Donald Riegle (D-Mich.), and John Glenn (D-Ohio), all of whom had received substantial campaign contributions from Keating, ranging from Riegle's $78,000 to Cranston's nearly $1 million. Gray indicated he did not know the specifics of the Lincoln S&L case and offered to arrange a meeting between the five senators and the regulators. When that meeting was held, DeConcini asked the regulators to lay off the Lincoln S&L until a lawsuit to determine the legality of the board's actions was settled. DeConcini cited the accountant's estimate of the good financial health of the S&L, asking, "You believe they'd prostitute themselves for a client?"[66] The regulators responded by noting that the Lincoln S&L case could involve criminal charges. At that point, the meeting adjourned and DeConcini suspended his inquiries. Later, DeConcini made repeated calls to Gray's successor and to another board member inquiring whether the Lincoln S&L could be sold. The day after his last phone call, Keating's Arizona company declared bankruptcy; then federal regulators took over the Lincoln S&L.

Sergy Shayerick/AP/Wide World Photos

Charles Keating, now out of prison, proclaims his innocence.

After the actions of DeConcini and the four other senators (called the **Keating 5**) came to light, they were the subject of a 14-month investigation by the Senate Ethics Committee, broadcast over C-SPAN. The senators defended their actions, noting that serving constituents is a routine part of their job. The investigating attorney argued that at least three of the group, including DeConcini, went far beyond the bounds of ethical behavior. Even though there was no actual exchange of money for favors, the arrangement gave the appearance of such an exchange and brought discredit to the Senate.

After the hearings, the committee found that Cranston, who was actively soliciting money from Keating even while he was intervening with the federal regulators, broke ethics rules linking "fund raising and official activities." The committee found that DeConcini and Riegle did not break rules but engaged in conduct that "gave the appearance of being improper." The committee noted that it "could not condone" their behavior. McCain and Glenn received the lightest sanction, merely being chastised for their "poor judgment."[67]

The collapse of Keating's S&L is estimated to be the largest in history. It cost the taxpayers $2.5 billion dollars to pay off the depositors whose accounts were insured. It was only a small but illustrative part of the shenanigans that led to the collapse of thousands of S&Ls all over the country (a drama that also spawned the Whitewater case). As one analyst indicated, "It's as though Jimmy Carter poured gasoline on the S&L house, a Democratically controlled Congress put a match to it, and the Reagan-Bush regime placed snipers on rooftops to shoot at firefighters."[68]

The pressure of the Keating 5 and other members of Congress delayed investigations of the failing S&Ls, postponing recognition of the magnitude of the savings and loan problem and thus escalating by many times the costs of bailing out depositors. Under pressure from constituents and donors, members also dragged their feet on legislation to begin the reorganization of the entire S&L industry. On average, each household in America will pay $5,000 for the bailout. As one commentator remarked, "Never has so much money gone to such key legislators who worked so hard for measures that cost taxpayers so dearly."[69]

Charles Keating was found guilty and sentenced to more than 12 years in prison for defrauding his savings and loan and its investors. However, he was released from prison after serving only five years of his term. To the outrage of his investors, a federal court found that Judge Lance Ito (of O. J. Simpson fame), who presided at Keating's trial, had bungled the job and that a later conviction was also gained illegally. Though technically no longer a convicted criminal, he does owe more than $5 billion in civil claims from his depositors and others.

Greed, criminality, and negligence led to this economic disaster. But, of course, it was not just the greed of public officials that brought about the S&L mess. Private enterprise contributed more than its share. In addition to the thousands of greedy and in some cases criminal S&L operators, real estate appraisers participated in the debacle by vastly inflating the estimates of the value of real estate that many S&Ls bought (thus making it look as if the S&Ls had more assets than they did). And, though DeConcini did not believe that the accountant who vouched for Lincoln S&L's financial health would prostitute himself for his clients, many did. That accountant took a job the next year with Keating's firm at a salary of $900,000. Economists, lawyers, and others were also willing to sell their good judgment. (Alan Greenspan, the economist who also testified to Lincoln S&L's financial strength, was paid by Keating's law firm to write the letter.)[70]

Has the Keating 5 scandal led to higher ethical standards in Congress and perhaps new campaign finance laws? Keating was quite open in acknowledging he was trying to buy influence with his campaign contributions. Asked if his financial support influenced several political figures to take up his cause, he replied, "I want to say in the most forceful way I can, I certainly hope so."[71] But even with this open acknowledgment of influence buying, no significant action has been taken to regulate campaign finance. The Democrats had their chance to limit campaign spending and blew it. The Republicans now have a chance but their leadership wants no part of this sort of reform. Thus, real reform seems unlikely in the near future.

The pressures against cleaning up the conflicts of interest that remain are strong. There are always members who want to make more money and always special interest groups that are happy to help them do so in exchange for access or more tangible favors. As one journalist noted, "The mutual affinity of the wealthy and the politically powerful offers a seduction that not all members of Congress are able to resist."[72]

For this reason, it is not surprising that most Americans believe that members lie, put the needs of special interests above the needs of the average citizen, and profit improperly from their positions.[73]

Despite all this, Congress is probably cleaner today than in the past. In earlier decades, these activities would not excite the least discussion. In the nineteenth century, Daniel Webster received a cash retainer from the Second Bank of the United States while chairing the Senate Finance Committee. At the height of the debate over the bank's rechartering, he complained to its president that his retainer was too low![74]

KEY TERMS

Muckrakers
Teapot Dome scandal
political action committees (PACs)
Federal Election Campaign Act
independent spending
soft money
conflicts of interest
junkets
influence peddling
Keating 5

FURTHER READING

John M. Barry, *The Ambition and the Power* (New York: Viking, 1989). The fall of Speaker Jim Wright set in the context of his successes as speaker and the enemies they created.

Larry J. Sabato and Glenn Simpson, *Dirty Little Secrets: The Persistence of Corruption in American Politics* (New York: Times Books, 1996). An up-to-date look at corruption in politics.

Frank Sorauf, *Inside Campaign Finance: Myths and Realities* (New Haven, Conn.: Yale University Press, 1992). An overview that challenges conventional wisdom.

ELECTRONIC RESOURCES

http://www.commoncause.org/issue_agenda/issues.htm
The home page of Common Cause, the public interest group whose major focus is reforming the campaign finance system. Linked to the page are the group's reports tracking relevant legislation, periodic reports on campaign spending, and reports on financial ties of those voting against major regulatory legislation such as the tobacco bill.

http://www.pbs.org/wgbh/pages/frontline/president/
The home page for a PBS special "So You Want to Buy a President." Contains much useful data on how much is contributed and who the contributors are.

http://www.fec.gov/index.html
The Federal Election Commission does not have much regulatory power, but it does publish useful reports of campaign spending. This page describes election rules and links to FEC reports on campaign spending and on voter turnout.

INFOTRAC CITATIONS

"Political Money What For"
"Financial Spending by Political Action Committees"
"Money Walks"
"Spending Limits a Good Idea"

NOTES

1. Material on DeConcini and Keating is drawn from John R. Cranford, "Keating and the Five Senators: Putting the Puzzle Together," *Congressional Quarterly Weekly Report* (January 26, 1991), p. 221; Jim Calle and Bill Roberts, "Who Was Asleep When Keating Went Astray?" *Palm Beach Post*, January 8, 1990, p. 18; "Bonfire of the S&Ls," *Newsweek*, May 21, 1990, pp. 20–30.
2. "Bonfire," p. 27.
3. Ibid.
4. Ibid.
5. Phil Kuntz, "Senators Ponder How to Treat Appearance of Wrongdoing," *Congressional Quarterly Weekly Report* (January 26, 1991), p. 229.
6. Jimmy Breslin, *How the Good Guys Finally Won: Notes from an Impeachment Summer* (New York: Ballantine Books, 1974), p. 14.
7. Congressional Quarterly, *Dollar Politics*, 3d ed. (Washington, D.C.: CQ Press, 1982), p. 3.
8. Ibid.
9. James Madison, *The Federalist Papers*, #10.
10. Haynes Johnson, "Turning Government Jobs into Gold," *Washington Post National Weekly Edition*, May 12, 1986, pp. 6–7.
11. Quoted in Richard Hofstadter, *The American Political Tradition* (New York: Vintage Books, 1958), p. 165.
12. Congressional Quarterly, *Dollar Politics*, p. 3.
13. Larry J. Sabato, *Feeding Frenzy* (New York: Free Press, 1991).
14. Elizabeth Drew, *Politics and Money* (New York: Collier, 1983), p. 9.
15. *Buckley v. Valeo*, 424 U.S. 1 (1976).
16. See Marick Masters and Gerald Keim, "Determinants of PAC Participation among Large Corporations," *Journal of Politics* 47 (November 1985), pp. 1158–1173; J. David Gopoian, "What Makes PACs Tick?" *American Journal of Political Science* 28 (May 1984), pp. 259–281; Larry Sabato, *PAC Power* (New York: W. W. Norton, 1984), chapter 3; Theodore Eismeier and Philip H. Pollock, "Political Action Committees," in Michael Malbin, ed., *Money and Politics in the United States* (Chatham, N.J.: Chatham House, 1984); John Peters, "Political Action Committees and the 1984 Congressional Elections," paper prepared for delivery to the Research Committee on Political Finance and Political Corruption at the World Congress, International Political Science Association, Paris, France, 1985.
17. *Federal Election Commission v. National Conservative PAC*, 470 U.S. 480 (1985).
18. Ruth Marcus, "Taking Issue with Advocacy," *Washington Post National Weekly Edition*, April 15–21, 1996, p. 13.
19. Drew, *Politics and Money*, p. 105. See also "Please Hold for the President," *New York Times*, March 14, 1993, p. E16; Michael Wines, "Snapping at the Hand That Fed Clinton Well," *International Herald Tribune*, March 5, 1993, p. 3; Peter Stone, "Return of the Fat Cats," *National Journal*, October 17, 1992, p. 2352.
20. Peter Overby, "Back Pocket PACs," *Common Cause*, July/August 1990, p. 26.
21. Ruth Marcus and Charles Babcock, "Feeding the Election Machine," *Washington Post National Weekly Edition*, February 17, 1997, pp. 6–10.
22. Jill Abramson, "After 1996, Campaign Finance Laws in Shreds," *New York Times*, November 2, 1997, p. 1; Marcus and Babcock, "Feeding the Election Machine."
23. Alison Mitchell, "Time Passes, Money Flows," *New York Times*, June 16, 1996, p. E5. The quotation from the NRA spokesperson is from Ruth Marcus, "Off the Ballot, but in the Contest," *Washington Post National Weekly Edition*, July 6, 1998, p. 13.
24. Marcus and Babcock, "Feeding the Election Machine."
25. Ibid.
26. Carol Matlock, "Lobbying Focus," *National Journal*, November 5, 1988, p. 2868.
27. Larry Makinson and Joshua Goldstein, *Open Secrets: The Encyclopedia of Congressional Money and Politics* (Washington, D.C.: Congressional Quarterly, Inc., 1994).

28. Michael Weisskopf, "To the Victors Belong the PAC Checks," *Washington Post National Weekly Edition*, January 2–5, 1995, p. 13. The remainder of the paragraph is also drawn from this source.

29. Jennifer Babson and Kelly St. John, "Momentum Helps GOP Collect Record Amounts from PACs," *Congressional Quarterly Weekly Report*, December 3, 1994, pp. 3456–3459.

30. See Kevin Grier and Michael Mangy, "Comparing Interest Group PAC Contributions to House and Senate Incumbents," *Journal of Politics* 55 (August 1993), pp. 615–643.

31. J. David Gopoian, "Change and Continuity in Defense PAC Behavior," *American Politics Quarterly* 13 (July 1985), pp. 297–322; Richard Morin and Charles Babcock, "Off Year, Schmoff Year," *Washington Post National Weekly Edition*, May 14–20, 1990, p. 15.

32. Gary Wasserman, "The Uses of Influence," *Washington Post National Weekly Edition*, January 11–17, 1993, p. 35.

33. Makinson and Goldstein, *Open Secrets*, p. 23.

34. Drew, *Politics and Money*, p. 68; Thomas B. Edsall, "More Than Enough Is Not Enough," *Washington Post National Weekly Edition*, February 9, 1987, p. 13. See also Edward Handler and John Mulkern, *Business in Politics* (Lexington, Mass.: D. C. Heath, 1982), pp. 1–34.

35. Johnson, "Turning Government Jobs into Gold," p. 7; Sabato, *PAC Power*, p. 84.

36. Amy Dockser, "Nice PAC You've Got There . . . A Pity if Anything Should Happen to It," *Washington Monthly* (January 1984), p. 21.

37. Meg Greenfield, "The Political Debt Bomb," *Newsweek*, April 1987, p. 76.

38. Quoted in *New York Times*, June 13, 1998, p. A7.

39. Gary Jacobson, *Money in Congressional Elections* (New Haven: Yale University Press, 1980), p. 61.

40. David Broder, "The High Road to Lower Finance?" *Washington Post National Weekly Edition*, June 29, 1987, p. 4; Diane Granat, "Parties' Schools for Politicians or Grooming Troops for Election," *Congressional Quarterly Weekly Report*, May 5, 1984, p. 1036.

41. Gary Orren, "The Nomination Process," in Michael Nelson, ed., *The Elections of 1984* (Washington, D.C.: CQ Press, 1986), chapter 2. See also Michael J. Robinson and Austin Ranney, eds. *The Mass Media in Campaign 1984* (Washington, D.C.: American Enterprise Institute, 1985); Michael Robinson, Clyde Wilcox, and Paul Marshall, "The Presidency: Not for Sale," *Public Opinion* (March/April 1989), pp. 49–52.

42. Nelson Polsby and Aaron Wildavsky, *Presidential Elections* (New York: Charles Scribner's Sons, 1984), p. 56.

43. David Nice, "Campaign Spending and Presidential Election Results," *Polity* 19 (Spring 1987), pp. 464–476, shows that presidential campaign spending is more productive for Republicans than Democrats.

44. Gary Jacobson, *Money in Congressional Elections*; Jacobson, "Public Funds for Congressional Campaigns: Who Would Benefit?" in Herbert E. Alexander, ed., *Political Finance* (Beverly Hills, Calif.: Sage Publications, 1979); Jacobson, "Parties and PACs in Congressional Elections," in Lawrence C. Dodd and Bruce I. Oppenheimer, eds., *Congress Reconsidered*, 3d ed. (Washington, D.C.: CQ Press, 1985); Jacobson, *The Politics of Congressional Elections*, 2d ed. (Boston: Little, Brown, 1987), chapter 4; Jacobson, "The Effects of Campaign Spending in House Elections," *American Journal of Political Science* 34 (May 1990), pp. 334–362; Christopher Kenny and Michael McBurnett, "A Dynamic Model of the Effect of Campaign Spending on Congressional Vote Choice," *American Journal of Political Science* 36 (November 1992), pp. 923–937; Donald Green and Jonathan Krasno, "Salvation for the Spendthrift Incumbent," *American Journal of Political Science* 32 (November 1988), pp. 884–907.

45. "Campaign Spending in '93–'94: The Senate, The House," *Washington Post National Weekly Edition*, January 30–February 5, 1995, pp. 14–15.

46. The survey of donors is reported in Bob Hebert, "The Donor Class," *New York Times*, July 19, 1998, p. 15; Woodrow Jones and K. Robert Keiser, "Issue Visibility and the Effects of PAC Money," *Social Science Quarterly* 68 (March 1987), pp. 170–176; Janet Grenzke, "PACs and the Congressional Supermarket," *American Journal of Political Science* 33 (February 1989), pp. 1–24, found little effect of PAC money on a series of votes that were not obscure. Laura Langbein, "Money and Access," *Journal of Politics* 48 (November 1986), pp. 1052–1064, shows that those who received more PAC money spend more time with interest group representatives.

47. Jean Reith Schroedel, "Campaign Contributions and Legislative Outcomes," *Western Political Quarterly* 39 (September 1986), pp. 371–389; Richard L. Hall and Frank Wayman, "Buying Time: Moneyed Interests and the Mobilization of Bias in Congressional Committees," *American Political Science Review* 84 (September 1990), pp. 797–820.

48. "Running with the PACs," *Time*, October 25, 1982, p. 20. The quotation is from Representative Thomas Downey (D-N.Y.).

49. "Congress Study Links Funds and Votes," *New York Times*, December 30, 1987, p. 7.

50. John Frendreis and Richard Waterman, "PAC Contributions and Legislative Behavior: Senate Voting on Trucking Deregulation," *Social Science Quarterly* 66 (June 1985), pp. 401–412. See also W. P. Welch, "Campaign Contributions and Legislative Voting," *Western Political Quarterly* 25 (December 1982), pp. 478–495; Jonathan Silberman and Garey Durden, "Determining Legislative Preferences on the Minimum Wage," *Journal of Political Economy* 84 (April 1976), pp. 317–329.

51. Laura Langbein, "PACs, Lobbies and Political Conflict: The Case of Gun Control," *Public Choice* 75 (1993), pp. 254–271; Laura Langbein and Mark Lotwis, "The Political Efficacy of Lobbying and Money: Gun Control in the House, 1986," *Legislative Studies Quarterly* 15 (1990), pp. 413–440; Jean Schroedel, "Campaign Contributions and Legislative Outcomes," *Western Political Quarterly* 39 (1986), pp. 371–389.

52. Adam Clymer, " '84 PACs Gave More to Senate Winners," *New York Times*, January 6, 1985, p. 13.

53. Kirk Brown, "Campaign Contributions and Congressional Voting," paper prepared for the annual meeting of the American Political Science Association, 1983, cited in Malbin, *Money and Politics*, p. 134.

54. Drew, *Politics and Money*, p. 79.

55. See Grenzke, "PACs and the Congressional Supermarket"; also see Frank Sorauf, *Money in American Elections* (Glenview, III.: Scott, Foresman, 1988).

56. Janet Grenzke, "Political Action Committees and the Congressional Supermarket"; John Wright, "Contributions, Lobbying and Committee Voting in the US House of Representatives," *American Political Science Review* 84 (1990), pp. 417–438; Henry Chappel, Jr., "Campaign Contributions and Voting on the Cargo Preference Bill," *Public Choice* 36 (2, 1981), pp. 301–312.

57. Jasper Shannon, *Money and Politics* (New York: Random House, 1959).

58. "Study: Bush Donors Get Government Favors," *Lincoln Journal*, May 28, 1992. A *Los Angeles Times* news release.

59. Charles Lewis quoted in "Book Details Candidates' Extensive Financial Alignments," *Lincoln Journal* (Tribune Media Sources), January 12, 1996, p. 5A.

60. Tom Kenworthy, "The Color of Money," *Washington Post National Weekly Edition*, November 6–12, 1989, p. 13.

61. Susan Welch and John Peters, "Private Interests in the U.S. congress," *Legislative Studies Quarterly* 7 (November 1982), pp. 547–555. See also John Peters and Susan Welch, "Private Interests and Public Interests," *Journal of Politics* 45 (May 1983), pp. 378–396.

62. "Having It All, Then Throwing It Away," *Time*, May 25, 1987, p. 22.

63. Elizabeth Drew, "Letter from Washington," *New Yorker*, May 1, 1989, pp. 99–108; see also Don Bolz, "Tales of Power and Money," *Washington Post National Weekly Edition*, May 1–7, 1989, pp. 11–12.

64. "Having It All," p. 22.

65. "100 Leading National Advertisers; US Ad Spending Totals," *Advertising Age*, September 27, 1995, p. 2.

66. "Bonfire of the S&Ls," p. 28.

67. Helen Dewar, "Much Ado About What?" *Washington Post National Weekly Edition*, March 11–17, 1991, p. 14.

68. Donald Kaul, "S & L Mess Response Baffling," *Sunday Journal-Star*, November 11, 1990, p. 3A, Tribune Media Services syndicate.

69. "Bonfire of the S&Ls," p. 28.

70. Ibid.

71. Jack Germond and Jules Witcover, "Looking for a Smoking Gun on Campaign Funds?" *National Journal*, December 2, 1989, p. 2956.

72. Drew, "Letter from Washington," p. 108.

73. Richard Morin, "They're All Crooks—Whatever Their Names Are," *Washington Post National Weekly Edition*, May 29–June 4, 1989, p. 39.

74. James Glassman, "Ethics, Schmethics—Congress Has Never Been Cleaner," *Washington Post National Weekly Edition*, June 5–11, 1989, p. 23.

President Bill Clinton addressing Congress, with former Speaker of the House Newt Gingrich and Vice President Al Gore (center). Newt Gingrich at age 7 (above). Bill Clinton near his childhood home of Hope, Arkansas (below).

Laura Pedrick

Reuters/Corbis-Bettmann

Reuters/Corbis-Bettmann

PART THREE INSTITUTIONS

Former Speaker of the House Newt Gingrich looking satisfied before the 1998 elections.

Gregory Heisler/outline

10 CONGRESS

Should You Risk Your Career?

It is August 1993 and the House of Representatives is considering Bill Clinton's first budget bill. The bill, which includes a plan to substantially reduce the deficit, has been portrayed as a "make or break" moment in Clinton's presidential term. Failure to get the bill passed will further reduce his persuasive power and stature, perhaps (the hyperbolic media pronounced) ruin his presidency, because he is already seen as weak. On the other hand, the media and the interested public will see passage of the bill as a huge victory, the first step in bringing the nation's deficit under control.

You are Marjorie Margolies-Mezvinsky, a freshman Democratic member of Congress from suburban Philadelphia. You are faced with a representative's worst nightmare: On an important, well-publicized vote, you must either stand with the president of your party against the wishes of the majority of your district's voters, or vote with your district but contribute in large part to your president's defeat.

You are not a typical member of Congress. A graduate of Columbia University, you are a television news reporter married to a former Iowa congressional representative. You have 11 children, including biological children, stepchildren, adopted children from Korea and Vietnam, and refugee foster children. After covering the Clarence Thomas–Anita Hill hearings as a journalist, you decided to run for Congress yourself. Your opponent, a former state representative and county commissioner, is well known for his constituency work (called a "zen master of constituency service" by the local paper), but you attacked him for feeding at the public trough and for waffling ("pro-choice, that's me; multiple choice, that's Jon Fox").[1] You supported abortion rights, improved health care programs, and a middle-class tax cut.

You are finishing your first term in office, and like most other members, are greatly concerned about your reelection chances. Your district had been continuously represented by Republicans since 1916 (!) before you were elected. But in 1992, the voters of the district gave you a razor-thin majority (you won by only 1,300 votes out of 254,000 cast) and a plurality to Bill Clinton, largely because of economic concerns and partly because of an anti-incumbent mood. Since coming to Congress, you have positioned yourself well. You are one of only five freshmen appointed to the powerful Energy and Commerce Committee. A position on that committee has given you access to important interests who have already contributed to your reelection campaign.

Clinton's budget bill calls for a combination of tax increases and spending cuts. It pleases no one entirely, but is the first significant move toward reducing the deficit since the 1960s. But the bill is in jeopardy for two reasons. First, the Republicans, the minority party in the House, are united in opposition. Many Republicans had supported similar budget measures when they were proposed by George Bush. But now that it is Clinton's budget bill, they sensed an opportunity to deal a major blow to his presidency by defeating this key economic package. The Republicans have traditionally positioned themselves as fiscally conservative (even though it was a Republican president, Ronald Reagan, who ran the largest deficits in U.S. history), and they do not wish to relinquish this advantage to the Democrats. But many conservative Democrats are defecting because they oppose the various tax increases, including a proposed tax on fuel as an energy-saving measure.

You initially voted against the bill because you have told your constituents you will not support the bill. You had

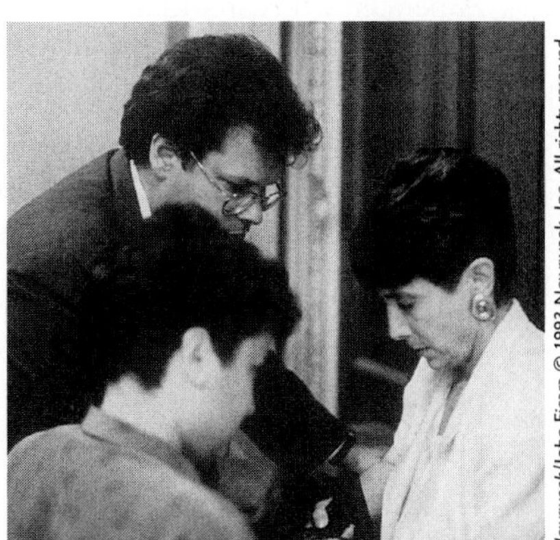

Representative Margolies-Mezvinsky with her aides moments before she must vote.

mixed emotions when it passed by six votes. The bill has come back to the House after House and Senate representatives reached agreement in a conference committee (when the Senate and House versions of a particular bill are not identical, a committee is set up to negotiate a common version of the bill, which is then sent to each house for ratification). Now the House must ratify the results of that negotiation. You have already prepared a statement explaining your "no" vote on the budget bill. You think it does not go far enough to reduce the deficit. In particular, you believe that it does not pare enough away from entitlements, those programs like Medicare, welfare, and Social Security. As part of your justification for the no vote, you indicate that you believe the president should call a "summit" meeting to discuss entitlement spending.

But now the president has spoken to you at length, pleading for your support. He, and anyone who follows the news, knows the vote is extremely close. He needs every vote, including yours. Given the unanimous opposition of the Republicans, most Democrats must stand firm or the bill will be defeated. You know that a defeat on this bill could have serious repercussions for his entire presidency.

But you do not really favor the bill. It does not go as far as you want on spending cuts, and it contains too many tax increases. Moreover, you think your constituents are not in favor of it either. You want to be reelected, and you fear that because you have told your constituents you will not support the bill, your constituents will think you have sold out. To vote for the bill could mean committing political suicide in your Republican district; even under the best of circumstances, you will have an uphill race. To waffle on this key issue could move your reelection chances from marginal to hopeless. What do you do?

Many Americans are angry at government, and they are most angry at Congress. Americans profess a love for democracy in the abstract, but paradoxically it is the very visibility of democratic processes that makes Congress the least loved branch of government.[2]

The public has the highest level of support for the Supreme Court, the institution that is the least democratic (Figure 1). The Court is most isolated from the public. Little of the disagreement, negotiation, and compromise that takes place on the Court becomes public. The public gives the president the next highest level of support. The president is certainly the most visible symbol of national government, but within the executive office, disagreement, negotiation, and compromise are somewhat concealed.

The public is least supportive of Congress, where the processes of democracy are exposed for all to see. C-SPAN and news broadcasts bring debate, disagreement, and compromise alive. The media also bring to every American who cares to listen the arguments of lobbyists and special interest groups, each trying to pull Congress in a particular direction. The public sees Congress as too powerful, impeding the president from carrying out his duties. Too often, for the public's taste, the debate is rancorous rather than calm, and focused on how prospective legislation will affect private interests rather than the public interest. None of this is surprising, of course, in a complex society where people and groups do have quite different interests and views of the world. But, as two political scientists recently commented, "The people want democracy without the mess and Congress is a tangible reminder that democracy is messy."[3]

That being said, however, public attitudes about Congress are themselves complex. One famous political scientist once observed that Americans hate their Congress, but love their own member of Congress.[4] This is true, but attitudes are not that simple. Two-thirds of the public approve of their own representative, compared to about one-fourth who approve of the members of Congress as a whole and about the same percentage who approve of congressional leaders.

The public thinks that most members of Congress care more about power than about the best interests of the nation, care more about special interests than the people, and lose touch with the people quickly after being elected. Although almost half think that most members of Congress are doing the best job they can, only 30% believe that members have high personal moral codes and even fewer believe that members care deeply about the problems of ordinary citizens. In other words, the public thinks members of Congress are a rather crass and self-interested group.

Despite all this, nearly 90 percent approve of Congress as an abstract institution, separate from the people in it.[5] The idea of a Congress as enshrined in the Constitution is important and esteemed. It is the people *in* Congress and the way Congress works that the public dislikes.

In addition to the public's dislike for Congress's messy processes, Congress seems to be blamed for the nation's problems, and for taxes and government wastefulness. Conflicts of interest also mar its reputation. Members themselves greatly contribute to the poor image of Congress by belittling the institution and promising voters a change when they campaign for office. They denigrate Congress to get themselves elected.[6]

And if that were not bad enough, the public tends to believe there is one "public interest," and if Congress is not passing legislation to pursue that interest, there must be something wrong. Only a minority of

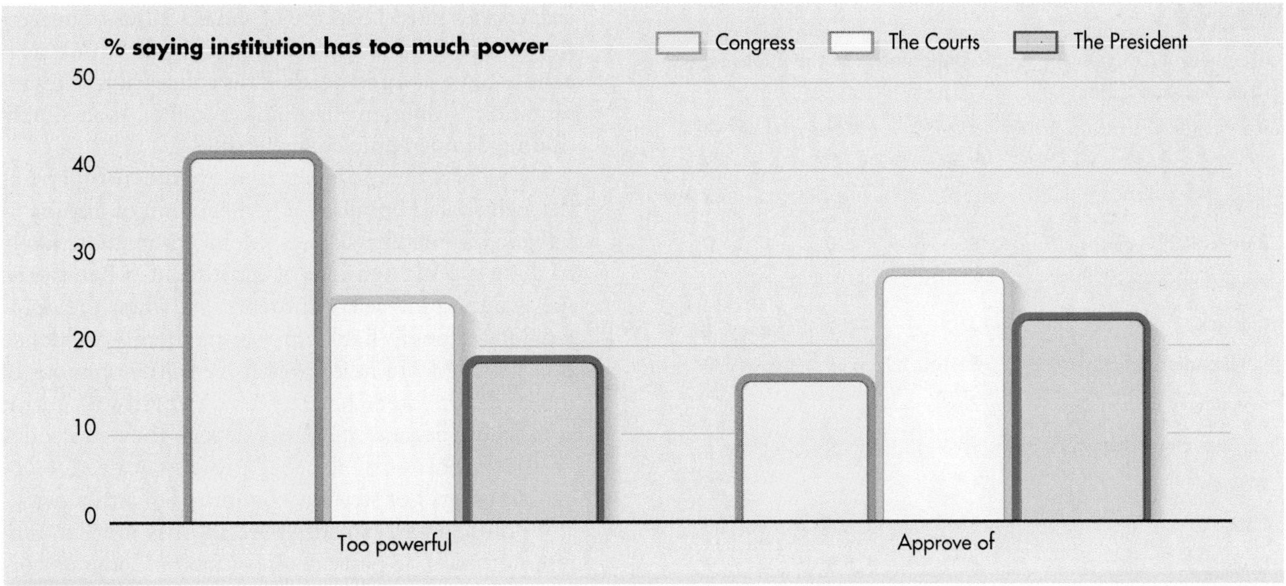

FIGURE 1

Public Perceives Congress as Most Powerful National Institution, and Likes It the Least

SOURCE: John Hibbing and Elizabeth Theiss-Morse, *Congress as Public Enemy* (Cambridge: Cambridge University Press, 1995). Data are from 1993.

the public, it seems, has a sophisticated understanding that there are many different interests in American society, and that Congress is the focus of controversy over which version of the public interest is adopted.

Individual members seem to be judged by other criteria than the whole Congress.[7] Members who work hard for their constituencies, doing favors for individual constituents and winning economic benefits for the district, usually are reelected. Policy failures of the institution do not seem to hurt them.

In this chapter, we try to understand this paradoxical pattern of citizen attitudes toward their representatives and their Congress by looking at the members of Congress and their backgrounds, elections, and behaviors. What do members of Congress do that makes them so popular back home? Then we look at Congress itself, how it works, and why it is a focus of public criticism.

MEMBERS AND CONSTITUENCIES

Alexis de Tocqueville was not impressed with the status of members of Congress, noting that they were "almost all obscure individuals, village lawyers, men in trades, or even persons belonging to the lower class." De Tocqueville would still find lawyers, but in the modern Congress he would find none belonging to the lower class.

Members

The Constitution places few formal restrictions on membership in Congress. One must be 25 years old to serve in the House and 30 in the Senate. One has to be a citizen for 7 years to be elected to the House and 9 to the Senate. Members must reside in the states from which they were elected, but House members need not reside in their own districts.

SOCIAL CHARACTERISTICS

Despite these rather loose requirements, Congress is not very representative of society. The process of recruiting, nominating, and selecting ensures that only certain types of individuals serve in Congress. Members tend to be very high in education, income, and occupational status compared to the rest of the population (see Table 1). Nearly all have college degrees, and a majority have graduate or professional degrees. Members are also quite well-off financially. Over one-fourth of the senators and one-ninth of the representatives are estimated to be millionaires. Although blue-collar workers constitute nearly one-third of the working population, there are no blue-collar workers in Congress. More than half the members of the House have served in their state legislature.[8]

By far the most common occupation of both senators and representatives is the law. Over the past decade, about 40% of the members of the House and over 50% of the Senate were lawyers. Law and politics

TABLE 1

Members of Congress Are Not Representative of the Public in Race, Sex, and Color

	POPULATION (%)	HOUSE (%)	SENATE (%)
Lawyer[a]	.6	40	54
Blue-collar[a]	30	0	0
Race & ethnicity*[b]			
Black	12	9	1
Hispanic	8	4	0
Asian	2	1	2
American Indian	1	0	1
Women[b]	51	12	9
Catholic[a]	23	26	20
Jewish[a]	4	5	9
Millionaires[a]	**	12	28
Mean age[a]	33	51	58

[a]Data are for 1993–1994. [b]Data are for 1997–1998.

* Does not include nonvoting Hispanic members from Puerto Rico, Guam, Samoa, and the Virgin Islands or the black nonvoting members from the District of Columbia.

**.05% (one-twentieth percent)

SOURCES: *Congressional Quarterly Weekly Report,* November 12, 1994, pp. 7–12; Glenn R. Simpson, "Representative Moneybags," *Washington Post National Weekly Edition,* May 2–8, 1994, p. 25; *Congressional Quarterly Weekly Report,* supplement to No. 45, November 9, 1996.

are closely linked. Many people enter law specifically because they see it as a stepping-stone to a political career. Lawyers can take time out from a legal practice to pursue a political career whereas most salaried or wage-earning individuals cannot. The personal contacts developed in law also can be invaluable in politics, and many former members of Congress enter law firms at salaries far higher than they commanded before serving in Congress.

Congress always has been predominantly white, Anglo (that is, not Hispanic), and male. It is only slightly less so today, as Table 1 shows. White, non-Hispanic males, who make up less than 40% of the total population, comprise about 80% of the House and 90% of the Senate. Thus, Congress is not very representative in its demographic characteristics.

OPINIONS AND PARTY IDENTIFICATION

Members of Congress seek to represent their **constituencies.** Those in districts filled with farmers must represent farmers, whether or not they know anything about farming. Representatives of districts with large universities must be aware of the reactions of university constituents even if they personally think academics have pointed heads. This conception of representation is different and more complex than simply sharing demographic characteristics.

One way members represent their constituents is through shared opinions. The liberalism of districts is reflected in members' votes. Members are more likely to share specific opinions of constituents when the issue is important to constituents and when the opinions are strongly held.[9] However, there is evidence that members are more responsive to the opinions of independent voters than to their own partisans.[10] This is probably because members believe they can count on the support of their own partisans but need to appeal to voters not strongly committed to either party.

Political party loyalties are another route to representation. The party composition of Congress corresponds rather well with the party identification of the public. Just as Democrats have been more numerous than Republicans in the public, Democrats have held majorities in both houses of Congress most of the years since World War II (see endpapers). The Republican victory in 1994 corresponded with the increase in Republican partisans during the 1980s, though there are still more Democrats than Republicans in the population.

Constituencies

Senators' constituencies include all the residents of their respective states; each state elects two senators. The number of each state's representatives is based on its population. Most members of the House are elected from districts within states, although six states have only one representative.

Initially, the House of Representatives had 59 members, but as the nation grew and more states joined the Union, the size of the House increased too. Since 1910, it has had 435 members except in the 1950s, when seats were temporarily added for Alaska and Hawaii. Every 10 years, in a process called **reapportionment,** the 435 seats are distributed among the states based on population changes.

Within a constant 435-seat House, states with fast-growing populations gain seats, while those with slow-growing or declining populations lose seats. Since World War II, population movement in the United States has been toward the South, West, and Southwest and away from the Midwest and Northeast. This has been reflected in the allocation of house seats. Since 1950, California has gained 22 seats and New York has lost 12, for example. In the next reapportionment after the 2000 census, Sunbelt states will continue to gain seats.

States that gain or lose seats and other states with population shifts within the state must redraw their district boundaries, a process called **redistricting.** This is always a hot political issue. The precise boundaries of a district can influence the election prospects of candidates and parties. In fact, districts often are formed with weird shapes to benefit the party in control of the state legislature. The term **gerrymander** is used to describe a district that is designed to maximize the political advantage of a party or a racial group (see also Chapter 7).

Majority parties in state legislatures continue to secure political advantage by drawing districts of bizarre shapes, although the Supreme Court requires all congressional districts to be approximately equal in population. Before 1960, states were often reluctant to redistrict their state legislative and congressional boundaries to conform to population changes within the state. Such redistricting would endanger incumbents and threaten rural areas whose populations were declining. After decades without reapportioning, some legislative districts in urban areas were as much as 19 times the population of rural districts.

When state legislatures, frequently dominated by rural representatives, still refused to reapportion themselves, the Supreme Court in *Baker v. Carr* (1962) issued the first in a series of rulings forcing states to reapportion their legislative districts.[11] In 1964, the Court required congressional districts to be approximately equal in population, thus mandating the principle of "one person, one vote."[12] As a result, most states had to redraw district lines, some more than once, during the 1960s. These decisions fueled heated controversy, including a proposed constitutional amendment to overturn them. But after a while the principle of "one person, one vote" came to be widely accepted.

Because of the important role state legislatures play in the redistricting process in most states, both parties see the 2000 state legislative elections as crucial. In the early 1980s, Democratic-controlled state legislatures were able to help Democratic candidates in states like California by drawing lines that concentrated Republican strength in a few areas and created districts with small Democratic majorities.[13] After the 1990 state legislative elections, which gave Republicans more clout, many states drew boundaries favoring Republicans, a factor in the Republicans' victories in 1994.

Another important aspect of redistricting is representation of women and minorities. Inroads into the House by women have been slow because of the large proportion of incumbents and their nearly perfect record of getting reelected. In 1992, however, there were many more open seats than usual, partly due to redistricting, and women were able to win about one-third of open seats.

Different factors influence the impact of redistricting on minority representation. A significant increase in the proportion of blacks or Hispanics serving in Congress will most likely depend on whether any more majority black or Hispanic districts are created. As we saw in Chapter 7, in 1992, 11 new districts were created with black majorities and 6 with Hispanic majorities; all but 1 were won by blacks and Hispanics. However, recent Supreme Court decisions have suggested that using race as a primary basis for creating districts is unconstitutional.[14]

The racial redistricting issue also affects the partisan composition of Congress. In some southern states, several Democratic districts were weakened in order to create one or two new majority black districts; Democratic black voters were redistricted from newly solid Democratic districts, leaving these districts with fewer Democrats and thereby creating Republican majorities.[15] The exact impact of this change is still being debated, but clearly the overall effect was to substantially weaken Democratic electoral strength in several states.[16]

This outcome was part of a deliberate strategy of the Republican Party in several southern states. The party often worked in concert with civil rights groups to encourage this redistricting, believing that it could result in new conservative Republican districts. Partly as a result, Republicans won 18 congressional seats for the first time in 1994.

CONGRESSIONAL CAMPAIGNS AND ELECTIONS

To understand Congress, one must understand the process by which its members are elected.[17] Because reelection is an important objective for almost all members of Congress and *the* most important objective for many, members work at being reelected throughout their terms. Most are successful, though senators are not as secure as members of the House. In 7 of the last 15 elections, over 20% of Senate incumbents were defeated; only twice were comparable House rates as large as 10%.

The Advantages of Incumbency

Before they even take the oath of office, newly elected representatives are given an introduction to the advantages of incumbency. At meetings arranged by the Democratic and Republican leadership and by the House Administrative Committee, new members learn about free mailing privileges, computers and software to help them target letters to specialized groups of constituents, facilities to make videotapes and audiotapes to send to

SYMBOLIC SOLUTIONS FOR COMPLEX PROBLEMS?

TERM LIMITS

"Throw the rascals out!" has been the battle cry of the 1990s. Fed up with politicians and politics, voters are calling for limits to the years that legislators can serve. Members of Congress and state legislators are the focus of voter anger, symbolizing everything that voters do not like about politics.

Over 70% of the public say they favor term limits.[1] Consequently, in 23 of 24 states that allow citizens to vote directly on bills, voters have adopted term limits for their members of Congress and state legislators. In New Hampshire and Utah the state legislatures themselves passed term limits. In most states, the limits are 12 years; for Congress, that means a limit of two Senate and six House terms.

Though Congress narrowly defeated term limit legislation, several states passed legislation that would have imposed term limits on the congressional delegations in their states. But in 1995, in a 5–4 vote, the Supreme Court held term limits for members of Congress unconstitutional. The majority argued that permitting individual states to have diverse qualifications for Congress would "result in a patchwork of state qualifications, undermining the uniformity and national character that the Framers envisioned and sought to ensure."[2] The Court indicated that state laws added to the qualifications spelled out in the Constitution (age and citizenship), therefore, in effect, "amending" the Constitution. Only a constitutional amendment can amend the Constitution, and supporters of term limits continue to push for such an amendment.

Are term limits merely a symbolic solution, perhaps assuaging the feelings of those who think government is out of control without changing the behavior of legislators at all? Or are term limits a good solution to a real problem of entrenched legislators forgetting about their constituency and building personal empires? Or will term limits actually be a negative factor, exacerbating problems that already exist with government?

Term limits were part of our original governing document, the Articles of Confederation, but were not adopted by the framers of the Constitution. Why do many people now favor term limits?

Some supporters cling to the mid-nineteenth century image of "citizen lawmakers," who set aside their personal business for a few years to attend to the public's business and then return home. Most supporters believe that by not having to worry about continuing to be elected, legislators can be free to consider the "public interest," not the "special interests," and will have no desire to build personal empires. Others also see term limits as a way to weaken the power of government by having a more rapid turnover of members of legislatures. Members without experience, this argument holds, could not learn the ropes fast enough to be able to wield power effectively. Still others saw term limits as a way to break the 60-year-old stranglehold of the Democrats on Congress, a rationale that was undercut by the Republican victories in 1994.

Opponents, including many Republicans, argue that term limits are a very bad, and very radical, idea. Term limits are antidemocratic in that they restrict the ability of voters to elect whomever they please to Congress. If Congressman Smith is not doing a good job, his constituents can elect someone else. Term limits allow Congresswoman Jones to tell Congressman Smith's constituents they cannot elect Smith. Even though the results of democracy are not always ideal, as one commentator remarked, "democracy is like blowing one's nose—you should do it yourself, even if you do it badly."[3]

Opponents also point out that the world is a much more complex place than in the early nineteenth century when many legislators were "citizen legislators." Today, most people want their heart surgery done by "career cardiac surgeons," not by people who sell real estate or teach school for a career and take two years off to try being surgeons. They want their legal problems handled by "career lawyers," their teeth pulled by "career dentists," and their bridges designed by "career engineers." Likewise, opponents of term limits argue, it is appropriate to have laws drafted by "career legislators," or at

hometown media, and other "perks" designed to keep members in touch with their constituencies and not coincidentally to help win reelection.

Incumbents win because, for a number of reasons, they are better known than nonincumbents and voters evaluate them more positively. Almost all voters can recognize the name of their representatives; they have seen the representatives on television or received mail from them, and they can give a general rating of their performances (see Figure 2).[18] Although most voters can correctly identify their representatives as liberal or conservative, only a small minority know how their representatives voted on any issue.[19] Therefore, representatives have the advantage of name recognition without the disadvantage of having voters know how they really voted.

Representatives' high level of public recognition is not so surprising given that members of Congress spend most of their time and energy looking for and using opportunities to make themselves known to their con-

least legislative bodies with a significant membership of experienced legislators.

Term limits also attack a problem that does not exist. They are a response to the very high reelection rates of the late 1980s, when the reelection rate of House incumbents was over 90%. However, the elections of 1992 and 1994 show that when voters want change, they can effect change by voting incumbents out. In 1995, 45% of the members of the House and 25% of the Senate were first elected in 1992 or 1994. In other words, there is already considerable turnover in legislatures without term limits.

Term limits also break the tie between citizens and their representatives. If representatives are not responsible to their voters, to whom are they responsible? Opponents of term limits fear that these limits will strengthen the power of lobbyists, bureaucrats, and committee staffs. These unelected officials will have the knowledge about policies and procedures that legislators elected for only a few years cannot possibly have. It is sometimes said that it takes members four years to learn when they are being snookered by lobbyists or bureaucrats; it takes six years to begin to accomplish something.[4] Term limits of six or eight years would ensure a legislature full of individuals with less knowledge than the professional bureaucrats have. As one long-term Republican congressman noted about term limits: "Career politician is an epithet. But pass term limits, and professionals . . . will run this government. Only they will not be elected: they will be the faceless, nameless, try-to-get-them-on-the-phone, unaccountable permanent bureaucracy."[5] It is unlikely that this is the outcome favored by those who prefer term limits.

About one-third of the nation's legislators are serving under term limits.[6] In Michigan, where term limits have been in effect, observers believe that lobbyists have more influence than before.[7] Moreover, some newly elected members, knowing they can only serve six years, have already started looking for their next jobs—by currying favor with lobbyists.

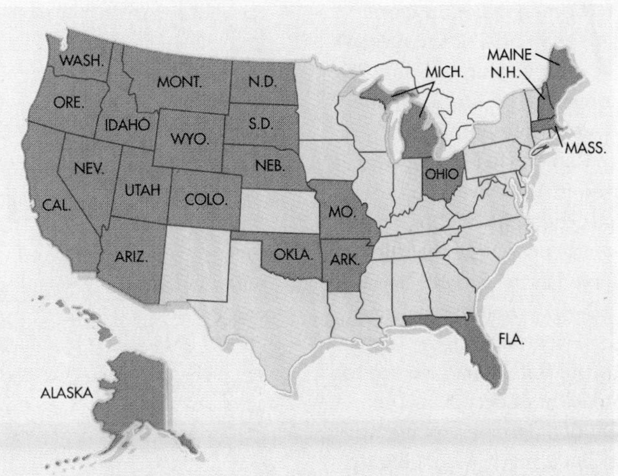

Blue areas show states that have passed term limits.

1. David Broder, "Dumbing Down Democracy," *Lincoln Journal,* April 5, 1995, p. 18.
2. Quoted in Kenneth J. Cooper and Helen Dewar, "No Limits on the Term Limits Crusade," *Washington Post National Weekly Edition,* May 29–June 4, 1995, p. 14. The majority of the Court included John Paul Stevens, Anthony Kennedy, David Souter, Ruth Bader Ginsburg, and Stephen Breyer.
3. Garry Wills, "Term Limits Attack Corrupt Electorate," *Lincoln Journal,* March 16, 1992, p. 6.
4. James J. Kilpatrick, "Cincinnatus' Time Is Past: Term Limits Are a Bad Idea," *Lincoln Journal,* September 3, 1992, p. 16.
5. Broder, "Dumbing Down Democracy."
6. Lois Romano, "Setting the Stage for Amateur Hour," *Washington Post National Weekly Edition,* 1998.
7. Arlene Levinson, "Michigan First among 20 States Dealing with Term Limits," *Centre Daily Times,* April 23, 1995, p. 9A.

stituents. Members visit their home districts or states an average of 35 times a year—at taxpayers' expense.[20]

Sometimes members take unusual steps in an attempt to become better known. One member stood on the Capitol steps "dressed in an exterminator's outfit with plastic cockroaches glued to his shoulders." He then jumped up and down, shouting "squash one for the Gipper." This was to endear himself to owners and workers of an insecticide manufacturer in his district.[21]

FRANKING

Members gain name recognition by free mail privileges called **franking.** In just six months during 1989, Senator Alfonse D'Amato (R-N.Y.) sent out nearly 17 million pieces of mail at a cost of $2.65 million. With the exception of 1990, congressional mailings have increased in volume every election year and fallen in the off-year.

Some restrictions are designed to make franking less blatantly political. For example, mass mailings

AMERICAN DIVERSITY

WOMEN IN CONGRESS

Women make up more than 50% of the nation's population but only 9% of the Congress. The first woman in Congress was Representative Jeannette Rankin (R-Mont.), who was elected in 1916 even before women got the right to vote nationally. It was not until 1932 that the first woman served in the Senate. Hattie Caraway (D-Ark.) won the seat after the death of her husband, the former occupant. The first woman elected to the Senate without occupying the Senate seat of a deceased spouse was Margaret Chase Smith, a Republican from Maine who spent a distinguished career in the Senate from 1949 to 1973.

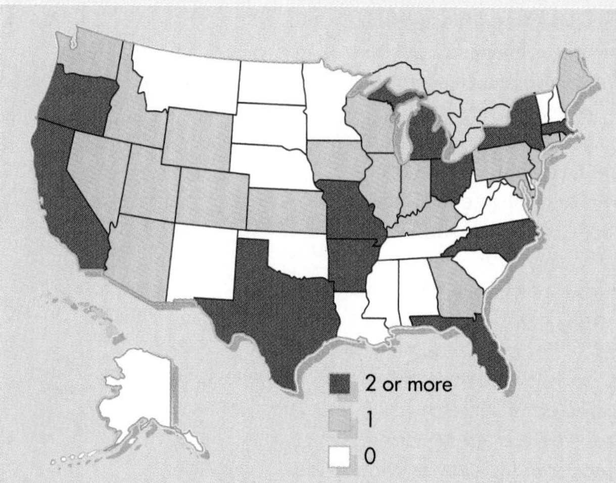

Number of women representatives by state.

SOURCE: Data from *Congressional Quarterly,* November 12, 1994, p. 10.

Many called 1992 "The Year of the Woman." Despite gains then and in succeeding elections, women make up only 9% of the Senate and 11% of the House. These paltry proportions are a large increase from the 1980s when the percentage of women in the House remained around 5% for many years. Twenty-three states have at least one woman in their delegation.

The women in Congress are racially heterogeneous. One-quarter of the women members of the House and one of the nine women Senators are black, Hispanic, or Asian.

In 1992, the proportion of women in the House increased because women targeted the extraordinarily large numbers of open seats available. Indeed, of the 65 open seats in the 1992 election, 22 were won by women. However, 6 of these new incumbents were swept out of office in the 1994 Republican landslide.

Although gains were small in 1994 and 1996, we may expect a growing proportion of women in Congress because more women are being elected to state legislatures and other offices that traditionally have been stepping-stones to Congress. Women fare about as well as men when they run for congressional seats.[1]

Women's problems are not over when they are elected, however. Women feel out of the congressional mainstream in many ways. These include small inconveniences, such as the lack of a women's restroom within 100 yards of the House floor and none at all in the Senate chamber. Only in recent years has the lavish congressional gym been open to women; before that the "ladies' health facility consisted of 10 hair dryers and a ping-pong table." More substantively, the leadership of both houses is all male. Said one woman who has tried for a seat on the prestigious Appropriations Committee three times, "Each time I've been nicely told that the women's slot is already filled on that committee." And in 1993, Nancy Johnson (R-Conn.), one of the Republicans' leading health care experts, was told by her subcommittee chair at a public hearing that she must have learned about a particular health issue through "pillow-talk" with her physician husband. The chair later apologized, but the incident was not forgotten.[2]

But women do seem to be making a substantive difference. The Congressional Caucus for Women's issues reported that in 1993–1994, Congress passed a record 66 bills of special importance to women. That nearly equals the number of such bills passed in the entire previous decade.[3]

1. For a recent analysis of Senate voting, see Philip Paolino, "Group-Salient Issues and Group Representation: Support for Women Candidates in the 1992 Senate Elections," *American Journal of Political Science* 39 (May 1995), pp. 294–313; Barbara Burrell, "Did We Get More than One 'Year of the Woman'?" paper presented at the 1995 Annual Meeting of the Midwest Political Science Association, Chicago.
2. Kevin Merida, "A Woman's Place on the Hill," *Washington Post National Weekly Edition,* April 11–17, 1994, p. 15.
3. Leslie Laurence, "Congress Makes Up for Neglect," *Lincoln Journal* (December 5, 1994), p. 8.

cannot be sent out close to an election. Regardless, one political consultant estimates that the frank is worth at least $350,000 in campaign funds.[22]

Franking privileges become even more useful when combined with sophisticated word processing systems to target very specific constituency groups with "personalized" letters. Members can maintain incredibly specialized lists, not just of Republicans and Democrats but of those living near federal prisons, small-business owners, veterans, teachers, and government employees, for example. No group is too specialized or ostensibly apolitical to be targeted. Senator Charles Grassley (R-Iowa) even sent a letter to a thousand Iowans with abbreviated intestinal tracts in honor of Ostomy Awareness Month.[23]

This system can help keep representatives in touch with their constituents. But the frank and the computer together have turned most congressional offices into full-time public relations firms. Their value in reelection is reflected in the fact that members send out much more mail in their reelection year than in other years (see Figure 3).[24]

MEDIA ATTENTION

In addition to "old-fashioned" mail, members use increasingly sophisticated production equipment and technology to make television and radio shows to send home. For example, one evening, on any of three local television news shows, residents of Boise, Idaho, might have seen their congressional representative, Larry Craig (R-Idaho), state in an interview that he was strongly opposed to a pay increase for Congress and would not take it if it were passed. The viewers were not told that the "interviewer" was one of Craig's congressional staffers and that the camera crew was that of the Republican Congressional Campaign Committee, which also paid for the broadcast.[25]

Members also like to tape themselves at committee meetings asking questions or being referred to as "Mr. (or Madam) Chairman" (because many members are chairs of at least a subcommittee). The tape then is edited to a 30-second sound bite to be sent to local television stations. Often stations run these productions as news and do not tell their viewers that they are essentially campaign features prepared by the members. But television is not alone in portraying members' self-publicity as "hard news." Congressional staffers write press releases about accomplishments of the member and fax them to local newspapers, which often print them as written. Local media, whether print or television, are often short of news with a local flavor and eagerly take whatever members give them.

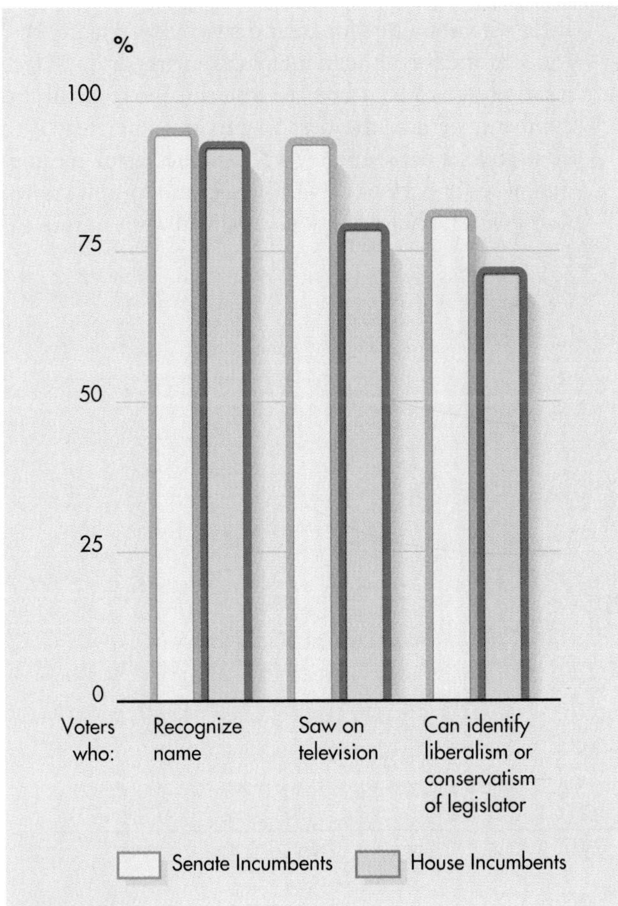

FIGURE 2

Senate and House Incumbents Are Well Known to Voters

SOURCE: John Alford and John Hibbing. "The Disparate Electoral Security of House and Senate Incumbents," paper presented at the American Political Science meetings, September 1989, Atlanta, Georgia.

CONSTITUENCY SERVICE

Members of Congress make themselves known in more routine ways. One is by providing **constituency service:** answering questions and doing personal favors for constituents who write or call for help.

This function, also called **casework,** is crucial for members and their staffs, who function as red-tape cutters for everyone from elderly citizens having difficulties with Social Security to small-town mayors trying to get federal grants for new sewer systems. Members provide information to students working on term papers and citizens puzzled about which federal agency to ask for assistance. Members can provide gifts of calendars, U.S. flags that were flown over the Capitol, and brochures and publications of the federal government.

Requests for service often come by mail. More than half the congressional office staffs work on the flood of mail that pours in. Some offices get 5,000 to 10,000 requests per year for assistance.[26] In addition to handling casework in Washington offices, most senators and representatives have one or more state or home district offices to deal personally with constituents and their casework. More than 35% of senators' staffs and 40% of all representatives' staffs are located in their home state or district.[27]

Citizens turn to their congressional representatives because they see them as allies in their struggles with bureaucracy.[28] Members of Congress, who are in large part responsible for the establishment of the huge Washington bureaucracy, are able to score with voters by helping them cope with the bureaucracy they have created.[29] Individual members may have limited power in trying to get important legislation passed, but in dealing with a constituent's problems, their power is much greater because of their clout with bureaucrats. A phone call or letter to a federal agency will bring attention to the constituent's problem.

Of course, not all casework is directed toward winning reelection. Some members say they enjoy their casework more than their policy roles, perhaps because the results of casework are often more immediate and tangible. Certainly, casework allows members to build nonpartisan and seemingly nonpolitical ties with their constituents, an advantage in this antipolitical era.

PORK BARREL

Another way members gain the attention of constituents is to obtain funds for special projects, new programs, buildings, or other public works in their districts or states. Such benefits, often called **pork barrel** projects, comprise about a seventh of the budget not devoted to entitlements and interest. They are sometimes defined as "federal spending with a zip code attached."[30] In the final days of one session of Congress, for example, a few of the last-minute pork barrel projects approved included a $3.6 million irrigation project for Maine's potato growers and a $400,000 fuel dock for a Hawaiian hotel.[31] These projects are desired by constituents because they provide jobs and business in the local district.

Because members consider pork barrel projects crucial to reelection chances, there is little support in Congress for eliminating projects known to be unwise or wasteful. Liberals and conservatives, Democrats and Republicans, protect these kinds of projects. Former Senator Alfonse D'Amato (R-N.Y.) was called "Senator Pothole" for his ability to win highway and transportation projects for New York. One conservative Kentucky Republican argued for a freeway in his district in 1995: "This project is not pork, [it is] a vital infrastructure necessity."[32] David Stockman, former President Reagan's director of the Office of Management and Budget, observed, "There's no such thing as a fiscal conservative when it comes to his district."[33]

FUND-RAISING

Another advantage of incumbency is the opportunity to raise funds from the hundreds of PACs that populate Washington. Eager to gain access to members of Congress, PACs make fund-raising much easier for incumbents than challengers, as we pointed out in Chapter 9.

Unsafe at Any Margin?

Most members are reelected even if they have done relatively little constituency work or have obtained little federal money for their districts (see Figure 4).[34] Indeed, one Republican member remarked, "Let's face it, you have to be a bozo to lose this job."[35] Still, incumbents believe the best way to ensure victory is to be so good at constituency work, so successful in bringing pieces of pork to their districts, and so well known to the voters that no serious rival will want to run. In-

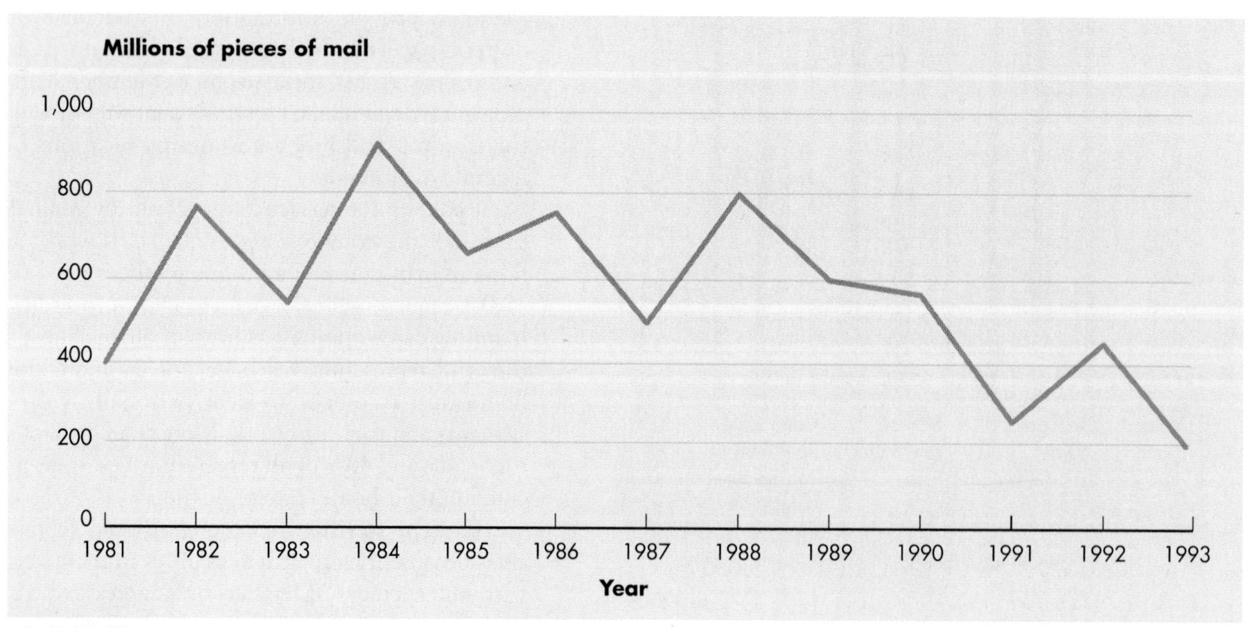

FIGURE 3

Members of Congress Send More Mass Mail in Election Years

SOURCE: Norman Ornstein, Thomas Mann, and Michael Malbin, *Vital Statistics of Congress, 1995–1996* (Washington, D.C.: CQ Press, 1996), p. 170.

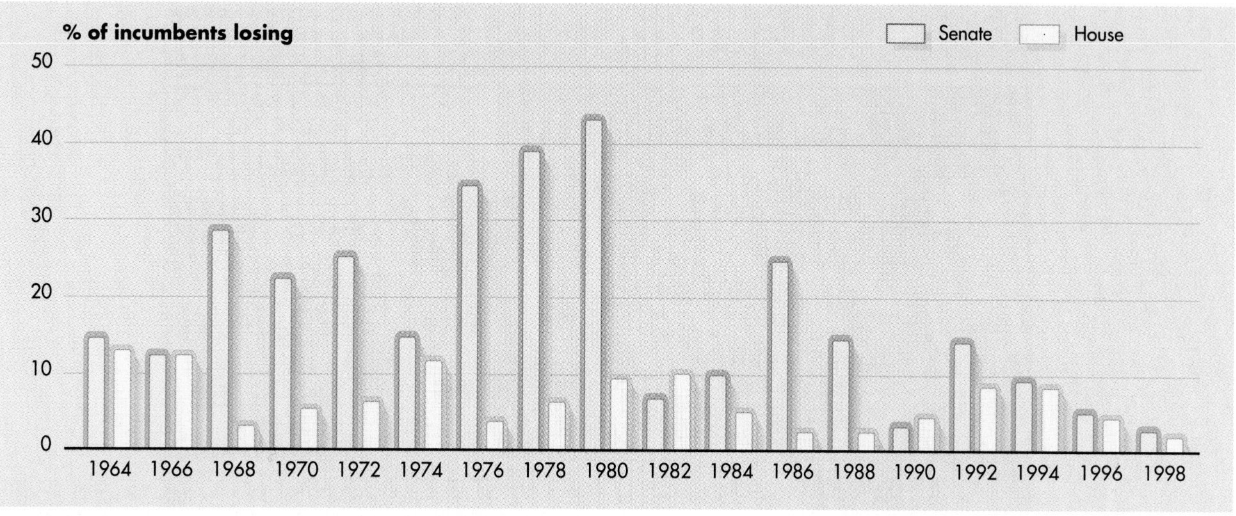

FIGURE 4

House Incumbents Have Had Secure Jobs in Recent Years

Notice that in the 1980s more House incumbents lost in the reapportionment year of 1982. In the 1970s more lost in the Watergate year, 1974, when many Republican defenders of President Nixon were defeated. In the 1960s reapportionment did not start until after 1962, so the elections of 1964 and 1966 reflected reapportionment.

SOURCES: *Congressional Quarterly Weekly Report,* November 19, 1988, p. 18, and November 10, 1990, p. 3801; "Women, Minorities Join Senate," *CQ Almanac,* 1992, pp. 8A–14A; "Wave of Diversity Spared Many Incumbents," *CQ Almanac,* 1992, pp. 15A–21A, 24A.

cumbents hope potential rivals will bide their time and wait for a better year or run for some other office.[36]

Given their advantages, you may wonder why incumbents worry about losing. But worry they do. One political scientist proclaimed that members feel "unsafe at any margin."[37] No matter how big their last victory, they worry that their next campaign will bring defeat. And despite the high reelection rate of incumbents, some are defeated. This fear prompts them to spend even more of their energies preparing for the next campaign.

But this fear is fairly remote. Even in the anti-incumbent elections of 1994, only 9% of House incumbents lost (all of them Democrats). In 1998, less than 2% did. Senators are usually somewhat more vulnerable. Fifteen percent lost in 1992 and 10% in 1994, but only 3% lost in 1998. Clearly, the electoral benefit of incumbency still exists for the great majority of candidates who choose to run for reelection.[38] Turnover in Congress comes primarily from those who decide not to run, sometimes from fear of losing.

Challengers

Another reason for the uneasiness of incumbents is that as their media and public relations sophistication has grown, so has that of challengers. Still, without the advantages of the free frank and other opportunities to become well known to constituents, challengers have a difficult time. The best advice to someone who wants to be a member of Congress is to find an open seat.

To beat an incumbent, challengers need money. The more they spend, the more likely they are to win. In recent House campaigns, a challenger needed to spend at least $250,000 to have even a one in four chance of winning—and the cost continues to rise.[39]

Spending is important for challengers because they must make themselves known in a positive way, and they must suggest that something is wrong with the incumbent. Usually, challengers will charge incumbents with ignoring the district, being absent from committee hearings or floor votes, being too liberal or too conservative, or voting incorrectly on a key issue. Sometimes, of course, the incumbent has been involved in a scandal, which offers a ready target for the challenger.[40]

Sometimes challengers will try unusual tactics to make themselves known. Tom Harkin (D-Iowa) worked in a series of blue-collar jobs when running for the House to show people in his district that he understood their problems. Meanwhile he got a lot of free publicity.

Senate challengers have a slightly better chance than House challengers. One reason is that there are stronger candidates to challenge incumbent senators because Senate seats are a bigger prize and because in a statewide constituency there are more potential challengers. Senate challengers are better known than House challengers.[41] They are often former governors or members of the House with a statewide reputation. For example, in 1988, about 80% of voters recognized

the name of the person running against their incumbent senator; less than 60% recognized the challenger to their House incumbent.[42] Senate challengers can attract more money because they are better known.

Another reason Senate challengers have greater success is that most incumbents have constituencies (i.e., states) much larger than House districts. The greater population means that senators cannot have personal contact with as high a proportion of their constituents. Also they cannot satisfy as high a proportion since their constituencies are much more heterogeneous than House district constituencies.[43] Evidence indicates that senators from the largest states have about a six- or seven-point electoral disadvantage compared to senators from the smallest states. Senators from the smallest states do about as well as House members from their states.[44]

Campaigns

In the nineteenth century, political campaigns were organized largely by political parties, and the candidates had relatively little to do. Today, however, congressional campaigns are candidate-centered. Most candidates hire workers, raise money, and organize their own campaigns. They may recruit campaign workers from local political parties; interest groups they belong to; unions; church, civic, or other voluntary organizations; or simply groups of friends and acquaintances.[45]

Political parties do have a significant role, however. National and local parties also recruit potential candidates. Presidents make personal appeals to fellow party members who they think can run strong races, and national campaign committees also recruit aggressively. Said one Democratic congressional campaign chair, "I'm not looking for liberals or conservatives. That's not my bag. I'm looking for winners."[46] Parties also provide campaign money and assistance to candidates for polling, mailing, issue research, and getting out the vote.[47] Parties redouble their efforts when, as in 1998, control of Congress may be at stake.[48]

THE MEDIA CAMPAIGN

To wage a serious campaign, the challenger or a contender for an open seat must wage a media campaign. Candidates hire media consultants and specialists in polling, advertising, and fund-raising.

Media campaigning has attracted a new type of congressional candidate and hence a new type of congressional incumbent. The old-style politician who might have been effective in small groups but who cannot appear poised and articulate on television has given way to one who can project an attractive television image. Candidates are elected on the basis of their media skills, which may not be the same skills as those of a good lawmaker.

Candidates have become less closely linked to parties than before and, once elected, are not as indebted to their party nor as obligated to reflect party views.[49] Political parties, however, recognize this problem. Since the early 1980s, national parties have increasingly provided useful services to congressional candidates—helping them manage their campaigns, develop issues, advertise, raise money, and conduct opinion polls. National parties also give substantial sums of money to congressional candidates.[50]

CAMPAIGN MONEY

The old adage says, "Half the money spent on campaigns is wasted. The trouble is, we don't know which half." This bromide helps explain why congressional campaigns are expensive. There is a kind of "campaign arms race" as each candidate tries to do what the other candidate does and a little more, escalating costs year by year.

In 1996, winners of open seats in the House spent $670,000 on average. Successful campaigns against incumbents cost more. Million-dollar campaigns are no longer unusual. Because they are statewide, Senate races are much more expensive than House races. In 1992, winning Senate candidates spent more than $4.7 million, on average.

Voting for Congress

Just as for presidential elections, party loyalties, candidate evaluations, and issues are important factors in congressional elections.[51]

Courtesy of Ailes Communications

Until this television ad ran, former Senator Walter Huddleston (D-Ky.) was substantially ahead of his opponent. The ad pointed out that Huddleston had a poor attendance record (hence sending out bloodhounds to find him). When the local media focused on this ad, it helped bring victory to his challenger, Mitch McConnell. After Senator McConnell's victory in 1984, Senate attendance on roll-call votes was at all-time highs.

Party loyalties are even more important for congressional than for presidential elections because congressional elections are less visible, so more people base their vote on traditional party loyalties. Incumbency is also more important than in presidential races. The result is that increasingly, since about 1960, voters have split their tickets in voting for presidential and congressional candidates. This is both because voters favor congressional incumbents and because many Democrats desert their party when casting a vote for president but not for lesser offices. For example, one out of five Reagan voters in 1984 voted for a Democratic member of the House, leaving Reagan with only a 41% Republican House despite his commanding personal victory.

Normally, the party of a winning presidential candidate gains seats during a presidential election year and loses a number of seats in the midterm election. This maintains a sort of equilibrium in party control of Congress.[52] In most recent elections these losses have been modest. In 1998, however, the Democrats actually gained seats in the House and lost no seats in the Senate. To some extent, midterm election results are a referendum on how well citizens think the president is doing. The more popular the president, the better his party's candidates for Congress do. In 1998, Clinton was given credit for the economic good times the country was experiencing. The Republicans were viewed by many as not having a positive program but rather simply being against Clinton.

THE REPRESENTATIVE ON THE JOB

Informal Norms

In addition to the formal requirements of the representative's job—which are few—there are **informal norms** learned from colleagues, staff, and the press. Like the subtle socialization of young people, new members of Congress learn the ways of their elders.[53] These norms help keep the institution running smoothly by attempting to diminish friction and competition among members. As in other American institutions, the norms of Congress have changed.

Thirty years ago, the most important norm was **institutional loyalty,** the expectation that members would respect their fellow members and the Congress itself, especially their own house. Personal criticism of one's colleagues was to be avoided, and mutual respect was fostered by such conventions as referring to colleagues by title, such as "The distinguished senator from New York," rather than by name. This norm has seriously eroded in the last two decades, leading some to call for a return to "civility."

Reciprocity, also called "logrolling," is reflected in the statement, "you support my bill and I'll support yours." This is another norm that is increasingly threatened. Sam Ervin, the late Democratic senator from tobacco-growing North Carolina, is reported to have told an audience from North Dakota, "I got to know Milt Young [then a senator from North Dakota] very well. And I told Milt, 'Milt, I would just like you to tell me how to vote about wheat and sugar beets and things like that, if you just help me out on tobacco.' "[54]

Tied to the norm of reciprocity is the norm of **specialization.** Members cannot be knowledgeable in all areas, so they specialize in some area related to their committee work. The Senate traditionally has been more individualistic than the House and less willing to give priority to specialists. Many senators see themselves as potential presidential candidates who need to be well versed on a variety of issues. The Senate is also much smaller so there are fewer members to cover all the issues.

Specialization and reciprocity increase the influence of individual members but also facilitate the smooth running of the institution. By specializing, a member can become an expert. Reciprocity helps members' work be accepted by their colleagues.

Norms have changed as decentralization and a "go your own way" sentiment are typical. Open meetings and media scrutiny have made it more difficult for members to "go along" on bills unpopular in their constituency. The increased fears of members for their electoral security reaffirm this basic caution and individualism.

Members have also become more willing to challenge the work of their colleagues, making it difficult for anyone to control Congress and direct its energies to the solution of public problems. On the other hand, the decline of these norms means that the institution is more democratic, because new members can have influence without being under the thumb of more senior members.

Working Privately and "Going Public"

A member's routine traditionally involved bargaining with other members, lobbyists, and representatives of the administration. Working privately, one-on-one in small groups, or in committees, members and staff discussed and debated issues, exchanged information, and planned strategies. Twenty years ago most issues were probably resolved this way. Even though many issues still are resolved through these private channels, much has changed in the way Congress operates.

Today members believe it is as important to "go public" as it is to engage in private negotiation.[55] **Going public** means to carry an issue debate to the public through the media. Congress goes public by televising floor debates and important hearings, and leaders and individual members go public by using the media to further their goals.

C-SPAN

From time to time, television networks broadcast important hearings, such as those for the Watergate scandal and for the Iran-contra affair. But more regular exposure comes daily on C-SPAN. In 1979, after considerable controversy and anxiety, the House began routinely to televise its proceedings. Fearful of being overshadowed by the House, and mindful of Ronald Reagan's advice on how to deal with televised coverage ("Learn your lines, don't bump into furniture, and, in kissing, keep your mouth closed"), in 1986 the Senate followed suit.[56] This coverage is available to more than 60 million people on cable television through C-SPAN. Estimates are that more than one-third of C-SPAN subscribers watch their legislators at least one hour a month.[57] Even more see them in session when network news programs use footage of members making speeches.[58]

OTHER USE OF THE MEDIA

During the 1980s, other use of the media by congressional leadership increased tremendously. Newt Gingrich's (R-Ga.) rise to power was attributed in part to his strategic use of television. He understood the potential of television and other technology. He used

WHAT GOVERNMENT DOES RIGHT

MUDDLING THROUGH TO COMPROMISE—AND SUCCESS

As we have noted, one of the most frustrating things about Congress for the average citizen is the "messiness" of the legislative process. Not only is the process of crafting laws incredibly complex, but it provides so many places along the way where individual legislators and interest groups, often for seemingly selfish motives, can exact concessions from the people who want to pass the bill. Add to that the partisan bickering, with Democrats picking a proposal apart simply because a Republican introduced it, for example, and casual observers are ready to throw up their hands in exasperation. How can we get good legislation when special interests, partisan concerns, and pork-hungry legislators dominate the lawmaking process?

Perhaps surprisingly, Congress legislates better than people commonly think. It has brought down the federal deficit dramatically—modest surpluses are expected for the next several years. It has made voter registration easier by allowing states to register voters when they apply for drivers' licenses. It has changed the telecommunication industry, providing for greater competition among telephone, cable, and television companies.

And Congress has usually accomplished these legislative goals *because* of its frustrating procedures, not in spite of them. The legislative process in Congress sometimes works well *because* individual legislators (especially senators) can derail bills, *because* interest groups can make their voices heard effectively, and *because* parties nitpick at each others' proposals. Moreover, because the process is slow, people who may be affected by a piece of legislation have time to let their representatives know about their concerns before the bill is passed.

Laws are effective if people accept them. That means that representatives have to try to build a consensus for their legislation. With no consensus, the losing side would simply work harder the next time to overturn the law, and if it wins, the other side would work to change things back again in following years. But if legislators build a consensus, all sides, and in complex matters there may be more than two, have an incentive to make the outcome work. After all, a reconsideration may lead to a worse result, so why risk it?

When individual legislators and lobbyists raise objections to a bill, their views suggest that a consensus has not emerged, that there are still some unresolved problems with the bill that need to be worked out. When the concerns are minor, they can either be taken care of quickly with a trivial amendment or ignored. If the representative has a strong power base, such as the chair of a relevant subcommittee, the objection can rarely be ignored. When the concerns are more significant, then reworking of the bill becomes the best path to a consensus.

Parties play a somewhat different role. Parties institutionalize criticism. By that we mean that parties see criticizing the opposition's proposals as important, and they have an incentive to find chinks in the other party's armor. When legislation is introduced in Congress, a group of legislators are ready and willing (some would say eager) to find fault with the bill. Frequently, the difficulties they find are minor and rarely heard of again. But just as frequently, the opposition party discovers that some elements of the proposal hurt significant segments of the population in unacceptable ways. By voicing such concerns, one party forces legislative attention on the suspect sections of the bill, leading, it hopes, to changes. Without parties playing this role, legislation may not always be examined in as much detail or with as critical an eye.

Consensus takes time to develop. When Congress passed a bill that reorganized many worker training programs and moved their administration to the states in 1995, the Senate voted 95–2 and the House 345–79 in favor. These margins show widespread satisfaction with the bill, but that acceptance was a long time developing. "Such victories," political commentator David Broder said, "are the result of hours (or in this case, years) of hard work by members of Congress and their staffs, negotiating with each other and with representatives of the affected constituencies."[1]

You and I rarely hear of such successes. What we learn from the media about Congress reflects conflict, not compromise. Yet by resolving conflicts and developing a consensus, Congress legislates effectively. It might well be said that the faults people find with Congress are in fact its greatest strengths, for those "shortcomings" allow Congress to accomplish its objective: legislation that has widespread support.

1. David S. Broder, "Manpower Bill Shows Good Intentions Sometimes Survive," *Lincoln Journal-Star,* October 18, 1995, p. 9B.

language that appeals to the public (as one reporter noted, he's "absolutist, aggressive, hyperbolic, informed, topical, unpredictable, and studied in his use of supercharged symbolic language").[59] His stated goal was to shape the entire nation through the news media.

Even before becoming a party leader, Gingrich illustrated strategic use of the media. He regularly stood on the House floor denouncing Democrats; because the camera is stationary, on TV it looked as if he were speaking to an interested audience of members. In reality he was talking to an empty chamber. The former Speaker of the House, Tip O'Neill, once ordered the House cameras to pan the chamber to expose Gingrich's make-believe performance, although the ensuing debate between Gingrich and O'Neill gave Gingrich even more publicity.

As leader, Gingrich continued to make use of the media to set the agenda for public debate, and he often put Bill Clinton on the defensive. As one observer noted, "Bill Clinton is the Jello, Newt is the mold."[60] However, Clinton may have had the last laugh when the poor Republican showing in the 1998 elections led Republicans to question Gingrich's leadership and, in turn, led Gingrich to resign.

The congressional leadership of both parties now goes public too. Leaders regularly call producers of television talk shows to suggest guests. They meet with the press and often have prepared statements. Before important congressional votes on key issues, the leadership plans letters to the editors of important newspapers and floor speeches designed for maximum television coverage.

The more media-oriented among the rank-and-file members are also experts in providing short and interesting comments for the nightly network news, writing articles for major newspapers, and appearing on talk shows and as commentators on news programs.

Voting by Members

We have seen that members of Congress represent their constituents through service and by obtaining special benefits for the district or state. A third major kind of representation is policy representation. In the eyes of most people, members are sent to Washington to make laws. By casting hundreds of votes each year, members try to represent the interests of their constituencies as they see them and in the process win support for reelection. Increasingly, constituents are becoming more active in communicating with their legislators. Members are flooded with faxes, poll results, and mailgrams, often stimulated as a result of radio or television talk shows. These individuals, however, do not represent the entire constituency. Talk show callers and listeners, for example, are more likely than other voters to be conservative, Republican, and male.[61]

Constituency opinion is often uninformed, divided, or apathetic. Because most votes in Congress are not on subjects the electorate knows little about, members cannot, and often do not want to, rely on a simple polling of constituents to tell them how to vote. The opinions of constituents do matter, but other influences are also important: the party, the president, the members' ideology, staffers, and other members' recommendations. Members look to these sources for cues as to how to vote.

PARTY AND CONSTITUENCY

Forty to 60% of the ballots in Congress are party votes; that is, a majority of one party opposes a majority of the other. In these votes, party members support their party between 70% and 90% of the time. Party support increased during the 1980s and is now at near record highs.

There are several reasons for the continuing importance of party. All members of Congress are elected on a partisan ballot, and Congress organizes itself on a partisan basis. Members tend to have policy views similar to others in their party, at least more similar than to those in the opposite party. Many members receive significant campaign support from the party, and party leaders try hard to influence party members to vote the "right" way. Party votes reflect different constituency needs, too, because Democratic and Republican constituencies are different.

Members must also be responsive to their constituents. Members have several constituencies, including not only their entire district but also constituencies within the district, such as voters of their party, major socioeconomic groups, and their own personal supporters.[62] Sometimes these constituencies may be in conflict. The representatives' personal constituency may be more liberal or conservative than the district as a whole. When members vote in conflict with what seems to be the sentiments of the majority of voters in the district, it may be that they are responding to their own supporters or partisans. Of course, in those rare instances where most of the representative's constituents feel strongly about an issue, the member cannot buck an overwhelming majority and expect to win reelection.

When neither the member or the member's constituents have strong feelings on an issue, it is certainly in the member's interest to go along with party leaders, who have some "perks" to dispense or pressure to exert. Although their efforts are usually low-key, party leaders sometimes turn on the heat. In a successful vote to override a Reagan veto, Democratic Senate leaders adopted a "baby-sitting" strategy to make sure that wavering Democrats did not get near anyone who might persuade them to uphold the president's veto. These Democrats were accompanied at all times by two other Democrats with the "right" views. For their part, Republicans called on Reagan to make personal appeals to wavering Republicans.

IDEOLOGY

The member's own ideology usually reflects both the party and the constituency, but it can be an independent influence.[63] In each party, some members are quite a bit more liberal—or conservative—than others.

On the whole, Democrats vote for more liberal measures than do Republicans. Historically, this has not always been true of southern Democrats, who often deserted the Democratic leadership and voted with Republicans because they shared the more conservative Republican outlook. Thus, the Democrats, even when a majority in Congress, often did not have a "working majority," as President Clinton learned early in his term.

The tendency of southern Democrats to vote as conservatives has diminished and probably will dwindle further. Today, southern conservatives run as Republicans and have a good chance of winning. A number of southern conservative Democrats have switched parties in recent years. Also, many southern districts are increasingly urban and contain voters who are more liberal than those of 30 years ago. African Americans, for instance, are now an important factor in many southern districts. These changes have combined to make the southern Democratic Party somewhat more liberal than it used to be, though it is still more conservative than the Democratic Party in the North.

THE PRESIDENT

The president is also a factor in congressional voting, due in part to his role as party leader.[64] The president appeals to fellow partisans to support a program and tries to persuade those in the other party to go along as well. Presidents can win support by granting or withholding favors, such as support for a member's proposed policy or pet project in his or her district.

INTEREST GROUPS

Interest group lobbyists are most effective when their interests overlap constituency interests or when the issue is technical or little publicized. They are also more likely to be effective when a bill is still in committee than when it is being debated on the floor of the House or the Senate.

STAFFERS

Staff can be a very important influence on a member's vote. Staff members are likely to have done the research and briefed the member on an issue. They probably have the greatest influence on technical issues or those the member does not care much about.

OTHER MEMBERS

Members also are influenced by other members of their party or their state's delegation. Members also may turn to colleagues whose judgment or expertise they respect or whose ideology or background they share. In fact, on most routine bills, cues from trusted fellow members are the most important influence on members' votes.

HOW CONGRESS IS ORGANIZED

An institution of 535 members without a centralized leadership that must make decisions about thousands of proposed public policies each year is not an institution that can work quickly or efficiently. Each year in the past decade, from 2,000 to 10,000 bills have been introduced in Congress, and 250 to 2,000 have been passed.

Although many of these bills are trivial, such as those proclaiming "National Prom Graduation Kickoff Day" or naming local courthouses, others deal with crucial issues. In addition to these bills, Congress must oversee the performance of the federal bureaucracy in implementing bills previously passed.

How Congressional Organization Evolved

Like all organizations, legislatures need some structure to be able to accomplish their purposes. Congress has a leadership system and a committee system, both organized along party lines. The Constitution calls for the members of the House of Representatives to select a **Speaker of the House** to act as its presiding officer and for the vice president of the United States to serve as president (or presiding officer) of the Senate. But the Constitution does not say anything about the powers of these officials, nor does it require any further internal organization.

The first House, meeting in New York in 1789, had slow and cumbersome procedures, but soon permanent committees were created, each with continuing responsibilities in one area, such as taxes or trade.[65] As parties developed, the selection of the Speaker became a partisan matter, and the Speaker became as much a party leader as a legislative one. As Speaker, Henry Clay (Ky.) used his powers to appoint committee members and chairs to maintain party loyalty and discipline. In the nation's early years, the House was the dominant branch, but its influence declined when it, like the rest of government, could not cope with the divisiveness of the slavery issue. By 1856 it took 133 ballots to elect a Speaker. In many instances there were physical fights on the House floor and duels outside.[66]

The Senate, a smaller body than the House, was less tangled in procedures and more informal and effective in its operation. Its influence rose as visitors packed the Senate gallery to hear the great debates over slavery waged by Daniel Webster (Mass.), John C. Calhoun (S.C.), and Henry Clay (who had moved from the House). During this era, senators were elected by state legislatures, not directly by the people.

Vitriolic exchanges in Congress are not just a phenomenon of the 1990s. Shown here is a fight in the House in 1798. After Representative Matthew Lyon (R-Vt.) spit on Representative Roger Griswold (Fed-Conn.), and the House refused to expel Lyon, Griswold attacked Lyon with a cane. Lyon defended himself with fire tongs as other members of Congress looked on (not without amusement, it seems).

Library of Congress

Thus, they had strong local party ties and often used their influence to get presidential appointments for home state party members. But the Senate too became ineffective as the nation moved toward civil war. Senators carried arms to protect themselves as the eloquent debates over slavery turned to violence.

After the Civil War, strong party leadership reemerged in the House, and it again became an effective legislative body. Speaker Thomas Reed (Me.) assumed the authority to name members and chairs of committees and to chair the Rules Committee, which decided which bills were to come to the floor for debate. A major consequence of the Speaker's extensive powers was increased party discipline. Members who voted against their party might be punished by a loss of committee assignments or chairships.

At the same time, both the House and the Senate became more professional. The emergence of national problems and an aggressive Congress made a congressional career more prestigious. Prior to the Civil War, membership turnover was high; members of the House served an average of only one term, senators only four years. After the war, the strengthening of parties and the growth of the one-party South made reelection easier.

This desire for permanent careers in the House produced an interest in reform. Members wanted a chance at desirable committee seats and did not want to be controlled by the Speaker. Resistance against the dictatorial practices of Reed and his successor Joseph Cannon (Ill.) grew. Cannon, more conservative than many of his fellow Republicans, used his powers to block legislation he disliked, to punish those who opposed him, and even to refuse to recognize members who wished to speak. In 1910 there was a revolt against "Cannonism," a synonym for the arbitrary use of the Speaker's powers.

The membership voted to strip the Speaker of his authority to appoint committees and their chairs and to remove the Speaker from the Rules Committee. The revolt weakened party influence because it meant party discipline could no longer be maintained by the Speaker punishing members through loss of committee assignments. And it gave committees and their chairs a great deal of independence from leadership influence.

The Senate also was undergoing a major reform. As part of the Progressive movement, pressure began to build for the direct popular election of senators. The election of senators by state legislatures had made many senators pawns of special interests—the big corporations (called "trusts") and railroads. In a day when millionaires were not as common as now, the Senate was referred to as the "Millionaires Club."

Not surprisingly, the Senate first refused to consider a constitutional amendment providing for its direct election, although in some states popular balloting on senatorial candidates took place anyway. Finally, under the threat of a call for a constitutional convention, which many members of Congress feared might consider other changes in the Constitution, a direct election amendment was passed in the House and Senate in 1912 and ratified by the states a year later.

These reforms of the early twentieth century dispersed power in both the House and Senate and weakened leadership. House members no longer feared the kind of retribution levied by Speaker Cannon on members who deviated from party positions. In the Senate, popular elections made senators responsive to diverse constituencies rather than to party leaders.

Leaders

Members of each party in each house meet to choose their leaders. The Speaker of the House is chosen by the majority party members and presides over the House. Typically someone who has served in the House a long time, the Speaker is usually a skilled parliamentarian and an ideological moderate. The new Speaker, Robert Livingston (R-La.), is partly an exception: he is a strong conservative, but also a capable negotiator. The institutional task of the Speaker is to see that legislation moves through the House. His (all speakers have been men so far) partisan task is to secure the passage of measures preferred by his party.

Trying to win partisan support is often difficult. The Speaker has some rewards and punishments to mete out for loyalty and disloyalty, but they are mild compared to the power wielded by Reed and Cannon. The Speaker, however, does have influence on which committees members will be assigned to, on which committees will be given jurisdiction over complex bills, on what bills will come to the House floor, and on how campaign funds are allocated. He also has the sole power to decide who will be recognized to speak on the floor of the House and whether motions are relevant. He has the authority to appoint members to the Rules Committee and to certain special committees, and he controls some material benefits, such as the assignment of extra office space. Despite these formal powers, the Speaker's main weapon is persuasion.

The party leadership in the House also includes a **majority leader,** a **minority leader,** and majority and minority **whips.** The majority leader is second in command to the Speaker, and the minority leader is, as the name suggests, the leader of the minority party. Whips originated in the British House of Commons, where they were named after the "whipper in," the rider who keeps the hounds together in a fox hunt. This aptly describes the whips' role in Congress. Party whips try to maintain contact with party members, see which way they are leaning on votes, and attempt to gain their support. Both parties have several assistant whips who keep tabs on their assigned state delegations.

The party apparatus in the House also includes committees to assign party members to standing committees, discuss policy issues, and allocate funds to party members running for reelection.

The party organization in the Senate is similar to that of the House except that there is no leader comparable to the Speaker of the House. The vice president is formally the presiding officer but in reality attends infrequently and has relatively little power. He is allowed to cast the tie-breaking vote in the rare instances in which the Senate is split evenly. Vice President Gore had such an opportunity in 1993. The Senate has an elected president pro tempore, a mostly honorific post with few duties except to preside over the Senate when the vice president is absent. Because presiding over the Senate on a day-to-day basis is considered boring, junior members usually do it.

George Tames/NYT Permissions

Senate majority leader Lyndon Johnson, persuading. LBJ "used physical persuasion in addition to intellectual and moral appeals. He was hard on other people's coat lapels. If one were shorter than Lyndon he was inclined to move up close and lean over the subject of his persuasive efforts." Here that subject is Senator Theodore Green (D-R.I.). "If a Senator were taller than [Johnson], he would come at him from below, somewhat like a badger." Senator Edmund Muskie (D-Me.), who was taller, "emerged from a meeting with Johnson with the observation that he had not known until this meeting why people had the hair in their nostrils trimmed." Quotes are from Eugene McCarthy, Up 'Til Now *(New York: Harcourt Brace, 1987).*

The real leader in the Senate is the majority leader, a position now held by Trent Lott (R-Miss.). The minority party leader, now Tom Daschle (D.-S. Dak.), is normally in line to assume the majority leadership post when his or her party gains a majority of the Senate.

Committees

STANDING COMMITTEES

Most of the work of Congress is done in committees. Observers of American politics take this for granted; yet the power of legislative committees is rather rare among western democracies. In Britain, for example, committees cannot offer amendments that change the substance of a bill.

Soon after its establishment, Congress set up four permanent committees; over the years the number slowly grew. Today there are 19 **standing committees** in the House and 17 in the Senate. Each deals with a different subject matter, such as finance or education or agriculture. Each has a number of subcommittees, totaling 84 in the House and 69 in the Senate. Nearly all legislation introduced in Congress is referred to a standing committee and then to a subcommittee. Subcommittees hold public hearings to give interested parties a chance to speak for or against a bill. They also hold **markup** sessions to provide an opportunity for the committee to rewrite the bill. Following markup, the bill is sent to the full committee, which also may hold hearings. If approved there, it goes to the full House or Senate.

Standing committees vary in size from 9 members to 73. Trying to accommodate members' desires for committee seats that allow them to help constituents has led to ever larger committees. Party ratios—that is, the number of Democrats relative to Republicans on each committee—are determined by the majority party. The ratios are generally set in rough proportion to party membership in the particular house, but the majority party gives itself a disproportionate number of seats on several key committees in order to ensure control. Conflict between the parties flared in 1995, when Republicans offered a seat on an influential committee to a Democrat if he would switch parties. He did, and the extra Republican seat further unbalanced the partisan makeup of the committee.

COMMITTEE MEMBERSHIP

New members and those members seeking committee changes express their preferences to their party's selection committee. As a general rule, preferences will be granted, although there is a self-selection process whereby junior members usually do not ask for the most prestigious posts.

Seats on some committees are sought after; others are shunned. The committees dealing with budgets and appropriations are always popular because having money to allocate gives members power and the ability to help their districts. Most members want committees that allow them to tell constituents that they are working on problems of the district. For example, members from agricultural districts strive to get on the agriculture committees.

The practice of filling committees with representatives whose districts have an especially strong economic interest in the subject matter makes committees rather parochial in their outlook and fills them with members who have financial interests in the businesses they make policies for.[67] Most members who sit on the banking committees own bank stock, the agriculture committees agribusiness stock, and the armed services committees stock in military contractors.[68]

In the media age, another criterion has become important for choosing a committee: media coverage. The work of some committees is more likely to be covered by television. In a five-year period, the Senate Foreign Relations Committee had 522 network television cameras covering it, whereas the Indian Affairs Committee had 0.[69] Getting on the right committee is important to those who want to become nationally known. When a journalist once asked Senator Joseph Biden (D-Del.) why he was so newsworthy, Biden replied, "It's the committees, of course." Biden had served on the three most publicized committees.

COMMITTEE CHAIRS

The chair is the leader and most influential member of a committee. Chairs have the authority to call meetings, set agendas, and control the committee staff and funds. In addition, chairs are usually very knowledgeable about matters that come before their committee, and this too is a source of influence. Some chairs have used their power to rule their committee with an "iron hand."

Usually, the member of the majority party with the longest service on a committee becomes its chair—the so-called **seniority rule.** Before the early 1900s, powerful Speakers of the House often would use their authority to reward friends and allies by appointing them as committee chairs. To protect themselves, committee members adopted seniority as the basis for selecting chairs. Chairs might be completely out of touch with most of the party, senile, alcoholic, or personally disliked by every member of the committee, but if they had served the longest and their party had a majority in the House, they were chairs regardless.

THE RISE AND FALL OF SPEAKER GINGRICH

When the Republicans took control of Congress after the 1994 midterm elections, Newt Gingrich of Georgia became Speaker of the House and soon wielded power reminiscent of the days of Thomas Reed and Joseph Cannon. Within months of taking office, he not only transformed the Speakership into a position from which he could rival President Clinton for national attention, but also led the Republican majority in an effort to change the direction of the federal government. In 1997, however, he was almost deposed in a revolt of party members, and he resigned after dismal GOP results in the 1998 elections. Why was he able to galvanize the Republican majority, and why did he lose his position?

His power in his first year derived from the fact that Republicans recognized that they owed their majority status to Gingrich and his efforts. During the previous 10 years, Gingrich had personally recruited and trained an army of new Republicans who were remarkably loyal to him and his conservative vision. Funding for these efforts came from Gingrich's political action committee, GOPAC.

About half the Republicans in Congress were recruits from his so-called farm team. Gingrich held training sessions on campaign tactics and issued campaign manuals and tapes with detailed campaign "dos" and "don'ts." Word lists coached candidates on how to talk like Newt.

The most famous GOPAC document is "Language, a Key Mechanism of Control," in which Gingrich provided a list of words tested in focus groups to use in discussing the opposition. Democrats were to be associated with decay, sick, pathetic, stagnation, corrupt, waste, and traitors. Republicans were to be identified with share, change, truth, moral, courage, family, peace, and duty.

Gingrich prepared audiotapes that prospective candidates listened to as they drove across their states. Former House member and now U.S. senator from Pennsylvania, Rick Santorum, said, "I listened to those tapes all the time driving around in the car. They taught tactics you should use, basic philosophy, how to discuss the issues. I was a *disciple.*"[1]

For the first two years of the Republican majority in the House, Gingrich's relationship with his Republican colleagues was his strongest base. "There is a personal loyalty to him that is without precedent in recent history," said former Republican representative Bill Gradison. "I don't think anyone ever felt they owed their seat to Jim Wright, Tom Foley, or Tip O'Neill."[2]

But, by 1997, Gingrich and the Republicans faced a President Clinton with strong public approval ratings, in part because Clinton had outmaneuvered the Republicans over the budget stalemate in 1995 that closed government for a while. Gingrich's own public approval had fallen, and the 1996 election left the GOP with a reduced majority (228 seats out of 435). The handwriting was on the wall: to get anything done, Republicans would have to compromise.

And that's what Gingrich did, most notably in a budget agreement during the spring of 1997. But compromise did not sit well with the "farm team." From the perspective of the newer Republican members who formed the base of Gingrich's support in the previous Congress, Gingrich had deserted the "Republican revolution" for accommodation with Clinton. In their view, principle had given way to expediency. The fact that Gingrich had consulted with few of his colleagues seemed to make matters worse.

In a most unusual occurrence, disgruntled Republicans plotted to replace Gingrich as Speaker, walking the thin line "somewhere between talk and treason."[3] In the end, the revolt was aborted; Gingrich got word of it and marshaled support from, somewhat ironically, moderate Republicans. "Imagine that," said one such member, "we're going to be the ones who save Gingrich."[4]

After Republicans lost five seats in the 1998 congressional elections, Gingrich lost the support he needed to remain as Speaker. Strong conservatives blamed him for not following their agenda of tax cuts and clear conservative positions. Moderates were disturbed at the loss of seats. After Gingrich resigned, Bob Livingston (R-La.) won the Speakership, hoping to unify the GOP once again. Gingrich's difficulties demonstrate that winning a majority and using that majority to govern are not the same thing. To participate in governing, a Speaker must maintain support among his party's rank-and-file, and he must continually cultivate their support. Compromise is part of the package. As Speaker, Livingston said, "I've got to work with people who don't believe the same way I do." Ultimately, Gingrich could not.

1. Quoted in Connie Bruck, "The Politics of Perfection," *The New Yorker,* October 9, 1995, p. 63 (emphasis in original).
2. Quoted in Roger H. Davidson and Walter J. Oleszek, *Congress and Its Members,* 5th ed. (Washington, D.C.: CQ Press, 1996), p. 169.
3. Ceci Connolly, David S. Broder, and Dan Balz, "A GOP House Divided," *Washington Post National Weekly Edition,* August 4, 1997, p. 6.
4. Quoted in E. J. Dionne, Jr., "Gingrich Survived, but the Party Festers," *Los Angeles Times,* July 20, 1997, p. M5.
5. Alison Mitchell, "A Move for Pragmatism," *New York Times,* November 9, 1988, p. A14.

Many members believed the custom of seniority led to chairs who were out of step with the rest of the party and dictatorial in their committees. In response to those complaints, in the early 1970s both parties agreed that the seniority rule no longer had to be followed. A Committee on Committees in the Republican Party and a Steering and Policy Committee in the Democratic Party now recommend chairs. Then the members of the party vote on these recommendations.

In 1975, in a striking break with precedent, the Democratic membership stripped three senior Democrats of

IMPEACHING THE PRESIDENT?

One of the powers of Congress is the right to remove a president from office. The Constitution gives the House of Representatives the authority to draw up impeachment charges, and the Senate to try the president on these charges. A two-thirds vote is necessary to convict.

Impeachment is a rare event, yet it was a popular topic of conversation in 1998. The target, President Bill Clinton, had given a deposition under oath in the sexual harassment suit Paula Jones had filed against him. In that deposition he seemed to deny any sexual relationship with former White House intern Monica Lewinsky. With permission from supervising judges, Independent Counsel Kenneth Starr, who had been investigating several matters loosely labeled "Whitewater," extended his investigation to determine whether President Clinton committed perjury in the Jones case. By August, after he testified before the Starr grand jury, the president admitted to a national television audience that he had indeed had an improper relationship with Ms. Lewinsky. Soon thereafter, Starr submitted boxes of evidence to the House of Representatives as it considered articles of impeachment.

Republicans voted unanimously to empower the Judiciary Committee to proceed with its own evaluation of the evidence, with most, but not all, Democrats opposed. For an impeachment to go forward, most observers believed that the public would have to support such a move.

In order to develop support for impeachment, the House GOP leadership, especially Speaker Newt Gingrich, pushed to make Clinton's alleged perjury a major issue in the 1998 congressional campaigns. To sway public opinion, they released the Starr report, with its graphic sexual detail, to the public through print and through the Internet. Public opinion polls, however, showed that most citizens thought the matter was relatively inconsequential. Many do not expect people to tell the truth about extramarital sex. Nevertheless, Republicans broadcast political ads in many areas of the country urging a vote for Republican candidates based on disapproval of Clinton's behavior. They expected to win more seats in the House and Senate. Such a victory could be evidence that the public did indeed want the House to impeach President Clinton and could strengthen the likelihood of an impeachment vote.

Surprisingly, however, Democrats gained five seats in the House (and lost no seats in the Senate). This was the first time since 1934 that the president's party won seats in a midterm election. Dissatisfaction with these results among Republicans in the House forced Speaker Gingrich to resign his post. Instead of strengthening impeachment prospects, the election reduced them.

Impeachment is a serious step, and the Constitution is little help in determining whether Clinton's perjury, if proven, is of sufficient importance to warrant removing him from office. The constitutional standard is "high crimes and misdmeanors," a very ambiguous phrase. In the past, this has been interpreted as meaning misuse of official powers rather than personal crimes. Politically, the relevant criterion is public support for impeaching a president: for what kinds of mistakes, criminal or otherwise, would the public accept impeachment?

their chairs. They did so again in 1985 and 1994. The Republicans also violated the seniority principle in their choice of chairs in 1995.[70] In the House, Speaker Gingrich elevated less senior members who were more conservative over other Republicans on the committees. Still, the seniority principle applies most of the time.

Why does Congress usually follow the seniority rule? It assumes that members with long service on the committee will have expertise in its subject matter, and that is usually true. It also eliminates potentially damaging intraparty fights over who will be chairs of important committees. Some people believe the seniority system is also the best protection for women and minorities as they gain seniority in the institution, although in this white male-dominated institution this is more a side effect than a reason for the system's persistence.

Choosing chairs by means other than strict seniority has ended the days of the autocratic chair. And the reform has brought about an interesting change in the behavior of senior members. Before 1975, committee chairs were much lower in support for their party in roll-call votes than other party members.[71] Since 1975, committee chairs have been much more likely to vote with their party than other members. The same pattern holds true of those who are second, third, and fourth in seniority on each committee. Thus, removing seniority as a sole criterion for choosing committee chairs has meant that senior party members are much less likely to deviate from their party's position. In that sense, the reforms have strengthened party influence in Congress.

SUBCOMMITTEES

Each committee is divided into subcommittees with jurisdiction over part of the committee's subject. The House International Relations Committee, for example, has five subcommittees—one for Africa, one for Asia and the Pacific, and one for the Western Hemisphere, as well as one on trade and one on human rights.

Committee chairs traditionally dominated not only their committee but its subcommittees as well. Chairs chose the chairs of the subcommittees and controlled the subcommittees' jurisdiction, budget, and staff. Chairs thus could manipulate the subcommittees' action on proposed legislation as they saw fit. In

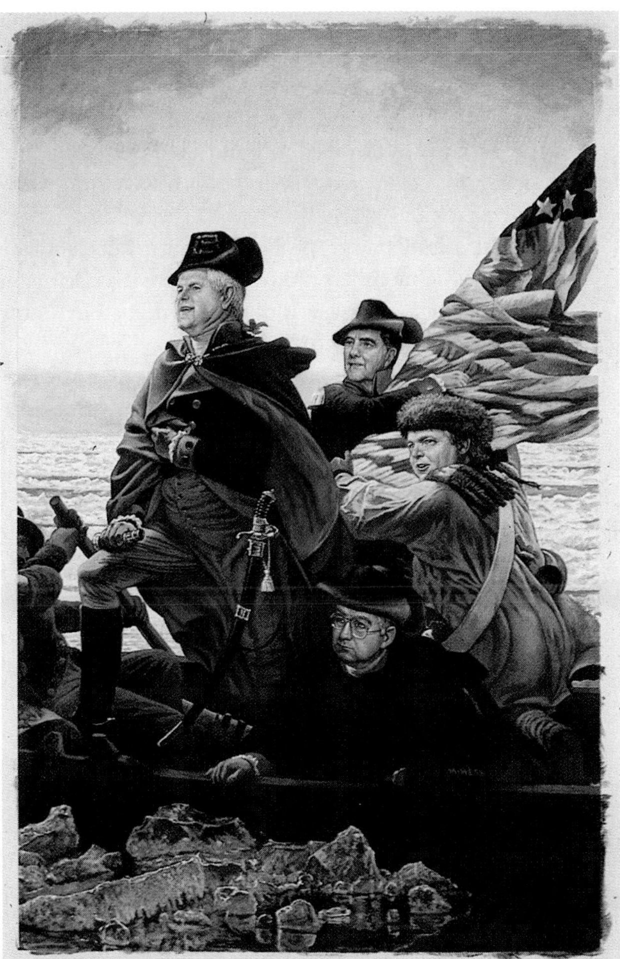

After they captured the majority in Congress in 1994, Republicans had high hopes for a Republican revolution. Here their leaders are pictured in the style of Washington crossing the Delaware River. Unlike the success of Washington, the Republicans found change slow going.

the 1950s, southern chairs bottled up important civil rights legislation for years.

In another rejection of domineering committee chairs, House Democrats made a number of rules changes in 1973 and 1974, sometimes called the **subcommittee bill of rights.** These measures reduced the control of the whole committee, especially its chair, over the subcommittees. Similar changes took place in the Senate. These reforms allow more members, especially newer members, to share in important decisions. In this way they make Congress more democratic.

But by diffusing power, they also make it less efficient. Each subcommittee can operate semi-independently of the parent committee. The multiplicity of subcommittees also contributes to government gridlock. Complex legislation might be sent to several subcommittees, each with its own interests and jurisdiction. In response, rule changes under the new Republican majority in Congress cut the number of subcommittees significantly, streamlining the legislative process and leaving fewer chairs with independent authority.

With so many committees and subcommittees, the average member is spread pretty thin. The typical senator sits on 11 committees and subcommittees; the average representative about 7. These multiple assignments mean that members have impossible schedules, and committees cannot obtain quorums because members have other committee hearings to attend. This leaves it to the committee chair, a few colleagues, and staff to do the work and make many of the decisions. This, too, increases the de facto influence of the chair.

OTHER COMMITTEES

There are a few other types of congressional committees. Select or special committees, such as the Senate Watergate Committee, are typically investigative committees organized on a temporary basis to investigate and make recommendations. Joint committees include members from both houses. Another committee is the Conference Committee, which we will discuss later.

EVALUATING COMMITTEE GOVERNMENT

The division of labor provided by committees and subcommittees enables Congress to consider a vast number of bills each year. If every member had to review every measure in detail it would be impossible to deal with the current workload. Instead, most bills are killed in committee, leaving many fewer for each member to evaluate before a floor vote. Committees also help members develop specializations. Members who remain on the same committee for some time gain expertise and are less dependent on professional staff and executive agencies for information.

But committee government also has disadvantages. In addition to the inefficiencies mentioned already, committees and especially subcommittees are often unrepresentative of Congress as a whole. As a result, they tend to be more responsive to narrow interests and constituencies and less responsive to national objectives, while making national policy.

Over time, members of congressional subcommittees develop close relationships with the interest groups and executive branch agencies affected by their work. These three sets of participants share a concern with a specific policy area. Over the years, the people in these three groups get to know each other, probably come to like and respect one another, and seek to accommodate each other's interests. Personal relationships foster favorable treatment of special interest groups.

The freedom and authority of individual members mean that Congress as a whole often cannot get things done because power is fragmented. Most members of the majority party in the Senate and about half of those in the House chair committees or subcommittees.

These centers of power are somewhat independent from party leaders. Thus, Congress often has difficulty mounting a coherent alternative to the president.

On the other hand, the fragmentation of power means it is relatively easy for Congress to block presidential initiatives. In this sense, Congress remains a conservative institution, protecting the status quo. Whether one thinks this is a good idea or not depends on the particular nature of the changes being proposed. Congress has frustrated both conservative and liberal presidents.

CRUMBLING COMMITTEES?

Over the past 15 years, there have been changes in the way Congress deals with important issues. Committee chairs and committees do not always have the power they used to. There is evidence of greater centralization, though not as much as at the turn of the century. Power is gravitating to all members of a few "power" committees, such as the Appropriations, Ways and Means, and Energy and Commerce committees in the House and the Finance Committee in the Senate. The power of these committees lies in their ability to control spending and raise revenue (as we will see later). As one observer commented, even the most senior member of Public Works finds it difficult to accomplish what the most junior member of Appropriations can do in winning home district pork barrel projects. The former chair of the Senate Appropriations Committee, Robert Byrd (D-W.Va.), was called the "Prince of Pork" for his success in bringing federal money to West Virginia.[72]

Power has also gravitated to party leaders. The formal leader of the House, the Speaker, has gained power, and party unity is on the upswing. Leaders, including some committee chairs, are also more powerful because more and more negotiations over important bills are taking place directly among the leaders of Congress and administration officials. For example, the recent attempt to pass legislation regulating tobacco originated in negotiations between tobacco companies and the states. When their agreement reached Congress, the leadership, President Clinton, and key legislators such as Senator John McCain (R-Ariz.) worked outside the committee system to draft an acceptable bill. Although no tobacco bill passed, in large part because the tobacco industry "went public" with an advertising campaign against the bill, it is doubtful that a committee-drafted bill would have fared better. Other issues, such as an anticrime bill, campaign finance legislation, and a congressional ethics package also have been developed outside formal committee structures.

These new arrangements have some advantages. They overcome the paralysis that sometimes results from the divided partisan control of Congress and the presidency. Direct negotiations between the White House and congressional leaders can sometimes break long-standing deadlocks.

On the other hand, these new arrangements bypass mechanisms for accountability to the public and to most rank-and-file members. Bills are written without formal hearings and the opportunities to point out potential pitfalls and problems of the legislation. Rank-and-file members often are faced with voting on a huge package of legislation about which they know only what they read in the newspaper.

Moreover, without powerful committees, if the majority leaders are not strong, bargaining over legislation can become a complete free-for-all, with dozens of legislators striking individual deals for their favorite program. Without strong committees or leaders, individual members of Congress, often with no expertise or interest beyond a special interest, can hold a piece of legislation hostage in exchange for a tax loophole or bit of pork.

Thus, many people believe that Congress is still ripe for reform. The Republicans did make several changes when they took over in 1995, including abolishing three House committees and several subcommittees, eliminating proxy committee voters, and planning for a substantial reduction in staff. Despite this modest streamlining, the basic functioning of the Congress is unchanged. However, its burst of legislative energy early in 1995 suggests that when Congress fails to get things done, committee structure is only part of the reason. A cohesive House majority with strong leadership can pass legislation even with a complex committee structure. Conversely, if the public is divided and there is little strong leadership or incentive for members to carry out a legislative agenda, congressional structure only reinforces other impediments to action. As one member remarked, "How is a committee overhaul going to make me more courageous to do things I don't want to do now?"[73]

Staff

The term "Congress" encompasses not only our 535 elected representatives but also their staff of nearly 30,000 people.

Congress hires far more staff members than any other legislative body. Even with recent cuts, it is still by far the largest. The Canadian legislature, which is second in staff size, has only about 3,300 people.[74]

TYPES OF STAFF

Congressional staff members include those working in members' Washington and district offices, defined as "personal" staff, those working for congressional committees, those working for the special support agencies

AMERICAN DIVERSITY

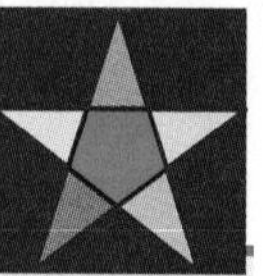

BLACK POWER IN CONGRESS

Special interest caucuses are groups of members united by some personal interest or characteristic. There are more than 60 House caucuses, representing partisan, ideological, policy, or regional interests. One of these, the Black Caucus, was organized in 1969 by black members of Congress determined to gain some clout. This organization, which includes most African-American members of Congress, has grown to 40 members and meets regularly, usually weekly. It also has more than 80 white associate members. Before 1994, the caucus, like other caucuses, had its own small staff. However, the Republican majority eliminated staff support for special interest caucuses, so now the caucus relies on its members to provide support from their staffs.

Paradoxically, at a time when the caucus is at its all-time high in number of members, it is perhaps the weakest it has been in two decades. The reason is that all of its members are Democrats, and now they are the minority party in both houses. When the Democrats controlled the House, many black members had positions of power, chairing, in 1994, 26% of all House committees and many subcommittees too. Now with their party out of power, they chair no committees or subcommittees. Moreover, the caucus has little influence with the Republican majority because of its lack of Republican membership and the Democratic predilections of the black constituents of Republican members of Congress.

As we have discussed, the success of blacks in getting several southern states to redistrict to form majority black districts helped weaken Democratic congressional representation in the South and contributed to the Republican majority. One analyst notes that "A lot of people say redistricting was a means to an end of getting more power for black people by getting more blacks in Congress; if redistricting was a means to an end, it turned out to be a dead end."[1] Others, such as Jesse Jackson, urge a continuation of the majority-minority redistricting strategy, arguing that the Democrats did poorly in 1994 and 1996 partly because of low black turnout, which can be increased if voters are mobilized.

To be influential in these new circumstances, Black Caucus members will have to negotiate and find new allies. Yet they must also continue speaking for their constituency. In today's climate, this is a very difficult task.

1. Juan Williams, "How Black Liberal Strategy Failed Its Followers," *Washington Post National Weekly Edition*, November 28–December 3, 1994, p. 25; Steven Holmes "Did Racial Redistricting Undermine Democrats?" *New York Times*, November 13, 1994, p. 32.

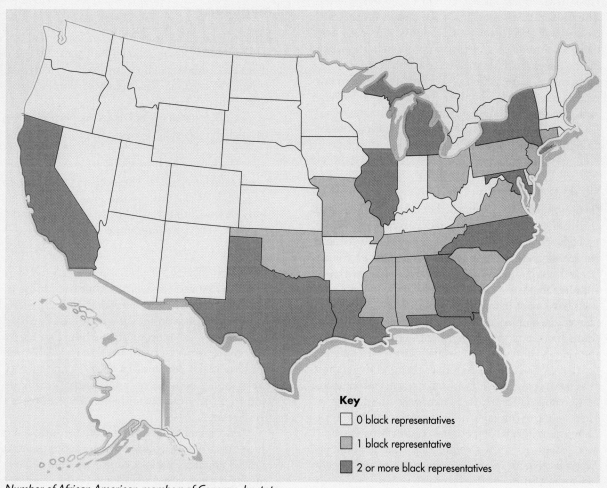

Key

0 black representatives

1 black representative

2 or more black representatives

Number of African American members of Congress, by state.

of Congress (the Congressional Research Service, Office of Technology Assessment, Congressional Budget Office, and the General Accounting Office), and auxiliary staff such as police.

House members have about 16 personal staff members, and the average senator has more than 40. Senators from states with larger populations have a larger staff than senators from smaller states. Leaders have many more staff than rank-and-file members. By far the largest proportion of members' personal staffs works on constituency service, both in the district offices and in Washington. Other staff members will be assigned to legislative duties, and one or more will do media work.

One of the reasons for the tremendous growth and size of staff is the increasing demand for constituency service. As more citizens turn to Congress for help with the bureaucracy, Congress hires more staff to take care of them. Another reason is that Congress has attempted to develop its own expertise and sources of information so it will not have to rely on the executive branch. Thus, its committees have staff members who research and draft legislation as well as develop support for it.

Staff in the support agencies of Congress carry out various research functions, again enabling Congress to be independent of the executive branch. The General Accounting Office checks on the efficiency and effectiveness of executive agencies. The Congressional Research Service conducts studies of public issues and does specific research at the request of members. The Office of Technology Assessment provides long-range analyses of the effects of new and existing technology, and the Congressional Budget Office provides the expertise and support for Congress's budgeting job.

IMPACT OF STAFF

Some scholars have argued that although increased congressional staff may be necessary, it has created more problems than it has solved.[75] Large staffs create more paperwork and have a tendency to produce ever more research, committee work, and hearings. Information is collected that is impossible for members to digest. Large staffs have made members into executives who need to manage their offices rather than legislators with time to think about policy. Congressional staffs have reduced the amount of discussion members have with one another over policy issues. As former Senator David Boren (D-Okla.) complained, "Very often, I will call on a senator on an issue, and he won't know anything about it. He'll ask me to get someone on my staff to call someone on his staff. It shuts off personal contact between senators."[76] This means the compromises and adjustments necessary to make policy are sometimes made by technicians rather than elected representatives.

WHAT CONGRESS DOES

The Founders intended Congress to be the dominant branch of government. The powers and role of Congress are spelled out in Article I of the Constitution, before attention is given to the president. Almost half the Constitution is devoted to a discussion of Congress. The importance of Congress also is reflected in the major, explicit constitutional powers the Founders gave it: to lay and collect taxes, coin money, declare war and raise and support a military, and regulate commerce with foreign governments and among the states. Essentially, most of the powers the Constitution gives to the national government were given to Congress. These and other powers specifically mentioned in the Constitution are called the enumerated powers of Congress.

Congress also has implied powers; that is, it can make all the laws "necessary and proper" to carry out its enumerated powers. Although the Founders did not necessarily foresee it, this tremendous grant of power covers almost every conceivable area of human activity.

Lawmaking

High school civics students learn the formal steps by which a bill becomes a law (see Figure 5). Although these procedures are important, at every step there are compromises, trade-offs, and understandings. In other words, there is politics.

A bill becomes a law if its supporters can get it through an obstacle course. Approval must be obtained at each obstacle or the bill fails. Those opposing a bill have an advantage because it is easier to defeat a bill than pass it. The need to win a majority at each stage of the process also means that individuals with varying interests must be satisfied. The end result is almost always a compromise.

INTRODUCTION

Bills may be introduced in either the House or the Senate, except for tax measures (which according to the Constitution must be introduced initially in the House) and appropriations bills (which by tradition are introduced in the House). This reflects the Founders' perceptions that on tax issues Congress should be especially responsive to the people and that the House would be more responsive than the Senate.

Only members of Congress are permitted to introduce bills. Interest groups or the president must find a congressional sponsor for a proposed bill. About half the legislation passed is initiated by the president.[77]

	HOUSE	SENATE	PRESIDENT
Bill Introduction ↓	Given a number Referred to committee	Given a number Referred to committee	
In Committee ↓	Referred to subcommittee Hearings held Markup Recommend passage or kill the bill Rules committee action (setting terms of debate)	Referred to subcommittee Hearings held Markup Recommend passage or kill the bill	
On the Floor ↓	Debate and amendment, if allowed under rule Vote on passage	Debate and amendment Vote on passage	
In Conference ↓	Conference Committee reconciles different versions Conference report adapted	Conference report adapted	
To President	Veto override (if necessary)	Veto override (if necessary)	Signs or vetoes

FIGURE 5

How a Bill Becomes a Law

These formal steps do not include the informal negotiations, discussions, and compromises that take place throughout the process. Neither do they include the efforts interest groups make to influence the decisions or the information legislators receive from their constituents.

REFERRAL AND COMMITTEE ACTION

After a bill's introduction, it is referred to a standing committee by the Speaker of the House or the presiding officer in the Senate. The content of the bill largely determines where it will go, although the Speaker has some discretion, particularly over complex bills that cover more than one subject area. Many of these are referred to more than one committee simultaneously.

Once the bill reaches a committee, it is assigned to a subcommittee. Bills receiving subcommittee approval go to full committee and if approved go to the whole House. Bills that get out of committee usually become law. Most bills, however, die in committee or subcommittee. Indeed, one of the main functions of committees is to screen bills with little chance of passage. (If a committee kills a bill, there are procedures that members can use to try to get the bill to the floor, but these are used infrequently.)

The committee and subcommittee markup stage is legally open yet barely visible to the public. Consequently, lobbyists attend hearings. For critical meetings, lobbyists will hire messengers to stand in line for them, sometimes all night, and then pack the hearing room. Members dependent on particular groups for financial or other support often face intense and direct pressure to vote a particular way in committee and are sometimes mobbed by lobbyists when they leave the hearing room.

SCHEDULING AND THE RULES COMMITTEE

Once a bill is approved by committee, it is placed on one of five "calendars," each of which contains a particular type of bill (for example, all bills considered to be noncontroversial are placed on one calendar). Bills from each calendar are generally considered in the order that they are reported from committee. In the House, the **Rules Committee** sets the terms of the debate over the bill by issuing a rule on it. The rule either limits or does not limit debate and determines whether amendments will be permitted. A rule forbidding amendments means that members have to vote Yes or No on the bill; there is no chance to change it. If the committee refuses to issue a rule, the bill dies.

The Rules Committee is not as independent or powerful as it once was. In earlier years the committee was controlled by a coalition of conservative Democrats and Republicans who used the committee to block liberal legislative proposals. It now functions as an arm of the majority leadership.[78] Members are nominated by the Speaker, and the leadership uses the committee to fashion rules to control and expedite floor action.

DEBATE IN THE HOUSE

Debate on a bill is controlled by the bill managers, the senior committee supporters of the bill. The opposition too has its managers who schedule opposition speeches. "Debates" are hardly a series of fiery speeches of point and counterpoint. They are often boring, given to sparse audiences, some of whom are reading, conversing, or walking around. After the agreed-upon time for debate is over, the bill is reported for final action.

THE SENATE

Because the Senate is a smaller body, it can operate with fewer rules and formal procedures. It does not have a rules committee. A lot of work is accomplished through the use of unanimous consent agreements, which allow the Senate to dispense with standard rules and limit debate and amendments. As the Senate's workload has increased and its sense of collegiality decreased, unanimous consent agreements are both more desirable and more difficult to gain from opponents of a bill. A few senators can delay or kill important bills. (Table 2 summarizes House and Senate differences.) As one observer remarked, "The Senate has the same procedural rules as you would find on Monkey Island in the San Francisco Zoo."[79]

Without unanimous consent, there is no rule limiting debate and no restrictions on adding amendments. Opponents can add all sorts of irrelevant amendments to pending legislation. One senator held up an antibusing bill for eight months with 604 amendments.

The other major mechanism for delay in the Senate is the **filibuster.** This is a continuous speech made by one or more members to prevent the Senate from taking action. Before 1917, only unanimous consent could prevent an individual from talking. Today a **cloture** vote of three-fifths of the members can limit debate to only 20 more hours.

Like nongermane amendments, filibusters are used by both liberals and conservatives. The filibuster developed in the 1820s when the Senate was divided between slave and free states. Unlimited debate maintained the deadlock.[80] For over a century the filibuster was used primarily to defeat race and civil rights legislation; the 1964 Civil Rights Act was passed only after a cloture vote. Recently, filibusters have occurred on many different types of legislation.

During Clinton's first year in office, Republicans used the filibuster quite frequently to block the Democratic Senate majority. After Republicans captured the Senate in 1994, the new majority leader, Trent Lott (R-Miss.), found himself frustrated by Democratic filibusters. "We are completely balled up and it's not my fault. I want us all to sober up here now and get on with the business of the Senate," he complained.[81]

Filibusters protect the rights of congressional minorities and help ensure that controversial issues will get full consideration. On the other hand, they deny the majority the right to legislate, and contribute mightily to gridlock.[82] In the last decade, they have been used far more frequently than in the past. In 1991–1992 alone they were used 35 times, compared with only 16 times during the entire nineteenth century. By in effect requiring 60 votes to pass controversial legislation, they make it difficult for a majority to legislate.

CONFERENCE COMMITTEE

Under the Constitution, the House and Senate must pass an identical bill before it becomes law. Thus, the House and Senate versions of the bill must be reconciled. Sometimes the house that passed the bill last will simply send the bill to the other house for minor modifications. But if the differences between the two versions are not minor, a **Conference Committee** is set up to try to resolve them. The presiding officers of each house, in consultation with the chairs of the standing committees that considered the bill, choose the members of the committee. Both parties are represented.

To win approval, majorities of members from each house must agree to the Conference Committee version. Sometimes the bill is rewritten fairly substantially, and occasionally a bill is killed.

TABLE 2

Important Differences between the House and Senate

HOUSE	SENATE
CONSTITUTIONAL DIFFERENCES	
Must initiate revenue bills.	Must give approval to many major presidential appointments.
Initiates impeachment and passes impeachment bills.	Tries impeached officials.
Apportioned by population.	Approves treaties.
	Two senators from each state.
DIFFERENCES IN OPERATION	
More centralized, more formal:	Less centralized, less formal:
Speaker's assignment of bills to committee hard to challenge.	Assignment of bills to committee appealable.
Rules Commitee fairly powerful in controlling time and rules of debate (works with majority leaders).	No rules committee; limits on debate come through unanimous consent or cloture of filibuster.
Nongermane amendments forbidden.	Nongermane amendments permitted.
Majority party controls scheduling.	Schedule and rules negotiated between majority and minority leaders.
More impersonal.	More personal.
Power less evenly distributed.	Power more evenly distributed.
Members are highly specialized.	Members are generalists.
Emphasizes tax and revenue policy.	Emphasizes foreign policy.
CHANGES IN THE INSTITUTION	
Power is becoming centralized in the hands of key committees and the leadership.	Senate workload increasing and informality breaking down.
House procedures are becoming more efficient with less debate and fewer amendments.	Members are becoming more specialized; debate and deliberation are less frequent.

SOURCES: Louis A. Froman, *The Congressional Process: Strategies, Rules, and Procedures* (Boston: Little, Brown, 1967); Norman Ornstein, "The House and Senate in a New Congress" in Thomas Mann and Norman Ornstein, eds., *The New Congress* (Washington, D.C.: American Enterprise Institute, 1981), pp. 363–384.

Once the Conference Committee reaches an agreement, the bill goes back to each house for ratification. It cannot be amended at that point so Congress must either "take it or leave it." This means the Conference Committee can be very influential.

PRESIDENTIAL ACTION AND CONGRESSIONAL RESPONSE

The president may sign the bill, in which case it becomes law. The president may veto it, in which case it returns to Congress with the president's objections. The president also may do nothing, which means the bill becomes law after 10 days unless Congress adjourns.

Presidents infrequently veto legislation, but when they do, they usually are not overridden by Congress. A two-thirds vote in each house is required to override a presidential veto. Congress voted to override only 9 of former President Reagan's 78 vetoes, and only 1 of President Bush's 46.

Overseeing the Federal Bureaucracy

As part of the checks and balances principle, it is Congress's responsibility to make sure the bureaucracy is carrying out the intent of Congress in administering federal programs. This congressional **oversight** has become more important as Congress continues to delegate authority to the executive branch. For a variety of reasons, Congress is not especially well equipped, motivated, or organized to carry out its oversight function. Nevertheless, it does have several tools for this purpose.

One tool is the General Accounting Office, created in 1921, which functions as Congress's watchdog in oversight and is mostly concerned with making sure that money is used properly.

Another tool is the **legislative veto.** Used since 1933, it allows one or both houses of Congress, or on occasion a congressional committee, to block executive action. Congress adds the veto provision to some legislation. In the 1970s, it did much more than in the past in order to restrict agency activities. For example, all Federal Trade Commission rulings were subject to a legislative veto.

In 1983, the Supreme Court declared the legislative veto unconstitutional as a violation of the separation of powers principle. Legislation, the Court ruled, must be passed by both houses and signed by the president. Congress cannot take over executive functions. Even so, since that decision, more than 100 bills have passed with provisions for a legislative veto.[83] Though presumably they could not be enforced, legislative vetoes continue to be honored by federal agencies unwilling to risk congressional wrath by doing something Congress has vetoed.

Yet another method of oversight is committee hearings, although they are not very effective. Members can quiz representatives from agencies on the operation of their agencies, but often the hearings go into great detail about some particular problem of minor importance and neglect broader policy questions. Poor attendance and the pressure of other business mean that members' attentions are usually not focused on congressional hearings. Nevertheless, officials in agencies view hearings as a possible source of embarrassment for their agency and spend a great deal of time preparing for them.

Political considerations also influence oversight. For example, Congress held well-publicized hearings into alleged abuses at the Internal Revenue Service (IRS) with vivid testimony from taxpayers about the high-handed tactics the IRS has used in the past. Newscasts throughout the nation carried snippets of the most sensational allegations. Not surprisingly, these hearings were held in April, when many Americans were busy preparing their income tax returns.

Congress's control over the budget is the major way it exercises oversight. Congress can cut or add to agencies' budgets and thereby punish or reward them for their performance.

Informal oversight is a common tool.[84] This can include requiring reports on topics of interest to members or committees. In a recent year the executive branch prepared 5,000 reports for Congress.[85] Moreover the chair and staff of the committee or subcommittee relevant to the agency's mission are consulted regularly by the agency. But one can question whether much actual oversight gets done informally. Members of congressional committees and subcommittees with authority over an agency's budget get benefits for their constituents from that agency. By responding to congressional wishes, agencies get a favorable budget. There are few electoral or other incentives for members to become involved in the drudgery of more thorough oversight.[86]

Budget Making

An increasingly large part of the job of Congress is to produce a budget. The Constitution gives Congress the authority to control the federal purse by collecting taxes and spending money.

The topic of making budgets sounds dull and can be tedious. However, without money to implement laws, laws themselves would mean very little. It is one thing to pass legislation that provides funding for day care, improves Medicare benefits, combats drug addiction, regulates health and safety standards for workers, and provides financial aid to students. But without money in the budget to fund these programs, the programs are empty rhetoric. And, in fact, sometimes laws are passed to give the impression that government is really doing something about a problem when in reality it is not doing much. Much of the "War on Drugs" fits this category. In other cases, those who support legislation do see that it is reasonably well funded initially, but later it may lose support and suffer funding cuts. During the Reagan administration, for example, many regulatory programs established during the 1970s, such as the Consumer Product Safety Commission and the Environmental Protection Agency, lost substantial parts of their funding and were forced to cut back their activities. Thus, budgets are crucial in determining what government actually does.

There are two major features of congressional spending patterns. First, the process is usually incremental; that is, budgets of one year are usually slightly more than budgets of the past year. Normally, Congress does not radically reallocate money from one year to the next; members assume agencies should get about what they received the previous year. This simplifies the work of all concerned. Agencies do not have to defend, or members scrutinize, all aspects of the budget.[87]

A second feature is that Congress tends to spend slightly more on federal agencies in election years.[88] This tendency increases in times of unemployment and moderates in times of inflation. Members are also more likely to vote for increasing federal payments to individuals (such as veterans' benefits or Social Security) in the years they are up for reelection.[89]

These general tendencies cannot account for every year's budgeting. Reagan's domestic budget cuts and increased military spending in 1981 were clearly an exception to incrementalism. But his failure to win further cuts and increases in succeeding years testifies to the persistence of incrementalism.

Budget legislation goes through a similar but more complicated process as other bills.[90] To grasp the complexity, we have to understand the distinction between budget authorizations and budget appropriations. **Authorizations** provide agencies and departments with the legal authority to operate. Although authorizations also might specify funding levels, they do not actually provide the funding. **Appropriations** are the authority to spend money.

Typically, authorization requests are reviewed by the particular standing committee whose subject matter encompasses the activities of a particular agency. In essence, almost all standing committees are authorization committees for those agencies whose work they oversee. The House Interior and Insular Affairs Committee and the Senate Energy and National Resources Committee, for example, review the authorization of the Park Service in the Department of Interior; the agriculture committees are authorization committees for the Department of Agriculture.

In reviewing an agency, the authorizing committee is not bound by the administration's request. It is free to expand, shrink, or eliminate it altogether. However, the authorizing committee and the agency being reviewed will have developed close ties over the years so authorizations are likely to be more generous than appropriations.

Appropriations are reviewed by the Appropriations Committee. There is only one appropriations committee in each house and it makes recommendations on the entire budget. Although appropriations subcommittees develop close ties with the agencies they review, the committee as a whole does not have these ties, and thus its recommendations for funding tend to be lower than authorized. Conflicts occur frequently between authorizing committees and the Appropriations Committee.

Both authorizing and appropriations bills must pass each house, and differences must be resolved in a conference. The separation of the authorization and appropriations process is complex and rather uncoordinated. Authorizing committees often make decisions without considering the total budget picture and so the real power to control spending passes to the Appropriations Committee, thus weakening the authorizing committees.

Congress is aided in its budget setting by the Congressional Budget Office (CBO), which provides expertise to Congress on matters related to the budget and economy. Before the establishment of the CBO, members of Congress felt they were junior partners in budget making because they had to depend on information provided by the president, his budget advisers, and the Office of Management and Budget. Because the CBO is responsible to both parties in Congress, it provides a less politically biased set of forecasts about the budget than does the administration.

In years when the president's party does not control Congress, the congressional majority produces its own budget, with priorities distinctly different from the president's. For example, since 1994, Republicans in the House have been more interested in cutting spending for domestic programs and possibly reducing taxes than has President Clinton. Because they control Congress, the Republicans' priorities, not the president's, have become the starting point for budget decisions. Led by Budget Committee Chair John Kasich (R-Ohio), Republicans have set the agenda for debate on the budget.

The budget process is now less tied to committees than in the past. Recent budgets have been produced after months of direct negotiations among congressional leaders, their staffs, administration aides, individual members, and the president. Committee hearings have become a sideshow, with the real decisions made in private negotiations. Congress is then presented with a "take it or leave it" budget package.

Since 1997 budget decisions have taken on a much different flavor. For the first time in 30 years, the federal budget is running a surplus, not a deficit. Under President Bush, one year the federal deficit was almost $300 billion; fiscal 1998 (which ended on September 30, 1998) finished with a surplus of about $70 billion. Debate among budget makers now is how to use the extra funds. President Clinton wants to commit the surplus to strengthening Social Security. Others want government to reverse some of the spending cuts in domestic programs, such as environmental protection, since the 1980s. Many Republicans want to return much of the surplus to taxpayers by cutting taxes. Still others want to use the extra funds to lower the national debt, thereby reducing the interest the government pays each year.

CONCLUSION: IS CONGRESS RESPONSIVE?

Congress is certainly responsive to many individuals with individual problems. The primacy given to constituency service practically guarantees this kind of responsiveness. But is Congress responsive to the nation's policy demands? The primary policy function of Congress seems to be to serve as a check on the president, reviewing, revising, and perhaps killing his policy proposals. The efficiency of Congress in producing its own legislation varies greatly and may be declining.

The media attention that Congress receives probably is eroding its ability to make public policy. Some media attention is good, because we prize open government in a democracy. But some of it is not so good, because in a heterogeneous society we rely on compromise to achieve our public goals and, under the harsh glare of media, there are fewer opportunities to compromise and deliberate without fear of losing votes back home.

Members often feel they have to be too responsive. Now, as never before, every step—or misstep—that members of Congress take is carried to every part of the nation. Or as the *New York Times* commented, "Modern Washington is wired for quadrophonic sound and wide-screen video, lashed by fax, computer, 800 number, overnight poll, FedEx, grassroots mail, air shuttle and CNN to every citizen in every village on the continent and Hawaii too. Its every twitch is blared to the world, thanks to C-SPAN, open meetings laws, financial-disclosure reports, and campaign spending rules, and its every misstep is logged in a database for the use of some future office seeker."[91] As a response to media scrutiny and partisan deadlock, more legislation is being written in secret negotiations between congressional and executive leaders and staffers. This trend is hailed by some but criticized by others who are shut out of the process.

The pressures of elections and of constituency service also undermine Congress's ability to focus on public policy. Said one long-term member, "We see people coming here who do nothing but public relations . . . and that's not good."[92] Pressure to be in the home district meeting constituents competes with legislators' desires to do a good job at lawmaking and to work more efficiently (such as by expanding the work week from three days to five). Pressure to raise money for reelection campaigns incurs obligations to interest groups that may not be consistent with either the members' or constituents' views.

Indeed, part of the congressional Democratic leadership's problems in articulating a clear vision and supporting Clinton's initiatives is that so many of its members have become dependent on the contributions of PACs for their campaign funding. This puts them in the position of having to support some interests that are not consistent with the Democratic voters' views or interests. The lengthy debate and foot dragging by some congressional Democrats on health care reform illustrated this tension, with many major interest groups (insurance companies, hospitals, drug companies, physicians) adamantly opposed to further government involvement in health care, but a huge Democratic constituency desperate for some change that would allow them access to quality health care. For the Republicans, reliance on PACs is not so contradictory, since Republicans have traditionally been the party of the better-off and of business.

The procedures and organization of Congress also give individuals and small groups opportunities to block or redirect action. This is particularly true in the Senate, where procedures allow a minority of senators to engage in unlimited debate, unless an overwhelming majority vote to stop it. The fragmented committee and subcommittee structure in both houses offers many points for action to be killed. Political parties have been strengthened in recent years but are not strong enough to protect against the pressure of lobbyists or outraged constituents. All of these factors mean that Congress continues to be more responsive to individual needs than to more general societal ones.

It is perhaps this nonresponsiveness to overall societal needs that has given rise to the disdain for government expressed so vehemently in the 1994 election (see Figure 6). The public wants their Congress to be responsive to their individual needs and those of their group, and then looks down on the institution because this responsiveness leads to inaction and conflict. Moreover, public disdain is fueled by an unrealistic public expectation that there really is one public interest, one majority, and it is only the malfeasance and inefficiencies of Congress that keeps "good" policies from being enacted. The truth is, of course, that there is no set of policies on which everyone agrees. The public does not always agree on the aims of public policy (Are we interested in saving money, or making sure

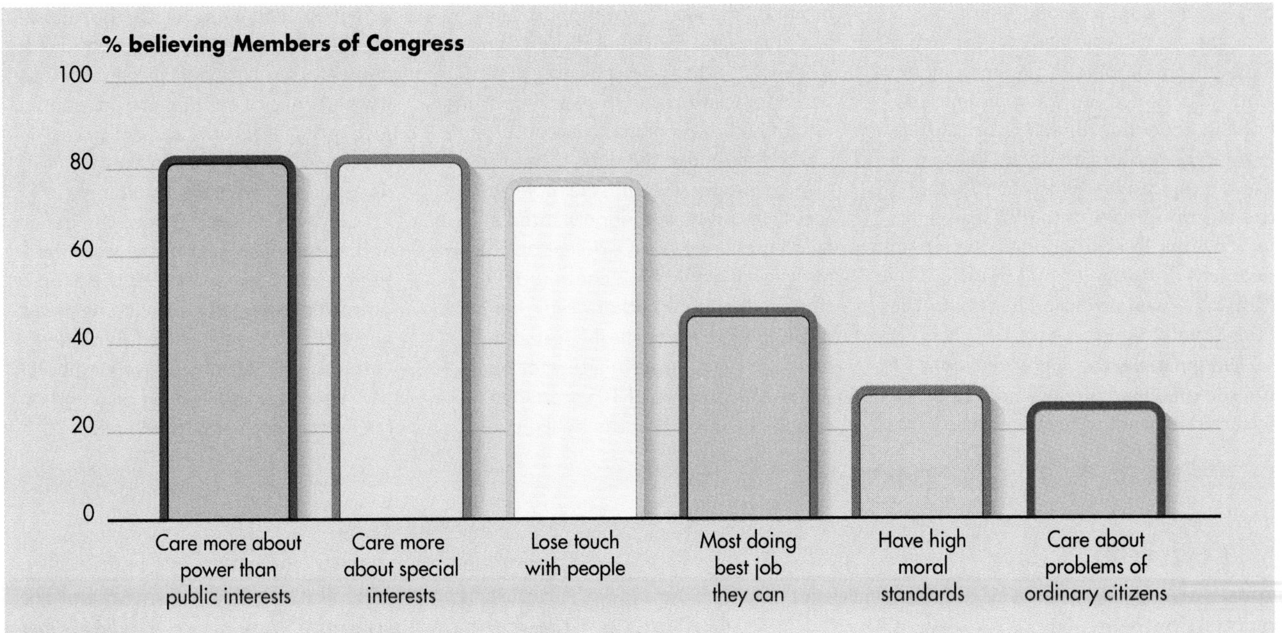

FIGURE 6

Public Holds Low Opinion of Congress

SOURCE: *Washington Post*-ABC Polls, reported July 11–17, 1994, p. 7.

every child has access to health care? Are we interested in making public schools better, or encouraging more education to be taken over by private schools? Are we interested in promoting a woman's right to choose an abortion, or closing off that choice?), let alone how to accomplish those aims.

Moreover, most of the public does not know what Congress has done. They are much more likely to know about bounced checks and sexual improprieties of members of Congress than they are about legislation. For example, in 1994, although two-thirds were aware of new handgun regulations and family leave policy (granting most employees the right to take an unpaid leave for a new baby or family illness), less than one-third of the public knew that Congress had passed a budget bill cutting the deficit by billions, reduced taxes on the working poor and raised them on the very rich, made voting registration nearly automatic when individuals sign up for their driver's licenses, and given federal workers the right to get involved in politics.[93] Thus, the public evaluation of Congress as having accomplished "not much" or "nothing at all" (from the same poll) was based on the public's lack of awareness of what Congress actually did.

Congress, as confused, inefficient, and conflict-ridden though it may be, is really a reflection of our society. And yet, few would want to replace this crucial democratic institution. The public takes pride, in the abstract, in this feature of constitutional government.

The new Republican majority has so far been unable to change the public's perception of Congress. Both congressional conflict with the president and some misreading of the national mood have made it difficult for Republicans to restore public confidence in this key democratic institution.

EPILOGUE

Margolies-Mezvinsky Supports the President and Loses Her Job

Representative Margolies-Mezvinsky told the president she would vote for the bill only if he was one vote short and hers was the swing vote, and only if he agreed to the entitlement summit. Unfortunately for her, the president needed her vote to pull out a one-vote victory. While many Democrats with safer seats "took a walk" away from supporting Clinton, Margolies-Mezvinsky supported him. As soon as she cast her ballot, some Republicans in the House stood up and waved "Goodbye, Marjorie."

Friends, members of the administration, and some media praised her courage for taking a fiscally responsible but politically dangerous position ("Courageous Freshman Saves the President"), but her constituents were infuriated. "Just another run-of-the-mill, cheap, soiled, ward-heeling politician whose word was not worth a spit stain in the street," said one local paper.[94] Phone lines to her offices were tied up for hours with angry constituents. Her proposals to cut entitlements were unpopular and so were tax increases in the bill. Focus groups found most voters thought she had sold her vote for an ambassadorship or some other emolument, when all she received was a promise to hold an economic summit in her district.

Margolies-Mezvinsky was swept out in the Republican landslide of 1994, losing the election by a 45% to 49% margin to Jon Fox, her 1992 opponent. She ran an excellent campaign to pull that close. Most observers attributed her loss to the budget vote.

Did she make the "right" decision? On the one hand, she was not responsive to some demands of her constituents. She promised she would not support Clinton's plan, and she did. But she was responsive in other ways. Her constituents voted for Clinton and she was supporting one of his key programs. Her constituents wanted to reduce the deficit, and the Clinton proposal would. Her constituent focus groups showed none wanted a failed presidency, and a defeat on the budget bill would have contributed to that perception. In other words, her constituents were as torn as she was about what was right. Unfortunately for Margolies-Mezvinsky, 9 of 10 voters erroneously believed that the deficit could be cut by eliminating waste, thus allowing them to reconcile their contradictory desires for tax cuts, deficit reduction, and maintenance of entitlement programs such as Social Security and Medicare.[95] Mezvinsky knew that belief was an illusion, and cast her vote accordingly.

Clinton's plan did reduce the deficit, and, contrary to Republican warnings, stimulated the economy. As the economy strengthened, the deficit declined and ultimately disappeared. Whether voters will eventually forgive members who voted for the Clinton plan and its tax increases remains to be seen.

KEY TERMS

constituencies
reapportionment
redistricting
gerrymander
franking
constituency service
casework
pork barrel
informal norms
institutional loyalty
reciprocity
specialization
going public
Speaker of the House
majority leader
minority leader
whips
standing committees
markup
seniority rule
subcommittee bill of rights
special interest caucuses
Rules Committee
filibuster
cloture
Conference Committee
oversight
legislative veto
authorizations
appropriations

FURTHER READING

Michael Barone et al., *The Almanac of American Politics* (Washington, D.C.: National Journal, since 1980). A description of each member, his or her district, and voting record. Revised every two years since 1980. A volume similar in format and publication schedule is Alan Ehrenhalt's *Politics in America* (Washington, D.C.: CQ Press).

Congressional Quarterly Weekly Report. Published weekly, provides analyses of the workings of Congress and its members. The Congressional Quarterly also publishes a yearly summary of congressional action called the *Congressional Quarterly Almanac*.

Timothy Cook, *Making Laws and Making News* (Washington, D.C.: Brookings, 1989). A revealing account of how media coverage has affected the legislative process in the U.S. House.

Elizabeth Drew, *Senator* (New York: Simon & Schuster, 1979). Describes the day-to-day life of a former U.S. senator, John Culver, working in his state and Washington.

Richard Fenno, *Home Style* (Boston: Little, Brown, 1978). A readable book based on Fenno's travels with House members to their home districts. Fenno offers interesting and valuable insights into how members present themselves to the home folks. In *The United States Senate: A Bicameral Perspective* (Washington, D.C.: The American Enterprise Institute, 1982), Fenno gives the same attention to senators.

Morris Fiorina, *Congress: Keystone of the Washington Establishment*, 2d ed. (New Haven: Yale University Press, 1989). A small and significant book that argues that members of Congress love the big bureaucracy because it helps their constituents and thereby helps them win reelection.

Linda Fowler, *Candidates, Congress, and the American Democracy* (Ann Arbor: University of Michigan Press, 1993). How the political system affects the recruitment of congressional candidates, and how the candidates affect the system.

Marjorie Margolies-Mezvinsky, *A Woman's Place: The Freshmen Women Who Changed the Face of Congress* (New York: Crown, 1994). Representative Margolies-Mezvinsky reflects on the changes brought about in Congress by the largest group of women representatives ever.

Timothy Phelps and Helen Winternitz, *Capitol Games: Clarence Thomas, Anita Hill and the Story of a Supreme Court Nomination* (New York: Hyperion, 1992). A close look at the Senate hearings on Clarence Thomas's nomination to the Supreme Court.

Pat Schroeder, *24 Years of House Work . . . and the Place Is Still a Mess* (Kansas City, Mo.: Andrews McMeel Publishing, 1998). One of the most outspoken women in Congress from 1973 to 1995, Schroeder tells how a woman politician succeeded in this male-dominated institution.

Steven Waldman, *The Bill: How the Adventures of Clinton's National Service Bill Reveal What Is Corrupt, Comic, Cynical—and Noble—about Washington* (New York: Viking, 1995). How a bill becomes a law in the 1990s, with a focus on Clinton's national service and student loan proposals.

ELECTRONIC RESOURCES

http://www.whitehouse.gov/WH/html/legi.html

This link takes you to the official U.S. House and U.S. Senate pages. On them you can find information about the membership of each branch, roll-call votes, hearing schedules, historical information, and much more. The site contains links to individual members' pages too. The site also links to agencies of Congress, such as the General Accounting Office and the Library of Congress, and to other federal agencies.

http://www.washingtonpost.com/

This is the Web site of the Washington Post, *whose news coverage of Congress is unrivaled.*

http://thomas.loc.gov/home/thomas.html

Links to texts of bills, the congressional record (reporting the entire floor debates), and committee hearings and reports.

http://lcweb.loc.gov/global/legislative/congress.html

Want to know how many Asian Americans are in Congress and who they are? How much members of Congress make? Who the leadership is? This page links to all kinds of statistics about Congress, along with links to the home pages and e-mail addresses of members.

INFOTRAC CITATIONS

"Same as the Old Boss—Term Limits"
"America's Town Crier"
"Newt's Heir Apparent"
"While Congress Plays Games"

NOTES

1. These quotations, and much of this background information, are from Michael Barone and Grant Ujifusa, *The Almanac of American Politics* (Washington, D.C.: National Journal, 1994), pp. 1108–1109; other sources include "Special Report," *Congressional Quarterly Weekly Report* (October 22, 1994), p. 3048; "The Last Stretch," *Congressional Quarterly Weekly Report,* August 7, 1993, pp. 2125, 2129. See also Marjorie Margolies-Mezvinsky, *A Woman's Place: The Freshmen Women Who Changed the Face of Congress* (New York: Crown, 1994).

2. John Hibbing and Elizabeth Theiss-Morse, *Congress as Public Enemy* (Cambridge, Mass.: Cambridge University Press, 1995). The next three paragraphs draw from this source.

3. Ibid.

4. Richard Fenno, "U.S. House Members and Their Constituencies: An Exploration," *American Political Science Review* 71 (September 1977), pp. 883–917. The data in this paragraph are from the Washington Post/ABC Polls, reported in *Washington Post National Weekly Edition,* July 11–17, 1994, p. 7.

5. Hibbing and Theiss-Morse, *Congress as Public Enemy.*

6. Fenno, "U.S. House Members and Their Constituencies."

7. Richard Fenno, "If, as Ralph Nader Says, Congress Is 'The Broken Branch,' How Come We Love Our Congressmen So Much?" in Norman Ornstein, ed., *Congress and Change* (New York: Praeger, 1974), pp. 277–287.

8. Michael Berkman, "State Legislators in Congress," *American Journal of Political Science* 38 (November 1994), pp. 1025–1055.

9. Robert Erikson and Gerald Wright, Jr., "Policy Representation of Constituency Interests," *Political Behavior 2* (1980), pp. 91–106; Erikson and Wright, "Voters, Candidates, and Issues in Congressional Elections," in Lawrence Dodd and Bruce Oppenheimer, eds., *Congress Reconsidered,* 3d ed. (Washington, D.C.: CQ Press; Wright, "Policy Voting in the U.S. Senate: Who Is Represented?" *Legislative Studies Quarterly* 14 (November 1989), pp. 465–486. See also Robert Erikson and Norman Luttbeg, *American Public Opinion* (New York: John Wiley & Sons, 1973), p. 257; William Shaffer, "The Ideological and Partisan Linkages between U.S. Senators and Their Constituents," paper prepared at the Annual Meeting of the Midwest Political Science Association, Chicago, 1987; Warren Miller and Donald Stokes, "Constituency Influence in Congress," *American Political Science Review* 56 (March 1963), pp. 45–56.

10. Wright, "Policy Voting in the U.S. Senate."

11. 369 U.S. 186 (1962).

12. *Wesberry v. Sanders,*376 U.S. 1 (1964).

13. Bruce Cain and Janet Campagna, "Predicting Partisan Redistricting Disputes," *Legislative Studies Quarterly* 12 (1987), pp. 265–274.

14. See report on *Miller* v. *Johnson,* 515 U.S. 900 (1995), in *New York Times,* July 2, 1995, pp. E1, E4.

15. Steven A. Holmes, "Did Racial Redistricting Undermine Democrats?" *New York Times,* November 13, 1994, p. 32.

16. Kevin A. Hill, "Does the Creation of Majority Black Districts Aid Republicans? An Analysis of the 1992 Congressional Elections in Eight States," *Journal of Politics* 57 (May 1995), pp. 384–401; Holmes, "Did Racial Redistricting Undermine Democrats?"; Juan Williams, "How Black Liberal Strategy Failed Its Followers," *Washington Post National Weekly Edition,* November 28–December 3, 1994, p. 25.

17. See Thomas E. Mann, "Elections and Change in Congress," in Thomas Mann and Norman Ornstein, eds., *The New Congress* (Washington, D.C.: American Enterprise Institute, 1981), pp. 32–54; David Mayhew, *The Electoral Connection* (New Haven: Yale University Press, 1974); Glenn Parker and Roger Davidson, "Why Do Americans Love Their Congressmen So Much?" *Legislative Studies Quarterly* (February 1979), pp. 53–62.

18. Thomas Mann and Raymond Wolfinger, "Candidates and Parties in Congressional Elections," *American Political Science Review* 74 (September 1980), pp. 617–632; Patricia Hurley and Kim Q. Hill, "The Prospects for Issue Voting in Contemporary Congressional Elections," *American Politics Quarterly* 8 (October 1980), p. 446.

19. John Alford and John Hibbing, "The Disparate Electoral Security of House and Senate Incumbents," paper presented at the American Political Science meetings, Atlanta, Georgia, September 1989.

20. Richard Fenno, *Home Style* (Boston: Little, Brown, 1978).

21. Susan Trausch, *It Came from the Swamp: Your Federal Government at Work* (New York: Houghton Mifflin, 1986).

22. Tim Miller, "Frankly Free Mail Seems to Help Incumbents," *Washington Post National Weekly Edition,* August 8, 1985, pp. 13–14. For an investigation of the impact of franked mail, see Albert Cover, "The Electoral Impact of Franked Congressional Mail," *Polity* 17 (Summer 1985), pp. 649–663.

23. Miller, "Frankly Free Mail Seems to Help Incumbents."

24. See Glenn Parker, "Sources of Change in Congressional District Attentiveness," *American Journal of Political Science* (February 1980), pp. 115–124.

25. Carol Matlack, "Live from Capitol Hill," *National Journal,* February 18, 1989, p. 390.

26. *Setting Course: A Congressional Management Guide* (Washington, D.C.: American University Congressional Management Program, 1984); Norman Ornstein, Thomas E. Mann, and Michael Malbin, *Vital Statistics on Congress, 1991–1992* (Washington, D.C.: American Enterprise Institute, 1992), p. 161.

27. Ornstein, Mann, and Malbin, *Vital Statistics*,1992, tables 5-3, 5-4.

28. Morris Fiorina, "Congressional Control of the Bureaucracy: A Mismatch of Incentives and Capabilities," in Lawrence C. Dodd and Bruce I. Oppenheimer, eds., *Congress Reconsidered*, 2d ed. (Washington, D.C.: CQ Press, 1981), p. 341.

29. Morris Fiorina, *Congress: Keystone of the Washington Establishment* (New Haven: Yale University Press, 1977), especially pp. 48–49.

30. Robert Sherill, "Squealing on Porcine Politics," *Washington Post National Weekly Edition*, September 7–12, 1992, p. 35; the quote is by Alan Schick from Brian Kelly, "Pigging Out at the White House," *Washington Post National Weekly Edition*, September 14–20, 1992, p. 23.

31. Cass Peterson, "Despite Gramm-Rudman Diet, the House Still Likes Its Pork," *Washington Post National Weekly Edition*, November 25, 1985, p. 13.

32. Michael Wines, "Watch out with that Budget Ax. My District NEEDS That Dam," *New York Times*, July 30, 1995, p. E7. "Hypocrites of Pork," *Newsweek*, April 12, 1993, p. 26.

33. Quoted in Kenneth Shepsle, "The Failures of Congressional Budgeting," *Social Science and Modern Society* 20 (1983), pp. 4–10. See also Howard Kurtz, "Pork Barrel Politics," *Washington Post*, January 25, 1982, reported in Randall Ripley, *Congress*, 3d ed. (New York: W. W. Norton, 1983).

34. See Paul Feldman and James Jondrow, "Congressional Elections and Local Federal Spending," *American Journal of Political Science* 28 (1984), p. 152; Glenn R. Parker and Suzanne Parker, "The Correlates and Effects of Attention to District by U.S. House Members," *Legislative Studies Quarterly* 10 (1985), p. 239.

35. Christopher Buckley, "Hangin' with the Houseboyz," *Washington Monthly*, June 1992, p. 44.

36. Linda L. Fowler, *Who Decides to Run for Congress?* (New Haven: Yale University Press, 1989); Linda L. Fowler, *Candidates, Congress and the American Democracy* (Ann Arbor: University of Michigan Press, 1993).

37. Thomas Mann, *Unsafe at Any Margin: Interpreting Congressional Elections* (Washington, D.C.: American Enterprise Institute, 1978).

38. "Women, Minorities Join Senate," *CQ Almanac*, 1992, pp. 8A–14A; "Wave of Diversity Spared Many Incumbents," *CQ Almanac*, 1992, pp. 15A–21A, 24A; "The Elections" *CQ*, November 12, 1994, p. 3237.

39. Gary Jacobson, *The Politics of Congressional Elections*, 2d ed. (Boston: Little, Brown, 1987), p. 51.

40. Ibid.

41. Barbara Hinckley, "The American Voter in Congressional Elections," *American Political Science Review* 74 (September 1980), pp. 641–650; Hinckley, "House Reelections and Senate Defeats: The Role of the Challenger," *British Journal of Political Science* 10 (October 1980), pp. 441–460; Mann and Wolfinger, "Candidates and Parties"; Alan I. Abramowitz, "A Comparison of Voting of U.S. Senators and Representatives in 1978," *American Political Science Review* 74 (September 1980), pp. 633–640.

42. Alford and Hibbing, "The Disparate Electoral Security of House and Senate Incumbents."

43. A good review of these arguments is found in John R. Hibbing and Sara L. Brandes, "State Population and the Electoral Success of U.S. Senators," *American Journal of Political Science 27* (November 1983), pp. 808–819. See also Eric Uslaner, "The Case of the Vanishing Liberal Senators: The House Did It," *British Journal of Political Science* 11 (January 1981), pp. 105–113; Abramowitz, "A Comparison."

44. Hibbing and Brandes, "State Population." See also Glenn Parker, "Stylistic Change in the U.S. Senate," *Journal of Politics* 47 (November 1985), pp. 1190–1202.

45. Edie Goldenberg and Michael Traugott, *Campaigning for Congress* (Washington, D.C.: CQ Press, 1984); Gary Jacobson and Samuel Kernell, *Strategy and Choice in Congressional Elections*, 2d ed. (New Haven: Yale University Press, 1983).

46. Edward Walsh, "Wanted: Candidates for Congress," *Washington Post National Weekly Edition*, November 25, 1985, p. 9.

47. Paul Herrnson, "Do Parties Make a Difference? The Role of Parties in Congressional Elections," *Journal of Politics* 48 (August 1986), pp. 589–615.

48. Ceci Connolly, "GOP Hold on House Hazier," *Washington Post*, June 8, 1998, p. A1.

49. Alan Ehrenhalt, "Technology, Strategy Bring New Campaign Era," *Congressional Quarterly Weekly Report*, December 7, 1985, p. 2561; Mann, "Elections and Change in Congress"; Jacobson, *The Politics of Congressional Elections*.

50. Paul Hernson, *Party Campaigning in the 1980s* (Cambridge, Mass.: Harvard University Press, 1988).

51. See Gerald Wright, Jr. and Michael Berkman, "Candidates and Policy in United States Senate Elections," *American Political Science Review* 80 (June 1986), pp. 567–588; Erikson and Wright, "Voters, Candidates, and Issues in Congressional Elections."

52. See James Campbell, "Explaining Presidential Losses in Midterm Elections," *Journal of Politics* 47 (November 1985), pp. 1140–1157. See also Barbara Hinckley, "Interpreting House Midterm Elections," *American Political Science Review* 61 (1967), pp. 694–700; Samuel Kernell, "Presidential Popularity and Negative Voting," *American Political Science Review* 71 (1977), pp. 44–66; Edward Tufte, "Determinants of the Outcomes of Midterm Congressional Elections," *American Political Science Review* 69 (1975), pp. 812–826; Alan Abramowitz, "Economic Conditions, Presidential Popularity and Voting Behavior in Midterm Elections," *Journal of Politics* 47 (February 1985), pp. 31–43.

53. Herbert Asher, "Learning of Legislative Norms," *American Political Science Review* 67 (June 1973), pp. 499–513. Michael Berkman points out that those freshmen who have had state legislative experience—now more than half of all House members—adapt to the job faster than other members. See "Former State Legislators in the U.S. House of Representatives: Institutional and Policy Mastery," *Legislative Studies Quarterly* 18 (February 1993), pp. 77–104.

54. Minot (North Dakota) *Daily News*, June 17, 1976, quoted in Ripley, *Congress*.

55. Samuel Kernell, *Going Public* (Washington, D.C.: CQ Press, 1986).

56. Quoted in W. Mark Crain and Brian Goff, *Televised Legislatures: Political Information Technology and Public Choice* (Boston: Kluwer, 1988), p. 19. See also R. E. Cohen, "The Congress Watchers," *National Journal*, January 26, 1985, p. 215. For an examination of the Senate debate, see Richard Fenno, "The Senate Thru the Looking Glass: The Debate over Television," *Legislative Studies Quarterly* 14 (August 1989), pp. 313–348.

57. Cohen, "The Congress Watchers."

58. Ronald Garay, *Congressional Television: A Legislative History* (Westport, Conn.: Grenwood Press, 1984), p. 143; Michael Robinson, "Three Faces of Congressional Media," in Thomas Mann and

Norman Ornstein, eds., *The New Congress* (Washington, D.C.: American Enterprise Institute, 1981), p. 68.

59. Katharine Q. Seelye, "Gingrich Used TV Skills to Be King of the Hill," *New York Times*, December 14, 1994, p. A14.

60. Ibid.

61. Diane Duston, "They're Angry, Conservative, and They're Dialing Right Now," *Centre Daily Times* (AP Release), July 16, 1993, p. 1. The study was done by the Times- Mirror Center for the People and the Press.

62. Richard Fenno, "U.S. House Members and Their Constituencies: An Exploration," *American Political Science Review* 71 (1977), pp. 883–917; and Fenno, *Home Style*.

63. Benjamin Page et al., "Constituency, Party and Representation in Congress," *Public Opinion Quarterly* 48 (Winter 1984), pp. 741–756; Jerrold E. Schneider, *Ideological Coalitions in Congress* (Westport, Conn.: Greenwood Press, 1979).

64. John Kingdon, *Congressmen's Voting Decisions* (New York: Harper & Row, 1973).

65. Congressional Quarterly, *The Origins and Development of Congress* (Washington, D.C.: CQ Press, 1976).

66. Neil McNeil, *Forge of Democracy* (New York: McKay, 1963), pp. 306–309.

67. Susan Welch and John G. Peters, "Private Interests in the U.S. Congress," *Legislative Studies Quarterly* 7 (November 1982), pp. 547–555.

68. See Roger Davidson, "Subcommittee Government," in Mann and Ornstein, *The New Congress*, pp. 110–111. Some of this occurs because members of Congress tend to be wealthy, and the wealthy make investments in corporations. It also occurs because members' financial interests are often similar to the interests in their districts (e.g., representatives of farm districts are likely to be involved in farming or agribusiness).

69. Alan Ehrenhalt, "Media, Power Shifts to Dominate O'Neill's House," *Congressional Quarterly Weekly Report*, September 13, 1986, pp. 2131–2136; Stephen Hess, "Live from Capitol Hill, It's . . . ," *Washington Monthly* (June 1986), pp. 41–43. The Biden quotation is from this article. See also Steven Smith and Christopher Deering, *Committees in Congress* (Washington, D.C.: CQ Press, 1984), p. 67.

70. Eric Planin, "David Obey Appropriates a New Fiefdom," *Washington Post National Weekly Edition*, May 9–15, 1994, p. 11.

71. John Hibbing and Sara Brandes-Crook, "Congressional Reform and Party Discipline: The Effects of Changes in the Seniority System on Party Loyalty in the U.S. House of Representatives," *British Journal of Political Science* 15 (April 1985).

72. Eleanor Clift, "The Prince of Pork," *Newsweek* (April 15, 1991), p. 35.

73. John Fairhall, quoting Thomas Downey (D-N.Y.), "Bureaucratic Bloat Crippling Congress," *Lincoln Journal-Star*, June 7, 1992, p. 7B.

74. Michael J. Malbin, "Delegation, Deliberation, and the New Role of Congressional Staff," in Mann and Ornstein, *The New Congress*, p. 135.

75. Ibid. pp. 170–177.

76. Alan Ehrenhalt, "In the Senate of the '80s, Team Spirit Has Given Way to the Rule of Individuals," *Congressional Quarterly Weekly Report*, September 4, 1982, p. 2175.

77. Ronald Moe and Steven Teel, "Congress as a Policy-Maker: A Necessary Reappraisal," *Political Science Quarterly* 85 (September 1970), pp. 443–470.

78. Bruce Oppenheimer, "The Rules Committee," in Lawrence Dodd and Bruce Oppenheimer, eds., *Congress Reconsidered* (New York: Praeger, 1977), p. 96–116.

79. Stanley Cloud, "Return of the Lions," *Time*, May 31, 1993, p. 28. The quote is by John Dingell (D-Mich.).

80. Thomas Geoghegan, "Bust the Filibuster" *Washington Post National Weekly Edition*, July 12–18, 1994, p. 25.

81. Quoted in Sarah A. Binder and Steven S. Smith, "The Politics and Principle of the Senate Filibuster," in *Extensions* (Norman, Okla.: University of Oklahoma, Carl A. Albert Center, Fall 1997), pp. 15–16.

82. Michael Malbin, "Leading a Filibustered Senate," in *Extensions* (Norman, Okla.: University of Oklahoma, Carl A. Albert Center, Spring 1985), p. 3.

83. Louis Fisher, "A Washington Guidebook," *Public Administration Review* (January/February 1989), p. 86.

84. Morris Ogul, "Congressional Oversight: Structures and Incentives," in Dodd and Oppenheimer, *Congress Reconsidered*. See also Loch Johnson, "The U.S. Congress and the CIA: Monitoring the Dark Side of Government," *Legislative Studies Quarterly* 5 (November 1980), pp. 477–501.

85. Joseph Califano, "Imperial Congress," *New York Times Magazine*, January 23, 1994, p. 41.

86. Morris Fiorina, "Congressional Control of the Bureaucracy: A Mismatch of Incentives and Capabilities," in Dodd and Oppenheimer, *Congress Reconsidered*, pp. 332–348.

87. Aaron Wildavsky, *The Politics of the Budgetary Process* (Boston: Little, Brown, 1964).

88. D. Roderick Kiewiet and Matthew McCubbins, "Congressional Appropriations and the Electoral Connection," *Journal of Politics* 47 (February 1985), pp. 59–82.

89. John Hibbing, "The Liberal Hour: Electoral Pressures and Transfer Payment Voting in the United States Congress," *Journal of Politics* 46 (August 1984), pp. 846–865.

90. Allen Schick, *Congress and Money* (Washington, D.C.: Urban Institute, 1980).

91. Michael Wines, "Washington Really Is in Touch. We're the Problem," *New York Times* (October 16, 1994), section 4, p. 2.

92. Broder, "Who Took the Fun?"

93. Richard Morin and Thomas Edsall, "Bumping Up against the Public Perception," *Washington Post National Weekly Edition*, April 17–23, 1995, p. 14. See also John Hibbing and Elizabeth Theiss-Morse," Civics Is Not Enough," *PS* 29 (March 1996), pp. 57–62.

94. Bill Turque, "Housebroken," *Newsweek*, November 29, 1993, pp. 32ff.

95. Ibid. See also Margolies-Mezvinsky's story in "Freshman Rush—First You Run to Get Elected, Then You Just Keep Running," *Washingtonian Magazine* (April 1993), pp. 76–80.

President Clinton has been on the hot seat during his second term because of investigations into his personal and political behavior.

Cynthia Johnson/*Time* magazine

11 THE PRESIDENCY

Stand by Your Man?

It is January 1998, and the *Washington Post* has broken another story about President Clinton's personal life. Now the special prosecutor is investigating the possibility that the president obstructed justice by encouraging a White House intern, Monica Lewinsky, to lie under oath about his relationship with her. Some people in the press and a few in Congress are actually talking about the possibility of impeachment hearings, and the president and White House staff are in a grim mood about having to devote time and resources to fight another attack on the administration.

You are the second in command, Albert A. Gore, Jr., vice president of the United States. The press is dogging the president's every move, but they have an eye on you, too. As the president maps out his strategy for handling the allegations and related legal problems, you also have to consider how to respond. Almost everyone believes you will be running for president in two years. You have already built the basis of a formidable campaign organization and have more than a leg up on any challenger in the Democratic primaries.

Despite these advantages, your election is far from guaranteed. Although six of the last nine vice presidents have been nominated for the presidency, George Bush was the first sitting vice president to win the presidency since 1836 when Martin Van Buren did it. Common wisdom says this is because vice presidents get saddled with the negatives of the presidents they have served without being able to take credit for the successes. How will you maintain your claim to a share in Clinton administration successes without being associated with the allegations of ethical and personal wrongdoing that have dogged the president? Will you stand by your man through this new crisis, or will you try to put some distance between yourself and the president so that, whatever happens, the damage to your future candidacy will be minimized?

The president is about to embark on his first trip outside Washington since the Lewinsky scandal hit the papers. As usual he is following up his State of the Union address by taking his message directly to the people, this year to Illinois and Wisconsin. You helped pick the sites for this year's visits, and the suggestion that you should accompany the president was meant to benefit you.[1] For the first time in your career you had been accused of serious—possibly criminal—wrongdoing, violating campaign finance laws by accepting money from foreign nationals. When questioned by the press, you appeared completely flustered and answered the questions poorly. To boost your image , the president agrees that you should travel with him to the Midwest after his State of the Union address. The administration has been riding high on good economic news, including the lowest unemployment and inflation rates in a quarter century. Clinton's popularity ratings are unusually high for a minority president halfway through the second term of an administration that has been plagued by scandals. He hopes some of the ratings gloss will rub off on you.

But now, quickly, the tables are turned. The Justice Department has cleared you of any wrongdoing in fundraising, while the president is reeling from the new charges against him. Now it seems that your presence on the trip may be a boon to him. Is it time to lie low, even at the risk of appearing self-serving and disloyal, or is it time to go to the mat for a friend and political ally?

No president and vice president in the history of the country have had a closer working relationship than you and Clinton. You are both southerners, moderate Democrats, Ivy Leaguers, babyboomers, and rock-and-rollers, and you have both spent most of your adult lives in electoral politics. You complement the president in many ways: your work on environmental issues shored up his mediocre record on environmental protection as governor of Arkansas; you have a special interest in the role of high technology in economic development whereas he has been slow to adapt to the computer age; you served in Vietnam and he evaded the draft; you are a Washington insider while he is an outsider; you have a squeaky clean image in both your public and personal life, while the president has been seen as a

SOMETIMES I MISS THE BUSH ADMINISTRATION.
IF THIS LIMO'S ROCKIN' DON'T COME A-KNOCKIN'

Reprinted with permission of King Features Syndicate

deal-maker and political compromiser and as someone with a rather undisciplined personal life.

In return, Clinton complements your many weaknesses as a campaigner. In contrast to your oft-described wooden demeanor and speaking style, he appears open and accessible and is a master of working the fence and extemporaneous speaking; and in his years of leading the Democratic Council, he gained a reputation as a policy wonk to match or surpass yours as an "eco-techno-nerd." You made a run for the presidency and failed; running for vice president on the ticket with Clinton has revitalized your political career. You owe him.

On the other hand, Clinton owes you. You have been a loyal stand-in, friend, and adviser. He has been accused of zigzagging across the policy map, but you stayed right with him, never striking out an independent policy line or even hinting at it. Through all his troubled times, you have been at his side in public saying great things about him. But Clinton has not been ungrateful. Whereas many presidents have refused their vice presidents any significant policy or advising role, and sometimes even shut them out of the information loop completely, Clinton has made you a full partner in his administration. You are in on the big meetings and have become one of his closest advisers; his staff and yours work closely to coordinate activities of the two offices. During his first term, he put you in charge of some priority issues, such as downsizing government and environmental and high-tech policy. He has let you be out front with the press and has helped you make the vice presidency as visible as the office has ever been. Never appearing insecure about a possible contender within his own ranks, Clinton shows little reluctance to add to your political capital at every opportunity. He has let you use the vice presidency in an unprecedented way to prepare for your own run for the presidency in 2000.

But as a politician, Clinton knows that if scandal overtakes his administration it could ruin your chances in the primaries in 2000. As a friend and a political realist, he would certainly cut you some slack. So he would surely understand if you tried to carve out some space for yourself to ensure that your campaign is not taken out by flying debris before you even announce your candidacy. Do you accompany the president into untested waters, stand by his side, and reaffirm your faith in his leadership? Or do you have a scheduling conflict and stay in Washington?

Pharaohs, consuls, kings, queens, emperors, czars, prime ministers, and councils of various sizes served as executives in other governments before 1789. But no national government had a president, an elected executive with authority equal to and independent of a national legislature, until we elected George Washington.

The Founders viewed their creation as a chief executive officer, someone who would serve as both a check on bills passed by Congress and the administrator of those enacted into law. He would also be head of state, chief diplomat, and commander of the armed forces. At its inception the presidency was a not-very-powerful office of a fledgling country with few international ties and virtually no standing army. The office's first occupants were drawn from among the Founders; a few of them, Washington and Jefferson especially, served with some reluctance. Nevertheless, they were willing to lend their reputations and abilities to the cause of stabilizing the new government, and as a result, they had the opportunity to influence the direction of its development.

Throughout the nineteenth century, except for the Civil War period, real power at the national level resided in Congress, so much so that Woodrow Wilson characterized the federal arrangement in the 1880s as "congressional government." Thus, between Andrew Jackson and Franklin Roosevelt, many who sought the presidency were "ordinary people, with very ordinary reputations."[2] There were powerful exceptions, such as Abraham Lincoln, Theodore Roosevelt, and Woodrow Wilson, and a few, such as Civil War hero Ulysses S. Grant, who were able to convert military achievement into political victory.

Today the president of the United States is among the most powerful people in the world. By the 1970s the scope of that power led one historian to write about an "imperial" presidency.[3] Yet most recent presidents have suffered reelection defeats and at times have seemed almost powerless to shape events affecting the national interest and their own reputations. A conservative Congress frustrated John Kennedy's policy initiatives before his assassination. Lyndon Johnson's bid for reelection was killed by a war that took Richard Nixon six years to end. And Nixon had to resign from office because of his Watergate cover-up. Ronald Reagan, one of our most popular presidents, was so frustrated when Congress thwarted his foreign policy initiatives that he condoned illegal activities, producing the Iran-contra scandal and a tarnished personal reputation. Gerald Ford, Jimmy Carter, and George Bush failed to get reelected, the latter hurt by economic problems and doubts about his leadership on domestic issues. And now Bill Clinton is finding out that instead of an imperial presidency, we may have an "impossible" or "imperiled" presidency.[4] Little wonder that a survey found that 52% of Americans would rather spend one week in jail than serve one term as president and that many Americans, instead of believing the president is too powerful, believe he is too weak to battle Congress and interest groups.[5]

In this chapter we will consider the paradox of presidential power and presidential weakness. After describing the growth of the modern presidency, we look at the constitutional provisions—the qualifications for the office and its responsibilities. We explain why a bureaucracy grew up around the presidency at the same time the president was becoming a more personal and accessible representative of the American people. Inevitably, the growth of the modern presidency has affected the balance of power between the executive and legislative branches, and that is another topic of this chapter.

THE GROWTH OF THE PRESIDENCY

Someone once said that Americans were lucky because we always got presidential leadership when we needed it: during the birth of the nation, the Civil War, and foreign crises. This implies that our needs change, that we need more government and executive leadership during crises and less at other times. Presidential power was traditionally supposed to return to its "normal" low profile after we resolved special problems.

This expectation may have been realistic before the United States became a unified country that accepted Washington as the center of governmental power. But once the country stretched from Mexico to Canada and from the Atlantic to the Pacific, once it had a standing army and the ambition to control foreign intervention in the hemisphere, and once it developed international trade aspirations, governmental power gravitated to Washington. The image of Thomas Jefferson sitting at his desk in isolation week after week conducting the presidency by personal correspondence was a quaint memory even twenty years later when Andrew Jackson was dubbed the "people's president."[6] Jackson was the first to act assertively to fulfill the popular mandate he saw in his election—the first to veto a bill because *he* did not like it. Thirty years later Lincoln boldly interpreted the Constitution to say individual states could not legally leave the Union, thereby setting the stage for the Civil War.

Teddy Roosevelt, who has been called the "preacher militant," used the presidency in an unprecedented way to challenge corporate power and to argue for labor reform and better living conditions for average Americans. He also saw an imperial role for the United States in world politics, especially through military expansion, and led the country toward those "entangling alliances" that Thomas Jefferson had warned against. Eight years after Roosevelt left office, Wilson became the first twentieth-century president to lead us into a major foreign involvement, World War I.

The Granger Collection, New York

Although political scientists rank Jefferson as a great president, he did not consider the office, or his performance in it, very important. His instructions for an epitaph listed what he thought were his three main accomplishments in life: authoring the Declaration of Independence and a Virginia law guaranteeing religious freedom and founding the University of Virginia. He did not include his two terms as president.

As we have already seen in Chapter 3, the Great Depression led to a large expansion in the role of the national government and tremendous growth in presidential power. Franklin Roosevelt was elected president in 1932 because people thought he would help them. His policies, which he called the New Deal, put the national government and the presidency in direct contact with many citizens for the first time. People saw presidential leadership as a way to deal with national needs. It was Roosevelt, not Congress, who provided the vision and legislative program to cope with the economic emergencies of the Great Depression. In his first inaugural address, he told Americans that he would ask Congress for "broad executive power" to fight the crisis, equivalent, he said, to what he might be granted if an enemy had invaded the country. The enactment of the New Deal programs led to an expansion of the executive branch because new agencies had to be created and new civil servants hired. This increased the president's power by making him more important as a manager and policymaker.

Radio and television also contributed to the expansion of presidential power. As an integral part of national life by the 1930s, broadcasting made the news seem more immediate and compelling. Along with the wire services, it gave people a way to follow presidents and a way for presidents to "sell" their policies and provide leadership. Because it is easier to follow one person than many (as in Congress), the media helped make the presidency the focal point of national politics. With his radio broadcasts during the Great Depression, Roosevelt became a kind of national cheerleader, a one-man band of optimism, persuading the public that solutions were at hand.

Congress is not structured to provide this kind of national leadership. Its 535 members are divided into two houses and hundreds of committees and subcommittees and come from both political parties. It is difficult for either the majority or minority leadership to develop, articulate, or keep its members faithful to national policy goals.

Even after the fifteen years of crisis receded, Roosevelt's successors had little opportunity to shrink the presidency. With the United States emerging from World War II as the preeminent world power, and with the onset of the Cold War, Congress was willing to cede even more leadership to the president to counter Soviet rivalry. Responsibilities as chief diplomat and commander in chief of the world's largest military establishment have made the president a principal actor in world politics, a platform not afforded to any other government official or institution.

Of his postwar administration Harry Truman said, "Being president is like riding a tiger. You have to stay on or get swallowed." And thus we have today's presidency, with everyone looking to see if the man is riding the tiger or the tiger is riding the man.

TERMS OF OFFICE

Qualifications

There are formal, constitutional qualifications to be president: one must be a "natural born citizen," at least 35 years old, and a resident of the United States for at least 14 years before taking office.

Informally, it also helps to be a white male with roots in small-town America, a Protestant of English, German, or Scandinavian background, a resident of a state with a large population, and a good family man. In recent years, however, this profile has broadened considerably as society has become more tolerant of diversity. Nevertheless, some gender and racial barriers remain, although they are eroding.

Rewards

In return for services rendered, the Constitution authorized Congress to award the president "a Compensation," which could be neither increased nor decreased during a president's term of office. The annual salary now stands at $200,000 plus a $50,000 expense allowance. This is quite small when compared to the compensation of a CEO of a major corporation, but no one runs for the presidency because of the money, and there are *substantial* fringe benefits. These include living quarters in one of the world's most famous mansions, a rural retreat in Maryland (Camp David), the best health care money can buy, and fleets of cars and aircraft. After leaving office, the president is entitled to a generous pension, as well as a security detail and money for an office and staff.

Tenure

Presidents serve four-year terms. The Twenty-second Amendment limits them to serving two terms, or 10 years if they complete the term of an incumbent who dies or resigns. Four presidents have died in office from illness (Harrison, Taylor, Harding, and Franklin Roosevelt), and four were assassinated (Garfield, McKinley, Lincoln, and Kennedy).

Presidents can be removed from office for "Treason, Bribery, or other high Crimes and Misdemeanors" (Article 2). The Founders established the impeachment option as part of the system of checks and balances, a final weapon against executive abuse of power. Impeachment is fundamentally a legal, not a political, instrument. The procedure is cumbersome and meant to be; the Founders did not intend for the president, as head of state and the only nationally elected official in government, to be removed from office easily. Like the other major powers, the impeachment process is divided. The House has the power of **impeachment,** that is, the authority to bring formal charges against the president (similar to an indictment in criminal proceedings), but the Senate has the power of removal. The House holds hearings to determine whether there is sufficient evidence to impeach, and if a majority votes yes, the process moves to the Senate, where a trial is held. Conviction requires a two-thirds vote of members present in the Senate and results in removal from the presidency and loss of the right to hold other federal office. The Senate can assign no additional punishment. Where applicable, however, a president removed from office can be subject to criminal charges and prosecuted through the court system.

Only three presidents have been targets of full impeachment proceedings. Andrew Johnson, who came to office on Lincoln's assassination, was a southerner who was unpopular in his own party; he was impeached by the House in a dispute over enforcement of Reconstruction policies in the post–Civil War South. He failed to be convicted in the Senate by a single vote. A century later the House Judiciary Committee voted to impeach Richard Nixon on obstruction of justice and other charges stemming from the Watergate scandal, but by resigning, Nixon prevented a vote by the full House and almost certain conviction in the Senate. Once out of office he avoided possible indictment on criminal charges through a full pardon granted by his successor, Gerald Ford. In 1998 Bill Clinton became the third target of the process when the House voted to open an unrestricted inquiry into possible grounds for his impeachment. The process was set in motion by allegations that Clinton obstructed justice when he lied under oath while giving testimony in a civil suit about a sexual relationship with a White House intern.

Succession

The original wording of the Constitution provided only that presidential powers "shall devolve on the Vice President" should the president die, resign, be removed, or become incapacitated. At the time the Constitution was written, it was assumed that the vice presidency would be occupied by the man who had been the runner-up in the presidential election. It was left to Congress to make provisions for a situation in which both the presidency and the vice presidency had been vacated. Not until 1947, two years after the death of Franklin Roosevelt had put the virtually unknown Harry Truman in the White House, did Congress pass the Presidential Succession Act. It establishes the order of succession of federal officeholders should both the president and the vice president be unable to serve. The list begins with the Speaker of the House, followed by the president pro tempore of the Senate, and then proceeds through the secretaries of the cabinet departments in the order in which they were created.

The Succession Act has never been used because we have always had a vice president when something happened to the president. The Twenty-fifth Amendment was ratified in 1967 to ensure, as much as possible, that this will always be the case. In the event that the vice presidency falls vacant, the amendment directs the president to name a new vice president acceptable to majorities in the House and Senate. The amendment has been used twice. Nixon chose Gerald Ford to replace Spiro Agnew, who resigned after pleading no contest to charges of taking bribes when he was a public official in Maryland. After Nixon resigned and Ford became president, he then named Nelson Rockefeller, the former governor of New York, as vice president.

The Twenty-fifth Amendment also charges the vice president and a majority of the cabinet—or some other body named by Congress—to determine, in instances where there is doubt, whether the president is mentally or physically incapable of carrying out his duties. This provision was meant to provide for situations in which it is unclear who is or should be acting as president such as when James Garfield was shot in July 1881. He did not die until mid-September, and during this period he was completely unable to fulfill his duties. In 1919, Woodrow Wilson had a nervous collapse in the summer and a stroke in the fall and was partially incapacitated for months. No one was sure about his condition, however, because his wife restricted access to him.

Under the amendment's provisions, the vice president becomes "acting president" if the president is found mentally or physically unfit to fulfill his duties. As the title suggests, the conferral of power is temporary; the president can resume office by giving Congress written notice of his recovery. Reagan followed the spirit of this section in 1985. Before undergoing cancer surgery, he sent his vice president, George Bush, a letter authorizing him to act as president while Reagan was unconscious.

If the vice president and other officials who determined the president unfit do not concur in his judgment that he has recovered, they can challenge his return to office by notifying Congress in writing. Then it falls to Congress to decide whether the president is capable of resuming his duties.

DUTIES AND POWERS OF OFFICE

The original source of presidential power lies in the formal duties assigned by the Constitution. Additional authority stems from powers the federal courts have ruled are implied by the president's constitutional mandate, delegated authority from Congress, and informal powers acquired through the exercise of office.

Chief Executive

The enumeration of the president's formal duties begins with the simple statement that "Executive power shall be invested in a President. . . ." The Founders expected Congress to make policy and the president to administer it. The Constitution has few provisions that describe the president's administrative duties, but it does invest the president with the authority to demand written reports from his "principal officers." The Constitution also directs the president to nominate the most important officers of the executive branch.

The president was given power neither to create executive branch departments and agencies nor to fund them—this authority resides with Congress—so his means for controlling the bureaucracy over which he presides lies in his formal powers of appointment, his implied power to remove those he appoints, and his delegated authority to reorganize agencies and make budget recommendations.

APPOINTING OFFICIALS

The president nominates about 1,300 people to policy-making jobs in executive agencies and to positions as U.S. attorneys and marshals, ambassadors, and members of part-time boards and commissions. All appointments to these positions require Senate confirmation. Another 1,140 presidential appointments to senior civil service jobs do not need Senate approval.

In practice, the president's freedom to name people to some positions is limited by the custom of **senatorial courtesy.** This gives senators from the president's party a virtual veto over appointments to positions, including judicial appointments, in their states. As the leader of his party, the president has a political (not governmental) obligation to help senators from his party get reelected. So he usually defers to their political needs and wishes when making federal appointments in their home states, even though doing so limits to some extent his freedom to choose.

Presidents have more latitude in nominating people to positions with national jurisdictions, such as cabinet posts and seats on regulatory boards and independent agencies. It has become customary to give preference in some appointments to people with politically useful backgrounds, such as naming a westerner secretary of the interior, a person with union ties to be labor secretary, or a close associate of the president to be attorney general. But these considerations were never confining and, as traditions, seem to be weakening.

It has also been customary for the Senate, no matter which party controls it, to approve the president's nominations to policymaking positions on the grounds that, having won the election, he is entitled to surround himself with people who can help put his policies in place. In the contentiousness of recent years, this practice also seems to be weakening. A Democrat-controlled Congress challenged several high-profile appointments made by Reagan and Bush, and under Republican control Congress has tabled or defeated many of Clinton's nominations.

REMOVING OFFICIALS

Although the power to remove appointees is not in the Constitution, presidents have it. Their power to name people they trust implies a power to remove those they find wanting. In 1935, the Supreme Court tried to define this power by saying that presidents can remove appointees from purely administrative jobs but not from those with quasi-legislative and judicial responsibilities. Although this ruling protects many appointees, distinguishing quasi-legislative and judicial positions from those with no policymaking authority can be subjective.[7]

Of course, presidents can appoint and remove their political aides and advisers at will; none of these appointments require Senate approval. Presidents also have wide latitude in replacing cabinet heads and some agency directors—even though these positions do require Senate confirmation—because they are seen as agents of presidential policy. But presidents cannot remove the people they appoint to policymaking bodies on fixed term appointments, as is the case with regulatory boards, the Federal Reserve Board, and the federal courts. To grant the president this power would interfere with the system of checks and balances among the executive, legislative, and judicial functions of government.

REORGANIZING EXECUTIVE BRANCH AGENCIES

When the president enters office, a huge bureaucracy is already in place. Each new president has to be able to reorganize offices and agencies to fit his administrative and working style and to be consistent with the issue priorities he has set.[8]

Since the 1930s, presidents have had the authority to submit plans to Congress to reorganize parts of the executive branch. This means redrawing agency boundaries to promote coordination when actions overlap or duplicate each other. It may involve merging or abolishing offices or creating new ones. If Congress approves the plan, the president issues a directive that puts the new organization, councils, or offices in place. (Within the White House Office itself, the president has a fairly free hand to reshuffle staff and offices; see the discussion of the White House Office below.) Nixon, for example, merged a number of offices to create the Domestic Policy Council to improve White House coordination of domestic programs. Clinton created the National Economic Council to coordinate departments and agencies that shape economic policy and to show that economic issues are a high priority for him.

BUDGET MAKING

The Founders gave Congress, and particularly the House of Representatives, the power of the purse. For many years the president had a negligible role in managing executive branch budgets. Agency funding requests went to the House unreviewed and unchanged by the White House. But by the end of World War I, a general awareness had developed that a larger government required better management. In the Budget and Accounting Act of 1921, Congress delegated important priority-setting and managerial responsibilities that have contributed to the president's dominance in budgetary politics.

The 1921 act requires the president to give Congress estimates of how much money will be needed to run the government during the next fiscal year. The president's annual budget message contains recommendations for how much money Congress should appropriate for every program funded by the national government. Formulating the message requires the White House to examine all agency budget requests and to decide which to support or reject. This exercise allows the president and his staff to initiate the annual budget debate on their own terms.

In addition, the act created the Bureau of the Budget, or BOB. Originally a part of the Treasury Department, BOB was meant to be the president's primary tool in developing budget policy. It was made a part of the newly created Executive Office of the President in 1939. Nixon changed BOB's name to the Office of Management and Budget (OMB) to stress its function of helping the president manage the executive branch.

The process of writing and passing the annual budget resolutions is one of the greatest sources of friction in presidential-congressional relations. Without funding, little is possible. Having the OMB within the Executive Office of the President gives the president an edge in dealing with Congress on budget issues because its hundreds of experts work only for the president. Congress's nonpartisan budget office (the Congressional Budget Office, or CBO) prepares budget reports that are regarded as substantially more reliable than those of the OMB, but the policy initiative lies with the OMB and the White House because they prepare the first budget draft. The annual budget is huge, hard to read and understand. Because the president presents it to Congress and the public, he has the opportunity to shape the debate over spending priorities. Presidents who are little interested in the details of domestic policy, such as Reagan and Bush, do not get maximum political leverage out of the budgetary powers Congress has delegated them. But a president whose strength lies in the mastery of detail may be able to use those powers as Clinton has to dominate budgetary politics and the debate over deficit reduction.

The OMB not only proposes allocations for each department, agency, and program of the federal government, but it also monitors how and when executive branch agencies spend appropriated funds, their operating procedures, and the policies they develop. This gives the president another advantage over Congress, one that Reagan used to great advantage. By appointing agency and department heads who oppose policies he opposes, but which Congress has funded, the president can issue directives that effectively bring policy implementation to a halt.

OTHER EXECUTIVE POWERS

In addition to the formal administrative powers granted under Article II and those delegated by Congress, federal courts have upheld additional powers that presidents have claimed are necessary to the administration of the executive branch.

EXECUTIVE PRIVILEGE Since the 1970s the courts have upheld the presidential claim to **executive privilege,** the right of a president to refuse to make public some internal documents and private conversations.

The rulings have argued that executive privilege is a power inherent in the president's duty as chief executive because without it a president would not be able to get full and frank advice from his aides. Although ruling that the power is limited rather than absolute in scope, the courts have not defined its limits. In the landmark ruling ordering President Nixon to turn over tapes of Oval Office conversations to the Watergate special prosecutor (see Chapter 2 You Are There), the Supreme Court did establish that executive privilege cannot be invoked to withhold evidence material to an investigation of criminal wrongdoing.

In the 1970s the federal courts requested that Congress specify the limits of the privilege but it declined, leaving it to the courts to resolve each invocation of privilege that the president and Congress cannot resolve. President Clinton interpreted this power very broadly. He claimed that senior aides could not be required to answer certain questions put to them by a grand jury convened by the special prosecutor investigating possible obstruction of justice charges against the president. His reason was that their answers would make public the content of privileged conversations with the president. Clinton asked the federal courts to extend the cover of executive privilege to his conversations about political strategy with his aides and to those between his aides and the First Lady, whom he regards as a political adviser and whom the courts had already recognized as serving a quasi-official role. In 1998 the lower federal courts again confirmed the right to executive privilege and its application to conversations between the president, aides, and the First Lady. But it ruled against the president on the circumstances under which he invoked the privilege (withholding information from a grand jury hearing evidence about possible criminal wrongdoing), saying the aides' testimony might be relevant to the investigation. The administration did not appeal the ruling.

EXECUTIVE ORDERS Because the Constitution charges the president with ensuring that "the laws be faithfully executed," the courts have ruled that the president has inherent power to take actions and issue orders to fulfill that duty. This gives the president the authority to issue directives or proclamations, called **executive orders,** that have the force of law and are therefore a form of legislative power residing in the executive branch. In arguing for these powers, presidents have claimed that "Article II of the Constitution grants them inherent power to take whatever actions they judge to be in the nation's best interests as long as those actions are not prohibited by the Constitution or by law." The rationale is that Congress often lacks the expertise and ability to act quickly when technological or other developments require fast action and flexibility.[9]

The recording and numbering of executive orders did not begin until 1907, and although an effort was made to identify and retroactively number orders issued back to the Lincoln administration, it is uncertain how many have been issued over the years. Since 1946 Congress has required all executive orders, except those dealing with classified national security issues, to be published in the *Federal Register*.[10] Many of these orders have had a significant impact. Truman, for example, used an executive order to integrate the armed forces, Kennedy to end racial discrimination in public housing, and Lyndon Johnson to require affirmative action hiring by firms with federal contracts.

Executive orders are used to implement the provisions of treaties and legislative statutes that are ambiguously stated (perhaps deliberately) by Congress. In fact, presidents have used executive orders to make policies opposed by congressional majorities. Reagan and Bush used this power to ban abortion counseling in federally financed clinics and financial aid to United Nations–sponsored family planning programs. Clinton canceled these orders in his first week in office. Thus, through the exercise of this inherent power of office the presidency has acquired significant legislative authority.

Executive orders are also commonly used by presidents to carry out more purely administrative duties in the form of directives issued to executive branch offices. These often deal with organizational problems and internal procedures, such as restructuring executive branch departments and agencies (discussed above). The controversial system used to classify government documents and withhold information from the public was established by executive order.

Head of State

As chief executive, the president is the presiding officer or head of government. But in our form of republic, the head of government is also the head of state; this arrangement is not common among Western democracies. A **head of state** is the official representative of a country, the person whose office symbolizes the collective unity and identity of the nation. When our president stands in public behind the Great Seal of the United States of America, he is not just a politician who was elected to govern but a nonpartisan representative of all the people, entrusted with the symbols, emblems, and traditions of the country. The unifying, nonpolitical nature of the role that the head of state is meant to serve is the reason why some countries separate this office (sometimes filled by a king or queen) from that of head of government. The latter is usually filled by the leader of a political party, who is by definition partisan. But the American president has to wear two hats, and members of Congress, the press, or the public who may attack him freely in his partisan role as head of government usually show more deference when the president is acting in his capacity as head of state.

As symbolic leaders, presidents often congratulate national sports heroes. Here, President Calvin Coolidge (a Republican, who served from 1923 to 1928 and was aptly known as "Silent Cal") presents a trophy to a Marine football team after its victory over Army.

New York Times

These duties include serving as official representative of the United States at a variety of state and ceremonial occasions both at home and abroad. It could be opening the Olympic Games, lighting the White House Christmas tree, attending the swearing in, coronation, or funeral of a foreign head of state, or serving as official greeter when a foreign head of state visits this country. The head of state is also empowered to take actions that symbolize national sentiment, such as issuing proclamations to commemorate events, or making gestures that express a humane national spirit, as in the granting of reprieves and pardons to people convicted of federal crimes.

As head of state, the president is required by the Constitution to address Congress and the country about the "State of the Union" at the start of each congressional session. He notes the successes of the past year, addresses problems, and outlines his policy agenda for the coming year. Part of the speech inevitably deals with the mood of the country and identifies goals for maintaining or increasing national unity.

In these televised addresses, delivered in the House of Representatives before a joint session of Congress, the president is received as head of state, rather than as partisan head of government. Even when presidents are mired in political controversy at the time of the speech—Nixon during the Watergate investigation, or Clinton, delivering the State of the Union address just weeks after the revelation of allegations of personal wrongdoing—congressional leaders usually caution the membership to show due respect to a person who is speaking in his constitutional role as head of state.

Chief Diplomat

As head of state, the president is given ceremonial powers "to receive Ambassadors and other public Ministers." In practice this means that when a country appoints a person to represent its interests to the United States, that ambassador must present his or her credentials to the president and have them accepted before taking up office. What appears to be a ceremonial duty has real potential for the making of foreign policy because the power to accept or reject foreign ambassadors, by extension, gives the president the power to decide which governments we will recognize and which we will shut out. Recognition is not automatic. We did not recognize the Soviet government until 16 years after the Bolshevik Revolution of 1917 or that of the communist government of mainland China until almost 25 years after it took power.

Article II also gives the president the power to make treaties with other countries, subject to Senate approval, and to appoint ambassadors and consuls to represent us abroad. In addition, the article contains implied powers, which were acknowledged by the Supreme Court in a 1936 decision.[11] Congress had authorized Franklin Roosevelt to ban arms sales to warring Bolivia and Paraguay, but a military aircraft manufacturer claimed that Congress lacked the constitutional authority to delegate such power. The Court ruled against the corporation, saying that the United States, like every nation, has implied powers to promote its interests in the world. The Court said there is a logic behind presidential power in foreign policy. A nation's government must be able to speak with one voice because having more than one voice can lead to confusion about what is official policy and therefore about what actions might be taken.

Commander in Chief

Using the military to achieve national goals is one way presidents conduct foreign policy. The Founders made the president "commander-in-chief." By this they meant that the president would be the "first general" and "first admiral," as Alexander Hamilton wrote in *Federalist* #69.

But the Founders did not want to give the president the sole power to make war. In the words of Connecticut's Roger Sherman, they believed "the Executive should be able to repel and not to commence war." The Founders feared that presidents, like the British kings from whom they had recently freed themselves, would be too eager to go to war.[12] So they gave Congress the power to declare war. James Madison expressed the view of several of the Founders when he argued that "the executive is the branch of power most interested in war and most prone to it. [The Constitution] has, accordingly, with studied care, vested the question of war in the legislature."[13] Thus, the Founders created a system of checks and balances in military affairs; the president commands the troops, but Congress has the power to declare war and to decide whether to authorize funds to pay for it. Thomas Jefferson thought this arrangement would be an "effectual check to the dog of war, by transferring the power of letting him loose from the executive to the legislative body, from those who are to spend to those who are to pay."[14]

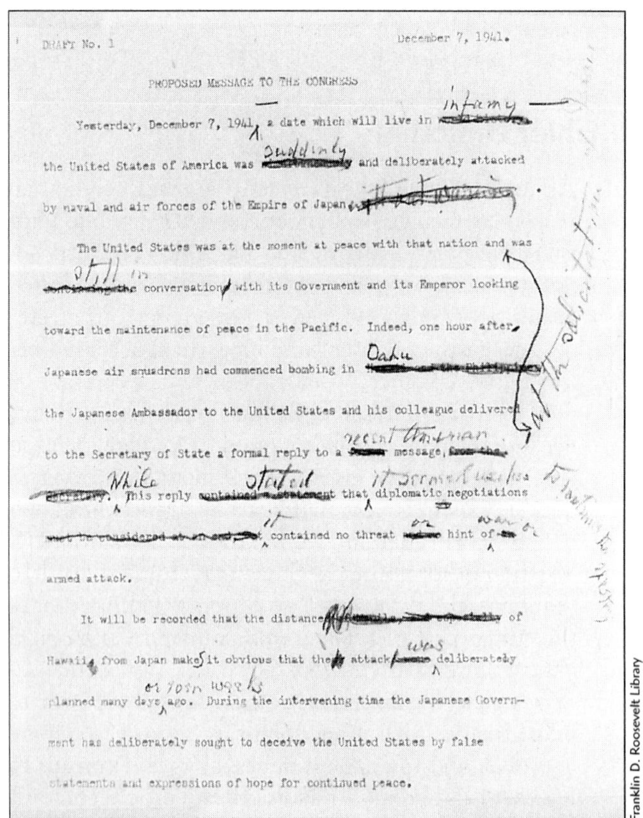

DRAFT No. 1 December 7, 1941.

PROPOSED MESSAGE TO THE CONGRESS

Yesterday, December 7, 1941, a date which will live in the United States of America was and deliberately attacked by naval and air forces of the Empire of Japan.

The United States was at the moment at peace with that nation and was conversation with its Government and its Emperor looking toward the maintenance of peace in the Pacific. Indeed, one hour after Japanese air squadrons had commenced bombing in the Japanese Ambassador to the United States and his colleague delivered to the Secretary of State a formal reply to a message. This reply that diplomatic negotiations contained no threat hint of armed attack.

It will be recorded that the distance of Hawaii from Japan make it obvious that the attack deliberately planned many days ago. During the intervening time the Japanese Government has deliberately sought to deceive the United States by false statements and expressions of hope for continued peace.

Franklin D. Roosevelt Library

As the nation's foreign policy leader, President Franklin Roosevelt edited his own speech to Congress about the Japanese attack on Pearl Harbor. He added the word that made memorable his phrase, "a date which will live in infamy."

Although every president is commander in chief, no sitting president has ever led troops into battle. However, modern weapons have led to more presidential involvement. The decision to use certain weapons has become important politically as well as militarily. The decision to wage a "limited" war in Vietnam, that is, not to use nuclear weapons, was political and based on presidential beliefs that defeating North Vietnam was not worth risking a nuclear holocaust.

Other technological developments have also given presidents more military leadership opportunities. Johnson and Nixon used sophisticated communications equipment to select targets in Vietnam. In the Persian Gulf War, Bush used modern transportation facilities to send large numbers of troops to the Gulf quickly with the latest "smart" weapons. His White House sent so many orders to General Norman Schwarzkopf in the Gulf (from how to stop a blockade-running Iraqi tanker to ending the ground war before Iraq's army was destroyed) that the general complained of "a total vacuum of guidance" when disagreements in Washington stopped the flow of instructions.[15]

Despite congressional oversight of military policy, presidential power is wide ranging and increasingly controversial as troops frequently are used without a declaration of war or even congressional approval. But presidents have historically assumed and exercised the most power during wars endangering our national survival. During the Civil War, Lincoln suspended the use of writs of habeas corpus, seized control of some eastern railroads, and blockaded southern ports. He took these actions as commander in chief and without congressional authorization. The war jeopardized national unity, and Lincoln believed he had to take extraordinary measures. Because most people in the North agreed with him, he was able to do what he thought necessary.

Acting under his self-defined authority as commander in chief, Franklin Roosevelt put 100,000 Amer-

National Archives

President Lincoln, as commander in chief, consults his generals at the Antietam battlefield during the Civil War. Lincoln wanted a more active role in Civil War battles, but his generals worried about his safety and made sure he was gone when there was fighting. Limited by an inability to maintain close communications with field commanders, he could not direct ongoing battles.

icans of Japanese descent into camps during World War II. He had the government seize and operate more than 60 industries important to the war effort and vulnerable to union strikes. In addition, he created special agencies to control the consumption and price of important materials such as gasoline, meat, and shoes.

Wars not threatening our national survival tend not to generate high levels of support for executive actions. When Truman had his secretary of commerce seize most of the nation's steel mills during the Korean conflict to keep them operating in the face of a possible labor strike, one of the steel companies took him to court to stop him. In 1952, the Supreme Court sided with the company by ruling that Truman had not exhausted other, legal remedies to the problem.[16]

The extent of the war-making power exercised by Presidents Johnson and Nixon during the undeclared war in Vietnam inspired the 1970s characterization of the presidency as "imperial" and led Congress to take action to limit the power of the president to take unilateral military action (see The President and Congress later in the chapter).

PRESIDENTIAL STAFF AND ADVISERS

For the first 150 years of the presidency, staff size was small. George Washington paid a nephew out of his own pocket to be his only full-time aide. Congress did not appropriate funds for a presidential clerk until 1857. Lincoln's staff "exploded" to four people, but he often opened and answered the daily mail himself. Cleveland answered the White House telephone, and Wilson typed many of his own speeches.[17] Today, as presiding officer of the executive branch, the president heads a bureaucracy of fourteen cabinet departments and several million civil servants, whose work is described in Chapter 12. But to carry out the day-to-day duties of his office, the president has a large staff of policy specialists and liaisons to other branches and agencies of government, as well as to his national constituencies.

The Executive Office of the President

The bureaucracy that surrounds the modern president had its origins in the administration of Franklin Roosevelt. Because his small staff was overwhelmed by the workload of administering New Deal agencies and programs, FDR called in a team of public administration experts to help restructure his office. In 1937, they recommended the creation of the Executive Office of the President (EOP), but FDR had to wait until 1939 before issuing the executive order that established the EOP. Angry at FDR for his court-packing scheme, Congress withheld approval for two years.

The size of the EOP grew rapidly in the Nixon administration and continued to grow until 1993. Bush's EOP employed more than 1,700 people, over 400 times the size of Lincoln's staff. Clinton cut this number by 25% in his first year in office to show his commitment to downsizing government and deficit reduction.

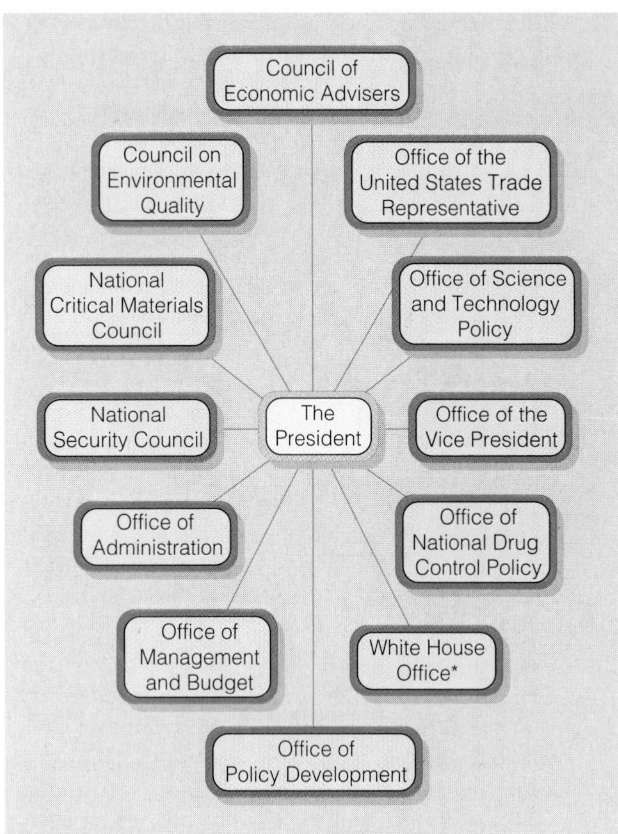

FIGURE 1

The Executive Office of the President in 1998

*Includes staff assistants to the First Lady.

SOURCE: Adapted from *United States Government Manual, 1997–1998* (Washington, D.C.: U.S. Government Printing Office, 1997).

The White House staff, a part of the EOP, has also grown, from 64 when Truman took office to more than 350 today. To put staff growth in perspective, Nancy Reagan's staff was larger than Roosevelt's at the height of the New Deal.[18]

Since FDR's administration, the EOP has been reorganized many times to reflect changing national problems and the issue priorities of individual presidents. The EOP is not a single office but a group of offices, councils, and boards devoted to specific functional or issue areas such as national security, trade, the budget, and drug abuse (see Figure 1). Their offices are divided among the White House and the two Executive Office Buildings, except for the Office of Management and Budget (OMB), which has its own building. Many EOP staffers are career civil servants, but the president appoints those who fill the top policymaking positions, and these are the most influential people in the EOP. Given the centrality of budget issues, the head of the OMB is an influential adviser in almost every administration. The influence of other EOP heads varies with the president's issue priorities, but those who count as the president's closest advisers are usually concentrated in the White House Office.

The EOP is essentially the president's bureaucracy, sitting atop the executive branch and monitoring the work done in cabinet departments and agencies to see that the president's policies are carried out. Although the president also appoints cabinet secretaries and directors of independent agencies, some of them head huge bureaucracies with vested interests that may be at odds with the president's agenda. Not surprisingly then, some scholars see the growth in influence of EOP officials as having come at the expense of cabinet secretaries.[19]

The White House Office

Presidents seek advice from different people depending on the issue, but they tend to consult some more than others. Andrew Jackson was the first to call the advisers he consulted frequently his "kitchen cabinet."

Jimmy Carter and Bill Clinton are notable among recent presidents for their degree of reliance on longtime associates. Unlike Kennedy, Nixon, Johnson, and Bush, neither had experience in Washington, and they filled their top staff positions with old friends and political operatives from Georgia and Arkansas. George Bush was a consummate Washington insider but relied heavily on his fellow Texan and longtime friend James Baker to serve on the White House staff, in the cabinet, and as his campaign manager. Of recent presidents, only Ronald Reagan, a man not known to have close personal friends in politics, did not fill his top staff positions with longtime friends and close associates.

Among their most trusted advisers, presidents often count friends who do not hold official positions but whom they have come to trust for candid, unguarded conversation. The lawyer and former civil rights activist Vernon Jordan, for example, has become well known as Clinton's "first friend." Richard Nixon had businessman Bebe Rebozo as a confidante, and Lyndon Johnson had lawyer and lobbyist Abe Fortas, whom he eventually appointed to the Supreme Court. Many presidents have counted their wives among their closest advisers (see "Who Elected Her?").

Members of the White House Office have greater influence than most advisers because the president appoints all of them, works daily with them, and tends to trust them more than others. They are often people who helped him get elected or worked for him when he held other offices.

Presidents have used different styles in running the White House Office. Roosevelt and Kennedy cared little for rigid lines of responsibility. They gave staffers different jobs over time and fostered a competitive spirit: Who could serve the president best?

Eisenhower and Nixon valued formal lines of authority. Eisenhower's military experience led him to rely on a chief of staff, Sherman Adams. Adams so dominated White House routine that one newspaper story was headlined, "Adams Insists Ike Is Really President."[20] Nixon's chief of staff, H. R. Haldeman, saw his job this way: "Every president needs a son of a bitch, and I'm Nixon's. I'm his buffer and his bastard. I get done what he wants done and I take the heat instead of him."[21]

The Watergate scandal led presidents Ford and Carter to avoid the appearance of strong staff chiefs, although both eventually saw a need for a chief of staff to manage their schedules and the huge flow of paper that passes through the White House. Reagan prided himself on delegating authority to the best people and letting them do their work without interference.[22] Serious problems developed, however, because no one had authority to make final decisions on more important matters and Reagan was too removed from daily affairs to do so. This detached management style had its costs, most noticeably the Iran-contra scandal.[23] Problems produced by his detached management style led Reagan to appoint a series of strong staff chiefs whose coordination of White House operations helped restore his image.

George Bush had more hands-on involvement in policy, but he spent more time on foreign policy and delegated domestic issues to his staff. Clinton's White House organization puts him in the center of decision making. He directed his first staff chief to channel all paperwork to him so his appointees would not repeat the frustration of a Bush cabinet member who had to mail his views to Bush because Bush's first staff chief, John Sununu, sat on them.

UPI/Corbis-Bettmann

President Kennedy's closest adviser was his brother Robert, whom he appointed Attorney-General.

Thus, Clinton's choice of many staffers with little Washington experience and diverse views, and his choice of his wife, Hillary Rodham Clinton, to develop and help sell his health reform proposal, showed his determination to be in command and to immerse himself in policy details. However, running the White House this way made it difficult for Clinton to keep his and the nation's focus on important issues. He got so bogged down in details that his wife complained that he had become the "mechanic-in-chief."[24] Four months into his term, he directed that low-priority issues be kept off his desk.

Under Clinton's second and third staff chiefs, lines of authority and communication were tightened and the flow of paper to Clinton more closely monitored. But Clinton's White House operation still reflects his love of policy details and an inability to stick to a few clear policy themes in communicating with the public and the media. A pundit wrote, "Each White House reflects the personality of its leader, and [Clinton], immune to punctuality and discipline, will always have a Pigpen cloud of chaos around him."[25]

OFFICE OF THE FIRST LADY

A small number of special presidential assistants on the White House Office staff are assigned to work full-time for the First Lady.[26] The First Lady's role is ill-defined: there is no mention of a presidential spouse in the Constitution, and she has no official position, no title, and no salary. Yet she is definitely expected to serve, especially as what Martha Washington called "the hostess of the nation."[27]

The visibility of the First Lady increased enormously after the arrival of photography in the mid-nineteenth century; mass circulation newspapers and magazines provided new means for satisfying public curiosity about the president's private life. There was heightened interest in seeing presidents' wives in public, and early in the twentieth century First Ladies began accompanying their husbands at official functions.

A quantum leap in the conception of the First Lady's role occurred during the administration of Franklin Roosevelt. Eleanor Roosevelt held press conferences (for women journalists shut out of the president's briefings), wrote a syndicated newspaper column read by millions, and made regular radio broadcasts. She discussed policy with her husband, bombarded him with memos, and brought supporters of the causes she advocated into the White House. She served on countless committees and traveled around the world promoting racial equality, women's and social welfare issues, and the war effort.

"WHO ELECTED HER?"

Does this sound familiar: a president's wife is accused of being a radical, more activist than her husband, and in danger of leading him in policy directions his opponents, and perhaps even his own party, do not support? Voters, pundits, and political columnists ask, "Who elected her?" The name of Hillary Rodham Clinton may come to mind, or Eleanor Roosevelt. Yet the controversy over the First Lady and how her proximity to the president and the special confidence she shares with him might affect policy decisions has been with us since the administration of John Adams.

The president's wife has always had to walk a fine line, presiding over state social functions and being supportive of her husband without looking as though she is politically out in front of him. Martha Washington and Louisa Adams (wife of John Quincy Adams) were just two First Ladies who felt they were in a prison, hemmed in by the limits of acceptable behavior.[1] Barbara Bush's chief of staff described the position as "filled with banana peels and land mines."[2]

The first and second presidential wives—they did not yet have a formal title—Martha Washington and Abigail Adams, were preoccupied with the problems of keeping their families afloat economically while their husbands led public lives. Abigail Adams managed the family farm in Massachusetts, and Martha Washington ran the plantation at Mount Vernon, as earlier she had managed the land inherited from her first husband. Although not always happy with it, neither rejected the role of manager of the domestic sphere and hostess for state social occasions. But whereas Martha Washington was basically unschooled and not much interested in public affairs, Abigail Adams was an accomplished writer with strong political opinions and not afraid to express them (for example, that women would "foment a Rebellion" if they were made subject to laws without representation). Her views on women's rights and other issues, coupled with the fact that her long and happy marriage to John Adams made her his principal adviser, led both supporters and opponents of the president to believe she might have "undue" influence on policy decisions. When Adams's opponents referred to his wife as "Mrs. President," they meant something other than her marital status.

Abigail's daughter-in-law, Louisa Adams, and Dolley Madison are other nineteenth-century First Ladies who played crucial roles in their husbands' political careers. Dolley Madison was so highly regarded among Washington's influential that in 1844 Congress reserved a seat for her whenever she chose to attend sessions.[3]

Influential First Ladies of the early twentieth century include Edith Wilson, who decoded classified diplomatic and military messages, encoded presidential responses, and served what she called a "stewardship" during a six-week period when her husband was completely disabled by a stroke. Much of the work organizing and financing Warren Harding's presidential campaign was done by Florence Harding, which explains her widely repeated query: "I got you the presidency; now what are you going to do with it?"

Although many First Ladies since have been political advisers to their husbands, no one did it quite so publicly,

Historical Pictures Chicago/Stock Montage

Many people believed that Edith Wilson, the president's wife, was making the decisions during President Wilson's illness.

or from such an independent platform, as Eleanor Roosevelt. Her tenure as First Lady was unique in that she had a policy agenda that sometimes was at odds with the president's; she had her own coterie of supporters and direct access to the public through her news conferences, broadcasts, and newspaper column. In later years she served as a delegate to the United Nations and was a member of John Kennedy's Committee on the Status of Women. Her efforts for human rights and international cooperation earned her the title "First Lady of the World." More than any other First Lady, she can be said to have developed a reputation independent from her husband's legacy as president. Although some thought her too powerful, Mrs. Roosevelt never differed with her husband publicly and always deferred to him in joint appearances. It was the job of a wife, she said, to offer no personal opinions, limit her appearances, and "lean back in an open car so voters [can] always see *him*."[4]

Mrs. Roosevelt's term may have been a type unto itself, but it has not been the general rule for this office to be filled by traditional wives who limited themselves to the domestic sphere and detached themselves completely from policy issues. In modern times, Bess Truman, Mamie Eisenhower, Pat Nixon, and Barbara Bush come closest to the image of traditional wife. But these were hardly women without influence on their husbands. Despite her lack of interest in electoral politics, Bess Truman was called "The Boss" by Harry, who said he frequently consulted her on the content of his speeches and in making important decisions. Mamie ("Ike runs the country; I turn the pork chops") Eisenhower cut as traditional a figure as possible in the 1950s, but that did not keep her husband from listening to her opinion when she gave it, or from wearing an "I Like Mamie" button when campaigning. Presidential husbands and wives who have led relatively separate lives, such as John and Jacqueline Kennedy—she having no interest in electoral politics—are not that common among first couples. In most long and close marriages, it is natural for husbands and wives to become confidantes and to rely on one another's judgment.

A number of strong-willed women followed Jacqueline Kennedy into the White House. Lady Bird (Claudia) Johnson helped finance her husband's congressional campaigns and in his presidential race had her own campaign train to tour the South while her husband worked on in Washington. She is said to have greeted him in the evenings with the query, "Well, what did you do for women today?" Betty Ford was an outspoken supporter of the Equal Rights Amendment and abortion rights in defiance of her party's position, and argued for a salary for her successors as First Lady. Her popularity often surpassed her husband's. Rosalynn Carter sat in on cabinet meetings, had weekly policy lunches with her husband, met with foreign heads of state to discuss policy, chaired the Commission on Mental Health Reform, and was at times derisively referred to as "co-president." Nancy Reagan's stepfather helped shape her husband's political philosophy, and she often controlled access to the Oval Office and weighed in on the hiring and firing of key advisers. The term *co-president* was revived for Hillary Clinton, a lawyer and lobbyist for child welfare causes, who has been one of her husband's closest advisers and strategists throughout his career in elective office, while also serving as the family's principal wage earner.

Although some political commentators and at least part of the public appear leery of activist First Ladies, it does not seem to bother many of their husbands. FDR often disagreed with Eleanor's policy positions, but he depended on her to fill a public role he was physically unable to sustain, and the political circle that developed around her never appeared to threaten him. Reagan depended heavily on Nancy's advice. Carter called Rosalynn a "full partner" and his co-strategist in the presidential campaign.[5] And Clinton clearly sees his wife's activist role as a natural continuation of the political partnership they have had throughout their marriage. "It doesn't bother me for people to get excited and say she could be president. I always say she could be president, too."[6] An exception perhaps was Gerald Ford who told his wife that her outspokenness cost him millions of votes in the 1976 election.[7]

Although Rosalynn Carter had more public hands-on involvement in policy, Hillary Clinton has prompted greater opposition to the activist conception of the office than anyone since Eleanor Roosevelt. During his first campaign, Clinton said that the American people would be getting "two for the price of one" and that he and Hillary would have an "unprecedented partnership," surpassing that of the Roosevelts.[8] He appointed the First Lady to head a task force on health care reform, but in response to public criticism, she retreated from this quasi-official role as policy adviser before the 1996 reelection campaign.

In some ways the concern over the influence and accountability of presidential spouses is moot. The First Lady is not subject to congressional approval, but neither are the members of the White House staff nor the president's close advisers outside government. But as Hillary Clinton has found, First Ladies are not immune from investigation of criminal wrongdoing, and when they serve by official appointment, as she did on the health care task force, they are subject to the same rules as other public officials.

How is issue advocacy of a presidential spouse different from that of any lobbyist? In cases where wives have played active roles in getting their husbands nominated and elected, how realistic is it that they will expect that their advice will no be longer needed after the election? And how realistic is it to expect that their advice will no longer be offered when the decisions being made carry much higher stakes? Yet some seem to worry that the special nature of a marital relationship provides opportunities to influence—the kind Betty Ford called "pillow talk"—unavailable to others. We frequently refer to lobbyists as "getting into bed" with politicians, but wives do not have to pay to get there, and if they are successful in changing their husband's views, it is not likely that money will have had anything to do with it. But neither Gerald Ford nor George Bush, whose wife also supported abortion rights, adopted his wife's views in defiance of official party policy. John Adams did not try to get women's suffrage into the Constitution, and FDR rejected many of his wife's policy recommendations.

Will the president's wife still be the "First Lady" in the next century? There probably will not be many more in the mold of Bess Truman or Mamie Eisenhower. Professional couples like the Clintons and Robert and Elizabeth Dole are more likely to occupy the White House. And inevitably there will be a First Gentleman. Will his influence be as feared as that of a presidential wife?

1. Edith P. Mayo, ed., *The Smithsonian Book of First Ladies* (Washington, D.C.: Smithsonian Institution, 1996), pp. 11, 43.
2. Henry Louis Gates, Jr., "Hating Hillary," *The New Yorker,* (February 26 and March 4, 1996), p. 121.
3. Mayo, *Smithsonian Book of First Ladies,* p. 31.
4. Carl Sferrazza Anthony, "The First Ladies: They've Come a Long Way, Martha," *Smithsonian Magazine,* October 1992, p. 150.
5. Gil Troy, *Affairs of State: The Rise and Rejection of the First Couple since World War II* (New York: Free Press, 1997), pp. 236–272.
6. Mayo, *Smithsonian Book of First Ladies,* p. 277.
7. Troy, *Affairs of State,* p. 222.
8. Troy, *Affairs of State,* p. 352.

OTHER SOURCES: Carol Chandler Waldrop, *Presidents' Wives: The Lives of 44 American Women of Strength* (Jefferson, N.C.: McFarland & Co., 1989); *The Presidency A to Z: A Ready Reference Encyclopedia* (Washington, D.C.: Congressional Quarterly, Inc., 1992), pp. 179–182; Lewis L. Gould, ed., *American First Ladies* (New York: Garland, 1996).

Mrs. Roosevelt's stature was attained under the exceptional circumstances of her husband's long tenure in the White House during a period of national crisis (the Great Depression and World War II). Furthermore, after his incapacitation from polio years earlier, FDR had become dependent on Eleanor to keep his political career afloat by serving as his stand-in and surrogate campaigner. In combination with their strained marriage, this meant that Mrs. Roosevelt entered the White House as much FDR's political partner as his wife.

But the evolution of the role of First Lady cannot be described as a simple incremental growth of duties and staff over time. What is made of the position is to a large extent dependent on the personality and orientation of the woman who fills it and on the dynamics of the relationship she has developed with her husband. It also depends on her style and how it fits with the times and how she is regarded by those with power and influence in Washington. Eleanor Roosevelt's successor, Bess Truman, saw herself more as Harry Truman's wife than as First Lady. Uninterested in Washington politics or social life, she was as aloof as Eleanor Roosevelt had been visible. She carried out as few functions as her title allowed and spent as much time as possible away from the capital.

With the era of television campaigns, the wives of presidential candidates began to figure much more prominently in campaign strategy. Even those not interested in electoral politics were used to great effect in getting votes, most famously, Mamie Eisenhower and Jacqueline Kennedy. Dwight Eisenhower considered his wife a better campaigner than he was, and Jacqueline Kennedy attained a level of popularity and celebrity that surpassed her husband's. First Ladies have been fixtures on the campaign trail ever since.

In many instances the greater visibility of First Ladies only made public the behind-the-scenes reality of their hands-on campaign involvement. From the earliest administrations, some First Ladies worked to engineer their husbands' nominations and helped run their campaigns. Not surprisingly, many continued to exert political influence after the election. The extent of this influence and the way it is exercised both in and outside the White House continue to be the most controversial and most ambiguous aspects of the First Lady's position.

It has become the custom for First Ladies to identify causes, usually nonpartisan, on which they will focus special effort. Jacqueline Kennedy devoted herself to historic preservation; Lady Bird Johnson to environmental issues; Betty Ford to the creative arts and welfare of the elderly; Nancy Reagan to drug prevention; Barbara Bush to literacy; and Hillary Rodham Clinton to child welfare.

In addition, all First Ladies have the domestic staff of the White House residential quarters to oversee, as well as an intense schedule of state social functions. These traditional duties, combined with charity and issue-oriented work and the heavy demand for public appearances, have made the First Lady into a formal, if not an institutionalized, role, complete with office, staff, and budget—but still no salary. For decades, funding her office presented legal problems since, officially, the First Lady is a private citizen and government funds could not be used to pay her staff. It was not until 1978 that Congress made formal budgetary provisions for the office.[28]

Nixon made a concerted attempt to modernize the office, located in the East Wing of the White House, and to integrate the activities of the First Lady's staff with those of the West Wing (site of the Oval Office). He wanted the office to focus less on social functions and more on supporting the president. The Carter administration made more substantial changes to accommodate Rosalynn Carter's expanded policy role. Whereas most First Ladies had done most of their work from the private quarters, Rosalynn Carter joined her seventeen aides in the East Wing of the White House. Hillary Rodham Clinton, wanting to integrate her work more closely with that of the Oval Office, moved into the West Wing. She has sixteen personal aides, including schedulers, publicity handlers, and a chief of staff, whose duties she has described as equivalent to those of the president's chief of staff.

Office of the Vice President

The Office of the Vice President was made part of the EOP in 1972. Not long afterward an official residence was established in the Admiral's House at the U.S. Naval Observatory. Vice presidents also have their own budgets and a staff housed in the old Executive Office Building adjacent to the White House. In the Carter and Clinton administrations, when the president and vice president have had close working relationships, Walter Mondale and Al Gore set up personal offices in the West Wing of the White House.

That vice presidents have succeeded to office unexpectedly nine times (eight presidential deaths and one resignation) may be responsible for the growing importance of the office.[29] Most recent vice presidents have been seasoned public servants with considerable experience and personal records of achievement. That they were willing to take the job suggests that it has become more than "standby equipment," as Nelson Rockefeller called it. Perhaps the furor over the qualifications (or lack of them) of Dan Quayle, Bush's vice president, reflects the fact that the public thinks the vice presidency deserves a highly qualified candidate.

The only formal duties the vice president has are to preside over the Senate, cast tie-breaking votes, and succeed to the presidency should it be vacated. Presidents have traditionally given their vice presidents little information and few opportunities to prepare for succession. Harry Truman did not even know about the atom bomb until after Franklin Roosevelt's death, but within months he had to decide whether to use it against Japan.

Woodrow Wilson's vice president, Thomas R. Marshall, said that holding the job was like being "a man in a cataleptic fit. He cannot speak, he cannot move. He suffers no pain. He is perfectly conscious of all that goes on. But he has no part in it." Franklin Roosevelt's first vice president, John Nance Garner, was less elegant in observing that his job was not worth a "pitcher of warm spit." Roosevelt had told Garner, "You tend to your office and I'll tend to mine."[30] The problem was that Garner had little to tend.

Historically, presidents have had difficulty delegating important jobs to their vice presidents. One reason is that vice presidential candidates have often been chosen to balance a ticket geographically and ideologically, not because of closeness to the presidential candidate. (In the first elections, before the Twelfth Amendment, when the vice presidency was filled by the runner-up in votes to the president, the vice president was actually an electoral opponent of the president.) And once in office, some vice presidents have used the position to build an independent political base from which to run for the presidency. This has not always made them the most loyal supporters of the president's agenda.

Until the Carter administration, vice presidents were asked to deal mainly with partisan or ceremonial matters. Jimmy Carter, who said that "the country loses when a competent Vice President is deprived of any opportunity to serve in a forceful way,"[31] was the first president to use his vice president for important work. Carter had no national experience before his election and considered Mondale, a former U.S. senator, a major asset. Carter gave Mondale a White House office, scheduled weekly lunches with him, included him in all White House advisory groups and all important meetings, and asked him to lobby Congress and read the paperwork that crossed Carter's desk. Ronald Reagan and George Bush did much the same with their vice presidents, and Bill Clinton has added to this new tradition.

The relationship between Bill Clinton and Al Gore is surely one of the closest in the history of the presidency (see You Are There at the beginning of the chapter). Gore has become so influential in the Clinton White House that he has been referred to as a "shadow president" and his staff as a "shadow cabinet." There is no legal basis for institutionalizing such an expansion of the office because, beyond the few duties specified in the Constitution, whatever duties vice presidents assume, and whatever advising or policymaking authority they acquire, are at the president's discretion. Therefore much depends on the personal relationship of the two people filling the positions and how needy the president is for assistance or how generous he is about sharing power.

THE PRESIDENT AND THE PEOPLE

Our earliest presidents had little contact with the general public and even communicated with Congress in writing. George Washington averaged only three speeches a year to the public while John Adams averaged one and Thomas Jefferson three.[32]

Abraham Lincoln thought it prudent to avoid giving speeches. He told people gathered at Gettysburg the night before his famous address, "I have no speech to make. In my position it is somewhat important that I should not say foolish things. It very often happens that the only way to help it is to say nothing at all."[33] It has been many years since we have had such a diffident public speaker in the White House.

Until the advent of radio and television, presidents had to speak to the nation indirectly through newspapers. The development of new transportation and communication technologies has given presidents more opportunities to utilize the presidency as a "bully pulpit," as Teddy Roosevelt called it.

Franklin Roosevelt's fireside chats were the first presidential effort to use the media to speak directly and regularly to the nation. They helped make him, and his office, the most important link between people and government. In a personalized style he began, "My friends . . ." People felt Roosevelt was talking to each of them in their own homes, and they gathered around their radios whenever he was on. Whereas President Herbert Hoover had received an average of 40 letters a day, Roosevelt received 4,000 letters a day after beginning his chats.[34] He even received some addressed not to "The President" but simply to "My Friend, Washington, D.C."

The Personal Presidency

Political scientist Theodore Lowi believes that we have had a **personal presidency** since the New Deal era.[35] He argues that, consciously or unconsciously, the American people have had a "new social contract" with the president since the 1930s. In return for getting more power and support from us than we give to other parts of government, the president is supposed to make sure we get what we want from government.

The personal presidency ties government directly to the people and gives us someone to rally around during times of crisis. To the extent that it serves as a focal point for national unity, the personal presidency also contributes to our ability to achieve national goals.

Polls have consistently shown that Americans consider "leadership" very important in evaluating presidents.[36] Somewhat paradoxically in light of their fear of "big government," most people want a president who can get government to "do" things.

Franklin Roosevelt was the first president to use survey data to identify public needs and to use the media to tell people that he would give them what they wanted. Making himself the major link between public opinion and government often enabled him to overcome the inertia and divisions associated with a system of fragmented powers.

However, Roosevelt's actions also revealed a cost of the personal presidency: Presidents with great power often seek more. Roosevelt won reelection in 1936 by a landslide, confirming popular support for his New Deal. This led him to seek more power by trying to expand the size of an unfriendly Supreme Court so he could appoint judges who supported him. He also tried to get local and state parties to nominate congressional candidates he favored by using federal funds as a carrot. The defeat of pro-Roosevelt congressional candidates in 1938 ruined both his plans. People did not want to politicize the Court, and state and local parties wanted to pick their own nominees.

Nixon and Reagan also tried to override constitutional limitations on their power after their landslide reelections in 1972 and 1984, as evidenced in the Watergate and Iran-contra scandals. The use of popular mandates to amass power in the Oval Office illustrates the relationship between the growth of the modern presidency and the rise of the personal presidency.

Practitioners of the personal presidency have sought more power because they promised more than they could deliver. To win approval for their programs, they needed more power to compete successfully with other parts of government and maintain their public support. Thus, they were caught in a cycle of making great promises, seeking more power to honor them, and making even greater promises to get more power. Inevitably, they promised more than they could deliver. Bush promised to send astronauts to Mars, protect the environment, be the "education president," and do many other things while cutting the budget deficit without raising taxes. Today promising *less* from government has become the tactic of the personal presidency. So while Clinton also began by making promises and saying he wanted "to do it all as quick as we can," he started his second term by announcing that "the day of big government is over."[37]

Lowi might have been right in calling the personal presidency the "victim" of democracy, but irresponsible leadership is not a requisite of democracy in the age of mass media nor an inevitable consequence. The separation of powers and the vote should check the short-term excesses of presidents. However, every president since the 1960s has needed and sought media exposure and in turn has had to submit to intense scrutiny by media that delve into every detail of his personal life, as well as his performance of official duties.

When President Franklin D. Roosevelt died, most Americans felt a personal loss, as these people showed, watching his body being loaded on the train.

Few people could withstand such prolonged exposure without losing public esteem. Since Roosevelt's death in 1945, only three of eight presidents have left office without experiencing permanently lowered public opinion ratings: Eisenhower, Kennedy (who was assassinated in mid-term), and Reagan.[38]

The question is whether the office of the president will suffer because its occupants' every human flaw, not just their policy mistakes, is reviewed daily in the press.

Persuading the Public

The relationship of the president to the people starts well before inauguration day. Changes in electoral laws have established a relationship with the public quite different from the one that the Founders saw for their head of state. The president is no longer just an elder statesman chosen by the Electoral College or a politician selected by party professionals to run for the presidency; he is a politician with a national constituency who convinced the rank-and-file voters in his party to choose him in the primaries and at least a plurality of the general population to vote for him in the general election. The modern president comes into office with extensive experience in persuading the public.

As presidential scholar Richard Neustadt pointed out long ago, presidents need more than their formal powers to achieve their goals. They need the **power to persuade.**[39] In addition to the public, presidents must be able to win over interest group leaders; newspaper and magazine publishers, reporters, and columnists; judges who hear challenges to their policies; and a majority in Congress. These policymakers and opinion elite, who Neustadt called Washingtonians, are, in short, the people the president needs to get his policies enacted. Because the Washingtonians also need him to get what they want, a president can bargain and persuade.

The effective president is "one who seizes the center of the Washington bazaar and actively barters . . . to build winning coalitions."[40] Presidents "remember" their friends by putting their pet projects in the budget, by campaigning for them, and by naming the people they want to public office.

In pursuit of his policy agenda, a president can use his powers to persuade the public as a means to bring pressure on reluctant Washingtonians, or when the public is disinterested or slow to accept, he can try to persuade Washingtonians to shape public opinion. In doing so he has much more to rely on than his rhetorical skills. A president's powers give him considerable favors and penalties to dispense. As the chief maker of foreign policy, he can seek support from Irish and Jewish Americans by supporting their objectives in Northern Ireland and the Middle East. As de facto leader of his party, he can use the symbolic resources of the presidency in campaigning for candidates he supports. And as chief budget maker, he has many favors to give and withhold, including support for hundreds of pork barrel projects.

The strategy of making a direct presidential appeal to the people to gain cooperation from Washingtonians is called going public.[41] The strategy includes giving prime-time television and radio addresses, holding press conferences, making speeches at events around the country, and using satellite technology to give interviews to local television stations, conventions, and other audiences.

Why have some presidents found "going public" attractive? One reason is that the weakness of party identification forces presidential candidates to appeal as widely as they can for support. They continue doing so after taking office because they have seen its value. In addition, national parties have been unable to represent the larger number of interests produced by government's larger role in society. This has helped to disperse power among alliances interest groups form with congressional committees, subcommittees, and executive agencies that write and administer the laws they lobby for and against. It is difficult for presidents to know, bargain with, and persuade all these Washingtonians. It is often easier to go public.

Finally, as outsiders, or presidential candidates without national political experience, Carter, Reagan, and Clinton have used the strategy of going public because they lacked ties with the Washingtonians they needed to govern.[42] In a 1981 television address to stimulate support for major tax cuts, Reagan asked viewers "to put aside any feelings of frustration . . . about our political institutions . . . [and] contact your senators and congressmen."[43] The public's reaction was swift and overwhelming. Many Democrats decided to support the president and the cuts passed.

Ronald Reagan Library

Although the public did not always agree with President Reagan's policies or views, he was popular in part because of his image as a rugged individualist.

Going public has a number of important effects. It makes the workings of the presidency resemble an election campaign because presidents fly around the country to get their views in the media. Seeking coverage and support, they use the same simple, dramatic style to oversell their positions that they used as candidates. To identify public reactions, presidential staff regularly gather data just as they did on the campaign trail. A White House aide described the Reagan administration as "a P.R. outfit that became President and took over the country."[44]

Going public leads presidents to use "sound bites" to simplify their positions to build public support while working behind the scenes to build congressional and interest group support. This worked for Reagan, who publicly described his 1982 budget package as "a line drawn in the dirt" to stress his resolve. He traveled around the country to generate public support, and his staff used focus groups to identify popular reactions to his proposals. These analyses told his advisers where he could hold firm and where he should compromise. And he made the necessary changes in his package to build congressional support for it.

Clinton used Reagan's sound-bite and compromise strategy to gain congressional passage of the North American Free Trade Agreement and a ban on assault weapons. When Clinton tried to sell health care reform to the nation and to Congress, however, an observer likened him to "a home-run hitter with a .200 batting average."[45] In his 1994 State of the Union address, Clinton threatened to veto any reform that did not offer universal coverage. However, his proposal was complex and difficult to understand. This made it an easy target for interest groups to oppose by playing on fears of an unknown plan. Despite focus groups, his effort to build support for his position could not overcome the problem, and Congress defeated his bill.

Going public may sometimes lead presidents to emphasize public relations over results and to blame the media rather than themselves for low poll scores. For example, Nixon and his supporters claimed the media had hounded him from office, Reagan blamed the media for exaggerating the importance of the Iran-contra scandal, and Clinton blamed the media for not giving him credit for his first-year accomplishments. He complained, "I have fought more damn battles than any president has in 20 years with the possible exception of Reagan's first budget and not gotten one damn bit of credit from the knee-jerk liberal press. I

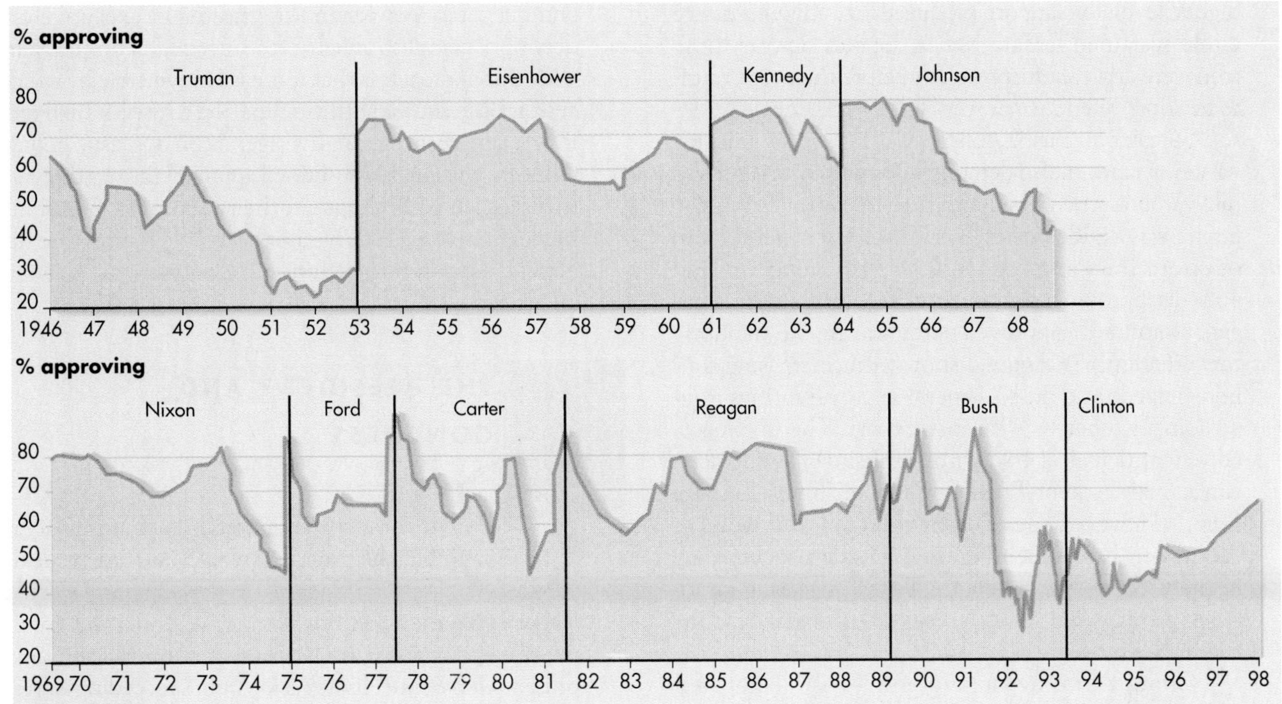

FIGURE 2

Presidential Popularity Usually Declines over Time

Eisenhower and, to some extent, Reagan are exceptions to the post–World War II tendency for presidential popularity to fall during their tenures. Although Reagan's popularity plunged 20 points at the end of 1986 because of the Iran-contra scandal, it partly rebounded by the end of his term. Most commentators thought this reflected popular fondness for Reagan as a person and Reagan's early successes rather than policy achievements late in his term. Bush began his term with high ratings typical of new presidents; after falling in 1990, his ratings rebounded to record heights during the Persian Gulf War, then began falling dramatically in 1991. Clinton's comparatively low first-year popularity reflects the minority share (43%) of the popular vote he received in 1992, reactions to his positions on controversial issues, and the first of the scandals to hit his administration. Despite his modest showing at the polls (49%) in 1996 and continuing scandals, Clinton's approval ratings soared to 67% in 1998.

SOURCES: Caption: William Schneider, "Reagan Now Viewed as an Irrelevant President," *National Journal*, November 28, 1987, p. 3051. See also George Gallup, Jr., and Alec Gallup, "The Former President," *The Polling Report*, January 30, 1989, pp. 1 and 5. Figure data: Gallup Polls, reported in *Public Opinion*, January/February 1989, and updated. The question asked is: "Do you approve or disapprove of the way [name of president] is handling his job as president?"

am sick and tired of it, and you can put that in the damn article."[46]

Bush used going public as a strategy in his handling of events leading up to the Persian Gulf War. He decided to use military force soon after Iraq invaded Kuwait in August 1990. Until January, when Congress approved this option, Bush made many speeches comparing Iraq's Suddam Hussein to Hitler, condemning Hussein's use of chemical and biological weapons on his own people, and warning that Hussein would soon have nuclear weapons. Bush's efforts won more public support for using force and made congressional support more likely.

Public Opinion and Effectiveness in Office

Americans pay more attention to the president than to other public officials, and we typically link government's success to the effectiveness of his leadership. Although many factors affect public opinion about presidential effectiveness, a positive image of a president's leadership skills helps protect his ratings after serious policy failures.

Many people are predisposed to support the president and to look at his overall record rather than his short-run successes.[47] Failure on specific issues does not always produce low scores on general performance. For example, majorities of respondents simultaneously disapproved of Reagan's handling of environmental and foreign policy issues, which the public thinks are important, *and* registered approval of his overall performance.

Crises called "rally events" affect presidential popularity.[48] President Clinton's approval ratings increased after the bombing of the federal building in Oklahoma City. Public support rises significantly at such times because people do not want to hurt the president, the symbol of national unity. However, the higher levels of support produced by rally events are rarely sustained.[49] The rise in support among those who were critical of a president before the event tends to be short-lived.

Support for Bush's policies toward Iraq after its invasion of Kuwait also demonstrates public readiness to rally around the president. In November 1990, the public was divided over Bush's decision to send more troops to the Persian Gulf, with 47% approving and 46% disapproving. By January 1991, after fighting began, almost 90% approved of the way he was handling the situation. As Figure 2 shows, this increasing support helped raise Bush's general approval ratings from 54% in October to 89% in February. The unexpectedly swift defeat of Iraq with surprisingly few American casualties kept Bush's poll scores high for some time.[50] However, the effect of the Gulf War faded as Americans began focusing on domestic concerns, especially economic problems. Bush's approval rating fell to 33% by mid-1992, leading to his defeat by Clinton in November.[51]

Clinton's rating at midterm (47%) compared well with the midterm ratings of recent presidents (Ford was at 45%, Carter 43%, and Reagan 37%). But he also had the lowest ratings of any president in their first two years.[52] His up and down scores in this period reflected public anxiety about his leadership skills. In 1995 polls 56% of Americans described Clinton as a weak president, and 80% expected the Republican Congress would have more influence than Clinton on the nation's direction.[53] But Clinton was far more adept at going public than the Republican leadership, and by the end of his first term, his approval rating was at 53% and Congress was in legislative retreat.

Winning consistently good ratings when public anger and frustration with government are widespread is difficult. Although short-term crises or rally events can help a president's ratings, long-term conditions will continue to influence them. From the time Clinton began to compete for his party's nomination, he has faced an almost steady stream of accusations of sexual impropriety, financial misdealings, and cover-ups. Yet in the aftermath of the most serious allegations, his approval rating rose to 67%. Clinton may have benefited again from a public backlash against the salaciousness of congressional and media commentary, but it is more likely that he got a positive bounce from public confidence in the overall state of the economy.

The more important issue is whether a president with high approval ratings can translate them into policy successes. Reagan had only qualified success in using his popularity to get Congress to enact his legislative proposals. He relied heavily on his own appointment and budgetary powers and the issuing of executive orders to accomplish much of his agenda. The problem with this approach is that it is easily reversible by a successor. Bush showed little inclination to use his high ratings to pursue any legislative agenda on domestic policy. Clinton, with higher sustained approval ratings than either Reagan or Bush late in their terms and a substantial legislative agenda, has not been able to translate his popular support into victories in Congress.

THE PRESIDENT AND CONGRESS

One thing the Founders did not anticipate is that the president would one day be dealing with Congress as the popularly elected leader of a national political party. Winning the nomination of a major political party is currently the only route to the White House (aside from succeeding a president who dies in office), and the victor does become the nominal head of the party and chief advocate for its policy agenda. This adds another dimension to the relationship between the executive and legislative branches: the president is never just the head of state or chief executive; he is also an electoral adversary of members of the House and Senate who do not belong to his party. He may use his reputation and the weight of his office to unseat them.

Party Leadership

To improve the electoral chances of their party, presidents try to help recruit good candidates for House and Senate races. In addition, presidents help raise money by being the headliner at fund-raising events and by staying on good terms with major contributors. They also send their aides around the country to help fellow Democrats or Republicans with their campaigns and sometimes even go themselves. Seeing a president in person—seeing a little history in the making—is exciting, and they almost always draw a crowd and good media coverage. Candidates for any office are usually eager for a presidential visit, although in 1992 some Republican candidates avoided being photographed with Bush when he visited their districts, and in 1994 and 1998 some Democratic congressional candidates preferred to campaign without Clinton's support.

Presidential partisanship has a purpose: The more members of a president's party who sit in Congress, the more support he gets for his policies. However, a president's support, when he chooses to give it, is no guarantee of electoral success for congressional candidates, especially in off-year elections (see Table 1). Since 1932, the president's party has lost an average of 29 House and 4 Senate seats in off-year elections; in presidential election years, the average gains for the winning presidential candidate's party in Congress are almost a mirror image, 21 in the House and 3 in the Senate. The 1988 and 1992 elections were unusual. The Republicans lost three House seats and one Senate seat when Bush was elected, and the Democrats lost 10 House seats with no change in the Senate when Clinton was elected. The off-year election of 1998 was also an anomaly. The Democrats actually gained House seats, the first time since 1934 that the president's party increased its seats in an off-year election.

The president usually tries to camouflage his actions as party leader when trying to persuade people to support him or to vote for his party's candidates. People are more likely to listen to a president when they see him in one of his other roles, such as head of state.

TABLE 1

Congressional Candidates Fall Off the President's Coattails in Off-Year Elections

YEAR	PRESIDENT	SEATS GAINED OR LOST BY PRESIDENT'S PARTY IN HOUSE	SENATE
1934	Roosevelt (D)	+9	+10
1938	Roosevelt (D)	−71	−6
1942	Roosevelt (D)	−45	−9
1946	Truman (D)	−55	−12
1950	Truman (D)	−29	−6
1954	Eisenhower (R)	−18	−1
1958	Eisenhower (R)	−47	−13
1962	Kennedy (D)	−4	+4
1966	Johnson (D)	−47	−3
1970	Nixon (R)	−12	+2
1974	Ford (R)	−48	−3
1978	Carter (D)	−11	−3
1982	Reagan (R)	−26	0
1986	Reagan (R)	−6	−8
1990	Bush (R)	−8	−1
1994	Clinton (D)	−52	−9
1998	Clinton (D)	+5	0
Average, all off-year elections		−27	−4
Average, all presidential election years		+21	+3

D = Democrat; R = Republican.

SOURCES: *Congressional Quarterly Guide to U.S. Elections, 1985,* p. 1116; Harold W. Stanley and Richard G. Niemi, *Vital Statistics on American Politics,* 3d ed. (Washington, D.C.: CQ Press, 1992), table 7-4; and *Congressional Quarterly Guide to Current American Government Spring 1991* (Washington, D.C.: CQ Press, 1991), p. 1. *Lincoln Star,* November 10, 1994, p. 1.

Divided Government

Presidents are normally active in support of House and Senate candidates not just because they are policy leaders, but also because one of the major factors influencing the working relationship between the president and Congress is whether the president's party controls the House and Senate. For all but two years since 1981, one party has controlled the White House and the other the Congress. This is called **divided government.** The Founders made divided government possible by dividing authority between the executive and legislative branches and providing that members of each would be elected in different ways and for different terms. This contrasts with parliamentary systems, in which voters elect members of the legislative branch and they in turn choose the executive leaders of the nation.

In the first half of the twentieth century, divided government did not occur very often. From 1900 to 1950, only 4 of 26 presidential and midterm elections resulted in divided government. From 1952 to 1994, however, 14 of 22 elections did.[54] Even with Reagan's overwhelming victory in 1980, the Republicans captured only the Senate. Their dominance lasted only until 1986, when the Democrats regained majority control. President Bush faced both a House and a Senate controlled by the Democrats, and now President Clinton has a Republican Congress.

Some believe that divided government is partially responsible for our failure to solve many of our important problems. The term *gridlock* has often been used to suggest this policy stalemate. The president presents a program and Congress does not accept it. Or Congress passes a bill and the president vetoes it. The result can be a lot of squabbling and little action. In 1998 when a period of especially bitter rivalry between the White House and Congress brought legislative action to a halt, President Clinton joked that C-SPAN coverage of Congress would be a good replacement for the *Seinfeld* TV sitcom because it was also "about nothing."

But united government does not always eliminate gridlock. From 1946 to 1990, as many major laws passed during periods of divided government as in periods of united government. Adoption of policies that address major problems is usually the result of strong presidential leadership, national crisis, policy failure, or a change in public opinion rather than united government.[55]

PRESIDENTS AND PRIME MINISTERS

Many Americans are frustrated by our system's fragmentation and by "gridlock," the inability of our elected officials to agree about how to solve our nation's problems. These differences can be exacerbated when different parties control the White House and Congress, as has been the case most years since World War II. Divided government makes it more likely that the president and congressional leaders will advocate different policies and priorities. It also makes it easier for elected officials to play the "blame game" and avoid taking responsibility for failed policies and inaction. We even have problems when the White House and Congress are controlled by the same party. The president and members of Congress often have different interests because they are elected by different constituencies at different times. And they can use the system's checks and balances to thwart each other's efforts.

In contrast, British heads of government, called prime ministers, seem to be better leaders and more accountable to the public. Like most democratic nations, Britain has a **parliamentary government,** that is, a system in which the executive is chosen by the legislature. The British government is marked by a unity of authority. The prime minister, or PM, is an elected member of the House of Commons, the lower house of Britain's national legislature called the Parliament. (Parliament's other house, the House of Lords, is unelected and has limited power.) The PM is elected like other members of the Commons—by the voters of a constituency—and then is chosen by his or her party as its leader. The PM is always the leader of the majority or plurality party in the Commons and usually decides when elections to the Commons will occur. However, elections must take place within five years of the last election. As members of the Commons, the PM and the cabinet ministers appointed by the PM must argue for their policies and respond to criticism from minority party members in debate.

Rank-and-file members of the Commons have very little independent power and often do not live in the constituencies that elect them. National party organizations have a great deal of influence over who is selected to run for election to the Commons. Members who do not vote the party line sometimes lose their party's support for reelection. This helps explain why 97% of the bills sponsored by the PM and cabinet from 1945 to 1987 were enacted.[1]

Although this is an attractive picture in some respects, the Founders designed our system to represent the diverse interests of a large, heterogeneous population. While more effective leadership in government is appealing, greater centralization can mean less opportunity to accommodate diverse local interests. Many Americans would not like a party organization to have the major influence on nominations for congressional office. Some would also be angry if representatives advocated positions contrary to local majority opinion on an important issue. America is a much more diverse society than Britain, perhaps making centralization less workable.

Diversity in America is also represented by powerful interest groups. Their close ties to congressional committees and subcommittees and executive branch officials give these interest groups considerable power to obstruct government. While these groups might be weakened by parliamentary-style arrangements, the interests they represent would still exist, as would their ability to lobby Congress and the executive branch.

Considering whether parliamentary forms would improve the workings of our government requires us to weigh some difficult trade-offs. Do we want to pay the costs of frequent gridlock and inefficiency to keep a system that is more responsive to diverse local and other interests?

1. Richard Rose, *Politics in England: Change and Persistence,* 5th ed. (London: Macmillan, 1989), p. 113.

Legislative Leadership

Because he is the head of a political party with an issue agenda, and because the public has come to expect policy leadership from the White House, a president usually takes office with legislative goals. This can mean a few key proposals such as for tax cuts, tax reforms, or downsizing government, or it can mean a comprehensive package of proposed legislation, such as Teddy Roosevelt's Square Deal, Wilson's New Freedom, Franklin Roosevelt's New Deal, and Johnson's Great Society. People often evaluate presidential leadership in terms of the content and impact of these programs.

All presidents have advisers who serve as congressional liaisons; they lobby for the president's agenda and facilitate exchange of information with members of Congress on pending legislation. How active the president's personal role is depends on his involvement in policy detail, knowledge of congressional operations, and powers of persuasion. Among post–World War II presidents, only the three governors, Carter, Reagan, and Clinton, had not served in Congress (Clinton ran for the House but lost). Truman, Kennedy, and Bush had short and undistinguished congressional careers, while Nixon used his short time in the House and Senate to build a national reputation. In their long years of congressional service, Johnson and Ford rose to leadership positions. As a former Senate majority leader of legendary persuasiveness, Johnson is the classic example of president as inside-dopester and congressional coalition builder. He knew how to approach members and was a masterful lobbyist. In working for a foreign aid bill, he invited key members to the White House for one-on-one talks described by an aide as "endless talking, ceaseless importuning, torrential laying on of the facts . . . for several days."[56]

Sometimes presidents are more heavy-handed in seeking support. A Reagan aide described how the White House changed one senator's vote: "We just beat his brains out. We stood him in front of an open grave and told him he could jump in if he wanted to [oppose Reagan]."[57] Such tactics can succeed but can also make a president look bad. In 1990, Bush was criticized for the way White House staff lobbied Congress for a budget plan. His chief of staff, John Sununu, called Trent Lott (R-Miss.), who is now majority leader of the Senate, "insignificant" on television after Lott refused to support the plan. And Sununu alienated others with petty reprisals.

Presidents also use the prestige of their office as an instrument of persuasion. In 1975, Ford persuaded 18 House members to change their votes to support one of his vetoes. He took them on his jet, *Air Force One*, and "lectured" them.[58] Because many members rarely, if ever, talk to a president, most consider these conversations memorable events and listen.

Reagan's leadership style in dealing with Congress involved going public to pressure it for support. In contrast, Bush used White House staff to negotiate policy matters directly with congressional leaders. Bush lacked Reagan's media skills and, as an insider, already had working relationships with Washington's influentials.

Clinton tries to generate congressional support for his policies by personally lobbying individual members and by trying to get backing in those parts of the country and from those interest groups most affected by the policies. One way he and his aides do this is to give interviews to journalists whose work reaches those he wants to influence. Clinton then tries to use popular support to build congressional backing by lobbying members both directly and indirectly, through intermediaries such as business and union leaders.

Presidents cannot always get the support they need, however. Members of Congress have their own constituencies and careers. And presidential persuasion does not always involve bargaining. Presidents also remind fellow Republicans or Democrats of the need to stick together to promote their party platform and achieve party goals. Bipartisan appeals can be effective, too, especially in foreign affairs.

VETO POWER

No president has to rely solely on his persuasive powers to affect legislation. The Constitution has given the chief executive veto power over bills passed by Congress. The veto power is not listed among the president's formal powers in Article II, but rather is included in Article I as a check on Congress's power to legislate.

When the president receives a bill passed by Congress, he has three options: he can sign it into law; he can veto it and send it back to Congress along with his objections; or he can take no action, in which case the bill becomes a law after 10 congressional working days. An unsigned bill returned by the president can be passed into law if two-thirds of both houses vote to override the veto. But if Congress adjourns within 10 working days after sending legislation to the White House, and the president chooses to pocket the bill, that is, not to act on it, the legislation dies. This option, called a pocket veto, is a means by which the president can kill a bill without facing an override attempt in Congress.

Given the presence of White House supporters in Congress and the president's ability to go public, mobilizing two-thirds majorities in both houses to override a veto is usually very hard. As a result, presidents can try to influence the content of bills by threatening to veto them if they do not conform to presidential wishes.

Only eight presidents never vetoed a bill. Franklin Roosevelt holds the record for most vetoes with 635 vetoes in 14 years, only 9 of which were overridden. Eisenhower vetoed 181 bills in 8 years. Congress overrode only 2, even though his party was in the minority for 6 of those years. Reagan vetoed 78 bills with 9 overridden, and Bush vetoed 46 bills with 1 overridden. Clinton did not use the veto until his third year in office, casting only 17 during his first full term. That was the lowest number for a full term since Woodrow Wilson's administration. In his second term Clinton briefly gained the additional power of the line-item veto (see the Symbolic Solutions box).

Presidents who use the veto too often may appear isolated or uncooperative or seem to be exercising negative leadership. But the fact that presidents are rarely overridden reminds us of their power when they decide they really want something.

CONGRESSIONAL SUPPORT

A president's reputation for effectiveness is based in part on how successful he is in getting congressional support. Franklin Roosevelt's ranking as one of our great presidents can be attributed in part to his legislative effectiveness. He was able to persuade Congress to enact much of his legislative program within the first 100 days of his administration. Those were extraordinary times, and few presidents since have been able to match his success in Congress.

Reagan's effectiveness with Congress was greatest in his first year in office when he got Congress to approve a major tax cut and increase military spending.

SYMBOLIC SOLUTIONS FOR COMPLEX PROBLEMS?

THE LINE-ITEM VETO

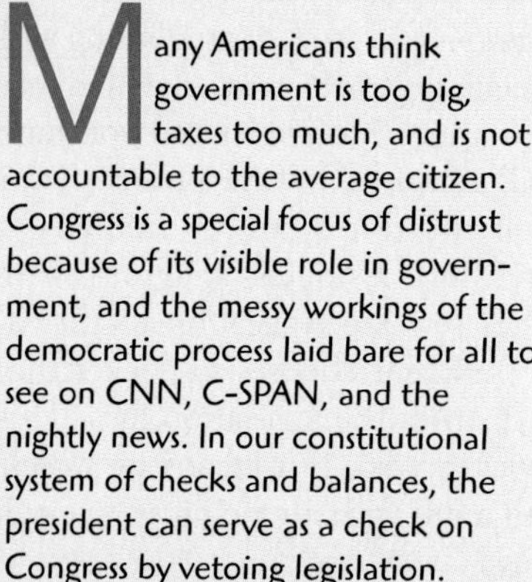

Many Americans think government is too big, taxes too much, and is not accountable to the average citizen. Congress is a special focus of distrust because of its visible role in government, and the messy workings of the democratic process laid bare for all to see on CNN, C-SPAN, and the nightly news. In our constitutional system of checks and balances, the president can serve as a check on Congress by vetoing legislation.

Presidents have been able to veto entire bills passed by Congress, but have not had the same power that most governors have to strike down specific provisions or parts of bills passed by their state legislatures. The purpose of the **line-item veto** is to give the president authority to veto one or more provisions of individual bills while allowing the remaining provisions to become law. Congress could override a line-item veto if majorities of both houses disapprove of the president's action.

Congressional Republicans and all recent presidents have been strong advocates for the line-item veto. But can the line-item veto work? Or is it a symbolic solution that cannot work but would make some elected officials look good?

Supporters of the line-item veto say its enactment would allow presidents to impose a discipline on Congress that Congress has been unable to impose on itself and thus reduce pork barrel spending. Knowing that the president has the power to veto spending items that primarily benefit special interests, members might be less likely to pass such proposals. And the president would have a weapon to use against opponents in Congress who add spending items he does not want to bills he does support (in these cases the president often swallows hard and signs the bill).

Opponents of giving the president a line-item veto counter that Congress would be even less inclined to act responsibly because presidents would have the final word in the budget process. Congress would vote to fund pork barrel projects, believing that the president would veto them. This would put the pressure on the president to make decisions that would deny benefits to their constituencies and leave him to suffer the political consequences.

In addition, opponents say that effective presidents have gotten most, though not all, of what they wanted without the line-item veto. Thus, they argue that the line-item veto is an unneeded or symbolic solution when we have effective presidents. And it would not be a more realistic solution when we have weak presidents because they, by definition, would avoid tough decisions that deny benefits to organized constituencies. In fact, the veto could give too much power to already effective presidents and produce executive excesses. "It doesn't take much imagination to consider how much more persuasive [the president] would be if his words were buttressed with a veto stamp over individual projects and activities within our districts," Senator Mark Hatfield (R-Ore.) noted.[1] Opponents have also argued that the president *is* as likely as Congress to use pork barrel spending and special tax breaks to win majorities for his programs. It will still be necessary "to buy votes with money for parochial projects," but the coalitions "will simply be packaged in the White House instead of Capitol Hill

Economic problems produced in part by these changes and a growing public awareness that he was uninformed about, and uninvolved in, White House routine led to a drop in his effectiveness with Congress during the remainder of his administration. As Figure 3 shows, Reagan's congressional support fell after 1981 and was low compared to other presidents.

Congressional support for Bush was weak throughout his term. Figure 3 shows that his first-year success with Congress was the lowest of any elected president since 1953, when scores were first computed. He also has the lowest two-year record. In part, these scores are products of partisanship. Bush had fewer congressional Republicans to work with than any GOP president in this century. However, low support for Bush among congressional Republicans may have resulted from the absence of a well-articulated White House legislative program. He also failed to capture the public's attention with clear themes, what he once called the "vision thing." This prevented Bush from securing more congressional support, even after the Persian Gulf War when his popularity was very high.

Clinton had some early setbacks in dealing with Congress (over his first two nominees to be attorney general, lifting the ban on gays in the military, and parts of his economic stimulus package), which raised doubts about his likely effectiveness. He tried, with mixed success, to emulate Reagan's successful first-year strategy of asking Congress to vote on a few high-priority bills. This strategy lets presidents define their positions in relatively simple terms and seek congressional support when they are in their postelection honeymoon periods and before other influences on Congress have time to make mobilizing majorities more difficult. Enjoying early successes with Congress can help presidents build their professional reputations.

committee rooms."[2] If so, the line-item veto may be little more than a symbolic solution.

A line-item veto, giving the president power to reject any specific appropriation or any tax break that affects fewer than 100 individuals or 10 businesses, became law in January 1997. As a counterweight, Congress gave itself the power to attach wording exempting funding provisions of a bill from application of the line-item veto. The use, or overuse, of such exemptions could have political costs however, since they would immediately be brought to public attention by opponents of the provisions. Long-time Republican supporters of the line-item veto could be especially vulnerable to the charge of supporting symbolic solutions if they used the exemption to curtail Clinton's exercise of veto powers.

Before Clinton could exercise the law, it was challenged in federal court by members of Congress. One of the group's leaders said that the line-item veto "may be suitable for royalty, but it is an unconstitutional insult to the principle of representative democracy." In its first court test, a federal judge agreed, overturning the legislation as unconstitutional because it delegated to the president powers the Constitution vested in the legislative branch. But on appeal by the Clinton administration, the Supreme Court—without addressing the merits of the constitutional issue—reinstated the law by ruling that the petitioners had no legal grounds to bring the suit (because they had suffered no material loss).

In 1997, Clinton used his new authority 82 times, cutting funding for 38 military construction projects; all 38 were restored by Congress. In all, Clinton's use of the veto cut less than $2 billion from the next five years of spending, or about .02% of total expected outlays for that period.[3] Once Congress showed its intent to undo any use of the veto that it did not approve, Clinton began using it much more sparingly, cutting nothing from welfare, education, or health appropriations. In its first year of use, the line-item veto did not look like a powerful new weapon for the executive branch.

Soon after the first veto was exercised, citizens affected by the funding cuts filed suit in federal court, and in 1998 the lower court again overturned the veto. The Clinton administration appealed to the Supreme Court, but the Court majority did not accept the administration's argument that the line-item veto is simply the exercise of spending authority delegated by Congress. In killing the legislation, the Court ruled that the line-item veto gives the president power to veto parts of a bill whereas the Constitution requires that bills presented by Congress must be accepted or rejected in their entirety. Congressional supporters of the line-item veto vowed to reword and resubmit the legislation, but the Court's decision cautioned that the only means of granting partial veto power to the president was by constitutional amendment.

1. Quoted in Roger H. Davidson and Walter J. Oleszek, *Congress and Its Members*, 5th ed. (Washington, D.C.: CQ Press, 1996), p. 302.
2. Marshall Ingwerson, "GOP Irony: Delivering Power Back to President," *Christian Science Monitor*, February 10, 1995, p. 5, Davidson and Oleszek, *Congress*, p. 305.
3. "Line-Item Vetoes Yield Savings Plus Headaches," *The News-Gazette*, December 3, 1997, p. D-2.

Clinton had an advantage in the first half of his first term that Reagan and Bush lacked. With both houses of Congress controlled by the Democratic majorities, he did not have to deal with a divided government. Despite substantial disagreements among congressional Democrats, Clinton succeeded in getting majority support for most of his early economic proposals. In fact, Clinton had the highest first-year success score with Congress (86%) since Eisenhower's 89% in 1953 and Johnson's 88% in 1964. And he got more out of Congress in his first two years than Kennedy, Ford, Carter, and Bush combined. Clinton's two-year record of congressional success exceeded that of every president since Johnson, a record that no doubt surprises many people.

Clinton's legislative record was impressive but it did not give him a reputation for effectiveness. His success was overshadowed by the scandals that followed him into his second term and by his failure to articulate larger goals so the American people knew where he wanted to lead them. The defeat of his health care bill in 1994 after he made it his top priority convinced many Americans that he was an inept leader who could not take advantage of Democratic majorities in Congress when he had them.

Foreign Policy and Military Leadership

Over the years, the president has become more powerful than Congress in foreign policy, assuming powers that were not explicitly given to either the legislative or the executive branch. One reason for this dominance is that in foreign policy, more than in domestic, the president has more information than others do. He can often stifle debate by citing classified

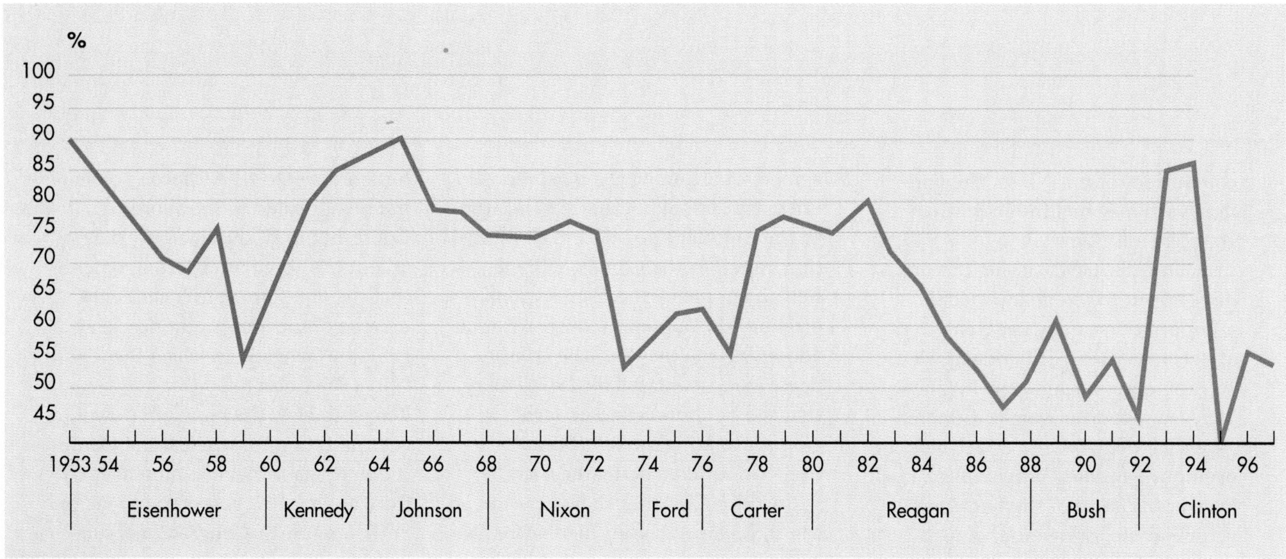

FIGURE 3

Presidential Success on Congressional Votes Often Declines over Time

Presidents usually have the most success with Congress early in their first terms. This figure shows the percentage of votes that presidents have won when they took a position. Clinton's 86.4% score ranks the highest of any president in his first year since Johnson's 88% in 1964 and Eisenhower's 89% in 1953 while his 1995 score of 36.2% was a record low. President Bush had the smallest first-year success of any of these presidents.

SOURCES: *Congressional Quarterly Weekly Report,* October 17, 1992, p. 3249; December 18, 1993, pp. 3427–3431; December 21, 1996; p. 3455; January 3, 1998, p. 27.

or secret information from the CIA, Defense Department, State Department, and other agencies and saying, "If you knew what I knew, you would agree with me." The president can also share certain information with Congress (and the public) while withholding other material. Members of Congress must often rely on the media and are at a distinct disadvantage in dealing with the president. In 1984, the Reagan administration mined harbors in Nicaragua after telling the Senate Intelligence Committee it was not doing so. When the facts became known, the chair of that committee, Barry Goldwater (R-Ariz.), wrote a blistering public letter to the head of the CIA saying, not so formally, "I am pissed off."[59]

The administration also has a large role in shaping the agenda of debate. Alternatives acceptable to the administration are advanced through public statements, background briefings of the press and Congress, and "national" newspapers such as the *New York Times* or *Washington Post*. Many reasonable alternatives may never be suggested or receive support. Thus, media outlets did little to initiate discussions of our goals in the Persian Gulf, choosing instead to cover troop commitments largely as a logistical challenge and human interest story. Media acceptance of Pentagon restrictions on news gathering also helped Bush generate support for his policies by producing news of successful, not unsuccessful, attacks and by concealing information describing casualties on both sides.

Although different presidential advisers sometimes advocate conflicting views publicly, it is much easier for a president than for Congress to have a coherent policy. Thus, another advantage the president has over Congress is that he can act decisively, whereas Congress must reach agreement and vote in order to act and this takes time. President Bush ordered American troops to Somalia in December 1992, but the House Foreign Affairs Committee did not meet until May 1993 to authorize this action—the day after the United Nations had assumed responsibility in Somalia and most of our troops had come home.

Because the president is one and Congress is many, the president is usually more effective in appealing for public support. There is almost always a "rally 'round the flag" effect on both Congress and the public when the president takes a strong stance in foreign policy, especially if troops are involved. In these cases, Congress may hesitate to oppose the president because it fears doing so may be seen by other nations as a sign of United States weakness.

Vietnam is a good example of presidential dominance in foreign policy. Presidential policy dominated even with demonstrations, mass arrests, opposing editorials, negative opinion polls, and congressional criticism.

The Vietnam War raised major questions about presidential authority in foreign and military policy. Although Congress never declared war in Vietnam, it routinely appropriated money for it. Nonetheless, many members of Congress believed that Johnson and

Nixon exceeded their authority in pursuing the war. This painful experience led Congress to try to supervise use of military force more closely.

In 1973, Congress passed the **War Powers Act** to limit the president's ability to commit troops to combat. It says the president can use troops abroad under three conditions: when Congress has declared war, when Congress has given him specific authority to do so, or when an attack on the United States or its military creates a national crisis. If a president commits troops under the third condition, he is supposed to consult with Congress beforehand, if possible, and notify it within 48 hours afterward. Unless Congress approves the use of troops, the president must withdraw them within 60 days, or 90 days if he needs more time to protect them. Congress can pass a concurrent resolution (not subject to presidential veto) at any time ordering the president to end the use of military force.

Congress passed the War Powers Act over Nixon's veto. He believed it violated his constitutional authority to protect the nation from military threats. Although presidents have not questioned Congress's constitutional authority to declare war, all have fought congressional involvement in the use of troops. As a result, enforcement of the act has proved difficult. For example, President Carter did not inform, let alone consult, Congress before using U.S. troops in an attempt to free the Iranian hostages in 1980. Congress did not protest. Neither did it protest after Bush sent troops to invade Panama in 1989. Bush did not even refer to the War Powers Act in the two-page letter he sent to Congress justifying the invasion 60 hours after it began.

On the whole, then, the War Powers Act has not stopped presidents from sending American troops abroad. This was certainly true in the Persian Gulf. President Bush sent 250,000 troops to the Gulf between August and November 1990 on his own authority. He also delayed announcing his decision to double this number until after the November elections, although he had made the decision in October. This kept the decision that changed our mission from defense (Operation Desert Shield) to offense (Operation Desert Storm) from coming to Congress until he had mobilized United States and world opinion and gained United Nations support. By the time Congress authorized using force in January 1991, the question of whether to do so was, practically speaking, already decided.

Congress has special need to be vigilant in election years because a president's public opinion scores, especially before national elections, can influence the use of military force abroad.[60] Presidents may be tempted to use rally events to increase their popularity and congressional support for their policies (see Figure 4). A White House aide, acknowledging low presidential popularity in October 1983, said Reagan needed "a major victory somewhere to show that we can manage foreign policy." Another added, "We need a win . . . whether it's in Central America, the Middle East or with the Russians."[61] The United States invaded Grenada that month. When Bush's scores were falling in 1990, his staff chief told associates that a short successful war against Iraq would guarantee Bush's reelection (he was wrong!).[62]

Historically, a president's use of military force tends to raise his congressional support for about a month.[63] This led one observer to note that, based on U.S. experiences in Vietnam and Grenada, presidents who start military actions abroad must win them in a hurry if they want to stay popular.[64]

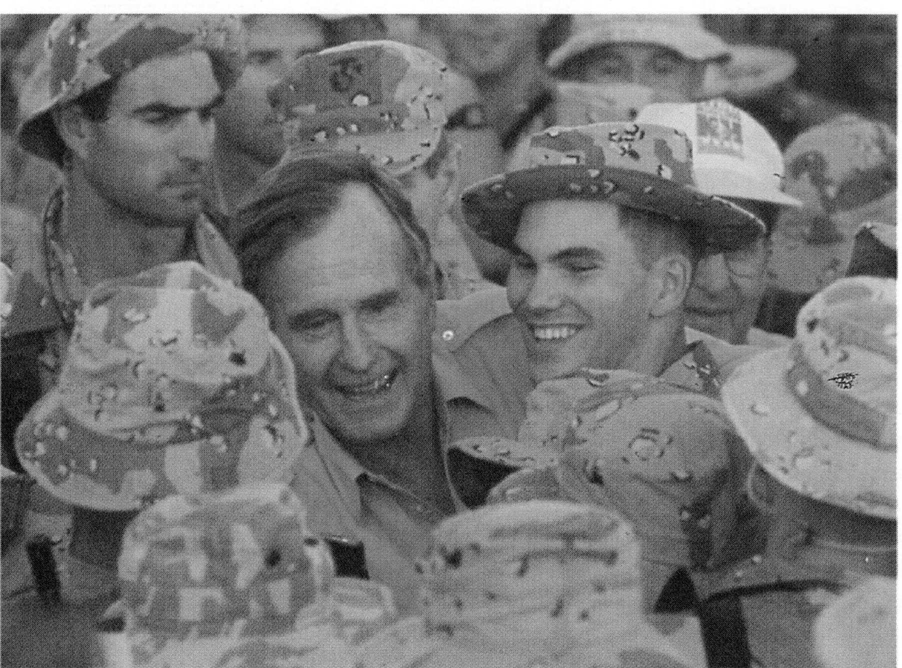

President Bush, as commander in chief, greets the troops in the Persian Gulf.

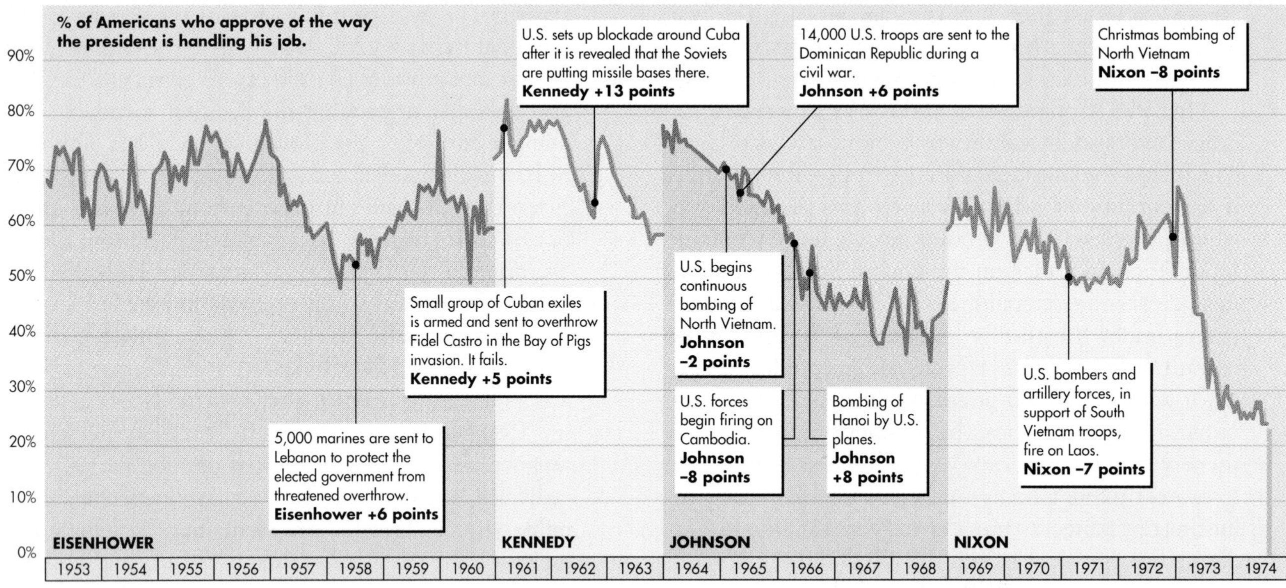

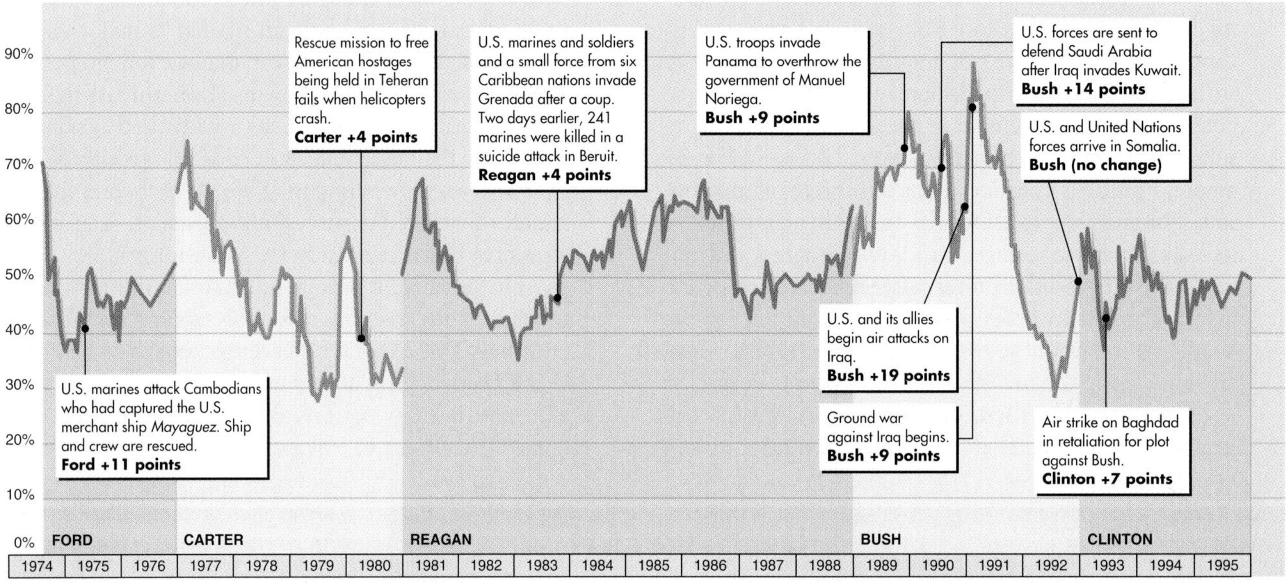

FIGURE 4

Presidential Support Rises with Military Action

Americans normally rally around the president when he uses military action, sometimes even when the action fails. (Vietnam was an exception because the war dragged on for so long.) Yet the increased support for the president does not last long because of other problems back home.

SOURCE: Based on Gallup Polls. *The New York Times*, Sunday, September 18, 1994, pp. E4–E5.

A president needs to be able to act decisively in international affairs. But we want to make sure the president does not act against our wishes. Congress has historically served as the most important check on the president, but its power to influence military policy is limited in emergency or crisis situations. An uneasy balance exists between presidential powers adequate to do the job and controls necessary to prevent abuse.

Although Congress has been reluctant to challenge presidential policies that were justified in terms of protecting national security, it has often refused to give its backing to presidential initiatives. Current studies suggest that even the widely held support for the "two presidencies" thesis—that presidents have substantially more success in winning support from Congress on foreign policy votes than on domestic policy—was largely unjustified if one looks at all the relevant votes cast by Congress.[65]

Since the end of the Vietnam War, Congress has sought to reassert its authority in foreign policy in a number of ways, including closer monitoring of intelligence operations, limiting the president's authority to enter into trade or other agreements with foreign countries, refusing to approve arms control and other treaties negotiated by presidents, and requiring congressional approval of major arms sales. Perhaps the greatest threat to presidential foreign policy dominance, however, will turn out to be the end of the Cold War. Without the threat of a challenging external enemy of superpower status, Congress is unlikely to give the president the benefit of the doubt in major foreign policy initiatives, certainly not those involving a commitment of military forces. There is evidence of this with Clinton's administration. Clinton, the first post–Cold War president, has not been able to count on congressional support even when he has committed troops, as in Bosnia and Haiti. Many of his trade and economic initiatives (loans to Mexico, NAFTA, fast-track trading authority) have met with similar resistance.

WHAT MAKES AN EFFECTIVE PRESIDENT?

Every president develops a track record of his effectiveness as a leader. Richard Neustadt calls it the president's professional reputation.[66] A president with an effective reputation has a record of getting what he wants, helping his allies, and penalizing the opposition. This reputation contributes to his continuing ability to persuade the public, Congress, and other Washingtonians. Few modern presidents were more adept at getting what they wanted from Congress than Lyndon Johnson, yet Johnson does not rank among the great presidents. A president's professional reputation is of great importance to him while he is in office and is a commentary on his political and administrative skills. But having the ability to get what he wants is not the same as being able to do what is best for the country, and therefore presidents seen as highly effective in office are not always judged by history to have been great presidents.

It is not always immediately clear how deep an impact a president's tenure has had on the direction of the country, and over time assessments of presidential performance do change. Truman is an example of a president who was very unpopular during his tenure and in the immediate years afterward, but who left a legacy of directness, personal integrity, and decisiveness on key decisions during an extremely difficult time (the national trauma of FDR's death while we were engaged in a world war). The "Buck Stops Here" sign that Truman kept on his desk illustrated both his sense of accountability and his no-nonsense rhetoric. In historical perspective his leadership skills have looked more impressive than they did while he was in office, and this has helped move him to the ranks of near-great presidents.

Scholarly assessment of Eisenhower's administrations has also changed significantly. Early on after he left office, he was judged an average president, a good and honest man with strong administrative skills, but one who took few chances and lacked an overall vision for the country. In retrospect analysts see as levelheaded and prescient his leadership during an extremely volatile period in the nuclear arms race and his warnings about the dangers of the military-industrial complex to the economy and national purpose.

How can presidential performance be measured? In characterizing the role of the president, the nineteenth-century historian Henry Adams wrote that he "resembles the commander of a ship at sea. He must have a helm to grasp, a course to steer, a port to seek."[67] That is, the incumbent must have a goal, a destination where he is leading the nation; he must have programs and a course of action to enable the nation to get there; and he must be a leader who is willing and able to use the instruments of office to achieve his goals.

Franklin Roosevelt characterized our great presidents as "leaders of thought at times when certain ideas in the life of the nation had to be clarified."[68] This reminds us that an opportunity factor is involved in rising to the highest ranks of performance. FDR's examples—"Washington embod[ying] the idea of the federal union, Jefferson and Jackson the idea of democracy, Lincoln union and freedom"—are of men who served at critical times in the country's development.[69] These are presidents whom almost all scholars rank among our greatest, and they are associated with ideas and policies that took root and affected the course of our country.

Any concept of presidential effectiveness inevitably involves the "vision thing." A president will likely be seen as effective only if he has a clear idea of where he wants to take the country. This is why Reagan is regarded by much of the public as a more effective president than Bush, even though scholars of the presidency give Reagan and Bush comparable rankings. To rank with the "greats," however, vision must be coupled with the political and administrative skills necessary to achieve it. In the scholarly consensus, Bush was willing and able to grab the helm but was steering to no port in particular; Reagan had a fixed destination but no firm hand on the helm and insufficient knowledge or interest to steer the ship. Like Bush, Reagan had a mediocre legislative record and an abysmal fiscal record, but in the public eye Reagan had a clear vision of what he wanted for the country. In contrast, Clinton has all the political and administrative skills to steer the ship, but keeps changing his destination. He has been unsuccessful in projecting to the public a clear and consistent vision of where the country should be headed. In a recent survey, Reagan, Bush, and Clinton were all ranked as average presidents (see the box "Rating the Presidents").

LIMITS ON PRESIDENTIAL POWER

As government grew during the first 75 years of the twentieth century, so did the office of the president. Some of these new powers came at the expense of Congress, but in large part they were delegated (e.g., budget making), voluntarily ceded to the president (e.g., foreign policymaking during the Cold War), or assumed by default through congressional inaction. What the executive branch gained was not the simple sum of what the legislative branch lost, as if the president and Congress were contestants in a zero-sum game. Much of the power FDR assumed in dealing with the Great Depression and World War II had not been exercised by any branch of the national government before. Crises arose, presidential incumbents responded, and in the process they assumed powers of government not yet established at the federal level.

Today a person elected to the presidency becomes the recipient of the respect bestowed on the office itself: people stand when the president enters a room; "Hail to the Chief" is played when he appears on a dais or at ceremonial events; men and women in uniform salute him; and

RATING THE PRESIDENTS

As children, we learned that George Washington, Abraham Lincoln, and Franklin Roosevelt were great presidents, but few of us think about most of the other presidents. How do they rate?

Presidential ratings surveys have been taken periodically since the historian Arthur Schlesinger Sr. first polled 55 leading historians in 1948. In the many surveys since, some presidents have improved their showing remarkably, most notably Eisenhower, who rose from 22nd place in a 1962 Schlesinger poll, to 12th in a 1981 poll by David Porter, to 9th in a 1997 poll of 719 historians and political scientists shown here.[1]

While presidents ranked between the bottom and top tiers may move up and down the rankings over the years, almost all polls agree on Washington, Lincoln, and Franklin Roosevelt as the Greats, and Jefferson, Jackson, Theodore Roosevelt, Wilson, and Truman as the Near Greats. The placement of Madison in the top 10 in the ranking shown here differs sharply from a 1996 *New York Times* poll of 32 presidential scholars; they rated Madison average.[2] Some presidents—Taylor, Harding, Kennedy, Ford—spent such short periods in office that they are hard to rank. The public has its own views, often placing Lyndon Johnson near the bottom and Kennedy near the top, while scholars tend to rank both as average to above average.

1. *Champaign-Urbana News Gazette*, February 8, 1997, p. D-2, citing William J. Ridings Jr. and Stuart R. McIver, *Rating the Presidents* (Secaucus, N.J.: Citadel Press, 1997).
2. Arthur M. Schlesinger Jr., "The Ultimate Approval Rating," *New York Times Magazine*, December 18, 1996, pp. 46–51.

Ranking U.S. Presidents

THE GREATS

U.S. PRESIDENT IN ORDER OF OVERALL RANKING	LEADERSHIP QUALITIES	ACCOMPLISHMENTS AND CRISIS MANAGEMENT	POLITICAL SKILL	APPOINTMENTS	CHARACTER AND INTEGRITY
1 Lincoln	2	1	2	3	1
2 F. Roosevelt	1	2	1	2	15
3 Washington	3	3	7	1	2
4 Jefferson	6	5	5	4	7
5 T. Roosevelt	4	4	4	5	12
6 Wilson	7	7	13	6	8
7 Truman	9	6	8	9	9
8 Jackson	5	9	6	19	18
9 Eisenhower	10	10	14	16	10
10 Madison	14	14	15	11	6

THE FAILURES (LISTED CHRONOLOGICALLY)

Pierce, Buchanan, A. Johnson, Grant, Harding, Hoover, Nixon

SOURCE: *Champaign-Urbana News-Gazette*, February 8, 1997, p. D-2.

for the remainder of his life, he can be addressed as "Mr. President." He is surrounded by bodyguards and aides, and the public and media scrutinize every detail of his personal life and public performance. He is almost universally regarded as the most powerful person in the world. Yet some presidents have become so frustrated by limitations on their power that they try to overcome those limitations by exceeding their constitutional authority.

The most famous examples of illegal presidential action in the face of perceived frustrations are Nixon's secret attempts to learn what his "enemies" were doing: invading individual privacy with phone taps, break-ins, and unauthorized reviews of income tax returns, and then obstructing justice by trying to cover up evidence of these acts. Reagan, frustrated in trying to free American hostages in Lebanon, authorized covert arms sales to Iran and supported covert and illegal aid to the Nicaraguan Contras (see the box "Presidential Abuse of Power: The Iran-Contra Affair.")

There have been many extraordinary extensions of presidential authority, especially in wartime or crises, including Lincoln's suspension of habeas corpus, Franklin Roosevelt's attempts to pack the Supreme Court, and Lyndon Johnson's conduct of an undeclared war. But even the most persuasive presidents like FDR, Reagan, and Johnson do not get everything they want. There are many formal checks on their constitutional powers as well as many limitations inherent in the office or the men who have served there.

Formal checks on the power of the presidency include the independence of the federal judiciary; the budgetary, confirmation, oversight, and removal powers of Congress; term limitations; and the power of the electorate to throw an incumbent out of office. When formal checks do not work, or do not work quickly enough, there is also the power of a free press. The abuses of office during the Nixon administration are instances where Congress and the public did not initially serve as a check on the president; illegalities might never have been revealed had it not been for investigative reporting by the *Washington Post*. Only after evidence was uncovered by the press did the Democratically controlled Congress deal seriously with accusations of wrongdoing.

There are also many idiosyncratic and situational factors that can impose restrictions on executive power, including the president's competence, personality, and attitude toward the exercise of power; the opportunity to exercise power presented by international or domestic crises, including warfare; the president's popularity and his reputation in Congress and with other Washingtonians; and the mood of Congress to fully use its powers to check the president.

In the last 25 years of the twentieth century, the power of the presidency has appeared to wane. The decline began in reaction to the sometimes arrogant or imperial exercise of power during the Johnson and Nixon administrations, especially with respect to the conduct of the Vietnam War and abuses of the electoral process during Nixon's reelection campaign. Reagan's personal popularity and conception of the office of presidency—emphasizing the head of state and symbolic roles of the office over governance—restored some of the prestige or grandeur of the presidency, but the illegalities of the Iran-contra affair and ethics scandals involving his appointees eroded public confidence again.

The end of the Cold War has also restricted the president's freedom to act unilaterally in international affairs and reduced his role as a rally figure to mobilize public opinion against foreign enemies. In domestic affairs, decades of budget deficits, the return of many responsibilities to the states, and a tendency toward downsizing national government have limited how much the personal presidency can credibly promise or deliver to the American public. As the presidency grew with the expanding role of national government, so it may shrink if power continues to gravitate away from the center.

The Clinton presidency suggests that the personal presidency may be imploding and contributing to the shrinking of presidential power. Six years of ethics investigations, a record number of special prosecutors, sensational headlines, and constant scrutiny of the First Family's personal lives have contributed to the diminution of the office, although it can be argued that media attention might have been substantially less had the power of the office not already been receding.

If the presidency *is* declining in power, there is no reason to believe that the decline will be permanent. Formal powers have remained fairly stable throughout the history of the office; it is how the inherent powers and the political role of the presidency are utilized by the incumbent, as well as the opportunities domestic and international political affairs afford him for the exercise of his office, that set the inner and outer limits of presidential power.

CONCLUSION: IS THE PRESIDENCY RESPONSIVE?

The presidency has become the most consistently visible office in government as well as one of the most personalized and responsive. Americans expect leadership from the president even in these days of "less" government.

Neustadt called twentieth-century public opinion about the presidency "monarchical." Johnson's and Nixon's "imperial" styles certainly were consistent with it. After a ceremony for Marines going to Vietnam, Johnson was directed to a helicopter by an airman who said, "That's your helicopter over there, sir." Johnson responded, "Son, they are all my helicopters." He once called the State of the Union speech the "State of My Union address."

PRESIDENTIAL ABUSE OF POWER: THE IRAN-CONTRA AFFAIR

During the early 1980s, eight Americans were kidnapped and held hostage in Lebanon by Muslim extremist groups, some of whom were supported by Iran and its leader, the Ayatollah Khomeini. One hostage, a Central Intelligence Agency (CIA) operative assigned to our Beirut embassy, was killed.

This situation was an embarrassment to President Reagan who, in the 1980 election, belittled his predecessor Jimmy Carter for not being able to free hostages who had been kidnapped from the American embassy in Iran. In 1984, when Reagan campaigned for reelection using slogans such as "America is back, and standing tall," our continuing inability to secure the release of the hostages appeared inconsistent with that message.

In an attempt to free the hostages, President Reagan decided to let the CIA secretly sell weapons to Iran for use in its war against Iraq. He hoped this would convince the Iranians to release the hostages. The sale was opposed by Reagan's secretary of state, George Schultz, and his secretary of defense, Caspar Weinberger, but was urged by national security adviser John Poindexter and his subordinate, Lt. Col. Oliver North.

According to federal law, Reagan was required to notify Congress of the secret arms sale. At the urging of North, and perhaps others, he did not do so.[1]

As a result of Reagan's decision, 2,008 antitank missiles were sent to Iran along with parts for antiaircraft missiles.[2] Everything was kept secret until a pro-Syrian Lebanese publication broke the news in November. This led to more revelations. News surfaced that we had also shipped arms to Iran earlier, in September 1985. Robert McFarlane, then national security adviser, told a congressional committee the president had approved these sales orally. Reagan said he did not remember. And Attorney General Edwin Meese revealed that profits from the sales were used to aid the Nicaraguan Contras, again in violation of the law.

Reactions were overwhelmingly negative. Reagan's popularity plummeted.[3] Media analyses began comparing the Iran-contra scandal to Watergate. The public and Congress asked what the president knew and when he knew it. At first the president called North a "national hero." Then he fired him.

For the next several years, various investigations tried to find out if the president had authorized breaking the law (and hence violated his constitutional oath) and if Vice President George Bush knew about it. A presidential fact-finding commission reported that Reagan was removed from day-to-day business and that his management of foreign policy was lax and ineffective. Reagan reported to the commission that he could not remember when he authorized arms sales to Iran and that he knew nothing about diversion of funds to the contras. But in 1987, Reagan contradicted his earlier claim by declaring, "I was very definitely involved in the decisions about support to the freedom fighters [the Contras]—my idea to begin with."

The congressional hearings investigating the matter suggested that Reagan did know what was going on, and opinion surveys continued to report that most people thought Reagan was lying when he said he didn't remember.[4]

In well-publicized criminal trials, North and Poindexter claimed they had followed the orders of their superiors,

Most recent presidents eventually learned hard lessons about the limits of presidential power. Indeed, the moral of the personal presidency suggests we have an "impossible" or "imperiled" presidency. Presidents who become popular by making exaggerated promises have trouble keeping them and their popularity in a system of fragmented power.

The presidency is responsive in that the president has an almost direct relationship with the public. Using the media, the president can tell us what he wants and attempt to shape our opinion. Through public opinion polls and the ballot box, we tell the president what we think. In this relationship there is a danger of overreponsiveness. To remain popular, a president may seek short-term solutions to the nation's problems and neglect long-term interests. Short-term responsiveness that caters to public opinion can siphon off the attention and resources a president should be devoting to the real needs of the nation.

EPILOGUE

"Every Step of the Way"

Al Gore made the trip to Illinois and Wisconsin with the president, and he did not go quietly. At public assemblies, his introductions of Clinton were so rousing and emotion-laden that they almost upstaged the president's talks. Evening news coverage focused on Gore's departure from his usual tepid delivery. Given his political situation, Clinton drew unusually receptive audiences, but Gore was not simply responding to vibrations from the audience. He and his staff had carefully considered their options before Gore decided on the tenor of his remarks.[70]

In many ways Gore's decision was a foregone conclusion given his political alliance with the president and friendship with both of the Clintons. When Clinton has needed Gore, he has been there, and when Gore has needed Clinton, the president has reciprocated. Aside from his personal feelings of loyalty, Gore had little to gain, and a lot to lose, in distancing himself from Clinton. Since everyone knows Gore wants the presidency, stepping back from Clinton, who has been unprecedentally generous including Reagan. North also said that Bush knew about illegal Contra supply efforts and had helped get other countries to assist the Contras in return for U.S. aid. Thus, the North and Poindexter trials also became Reagan's and Bush's. Evidence showed that Bush had not been "out of the loop," as he had claimed earlier. Bush regularly attended meetings from 1984 to 1986 dealing with the arms sales, hostages, and Contra aid.[5]

Fearing what some of his aides described as a "political witch hunt" after his defeat by Clinton,[6] Bush pardoned six Reagan-era officials, each of whom had been charged with or convicted of crimes related to the Iran-contra scandal. Bush decried what he saw as the "criminalization of policy differences" and argued that "the common denominator of their motivation—whether their actions were right or wrong—was patriotism. . . . [and] they did not profit or seek to profit from their conduct."[7]

Reactions to the pardons were quick and critical. Some critics charged that Bush had misused his pardon power. Others rebuked him for arguing that the prosecutor had criminalized policy differences when those who were pardoned had been accused or convicted of lawbreaking and lying to congressional and other investigators. A poll found that only 15% of those surveyed thought Bush's main reason for issuing the pardons was "to protect people he felt acted honorably and patriotically from unfair prosecution."[8]

The Iran-contra incident reveals the temptations offered to presidents to use illegal means to increase their power to make foreign policy. Although presidents have an inherent advantage over Congress in making foreign policy, they cannot legally operate in defiance of Congress. The Iran-contra affair raised serious questions about the accountability of the personal presidency that some thought had been resolved by the outcome of the Watergate scandal.

1. Much of the information in this section comes from James M. McCormick and Steven S. Smith, "The Iran Arms Sale and the Intelligence Oversight Act of 1980," *PS* 20 (Winter 1987), pp. 29–37.
2. Robert Pear, "The Story Thus Far: Assembling Some of the Pieces of the Puzzle," *New York Times*, December 14, 1986, Section 4, p. 1. "Reagan's Crusade," *Newsweek*, December 15, 1986, pp. 26–28.
3. Elizabeth Drew, "Letter from Washington," *The New Yorker*, August 31, 1987, p. 72.
4. For a critique of the congressional hearings, see Seymour M. Hersh, "The Iran-Contra Committees: Did They Protect Reagan?" *New York Times Magazine*, April 29, 1990, pp. 46–78; Louis Harris, "Iran-Contra Hearings Erode Faith in Reagan," *Lincoln Star*, May 25, 1987.
5. See Tom Blanton, "Iran-Contradictions: It's Time to Ask Where George Was," *Washington Post National Weekly Edition*, June 18–24, 1990, pp. 24–25; Richard Cohen, "What Did Bush Know?"; and Walter Pincus, "Has Bush Come Clean about Iran-Contra?" *Washington Post National Weekly Edition*, September 28–October 4, 1992, pp. 29 and 31–32.
6. "Pardon Me," *Newsweek*, January 4, 1993, p. 15.
7. Leslie H. Gelb, "Bush's Ethical Manure," *New York Times*, December 27, 1992, p. E11.
8. "Pardon Me." See also George Lardner, Jr., and Walter Pincus, "Dear Diary: Now, about Iran-Contra . . . ," *Washington Post National Weekly Edition*, January 25–31, 1993, p. 31; see also George Lardner, Jr., and Walter Pincus, "The Source of the Iran-Contra Mess Is Tracked to Reagan," *Washington Post National Weekly Edition*, January 24–30, 1994, p. 13.

to his vice president, would only look crass and calculating. But did Gore have to go as far as he did, practically screaming his loyalty, emphasizing their personal friendship, and cajoling the public to "stand by his side"?

Gore's career has been built on personal character and credibility, as well as on devotion to policy detail. His reputation had taken some hard hits from the fund-raising allegations and his ties to the tobacco industry; he did not need any more questions about his character and credibility. After saying publicly that if he ran for the presidency, he would not try to separate himself from Clinton because he had been with him "every step of the way," Gore would have a lot of explaining to do. After the Lewinsky scandal broke, Tipper Gore had said, "I don't anticipate anybody being able to divide the Clintons and the Gores. Ever."[71] With this said, Gore was in a situation where half-measures or sitting on the fence, might not have worked.

In addition, Gore has been through this before. The Lewinsky scandal could turn out differently from other ethics crises the administration has weathered, but to Gore it may have had the feel of just one more partisan assault. Not for nothing has Clinton been known as the "Comeback Kid." And in the unlikely event it did lead to a resignation, Gore would walk into the Oval Office as a man to whom personal and political loyalty meant something, as someone irrevocably tied to Clinton's policies, but whose personal life was never in danger of being confused with his predecessor's.

In reaffirming his support for the president, Gore was boosting confidence in someone from whom he probably can no longer be distanced, as well as in an administration on whose accomplishments he will run. And, unlike many vice presidents, Gore will have every right to do this since he has had a hand in shaping most of its major policy. This is both the advantage and the price of the partnership he has developed with the president.

KEY TERMS

impeachment
senatorial courtesy
executive privilege
executive orders
head of state
personal presidency
power to persuade
divided government
parliamentary government
line-item veto
War Powers Act

FURTHER READING

Michael R. Beschloss, ed., *Taking Charge: The Johnson White House Tapes*, 1963–64 (New York: Simon & Schuster, 1997). Listen in on White House conversations President Johnson taped during his first year in office and see how one of the legendary exercisers of legislative and executive powers used his powers of persuasion in the conduct of office and hear his thoughts on the assassination of President Kennedy.

Colin Campbell and Margaret Jane Wyszomirski, eds., *Executive Leadership in Anglo-American Systems* (Pittsburgh: University of Pittsburgh Press, 1991). Comparisons of presidential government in the United States and British and Canadian cabinet government with respect to domestic and foreign policymaking, the roles of political appointees and civil servants, and media relations.

Joseph J. Ellis, *American Sphinx: The Character of Thomas Jefferson* (New York: Knopf, 1997). A fascinating look at the mind and presidential style of one of America's greatest presidents.

Doris Kearns Goodwin, *No Ordinary Time* (New York: Simon & Schuster, 1994). An engaging study of life in the White House and the leadership of Franklin Roosevelt during World War II.

Charles O. Jones, *The Presidency in a Separated System* (Washington, D.C.: Brookings Institution, 1994). A book for post–Cold War times, it argues that constitutional limits make popular expectations of presidential leadership unrealistic and that responsibility for public policy must be shared by all branches of government.

Richard E. Neustadt, *Presidential Power and the Modern Presidents* (New York: Free Press, 1990). The most cited book on the presidency, it argues that presidential power is based on the ability to persuade.

Bradley H. Patterson, Jr., *The Ring of Power: The White House Staff and Its Expanding Role in Government* (New York: Basic Books, 1988). This book sees White House operations as so complex and involving so many officials that "the only decision a president carries out himself is to go to the bathroom."

Robert B. Reich, *Locked in the Cabinet* (New York: Knopf, 1997). The former secretary of labor's diary of his years of service in the Clinton cabinet. Although his memory of events has been challenged, it is an informative and witty account of life in the executive branch.

Bob Woodward, *The Commanders* (New York: Simon & Schuster, 1991). An account of how Bush's White House brought the nation to war in the Persian Gulf that reveals high-level differences of opinion that did not surface in the months before the war.

ELECTRONIC RESOURCES

http://www.pbs.org/wgbh/pages/amex/presidents/indexjs.html

The American Presidents Series from PBS's American Experience. The "Decision Interactive" page allows users to make voting decisions in a simulated presidential campaign. The site also has transcripts of the televised biographies of Theodore and Franklin Roosevelt, Truman, Eisenhower, Kennedy, Johnson, Nixon, and Reagan.

http://whitehouse.gov/

The White House home page has links to the Office of the Vice President, the First Lady, and all other EOP offices. You can tour the White House, read presidential speeches, and e-mail the president. The link to the First Lady's home page allows viewers to send e-mail, look at the work of the office, and link to biographies of each of America's First Ladies.

http://www.pbs.org/wgbh/pages/frontline/shows/arkansas

Contains the transcript of Frontline's documentary "Once Upon a Time in Arkansas: The Deals and Relationships at the Heart of the Whitewater Scandal." Also at the Frontline site is its documentary on the office of the special prosecutor.

INFOTRAC CITATIONS

"Prospects for the 2000 Democratic Nomination"
"Congressional Sausage"
"Hillary's Resurrection"

NOTES

1. Richard L. Berke, "The Gore Guide to the Future," *New York Times Magazine*, February 22, 1998, pp. 30–35, 46–70. Other sources for this section include Richard L. Berke, "Gore Is No Typical Vice President in the Shadows, *New York Times*, February 19, 1995, pp. 1, 16; L. Edward Purcell, ed., *The Vice Presidents: A Biographical Dictionary* (New York: Facts on File, 1998), pp. 401–407.

2. Theodore J. Lowi, *The Personal President* (Ithaca, N.Y.: Cornell University Press, 1985).

3. Arthur M. Schlesinger, Jr., *The Imperial Presidency* (Boston: Houghton Mifflin, 1973).

4. Harold M. Barger, *The Impossible Presidency* (Glenview, Ill.: Scott-Foresman, 1984).

5. Richard Morin, "A Pollster's Worst Nightmare: Declining Response Rates," *Washington Post National Weekly Edition*, July 5–11, 1993, p. 37; John Hibbing and Elizabeth Theiss-Morse, *Congress as Public Enemy* (Cambridge: Cambridge University Press, 1995).

6. Jefferson's management of the presidency is described in Joseph J. Ellis, *American Sphinx: The Character of Thomas Jefferson* (New York: Knopf, 1997), pp. 186–228.

7. For discussion of the president's removal powers in light of a 1988 Supreme Court decision regarding independent counsels, see John A. Rohr, "Public Administration, Executive Power, and Constitutional Confusion," and Rosemary O'Leary, "Response to John Rohr," *Public Administrative Review* 49 (March/April 1989), pp. 108–115.

8. Charles O. Jones, *The Presidency in a Separated System* (Washington, D.C.: The Brookings Institution, 1994), p. 53.

9. *The Presidency A to Z: A Ready Reference Encyclopedia* (Washington, D.C.: Congressional Quarterly, 1992), p. 169.

10. Ibid., p. 170.

11. *United States v. Curtiss-Wright Export Corporation*, 299 U.S. 304 (1936).

12. See the discussion in the *Federalist Paper* #69, written by Alexander Hamilton.

13. Quoted in "Notes and Comment," *New Yorker*, June 1, 1987, p. 23.

14. Ibid.

15. John Barry, "What Schwarzkopf's Book Leaves Out," *Newsweek*, September 28, 1992, p. 68.

16. *Youngstown Sheet and Tube Co. v. Sawyer*, 343 U.S. 579 (1952).

17. Thomas F. Cronin, *The State of the Presidency* (Boston: Little, Brown, 1975), p. 118.

18. James Reston, "Cut the Public Relations Budget," *Lincoln Star*, February 7, 1989, p. 6.

19. Jones, *The Presidency*, pp. 56–57.

20. Fred I. Greenstein, *The Hidden-Hand Presidency* (New York: Basic Books, 1982), p. 139.

21. Quoted in Richard Pious, *The American Presidency* (New York: Basic Books, 1979), p. 244.

22. Ann Reilly Dowd, "What Managers Can Learn from Manager Reagan," *Fortune*, September 15, 1986, pp. 32–41.

23. See John H. Kessel, "The Structures of the Reagan White House," *American Journal of Political Science* 28 (May 1984), pp. 231–258.

24. Hillary Rodham Clinton quoted in Carol Gelderman, *All the Presidents' Words: The Bully Pulpit and the Creation of the Virtual Presidency* (New York: Walker, 1997), p. 160.

25. Maureen Dowd, "On Washington: Beached," *New York Times Magazine*, June 19, 1994, p. 18.

26. "The White House Office," *U.S. Government Manual, 1997–1998*, pp. 90–93.

27. Edith P. Mayo, ed., *The Smithsonian Book of First Ladies* (Washington, D.C.: Smithsonian Institution, 1996), p. 11.

28. Gil Troy, *Affairs of State: The Rise and Rejection of the First Couple since World War II* (New York: Free Press, 1997), p. 250. Troy also discusses attempts at reorganizing the First Lady's office. See especially pp. 178–188, and pp. 248–258.

29. For a review of the backgrounds of men who have served in the vice presidency and the roles they have played, see Purcell, *The Vice Presidents*.

30. Michael Nelson, *A Heartbeat Away* (New York: Priority Press, 1988). For more on the vice presidency, see Paul C. Light, *Vice-Presidential Power: Advice and Influence in the White House* (Baltimore: Johns Hopkins University Press, 1984), and George Sirgiovanni, "The 'Van Buren Jinx': Vice Presidents Need Not Beware," *Presidential Studies Quarterly* 18 (Winter 1988), pp. 61–76.

31. Purcell, *The Vice Presidents*, p. 380.

32. Jeffrey K. Tulis, *The Rhetorical Presidency* (Princeton, N.J.: Princeton University Press, 1987).

33. Garry Wills, *Lincoln at Gettysburg* (New York: Simon & Schuster, 1992), p. 31.

34. David Halberstam, *The Powers That Be* (New York: Dell, 1980), p. 30.

35. Lowi, *The Personal President*.

36. Associated Press, "Poll Shows Americans Want a Strong Leader," *Lincoln Journal*, June 16, 1992, p. 5.

37. "A Talk with Clinton," *Newsweek*, January 25, 1993, p. 37.

38. Bush's ratings fluctuated considerably. They achieved record highs during the Persian Gulf War after being fairly low in mid-1990.

39. Richard E. Neustadt, *Presidential Power: The Politics of Leadership from FDR to Carter* (New York: John Wiley & Sons, 1980).

40. Samuel Kernell, *Going Public: New Strategies of Presidential Leadership* (Washington, D.C.: CQ Press, 1986), p. 15.

41. Ibid.

42. Ibid., pp. 38–42.

43. Ibid., p. 120.

44. "Notes and Comments," *The New Yorker*, November 7, 1988, p. 29.

45. From presidential scholar Fred I. Greenstein, quoted in "White House Notebook: When Clinton Speaks . . . Does Anyone Listen?"*National Journal*, February 11, 1995, p. 378.

46. "The Presidency," *Newsweek*, December 20, 1993, p. 46.

47. George C. Edwards III, *The Public Presidency* (New York: St. Martin's Press, 1983), p. 253.

48. John Mueller, *War, Presidents and Public Opinion* (New York: John Wiley & Sons, 1970).

49. For example, see Edwards, *The Public Presidency*, pp. 239–247.

50. Poll scores reported here are from the following *National Journal* issues: December 8, 1990, p. 2993; January 19, 1991, p. 185; and February 16, 1991, p. 412.

51. For more on the Gulf War's impact on Bush's ratings, see John A. Krosnick and Laura A. Brannon, "The Impact of the Gulf War on the Ingredients of Presidential Evaluations: Multidimensional Effects of Political Involvement," *American Political Science Review* 87 (December 1993), pp. 963–975.

52. Richard Morin, "A-Not-So-Bad Midterm Grade," *Washington Post Weekly Edition*, February 20–26, 1995, p. 37.

53. These survey results are from "Opinion Outlook," *National Journal*, February 18, 1995, p. 452.

54. M. Fiorina, *Divided Government* (New York: Macmillan, 1992), p. 7.

55. D. R. Mayhew, "Divided Party Control: Does It Make a Difference?" *PS: Political Science and Politics*, December 1991, pp. 637–640.

56. Reported in George C. Edwards III, *Presidential Influence in Congress* (San Francisco: W. H. Freeman, 1980), p. 125.

57. Quoted in Dick Kirschten, "Reagan Warms Up for Political Hardball," *National Journal*, February 9, 1985, p. 328.

58. Edwards, *Presidential Influence*, p. 127.

59. "A Furor over the Secret War," *Newsweek*, April 23, 1984, p. 22.

60. Charles W. Ostrom, Jr., and Brian I. Job, "The President and the Political Use of Force," *American Political Science Review* 80 (June 1986), pp. 541–566.

61. Quoted in Lowi, *The Personal President*, p. 133.

62. Elizabeth Drew, "Letter From Washington," *The New Yorker*, February 4, 1991, p. 83.

63. Richard J. Stoll, "The Sound of the Guns," *American Politics Quarterly* 15 (April 1987), pp. 223–237.

64. Richard J. Barnet, *The Rockets' Red Glare: When America Goes to War—The Presidents and the People* (New York: Simon & Schuster, 1990).

65. Karen Toombs Parsons, "Exploring the 'Two Presidents' Phenomenon: New Evidence from the Truman Administration," *Presidential Studies Quarterly* 24 (Summer 1994), pp. 495–514.

66. Richard E. Neustadt, *Presidential Power: The Politics of Leadership from FDR to Carter* (New York: John Wiley & Sons, 1980).

67. Quoted in Arthur M. Schlesinger Jr., "The Ultimate Approval Rating," *New York Times Magazine*, December 18, 1996, p. 50.

68. Ibid.

69. Ibid.

70. Berke, "The Gore Guide to the Future," p. 32.

71. Quoted in ibid., p. 34.

Bureau of Engraving and Printing employees check the quality of $20 bills. The woman on the right is holding $8,000 of mistakes.

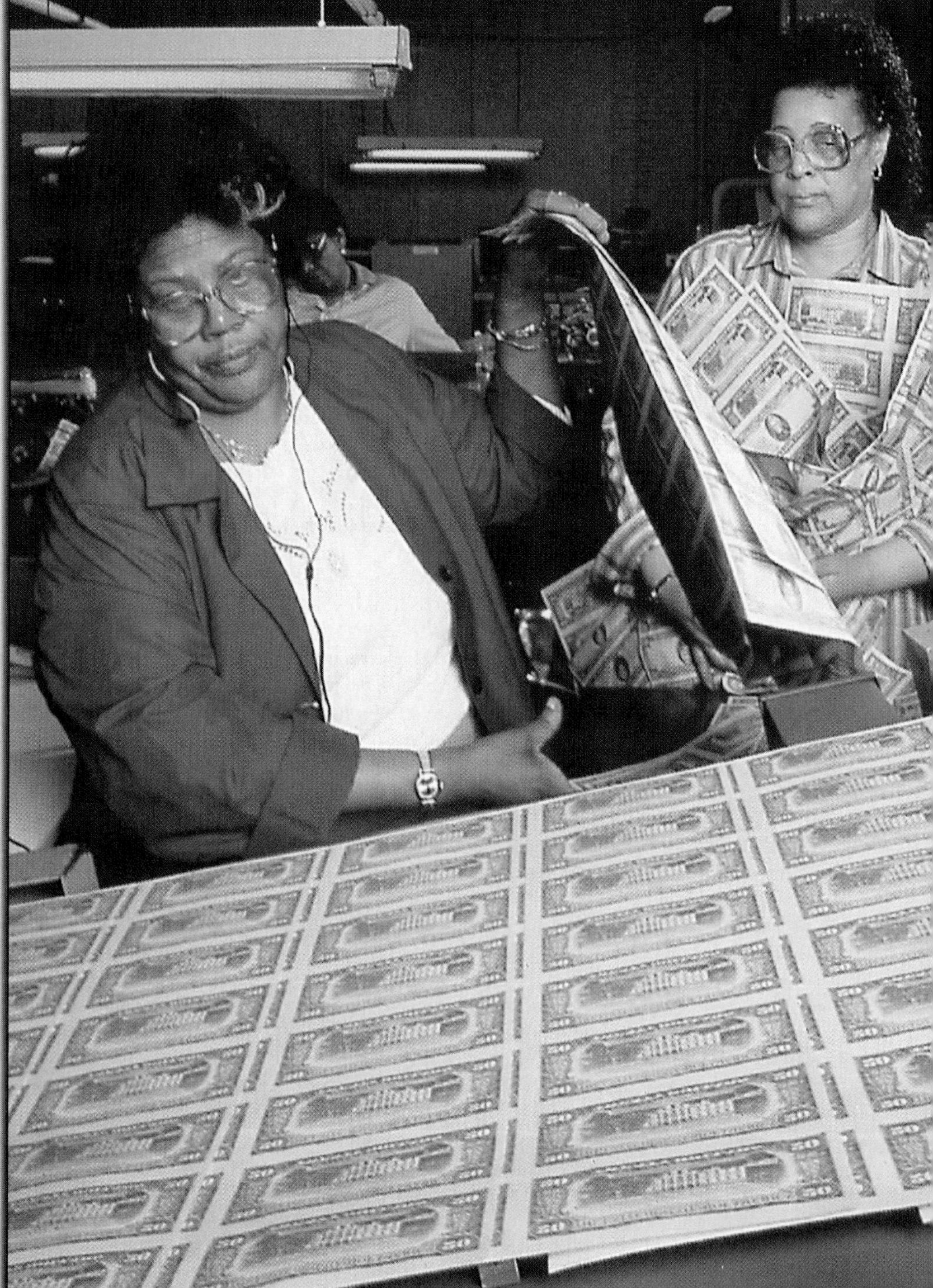

Ted Thai/*Time* magazine

12 THE BUREAUCRACY

OUTLINE

- **Bureaucracy**
  - Nature of Bureaucracy
  - Public and Private Bureaucracies
- **Federal Bureaucracy**
  - Growth of the Bureaucracy
  - Why the Bureaucracy Has Grown
  - Types of Bureaucracy
- **Bureaucratic Functions**
  - Making Policy
  - Administering Policy
  - Other Functions
- **Expectations about the Federal Bureaucracy**
  - Responsiveness
  - Neutral Competence
- **Controlling the Bureaucracy**
  - President
  - Congress
  - Courts
  - Interest Groups and Individuals
- **Conclusion: Is the Bureaucracy Responsive?**

YOU ARE THERE

Attacking AIDS

You are the government's top medical officer, the surgeon general of the United States, C. Everett Koop. It is 1986 and President Reagan has asked you to report to him on what has become a major problem: AIDS, or acquired immune deficiency syndrome. AIDS involves a virus that weakens the body's immunity, making it vulnerable to deadly infections.

There have been more than 35,000 cases of AIDS so far in the United States, 493 of them children. Those who contract AIDS inevitably die, as 20,000 Americans have so far. You estimate that 1.5 million people have been exposed to the virus and that 270,000 will develop AIDS by 1991.[1] In the United States, people at most risk of getting it are intravenous drug users and homosexual men.[2] However, AIDS has begun to appear among heterosexual men and women through contact with intravenous drug users, prostitutes, bisexuals, and those who had multiple blood transfusions before the spring of 1985, when blood banks began testing for AIDS.

As long as almost all the victims came from the first two groups, most people did not worry about AIDS. As it began to spread, however, it became a major issue arousing considerable public anxiety. For example, real estate agents trying to sell Rock Hudson's house found that clients would not enter it because they knew he had died of AIDS. And some parents have tried to bar child victims of AIDS from the schools their children attend.

Now the president has asked for a report advising him what to do. You do not expect an effective vaccine to be available until the mid-1990s at the earliest. A major issue that your report must deal with is whether we should require mandatory testing for AIDS. A blood test can reveal exposure to the AIDS virus, but it cannot predict who will get the disease because some who carry the virus will not contract the disease. Still, finding out who has been exposed to the virus can help limit the exposure of others to it.

Already, military recruits and Foreign Service officers must take a blood test to determine if they have been exposed to AIDS. Proposals have been made to test many others, such as convicted prostitutes and intravenous drug users, hospital patients from 15 to 49 years of age, venereal disease patients, and couples seeking marriage licenses. Secretary of Education William Bennett, whose views often echo the president's, also wants to include prison inmates and people planning to immigrate here. He says the government should notify spouses and past sexual partners if test results are positive—that is, if evidence of exposure to AIDS is found.

Many conservatives view AIDS as a moral issue. They think AIDS is a punishment for homosexuality and drug use. Some charge that public health officials are "intimidated by the homosexual lobby." One called AIDS the "first politically protected disease in the history of mankind."[3] They want you to recommend mandatory testing to identify who is infected so government can quarantine those who will not change their sexual or drug habits to protect society.

Most public health experts reject mandatory testing as unworkable. They argue that many people will go underground to avoid being tested. They also say mandatory testing of huge numbers of people will produce mistakes in test results. Further, most experts oppose mandatory testing as a violation of doctor/patient confidentiality and doubt that most people will identify their sexual partners. They add that mandatory testing will only increase discrimination against homosexuals and others who have been exposed to AIDS and who may or may not contract it.

Few experts agree with Secretary Bennett, who argues that the key to stopping AIDS is to teach sexual abstinence to our children. Most experts recommend educating young people about "safe sex" and contraception. They say abstinence as a policy is unrealistic given the emphasis on sex in our society, as illustrated by studies showing that television programming refers to sexual intercourse at least once an hour. Their views reflect Senator Paul Simon's (D-Ill.)

Former Surgeon General Koop visits an AIDS patient.

remark that, "It's been too long since [Bennett] was a teenager."

Many conservatives object strongly to sex education in schools. Referring to "safe sodomy" instead of "safe sex," they say "condomania" means we have given up trying to raise our children properly.

The president is comfortable with conservative views on AIDS. When he appointed you, you were a surgeon in Philadelphia, known for having pioneered techniques to separate Siamese twins and for being a born-again Christian with conservative views on abortion and birth control. You know your views were more important to the president than your surgical innovations. You agree with him on many issues and want to write a report he will like. Your political instincts push you this way.

On the other side of the coin, and in government there is always another side to the coin, you are a doctor who respects the views of health care professionals. You want to write a report that will help fight AIDS, without political interference. What should you do?

Americans expect their government to deliver billions of dollars worth of services to them, from highways for fast-moving cars to Social Security payments on time, from clean running water to safe neighborhoods, from protection from foreign enemies to cures for cancer. At the same time, most Americans denigrate their government and its bureaucracy, and some even express hatred toward it. In 1995, in Oklahoma City, scores of people were murdered because they were federal bureaucrats (or happened to be in the same building with bureaucrats).

Despite the strong emotions sometimes directed toward them, federal bureaucrats are ordinary people. But the jobs they are asked to do and the number of different groups to which they are responsible make them a target for public distress with society's problems.

The federal bureaucracy employs nearly 3 million civilians, who work in more than 800 different occupations in 100 agencies, and over 2 million uniformed military personnel. The bureaucracy executes or enforces policies made by Congress and the president. Because policymakers have given government many different goals, the bureaucracy has many different jobs. It analyzes the soil, runs hospitals and utilities, fights drug abuse, checks manufacturers' claims about their products, to mention only a few bureaucratic responsibilities.

To some, the bureaucracy is the fourth branch of government—powerful, uncontrollable, and often seeming to have a life of its own. As the part of government that carries out the law, the bureaucracy is also political. People disagree about whether it does its job well, largely because they disagree about the goals policymakers set for it. One person's lazy, red tape–ridden, uncaring bureaucracy is another's responsive agency.

BUREAUCRACY

Around the turn of the century, the German social scientist Max Weber predicted that bureaucracy would someday dominate society. That future is now. Bureaucracy affects almost everything we do.

Nature of Bureaucracy

Although individual bureaucracies differ in many ways, all share some common features.[4] For example, all have hierarchies of authority; that is, everyone in a bureaucracy has a place in a pyramidal network of jobs with fewer near the top and more near the bottom. Almost everyone in a bureaucracy has a boss and, unless one is at the bottom of a hierarchy, some subordinates.

Individuals with more expertise and experience tend to have more authority. As a result, bureaucracy is not always consistent with democratic principles, which hold that everyone should have the same opportunity to influence events. Indeed, bureaucracy can endanger individual opportunities to express opinions, raise doubts about the value of individual opinions, and jeopardize the availability of information to individuals. In effect, bureaucratic tendencies, if unrestrained, can transform "citizens" into "subordinates."

Public and Private Bureaucracies

Many people associate public bureaucracies with monotony and inefficiency. A Virginia company sold a

"Bureaucrat" doll, calling it "a product of no redeeming social value. Place the Bureaucrat on a stack of papers on your desk, and he will just sit on them."[5]

Although stereotyping the public service can produce some laughs, it misses the similarities shared by public and private bureaucracies. For example, both involve a good deal of routine. Auditing expense vouchers is as routine in a business firm as in a public agency. Both also have workers who are productive and efficient and others who are not. Executives in the Defense Department bought $600 toilet seats and spent more than $75 apiece for metal screws sold elsewhere for 57 cents. Their private counterparts at Chrysler, Lockheed, Penn Central, and hundreds of banks and savings and loans ran their businesses into the ground.

To some extent, the distinction between private and public bureaucracies has become blurred.[6] However, Americans typically distinguish public from private bureaucracies by looking at goals and openness.

GOALS

Businesses are supposed to make a profit while public agencies are supposed to promote the "public interest." Although people disagree over what the "public interest" is, they know public agencies do not exist to make a profit.

Public and private bureaucratic goals differ in another way too. It is usually easier to measure and put a value on efforts to achieve private goals than public ones. We can identify the value of a chair or a house by computing the cost of building them. Placing a value on such public goals as consumer safety or education is much harder. How many children must die from eating the contents of medicine bottles before government should require pharmaceutical manufacturers to use childproof caps on bottles? How many lives saved make it worthwhile for government to require auto manufacturers to install side-impact beams, thereby raising auto prices?

Difficulties in measuring what government agencies do and disagreements over defining the public interest often produce charges that public bureaucracy is wasteful. Indeed, over two-thirds of the American public believes government programs are usually inefficient and wasteful.[7] Of course, private corporations may waste far more than government.[8] But government spending is so great that even if it wastes only proportionally as much money as a typical citizen does, the sums are vast.

Discussions of government "waste" are confusing because they refer to two quite different things. One involves inefficient or corrupt government agencies, those that, for example, do not get competitive bids and therefore pay more than they need to for supplies. Waste also occurs when more employees are hired than are necessary to do a job, when consultants are paid to do little, or when errors are made in calculating welfare or farm subsidy payments so that recipients are overpaid.

"I'm sorry, dear, but you knew I was a bureaucrat when you married me."

The Under Secretary of Energy
Washington, D.C. 20585

December, 1992

MEMORANDUM FOR SECRETARIAL OFFICERS

SUBJECT: NE/NE-60 Concurrence

Recently, memoranda have been prepared for my signature or directed to departmental offices from other departmental offices which contain statements regarding whether the direction contained in the memorandum is applicable to Naval Reactors (NE-60). Several memoranda have been incorrect in their assumption regarding the effects on NE-60, resulting in unnecessary further correspondence to correct the misunderstanding.

Applicability to NE-60 of a contemplated action is not always obvious. In many cases, the impact is either indirect or the direct impact is not appreciated due to lack of understanding of the scope of NE-60 responsibility. To avoid misunderstandings in the future, you are requested to consult NE regarding applicability statements before they are made and before memoranda are presented to me, the Secretary, or Deputy Secretary for signature.

I appreciate your attention to this matter.

Hugo Pomrehn
Hugo Pomrehn

Sometimes real examples of bureaucratic thinking are stranger than ones we might imagine. Every issue, Washington Monthly *reprints a memo containing an especially striking example of bureaucratic language. Is it any wonder ordinary people do not trust—or understand—the bureaucracy?*

A second kind of government "waste" is a program that some people find objectionable, no matter how well run it is. This meaning of waste has little to do with mismanagement or fraud. Waste in this sense may mean that a particular program serves relatively few people at a large cost. For example, a government commission labeled the operation of hundreds of very small post offices "wasteful." The commission did not allege fraud or mismanagement but said the post offices cost a lot for the small number of people served. However, residents of small communities argued that their post offices were not a waste but an important source of community pride.

The average citizen probably does not think much about waste, particularly this second kind, in private bureaucracies. If a business or industry makes a profit, we assume it is not being wasteful. We may not like chocolate-covered raisins, but we do not consider their manufacturer wasteful for making them as long as the product is profitable.

OPENNESS

The openness of public bureaucracy is a second way of distinguishing it from private bureaucracy. Both often have internal disagreements about their goals, but differences about public agency goals are usually more visible. This visibility, or openness, helps to make public agencies responsive. Only by having knowledge of both the process and the content of public decisions can interested groups and individuals express their preferences effectively.

The question, of course, is openness to whom? Because the bureaucracy is doing the public's business, one answer is being open to the public. But being open to the public also means being open to the media who want to report significant conflicts and decisions made in the executive branch and open to interest groups who want to influence agencies' decisions.

In the Sunshine Act of 1977 and the Freedom of Information Act of 1966, as amended in 1974, Congress recognized the importance of keeping public bureaucracies open. The Sunshine Act requires regulatory agencies, such as the Food and Drug Administration, to give advance notice of the date, time, place, and agenda of their meetings and to follow certain rules to prevent unwarranted secrecy. The Freedom of Information Act lets people obtain information from agencies if it is not classified or concerned with sensitive matters.

The Freedom of Information Act was intended to make agencies more open to the public, but most requests for information come from businesses, interest groups, lawyers, and the media. Very few members of the general public take advantage of it. But groups that are directly affected by an agency's decisions have a strong incentive to use the act. Thus, in 1985, 85% of the requests for information submitted to the Food and Drug Administration came from companies that it regulates. That information enables those companies to evaluate their strategies for influencing the agency's decisions that affect them. And media want to uncover disagreements and conflicts in the agency's internal decision-making process, something no agency would welcome.

Efforts to make government agencies more open often run up against a desire to limit the distribution of critical or embarrassing information. It is the rare public or private bureaucracy that wants to reveal its failures. Thus, an evaluation of the Freedom of Information Act found that agencies used many tactics to discourage people from seeking information, such as delaying responses to requests, charging high fees for copies of records (the State Department once charged $10 a page for copying records), and requiring detailed descriptions of material in requests for information.[9] In 1993, the Federal Bureau of Investigation (FBI) refused to expedite the release of information to a prisoner on death row who was afraid he would be executed before the information was available. (The FBI's judgment that his situation did not show "exceptional need or urgency" was overruled by a federal court.)[10]

As the chief executive, a president's views on the openness of agencies have also been important. Recent presidents have had different views. Under Reagan and Bush, federal agencies adopted a narrow reading of the act, making it more difficult to get information.[11] Carter and Clinton attempted, somewhat unsuccessfully, to open the bureaucracy more and to classify fewer pieces of information. President Carter banned the classification of files lacking a clear relation to national security. In 1995, President Clinton issued an executive order that directed that most documents 25 years old or older be declassified and put a 10-year limit on how long documents can remain classified unless a review determines that they should remain so.[12]

Finally, problems with the Freedom of Information Act have surfaced because it was written with the expectation that all information would be on paper. But the federal government, like private businesses, stores an increasing amount of information electronically. The federal bureaucracy now has millions of computers, compared to only 17,500 in 1985. Retrieving the growing mass of information stored on computer can be easier than finding information on paper. However, the act neither defines when electronic information is in the public domain nor requires agencies to save and release it. Thus, the act does not say whether electronic messages used by officials to schedule meetings or exchange opinions are their private property or public records. Reagan, Bush, and Clinton aides used e-mail extensively. Bush took his aides' e-mail tapes with him when he left office and argued that the tapes were not public property. A federal appeals court ruled that these tapes are public records and must be preserved. The Clinton administration sided with Bush and argued that White House officials have a right to erase the e-mail messages they send to each other.[13] Defining such messages as public helps hold officials accountable. The act also fails to address problems created by the loss of data over time because tapes and disks deteriorate or are incompatible with new generations of hardware and software. Congress has been trying to remedy computer-related problems for several years without success.

Some agencies are more open than others. Agencies that depend on public support and agreement with their goals are more likely to respond to media requests for information and news. The Food and Drug Administration, for instance, is much more accessible than the State Department.[14] Other agencies prefer less coverage. For them, no news is good news. The balance between openness and responsiveness to the public and undue access for interest groups and the media has been difficult to strike.

Despite the limitations of the Freedom of Information Act, it has enabled individuals and groups to gain important, useful, and even entertaining information. Citizens have used the Freedom of Information Act to gather injury and fatality information on defective cars, to assess dangerous infant formulas, to reveal a link between aspirin and a disease known as Reye's syndrome, to learn that J. Edgar Hoover and the FBI had planted a rumor that Jane Fonda proposed killing Richard Nixon, and to reveal that Elvis Presley volunteered to become an FBI informant but was not accepted.[15]

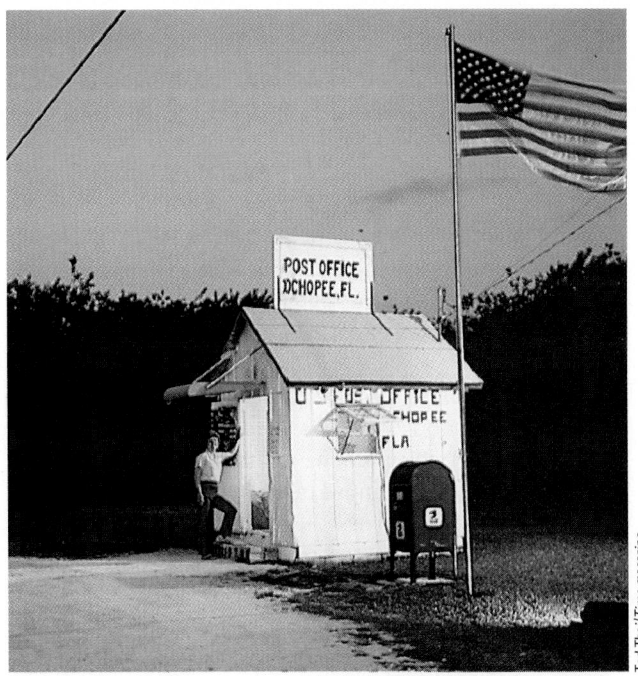

Ted Thai/*Time* magazine

Some local post offices are economically inefficient, but residents of small towns lobby Congress to keep them open.

FEDERAL BUREAUCRACY

Growth of the Bureaucracy

The Founders did not discuss the federal "bureaucracy," but they did recognize the need for an administration to carry out laws and programs. They envisioned administrators with only a little power, charged with "executive details" and "mere execution" of the law. But the growing size and complexity of modern society and increasing demands that government do more have dramatically changed the nature of the federal bureaucracy.

George Washington's first cabinet included only three departments and the offices of attorney general and postmaster general, employing a few hundred people.

SYMBOLIC SOLUTIONS FOR COMPLEX PROBLEMS?

SLASHING THE BUREAUCRACY

Government bureaucrats have a long history of getting under Americans' skins (recall that opposition to the king's tax collectors helped to fuel the American Revolution). Despite this perennial irritation, government continues to grow. Most Americans think government is too big, and there are many proposals to cut it. The Clinton administration plans to cut nearly 300,000 federal government positions by 1999. Republicans have proposed the end of the Departments of Education, Commerce, Housing and Urban Development, and Labor, as well as scores of government programs located in other agencies. But is cutting the size of the bureaucracy a real solution to our country's problems? Or is it a symbolic solution?

Cutting the size of the bureaucracy is a real solution if it would make government more efficient, save money, and allow us to direct more resources to attack the nation's problems or to reduce the deficit. For example, Clinton's proposed "reinvention of government," led by Vice President Gore, would cut 2,400 jobs from Health and Human Services by eliminating a layer of management, consolidating dozens of programs, turning some work over to private business, and giving states a bigger role in these programs. The vice president argues that this would create a more "customer friendly" agency.[1]

Some of those who wish to cut some of the federal agencies mentioned above believe that services can be improved by merging programs that duplicate each other, cutting some programs that no longer serve an urgent need, and increasing resources for other, more pressing needs, including deficit reduction.

Other institutions, particularly some large corporations, have found that they can operate more efficiently and serve their customers better by consolidations, cutting, and reducing the layers of management. If government achieves these successes, cutting government could be a real solution.

On the other hand, cutting government may be mostly a symbolic solution that does not really help us solve our nation's problems more effectively. Cutting government might not save money. For example, if private firms take over the provision of services, costs could fall, but they could also increase. Those who can pay will get the services, though not necessarily at a lower cost.[2]

Some advocates of cutting the size of government think local government can handle problems more efficiently. This may be true in some instances but not in others. After all, the federal government got into the programs it did because some constituencies were not satisfied with local or state handling of programs.

And, though we can all point to some agencies that seem ineffective, many agencies do their jobs well, and eliminating them would increase, not decrease, problems—for example, the Social Security Administration, the Securities and Exchange Commission, the air traffic control system, the Secret Service, among others. In fact, there is little evidence that, on the whole, public bureaucracies are less effective than private ones.[3]

Moreover, if we eliminated those agencies the Republicans have targeted, would our nation's problems be closer to solution? Would crime be reduced, more families be intact, our country's defense strengthened, teenage pregnancies decreased, or racism ameliorated? Probably not. Perhaps eliminating some federal agencies might be a good idea, but doing so in and of itself is not a solution to the country's most pressing problems.[4]

Despite years of vociferous debate about whether government is too big, too intrusive, and too expensive, it is difficult to reach a conclusion about what the "right" size of government

More people worked at Mount Vernon, his plantation, than in the executive branch in the 1790s.[16] The Department of State had just nine employees. By 1800, the bureaucracy was still small, with only 3,000 civil servants. Since then, the bureaucracy has grown continuously, though not always at the same rate. Three eras of especially large growth have occurred.

The first period of rapid growth followed the Civil War. This era of industrialization, westward expansion, and population growth saw increasing demands for government to provide benefits to business, labor, and farmers. So Congress established the Departments of Commerce, Labor, and Agriculture. Worries about abuses by big business also led to the creation of new bureaucracies, such as the Interstate Commerce Commission, and expanded powers for others, such as antitrust law enforcement in the Justice Department.

A second surge of bureaucratic growth took place during the Great Depression. With New Deal programs, such as Social Security and bank deposit insurance, came an expansion of bureaucracy to administer them.

A third era of bureaucratic growth came during the 1960s and 1970s as a response to public demands that government do more to fight poverty, protect the environment, promote civil rights, and ensure consumer and worker safety. During this time Congress created several new cabinet departments (Housing and Urban Development, Transportation, Energy, and Education) and agencies (Environmental Protection Agency [EPA], Occupational Safety and Health Administration [OSHA], and the Equal Employment Opportunity Commission [EEOC]).

Ironically, despite President Reagan's desire to slash the size of government, Congress named the largest federal building (except for the Pentagon) after him.

is. Government has grown considerably over the past 60 years, but so have the size and wealth of the nation. The federal government employs about 2% of all employees in the United States; excluding the Department of Defense, it employs 1%. Whether this is too big probably depends on your view of what government should be doing rather than of the size of government itself. That being the case, slashing the bureaucracy is likely to be predominantly a symbolic solution.

After all, if we agree that government is an appropriate agency to solve an important problem, but does it poorly, we should think about fixing the bureaucracy, not eradicating it. For example, if the military slips up (consider Pearl Harbor, the Bay of Pigs, or the bombing of the Marine barracks in Beirut), we do not argue that we should do away with it. We look for ways to make it work better.[5]

This sounds like a sensible approach. But it is easier to agree with than to implement. For example, most Americans criticize the bureaucracy in the abstract but say they are satisfied with the services they receive from particular agencies (e.g., the Postal Service and Social Security Administration).[6]

Agreeing to fix the bureaucracy will not work if we do not agree on what government should do and if we do not admit that some agencies work well—that government can work—and that our attention must be on agencies that work poorly.

1. For more about "reinventing" government, see Al Gore, Jr., "The New Job of the Federal Executive," *Public Administration Review* (July/August 1994), pp. 317–321; Ronald C. Moe, "The 'Reinventing Government' Exercise: Misinterpreting the Problem, Misjudging the Consequences," *Public Administration Review* (March/April 1994), pp. 111–122; James Q. Wilson, "Reinventing Public Administration," *PS: Political Science & Politics* (December 1994), pp. 667–673; and "Clinton Team Plans to Redesign HHS," *Omaha World-Herald,* May 12, 1995, p. 5.
2. Rob Gurwit, "Social Services and Reality," *Governing* (May 1995), p. 13.
3. Nicolas Lemann, "Government *Can* Work," *Washington Monthly* (January/February 1994), p. 37; see also Charles Goodsell, *The Case for Bureaucracy,* 3d ed. (Chatham, N.J.: Chatham House, 1994).
4. This point is drawn from Herbert Stein, "Shrinking Government May Not Be the Answer," *Washington Post National Weekly Edition,* March 6–12, 1995, p. 28.
5. Lemann, "Government *Can* Work," p. 36.
6. Goodsell, *The Case for Bureaucracy,* Chapter 2.

Why the Bureaucracy Has Grown

President Reagan once expressed the popular dissatisfaction with big government by noting that he liked flying over Washington because being in the air made government look smaller. Despite Reagan's pronounced feelings about the bureaucracy, it grew by over 200,000 employees during his administration. Although many agencies lost personnel (the biggest loser was the Department of Housing and Urban Development), others such as the Defense, Justice, and Treasury Departments gained. The continued growth of the bureaucracy suggests that powerful forces in society view it as a source of benefits.

One scholar explained the bureaucracy's growth by pointing to Americans' discovery that "government can protect and assist as well as punish and repress."[17] Thus, at the same time we criticize government's growth, we demand educational services, irrigation projects, roads, airports, job training, consumer protection, and many other benefits. Each of us might be willing to cut benefits for someone else, but most of us want government benefits for ourselves.

Sometimes bureaucracies grow in response to external threats. Though World War II was won 50 years ago, our Department of Defense has never returned to its prewar size or scope. The Cold War gave us a new reason to support a massive military establishment. And, of course, from the war as well as later ones came demands for services for veterans, another area of government growth.

Because the bureaucracy has grown in response to demands for public services, its growth has not been uncontrolled as some have charged. Every agency needs congressional and presidential approval of its programs, appropriations, staffing, and procedures. In fact, government also grows, ironically, because the president and Congress want it to be more accountable. The number of managerial layers in it has almost doubled in the last 30 to 40 years because of presidential and congressional efforts to control agency rulemaking and enforcement. This has produced waste, inefficiency, and, ironically, more difficulty in holding agencies accountable.[18] Bureaucrats cannot produce growth on their own. Every agency exists because it is valuable to enough people with enough influence to sustain it.

The growth of the bureaucracy should be seen in the perspective of the overall growth of our economy and population. For example, the number of federal bureaucrats for every 1,000 people in the United States decreased from 16 in 1953 to 11.2 in 1994.[19] This trend will continue. A 1994 law requires cuts of almost 273,000 bureaucratic jobs by 1999. By 1996, nearly 100,000 people had left the bureaucracy as a result of hiring freezes, buyouts, and layoffs. Total personnel costs were only 15% of total federal spending in 1994.

The major growth in public employment has been at the state and local levels. Over 37% of all government workers were federal employees in 1953; in 1994 only 14% were. Only 12% of these federal civil servants work in the Washington, D.C., metropolitan area.

Some of these trends are illustrated in Figure 1, which shows the growth in the size, cost, and regulatory activities of the executive branch. Although the size of the bureaucracy has been relatively stable, its production of regulations has grown more, especially from about 1968 to 1980, and its expenditure of funds has doubled since 1961.

Types of Bureaucracy

Although the Constitution says little about the organization of the executive branch, the Founders probably expected all bureaucratic jobs to be included in only a few departments, each headed by one person. Yet the bureaucracy has become much more complex than this. There are several major types of federal bureaucracy.[20]

DEPARTMENTS

Fourteen departments are directly responsible to the president and headed by his appointees. Thirteen of these appointees, called secretaries, comprise the president's cabinet, along with the attorney general who runs the Justice Department. Departments constitute the lion's share of the executive branch, with over 60% of all civilian workers. The largest employer is the Defense Department. The Department of Veterans

National Archives

In its early years Washington was described as "a miserable little swamp." When this photo was taken in 1882, the government was still comparatively small.

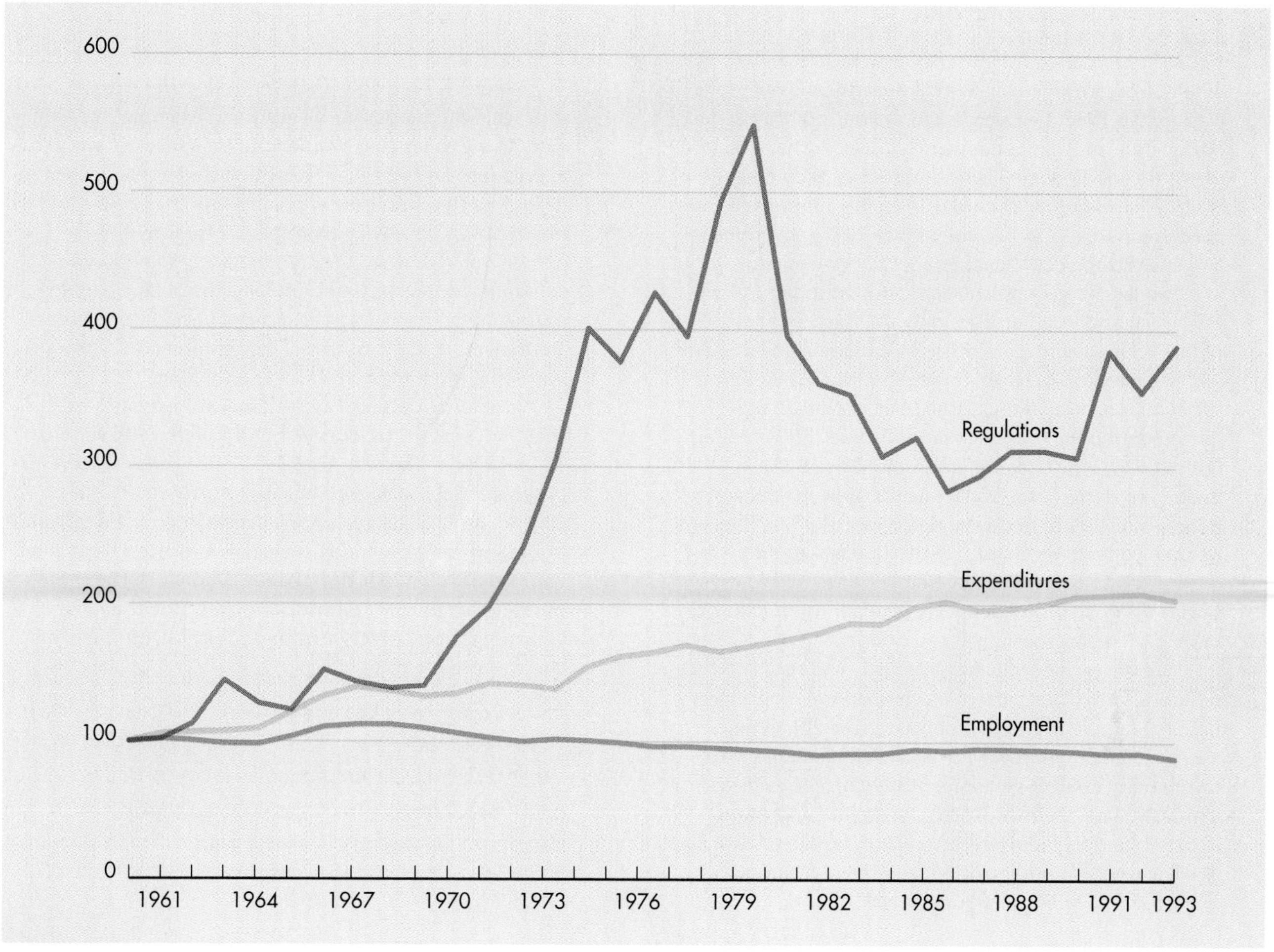

FIGURE 1

Federal Government Growth: Money, Rules, and People

The numbers listed vertically on the left are percentages, comparing each year with 1961. They indicate the growth of federal regulatory activity, federal spending, and the size of the civil service, each on a per person basis.

SOURCES: Idea for chart from Hugh Heclo, "Issue Networks and the Executive Establishment," in Anthony King, ed., *The New American Political System* (Washington, D.C.: American Enterprise Institute, 1978), p. 90. Federal employment statistics are from the Bureau of Economic Analysis, Department of Commerce, *Budget of the United States Government: Fiscal Year 1994* (Washington, D.C.: U.S. Government Printing Office, 1993), p. 42. Data on expenditures are from *Budget of the United States Government: Fiscal Year 1994*, p. 101, and *Budget of the United States Government: Fiscal Year 1995*, p. 251. Federal regulations information is based on the number of pages in the *Federal Register* for each year.

Affairs is the newest department, created in 1989 from an independent agency.

INDEPENDENT AGENCIES

Independent agencies are independent only in that they are not parts of departments. Their heads are appointed by and responsible to the president. In this, independent agencies resemble departments. They differ from departments, however, in that they are often smaller and their heads do not sit in the cabinet. The largest of these agencies are the National Aeronautics and Space Administration and the General Services Administration.

INDEPENDENT REGULATORY BOARDS AND COMMISSIONS

These boards and commissions regulate some aspect of the economy. Five to 10 presidential appointees head every independent regulatory board and commission. By law, each board and commission must be balanced with members of both major political parties. Appointees serve staggered terms and cannot be removed by presidents who dislike their decisions. Examples of such boards include the Federal Communications Commission, which regulates the electronic media and interstate telephone and telegraph rates. The Securities and Exchange Commission makes and enforces

ARE BUREAUCRATS THE ENEMY?

When George Wallace ran as a third-party candidate for president in 1968, he campaigned against "pointy-headed bureaucrats" in Washington making decisions that regulated good people's lives. Bureaucrats, according to Wallace, were out of touch with everyday citizens and their concerns. Bureaucrats became symbols of big government and everything people dislike about big government.

Similar charges and criticisms abound today. Patrick Buchanan and Ross Perot are only the latest in a long line of politicians who run for office by criticizing government and the people who work for it. When they refer to "Washington," we all understand the reference: Big government using too much money to do things that are not needed. Why does big government do so many unneeded things? These critics would answer, "Because bureaucrats do not understand how people live. They are not like you and me." Instead, they are busybodies committed to expanding government's size, spending taxpayers' money, and designing regulations to make life more difficult for individuals and business.

Are government bureaucrats really like this? Are they different from other citizens? A comparison using a large national sample found that public employees are like everyone else in most ways. They are no more likely to favor raising taxes or government spending; they have about the same confidence in government and other institutions—such as organized religion, business, labor, and the press—as other citizens; and they are about as likely to favor busing and gun control.

When civil servants do differ from other citizens, they seem more open to diversity. For example, they are more likely to say they would vote for a black or woman as president and less likely to accept traditional gender roles. And they are somewhat *less* likely than other Americans to approve government intrusions into people's private lives. They are less likely to approve censoring people with unpopular views or laws banning pornography or interracial marriage. On only one issue are they more liable to favor "big government." They are somewhat more likely to favor wiretapping.

Not only do federal bureaucrats resemble us, they live around us, too. A small number—fewer than 10%—work in Washington, D.C.,[1] but the rest work in branch offices scattered throughout the nation. Check the U.S. Government listing in your telephone book and see how many offices are located in or near your hometown. All the people who work there are bureaucrats in one sense or another. But they are your neighbors, pretty ordinary people you meet on the street every day.

1. U.S. Department of Commerce, Bureau of the Census, *Statistical Abstract of the United States, 1995,* 115th ed. (Washington, D.C.: U.S. Government Printing Office, 1995), p. 352, table 544.

SOURCE: Gregory B. Lewis, "In Search of the Machiavellian Milquetoasts: Comparing Attitudes of Bureaucrats and Ordinary People," *Public Administration Review* (May/June 1990): 220–227.

rules regarding stocks, bonds, and securities. And the National Labor Relations Board regulates labor-management relations.

These and other regulatory agencies are "independent" because they are supposed to work free of partisan influences and presidential control. Many people believe regulatory problems are technical, not political, and should be removed from politics insofar as possible. Others point out that technical decisions may also be political. Just how strict or lax the regulations for nuclear power plants should be is a political as well as a technical question because it involves value judgments, weighing costs, health, and safety. Because the voice of the public is heard through elected officials, the immunity of regulators from "politics" means immunity from public, as well as presidential or congressional, control.

As a result, in recent years Congress has tended to place regulatory functions in the hands of agencies within the executive branch, which are more responsive to the president through his power of removal.

GOVERNMENT CORPORATIONS

Although government corporations charge for their services or products like private firms, their charges are not meant to make a profit. Historically, these corporations were created when government decided a service was important to the public interest but no private company could profit from providing it. The first government corporation, the Tennessee Valley Authority, supplies electricity to its part of the country. COMSAT markets satellite communications capabilities to businesses and other governments. The Postal Service and AMTRAK (passenger railroad service) are other examples.

The operating costs and incomes of government corporations are not counted as expenditures and revenues in the annual budget. Thus, they have become an attractive device for elected officials who want to spend without enlarging the deficit. Real spending and deficits are put "off budget" to make the deficit look smaller. For example, when the Post Office showed a projected $2 billion deficit in 1990, it was taken out of the official budget.[21] Moving spending off the budget can be done with any government program, but officials find it easier to do with government corporations.

BUREAUCRATIC FUNCTIONS

After elected officials make a law, someone must carry it out. That is the job of the bureaucracy. Bureaucrats convert laws passed by Congress and signed by the president into rules and activities that have an actual impact on people and things. We call this process **policy implementation.**

For example, the Americans with Disabilities Act directs employers to make a "reasonable accommodation" for a competent worker with a disability that "substantially limits" a major life activity such as seeing or walking, except when this causes "undue hardship."[22] Although the act went into effect in 1992 and a bureaucracy, the Equal Employment Opportunity Commission (EEOC), is still trying to determine what the act means, much is unclear. What is the difference between a "reasonable accommodation" and an "undue hardship"? When voters want local governments to spend less, is the $2 million Des Plaines, Illinois, spent for sidewalks and curb cuts an "undue hardship" or not?[23] Will the EEOC let colleges and universities make only some classrooms accessible to students and staff in wheelchairs or must every classroom be accessible to people with disabilities, by elevators, for example, at a cost of millions of dollars on older campuses?

After the answers to such questions are developed and formulated into rules, implementation involves carrying out the rules and negotiations over interpretations of the rules. State and local counterparts of the EEOC and their clients must be informed of the rules, assisted in their attempts to use the rules, and monitored in their progress. Bills must be paid, disputes resolved, and information collected as to how successful the program is.

As this example illustrates, the general process of policy implementation has two major components: making policies and administering them.

Making Policy

Over time, the policymaking functions of public bureaucracies have grown. Industrialization, population growth, urbanization, and profound changes in science, transportation, and communications have put problems of a more complex nature on government's agenda. The large number and technical nature of these problems, as well as policy differences among its members, have often limited Congress's ability to draft specific policy responses.

Congress often responds to this situation by enacting a general statement of goals and identifying actions that would help achieve them. Congress then has an agency with the relevant expertise draft specific rules that will achieve these goals. Thus, Congress gives agencies **delegated legislative authority,** the authority to draft, as well as execute, specific policies. The Tax Reform Act of 1986, for example, required thousands of rules to be written by the Internal Revenue Service (IRS) and the Treasury Department.

Agency-made policy is just as binding as acts of Congress because agencies make it on Congress's behalf. In strictly numerical terms, agencies make much more policy than Congress. On average, for example, executive agencies issue about 7,000 new rules and regulations a year compared to Congress's annual production of about 300 new laws.

Many political scientists believe Congress abdicates its authority and acts in an irresponsible manner by refusing, because of political pressures and its heavy workload, to develop specific guidelines for agencies.[24] This congressional inaction has contributed to partisan conflicts. From 1980 to 1993, intense policy differences divided Democratic congressional majorities and Republican executive branch officials. Committed to cutting domestic spending, the latter ignored or only partially implemented legislative directives they disliked. The administration justified this by arguing that Congress's directions were unclear. This was sometimes true. For example, a section of a bill prohibiting discrimination against people with disabilities in federally subsidized programs had no congressional hearings, no mention in committee reports and floor debates, and no explanation elsewhere.[25]

Sometimes, however, these complaints about Congress were just an excuse not to implement disliked policies. In response, Congress began to adopt more detailed directives to agencies. Although this resulted in less agency-made policy (see Figure 1), executive officials still argued that congressional directives they disliked were too complex and unrealistic to follow.

In effect, the competition associated with legislative policymaking continued when Congress delegated legislative authority to agencies. This competition subsided when the Democrats won the White House in 1992 and reemerged after the Republicans won congressional majorities in 1994. The competition will likely continue regardless of who controls the White House and Congress because officials in both branches often have different priorities and policy positions. This puts agencies in the difficult position of

AMERICAN DIVERSITY

WOMEN AND MINORITIES IN THE CIVIL SERVICE

Americans expect their public bureaucracies to be open and responsive. Andrew Jackson recognized this when he opened the civil service to frontiersmen of "common" origins. He hoped to make the bureaucracy more responsive and more representative by putting his frontier supporters in office. In the twentieth century, the expectation that public agencies should be open to all qualified applicants has given some groups, such as the Irish, Jews, and blacks, more job opportunities than in the more restricted private corporate world.

Although progress has been made, the federal bureaucracy does not yet fully reflect the diversity of the American people. The bureaucracy seems to have a "glass ceiling" that keeps women and minority men out of top management positions.[1] Most women work in lower civil service grades doing mostly clerical and service jobs. Women tend to earn several thousand dollars less and to be in jobs one to three grades lower than men with the same levels of education and federal job experience. Women are also less likely to be promoted in their first five years of federal employment than men with the same qualifications and background. And fewer women than men get to Grade 13, the gateway to supervisory jobs. Thus, women are less likely than men to be in grades from which they can be promoted to top-level jobs. Similarly, blacks, Hispanics, and other minorities hold few top-level jobs in the federal government. A government report found that minority workers are almost three times as likely to be fired as white workers.[2]

In the 1970s, both women and minorities made progress in filling high-level civil service jobs. In the 1980s, women made more progress than minorities, though in relation to their proportion of the population, minorities are better represented than women. In 1990, women comprised about 52% of the total population, while blacks totaled over 12%, Hispanics 9%, Native Americans 0.8%, and Asians 3%.[3] As the accompanying table indicates, the representation of women and minorities among top-level federal executives, while improving, remains far from being proportional to their share of the total U.S. population.

Major discrepancies remain, in part, because those who enforced equal opportunity and nondiscrimination regulations were white men opposed to affirmative action policies. Indeed, the Justice Department backed white males who sued the government for reverse discrimination.

Problems also remain because performance evaluations in the bureaucracy favor employees who work overtime and who have worked in different offices as a result of transfers. These criteria limit the careers of many women. For example, the government's poor record of providing job-site child care means that many women cannot work overtime because they, more than men, must juggle work and family commitments. Moreover, for many women the work environment is still hostile. They

Percentage of Women and Minorities in High-Level Executive Jobs in the Federal Civil Service

	1985	1990	1995
Women	8	12	16*
Blacks	4	5	7
Hispanics	1	2	3
Asians/Pacific Islanders	1	1	1

*1994 data

SOURCE: Equal Employment Opportunity Commission, *Annual Report on the Employment of Minorities, Women and People with Disabilities in the Federal Government, for the Fiscal Year Ending 1994,* Table I-15. 1995 data from U.S. Census, *Statistical Abstract* of the *United States, 1997* (Washington, D.C.: Government Printing Office, 1997) Table 538.

having to satisfy diverse interests. To figure out what Congress, the president, and others want, agency officials read congressional debates and testimony and talk to members of Congress, committee staffers, White House aides, lobbyists, and others. While agencies also try to determine what the public wants, they are more likely to respond to well-organized and well-funded interests that closely monitor their actions. As a result, agency-made policy is often less responsive to the general public than to particular interests.

REGULATION

A special kind of policymaking is called **regulation.** Though regulation is hard to define, in general, it is an action of a regulatory agency. Regulatory agencies have authority to establish standards or guidelines conferring benefits and imposing restrictions on business conduct, have heads or members appointed by the president, and have legal procedures generally governed by the Administrative Procedure Act (discussed later). Regulatory agencies include not only inde-

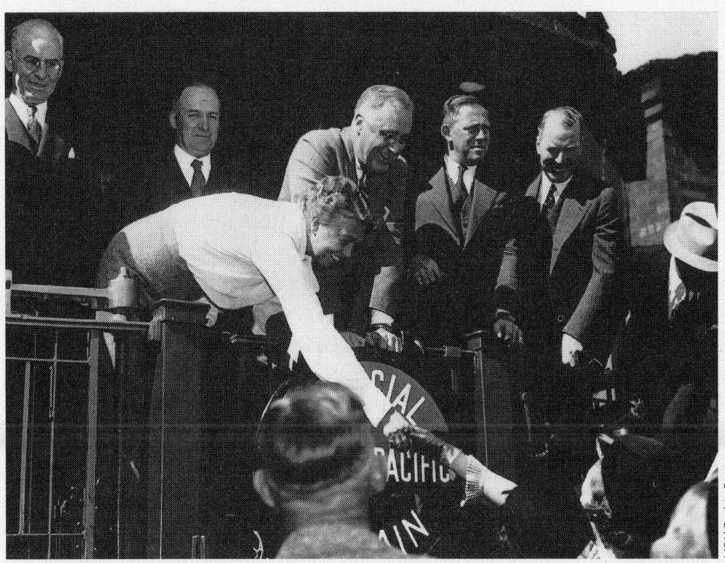
UPI/Corbis-Bettmann

A shy woman who once said, "I hate politics," Eleanor Roosevelt became the most influential First Lady ever. In her role as wife and advisor to her husband, Franklin Delano Roosevelt, Mrs. Roosevelt prodded him to appoint women to high levels of the federal government.

believe they are not as respected as men and have to meet higher standards to be promoted and rewarded.[4]

Some factors limit the ability of policymakers to diversify public service employment. For example, offices in parts of the country with small minority populations may have problems hiring minorities.[5] However, other factors suggest that the diversification of the public service is inevitable. By the year 2000, a majority of new entrants into the labor force will be women, including many Hispanic and black women. What is not inevitable is that more women and minorities will hold top-level jobs. For this to happen, policymakers must set clear goals, adopt effective recruitment and training programs, and treat complaints of discrimination sympathetically.

1. For summaries of the studies see Joanne Desky, "Women Bump into Glass Ceiling in Government," *PA Times,* December 1, 1992, pp. 1 and 16; Pan Suk Kim and Gregory B. Lewis, "Asian Americans in the Public Service: Success, Diversity, and Discrimination," *Public Administration Review* (May/June 1994), pp. 285–290; Gregory B. Lewis, "Is It Time to Drop the Glass Ceiling Metaphor?" and Katherine C. Naff, "A Question of Equity in the Federal Government," both in *PA Times,* November 1, 1992, p. 8; Bill McAllister, "Female Bureaucrats, Up Against It," *Washington Post National Weekly Edition,* November 9–15, 1992, p. 34; Mary E. Guy, "Three Steps Forward, Two Steps Backward: The Status of Women's Integration into Public Management," *Public Administration Review* (July/August 1993) pp. 285–292.
2. Stephen Barr, "In the Line of Firings," *Washington Post National Weekly Edition,* February 21–27, 1994, p. 34; Craig Zwerling and Hilary Silver, "Race and Job Dismissals in a Federal Bureaucracy," *American Sociological Review* (October 1992), pp. 651–660.
3. *Statistical Abstract of the United States, 1997,* Table 30. For a report on minority and especially African American progress, see Sylvester Murray et al., "The Role Demands and Dilemmas of Minority Public Administrators," *Public Administration Review* (September/October 1994), pp. 409–416.
4. Katherine C. Naff, "Through the Glass Ceiling: Prospects for the Advancement of Women in the Federal Civil Service," *Public Administration Review* (November/December 1994), p. 513.
5. J. Edward Kellough, "Integration in the Public Workplace: Determinants of Minority and Female Employment in Federal Agencies," *Public Administration Review* (September/October 1990), pp. 557–566. For more on this see Lois Recascino Wise, "Social Equity in Civil Service Systems," *Public Administration Review* (September/October 1990), pp. 567–575.

pendent regulatory boards and commissions but also some independent agencies, such as the Environmental Protection Agency (EPA), and some agencies within cabinet departments, such as the Food and Drug Administration in Health and Human Services and OSHA within the Labor Department.

Some regulatory policies require businesses to meet standards, such as for clean air, safe disposal of toxic wastes, or safe workplaces. Failure to do so results in legal penalties. Other regulations control who can own certain goods. For example, the Federal Communications Commission licenses people to own and operate radio and television stations. Regulations may require businesses to provide information, such as the cancer warnings on cigarette packages and the labels noting sugar, salt, and vitamin content on packaged food.

Regulatory actions include two steps: making rules and adjudicating their enforcement. Rulemaking is the establishment of standards that apply to a class of individuals or businesses. For example, the Surface Transportation

Board, formerly the Interstate Commerce Commission, sets standards that apply to interstate carriers such as railroads, trucking firms, and bus lines. Adjudication occurs when agencies try individuals or firms charged with violating standards. To do this, they use procedures that are very similar to those of courts.

Because of the dangers inherent in having one agency be the lawmaker, judge, and jury, in 1946 Congress passed the Administrative Procedure Act (APA) to establish fair and open procedures. For example, agencies must publish a description of their rulemaking procedures in the *Federal Register* and hold open hearings on proposed rules or provide for another means of public input. Those who believe they have been treated unfairly by an agency have the right to take their case to court.

Antiregulation feeling helps to fuel public distrust of government. Surveys report that the number of people who think government controls too much of our daily lives has risen from 57% to 69% since 1987.[26] As Figure 1 shows, regulation has increased since then. This is largely because of the passage of the Clean Air Act, the Civil Rights Act, and the Americans with Disabilities Act during the Bush years plus a reversal by Bush and Clinton appointees of the antiregulatory fervor of the Reagan years. Most Americans support the goals of these laws (e.g., 78% of the public says government should do "whatever it takes to protect the environment").[27] But many also think that the regulations to implement these and other laws result in wasteful paperwork and more costs than benefits. For example, officials in Madison, Wisconsin, report that they spend 14% of their transit budget obeying regulations to ensure bus service to the disabled, who make up 1.5% of their users.[28]

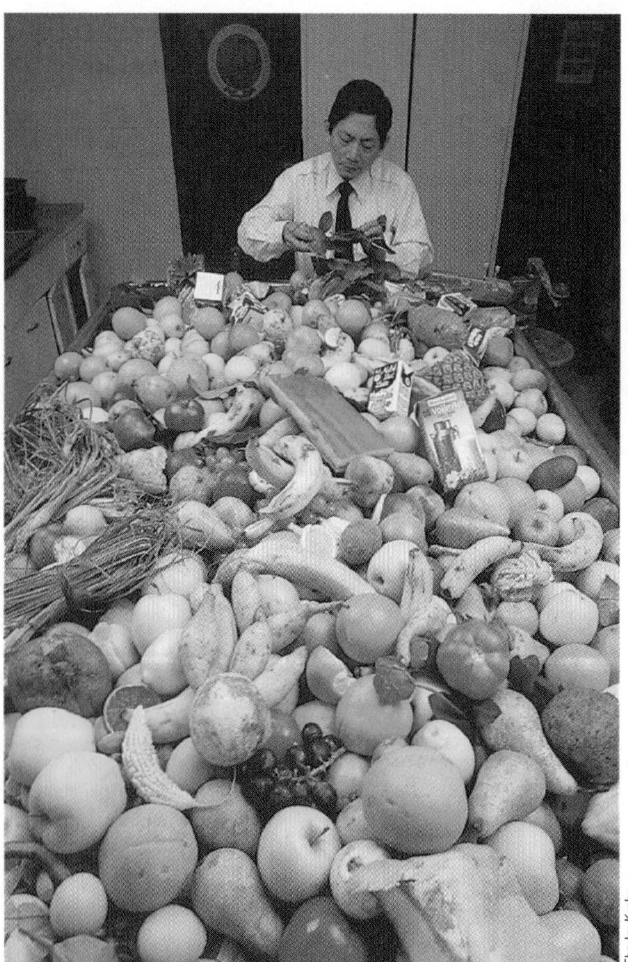

Charles Krebs

At JFK International Airport in New York, a Department of Agriculture inspector searches for illegal immigrants—insects—in fruits and vegetables that travelers bring into the United States.

Most regulations are based on laws that direct agencies to take certain actions to accomplish certain ends. Thus, Congress gave the EPA authority to tell business to use or not use certain processes to reduce pollution. This "command and control" strategy is expensive because agencies have to employ many experts to design rules to achieve the desired ends and then have to get those they regulate to obey the rules. The strategy also allows little flexibility for the agencies and the people they regulate.

Many people believe there may be better ways to achieve the goals of clean air, fairness to the disabled, and other desirable objectives.[29] Some argue that we should eliminate agency regulations and rely on lawsuits by private citizens to protect public health and safety by proving in court that they have been harmed by something, such as pollution. A problem with this idea is that it could pit individuals with limited means against industries with vast resources. It also moves problems to the courts more quickly. Other critics say we should entrust regulation to the states, which would finance their own efforts. Still others call for Washington to give block grants to states and allow them to set their own priorities and devise solutions consistent with broad goals set at the federal level. And others argue we should make business and industry comply with goals and standards (for example, in environmental cleanups) but leave them more discretion on how to do it.

Since the election of Republican majorities in the House and the Senate in 1994, some change, perhaps significant, in the regulatory process seems certain. Congress signaled its opposition to command-and-control regulation by threatening to pass bills that would stop the making of new regulations for one year and force agencies to give greater weight to the costs of new regulations (to kill those based on "minute or exaggerated risks").[30] And Clinton issued an executive order to cut paperwork, void many regulations,

YOUR HAMBURGER: 41,000 REGULATIONS

Protesting "overregulation" is a popular pastime of Americans. The 41,000 regulations that accompany a hamburger may seem an obvious example of the absurdity of too much regulation. But the issue is more complicated than it seems at first glance. If government does not regulate pesticide use on crops, there is a significant risk of serious illness to consumers who eat the crops. If the government does not inspect to make sure livestock are free of tuberculosis, the incidence of TB bacteria in meat will be higher.

When examined closely, most of the regulations have a plausible rationale. But regulation is not free. The cost of regulating hamburger is about 8 to 11 cents per pound. Is this a high cost? It depends on the probability of contracting a serious disease and the value you as a consumer place on having some confidence in the quality of products you buy. Recently, after outbreaks of potentially deadly food poisoning from *E. coli* bacteria in ground beef, government officials have considered adopting additional regulations in response to consumers' concerns.

And then, of course, there are some regulations that are mystifying even to those not especially opposed to government regulation. What is the danger in eating a pickle sliced too thin? Only Uncle Sam knows!

SOURCES: *U.S. News & World Report,* February 11, 1980, p. 64. Copyright 1980, U.S. News & World Report, Inc.; Carole Sugarman, "A Beef with the Cattlemen," *Lincoln Journal Star,* September 15, 1997, p. 32.

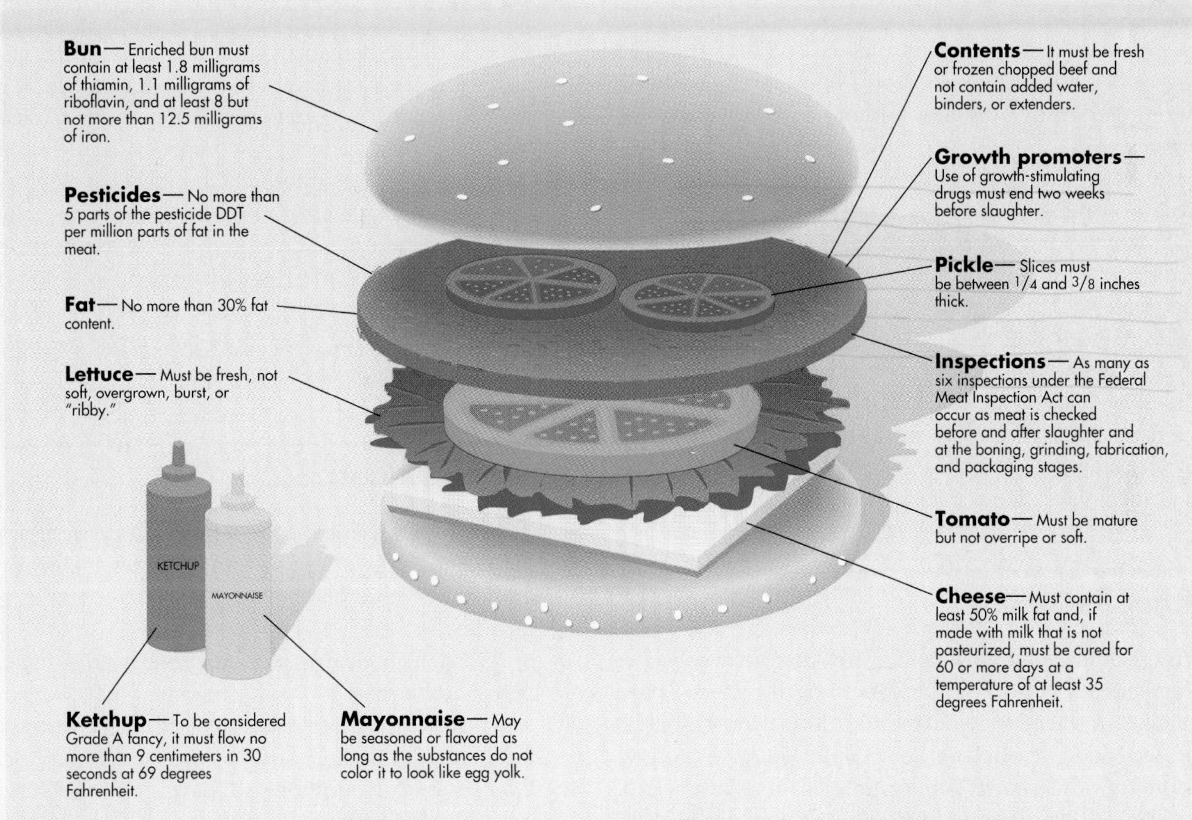
Bun— Enriched bun must contain at least 1.8 milligrams of thiamin, 1.1 milligrams of riboflavin, and at least 8 but not more than 12.5 milligrams of iron.
Pesticides— No more than 5 parts of the pesticide DDT per million parts of fat in the meat.
Fat— No more than 30% fat content.
Lettuce— Must be fresh, not soft, overgrown, burst, or "ribby."
KETCHUP
MAYONNAISE
Ketchup— To be considered Grade A fancy, it must flow no more than 9 centimeters in 30 seconds at 69 degrees Fahrenheit.
Mayonnaise— May be seasoned or flavored as long as the substances do not color it to look like egg yolk.
Contents— It must be fresh or frozen chopped beef and not contain added water, binders, or extenders.
Growth promoters— Use of growth-stimulating drugs must end two weeks before slaughter.
Pickle— Slices must be between 1/4 and 3/8 inches thick.
Inspections— As many as six inspections under the Federal Meat Inspection Act can occur as meat is checked before and after slaughter and at the boning, grinding, fabrication, and packaging stages.
Tomato— Must be mature but not overripe or soft.
Cheese— Must contain at least 50% milk fat and, if made with milk that is not pasteurized, must be cured for 60 or more days at a temperature of at least 35 degrees Fahrenheit.

The hamburger, staple of the quick, inexpensive meal, is the subject of 41,000 federal and state regulations, many of them stemming from 200 laws and 111,000 precedent-setting court cases. These rules, cited in a three-volume study by Colorado State University, touch on everything involved in meat production, including cattle-grazing practices, conditions in slaughterhouses, and methods used to process meat for sale to supermarkets, restaurants, and fast-food outlets. Here is just a sampling of the rules and regulations governing the burger.

and create a pilot program to give business more flexibility to comply with clean air and water requirements. These actions indicate that less regulatory activity is likely now given the influence of policymakers' preferences. However, titanic political battles lie ahead because advocates of a cleaner environment, more rights for the disabled, and other interests protected by regulations point out that giving businesses more flexibility and weakening regulations is likely to erode progress toward goals they desire.

Administering Policy

Public bureaucracy's oldest job is to administer the law. To "administer" is to execute, enforce, and apply the rules that have been made either by Congress or the bureaucracy itself. Thus, if policymakers decide to go to war, they must empower an agency to acquire weapons, recruit and train soldiers, and lead them in battle with a winning strategy. Policymaking without administration is usually tantamount to having no policy at all.

Administration includes thousands of different kinds of activities. It involves writing checks to farmers who receive payments for growing—or not growing—crops, providing direct services to the public, evaluating how well programs are working, prosecuting those who try to defraud the government, and maintaining buildings and offices. For forest rangers, administration involves helping backpackers in the Grand Canyon or putting out a forest fire in northern Minnesota. For postal employees, it includes delivering the mail or repairing an automatic sorting machine.

Other Functions

In the course of policymaking and administration, the bureaucracy performs other functions. It collects data, such as in the census, and makes information available to us. Much of what we know about ourselves comes from the government's collection of data on births and deaths, occupations and income, housing and health, crime, and many other things.

The bureaucracy engages in research too. A prime example is the Department of Agriculture, which for over 100 years has conducted research on how to grow bigger and better crops, raise healthier animals, and transport and market products more effectively.

In addition, providing continuity is an important offshoot of the bureaucracy's activities. Presidents and members of Congress come and go, and political appointees in the bureaucracy stay an average of two years. Many barely learn their jobs by the time they leave. Career civil servants tend to know more about government's past and current efforts, which can make government more productive. At the same time, the presence of careerists can make the bureaucracy less responsive.

Bureaucracy also teaches citizens about government. First, it informs us about public policies and programs. For example, we contact the National Park Service if we want to know the rules governing camping in national parks. The bureaucracy also performs a socialization function. It helps us learn about government and our role as citizens.

EXPECTATIONS ABOUT THE FEDERAL BUREAUCRACY

Historically, Americans have had two sometimes contradictory expectations about public bureaucracy. They have wanted bureaucracies to be responsive to their needs, which often means responsive to majority views. But they have also wanted bureaucracies to be competent enough to do an effective job. They want fair, apolitical competence applied so that, for example, Social Security recipients who are Democrats do not receive favors when Democrats are in office and Republican recipients do not receive favors when Republicans are in office. For the bureaucracy to have both political responsiveness and neutral competence is often difficult.

Responsiveness

Responsiveness refers to a democratic desire that public agencies do what we want. We have shown how highly we value bureaucratic responsiveness in three major ways.

First, Americans elect more bureaucrats than citizens of other nations do. By the mid-1800s voters were electing numerous state and local executive officers from ballots (called long ballots) having hundreds of names. Many states and localities still have long ballots electing not only chief executives, such as governors and mayors, but also treasurers, clerks, sheriffs, surveyors, auditors, engineers, and other administrative officers. Electing rather than appointing these officials is supposed to make them responsive, though in reality it may have the opposite effect by making it unclear who is really in charge.

The second way Americans have encouraged bureaucratic responsiveness is through **patronage.** Under the patronage system, elected officials appoint their supporters to administrative jobs in order to build their own political strength. Newly elected presidents and other executives replace everyone appointed by their predecessors with their own supporters: "To the victor belong

The Granger Collection, New York

Andrew Jackson opened the doors to the White House as well as to the government bureaucracy. The guests at a White House party open to the public consumed or carried away much of a 1,400-pound cheese.

the spoils." Andrew Jackson's presidential election in 1828 was a watershed in using the patronage system. Jackson and others believed that any white male citizen of average intelligence and goodwill could do a government job well. So he reversed the existing practice of naming mostly well-off people from the East Coast by appointing less well-off supporters from frontier areas.

A major problem with patronage is that it can lead to corruption, in particular to deal making between candidates and voters or, more unfortunately, individuals who control blocks of voters. Voters may support candidates who promise them jobs or other favors. Such corruption increasingly sullied city councils, state legislatures, and Congress during the 1800s.

Another problem with patronage is incompetence. People got bureaucratic jobs because they supported winning candidates, not because they knew how to do the jobs. This became a major problem as government jobs became more technical.

The third way Americans have sought bureaucratic responsiveness is by giving legislatures great authority over the bureaucracy. Before the Revolution and for a long time after, the bureaucracy performed a few relatively simple jobs and was relatively easy to control. Now the job of controlling the bureaucracy is much more difficult as government has become larger and more complex.

Neutral Competence

Neutral competence can be a contradictory objective to responsiveness. It holds that bureaucrats should be uninvolved or neutral in policymaking and chosen only for their expertise in executing policy. It assumes that there is no Republican or Democratic way to build a sewer, collect customs, or fight a war. In effect, it says politics has no place in bureaucracy. It also implies that bureaucrats should not profit personally from the decisions they make.

Woodrow Wilson, a major advocate of neutral competence, wrote that we can learn to execute policy both expertly and responsively.[31] He believed that government jobs are either political or administrative in nature and that if we know which is which, we can create a bureaucracy that policymakers can control. Most current observers believe it is impossible to separate politics from administration completely, however.[32] The accompanying boxes on the census and on breast implantation illustrate the difficulties that can arise when we try to have full measures of both political responsiveness and neutral competence.

The first impact of the desire for neutral competence was the creation of the **Civil Service Commission** by the Pendleton Act in 1883. Patronage was a serious problem by the 1880s. Given the strength of political machines that had grown powerful through its use, Congress did not act until the 1881 assassination of President James Garfield by an unsuccessful job seeker.

The commission filled certain bureaucratic jobs with people who had proved their competence in competitive examinations and then protected these people from having to support or oppose particular candidates. Jobs under the commission's jurisdiction were part of the **merit system.**

The Pendleton Act authorized the president to extend merit system coverage to additional federal jobs by executive order. The merit system covered about 10% of the jobs in the federal bureaucracy in 1884. That figure is over 90% today; most of the remainder are covered by some other merit system such as that in the State Department's Foreign Service.

A merit system protects individuals from dismissal for partisan reasons. However, the system does not give "merit" a monopoly. The system favors veterans by adding a 5-point bonus to their test scores (disabled veterans get 10 points). People already in the system are also favored because they know about job openings first. Sometimes, job descriptions are written to fit particular individuals.

Another result of the push for neutral competence was the creation of independent regulatory boards and commissions. In 1887, Congress created the Interstate Commerce Commission to decide, on the basis of expert, not partisan, factors, such things as interstate freight rates, railroad ticket prices, conditions of service, and which companies could operate between different places. Some partisan influences remain: the president names and the Senate confirms board and commission members, and Congress and the president determine their funding. But partisanship is supposed to end there.

NEUTRAL COMPETENCE VERSUS POLITICS IN THE U.S. CENSUS

The Constitution directs that a count of all residents, called the census, be completed every 10 years. The Census Bureau prepares for the next census far in advance in order to carry it out with the greatest accuracy. Conducting a census is neither easy nor inexpensive.

In the mid to late 1990s, a battle over the census arose that provides a classic example of the conflict between political responsiveness and neutral competence. The census is supposed to include all residents in the United States. Some citizens, however, lacking a permanent address of their own, move from friend to friend or relative to relative. Others are homeless. Obtaining an accurate count of these people is nearly impossible. So the Census Bureau has proposed to use a widely accepted form of scientific sampling to correct the census count in the year 2000. By using sampling, a more accurate count of these individuals, many of whom tend to be very poor or minorities, could be achieved.

Republicans, concerned with maintaining their majority in the House of Representatives, have strenuously objected. Knowing that undercounted persons tend to live in areas where Democratic candidates win elections, Republicans fear that adjusting the census through sampling will result in higher populations in Democratic areas and thus more congressional seats in those areas. As a consequence, the Republicans might lose control of the House to the Democrats. To forestall this possibility, Republicans in the House have attempted to amend several bills to require that the Census Bureau not utilize these methods of correcting the census. They have also attempted to delay funding for the census.

Barbara E. Bryant, the Republican-appointed director of the 1990 census, supports the plans of the Census Bureau to correct for the undercounting of many poor and minority residents. She wrote to the Republican leadership in Congress, expressing her support for the Census Bureau's plans, but received no response from the House Republican leaders.

Who should prevail—the bureaucratic experts using scientific methods in pursuit of neutral competence or politicians who fear loss of power? Should neutral competence or political reality determine the outcome? Questions such as these are seldom easily answered.

SOURCES: David S. Broder, "Republicans Trying to Bar Census Bureau from Using Sampling," *Lincoln Journal Star,* August 19, 1997, p. 4A; Bill McAllister, "Just a Sampling of Battles to Come," *Washington Post National Weekly Edition,* July 28, 1997, p. 12.

Limits on the partisan political activities of federal workers resulted from attempts to achieve neutral competence. The **Hatch Act** of 1939 says that federal employees can do very little in partisan campaigns, even in state and local ones. They can vote, attend rallies, and talk privately to others. But they cannot participate in party-sponsored voter registration drives, endorse party candidates, or work for or against them in any way. These prohibitions also apply to state and local government workers supported by federal funds.

The Hatch Act has been the subject of considerable controversy. Supporters argue that it protects the neutral competence of civil servants from partisan influences. Critics of the act say it makes civil servants second-class citizens by denying them the First Amendment guarantees of freedom of speech and association. In 1993, Congress changed the law to allow most federal employees to run for office within political parties, to participate in political campaigns, and to raise funds for political action committees when they are off-duty. However, all employees of law enforcement and national security agencies remain under the earlier, more stringent prohibitions.[33]

The 1980s were troubled years for the entire civil service. Reagan's belief that "government isn't the solution, it's the problem" endorsed negative views of the public service and indicated a commitment to cut government activity. This and publicity glorifying private business made hiring and keeping good people in government difficult; the work of many agencies suffered. For example, the Food and Drug Administration (FDA) tests products that represent about a quarter of consumer spending. Yet in a decade that saw the onset of AIDS and the development of many new products, FDA staffing dropped 9% and food and drug inspections fell 40%. In 1990, the FDA took 31 months, not the 6 months required by law, to review new drug applications.[34]

Although Bush noted his "very high regard for the overall competence of career civil servants and for [their] vital role,"[35] he did little to overcome the trends of the 1980s. Clinton sent mixed signals to the bureaucracy. He described government, and by implication the bureaucracy, as a valuable tool for social change, but recommended freezing civil service salaries and vowed to cut 100,000 federal jobs. The number of new workers is declining in the 1990s as the "baby bust" generation enters the job market and as one-quarter of the federal workforce reaches retirement age. Government will have trouble competing with the private sector for workers because federal salaries lag behind comparable nongovernment jobs and this gap widens at higher levels.

Neutral competence also includes the idea that bureaucrats should not profit personally from their decisions. Civil servants should be experts in what they do but should not have a personal stake in it. For example, bureaucrats who are stockholders in chemical companies should not make policy about chemical waste. Even if policymakers could completely divorce themselves from their financial interests, their ties with a regulated firm would still produce an appearance of conflict of interest. Critics of policy could point to it, lowering public confidence in government.

Responding to concerns about conflicts of interest, Congress passed the Ethics in Government Act in 1978. The act sought to prevent ex-public officials with inside information about specific issues from using it and their contacts to give their private employers an unfair competitive advantage. The act barred ex-public servants from lobbying their former agencies for one year and, on matters in which they "personally and substantially" participated as public officials, for life. In 1989, news that ex-Reagan officials had used their government service for substantial financial gain led to the passage of a law designed to strengthen the 1978 act. It will have little impact if it is enforced as weakly as its predecessor.

To address these concerns, President Clinton signed an executive order requiring many of his political appointees to sign a pledge that they will not lobby the agencies in which they worked for five years and will never lobby for foreign political parties and governments. Analysts noted that the rules apply to only one-third of his appointees, that lobbying for foreign corporations is unaffected, and that Clinton said nothing about how he will enforce the rules. These points suggest that the new rules may have little more impact than the old ones.[36]

Although responsiveness and neutral competence contribute to an effective bureaucracy, each has problems and ultimately works against the other. The most neutrally competent bureaucracy is not always the most responsive one and vice versa.

The Granger Collection, New York

A disappointed office seeker assassinates President Garfield.

THE POLITICS OF BREAST IMPLANTS

Bureaucracies affect most things in life, including sometimes the shape of one's body. The debate over how government should regulate silicone-gel breast implants illustrates the pervasiveness, slowness, and political responsiveness of the regulatory process.

Breast surgery is a $300 million industry and accounts for more than 130,000 surgical operations annually. It is one of the most frequently used forms of plastic surgery in the United States. Some plastic surgeons obtain more than 50% of their income from this operation.[1] Fifteen to 20% of these operations involve replacing breast tissue lost to cancer surgery. The rest are elective surgeries to augment the size and change the shape of the breasts of women who are not pleased with their natural shape.[2]

When silicone-gel implants were introduced in the 1960s, the Food and Drug Administration (FDA), which has the regulatory responsibility for food and drugs, did not have specific legislative authority to regulate medical devices such as implants. Thus, manufacturers did not have to obtain FDA approval before marketing implants. In 1976, Congress gave the FDA responsibility for regulating the safety of medical devices but exempted more than 100,000 existing medical devices. The FDA could, however, ask manufacturers to submit safety data on existing devices for the purpose of deciding if regulation was needed.[3]

In 1987, the FDA asked silicone-gel implant manufacturers to provide evidence of their safety by 1991. If the devices were found safe, the FDA would allow them to be sold and used as in the past.[4] If not, the FDA could impose restrictions on their use or even ban them all together. The FDA requested this safety information after the medical literature began to report that the implants did not always perform as advertised (they sometimes leaked or became lumpy or hard). Even more seriously, silicone from leaky or ruptured implants appeared to be causing arthritic conditions and autoimmune diseases.

In 1991, three of the four manufacturers of the implants submitted millions of pages of documentation on implant safety (the fourth manufacturer discontinued the product). They argued that these studies of patients' medical records and their other research found silicone-gel implants harmless. The American Society of Plastic and Reconstructive Surgeons reported that over 90% of breast implant patients were happy with the results.[5]

Critics presented a different picture. They pointed out that despite the documentation presented, manufacturers had not studied many patients. Dow Chemicals, one of the largest manufacturers, had studied only about 1,000 women. More important, the patients had not been studied over a long time period. Most were followed only a year or two after the operation, a time that would not begin to reveal long-term effects. Only one-third of the subjects in the biggest test had been studied more than two years, and only 46 women were checked after

Reuters/Corbis-Bettmann

Karen Berger holds a silicone-gel breast implant. Berger, an author of a book on implants, testified at an FDA hearing on the safety of implants.

CONTROLLING THE BUREAUCRACY

To whom is the bureaucracy responsible? Although many bureaucratic decisions significantly affect our lives, most are not made in the public eye, and most citizens know little about them. No "ADM-SPAN" channel televises agency activities as C-SPAN covers Congress.[37] Nevertheless, many compete to influence public agencies: the president, parts of Congress, interest groups, and individual citizens. Whether they succeed depends on their resources, agency reactions, and agency ability to resist unwanted outside influence.[38]

President

The development of the bureaucracy led to demands for **executive leadership.** The president, constitutionally the "chief executive," has several tools to control the bureaucracy. One is budgeting. Presidents can try to limit agency appropriations to keep agencies from doing certain things, or they can tie conditions to appropriations to make them do things. Using these strategies effectively can be difficult, although President Reagan was able to weaken some regulatory agencies by significantly cutting their budgets.[39] President Bush's 1991 budget for the Internal Revenue Service proposed that the IRS target middle- and lower-income tax-

seven years. Even without long-term studies, the companies' data showed problems with one-third of the implants.[6] And there were many personal accounts from women who told stories of pain and serious disease after implant surgery.[7]

When it was apparent that serious regulation was contemplated, the American Society of Plastic and Reconstructive Surgeons launched a multimillion-dollar lobbying initiative to fight proposed regulations. Each member was assessed $1,050 to pay for the campaign, which included recruiting 400 women to travel to Washington to state how important the breast implants were to their health and well-being.[8] On the other side, a network of women whose implants were unsuccessful formed a group called Command Trust Network to continue to publicize the negative aspects of implants.

After committee hearings highlighting these disagreements and in the context of a larger discussion over whether government agencies were giving women's health concerns equal weight to those of men, the FDA commissioner decided that silicone-gel breast implants would be restricted while additional safety data were collected. Implants will be limited to women who are part of FDA-approved safety studies. The studies will be open to all women seeking implants following breast cancer surgery, but the number of implants for cosmetic purposes will be drastically reduced until safety questions are answered.[9]

In June 1994, the prestigious *New England Journal of Medicine* published the results of a Mayo Clinic study that found no increased risk of connective-tissue damage and other disorders among women with silicone implants. A bit later, other studies supported the finding that these disorders were no more likely to occur in women with implants than in women without implants. As Dr. Marcia Angell, the executive editor of this journal, explained, "About 1 percent of women [in the United States] have breast implants and about 1 percent of American women have connective-tissue diseases, the most common being rheumatiod arthritis. So if you do the arithmetic, you find that in this country you can expect about 10,000 women will have both, just by coincidence."[10]

Many believers in the dangers of silicone implants continue to pursue legal remedies. Some accuse medical researchers of being paid by the manufacturers of these devices. Women and their lawyers continue to seek sizable monetary settlements from implant manufacturers.

The FDA only slowly responded to initial complaints about breast implants. But, ultimately, this government agency did respond to concerned citizens by insisting that breast implantation be limited until further and more definitive studies could be completed. As this experience demonstrates, finding an appropriate balance between responsiveness and neutral expertise can be very difficult and time-consuming.[11]

1. Jean Seligmann, Mary Hager, and Karen Springen, "Another Tempest in a C Cup," *Newsweek*, March 23, 1992, p. 67.
2. Diana McLellan, "Rethinking Big," *The Washingtonian* (June 1991), pp. 57–59; Laura Shapiro, Karen Springen, and Jeanne Gordon, "What Is It with Women and Large Breasts?" *Newsweek*, January 20, 1992, p. 57.
3. Malcolm Gladwell, "FDA Set to Begin Hearings on Silicone Breast Implants," *Washington Post*, February 17, 1992, p. A1.
4. Malcolm Gladwell, "Silicone Breast Implants," *Washington Post* (Health Supplement), March 3, 1992, p. 10.
5. McLellan, "Rethinking Big," p. 57.
6. Philip Hilts, "Under Pressure, US Weighs Ban on Use of Breast Implants," *New York Times*, October 21, 1991, p. 1.
7. "Reprieve for Breast Implants," *Time*, November 25, 1991, p. 81.
8. Hilts, "Under Pressure."
9. Malcolm Gladwell, "FDA Will Allow Limited Use of Silicone-Gel Breast Implants," *Washington Post*, April 17, 1992, p. A2.
10. PBS, "Breast Implants on Trial," *Frontline*, February 27, 1996. Available online at **www2.pbs.org/wgbh/pages/frontline/implants/implantscript.html**
11. Ibid.

payers for audits (to check the honesty of their tax returns) rather than wealthy individuals and companies. He cut the IRS's budget request to target rich tax cheats by over 90%.[40]

Second, presidents can try to control agencies by appointing people to them with views like their own. This is obvious in the case of cabinet departments. Reagan and Bush filled health care–related positions in the Department of Health and Human Services with people who were pro-life.[41] Clinton filled these jobs with people who are pro-choice. In appointments to regulatory agencies, Republican presidents tend to appoint pro-business people and Democratic presidents pro-consumer and prolabor individuals.[42] Reagan's appointees to regulatory agencies such as OSHA, the Consumer Products Safety Commission, and the EPA agreed with his goal of reducing government regulation. Clinton's appointees to these agencies believe, with him, that government can be a valuable agent of social change.

Often, however, presidential appointees end up representing agency interests rather than presidential ones. This can happen because most appointees have less expertise and experience in agency operations than career civil servants and often come to rely on career officials for information about agency history, procedures, and policy questions.

Administrative reform is a third presidential opportunity to control the bureaucracy. Generally, the more sweeping a president's recommendation for change, the more he must anticipate congressional and interest group resistance. For example, Reagan wanted to abolish the Departments of Education and

AMERICAN DIVERSITY

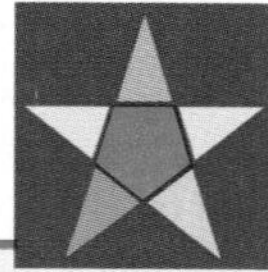

PRESIDENTIAL ADMINISTRATIVE APPOINTMENTS

Bill Clinton, as a candidate for the presidency, promised that his administration would reflect American diversity. After one year, with more than two-thirds of his appointments filled, Clinton's choices almost exactly represented gender and minority groups, with small exceptions for women and Hispanics.

Perhaps even more importantly for the representation of these groups, many were also included among top-level appointees. These are the officials who participate in the shaping of policy, rather than serving in low-level service positions. If we examine the proportion of top-level appointees in each group and compare it with that group's population of college-educated, 30- to 64-year-olds, we find both women and minorities to be reasonably well represented among the higher echelons of the Clinton administration when compared with the overall population and very well represented when compared with the highly educated population. This level of representation also exists in the president's cabinet, those persons whom he chooses to head agencies and departments in the government.

Clinton Administration Appointments of Minorities and Women

	% OF TOTAL APPOINTMENTS	% OF TOTAL POPULATION
Women	46	50
African Americans	14	12
Hispanics	6	10
Asian Americans	3	3
Native Americans	1	1

	% OF TOTAL TOP-LEVEL APPOINTMENTS	% OF TOTAL COLLEGE-EDUCATED POPULATION, AGES 30–64
Women	30	35
African Americans	14	6
Hispanics	5	3
Asian Americans	3	5
Native Americans	3	0.3

CLINTON'S CABINET	% IN 1993	% IN 1998
Women	22	30
African Americans	15	15
Hispanics	7	7

SOURCES: Martha Farnsworth Riche, "An Administration That Mirrors America," *Washington Post National Weekly Edition*, January 31–February 6, 1994, p. 25; *The United States Government Manual 1997/1998* (Washington, D.C.: National Archives and Records Administration, 1997); Jeffrey B. Trammell and Gary P. Osifchin, eds., *The Clinton 500: The New Team Running America* (Washington, D.C.: Almanac Publishing, 1994); *Federal Staff Directory* (Washington, D.C.: C.Q. Staff Directories, 1998).

Energy and merge the Commerce and Labor Departments, but Congress would not support him.

Fourth, the White House can try to influence agencies not under presidential control by lobbying and mobilizing public opinion. For example, presidents try to influence Federal Reserve Board decisions on interest rates.

Despite these powers, there are many limits on the president's ability to control the bureaucracy. Given its size and complexity, the president cannot possibly control every important decision. Moreover, presidents have found it increasingly difficult to lead an executive branch containing large numbers of merit system employees deliberately insulated from presidential control.

Presidential control problems became much more serious in the 1930s with the establishment of many new programs and agencies. In 1935, Franklin Roosevelt appointed the Brownlow Committee, named after its chair and composed of public administration specialists, which wrote an excellent statement of the principles of executive leadership in its 1937 report.

The report was very influential. At its suggestion, the Bureau of the Budget, created in 1921, was put into the new Executive Office of the President to help the president cope with the bureaucracy. Congress also passed legislation in 1939 permitting the president to create, merge, or dissolve agencies subject to Congress's disapproval.

In 1978, the Civil Service Reform Act replaced the Civil Service Commission with two agencies. One promotes executive leadership by working with the president in writing and administering civil service regulations. The other is supposed to protect civil servants from violations of these regulations. In addition, the act gave managers more opportunity to fire incompetent subordinates, authorized bonuses and a new pay scale for managers to encourage better performance, and created the Senior Executive Service (SES).

Despite this legislation, executive leadership is still thwarted by the difficulty of removing incompetents from the civil service. Although job security is not meant to shield public servants who do poor work, it does make firing incompetent workers difficult and time-consuming. The organization of public employees into unions contributes to this. The government's rate of discharging people for inefficiency is .01% a year. The 1978 reform has made little difference. As one public employee said, "We're all like headless nails down here—once you get us in you can't get us out."[43]

Agencies' connections to strong allies provide another limit to presidential leadership. Presidents have more success trying to control agencies that lack strong congressional allies and domestic clientele groups, such as the Treasury and State Departments, than agencies *with* such allies, such as the Agriculture and Health and Human Services Departments.

Congress

Creating and reorganizing agencies and enacting laws give Congress opportunities to tell agencies what to do and how to do it. In recent years, Congress took away some of the powers of the Federal Trade Commission to regulate used-car sales, practices of the insurance industry, and television advertising aimed at children. In doing so, Congress was responding to complaints (and campaign donations) from used-car dealers, the insurance industry, and other businesses that found their actions being circumscribed by the commission's new or proposed regulations. In 1995, congressional interest in cutting the bureaucracy and regulatory activity led Clinton to propose and later approve the elimination of the Interstate Commerce Commission, the original independent regulatory commission. Despite these examples, however, the existence of complex, technical issues and the tendency to state congressional goals in general terms often give agencies considerable leeway in doing their jobs.

Legislative oversight is another congressional tool of control, but it too has problems. Just as an agency's connections can work to thwart presidential control, they can also limit congressional oversight. Agencies frequently work closely with certain congressional committees and interest groups for mutual support; agencies adjust their actions to the preferences of the congressional committees that authorize their programs and appropriate their funds. For example, decisions by members of independent regulatory commissions are sensitive to the views of members of their congressional oversight committees. When the membership of the committees becomes more liberal, so too do the decisions regulators make.[44]

Constituent service is also a congressional tool for controlling the bureaucracy. Members of Congress often try to influence agencies on behalf of constituents. This becomes a problem when it leads to inefficiencies such as keeping unneeded military bases open to boost the economy of a member's district or when it impedes necessary government regulation, as it did when several prominent senators delayed investigation of corrupt and careless savings and loan operations.

Courts

The courts also influence the bureaucracy. Judicial decisions shape agency actions by directing agencies to follow legally correct procedures. Of course, the courts cannot intercede in an agency's decision making unless some aggrieved person or corporation files a suit against the agency. Nevertheless, in almost any controversial agency action, there will be aggrieved parties, and possibly some with sufficient resources to bring a court action.

The courts interpret lawmakers' intentions by deciding what congressional majorities and the president had in mind when they made a law. This can be difficult. Sometimes, in their haste, lawmakers may have left out parts of a law or, as a Supreme Court justice put it, "agreed to disagree."[45] Lawmakers may also have written a law so agencies can adapt it to unknown future conditions. How the courts read a law may add to or reduce the relative power of Congress and the president or expand the courts' own powers. We discuss these issues in Chapter 13.

Regulators as well as other agency policymakers appear to be quite sensitive to court decisions. For example, when the courts begin overturning the National Labor Relations Board's decisions in a pro-labor direction, NLRB decisions soon become more pro-labor. Similarly, decisions drift the other way when courts begin to overturn decisions in a pro-business direction.[46]

Interest Groups and Individuals

Interest groups want to make sure bureaucracies adopt rules and enforcement practices they favor. A law

THE FBI RUNS AMOK

J. Edgar Hoover helped the Federal Bureau of Investigation (FBI) develop a reputation for being *the* leading crime fighter in America. Hollywood made movies about the FBI, and television carried a popular weekly series describing its exploits. What became known only later is that under Hoover's leadership the FBI consistently did things that were illegal and violated citizens' rights:

- It conducted over 500,000 investigations of "subversive" activity between 1960 and 1974, none of which resulted in a prosecution. Those investigated included Washington, D.C. high school students who had complained about the quality of school food, the women's liberation movement, all black student groups, and antiwar activists.
- It played "dirty tricks" on what it thought were subversive people. For example, it harassed Martin Luther King, Jr., by discouraging colleges from giving him honorary degrees; putting wiretaps and bugs in his hotel rooms, home, and offices; circulating information obtained with these devices to the media and executive branch officials; and mailing King a tape suggesting he kill himself or face public exposure of material on his extracurricular sex life the agency had collected about him. (After King's assassination, the FBI worked against congressional proposals to commemorate him with a national holiday.)
- Hoover "blackmailed" President Kennedy into signing an order permitting wiretapping of King by threatening to expose Kennedy's extracurricular sex life to the public. Hoover had gotten this evidence by tapping White House telephone conversations between Kennedy and a woman with Mafia ties.
- It conducted burglaries, forged letters, disrupted marriages, got people fired from jobs and ousted from apartments, and supplied violent groups like the Ku Klux Klan with arms and explosives.

The FBI's usual justification for doing these things was that they were necessary to fight those wanting to overthrow the government. But, in fact, the agency directed its efforts at anyone Hoover disliked—people such as Albert Einstein, Ernest Hemingway, and John Lennon. Hoover had the FBI keep files on leading political figures to protect himself and the agency from criticism.

Hoover led the FBI for 48 years, until 1972. "Hoover used his confidential files to hang on to power long past retirement age. Once when an aide suggested Johnson get rid of Hoover, the President replied, 'Son, when you have a skunk it is better to have him inside the tent pissing out than outside pissing in.' "[1]

Although his successors have acknowledged the need to prevent abuses, progress is slow. For example, from 1981 to 1985, the FBI harassed labor unions, churches, and individuals (including nuns and students) opposed to White House Central American policies. It infiltrated their meetings and took and circulated photographs of them without finding any criminal activity. In 1988, criticism that the FBI was violating privacy rights forced it to retreat from looking for Soviet spies by asking librarians to finger library users with foreign-sounding names or accents and those who acted in "suspicious" ways.[2] And, during the Persian Gulf crisis, FBI investigations into the political beliefs of Arab Americans frightened many into recalling the internment of Japanese Americans during World War II.

Fred Ward/Black Star

Hoover was a master organizer who created a paranoid agency environment that stifled those who disagreed with him or did not conform to his idea of what an FBI agent should do or look like. He hired agents who would adapt to this environment and, as an opponent of the civil rights movement, hired mostly whites. His preferences still dominate the agency.

Before we can control an agency, we need to know what it is doing. Most Americans had little idea these activities were taking place. This indicates that controlling the bureaucracy is a never-ending job.

1. Hugh Sidey, "Reach Out and Twist an Arm," *Time*, December 13, 1993, p. 43.
2. Herbert N. Foerstel, *Surveillance in the Stacks* (Westport, Conn.: Greenwood Press, 1991).

SOURCES: Robert Justin Goldstein, "The FBI and American Politics Textbooks," *PS* 18 (Spring 1985), pp. 237–246. For more on Hoover and the FBI, see Taylor Branch, *Parting the Waters: America in the King Years, 1954–1963* (New York: Simon & Schuster, 1988), which examines the FBI and the civil rights movement; Herbert Mitgang, *Dangerous Dossiers* (New York: Donald I. Fine, 1988); Kenneth O'Reilly, *"Racial Matters": The FBI's Secret File on Black America, 1960–1972* (New York: Free Press, 1989).

establishing new safeguards in toxic waste disposal may be applauded by environmental and citizen groups, but the job of these groups is not over until they make sure the Environmental Protection Agency writes strict rules to carry out the law and then enforces them. Thus, it is not enough to get a law passed that responds to your interests; the law must be implemented in a responsive way too.

How do groups seek to make sure this happens? One way is through relationships with Congress. If an agency seems to be sabotaging the intent of Congress, interest groups can work with friendly congressional committees to put pressure on the agency to mend its ways. Interest groups can also try to rally public opinion to their side and pressure Congress or the president to do something about the agency.

Interest groups try to influence agencies directly, too. For example, the broadcasting industry tries to shape Federal Communications Commission decisions to enable the industry to compete more effectively with cable television companies. Sometimes interest groups pressure an agency so effectively that the agency is said to be "captured."[47] This term is used most frequently in referring to regulatory agencies said to be controlled by the groups they are supposed to be regulating. Thus, the Nuclear Regulatory Commission looks out for the interests of the nuclear industry, which it is supposed to be regulating.

Studies of voting by regulatory commissioners also show an indirect influence of industry. Some commissioners come to their regulatory agencies from the industry they are regulating. These commissioners are more likely than others to take a pro-industry position in cases before the agency. Furthermore, commissioners leaving a regulatory agency to take jobs in a regulated industry become more pro-industry in their last year as regulators than others who are not leaving for such jobs.[48] They apparently anticipate a move to industry and, in a sacrifice of their neutral competence, try to make their decisions more acceptable to possible employers.

Can individual citizens influence the bureaucracy too? It is difficult for citizens acting as individuals to influence public agencies. Not surprisingly, as we have seen, few individuals take advantage of their right to information from the bureaucracy.

However, individual bureaucrats, called **whistleblowers,** can sometimes open their agencies to public view. Their purpose is usually to expose mismanagement and abuse of discretion to make their agencies more responsive and productive. The most famous whistleblower is Ernest Fitzgerald. In 1968, as an Air Force cost accountant, he exposed bad management by revealing problems with the Lockheed C-5A transport plane. The plane vibrated so much in flight that its wings actually fell off if they were not replaced after only 200 hours of flying time. Saying it wanted "to save expenses"—his $32,000 salary—the Air Force reacted by firing Fitzgerald. He sued to get his job back and won, but all he got was his title, office, and pay. The Air Force gave him nothing to do, and he had to wait for a court order in 1982 before the Air Force gave him responsibilities equal to his qualifications. The wings were repaired, and the C-5A operated successfully for many years.[49] In 1987, the Air Force was still trying to neutralize what one Pentagon veteran called "the most hated man in the Air Force" by juggling staff assignments.[50]

The 1978 Civil Service Reform Act created an agency to protect whistleblowers. During its first decade, the agency was ineffective because the act defined whistleblowers' rights narrowly and because of budget cuts and morale problems in the 1980s. In 1988, Reagan vetoed a bill designed to strengthen it. Congress passed the bill again in 1989 and Bush signed it into law. It gives whistleblowers more protection from agencies they accuse of mismanagement and harassment. A law passed in 1986 allows private citizens to be whistleblowers too by suing companies with government contracts that defraud the government.[51]

Relying on brave people like Fitzgerald to get agencies to operate properly is a mistake. In 1993, a study reported that over one-third of federal whistleblowers alleged they suffered some form of reprisal or threat of reprisal.[52] It is the rare person who will set aside ambition for promotion and cordial relations with colleagues to challenge the status quo. Most people, whether in the private or the public sector, find it difficult to expose the dirty laundry of the bureaucracy employing them.

"It's not mailmen per se. I'm just very anti-government these days.

CONCLUSION: IS THE BUREAUCRACY RESPONSIVE?

Is the federal bureaucracy the uncontrollable fourth branch of government as some portray it? Our fragmented political system has created an environment of uncertainty and competition for public agencies. They have many bosses: a president, his appointees, Congress, and its many committees and subcommittees. In addition, numerous interest groups try to influence them. The often contradictory expectations of responsiveness and neutral competence contribute to the uncertainty of the bureaucracy's environment too.

As a result, agencies try to protect themselves by cultivating the support of congressional committees and interest groups. Even presidents have trouble influencing agencies because of these alliances. Although some presidents, such as Franklin Roosevelt and Lyndon Johnson, have occasionally rearranged the status quo, their successes in representing a vision of national priorities are more the exception than the rule.

Well-organized interest groups and Congress can also influence agencies, often through the iron triangles that help stabilize agency environments. But interest groups do not represent everyone. Likewise, not everyone feels represented by members of Congress or can take advantage of the Sunshine and Freedom of Information Acts. As a result, agencies may not represent those who fall through the "safety net" of interest group and congressional representation.

Thus, diverse expectations of what government should do make the federal bureaucracy seem unresponsive. Even well-run agencies represent waste, and therefore a lack of responsiveness and executive leadership, to people unaware of, lacking need of, or opposed to their services.

Despite people's negative feelings about the bureaucracy, the mail is delivered, bridges get inspected, and passports are issued. As Charles Goodsell points out, "Unmistakably, . . . bureaucracy works most of the time."[53] It usually does what it is supposed to do. But when what the bureaucracy is supposed to do is unclear, it is harder for the bureaucracy to respond to our wishes.

EPILOGUE

The Surgeon General Chooses Neutral Competence

In 1986 Surgeon General Koop issued a report proposing expanded sex education and better education on the dangers of AIDS for schoolchildren. The 36-page report ignored conservative views. It concluded that a lack of sex education impedes the effort to stop AIDS in the absence of a vaccine or cure. The report noted that testing all hospital patients is unnecessary because many of the 37 million people hospitalized each year are children or the elderly, who face low risks of infection.

Later, in a radio broadcast, Koop called on the nation's networks to lift their self-imposed ban on condom advertising. He argued that "anyone who is sexually active should use a condom from start to finish. AIDS kills and sexually active people have to be told this." The networks indicated they would leave policy changes to their local affiliates.

The government's most visible response to AIDS was a brochure mailed to 107 million households in 1988 describing how AIDS is contracted and how to avoid it. That same year, a presidential commission and a National Academy of Sciences panel made recommendations about dealing with AIDS that echoed Koop's. Both criticized the government, and especially Reagan's White House, for a lack of leadership. At the same time, many conservatives were disappointed and angry, accusing Koop of not promoting chastity.

By 1995, AIDS had killed more than 204,000 people. And the demographics of the disease were changing. A majority of victims were still gay men, but there were signs that the spread of AIDS among gays had peaked. Increasingly, the new high-risk populations were intravenous drug users and poor inner city blacks and Hispanics. In 1993, over 40% of all Americans with the disease were minorities. It is now the second leading cause of death of men and the fourth leading killer of women aged 25 to 44. It is also the seventh leading cause of death of young children. Koop acknowledged that health workers have been "singularly unsuccessful in penetrating

Courtesy of New York City Department of Health

the drug-addicted culture" with educational messages.[54] An observer noted that heterosexual AIDS is becoming a "poor people's disease."[55]

Civil servants are supposed to be responsive to public opinion and their superiors, in Koop's case the president. At the same time, they are supposed to do their jobs in a neutrally competent way. As surgeon general, Koop said, "I'm not afforded the luxury of bringing ideology or morals into my job, especially with the sort of threat we have with AIDS."[56] He could not satisfy presidential expectations because his professional expertise led him to different conclusions.

KEY TERMS

independent agencies
policy implementation
delegated legislative authority
regulation
patronage
neutral competence
Civil Service Commission
merit system
Hatch Act
executive leadership
whistleblowers

FURTHER READING

David Burnham, *A Law unto Itself: Power, Politics and the IRS* (New York: Random House, 1990). An analysis of the enforcement of the federal tax code, a code so complex it seems to invite bureaucratic inefficiency and abuses.

Irving L. Janis, *Victims of Groupthink* (Boston: Houghton Mifflin, 1972). Explaining why people often prefer getting along to making hard decisions, he helps us see why whistleblowers are rare souls.

James H. Jones, *Bad Blood* (New York: Free Press, 1981). Award-winning account of the Public Health Service's experiment in which black men with syphilis were left untreated so doctors could see the effects of the disease. The book is revealing about the nature of both bureaucratic behavior and racial discrimination.

Robert N. Kharasch, *The Institutional Imperative: How to Understand the United States Government and Other Bulky Objects* (New York: Charterhouse Books, 1973). A witty and insightful study of such topics as the "irrelevance" of bureaucratic morality and purpose, Pentagon "busyness," and the "Sweet Uses of Stupidity."

Jonathan Kwitny, *Acceptable Risks* (New York: Poseidon Books, 1992). A fast-paced and well-written story of two men who prodded and fought the Food and Drug Administration to make potentially helpful medicines available to AIDS patients. A good illustration of both agency rigidity and, ultimately, responsiveness.

ELECTRONIC RESOURCES

(http://www.whitehouse.gov/WH/Cabinet/html/cabinet_links.html and **http://www.whitehouse.gov/WH/Independent_Agencies/html/independent_links.html**

Each federal agency has its own Web page. The first page listed here links to all cabinet departments, and the second to independent agencies and commissions. These sites provide information about the policies of the agency, relevant statistics, current activities and priorities, and leadership within the agency.

http://www.fedstats.gov/

Federal agencies collect many statistics about the American population, the economy, housing, employment, and many other areas of life. This Web site provides a guide to finding and using those statistics, whether they involve the mean household income of American families or last year's export trade data.

http://www.usajobs.opm.gov/

At this site, you can see what jobs are open in the federal government and make an online application.

INFOTRAC CITATIONS

"Has the White House Delivered on Promises to Reinvent Government?"
"Why Deregulation Has Gone Too Far"
"Civil Rights Group Makes Stand"
"Court Makes It Harder for Corporations"

NOTES

1. "AIDS:" Who Should Be Tested?" *Newsweek*, May 11, 1987, pp. 64–65.
2. Stephen Jay Gould, "The Exponential Spread of AIDS Underscores the Tragedy of Our Delay in Fighting One of Nature's Plagues," *New York Times Magazine*, April 19, 1987, p. 33.
3. "AIDS Becomes a Political Issue," *Time*, March 23, 1987, p. 24.
4. For a description of Weber's view of bureaucracy, see H. H. Gerth and C. Wright Mills, trans., *From Max Weber: Essays on Sociology* (New York: Oxford University Press, 1946), pp. 196–239.
5. Taken from Bruce Adams, "The Frustrations of Government Service," *Public Administration Review* 44 (January/February 1984), p. 5. For more discussion of public attitudes about the civil service, see Herbert Kaufman, "Fear of Bureaucracy: A Raging Pandemic," *Public Administration Review* 41 (January/February 1981), p. 1.
6. Barry Bozeman, *All Organizations Are Public: Bridging Public and Private Organizational Theories* (San Francisco: Jossey-Bass, 1987).
7. Donald S. Kellermann, Andrew Kohut, and Carol Bowman, *The People, The Press and Politics on the Eve of '92: Fault Lines in the Electorate* (Washington, D.C.: Times Mirror Center for The People & The Press, December 4, 1991), p. 39.
8. Mark Green and John Berry, *The Challenge of Hidden Profits: Reducing Corporate Bureaucracy and Waste* (New York: Wm. Morrow, 1985).
9. Reported in Sam Archibald, "The Early Years of the Freedom of Information Act—1955–1974," *PS: Political Science & Politics* (December 1993), p. 730.
10. Debra Gersh Hernandez, "Many Promises, Little Action," *Editor & Publisher* (March 26, 1994), p. 15.

11. General Accounting Office, *Freedom of Information Act: State Department Request Processing* (Washington, D.C.: U.S. Government Printing Office, January 23, 1989).

12. "President Declassifies Old Papers," *Omaha World-Herald*, April 18, 1995, p. 1.

13. Hernandez, "Many Promises, Little Action," p. 12; and George Lardner Jr., "Hit That 'Save' Button," *Washington Post National Weekly Edition*, August 23–29, 1993, p. 32.

14. Stephen Hess, *The Government/Press Connection: Press Officers and Their Offices* (Washington, D.C.: Brookings Institution, 1984), p. 101.

15. Evan Hendricks, *Former Secrets: Government Records Made Public through the Freedom of Information Act* (Washington, D.C.: Campaign for Political Rights, 1982).

16. Joyce Appleby, "That's General Washington to You," *New York Times Book Review*, February 14, 1993, p. 11. This is a review of Richard Norton Smith, *Patriarch* (Boston: Houghton Mifflin, 1993).

17. Leonard D. White, *Introduction to the Study of Public Administration*, 4th ed. (New York: Macmillan, 1955), p. 4.

18. Paul C. Light, *Thickening Government: Federal Hierarchy and the Diffusion of Accountability* (Washington, D.C.: Brookings Institution, 1995).

19. Office of Management and Budget, *Special Analyses: Budget of the United States: Fiscal Year 1990* (Washington, D.C.: U.S. Government Printing Office, 1989), pp. 1–13; *Historical Tables: Budget of the United States: Fiscal Year 1996* (Washington, D.C.: U.S. Government Printing Office, 1995), p. 245.

20. Harold Seidman and Robert Gilmour, *Politics, Position and Power: The Dynamics of Federal Organization*, 4th ed. (New York: Oxford University Press, 1986), pp. 249–292. See also Herbert Kaufman, "Emerging Conflicts in the Doctrines of Public Administration," *American Political Science Review* 50 (December 1956), pp. 1057–1073, for a study of the growth of American public bureaucracy focusing on the conflicting expectations people have of it.

21. See Lawrence J. Haas, "Dodging the Budget Bullet," *National Journal*, October 1, 1988, pp. 2465–2469; Donald F. Kettl, "Expansion and Protection in the Budgetary Process," *Public Administration Review* 49 (May/June 1989), pp. 231–239; Seidman and Gilmour, *Politics, Position, and Power*, pp. 281–292.

22. For a discussion of these issues see Peter T. Kilborn, "Big Change Likely as Law Bans Bias toward Disabled," *New York Times*, July 19, 1992, pp. 1 and 16.

23. Jill Smolows, "Noble Aims, Mixed Results," *Time*, July 31, 1995, p. 54.

24. Theodore Lowi, *The End of Liberalism* (New York: W. W. Norton, 1969).

25. Thomas J. Anton, *American Federalism and Public Policy* (Philadelphia: Temple University Press, 1989).

26. Virginia I. Postrel, "Red (Tape) Alert," *Washington Post National Weekly Edition*, February 20–26, 1995, p. 23.

27. Ibid.

28. John M. Goshko, "The Big-Ticket Costs of the Disabilities Act," *Washington Post National Weekly Edition*, March 20–26, 1995, p. 31.

29. For more, see Margaret Kriz, "A New Shade of Green," *National Journal*, March 18, 1995, pp. 661–665.

30. Gary Lee, "Deregulating Regulations," *Washington Post National Weekly Edition*, February 20–26, 1995, pp. 6–7.

31. Woodrow Wilson, "The Study of Administration," *Political Science Quarterly* 56 (December 1941), pp. 481–506. This was reprinted from the article's original publication in *The Academy of Political Science* in 1887.

32. See David H. Rosenbloom, "Editorial: Have An Administrative Rx? Don't Forget the Politics!" *Public Administration Review* (November/December 1993), pp. 503–507.

33. "Hatch Act Revamped," *PA Times*, November 1, 1993, p. 3; "Hatch Act Political Curbs Retained for Some Workers," *Lincoln Star*, July 16, 1993, p. 3.

34. Walter Williams, "So, You Like Government on Cheap?" *Lincoln Sunday Journal-Star*, October 21, 1990, p. 6B. See also E. J. Dionne, Jr., "Are We Getting the Kind of Public Servants We Deserve?" *Washington Post National Weekly Edition*, August 13–19, 1990, p. 31; Gregory B. Lewis, "Turnover and the Quiet Crisis in the Federal Civil Service," *Public Administration Review* (March/April 1991), pp. 145–155.

35. Reported in "Bush Commits to Support the Public Service," *PA Times*, November 25, 1988, p. 1. See also Judith Havemann, "Panel Seeks Raises for Civil Service," *Washington Post*, March 30, 1989, p. A20.

36. Information about conflict-of-interest matters is in Ronald Brownstein, "Agency Ethics Officers Fear Meese Ruling Could Weaken Conflict Laws," *National Journal*, March 23, 1985, pp. 639–642; W. John Moore, " Ethics Plan: Too Stingy or Humbug?" *National Journal*, December 19, 1992, p. 2898.

37. Steven Maynard-Moody, "Beyond Implementation: Developing an Institutional Theory of Administrative Policy Making," *Public Administration Review* 49 (March/April 1989), p. 139.

38. B. Dan Wood, "Principals, Bureaucrats, and Responsiveness in Clean Air Enforcements," *American Political Science Review* 82 (March 1988), pp. 213–234.

39. George C. Eads and Michael Fix, *Relief or Reform?* (Washington, D.C.: Urban Institute Press, 1984), chapter 7.

40. David Ellis, "White House to IRS: Hands Off the Rich," *Time*, April 1, 1991, p. 15.

41. Richard Lacayo, "Pro-Choice? Get Lost," *Time*, December 4, 1989, pp. 43–44.

42. Jeffrey Cohen, "The Dynamics of the Revolving Door," *American Journal of Political Science* 30 (November 1986), pp. 689–708.

43. Charles Peters, *How Washington Really Works* (Reading, Mass.: Addison-Wesley, 1980), pp. 46–47.

44. Terry Moe, "Regulators' Performance and Presidential Administrations," *American Journal of Political Science* 26 (May 1982), pp. 197–224; Terry Moe, "Control and Feedback in Economic Regulation," *American Political Science Review* 79 (December 1985), pp. 1094–1116.

45. Joan Biskupic, "Asking the Court to Read between the Lines," *Washington Post National Weekly Edition*, May 9–15, 1994, p. 32.

46. Moe, "Control and Feedback."

47. The term *capture* is widely used, but its use by political scientists studying regulation seems to have originated with Samuel Huntington, "The Marasmus of the ICC," *Yale Law Journal* 61 (April 1952), pp. 467–509; it was later popularized by Marver Bernstein, *Regulating Business by Independent Commission* (Princeton, N.J.: Princeton University Press, 1955).

48. Bernstein, *Regulating Business;* William Gormley, "A Test of the Revolving Door Hypothesis in the FCC," *American Journal of Political Science* 23 (November 1979), pp. 665–683; Jeffrey Cohen, "The Dynamics of the Revolving Door," *American Journal of Political Science* 30 (November 1986), pp. 689–708.

49. See "C-5As with Wing Modifications Planned for September Delivery," *Aviation Week & Space Technology*, December 22, 1969, p. 13; "Whatever Happened to the C-5A 'White Elephant'?" *U.S. News and World Report*, June 19, 1972, p. 63.

50. David C. Morrison, "Extracting a Thorn, Air Force-Style," *National Journal*, March 7, 1987, p. 567. For more on Fitzgerald's experiences, see A. Ernest Fitzgerald, *The Pentagonists: An Insider's View of Waste, Mismanagement, and Fraud in Defense Spending* (Boston: Houghton Mifflin, 1989).

51. W. John Moore, "Citizen Prosecutors," *National Journal*, August 18, 1990, pp. 2006–2010.

52. Merit Systems Protection Board, Office of Policy and Evaluation, "Whistleblowing in the Federal Government: An Update" (Washington, D.C., 1993).

53. Charles T. Goodsell, *The Case for Bureaucracy: A Public Administration Polemic*, 2d ed. (Chatham, N.J.: Chatham House, 1985), p. 140.

54. Lawrence K. Altman, "Who's Stricken and How: AIDS Pattern Is Shifting," *New York Times*, February 5, 1989, pp. 1 and 16. See also Sandra Panem, *The AIDS Bureaucracy* (Cambridge, Mass.: Harvard University Press, 1988).

55. Ibid.

56. Koop's 1987 remark is quoted in Julie Kosterlitz, "Health Focus," *National Journal*, January 28, 1989, p. 259.

Inside the Supreme Court after an oral argument.

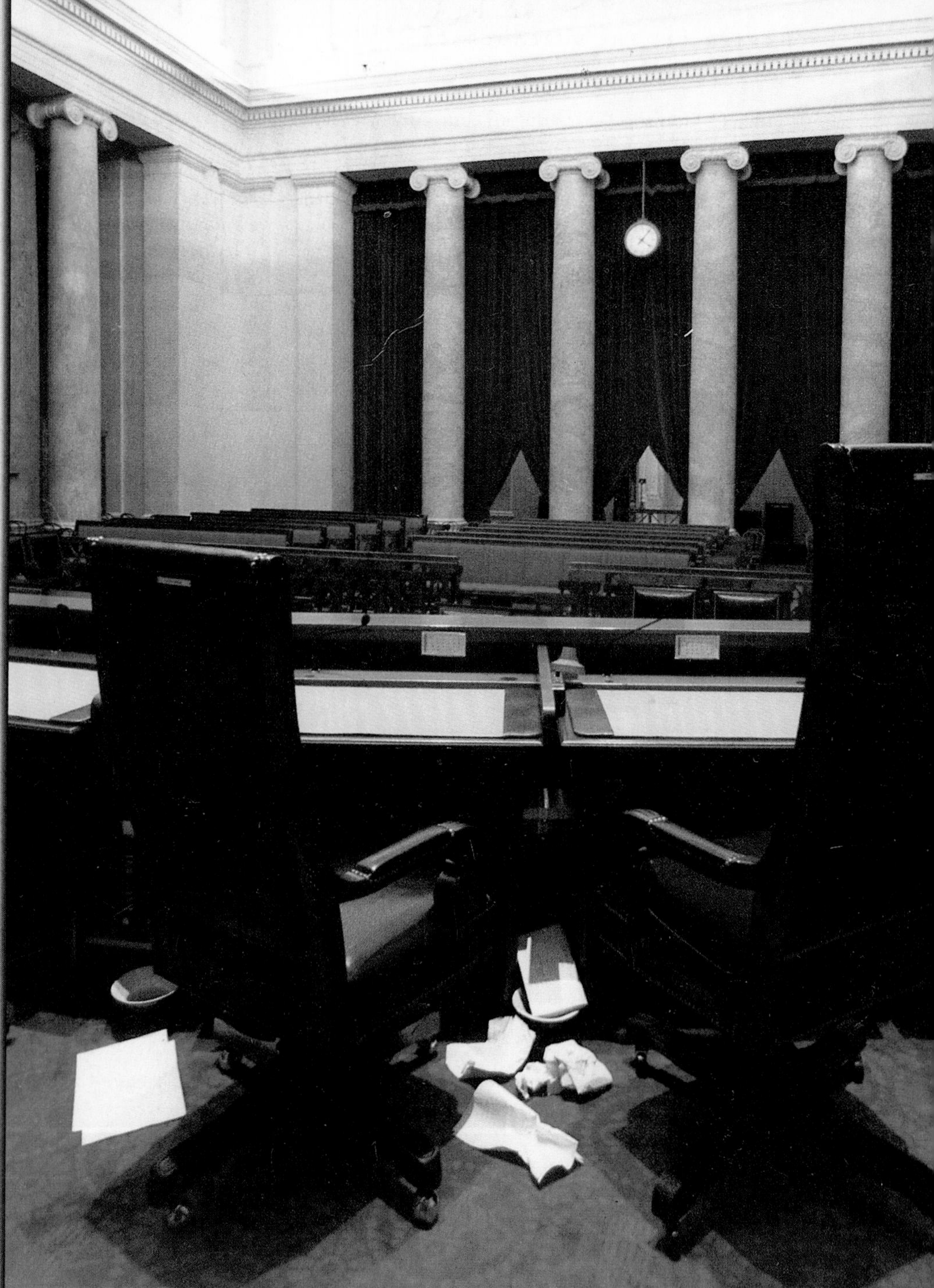

Lynn Johnson/Aurora

13 THE JUDICIARY

OUTLINE

- **Development of the Courts' Role in Government**
  - Founding to the Civil War
  - Civil War to the Depression
  - Depression to the Present
- **Courts**
  - Structure of the Courts
  - Jurisdiction of the Courts
- **Judges**
  - Selection of Judges
  - Tenure of Judges
  - Qualifications of Judges
  - Independence of Judges
- **Access to the Courts**
  - Wealth Discrimination in Access
  - Interest Group Help in Access
  - Restrictions on Access
  - Proceeding through the Courts
- **Deciding Cases**
  - Interpreting Statutes
  - Interpreting the Constitution
  - Restraint and Activism
  - Following Precedents
  - Making Law
- **The Power of the Courts**
  - Use of Judicial Review
  - Use of Political Checks against the Courts
- **Conclusion: Are the Courts Responsive?**

YOU ARE THERE

Is the President Immune?

You are Justice John Paul Stevens, and you must decide how to vote on a sensitive constitutional issue facing the U.S. Supreme Court in 1997: Is a president, during his term in office, immune from a lawsuit based on alleged actions he took before becoming president?

Paula Jones, a clerical worker in an Arkansas state agency, claims that Bill Clinton, as governor of Arkansas in 1991, made a sexual advance toward her—"He exposed himself"—at a conference in a hotel, where she staffed the registration desk and he delivered a speech. After she refused his overture, Jones claims that she suffered hostility from her superiors and a change in her duties. Essentially, Jones argues that Clinton sexually harassed her.[1] She is suing for $700,000.

President Clinton denies that the incident or the treatment after the conference ever occurred. Regardless, he maintains that as president he is immune—that is, he cannot be sued—during his term in office. He acknowledges that as a private citizen he could be sued after he leaves the White House.[2]

This case is unique. Only three prior presidents have been sued for incidents occurring before taking office. The suits against Theodore Roosevelt and Harry Truman were dismissed before these men were inaugurated. Two suits against John Kennedy, arising from an automobile accident involving staff members in the campaign, were settled out of court after Kennedy took office.

Some presidents have been sued for incidents occurring during their term, but there are few court rulings to guide you. The primary precedent is a Supreme Court ruling in 1982 involving President Richard Nixon.[3] During his term, Nixon had ordered the firing of a Pentagon accountant who had told Congress that an Air Force cargo plane was costing more, and performing worse, than it was supposed to. (Its wings were falling off after 200 hours of flight time.) The firing was unlawful, so the accountant sued the president. The Court ruled that although the Constitution does not mention **presidential immunity,** the concept of separation of powers entails such immunity. Presidents must be free to make decisions without worrying about lawsuits or spending time defending themselves against lawsuits. Otherwise, presidents might be weaker than our constitutional framework envisions.

More specifically, the Court ruled that presidents have immunity, forever, for acts that occur while in office and that relate to their official responsibilities. This precedent does not indicate whether immunity exists for decisions made before taking office or for decisions unrelated to a president's official responsibilities.

The president's lawyer has argued that a key rationale for immunity—to shield presidents from diverting their attention and energy from governmental matters in the process of defending themselves against private suits—would apply to Clinton's situation just as it did to Nixon's. The lawyer has cited additional reasons that seem plausible in the 1990s: that Jones's suit, if allowed to continue, might inspire copycat suits; that it might prompt others to seek the fame that it has brought her; and that it might tempt interest groups to tie up and possibly bring down presidents they oppose. Presidents might feel pressure to defend themselves against politically motivated suits rather than attend to the country's business.

Jones's lawyers have countered that nobody, not even a president, is above the law. Moreover, his alleged tawdry behavior was not related to his official responsibilities and did not occur during his presidential term. Although Jones could sue after Clinton left office, even if the Court rules against her now, the lawyers have pointed out that a suit would be harder to win if key evidence is lost or an important witness dies in the intervening years.[4]

You have several options. You could grant or deny the president's request for temporary immunity. Or, like the federal trial court, you could grant partial temporary immunity. This judge ruled that the president was immune from trial but not from "discovery"—the process of disclosing information and establishing facts to be used at trial. This compromise would allow Jones to preserve a record of crucial evidence and testimony but allow Clinton to avoid a trial while in office.

You are a Republican, appointed by President Gerald Ford, but you have become a liberal on the bench. And, like other Americans, you have your own opinions about Bill Clinton. Yet you realize that your partisan ties or ideological views or personal feelings about him should not determine your decision in this important case. How do you decide? And why?

Most people assume that courts are nonpolitical and that judges are objective. People say we have "a government of laws, not of men." This is a myth. At any time in our history, "It is individuals who make, enforce, and interpret the law."[5] When judges interpret the law, they are political actors and courts are political institutions.

As political institutions, courts make policy, although not all make policy to the same degree. The Supreme Court makes national policy in most of its cases. The lower courts make regional and local policy in some of their cases, although most of their cases are routine because the law is clear and the decisions are of little consequence except to the litigants.

The public expresses more support for the Supreme Court than for the president or Congress.[6] The public is turned off by the disagreements and debates and the negotiations and compromises among officials and by the efforts of interest groups to influence policies. These messy features of democratic government, which are so visible in the executive and legislative branches, are not very visible in the judicial branch. As a result, most people assume that these things do not occur in the judicial branch. In reality, they do occur; they just are not as apparent.

That the judiciary is part of the political process can be seen in all of the topics this chapter covers—the history, structure, jurisdiction, composition, operation, and impact of the courts.

DEVELOPMENT OF THE COURTS' ROLE IN GOVERNMENT

The Founders expected the judiciary to be the weakest branch of government. In the *Federalist Papers*, Alexander Hamilton wrote that Congress would have power to pass the laws and appropriate the money; the president would have power to execute the laws; but the courts would have "merely judgment," that is, only power to resolve disputes in cases brought to them. In doing so, they would exercise "neither force nor will." They would not have any means to enforce decisions, and they would not use their own values to decide cases. Rather, they would simply apply the Constitution and laws as written. Consequently, the judiciary would be the "least dangerous" branch.[7]

This prediction was accurate for the early years of the Republic. The Supreme Court was held in such low esteem that some distinguished men refused to accept appointment, or they accepted appointment but refused to attend sessions. The first chief justice thought the Court was "inauspicious,"[8] without enough "weight and dignity" to play an important role.[9] So he resigned to be governor of New York. The second chief justice resigned to be envoy to France. To add insult, when the capital was moved to Washington in 1801, the planners overlooked the Court and forgot to provide a place for it to hold sessions. It had to meet in the office of the clerk of the Senate for some years.

However, the status of the Court changed after the appointment of the third chief justice—John Marshall. Under the leadership of Marshall and later chief justices, the Court gradually developed "weight and dignity" and came to play an important role in government. The lower courts eventually did as well.

The development of the courts' role in government can be shown by dividing the courts' history into three eras—from the founding to the Civil War, from the Civil War to the Great Depression, and from the depression to the present.

Founding to the Civil War

The primary issue for the courts in the era from the country's founding to the Civil War was the relationship between nation and state. In addressing this issue, the Supreme Court established judicial review and national dominance.

JUDICIAL REVIEW

Judicial review is the authority to declare laws or actions of government officials unconstitutional. The Constitution does not mention judicial review, but the Founders apparently expected the courts to exercise it. In the *Federalist Papers*, Hamilton said the courts would have authority to void laws contrary to the

Chief Justice John Marshall.

Constitution,[10] and at the time some state courts had such authority. Yet the Founders did not expect the courts to exercise it vigorously.

The Supreme Court articulated judicial review in the case of ***Marbury v. Madison*** in 1803.[11] The case had its origins in 1800, when the Federalist president John Adams was defeated in his bid for reelection by Thomas Jefferson and Federalist members of Congress were defeated by Jeffersonians. With both the presidency and Congress lost, the Federalists tried to ensure continued control of the judiciary. The lame duck president and Congress added more judgeships, which actually were not needed, and appointed Federalists to fill them. They hoped to install these "midnight judges" before the new president and Congress took over. In addition, Adams named his secretary of state, John Marshall, to be chief justice. At the time, though, Marshall was still secretary of state and was responsible for delivering the commissions to the new appointees. But he ran out of time and failed to deliver 17 of the 42 commissions for District of Columbia justices of the peace. He assumed that his successor would deliver the rest. But Jefferson, angry at the Federalists' efforts to pack the judiciary, told his secretary of state, James Madison, not to deliver the commissions. Without the signed commissions, the appointees could not prove that they had in fact been appointed.

William Marbury and three other appointees petitioned the Supreme Court for a writ of mandamus, a writ that orders government officials to do something they have a duty to do. In this case it would order Madison to deliver the commissions.

As chief justice, Marshall was in a position to rule on his own failure to deliver the commissions. Today this would be considered a conflict of interest, and he would be expected to disqualify himself. But at the time people were not as troubled by such conflicts.

Marshall could issue the writ, but Jefferson would tell Madison to disobey it and the Court would be powerless to enforce it. Or he could not issue the writ, and the Court would appear powerless to issue it. Either way the Court would demonstrate weakness rather than strength. But Marshall shrewdly found a way out of the dilemma.

Marshall interpreted a provision of a congressional statute in a questionable way and then a provision of the Constitution in a questionable way as well. Marbury had petitioned the Court for a writ of mandamus under the authority of a provision of the Judiciary Act of 1789 that permitted the Court to issue such a writ. Marshall maintained that this provision broadened the Court's original jurisdiction and thus violated the Constitution. (The Constitution allows the Court to hear cases on appeal, and it gives the Court original jurisdiction—that is, the authority to hear cases that have not been heard by any other court before—in cases involving a state or foreign ambassador. Marbury's involved neither.) Actually, it is not clear that the provision of the act did broaden the Court's original jurisdiction. Further, even if the provision did broaden the Court's original jurisdiction, it is not clear that this would violate the Constitution. (The Constitution does not say the Court shall have original jurisdiction *only* in cases involving a state or foreign ambassador.) Many members of Congress who had drafted and voted for the Judiciary Act had been delegates to the Constitutional Convention, and it is unlikely that they would have initiated a law that contradicted the Constitution. But these interpretations allowed Marshall a way out of the dilemma.

Marshall concluded that the Court could not order the administration to give the commission because the provision of the act was unconstitutional. Thus, Marshall exercised judicial review. He wrote, in a statement that would be repeated by courts for years to come, "It is emphatically the province and duty of the judicial department to say what the law is."

Marshall justified judicial review this way: The Constitution is the supreme law of the land. If other laws contradict it, they are unconstitutional. So far, few of his contemporaries would quarrel with his reasoning.

Marshall continued: Judges decide cases, and to decide cases they have to apply the Constitution. To apply it, they have to say what it means. They can be trusted to say what it means because they take an oath to uphold it. Here many would quarrel with his reasoning. Other officials have to follow the Constitution and take an oath to uphold it, and they could interpret it as appropriately as judges could.

But Marshall was persuasive enough to convince many people. A sly fox, he sacrificed the commissions—he could not have gotten them anyway—and established the power of judicial review instead. In doing so, with one hand he gave the Jeffersonians what they wanted, while with the other he gave the Federalists something much greater. And all along he claimed he did what the Constitution required him to do.

Jefferson saw through this. He said the Constitution, in Marshall's hands, was "a thing of putty."[12] But the decision did not require Jefferson to do anything, so he could not do anything but protest. Most of Jefferson's followers were satisfied with the result. They were not upset that the Court had invalidated a Federalist law or especially concerned with the means used to do so.

Of course, they were shortsighted because this decision laid the cornerstone for a strong judiciary. Thus, the case that began as a "trivial squabble over a few petty political plums"[13] became perhaps the most important case the Court has ever decided.

Supreme Court Historical Society

This portrait of William Marbury reflects the importance of Marbury v. Madison. *It is the only portrait of a litigant owned by the Supreme Court Historical Society.*

NATIONAL DOMINANCE

After *Marbury* the Court did not declare any other congressional laws unconstitutional during Marshall's tenure, although it did declare numerous state laws unconstitutional.[14]

The Court also furthered national dominance by broadly construing Congress's power. In *McCulloch v. Maryland*, explained in Chapter 3, the Court interpreted the "necessary and proper clause" to allow Congress to legislate in many matters not mentioned in the Constitution. The Court also furthered national dominance by narrowly construing states' power to regulate commerce.[15]

When President Andrew Jackson named Roger Taney to replace Marshall, proponents of a strong national government worried that Taney would undo what Marshall had done. But, although Taney did not further expand national power, he upheld national supremacy and thus solidified most of Marshall's doctrine.

Even so, in one case Taney severely undermined the Court's reputation and effectiveness. In the Dred Scott case,[16] the Court jumped into the thick of the slavery conflict and declared the Missouri Compromise of 1820, which controlled slavery in the territories, unconstitutional.

This was only the second time the Court had declared a congressional law unconstitutional, and it could not have come in a more controversial area or at a less opportune time. The slavery issue had polarized the nation, and the ruling polarized it further. Southerners were disenchanted with the Court because of its emphasis on a strong national government. Now northerners became disenchanted too. The Court's prestige dropped so precipitously that it could play only a weak role for two decades. President Abraham Lincoln refused to enforce one of its rulings,[17] and Congress withdrew part of its jurisdiction.[18] As a result, the Court avoided important issues.

The Taney Court naively thought it could resolve the clash over slavery and thereby resolve the conflict between nation and state. But no court could achieve this. It took the Civil War to do so.

Civil War to the Depression

With the controversy between nation and state dampened, the next primary issue for the courts was the relationship between government and business in cases involving regulation of business.

After the war, industrialization proceeded at a breakneck pace, bringing not only benefits but many

Courtesy of the Utah State Historical Society

Although many children worked long days in unhealthy conditions, the Supreme Court declared initial laws prohibiting child labor unconstitutional. This boy worked in the coal mines in the early 1900s.

problems. Some corporations abused their power over their employees, their competitors, and their customers. Although legislatures passed laws to regulate these abuses, the corporations challenged the laws in court. The Supreme Court, dominated by justices who had been lawyers for corporations, reflected the views of corporations and struck down laws regulating them.

Beginning in the 1870s, intensifying in the 1890s, and continuing in the 1900s, the Court invalidated laws that regulated child labor,[19] maximum hours of work,[20] and minimum wages for work.[21] It also discouraged employees from joining unions and striking,[22] and it limited antitrust laws.[23] In just one decade, the Court invalidated 41 state laws that regulated railroads.[24]

In 1935 and 1936, the Court struck down 12 congressional laws,[25] nearly nullifying President Franklin Roosevelt's New Deal program to help the country recover from the Great Depression.

The Court's action precipitated another major crisis. Roosevelt was reelected resoundingly in 1936. Heady from his victory and frustrated by the Court's decisions and his lack of opportunities to appoint new justices in his first term, he retaliated against the Court by proposing what was soon labeled a **court-packing plan.** The plan would have authorized the president to nominate and the Senate to confirm a new justice for every justice over 70 who did not retire, up to a total of 15. At the time, there were 6 justices over 70, so Roosevelt could have appointed 6 new justices and assured himself a friendly Court. Roosevelt claimed the plan was to help the Court cope with its increasing caseload, but virtually everyone could see through this. Even many of his supporters criticized him for tampering with the Court.

Before Congress could vote on the plan, two justices who often sided with four conservative justices against New Deal legislation switched positions to side with three liberal justices for similar legislation. Chief Justice Charles Evans Hughes and Justice Owen Roberts apparently thought the Court would suffer if it continued to oppose the popular president and his popular programs. Their "conversion" tipped the scales from votes of 6 to 3 against New Deal legislation to 5 to 4 for similar legislation. As a result, Roosevelt's plan became unnecessary, and Congress scuttled it. Hughes's and Roberts's switch was dubbed "the switch in time that saved nine."

Thus, the Court resolved this issue in favor of government over business. Since then it has permitted most efforts to regulate business.

Depression to the Present

With the controversy between government and business subdued, the next primary issue for the courts has been the relationship between government and the individual in cases involving civil liberties and rights. Often this issue has featured a conflict between the majority, whose views were reflected in government policy toward civil liberties and rights, and a minority individual or group who challenged the policy.

Individuals and groups, especially since the 1950s, have demanded an expansion of both the rights in the Bill of Rights and the guarantees of due process and equal protection in the Fourteenth Amendment.

Traditionally, the Supreme Court had not supported civil liberties and rights very much. But in 1953 President Dwight Eisenhower appointed Earl Warren to be chief justice. For the rest of the 1950s and the 1960s, Warren led the Court more effectively than any chief justice since Marshall. The **Warren Court** completely overhauled doctrine in the areas of racial segregation, criminal defendants' rights, and reapportionment. It also significantly altered doctrine in the areas of libel, obscenity, and religion. In the process it held many laws

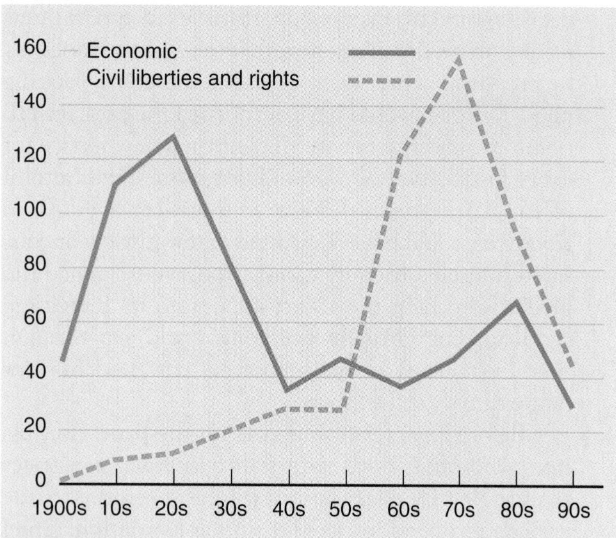

FIGURE 1

Number of Laws Regulating Economic Activity and Restricting Civil Liberties and Rights Declared Unconstitutional by the Supreme Court since 1900

The Supreme Court was nearly as activist in striking down laws in the 1910s, 1920s, and 1930s as it was in the 1950s, 1960s, and 1970s. But in the former years it was activist in economic cases (usually ones involving governmental regulation of business), while in the latter years it was activist in civil liberties and rights cases.

SOURCES: Congressional Research Service, *The Constitution of the United States: Analysis and Interpretation and 1990 Supplement* (Washington, D.C.: U.S. Government Printing Office, 1987 and 1991); Lawrence Baum, *The Supreme Court*, 6th ed. (Washington, D.C.: CQ Press, 1998), p. 213. Data are through 1996 and were multiplied by 1.43 to create a 10-year rate for the decade.

unconstitutional. It was more activist in these areas than the Court had ever been (see Figure 1).

The Warren Court was activist in favor of individuals from unpopular and powerless groups—racial minorities, religious minorities, criminal defendants, and alleged subversives—when they challenged governmental policies. Thus, the most elite institution in our government used its power to benefit many nonelites in our society. In its sympathies, the Warren Court sharply differed from previous Courts, which historically favored the haves over the have-nots and efforts to preserve the status quo over struggles to change it.

The Warren Court's decisions brought about a backlash that peaked in the late 1960s. President Richard Nixon vowed to change the direction of the Court, and in 1969 he appointed Warren Burger to be chief justice after Warren retired. Then Nixon and his former vice president, President Gerald Ford, appointed four more justices when vacancies occurred. They wanted to slow, halt, or even reverse the Warren Court's actions. They expected the **Burger Court** to make a "constitutional counter-revolution."

But the Court did not. Although it eroded some of the Warren Court's doctrine, particularly in the area of criminal defendants' rights, it left most of the doctrine intact. Further, it overhauled doctrine in two areas where the Warren Court was silent—sexual discrimination and abortion. In these and other areas, the Burger Court held numerous laws unconstitutional. Although not as committed to civil liberties and rights as the Warren Court, the Burger Court was more committed to them than any earlier Court.

President Ronald Reagan sought to erode the Warren Court's doctrine further, and now the Burger Court's liberal doctrine as well, by appointing three more conservatives and, in 1986, by naming William Rehnquist, the most conservative associate justice, to be chief justice after Burger retired. President George Bush also sought to erode the previous Courts' doctrine further by appointing two more conservatives when the only two consistent liberals retired. By the end of his administration, Republican presidents had named 10 straight justices and the **Rehnquist Court** had seven conservatives. The election of President Clinton led to the appointment of the first Democratic justices since 1967. Although these two moderates have prevented any further swing to the right, the conservatives retain control of the Court. But conflicts among the conservatives—some are willing to uphold precedents they would not have agreed to set in the first place, while others vote to sweep them away—have splintered the bloc. In some terms, the former group has dominated, but in other terms the

Dennis Brack, Black Star

Chief Justice Earl Warren, flanked by Justices Hugo Black (left) *and William Douglas.*

INTO THE 21ST CENTURY

THE NEXT ERA

If the third era is over, what controversy will the fourth era address? It is too soon to know. We probably will not know for many years, until we can look back with more perspective than we have now, but it is interesting to speculate. Might the fourth era focus on information technology, including computers, the software they use, and the data they store? And might it resolve disputes about which people have access to this technology, when people have access to it, how people can use it—in short, in what ways and to what extent the government and the private sector can impose restrictions on the new technology? These questions would be similar to ones the Court answered about freedom of speech, freedom of the press, libel, and obscenity in the third era. Or perhaps the emphasis will be on privacy from all the intrusions of this new technology. The Court only tentatively addressed invasion of privacy in the third era. Eventually, it will have to face this problem squarely. (Chapter 14 explains the Court's doctrine in these areas.)

latter group has dominated. Overall, the Rehnquist Court, though markedly more conservative than the Burger Court, has not overturned most of the previous Courts' doctrine.

Yet the Rehnquist Court has altered some of the previous Courts' doctrine. The conservative justices have made it harder for racial minorities to use affirmative action to overcome past discrimination, and they have made it harder for religious minorities to follow the tenets of their religion. At the same time, the conservative justices have made it somewhat easier for Christian denominations to play a prominent role in public settings. In two less obvious areas, the Rehnquist Court has altered doctrine in more fundamental ways. It has tightened access to the courts for individuals and groups trying to challenge government policies. And it has restricted some efforts by the federal government to impose new regulations on the states, thus affecting the balance between the two levels of the federal system. In these ways the Republican justices have mirrored the views of the Republican presidents and members of Congress in the 1980s and 1990s.

In sum, throughout its history the Court's role in government has been that of a policymaker—in relationships between nation and state, government and business, and government and the individual. In the first and second eras, the Court was a solidly conservative policymaker, protecting private property rights and limiting government regulation of business; in the third era, under the leadership of Warren and Burger, the Court was a generally liberal policymaker, permitting government regulation of business and supporting civil liberties and rights for individuals. It now appears that the third era is over. Although the Rehnquist Court has not overturned most of the previous Courts' doctrine, it has refused to expand individual rights (except freedom of speech).

COURTS

Most countries with a federal system have one national court over a system of regional courts. In contrast, the United States has a complete system of national courts side by side with complete systems of state courts, for a total of 51 separate systems. This makes litigation far more complicated than in other countries.

Structure of the Courts

The Constitution mentions only one court—a supreme court—although it allows Congress to set up additional, lower courts, which it did in the Judiciary Act of 1789. The act was a compromise between Federalists, who wanted a full system of lower courts with extensive jurisdiction—authority to hear and decide cases—in order to strengthen the national government, and Jeffersonians, who wanted only a partial system of lower courts with limited jurisdiction in order to avoid strengthening the national government. The compromise established a full system of lower courts with limited jurisdiction. These courts were authorized to hear disputes involving citizens of more than one state but not disputes relating to the U.S. Constitution and laws. The state courts were permitted to hear all these cases.

In 1875, Congress granted the federal courts extensive jurisdiction. Sixteen years later Congress created another level of courts, between the Supreme Court and the original lower courts to complete the basic structure of the federal judiciary.

The **district courts** are trial courts. There are 94, based on population but with at least one in each state.

They have multiple judges, although a single judge or jury decides each case.

The **courts of appeals** are intermediate appellate courts. They hear cases that have been decided by the district courts but are appealed by the losers. There are 12, based on regions—"circuits"—of the country. They have numerous judges, although a panel of three judges decides each case.

The Supreme Court is the ultimate appellate court. It hears cases that have been decided by the courts of appeals, district courts, or state supreme courts. (Although it can hear some cases—those involving a state or diplomat—that have not proceeded through the lower courts first, in practice it hears nearly all of its cases on appeal.) The group of nine justices decides its cases.

The district courts conduct trials. The courts of appeals and Supreme Court do not; they do not have juries or witnesses to testify and present evidence—just lawyers for the opposing litigants. Rather than determine guilt or innocence, these courts evaluate arguments about legal questions arising in the cases.

The state judiciaries have a structure similar to the federal judiciary. In most states, though, there are two tiers of trial courts. Normally, the lower tier is for criminal cases involving minor crimes, and the upper tier is for criminal cases involving major crimes and for civil cases. In about three-fourths of the states, there are intermediate appellate courts, and in all of the states there is a supreme court (although in a few it is called another name).

Jurisdiction of the Courts

Jurisdiction is the authority to hear and decide cases. According to the Constitution, the federal courts exercise jurisdiction over cases in which the subject involves either the U.S. Constitution, statutes, or treaties; maritime law; or cases in which the litigants include either the U.S. government, more than one state government, one state government and a citizen of another state, citizens of more than one state, or a foreign government or citizen. The state courts exercise jurisdiction over the remaining cases. These include most criminal cases because the states have authority over most criminal matters and pass most criminal laws.

Despite this dividing line, some cases begin in the state courts and end in the federal courts. These involve state law and federal law, frequently a state statute and a federal constitutional right. For these cases there are two major paths from the state judiciary to the federal judiciary. One is for the litigant who lost at the state supreme court to appeal to the U.S. Supreme Court.

The other path, available only in a criminal case, is for the defendant who has exhausted appeals in the state courts to appeal to the local federal district court through a writ of **habeas corpus.** Latin for "Have ye the body!" this writ demands that the state figuratively produce the defendant and justify his or her incarceration. If the district court decides that the state courts did not grant the defendant's federal constitutional rights, it will reverse the conviction. From the district court's decision, the losing side can try to appeal to the courts of appeals and Supreme Court. Jurisdiction in these cases is complicated, and appeals may be numerous (see Figure 2).

JUDGES

Selection of Judges

Benjamin Franklin proposed that judges be selected by lawyers because lawyers would pick "the ablest of the profession in order to get rid of him, and share his practice among themselves."[26] The Founders rejected this unique idea in favor of a plan whereby the president nominates judges and the Senate confirms them. There are no other requirements in the Constitution, although there is an unwritten requirement that judges be lawyers and an expectation that they be members of the president's political party. Most have been active party members who have served in office or contributed to candidates. In this century presidents nominated members of their party from 82% of the time (Gerald Ford) to 99% of the time (Woodrow Wilson). Thus, the process of selecting federal judges is highly political.

MECHANICS OF SELECTION

For lower court vacancies, administration officials recommend candidates, but senators also play a key role through the practice of senatorial courtesy. This tradition allows senators of the president's party to veto candidates for positions in their state and to recommend other candidates instead.

Senatorial courtesy can tie the president's hands. In deference to southern senators, President John Kennedy, who advocated civil rights, appointed southern judges who advocated segregation. One characterized the Supreme Court's desegregation ruling as "one of the truly regrettable decisions of all time," and another called blacks "niggers" and "chimpanzees" in court.[27]

Senatorial courtesy applies not only to district courts, which lie within individual states, but also to courts of appeals, which span several states. For these courts, senators informally divide the seats among the states in the circuit. The practice does not apply to the

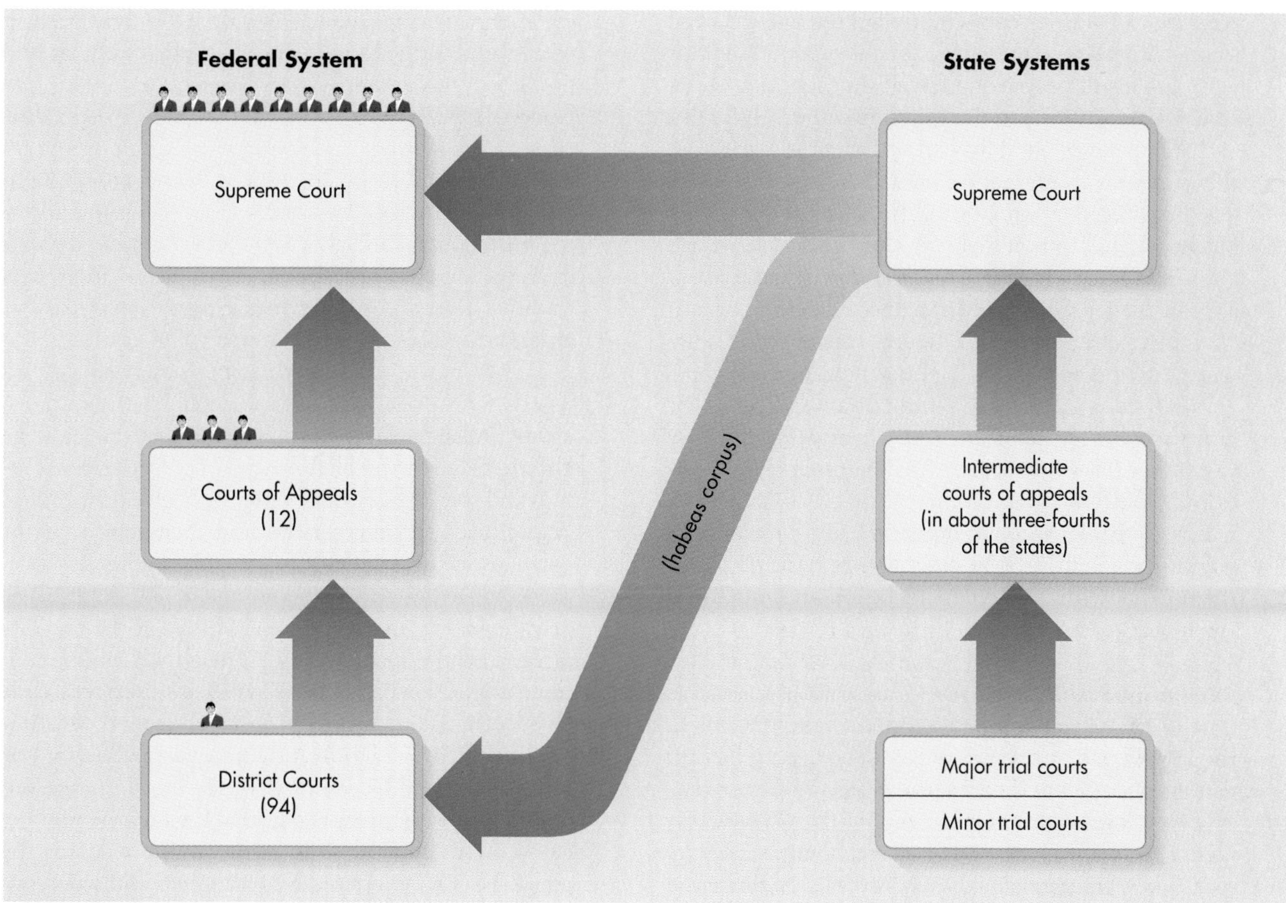

FIGURE 2

Federal and State Court Systems

The arrows indicate the primary avenues of appeal, and the heads indicate the usual number of judges who hear cases in the federal system.

Supreme Court, however, because this court is a national court and there are too few seats to divide among the states.

For Supreme Court vacancies, administration officials conduct a search for acceptable candidates. Prominent politicians and lawyers recommend persons, and interest groups lobby for their preferences.

Once the president has settled upon a candidate, he submits the nomination to the Senate, where it goes to the Judiciary Committee for hearings. Senators question the nominee about his or her judicial philosophy, and interest groups voice their concerns. If a majority of the committee consents, the nomination goes to the whole Senate. If a majority of the Senate consents, the nomination is confirmed.

CRITERIA USED IN SELECTION

The Founders expected judges to be selected by merit; they did not foresee the policymaking role of the courts or the development of political parties and senatorial courtesy, which have thrust political criteria into the process of selection.

CRITERIA USED BY PRESIDENTS Although presidents prefer judges with merit, usually they select them on the basis of other factors—friendship, favors, political experience, or ideological views. President Reagan emphasized ideology in an effort to mold the bench more than any president since Franklin Roosevelt. His administration screened candidates for conservative views on controversial issues. For example, the administration looked for those who, in the language of the Republican Party platform, "respect the sanctity of innocent human life"—code words for opposition to Supreme Court decisions allowing abortion. President Bush also sought candidates with conservative views.

Presidents sometimes select justices to balance representation on the Supreme Court. They choose persons from groups who do not have a member, or many members, on the Court already. Presidents have nominated Catholics, Jews, blacks, and women due to pressure to balance representation. They have bowed to pressure because they have sought support from diverse groups of people and feared that ignoring them would make confirmation of their nominees difficult.

When Thurgood Marshall, the first black to sit on the Supreme Court, retired in 1991, President Bush felt obligated to nominate another black for this seat, but he wanted to nominate another conservative. He chose Clarence Thomas, a black conservative court of appeals judge. Whereas Marshall had been an ardent champion of civil rights, Thomas had opposed affirmative action and drawn the ire of most black leaders.

Individual justices do not always reflect their group's views. In abortion cases Justice Sandra Day O'Connor has voted against the feminist groups' position in some cases, and former Justice William Brennan, a Catholic, voted against the Catholic Church's policy consistently. Sometimes groups have to satisfy themselves with the symbolic benefits of having a "member" on the Court.

CRITERIA USED BY SENATORS Historically, senators usually have been willing to confirm nominations to the lower courts but occasionally have been reluctant to confirm nominations to the Supreme Court. Because the high court is more important and appointments to it are more visible, these nominations are more likely to become embroiled in politics. Since the late 1960s senators have rejected six nominations to the Court—two by President Lyndon Johnson, two by President Nixon, and two by President Reagan.[28]

Senators decide whether to confirm a nomination primarily on the basis of the qualifications and ideology of the nominee.[29] If the qualifications are good, they usually approve, regardless of the ideology. But if the qualifications are questionable, they often consider how closely the nominee's ideology matches theirs. (However, they are reluctant to admit this because doing so would reveal the politics involved, and most of the public thinks politics is not or at least should not be involved.)

When Nixon chose court of appeals judge G. Harold Carswell, law scholars familiar with his record were dismayed. At Senate hearings they testified that he was undistinguished, as well as opposed to civil rights. Nixon's floor manager for the nomination, Senator Roman Hruska (R-Neb.), blurted out in exasperation, "Even if he is mediocre there are a lot of mediocre judges and people and lawyers. They are entitled to a little representation, aren't they and a little chance? We can't have all Brandeises, Cardozos, and Frankfurters, and stuff like that there."[30] This was the kiss of death. Once Carswell's supporters acknowledged his mediocrity, senators who objected to his views on civil rights could vote against him freely, and his nomination was doomed.

Yet when presidents nominated conservatives with unquestioned qualifications, they rarely faced a problem. One exception was Reagan's nomination of Robert Bork in 1987. Bork had criticized Court doctrine in his writings and speeches, and the debate focused on his ideology. In addition to rejecting a right to privacy, which is the basis of Court decisions allowing birth control and abortion, he had criticized Court decisions and congressional laws advancing racial equality. Bork's positions struck many Americans as extreme, and his nomination was voted down.

This battle prompted some observers to ask whether anyone with a record could be nominated again. Indeed, when Bush had his first vacancy, he chose a man who had left no trail of controversial writings and speeches. David Souter, though a former New Hampshire attorney general and then state supreme court justice, was called the "Stealth candidate" (after the bomber designed to elude radar).[31] Souter was a private person, living alone in a house at the end of a dirt road and not answering his neighbors' phone calls some nights. He had expressed few positions and made few decisions reflecting his views on federal constitutional doctrine. Even in his confirmation hearings he refused to reveal his views. It was assumed that he was another conservative, because of his lifestyle and because of his support from conservative aides to the president, yet he offered a small target and won confirmation easily.

When Bush had his second vacancy and chose Thomas, he realized that the nomination could be controversial (even before the charges of sexual harassment surfaced) but saw that it would split the Democratic coalition: some Democrats would be sympathetic because of Thomas's race, while others would be critical because of his views. For insurance the administration instructed Thomas to soft-pedal his views. Thomas told senators he made his previous statements as a representative of the administration but would be impartial as a justice. On abortion he insisted, incredibly, that he had no position and, in fact, had never discussed the issue with anyone.

Both Souter and Thomas said they could not reveal their views because they would have to decide these issues and so would need to preserve their impartiality. Yet both stated their support for capital punishment, although they would also have to decide these cases. The difference is that their view on capital punishment coincided with that of three-fourths of the public, whereas their views on other issues probably did not.

When Clinton had his first vacancy, he was wary because the Senate had forced him to withdraw several nominations to other positions and because Republicans had vowed to avenge Bork's defeat. The president chose Ruth Bader Ginsburg, a court of appeals judge for

AMERICAN DIVERSITY

DO WOMEN JUDGES MAKE A DIFFERENCE?

Some argue that there should be more women judges because women are entitled to their "fair share" of all governmental offices, including judgeships. Others argue that there should be more so that women as well as men will feel that courts represent them and make decisions that are fair and legitimate. Still others argue that there should be more because women, compared to men, have somewhat different views and would make somewhat different decisions.

A study of Justice Sandra Day O'Connor's behavior shows that although she generally votes on the conservative side of issues, she usually votes in a liberal direction in sex discrimination cases. Moreover, her presence on the Court apparently sensitizes her male colleagues to gender issues. All but two of them began to vote against sex discrimination more frequently after she joined the Court.[1]

Some studies reflect similar results for women justices on state supreme courts. These justices tend to support a broad array of women's rights in cases ranging from sex discrimination to child support and property settlement. On these issues even women justices from opposing political parties tend to agree.[2]

But studies that compare voting patterns on issues less obviously related to gender have less clear findings. Women judges appear more liberal than men in cases involving employment discrimination and racial discrimination. Perhaps the treatment they have experienced as women has made them more sympathetic to the discrimination others have faced. On the other hand, women judges do not appear more liberal or conservative than men in cases involving criminal rights or obscenity.[3]

A study of the sentences of state trial court judges found that women judges, compared to men judges, sentenced male defendants the same way, but they sentenced female defendants to prison more frequently. That is, in borderline cases, women judges ordered female defendants to prison, while men judges gave them probation. Where women judges treated male and female defendants equally, men judges treated female defendants more leniently and more paternalistically, permitting them to avoid prison.[4]

In addition, women judges seem to make a difference in a less direct way. They help protect the credibility of women lawyers and witnesses. In court occasionally men judges and lawyers refer to women lawyers and witnesses by their first names or by such terms as "young lady," "sweetie," or "honey." Or the men, in the midst of the proceedings, comment upon the women's perfume, clothing, or appearance. "How does an attorney establish her authority when the judge has just described her to the entire courtroom as 'a pretty little thing'?"[5] Even if the men consider their remarks harmless compliments rather than intentional tactics, their effect is to undermine the credibility of women lawyers and witnesses in the eyes of jurors. Women judges have attempted to squelch such remarks.[6]

1. Karen O'Connor and Jeffrey A. Segal, "Justice Sandra Day O'Connor and the Supreme Court's Reaction to Its First Female Member," in Naomi B. Lynn, ed., *Women, Politics and the Constitution* (New York: Haworth Press, 1990), pp. 95–104.
2. David W. Allen and Diane E. Wall, "Role Orientations and Women State Supreme Court Justices," *Judicature* 77 (November/December 1993), pp. 156–165.
3. Sue Davis, Susan Haire, and Donald R. Songer, "Voting Behavior and Gender on the U.S. Courts of Appeals," *Judicature* 77 (November/December 1993), pp. 129–133; Thomas G. Walker and Deborah J. Barrow, "The Diversification of the Federal Bench," *Journal of Politics* 47 (1985), pp. 596–617.
4. John Gruhl, Cassia Spohn, and Susan Welch, "Women as Policymakers: The Case of Trial Judges," *American Journal of Political Science* 25 (May 1981), pp. 308–322.
5. William Eich, "Gender Bias in the Courtroom: Some Participants Are More Equal Than Others," *Judicature* 69 (April/May 1986), pp. 339–343.
6. Georgia Dullea, "Women on the Bench Increase," *New York Times*, April 26, 1984.

13 years. The nomination satisfied Republicans because Ginsburg had often voted with Republicans on the bench, yet it also pleased some Democratic constituencies. Women's groups, of course, expected more seats, and Jews, who had not had a representative on the Court since 1969, also wanted a seat.

Ginsburg refused to discuss doctrine at her hearings, but her record showed a commitment to abortion rights and sexual equality. Although she had tied for first in her graduating class from Columbia Law School in 1959, she was turned down for a clerkship by Justice Felix Frankfurter and for a job by New York City law firms. The firms, just beginning to hire Jews, were not ready to hire mothers with young children. She taught law and then served as an attorney for the American Civil Liberties Union (ACLU). In the 1970s she argued six sex discrimination cases before the Supreme Court and, with an innovative approach, won five.

When Clinton had his second vacancy, he was still wary of a confirmation fight. Instead of the people he most desired, he chose Stephen Breyer, a court of appeals judge with a reputation as a moderate.

Nominations to the Court, which were contentious during the nineteenth century but not during the first half of the twentieth century, have become contentious again partly because of the Court's activism—both liberals and conservatives have seen what the Court can do—and partly because of the struggle for control of the divided government since the late 1960s. In most years Republicans have dominated the presidency while Democrats have dominated Congress (though in the 1990s, the situation has been just the reverse), so both have fought over the judiciary to tip the balance. Republicans, especially, have been frustrated by their inability to push their civil liberties and rights policies through Congress, so they have hoped that their appointees to the Court would do what their members in Congress have not been able to do.

Even nominations to the lower courts have become contentious in recent decades. The Senate has confirmed fewer nominations to the lower courts in the fourth year of a president's term, especially when the Senate has been controlled by the other party.[32] Senators in the other party hope their candidate will capture the White House in the next election. They delay confirmation so there will be numerous vacancies for the new president and, through senatorial courtesy, for themselves to fill as well.

Efforts to delay confirmation have become more pronounced since the Republicans won control of the Senate in 1994. They dragged their feet even at the beginning of President Clinton's second term, following a pace that keeps about 100 seats vacant.[33] These vacancies contribute to backlogs in the courts' dockets, prompting Chief Justice Rehnquist to complain about the Senate's inaction. The Republicans respond that the president has been slow to submit nominations and that the Judiciary Committee needs to scrutinize nominees to make sure they are not "liberal activists." In reality, Clinton, who appears unwilling to risk a confirmation fight over any judicial nominee, has nominated moderates almost exclusively, disappointing liberals by not trying to balance the conservatives still on the bench from the Reagan and Bush years.[34]

The Republicans' tactics serve several goals. Their efforts to delay confirmation and their complaints about liberal activists are like brushback pitches in baseball: they warn the president, as he steps up to the plate to choose his candidates, not to be aggressive and not to get close in selecting the ones he might prefer. They also warn sitting judges not to decide cases as they might prefer. One Republican leader, who has called for impeaching judges, said, "The judges need to be intimidated."[35]

Republican strategists have told Republican officials that complaining about liberal activists is a winning political issue. One said, "You can both channel populist anger at the notion of elitist judges with a general sense of resentment that the federal government is controlling people's lives too much."[36] In addition, complaining about liberal activists helps raise money for conservative organizations. One conservative group is circulating a videotape attacking federal judges and asking for donations to block Clinton's nominations.[37]

The immediate result of these tactics, according to a political scientist who studies the nomination and confirmation process, is a polarization and a delay "unprecedented in its scope." He analogizes the Republicans' efforts to President Franklin Roosevelt's court-packing plan.[38]

RESULTS OF SELECTION

Judges are drawn primarily from the lower federal and state courts, the federal government, or large law firms. These established legal circles are dominated by white men so, not surprisingly, most judges have been white men. Before President Jimmy Carter took office, only eight women had ever served on the federal bench at any level.[39] Carter, however, made a concerted effort to appoint more women and racial minorities. Sixteen percent of his appointees were women, and 21% were racial minorities. President Reagan, despite the impression he created by naming the first woman to the Supreme Court, named mostly white men to the lower courts. Eight percent of his appointees were women, and 6% were racial minorities.[40] President Clinton nominated 30% women, 19% blacks, and 7% Hispanics.[41]

Most judges have been wealthy. Most of Bush's appointees to the lower courts were worth more than half a million dollars; a third were millionaires. Five or six of the justices on the Supreme Court are millionaires.[42]

Despite some efforts to balance representation on the Supreme Court, presidents have not sought actual representatives of all socioeconomic groups. Throughout history, justices have come from a narrow, elite slice of society. Most have been born into families of Western European stock (especially English, Welsh, Scotch, and Irish), profess the Protestant religion (especially Episcopalian, Presbyterian, Congregational, and Unitarian), and are upper middle or upper class. Moreover, they have been born into families with traditions of political or even judicial service, families with prestige and connections as well as expectations for achievement.[43]

With the power to nominate judges, presidents have a tremendous opportunity to shape the courts and their decisions. By the time Carter finished his term, he had appointed about 40% of the lower court judges, although he had no opportunity to appoint Supreme Court justices. By the time Bush finished his term, he and Reagan had appointed about 65% of the lower court judges and five Supreme Court justices (in

TABLE 1

Appointees of Democrats and Republicans Think Differently

	PERCENT WHO AGREE		
	DEMOCRATIC APPOINTEES	REPUBLICAN APPOINTEES	DIFFERENCE
Big corporations should be taken out of private ownership.	10%	2%	8%
U.S. institutions need complete restructuring.	24	13	11
The more able should earn more.	86	98	12
America would be better off if it moved toward socialism.	19	4	15
Private enterprise is fair to workers.	70	87	17
The poor are such due to circumstances beyond their control.	50	33	17
America offers an opportunity for financial security to all who work hard.	59	85	26
Government should ensure a good standard of living.	57	27	30
Less regulation of business is good for the country.	54	85	31
Government should not guarantee jobs.	36	70	34
Government should reduce the income gap between rich and poor.	78	44	34

A survey of the economic attitudes of federal lower court judges shows that most hold opinions accepting the economic status quo. Even so, there are significant differences according to the political party of the appointing president. Judges appointed by Republican presidents tend to think individuals are largely responsible for their financial success or failure and that government should do less to equalize conditions.

SOURCE: Althea K. Nagai, Stanley Rothman, and S. Robert Lichter, "The Verdict on Federal Judges." *Public Opinion* (November/December 1987), p. 54.

addition to elevating Rehnquist from associate to chief justice). Most of Carter's appointees were moderates or liberals, whereas most of Bush's and Reagan's were conservatives (see Tables 1 and 2).

In addition to ideological differences in broad categories of cases, appointees of recent presidents also reflect differences in the narrower categories of abortion and the environment. Carter's appointees to the district courts voted against abortion rights in just 13% of their cases, whereas Reagan's appointees voted against abortion rights in 77% of their cases.[44] Carter's appointees to the appellate courts sided more often with environmental groups, whereas Reagan's and Bush's appointees sided more often with businesses.[45] Reagan's appointees voted to narrow existing air and water pollution laws.[46]

Tenure of Judges

Once appointed, judges can serve for "good behavior." This means for life, unless they commit "high crimes and misdemeanors." These are not defined in the Constitution but are considered serious crimes or, possibly, political abuses. Congress can impeach and remove judges as it can presidents, but it has impeached only 13 and removed only 6.[47] The standard of guilt—"high crimes and misdemeanors"—is vague, the punishment drastic, and the process time consuming, so Congress has been reluctant to impeach judges.

As an alternative, in 1980 Congress established other procedures to discipline lower federal court judges. Councils made up of district and appellate court judges can ask judges to resign or can prevent them from hearing cases, but cannot actually remove them. The procedures have been used infrequently, although their existence has prompted some judges to resign before being disciplined.

Qualifications of Judges

Given the use of political criteria in selecting judges, are judges well qualified?

Political scientists who study the judiciary consider federal judges generally well qualified. This is especially true of Supreme Court justices, apparently because presidents think they will be held responsible for the justices they nominate and do not want to be embarrassed by them. Also, because presidents have so few vacancies to fill, they can confine themselves to persons of their party and political views, and even to persons of a particular region, religion, race, and sex, and still locate good candidates. This is less true of lower court judges. Presidents and senators jointly appoint them, so both can avoid full responsibility for

TABLE 2

Appointees of Democrats and Republicans Vote Differently

A study of the votes of federal district court judges appointed by President Nixon through President Clinton shows differences according to the political party of the president. The study also shows some differences, in criminal justice and in civil rights and liberties cases, among appointees of Republicans. Compare the appointees of Bush and Reagan with those of earlier Republicans. These results reflect the effort that the Bush and Reagan administrations made to nominate candidates who held conservative views on these issues.

	PERCENTAGE OF LIBERAL* VOTES BY APPOINTEES OF					
ISSUE	NIXON (R)	FORD (R)	CARTER (D)	REAGAN (R)	BUSH (R)	CLINTON (D)
Criminal justice	30%	32%	38%	23%	29%	34%
Civil rights and civil liberties	37	39	52	33	33	39
Labor and economic regulation	48	55	62	49	51	62

*Liberal votes were defined as ones in favor of criminal defendants' or prisoners' rights in criminal justice cases; individuals' rights, involving freedom of expression or religion and equality between the races or sexes, in civil rights and liberties cases; and workers' or economic underdogs' interests, rather than businesses' or economic upper-dogs' interests, in labor and economic regulation cases. Cases from 1992–1996 are included.

SOURCE: Ronald Stidham, Robert A. Carp, and Donald R. Songer, "The Voting Behavior of President Clinton's Judicial Appointees," *Judicature* 80 (July/August, 1996), pp. 16–20.

them. These judges are also less visible, so a lack of merit is not as noticeable.

Presidents do appoint some losers. President Truman put a longtime supporter on a court of appeals who was "drunk half the time" and "no damn good." When asked why he appointed the man, Truman candidly replied, "I . . . felt I owed him a favor; that's why, and I thought as a judge he couldn't do too much harm, and he didn't . . . he wasn't the worst court appointment I ever made. By no means the worst."[48]

Sometimes presidents appoint qualified persons who later become incompetent. After serving for many years they incur the illnesses and infirmities of old age, and perhaps one-tenth become unable to perform their job well.[49] Yet they hang on because they are allowed to serve for "good behavior." The situation has prompted proposals for a constitutional amendment setting a mandatory retirement age of 70. This would have a substantial impact because fully one-third of all Supreme Court justices, for example, have served past 75. But constitutional amendments are difficult to pass, and mandatory retirement ages are out of favor now. Further, some of the best judges have done some of their finest work after 70.

Independence of Judges

Given the use of political criteria in selecting judges, can judges be independent on the bench? Can they decide cases as they think the law requires? Or do they feel pressure to decide cases as presidents or senators want them to?

Because judges are not dependent upon presidents for renomination or senators for reconfirmation, they can be independent to a great extent. In the Watergate tapes case, three Nixon appointees joined the decision against President Nixon. In a case involving a law authorizing a special prosecutor to investigate and prosecute misconduct by governmental officials, Chief Justice Rehnquist wrote the majority opinion and another Reagan appointee joined the decision upholding the law against a challenge by President Reagan (whose aides had been prosecuted under the law).[50]

After surveying Warren and Burger Court decisions involving desegregation, obscenity, abortion, and criminal defendants' rights, one scholar observed, "Few American politicians even today would care to run on a platform of desegregation, pornography, abortion, and the 'coddling' of criminals."[51]

Presidents have scoffed at the notion that their appointees become their pawns. A study concluded that one-fourth of the justices deviated from their president's expectations.[52] Theodore Roosevelt placed Oliver Wendell Holmes on the Court because he thought Holmes shared his views on trusts. But in an early antitrust case, Holmes voted against Roosevelt's position, which prompted Roosevelt to declare, "I could carve out of a banana a judge with more backbone than that!"[53] Holmes had plenty of backbone; he just did not agree with Roosevelt's position in this case. Likewise, President Eisenhower placed Earl Warren on the Court, in part because he thought Warren was a moderate. But Warren turned out to be a liberal. Later Eisenhower said his appointment of Warren was "the biggest damn fool thing I ever did."[54] President Truman concluded that "packing the Supreme Court simply can't be done . . . I've tried it and it won't work. . . . Whenever you put a man on the Supreme Court he ceases to be your friend."[55]

Truman exaggerated, although some presidents have had trouble "packing" the courts. They have not been able to foresee the issues their appointees would have to rule on or predict the ways their appointees would change on the bench. Nevertheless, presidents who have made a serious effort to find candidates with similar views usually have not been disappointed.

ACCESS TO THE COURTS

In this litigation-prone society, many individuals and groups want courts to resolve their disputes. Whether these individuals and groups get their "day in court" depends on their type of case, their wealth, and the level of court involved.

Courts hear two kinds of cases. **Criminal cases** are those in which governments prosecute persons for violating laws. **Civil cases** are those in which persons sue others for denying their rights and causing them harm. Criminal defendants, of course, must appear in court. Potential civil litigants, however, often cannot get to court.

Wealth Discrimination in Access

Although the courts are supposed to be open to all, most individuals do not have enough money to hire an attorney and pay the related costs necessary to pursue a case. Only corporations, wealthy individuals, or seriously injured victims suing corporations or wealthy individuals do. (Seriously injured victims with a strong case can obtain an attorney by agreeing to pay him or her a sizable portion of what they win in their suit.) In addition, a small number of poor individuals supported by legal aid programs can pursue a case.

The primary expense is paying an attorney. In 1996 new lawyers in law firms charged an average of $95 per hour, while established partners charged an average of $183 per hour.[56] Other expenses include various fees for filing the case, summoning jurors, paying witnesses, and also lost income from the individual's job due to numerous meetings with the attorney and hearings in court.

Even if individuals have enough money to initiate a suit, the disparity continues in court. Those with more money can develop a full case, whereas others must proceed with a skeletal case that is far less likely to persuade judges or jurors. Our legal system, according to one judge, "is divided into two separate and unequal systems of justice: one for the rich, in which the courts take limitless time to examine, ponder, consider, and deliberate over hundreds of thousands of bits of evidence and days of testimony, and hear elaborate, endless appeals and write countless learned opinions" and one for the nonrich, in which the courts provide "turnstile justice."[57] (During the week that one judge spent conducting the preliminary hearing to determine if there was sufficient evidence to require O. J. Simpson to stand trial for murdering his ex-wife and her friend, other judges in Los Angeles disposed of 474 preliminary hearings for less wealthy defendants.) Consequently, many individuals are discouraged from pursuing a case in the first place.

Michael Tighe/Outline

AP/Wide World Photos

Both sides in Paula Jones's suit against President Clinton used the media to influence public opinion. They expected the jurors to reflect the public's views. Jones's team had her made over (from left to right) to appear more appealing.

Interest Group Help in Access

Interest groups, with more resources than most individuals, help some individuals gain access. The groups sponsor and finance these individuals' cases. Of course, the groups do not act purely out of altruism. They choose selected cases they hope will advance their goals. An attorney for the American Civil Liberties Union (ACLU), which takes cases as a way to prod judges to protect constitutional rights, admitted that the criminal defendants the ACLU represents "sometimes are pretty scurvy little creatures, but what they are doesn't matter a whole hell of a lot. It's the principle that we're going to be able to use these people for that's important."

Some liberal groups, especially civil liberties organizations such as the ACLU, civil rights organizations such as the National Association for the Advancement of Colored People (NAACP), environmental groups such as the Sierra Club, and consumer and safety groups such as Ralph Nader's organizations, use litigation as a primary tactic. Other groups use it as an occasional tactic. In the 1980s and 1990s, some conservative groups began to use litigation as aggressively as these liberal groups. The Rutherford Institute, for example, arose to help persons who claimed their religious rights were infringed, representing children who were forbidden from reading the Bible on the school bus or praying in the school cafeteria. The institute then took on Paula Jones's suit after her previous attorneys quit when she rejected a settlement offered by President Clinton. The institute steered her to other lawyers (a Dallas firm that had fought to reinstate the Texas sodomy statute after it had been found unconstitutional) and funded her case. Interest groups have become ubiquitous in the judicial process. About half of all Supreme Court cases involve a liberal or conservative interest group,[58] and many lower court cases do as well. Even so, interest groups can help only a handful of the individuals who lack the resources to finance their cases.

Restrictions on Access

Even if litigants have enough wealth or interest group help, they must overcome various restrictions on access imposed by the courts. According to the Constitution, litigants can get access only for a "case" or "controversy." Courts interpret this to mean a real dispute—one in which the litigants themselves have lost rights and suffered harm. This major restriction is called **standing to sue.**

This principle is illustrated by a series of cases challenging Connecticut's birth control law. Passed in 1879, the law prohibited giving advice about, or using, birth control devices. Actually, the law was not enforced much; women with a private doctor could get advice and a prescription. But the law effectively prevented opening birth control clinics that would help poor women without a private doctor or young women who did not want to go to their family doctor.

In the 1940s a doctor challenged the law, arguing that it prevented him from advising patients whose health might be endangered by childbearing. The courts said he did not have standing because he could not point to any injury he had suffered.[59] In the 1960s a doctor and two patients, who had experienced dangerous pregnancies in the past, challenged the law, claiming that it forced them to choose between stopping sexual activity or risking dangerous pregnancies. Again the courts said they did not have standing because they could not point to any injury they had suffered, or would suffer, because the law was rarely enforced.[60] Finally, the head of Connecticut's Planned Parenthood League and the head of Yale's obstetrics and gynecology department opened a birth control clinic. Within days they were arrested. Although they could not get access in a civil suit, they could in the criminal case. In the process of defending themselves, they claimed the law was unconstitutional, and the Supreme Court agreed.[61]

Although this doctrine is technical, its implications are highly political. Without access, of course, individuals and groups have no chance to get courts to rule in their favor. And whether they get access depends, to a considerable extent, on the ideology of the judge presiding. According to one study, Reagan's appointees to the district courts denied access to underdogs (individuals, groups representing individuals, or unions) in 78% of the cases in which they sued but denied access to upper-dogs

USING MALPRACTICE SUITS FOR POLITICAL GOALS

Interest groups use the courts to attain their goals in various ways. Some pro-life groups, for instance, help draft antiabortion laws for legislators, while others provide lawyers for protestors arrested at abortion clinics. Now, one group, Life Dynamics, Inc. (LDI) of Denton, Texas, encourages malpractice suits against doctors who perform abortions. The suits are targeted at doctors who botch abortions—for example, leaving some part of the fetus in the uterus.[1]

Proclaiming that "abortion malpractice is poised to become the most prolific litigation opportunity of a decade," LDI has recruited lawyers in the pro-life movement and lawyers who specialize in personal injury cases. It has sent how-to videos to those lawyers, and it offers ads and brochures to attract clients, expert witnesses to testify, and 3-D animation to illustrate the operation and the mistakes to judges and jurors.

The goal? Unlike normal malpractice suits intended to compensate patients for injuries and to hold doctors accountable for mistakes, LDI's primary goal, according to its publication subtitled, "A Guerrilla Strategy for Pro-Life America," is to "force abortionists out of business by driving up their insurance rates."

This strategy illustrates the split between conservative groups. Business and medical groups are trying to reduce the number of lawsuits and the size of awards to cut their rates for insurance, while antiabortion groups are trying to increase them. This split reflects the uneasy marriage of conservative groups within the Republican Party. Traditional Republicans, such as business executives and doctors, think of the economy and demand that government intervene less. But religious right Republicans think of personal morality and demand that government intervene more. The different opinions about lawsuits, then, reflect the general divergence among these groups and within the party.

1. The group also intends to sue doctors who perform abortions properly but whose patients develop "postabortion trauma." However, this emotional reaction to one's abortion is not now accepted as a basis for a malpractice suit.

SOURCE: Christopher John Farley, "Malpractice as a Weapon," *Time*, March 13, 1995, p. 65.

USING RACKETEERING LAWS FOR POLITICAL GOALS

When Congress passed the Racketeer Influenced and Corrupt Organizations (RICO) statute in 1970, it intended to target organized crime. The law permits prosecution of all members of a "criminal enterprise" rather than only the perpetrators of particular crimes, and it provides for long prison terms. When civil suits are brought by people who lost money or property because of the criminal acts, it allows triple damages—that is, three times what they lost. Thus, the law was designed to cripple organized crime by putting its members in prison and confiscating its wealth. The law was written so broadly that it worked very effectively for prosecutors.

Once prosecutors realized how general the language was, they began to use RICO in cases besides organized crime. The National Organization for Women (NOW), searching for a "statutory guard dog that might take a bite out of not only antiabortion foot soldiers but also their leaders,"[1] whom they were calling "kingpins," decided to use the law to bring a civil suit against two of the largest pro-life groups—Operation Rescue and Pro-Life Action Network. The goal was to connect these groups with the antiabortion protesters who committed crimes, from blockading clinics to burning and bombing them. Ultimately, NOW hoped to curtail the activity of the groups by extracting money from them.

The pro-life groups claimed the law did not apply to them, because it was intended to apply to organized syndicates rather than to nonprofit groups. But the statute did not specify this, and the Supreme Court unanimously ruled that it did not require this.[2] The Court allowed the law to be used against these groups. However, the people who bring these suits still must prove that the perpetrators were connected with the leaders and that the protests were not protected by the First Amendment.

In 1998, a federal jury in Chicago ruled for NOW and against Operation Rescue and Pro-Life Action Network, ordering them to pay a quarter of a million dollars to two clinics. More suits involving other clinics could follow.

1. David Van Biema, "Your Activist, My Mobster," *Time,* February 7, 1994, p. 32.

2. *National Organization for Women v. Scheidler,* 127 L.Ed.2d 99 (1994).

(governments or corporations) in only 41% of the cases in which they sued. These rulings contrast with those of Carter's and Nixon's appointees, who were both less strict in denying access and more evenhanded in treating underdogs and upper-dogs.[62]

Proceeding through the Courts

Cases normally start in a district court. Individuals who lose have a right to have their case decided by one higher court to determine if there was a miscarriage of justice. They normally appeal to a court of appeals. Individuals who lose at this level have no further right to have their case decided by another court, but they can appeal to the Supreme Court. However, the Court can exercise almost unlimited discretion in choosing cases to review. No matter how important or urgent an issue seems, the Court does not have to hear it.

Litigants who appeal to the Supreme Court normally file a petition for a **writ of certiorari** (Latin for "made more certain"). The Court grants the writ—that is, the Court agrees to hear the case—if four of the nine justices vote to do so. The rationale for this "rule of four" is that a substantial number, but not necessarily a majority, of the justices should think the case is important enough to review. Generally, the Court agrees to review a case when the justices think an issue has not been resolved satisfactorily or consistently by the lower courts.

From about 8,000 petitions each year, the Court selects less than 100 to hear, thus exercising considerable discretion.[63] The oft-spoken threat, "We're going to appeal all the way to the Supreme Court," is usually just bluster. Likewise, the notion that the Court is "the court of last resort" is misleading. Most cases never get beyond the district courts or courts of appeals.

That the Supreme Court grants so few writs means the Court has tremendous power to control its docket and therefore to determine which policies to review. It also means the lower courts have considerable power because they serve as the court of last resort for most cases.

DECIDING CASES

In deciding cases judges need to interpret statutes and the Constitution and determine whether to follow precedents. In the process they make law.

Interpreting Statutes

In deciding cases judges start with statutes—laws passed by legislatures. If the statutes are ambiguous, judges need to interpret them in order to apply them to their cases.

Sometimes statutes are ambiguous because of their nature. To be broad enough to cover many situations, their words and phrases must be so general that they might not be clear. Other times statutes are ambiguous because of the nature of the legislative process. To satisfy public demand for action on problems, legislators are urged to move quickly, even if they are not prepared. They are encouraged to act symbolically, even if they cannot alleviate the problems this way. They are pressed to compromise, even if they must include fuzzy provisions in statutes to avoid upsetting fragile agreements negotiated among themselves. Thus, a member of Congress, tongue in cheek, told one justice that they purposely use "unintelligible language" in statutes so the courts will "tell us what we mean."[64]

When statutes are ambiguous, judges try to ascertain the legislators' intent in passing them. They scrutinize the legislators' remarks and debates. But they often find that different members said different things, even contradictory things, and most members said nothing about the provisions in question. This gives judges considerable leeway in construing statutes.

Congress passed a statute that imposes a minimum sentence of five years in prison for anyone convicted of a violent crime or a drug trafficking crime in which he or she "uses" a gun. The question arose: What does "uses" mean? The Supreme Court had to interpret this provision in 1995. After police arrested a man for possession of cocaine, they found a gun in a bag in the trunk of his car. Although the man had not directly employed the gun when he had obtained the cocaine, lower courts concluded that he had used it by having it accessible to himself and near the cocaine, and they imposed the sentence under the statute. The Supreme Court unanimously reversed.[65] Justice O'Connor illustrated the problem by posing this statement: "I use a gun to protect my house, but I've never had to use it." That is, people mean different things by the word "use." The lower courts interpreted the word essentially as a synonym for "possess." But Justice O'Connor observed that the same statute has another provision that refers to a person who "carries" a gun, and another statute has a provision that refers to a person who "possesses" a gun. Therefore, Congress must have intended "use" to mean something different than "carry" or "possess." So the Supreme Court ruled that "use" means active use, whether brandishing, striking, or firing the gun or even making reference to having a gun.

Interpreting the Constitution

After interpreting statutes, judges determine whether they are constitutional. Or, if the cases involve actions of government officials rather than statutes, judges determine whether the actions are constitutional. For either, they need to interpret the Constitution.

Compared to constitutions of other countries, our Constitution is short and therefore necessarily ambiguous. It speaks in broad principles rather than in narrow details. The Fifth Amendment states that persons shall not be "deprived of life, liberty, or property without due process of law." The Fourteenth Amendment states that persons shall not be denied "the equal protection of the laws." What is "due process of law"? "Equal protection of the laws"? Generally, the former means that people should be treated fairly and the latter means that they should be treated equally. But what is fairly? Equally? These are broad principles that need to be interpreted in specific cases.

Sometimes the Constitution uses relative terms. The Fourth Amendment provides that persons shall be "secure . . . against unreasonable searches and seizures." What are "unreasonable searches and seizures"? Other times the Constitution uses absolute terms. These appear more clear-cut but are deceptive. The First Amendment provides that there shall be "no law . . . abridging the freedom of speech." Does "no law" mean literally no law? Then what about the proverbial example of the person who falsely shouts "Fire!" in a crowded theater? Whether relative or absolute, the language needs to be interpreted in specific cases.

Occasionally, politicians assert that judges ought to be "strict constructionists"; that is, they ought to interpret the Constitution "strictly." This is nonsense. Judges cannot possibly interpret ambiguous language strictly.

When the language does not give sufficient guidance, some judges believe they should follow the intentions of the framers.[66] Yet these intentions are difficult to ascertain. James Madison's notes of the Constitutional Convention or the *Federalist Papers* are considered the most authoritative sources, but relying upon them is fraught with problems. Because Madison edited his notes many years after the convention, his experiences in government or lapses of memory might have colored his version of the intentions of the delegates. Because Madison, Hamilton, and Jay published the *Federalist Papers* to persuade New York to ratify the Constitution, their motive might have affected their account of the intentions of the delegates. Further, there were 55 delegates to the Constitutional Convention and many more to the state ratifying conventions, and the sources do not indicate what most thought about any of the provisions. Undoubtedly, all did not think the same.

Other judges believe they need not follow the intentions of the framers. They maintain that the Constitution was designed to be flexible and adaptable to changes in society.[67] These judges try to distill the general meaning of the provisions of the Constitution and apply this meaning to the contemporary situations facing them. The Fourteenth Amendment's equal protection clause does not refer to schools, and its framers did not intend it to relate to schools. However, they did intend it to grant blacks greater equality than before, and therefore the Court applied this meaning to segregated

Ken Regan/Camera 5

Chief Justice William Rehnquist dons his robe in the Supreme Court's robing room.

schools. Then the Court applied it to other segregated facilities, then to other racial minorities, and then to women. In short, the Court extracted the general meaning of equality and extended it to prohibit discrimination in many situations. In this way the Court put into practice Chief Justice John Marshall's statement that the Constitution is "intended to endure for ages to come."[68]

When judges interpret the Constitution, they exercise discretion. As former Chief Justice Hughes candidly acknowledged, "We are under a constitution, but the Constitution is what the Supreme Court says it is."[69]

Restraint and Activism

All judges exercise discretion, but not all engage in policymaking to the same extent. Some, classified as restrained, are less willing to declare statutes or actions of government officials unconstitutional, whereas others, classified as activist, are more willing to do so.

Restrained judges argue that the judiciary is the least democratic branch because judges are appointed for life rather than elected and reelected. Consequently, they should be reluctant to overrule the other branches. "Courts are not the only agency of government that must be presumed to have the capacity to govern," Justice Harlan Stone said. "For the removal of unwise laws from the statute books appeal lies not to the courts, but to the ballot and the processes of democratic government."[70] Restrained judges also contend that the judiciary is the branch least capable of making policy because judges are generalists. They lack the expertise and resources that many bureaucrats and legislators use to help make policy. Restrained judges further maintain that the power to declare laws unconstitutional is more effective if it is used sparingly. Justice Louis Brandeis concluded that "the most important thing we do is not doing."[71] That is, the most important thing judges do is declare laws constitutional and thereby build up political capital for the occasional times that they declare laws unconstitutional.

Activist judges do not share these qualms. Instead, they seem more outraged at injustice. Court of appeals

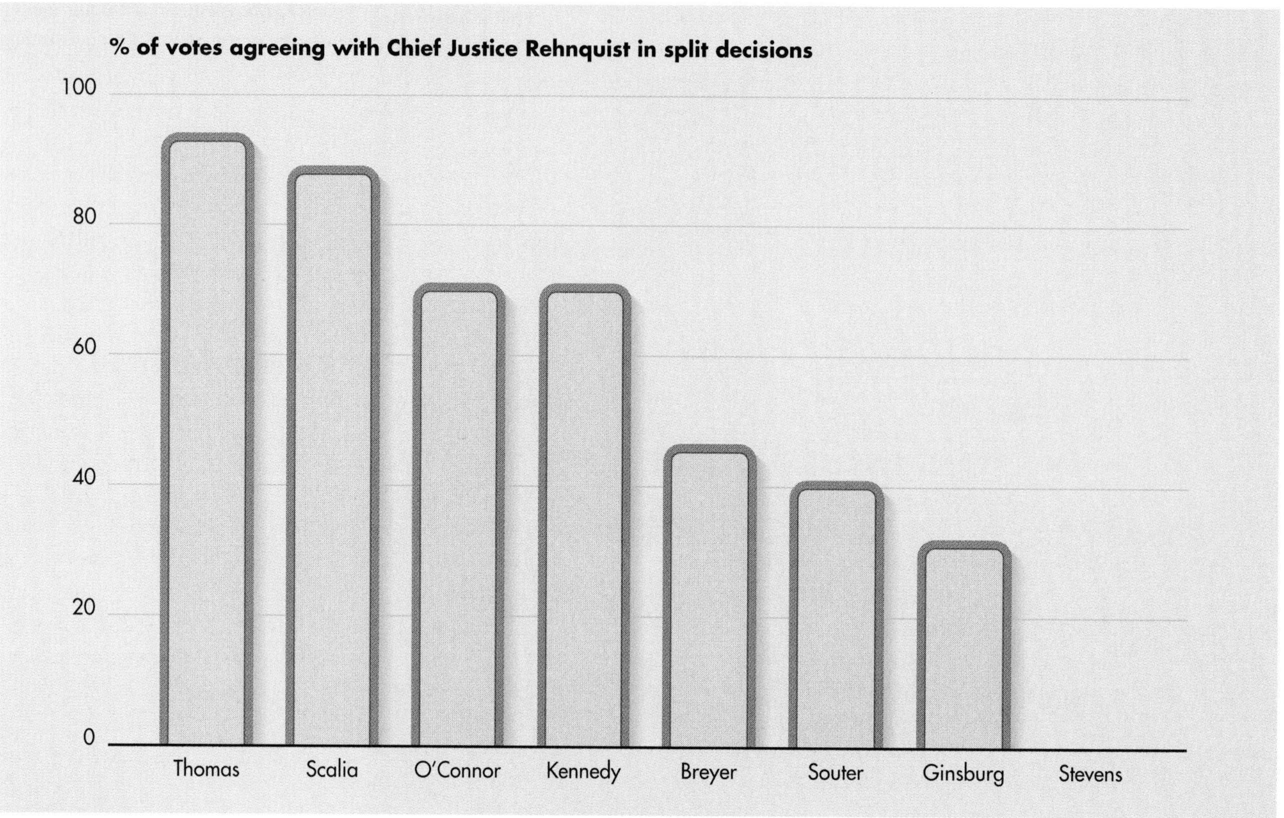

FIGURE 3

Ideological Blocs on the Rehnquist Court

Now the Court has a very conservative bloc of Chief Justice Rehnquist and Justices Thomas and Scalia; a fairly conservative bloc of Justices O'Connor and Kennedy; a moderate bloc of Justices Breyer, Souter, and Ginsburg; and the fairly liberal Justice Stevens. (There are no very liberal justices since the retirements of Justices Brennan and Marshall.) As a result of these blocs, the conservative side usually wins. However, Justice O'Connor or Kennedy occasionally switches, providing the margin of victory for the liberal side.

SOURCE: *New York Times*, July 3, 1995, Section 3, p. 1 ff. Based on 35 votes on which Justices Rehnquist and Stevens disagreed in 1995.

judge David Bazelon, of the District of Columbia, said the test should be "Does it make you sick?" If so, the law or action should be struck down.[72] Activist judges also seem more concerned about obtaining results than following technical procedures. Chief Justice Warren asked lawyers who emphasized technical procedures during oral arguments, "Yes, yes, yes, but is it right? Is it good?"[73] In addition, activist judges seem more pragmatic. District court judge Frank Johnson, who issued sweeping orders for Alabama's prisons and mental hospitals, replied to critics, "I didn't ask for any of these cases. In an ideal society, all of these . . . decisions should be made by those to whom we have entrusted these responsibilities. But when governmental institutions fail to make these . . . decisions in a manner which comports with the Constitution, the federal courts have a duty to remedy the violation."[74]

The distinction between restrained and activist judges does not necessarily parallel that between conservative and liberal judges. In the 1950s and 1960s, it did; the Supreme Court was both activist and liberal. But in the early 1930s, the Court was activist and conservative; it struck down regulations on business. In the late 1930s, it was restrained and liberal; it upheld similar regulations on business.

But we should not make too much of the distinction between restraint and activism. It is usually more important to know whether a judge is conservative or liberal. Although a restrained conservative might vote differently than an activist conservative in some cases, the two conservatives are likely to vote the same in most cases. A study of the justices appointed to the Supreme Court from 1953 through 1987 found that their conservative or liberal attitudes accounted for most of their individual votes, regardless of their restraint or activism (and regardless of the existence of relevant precedents or unique facts in the cases).[75] Some researchers conclude that "judicial restraint" is little more than "a cloak for the justices' policy preferences."[76] That is, it enables them to proclaim their "restraint" while actually voting on the basis of their ideology—without ever admitting this to the public. For example, the conservative justices on the Rehnquist Court, many of whom profess their "restraint" and all of whom were appointed by presidents who touted their "restraint," have been conservative activists at times (Figure 3 shows the ideological blocs on the Rehnquist Court). They have struck down laws implementing affirmative action programs, laws establishing legislative districts to benefit racial minorities, and laws regulating gun registration and possession. Thus, although restraint and activism are useful concepts—they help us understand the roles judges can play—we should be skeptical when we hear these terms used, especially by judges and by politicians trying to pacify or inflame the public.

Following Precedents

In interpreting statutes and the Constitution, judges are expected to follow precedents established by their court or higher courts in previous cases. This is the rule of **stare decisis** (Latin for "stand by what has been decided").

When in 1962 the Supreme Court held unconstitutional a New York law that required public school students to recite a nondenominational prayer every day, the ruling became a precedent.[77] Then in 1963 the Court held unconstitutional a Baltimore school board policy that required students to recite Bible verses.[78] The Court followed the precedent it had set the year before. Then in 1980 the Court held unconstitutional a Tennessee law that forced public schools to post the Ten Commandments in all classrooms.[79] Although this law differed from the previous ones in that it did not require recitation, the majority concluded that it reflected the same goal—to use the public schools to promote the Christian religion—so it violated the same principle, separation of church and state. Then in 1992 the Court ruled that clergy cannot offer prayers at graduation ceremonies for public schools.[80] Although this situation, too, differed from the previous ones in that it did not occur every day at school, the majority reasoned that it, too, reflected the same goal and violated the same principle. Thus, for three decades the Court followed the precedent it originally set when it initially addressed this issue.

The primary advantage of stare decisis is that it provides stability in the law. If different judges were to decide similar cases in different ways, the law would be unpredictable, even chaotic. "Stare decisis," Justice Brandeis said, "is usually the wise policy; because in most matters it is more important that the applicable rule of law be settled than that it be settled right."[81] Another advantage of this practice is that it promotes equality in the law, ensuring that judges treat comparable cases similarly. Otherwise, judges might appear to be arbitrary and discriminatory.

The primary disadvantage of stare decisis is that it produces excessive stability—inflexibility—in the law when it is adhered to strictly. Times change and demand new law, but precedents of past generations bind present and future generations. Justice Holmes declared, "It is revolting to have no better reason for a rule of law than that it was laid down in the time of Henry IV. It is still more revolting if the grounds upon which it was laid down have vanished long since, and the rule simply persists from blind imitation of the past."[82]

Even when judges agree to follow precedents, sometimes they have discretion to decide which ones to follow. There might not be any that are controlling but several that are relevant, and these might point in contrary directions. This situation often arises when courts face technological changes in society. In 1996 the justices weighed government regulation of indecent programming on cable television. They had precedents that governed broadcast television, telephones, and bookstores. But, as Justice Breyer observed, none of these really paralleled cable television, which looks like broadcast television but uses telephone lines rather than airwaves to transmit its signals. Thus, he was uncertain which precedents to use. Apparently, the others were uncertain also, as the nine justices split three ways and wrote six opinions while upholding one section and striking down two other sections of the law.[83]

Making Law

Many judges deny that they make law. They say that it is already there, that they merely "find" it or, occasionally, "interpret" it with their education and experience. They imply that they use a mechanical process. Justice Roberts wrote for the majority that struck down a New Deal act in 1936:

> *It is sometimes said that the Court assumes a power to overrule . . . the people's representatives. This is a misconception. The Constitution is the supreme law of the land. . . . All legislation must conform to the principles it lays down. When an act of Congress is appropriately challenged in the courts as not conforming to the constitutional mandate, the judicial branch of government has only one duty—to lay . . . the Constitution . . . beside the statute . . . and to decide whether the latter squares with the former.*[84]

In other words, the Constitution itself dictates the decision.

However, by now it should be apparent that judges do not use a mechanical process—that they do exercise discretion. They *do* make law—when they interpret statutes, when they interpret the Constitution, and when they determine which precedents to follow or disregard.

In doing so, they reflect their own political preferences. As Justice Benjamin Cardozo said, "We may try to see things as objectively as we please. Nonetheless, we can never see them with any eyes except our own."[85] That is, judges too are human beings with their own perceptions and attitudes and even prejudices. They do not, and cannot, shed these the moment they put on their robes.

But to say that judges make law is not to say that they make law as legislators do. Judges make law less directly. They make it in the process of resolving disputes brought to them. They usually make it by telling governments what they cannot do, rather than what they must do and how they must do it. And judges make law less freely. They start not with clean slates but with established principles embodied in statutes, the Constitution, and precedents. They are expected to follow these principles. If they deviate from them, they are expected to explain their reasons.

THE POWER OF THE COURTS

Alexis de Tocqueville observed that unlike in other countries, "Scarcely any political question arises in the United States that is not resolved, sooner or later, into a judicial question."[86] Because Americans are more inclined than other people to bring suits, courts have many opportunities to try to wield power.

This inclination does not in itself guarantee that the courts can wield power, but they have been able to because the public venerates the Constitution and the courts interpret it, and because the courts enjoy relative, though not absolute, independence from the political pressures on the other branches.

The use of judicial review and the use of political checks against the courts reveal the extent of the power of the courts.

Use of Judicial Review

Judicial review—the authority to declare laws or actions of government officials unconstitutional—is the tool that courts use to wield power. When courts declare a law or action unconstitutional, they not only void that particular law or action, but they also might put the issue on the public agenda, and they might speed up or slow down the pace of change in government policies.

When the Supreme Court declared a Texas abortion law unconstitutional in *Roe v. Wade* in 1973, the Court put abortion on the public agenda.[87] The issue had not been a national controversy before the decision.

The Court used judicial review as a catalyst to speed up change in the desegregation cases in the 1950s. At the time President Eisenhower was not inclined to act, and although many members of Congress were, they were unable to act because the houses were dominated by southerners who, as committee chairs, blocked civil rights legislation. The Court broke the logjam.

The Court used judicial review as a brake to slow down change in the business regulation cases in the first third of the twentieth century. The Court delayed some policies for several decades.

Judicial review, an American contribution to government, was for years unique to this country. It is now used in numerous other countries but not as extensively or as effectively as in the United States.

The Supreme Court alone has struck down more than 100 provisions of federal laws and more than 1,000 provisions of state and local laws (see Figure 4). The Court has struck down more of the latter for several reasons: State and local legislatures enact more laws; these legislatures reflect parochial, rather than national, interests, so they enact more laws that the national Court considers in conflict with the national Constitution; and these legislatures are less risky to confront than Congress.

The number of laws struck down, however, is not the true measure of the importance of judicial review. Instead, the ever present threat of review has undoubtedly prevented legislatures from enacting many laws they feared would be struck down.

By using judicial review to play a strong role in government, the Court has contradicted the Founders' expectation that the judiciary would be the weakest branch. Although it has been the weakest at times, it has been the strongest at other times. Arguably, these include some years during the early nineteenth century, when the Court established national dominance; the late nineteenth century and early twentieth century, when the Court thwarted efforts to regulate business; and the 1950s and early 1960s, when the Court extended civil liberties and rights.

Nevertheless, the extent to which the Court has played a strong role in government should not be exaggerated. The Court has not exercised judicial review over a wide range of issues; in each of the three eras of its history, it has exercised review over one dominant issue and paid relatively little attention to other issues. Moreover, the one dominant issue always has involved domestic policy. Traditionally the Court has been reluctant to intervene in foreign policy.[88] Even when the war in Vietnam was the most contentious issue in the country, with many people questioning its constitutionality and numerous men challenging the draft, the Court refused to review the issue.

Even when the Court has tackled an issue, it has been cautious. Of the provisions of congressional laws held unconstitutional, more than half were voided more than 4 years after they had been passed, and more than one-fourth were voided more than 12 years after they had been passed.[89] These laws were voided after many members of Congress who had initiated and voted for them had left Congress. The Court confronted Congress when it was safer to do so.

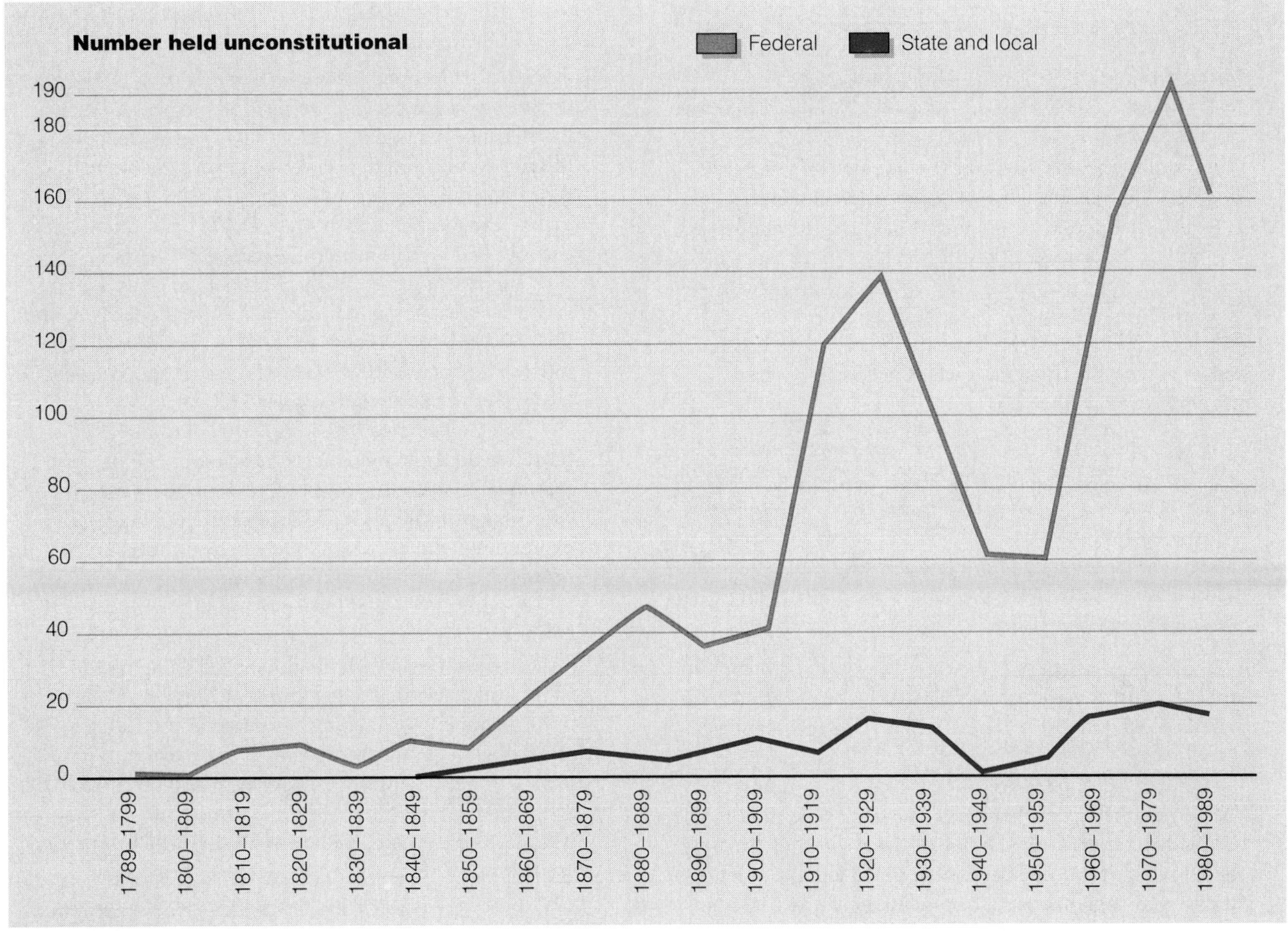

FIGURE 4

The Supreme Court Has Declared Unconstitutional More State and Local Laws than Federal Laws

SOURCE: Harold W. Stanley and Richard G. Niemi, *Vital Statistics on American Politics,* 4th ed. (Washington, D.C.: CQ Press, 1994), p. 308.

Use of Political Checks against the Courts

Although the courts enjoy relative independence from the political pressures on the other branches, they certainly do not enjoy absolute independence. Because they are part of the political process, they are subject to political checks, which limit the extent to which they can wield judicial review.

CHECKS BY THE EXECUTIVE

Presidents can impose the most effective check. If they dislike judges' rulings, they can appoint new judges when vacancies occur. And a sizable proportion of these appointees remain on the bench even two decades after presidents leave the White House.[90] Even so, it can be difficult to get judges to reverse precedents or to make decisions beyond the existing political consensus, as Presidents Reagan and Bush discovered.

Presidents and state and local executives, such as governors and mayors and even school officials and police officers, can refuse to enforce courts' rulings. School officials have disobeyed decisions requiring desegregation and invalidating class prayers. Police officers have ignored decisions invalidating some kinds of searches and interrogations.

Yet executives who refuse to enforce courts' rulings risk losing public support, unless the public also opposes the rulings. Even President Nixon complied when the Court ordered him to turn over the incriminating Watergate tapes.

CHECKS BY THE LEGISLATURE

Congress and the state legislatures can overturn courts' rulings by adopting constitutional amendments. They have done so four times (Eleventh, Fourteenth, Sixteenth, and Twenty-sixth Amendments).[91] They can also overturn courts' rulings by passing new statutes. When courts base decisions on

THE SUPREME COURT DECIDES A CASE

When the Supreme Court agrees to hear a case, it asks the litigants to submit written arguments. These "briefs" identify the issues and marshal the evidence—statutes, the Constitution, precedents—for their side. After the Court receives the briefs, it sets a date for oral arguments.

On that date the justices gather in the robing room behind the courtroom. They put on their black robes and, as the curtains part, file into the courtroom and take their places at the raised half-hexagon bench. The chief justice sits in the center, and the associate justices extend out in order of seniority. The crier gavels the courtroom to attention and announces:

The Honorable, the Chief Justice and Associate Justices of the Supreme Court of the United States! Oyez, oyez, oyez! [Give ear, give ear, give ear!] All persons having business before the Honorable, the Supreme Court of the United States are admonished to draw near and give attention, for the Court is now sitting. God save the United States and this Honorable Court.

The chief justice calls the case. The lawyers present their arguments, although the justices interrupt with questions whenever they want. When Thurgood Marshall, as counsel for the NAACP before becoming a justice, argued one school desegregation case, he was interrupted 127 times. The justices ask about the facts of the case. "What happened when the defendant . . . ?" They ask about relevant precedents that appear to support or rebut the lawyers' arguments. "Can you distinguish this case from . . . ?" They ask about hypothetical scenarios. "What if the police officer . . . ?" With these questions the justices want to know what is at stake, how a ruling would relate to existing doctrine, and how a ruling might govern future situations. They are experienced at pinning lawyers down. Chief Justice Rehnquist, who is affable toward his colleagues, is tough on the lawyers appearing before him. When asked if the lawyers were nervous, he replied, "I assume they're all nervous—they should be."[1] Occasionally, a lawyer becomes unnerved and faints on the spot.

The chief justice usually allots half an hour per side. When time expires, a red light flashes on the lectern, and the chief justice halts any lawyer who continues. Chief Justice Hughes was so strict that he reportedly cut off one lawyer in the middle of the word "it."

The Court holds Friday conferences to make a tentative decision and assign the opinion. The decision affirms or reverses the lower court decision; it indicates who wins and who loses. The opinion explains why. It expresses principles of law and thereby establishes precedents for other cases, so it is very important.

A portrait of Chief Justice Marshall presides over the conference. To ensure secrecy, no one is present but the justices. They begin with handshakes. (During his tenure Chief Justice Marshall suggested that they begin with a drink anytime it was raining anywhere in the Court's jurisdiction. Perhaps this accounts for his extraordinary success in persuading his colleagues to adopt his views.) Then the justices battle. The chief justice initiates the discussion of the case. He asserts what he thinks the issues are and how they ought to be decided, and he casts a vote. The associate justices follow in order of seniority. The discussion might become heated. When the justices reach a tentative decision, if the chief justice is in the majority, he assigns a justice to write the opinion of the Court. If not, the most senior associate justice in the majority assigns one to write it.

These procedures reveal the chief justice's power. Although his vote counts the same as each associate justice's vote, his authority to initiate the discussion and assign the opinion is significant. The former can influence what the other justices think about the case; the latter can determine what the opinion expresses.

Before Marshall became chief justice, each justice wrote his own opinion. But Marshall realized that one majority opinion would have more clout. He often convinced the other justices to forsake their own opinions and subscribe to his; he authored almost half of the Court's approximately 1,100 opinions during his years. Chief Justices Warren and Burger assigned more than 80% of the Court's opinions during their years, though they wrote only some of them.[2] Burger reportedly used his authority to punish several colleagues who voted opposite him in other cases. Justice Powell told another justice, "I'm resigned to writing nothing but Indian affairs cases for the rest of my life."[3] Chief Justice Rehnquist is so

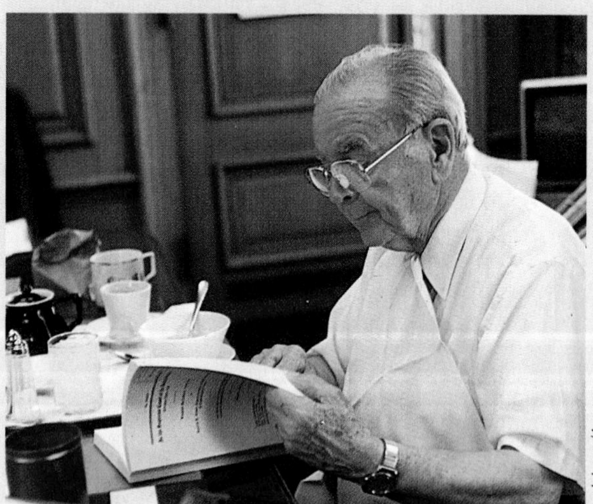

Lynn Johnson/Aurora

The job of a justice is unlike that of other political officials. Even after three decades of experience, Justice William Brennan often ate at his desk so he could finish his work.

conservative that he has dissented more than most chief justices and consequently has left the most senior associate to assign numerous opinions.[4]

After the conference the Court produces the opinion. This is the most time-consuming stage in the process. Because the justices are free to change their vote anytime until the decision is announced, there is much maneuvering and politicking. The justice assigned the opinion tries to write it to command support of the justices in the original majority and possibly even some in the original minority. The writer circulates the draft among the others, who suggest revisions. The writer circulates more drafts. These go back and forth, as the justices attempt to persuade or cajole, nudge or push their colleagues toward their position.

These inner workings underscore the politicking among the justices. Justice William Brennan, a liberal activist on the Warren and Burger Courts, was a gregarious and charming Irish American who was well liked by his colleagues. After drafting an opinion, he sent his clerks to other justices' clerks to learn if the other justices had any objections. Then he tried to redraft it to satisfy them. If they still had qualms, he went to their offices and tried to persuade them. If necessary, he compromised. "He [didn't] want to be 100% principled and lose by one vote," a law professor observed.[5] Brennan was so adept at persuasion that some scholars consider him "the best coalition builder ever to sit on the Supreme Court."[6] In fact, some say the Warren and Burger Courts should have been called the Brennan Court.

Justice Antonin Scalia, a conservative activist on the Rehnquist Court, is a brilliant and gregarious Italian American who, when appointed by President Reagan, was expected to dominate his colleagues and become the leader of the Court. Yet he has not fulfilled this expectation. He has been brash and imprudent, appearing to take more pleasure in insulting his colleagues than in persuading them.[7] In a case in which Justice O'Connor, also conservative but more cautious, did not want to go as far in limiting abortion rights as he did, Scalia wrote that her arguments "cannot be taken seriously."[8] In another case in which Chief Justice Rehnquist, who usually votes with Scalia, voted opposite him, Scalia wrote that his arguments were "implausible" and suggested that any lawyer who advised his client as Rehnquist urged should be "disbarred."[9] As a result, Scalia has not been as effective in forging a consensus among conservatives as Brennan was among liberals.

If the opinion does not command the support of some of the justices in the original majority, they write a concurring opinion. This indicates that they agree with the decision but not the reasons for it. Meanwhile, the justices in the minority write a dissenting opinion. This indicates that they do not agree even with the decision.

My dissenting opinion will be brief. "You're all full of crap."

Both concurring and dissenting opinions weaken the force of the majority opinion. They question the validity of it, and they suggest that at a different time with different justices there might be a different ruling. Chief Justice Hughes used to say that a dissenting opinion is "an appeal to the brooding spirit of the law, to the intelligence of a future day."

The Court's own print shop in the basement prints the opinions. Then the Court announces the decision and opinions in the hushed courtroom.

1. David J. Garrow, "The Rehnquist Reins," *New York Times Magazine*, October 6, 1996, p. 70.
2. David W. Rhode and Harold J. Spaeth, *Supreme Court Decision Making* (San Francisco, W. H. Freeman, 1976), p. 177; Harold J. Spaeth, "Distributive Justice: Majority Opinion Assignments in the Burger Court," *Judicature* 67 (December/January 1984), pp. 299–304.
3. Nina Totenberg and Fred Barbash, "Burger's Colleagues Won't Be Sorry to See Him Go," *Washington Post National Weekly Edition*, July 7, 1986, p. 8.
4. Al Kamen, "The Scalia Surprise," *Washington Post National Weekly Edition*," March 23,1987, p. 6.
5. Michael S. Serrill, "The Power of William Brennan," *Time*, July 22, 1985, p. 62.
6. Ibid.
7. David J. Garrow, "One Angry Man," *New York Times Magazine*, October 6, 1996, pp. 68–69.
8. *Webster v. Reproductive Health Services*, 492 U.S. 445 (1989).
9. *U.S. v. Virginia*, 135 L.Ed.2d 735, 787–789 (1996).

WHAT GOVERNMENT DOES RIGHT

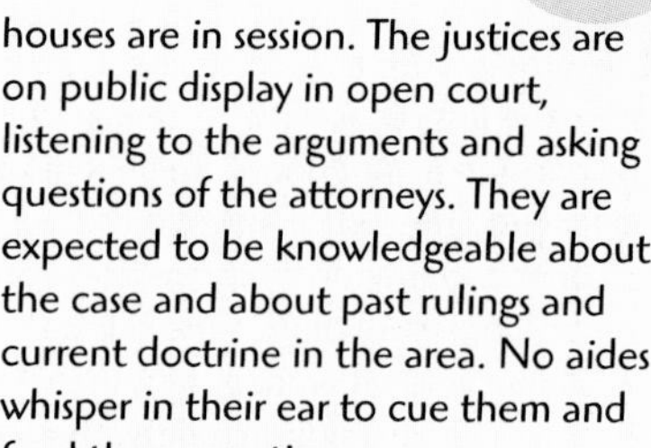

THE JUSTICES DO THEIR OWN WORK

The process of deciding cases shows that the Supreme Court operates very differently than the presidency or Congress. The justices take responsibility for their decisions. As Justice Brandeis observed decades ago, "the reason the public thinks so much of the justices of the Supreme Court is that they are almost the only people in Washington who do their own work."

Presidents have numerous aides and a large White House staff. Although presidents are responsible for their policies, aides do much of their work for them, deciding what subjects they will address at which times, what answers they will give to reporters' questions, what speeches they will give to which audiences, and, of course, what language they will use in these speeches. Presidents even turn to their pollsters to determine what positions they should take in light of the opinions the public holds. Members of Congress, who also are pulled in many directions at once, rely upon their aides and committee staffers when deciding how to interact with constituents, lobbyists, and colleagues throughout the day, how to position themselves on issues, and how to vote on legislation.

Justices do have their clerks, who are recent graduates of law schools, usually the most elite students from the most prestigious institutions. Each year each justice can hire four clerks to help read petitions asking the Court to hear new cases, research statutes and precedents for pending cases, and draft opinions in these cases. Periodically, a fuss is made about the clerks' role and influence. Sometimes critics of decisions suspect that the clerks manipulated the justices.[1] But most observers discount such assertions. A law professor who was a clerk to Justice Blackmun said, "They are like the students of Michelangelo. They may put the ink on paper, but it is according to the justices' design."[2] A former clerk who was also a congressional committee staffer and a vice presidential aide thinks that clerks, who are young and inexperienced, have less impact than staffers and aides in the other two branches.[3]

Much of the business of the Supreme Court is conducted in public, unlike that of Congress, whose chambers are nearly deserted even when its houses are in session. The justices are on public display in open court, listening to the arguments and asking questions of the attorneys. They are expected to be knowledgeable about the case and about past rulings and current doctrine in the area. No aides whisper in their ear to cue them and feed them questions.

When the justices decide their cases, they not only cast a clear vote, but they state their reasons. They consider, very carefully, whether to join the majority opinion or a concurring or dissenting opinion. Even then, they make fine distinctions. In one case, Justice O'Connor joined a concurring opinion except for one sentence. In another case, Justice Thomas joined the majority opinion except for one footnote.[4] Each justice, then, is open to scrutiny and criticism of his or her reasoning. Although justices exercise discretion when they interpret statutes, constitutional provisions, and precedents, the expectation that they justify their conclusions makes them accountable. They realize that lower court judges, lawyers, law professors, law students, and sometimes the general public will evaluate their work.[5]

their interpretations of statutes, or when they make decisions in the absence of statutes, legislatures can pass new statutes to negate the decisions. In 1986 the Supreme Court ruled that the Air Force did not have to allow an ordained rabbi to wear his yarmulke with his uniform.[92] The next year Congress passed a statute permitting military personnel to wear some religious apparel while in uniform. From 1967 through 1990, Congress passed statutes to negate 121 Supreme Court rulings.[93]

Legislatures can refuse to implement courts' rulings, especially when money is needed to implement them. The legislators simply do not appropriate the money.

Although these checks are the most common, Congress has invoked others, although only rarely: it can alter the structure of the lower federal courts; it can limit the appellate jurisdiction of the Supreme Court; and it can impeach and remove judges.

CHECKS BY THE PUBLIC

Judges, chosen by officials who are elected by the public, tend to reflect the views of the public. A study that compared 110 Supreme Court rulings from 1936 through 1986 with public opinion polls on the same issues found that the rulings mirrored the polls in 62% of the cases.[94]

But when court rulings do not reflect the views of the public, opinion toward the courts can turn negative. Although research shows that citizens know little about the cases, they do remember controversial decisions, and they do recognize broad trends. A study of opinion toward the Supreme Court from 1966 to 1984 found that opinion became more negative when

Two clerks meet with Justice Stevens.

Contrast this accountability with the difficulty of determining responsibility in Congress. Even when votes are recorded in Congress, it is often unclear how particular members acted on the issues. Many bills are so complex and so loaded with diverse provisions that it is hard to know what a vote "for" or "against" them means. When amendments to bills are proposed, it is hard to know whether members' votes reflect their views on the amendment or represent their efforts to bolster or torpedo the overall bill. Sometimes members vote to authorize a program but later vote against appropriating money for the program.

It is easier for the justices to do their own work because they are not pulled in as many directions as presidents and members of Congress. It is easier for the justices to take responsibility for their own work because they have judicial independence. They do not need to be as responsive to the public as presidents and members of Congress do. Although the justices do not always make wise decisions, at least the process of making judicial decisions allows the legal profession and sometimes the public to hold them accountable.

1. The machinations of conservative clerks in the 1980s are revealed by Edward Lazarus, *Closed Chambers* (New York: Times Books, 1998), while the possible influence of liberal clerks in the 1970s is examined by Bob Woodward and Scott Armstrong, *The Brethren* (New York: Simon & Schuster, 1979).
2. Harold Koh, quoted in Tony Mauro, "Justices Give Pivotal Role to Novice Lawyers," *USA Today*, March 13–15, 1998, p. 2A.
3. Ibid.
4. Ronald Suresh Roberts, *Clarence Thomas and the Tough Love Crowd* (New York: New York University Press, 1995), p. 84.
5. Even when a justice sits out a case due to illness or possible conflict of interest, his or her absence is announced and then recorded with the justices' opinions.

the Court struck down more congressional laws and when it upheld more criminal rights.[95]

When opinion toward the courts does turn negative, the president or Congress is more likely to impose checks on the courts. This possibility has made the courts wary. As one political scientist concluded, the Supreme Court has "learned to be a political institution and to behave accordingly." It has "seldom lagged far behind or forged far ahead" of public opinion.[96] When it has, notably in the Dred Scott case and in the business regulation cases in the 1930s, it has lost some of its support and consequently some of its power.

In response to the occasional checks threatened or imposed on them, the courts have developed a strong sense of self-restraint to ensure self-preservation. This, more than the checks themselves, limits their use of judicial review.

CONCLUSION: ARE THE COURTS RESPONSIVE?

The judiciary, appellate court judge Learned Hand said, stands as a bulwark against "the pressure of public panic." It provides a "sober second thought."[97] The Founders did not intend the judiciary to be responsive. They gave judges life tenure so courts would be relatively independent.

Indeed, the judiciary is more independent of pressures from the rest of the political process than the other branches are. This enables courts to act on behalf of minorities, whether wealthy businesses, as in the early twentieth century, or unpopular individuals, as in the mid-twentieth century. In either case, courts can be unresponsive to public opinion for some time. Chapters 14 and 15 will show how courts have extended important civil liberties and rights to unpopular individuals who have lacked clout with the executive and legislative branches and support from the majority of the public.

Although relatively independent, the judiciary is part of the political process and is sensitive to others in the process. Ultimately, it is responsive to the president and Congress—or at least to one of these—and to the majority of the public. Thus, in most cases, decisions by the courts reflect the attitudes of society.

EPILOGUE

The Court Allows the President to Be Sued and the Government to Be Disrupted

During oral arguments for *Clinton v. Jones,* the justices signaled their decision in the case. Their questions reflected their skepticism that a lawsuit would occupy much of a president's time or absorb much of his energies. Justice O'Connor suggested that the only aspect of a trial that would take very long would be "the concern about damage control." Justice Scalia snickered that "we see presidents riding horseback, chopping firewood, fishing, playing golf and so forth and so on."[98]

The justices rejected the trial court's careful compromise, that Jones could establish a record of facts now but could not sue Clinton until he left office, and ruled against the president unanimously.[99] They held that presidents do not have immunity for actions that occur before their term in office or that involve personal matters rather than presidential responsibilities. Justice Stevens wrote the opinion, expressing doubt that a trial would take "any substantial amount" of time or prompt other suits that would "engulf the Presidency." Stevens did say that the trial judge could schedule the trial and the president's testimony around his other obligations. Only Justice Breyer, who authored a concurring opinion, expressed concern that the ruling understated the potential for lawsuits to undermine the presidency.

The justices concluded that providing immunity for presidents would disregard the interests of litigants. But the justices ignored the interests of the public in having unfettered presidents who could exercise effective leadership. On the day the Court issued its ruling, President Clinton and Russian president Boris Yeltsin were in Paris to sign an agreement that would allow the NATO alliance to expand into Eastern Europe. That night American television networks highlighted the Court ruling and downplayed the NATO agreement. The next morning American newspapers did the same.

In preparation for the trial, the process of discovery began, with the attorneys asking questions of the two litigants and potential witnesses. When Clinton's attorney questioned Jones in Arkansas, the president, who as a litigant normally would be present to advise his attorney, was in Washington preparing the United States' response to Iraq's expulsion of United Nations weapons inspectors, a response that envisioned military retaliation and, possibly, another Middle Eastern war. Also during these days, the president was conferring with the president of Mexico, negotiating with Congress over its refusal to provide the United States' contribution to the International Monetary Fund for a loan to prop up the sagging Asian economies, and defending against congressional critics his nominee to head the Justice Department's civil rights division.[100] When Jones's attorneys questioned Clinton, the president was in the midst of preparing his State of the Union address. Regardless, he became the first sitting president to be a defendant and to be questioned under oath.[101]

Jones's attorneys leaked rumors and information from discovery to reporters. The result was a titillating sideshow, with talk about "distinguishing characteristics" of the president's genitals and speculation as to what these might be and how they might be confirmed in court. Although some media treated these leaks as facts, they were just rumors, and apparently false ones at that.

To bolster Jones's claims about Clinton's behavior, her attorneys investigated reports about other women who allegedly had sexual relationships with him. Although consensual relationships might have been irrelevant and inadmissible in Jones's suit, her attorneys passed along this information, encouraging the media to report it and the special prosecutor to expand his investigation to encompass it. Without Jones's suit, the public would probably not have had knowledge of allegations of a relationship with Monica Lewinsky or an encounter with Kathleen Willey, nor would the media have paid attention to such allegations.

In short, the suit took considerable time and energy to defend against, and it undermined the president's effectiveness. It also distracted the media and the public—when they were not cracking jokes, people were scolding him as immoral or sympathizing with him as a victim. They seemed only dimly aware of his performance in office.

In the meantime, the two sides tried to negotiate a settlement before trial, as happens in most civil suits. Clinton ultimately offered $700,000—the entire sum Jones originally sued for—but Jones rejected the money, apparently on the advice of her husband or that of a political activist who had become her confidante and adviser. They wanted a trial to humiliate the president.[102]

As the trial date neared, however, the trial judge, Susan Webber Wright, a Republican appointed by President Bush, dismissed Jones's suit. Although Wright did not exonerate Clinton, she concluded that Jones had too little evidence to prove her contentions—too little even for a jury to weigh.[103] Moreover, the incident, if it happened, was "boorish and offensive," she wrote, but it did not constitute sexual harassment. (Chapter 15 will discuss sexual harassment in more detail.)

But Jones appealed the ruling. Soon after, the president's affair with Monica Lewinsky became public, and the lawyers for both Jones and the president realized that although this affair did not involve sexual harassment this news might influence the appellate court. Jones demanded money to settle the case, and the president agreed to pay $850,000. Although this settlement extricated the president from any further proceedings in this case, his effectiveness will be diminished for the rest of his term, and his reputation will be besmirched in history. The suit inflicted much damage.

The Supreme Court's reputation might be tarnished as well. The justices' ruling proved to be shortsighted, even naive about the nature of our political system. To think that such a suit could go to trial today without disrupting the president and the rest of the political process was wishful thinking.

The Supreme Court's ruling, of course, serves as a precedent, despite Judge Wright's decision to dismiss Jones's suit. Other persons can sue future presidents—whether for real or imagined injuries, and whether out of personal or political motives. The ruling, then, could weaken the presidency.

Yet the Court's ruling does illustrate a desirable feature of our constitutional system. The judiciary has so much independence that the justices felt free to challenge the most powerful official in the government. Even Clinton's two appointees felt free to rule against him. And then the trial judge, a member of the opposite party and an appointee of the president whom Clinton beat, felt free to rule in his favor.

KEY TERMS

presidential immunity
judicial review
Marbury v. Madison
court-packing plan
Warren Court
Burger Court
Rehnquist Court
district courts
courts of appeals
jurisdiction
habeas corpus
criminal cases
civil cases
standing to sue
writ of certiorari
restrained judges
activist judges
stare decisis

FURTHER READING

Robert Chrisman and Robert L. Allen, eds., *Court of Appeal: The Black Community Speaks Out on the Racial and Sexual Politics of Thomas vs. Hill* (New York: Ballentine, 1992). Passionate and provocative essays by black writers reflecting on the nomination and confirmation of Justice Thomas.

Richard D. Kahlenberg, *Broken Contract* (Boston: Faber & Faber, 1992). A memoir by a student at Harvard Law School that tells you a lot about law schools, the legal profession, and the nature of American law.

David M. O'Brien, *Storm Center*, 3d ed. (New York: W. W. Norton, 1993). A lively account of the Supreme Court and its very human justices.

Bob Woodward and Scott Armstrong, *The Brethren* (New York: Simon & Schuster, 1979). A behind-the-scenes look at the politicking among Supreme Court justices for major cases during the 1970s.

ELECTRONIC RESOURCES

http://oyez.nwu.edu/

This excellent site has biographies of all the Supreme Court justices, current and previous. It is a multimedia site, where you can hear the marshal cry "Oyez, oyez," listen to oral arguments in important cases, take a virtual tour of the Court, and search for Court decisions by subject, date, or citation.

http://www.courttv.com/library/supreme/

This site, developed by a private company, contains biographies of all the Supreme Court justices. It provides links to summaries of recent key decisions and the text of actual decisions. A similar site operated by Cornell University is http://supct.law.cornell.edu/supct/justices/fullcourt.html

INFOTRAC CITATIONS

"RFRA Coalition Frays in Wake of Ruling"
"Is the GOP Causing a Vacancy Crisis in the Federal Judiciary?"
"The Lawyers Are at It Again"
"The Supreme Court's Relaxed Work Ethic"

NOTES

1. Technically, Jones could not sue on the basis of sexual harassment, however, because the statute of limitations had expired. Instead, she sued on the basis of denial of civil rights, intentional infliction of emotional distress, and defamation. (The latter stemmed from assertions by presidential aides that the incident had not occurred and the resulting implication that she had lied.) Yet the evidence relevant to these claims would be nearly the same as for a sexual harassment suit.

2. This conclusion would parallel the conclusion of many legal scholars about immunity from criminal prosecution. Although presidents, of course, can be impeached for criminal (or noncriminal) behavior, they might have immunity from prosecution while remaining in office. Thus, the special prosecutor told the grand jury that it could not indict President Nixon for Watergate crimes. (Instead, the grand jury cited the president as an "unindicted co-conspirator.") The Supreme Court initially agreed to address this question in the Watergate tapes case but ultimately avoided it. At least it is clear that presidents can be prosecuted after leaving office. Hence, President Nixon's effort to arrange a pardon for himself before agreeing to step down.

3. *Nixon v. Fitzgerald*, 457 U.S. 731.

4. The federal appellate court cited these possibilities when it ruled against the president.

5. John R. Schmidhauser, *Justices and Judges* (Boston: Little, Brown, 1979), p. 11.

6. John Hibbing and Elizabeth Theiss-Morse, *Congress as Public Enemy: Public Attitudes toward American Political Institutions* (Cambridge University Press, 1995), chapters 2 and 3.

7. *Federalist Paper* #78.

8. Henry J. Abraham, *Justices and Presidents* (New York: Oxford University Press, 1974), p. 74.

9. Henry J. Abraham, *The Judicial Process*, 3d ed. (New York: Oxford University Press, 1975), p. 309.

10. *Federalist Paper* #78.

11. 1 Cranch 137 (1803). Technically, *Marbury* is not considered the first use of judicial review, but it is the first clear example.

12. Walter F. Murphy and C. Herman Pritchett, *Courts, Judges, and Politics*, 3d ed. (New York: Random House, 1979), p. 4.

13. John A. Garraty, "The Case of the Missing Commissions," in John A. Garraty, ed., *Quarrels That Have Shaped the Constitution* (New York: Harper & Row, 1962), p. 13.

14. *Fletcher v. Peck*, 6 Cranch 87 (1810); *Martin v. Hunter's Lessee*, 1 Wheaton 304 (1816); *Cohens v. Virginia*, 6 Wheaton 264 (1821).

15. *Gibbons v. Ogden*, 9 Wheaton 1 (1824).

16. *Scott v. Sandford*, 19 Howard 393 (1857).

17. *Ex parte Merryman*, 17 Federal Cases 9487 (1861).

18. *Ex parte McCardle*, 7 Wallace 506 (1869).

19. *Hammer v. Dagenhart*, 247 U.S. 251 (1918).

20. *Lochner v. New York*, 198 U.S. 45 (1905).

21. *Adkins v. Children's Hospital*, 261 U.S. 525 (1923).

22. *Adair v. United States*, 208 U.S. 161 (1908). *In re Delis*, 158 U.S. 564 (1895).

23. *United States v. E. C. Knight Co.*, 156 U.S. 1 (1895).

24. Lawrence Baum, *The Supreme Court*, 2d ed. (Washington, D.C.: CQ Press, 1985), p. 177.

25. C. Herman Pritchett, *The American Constitution*, 2d ed. (New York: McGraw-Hill, 1968), p. 166.

26. Henry Abraham, "A Bench Happily Filled," *Judicature* 66 (February 1983), p. 284.

27. Victor Navasky, *Kennedy Justice* (New York: Atheneum, 1971), pp. 245–246.

28. One of President Reagan's nominees, Douglas Ginsburg, withdrew his nomination due to widespread opposition in the Senate, so officially his nomination was not denied.

29. Charles M. Cameron, Albert D. Cover, and Jeffrey A. Segal, "Senate Voting on Supreme Court Nominees: A Neoinstitutional Model," *American Political Science Review* 84 (June 1990), pp. 525–534.

30. Abraham, *Justices and Presidents*, pp. 6–7.

31. Ruth Marcus and Joe Pichirallo, "The Noncontemporary Judge," *Washington Post National Weekly Edition*, September 17–23, 1990, p. 6; Margaret Carlson, "An 18th Century Man," *Time*, August 6, 1990, p. 19; Richard Lacayo, "A Blank Slate," *Time*, August 6, 1990, p. 16.

32. Jeffrey Segal and Harold Spaeth, "If a Supreme Court Vacancy Occurs, Will the Senate Confirm a Reagan Nominee?" *Judicature* 69 (1986), pp. 188–189.

33. Al Kamen, "Switching Sides to Court Victory," *Washington Post National Weekly Edition*, July 14, 1997, p. 15.

34. Neil A. Lewis, "Impeach Those Liberal Judges! Where Are They?" *New York Times*, May 18, 1997, p. E5.

35. House Majority Whip Tom DeLay (Tex.). Joan Biskupic, "Objecting to Judicial Activism," *Washington Post National Weekly Edition*, September 22, 1997, p. 6.

36. Lewis, "Impeach Those Federal Judges!"

37. Neil A. Lewis, "Stalled Judicial Nominee Feels the Personal Pain of Politics," *New York Times*, November 16, 1997, p. 22. One nonpartisan research center—the Miller Center of Public Affairs at the University of Virginia—has attributed these tactics, in general, to the Republicans' reliance on conservative interest groups that focus primarily on the judiciary. Garland W. Allison, "Delay in Senate Confirmation of Federal Judicial Nominees," *Judicature*, 80 (July/August 1996), p. 14.

38. Sheldon Goldman. Biskupic, "Objecting to Judicial Activism."

39. M. Nejelski, *Women in the Judiciary: A Status Report* (Washington, D.C.: National Women's Political Caucus, June 1984).

40. Sheldon Goldman, "Reagan's Second Term Judicial Appointments," *Judicature* 70 (April/May 1987), pp. 324–339; Al Kamen and Ruth Marcus, "The Next Species for the Endangered List: Liberal Judges," *Washington Post National Weekly Edition*, February 6–12, 1989, p. 31; "Clinton Begins Undoing the Reagan-Bush Judiciary," *Time*, January 10, 1994, p. 10.

41. Sheldon Goldman and Elliot Slotnick, "Clinton's First Term Judiciary: Many Bridges to Cross," *Judicature* 80 (1997), pp. 261, 269.

42. Breyer, Ginsburg, O'Connor, Souter, Stevens, and possibly Scalia.

43. Schmidhauser, *Justice and Judges*, pp. 55–57.

44. Steve Alumbaugh and C. K. Rowland, "The Links between Platform-Based Appointment Criteria and Trial Judges' Abortion Judgments," *Judicature* 74 (October/November 1990), pp. 153–162.

45. Lettie M. Wenner and Cynthias Ostberg, "Restraint in Environmental Cases by Reagan-Bush Judicial Appointees," *Judicature* 77 (January/February 1994), pp. 217–220.

46. William E. Kovacic, "The Reagan Judiciary and Environmental Policy," *Environmental Affairs* 18 (1991), pp. 669–713.

47. These numbers include a recent impeachment that was overturned by a district court because the Senate, to streamline procedures, had only the Judiciary Committee hear the charges and then allowed all senators to vote. The removal was reinstated by a court of appeals.

48. Merle Miller, *Plain Speaking* (New York: Berkeley Publishing/G. P. Putnam's Sons, 1974), p. 121.

49. Harold W. Chase, *Federal Judges* (Minneapolis: University of Minnesota Press, 1972), p. 189.

50. *Morrison v. Olson*, 487 U.S. 654 (1988).

51. Martin Shapiro, "The Supreme Court: From Warren to Burger," in Anthony King, ed., *The New American Political System* (Washington, D.C.: American Enterprise Institute, 1978), pp. 180–181.

52. Robert Seigliano, *The Supreme Court and the Presidency* (New York: Free Press, 1971), pp. 147–148.

53. Abraham, *Justices and Presidents*, p. 62.

54. Earl Warren, *The Memoirs of Earl Warren* (Garden City, N.Y.: Doubleday, 1977), p. 5.

55. Abraham, *Justices and Presidents*, p. 63.

56. "How Much Do Lawyers Charge?" *Parade*, March 23, 1997, p. 14.

57. Lois G. Forer, *Money and Justice* (New York: W. W. Norton, 1984), pp. 9, 15, 102.

58. Karen O'Connor and Lee Epstein, "The Rise of Conservative Interest Group Litigation," *Journal of Politics* 45 (May 1983), p. 481. See also Richard C. Cortner, *The Supreme Court and the Second Bill of Rights* (Madison: University of Wisconsin Press, 1981), p. 282.

59. *Tileston v. Ullman*, 318 U.S. 44 (1943).

60. *Poe v. Ullman*, 367 U.S. 497 (1961).

61. *Griswold v. Connecticut*, 381 U.S. 479 (1965).

62. C. K. Rowland and Bridget Jeffery Todd, "Where You Stand Depends on Who Sits," *Journal of Politics* 53 (February 1991), pp. 175–185.

63. Although the Court accepted about 150 cases for oral argument and written opinions (and about an equal number to decide summarily—without oral arguments and written opinions) each term during the mid-1980s, the Rehnquist Court has shrunk the docket. It heard only 84 cases in the 1994 term.

64. Fred Barbash and Al Kamen, "Supreme Court, 'A Rotten Way to Earn a Living,'" *Washington Post National Weekly Edition*, October 1, 1984, p. 33.

65. *Bailey v. U.S.*, 133 L.Ed.2d 472 (1995).

66. Robert Bork, *The Tempting of America* (New York: Touchstone/Simon & Schuster, 1990).

67. Lawrence Tribe, *On Reading the Constitution* (Cambridge, Mass.: Harvard University Press, 1992).

68. *Osborn v. U.S. Bank*, 9 Wheaton 738 (1824), at 866.

69. Abraham, *Judicial Process*, p. 324.

70. *U.S. v. Butler*, 297 U.S. 1, at 94.

71. Murphy and Pritchett, *Courts, Judges, and Politics*, p. 586.

72. "Judicial Authority Moves Growing Issue," *Lincoln Journal*, April 24, 1977.

73. Alexander Bickel, *The Morality of Consent* (New Haven: Yale University Press, 1975), p. 120.

74. "Judicial Authority Moves Growing Issue."

75. Jeffrey A. Segal and Albert D. Cover, "Ideological Values and the Votes of U.S. Supreme Court Justices," *American Political Science Review* 83 (June 1989), pp. 557–564. For different findings for state supreme court justices, see John M. Scheb II, Terry Bowen, and Gary Anderson, "Ideology, Role Orientations, and Behavior in the State Courts of Last Resort," *American Politics Quarterly* 19 (July 1991), pp. 324–335.

76. Harold Spaeth and Stuart Teger, "Activism and Restraint: A Cloak for the Justices' Policy Preferences," in Stephen P. Halpern and Clark M. Lamb, eds., *Supreme Court Activism and Restraint* (Lexington, Mass.: Lexington, 1982), p. 277.

77. *Engel v. Vitale*, 370 U.S. 421 (1962).

78. *Abington School District v. Schempp*, 374 U.S. 203 (1963).

79. *Stone v. Graham*, 449 U.S. 39 (1980).

80. *Lee v. Weisman*, 120 L.Ed.2d 467 (1992).

81. *Burnet v. Coronado Oil and Gas*, 285 U.S. 293 (1932), at 406.

82. Abraham, *Judicial Process*, p. 13.

83. *Denver Area Educational Telecommunications Consortium v. Federal Communications Commission*, 116 S.Ct. 2374 (1996).

84. *U.S. v. Butler*, 297 U.S. 1 (1936), at 79.

85. Murphy and Pritchett, *Courts, Judges and Politics*, p. 25.

86. Baum, *The Supreme Court*, p. 4.

87. 410 U.S. 113.

88. Craig R. Ducat and Robert L. Dudley, "Federal Appellate Judges and Presidential Power," paper presented at the Midwest Political Science Association Meeting, April 1987.

89. Baum, *The Supreme Court*, p. 158.

90. Sheldon Goldman, "How Long the Legacy?" *Judicature*, 76 (April/May 1993), p. 295.

91. The Eleventh Amendment overturned *Chisholm v. Georgia* (1793), which had permitted the federal courts to hear suits against a state by citizens of another state. The Fourteenth overturned the Dred Scott case, *Scott v. Sandford* (1857), which had held that blacks were not citizens. The Sixteenth overturned *Pollock v. Farmers' Loan and Trust* (1895), which had negated a congressional law authorizing a federal income tax. The Twenty-sixth overturned *Oregon v. Mitchell* (1970), which had negated a congressional law allowing 18-year-olds to vote in state elections.

92. *Goldman v. Weinberger*, 475 U.S. 503 (1986).

93. William N. Eskridge, Jr., "Overriding Supreme Court Statutory Interpretation Decisions," *Yale Law Journal* 101 (1991), p. 338.

94. Thomas R. Marshall, "Public Opinion, Representation, and the Modern Supreme Court," *American Politics Quarterly* 16 (July 1988), pp. 296–316.

95. Gregory A. Caldeira, "Neither the Purse nor the Sword," paper presented at the American Political Science Association Meeting, August 1987.

96. Robert G. McCloskey, *The American Supreme Court* (Chicago: University of Chicago Press, 1960), p. 225.

97. Abraham, *Justices and Presidents*, pp. 342–343.

98. Excerpts of oral arguments are from "The Ruling That Entangled the President," *New York Times*, March 15, 1998, Week in Review, p. 7.

99. 137 L.Ed.2d 945 (1997).

100. Vincent Bugliosi, *No Island of Sanity: Paula Jones v. Bill Clinton* (New York: Ballantine, 1998). This book is an extended critique of the Supreme Court's ruling in this case.

101. Richard Lacayo, "The Big Face-off," *Time*, January 26, 1998, p. 46.

102. Jeffrey Toobin, "Casting Stones," *New Yorker*, November 3, 1997, pp. 55–57.

103. Jones's lawyers seemed so obsessed with the possible affairs of the president that they paid little attention to the purported employment discrimination that Jones claimed. This charge—that she suffered at work because she rebuffed the president—would, if proved, establish her harassment charge. Yet during her deposition she said that her lawyers had not reviewed her employment records with her. And during the president's deposition, her lawyers made little effort to probe this possibility. Jeffrey Toobin, "How Paula Jones's Defenders Left Her Defenseless," *New Yorker*, April 13, 1998, p. 27.

PART FOUR CIVIL LIBERTIES AND RIGHTS

Ernesto Pichardo, priest of the Church of the Lukumi Babalu Aye.

Tom Salyer

14 CIVIL LIBERTIES

YOU ARE THERE

Does Religious Liberty Include Animal Sacrifice?

You are Justice Anthony Kennedy of the U.S. Supreme Court facing an unusual case from Hialeah, Florida. The Church of the Lukumi Babalu Aye has brought suit against the city because of ordinances that restrict the church's practices.

The church follows the Santeria religion, which originated in Nigeria 4,000 years ago. The religion spread to Cuba when Nigerians were brought as slaves and eventually to Florida when Cubans fled their communist government. Santeria now blends ancient African rites and Roman Catholic rituals, but its distinguishing and most provocative practice is animal sacrifice. Adherents believe animal sacrifice is necessary to win the favor of the gods, and they practice it at births, marriages, and deaths, and at initiations of new members and priests. Chickens, ducks, doves, pigeons, sheep, goats, and turtles are killed by knife, their blood is drained into pots, and their meat is prepared for eating.

Santeria long existed underground, but the church decided to bring it into the open in 1987, leasing a used-car lot and announcing plans for a church building, cultural center, museum, and school in the Miami suburb. Then "the neighborhood went ape," according to one resident.[1] The city council held an emergency session, at which one council member stated that devotees "are in violation of everything this country stands for," while another quoted the Bible in opposition. The council president asked, "What can we do to prevent the church from opening?"

The city attorney's office drafted a series of ordinances, which the city council passed, that essentially deny adherents the opportunity to practice their religion. Although the ordinances do not explicitly refer to Santeria, they prohibit ritualistic animal sacrifice. They make exception for kosher slaughter for persons who follow Jewish dietary laws.

The church filed suit, claiming that the ordinances impinge on members' free exercise of their religion guaranteed by the First Amendment of the Constitution. The free exercise clause allows individuals to practice their religion as they see fit. Governments cannot restrict a particular religion or practice, unless there is a compelling reason to do so. The city countered that there were compelling reasons: First, animal sacrifice presents a health risk to the adherents, because the animals are uninspected and might be unsanitary, and to the public, because the carcasses sometimes are found rotting in the streets and floating in the canals. (The church responded that it properly disposes of the remains but that adherents of Santeria who are not members of the church might not.) Second, animal sacrifice entails cruelty to animals. (The church responded that it humanely kills the animals by slicing their carotid artery, as kosher slaughter does.) Third, animal sacrifice results in emotional injury to children who witness it.

The church's priest, Ernesto Pichardo, suggested that town officials were hypocrites. "You can kill a turkey in your backyard, put it on the table, say a prayer, and serve it for Thanksgiving. But if we pray over the turkey, kill it, then eat it, we violated the law."[2]

But the federal district court ruled for the city, and the federal court of appeals affirmed. Now it is 1993, and the Supreme Court is deciding the case.

You were appointed by President Reagan because of your conservatism. Actually, you were not Reagan's first choice for this seat. Robert Bork was, but he was denied confirmation because of his more extreme conservatism. Eventually, you were nominated because you were less flamboyant and less likely to antagonize the groups and senators who opposed Bork. But in most cases you have voted the way observers predicted Bork would have voted—generally against individual rights and for government authority. (Even now you are relatively unknown. A group of tourists of the Court, thinking you were also sightseeing, asked you to take their picture.)

You are a Roman Catholic, a former altar boy, and you seem inclined to accommodate people's religious desires or demands, yet your views appear uncertain. A year ago, for instance, you wrote the majority opinion that invalidated prayers at graduation ceremonies for public elementary, middle, and high schools.[3] In cases involving minority religious practices, you voted to allow Hare Krishnas the right to distribute literature at public airports, yet you voted to deny members of the Native American church the right to use peyote, a hallucinogen, in worship ceremonies.[4] In that case you joined an opinion that could make it difficult for members of minority religions to adhere to their practices.

So how do you decide this case?

Americans value their "rights." Eighteenth-century Americans believed that people had "natural rights" by virtue of being human. Given by God, not by government, the rights could not be taken away by government. Contemporary Americans do not use this term, but they do think about rights much as their forebears did.

Yet Americans have a split personality about their rights. As Chapter 4 described, most people tell pollsters they believe in various constitutional rights in the abstract, but many do not accept these rights when applied to concrete situations. For example, most people say they believe in free speech, but many would not allow communists, socialists, or atheists to speak in public or teach in schools.

Surveys in the 1990s show that Americans remain divided over their support for civil liberties. Thirty-one percent say freedom of expression should not apply to network television; 28% say it should not apply to newspapers; and 26% say it should not apply to art, film, or music. Fifty-five percent think songs with sexually explicit lyrics should be barred from radio and television, and 50% think books with "dangerous ideas" should be banned from school libraries.[5] Forty percent believe police should be able to search homes of suspected drug dealers without search warrants.[6]

Conflicts over civil liberties and rights have dominated the courts since the Great Depression. This chapter, covering civil liberties, and the next, covering civil rights, describe how the courts have interpreted these rights and tried to resolve these conflicts. We will explain the most important rights and recount the struggles by individuals and groups to achieve them. We will see how judges act as referees between litigants, brokers among competing groups, and policymakers in the process of deciding these cases.

THE CONSTITUTION AND THE BILL OF RIGHTS

Individual Rights in the Constitution

Although the term *civil liberties* usually refers to the rights in the Bill of Rights, a few rights are granted in the body of the Constitution. The Constitution bans religious qualifications for federal office and guarantees jury trials in federal criminal cases. It bans **bills of attainder,** which are legislative acts rather than judicial trials pronouncing specific persons guilty of crimes, and **ex post facto laws,** which are legislative acts making some behavior illegal that was not illegal when it was done. The Constitution also prohibits suspension of the writ of habeas corpus, except during rebellion or invasion of the country. These rights are significant, but they by no means exhaust the rights people believed they had at the time the Constitution was written.

The Bill of Rights

ORIGIN AND MEANING

The Constitution originally did not include a bill of rights; the Founders did not think traditional liberties needed specific protections because federalism, separation of powers, and checks and balances would prevent the national government from becoming too powerful. But to win support for ratification, the Founders promised to adopt amendments to provide such rights. James Madison proposed 12, Congress passed them, and in 1791 the states ratified 10, which came to be known as the Bill of Rights.[7] Of these, the first eight grant specific rights. (The Ninth says the listing of these rights does not mean they are the only ones the people have; and the Tenth says the powers not granted to the federal government are reserved for the state governments.)

The Bill of Rights provides rights against the government. According to Justice Hugo Black, it is "a collection of Thou shalt nots" directed at the government.[8] Essentially, the Bill of Rights provides rights for minorities against the majority, because government policy concerning civil liberties tends to reflect the views of the majority.

As Chapter 2 explained, the Founders set up a government to protect property rights for the well-to-do minority against the presumably jealous majority. Separation of powers, checks and balances, and various specific provisions of the Constitution were intended to limit the ability of the masses to curtail the rights of the elites. However, as Americans became more egalitarian and got more opportunity to participate in politics, the importance of property rights has declined while the importance of other rights has increased. At the same time, the role of the Bill of Rights has increased to protect the "have-nots" of society—the unpopular, powerless minorities in conflict with the majority.

Responsibility for interpreting the Bill of Rights generally falls on the federal courts. Because their judges are appointed for life, they are more independent from majority pressure than elected officials are.

APPLICATION

For many years the Supreme Court applied the Bill of Rights only to the federal government—not to state governments (or local governments, which are under the authority of state governments). The Court ruled that the Bill of Rights restricted only what the federal government could do.[9]

The Founders thought that states, being closer to the people, would be less likely to violate their liberties. Also, they knew that many states had their own bills of rights, and they expected the rest to follow.

The Founders did not realize that states would come to violate people's liberties more frequently than the federal government. The state governments, representing smaller, more homogeneous populations, tended to reflect majority sentiment more closely than the federal government, and they often rode roughshod over criminal defendants or racial, religious, or political minorities. When disputes arose, state courts tended to interpret their bills of rights narrowly.

However, starting in 1925[10] and continuing through 1972,[11] the Supreme Court gradually applied most provisions of the Bill of Rights to the states, using the Fourteenth Amendment's due process clause as justification. This clause, adopted after the Civil War to protect blacks from southern governments, reads, "Nor shall any state deprive any person of life, liberty, or property, without due process of law." The clause refers to states and "liberty." It is ambiguous, but the Court interpreted it to mean that states also have to provide the liberties in the Bill of Rights.

The Court has applied all but two provisions of the First and the Fourth through the Eighth Amendments to the states: guarantee of a grand jury in criminal cases and guarantee of a jury trial in civil cases. In addition, the Court has established some rights not in the Bill of Rights, and it has applied these to the states, too: presumption of innocence in criminal cases, right to travel within the country, and right to privacy. Thus, most provisions in the Bill of Rights, and even some not in it, now restrict what both the federal and state governments can do.

To see how the Court has interpreted these provisions, we will look at three major areas—freedom of expression, rights of criminal defendants, and right to privacy.

CIVIL LIBERTIES IN THE BILL OF RIGHTS

- First Amendment
  freedom of religion
  freedom of speech, assembly, and association
  freedom of the press
- Second Amendment
  right to keep and bear arms (for individuals in a militia at a time when there was no standing army to protect the country)
- Third Amendment
  forbids quartering soldiers in houses during peacetime
- Fourth Amendment
  forbids unreasonable searches and seizures
- Fifth Amendment
  right to grand jury hearing in criminal cases
  forbids double jeopardy (more than one trial for the same offense)
  forbids compulsory self-incrimination
  right to due process
  forbids taking private property without just compensation
- Sixth Amendment
  right to speedy trial
  right to public trial
  right to jury trial in criminal cases
  right to cross-examine adverse witnesses
  right to present favorable witnesses
  right to counsel
- Seventh Amendment
  right to jury trial in civil cases
- Eighth Amendment
  forbids excessive bail and fines
  forbids cruel and unusual punishment

FREEDOM OF EXPRESSION

The First Amendment provides freedom of expression, which includes freedom of speech, assembly, and association;[12] freedom of the press; and freedom of religion.

The amendment states that "Congress shall make no law" abridging these liberties. The language is absolute, but few justices interpret it literally. They cite the example of the person who falsely shouts "Fire!" in a crowded theater and causes a stampede that injures someone, and they say the amendment does not protect this expression. So the Court needs to draw a line between expression the amendment protects and that which it does not.

"The way I see it, the Constitution cuts both ways. The First Amendment gives you the right to say what you want, but the Second Amendment gives me the right to shoot you for it."

Freedom of Speech

Freedom of speech, Justice Black asserted, "is the heart of our government."[13] First, by allowing an open atmosphere, it maximizes the opportunities for every individual to develop his or her personality and potential to the fullest. Second, by encouraging a variety of opinions, it furthers the advancement of knowledge and discovery of truth. Unpopular opinions could be true or partially true. Even if completely false, they could prompt a reevaluation of accepted opinions. Third, by permitting citizens to form opinions and express them to others, it helps them participate in government. It especially helps them check inefficient or corrupt government. Fourth, by channeling conflict toward persuasion, it promotes a stable society. Governments that deny freedom of speech become inflexible; they force conflict toward violence.[14]

SEDITIOUS SPEECH

The first controversies to test the scope of freedom of speech involved **seditious speech,** speech that encourages rebellion against the government. The government historically prosecuted individuals for seditious speech during or shortly after war, when society was most sensitive about loyalty.

Numerous prosecutions came with World War I and the Russian Revolution, which brought the Communists to power in the Soviet Union in 1917. The Russian Revolution prompted a "Red Scare," in which people feared conspiracies to overthrow the U.S. government. Congress passed the Espionage Act of 1917, which prohibited interfering with military recruitment, inciting insubordination in military forces, and mailing material advocating rebellion; and the Sedition Act of 1918, which prohibited "disloyal, profane, scurrilous, or abusive language about the form of government, Constitution, soldiers and sailors, flag or uniform of the armed forces." Many states passed similar laws. In short, government prohibited a wide range of speech.

During the war the federal government prosecuted almost 2,000 and convicted almost 900 persons under these acts, and the states prosecuted and convicted many others. They prosecuted individuals for saying that war is contrary to the teachings of Jesus, that World War I should not have been declared until after a referendum was held, and that the draft was unconstitutional. Officials even prosecuted an individual for remarking to women knitting clothes for the troops, "No soldier ever sees those socks."[15]

These cases gave the Supreme Court numerous opportunities to rule on seditious speech. In six major cases, the Court upheld the federal and state laws and affirmed the convictions of all the defendants.[16] The defendants advocated socialism or communism, and some advocated the overthrow of the government to achieve it. Except for one—Eugene Debs, the Socialist Party's candidate for president—the defendants did not command a large audience. Even so, the Court concluded that these defendants' speech constituted a

UPI/Corbis-Bettmann

Eugene Debs, the Socialist Party's candidate for president, criticized American involvement in World War I and the draft. He was convicted for violating the Espionage Act and sentenced to 10 years in prison. When President Harding pardoned him early, Debs commented, "It is the government that should ask me for a pardon."

"clear and present danger" to the government. Justice Edward Sanford wrote, "A single revolutionary spark may kindle a fire that, smouldering for a time, may burst into a sweeping and destructive conflagration."[17] In reality, there was nothing clear or present about the danger; the defendants' speech had little effect.

More prosecutions came after World War II. In 1940, Congress passed the Smith Act, which was not as broad as the World War I acts because it did not forbid criticizing the government. But it did forbid advocating overthrow of the government by force and organizing or joining individuals who advocated overthrow.

The act was used against members of the American Communist Party after the war. The uneasy alliance between the United States and the Soviet Union had given way to the Cold War between the countries. Politicians, especially Senator Joseph McCarthy (R-Wis.), exploited the tensions. McCarthy charged various government officials with being Communists. He had little evidence, and his tactics were called "witch-hunts" and, eventually, **McCarthyism.** Other Republicans also accused the Democratic administration of covering up Communists. They goaded it into prosecuting members of the Communist Party so it would not appear "soft on communism."

In 1951, the Court upheld the Smith Act and affirmed the convictions of 11 top-echelon leaders of the Communist Party.[18] These leaders organized the party and the party advocated overthrowing the government by force, but the leaders had not attempted overthrowing it. (If they had, they clearly would have been guilty of crimes.) Even so, the Court majority concluded that they constituted a clear and present danger, and Chief Justice Fred Vinson wrote that the government does not have to "wait until the putsch is about to be executed, the plans have been laid and the signal is awaited" before it can act against the party. The minority argued that the Communist Party was not a danger. Justice William Douglas said that the party was "of little consequence. . . . Communism has been so thoroughly exposed in this country that it has been crippled as a political force. Free speech has destroyed it as an effective political party." Following the Court's decision, the government prosecuted and convicted almost 100 other Communists.

But the Cold War thawed slightly, the Senate voted to condemn McCarthy, and two new members, including Chief Justice Earl Warren, joined the Court. In a series of cases in the 1950s, the Court made it more difficult to convict Communists,[19] thereby incurring the wrath of the public, Congress, and President Eisenhower. In a private conversation, Warren asked Eisenhower what he thought the Court should do with the Communists. Eisenhower replied, "I would kill the S.O.B.s."[20]

The government took other action against Communists. The federal government ordered Communists to register, and then some state governments banned them from public jobs such as teaching, or private jobs such as practicing law or serving as union officers. Legislative committees held hearings to expose and humiliate them. The Court heard numerous cases involving these actions and usually ruled against the government.

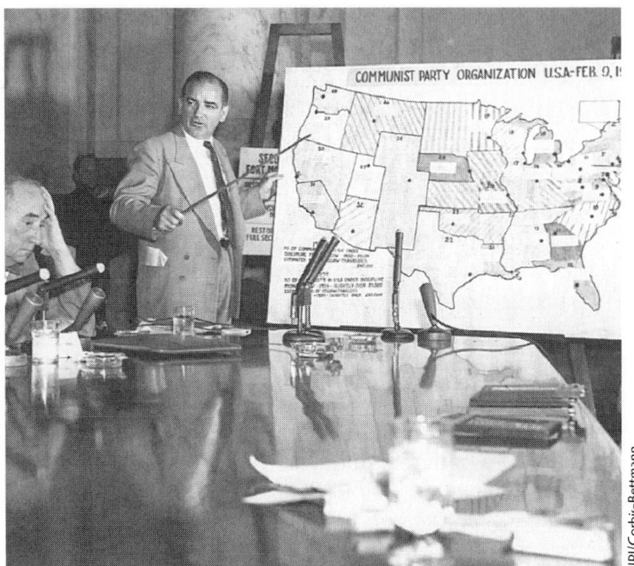

UPI/Corbis-Bettmann

At congressional hearings Senator Joseph McCarthy identified locations of alleged Communists and "fellow travelers."

The Vietnam War did not prompt the same fears that World Wars I and II did. Congress did not pass comparable laws, perhaps because many "respectable" people opposed this war and also because the Court in the 1950s and 1960s increasingly allowed seditious speech.

The Court developed new doctrine for seditious speech in 1969. A Ku Klux Klan leader said at a rally in Ohio that the Klan might take "revengeance" on the president, Congress, and Supreme Court if they continued "to suppress the white, Caucasian race." The leader was convicted under a statute similar to those upheld after World War I, but this time the statute was unanimously struck down by the Court.[21] The justices said people can advocate—enthusiastically, even heatedly—as long as they do not incite illegal action. This broad protection for seditious speech remains in effect today.

Thus, after many years and many cases, the Court concluded that the First Amendment protects seditious speech as much as other speech. Justice Douglas noted that "the threats were often loud but always puny."[22] Even the attorney general who prosecuted the major Communist cases later admitted that the cases were "squeezed oranges. I didn't think there was much to them."[23] Nevertheless, the Court had permitted a climate of fear to overwhelm the First Amendment for many years.

Although the country is at peace today, these precedents will be important again. Already they have had some effect on government action against right-wing militia groups. Since the Oklahoma City bombing in 1995, government surveillance of these groups and enforcement of gun laws have stepped up, but prosecution of the members, under terrorism laws, has been limited because most of the "evidence" is fiery rhetoric, which is protected speech (unless it reflects concrete plans to violate any laws).

Now we will turn to other speech—nonseditious speech—to see how the Court has interpreted the First Amendment in these situations.

PUBLIC FORUM

People usually communicate with each other in private. But sometimes speakers want more listeners and they use public places where people congregate. This means speakers will be heard by some listeners who do not like their message or their use of public places to disseminate it, and it also means speakers might disrupt the normal purposes of these places.

The Court holds that individuals have a right to use public places, such as streets, sidewalks, and parks, to express their views on public issues. These places constitute the **public forum** and serve as "the poor person's printing press."

When speakers seek to use other public facilities, the Court has to determine which ones are also part of the public forum. It decided that federal and state capitol grounds,[24] Supreme Court grounds,[25] and public school grounds[26] are part of the forum. It decided that blacks could protest library segregation at a public library[27] and promoters could show the rock musical *Hair* at a public theater[28] because these too are part of the forum.

On the other hand, the Court decided that civil rights activists could not demonstrate against jail segregation outside a jail because of the need for security,[29] and that Dr. Benjamin Spock—the baby doctor—and other antiwar activists could not encourage opposition to the Vietnam War at an army base because of the need for discipline in the army.[30]

Normally, only publicly owned facilities are considered part of the public forum, but the proliferation of shopping centers and malls prompted speakers to use these privately owned facilities to reach crowds of shoppers. The Warren Court permitted them to do so, saying that shopping centers and malls are similar to downtown shopping districts where streets and sidewalks are part of the public forum.[31] But the Burger Court overruled the Warren Court; it allowed the shopping centers and malls to prohibit speech. Thus, the Burger Court emphasized property rights rather than First Amendment rights in this situation.[32]

Even in public forums people cannot speak whenever and however they want. The Court has divided speech into three kinds—pure speech, speech plus conduct, and symbolic speech—and established doctrine for each.

PURE SPEECH

Pure speech is speech without any conduct (besides the speech itself). Individuals can say what they want as long as they do not cause a breach of the peace or a riot, or hurl "fighting words" at specific persons, except at police officers, who are supposed to be trained and disciplined to take abuse.[33]

Before the Court's ruling in 1972, arrests for swearing were common. In the District of Columbia, for example, more than half of the 15,000 to 20,000 arrests for "disorderly conduct" each year involved swearing, usually at police.[34]

Individuals can use offensive language in many situations.[35] During the Vietnam War, a man walked through the corridors of the Los Angeles County courthouse wearing a jacket with the words "Fuck the Draft" emblazoned on the back. Police arrested him. The Court reversed his conviction, and 72-year-old Justice John Harlan remarked that "one man's vulgarity is another's lyric."[36]

The media, however, cannot broadcast some offensive language. A California radio station broadcast a monologue by comedian George Carlin. Titled "Filthy Words," it lampooned society's sensitivity to seven words that "you couldn't say on the public airwaves . . . the ones you definitely wouldn't say, ever." The seven words, according to the Federal Communications Commission report, included "a four-letter word for excrement" repeated 70 times in 12 minutes.

In a close vote, the Court ruled that although the monologue was part of a serious program on contemporary attitudes toward language, it was not protected under the First Amendment because people, including children, tuning the radio could be subjected to the language in their home.[37]

Yet the Court struck down a Utah law restricting "indecent material" on cable television. The difference apparently is that people choose to subscribe and pay for cable television.[38]

SPEECH PLUS CONDUCT

Speech plus conduct is speech combined with conduct that is intended to convey ideas—for example, a demonstration in which protesters chant slogans or carry signs with slogans (the speech) and march, picket, or sit in (the conduct).

Individuals can demonstrate, but they are subject to some restrictions. Places in the public forum are used for other purposes besides demonstrating, and individuals cannot disrupt these activities. They cannot, Justice Arthur Goldberg remarked, hold "a street meeting in the middle of Times Square at the rush hour."[39] Thus, abortion protesters can demonstrate on public streets and public sidewalks by abortion clinics, and they can approach staffers and patients who come and go. But protesters cannot block access (and, to ensure this, judges can order them not to come within a certain distance—for example, 15 feet—of driveways and doorways).[40]

To help enforce the restrictions, governments can require groups to obtain a permit, which can specify the place, time, and manner of the demonstration. However, officials cannot allow one group to demonstrate but forbid another, no matter how much they dislike the group or its message. They cannot forbid the group even if they say they fear violence, unless the group actually threatens violence. In short, officials may establish restrictions to avoid disruption, but they may not use these restrictions to censor speech.

Accordingly, lower federal courts required the Chicago suburb of Skokie to permit the American Nazi Party to demonstrate in front of the town hall in 1978.[41] About 40,000 of Skokie's population of 70,000 were Jews. Of these, hundreds had survived the German Nazi concentration camps during World War II, and thousands had lost relatives who died in the camps. The city, edgy about the announced demonstration, passed ordinances that prohibited wearing "military-style" uniforms and distributing material that "promotes and incites hatred against persons by reason of their race, national origin, or religion." These ordinances were thinly disguised attempts to bar the demonstration, and the courts threw them out. One quoted Justice Oliver Wendell Holmes's statement that "if there is any principle of the Constitution that more imperatively calls for attachment than any other it is the principle of free thought—not free thought for those who agree with us but freedom for the thought we hate."[42]

The Rehnquist Court, however, did uphold a Milwaukee suburb's ordinance that prohibited picketing at a residence.[43] The city passed the ordinance after antiabortionists had picketed, six times in one month, the home of a doctor who performed abortions. Although protesters can march through residential neighborhoods, the Court said, a city can prohibit them from focusing on a particular home. Thus, the Court emphasized the right to privacy at home over the right to demonstrate in this situation.

SYMBOLIC SPEECH

Symbolic speech is the use of symbols, rather than words, to convey ideas.

During the Vietnam War, men burned their draft cards to protest the draft and the war. This was powerful expression, and Congress tried to stifle it by passing a law prohibiting destruction of draft cards. The Supreme Court was uncomfortable with symbolic speech and reluctant to protect it. Even Chief Justice Warren worried that this would mean that "an apparently limitless variety of conduct can be labeled 'speech.' " The Court upheld the law.[44]

One year later, however, the Court was willing to protect symbolic speech. A junior high and two senior high school students in Des Moines, Iowa, including Mary Beth Tinker, wore black armbands to protest the war. They were suspended, and they sued school officials. Public schools, Justice Abe Fortas said, "may not

UPI/Corbis-Bettmann

Mary Beth Tinker, here with her mother and brother, wore a black armband at school to protest the Vietnam War.

HATE SPEECH ON CAMPUS AND THE FIRST AMENDMENT

A student puts a sign on her dorm room door that announces, "People who will be shot on sight—preppies, bimbos, men without chest hair, and homos."

A fraternity holds a "slave auction" as a fund-raiser. White pledges in blackface and Afro wigs perform skits. Afterward, audience members bid on the performers.

Two black students find the letters "KKK" carved into their dorm room door and a note saying, "African monkeys, why don't you go back to the jungle."

After a class discussion of media treatment of African Americans, a black woman receives a card asking her to have "a very bad Christmas" and calling her a "nigger."

Such incidents have forced members of college and university communities—students, faculty, and administrators—to consider in a real and personal way the meaning of the First Amendment. Many conclude that hate speech should be prohibited and that students who engage in it should be punished. They argue that students who hurl epithets or slurs at others, especially anonymously, are more interested in intimidating than in initiating a dialogue about issues. They also argue that civility and tolerance must be maintained. Otherwise, victims of such speech are made to feel unwelcome on campus and in some cases are kept from concentrating on their studies. A student who was jeered nightly by students taunting "Faggot!" said, "When you are told you are not worth anything, it is difficult to function."[1]

Some legal scholars believe hate speech could be a violation of the Fourteenth Amendment's equal protection clause—which guarantees "equal protection of the laws" and restricts discrimination in society—if it creates a hostile and intimidating environment for minority students.[2]

Other scholars, however, believe such speech is protected by the First Amendment. Precedents described in this chapter emphasize that even repulsive speech is allowed. Indeed, the First Amendment would be meaningless if only speech acceptable to everybody were protected.

Critics of speech codes point to history: The First Amendment has helped minorities make their case against discrimination. By thwarting southern law enforcement officials' efforts to censor and intimidate the media, the amendment helped the civil rights movement gain national support. On the other hand, censorship has been used against minorities. It is shortsighted to expect new censorship to be used primarily for minorities against majorities. New censorship could be directed at students and speakers who say the sorts of things Malcolm X once said. During the year and a half that the University of Michigan's speech code was in effect, more than 20 black students were charged with violations by white students, and no white students were charged with violations.[3]

Critics also say the codes could be directed at students who make relatively innocuous comments. A Brown University student was the first casualty. He was expelled for shouting "nigger" and "faggot" to no one in particular while drunk. A University of Pennsylvania student faced disciplinary action for yelling, "Shut up, you water buffalo. If you're looking for a party, there's a zoo a mile from here," to a dozen sorority sisters singing loudly outside his dorm window while he was writing a paper one night. It turns out that the women were black and the remark was considered a racial slur.[4] (The women who filed the grievance later dropped it.)

Critics observe that more than any other institutions, colleges and universities traditionally have fostered free inquiry and free expression. They have allowed, even encouraged, a variety of views so the views could be debated.

The answer to the problem, these critics contend, is more, not less, speech. According to the theory of free expression, the remedy for bad ideas is more speech to demonstrate why the ideas are wrong. Four black women at Arizona State University passed a dorm room door with a "job application form" for minority applicants. The form asked for:

---

be enclaves of totalitarianism." They must allow students freedom of speech, providing students do not disrupt the schools.[45]

In the 1960s and 1970s, many students wore long hair or beards in violation of school policy. Some claimed they did so to protest "establishment culture." Blacks and Indians claimed they wore Afros and braids to show racial pride. Federal courts of appeals split evenly as to whether this was symbolic speech. The Supreme Court refused to hear any of these cases, so there was no uniform law across the country.

Some individuals treated the American flag disrespectfully to protest the Vietnam War. A Massachusetts man wore a flag patch on the seat of his pants and was sentenced to six months in jail. A Washington student taped a peace symbol on a flag and then hung the flag, upside down, outside his apartment. The Court reversed both convictions.[46]

When a member of the Revolutionary Communist Youth Brigade burned an American flag outside the Republican National Convention in Dallas in 1984, the justices faced the issue of actual desecration of the flag. The Rehnquist Court surprisingly permitted this symbolic speech.[47] Two Reagan-appointed conservatives joined the three most liberal members of the Court to forge a bare majority. The foremost free speech advocate on the bench, Justice William Brennan, wrote that the First Amendment cannot be limited just because this form of expression offends some people. "We do not consecrate the flag by punishing its desecration, for in doing so we dilute the freedom that this cherished

- Sources of income: (1) theft, (2) welfare, (3) unemployment;
- Marital status: (1) common law, (2) shacked up, (3) other;
- Number of legitimate children (if any).

Although ASU had a speech code, the women did not try to invoke it or even approach the administration. First they knocked on the door and told one of the occupants what they thought of the form. Then they organized an open meeting in the dorm. Eventually, a news conference and a rally were held, and a program on African American history was instituted in the dorm. All along there was a lively exchange in the campus newspaper. The women accomplished more and, in the process, kept the focus on racism rather than on a speech code.[5]

Supporters of speech codes are not convinced that more speech is the answer. They think that minorities who talk back will be perceived as making a direct challenge and that a verbal confrontation could escalate into a violent one. They argue that codes are necessary to dampen such potential conflict.[6]

Many schools have enacted speech codes, but federal district courts struck down codes at the Universities of Michigan and Wisconsin on grounds that they were overly broad and inherently vague.[7] The Supreme Court has not ruled on the constitutionality of these codes, but it struck down a St. Paul, Minnesota, ordinance that prohibited people from writing graffiti and displaying objects such as a Nazi swastika or a burning cross on public or private property.[8] This ruling probably means that the Court would invalidate campus speech codes as well.

Now some schools are reinventing their speech codes and applying them to computers. George Mason University has a policy prohibiting students from using computers to "harass, threaten, or abuse others." Virginia Tech has a policy also prohibiting students from using computers to "annoy another person." Although this policy probably would be struck down, the school used it to discipline a student for posting a message on the Internet home page of a gay men's group calling for gays to be castrated and to "die a slow death."[9]

The Supreme Court has said that illegal *conduct* associated with hate speech can be punished. A person who erects a burning cross on private property can be prosecuted for trespassing, starting an open fire, and littering, or for such major crimes as arson and making terroristic threats. Similarly, students who engage in hate speech in some situations might be punished for defacing public property or making terroristic threats.

1. Mary Jordan, "Free Speech Starts to Have Its Say," *Washington Post National Weekly Edition*, September 21–27, 1992, p. 31.
2. Mary Ellen Gale, "On Curbing Racial Speech," *The Responsive Community* (Winter 1990–91), pp. 53, 57.
3. Nadine Strossen, *Defending Pornography: Free Speech, Sex, and the Fight for Women's Rights* (New York: Scribners, 1995).
4. Mike Littwin, "Penn's Water Buffalo Debate," *Lincoln Journal* (Baltimore Sun), May 13, 1993.
5. Nat Hentoff, "The Right Thing at ASU," *Washington Post National Weekly Edition*, July 1–7, 1991, p. 28.
6. Richard Delgado and David H. Yun, "Pressure Valves and Bloodied Chickens: An Analysis of Paternalistic Objections to Hate Speech Regulation," *University of California Law Review* 82 (1994), p. 716.
7. *Doe v. University of Michigan*, 721 F.Supp. 852 (E.D. Mich., 1989); Jordan, "Free Speech Starts to Have Its Say." A California court also struck down Stanford University's antiharassment code, which was similar to a speech code.
8. *R.A.V. v. St. Paul*, 120 L.Ed.2d 305 (1992). Yet the Court has upheld state laws that provide longer sentences for violent crimes motivated by bias than for the same crimes without evidence of bias. *Wisconsin v. Mitchell*, 124 L.Ed.2d 436 (1993).
9. Michael D. Shear, "A Tangled World Wide Web," *Washington Post National Weekly Edition*, October 30–November 5, 1995, p. 36.

emblem represents." The ruling invalidated laws of 48 states and the federal government.

Chief Justice Rehnquist emotionally criticized the decision. He said the First Amendment should not apply because the flag is a unique national symbol. He recounted the history of the "Star-Spangled Banner" and the music of John Philip Sousa's "Stars and Stripes Forever"; he quoted poems by Ralph Waldo Emerson and John Greenleaf Whittier that refer to the flag; and he discussed the role of the "Pledge of Allegiance."

Civil liberties advocates praised the decision. One lawyer for the defendant said, "If free expression is to exist in this country, people must be as free to burn the flag as they are to wave it." Another said veterans should cheer the decision because it shows that the values in the Bill of Rights that they fought for are intact. Yet veterans groups were outraged.

After administration officials assessed public opinion by monitoring talk shows, President Bush stood in front of the Iwo Jima Memorial and proposed a constitutional amendment to override the decision.[48] Members of Congress, always anxious to appear patriotic, lined up in support. But some, especially Democrats, later came out in opposition. They criticized the proposal for creating an unprecedented exception to the First Amendment. Instead of the proposed amendment, Congress passed a statute prohibiting flag desecration. Apparently, a majority felt that this less permanent substitute would be an adequate shield against the public's wrath. Yet in 1990, the justices, dividing the same way, declared the statute unconstitutional

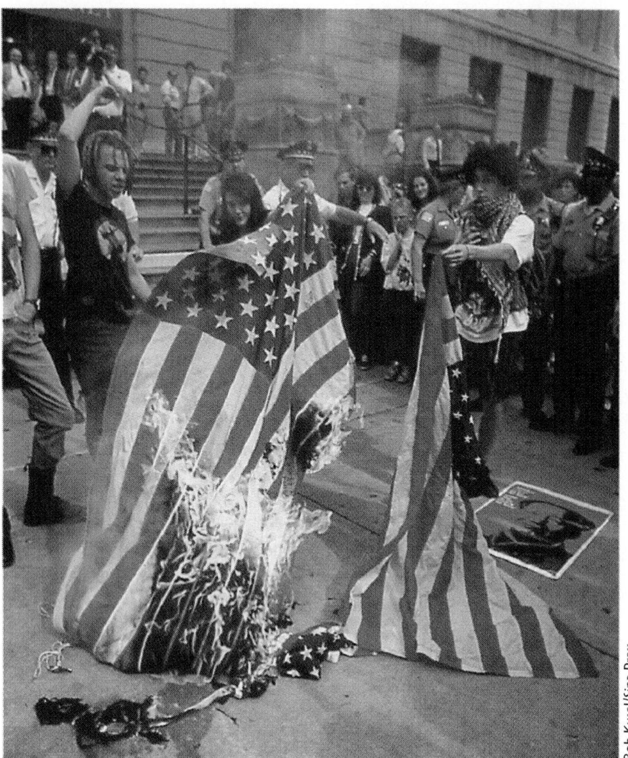
Bob Kusel/Sipa Press

Protesters torch flags in Chicago.

for the same reasons they reversed the Dallas conviction.[49] President Bush, this time waving a model of the Iwo Jima Memorial, proposed another constitutional amendment, and Senate Republican Leader Robert Dole (Kan.) warned Democrats that their opposition to the amendment "would make a good 30-second spot" for the upcoming elections, but Congress rejected the amendment. Members sensed less pressure from the public. By this second year of debate on this issue, the initial emotional reaction of the public had ebbed. More voices had spoken out against dilution of the First Amendment. Then in 1995, after Republicans became the majority in Congress, they renewed efforts to adopt a constitutional amendment but fell three votes short in one house.

Freedom of the Press

Unlike most civil liberties cases, which pit a relatively powerless individual or group against the government, freedom of press cases usually feature a more powerful publisher or broadcaster against the government. Even so, these cases still involve rights against the government.

PRIOR RESTRAINT

The core of freedom of the press is freedom from **prior restraint**—censorship. If the press violates laws prohibiting, for example, libelous or obscene material, it can be punished after publishing such materials. But freedom from prior restraint means the press at least has the opportunity to publish what it thinks is appropriate.

Freedom from prior restraint is not absolute. At the height of the Vietnam War, the secretary of defense in the Johnson administration, Robert McNamara, became disenchanted with the war and ordered a thorough study of our involvement. The study, called "The Pentagon Papers," laid bare the reasons the country was embroiled—reasons not as honorable as the ones officials had been giving the public—and it questioned the effectiveness of military policy. The study was so revealing that McNamara remarked to a friend, "They could hang people for what's in there."[50] He printed only 15 copies and classified them "Top Secret" so few persons could see them. One of the 36 authors, Daniel Ellsberg, originally supported the war but later turned against it. To prod the government into stopping it, he photocopied the papers and gave them to the *New York Times* and *Washington Post*, which published excerpts.

Although the papers embarrassed the Kennedy and Johnson administrations, President Nixon, who was in office at the time, was continuing to fight the war, so the excerpts infuriated him. Meeting with his chief of staff and his national security adviser, he demanded, "I have a project I want somebody to take. . . . This takes 18 hours a day. It takes devotion and loyalty and diligence such as you've never seen. . . . I really need a son of a bitch . . . who will work his butt off and do it dishonorably. . . . And I'll direct him myself. I know how to play this game and we're going to start playing it. . . . I want somebody just as tough as I am for a change. . . . We're up against an enemy, a con-

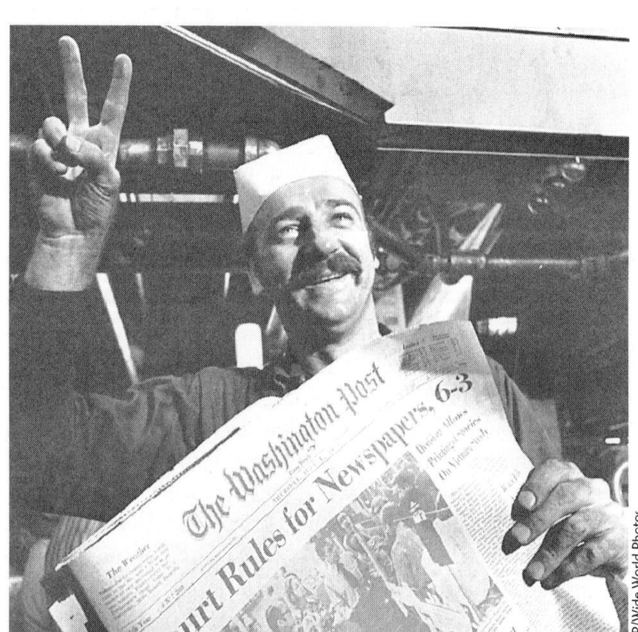

AP/Wide World Photos

The chief of the presses of the Washington Post *hails the Supreme Court's decision allowing publication of the Pentagon Papers.*

spiracy. They're using any means. We're going to use any means."[51] This tirade set in motion the developments that eventually would culminate in the Watergate scandal.

But immediately Nixon sought injunctions to restrain the newspapers from publishing more excerpts. However, the Supreme Court refused to grant them.[52] Most justices said they would grant injunctions if publishing the papers clearly jeopardized national security. But information in the papers was historical; it did not directly hinder the war effort. Thus, the rule remained—no prior restraint—but exceptions were possible.

The Rehnquist Court did approve prior restraint in a situation far removed from national security. When journalism students at a St. Louis high school wrote articles for their newspaper about the impact of pregnancy and of parents' divorce on teenagers, the principal deleted the articles and three of the students sued. The Court, noting that students below the college level have fewer rights than adults, decided that officials can censor school publications.[53]

Principals typically have exercised their authority over articles covering school policies or social issues. A Colorado principal blocked an editorial criticizing his study hall policy while allowing another editorial praising it. A Texas principal banned an article about the class valedictorian who succeeded despite the death of her mother, the desertion of her father, and her own pregnancy. An editorial urging students to be more responsible about sex was censored by a Kentucky principal, who feared it could be interpreted as condoning sex, while a survey on AIDS was censored by a Maryland principal, who prohibited students from defining the term "safe sex." A North Carolina high school newspaper was shut down and its adviser was fired because of three articles, including a satirical story about the "death" of the writer after eating a cheeseburger from the school cafeteria.

High school newspaper advisers say that principals have tightened their control in recent years. Over a third of the advisers report that principals have rejected articles or required changes in articles for their paper.[54]

Some principals have disciplined students who have used the Internet to criticize school officials or policies. But, like underground newspapers of the 1960s and 1970s, Web pages created off campus (rather than in computer class) cannot be censored by administrators. Web pages cannot be used to make terroristic threats, however. A Georgia student was arrested for suggesting that the principal be shot, his daughter kidnapped, his car scratched with keys, and its locks clogged with superglue.

Despite these exceptions to freedom from prior restraint, the press in the United States is freer than that in Great Britain, where freedom from prior restraint

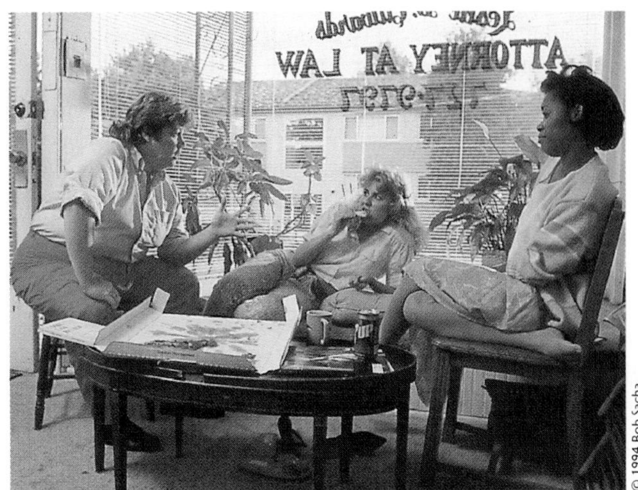

Leanne Tippell and Leslie Smart, two of the St. Louis high school students who sued their school for suppressing their student newspaper story, meet with their attorney, Leslie Edwards (left).

began. Britain has no First Amendment and tolerates more secrecy. In 1987, the government barred publication of controversial and embarrassing memoirs by a former security service agent, even though they were being published in the United States at the time. A year later the government banned radio and television interviews with all members of the outlawed Irish Republican Army (IRA) and its political party, including its one representative in Parliament.[55] The government even banned broadcast of a song by a popular folk group because the lyrics supported people convicted of IRA bombings. During the Persian Gulf War, the French government banned sale of a song—"Go for It Saddam"—that criticized the West. After neo-Nazi violence in 1992, the German government banned the sale of music by skinhead groups.

RESTRICTIONS ON GATHERING NEWS

Although prior restraint is an obvious limitation on freedom of the press, restrictions on gathering news in the first place are less obvious but no less serious. They also keep news from the public.

The Burger Court was not vigilant in guarding the press from these restrictions. Most important, it denied reporters a right to keep the names of their sources confidential. In investigative reporting, reporters frequently rely on sources who demand anonymity in exchange for information. The sources might have sensitive positions in government or relations with criminals that would be jeopardized if their names were publicized. A Louisville reporter was allowed to watch persons make hashish from marijuana if he kept their names confidential. But after publication of the story, a grand jury demanded their names. When the reporter refused to reveal them, he was cited for contempt of court, and his conviction was upheld by the

Supreme Court.[56] The majority said reporters' need for confidentiality is not as great as the judicial system's need for information about crimes. So either reporters cannot guarantee a potential source anonymity, or they may have to choose between breaking their promise or being cited for contempt and jailed for an indefinite period of time.

INVASION OF PRIVACY

The right to a free press can conflict with an individual's right to privacy when the press publishes personal information. The Supreme Court has permitted the press to publish factual information. For example, although a Georgia law prohibited the press from releasing names of crime victims to spare them embarrassment, an Atlanta television station announced the name of a high school girl who was raped by six classmates and left unconscious on a neighbor's lawn to die. The girl's father sued the station, but the Court said the press needs freedom to publish information that is a matter of public record so citizens can scrutinize the workings of the judicial system.[57]

In 1975, a man in a crowd of people watching President Gerald Ford noticed a woman pull out a gun. He grabbed the gun and prevented the assassination. Reporters wrote stories about this hero, including the fact that he was a homosexual. This caused the man embarrassment and some practical problems and he sued. The courts sided with the press again. The man's good deed made him newsworthy, whether he wanted to be or not.[58] Persons who become newsworthy are permitted little privacy. Justice Brennan said this is a necessary evil "in a society which places a primary value on freedom of speech and of press."[59]

Libel and Obscenity

Despite broad protection for the press overall, courts grant much less protection for libelous and obscene material. Traditionally, they considered such material irrelevant to the exposition of ideas and search for truth envisioned by the framers of the First Amendment. Whatever benefit such material might have was outweighed by the need to protect persons' reputations and morals. Courts thus allowed states to adopt and implement libel and obscenity laws as they saw fit.

LIBEL

Libel consists of printed or broadcast statements that are false and that tarnish someone's reputation. Victims are entitled to sue for money to compensate them for the damage.

The Warren Court decided that traditional state libel laws infringed on freedom of the press too much and forced radical changes in these laws. Its landmark decision came in *New York Times v. Sullivan* in 1964.[60]

The *Times* ran an ad by black clergymen who criticized Montgomery, Alabama, officials for their handling of racial protests. The ad contained some trivial inaccuracies. It did not mention any officials by name, but the commissioner of police claimed it referred to him implicitly, and he sued. The local jury ordered the *Times* to pay him a half million dollars! The Court could see that the law was used to punish a detested northern newspaper for an ad that criticized the handling of controversial civil rights protests. And the Court could not ignore the size of the award or the fact that another jury had ordered the *Times* to pay another commissioner a half million dollars for the same ad. It was apparent that libel laws could be used to wreak vengeance on a critical press.

The Court ruled against the police commissioner and made it harder for public officials to win libel suits. It said officials must show not only that the statements about them were false but also that the statements were made with "reckless disregard for the truth." This provides the press some leeway to make mistakes and print false statements, as long as the press is not careless to the point of recklessness.

This protection for the press is necessary, according to Justice Brennan, because "the central meaning of the First Amendment" is that individuals should have the right to criticize officials' conduct. This statement prompted one legal scholar to herald the decision as "an occasion for dancing in the streets."[61]

In later cases the Court extended this ruling to public figures—persons other than public officials who have public prominence or who thrust themselves into public controversies. The court held several persons to be public figures: candidates for public office,[62] a retired general who spoke for right-wing causes,[63] a real estate developer,[64] and a university athletic director.[65] The Court justified making it harder for public figures to win libel suits by saying that they sometimes influence public policy as much as public officials do. They also are newsworthy enough to get coverage to rebut any false charges against them.

The Burger Court was less inclined to consider various persons public figures,[66] but it maintained the core of the Warren Court's doctrine, which shifted the emphasis from protection of personal reputation to protection of press freedom.

This shift in emphasis has aided the press tremendously at a time when its coverage of controversial events has angered much of the public. Increasingly, since the 1960s, individuals and groups have sued the press not primarily to win compensation for damage to personal reputations but to punish it. A lawyer for a conservative organization admitted that the organization sought "the dismantling" of CBS by suing the network for its depiction of the army general commanding the U.S. military in Vietnam.[67]

Although the press has an advantage in the law when public officials or figures bring suits, lawsuits are expensive to defend against. One case cost the *Washington Post* more than a million dollars in defense expenses at the trial court level alone.[68] The expense puts pressure on the press to refrain from publishing controversial material. Large news organizations can withstand most of this pressure, but many small ones cannot. After 12 libel suits in as many years, the publisher of six weekly newspapers in suburban Philadelphia halted his papers' investigative reporting. "I found myself vigorously defending the First Amendment and watching my business go to hell," he said. "Now the communities our papers serve no longer learn about the misconduct of their officials."[69]

OBSCENITY

Obscenity also pits conservative groups against the media, albeit a small and specialized part of the media. Yet there are important differences. Whereas it is relatively clear what libel is and who the victim is, it is not at all clear what obscenity is and who, if anyone, the victim is. It is not even clear why the law needs to deal with it. Some say it is necessary because obscenity is immoral; others say it is necessary because obscenity leads to improper behavior (although this link is uncertain). The justices themselves have disagreed, perhaps more than in any other area, and their decisions reflect this. They have been neither clear nor consistent.

The Warren Court decided that state obscenity laws restricted publication of sexual material that should be allowed. While maintaining that the First Amendment does not protect obscenity, the Court narrowed the definition of obscenity in a series of cases in the 1950s and 1960s.[70]

The Burger Court, however, thought the Warren Court went too far. When a man and his mother received an ad for a book entitled *Orgies Illustrated*, their suit prompted the justices to broaden the definition of obscenity somewhat.[71] Now the Court defines obscenity as sexual material that is patently offensive to the average person in the community and that lacks any serious literary, artistic, or scientific value. The Court generally permits state legislatures and local juries, in passing statutes and deciding cases, to determine if this definition applies to certain types of material.

But some local officials got carried away. A prosecutor in Charlottesville, Virginia, announced that he would prosecute persons who sold *Playboy* magazine. Jurors in Albany, Georgia, convicted a theater manager who showed the movie *Carnal Knowledge*. The movie, which featured explicit language and occasional nudity, was nominated for an Academy Award as the best film of the year. The Burger Court reversed the conviction and announced that local communities have discretion but not "unbridled discretion."[72]

A prosecutor in Cincinnati put the director of an art gallery on trial for an exhibit of photographs by Robert Mapplethorpe. The homoerotic pictures, which the director called "tough, brutal, sometimes disgusting," included three showing penetration of a man's anus with various objects. Yet the prosecutor could not prove that the photographs lacked serious artistic value, because the photographer has received praise from art critics and the pictures, of course, were displayed in an art gallery, so the jury acquitted the director.

The Burger Court did not succeed in its efforts to reduce the availability of sexual material. Prosecutors report that they actually prosecute fewer cases, because the public is less concerned than in earlier eras about obscenity, so jurors are less likely to convict.[73]

The continuing flow and increasing violence of pornography prompted some radical feminists, in alliance with religious fundamentalists, to advocate new antipornography statutes. They maintain that pornography discriminates against women by degrading them and portraying them as willing targets for violent sex. In response, Indianapolis passed a statute that defined pornography as "the sexually explicit subordination of women"—material in which women were "sexual objects for domination . . . or use" or depicted in "positions of servility or submission or display." The statute allowed women who believed themselves victims of pornography to sue for a court order banning such material and, possibly, for monetary damages. The proponents' aim was to encourage enough women to sue to drive the purveyors out of business.

A coalition of book and magazine publishers, distributors, and sellers challenged the law. They said it was so broad and vague it could apply to many nonpornographic books and magazines. The American Civil Liberties Union (ACLU) maintained that it could apply to books such as Ian Fleming's James Bond stories and movies like *Last Tango in Paris*. Some feminist writers said it could apply to feminist literature.

The federal district court judge, a woman, ruled the statute unconstitutional. She said its breadth and vagueness would prohibit much sexual material now permitted by the Supreme Court and would severely restrict the First Amendment. The Supreme Court affirmed the decision.[74]

Despite the Court's refusal to broaden its definition of obscenity further, it does allow cities, through zoning ordinances, to scatter "adult" theaters and bookstores to avoid seedy districts that might attract criminals, or to concentrate them to avoid location in neighborhoods where they might offend residents or passersby.[75] The Court acknowledged that such ordinances help preserve the quality of urban life.

INTO THE 21ST CENTURY

REGULATING CYBERPORN

The Internet enables people to get pornography in the privacy of their home, without having to go to a seedy adult bookstore or movie theater and without risking the embarrassment that might occur. Users can type in key words, such as "sex," and easily find their way to "Bianca's Smut Shack." Perusing pornography is one of the most common, if not the most common, recreational uses of computers. (At one university, 13 of the 40 most visited sites had names like "rec.arts.erotica.")[1] Much of this pornography depicts sex with children or animals, or other deviant practices such as bondage or sadomasochism.

Shocked by the amount and the nature of online pornography, and worried about its availability to children, Congress passed the Communications Decency Act in 1996. The law prohibited people from knowingly circulating "obscene" or "indecent" material online "in a manner available" to those under 18. Thus, the law banned sexual material that would be defined, under existing law, as "obscene" and additional material that would be considered "indecent." However, the latter was not clearly defined.[2]

A coalition of 47 groups filed suit to have the law declared unconstitutional. These included the American Civil Liberties Union (ACLU), the American Library Association, and the computer companies Microsoft and America Online. The U.S. Chamber of Commerce filed a supplementary brief arguing that the law threatened corporations' ability to compete globally in an age of new communications.

The new technology of the Internet has made the old laws under the First Amendment difficult to apply. A commentator observed that "it's one thing to support the free speech rights of bookstore owners, quite another to have an 'XXX' store open at the end of the block, and still another to have its contents available in your rumpus room."[3]

So what precedents should apply? Is the Internet like the print media, which have substantial freedom so long as they do not publish the narrow category of sexual material defined as obscenity? Or is the Internet more like the broadcast media, which have less freedom because they are pervasive and reach into people's homes? Or, because the goal is to protect children, is the law more analogous to child pornography laws that prohibit a broader range of material than regular obscenity laws?

A lower federal court recognized that the Internet is a different medium and is, in fact, the most participatory speech medium yet developed. As such, the judges concluded, it should be nurtured, not stifled. In 1997 the Supreme Court, in its initial effort to apply the First Amendment to cyberspace, agreed.[4] It did not want the Internet censored more than other media. Thus, the Internet would receive as much protection as books, magazines, and newspapers (and more than radio and television). As a result, the portion of the law banning "obscene" material was upheld, while the portion banning additional "indecent" material was struck down. This portion was too broad and too ambiguous. It might lead to prosecution of people for discussing homosexuality or prison rape. It could even lead to prosecution of parents for sending their child information about birth control. Or the stiff penalties, two years in prison and a $250,000 fine, might cause people to avoid subjects they should feel free to address. Then the law would have a chilling effect on speech, which the First Amendment is supposed to guard against.

Although the goal of protecting children was worthy, the justices said, the result would be to prevent adults from communicating with each other, because the nature of the Internet made it impossible to know who might receive the material. Adults might be prosecuted if children obtained the material even though the adults were unaware that the children were doing so.

The Court took a bold step. But, of course, this was just a first step. Evolving technology will force the Court to take more steps in coming years.

1. Philip Elmer-DeWitt, "On a Screen near You: Cyberporn," *Time*, July 3, 1995, p. 40.
2. In one section the law vaguely referred to images of "sexual or excretory activities."
3. John Schwartz, "The New Cultural Battleground Comes with a Mouse," *Washington Post National Weekly Edition*, February 23, 1998, p. 22.
4. *Reno v. American Civil Liberties Union*, 138 L.Ed.2d 874 (1997).

Freedom of Religion

Some people came to America for religious liberty, but once they got here, many did not want to allow others this liberty. Some communities here were as intolerant as the ones in the Old World from which people had fled. But people came with so many different religious views that the diversity gradually led to tolerance, and by the time the Bill of Rights was adopted there was widespread support for religious liberty. The First Amendment states, "Congress shall make no law respecting an establishment of religion, or prohibiting the free exercise thereof." The two clauses concerning religion—the establishment clause and the free exercise clause—were intended to work in tandem to provide freedom of religion and, by implication, freedom from others' religions.

The Founders' recoiled from the Europeans' experience of continuous conflict and long wars fought

Tom Defeo © 1965, The Des Moines Register and Tribune Co.

Amish children head for the cornfields to avoid school officials in Iowa.

over religious differences. Thus, Thomas Jefferson said, the clauses were designed to build "a wall of separation between church and state." Each would stay on its own side of the wall and not interfere or even interact with the other.

However, as society became more complex and government became more pervasive, church and state came to interact, sometimes interfere, with each other. Inevitably, the high wall began to crumble, and courts had to devise new doctrine to accommodate both church and state.

FREE EXERCISE OF RELIGION

The **free exercise clause** allows individuals to practice their religion without government coercion. Government occasionally has restricted free exercise of religion directly. Early in the country's history, some states prohibited Catholics or Jews from voting or holding office, and as late as 1961 Maryland prohibited nonbelievers from holding office.[76] In the 1920s, Oregon prohibited students from attending parochial schools.[77] More recently, prisons in Illinois and Texas prohibited Black Muslims and Buddhists from receiving religious publications and using the prison chapel.[78] The Supreme Court invalidated each of these restrictions.

Government also has restricted free exercise of religion indirectly. As society has become more complex, some laws inevitably have interfered with religion, even when not designed to. The laws usually have interfered with minority religions, which do not have many members in legislatures looking out for their interests.

At first the Court distinguished between belief and action: individuals could believe what they wanted, but they could not act accordingly if such action was against the law. In 1878, male Mormons who believed their religion required polygamy could not marry more than one woman.[79] The Court rhetorically asked, "Suppose one believed that human sacrifices were a necessary part of religious worship?" Of course, belief without action gave little protection and scant satisfaction to the individuals involved.

In the 1960s the Warren Court realized this and began to broaden protection by granting exemptions to laws. A Seventh-Day Adventist who worked in a textile mill in South Carolina quit when the mill shifted from a five- to six-day workweek that included Saturday—her Sabbath. Unable to find another job, she applied for unemployment benefits, but the state refused to provide them. To receive them she had to be "available" for work, and the state said she was not available because she would not accept jobs that required Saturday work. The Court ordered the state to grant an exemption to its law.[80] The Burger Court ruled that employers need to make a reasonable effort to accommodate employees' request to fit work schedules around their Sabbath.[81]

Amish in Wisconsin withheld their children from high school, although the law required attendance until age 16. The parents sent their children to elementary and junior high school to learn basic reading, writing, and arithmetic, but they complained that high school would subject their children to worldly influences that would interfere with their semi-isolated agricultural life. The Warren Court ruled that the Amish could be exempt from the additional one to two years the law required beyond junior high school.[82]

Congress too has granted some exemptions. It excused the Amish from participating in the Social Security program, because the Amish support their own elderly. And in every draft law it excused conscientious objectors from participating in war.

The Court has been most reluctant to exempt individuals from paying taxes. It did not excuse either the Amish[83] or Quakers, who as pacifists tried to withhold the portion of their income taxes that would go to the military.[84] The Court worried that many other persons would try to avoid paying taxes, too.

The Rehnquist Court has been especially reluctant to grant exemptions.[85] The Native American church uses peyote, a hallucinogen from a cactus, in worship ceremonies. Members believe the plant embodies their deity and eating it is an act of communion. Although peyote is a controlled substance, Congress has authorized its use on Indian reservations, and almost half the states have authorized its use off reservations by members of the church. But when two members in Oregon, a state that did not allow its use off reservations, were fired from their jobs and denied unemployment benefits for using the substance, the Court refused to grant them an exemption.[86] A five-justice majority rejected the doctrine and precedents of the Warren and Burger Courts. Justice Scalia, a Catholic, admitted that denying exemptions will put minority religions at a disadvantage but said that this is an "unavoidable consequence of democratic government." That is, denying minority rights is acceptable because of majority rule. This rationale, of course, could be used to emasculate not only the free exercise clause but other provisions of the Bill of Rights as well.

Although Congress overturned the narrow focus of the decision, involving Indians' use of peyote,[87] the broad implications of the decision remained. Some adherents of minority religions were not allowed to practice the tenets of those religions. Families of deceased Jews and Laotian immigrants who reject autopsies on religious grounds were overruled. Muslim prisoners whose religion forbids them from eating pork were refused other meat instead. Members of the Sikh religion, who wear turbans, had been exempted from the federal law requiring construction workers to wear hard hats, but the Occupational Safety and Health Administration (OSHA) rescinded the exemption in the wake of the ruling.[88]

Even mainstream churches worried about the implications of the ruling, and a coalition of religious groups lobbied Congress to overturn it. Congress passed and President Clinton signed an act that reversed the ruling and substituted the previous doctrine. But in 1997 the Rehnquist Court invalidated the act.[89]

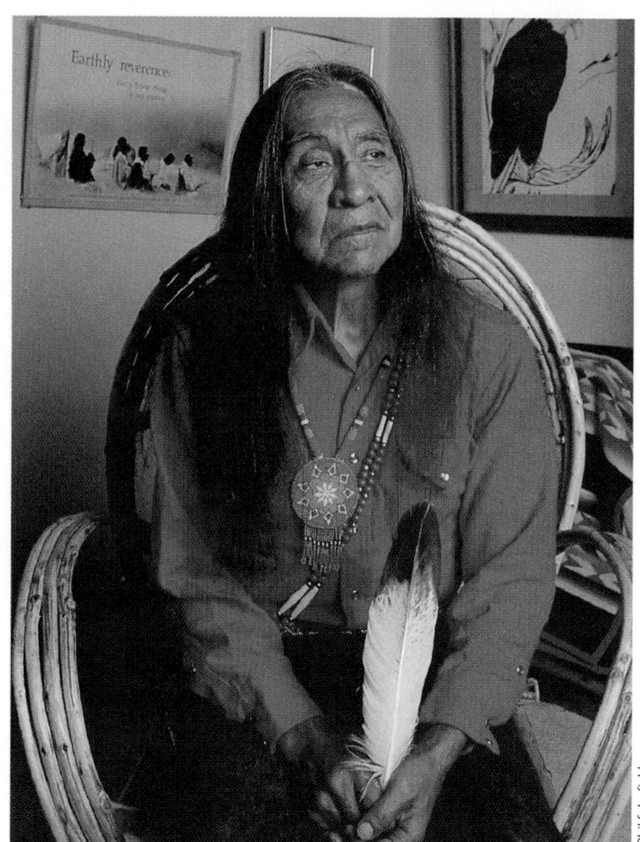

© Phil Schofield

Alfred Smith, fired for using peyote in religious ceremonies, challenged Oregon's law.

ESTABLISHMENT OF RELIGION

Two competing traditions regarding the role of government have led to conflict over the **establishment clause.** Many early settlers in America wanted government to reinforce their religion, yet the framers of the Constitution were products of the Enlightenment, which emphasized the importance of reason and deemphasized the role of organized religion. The two individuals most responsible for the religious guarantees in the First Amendment, Jefferson and Madison, wanted strict separation of church and state, advocating not only freedom *of* religion for believers but freedom *from* religion for others.[90]

Early decisions by the Supreme Court usually reflected the first of these traditions. In 1892, Justice David Brewer smugly declared that "this is a Christian nation."[91] But as the country became more pluralistic, the Court moved toward the second of these traditions. Since the early 1960s, the Court generally has interpreted the establishment clause not only to forbid government from designating an official church, like the Church of England in England, but also to forbid government from aiding one religion over another or even from aiding religion over nonreligion.

Courts have used the clause to resolve disputes about prayer in public schools. In 1962 and 1963, the Supreme Court issued its famous, or infamous, prayer rulings. New York had students recite a nondenominational prayer at the start of every day, and Pennsylvania and Baltimore had students recite the "Lord's Prayer" or Bible verses. The Court, with only one justice dissenting, ruled that these practices violated the establishment clause.[92] The prayers technically were voluntary; students could leave the room. But the Court doubted that the prayers really were voluntary. It noted that nonconforming students would face tremendous pressure from teachers and peers, and that leaving the room usually connotes punishment for bad behavior. Thus, the Court said the prayers fostered religion. According to Justice Black, "Government in this country should stay out of the business of writing and sanctioning official prayers and leave that purely religious function to the people themselves and to those the people choose to look to for religious guidance." Schools could teach about religion, but they could not promote it.

Many people sharply criticized the rulings. A representative from Alabama lamented, "They put the Negroes in the schools, and now they've driven God out."[93] Actually, the justices had not driven God out because students could pray on their own anytime they felt the need.

A survey of teachers two years after the rulings found that prayers and Bible readings had decreased but by no means disappeared. Schools in the West, East, and, to a lesser extent, the Midwest generally complied with the rulings, but schools in the South overwhelmingly refused to.[94] For example, just 1 of 121 districts in Tennessee fully complied. A local official said, "I saw no reason to create controversy," and another asserted, "I am of the opinion that 99% of the people in the United States feel as I do about the Supreme Court's decision—that it was an outrage. . . . The remaining 1% do not belong in this free world."[95]

Despite the passage of time, periodic news reports indicate that many schools, especially in the rural South, still use prayers or Bible readings in violation of the Court's rulings.

Congress considered a constitutional amendment to overturn the rulings but did not pass one for several reasons. Some people support the rulings. Others support the Court and do not want to challenge its authority and thereby set a precedent for other groups on other matters. Some religious leaders doubt that groups would ever agree about specific prayers. America's religious diversity means that the prayers would offend some students or parents. Prayers that suit Christians might not suit Jews; those that suit Jews might not suit persons of other faiths. Recent immigrants from Asia and the Middle East, practicing Buddhism, Shintoism, Taoism, and Islam, have made the country even more pluralistic. Now, according to one researcher, America's religious diversity is greater than that of any country in recorded history.[96] Thus, asking students in this country to say a prayer would be like "asking the members of the United Nations to stand and sing the national anthem of one country."[97] Other religious leaders expect that officials anxious to avoid

The country's religious diversity has led to demands for some exotic exemptions. Inspired by the Bible's statement that Jesus' followers "shall take up serpents" and "if they drink any deadly thing, it shall not hurt them," members of the Holiness Church of God in Jesus' Name handle snakes and drink strychnine. Some become enraptured and entranced to the point of hysteria, and occasionally some die. In 1975 the Tennessee Supreme Court forbade such practices, saying that the state has "the right to guard against the unnecessary creation of widows and orphans." However, the practices continue in some places.

Courtesy of National Archives

Peter Yates/SABA

A mosque appears in an Ohio cornfield as a reflection of our religious pluralism.

controversy would adopt the religious equivalent of canned peas—bland and watered-down prayers. And they expect that prayers would become rote exercises while students were daydreaming or checking out their classmates. In either event, the prayers would trivialize religious faith.

In lieu of an amendment, about half the states have passed laws providing for a "moment of silence" to begin each school day. Although the laws ostensibly are for meditation, some legislators admit they really are for prayer. The Supreme Court invalidated Alabama's law that authorized a moment of silence "for meditation or voluntary prayer" because the wording of the law endorsed and promoted prayer.[98] Yet a majority of justices indicated that they would approve a moment of silence if students were not encouraged to pray.

Although the Rehnquist Court's support for the prayer rulings was uncertain, the Court did reaffirm them and even extend them in 1992. It held that clergy cannot offer prayers at graduation ceremonies for public elementary, middle, and high schools.[99] The prayers in question were brief and nonsectarian, but the majority reasoned, "What to most believers may seem nothing more than a reasonable request that the nonbeliever respect their religious practices, in a school context may appear to the nonbeliever or dissenter to be an attempt to employ the machinery of the state to enforce a religious orthodoxy." Although attendance at the ceremony was voluntary, like participation in school prayers, the majority did not consider it truly voluntary. Justice Kennedy wrote, "Everyone knows that in our society and in our culture high school graduation is one of life's most significant occasions. . . . Graduation is a time for family and those closest to the student to celebrate success and express mutual wishes of gratitude and respect. . . ." The Court's decision was by a bare majority, but the opinion's wording was emphatic.

The Court's stance on student-led prayers at graduation, however, is ambiguous. In 1992, the Court refused to review a federal court of appeals ruling that allowed student-led prayers at graduation ceremonies.[100] A Texas school board permitted the senior class to decide whether to have a prayer and, if so, which student to give it. The appellate court held that this policy was not precluded by the Supreme Court's ruling, because the decision was not made by officials and the prayer was not given by a clergy member, so there would not be any official coercion. But in 1996 the Court also refused to review a federal court of appeals ruling from a different circuit that would prohibit student-led prayers at various school events.[101] The Court's reluctance to resolve this controversy means that the ruling of each court of appeals remains but applies only to schools in its circuit, and that no appellate ruling governs schools in the rest of the country.

The first appellate court's holding encouraged opponents of the Supreme Court's school prayer rulings to use the same approach to circumvent these rulings as well. Several southern states passed laws allowing student-led prayers. Some school officials, who selected the students, let them give the prayers over the intercom. Federal courts in Alabama and Mississippi invalidated these laws, because school officials were involved and because all students were required or at least pressured to listen to the prayers.

The public demand is fueled by the symbolism of school prayer and a nostalgia for the less troubling times before the 1960s. As one writer perceived, the demand "doesn't have much to do with prayer anyway, but with a time, a place, an ethos that praying and pledging allegiance at the beginning of school each day represent."[102] Many people echo the feelings of a Pennsylvania school board member who said, "The country has certainly gone downhill since they took it out."[103] For these people, reinstitutionalization of school prayer would be a symbol that our society stands for appropriate values. For some religious leaders, however, calls for school prayer are "a cynical exploitation" of the public by politicians who imply that "two-minute pieties" will make up for the decline of values in society.[104]

The public demand is also aggravated by occasional reports of school officials who mistakenly believe that court rulings require them to forbid all forms of religious expression. Thus, some confused administrators have prohibited a few students from wearing religious jewelry, reading the Bible while riding the bus, and praying before eating their lunch.

In another case, the Supreme Court said that the University of Missouri at Kansas City had to make its meeting rooms available to students' religious organizations on an equal basis with other organizations, even if the religious organizations used the rooms for prayer or worship.[105] Otherwise, the university would be discriminating against religion. After this decision, Congress passed a law that requires public high schools as well to allow meetings of students' religious, philosophical, or political groups outside class hours. The Court accepted this law in 1990.[106] Justice O'Connor said high school students "are likely to understand that a school does not endorse or support student speech that it merely permits on a nondiscriminatory basis." Students have established Bible clubs in a quarter of the public schools, according to an estimate in 1998.[107] Yet students' desires have not always been the driving force. Adults who are anxious to put prayers back into the schools have often taken the initiative. Organized networks encourage the clubs and provide advice, workshops, and handbooks for them.

The Rehnquist Court also said that the University of Virginia had to provide financial aid, from students' fees, to students' religious organizations on an equal basis with other campus organizations, even if a religious organization sought the money to print a religious newspaper.[108]

Despite its prayer rulings, the Court has been reluctant to invalidate traditional religious symbols. It has not questioned the motto "In God We Trust," on our money since 1865, or the phrase "One nation under God," in the Pledge of Allegiance since 1954.

The Rehnquist Court upheld the display of a nativity scene on government property, at least if it is part of a broader display for the holiday season.[109] Pawtucket, Rhode Island, had a crèche, Santa Claus, sleigh with reindeer, Christmas tree, and talking wishing well. Although the nativity scene was an obvious symbol of Christianity, the Court said it was a traditional symbol of a holiday that has become secular as well as religious. Moreover, the presence of the secular decorations diluted any religious impact the nativity scene would have. A crèche by itself, however, would be impermissible.[110]

Courts have also used the establishment clause to resolve disputes about teaching evolution in schools. In 1968, the Supreme Court invalidated Arkansas's 40-year-old law forbidding schools from teaching evolution.[111] Arkansas and Louisiana then passed laws requiring schools that teach evolution to also teach "creationism"—the biblical version of creation.[112] In 1987, the Court invalidated these laws, because their purpose was to promote the fundamentalist Christian view.[113] Yet teaching evolution remains controversial. Many science teachers skip it to avoid confrontations with conservative parents or religious groups.[114]

Steve Liss/*Time* magazine

A Christian Bible club meets in a Minneapolis school.

Courts have also used the establishment clause to resolve disputes about aid to parochial schools, most of which are Catholic. Millions of students attend these schools, and their parents pay tuition and other expenses. In recent decades, costs have risen and enrollments have dropped. Schools have asked legislatures to provide money to defray part of the costs of their nonreligious activities. Courts have had to decide whether providing the money helps religion or whether denying it hinders religion. In addition, courts have had to determine if providing the money leads to excessive entanglement of church and state because of the monitoring required to ensure that the money is not spent for religious purposes.

The Court has upheld some types of aid[115] but has rejected most types.[116] Yet the Court, reflecting shifting coalitions of justices, has not drawn a clear line separating permissible from impermissible forms of assistance.[117]

Despite frequent tensions and periodic conflicts, the effort to separate church and state over the years has enabled the United States to manage, and even nourish, its religious pluralism. The effort has kept much religious debate and potential religious fights out of the political arena. But this practical arrangement is opposed both by those who believe that their religion is so important that it should be reinforced by the government and by those who believe that religion should play no role in public life.

RIGHTS OF CRIMINAL DEFENDANTS

The Fourth, Fifth, Sixth, and Eighth Amendments provide numerous **due process** rights for criminal defendants. When the government prosecutes defendants, it must give them the process—that is, the procedures—they are due; it must be fair and "respect certain decencies of civilized conduct,"[118] even toward uncivilized people.

One defense attorney said many of his clients "had been monsters—nothing less—who had done monstrous things. Although occasionally not guilty of the crime charged, nearly all my clients have been guilty of something."[119] Then why do we give them rights? The reason is that we give all individuals rights. As Justice Douglas observed, "respecting the dignity even of the least worthy citizen . . . raises the stature of all of us."[120]

But why do we give all citizens rights? We do so because we have established the presumption of innocence. This presumption is "not . . . a naive belief that most or even many defendants are innocent, or a cavalier attitude toward crime. It reflects mistrust of the state. Requiring the state to prove guilt is a way of saying, 'We won't take your word for it.' "[121] Of course, when the crime rate is high or a crime is particularly heinous, many people fear the state less than the criminals. Then they want to give officials more authority and defendants fewer rights. But eventually this is the way people lose rights.

Search and Seizure

England fostered the notion that a family's home is its castle, but Parliament made exceptions for the American colonies. It authorized writs of assistance, which allowed customs officials to conduct general searches for goods colonists had imported without paying taxes to the crown. The English tradition combined with the colonists' resentment of the writs of assistance led to adoption of the Fourth Amendment, which forbids **unreasonable searches and seizures.**

One type of seizure is the arrest of a person. Police must have evidence to believe that a person committed a crime. Another type of seizure is the confiscation of illegal contraband. The general requirement is that police should get a search warrant from a judge by showing evidence that a particular thing is in a particular place.

However, the Supreme Court has made exceptions to this requirement that complicate the law. These exceptions account for the vast majority of searches. If persons consent to a search, police can conduct one without a warrant. If police see contraband in plain view, they can seize it; they do not need to close their eyes to it. If police have suspicion that a person is committing a crime but lack evidence to arrest him, they can "stop and frisk" the person—give him a pat-down search. If police have evidence to arrest someone, they can search her and the area within her control. If police face an emergency situation, they can search for weapons. And if police want to search motor vehicles in some situations, they can do so because vehicles are mobile and could be gone by the time police get a warrant.

Customs and border patrol officials can search persons and things coming into the country to enforce customs and immigration laws. Airport guards can search passengers and luggage to prevent hijackings. And prison guards can search prisoners to ensure security.

In defining reasonable and unreasonable searches and seizures, the Court has tried to walk a fine line between acknowledging officials' need for evidence and persons' need for privacy.

EXCLUSIONARY RULE

To enforce search and seizure law, the Court has established the **exclusionary rule,** which bars from court any evidence obtained in violation of the Fourth Amendment. The rule's goal is to deter police from illegal conduct.

Although the Court issued the rule for federal courts in 1914,[122] it did not impose the rule on state courts until 1961. Even so, the Warren Court's decision, in the case of *Mapp v. Ohio*,[123] was one of its most controversial. Until this time, police in many states had ignored search and seizure law.

The decision still has not been widely accepted. The Burger Court created an exception to it. In a pair of cases, the justices allowed evidence obtained illegally to be used in court because the police had acted in "good faith."[124] The Rehnquist Court is expected to define the scope of this exception more fully.

ELECTRONIC SURVEILLANCE

The Fourth Amendment traditionally applied to searches involving a physical trespass and seizures producing a tangible object. Electronic surveillance, however, does not require a physical trespass or result in a tangible object.

This posed a problem for the Supreme Court when it heard its first wiretapping case in 1928. Federal prohibition agents tapped the telephone of bootleggers by installing equipment on wires in the basement of the bootleggers' apartment building. The majority of the Court rigidly adhered to its traditional doctrine, saying this was not a search and seizure so the agents did not need a warrant.[125]

In a classic example of keeping the Constitution up to date, the Warren Court overruled this precedent in 1967.[126] Because electronic eavesdropping might threaten privacy as much as traditional searching, officials must get judicial authorization, similar to a warrant, to engage in such eavesdropping.

Self-Incrimination

The Fifth Amendment provides that persons shall not be compelled to be witnesses against themselves, that is, to incriminate themselves. Because defendants are presumed innocent, the government must prove their guilt.

This right means that defendants on trial do not have to take the witness stand and answer questions, and neither prosecutor nor judge can call attention to their failure to do so. Neither can suggest that defendants must have something to hide and thereby imply that they must be guilty. (But if defendants do take the stand and testify, this constitutes a waiver of their right, so the prosecutor can cross-examine them and they must answer.)

This right also means that prosecutors cannot introduce into evidence any statements or confessions from defendants that were not voluntary. However, the meaning of "voluntary" has changed over time.

For years law enforcement officials used physical brutality—"the third degree"—to get confessions. After 1936, when the Supreme Court ruled that confessions

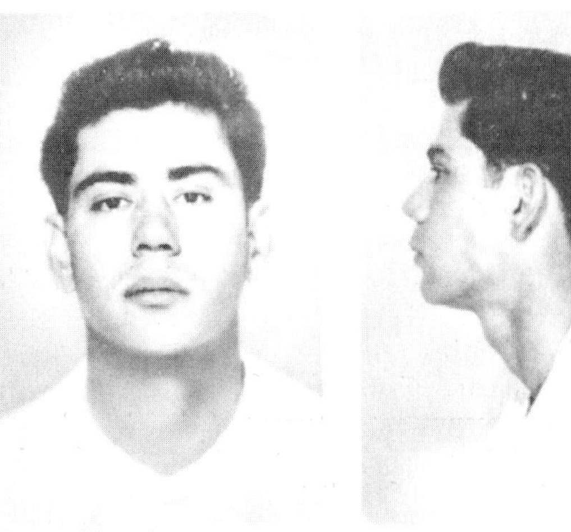

Mark Solomon/*Time* magazine

Ernesto Miranda.

obtained this way were invalid,[127] officials resorted to more subtle techniques. They held suspects incommunicado, so the suspects could not notify anyone about their arrest, and delayed bringing them to court, so the judge could not inform them of their rights.[128] Officials interrogated suspects for long periods of time without food or rest, in one case with alternating teams of interrogators for 36 hours.[129] They tricked suspects. In one case, police told a man they would jail his wife if he did not talk, although they knew she was not involved, and in another they told a woman they would take away her welfare benefits and even her children if she did not talk, although they did not have authority to do either.[130] The Court ruled that these techniques, designed to break the suspects' will, were psychological coercion, so the confessions were invalid.

The Warren Court still worried that many confessions were not truly voluntary, so it issued a landmark decision in 1966. Arizona police arrested a poor, mentally disturbed man, Ernesto Miranda, for kidnapping and raping a woman. After the woman identified him in a lineup, police interrogated him for two hours, prompting him to confess. He had not been told that he could remain silent or be represented by an attorney. In *Miranda v. Arizona*, the Court decided that his confession was not truly voluntary.[131] Chief Justice Warren, himself a former district attorney, noted the tremendous advantage police have in interrogation and said suspects needed more protection. The Court ruled that officials must advise suspects of their rights before interrogation. These came to be known as the **Miranda rights:**

- You have the right to remain silent.
- If you talk, anything you say can be used against you.
- You have the right to be represented by an attorney.
- If you cannot afford an attorney, one will be appointed for you.

The Burger and Rehnquist courts have not required police and prosecutors to follow *Miranda* as strictly as the Warren Court did but, contrary to expectations, have not abandoned *Miranda*.

Counsel

The Sixth Amendment provides the **right to counsel** in criminal cases. Historically, it permitted defendants to hire an attorney to help them prepare a defense and then to represent them at trial, but it was no help to most defendants because they were too poor to hire an attorney.

Consequently, the Supreme Court required federal courts to furnish an attorney to all indigent defendants as long ago as 1938.[132] But most criminal cases are state cases, and although the Court required state courts to furnish an attorney in some cases, it was reluctant to impose a broad requirement on these courts.[133]

In 1963, the Warren Court accepted the appeal of Clarence Earl Gideon. Charged with breaking into a pool hall and stealing beer, wine, and change from a vending machine, Gideon asked the judge for a lawyer. The judge refused to appoint one, leaving Gideon to defend himself. The prosecutor did not have a strong case, but Gideon was not able to point out its weaknesses. He was convicted and sentenced to five years. On appeal, the Warren Court unanimously declared that Gideon was entitled to be represented by counsel.[134] Justice Black explained that "lawyers in criminal courts are necessities, not luxuries." The Court finally established a broad rule: State courts must provide an attorney to indigent defendants in felony cases.

Gideon proved the Court's point. Given a lawyer and retried, he was not convicted. The lawyer did the effective job defending him that he had not been able to do himself.

In 1972, the Burger Court expanded the rule: State courts must provide an attorney to indigent defendants in misdemeanor cases too, except those that result in no incarceration at all,[135] because even misdemeanor cases are too complex for defendants to defend themselves. In addition, the Court decided that courts must provide an attorney for one appeal.[136]

Receiving counsel does not necessarily mean receiving effective counsel, however. Some assigned attorneys are inexperienced, some are incompetent, and most are overworked and have little time to prepare the best possible defense.

WHEN A COURT REVERSES A CONVICTION . . .

. . . the defendant does not necessarily go free. An appellate court normally only evaluates the legality of the procedures used by officials; it does not determine guilt or innocence. Therefore, when it reverses a conviction, it only indicates that officials used some illegal procedure in convicting the defendant—for example, they may have used evidence from an improper search and seizure. Then the prosecutor can retry the defendant, without this evidence, if the prosecutor thinks there is enough other evidence. Often prosecutors do retry the defendants, and in about half the cases judges or juries reconvict them.[1]

1. Robert T. Roper and Albert P. Malone, "Does Procedural Due Process Make a Difference? A Study of Second Trials," *Judicature* 65 (1981), pp. 136–141.

Jury Trial

The Sixth Amendment also provides the **right to a jury trial** in "serious" criminal cases. The Supreme Court has defined "serious" cases as those that could result in more than six months' incarceration.[137]

The right was adopted to prevent oppression by a "corrupt or overzealous prosecutor" or a "biased . . . or eccentric judge."[138] It also has served to limit governmental use of unpopular laws or enforcement procedures. Regardless of the extent of evidence against a defendant, a jury can refuse to convict if it feels the government has overstepped its bounds.

The jury is to be "impartial," so persons who have made up their minds before trial should be dismissed. It also is to be "a fair cross section" of the community, so no group should be systematically excluded.[139] But the jury need not be a perfect cross section and, in fact, need not have a single member of a particular group.[140] Most courts use voter registration lists to obtain names of potential jurors. These lists are not truly representative because poor people do not register at the same rate as others, but courts have decided that the lists are sufficiently representative. And Congress passed and President Clinton signed the "motor voter bill," which requires drivers' license and welfare offices to offer voter registration forms. Presumably, more poor people will register and be eligible to serve on juries.

Cruel and Unusual Punishment

The Eighth Amendment forbids **cruel and unusual punishment** but does not define it. The Supreme Court had defined it as torture or any punishment grossly disproportionate to the offense, but the Court had seldom used the provision until applying it to capital punishment in the 1970s.

Because the death penalty was used at the time the amendment was adopted and had been used ever since, it was assumed to be constitutional. In fact, in the nineteenth century the Court ruled that two methods of execution—the firing squad and the electric chair—were not so inhumane as to be torture.[141]

Courtesy of the National Archives

Clarence Earl Gideon, convinced he was denied a fair trial because he was not given an attorney, read law books in prison so he could petition the Supreme Court for a writ of certiorari. Although he had spent much of his life in prison, he was optimistic. "I believe that each era finds an improvement in law each year brings something new for the benefit of mankind [sic]. Maybe this will be one of those small steps forward."

No. 990 Misc.
OCT. TERM 1961
U.S. Supreme Court

DIVISION OF CORRECTIONS

CORRESPONDENCE REGULATIONS

MAIL WILL NOT BE DELIVERED WHICH DOES NOT CONFORM WITH THESE RULES

No. 1 -- Only 2 letters each week, not to exceed 2 sheets letter-size 8 1/2 x 11" and written on one side only, and if ruled paper, do not write between lines. *Your complete name* must be signed at the close of your letter. *Clippings, stamps, letters from other people, stationery or cash must not be enclosed* in your letters.

No. 2 -- All *letters* must be addressed in the *complete prison name* of the inmate. *Cell number*, where applicable, and *prison number* must be placed in lower left corner of envelope, with your complete name and address in the upper left corner.

No. 3 -- *Do not send any packages without a Package Permit.* Unauthorized *packages* will be destroyed.

No. 4 -- *Letters* must be written in English only.

No. 5 -- *Books, magazines, pamphlets,* and newspapers of reputable character will be delivered *only if* mailed direct from the publisher.

No. 6 -- *Money* must be sent in the form of *Postal Money Orders* only, in the inmate's complete prison name and prison number.

INSTITUTION ______ CELL NUMBER ______

NAME ______ NUMBER ______

RECEIVED
JAN 8 1962
OFFICE OF THE CLERK
SUPREME COURT, U.S.

In the Supreme Court of the United States
Washington D.C
Motion for leave to proceed in Forma Paupers
Clarence Earl Gideon, Petitioner
VS.
H. G. Cochran Jr, Director, Divisions of corrections State of Florida Respondent

Petitioner, Clarence Earl Gideon, who is now held in the Florida state penitentiary, asks leave to file the attached petition for a Writ of Certiorari to the United States Supreme Court, directed to the Supreme Court of The State of Florida, without prepayment of costs and to proceed in Forma Pauperis. The petitioner's affidavit in support is attached hereto.

Clarence Earl Gideon
counsel for Petitioner

Affidavit in support of petition for leave to proceed in Forma Paperis
Clarence Earl Gideon, petitioner
VS.
H. G. Cochran Jr, Director, Divisions of corrections State of Florida, Respondent.

I, Clarence Earl Gideon, being duly sworn according to law, depose and say that I am

Courtesy of the National Archives

But the Burger Court, albeit with Chief Justice Burger and the other three Nixon appointees in dissent, held that capital punishment as it was then being administered was cruel and unusual.[142] The Court said the laws and procedures allowed too much discretion for those who administered the punishment and too much arbitrariness and discrimination for those who received it. It was imposed so seldom, according to Justice Potter Stewart, that it was "cruel and unusual in the same way that being struck by lightning is cruel and unusual." Yet when imposed, it was given to blacks disproportionately to their convictions for murder.

The decision invalidated the laws of 40 states and commuted the death sentences of 629 inmates. But because the Court did not hold capital punishment cruel and unusual in principle, about three-fourths of the states adopted new laws that permitted less discretion in an effort to be less arbitrary and discriminatory.

These changes satisfied a majority of the Court, which ruled that capital punishment is not cruel and unusual for murder if administered fairly.[143] But the death penalty cannot be imposed automatically for everyone convicted of murder, for the judge or jury must consider any mitigating factors that would call for a lesser punishment.[144] Also, capital punishment cannot be imposed for rape, because it is disproportionate to that offense.[145]

The new laws apparently have reduced but not eliminated discrimination. Although past studies showed discrimination against black defendants, recent studies show discrimination against black or white defendants who murder whites. People who affect the decision to impose the death penalty—prosecutors, defense attorneys, judges, and jurors—appear to value white lives more. Despite evidence that in Georgia those who kill whites are more than four times as likely to be given the death penalty as those who kill blacks, the Rehnquist Court, by a five to four vote, upheld capital punishment in the state.[146]

And the new laws have not addressed an equally serious problem—the inadequate representation provided for poor defendants who face the death penalty. In some states, especially in the South, incompetent or inexperienced attorneys are routinely assigned to defendants charged with murder, and the attorneys are normally

SYMBOLIC SOLUTIONS FOR COMPLEX PROBLEMS?

CAPITAL PUNISHMENT

Public opinion was opposed to capital punishment in the 1960s but reversed as the crime rate soared late in that decade. Since the 1970s, 70 to 80% of the people have supported capital punishment. They cite two arguments primarily—deterrence and retribution. Both reflect the symbolism of this punishment.

DETERRENCE

Many people believe the death penalty is a deterrent to the crime problem, especially to the homicide rate.[1] The theory of deterrence rests on the assumption that people are rational actors who weigh the costs and benefits of their actions. They try to avoid unpleasant or painful consequences. If society does not want them to do something, society imposes such consequences. If these do not work, society increases the severity of the consequences. Thus, because almost no one wants to die, capital punishment in theory ensures that almost no one will take a life. But does capital punishment actually deter murder?

The death penalty, of course, does deter the killer who receives it. But life in prison also would isolate the killer from society and prevent him or her from killing again (at least outside prison). Regardless, the killer is not likely to kill again. Most who have been paroled have not repeated this crime.[2]

But does the death penalty deter potential killers from killing in the first place? This is extremely difficult to assess. Many factors contribute to the homicide rate—poverty, unemployment, brutality at home, brutality in the community, availability of guns, number of males in their teens or early 20s (the most criminal- and violent-prone people in society), and so forth. It is difficult to identify, let alone take into account, all of the relevant factors. Thus, social science has not proved whether capital punishment is a deterrent.[3]

However, research suggests that capital punishment is not a deterrent. Comparisons of neighboring states with and without the death penalty found that the murder rates are similar and increase or decrease at about the same time, indicating that the rates reflect broad social trends rather than official executions.[4] Examinations of states that abolished or reinstated the death penalty and comparisons with neighboring states that did not change their punishment found that the murder rates seem unaffected by the changes.[5]

Numerous studies have looked at the possibility of deterrence in the murder of police officers. These murderers have a high rate of apprehension, and because the victims are officers, the killers have a good chance of facing the death penalty. And these crimes and their punishment receive much publicity. Thus, if capital punishment is a deterrent, it should be seen here. Yet the studies found no higher murder rates of police officers in states that have abandoned capital punishment.[6] Now most police chiefs (67%) say they do not think the death penalty is a deterrent.[7]

Some proponents of capital punishment have hypothesized that it would also deter crimes beside murder by educating people in general to obey the law or face the consequences. Yet a study found no such impact on other serious crimes.[8]

There are good reasons why we should not expect capital punishment to be a deterrent. Before defendants can be given this sentence, they must be arrested and convicted. Otherwise, the sentence on the books is irrelevant.

Further, the alternative sentence—life in prison, with or without the possibility of parole—already is steep. Perhaps it already provides as much deterrence as possible. Capital punishment presumably would be a deterrent only to the extent that a potential killer thought life in prison was acceptable but execution was not.

Moreover, consider the typical killers. Professional killers are rare and are rarely caught. Then they are usually offered leniency in exchange for information about the people who employed them.[9] Most killers are not "hit men" and do not plan their crime, let alone think about getting caught, being convicted, and receiving the death sentence. Many killers, like other criminals, are high on alcohol or drugs, so they are even less rational than they would be otherwise.

Murders frequently occur out of anger, often in an argument with an acquaintance, such as a partner or ex-partner in a sour domestic relationship. Murders also frequently occur in the drug trade. Drug dealers realize that rivals, wannabes, or others might kill them for money, territory, or "respect" any day, yet the dealers continue to traffic in drugs and sometimes commit violent acts. If their immediate fears do not prompt them to quit, the remote possibility of capital punishment is not likely to, either. If capital punishment is not a deterrent, then it is a symbolic rather than a real solution to crime.[10]

Some proponents argue that capital punishment is not a deterrent now because it is not used soon enough after arrest or conviction. There is, on average, a delay of 8 years between a murder and the execution. This is due to additional appeals afforded defendants who face this ultimate and irrevocable punishment. Although most convicted criminals do not take advantage of their appeals, those facing the death penalty have the most incentive to do so. Because the punishment is irrevocable—and reports of new evidence exonerating inmates on death row periodically surface—it is unlikely that society would tolerate much reduction in these safeguards.

RETRIBUTION

Many people also believe the death penalty is just retribution. The theory of retribution is the secular equivalent of the biblical phrase, "an eye for an eye." It is a payment to society, to satisfy the moral indignation of society, for the act the defendant committed. If the act was taking a life, the payment should be forfeiting one's life. (Taken literally, the execution should be performed in the same manner as the murder was committed.)

If capital punishment is considered just retribution, it is a symbolic reflection of society's morality and as such is also a symbolic solution to crime. This might be a sufficient basis to persuade many people to support capital punishment. Indeed, polls find that many people who support capital punishment do not want it used much. Apparently, they want it on the books as a symbol. But these people should not expect it to reduce the homicide rate, let alone the overall crime rate.

Regardless of one's own views on capital punishment, this issue reflects the inherent problems of symbolic solutions in our politics. Some sponsors of such solutions are merely trying to score political points, pointing out their stand in favor, or their opponent's stand against, the penalty. Other sponsors are sincerely hoping to do some good. Either way, the debate about symbolic measures usually takes precedence over and interferes with efforts to adopt more substantive solutions. Mario Cuomo, who as governor of New York vetoed capital punishment and lost reelection in part as a result, called it "the ultimate political cop-out." It lets legislators convince constituents that they are doing something about the crime problem. When Congress adopted the death penalty for federal courts in 1994, sponsors claimed that they made the country safer by allowing the penalty for 50 different crimes. But one crime was murder of egg inspectors, another was murder of poultry inspectors, and so on. Many members privately conceded that they voted for the penalty only to avoid appearing "soft on crime."[11] Yet many legislators who claim to be so worried about the crime problem refrain from proposing substantive solutions. Such programs would cost more money, require more taxes, and take years to reap the benefits. Instead, Cuomo said, "It is easier to hold out a quick fix, the idea that all will be well if we just burn people."[12] But the crime problem did not develop quickly, and it will not be resolved quickly.

1. K. M. Jamieson and T. J. Flanagan, *Sourcebook of Criminal Justice Statistics, 1988* (Albany, N.Y.: Hindelang Criminal Justice Research Center, 1989), p. 229.
2. Hugo Adam Bedau, ed., *The Death Penalty in America*, 3d ed. (New York: Oxford University Press, 1982), p. 180.
3. Victor E. Kappeler, Mark Blumberg, and Gary W. Potter, *The Mythology of Crime and Criminal Justice* (Prospect Heights, Ill.: Waveland, 1993), pp. 213–222; Samuel Walker, *Sense and Nonsense about Crime and Drugs*, 3d ed. (Belmont, Calif.: Wadsworth, 1994), pp. 103–108.
4. Thorsten Sellin, *The Penalty of Death* (Beverly Hills, Calif.: Sage, 1980).
5. Hans Zeisel, "The Deterrent Effect of the Death Penalty: Facts v. Faith," in Philip B. Kurland, ed., *The Supreme Court Review, 1976* (Chicago: University of Chicago Press, 1977).
6. See numerous sources cited in Kappeler, et. al., *Mythology of Crime and Criminal Justice*, p. 218. Isaac Ehrlich claimed that every execution from 1930 to 1969 deterred 7 or 8 murders. Although he took into account some variables that could affect the homicide rate, such as the probabilities of apprehension, conviction, and execution, flaws in the study led later researchers to dismiss his conclusions. See Ehrlich, "The Deterrent Effect of Capital Punishment," *American Economic Review* 65 (1975): 397–417; and numerous sources cited in Kappeler, et. al., *Mythology of Crime and Criminal Justice*, pp. 220–221.
7. Eric Pooley, "Death or Life?" *Time*, June 16, 1997, p. 33.
8. William C. Bailey, "The General Prevention Effect of Capital Punishment for Non-Capital Felonies," in R. M. Bohm, ed., *The Death Penalty in America: Current Research* (Cincinnati: Anderson Publishing and Academy of Criminal Justice Sciences, 1991).
9. John Kaplan, "The Problem of Capital Punishment," *University of Illinois Law Review* 31 (1963), pp. 565–570.
10. There is even some evidence that official executions slightly increase the homicide rate in the month or two afterward. Perhaps executions convey the message that violence is an acceptable solution to problems—just enough to push people already on the brink. Or perhaps executions show potential killers that they, too, can get public attention by committing such acts. W. J. Bowers, G. L. Pierce, and J. F. McDevitt, *Legal Homicide: Death as Punishment in America, 1864–1982* (Boston: Northeastern University Press, 1984), p. 284.
11. Helen Dewar, "It's Better to Look Good Than to Do Good," *Washington Post National Weekly Edition*, December 2–8, 1991, p. 12.
12. Michael Kramer, "Cuomo, the Last Holdout," *Time*, April 2, 1990, p. 20.

paid so little that they are discouraged from putting forth much effort. Due to this pattern of inadequate representation and to the pattern of racial discrimination, in 1997 the American Bar Association called for a moratorium on the use of capital punishment.

Rights in Theory and in Practice

Overall the Supreme Court has interpreted the Bill of Rights to provide an impressive list of rights for criminal defendants (although perhaps the greatest change from the Warren Court to the Burger and Rehnquist Courts has been a decline in support for criminal defendants—see Figure 1). Yet not all rights are available for all defendants in all places. Some trial court judges, prosecutors, and police do not comply with Supreme Court rulings. If defendants appeal to a high enough court, they probably will get their rights, but most defendants do not have the knowledge, the resources, or the perseverance to do this.

When rights are available, most defendants do not take advantage of them. About 90% of all criminal defendants plead guilty, and many of them do so as part of a **plea bargain.** This is an agreement between the prosecutor, the defense attorney, and the defendant, with the explicit or implicit approval of the judge, to reduce the charge or the sentence in exchange for a plea of guilty. A plea bargain is a compromise. For officials it saves the time, trouble, and uncertainty of a trial. For defendants it eliminates the fear of a harsher sentence. However, it also reduces due process rights. A plea of guilty waives defendants' rights to a trial by a jury of their peers, in which defendants can present their own witnesses and cross-examine the government's witnesses, and in which they cannot be forced to incriminate themselves. A plea of guilty also waives the right to counsel to some extent because most attorneys appointed to represent defendants are overworked and inclined to pressure defendants to plead guilty so they do not have to prepare a defense. Despite these disadvantages for due process rights, the Court allows plea bargaining because of its practical advantages.[147]

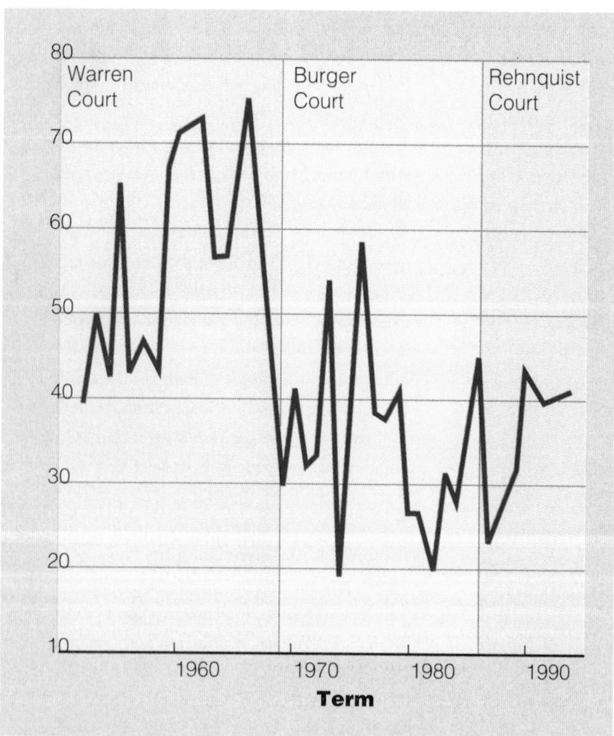

FIGURE 1

Support for Rights of Criminal Defendants Has Declined

Percentage of Supreme Court criminal rights cases decided in favor of the defendant.

SOURCE: Lee Epstein, Jeffrey A. Segal, Harold J. Spaeth, and Thomas G. Walker, *The Supreme Court Compendium: Data, Decisions, and Developments*, 2d ed. (Washington, D.C.: Congressional Quarterly, 1996), Table 3-8.

RIGHT TO PRIVACY

Neither the Constitution nor the Bill of Rights mentions "privacy." Nevertheless, the **right to privacy,** Justice Douglas noted, is "older than the Bill of Rights,"[148] and the framers undoubtedly assumed that people would have such a right. The framers did include amendments that reflect a concern for privacy: the First Amendment protects privacy of association, the Third privacy of homes from quartering soldiers, the Fourth privacy of persons and places where they live from searches and seizures, and the Fifth privacy of knowledge or thoughts from compulsory self-incrimination.

So far the Court's right-to-privacy doctrine reflects a right to autonomy—what Justice Louis Brandeis called "the right to be left alone"—more than a right to keep things confidential. As noted earlier in the chapter, the Court has been reluctant to punish the press for invasion of privacy.[149]

Birth Control

The Warren Court explicitly established a right to privacy in 1965 when it struck down a Connecticut law that prohibited distributing or using contraceptives.[150] To enforce the law the state would have had to police people's bedrooms, and the Court said the very idea of policing married couples' bedrooms was absurd. Then the Court struck down Massachusetts and New York laws that prohibited distributing contraceptives to unmarried persons.[151] "If the right of privacy means anything," Justice Brennan said, "it is the right of the individual, married or single, to be free from unwarranted governmental intrusion into matters so fundamentally affecting a person as the decision whether to bear or beget a child."[152]

Abortion

When 21-year-old Norma McCorvey became pregnant in 1969, she was divorced and already had a 5-year-old daughter, and she sought an abortion. But Texas, where she lived, prohibited abortions unless the mother's life was in danger. She discovered, "No legitimate doctor in Dallas would touch me. . . . I found one doctor who offered to abort me for $500. Only he didn't have a license, and I was scared to turn my body over to him. So there I was—pregnant, unmarried, unemployed, alone, and stuck."[153]

Too poor to go to a state that permitted abortions, McCorvey decided to put her baby up for adoption. But the state law still rankled her. With the help of two women attorneys recently out of law school, she used her case to challenge Texas's law. She adopted the name Jane Roe to conceal her identity.

In *Roe v. Wade* in 1973, the Burger Court extended the right to privacy from birth control to abortion.[154] The majority concluded that because doctors, theologians, and philosophers cannot agree when life begins, judges should not assert that life begins at conception, thus deeming a fetus a person and abortion murder. Amidst such uncertainty, the majority decided that a woman's right to privacy of her body is paramount.

The Court ruled that women can have an abortion during the first three months of pregnancy and, subject to reasonable regulations for health, during the middle three months. States can prohibit an abortion during the last three months. Thus, the right is broad though not absolute.

The justices, as revealed in memos discovered years later, acknowledged that their division of pregnancy into trimesters was "legislative," but they saw this as a way to balance the rights of the mother in the early stages of pregnancy with the rights of the fetus in the later stage.[155]

The Court's ruling invalidated the abortion laws of 45 states (see Figure 2). Far from settling the issue, however, it stimulated more controversy. The right-to-life movement, spearheaded initially by Catholics and later by fundamentalist Protestants, organized to protest the ruling. The movement also pressured legislators to overturn or circumvent the ruling. Although Congress failed to pass a constitutional amendment banning abortions or allowing states to regulate them, many state legislatures did pass statutes restricting abortions in various ways.

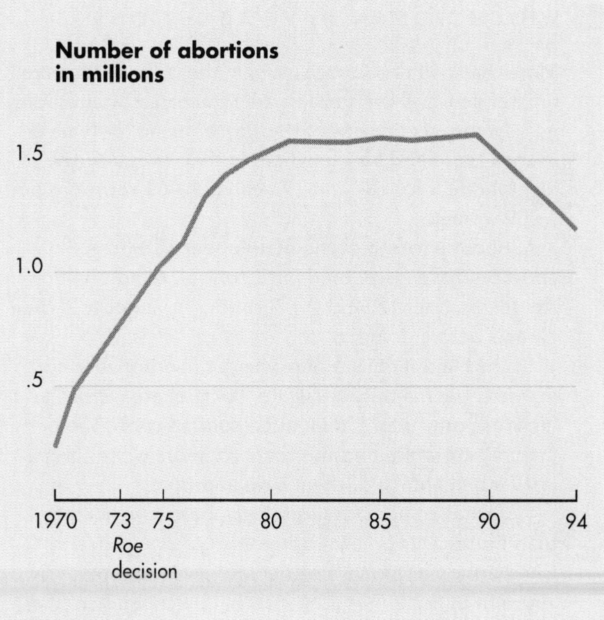

FIGURE 2

The Number of Abortions Has Declined

The number of abortions in the United States was already increasing before the Supreme Court's Roe *decision because some states had liberalized their laws. After the* Roe *decision, the number increased sharply but leveled off in the 1980s and declined in the 1990s.*

SOURCES: 1970–1972: Susan Hansen, "State Implementation of Supreme Court Decisions: Abortion Rates since *Roe v. Wade*," *Journal of Politics 42* (May 1980), pp. 372–395; 1973–1981: Stanley K. Henshaw and Ellen Blaine, *Abortion Services in the United States, Each State, and Metropolitan Area, 1981–1982* (New York: Alan Guttmacher Institute, 1985), p. 64; 1982–1983: Stanley K. Henshaw, "Characteristics of U.S. Women Having Abortions, 1982–1983," *Family Planning Perspectives* 19 (1987), pp. 6–7; 1984–1985: Stanley K. Henshaw, Jacqueline Darroch Forrest, and Jennifer Van Vort, "Abortion Services in the United States, 1984 and 1985," *Family Planning Perspectives* 19 (1987), p. 64; 1986–1988: *Abortion Fact Book* (New York: Alan Guttmacher Institute, 1992); "Number of Abortions at Lowest Level Since '79," *Lincoln Journal* (AP), June 16, 1994; 1993–1994: Tara Meyer, "Abortion Rate Lowest since 1976 in U.S.," *Lincoln Journal-Star* (AP), January 4, 1997.

The Burger Court invalidated most of these laws,[156] but it upheld a major restriction. It allowed laws that bar the use of government funds to pay for abortions for poor women. The Medicaid program, financed jointly by the federal and state governments, had paid for abortions for poor women. Before these laws, the program had paid for about one-third of the abortions in the country each year.[157] These laws put a safe abortion, by a doctor in a clinic or hospital, beyond the financial reach of some women. Regardless, a majority of the Burger Court ruled that governments have no obligation to finance abortions, even if this means that some women cannot take advantage of their right to have them.[158]

Congress and over half the states now prohibit use of their funds to pay for abortions for poor women, except for those whose pregnancy threatens their life or whose pregnancy is the result of rape or incest. However,

WHICH WOMEN HAVE ABORTIONS

More than half of all pregnancies in the United States are unintended, and half of these are terminated by abortions.

Twenty-six percent of the abortions are for females in their teens and 55% for those in their twenties. The highest rate is for 18- and 19-year-olds—64 abortions per 1,000 women.

About a fourth of the teens under 18 who get abortions have never used birth control. Almost half of the teens under 18 who get abortions have not told their parents before doing so.

The majority of women who get abortions are not married. The majority are white, but the rate is twice as high for nonwhites. (This is not a contradiction. The majority are white because there are more whites, but a smaller percentage of them have abortions.)

Catholics, perhaps surprisingly, have a higher rate than Protestants or Jews. Born-again or evangelical Christians do not have a higher rate; even so, one of six abortion patients in recent years has described herself as a born-again or evangelical Christian.

Almost all women have their abortion during the first trimester of pregnancy, when it is safest and easiest to obtain. Fifty percent have it within the first two months, and 39% more within the third month.

Why Women Have Abortions	
Child would change life (job, school)	76%
Cannot afford child	68
Problems with husband or partner, or do not want to be single parent	51
Do not want people to know I had sex or am pregnant	31
Too young, or cannot handle the responsibility	30
Husband or partner wants me to	23
Concerned for fetus's health	13
Concerned for own health	7
Pregnancy was due to rape or incest	1

SOURCE: Alan Guttmacher Institute, 1989 and 1992.

about a fifth of the states do provide funds for all poor women who want abortions.[159]

One effect of the laws barring use of government funds is to delay abortions, making them more risky and expensive, while the women search for the money.[160] Another effect is to deny abortions to an estimated 20% of the women who cannot obtain the money. The women, then, bear their unwanted children. As a result, state medical and welfare expenditures for the additional children increase. According to one analysis of states that do provide funds for poor women, the states incur the cost of the abortions initially but save money in the long run. For every $1 spent for the abortions, $4 is saved in medical and welfare expenses in what would have been just the first two years of the child's life.[161]

Presidents Reagan and Bush sought justices who opposed *Roe*, and after they filled their fifth vacancy on the Court, pro-life advocates expected the Court to overturn it. Yet the Rehnquist Court, while narrowing *Roe*, has not overturned it.[162] In 1992, a bare majority of five justices reaffirmed the right to abortion.[163] At the same time, the majority signaled a willingness to allow more restrictions on the right—as long as they do not place an "undue burden" on women seeking abortions.

The majority upheld Pennsylvania's 24-hour waiting period between the time a woman indicates her desire to have an abortion and the time a doctor can perform one. Although a 24-hour waiting period will not be much burden for many women, it will for some. Poor women who live in rural areas and must travel to cities to obtain abortions will have to make one trip, turn around and go home, then turn around and come back the next day. Or they will have to spend the night and pay for food and lodging. One woman in Mississippi hitch-hiked and planned to sleep on outdoor furniture in the K Mart parking lot across the street (until the clinic offered to pay for her motel room).[164]

Teenagers will also be affected. Pro-life groups often note the license numbers of cars driven to clinics by teenagers. They look up the name and address of the family and then inform the parents in the hope that the parents will pressure the daughter to change her mind during the waiting period.

The majority struck down Pennsylvania's requirement that a married woman notify her husband before having an abortion. This was an undue burden because a woman who fears physical abuse from her husband would be deterred from seeking an abortion. Justice O'Connor said a state "may not give to a man the kind of dominion over his wife that parents exercise over their children."

But the Court upheld numerous states' requirement that unmarried minors notify their parents before having an abortion.[165] If a daughter does not want to tell her parents, she can try to get permission from a judge. She must convince the judge that an abortion would be in her best interest or that she is mature enough to make the decision herself. If she is not mature enough, she must become a mother. These laws, Justice Marshall wrote in dissent, force "a young woman in an already dire situation to choose between two fundamentally unacceptable alternatives: notifying a possibly dictatorial or even abusive parent or jus-

TOOLS AND SYMBOLS

Norma McCorvey, a carnival barker, was used as a tool by pro-choice lawyers and then became a symbol fought over by both pro-choice and pro-life forces.

Young lawyers Sarah Weddington and Linda Coffee were planning to challenge anti-abortion laws when they met the pregnant McCorvey, who said she was gang-raped. She wanted an abortion, and although the lawyers knew how she could get an illegal one, they did not tell her. So she agreed to be the plaintiff in a test case. After signing a one-page affidavit and authorizing the suit, she was not involved or even informed of its progress. When the Supreme Court issued its ruling, she learned about it from newspapers.

She lived in anonymity, partly to protect her privacy and partly to conceal her lie: her pregnancy had been the result of romance rather than rape. In 1989, feeling proud of her involvement in the landmark case, she decided to go public. As a result, she received hate mail, found baby clothes scattered across her lawn, and was shot at through the window of her home.

Pro-choice groups considered her a useful symbol and gave her a job at an abortion clinic in Dallas. But otherwise they ignored her. Yet she had a difficult life and wanted more attention. She had been born to an alcoholic parent, sexually assaulted as a teenager, married at 16 but deserted soon after, and hooked on drugs. She was "so spiritually needy that she ran through religions as if channel surfing." She said, with dismay, that she could not remember any pro-choice representatives calling and asking, "Good morning, Norma, are you having any trouble in your life?" Indeed, when pro-choice groups hosted a twentieth anniversary party for *Roe v. Wade*, they did not bother to invite her.

She felt uncomfortable with the upper-middle-class women who predominated in the movement. "I am a rough woman," she said. "I don't have a degree from Vassar."

When Operation Rescue, a pro-life group, moved its headquarters into the same building that housed the abortion clinic where she worked, she called its workers "a pack of vultures." But their charismatic leader, Flip Benham, wooed McCorvey, and eventually she warmed to him. "He doesn't make me feel bad about myself," she said.

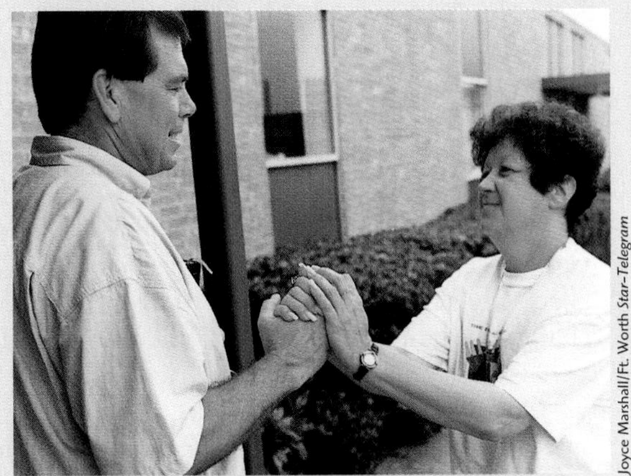
Joyce Marshall/Ft. Worth *Star-Telegram*

Operation Rescue's Flip Benham moved Norma McCorvey to his side.

In 1995, after watching a second trimester abortion, she quit her job at the abortion clinic and became a volunteer for Operation Rescue. She dramatically announced that she was "pro-life" (though at the same time she said that she favored the right to first trimester abortions). The head of another pro-life group gleefully remarked, "The poster child has jumped off the poster." So the woman whose case was used to further the pro-choice cause is now being used to advance the pro-life cause.

McCorvey says she wants to be "a regular person," but she has become too valuable as a public symbol in the abortion debate for that. Now both sides, with their eyes on the ambivalent views of the people in the ideological center of the spectrum, are nervous about McCorvey's own ambivalence on this contentious issue.

SOURCES: David Van Biema, "An Icon in Search Mode," *Time*, August 21, 1995, p. 36; Ellen Goodman, "Poster Child for Ambivalence," *Lincoln Journal-Star (Boston Globe)*, August 17, 1995.

tifying her profoundly personal decision in an intimidating judicial proceeding to a black-robed stranger."

Pro-life groups advocated these laws with the expectation that they would result in fewer abortions. They believed that many teenagers would go to their parents rather than face the forbidding atmosphere of a court hearing and that their parents would persuade or pressure them not to have the abortion. Some evidence indicates that the laws have had this effect.[166]

When teenagers do go to court, they routinely get waivers in some states but not in others. The Nebraska Supreme Court ruled that a 15-year-old was too immature to decide to have an abortion, because although she could discuss the consequences of keeping the baby or giving it up for adoption, discuss her philosophy of abortion, and explain the procedures involved in one, she was unable to explain the risks involved.[167]

Despite the dissatisfaction of some people, it is worth noting that the unelected, nonmajoritarian Supreme Court has come closer to forging a policy reflective of public opinion than have most politicians. Polls show the majority of the people want to keep the right to abortion but would like to discourage it somewhat.[168] The Court's doctrine now essentially articulates this view.

The pro-life movement, growing increasingly frustrated in recent years, has adopted more militant tactics. Organizations such as Operation Rescue engage in civil disobedience, blockading clinics and harassing workers and patients as they come and go. Some organizations spray chemicals inside clinics, ruining carpets and fabrics and leaving a stench that makes the clinics unusable. Such incidents occurred 50 times in one year alone.[169]

Protesters in Charleston, South Carolina, distributed fliers in the city's poorest neighborhood encouraging residents to rob an abortion clinic: "The killers accept only cash! They kill about 60 babies each week. That is $16,500 of CASH taken to the bank each week. That means that an average of $5,500 is waiting there each day of business in cash before closing hours."[170]

Organizations also target doctors, nurses, and other workers of the clinics. Operation Rescue runs a training camp in Florida that instructs members how to use public records to locate personal information about employees, how to tail them to their homes, and how to organize demonstrations at their homes. Organizations put up "Wanted" posters, with a doctor's picture, name, address, and phone number. They encourage others to harass the doctor, his or her spouse, and even their children. (One 13-year-old was confronted in a restaurant and was told that he was going to burn in hell.)[171] Some activists have come out in favor of killing abortion doctors. One organization released a "deadly dozen" list of abortion doctors—a quasi-hit list. One minister wrote a book—*A Time to Kill*—and markets a bumper sticker—"EXECUTE ABORTIONISTS-MURDERERS."[172]

In this climate, three doctors, two clinic receptionists, and one clinic volunteer have been killed, and seven other doctors, employees, and volunteers have been wounded.[173] Numerous clinics have been fire-bombed.

The tactics have had their intended effect on doctors (143 attacks from 1977 through 1996).[174] They have made the practice of providing abortions seem dangerous and even undesirable. Fewer medical schools offer abortion classes, fewer hospitals provide abortion training, fewer doctors study abortion procedures, and fewer gynecologists and obstetricians, despite most being pro-choice, perform abortion operations.[175]

One pro-life leader proclaimed, "We've found the weak link is the doctor." And another observed, "When you get the doctors out, you can have all the laws on the books you want and it doesn't mean a thing."[176]

Abortions remain available in most metropolitan centers but not in most rural areas. Eighty-three percent of U.S. counties have no doctor who performs abortions. Some states have only one or two places where women can obtain abortions.[177]

Meanwhile, *Roe v. Wade* remains controversial. Although it was not even the lead story in the news when it was decided, it has had an enormous impact on politics ever since. It put abortion on the public agenda, and it galvanized conservative groups, who saw it as a symbol of removing societal restraints and increasing social problems.[178] Disparate groups, such as evangelical Protestants and Roman Catholics (and some Orthodox Jews), rural residents and urban ethnics, who normally did not see eye to eye, coalesced around this issue and exercised leverage within the Republican Party.

Homosexuality

The Court has not extended the right to privacy to protect homosexual acts. Almost half the states have laws prohibiting sodomy—oral and anal sex. Although applicable to heterosexuals as well, these laws are seen as restrictions on homosexuals. Although they are primarily symbolic and rarely enforced, they can be invoked. For example, when police delivered a summons to residents of a house and discovered them violating the law of Georgia, police arrested them. Although prosecutors did not file charges, one of the men sued to have the courts declare the law unconstitutional. In 1986, the Supreme Court, by a one-vote margin, refused to do so.[179]

Justice Powell reportedly believed the law was unconstitutional, but after voting against the law in conference, he switched before the decision was announced in court because the man had not been prosecuted. After public reaction to the *Roe* ruling, Powell was leery of potential reaction to another controversial ruling, especially when the law might never be enforced. When he retired, however, he admitted he made a mistake.[180]

In Colorado, voters adopted a constitutional amendment prohibiting laws that bar discrimination against homosexuals, but in 1996 the Supreme Court found the amendment unconstitutional.[181] The majority said it singled out homosexuals and denied them the opportunity, enjoyed by everyone else, to seek protection from discrimination. Justice Kennedy said it was based on "animus" toward homosexuals. In dissent, Justice Scalia accused the majority of overriding the state's political processes and taking sides in the country's cultural wars. The ruling was a significant legal victory for gays and lesbians; it put the brakes on the movement to adopt similar provisions in other states, and it signaled the possibility of more sympathy from the justices in the future. However, the ruling did not extend the right to privacy to homosexual acts or affect any policies, such as those limiting spousal benefits to married couples, that gays and lesbians want to change.

Although some state and local legislatures have passed laws barring discrimination in employment, housing, credit, insurance, and public accommodations, in 1996 Congress, by one vote, rejected a bill

barring discrimination in employment. At the same time, it passed the Defense of Marriage Act, which forbids federal recognition of same-sex marriages and thus denies federal benefits, such as Social Security, for same-sex couples. The act also allows states to disregard same-sex marriages performed in other states. The act was prompted by speculation that the Hawaii Supreme Court might allow homosexual marriages and thereby encourage homosexual couples to flock to the islands to get married and then return to their states. (Under the full faith and credit clause of the Constitution, states normally must recognize the public records and judicial proceedings of other states.)[182]

Congress also blocked President Clinton's pledge to issue an executive order barring discrimination against homosexuals in the military.[183] Since World War II, the military has rejected recruits who admit to being homosexual and discharged troops who are found to be homosexual. According to the military, having homosexuals in the trenches or on ships would undermine the discipline and morale essential for combat.[184] However, when more troops were needed during the Korean, Vietnam, and Persian Gulf Wars, the military did not find this to be such a problem and relaxed its policy.[185] And most other democracies do not find this such a problem either. Western European countries, Canada, Japan, and Israel, which has a battle-tested military, tolerate homosexuals in their services.[186]

But strident opposition from military officials and members of Congress forced President Clinton to accept a compromise, a policy called "don't ask—don't tell." The military (including the Reserves and National Guard) is not allowed to ask questions about sexual orientation on enlistment or security questionnaires but is allowed to discharge members for statements admitting homosexuality or conduct reflecting homosexuality (or bisexuality). Such conduct is defined broadly to encompass not only sexual actions, but also holding hands, dancing, or trying to marry someone of the same sex. The restrictions apply off-base as well as on. They do not encompass reading gay publications, associating with gay people, frequenting gay bars or churches, or marching in gay rights parades.

The new policy does not resolve the issue and does not satisfy either side. Many commanders seem confused, and some seem unwilling to accept the policy; they continue to ask and pursue. The debate about the policy called attention to homosexuality. Consequently, "everyone from private to general openly speculated about who in their unit might be gay, and as a result there are some people who've had a bull's-eye on their back."[187] In this climate, more rather than fewer homosexuals have been discharged. Female homosexuals have been discharged at a disproportionate rate, probably because women in general have not been fully accepted in the services.[188]

Right to Die

The Court has broadened the right to privacy to provide a limited right to die. When Nancy Cruzan's car skidded off an icy road and flipped into a ditch in 1983, doctors were able to save her life but not her brain. She never regained consciousness. She lived in a vegetative state, similar to a coma, and was fed through a tube. Twenty-five at the time of the accident, she was expected to live another 30 years. When her parents asked doctors to remove the tube, the hospital objected and the state of Missouri, despite paying $130,000 a year to support her, also objected. This issue, complicated enough in itself, became entangled in other controversial issues. Pro-life groups said denying life support was analogous to abortion; disability groups said that her condition was merely a

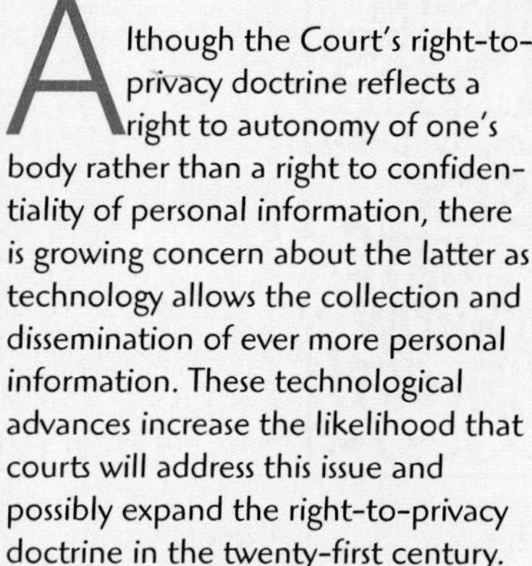

INTO THE 21ST CENTURY

A RIGHT TO KEEP INFORMATION CONFIDENTIAL?

Although the Court's right-to-privacy doctrine reflects a right to autonomy of one's body rather than a right to confidentiality of personal information, there is growing concern about the latter as technology allows the collection and dissemination of ever more personal information. These technological advances increase the likelihood that courts will address this issue and possibly expand the right-to-privacy doctrine in the twenty-first century.

Already technology has led to the erosion of privacy from law enforcement. Electronic surveillance is permitted with court authorization (and wiring an informant is permitted without authorization). Videocamera surveillance is extensive, not only in banks, but also at ATMs, stores, freeway tollbooths, and, increasingly, road intersections and housing projects in urban areas. Road checks for drunk drivers and urine tests for drug users are allowed in some situations. Courts have not interpreted the Fourth Amendment to restrict these practices very much.

Now technology is leading to an erosion of privacy far beyond the needs of law enforcement. Some companies collect data on individuals and then sell it to other businesses to use in marketing or hiring. Data are also made available to landlords, credit grantors, private investigators, and charitable organizations. Metromail Corporation, for example, has a massive database encompassing more than 90% of American households.

Individuals can be searched by their name, address, or telephone number; or by their professional affiliations, political contributions, medical conditions, or magazine subscriptions.

Driving records—including one's tickets, accidents, revocations, and height and weight—can be obtained easily. So can student loan records and bank records, including account numbers, deposits, withdrawals, balances, and the location of safe deposit boxes. So can records of long-distance calls and unlisted phone numbers.

Whenever customers use credit cards to order from catalogs or to pay at restaurants, or use discount cards to shop at supermarkets, every item they buy is recorded. Whenever people visit a Web site that asks personal questions, the responses are recorded.

With computer technology, searchers need very little to find out a lot. One computer program allows businesses to type in license plate numbers from a parking lot and get back their customers' name, address, and a demographic categorization from "Hardscrabble" to "Furs." Another program provides businesses with a detailed profile of each person who called an 800 number.

A writer gave a company the name of an acquaintance and only the facts that the man worked in the securities business and lived in the United States. Within 72 hours, the company had located the man, identifying his current and past addresses (tracing his moves from a lower-middle-class apartment to an upper-class condominium in New York City and his purchase of another condominium at a ski resort). The search also revealed a separate apartment in the city where this married man apparently kept his mistress. The company also could identify his salary and stocks and bonds; his medical history and insurance policies; the restaurants, hotels, and airlines he frequented; the cars he bought, the stores his wife shopped at (and the amount she spent), and his children's schools.

Information collected in one context can be used for other purposes, and information collected for legitimate users can be obtained by unscrupulous companies or scam artists as well. The debate, then, is about how the data may be used. Except for criminal laws applying to fraud and theft, few laws restrict how information may be used. Laws do govern income tax, Social Security, and credit records, and after reporters got Robert Bork's video-rental records during his Supreme Court confirmation hearings in 1987, a law was passed to protect privacy of these and cable television pay-per-view records. (But no law protects the privacy of book purchases, so the special prosecutor subpoenaed records of Monica Lewinsky's book purchases.)

Although polls show that a majority of people support more privacy, this group is relatively unorganized. In contrast, businesses that use these data are well organized and funded. In addition, the news media worry that restrictions will interfere with investigative reporting, and feminist groups worry that restrictions will impede efforts to track down deadbeat dads. Some groups fear that an increased concern for privacy might shield sex offenders who abuse children. Religious groups that oppose abortion and homosexuality worry that any heightened emphasis on information privacy will lead to an expanded right to bodily privacy. Yet the head of an organization that monitors this industry predicts, "Privacy will be to the information economy what consumer protection and product safety were to the industrial age."[1]

1. Nina Bernstein, "On Frontier of Cyberspace, Data Is Money, and a Threat," *New York Times*, June 12, 1997, p. A16.

SOURCES: Nina Bernstein, "On Frontier of Cyberspace, Data Is Money, and a Threat," *New York Times*, June 12, 1997, p. 1; John M. Broder, "F.T.C. Opens Hearings on Computers' Threat to Americans' Right to Privacy," *New York Times*, June 11, 1997, p. A20; Peter Maas, "How Private Is Your Life?" *Parade*, April 19, 1998, pp. 4–5; Peter Rooney, "UI Prof Urging Privacy Safeguards for Nation's Workers," *Champaign-Urbana News-Gazette*, April 23, 1996; Jeffrey Rosen, "Is Nothing Private?" *New Yorker*, June 1, 1998, p. 40.

disability and that withholding food and water from her would lead to withholding treatment from other people with disabilities.[189]

In this case the Rehnquist Court established a limited right to die.[190] The justices ruled that individuals can refuse medical treatment, including food and water, even if this means they will die. But states can require individuals to make their decision while competent and alert. (Presumably, individuals can also prepare a "living will" or designate another person as a proxy to make the decision in the event that they are unable to.)

Several months after the Court's decision, Cruzan's parents returned to a Missouri court with evidence that their daughter would prefer death to being kept alive by medical machines. Three of Cruzan's former co-workers testified that they recalled conversations in which she said she never would want to live "like a vegetable." Her parents asked for permission to remove her feeding tube and the court agreed. She died 12 days later.

Although the legal doctrine seems clear, practical problems persist. Many people do not indicate their decision. Approximately 10,000 people in irreversible comas now did not indicate their decision beforehand.[191] Some people who do indicate their decision beforehand waver when they face death. Some doctors, who are in the habit of prolonging life even when their patients have little chance of recovering or of enjoying life, resist their decision. The doctors try to persuade the patients or their families not to "pull the plug."[192]

The Rehnquist Court has resisted patients' pleas to extend the limited right to die to encompass a broader right to obtain assistance in committing suicide.[193] Thus, the Court has drawn a distinction between stopping treatment and assisting suicide; individuals have a right to demand the former but not the latter. The laws of 35 states that prohibit assisting suicide can be enforced, but the Court left open the possibility that exceptions might be made. The justices seemed tentative, as is typical with an issue new to the courts. Chief Justice Rehnquist emphasized, "Our holding permits this debate to continue, as it should in a democratic society."

The public, by a small margin, favors a right to assisted suicide,[194] but conservative religious groups oppose one. They insist that people should not take a life. Some ethicists worry that patients will be pressured to give up their life because of the costs, to their family or health care provider, of continuing it. Thus, they fear that a right will become a duty.

Meanwhile, the practice, even where officially illegal, is widely condoned, much as abortion was before *Roe*. Almost a fifth of doctors who treat cancer patients in Michigan admitted in a survey that they have assisted suicide, and over half of 2,000 doctors who treat AIDS patients in San Francisco also admitted that they have done so.[195]

CONCLUSION: ARE THE COURTS RESPONSIVE IN INTERPRETING CIVIL LIBERTIES?

The Supreme Court has interpreted the Constitution to provide many important civil liberties. The Warren Court in the 1950s and 1960s expanded civil liberties more than any other Court in history. It applied many provisions of the Bill of Rights to the states. It substantially broadened rights in the areas of speech, libel, obscenity, and religion. It enormously broadened rights of criminal defendants in the areas of search and seizure, self-incrimination, counsel, and jury trial. And it established a right to privacy.

Observers predicted the Burger Court would lead a constitutional counterrevolution. However, it did not. The Burger Court in the 1970s and 1980s narrowed rights in the areas of freedom of the press, libel, and obscenity. It narrowed rights of criminal defendants in the areas of search and seizure, self-incrimination, and jury trial. And it narrowed opportunities for convicted defendants to appeal on the basis that their rights were violated.[196] But the Court accepted the core of the Warren Court's doctrine and, in fact, even extended it in two areas—right to counsel and right to privacy.

Nor has the Rehnquist Court produced a constitutional counterrevolution. It has narrowed rights further in some areas, but it too has accepted most of the Warren Court's doctrine.

The decisions of these Courts show the extent to which the Supreme Court is responsive to the people in civil liberties cases. The majority of the people support civil liberties in general but not necessarily in specific situations. Elites support civil liberties more than the masses. As the Court has expanded civil liberties, it has not been very responsive to the majority. But it has been more responsive to elites, and it has been very responsive to minorities.

The Court, given relative independence from the rest of the political process, was not intended to be responsive to the majority. Therefore, it does not have to mirror public opinion, although it cannot ignore this opinion either. It must stay within the broad limits of this opinion, or it will be pulled back. Thus, the Warren Court went too far too fast for too many people. It produced a backlash that led to the Burger and Rehnquist Courts, which have been more responsive to majority opinion. At the same time, they have been less vigilant in protecting civil liberties.

EPILOGUE

The First Amendment Protects Animal Sacrifice

Although the case of *Church of the Lukumi Babalu Aye v. Hialeah* might seem bizarre, it did not prove difficult for the justices to decide. The justices unanimously struck down the ordinances.[197] Justice Kennedy wrote the opinion, concluding that the ordinances restricted the Santeria religion without compelling reasons.

Although the ordinances did not mention the Santeria religion, they were written in such a way that they restricted this religion and its practices but virtually no others. The ordinances exempted Jewish kosher slaughter and also a variety of other animal killings—slaughter primarily for food (not primarily for religious purposes), hunting, fishing, euthanasia, and eradication of insects. State law even allowed the use of live rabbits to train greyhound dogs for racing. Thus, the argument that restriction of animal sacrifice was necessary to prevent cruelty to animals rang hollow.

The ordinances also made no effort to regulate the disposal of carcasses from hunting and fishing or the disposal of garbage from restaurants, which would be more voluminous than the carcasses from Santeria ceremonies. Thus, the argument that restriction of animal sacrifice was necessary to prevent a public health risk also rang hollow.

In short, the Court concluded that Hialeah had targeted the Santeria religion because officials and citizens disapproved of it. "Although the practice of animal sacrifice may seem abhorrent to some," Kennedy wrote, "religious beliefs need not be acceptable, logical, consistent, or comprehensible to others in order to merit First Amendment protection." And, he reminded, "it was historical instances of religious persecution and intolerance that gave concern to those who drafted the free exercise clause."

KEY TERMS

bills of attainder
ex post facto laws
freedom of speech
seditious speech
McCarthyism
public forum
pure speech
speech plus conduct
symbolic speech
prior restraint
libel
obscenity
free exercise clause
establishment clause
due process
unreasonable searches and seizures
exclusionary rule
Miranda rights
right to counsel
right to a jury trial
cruel and unusual punishment
plea bargain
right to privacy

FURTHER READING

Dan T. Carter, *Scottsboro: A Tragedy of the American South* (Baton Rouge: Louisiana State University Press, 1979). An examination of the infamous Scottsboro, Alabama, rape case that prompted the Supreme Court to begin to provide counsel to poor defendants.

Fred W. Friendly, *Minnesota Rag* (New York: Random House, 1981). A lively chronicle of the Court's first important freedom of the press case—*Near v. Minnesota* in 1927.

David J. Garrow, *Liberty and Sexuality: The Right to Privacy and the Making of Roe v. Wade* (New York: Macmillan, 1994). An exhaustive account of the hard road to *Roe*.

Franz Kafka, *The Trial* (numerous editions, 1937). One of the great novels of the twentieth century, which shows, perhaps more dramatically than anything else written, what life without due process rights would be like.

James Kirby, *Fumble: Bear Bryant, Wally Butts, and the Great College Football Scandal* (New York: Dell, 1986). Law for football fans—the story of the libel suit against a national magazine for writing that the coach of Alabama and athletic director of Georgia fixed a football game between the two schools. The author, a lawyer, was hired by the Southeastern Conference to determine what really happened in the dispute.

Anthony Lewis, *Gideon's Trumpet* (New York: Vintage, 1964). A wonderful account of Clarence Earl Gideon's suit and the Court's landmark decision.

Patricia G. Miller, *The Worst of Times* (New York: HarperCollins, 1992). Recollections of woman who had abortions before *Roe* made them legal—and interviews with abortionists, doctors, and police who witnessed the effects.

ELECTRONIC RESOURCES

http://w3.trib.com/FACT/
A home page for the First Amendment, sponsored by the Casper, Wyoming, Star-Tribune, *and winner of a national award for best online newspaper services. Links to many resources on different issues involving the first amendment, including freedom of the press, internet censorship, state freedom of information laws, and others. Links to Supreme Court decisions and original documents.*

http://www.uark.edu/depts/comminfo/www/religion.html
A link to a variety of sources on freedom of religion, historical and contemporary, from the Christian Research Institute to the American Secular Union.

http://www.aclu.org/index.html
The home page of the American Civil Liberties Union, a group organized to protect civil liberties through legal and political action. Links to information and position papers on many issues covered in this chapter, including church and state, reproductive rights, flag burning, free speech, gay rights, and many others.

http://www.naral.org and **http://www.prolife.org/ultimate/**
The first site is the home page of the National Abortion Rights Action League, a pro-choice group, and the second site is a link to pro-life groups. Each provides perspectives on the conflict over abortion rights.

INFOTRAC CITATIONS

"Why Was I Thrown Out of the Hall?"
"First They Come for the Libraries"
"Blocking the Exits"
"The World Wide Web Never Forgets"

NOTES

1. Bob Cohn and David A. Kaplan, "A Chicken on Every Altar?" *Newsweek*, November 9, 1992, p. 79. Previously, Santeria had been practiced semi-openly in parts of New York City and Puerto Rico.
2. Ibid.
3. *Lee v. Weisman*, 112 S.Ct. 2649 (1992).
4. *International Society for Krishna Consciousness v. Lee*, 120 L.Ed.2d 541 (1992); *Employment Division v. Smith*, 494 U.S. 872 (1990).
5. Richard Morin, "Is There a Constitutional Right to Rap Rambunctiously?" *Washington Post National Weekly Edition*, September 24–30, 1990, p. 37.
6. "Poll: 33% of Americans Can Identify Bill of Rights," *Lincoln Journal-Star* (AP), December 15, 1991.
7. The states did not ratify a proposed amendment that would have required at least one representative in Congress for every 50,000 people. That amendment would have put about 5,000 members in today's Congress. The states did not ratify, until 1992, another proposed amendment that would have prohibited a salary raise for members of Congress from taking effect until after the next election to Congress.
8. *Reid v. Covert*, 354 U.S. 1 (1957).
9. *Barron v. Baltimore*, 32 U.S. 243 (1833).
10. *Gitlow v. New York*, 268 U.S. 652 (1925).
11. *Argersinger v. Hamlin*, 407 U.S. 25 (1972).
12. Freedom of association is not listed in the First Amendment, but the Court has interpreted freedom of speech and assembly to imply such a right.
13. *Milk Wagon Drivers Union v. Meadowmoor Dairies*, 312 U.S. 287 (1941).
14. Thomas I. Emerson, *The System of Freedom of Expression* (New York: Random House/Vintage, 1971), pp. 6–8.
15. Zechariah Chafee, Jr., *Free Speech in the United States* (Cambridge, Mass.: Harvard University Press, 1941), pp. 51–52.
16. *Schenk v. United States*, 249 U.S. 47 (1919); *Frohwerk v. United States*, 249 U.S. 204 (1919); *Debs v. United States*, 249 U.S. 211 (1919); *Abrams v. United States*, 250 U.S. 616 (1919); *Gitlow v. New York*, 268 U.S. 652 (1925); *Whitney v. California*, 274 U.S. 357 (1927).
17. *Gitlow v. New York*.
18. *Dennis v. United States*, 341 U.S. 494 (1951).
19. *Yates v. United States*, 354 U.S. 298 (1957); *Scales v. United States*, 367 U.S. 203 (1961).
20. Earl Warren, *The Memoirs of Earl Warren* (Garden City, N.Y.: Doubleday, 1977), p. 6.
21. *Brandenburg v. Ohio*, 395 U.S. 444 (1969).
22. *Brandenburg v. Ohio*.
23. *Esquire*, November 1974.
24. *Jeannette Rankin Brigade v. Chief of Capital Police*, 409 U.S. 972 (1972); *Edwards v. South Carolina*, 372 U.S. 229 (1963).
25. *United States v. Grace*, 75 L.Ed.2d 736 (1983).
26. *Grayned v. Rockford*, 408 U.S. 104 (1972); *Tinker v. Des Moines School District*, 393 U.S. 503 (1969).
27. *Brown v. Louisiana*, 383 U.S. 131 (1966).
28. *Southeastern Promotions v. Conrad*, 420 U.S. 546 (1975).
29. *Adderley v. Florida*, 385 U.S. 39 (1966).
30. *Greer v. Spock*, 424 U.S. 828 (1976).
31. *Amalgamated Food Employees v. Logan Valley Plaza*, 391 U.S. 308 (1968).
32. *Lloyd v. Tanner*, 407 U.S. 551 (1972); *Hudgens v. NLRB*, 424 U.S. 507 (1976).
33. *Gooding v. Wilson*, 405 U.S. 518 (1972); *Lewis v. New Orleans*, 408 U.S. 913 (1972).
34. C. Herman Pritchett, *The American Constitution*, 2d ed. (New York: McGraw-Hill, 1968), p. 476, n. 2.
35. *Rosenfeld v. New Jersey*, 408 U.S. 901 (1972); *Brown v. Oklahoma*, 408 U.S. 914 (1972).
36. *Cohen v. California*, 403 U.S. 15 (1971).
37. *FCC v. Pacifica Foundation*, 438 U.S. 726 (1968). In response, Congress and the FCC have considered several proposals to ban offensive speech except for hours when children are not likely to be listening. In 1993, a federal court of appeals ruled that a ban except from midnight until 6 A.M. was too broad. The court said it infringed on the rights of adults.
38. *Wilkinson v. Jones*, No. 86–1125, 1987.
39. *Cox v. Louisiana*, 379 U.S. 536 (1965).
40. *Schenk v. Pro-Choice Network*, 137 L.Ed.2d 1 (1997).
41. *Collin v. Smith*, 447 F.Supp. 676 (N.D. Ill., 1978); *Collin v. Smith*, 578 F.2d 1197 (7th Cir., 1978).
42. *U.S. v. Schwimmer*, 279 U.S. 644 (1929).
43. *Frisby v. Schultz*, 101 L.Ed.2d 420 (1988).
44. *United States v. O'Brien*, 391 U.S. 367 (1968).
45. *Tinker v. Des Moines School District*.
46. *Smith v. Goguen*, 415 U.S. 566 (1974); *Spence v. Washington*, 418 U.S. 405 (1974).
47. *Texas v. Johnson*, 105 L.Ed.2d 342 (1989).
48. Walter Isaacson, "O'er the Land of the Free," *Time*, July 3. 1989, p. 15; "What Price Old Glory?" *Time*, July 10, 1989, p. 23.
49. *U.S. v. Eichman*, 110 L.Ed.2d 287 (1990).
50. David Halbertstam, *The Best and the Brightest* (Greenwich, Conn.: Fawcett, 1969), p. 769.
51. From Watergate tapes released in 1996. For transcripts of tapes made public in 1996, see Stanley Kutler, ed., *Abuse of Power: The New Nixon Tapes* (New York: Free Press, 1998).
52. *New York Times v. United States*, 403 U.S. 713 (1971). In addition to seeking injunctions, the Nixon administration sent a telegram to the *New York Times* demanding that it cease publication of the excerpts, but the FBI had the wrong telex number for the newspaper, so the telegram went first to a fish company in Brooklyn. R. W. Apple, "Lessons from the Pentagon Papers," *New York Times*, June 23, 1996, p. E5.
53. *Hazelwood School District v. Kuhlmeier*, 98 L.Ed.2d 592 (1988).
54. William Glaberson, "Censors and Finances Curb Student Press, Report Says," *New York Times*, May 1, 1994, p. 19. However, a bigger problem for city schools has been a lack of money to publish a paper at all.
55. Then radio and television stations used actors with Irish accents to dub the comments made by IRA members. In 1994, the government lifted the ban.
56. *Branzburg v. Hayes*, 408 U.S. 665 (1972).
57. *Cox Broadcasting v. Cohn*, 420 U.S. 469 (1975).
58. This was not a Supreme Court case.
59. *Time v. Hill*, 385 U.S. 374 (1967).
60. 376 U.S. 254.
61. Harry Kalven, "The *New York Times* Case: A Note on 'the Central Meaning of the First Amendment,' " *Supreme Court Review* 1964, p. 221.
62. *Monitor Patriot v. Roy*, 401 U.S. 265 (1971).
63. *Associated Press v. Walker*, 388 U.S. 130 (1967).
64. *Greenbelt Cooperative Publishing v. Bresler*, 398 U.S. 6 (1970).
65. *Curtis Publishing v. Butts*, 388 U.S. 130 (1967).
66. *Gertz v. Robert Welch*, 418 U.S. 323 (1974), and *Time v. Firestone*, 424 U.S. 448 (1976).

67. Eric Press, "Westmoreland Takes on CBS," *Newsweek*, October 22, 1984, p. 62.

68. William A. Henry III, "Libel Law: Good Intentions Gone Awry," *Time*, March 4, 1985, p. 94.

69. Ibid., p. 71.

70. *Roth v. United States*, 354 U.S. 476 (1957); *Manual Enterprises v. Day*, 370 U.S. 478 (1962); *Jacobellis v. Ohio*, 378 U.S. 184 (1964); *A Book Named "John Cleland's Memoirs of a Woman of Pleasure" v. Attorney General of Massachusetts*, 383 U.S. 413 (1966).

71. *Miller v. California*, 413 U.S. 15 (1973).

72. *Jenkins v. Georgia*, 418 U.S. 153 (1974).

73. "Project—An Empirical Inquiry into the Effects of *Miller v. California* on the Control of Obscenity," *New York University Law Review* 52 (October 1977), pp. 810–939.

74. *Hudnut v. American Booksellers Association*, 89 L.Ed.2d 291 (1986).

75. *Young v. American Mini Theaters*, 427 U.S. 50 (1976); *Renton v. Playtime Theaters*, 89 L.Ed.2d 29 (1986).

76. *Torcaso v. Watkins*, 367 U.S. 488 (1961).

77. *Pierce v. Society of Sisters*, 268 U.S. 510 (1925).

78. *Cooper v. Pate*, 378 U.S. 546 (1963); *Cruz v. Beto*, 405 U.S. 319 (1972).

79. *Reynolds v. United States*, 98 U.S. 145 (1879).

80. *Sherbert v. Verner*, 374 U.S. 398 (1963).

81. Although a congressional statute mandates "reasonable accommodation," the Court interpreted it so narrowly that it essentially requires only minimal accommodation. *T.W.A. v. Hardison*, 432 U.S. 63 (1977). For analysis see Gloria T. Beckley and Paul Burstein, "Religious Pluralism, Equal Opportunity, and the State," *Western Political Quarterly* 44 (March 1991), pp. 185–208. For a related case see *Thornton v. Caldor*, 86 L.Ed.2d. 557 (1985).

82. *Wisconsin v. Yoder*, 406 U.S. 205 (1972).

83. *United States v. Lee*, 455 U.S. 252 (1982).

84. *United States v. American Friends Service Committee*, 419 U.S. 7 (1974).

85. *Goldman v. Weinberger*, 475 U.S. 503 (1986); and *O'Lone v. Shabazz*, 482 U.S. 342 (1986).

86. *Employment Division v. Smith*, 108 L.Ed.2d 876 (1990).

87. American Indian Religious Freedom Act of 1994.

88. Ruth Marcus, "One Nation, under Court Rulings," *Washington Post National Weekly Edition*, March 18–24, 1991, p. 33.

89. *Boerne v. Flores*, 138 L.Ed.2d 624 (1997).

90. William Lee Miller, "The Ghost of Freedoms Past," *Washington Post National Weekly Edition*, October 13, 1986, pp. 23–24.

91. *Church of Holy Trinity v. United States*, 143 U.S. 457 (1892).

92. *Engel v. Vitale*, 370 U.S. 421 (1962); *Abington School District v. Schempp*, 374 U.S. 203 (1963).

93. C. Herman Pritchett, *The American Constitution*, 3d ed. (New York: McGraw-Hill, 1977), p. 406.

94. Kenneth M. Dolbeare and Phillip E. Hammond, *The School Prayer Decisions* (Chicago: University of Chicago Press, 1971).

95. Robert H. Birkby, "The Supreme Court and the Bible Belt," *Midwest Journal of Political Science* 10 (1966), pp. 304–315.

96. J. Gordon Melton, quoted in Jon D. Hull, "The State of the Union," *Time*, January 30, 1995, p. 55.

97. Peter Cushnie, "Letters," *Time*, October 15, 1984, p. 21.

98. *Wallace v. Jaffree*, 86 L.Ed.2d 29 (1985).

99. *Lee v. Weisman*, 120 L.Ed.2d 467 (1992).

100. *Jones v. Clear Creek*, 977 F.2d 965 (5th Cir., 1992).

101. *Moore v. Ingebretsen*, 88 F.3rd 274 (1996).

102. Anna Quindlen, "School Prayer: Substitutes for Substance," *Lincoln Journal (New York Times)*, December 8, 1994.

103. Ibid.

104. James M. Wall, "Keep Faith Voluntarily," *Lincoln Journal-Star (Newsday)*, January 29, 1995.

105. *Widmar v. Vincent*, 454 U.S. 263 (1981). The law requires high schools that receive federal funds to allow meetings of students' religious, philosophical, or political groups if the schools permit meetings of any "noncurriculum" groups. Schools could prohibit meetings of all noncurriculum groups. Thus, a Salt Lake City high school banned all nonacademic clubs rather than let students form a homosexual organization in 1996.

106. *Board of Education v. Mergens*, 110 S. Ct. 2356 (1990).

107. David Van Biema, "Spiriting Prayer into School," *Time*, April 27, 1998, p. 28–31.

108. *Rosenberger v. University of Virginia*, 132 L.Ed.2d 700 (1995).

109. *Lynch v. Donnelly*, 79 L.Ed.2d 604 (1984).

110. *Allegheny County v. ACLU*, 106 L.Ed.2d 472 (1989).

111. *Epperson v. Arkansas*, 393 U.S. 97 (1968).

112. Some groups use the more sophisticated sounding term, "creation science." Although these groups do address the science of evolutionary theory, the courts consider "creation science" to be religion in the guise of science.

113. *Edwards v. Aguillard*, 482 U.S. 578 (1987).

114. Peter Applebome, "Seventy Years after Scopes Trial, Creation Debate Lives," *New York Times*, March 10, 1996, pp. 1, 12.

115. *Everson v. Board of Education of Ewing Township*, 330 U.S. 1 (1947); *Board of Education v. Allen*, 392 U.S. 236 (1968); *Meek v. Pittinger*, 421 U.S. 349 (1975).

116. *Lemon v. Kurtzman*, 403 U.S. 602 (1971); *Committee for Public Education and Religious Liberty v. Nyquist*, 413 U.S. 756 (1973).

117. For example, striking down tax credits but upholding tax deductions to reduce tuition costs for parents. *Lemon v. Kurtzman; Committee for Public Education and Religious Liberty v. Nyquist, Mueller v. Allen*, 463 U.S. 388 (1983).

118. *Rochin v. California*, 342 U.S. 165 (1952).

119. Seymour Wishman, *Confessions of a Criminal Lawyer* (New York: Penguin Books, 1981), p. 16.

120. *Stein v. New York*, 346 U.S. 156 (1953).

121. Wendy Kaminer, *It's All the Rage* (Reading, Mass.: Addison-Wesley, 1995), p. 78.

122. *Weeks v. United States*, 232 U.S. 383 (1914).

123. 367 U.S. 643 (1961).

124. *United States v. Leon*, 82 L.Ed.2d 677 (1984); *Massachusetts v. Sheppard*, 82 L.Ed.2d 737 (1984).

125. *Olmstead v. United States*, 277 U.S. 438 (1928).

126. *Katz v. United States*, 389 U.S. 347 (1967).

127. *Brown v. Mississippi*, 297 U.S. 278 (1936).

128. *McNabb v. United States*, 318 U.S. 332 (1943); *Mallory v. United States*, 354 U.S. 449 (1957); *Spano v. New York*, 360 U.S. 315 (1959).

129. *Ashcraft v. Tennessee*, 322 U.S. 143 (1944).

130. *Rogers v. Richmond*, 365 U.S. 534 (1961); *Lynumn v. Illinois*, 372 U.S. 528 (1963).

131. 384 U.S. 436 (1966).

132. *Johnson v. Zerbst*, 304 U.S. 458 (1938).

133. *Powell v. Alabama*, 287 U.S. 45 (1932).

134. *Gideon v. Wainwright*, 372 U.S. 335 (1963).

135. *Argersinger v. Hamlin*, 407 U.S. 25 (1972); *Scott v. Illinois*, 440 U.S. 367 (1974).

136. *Douglas v. California*, 372 U.S. 353 (1953).

137. *Baldwin v. New York*, 339 U.S. 66 (1970); *Blanton v. North Las Vegas*, 489 U.S. 538 (1989).

138. *Duncan v. Louisiana*, 391 U.S. 145 (1968).

139. *Taylor v. Louisiana*, 419 U.S. 522 (1975).

140. *Swain v. Alabama*, 380 U.S. 202 (1965).

141. *Wilkerson v. Utah*, 99 U.S. 130 (1878); *In re Kemmler*, 136 U.S. 436 (1890).

142. *Furman v. Georgia*, 408 U.S. 238 (1972).

143. *Gregg v. Georgia*, 428 U.S. 153 (1976).

144. *Woodson v. North Carolina*, 428 U.S. 289 (1976).

145. *Coker v. Georgia*, 433 U.S. 584 (1977).

146. McCleskey *v. Kemp*, 95 L.Ed.2d 262 (1987).

147. *Brady v. United States*, 397 U.S. 742 (1970).

148. *Griswold v. Connecticut*, 38 U.S. 479 (1965).

149. For a rare exception, see *Time v. Hill*, 385 U.S. 374 (1967).

150. *Griswold v. Connecticut*.

151. *Eisenstadt v. Baird*, 405 U.S. 438 (1972); *Carey v. Population Services International*, 431 U.S. 678 (1977).

152. *Eisenstadt v. Baird*.

153. Lloyd Shearer, "This Woman and This Man Made History," *Parade* (1983).

154. 410 U.S. 113 (1973).

155. Bob Woodward, "The Abortion Papers," *Washington Post National Weekly Edition*, January 30–February 5, 1989, pp. 24–25.

156. *Akron v. Akron Center for Reproductive Health*, 76 L.Ed.2d 687 (1983).

157. "The Supreme Court Ignites a Fiery Abortion Debate," *Time*, July 4, 1977, pp. 6–8.

158. *Beal v. Doe*, 432 U.S. 438 (1977); *Maher v. Roe*, 432 U.S. 464 (1977); *Poelker v. Doe*, 432 U.S. 519 (1977); *Harris v. McRae* 448 U.S. 297 (1980).

159. Margaret Carlson, "Abortion's Hardest Cases," *Time*, July 2, 1990, p. 25. These states provide funds to varying degrees. States with a higher proportion of Catholics or Protestant fundamentalists provide lower levels of funding. Kenneth J. Meier and Deborah R. McFarlane, "The Politics of Funding Abortion," *American Politics Quarterly* 21 (January 1993), pp. 81–101.

160. Benjamin Weiser, "The Abortion Dilemma Come to Life," *Washington Post National Weekly Edition*, December 25–31, 1989, pp. 10–11.

161. "Facts in Brief: Abortion in the United States" (New York. Alan Guttmacher Institute, 1992); Stephanie Meneimer, "Ending Illegitimacy as We Know It," *Washington Post National Weekly Edition*, January 17–23, 1994, p. 24.

162. *Webster v. Reproductive Health Services*, 106 L.Ed.2d 410 (1989).

163. *Planned Parenthood of Southeastern Pennsylvania v. Casey*, 120 L.Ed.2d 674 (1992).

164. William Booth, "The Difference a Day Makes," *Washington Post National Weekly Edition*, November 23–29, 1992, p. 31.

165. *Hodgson v. Minnesota*, 111 L.Ed.2d 344 (1990); *Ohio v. Akron Center for Reproductive Health*, 111 L.Ed.2d 405 (1990).

166. Carlson, "Abortion's Hardest Cases," p. 24.

167. Butch Mabin, "Supreme Court Says Teen Seeking Abortion Too Immature," *Lincoln Journal-Star*, December 13, 1997.

168. Joe Klein, "The Senator's Dilemma," *New Yorker*, January 5, 1998, p. 32.

169. Alissa Rubin, "The Abortion Wars Are Far from Over," *Washington Post National Weekly Edition*, December 21–27, 1992, p. 25.

170. Sandra G. Boodman, "Bringing Abortion Home," *Washington Post National Weekly Edition*, April 19–25, 1993, p. 7.

171. Richard Lacayo, "One Doctor Down, How Many More?" *Time*, March 22, 1993, p. 47.

172. Douglas Frantz, "The Rhetoric of Terror," *Time*, March 27, 1995, pp. 48–51.

173. Dan Sewell, "Abortion War Requires Guns, Bulletproof Vests," *Lincoln Journal-Star* (AP), January 8, 1995.

174. "Blasts Reawaken Fear of Domestic Terrorism," *Lincoln Journal-Star* (Cox News Service), January 17, 1997.

175. Richard Lacayo, "Abortion: The Future Is Already Here," *Time*, May 4, 1992, p. 29; Jack Hitt, "Who Will Do Abortions Here?" *New York Times Magazine*, January 18, 1998, p. 20.

176. Randall Terry, quoted in Anthony Lewis, "Pro-Life Zealots 'Outside the Bargain, " *Lincoln Journal-Star* (*New York Times*), March 14, 1993; Joseph Scheidler, quoted in Boodman, "Bringing Abortion Home," p. 6.

177. Cynthia Gorney, "Getting an Abortion in the Heartland," *Washington Post National Weekly Edition*, October 15–21, 1990, pp. 10–11.

178. David Von Drehle, "The Opinion That Ignited the Great Abortion War," *Washington Post National Weekly Edition*, April 11–17, 1994, p. 7.

179. *Bowers v. Hardwick*, 92 L.Ed.2d 140 (1986); see also *Doe v. Commonwealth's Attorney*, 425 U.S. 901 (1976).

180. "Ex-Justice's Second Thoughts to Make Heated Debate Hotter," *Lincoln Sunday Journal-Star*, October 28, 1990.

181. *Romer v. Evans*, 134 L.Ed.2d 855 (1996).

182. The House sponsor of the act, Robert Barr (R-Ga.), said the act was necessary because "The flames of hedonism, the flames of narcissism, the flames of self-centered morality are licking at the very foundation of our society, the family unit." At the time he was protecting the family unit, he was in his third marriage. Margaret Carlson, "The Marrying Kind," *Time*, September 16, 1996, p. 26.

183. President Clinton also ordered the FBI to end its policy that made it difficult for homosexuals to be hired.

184. The policy originally was based on psychoanalytic theory, which considered homosexuality a mental illness. This conclusion was rejected by the American Psychiatric Association some years later.

185. Randy Shilts, "What's Fair in Love and War," *Newsweek*, February 1, 1993, pp. 58–59.

186. Israel drafts every 18-year-old man and woman. It does consider homosexuality in the assignment of jobs. Gays who admit their orientation to their superiors confidentially are restricted from security-sensitive jobs for fear they are susceptible to blackmail. But gays who acknowledge their orientation openly could not be blackmailed, so they are treated the same as straights. Shilts, "What's Fair in Love and War," pp. 58–59; Eric Konigsberg, "Gays in Arms," *Washington Monthly*, November 1992, pp. 10–13; "Canada Had No Problems Lifting Its Military Gay Ban," *Lincoln Journal-Star* (AP), January 31, 1993. See also Randy Shilts, *Conduct Unbecoming: Gays and Lesbians in the U.S. Military* (New York: St. Martin's, 1993).

187. Philip Shenon, "New Study Faults Pentagon's Gay Policy," *New York Times*, February 26, 1997, A8.

188. "Group Says Gays Worse Off in Military since New Policy," *Lincoln Journal-Star*, (AP), February 28, 1996; Shenon, "New Study Faults Pentagon's Gay Policy."

189. Al Kamen, "When Exactly Does Life End?" *Washington Post National Weekly Edition*, September 18–24, 1989, p. 31; Alain L. Sanders, "Whose Right to Die?" *Time*, December 11, 1989, p. 80.

190. *Cruzan v. Missouri Health Department*, 111 L.Ed.2d 224 (1990).

191. Otto Friedrich, "A Limited Right to Die," *Time*, July 9, 1990, p. 59.

192. Tamar Lewin, "Ignoring 'Right to Die' Directives, Medical Community Is Being Sued," *New York Times*, June 2, 1996, p. 1.

193. *Washington v. Glucksberg*, 138 L.Ed.2d 772 (1997); *Vacco v. Quill*, 138 L.Ed.2d 834 (1997).

194. David E. Rosenbaum, "Americans Want a Right to Die. Or So They Think," *New York Times*, June 8, 1997, p. E3.

195. Ibid.

196. *Stone v. Powell*, 428 U.S. 465 (1976).

197. 124 L.Ed. 2d 472 (1993).

schools.

Michael Eastman

15 CIVIL RIGHTS

Compromise or Continue to Fight?

You are Fannie Lou Hamer, a leader of the Mississippi Freedom Democratic Party (MFDP), a group of mostly African Americans challenging the seating of the regular state Democratic Party delegates at the national Democratic Party Convention in 1964. You have to decide whether to accept a compromise offered by national party officials.

You have come a long way.[1] You were born the youngest in a family of 20 children in the small town of Ruleville, located in the heart of the Mississippi Delta. Like many other African Americans, your parents were sharecroppers, picking cotton on a white family's plantation in exchange for housing and a little money for food.[2] At the age of six, after the owner enticed you with treats from the plantation store, you began picking cotton too.

You were not satisfied with your life because you had little control over it. For instance, the owner of your house refused to fix the toilet, saying you did not need one indoors. (Yet his house had a separate bathroom for the dog.) And when you entered the hospital to have a small tumor removed, you were sterilized without your knowledge or permission.

So when the civil rights movement reached Ruleville in 1962, you were ready. You were 44 years old, yet you could not vote. At a meeting at church, a leader of the Student Non-Violent Coordinating Committee (SNCC) and a minister with Martin Luther King's Southern Christian Leadership Conference (SCLC) spoke. When they asked who would try to register to vote, you raised your hand. Two weeks later you and 17 others were driven to the county seat. You were confronted by many people, you recalled, "and some of them looked like the Beverly Hillbillies . . . but they wasn't kidding down there; they had on, you know, cowboy hats and they had guns; they had dogs."[3] The registrar pulled out a copy of the state constitution and asked you to explain one section. You could not, so he would not register you.

On the way back to Ruleville, the civil rights workers' bus was stopped and the driver was arrested. The charge? The bus was too yellow. (Police said it looked like a school bus.) Once home, the owner of the plantation where you had toiled for 18 years told you to go back and take your name off the registration forms or leave the plantation. You told him, "I didn't go down there to register for you. I went down to register for myself."[4] You left your house on the plantation and moved in with friends in town (and after the cotton season, your husband also was evicted from the plantation).

It became clear that getting your rights would not be easy. But you are deeply religious, and you told people, "Whether I want to do it or not, I got to. This is my calling. This is my mission."[5]

With help from the SNCC workers, you studied the state constitution and several months later returned to register again. This time you passed the "test." At the next election, however, you were not allowed to vote because you had not paid poll taxes in the previous years when you were not allowed to vote.

You were determined to get your right to vote and to help others get theirs. You attended an SCLC training course. While returning on the bus, you and others in the group sat at a whites-only lunch counter in the station and then complained when a white girl was moved ahead of you in the line. The driver explained that "niggers are not to be in front of the line."[6] When the bus reached the next town, the members of your group were arrested and severely beaten. For the rest of your life, you would be plagued by ailments from this beating.[7]

Yet you continued. You organized throughout the Delta, inspiring your neighbors to be strong and mocking those, such as the "chicken-eating preachers," who were less courageous. You traveled throughout the country to help raise funds for civil rights organizations. Although you are short and overweight and you have little education, you are a charismatic figure in the

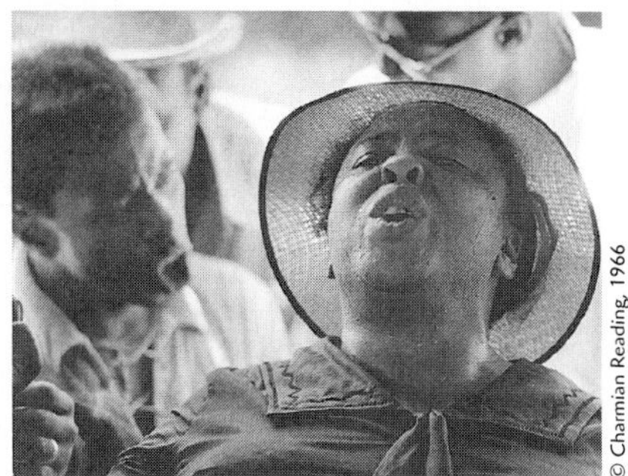
© Charmian Reading, 1966

Fannie Lou Hamer leads marchers in song.

movement—a rousing speaker, perhaps more than anyone except King, and a beautiful singer. After your speeches, you lead the audience in religious hymns and movement songs, breaking down the barriers among strangers.

"We're tired of all this beatin', we're tired of takin' this," you say to anyone who will listen. "All my life I've been sick and tired. Now I'm sick and tired of being sick and tired."[8]

Now, in 1964 you were permitted to vote for the first time in your life, but most blacks still are prevented from voting, and all are prevented from participating in the regular Democratic Party in Mississippi. The state party, whose platform endorsed segregation, controls the state legislature, whose laws make voting by blacks nearly impossible. So you and a few others decided to organize your own party.[9]

The Mississippi Freedom Democrats' immediate goal is to challenge the regular Democrats chosen as delegates to the national convention this year. The Freedom Democrats claim that the delegates are unlawful representatives of the state because they were chosen by unlawful means.

The MFDP held its own precinct, county, and state conventions and allowed whites as well as blacks to participate. You were elected as one of the delegates. But when you and the other members of the upstart delegation arrived in Atlantic City, New Jersey, for the Democratic National Convention, you learned that national party officials, though sympathetic to your cause, did not want you to challenge the regular delegation.

President Johnson, who took office after President Kennedy was assassinated, is running for his own term. Although a southerner—a Texan—he favors civil rights. He plans to tap Minnesota Senator Hubert Humphrey as his running mate. At the 1948 convention Humphrey gained attention by calling for government to open the door to people of all races. His speech caused many white southerners to walk out in protest.

Johnson will face the Republican, Arizona Senator Barry Goldwater, whose positions are closer to many white southerners' views. The Democrats are worried that, with the civil rights movement and the combination of Humphrey's liberalism and Goldwater's conservatism, southerners will not vote solidly Democratic this year as they have historically. Now Johnson and other officials are vexed that a challenge by the MFDP, even if unsuccessful, would attract publicity that would upset southerners still more.

So Johnson sent word that he might not pick Humphrey if the Freedom Democrats persisted. Clearly, you would prefer Humphrey to anyone else mentioned as a possible vice presidential candidate.

If you gave up your challenge, officials said you could sit as honored guests in the balcony. You rejected this offer; it sounded like the segregated seating in the movie theaters back home. Then officials made their final proposal: You could have two seats as at-large delegates. The regular delegates could keep their seats but would have to pledge loyalty to the national ticket. (It was likely that many would refuse and would leave.) Further, officials promised that in the future delegates would not be seated if their state party did not allow full participation by blacks.

Do you accept this compromise? Some national civil rights leaders urge you to. They stress that you are now involved in politics, not protest, and that politics is the art of compromise.[10]

Civil rights refer to equality of rights for persons regardless of their race, sex, or ethnic background. The Declaration of Independence proclaimed that "all men are created equal." The author, Thomas Jefferson, knew that all men were not created equal in many respects, but he sought to emphasize that they should be considered equal in rights and equal before the law. This represented a break with Great Britain where rigid classes with unequal rights existed; nobles had more rights than commoners. The Declaration's promise did not include nonwhites or women, however. Thus, although colonial Americans advocated equality, they envisioned it only for white men. Others gradually gained more equality, but the Declaration's promise remains unfulfilled for some.

RACE DISCRIMINATION

African Americans, Hispanics, and Native Americans all have endured and continue to face much discrimination.

Discrimination against African Americans

SLAVERY

The first blacks came to America in 1619, just 12 years after the first whites. The blacks, like many whites, initially came as indentured servants. In exchange for passage across the ocean, they were bound to an employer, usually for 4 to 7 years, and then freed. But later in the seventeenth century, the colonies passed laws requiring blacks and their children to be slaves for life. Once slavery was established, the slave trade flourished, especially in the South.

As a result of compromises between northern and southern states, the Constitution accepted slavery. It allowed the importation of slaves until 1808, when Congress could bar further importation, and it required the return of escaped slaves to their owners.

Shortly after ratification of the Constitution, northern states abolished slavery. In 1808 Congress barred the importation of slaves but did not halt the practice of slavery in the South. Slavery became increasingly controversial, and abolitionists called for its end.

Southerners began to question the Declaration of Independence and to repudiate its notion of natural rights. They attributed this idea to Jefferson's "radicalism."[11] The Supreme Court tried to quell the antislavery sentiment in the **Dred Scott case** in 1857.[12] Dred Scott, a slave who lived in Missouri, was taken by his owner to the free state of Illinois and the free territory of Wisconsin and, after five years, was returned to Missouri. The owner died and passed title to his wife, who moved but left Scott in the care of people in Missouri. They opposed slavery and arranged to have Scott sue his owner for his freedom. They argued that Scott's time in a free state and a free territory made him a free man even though he was brought back to a slave state. The owner, who also opposed slavery, had the authority to free Scott, so the purpose of the suit was not to win his freedom. Rather, she and others sought a major court decision to keep slavery out of the territories.

In this infamous case, Chief Justice Roger Taney stated that no blacks, whether slave or free, were citizens, and that they were "so far inferior that they had no rights which the white man was bound to respect." Taney could have stopped here—if Scott was not a citizen, he could not sue in federal court—but Taney continued. He declared that Congress had no power to control slavery in the territories. This meant that slavery could extend into the territories Congress already had declared free. It also raised the possibility that states could not control slavery within their borders.[13]

By this time, slavery had become the hottest controversy in American politics, and this decision fanned the flames. It provoked vehement opposition in the North and prompted further polarization, which eventually led to the Civil War. Meanwhile, Scott got his freedom from his owner.

The North's victory in the Civil War gave force to President Lincoln's Emancipation Proclamation ending slavery. But blacks would find short-lived solace.

The Granger Collection, New York

Dred Scott.

CIVIL WAR AMENDMENTS AND RECONSTRUCTION

After the war, Congress passed and the states ratified three constitutional amendments. The Thirteenth prohibited slavery. (Mississippi became the last state to ratify the amendment—in 1995.) The Fourteenth granted citizenship to blacks, thus overruling the Dred Scott decision, and also granted "equal protection of the laws" and "due process of law." The Fifteenth provided the right to vote for black men. The **equal protection clause** eventually would become the primary guarantee that government would treat people equally.

Congress also passed a series of Civil Rights Acts to reverse the "Black Codes" that southern states had enacted to deny the newly freed slaves legal rights. These Civil Rights Acts allowed blacks to buy, own, and sell property; to make contracts; to sue; and to be witnesses and jurors in court. They also allowed blacks to use public transportation, such as railroads and steamboats, and to patronize hotels and theaters.[14]

Even so, most freed blacks faced bleak conditions. Congress rejected proposals to break up plantations and give former slaves "40 acres and a mule" or to provide aid to establish schools. Without land or education, they had to work for their former masters as hired hands or sharecroppers. Their status was not much better than it had been. Landowners designed a system to keep the former slaves dependent. They allowed sharecroppers to sell half their crop and keep the proceeds, but paid so little, regardless of how hard the farmers worked, that the

AMERICAN DIVERSITY

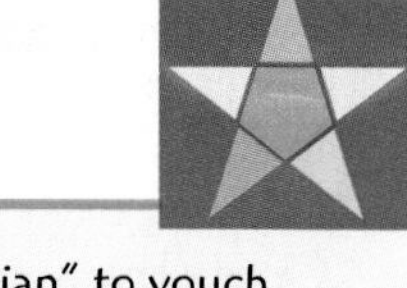

BLACK MASTERS

Although most slaveowners were white, some were black. William Ellison of South Carolina was one. Born a slave, he bought his freedom and then his family's by building and repairing cotton gins. Over time he earned enough to buy slaves and operate a plantation. With 60 slaves, Ellison ranked in the top 1% of all slaveholders, black or white.

Ellison was unusual, but he was not unique. In Charleston, South Carolina, alone, more than 100 African Americans owned slaves in 1860. Most, however, owned fewer than four.

Although part of the slave-owning class, black slaveholders were not much more acceptable to whites. Ellison's family was granted a pew on the main floor of the local Episcopal church, but they had to be on guard at all times. Failure to maintain the norms of black-white relations—acting deferentially—could mean instant punishment. And as the Civil War approached, whites trying to preserve the established order increasingly viewed free blacks, even slaveholders, as a threat. Harsher legislation regulated their lives. For example, they had to have a white "guardian" to vouch for their character, and they had to carry special papers to show their free status. Without these papers, they could be sold back into slavery.

Some black slaveowners showed little sign that they shared the concerns of black slaves. Indeed, Ellison freed none of his slaves.

SOURCE: Michael P. Johnson and James L. Roark, *Black Masters* (New York: W. W. Norton, 1984).

families had to borrow to tide them over the winter. The next year they had to work for the landowner to pay off their debt. The following year the cycle continued. And, lacking education, most sharecroppers did not keep records of how much they owed and how much the landowner owed them, and many were cheated.

During the period of Reconstruction, the Union army enforced the new amendments and acts. While the army occupied the South, military commanders established procedures to register voters, including the newly freed slaves; hold elections; and ratify the Fourteenth Amendment. The commanders also started schools for children of the newly freed slaves. But in state after state, the South resisted and eventually the North capitulated. After a decade, the two regions struck a deal to end what was left of Reconstruction. The 1876 presidential election between Republican Rutherford Hayes and Democrat Samuel Tilden was disputed in some states. To resolve the dispute, Republicans, most of whom were northerners, and Democrats, many of whom were southerners, agreed to a compromise: Hayes would be named president, and the remaining Union troops would be removed from the South.

In hindsight, it should not be a surprise that Reconstruction did not accomplish more. It was not easy to integrate four million former slaves into a southern society that was bitter in its defeat and weak in its economy. Northern citizens who expected progress to come smoothly were naive. When it did not come quickly, they became disillusioned.

Public attitudes during Reconstruction thus began a recurring cycle that continues to this day: The public gets upset about the treatment of African Americans and supports some efforts to improve conditions. But the public is naive, and when the efforts do not immediately produce the expected results, the public becomes disillusioned and dissatisfied with the costs. The public's lack of patience then forces officials to put the race problem on the back burner for some future generation to handle.[15]

SEGREGATION

In both the South and the North, blacks came to be segregated from whites.

SEGREGATION IN THE SOUTH The reconciliation between Republicans and Democrats—northerners and southerners—was effected at the expense of blacks. Removing the troops enabled the South to govern itself again, and this enabled the South to reduce blacks to near-slave status.

Before the Civil War, slavery itself had kept blacks down, and segregation would have been inconvenient when blacks and whites needed to live and work near each other. There was no residential segregation—not in rural areas, where former slaves' shacks were intermixed with plantation houses, and not in urban areas, where few blocks were solidly black. But after slavery, southerners established segregation as another way to keep blacks down. Initially, they did so haphazardly—one law here, another there. By the early 1900s, however, there was a pervasive pattern of **Jim Crow laws.**

Jim Crow laws segregated just about everything. Some segregated blocks within neighborhoods, others neighborhoods within cities. Laws in some small towns excluded blacks altogether. Some did so explicitly; others simply established curfews that required blacks to be off the streets by 10 P.M. Laws also segregated schools, which blacks had been allowed to attend during Reconstruction, and even textbooks (black schools' texts had to be stored separately from white schools' books). Many laws segregated public accommodations, such as hotels, restaurants, bars, and transportation. At first the laws required the races to sit in separate sections of streetcars; eventually, they required them to sit in separate cars; finally, they also forced them to sit in separate sections of waiting rooms. Other laws segregated parks, sporting events, and circuses. Laws segregated black and white checkers players in Birmingham and established districts for black and white prostitutes in New Orleans. They segregated drinking fountains, restrooms, ticket windows, entrances, and exits. They segregated the races in prisons, hospitals, and homes for the blind. They even segregated the races in death—in morgues, funeral homes, and cemeteries.

Blacks were forced to defer to whites in all informal settings as well, and failure to do so could mean punishment or even death. Blacks were "humiliated by a thousand daily reminders of their subordination."[16]

Meanwhile, northern leaders, who had championed the cause of the slaves before and during the Civil War, abandoned blacks a decade after the war; Congress did not pass new laws, presidents did not enforce existing laws, and the Supreme Court gutted the constitutional amendments and Civil Rights Acts. All acquiesced in "the southern way."

The Supreme Court struck down the Civil Rights Act allowing blacks to use public accommodations, including transportation, hotels, and theaters.[17] Where the Fourteenth Amendment said that "no state" shall deny equal protection, the Court interpreted this to mean that "no government" shall, but private individuals—owners of transportation, hotels, and theaters—could. The Court's interpretation might seem plausible, but it was clearly contrary to Congress's intent.[18]

Then the Court upheld segregation itself. Louisiana passed "an Act to promote the comfort of passengers," which mandated separate accommodations in trains. New Orleans black leaders sponsored a case to test the act's constitutionality. Homer Adolph Plessy bought a ticket and sat in the white car. When the conductor ordered him to move to the black car, Plessy refused. He maintained that the act was unconstitutional under the Fourteenth Amendment. In ***Plessy v. Ferguson*** in 1896, the Court disagreed, claiming that the act was not a denial of equal protection because it provided equal accommodations.[19] Thus the Court established the **separate-but-equal doctrine,** which allowed separate facilities if they were equal. Of course, government required separate facilities only because it thought the races were not equal, but the Court brazenly commented that the act did not stamp "the colored race with a badge of inferiority" unless "the colored race chooses to put that construction on it." Only Justice John Harlan, a former Kentucky slaveholder, dissented: "Our Constitution is color-blind, and neither knows nor tolerates classes among citizens."

Three years later the Court accepted segregation in schools.[20] A Georgia school board turned a black high school into a black elementary school. Although the board did not establish a new high school for blacks or allow them to attend the ones for whites, the Court did not object. This set a pattern in which separate but equal meant separation but not equality.

SEGREGATION IN THE NORTH Although Jim Crow laws were not as pervasive in the North as in the South, northerners imitated southerners to the point where one writer proclaimed, "The North has surrendered!"[21]

Job opportunities were better in the North. Southern blacks were sharecropping—by 1930 80% of those who farmed were still working somebody else's land[22]—and northern factories were offering jobs. Between 1915 and 1940, more than a million southern blacks headed north in the "Great Migration." But they were forced to live in black ghettos because they could not afford better housing and because they could not escape discrimination in the North, either.

DENIAL OF THE RIGHT TO VOTE

With the adoption of the Fifteenth Amendment, many blacks voted and even elected fellow blacks to office during Reconstruction, but southern states began to disfranchise them in the 1890s (as explained in Chapter 7). Thus, they were unable to elect black representatives or even pressure white officials to oppose segregation.

VIOLENCE

To solidify their control, whites engaged in sporadic violence against African Americans. In the 1880s and 1890s, whites lynched about 100 blacks a year. In the 1900s vigilante "justice" continued (Table 1). For example, a mob in Livermore, Kentucky, dragged a black man accused of murdering a white man into a theater. The ringleaders charged admission and hanged the man. Then they permitted the audience to shoot at the swinging body—those in the balcony could fire once; those in the better seats could empty

Lynching occurred not only in the South but also in northern cities such as Marion, Indiana, in 1930.

© Charmian Reading

TABLE 1

Why Whites Lynched Blacks in 1907

Whites gave the following reasons for lynching blacks, who may or may not have committed these acts.

REASON	NUMBER
Murder	5
Attempted murder	5
Manslaughter	10
Rape	9
Attempted rape	11
Burglary	3
Harboring a fugitive	1
Theft of 75¢	1
Having a debt of $3	2
Being victor over white man in fight	1
Insulting white man	1
Talking to white girls on telephone	1
Being wife or son of rapist	2
Being father of boy who "jostled" white women	1
Expressing sympathy for victim of mob	3
	56

SOURCE: Adapted from Ray Stannard Baker, *Following the Color Line* (New York: Harper & Row, 1964), pp. 176–177.

their revolvers.[23] In 1919 there were 25 race riots in six months. White mobs took over cities in the North and South, burning black neighborhoods and terrorizing black residents for days on end.[24]

The Ku Klux Klan, which began during Reconstruction and started up again in 1915, played a major role in inflaming prejudice and terrorizing blacks. It was strong enough to dominate many southern towns and even the state governments of Oklahoma and Texas. It also made inroads into some northern states.

Federal officials said such violence was a state problem—presidents refused to speak out, and Congress refused to pass legislation making lynching a federal offense—yet state officials did nothing.

For at least the first third of the twentieth century, white supremacy reigned—in the southern states, the border states, and many of the northern states. It also pervaded the nation's capital, where President Woodrow Wilson instituted segregation in the federal government.[25]

Overcoming Discrimination against African Americans

African Americans fought white supremacy primarily in three arenas—the courts, the streets, and Congress. In general, they fought in the courts first and Congress last, although as they gained momentum they increasingly fought in all three arenas at once.

THE MOVEMENT IN THE COURTS

The first strategy was to convince the Supreme Court to overturn the separate-but-equal doctrine of *Plessy v. Ferguson*.

THE NAACP In response to white violence, a group of blacks and whites founded the **NAACP**, the National Association for the Advancement of Colored People, in 1909. In its first two decades, it was led by W. E. B. DuBois, a black sociologist. In time it became the major organization fighting for blacks' civil rights.

Frustrated by presidential and congressional inaction and its own lack of power to force action, the NAACP decided to converge on the federal courts, which were less subject to pressures from the majority. The association assembled a cadre of lawyers, mainly from Howard University Law School, a black university in Washington, D.C., to bring lawsuits attacking segregation and the denial of the right to vote. In 1915 they persuaded the Supreme Court to strike down the grandfather clause (which exempted persons whose ancestors could vote from the literacy test),[26] and two years later they convinced the Court to invalidate laws prescribing residential segregation.[27] But the Court continued to allow most devices to disfranchise blacks and most efforts to segregate.

In 1938 the NAACP chose a 30-year-old attorney, Thurgood Marshall, to head its litigation arm.[28] In the next two decades, presidents appointed more liberals to the Supreme Court. These two developments led to the NAACP's success in the courts.

DESEGREGATION OF SCHOOLS Seventeen states and the District of Columbia segregated their schools (and four other states allowed it by local option). The states gave white students better facilities and paid white teachers more. Overall, they spent from 2 to 10 times more on white schools than on black ones.[29] Few of these states had graduate schools for blacks: As late as 1950, they had 15 engineering schools, 14 medical schools, and 5 dental schools for whites and none for blacks; they had 16 law schools for whites and 5 for blacks.

The NAACP's tactics were first to show that "separate but equal" really resulted in unequal schools and then to attack "separate but equal" head on, arguing that it led to unequal status.

The NAACP began by challenging segregation in graduate schools. Missouri provided no black law school but offered to reimburse blacks who went to out-of-state law schools. In 1938 the Supreme Court said the state had to provide a black law school.[30] Texas established a black law school clearly inferior to the white law school at the University of Texas in size of faculty, student body, library, and opportunities for students to specialize. In 1950 the Court said the black school had to be substantially equal to the white school.[31] Oklahoma allowed a black student to attend the white graduate school at the University of Oklahoma but designated a separate section of the classroom, library, and cafeteria for the student. The Court said this too was inadequate, because it deprived the student of the exchange of views with fellow students necessary for education.[32] The Court did not invalidate the separate-but-equal doctrine in these decisions, but it made segregation almost impossible to implement in graduate schools.

The NAACP continued by challenging segregation in grade schools and high schools. Marshall filed suits in two southern states, one border state, one northern state, and the District of Columbia. The suit in the northern state was brought against Topeka, Kansas, where Linda Brown could not attend the school just 4 blocks from her home because it was a white school. Instead, she had to go to a school 21 blocks away.

When the cases reached the Supreme Court, President Eisenhower pressured his appointee, Chief Justice Earl Warren, to rule in favor of segregation. Eisenhower invited Warren and the attorney for the states to the White House for dinner. When the conversation turned to the segregationists, Eisenhower said, "These are not bad people. All they are concerned about is to see that their sweet little girls are not required to sit in schools alongside some big overgrown Negroes."[33]

However, Warren not only voted against segregation but persuaded the other justices, some of whom had supported segregation, to vote against it too.

In the landmark case of ***Brown v. Board of Education*** in 1954, the Court ruled unanimously that school segregation violated the Fourteenth Amendment's equal protection clause.[34] In the opinion, Warren asserted that separate but equal not only resulted in unequal schools but was inherently unequal because it made black children feel inferior. In overruling the *Plessy* doctrine, the Court showed how revolutionary the equal protection clause was—or could be interpreted to be. The Court required the segregated states to change their way of life to a degree unprecedented in American history.

After overturning laws requiring segregation in schools, the Court overruled laws mandating segregation in such places as public parks, golf courses, swimming pools, auditoriums, courtrooms, and jails.[35]

In *Brown* the Court ordered schools to desegregate "with all deliberate speed."[36] This was a compromise between those who wanted schools to do so immediately and those who wanted schools to do so gradually.[37] The ambiguity of the phrase, however, allowed them to take years to desegregate. The ruling prompted much deliberation but little speed.

The South engaged in massive resistance. The Court needed help from the other branches of government to implement its ruling but failed to get any cooperation for some time. President Eisenhower was reluctant to tell the states to change. In fact, he joined their representatives in Congress in criticizing the decision. With his position and popularity, the president could have speeded implementation by speaking out in support of the decision, yet he did not do so for more than three years. When nine black students tried to attend a white high school under a desegregation plan in Little Rock, Arkansas, the governor's and state legislature's inflammatory rhetoric against desegregation encouraged local citizens to take the law into their own hands. Finally, President Eisenhower acted; he sent federal troops and federalized the state's national guard to quell the riot.

A few years later President Kennedy used federal marshals and paratroopers to quell violence after the governor of Mississippi blocked the door to keep James Meredith from registering at the University of Mississippi. Kennedy again sent troops when the governor of Alabama, George Wallace, proclaiming "segregation now, segregation tomorrow, segregation forever," blocked the door to keep blacks from enrolling at the University of Alabama.

After outright defiance, some states attempted to circumvent the ruling by shutting down their public schools and providing tuition grants for students to use at private schools, which at the time could segregate. They also provided other forms of aid, such as textbooks and public recreation facilities, for private schools. These efforts hindered desegregation and hurt black education because the black communities seldom had the resources to establish their own schools.

The states also tried less blatant schemes, such as "freedom of choice" plans, that allowed students to choose the school they wanted to attend. Of course, virtually no whites chose a black school, and due to strong pressure, few blacks chose a white school. The idea was to achieve desegregation on paper, or token desegregation in practice, in order to avoid real desegregation. But the Court rebuffed these schemes and even forbade discrimination by private schools.[38]

The Court's firm support gave blacks hope. Thurgood Marshall said, "Chief Justice Warren became the image [of the Court] that allowed the poor Negro sharecropper to say, 'Kick me around Mr. Sheriff, kick me around Mr. County Judge, kick me around Supreme Court of my state, but there's one person I can rely on.' "[39]

Nevertheless, progress was excruciatingly slow. If a school district was segregated, a group like the NAACP had to run the risks and spend the time and money to bring a suit in a federal district court. Judges in these courts reflected the views of the state or local political establishment they came from, so the suit might not be successful. If it was, the school board had to prepare a desegregation plan. Members of the school board reflected the views of the community and the pressures from the segregationists, so the plan might not be adequate. If it was, segregationists would

AP/Wide World Photos

Linda Brown's kindergarten class. Brown is in the back row, fourth from the right.

Outside the Supreme Court, NAACP attorneys George E. C. Hayes, Thurgood Marshall, and James M. Nabrit celebrate the Brown v. Board of Education *decision.*

challenge it in a federal district court. If the court upheld the plan, segregationists would appeal to a federal court of appeals. Judges in these courts came from the South, and they sat in Richmond and New Orleans. However, they were not as tied to the state or local political establishment, and they usually decided against the segregationists. But then segregationists could appeal to the Supreme Court. Segregationists knew they would lose sooner or later. But the process took several years, so they were able to delay the inevitable.

Thus, segregationists tried to resist, then to evade, and finally to delay. In this they succeeded. In 1964, a decade after *Brown*, 98% of all black children in the South still attended all-black schools.[40]

By this time, the mood in Congress had changed. Congress passed the Civil Rights Act of 1964, which, among other things, cut off federal aid to school districts that continued to segregate. The following year it passed the first major program providing federal aid to education. This was the carrot at the end of the stick: School districts began to comply to get the federal money.

Finally, by 1970 only 14% of all black children in the South still attended all-black schools. Of course, some went to mostly black schools. Even so, the change was dramatic. Since then, though, many white students have left the public schools for private schools, causing creeping resegregation of the public schools.

BUSING *Brown* and related rulings addressed **de jure segregation**—segregation enforced by law. This segregation can be attacked by striking down the law. *Brown* did not address **de facto segregation**—segregation based on residential patterns—typical of northern cities and large southern cities, where most blacks live in black neighborhoods and most whites live in white neighborhoods. Students attend their neighborhood schools, which are mostly black or mostly white. This segregation is much more intractable because it does not stem primarily from a law, so it cannot be eliminated by striking down a law.

Civil rights groups proposed busing some black children to schools in white neighborhoods and some white children to schools in black neighborhoods. They hoped to improve black children's education, their self-confidence and aspirations, and, eventually, their college and career opportunities. They also hoped to improve black and white children's ability to get along together.

Although Chief Justice Warren retired and President Nixon, who opposed busing, appointed Warren Burger to be chief justice, the Supreme Court unanimously upheld busing in Charlotte, North Carolina, in 1971.[41] The Court ruled that busing is appropriate within school districts—ordinarily cities—where there is a history of intentional segregation. The Court brushed off complaints that busing would be too burdensome for students. It noted that 39% of the public school students in the country were already bused for reasons other than desegregation.

Following this decision, the Court upheld busing in northern cities—Columbus, Dayton, and Denver.[42] Although these cities had mostly de facto segregation, school officials had located schools and assigned students in ways that perpetuated this segregation.

But no matter how extensive busing is within a city, it still cannot desegregate most large cities, where blacks and other minorities now are in the majority. There are not enough whites to desegregate the schools, largely because of "white flight" from the cities and their public schools. After World War II, affluent whites began to leave central cities for suburbs, and after the courts upheld busing, even more did so. In addition, others transferred their children out of public and into private schools.

Consequently, civil rights groups proposed busing some black children from the city to the suburbs and some white children from the suburbs to the city. This would provide enough of both races to achieve balance in both places.

The Burger Court rejected this proposal by a five to four vote in 1974.[43] It said busing between Detroit and its suburbs was not necessary, although Detroit schools were 70% black and suburban schools were 80% white. The Court said busing is not appropriate between school districts unless there is evidence of

MISSISSIPPI'S SECRET POLICE

Two years after the Supreme Court's *Brown* decision, the Mississippi legislature created a secretive agency to "protect the sovereignty of the State of Mississippi and her sister states." The Sovereignty Commission lasted until 1973. Little information about its practices came to light, however, until 1998, when a 21-year legal battle ended and a federal court required disclosure of the commission's records.

This tax-supported secret police force acted to preserve segregation. The Sovereignty Commission hired a public relations officer, established a speakers' bureau, and produced propaganda films to portray race relations in the segregated state in a positive light. It persuaded newspapers to kill stories it disapproved of and run stories it submitted. (For example, "Mississippi authorities have learned that the apparently endless 'freedom' rides into Mississippi and the South were planned in Havana, Cuba, last winter by officials of the Soviet Union.")

It also set up a network of spies—"eyes and ears" in each of the state's 82 counties—to collect information on everyone who posed a threat to segregation, from civil rights workers to ordinary white folks who made an improper comment at an inopportune time. The commission estimated that it had files on 10,000 people, tracing their whereabouts and detailing such personal information as their financial transactions and sexual practices.

The commission dispatched an investigator to the University of Southern Mississippi to determine if a white woman was dating a young man who was "said to be part Negro"; another investigator was sent out to determine whether an out-of-wedlock baby was the offspring of an interracial liaison.

The commission fed its information to the individuals' employers and to the Ku Klux Klan. Individuals were fired, and some apparently were beaten and killed as a result. (The commission circulated the license plate number of the car driven by three civil rights workers murdered in Neshoba County.) The commission also disseminated misinformation, smearing individuals and causing one early black applicant to the University of Southern Mississippi to be convicted and imprisoned on false charges.

Although the commission was an extreme incarnation of attitudes typical at the time, it was not alone. Commissioners shared information with officials in the FBI and members of Congress. Both of these institutions were investigating communists and other "subversives" and were skeptical about the patriotism of civil rights leaders and fearful of the changes sought by the civil rights movement.

Even in 1998, a former commissioner defended the commission's practices: "It was all-out warfare to keep the communists and the agitators from taking over Mississippi," he said. "We did what we had to do."

SOURCES: Calvin Trillin, "State Secret," *New Yorker*, May 29, 1995, pp. 54–64; John Cloud, "The KGB of Mississippi," *Time*, March 30, 1998, p. 30; "Files Provide Look at Infamous Panel," *Champaign-Urbana News-Gazette* (AP), March 15, 1998.

intentional segregation in both the city and its suburbs. Otherwise, such extensive busing would require too long rides for students and too much coordination by administrators. Although there has been intentional segregation by many cities and their suburbs,[44] the evidence is not as clear as that of the de jure segregation by southern states at the time of *Brown*, so it is difficult to demonstrate a pattern by the cities and their multiple suburbs to the extent expected by the judges. Consequently, the Court's ruling makes busing between cities and suburbs much less likely than within the cities alone.

Thurgood Marshall, by then on the Court, dissented and predicted that the ruling would allow "our great metropolitan areas to be divided up each into two cities—one white, the other black." Indeed, the ruling did contribute to this result. Only atypical metropolitan areas, such as Louisville, Kentucky, where the city and its suburbs formed a single school district, achieved significant desegregation.

During these years relatively few students were bused for desegregation—4% in one typical year. These students were far fewer than those bused, at public expense, to segregated public and private schools.[45]

Nevertheless, busing ran up against a wall of public opinion. White parents criticized the courts sharply. Their reaction stemmed from prejudice against blacks; bias against poor persons; fear of the crime in inner city schools; worry about the quality of inner city schools; and desire for the convenience of neighborhood schools. They also resented the courts for telling local governments what to do. In addition, some black parents opposed busing because it disrupted their children's lives and exposed them to the hostility of white students in their new schools. Black parents also resented the implication that their children could learn only if sitting next to white children. But other black parents favored busing because of the opportunity for their children to go to better schools.

Opponents, especially white parents, have been so strident that many people assume busing could not work. In Charlotte, where the Supreme Court first upheld busing, it suffered a rocky start; each of the 10 high schools closed because of racial fighting. But after a period of ad-

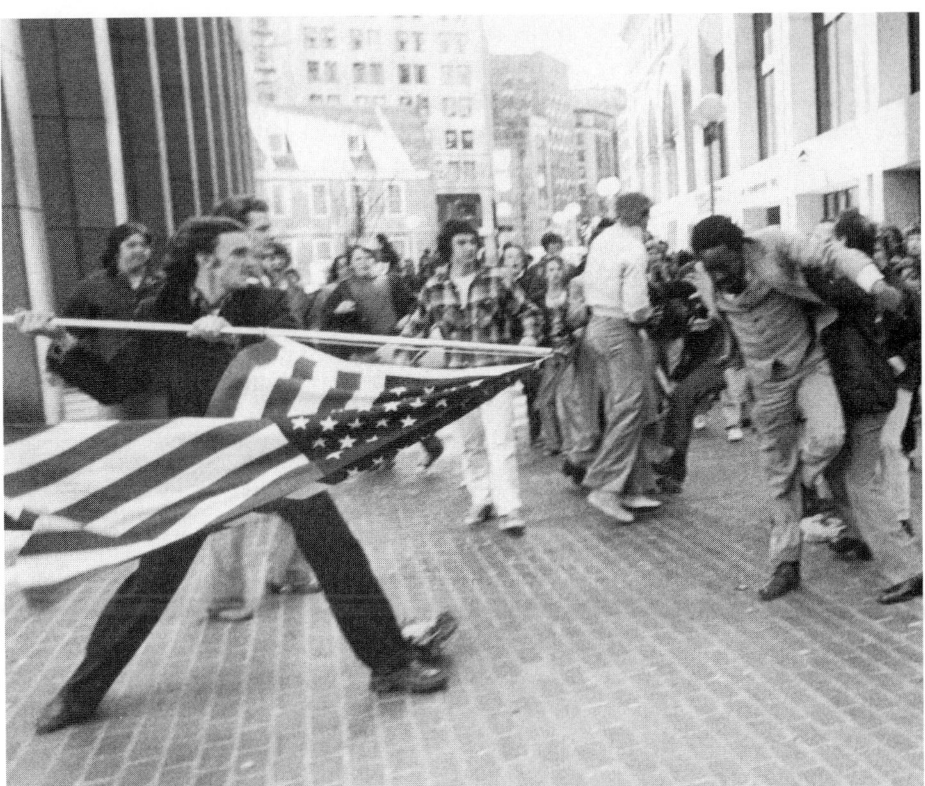

Stanley J. Forman, Pulitzer Prize, 1977

Busing led to rioting in some cities, such as Boston. Here protesters assault a black man in 1976.

justment, busing won the support of most students and parents.[46] Studies of some other cities, particularly small- and medium-size cities, show similar results.[47]

Busing had less success in big cities. It prompted an increase in white flight, with the result that there are fewer white students to balance enrollments and fewer middle-class students to provide stability in the cities' schools. It also contributed to the deterioration of minority communities, because it diminished the neighborhood schools that had helped define these communities and hold them together.[48]

Busing, only one part of the education equation, could not accomplish all that civil rights groups and federal judges expected—or at least hoped—it could. Busing could not compensate for massive residential segregation. It could not overcome students' poverty or their parents' lack of involvement in their education. Thus, studies of the performance of minority children bused to white schools show disappointing, mixed results.

In 1991, the Rehnquist Court reduced judicial pressure for even the limited busing that was occurring.[49] The majority said districts could stop busing when "the vestiges of past discrimination had been eliminated to the extent practicable."

As an alternative to busing, some districts established magnet schools, which receive extra resources and offer special programs, often in sciences, languages, or performing arts. These schools are located in the inner city but are designed to attract whites from throughout the city as well as blacks from the neighborhood. Magnet plans can produce some integrated schools, but they can enroll only a fraction of a city's students. These schools are expensive, and they cannot offset the imbalance in the number of whites and blacks in the city's system. Thus, most students continue to attend segregated schools.

A federal district court in Kansas City, Missouri, tried to address this problem by ordering officials to draw up a magnet plan that would lure whites from the suburbs as well as blacks in the city. The plan was ambitious and, of course, expensive—it required funding from the state in addition to the district—and it was challenged in court. In 1995, the Rehnquist Court invalidated it. The majority said federal judges could not order state or local officials to pay for school improvements to attract suburban students.[50]

The Rehnquist Court's rulings came at a time when more minorities began to question the goal of integration. Their communities have deteriorated so much that many minorities voice greater concern about improving the quality and safety of their schools than about sending their children to other schools or bringing white children to their schools.[51]

THE MOVEMENT IN THE STREETS

After the NAACP's early successes in the courts, other blacks, and some whites, took the fight to the streets. Their bold efforts gave birth to the modern civil rights movement.

The movement began in Montgomery, Alabama, in 1955, when Rosa Parks refused to move to the back of the bus. Her refusal and arrest prompted blacks to boycott city buses. For their leader they chose a young Baptist minister, Dr. Martin Luther King, Jr. The boycott catapulted the movement and King to national attention (as explained in Chapter 5).

King was the first charismatic leader of the movement. He formed the Southern Christian Leadership Conference (SCLC) of black clergy and adopted the tactics of Mahatma Gandhi, who had led the movement to free India from the British. The tactics included direct action, such as demonstrations and marches, and civil disobedience—intentional and public disobedience of laws considered unjust. The tactics were based on nonviolence, even when confronted with violence. This strategy was designed to draw support from whites by contrasting the morality of the movement's position with the immorality of discrimination and violence against blacks.

For a long time some whites, focusing on civil rights leaders such as King and even fearing foreign "communists," deluded themselves into thinking that "outside agitators" were responsible for the turmoil in their communities.[52] But the movement grew from the grass roots, and it eventually shattered this delusion.

Charles Moore/Black Star

Martin Luther King, under arrest in 1958.

The movement spread, especially among black students. In 1960, four black students of North Carolina A&T College sat at the lunch counter in Woolworth's and asked for a cup of coffee. The waitress refused to serve them, but they stayed and were arrested. On following days, as whites waved the Confederate flag and jeered, more students sat at the lunch counter. Within a year such sit-ins occurred in more than 100 cities.

When blacks asserted their rights, whites often reacted with violence. In 1963, King led demonstrators in Birmingham, Alabama, for desegregation of public facilities. Public Safety Commissioner Eugene "Bull" Connor had police unleash their dogs to attack the marchers. In 1964, King led demonstrators in Selma, Alabama, for voting rights. State troopers clubbed many of the marchers, and vigilantes beat and shot marchers.

In the summer of 1964, black and white college students mounted a voter registration drive in Mississippi. By the end of the summer, 1,000 had been arrested, 80 beaten, 35 shot, and 6 killed.[53] These included 1 southern black and 2 northern whites who were murdered by Klansmen, allegedly with aid from a sheriff and deputy sheriff, in Neshoba County. (This incident was fictionalized in the movie *Mississippi Burning*.)

Perpetrators of the violence usually were not caught. When they were, they usually were not punished. Law enforcement was frequently in the hands of bigots, and juries generally were all white. The Supreme Court had struck down discrimination in choosing juries,[54] but discrimination continued through informal means.

During these years, most whites told pollsters they disliked the civil rights movement's speed and tactics: "They're pushing too fast and too hard." At the same time, most said they favored integration more than ever. And they seemed repelled by the violence. The brutality against blacks generated more support for them.

Although the movement's tactics worked well against southern de jure segregation, they did not work as well against northern de facto segregation or against both regions' job discrimination. By the mid-1960s, a decade after the *Brown* decision, progress had stalled and dissatisfaction was growing. Young blacks from the inner city, who had not been involved in the movement, questioned two of its principles—interracialism and nonviolence. As James Farmer, head of the Congress of Racial Equality (CORE), later explained, these blacks began to say, "What is this we-shall-overcome, black-and-white together stuff? I don't know of any white folks except the guy who runs that store on 125th Street in Harlem and garnishees wages and repossesses things you buy. I'd like to go upside his head. [Or] the rent collector, who bangs on the door demanding rent that we ain't got. I'd like to go upside his

AP/Wide World Photos

When three civil rights workers were murdered in Neshoba County, Mississippi, no one was ever indicted by the state. After an investigation, 18 persons, including the sheriff (right) and deputy sheriff (left), here in court, were indicted by the federal government for the lesser charge of conspiracy. (There was no applicable federal law for murder.) Ultimately, 7 persons, including the deputy, were convicted by the federal court.

head."[55] These blacks criticized King and his tactics. In place of the integration advocated by King, some leaders began to call for "black power." This phrase meant different things to different people. To some it meant political power through the ballot box; to others, economic power through boycotts of segregated businesses or ownership of their own businesses. At least it implied black pride and self-reliance. And in place of the nonviolence practiced by King, some leaders began to urge violence in retaliation for the violence of whites. The movement splintered further.

THE MOVEMENT IN CONGRESS

As the civil rights movement expanded, it pressured presidents and members of Congress to act. Presidents Kennedy and Johnson supported civil rights but felt hamstrung by southerners in Congress who, through the seniority system, had risen to chair key committees and dominate both houses. As a result, the presidents considered civil rights leaders unreasonable and the movement a nuisance that alienated the southerners upon whom the presidents had to rely. But once the movement demonstrated its strength, it was able to prod officials to act. After 200,000 blacks and whites marched in Washington in 1963, President Kennedy introduced civil rights legislation, and President Johnson, with his consummate legislative skills, forged a coalition of northern Democrats and northern Republicans to overcome southern Democrats and pass the Civil Rights Act of 1964. After 1,000 blacks and whites had been arrested and many had been attacked in Selma, the public outcry led Johnson to introduce and Congress to pass the Voting Rights Act of 1965.

Within a span of four years, Congress passed legislation prohibiting discrimination in public accommodations, employment, housing, and voting.

DESEGREGATION OF PUBLIC ACCOMMODATIONS The Civil Rights Act of 1964 prohibits discrimination on the basis of race, color, religion, or national origin in public accommodations. This time, unlike after the Civil War, the Court unanimously upheld the act.[56]

The act does not cover private clubs, such as country clubs, social clubs, or fraternities and sororities, on the principle that the government should not tell people with whom they must associate in private. (The Court has made private schools an exception to this principle to help enforce *Brown*.)

DESEGREGATION OF EMPLOYMENT The Civil Rights Act of 1964 also prohibits employment discrimination on the basis of race, color, religion, national origin, or sex and (as amended) physical handicap, age, or Vietnam-era veteran status. The act covers employers with 15 or more employees and unions.[57]

In addition to practicing blatant discrimination, some employers practiced more subtle discrimination. They required applicants to meet standards unnecessary for their jobs, a practice that hindered blacks more than whites. A high school degree for a manual job was a common example. The Court held that standards must relate to the jobs.[58] However, standards that hindered blacks more than whites are not necessarily unlawful. Washington, D.C., required applicants for police officer to pass an exam. Although a higher percentage of blacks failed to pass, the Court said the exam related to the job.[59]

The Court has allowed employers to reduce their workforce by laying off workers with less seniority, even if these workers are disproportionately black.[60] The principle of "last hired, first fired" thwarts desegregation of employment when an employer hires more blacks to compensate for past discrimination but then lays off the newer workers when the economy slows.

© 1963 Charles Moore/Black Star

Civil rights demonstrators were pounded by fire hoses in some southern cities.

DESEGREGATION OF HOUSING Although the Supreme Court had struck down laws that prescribed segregation in residential areas, whites maintained segregation by making **restrictive covenants**—agreements among neighbors not to sell their houses to blacks. In 1948, the Court ruled that courts could not enforce these covenants because doing so would involve the government in discrimination.[61]

Realtors also played a role in segregation by practicing **steering**—showing blacks houses in black neighborhoods and whites houses in white neighborhoods. Unscrupulous realtors practiced **blockbusting.** After a black family bought a house in a white neighborhood, realtors would warn white families that more blacks would move in. Because of prejudice and fear that their houses' values would decline, whites would panic and sell to the realtors at low prices. Then the realtors would resell to blacks at higher prices. In this way neighborhoods that might have been desegregated were instead resegregated—from all white to all black.

Banks and savings and loans also played a role. They were reluctant to lend money to blacks who wanted to buy a house in a white neighborhood. Some engaged in **redlining**—refusing to lend money to those who wanted to buy a house in a racially changing neighborhood. The lenders worried that if the buyer could not keep up with the payments, the lender would be left with a house whose value had declined.

The government also played an important role. The Veterans Administration and the Federal Housing Authority, which guaranteed loans to some buyers, were reluctant to authorize loans to blacks who sought to buy a house in a white neighborhood. And the federal government, which funded low-income housing, allowed local governments to locate such housing in ghettos. In these ways the governments helped perpetuate segregation.[62]

But the **Civil Rights Act of 1968** bans discrimination in the sale or rental of housing on the basis of race, color, religion, national origin, and (as amended) on the basis of sex, having children, or being disabled. The act covers about 80% of the available housing and prohibits steering, blockbusting, and redlining.

RESTORATION OF THE RIGHT TO VOTE After years of skirmishing with the states, the Supreme Court and Congress barred measures designed to keep blacks from voting. The Voting Rights Act of 1965 permitted large numbers of blacks to vote for the first time (as explained in Chapter 7).

Continuing Discrimination against African Americans

African Americans have overcome much discrimination but still face continuing discrimination. Overt laws and blatant practices have been struck down, but subtle manifestations of old attitudes and habits persist—and in ways far more numerous and with effects far more serious than this one chapter can convey.[63] Moreover, African Americans must cope with the legacy of generations of slavery, segregation, and discrimination and, for many of them, the effects of generations of poverty. And they must cope with the attitudes of whites. Although few people say they want to return to the days of legal segregation, about half reject the dream of an integrated society.[64]

DISCRIMINATION IN EDUCATION

For blacks who can afford it, there has been a great deal of desegregation in education. Affluent parents who can pay for private schools or live in expensive neighborhoods with good public schools can send their children to integrated schools. However, for most blacks in big cities, medium cities, or areas where private schools predominate, there has been much less desegregation.

Although de jure segregation of schools has been eliminated, de facto segregation remains. In fact, this segregation is getting worse. After progress in the mid-1960s and 1970s, the trend toward desegregation slowed and then reversed itself in the 1980s. "For the first time since the *Brown v. Board* decision," according to one study, "we are going backwards."[65] (See Table 2.)

TABLE 2

School Segregation of Blacks Is Greatest in the North

The following states have the largest percentages of black students attending schools with 50% or more minority enrollment.

Illinois	89%
New York	86
Michigan	85
New Jersey	80
California	79
Maryland	76
Wisconsin	75
Texas	68
Pennsylvania	68
Connecticut	66

SOURCE: Gary Orfield and Franklin Montfort, "Status of School Desegregation: The Next Generation," a report to the National School Boards Association, reprinted in Karen De Witt, "The Nation's Schools Learn a 4th R: Resegregation," *New York Times*, January 19, 1992, p. E5.

The reversal is caused by massive residential segregation that is exacerbated by the flight of whites to the suburbs and the movement of whites to private schools. In our 47 largest cities, only one of four students in public schools is white. In Detroit, for example, the number of whites in public schools fell from 98,000 in 1970 to 14,000 in 1993; in Atlanta, from 50,000 in the 1960s to 4,000 in 1993.[66] To a lesser extent, the reversal is due to the Burger and Rehnquist Courts' decisions to restrict busing and financing for desegregation efforts and to the Reagan and Bush administrations' policies not to enforce desegregation orders. School districts got the message that school desegregation was no longer an important national goal.[67]

As a result, in much of the South, where segregation was de jure, desegregation has been substantial. But in the big cities of the South and in most of the North, where housing segregation is highest and thus school segregation is de facto, desegregation has been minimal. In fact, blacks in the Northeast and Midwest are more likely to attend predominantly minority schools than blacks in the South are.[68]

The persistence of de facto segregation and the waning of commitment to integration have led national, state, and local officials to adopt the attitude, "We still agree with the goal of school desegregation, but it's too hard, and we're tired of it, and we give up.[69]

Reforms proposed for urban schools rarely include desegregation. Officials speak of a ghetto school that is more "efficient" or one that gets more "input" from ghetto parents or offers more "choices" for ghetto children. But the existence of ghetto education as "a permanent American reality" appears to be accepted.[70]

A writer who visited many ghetto classrooms and talked with students, teachers, and administrators observed that Martin Luther King was treated as "an icon, but his vision of a nation in which black and white kids went to school together seemed to be effaced almost entirely. Dutiful references to 'The Dream' were often seen in school brochures and on wall posters in February, when 'Black History' was celebrated in the public schools, but the content of the dream was treated as a closed box that could not be opened without ruining the celebration."[71]

Indeed, many cities have a school named after King—a segregated school in a segregated neighborhood—"like a terrible joke on history," a 14-year-old, wise beyond her years, remarked.[72]

UNEQUAL FUNDING In areas where schools are segregated, the quality varies enormously—from "the golden to the godawful," in the words of a Missouri judge.[73] And, of course, minorities are more likely to be in the "godawful."

Schools are financed largely by property taxes paid by homeowners and businesses. Wealthy cities get more in property taxes than poor ones. In modern America, this means suburban school districts get more to spend per pupil than central city school districts. (And although many suburbs tax their residents at a lower rate than cities do, suburbs still bring in more revenue because their property is valued at a higher level. Thus, these suburbs ask their residents to sacrifice less but still provide their children with an education that costs more.)[74]

Thus, it is common for a city such as Detroit to spend $3,600 per pupil while a suburb spends $6,400 per pupil per year, or for Camden, New Jersey, to spend $3,500 per pupil while Princeton spends $7,700. In Illinois the range stretched from $2,100 per pupil to more than $10,000 per pupil in 1990.[75]

And spending per pupil figures do not take into account that the needs of poor children, after years of neglect and with scores of problems at home and in the neighborhood, are greater than the needs of other children. Schools for poor children would require *more* funding to provide their students an equal education.

So, many inner city schools are bleak institutions, reflecting disrepair and filth. A Camden school has a fire alarm system that has not worked in 20 years. An East St. Louis, Illinois, school has, a visitor discovered, a boys' bathroom in which "[f]our of the six toilets do not work. The toilet stalls, which are eaten away by red and brown corrosion, have no doors. The toilets have no seats. One has a rotted wooden stump. There are no paper towels and no soap. Near the door is a loop of wire with an empty toilet-paper roll." Yet the visitor was told, "This is the best school we have in East St. Louis." At another school in the city, sewage repeatedly backed up into the bathrooms and kitchen and flooded the gym and parking lot.[76]

Many inner city schools are overcrowded. Classes routinely are held in former coatrooms and closets. At one school two classes are held in converted coal bins while another is held in the current bathroom. Some cities in New Jersey literally ran out of classrooms and tried to rent space in vacant schools in the suburbs. But the cities were turned down because the suburbs did not want the mostly nonwhite children using the empty buildings.[77]

Many inner city schools do not have texts for all their students, texts that are at the appropriate grade levels, or texts that are up to date. A Chicago school has not had a library for 21 years. Some schools cannot afford to hire science, art, music, or physical education teachers. Almost all cannot afford to offer competitive salaries to hire good teachers in the subjects the schools do offer. A New York City principal says he is forced to take the "tenth-best" teachers. "I thank God they're still breathing."[78]

To save money, the Chicago school system relies on substitutes for a fourth of its teaching force. It cannot attract and hold enough substitutes, so on an average morning 5,700 students in 190 classrooms show up to find they have no teacher.[79]

A Chicago alderman, reflecting the prevailing middle-class view about local education, said, "Nobody in his right mind would send [his] kids to public school."[80]

Despite the pervasive pattern of unequal funding, cash alone would not solve all the problems. Cultural and economic factors in inner cities also restrict the quality of education available. But cash would help. According to one calculation, if New York City schools had been funded at the same level as the highest spending suburban schools on Long Island, a typical fourth grade class of 36 children would have had $200,000 more invested in their education in 1987. The difference would have been enough to divide the class in half, hire two excellent teachers, and provide the classrooms with computers, new texts, reference books, learning games, carpets, air conditioning, and new counselors to help the children cope with problems in their environment outside school.[81]

Some states have equalized funding, but moves to do so in other states have encountered fierce opposition. After the New Jersey Supreme Court in 1990 ordered the state to reduce disparities between districts, the Democratic governor and legislature increased some taxes and cut some spending in other areas. The governor also redirected a portion of state aid from suburban schools to inner city schools to comply with the order. Suburbanites were furious; the next year they elected veto-proof majorities of Republicans to both houses of the state legislature in an attempt to block the program, and in the next election they ousted the governor.

SECOND-GENERATION DISCRIMINATION Even where desegregation of schools has been achieved, segregation within schools exists. This "second-generation discrimination" isolates many minority students by placing them in separate programs or classes from white students. Black children are more likely to be put in "special education" classes for slow learners and

HOW MUCH IS WHITE SKIN WORTH?

"You will be visited tonight by an official you have never met. He begins by telling you he is extremely embarrassed. The organization he represents has made a mistake, something that hardly ever happens.

According to their records, he goes on, you were to have been born black—to another set of parents, far from where you were raised.

However, the rules being what they are, this error must be rectified, and as soon as possible. So at midnight tonight, you will become black. And this will mean not simply a darker skin, but the bodily and facial features associated with African ancestry. However, inside, you will be the person you always were. Your knowledge and ideas will remain intact. But outwardly you will not be recognizable to anyone you now know.

Your visitor emphasizes that being born to the wrong parents was in no way your fault. Consequently, his organization is prepared to offer you some reasonable recompense. Would you, he asks, care to name a sum of money you might consider appropriate? He adds that his group is by no means poor. It can be quite generous when the circumstances warrant, as they seem to in your case. He finishes by saying that their records show you are scheduled to live another 50 years—as a black man or woman in America.

How much financial recompense would you request?

A professor who puts this parable to white college students finds that most feel $1 million per year—$50 million total—would be appropriate. This much would protect them from, and reimburse them for, the danger and discrimination they would face if they were perceived as black. In acknowledging that white skin is worth this much, the students also are admitting that treatment of the races, even today, is not nearly equal.

SOURCE: Andrew Hacker, *Two Nations: Black and White, Separate, Hostile, Unequal* (New York: Charles Scribner's Sons, 1992), pp. 31–32.

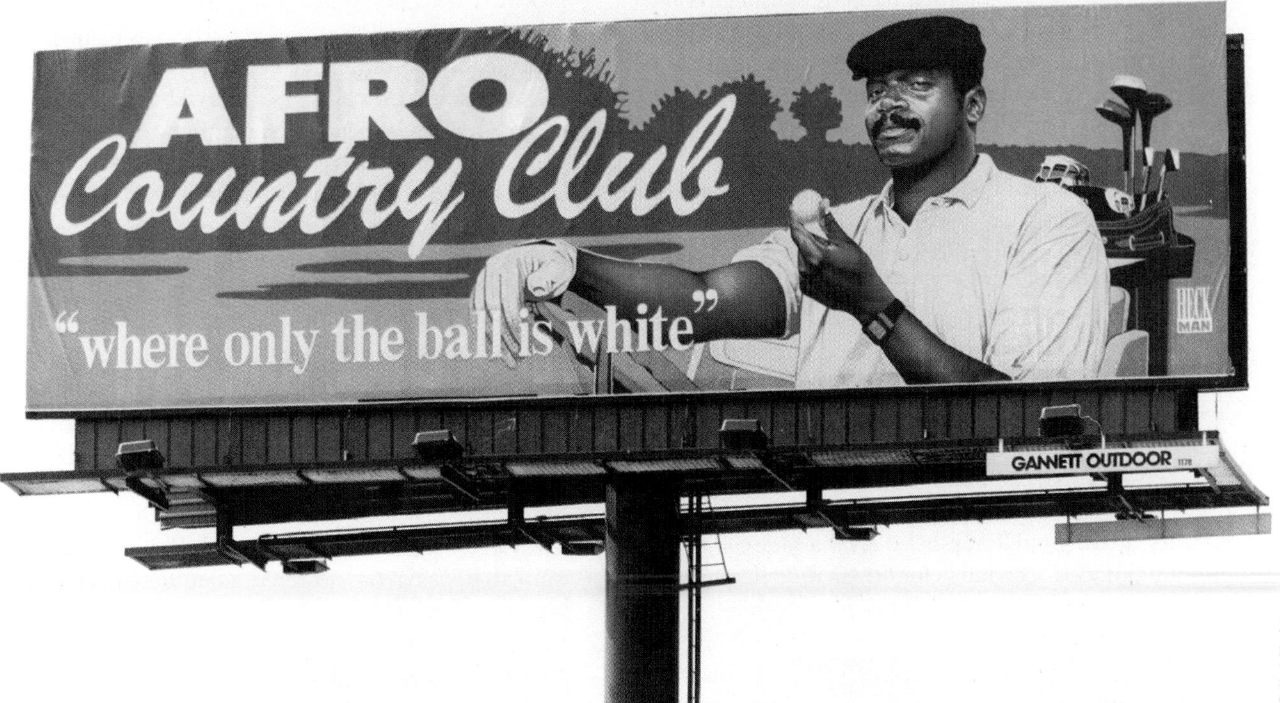

© Mark Heckman

A Grand Rapids artist put up this billboard to prompt white motorists to think about how they would feel if discrimination were directed at them instead. By the next day the word NIGER [sic] had been scrawled on the billboard, and the mayor had gotten so many complaints that the artist had to take the billboard down.

less likely to be put in programs for gifted students. They are more likely to be put in classes for the educable mentally retarded (EMR).[82]

These facts by themselves are not necessarily evidence of second-generation discrimination, because the long legacy of discrimination and the dismal living conditions of many blacks make it harder for them to succeed in school. However, in school districts where more minorities are school board members or are administrators or teachers, less disparate treatment occurs.[83] The presence of minorities in authoritative positions apparently sensitizes white administrators or teachers to this discrimination.

DISCRIMINATION IN PUBLIC ACCOMMODATIONS

Most businesses comply with the Civil Rights Act of 1964 prohibiting discrimination in public accommodations.[84]

However, Jim Crow still lives in some places. For example, numerous blue-collar bars and lounges in New Orleans operate as though the act is not on the books. One serves blacks through a side window while it allows whites to drink inside. Others keep separate rooms for blacks and whites. Others use separate entrances—blacks through a back or side door, whites through the front door. "I can go to the front door, now," a black patron says. "But no one is going to let me in. All I'll do is get my feelings hurt. If you want service, you go around to the back room—that's for blacks."[85] Although illegal, these practices persist if no one files a complaint or brings a lawsuit.

In recent years a Denny's restaurant in Maryland refused to serve a group of blacks—unbeknownst to the restaurant, Secret Service agents—and the Denny's chain in California faced a lawsuit for discriminating against blacks. The plaintiffs said Denny's refused to honor offers for free birthday meals, assessed them a $2 cover on top of the cost of their meals, and asked them to pay in advance for their meals.[86] An Avis franchise in North Carolina refused to rent cars to blacks.

Some businesses try to circumvent the act. For instance, some restaurants give blacks poor service so they will not return. A suburban mall refused to allow city buses from Buffalo in its parking lot, although it allowed Canadian buses to bring their shoppers from across the border. Mall executives assured shopkeepers that "you'll never see an inner-city bus on the mall premises."[87]

Even some businesses that try to comply with the act have employees who treat blacks differently and embarrassingly. As one writer notes, "You stroll into a shop to look at the merchandise, and it soon becomes clear that the clerks are keeping a watchful eye on you. Too quickly, one of them comes over to inquire what it is you might want, and then remains conspicuously close as you continue your search. It also seems that they take an unusually long time verifying your credit card. And then you and a black friend enter a restaurant, and find yourselves greeted warily, with what is obviously a more anxious reception than that given to white guests. Yes, you will be served, and your table will not necessarily be next to the kitchen. Still, you sense that they would rather you had chosen some other eating place."[88]

Because the Civil Rights Act does not apply to private clubs, many country clubs and golf clubs discriminate against blacks. One estimate is that three-fourths of these clubs have no black members, and many of the remainder have only one or a few token members.[89] Thus, the business, professional, and political elites who form the membership perpetuate inequality in their circles and also send a message that discrimination is acceptable for others in society.

DISCRIMINATION IN EMPLOYMENT

Although the Civil Rights Act of 1964 and affirmative action (discussed later in the chapter) have prompted more employers to hire and promote African Americans, discrimination remains.

A 1991 study of Chicago and Washington, D.C., used pairs of white and black male college students who were matched in education, experience, age, speech, demeanor, and physical build. The men applied for nearly 500 advertised jobs involving retail, service, clerical, or physical labor. The whites advanced farther in the hiring process 20% of the time, while the blacks did 7% of the time. (They were equal in the remainder.) The blacks found the most discrimination in white-collar jobs—one who had applied for a job as a hotel desk clerk was offered a job as a bellboy—and those requiring contact with customers.[90] These results not only reflect discrimination against blacks, but also contradict the perception that there is widespread reverse discrimination against whites.

A 1992 investigation by the Equal Employment Opportunity Commission (EEOC) uncovered discriminatory practices by employment agencies that hire workers for many companies. The agencies devised code phrases the companies could use to screen out applicants of a particular race or sex or age as a way to violate the law without being caught. If, for example, a business did not want any blacks, it was instructed to specify, "No Z." If it simply preferred whites, it was instructed to say, "Talk to Mary." Through these phrases, one Los Angeles agency alone discriminated against 3,900 applicants.[91]

Many blacks who are hired are passed over when they believe they should be promoted.[92] But discrimination at this point is more subtle and more difficult to prove. Black employees at Texaco filed suit but felt stymied until a white executive, who was being forced to retire early, disclosed secret tape recordings of a meeting at which top executives discussed the suit and admitted shredding documents and hiding others that had been subpoenaed by aggrieved employees. In the wake of the publicity, the company quickly settled the suit.

Many blacks are also subjected to racial slurs—in comments, notes, and graffiti—on the job. They face an unfriendly or hostile environment.

Upper-level executives realize that it is economically advantageous to have a diverse workforce, but some middle-level white managers, and lower-level white workers interact poorly with the black employees.

DISCRIMINATION IN HOUSING

The Civil Rights Act of 1968 prohibiting discrimination in housing has fostered some desegregation of housing, especially big apartment complexes, which are more visible and therefore more susceptible to pressure from civil rights groups and the government. And the act has resulted in large penalties on individuals found guilty of violations. Lawyers for fair-housing organizations say white jurors think discrimination has been eliminated—until they hear the testimony, which jars them into granting large awards. These awards prompt more lawyers to file more suits.[93]

But the act is working at a snail's pace to change housing patterns. One reason is economic. Most blacks do not have enough money to buy homes in white neighborhoods. This problem is aggravated by local zoning laws designed to establish a certain type of community. Often these laws require large lots and large houses, which command high prices.

Another reason is continuing discrimination. Occasional violence and considerable social pressure discourage blacks who try to move into white neighborhoods. Actual discrimination by homeowners, realtors, lenders, and insurers also stymies them. A study of 40 metropolitan areas found that blacks who try to buy a house face discrimination 75% of the time, and those who try to rent do so 62% of the time.[94]

Some realtors still practice steering. Many lenders apparently require extra proof that blacks will repay their home loans. A study by the Federal Reserve Board examined 5.3 million mortgage applications to 9,300 financial institutions in 19 major cities in 1990. It found that applications from blacks were denied more than twice as often as those from whites with comparable income. As a result, applications from high-income blacks were rejected about as often as those from low-income whites.[95] Some insurers evidently practice a version of redlining. A 1993 study of five large midwestern cities concluded that insurance companies charged blacks in inner cities twice the rate for homeowners' insurance that they charged whites with similar income.[96] Because lenders normally require borrowers to get homeowners' insurance to qualify for a home loan, higher-priced insurance makes it harder to buy the home.

For all of these reasons, residential segregation remains pervasive in metropolitan areas (see Table 3). However, segregation declined slightly in the 1980s. The percent of blacks living in nonblack neighborhoods, defined as areas with less than 10% blacks, inched from about 10% to 12%.[97] Still, Asians and Hispanics with third grade educations are more likely to live in integrated neighborhoods than blacks with Ph.D.s.[98]

Segregation does not continue because blacks "want to live by their own kind," as some whites insist. Surveys show that only about 15% want to live in segregated neighborhoods, while 85% would prefer mixed neighborhoods. (Many say the optimal level would be about half blacks and half whites.) Yet whites tend to move out, and new ones do not move in, when blacks reach 8–10%.[99] These very different views make integration an elusive goal, particularly because blacks make up 12–13% of the American population and a much larger percent of some cities.

These patterns and attitudes are all the more troublesome because residential segregation, of course, leads to further school segregation.

To add potential injury to the insult for blacks, a study of the Environmental Protection Agency's enforcement of air, water, and hazardous-waste pollution laws from 1985 to 1991 concluded that the government took longer to act in minority communities, imposed smaller fines against polluters in those communities, and required less stringent solutions in those communities.[100]

TABLE 3

Residential Segregation of Blacks Is Pervasive

The following major cities have the largest percentages of black residents who would have to change neighborhoods for the cities to have a desegregated residential pattern.

Gary	89%
Detroit	88
Chicago	86
Cleveland	85
New York	82
Philadelphia	77
Los Angeles	73
Birmingham	72
Miami	71
Boston	68
San Francisco	66
Washington	66
New Orleans	64
Dallas	63

SOURCES: Douglas Massey and Nancy Denton, *American Apartheid: Segregation and the Making of the Underclass* (Cambridge, Mass.: Harvard University Press, 1993), p. 222. Data from 1990 Census reported by Rodrick Harrison and Daniel Weinberg.

DISCRIMINATION IN OTHER WAYS

African Americans, especially males, experience discrimination from police officers. Sometimes officers stop black drivers without any evidence. Officers claim that blacks driving expensive cars might be stealing them and those driving other cars might be hauling drugs. On Interstate 95 in Maryland, for example, far more black drivers are stopped and far more searches of their cars are conducted, although there are many more white drivers.[101] African Americans speak of the moving violation "DWB"—Driving While Black. A Chicago journalist who was stopped at least every other time he traveled through the Midwest learned not to rent flashy Mustangs or wear his beret. Others avoid tinted windshields or expensive sunglasses—any flamboyance—to avoid the cops.[102]

Other discrimination from police officers is less common but more serious. Sometimes officers arrest black citizens without legal cause, and occasionally they use excessive force against them. Numerous examples attest to improper beatings.[103] Sometimes officers lie while testifying against black suspects in court. As a result, even prominent African Americans say their "worst fear is to have to go before the criminal justice system."[104] It is little wonder, then, that black jurors hearing the O. J. Simpson trial and black citizens following it put less faith in the police testimony than white observers did.

Most blacks, even those in the upper and middle classes and those in professional occupations, face insults because of their race. Black women tell of being mistaken for hotel chambermaids. One family therapist, invited to speak at a conference, was stopped in the hallway by a white attendee who asked where the restrooms were. When the therapist appeared taken aback, the attendee said she thought the woman worked at the hotel. Although the therapist was wearing her official name tag and presenter's ribbon, the attendee did not look past her black face.[105] Black women also tell of waiting for friends in hotel lobbies and being mistaken for prostitutes by white men and police officers. A distinguished black political scientist tells of people who assume he is a butler, in his own home. Black doctors tell of dressing up when they go shopping to avoid being regarded as shoplifters. But even dressing up is no guarantee. A black lawyer, a senior partner in a large law firm, arrived at work early one morning, before the doors were unlocked. As he reached for his key, a young white lawyer, a junior associate in the firm, arrived, blocked his entrance, and asked, repeatedly and demandingly, "May I help you?" The white associate had taken the black partner for an intruder.[106] Although in these encounters the insults were unintentional, the stings hurt just the same.

Overall, discrimination against African Americans continues. Whites speak of "past discrimination"—sometimes referring to slavery, sometimes to official segregation—but this phrase is misleading. True, there was more discrimination in earlier decades and there is a lot less discrimination now due to the civil rights movement and Supreme Court decisions and congressional acts. However, there is nothing "past" about much "past discrimination."[107] The effects linger and, indeed, the discrimination itself persists.

Even when blacks point out the discrimination, some whites insist there is little discrimination left. These whites apparently assume they know more than blacks do about what it is like to be black.

As African Americans have become frustrated with the slow pace of progress in the 1980s and 1990s, some have been attracted to the black separatist movement. These blacks, seeing themselves as realistic, consider integration a naive ideal from the 1950s and 1960s—an impossibility even in the future. They want to direct their energy toward building up the black community.[108] (Supreme Court Justice Clarence Thomas seems to hold this view.) But most blacks, remaining hopeful, consider separatism premature and risky; they fear it will play into the hands of the most prejudiced whites trying to perpetuate discrimination.

TABLE 4

Majority Dislike of Ethnic Minorities

People were asked whether they had "unfavorable" attitudes toward the principal minority in their country.

COUNTRY	MINORITY GROUP	PERCENT DISLIKING
East Germany	Poles	54
Czechoslovakia*	Hungarians	49
West Germany	Turks	45
Russia	Azerbaijanis	44
France	North Africans	42
Poland	Ukrainians	42
Ukraine	Azerbaijanis	42
Hungary	Romanians	40
Bulgaria	Turks	39
Lithuania	Poles	30
Spain	Catalans	22
Great Britain	Irish	21
United States	African Americans	13

*Now the Czech Republic and Slovakia.

SOURCE: Times Mirror Center for the People and the Press, *The Pulse of Europe: A Survey of Political and Social Values and Attitudes* (Washington, D.C.: Times Mirror Center, 1991), sec. VIII.

Improving Conditions for African Americans?

Despite continuing discrimination, African Americans have taken great strides toward achieving equal rights. These strides should have led to much better living conditions for them and to a healthier racial climate in society. If we look at the actual conditions and the actual climate today, we see that many African Americans are indeed better off, but others are no better off and some might be worse off than before the civil rights movement.

Since the 1960s, blacks' lives have improved in most ways that can be measured.[109] Blacks have a longer life expectancy and a lower poverty rate than before. They have completed more years of education, with larger numbers attending college and graduate school. They have attained higher occupational levels—for example, tripling their proportion of the country's professionals[110]—and income levels. (Yet their average income is only about half of whites' average income.) More have reached the middle class. About half of all blacks consider themselves middle class, and even more are classified as middle class or higher—fully 59% are "middle class" and another 11% are "affluent," according to one calculation.[111] A third have moved to the suburbs,[112] and many have bought their own homes.

The integration of African Americans into sports, music, and other forms of entertainment has been dramatic. In all these areas, they have become highly visible. In the mid-1980s, a Louisville sportswriter cracked that a Martian would sit in the White House before a black man would coach basketball at the University of Kentucky. But in 1998 the university hired a black man, Tubby Smith, who guided the team to a national championship in his first season.

During the same years that blacks' lives have improved, whites' racial attitudes have also improved. Although answers to pollsters' questions cannot be accepted as perfect reflections of people's views, especially on emotional matters such as racial attitudes, the answers can be considered general indicators of these views. Polls encompassing a wide variety of racial questions show that whites' views have changed significantly (even assuming that some whites gave

TABLE 5

Blacks and Whites Have Had More Social Contact since the 1960s

The percentages of respondents who say that members of the other race do the following:

	BLACKS	WHITES
Live in their neighborhood		
1964	66	20
1976	70	38
1994	83	61
Are friends of theirs		
1964	62	18
1976	87	50
1989	82	66
Are "good friends" of theirs		
1975	21	9
1994	78	73
Have been dinner guests in their home		
1973	39	20
1994	53	34
Attend their church		
1978	37	34
1994	61	44

SOURCE: Stephan Thernstrom and Abigail Thernstrom, *America in Black and White* (New York: Simon & Schuster, 1997), p. 521.

more socially acceptable answers than they really felt).[113] The percentage of whites who say they have an unfavorable view of blacks is significantly smaller than the percentage of the dominant group in several other countries who report disliking their principal minority group (see Table 4). Whites and blacks both report more social contact with members of the other race since the 1960s (see Table 5). And they both report more approval of interracial dating and marriage (see Table 6). The acceptance of interracial dating and marriage is especially significant, because these practices were the ultimate taboos in segregated society. Interracial couples represented the clearest breach and their potential offspring the greatest threat to continued segregation.

Some whites, of course, remain blatant racists (perhaps from 2% to 24%, according to various estimates by social scientists).[114] But blatant racist behavior occurs less frequently and is condemned more quickly than before.

Even so, blacks have pessimistic views of whites' attitudes. In 1989, one-fourth of blacks believed that at least a quarter of whites were in the Ku Klux Klan; one-fourth of blacks also believed that most whites shared the views of the KKK. In 1992, two-thirds of blacks believed that about half of whites were "basically prejudiced." (Whites also believed this about whites.)[115] One sociologist estimates that, despite the improvement in whites' attitudes, there are still two white racists for every African American. And, for socioeconomic reasons, blacks are more likely to come into contact with prejudiced whites, who live and work in closer proximity to blacks, than they are to come into contact with tolerant whites, who are more educated, prosperous, and suburban.[116] Further, some blacks have not experienced the overall improvements. It would be more surprising if they were not pessimistic.

When the push for civil rights opened doors, some blacks were not in a position to pass through. About a third of the black population lives in poverty—three times the rate among the white population—and about a tenth, the poorest of the poor, exists in a state of economic and social "disintegration."[117] This "underclass" is trapped in a cycle of self-perpetuating problems from which it is extremely difficult to escape. These people are isolated from the rest of society and demoralized about their prospects for improvement.

The problems of the lower class and underclass were exacerbated by economic changes that began in the 1970s and hit the poor the hardest. Good-paying manufacturing jobs in the cities—the traditional path out of poverty for immigrant groups—disappeared. Chicago lost over 300,000 jobs, New York over 500,000.[118] Many jobs were eliminated by automation, while many others were moved to foreign countries or to the suburbs. Although service jobs increased, most were outside the cities also. And most either required more education or paid lower wages than the manufacturing jobs had.

As a result, black men, especially, lost their jobs and lost their ability to support a family. This led not only to pressure on intact families but to a decrease in the number of "marriageable" black men and an increase in the number of households headed by black women.[119] The percentage of such households rose from about 20% in 1960 to nearly 50% in 1994.[120] And 60% of black children live in such households. These families are among the poorest in the country.

Meanwhile, the black middle class fled the inner cities to the suburbs. Their migration left the ghettos with fewer healthy businesses, strong schools, or other institutions to provide stability and fewer role models to portray mainstream behavior.[121] By 1996 one Chicago ghetto with 66,000 people had just one supermarket and one bank but 48 state-licensed lottery agents and 99 state-licensed liquor stores and bars.[122] The combination of chronic unemployment in the inner cities and middle-class migration from the inner cities created an

TABLE 6

Approval of Interracial Dating and Marriage Has Increased since the 1960s

The following percentages say it is all right for blacks and whites to date each other.

	BLACKS	WHITES
1963	NA	10
1987	72	43
1994	88	65
Ages 18–24	NA	85
Age 65 or over	NA	36

The following percentages say it is all right for blacks and whites to marry each other.

	BLACKS	WHITES
1958	NA	4
1968	48	17
1978	66	32
1983	76	38
1994	68	45

SOURCE: Stephan Thernstrom and Abigail Thernstrom, *America in Black and White* (New York: Simon & Schuster, 1997), pp. 524–525.

environment that offers ample opportunity and some incentive to use drugs, commit crimes, and engage in other types of antisocial behavior.

The development of crack, a cheap form of cocaine, in the mid-1980s aggravated these conditions. It led to more drug use and drug trafficking that overwhelmed whole neighborhoods. Crack ravaged the lives of users in ways that other drugs did not, and by producing steady demand by users and huge profits for dealers, it stimulated more violence. As drug gangs multiplied and tangled with each other for control of turf, drug executions and drive-by shootings became commonplace.[123]

The spread of AIDS, rampant among intravenous drug users, further aggravated these conditions.

Half of the victims of murder and more than half of those charged with murder are black, although the population is only 12% black.[124] Two-thirds of the defendants sent to state prisons for drug offenses are black. According to one study in Washington, D.C., one-fourth of black males born in the 1960s were charged with drug dealing between the ages of 18 and 24.[125]

The plight of young black men is worse than that of any other group in society. In 1990, almost one of every four black men between the ages of 20 and 29 was serving a criminal sentence in prison or was on probation or parole; by 1995 almost one of every three was.[126] And a black man in Harlem has less chance of living past 40 than a man in Bangladesh.[127]

After the riots in the 1960s, the Kerner Commission, appointed by President Johnson to examine the cause of the riots, concluded, "What white Americans have never fully understood—but what the Negro can never forget—is that white society is deeply implicated in the ghetto. White institutions created it, white institutions maintain it, and white society condones it." After the riots, however, governments did little to improve the conditions that precipitated the riots. Now the conditions in the ghettos are worse.

After the 1992 riots in Los Angeles that followed the trial of the police officers who beat Rodney King, there was more talk about improving conditions in the ghetto. But a columnist who had heard such talk before commented, "My guess is that when all is said and done, a great deal more will be said than done. The truth is we don't know any quick fixes for our urban ills and we lack the patience and resources for slow fixes."[128]

These problems are all the more difficult to resolve, because the cities have lost political power as they have lost population due to white flight and black migration. In 1992, for the first time, more voters lived in the suburbs than in the cities. These voters do not urge action on urban problems. Sometimes, in fact, they resist action if it means an increase in their taxes or a decrease in their services.

For the black lower class, and especially for the black underclass, it is apparent that civil rights are not enough. As one black leader said, "What good is a seat in the front of the bus if you don't have the money for the fare?"[129] But the lower class and underclass do not define all or most blacks, and the ghetto does not typify the environment of all or most blacks today.

Discrimination against Hispanics

Hispanics, also called Latinos, are people with Spanish-speaking backgrounds. The first Hispanics came to America from Spain in the 1500s. They settled in the Southwest, and when the United States took this land from Mexico in 1848, they became U.S. citizens. Other Hispanics came to America more recently.

Hispanics include groups with different cultural traditions. About 61% trace their ancestry to Mexico and live mainly in the Southwest, though some live in large cities in the Midwest. About 15% are from Puerto Rico, which is a commonwealth—a self-governing territory—of the United States. As members of the commonwealth, they are U.S. citizens. Most live in New York, Boston, Chicago, and other cities in the North. Another 6% are from Cuba. Following the establishment of a communist government in Cuba in

1959, many fled to the United States and settled in south Florida. In recent years, Hispanics from other Caribbean or Central American countries have immigrated to the United States to escape turmoil and oppression.

Despite the diversity of their origins, Latinos are heavily concentrated. More than half live in California and Texas.

Hispanics represent about 9% of the U.S. population. Already the United States has the seventh largest Hispanic population in the world, and within the United States this group is the second fastest growing minority (after Asians). Due to a high birthrate, they are predicted to equal blacks in 2020 even without the increased immigration that is likely.[130]

Hispanics never endured slavery, but they have suffered discrimination. Many Hispanics are Caucasian. However, many Puerto Ricans and Cubans have African ancestry, and many Mexicans have some Indian ancestry, so they have darker skin than non-Hispanic whites. Like blacks, Hispanics have faced discrimination in education, employment, housing, and voting.[131]

Hispanics also encounter discrimination due to continuing immigration. The illegal immigrants pouring in from Mexico exacerbate hostility and discrimination against Hispanics, especially in the Southwest. U.S. Border Patrol and local law enforcement officials, who cannot tell the difference between Hispanics who are citizens or legal residents and those who are not, often stop Hispanics for questioning not only at the border but inland as well. (Agents stopped the mayor of Pomona, California, more than 100 miles from the border, and ordered him to produce papers to prove that he is a legal resident.) Even if officials are well intentioned, their conduct is considered harassment by law-abiding legal residents.

DISCRIMINATION IN EDUCATION

For years Hispanic children in some areas were not allowed to attend schools at all. In other areas they were segregated into "Mexican" schools whose quality was not comparable with Anglo schools.[132]

In the 1940s, Mexican American organizations asked the courts to find that Mexican Americans were "white" so that they could not be segregated. The federal courts agreed. This strategy backfired, however, after the Supreme Court declared segregation by race illegal. Many school districts accomplished "integration" by combining blacks with Hispanics, leaving non-Hispanic whites in separate schools.[133]

Even when admitted to schools, Hispanics faced discrimination due to their language. Traditionally, teachers and administrators forbade students from speaking their native Spanish to each other in school. They reprimanded, spanked, or expelled those who did. Some even anglicized students' names in class and in school records so that "Jesus" became "Jesse" and "Miguel" became "Michael."[134]

Although de jure segregation has been struck down,[135] de facto segregation exists in northern and southwestern cities where Hispanics are concentrated, due to residential segregation and white flight to the suburbs. Many Hispanics attend schools with more than 90% minorities, and most attend schools with more than half minorities.[136] As a result, Latinos in Los Angeles, for example, are more likely to attend segregated schools than blacks in Alabama or Georgia.[137]

Predominantly Hispanic schools, like predominantly black schools, are not as well funded as other schools. Because minority schools are frequently in poor communities, they do not receive as much revenue from property taxes. In San Antonio, Hispanic families were concentrated in the poorest districts, while wealthy families were concentrated in a section that was incorporated as a separate district, though it was surrounded on four sides by the rest of the city. Its property taxes financed its schools only. When Hispanic parents sued, the Burger Court ruled that the Fourteenth Amendment's equal protection clause does not require states to equalize funding between school districts.[138] Although some states proceeded to equalize funding, other states have not.

Hispanics are gradually improving their status. This woman toils as a migrant farm worker, but her son graduated from college and now runs personnel management programs for farmers.

Even where Hispanics go to desegregated schools, they are often segregated within the schools. They face "second-generation discrimination," though not as much as blacks.[139] Some Hispanics also face a language barrier because of their inability to speak English. These children fail in school and drop out of school at higher rates than other students.[140]

Bilingual education was established to help such students. These classes use the students' native language to teach them English and also substantive subjects such as math. In 1968, Congress encouraged bilingual education by providing funding, and in 1974 the Supreme Court, in a case brought by Chinese parents, held that schools must teach students in a language they can understand.[141] This can be their native language, or it can be English if they have been taught English. These federal actions prompted many states to establish bilingual education programs.

More than 150 languages, from Chinese to Yapese, have been offered nationwide. Because almost three-fourths of the students who do not speak English are Hispanic, Spanish is the most common.[142]

Bilingual education programs have been controversial. Hispanic parents want their children to learn English, and to learn it well, as Chapter 2 explains. Whether these programs accomplish this goal is uncertain. The programs vary, being staffed at different levels and offered for different lengths of time, so research is difficult and conclusions tentative.

But the debate revolves around politics as much as education. Some Hispanic groups see bilingual education as a way to preserve their native language and culture. They consider it to be a component of multiculturalism. So they want it not as a temporary bridge until students learn English but as a permanent fixture through high school. Many Anglo citizens, especially those who fear the influx of immigrants, also see bilingual education as a way to preserve Hispanics' native language and culture. But these Anglos discount the need for multiculturalism. Instead, they want the students to be exposed only to English so that they will be more likely to assimilate into society. Some Hispanic leaders accuse these Anglo citizens of "cultural genocide."[143]

For both sides, then, bilingual education has become a symbolic issue. It prompts concerns, even fears, about the relative dominance of Anglo culture and Hispanic culture and about the extent to which Anglo Americans will make room for Hispanic Americans in society.

Economic and bureaucratic problems within bilingual programs have complicated the debate. The programs have been expensive because they require extra teachers and small classes. California officials estimated that the state had 21,000 fewer bilingual teachers than it needed in 1998.[144] As a result, only a third of the eligible students received bilingual instruction.[145] And the programs have been impractical for some languages in some places. "It's hard to find someone who can teach math in Korean," a Virginia educator explained.[146]

For all of these reasons, California citizens voted to abolish bilingual programs in 1998. Now non-English-speaking students will receive intensive immersion in English for one year and then will move into regular classes. Because half of all students in bilingual classes in the United States live in California, this change will affect bilingual education dramatically.

COMBATING DISCRIMINATION AGAINST HISPANICS

Hispanics have had some political success at the local level in places where they are heavily concentrated, but they have had less success at the national level. Except for Cesar Chávez, who led a coalition of labor, civil rights, and religious groups to obtain better working conditions for migrant farm workers in California in the 1960s, Hispanics have not had highly visible national leaders or organizations.

Hispanics are more diverse and less cohesive than blacks. Most do not even consider themselves part of a large group of Hispanics.[147] They profess strong loyalty to people of their national origin and have little contact with Hispanics with other ancestry. Thus, most do not call themselves "Hispanics" or "Latinos," but "Mexican Americans," "Puerto Ricans," or "Cuban Americans."[148] Also, they have different legal statuses. Puerto Ricans have American citizenship by birth, but many Hispanics do not have it at all. And they lack a common defining experience in their background, such as slavery for blacks, to unite them.

But they are moving up the ladder. More attend college and become managers and professionals. At least those who speak educated English appear to be following the pattern of Southern and Eastern European immigrants—arriving poor, facing discrimination, but eventually working their way up.

Discrimination against Native Americans

About one and a half million Native Americans live in the United States. Although some are Eskimos and Aleuts from Alaska, most are Indians, representing more than 500 tribes with different histories, customs, and languages. More than half live off reservations, mostly in urban areas.

Although Native Americans have faced some discrimination similar to that against blacks and Hispanics, they have endured much discrimination of a different nature.

GOVERNMENT POLICY TOWARD NATIVE AMERICANS

The government's policy toward Native Americans has varied over the years, ranging from forced separation at one extreme to forced assimilation at the other.

SEPARATION Initially, the policy was separation. For many years people believed the continent was so vast that most of its interior would remain wilderness, populated by Indians who would have ample room to live and hunt. The Constitution reflects this belief. It grants Congress authority to "regulate commerce with foreign nations, and among the several states, and with the Indian tribes." In early cases Chief Justice John Marshall described the tribes as "dependent domestic nations."[149] They were within U.S. borders but outside its political process.

Early treaties reinforced separation by establishing boundaries between Indians and non-Indians. The government thought these boundaries were necessary for its growth, the Indians for their survival. The boundaries were intended to minimize conflict. White hunters or settlers who ventured across the boundaries could be punished as the Indians saw fit.

But as the country grew, it became increasingly difficult to contain settlers within the boundaries. Mounting pressure to push Native Americans further west led to the Indian Removal Act of 1830, which authorized removal of tribes east of the Mississippi River and relocation on reservations west of the river. At the time people considered the Great Plains to be the great American desert, unfit for habitation by whites but suitable for Indians. At first, removal was voluntary, but eventually it became mandatory for most and was supervised by the U.S. cavalry.

ASSIMILATION AND CITIZENSHIP As more settlers moved west, the vision of separate Indian country far enough beyond white civilization to prevent conflict faded. In the 1880s, the government switched its policy to assimilation. Prompted by Christian churches, officials sought to "civilize" the Indians, that is, to incorporate them into the larger society, whether they wanted to be incorporated or not. In place of their traditional means of subsistence, rendered useless once the tribes were removed from their homeland, the government subdivided reservation land into small tracts and allotted these tracts to tribe members in hopes that they would turn to farming as white and black settlers had. (In the process, the government reclaimed "surplus" land and sold it to white settlers. Ultimately, the Indians lost about two-thirds of their reservation land.)[150] Bureau of Indian Affairs agents, who supervised the reservations, tried to root out Native American ways and replace them with white dress and hairstyles, the English language, and the Christian religion. Government boarding schools separated Native American children from their families to instill these new practices.

Early in the history of the United States, Native Americans were not considered citizens but members of separate nations. Treaties made exceptions for those who married whites and for those who left their tribes and abandoned their tribal customs. But in 1890, after government policy switched to assimilation, Congress permitted some who remained with their tribes on reservations to become citizens by applying to the U.S. government. Citizenship was sometimes marked by a formal ceremony. In one the Indian shot his last arrow and then took hold of the handles of a plow to demonstrate his assimilation.[151] After World War I, Congress granted citizenship to those who served in the military

Both courtesy of Smithsonian Institute

Tom Torlino, before and after his transformation at a boarding school in Carlisle, Pennsylvania. Native Americans were shorn of their hair and clothes and trained to adopt white ways.

Native Americans feel renewed cultural pride but also the lure of modern American technology.

during the war, and finally in 1924, Congress extended it to all those born in the United States.

Citizenship enabled Indians to vote and hold office, though some states effectively barred them from the polls for decades. Arizona denied them the right to vote until 1948, Utah until 1956.[152]

TRIBAL RESTORATION By the 1930s, the government recognized the negative consequences of coerced assimilation. Most Indians could speak English, but they were poorly educated in other respects. And with their traditional means of earning a living gone, most were poverty stricken. The policy led to destruction of Native American ways without much assimilation into white society. Consequently, in 1934 Congress implemented a new policy of tribal restoration that recognized Indians as distinct persons and tribes as autonomous entities that were encouraged to govern themselves once again. Traditional cultural and religious practices were accepted, and children, no longer forced to attend boarding schools, were taught some Indian languages.

The government even made an effort to settle claims for wrongful taking of tribal land. For several decades the Indian Claims Commission authorized the payment of money—not the return of property—to tribes whose land was illegally taken by the government anytime since 1776. But the commission faced an impossible task. Most tribes had a hazy conception of land ownership and did not keep written records. And how would disputed land be valued—according to the earlier subsistence living of the Indians or the later market value to farmers, ranchers, and miners? And how would religious land be valued? (Native religions focused on particular parcels of land or prominent features of the landscape, rather than on buildings such as churches.) Ultimately, the commission authorized as much money as it thought was politically feasible, but this amounted to less than $1,000 for every Native American.[153]

Reflecting the policy of tribal restoration and the efforts of other minorities in the 1960s and 1970s, Indian interest groups became active. Indian law firms pursued cases in court, seeking to protect not only tribal independence and traditional ways, but also land, mineral, and water resources. The diversity of the tribes—they are divided by geography and culture and located in many of the remotest and poorest parts of the country—makes it difficult for them to present a united front. Nevertheless, they have been able to wrest some autonomy from the government. In particular, they have gotten more authority over the educational and social programs administered by the Bureau of Indian Affairs for the tribes.[154]

In recent years Indians have fought for an end to digging up old gravesites and for a return of bones and artifacts unearthed from them. With little regard for Native American culture, "pothunters" have searched for artifacts to sell to collectors. Such looting raises the ire of archaeologists who say, "We'll never know what's been taken or how it relates to what remains in the ground. Everything has been scrambled." But digging for scientific purposes itself enrages some Indians, who say that archaeologists are "hardly any better than grave robbers themselves; only difference is they've got a state permit." Until recent years, in fact, many laws about exhumation of bones applied only to those of whites.[155]

Some tribes are enjoying renewed vitality with the income they receive from mineral rights or gambling casinos. After a Supreme Court ruling and a congressional law in the 1980s underscored tribal sovereignty on tribal land, tribes could establish gambling casinos on reservations, even if their state did not allow casinos.[156] Almost 300 tribes (of the 555 tribes recognized by the government) have done so, although less than a dozen have found a bonanza.[157] Even so, they have heard complaints about "rich Indians" (a very unlikely, and inaccurate, description of most Indians). With their new revenues, the tribes have begun to buy into the political process, as other groups have done. Threatened by gambling interests in Las Vegas and Atlantic City, which fear that tribal casinos will lure away potential customers, the tribes have formed their own lobby, the National Indian Gaming Association, and made their own contributions to politicians.

Overall, Native Americans enjoy renewed pride. From 1970 to 1990, according to birth and death records, the Indian population increased by 760,000. Yet, according to people's self-identification for the census, this population rose by 1.4 million.[158] Evidently, many people, including those with only distant Indian ancestry, who did not wish to identify themselves as Indians in 1970, did by 1990.

Now more Indians share the views of one activist who says, "You have a federal government, state governments, and tribal governments—three sovereigns in one country. This is . . . the civil rights movement of Native Americans."[159]

SEX DISCRIMINATION

Discrimination against Women

For many generations, people believed that natural differences between the sexes required them to occupy separate spheres of life. Men would dominate the public domain of work and government, while women would dominate the private domain of the home. Both domains were important, and men were considered superior in one while women were considered superior in the other. Unlike racial minorities, women were not held in disdain in every aspect of life.

Thomas Jefferson, the most egalitarian of the Founders, reflected this widespread view when he said, "Were our state a pure democracy there would still be excluded from our deliberations women, who, to prevent deprivation of morals and ambiguity of issues, should not mix promiscuously in gatherings of men."[160] That is, women are more moral than men, so they would be corrupted by politics, but also more irrational, so they would confuse the issues. For both reasons, they should not be involved in politics.

Women were denied the right to vote in most places, and married women were denied other rights. They did not have the right to manage property they owned before marriage, to manage wages they received from jobs, to enter into contracts, or to sue. Although some states eventually enacted laws granting women these rights, when disputes arose within families, male judges hesitated to tell other men how to treat their wives. Often, then, these rights did not exist in practice until well into the twentieth century.

Women were also barred from schools and jobs. Before the Civil War, they were not admitted to public high schools. Because they were being prepared for motherhood, education was considered unnecessary, even dangerous. According to the *Encyclopaedia Britannica* in 1800, women had smaller brains than men.[161] Education would fatigue them and possibly ruin their reproductive organs. Similarly, before the Civil War, women were not encouraged to hold jobs. Those who sought employment were shunted into jobs that were seen as extensions of the domestic domain, such as producing textiles, clothes, and shoes in sex-segregated factories.[162]

This traditional conception of gender roles created problems for women who did not fit the mold. Myra Bradwell ran a private school, founded a weekly newspaper, and worked for civic organizations. She was active in the women's suffrage movement and instrumental in persuading the Illinois legislature to expand women's legal rights. But after studying law, she was denied a license to practice law solely because she was a woman. In 1873, the U.S. Supreme Court upheld the Illinois policy.[163] Justice Joseph Bradley declared:

[L]aw as well as nature itself, has always recognized a wide difference in the respective spheres and destinies of

"Kemo sabe, I want you to be official greeter at my new casino."

man and woman. Man is, or should be the woman's protector and defender. The natural and proper timidity and delicacy which belongs to the female sex evidently unfits it for many of the occupations of civil life. . . . The constitution of the family organization . . . indicates the domestic sphere as that which properly belongs to the domain and functions of womanhood. The harmony . . . of interests and views which belong, or should belong, to the family institution is repugnant to the idea of a woman adopting a distinct and independent career from that of her husband. . . . The paramount destiny and mission of woman are to fulfill the noble and benign offices of wife and mother. This is the law of the Creator. And the rules of civil society must be adapted to the general constitution of things, and cannot be based upon exceptional cases.

Sometimes it was difficult to distinguish between this separate-but-equal view and discriminatory treatment. In the 1860s and 1870s, the doctors who practiced scientific medicine formed the American Medical Association (AMA) to drive out other people who offered medical services. These people included not only hucksters and quacks, but also women who served as midwives or abortionists. Although abortions had been widely available, the AMA, drawing upon popular fears about the women's suffrage movement, convinced male state legislators that abortions were "a threat to social order and to male authority." The woman who seeks an abortion, the AMA explained, "becomes unmindful of the course marked out for her by Providence, she overlooks the duties imposed on her by the marriage contract. She yields to the pleasure—but shrinks from the pains and responsibilities of maternity. . . . Let not the husband of such a wife flatter himself that he possesses her affection."[164]

Sometimes the discriminatory treatment was even more blatant. The Mississippi Supreme Court acknowledged a husband's right to beat his wife.[165] According to the "rule of thumb," a husband could not beat his wife with a weapon thicker than his thumb.

THE WOMEN'S MOVEMENT

Early feminists were determined to remedy these inequities. Many had gained political and organizational experience in the abolitionist movement. It was not considered "unladylike" for women to campaign for the end of slavery, because the movement was associated with religious groups. Yet women were barely tolerated by the male leaders of the movement and not allowed to participate fully in the major antislavery society. They formed their own antislavery society, but when they attended a convention of antislavery societies, they were not allowed to sit with the male delegates.

Angry at such treatment, the women held a meeting to discuss the "social, civil and religious rights of women." This first Women's Rights Convention in 1848 adopted a declaration of rights based on the Declaration of Independence. It said, "We hold these truths to be self-evident: that all men and women are created equal." The convention also passed a resolution in favor of women's suffrage.

Following the Civil War, women who had worked in the abolitionist movement expected that women, as well as blacks, would get legal rights and voting rights. When the Fourteenth and Fifteenth Amendments did not include women, they felt betrayed and disassociated themselves from the black movement. They formed their own organizations to campaign for women's suffrage. This movement, led by Susan B. Anthony and Elizabeth Cady Stanton, succeeded in 1920, when the Nineteenth Amendment gave women the right to vote.

Then dissension developed within the women's movement. Many groups felt the passage of the Nineteenth Amendment was but a first step in the struggle for equal rights. They proposed the Equal Rights Amendment to remedy remaining inequities. Other groups felt the battle had been won. They opposed the Equal Rights Amendment, arguing that it would overturn labor laws recently enacted to protect women. Because of this dissension and the conservatism in the country, the movement became relatively dormant.[166]

The movement reemerged in the 1960s. As a result of the civil rights movement, many women recognized their own inferior status. Numerous writers sensitized more women to this. A group of middle-class, professional women formed the National Organization for Women (NOW) in 1966 and installed Betty Friedan as its first president. They resolved "to bring women into full participation in the mainstream of American society now."

Other women, also middle class but veterans of the civil rights and antiwar movements, had developed a taste for political action and gained political experience. They formed other organizations. Where NOW fought primarily for women's political and economic rights, the other organizations fought more broadly for women's liberation in all spheres of life. Together these organizations pushed the issue of discrimination against women back onto the public agenda.

Nevertheless, they were not taken seriously for some years. In 1970, *Time* magazine reported, "No one knows how many shirts lay wrinkling in laundry baskets last week as thousands of women across the country turned out for the first big demonstration of the women's liberation movement. They took over [New York City's Fifth Avenue], providing not only protest but some of the best sidewalk ogling in years."[167]

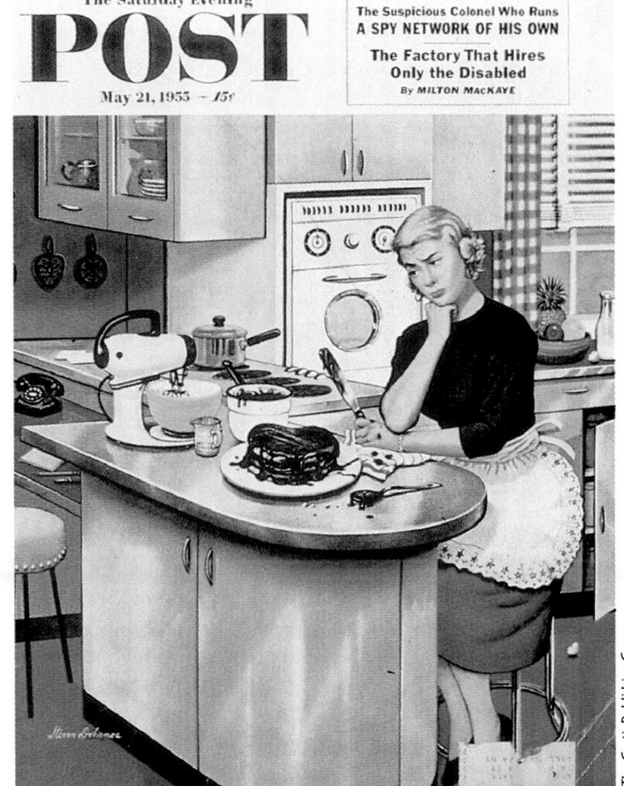

During World War II, women were urged into the labor force to replace men called to war. "Rosie the Riveter" became a symbol of women working in the war effort. Following the war, they were told that it was patriotic to go home and give their jobs to returning veterans. The 1955 magazine cover on the right depicts the stereotypical women's role in this postwar era before the beginning of the modern women's movement.

THE MOVEMENT IN CONGRESS AND THE COURTS

Congress initially did not take the modern women's movement seriously either. When civil rights proponents sponsored a bill to forbid racial discrimination in employment, 81-year-old Representative Howard Smith (D-Va.) proposed an amendment to add sex discrimination to the bill. A foe of equal rights for blacks, Smith thought his proposal so ludicrous and radical that it would help defeat the entire bill. Indeed, during debate on the amendment, members of Congress laughed so hard that they could barely hear each other speak.[168] But the joke was on them, because the amendment, and then the entire bill, passed.

Congress later adopted legislation to forbid sex discrimination in credit and education. Congress also passed the Equal Rights Amendment.

The **Equal Rights Amendment (ERA)** simply declared, "Equality of rights under the law shall not be denied or abridged by the United States or by any state on account of sex." Introduced in 1923 and every year thereafter, the amendment was passed by Congress in 1972.

It appeared the amendment would zip through the states. Both parties endorsed it, and the majority of the public supported it. But after about half the states ratified it, the amendment bogged down. Observers noted that it would make women subject to the draft and, possibly, combat duty. Opponents charged that it would result in unisex restrooms and homosexual rights. Legal scholars denied that it would lead to these latter consequences, but after the judicial activism of the 1950s, 1960s, and 1970s, some people distrusted the courts to interpret the amendment.

The main problem, however, proved to be the symbolism of the amendment. For many women the ERA represented an attack on the traditional values of motherhood, the family, and the home. Early feminists emphasized equality in employment so much that they gave some women the impression that they were against these values. Traditional women sensed implicit criticism for being housewives.[169] To underscore the symbolism, women in anti-ERA groups baked bread for state legislators about to vote on ratification. Because of the symbolism, even some women who favored equality opposed the amendment itself. Although many young women supported it, fewer of their mothers and grandmothers did; and although many working women supported it, fewer housewives did.

SEXUAL HARASSMENT AT WORK

Although the Supreme Court had ruled that sexual harassment was a form of job discrimination prohibited by the Civil Rights Act of 1964,[1] and Congress had passed a law allowing victims to collect monetary damages from employers for distress, illness, or loss of their job due to harassment, there was little public awareness of the law until Clarence Thomas's confirmation hearings for appointment to the Supreme Court in 1991.

The hearings propelled sexual harassment to the forefront of societal debate. For seven days the public was riveted to the televised hearings. Anita Hill's charges—that Thomas, as her supervisor at the Equal Employment Opportunity Commission, made lewd comments about her, about sex, about finding pubic hairs on Coke cans and watching animals have sex in films—led to many discussions around workplace water coolers.

After the hearings, more women recognized that behavior they had dismissed as merely annoying was actually harassment. The number of complaints filed with the EEOC doubled (though in recent years it has leveled off).

Courts recognize two types of sexual harassment. The most obvious is quid pro quo, in which a supervisor makes unwanted sexual advances and either promises good consequences (for example, a promotion) if the employee goes along or threatens bad consequences (for example, an undesirable reassignment) if the employee refuses. Less obvious is creating a hostile environment that interferes with the employee's ability to do the job. To prove a hostile environment, the employee must demonstrate that the conduct was severe or persistent.

Paula Jones's suit against President Clinton was dismissed because the alleged sexual advance was considered neither severe enough nor, as a single incident, persistent enough to constitute a hostile environment. If it happened, the judge said, it was "boorish and offensive" but not technically harassment.

Although many men seem to worry that innocuous comments will be classified as sexual harassment, Justice Antonin Scalia emphasized that the law did not create "a general civility code."[2]

Yet there is considerable confusion, because the law is relatively recent and different courts have issued varying interpretations. In addition, employers, who can be held responsible for sexual harassment by their employees (even if the employers are unaware of the harassment), can defend themselves by having policies to prevent such conduct.[3] Some have adopted "zero tolerance" policies to insulate them from employee lawsuits. These policies are stricter than the law, and they have led to the firing of a few men who would not have been convicted under the law.

Consultants who advise employers have observed that women in traditional female jobs, such as secretary, are more likely to be subjected to quid pro quo harassment from supervisors, whereas women in traditional male jobs, especially blue-collar jobs, are more likely to be subjected to hostile environment harassment from co-workers. Hundreds of women in the Mitsubishi auto plant in Normal, Illinois, experienced incidents ranging from finding plastic penises in tool buckets to being asked their sexual habits and preferences, being called "bitches," "sluts," and "whores," rather than their names, and being grabbed by their breasts, buttocks, and genitals. Some women had their

Women's organizations had not created an effective grassroots campaign to sway traditional women. Ultimately, the disaffection of many women allowed male legislators to vote according to their traditional attitudes. They did not need to worry that a strong majority of their female constituents would object.[170]

In 1980, the Republican Party became the first party not to endorse the ERA since 1940, and President Reagan became the first president not to support the amendment since Truman.

When the deadline set by Congress expired in 1982, the ERA fell three states short of ratification by the necessary three-fourths—38—of the states. Like the Nineteenth Amendment, it was not ratified primarily by southern states.

Courts traditionally upheld laws that limited women's participation in the public domain and occasionally even laws that diminished their standing in the private domain. As late as 1970, the Ohio Supreme Court held that a wife is a husband's servant with "no legally recognized feelings or rights."[171]

The Burger Court finally reversed this pattern of decisions. In 1971, for the first time, the Court struck down a law that discriminated against women,[172] heralding a long series of rulings that invalidated a variety of such laws. In these rulings the Court used the congressional statutes and also broadened the Fourteenth Amendment's equal protection clause to apply to women as well as to racial minorities.

The change was especially apparent in a pair of cases involving the selection of jurors. For the pool of potential jurors, some states drew the names of men, but not women, from voter registration or other lists. These states allowed women to serve only if they voluntarily signed up at the courthouse. Consequently, few women served. In 1961, the Court let Florida use these procedures because the "woman is still regarded as the center of home and family life."[173] In 1975, however, the Court forbade Louisiana from using similar procedures,[174] thus overturning a precedent only 14 years old.

The Court's rulings rejected the traditional stereotypes that men are the breadwinners and women work sabotaged to make their performance seem slow and shoddy.[4]

The dynamics of sexual harassment do not revolve around sex as much as they reflect abuse of power. A supervisor or co-worker makes a woman feel vulnerable and thus exercises psychological dominance over her.

Consultants have also observed that a very small percentage of men harass women but these men do it a lot. One consultant has found that perhaps 3 to 5 men out of 100 create problems but these men might affect 50 women in the same workplace. The harassers typically feel bitter toward women or threatened by them. Some have long been bullies toward men as well as women.[5]

Surveys show that a third of female workers say they have been sexually harassed on the job.[6] After 23 women acknowledged in 1992 and 1993 that they had to fend off sexual advances by Senator Bob Packwood (R.-Ore.), the *Washington Post* conducted a survey of women who worked as aides to members of Congress or staffers for congressional committees. It found the same results: A third of the women had been sexually harassed in the hallowed halls of Congress, and a third of these had been harassed by a member of Congress. (The others had been harassed by supervisors, co-workers, or lobbyists.)[7]

Yet few victims file formal complaints, let alone bring lawsuits, because they need their jobs. According to several studies, only 3% of women who have been harassed have filed formal complaints.[8] On Capitol Hill, 80% of the women surveyed said they would lose their job if they did; 80% said they would never find another job there if they did; and 70% said nothing would be done to the harasser anyway.[9]

Sexual harassment can be directed toward men as well.[10] About 15% of male workers say they have been sexually harassed by men or women on the job.[11]

Recently, a backlash has set in, apparently because of the legal confusion in the courts and zero tolerance policies of some employers. A majority—57% of men and 52% of women—say that "we have gone too far in making common interactions between employees into cases of sexual harassment."[12]

1. *Meritor Savings Bank v. Vinson*, 91 L.Ed.2d 49 (1986).
2. *Oncale v. Sundowner Offshore Services* (1998).
3. *Burlington Industries v. Ellerth* (1998).
4. Kirsten Downey Grimsley, Frank Swoboda, and Warren Brown, "Trouble on the Line," *Washington Post National Weekly Edition*, May 6–12, 1996, pp. 6–7.
5. Kirsten Downey Grimsley, "Confronting Hard-Core Harassers," *Washington Post National Weekly Edition*, January 27, 1997, p. 6.
6. Richard Morin, "Think Twice Before You Say Another Word," *Washington Post National Weekly Edition*, December 28, 1992–January 3, 1993, p. 37.
7. Richard Morin, "Jack and Jill Went Up the Hill," *Washington Post National Weekly Edition*, March 1–7, 1993, p. 37.
8. Daniel Goleman, "Sexual Harassment: About Power, Not Sex," *New York Times*, October 22, 1991, p. B8.
9. Morin, "Jack and Jill Went Up the Hill."
10. *Oncale v. Sundowner Offshore Services.*
11. Janice Castro, "Sexual Harassment: A Guide," *Time*, January 20, 1992, p. 37.
12. John Cloud, "Sex and the Law," *Time*, March 23, 1998, p. 49.

the childrearers in society. The Court invalidated Utah's law that required divorced fathers to support their daughters until age 18 but their sons until 21.[175] The state assumed that the daughters would get married and be supported by their husbands, whereas the sons would need to get educated for their careers. But the Court noted, "No longer is the female destined solely for the home."

EMPLOYMENT The Civil Rights Act of 1964 forbids discrimination on the basis of sex as well as race in hiring, promoting, and firing. It prohibits discrimination on the basis of sex, except where sex is a "bona fide occupational qualification" for the job. The Equal Employment Opportunity Commission (EEOC), which enforces the act, interprets it broadly and accepts sex as a legitimate qualification for very few jobs. For example, employers can seek a man or woman to be a restroom attendant, lingerie salesclerk, model, actor, or performer in the entertainment business where sex appeal is considered necessary. On the other hand, employers cannot seek a male for jobs men traditionally held, such as those that entail heavy physical labor, unpleasant working conditions, late-night hours, overtime, or travel.

Some employers are reluctant to comply. For matched pairs of men and women, résumés were sent to 65 Philadelphia restaurants in 1995. The men were more than twice as likely to get an interview and more than five times as likely to get the job at the higher-priced restaurants than the equally qualified women were.[176]

The **Equal Pay Act** of 1963 requires that women and men receive equal pay for equal work. The act makes exceptions for merit, productivity, and seniority. Yet working women earn only 76¢ for every $1.00 working men earn (although young women, from 16 through 24, earn more than 90¢ for every $1.00 young men earn).

Women make less partly because they have less education and experience than men in the same jobs; many stopped their schooling or working to marry and

"Some kids at school called you a feminist, Mom, but I punched them out."

have children. But they make less primarily because they have different jobs than men, and these jobs pay much less.

Traditionally, women have been shunted into a small number of jobs. These "pink-collar" jobs include secretaries (98% are women), household workers (97%), child care workers (97%), nurses (93%), bank tellers (90%), librarians (83%), elementary school teachers (83%), and health technicians (81%).[177] In contrast, few women are carpenters (1%), firefighters (2%), mechanics (4%), or truck drivers (5%).[178]

Although the Equal Pay Act mandates equal pay for essentially equal work, it does not require equal pay for comparable work—usually called **comparable worth.** According to a personnel study in Washington State, maintenance carpenters and secretaries performed comparable jobs, but the carpenters, mostly men, made about $600 a month more than the secretaries, mostly women. Overall, the study found that "men's jobs" paid about 20% more than comparable "women's jobs." These findings prompted unions representing government employees in the state to file a suit and demand an increase in pay for jobs held mostly by women. The federal court of appeals, in an opinion by Judge Anthony Kennedy, now on the Supreme Court, rejected comparable worth. Nevertheless, some state and city governments have begun to implement comparable worth plans for their employees after prodding by unions and women's groups. Most private companies, however, have not adopted comparable worth because it would require them to pay most of their women employees more.

Although formal barriers against women have been lifted, informal ones remain. Many women get hired, but some women do not get promoted as fast or as high as comparable men. They hit a "glass ceiling."

Many women in masculine workplaces feel pressure to submerge feminist beliefs. "You're not a feminist, are you?" is a familiar query. Women who seek career advancement say they would commit "professional suicide" if they spoke up for their rights or beliefs as women.[179]

Some women also face sexual harassment. "In college, they lied to us twice," one disillusioned young woman said. "They said it would be equal. And they said it would be safe."[180]

Mothers with young children confront more obstacles. Their male employers and co-workers think women should be responsible for child rearing, but these men do little to accommodate the demands of child rearing. Most companies do not provide paid maternity leaves, flexible schedules, or on-site day care. The United States lags far behind many other countries, 98 of which grant partly paid maternity leaves for at least three months.[181]

When Congress passed a bill requiring employers to grant unpaid maternity and paternity leaves, President Bush vetoed it, but then President Clinton signed a similar bill. Companies must allow unpaid leaves for up to three months for workers with newborn or recently adopted children or with seriously ill family members. The act applies to companies that have 50 employees and to workers who work 25 hours a week for a year.[182] This covers about half of American workers.

So far, however, relatively few workers have taken advantage of family leaves or flexible schedules where they are available. Most workers cannot afford to take unpaid leave. Moreover, managers often do not support such measures, and co-workers resent the additional burdens, so employees are reluctant to take advantage of them. At a time when many companies have laid off workers to cut costs, "If you look like you are not career-oriented, you can lose your job."[183]

Mothers and fathers with young children often face unreasonable time demands from employers accustomed to hiring married men who have a wife at home to rear the children, maintain the house, and run the errands. Now employers are putting the same demands on married women. Nobody is left to do the jobs of the housewife. Although women often continue to perform most of them, both spouses frequently feel stretched thin and stressed out.

Not surprisingly, among men with children, those who have a wife at home rise up the career ladder faster than those who have a wife working outside the home. (The latter men apparently put in less "face time" at work.) And executives who reach the higher rungs "almost always" are men who have a wife at home.[184] An executive of a Fortune 500 company, in a conversation with business professors at a southwestern university in a recent year, admitted that his company still prefers to hire men married to women who remain at home.[185]

Thus, women have gained some acceptance in the workplace, but they, and their spouses, have not yet overcome the expectations that developed long before they were ever allowed in the workplace.

CREDIT The Equal Credit Opportunity Act of 1974 forbids discrimination on the basis of sex or marital status in credit transactions. Historically, banks, savings and loans, credit card companies, and retail stores discriminated against women. Typically, these businesses determine how much money people can borrow according to how much they earn. Yet the lenders refused loans to single women, regardless of income, because they assumed that the women would work only until they got married and became pregnant. Likewise, the lenders did not count a wife's income as part of a couple's total income, again because they assumed the wife would work temporarily. Only if women were professionals or in their 40s would lenders count their income the same as men's. And when businesses lent money to a married couple, they put the transactions in just the husband's name. Upon divorce or widowhood, women had no credit record and little chance to obtain credit.

The Equal Credit Opportunity Act requires lenders to lend to single women and to count the wife's income as part of a couple's total income. It restricts lenders from asking women if they intend to bear children. And the act requires lenders to put accounts in the names of both spouses if they request.

EDUCATION The Education Amendments of 1972 (to the Civil Rights Act of 1964) forbid discrimination on the basis of sex in schools and colleges that receive federal aid. The amendments were prompted by discrimination against women by undergraduate and graduate colleges, especially in admissions and financial aid.

The language of the amendments, often referred to as "Title IX," is so broad that the Department of Education, which administers them, has established rules that cover more aspects of education than their congressional supporters expected.[186] The department has used the amendments to prod institutions into employing and promoting more female teachers and administrators, opening vocational training classes to women and home economics classes to men, and offering equal athletic programs to women. If institutions do not comply, the government can cut off their federal aid.

The amendments have affected athletic programs especially. Before the amendments, schools provided fewer sports for females than for males, and they spent far fewer dollars—for scholarships, coaches, and facilities—on women's sports. Now the department interprets the amendments to require a school either to have about the same percentage of female athletes as female undergraduates, to continually expand opportunities for female athletes, or to fully accommodate the interests and abilities of female students. (The latter would occur if a school's female students were satisfied that it offered sufficient opportunities for them, given their interests and abilities, even if the opportunities were not equal to those for men.)

Very few colleges meet the first requirement. To comply, most are trying to meet the second requirement by expanding the number of women's sports. But they worry that they will have to fulfill the first requirement eventually. And they fear that they will have to cap the squad size of their football team, which has the most players and costs the most money, to do so. Reducing the number of football players would lessen the imbalance in the numbers of male and female athletes, and it would free more money for women's teams (though in large schools with highly successful football programs, lost revenue from curtailing football might jeopardize women's programs).

Thus, some colleges have resisted enforcement of Title IX, partly because it comes at a time when athletic departments are struggling to stay out of "the red" and partly because it threatens deeply ingrained cultural values that are reflected in men's athletics.

Men resisted the expansion of women's athletics. The Boston Marathon traditionally was for men only, and when the first woman tried to participate in 1967, a marathon official assaulted her.

Administrators and boosters fear that women's sports will take money from men's sports and thereby weaken the primacy of men's athletics. They especially fear that enforcement will mean "the end" of major college football.

When Brown University tried to eliminate women's volleyball and gymnastics (at the same time it dropped men's golf and water polo), members of the women's teams sued. More than 60 schools filed briefs supporting Brown's decisions and criticizing the department's interpretations of Title IX. Lower courts ruled against Brown, and in 1997 the Supreme Court refused to hear the case, which left the lower courts' rulings intact. The Supreme Court's refusal signaled that the department's interpretations would remain and the schools would have to comply.

Already Title IX has had a major impact. Colleges have increased their women's teams, from an average of six to an average of eight in 1996.[187] The number of schools that offer women's soccer increased from 133 to 445 in the 1980s and 1990s.[188] Meanwhile, some colleges have reduced their men's teams in non-revenue-producing sports, such as wrestling, gymnastics, and swimming. Title IX has also had a major impact on high schools, which have increased their girls' teams, and on American Olympic teams, which have benefited from the women's training in college.

But supporters have a broader goal in mind as well. "If girls are socialized the way boys are to take part in sports," the editor of a women's sports magazine says, and "if boys and girls grow up with the idea that girls are strong and capable, it will change the way girls and women are viewed—by themselves and by society."[189]

Discrimination against Men

Although most sex discrimination has been directed at women, some has been directed at men. The traditional conception of gender roles has created problems for men who did not fit the mold either.

When the Burger Court rejected stereotypes that led to discrimination against women, it also rejected some that led to discrimination against men. It invalidated Mississippi's law that barred men from one of the state's university nursing schools.[190] It also invalidated Alabama's law that allowed just women to seek alimony upon divorce.[191] Thus, the Court rejected stereotypes that only women become nurses and only women are dependent upon their spouses.

On the other hand, the Burger Court upheld some laws that were designed to protect women but that discriminate against men. It affirmed laws that prohibit statutory rape—intercourse with a minor, with consent—by males but not by females.[192] It also affirmed draft registration, required for males but not for females.[193] In 1980, President Carter asked Congress to reinstate draft registration, though not the draft itself, to show our "toughness" to the Soviet Union and other communist countries. Carter urged Congress to include women in the program. Although Congress had admitted women to the military academies in 1975, it was not ready to include them here. The Court upheld the law, rationalizing that registration eventually could lead to the draft and the draft eventually could lead to combat. And it insisted that most women are not capable of combat. Thus, the Court accepted the stereotypes that only men initiate sex with underage partners and only men can fight in war.

In the absence of war, the most significant discrimination against men may occur in divorce cases, where the norm is to grant custody of children to mothers and require payment of support by fathers. Although courts give fathers visitation rights, they permit mothers to move miles away, making visitation difficult and sporadic. And although governments have taken steps to enforce support payments, they have done little to enforce visitation rights. This practice reflects the stereotype that fathers are capable of financing their children's upbringing but not of bringing them up themselves. The Supreme Court has ignored this problem.

Overall, however, Congress and the courts have moved steadily toward legal equality for the sexes. Women, and men, have accomplished through congressional and judicial action much of what they would have accomplished with the ERA. It is an indication of the success of the movement that young women in the 1990s take their equality for granted, that they focus on their personal life rather than see the need for further reform.

AFFIRMATIVE ACTION

Assume there is a track meet. A black runner and a white runner start together. But the officials force the black runner to carry heavy weights, and he falls behind. Eventually, the officials realize this is unfair, and they take the weights off. Of course the black runner is still behind. Would this be fair? Assume, instead, the officials not only take the weights off but allow him to catch up. Would this be more fair? Or would it be unfair to the white runner who was not responsible for the weights and who might have run faster than the black even without the weights?[194]

This scenario captures the dilemma of civil rights policy today. Although most race and sex discrimination has been repudiated by the courts and legislatures, the effects of past discrimination survive. Now the

AFFIRMATIVE ACTION FOR . . . ALUMS' CHILDREN?

Critics of affirmative action by colleges and universities charge that preferential treatment for racial minorities means that many better-qualified whites are denied admission. Critics claim that this lowers academic standards at the schools.[1]

But at most elite schools the number of students admitted through affirmative action does not come close to the number admitted because their parents are alums.[2] For more than 40 years, a fifth of Harvard's students have had preferential treatment in admission because their parents attended the school. In the 1980s Harvard's "legacies" were more than two times as likely to be admitted as blacks or Hispanics. A similar advantage exists at other Ivy League schools.[3] Yale's legacies were more than two-and-a-half times as likely to be admitted as nonlegacies. A former dean of admissions at Princeton asserts that having one or both parents as alums "doubles, even trebles the chances of admission."

This advantage exists at other selective schools. Notre Dame reportedly reserves 25% of its openings for legacies. The Universities of Virginia and California—Berkeley treat out-of-state legacies as in-state students, which gives them a competitive edge because most state universities favor state residents.

Schools say legacies have such a high rate of admission because their parents provide the upbringing that makes their children more qualified than other students. Yet the U.S. Department of Education's Office of Civil Rights, investigating Harvard for possible discrimination in admission, found that the average admitted legacy was significantly less qualified than the average admitted nonlegacy. In fact, the number of marginally qualified legacies was greater than the number of black, Mexican American, Puerto Rican, and Native American students combined.

Schools also justify their policies by saying they fear that alums will stop giving money if their children are denied admission. This probably is the main concern.

Regardless of the wisdom of the policies, hypocrisy toward affirmative action is widespread. Opponents ignore the many factors in addition to merit that have always gone into college admissions decisions. Some who have called for the end of affirmative action for minorities, such as a group of Dartmouth alumni, have at the same time demanded that it continue for their children.

1. Thomas Sowell, *Preferential Policies: An International Perspective* (New York: Morrow, 1990); Dinesh D'Souza, *Illiberal Education* (New York: Free Press, 1991).
2. The remaining text is drawn from John Larew, "Why Are Droves of Unqualified, Unprepared Kids Getting into Our Top Colleges?" *Washington Monthly*, June 1991, pp. 10–14.
3. Theodore Cross, "Suppose There Was No Affirmative Action at the Most Prestigious Colleges and Graduate Schools," *Journal of Blacks in Higher Education*, Spring 1994, pp. 47, 50.

question is whether civil rights policy should ignore race and sex or take race and sex into account to compensate for the effects of past discrimination. That is, should the policy require nondiscrimination only or **affirmative action** as well?

Affirmative action applies to employers in hiring and promoting minorities and women, governments in reserving a portion of their contracts for businesses owned by minorities and women, and colleges and universities in admitting minorities and women.

The Civil Rights Act of 1964, which bars discrimination in employment, does not mention affirmative action, but it does authorize the bureaucracy to make rules to help end discrimination. In 1969, the Department of Labor called for affirmative action by companies doing business with the federal government. Later the Equal Employment Opportunities Commission called for affirmative action by governments and the Office of Education by colleges as well. Despite public hostility to affirmative action, presidents from Nixon through Carter supported it with executive orders, and the Supreme Court sanctioned it in a series of cases.[195] Many state and local governments also adopted it.

Affirmative action applies most extensively to employment. It requires positive steps to ensure that qualified minorities and women receive a fair share of jobs at all levels. Just what the positive steps and the fair share should be are the subject of much controversy.

If the number of minorities and women in a company or government agency, at any level, is less than the number in the local labor force, the company or agency must agree to recruit more or, in serious cases, draw up an affirmative action plan. The plan must include goals to hire or promote more minorities or women and a timetable to reach these goals. If the company or agency does not reach them, it must explain why. Failure to satisfy the government can result in the loss of future contracts or aid.

Although the requirements for affirmative action plans speak of "goals," some people say they really mean quotas. Critics charge that quotas would result in both lower standards and reverse discrimination. But affirmative action usually does not require actual quotas. Admittedly, the terms blur; if employers are pressured to meet "goals," they might interpret them to be quotas. But only occasionally,

INTO THE 21ST CENTURY

THE FUTURE OF AFFIRMATIVE ACTION

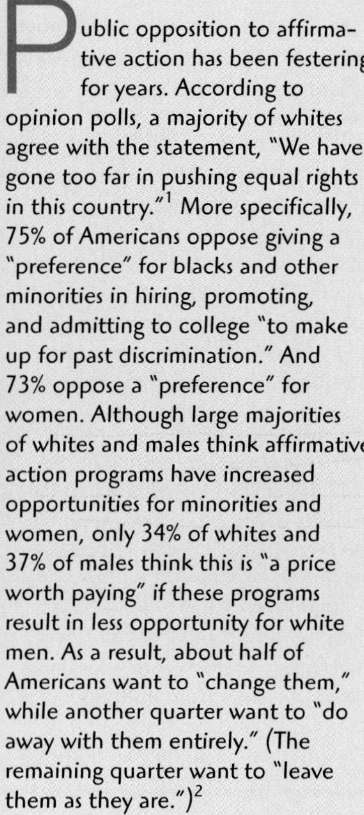

Public opposition to affirmative action has been festering for years. According to opinion polls, a majority of whites agree with the statement, "We have gone too far in pushing equal rights in this country."[1] More specifically, 75% of Americans oppose giving a "preference" for blacks and other minorities in hiring, promoting, and admitting to college "to make up for past discrimination." And 73% oppose a "preference" for women. Although large majorities of whites and males think affirmative action programs have increased opportunities for minorities and women, only 34% of whites and 37% of males think this is "a price worth paying" if these programs result in less opportunity for white men. As a result, about half of Americans want to "change them," while another quarter want to "do away with them entirely." (The remaining quarter want to "leave them as they are.")[2]

As with other racial issues, public opinion about affirmative action divides largely along racial lines. Although 81% of whites oppose affirmative action for minorities, 46% of blacks do too.[3] These blacks say affirmative action casts doubt on minorities' credentials—in whites' minds and in minorities' minds as well. One student complained, "I feel like I have AFFIRMATIVE ACTION stamped on my forehead." Other blacks believe affirmative action provides opportunities that they should have but would not have otherwise.

Despite the public opposition, the public debate over affirmative action had been muted until recently. In the late 1960s and 1970s, when affirmative action was introduced, government policy was initiated by executive orders, implemented by bureaucratic agencies, and sanctioned by judicial rulings. The legislative branch, controlled by Democrats sympathetic to civil rights, acquiesced, so Congress never staged a sharp debate on affirmative action as it has done for other controversial policies.

Republican candidates realized the volatility of this issue and reopened—some might say, reignited—the debate. When the Republicans wrested control of Congress from the Democrats in 1994, affirmative action was no longer protected. Republicans in Congress called for a review of affirmative action programs, with an eye toward shrinking or dismantling them. President Clinton, although a supporter of affirmative action, acknowledged the political climate and agreed to a review of the programs, but urged "mending, not ending" them.

Meanwhile, the University of California board of regents voted to eliminate the use of race and sex as factors for admission to the university.[4] Two California State University professors, prompted by a legislative proposal (which failed to pass) to establish quotas for admission to and graduation from state universities, launched a petition drive for a public vote to prohibit the use of race, sex, or national origin as "a criterion for either discriminating against, or granting preferential treatment to, an individual or group" in state education, employment, or contracting. This initiative passed in 1996. In the same year, the U.S. Court of Appeals for the Fifth Circuit, which covers Texas, Louisiana, and Mississippi, ruled that state universities in these states cannot use race or ethnicity in admissions.[5] These judges disregarded the *Bakke* precedent and acted as conservative activists. The Supreme Court refused to hear this case, thus leaving the ruling intact. Legal observers have speculated that the Rehnquist Court, which has not been sympathetic to affirmative action, might declare it unconstitutional in another case.

At the same time, many businesses, especially large corporations, which initially resisted affirmative action, have gradually come to support it.[6] By implementing affirmative action, or "diversity," policies, they have found new pools of untapped talent in overlooked groups, and they have reached new markets in these groups. That is, hiring more minority and female workers has led to insights that enable the corporations to sell products to more minority and female consumers.

Most universities also support affirmative action in admissions at least.[7]

Now that the debate has been reopened, the issue will have to be resolved. We would like to be able to say that affirmative action is no longer necessary, that the playing field is now level. But as this chapter has explained, the playing field is less tilted but not yet level. Minorities face continuing discrimination as well as the legacy of past discrimination.

In the meantime, what might become of affirmative action? The most common proposal is to base it

and only after a finding of deliberate and systematic discrimination, does affirmative action entail actual quotas.

The Supreme Court has issued mixed rulings on the legality of quotas. In *University of California Regents v. Bakke* in 1978, the Court upheld the policy of the medical school at the University of California at Davis to consider race as a factor in admissions, but it struck down the policy to establish a quota of 16 spaces for minorities out of 100 spaces in the class. On the other hand, the Court upheld quotas for skilled workers, firefighters, and state police.[196] The primary factor in de-on class rather than race. Thus, it would be available for poor whites as well as for poor minorities. It would not be available for middle-class or upper-class minorities or women. This proposal is more palatable to many people, including many opponents of affirmative action as it is now administered. They consider class to be a fairer and less divisive basis than race. But because racial minorities are disproportionately poor, it would still benefit them. Some observers see this proposal as a way to defuse the debate and at the same time continue the progress for racial minorities.[8]

The underlying assumption of this proposal is that numerous minorities, in the middle and upper classes, are benefiting from affirmative action but do not need it, while whites in the lower class are being shut out and do need it. Yet the number of middle-class beneficiaries probably is not as large as assumed, given the relative size of the black, Hispanic, and American Indian middle classes compared to their lower classes. And middle-class blacks, at least, face frequent affronts and some discrimination due to their race. Although they are financially better off than lower-class whites, it is not clear that they are generally better off in contemporary society.

Another underlying assumption of this proposal is that the class of applicants to schools and jobs can be determined. But defining class presents numerous conceptual and practical problems. Whose economic position would be measured—that of the individual or that of the individual's family or household? (These are not necessarily the same.) Would wealth be considered as well as income? For example, money from parents or relatives for a down payment on a house creates wealth for a family beyond what its income provides. Would other indices of class, such as occupation or education, be incorporated? How would education be measured? By number of years, type of schools, or grades or honors received by the student? Would indices such as an individual's class consciousness or buying habits be included? These reflect class but would be exceedingly difficult to measure. As one examination of this problem concluded, "Social scientists who specialize in . . . economic inequality have great difficulty in reaching agreement on its proper definition and measurement. [Creating] . . . a legal definition of economic inequality would be beyond the technical capacity of most social scientists, let alone most governmental agencies."[9] As a result, a very simplified index of class would probably be employed, but this ultimately might seem just as unfair as using race.

Nevertheless, it is appealing to think that a revised policy could help whites who have overcome disadvantages in their background as well. But revising the policy to do this would create a serious problem for nonwhites. Because whites are so numerous, and because there are more poor whites than blacks or other minorities, the whites would tend to squeeze out the minorities in these programs. That is, broadening the programs to apply to poor whites would significantly narrow the opportunities for poor minorities.

Thus, a proposal that has philosophical appeal to many people would create practical problems for schools, employers, and governments and have significant ramifications for racial progress that might diminish the initial appeal.

1. Richard Lacayo, "A New Push for Blind Justice," *Time*, February 20, 1995, p. 39.
2. Richard Morin and Sharon Warden, "Poll Says Americans Angry about Affirmative Action," *Washington Post*, March 24, 1995, p. A4. There appears to be majority support for the vague concept of "affirmative action," undefined, but the support evaporates when the questions use language indicating or implying any preference for minorities or women. Richard Morin, "No Place for Calm and Quiet Opinions," *Washington Post National Weekly Edition*, April 24–30, 1995, p. 34.
3. Morin and Warden, "Poll Says Americans Angry about Affirmative Action."
4. Yet several of the regents who voted to stop affirmative action had acted behind the scenes to get relatives, friends, and children of business partners enrolled at the UC schools. One had made 32 requests to UCLA alone. "UC Regents Aided Own, Paper Says," *San Diego Tribune*, March 17, 1996, p. A-3.
5. *Hopwood v. Texas*, 78 F.3d 932 (1996).
6. This "is one of the better kept secrets of the debate." Alan Wolfe, "Affirmative Action, Inc.," *New Yorker*, November 25, 1996, p. 107. And see numerous sources cited therein.
7. Susan Welch and John Gruhl, *Affirmative Action and Minority Enrollments in Medical and Law Schools* (Ann Arbor: University of Michigan, 1998).
8. Richard D. Kahlenberg, *The Remedy: Class, Race, and Affirmative Action* (New York: New Republic/Basic Books, 1996).
9. Deborah C. Malamud, "Class-based Affirmative Action: Look Carefully before You Leap," *University of Michigan Law Quadrangle Notes*, Fall/Winter, 1996, pp. 61–72.

termining the legality of quotas is whether the employer or union discriminated in the past. The University of California at Davis had no history of discrimination, but the other employers did.

In reviewing an affirmative action plan, the Court also looks at two crucial elements: the plan must not prevent all white men from being hired and promoted, and it must be temporary (usually until the percentage of black employees approaches the percentage of black workers in the community).

Because of concern that affirmative action should not pose too great a burden on innocent individuals, the Court has struck down affirmative action in laying off workers—that is, struck down protection for minorities and women when employers pare their workforce for economic reasons. Instead, the Court has accepted the traditional practice, based on seniority, that the last hired is the first fired.[197]

The Rehnquist Court, however, has signaled a change of direction in affirmative action doctrine. Although the Court has not barred affirmative action programs, a slim majority has made it more difficult for governments to adopt some programs.[198] Governments must demonstrate a "compelling" reason, which probably means they must have clear evidence of specific discrimination, rather than cite the general pattern of historical discrimination, and they must show how particular programs would ameliorate the problems.

Affirmative action requirements are not very stringent and are not strictly enforced. Employers who are required to file an affirmative action plan but fail to reach their goals ordinarily need to show only that they made a genuine effort to reach them. Employers rarely are penalized. Federal officials focus on discrimination complaints and have little time to investigate compliance with affirmative action policies. Thus, compliance depends on the good faith of some employers plus the strategic use of a few investigations and penalties to serve as a threat to others.

Some government pressure evidently is necessary. White men dominate public and private institutions, and as the personnel director of a Fortune 500 company observed, "People tend to hire people like themselves."[199] A study of Philadelphia companies found that over half were run by executives whose views on affirmative action ranged from "neutral" to "extremely resistant." They practiced affirmative action because they felt they had to.[200]

Affirmative action programs have helped minorities and women. Companies that do business with the federal government, and therefore are subject to affirmative action, have shown more improvement in hiring minorities and women than other companies. And state and local governments, also subject to affirmative action, have shown more improvement in hiring than private companies. Organizations subject to affirmative action have shown even more progress in promoting minorities and women previously kept in low-level positions.[201]

The state of Alabama, for example, made dramatic gains. After a court found that the state troopers had never employed any blacks, it ordered them to hire one new black for every new white until the force reached 25% black. The force became the most integrated force in the country. Faced with the threat of a similar order, other departments of the state government quickly hired more blacks at all levels.

Affirmative action has helped middle-class and some lower-class blacks get jobs in government and business.[202] It has noticeably increased the number of blacks in government agencies, police departments, fire departments, construction trades, and textile companies. Affirmative action has also helped women get jobs in government and business that traditionally went only to men.

But affirmative action has not pulled blacks out of the "underclass." Many, from families that have suffered long-term poverty, experience continual unemployment because they lack the education and the skills necessary to compete for available jobs.[203]

And affirmative action, of course, cannot create new jobs or better jobs. Thus, it is not as helpful to minorities or women as a flourishing economy is.

In short, affirmative action should not be credited by proponents for more benefits nor blamed by opponents for more harms than it actually causes. It has boosted some minorities and women, but it cannot help many others. It has displaced some white men, but it has not affected many others.

Thirteen percent of white men think they lost a job or promotion because of their race, and 10% think they did because of their sex.[204] Many others claim they "heard about" another white man who did. Yet affirmative action is neither as pervasive nor as rigidly enforced as many people assume. For instance, the number of black employees in 40 cities between 1973 and 1980, the peak years for affirmative action, increased only from 28% to 33% of the total employees. The number of black administrators increased from 9% to 16%, which was about half the proportion of black workers in these cities.[205]

Many people subconsciously view affirmative action as they do handicapped parking. When looking for a parking space in a crowded lot, numerous drivers see the handicapped space and think, "If it weren't for that reserved space, I could park here." In reality, if the space wasn't reserved, only one other driver could park there.[206] So it is with affirmative action. Many white men think they would get a particular job if it weren't for affirmative action, but only one would. Meanwhile, the rest feel victimized by the policy.

For both sides in the controversy, affirmative action has become a symbol. For civil rights leaders, it represents fairness and real progress toward equality. For critics, it represents unfairness and an attack on individuality and meritocracy. It is important to debate these values, but it is also important to recognize that affirmative action is neither the key public policy for racial and sexual equality nor the biggest stumbling block for individual achievement as supporters and detractors seem to assume.

CONCLUSION: IS GOVERNMENT RESPONSIVE IN GRANTING CIVIL RIGHTS?

Blacks and women have made tremendous progress in obtaining civil rights since the time when a federal official who fired competent blacks could insist, "A Negro's place is in the cornfield,"[207] or employers who refused to hire women could insist, "A woman's place is in the home." The black movement and the women's movement initiated the changes. They protested legal inequality and put the issue on the public agenda. As they grew and garnered support, they pressured the government. Finally, approximately one century after the first significant agitations for change, the government responded.

Within the government, the Supreme Court exercised decisive leadership. Historically, the Court was both activist and restrained toward blacks—whichever was necessary to deny their rights—while it was restrained toward women. Then in the 1950s and 1960s, the Warren Court was activist in striking down segregation. In the 1970s and 1980s, the Burger Court was somewhat less activist in upholding limited busing and affirmative action. At the same time, it was activist in striking down sex discrimination. As with the Warren Court's decisions against race discrimination, the Burger Court's decisions against sex discrimination may go down in history as its major achievement.

But the Court's rulings themselves did not guarantee the rights. Because the Court lacks the means to enforce its decisions, the president and Congress had to help overcome the resistance. The history of the government's efforts to grant civil rights, especially to blacks, shows the limits of the Supreme Court.

The changes in policy illustrate the responsiveness of government. In its subjugation of minorities until the 1950s and treatment of women until the 1970s, government was responding to the majority view. When minorities and women organized to protest their status, government began responding to them and to shifts in the majority view that their protest prompted.

In pressuring government to respond, blacks have benefited from being numerous, visible, and—with their common legacy of slavery, segregation, and discrimination—relatively cohesive. Their concentration in large northern cities and some southern states has helped them exercise political power. Their long legacy, though, has fostered debilitating ghetto conditions and denied them resources to make quicker and greater progress.

Hispanics are less numerous but growing in number rapidly. Their concentration in some western and southwestern states has enabled them to influence state and local governments. Their diversity and lack of cohesiveness, however, have hindered their ability to influence the national government.

Native Americans are the smallest, most isolated, and least organized minority, so they have had the poorest success in pressuring government to respond.

As minority groups grow in size, they will be able to pressure governments more effectively. In the 1980s, blacks increased their population 13%, Native Americans 39%, Hispanics 53%, and Asians 108%, while whites increased their population just 6%.[208]

But as minority groups expand, they will increasingly come into conflict with each other, especially when economic conditions are stagnant. Competition for scarce resources will widen the cracks in the coalition. Already there are tensions. Some blacks resent the faster progress of Hispanics and Asians. Blacks say they were here before most Hispanics and Asians, they suffered more and struggled more, and so they should reap the rewards sooner. On the other hand, some Hispanic leaders resent the reluctance of black groups to help them with their civil rights problems.[209] Sometimes there are conflicts over issues. Occasionally, there have been riots. Blacks have rioted in Miami from frustration with the Cuban-dominated leadership. Hispanics have rioted in Washington, D.C., out of anger with their lack of city services and jobs and with gerrymandering by the black power structure.

Nonminority women were never subjugated as much as minority men and women, so they have had less to overcome. Moreover, women are a majority, they vote as frequently as men, and they have well-organized and well-funded interest groups. Consequently, since the 1970s they have made the greatest strides toward equality.

EPILOGUE

Hamer Continues to Fight

Fannie Lou Hamer was not one to back down from a challenge, especially since the first time she tried to register to vote. Indeed, a frequent criticism levied against her, by supporters as well as opponents, was that she was unwilling to compromise. At the Democratic convention in 1964, she and two other women leaders of the Mississippi Freedom Democratic Party urged the delegation to reject the compromise offered by the national Democratic Party officials. "We didn't come all this way for no two seats," she declared.[210] She also criticized the proposal that the seats be given to two middle-class representatives of the delegation—a professor and a druggist—rather than to any of the poor sharecroppers who formed the bulk of the delegation.

The delegation voted to press its case before the credentials committee of the convention. But the FBI had infiltrated the MFDP and had wiretapped its phones to determine the delegation's plans, and then had forwarded this information to President Johnson. When the credentials committee began its hearing, the president called a press conference to preempt the hearing from television. Without the cameras present, the committee voted to seat the regular Democrats.

Furious, the Freedom Democrats entered the convention hall, using their tickets as "guests," and stood silently in a circle to call attention to their issue. The sergeants-at-arms tried to remove them but gave up when officials realized that the effort would cast the wrong image on television. Nevertheless, the protest attracted the press coverage that had been denied at the hearing.

Meanwhile, most of the regular Democrats left for Mississippi. They apparently went to the convention just to keep the Freedom Democrats from getting the seats.

When Johnson wrote his memoirs after retiring, he omitted any mention of the Freedom Democrats' challenge. "Atlantic City in August 1964," he wrote, "was a place of happy surging crowds and thundering cheers. To a man as troubled as I was by party and national divisions, this display of unity was welcome indeed.[211]

Hamer continued to fight. Following the election she challenged the seating of the five regular Democrats elected to the House of Representatives from Mississippi.

Change eventually came, however. In 1965 President Johnson pushed the Voting Rights Act through Congress, and in 1968 the Democratic Party propounded rules against seating delegations that denied full participation to blacks.

Yet Mississippi's regular Democrats resisted. A coalition including Hamer, other Freedom Democrats, and moderate whites challenged the seating of the regular Democrats at the national convention. This time Vice President Humphrey, running for president after Johnson retired, backed the challenge and it succeeded. Finally, an integrated delegation represented Mississippi.

Fannie Lou Hamer, with her boundless energy, still had battles to fight. She brought lawsuits to broaden interpretation of the Voting Rights Act, reconfigure electoral districts in the state, and desegregate schools in her town.

As African Americans began to overcome discrimination, she believed the next step was for the poor, blacks and whites alike, to overcome poverty. She arranged financing for 70 new homes in town and helped organize a farm co-op and a "pig bank." (She bought 40 pigs and loaned them to families who would care for them and keep the new piglets—the "dividends"—and then return the pigs—the "principal"—to the bank for other families the next year.)

In her declining years, she felt frustrated because she had not accomplished more, and forgotten because people had not come to see her as often when she no longer had the energy for their cause. In 1977 she died.

Yet Fannie Lou Hamer had achieved much. With the increased participation of black voters in Mississippi, black candidates ran for office, and many won; and white candidates began to court black voters as well. In 1986 the first black person to represent Mississippi in the House of Representatives since Reconstruction was elected.

Fannie Lou Hamer would not be forgotten. She showed people that although she had much to fear, her oppressors were the ones who came to fear her because she would not be silenced and could not be controlled. "She owed them nothing, and she gave them hell."[212]

KEY TERMS

- Dred Scott case
- equal protection clause
- Jim Crow laws
- *Plessy v. Ferguson*
- separate-but-equal doctrine
- NAACP
- *Brown v. Board of Education*
- de jure segregation
- de facto segregation
- Civil Rights Act of 1964
- restrictive covenants
- steering
- blockbusting
- redlining
- Civil Rights Act of 1968
- bilingual education
- Equal Rights Amendment (ERA)
- Equal Pay Act
- comparable worth
- affirmative action

FURTHER READING

Edward Ball, *Slaves in the Family* (New York: Farrar, Straus & Giroux, 1998). A search by the descendant of a plantation owner for the descendants of his family's slaves.

Taylor Branch, *Parting the Waters: America in the King Years, 1954–63* (New York: Simon & Schuster, 1988). A readable account of Martin Luther King, Jr., and the first decade of the civil rights movement.

Seth Cagin and Philip Dray, *We Are Not Afraid: The Story of Goodman, Schwerner, and Chaney and the Civil Rights Campaign for Mississippi* (New York: Macmillan, 1988). An American crime in the steamy summer of 1964.

Melissa Fay Greene, *Praying for Sheetrock* (Reading, Mass. Addison-Wesley, 1991). A nonfiction story about the clash between "good old boy politics" and black power in a Georgia county in the 1970s.

David Halberstam, *The Children* (New York: Random House, 1998). The lives of eight students who attended college in Nashville and helped launch the civil rights movement. The book shows how a small group of courageous students helped transform the country.

Jane Kramer, "Whose Art Is It?" *New Yorker*, December 21, 1992, pp. 80–109. A fascinating article about the interactions between a white artist, the poor black neighbors he uses as models for his lifelike sculptures, and the middle-class black officials in New York City who determine whether, and where, the controversial sculptures can be erected.

Susan Ware, *Still Missing: Amelia Earhart and the Search for Modern Feminism* (New York: W. W. Norton, 1994). The life of the famous pilot, who disappeared over the Pacific Ocean in 1937, as a reflection of American feminism between the two world wars.

Gregory Howard Williams, *Life on the Color Line: The True Story of a White Boy Who Discovered He Was Black* (New York: Dutton, 1995). How the life of a 10-year-old boy changed the day he learned that his father was black.

ELECTRONIC RESOURCES

http://www.naacp.org/
The Web site of the NAACP, the largest and oldest civil rights organization. Links to discussions of policy issues and information about the organization and its mission.

http://www.census.gov/prod/www/abs/cc97stab.html
The Statistical Abstract of the United States *online. Information about the state of the American people, their incomes, family structures, occupations, and many other characteristics. Includes detailed information about individual ethnic and racial groups as well as men and women.*

http://www.n-polk.k12.ia.us/pages/departments/Media/nat.html
A link to information about Native Americans and their cultures.

http://oyez.nwu.edu/ or
http://www.wolfenet.com/~dhillis/STATE3.HTM
Read important civil rights cases online from this Web page. Allows you to search for and access cases by name or topic.

INFOTRAC CITATIONS

"Clinton Opens School Doors for Little Rock Nine"
"Will You Lose Your Right to Vote?"
"Two Languages Are Better than One"
"Groping Toward Sanity"

NOTES

1. The information for this section is from Kay Mills, *This Little Light of Mine: The Life of Fannie Lou Hamer* (New York: Plume, 1994).

2. In the Delta, as in much of Mississippi, most blacks picked cotton or cleaned or cooked for white people. Black teachers had some status, but they were hired and usually controlled by the white officials of the segregated school systems. Only black preachers and funeral directors had any independence.

3. Mills, *This Little Light*, p. 36.

4. Ibid., p. 38.

5. Ibid., p. 18.

6. Ibid., p. 57.

7. This incident received little media coverage because no reporters were present. And this result prompted civil rights leaders to seek help from white college students, assuming, correctly, that if any of them were harmed there would be more coverage of the repression blacks encountered. Thus began the recruitment of northern college students for voter registration drives during the summer.

8. Mills, *This Little Light*, p. 93.

9. The Republican Party was not a viable party in the state at the time. There was a black wing of the party, called the "Black and Tans," but its only role was to help dispense patronage when there was a Republican president. In fact, the head of the Mississippi Black and Tans was an attorney who lived in Washington, D.C. Mills, *This Little Light*, p. 109.

10. Ibid., p. 128.

11. Russell Nye, *Fettered Freedom* (Lansing: Michigan State University Press, 1963), pp. 187, 227–229.

12. *Scott v. Sandford*, 19 How. 393 (1857).

13. Despite the ruling, Taney considered slavery "a blot on our national character." Three decades before the case, he had freed his own slaves, whom he had inherited from his parents. When the South seceded, Taney remained with the Union. Richard Shenkman, *I Love Paul Revere, Whether He Rode or Not* (New York: HarperCollins, 1991), p. 168.

14. Civil Rights Act of 1866; Civil Rights Act of 1871; Civil Rights Act of 1875.

15. See generally Eric Foner, *Reconstruction: America's Unfinished Revolution* (New York: Harper & Row, 1988).

16. C. Vann Woodward, *The Strange Career of Jim Crow*, 2d ed. (London: Oxford University Press, 1966), p. 44.

17. *Civil Rights Cases*, 109 U.S. 3 (1883).

18. C. Herman Pritchett, *The American Constitution*, 3d ed. (New York: McGraw-Hill, 1977), p. 486.

19. *Plessy v. Ferguson*, 163 U.S. 537 (1896). The Court's ruling prompted states to expand their Jim Crow laws. Before *Plessy* states segregated just trains and schools.

20. *Cumming v. Richmond County Board of Education*, 175 U.S. 528 (1899). Then the Court enforced segregation in colleges. It upheld a criminal conviction against a private college for teaching blacks together with whites. *Berea College v. Kentucky*, 211 U.S. 45 (1908).

21. Woodward, *Strange Career of Jim Crow*, p. 113. Before the Civil War northern states had passed some Jim Crow laws, which foreshadowed the more pervasive laws in southern states after the war. Leon F. Litwack, *Trouble in Mind: Black Southerners in the Age of Jim Crow* (New York: Knopf, 1998).

22. Jacqueline Jones, *The Dispossessed: America's Underclasses from the Civil War to the Present* (Basic Books, 1992), p. 83. And they were still being cheated. One sharecropper went to the landowner at the end of the season to settle up but was told he would not receive any money that year because the landowner needed it to send his son to college. The sharecropper moved North. Interview with sharecropper's son, "The Best of Discovery," Discovery Television Channel, June 11, 1995.

23. Richard Kluger, *Simple Justice* (New York: Alfred A. Knopf, 1976), pp. 89–90.

24. Woodward, *Strange Career of Jim Crow*, p. 114.

25. Wilson apparently opposed segregation in government but still allowed it to appease southerners who were a major portion of his Democratic Party and whose support was essential for his economic reforms.

26. *Guinn v. United States*, 238 U.S. 347 (1915).

27. *Buchanan v. Warley*, 245 U.S. 60 (1917).

28. In 1939 the NAACP established the NAACP Legal Defense and Educational Fund as its litigation arm. In 1957 the IRS, pressured by southern members of Congress, ordered the two branches of the NAACP to break their connection or lose their tax-exempt status. Since then they have been separate organizations,

and chapter references to the "NAACP" are to the NAACP Legal Defense and Educational Fund.

29. Kluger, *Simple Justice*, p. 134.

30. *Missouri ex rel. Gaines v. Canada*, 305 U.S. 337 (1938).

31. *Sweatt v. Painter*, 339 U.S. 629 (1950).

32. *McLaurin v. Oklahoma State Regents*, 339 U.S. 637 (1950).

33. Earl Warren, *The Memoirs of Earl Warren* (Garden City, N.Y.: Doubleday, 1977), p. 291.

34. 347 U.S. 483 (1954).

35. *Holmes v. Atlanta*, 350 U.S. 879 (1955); *Baltimore v. Dawson*, 350 U.S. 877 (1955); *Schiro v. Bynum*, 375 U.S. 395 (1964); *Johnson v. Virginia*, 373 U.S. 61 (1963); *Lee v. Washington*, 390 U.S. 333 (1968).

36. *Brown v. Board of Education II*, 349 U.S. 294 (1955).

37. Justice Tom Clark later told a political science conference that one justice had proposed desegregating one grade a year, beginning with kindergarten or first grade, but this concrete standard was rejected because the other justices felt it would take too long. In retrospect, it might have been quicker, and easier, than the vague standard used.

38. *Griffin v. Prince Edward County School Board*, 377 U.S. 218 (1964); *Norwood v. Harrison*, 413 U.S. 455 (1973); *Gilmore v. Montgomery*, 417 U.S. 556 (1974); *Green v. New Kent County School Board*, 391 U.S. 430 (1968).

39. James F. Simon, *In His Own Image* (New York: David McKay, 1974), p. 70.

40. William Cohen and John Kaplan, *Bill of Rights* (Mineola, N.Y.: Foundation Press, 1976), p. 622.

41. *Swann v. Charlotte-Mecklenburg Board of Education*, 402 U.S. 1 (1971).

42. *Columbus Board of Education v. Penick*, 443 U.S. 449 (1979); *Dayton Board of Education v. Brinkman*, 443 U.S. 526 (1979); *Keyes v. School District 1, Denver*, 413 U.S. 921 (1973).

43. *Milliken v. Bradley*, 418 U.S. 717 (1974).

44. For example, some suburbs of Kansas City, Missouri, did not allow black students to attend high schools. Some black families, then, moved back to the city, aggravating both school segregation and residential segregation. James S. Kunen, "The End of Integration," *Time*, April 29, 1996, p. 41.

45. Lee A. Daniels, "In Defense of Busing," *New York Times Magazine*, April 17, 1983, pp. 36–37.

46. Daniels, "In Defense of Busing," p. 34.

47. Ibid., p. 97; Susan Chira, "Housing and Fear Upend Integration," *New York Times*, February 14, 1993, p. E3.

48. Rob Gurwitt, "Getting Off the Bus," *Governing* (May 1992), pp. 30–36.

49. *Board of Education of Oklahoma City v. Dowell*, 112 L.Ed.2d 715 (1991).

50. *Missouri v. Jenkins*, 132 L.Ed.2d 63 (1995).

51. Gurwitt, "Getting Off the Bus"; Jervis Anderson, "Black and Blue," *New Yorker*, April 29 and May 6, 1996, p. 64.

52. FBI director J. Edgar Hoover ordered wiretaps that he hoped would link King with communists. When the taps failed to reveal any connection, Hoover had agents bug a hotel room, where they heard King having extramarital sex. Taylor Branch, *Pillar of Fire: America in the King Years 1963–65* (New York: Simon & Schuster, 1998).

53. Woodward, *Strange Career of Jim Crow*, p. 186.

54. *Norris v. Alabama*, 294 U.S. 587 (1935); *Smith v. Texas*, 311 U.S. 128 (1940); *Avery v. Georgia*, 345 U.S. 559 (1952).

55. Henry Louis Gates, Jr., "After the Revolution," *New Yorker*, April 29 and May 6, 1996, p. 60.

56. *Heart of Atlanta Motel v. United States*, 379 U.S. 421 (1964).

57. For discussion of organized labor's ambivalence toward enactment and enforcement of the employment provisions of the act, see Herbert Hill, "Black Workers, Organized Labor, and Title VII of the 1964 Civil Rights Act: Legislative History and Litigation Record," in Herbert Hill and James E. Jones, *Race in America* (Madison: University of Wisconsin Press, 1993), pp. 263–341.

58. *Griggs v. Duke Power*, 401 U.S. 424 (1971).

59. *Washington v. Davis*, 426 U.S. 229 (1976). When the Burger Court held that standards must relate to the job, it placed the burden of proof on employers. (They had to show that their requirements were necessary.) In *Wards Cove Packing v. Atonio*, 490 U.S. 642 (1989), the Rehnquist Court shifted the burden of proof to workers. This technical change had a substantial impact; it made it hard for victims to win in court. In 1991, Congress passed new legislation to override the ruling and clarify its intent that employers should bear the burden of proof.

60. *Firefighters Local Union v. Stotts*, 81 L.Ed.2d 483 (1984).

61. *Shelley v. Kraemer*, 334 U.S. 1 (1948).

62. Less directly, the numerous national and state policies that encouraged urban sprawl provided the opportunity for middle-class whites to flock to the suburbs—and leave the cities disproportionately black.

63. For more extensive examination, see Andrew Hacker, *Two Nations: Black and White, Separate, Hostile, Unequal* (New York: Charles Scribner's Sons, 1992).

64. Richard Morin, "Southern Discomfort," *Washington Post National Weekly Edition*, July 15–21, 1996, p. 35.

65. Gary Orfield, quoted in Mary Jordan, "Separating the Country from the *Brown* Decision," *Washington Post National Weekly Edition*, December 20–26, 1993, p. 33.

66. Mary Jordan, "On Track Toward Two-Tier Schools," *Washington Post National Weekly Edition*, May 31–June 6, 1993, p. 31.

67. Jordan, "Separating the Country from the *Brown* Decision."

68. J. Harvie Wilkinson, *From Brown to Bakke* (New York: Oxford University Press, 1979), pp. 118–125; "School Segregation Worsens, Study Says," *Lincoln Journal (Los Angeles Times)*, December 14, 1993; William Celis 3d, "Forty Years after *Brown*, Segregation Persists," *New York Times*, May 18, 1994, p. A1.

69. Kunen, "The End of Integration," p. 39.

70. Jonathan Kozol, *Savage Inequalities: Children in America's Schools* (New York: HarperPerennial, 1992), p. 4.

71. Kozol, *Savage Inequalities*, p. 3.

72. Ibid., p. 35.

73. "That's Quite a Range," *Lincoln Journal*, January 21, 1993.

74. In addition, cities have numerous nonprofit institutions—colleges, museums, hospitals—that benefit the entire urban area but do not pay property taxes. According to one estimate, 30% of the cities' potential tax base is tax exempt, compared with 3% of the suburbs'. Kozol, *Savage Inequalities*, p. 55.

75. Ibid., pp. 198, 137, 236, 57. (There are a few exceptions, such as Newark, New Jersey, which spent more than $9,000 per pupil in recent years. Jordan, "On Track Toward Two-Tier Schools," p. 31.)

76. Kozol, *Savage Inequalities*, pp. 140, 36, 23–24.

77. Ibid., pp. 155–156.

78. Ibid., pp. 53, 84.
79. Ibid., p. 52.
80. Ibid., p. 53.
81. Ibid., pp. 123–124.
82. Robert England and Kenneth Meier, "From Desegregation to Integration: Second Generation School Discrimination as an Institutional Impediment," *American Politics Quarterly* 13 (April 1985), pp. 227–247; Charles Bullock and Joseph Stewart, "Incidence and Correlates of Second-Generation Discrimination," in Marian Palley and Michael Preston, eds., *Race, Sex, and Policy Problems* (Lexington, Mass: Lexington Books, 1979); Stephen Wainscott and J. David Woodard, "Second Thoughts on Second Generation Discrimination," *American Politics Quarterly* 16 (April 1988), pp. 171–192.
83. Kenneth Meier and Robert England, "Black Representation and Educational Policy," *American Political Science Review* 78 (June 1984), pp. 392–403; Kenneth Meier, Joseph Stewart, and Robert England, *Race, Class, and Education: The Politics of Second-Generation Discrimination* (Madison: University of Wisconsin Press, 1989).
84. Suits claiming discrimination fell 51% from 1975 to 1984. Marc Galanter, "Beyond the Litigation Panic," in *New Directions in Liability Law, Proceedings of the Academy of Political Science* 37 (New York: Academy of Political Science, 1988), pp. 21, 23.
85. Gary Boulard, "Jim Crow Said Alive in the South," *Lincoln Journal* (*Los Angeles Times*), October 3, 1991.
86. Colleen Barry, "Denny's Accused of Discrimination," *San Diego Union-Tribune*, March 25, 1993, p. A–3.
87. Edward Barnes, "Can't Get There from Here," *Time*, February 19, 1996, p. 33.
88. Hacker, *Two Nations*, pp. 48–49.
89. William A. Henry III, "The Last Bastions of Bigotry," *Time*, July 22, 1991, pp. 66–67.
90. "Study Demonstrates Hiring Discrimination against Blacks," *Lincoln Star* (*Washington Post*), May 15, 1991.
91. "Deciphering a Racist Business Code," *Time*, October 19, 1992, pp. 21–22.
92. Earl G. Graves, *How to Succeed in Business without Being White* (New York: HarperBusiness, 1997).
93. Jerry DeMuth, "Fair-Housing Suits: Color Them Gold," *Washington Post National Weekly Edition*, August 11, 1986, p. 34.
94. Jonathan Kaufman, "In Big-City Ghettos, Life Is Often Worse Than in '60s Tumult," *Wall Street Journal*, May 23, 1980.
95. Jerry Knight, "Coloring the Chances of Getting a Mortgage," *Washington Post National Weekly Edition*, October 28–November 3, 1991, p. 26; "Racial Disparities Seen in Home Lending," *Lincoln Journal* (AP), October 22, 1991.
96. "Possible Redlining Investigated," *Urbana News-Gazette* (AP), February 15, 1993.
97. Barbara Vobejda, "Neighborhood Integration, Inch by Inch," *Washington Post National Weekly Edition*, March 23–29, 1992, p. 37.
98. Nancy Denton and Douglas Massey, "Residential Segregation of Blacks, Hispanics, and Asians by Socioeconomic Status and Generation," *Social Science Quarterly* 69 (December 1988), p. 259.
99. Hacker, *Two Nations*, pp. 35–38.
100. "Study Says EPA Penalties Smaller in Minority Areas," *Lincoln Journal* (*Newsday*), September 14, 1992. President Clinton issued an executive order intended to prevent minority neighborhoods from being burdened with an unfair share of dumps, incinerators, and other sources of pollution, but state governments and industrial groups are challenging the order.
101. " 'Driving While Black' on 95," *Washington Post National Weekly Edition*, November 25–December 1, 1996, p. 25.
102. Michael A. Fletcher, "May the Driver Beware," *Washington Post National Weekly Edition*, April 8–14, 1996, p. 29.
103. Pierre Thomas, "Bias and the Badge," *Washington Post National Weekly Edition*, December 18–24, 1995, pp. 6–9.
104. Henry Louis Gates, Jr., "Thirteen Ways of Looking at a Black Man," *New Yorker*, October 23, 1995, p. 59; Anderson, "Black and Blue," p. 64.
105. Laura M. Markowitz, "Walking the Walk," *Networker* (July/August 1993), p. 22.
106. William Raspberry, "The Little Things That Hurt," *Washington Post National Weekly Edition*, April 18–24, 1994, p. 29. And see Ellis Cose, *The Rage of a Privileged Class* (New York: HarperCollins, 1993).
107. Kozol, *Savage Inequalities*, pp. 179–180.
108. Juan Williams, "Why Segregation Seems So Seductive," *Washington Post National Weekly Edition*, January 24–30, 1994, p. 24. For an extended examination, see Derrick Bell, *Faces at the Bottom of the Well: The Permanence of Racism* (New York: Basic Books, 1992).
109. Stephan Thernstrom and Abigail Thernstrom, *America in Black and White: One Nation, Indivisible* (New York: Simon & Schuster, 1997), especially part 3. Some improvement began before the civil rights movement—when southern blacks migrated to northern cities in the 1940s.
110. Andrew Tobias, "Now the Good News about Your Money," *Parade*, April 4, 1993, p. 5.
111. James P. Smith and Finis Welch, "Race and Poverty: A 40-Year Record," *American Economic Review* 77 (1987), pp. 152–158.
112. Joel Garreau, "Candidates Take Note: It's a Mall World After All," *Washington Post National Weekly Edition*, August 10–16, 1992, p. 25.
113. Thernstrom and Thernstrom, *America in Black and White*, p. 500.
114. Ibid., p. 507.
115. Ibid., p. 506.
116. Orlando Patterson, quoted in ibid., p. 507.
117. Orlando Patterson, quoted in Anderson, "Black and Blue," p. 62.
118. From 1967 to 1987, according to calculations by William Julius Wilson. David Remnick, "Dr. Wilson's Neighborhood," *New Yorker*, April 29 and May 6, 1996, p. 98.
119. Sociologist William Julius Wilson develops this idea extensively in *The Truly Disadvantaged* (Chicago: University of Chicago Press, 1987).
120. U.S. Department of Commerce, *Statistical Abstract of the United States 1995* (Washington, D.C.: U.S. Government Printing Office, 1995), Table 70.
121. Wilson, *The Truly Disadvantaged*.
122. Remnick, "Dr. Wilson's Neighborhood," p. 98.
123. Samuel Walker, *Sense and Nonsense about Crime and Drugs*, 3d ed. (Belmont, Calif.: Wadsworth, 1994), pp. xviii, 3.
124. Thernstrom and Thernstrom, *America in Black and White*, p. 533.
125. Peter Reuter, "Why Can't We Make Prohibition Work Better: Some Consequences of Ignoring the Unattractive," in *Perspectives on Crime and Justice: 1996–1997 Lecture Series* (Washington, D.C.: National Institute of Justice, 1997), pp. 30–31.
126. Connie Cass, "More Young Black Men in Trouble with Law," *Lincoln Journal-Star* (AP), October 5, 1995.

127. "Doctor: Harlem's Death Rate Worse Than Bangladesh's," *Lincoln Journal* (AP), January 18, 1990.

128. Donald Kaul, "Only Surprise Is That Riots Didn't Happen Sooner," *Lincoln Journal* (Tribune Media Services), May 19, 1992.

129. *New York Times*, April 2, 1978.

130. C. Davis, C. Haub, and J. Willette, "U.S. Hispanics: Changing the Face of America," *Population Bulletin* 38 (1983), pp. 1–44.

131. Although Hispanics commonly are spoken of as though they are a separate race, they really are not. Most are an amalgam of European, African, and/or Indian ancestry that makes it impossible to identify a race. On the 1990 census forms, where individuals indicate their own race, half of the Hispanics left this line blank. Hacker, *Two Nations*, p. 6.

132. Guadaloupe San Miguel, "Mexican American Organizations and the Changing Politics of School Desegregation in Texas, 1945–1980," *Social Science Quarterly* 63 (1982), pp. 701–715. See also Luis R. Fraga, Kenneth J. Meier, and Robert E. England, "Hispanic Americans and Educational Policy: Structural Limits to Equal Access and Opportunities for Upward Mobility," unpublished paper, University of Oklahoma, 1985.

133. San Miguel, "Mexican American Organizations," p. 710.

134. Leo Grebler, Joan W. Moore, and Ralph C. Guzman, *The Mexican-American People* (New York: Free Press, 1970), p. 157.

135. And even children of illegal aliens have been given the right to attend public schools by the Supreme Court. The majority assumed that most of these children, although subject to deportation, would remain in the United States, given the large number of illegal aliens who do remain here. Denying them an education would deprive them of the opportunity to fulfill their potential and would deprive society of the benefit of their contribution. *Plyler v. Doe* 457 U.S. 202 (1982).

136. Fraga, Meier, and England, "Hispanic Americans," p. 6.

137. Karen De Witt, "The Nation's Schools Learn a 4th R: Resegregation," *New York Times*, January 19, 1992, p. E5.

138. *San Antonio Independent School District v. Rodriguez*, 411 U.S. 1 (1973).

139. Luis Ricardo Fraga, Kenneth Meier, and Robert England, "Hispanic Americans and Educational Policy: Limits to Equal Access," *Journal of Politics* 48 (November 1986), pp. 850–873.

140. Hispanics have a higher dropout rate than blacks; over a quarter leave high school. "High Hispanic Dropout Rate Language-Related," *Lincoln Journal*, September 14, 1994.

141. *Lau v. Nichols*, 414 U.S. 563 (1974).

142. "Many-Tongued Classes," *Newsweek*, February 11, 1991, p. 57.

143. Margot Hornblower, "No Habla Espanol," *Time*, January 26, 1998, p. 63.

144. "Bilingualism's End Means a Different Kind of Change," *Champaign-Urbana News-Gazette* (Knight Ridder), June 7, 1998.

145. Hornblower, "No Habla Espanol."

146. Paul Gray, "Teach Your Children Well," *Time*, Fall, 1993, p. 70.

147. "Survey: Hispanics Reject Cohesive Group Identity," *Lincoln Journal* (AP), December 15, 1992.

148. Lynne Duke, "English Spoken Here," *Washington Post National Weekly Edition*, December 21–27, 1992, p. 37.

149. *Cherokee Nation v. Georgia*, 5 Peters 1 (1831); *Worcester v. Georgia*, 6 Peters 515 (1832).

150. Alfonso Ortiz, *The Pueblo* (New York: Chelsea House, 1994), p. 10.

151. Vine Deloria, Jr. and Clifford M. Lytle, *American Indians, American Justice* (Austin: University of Texas Press, 1983), p. 221.

152. Ibid., pp. 222–225.

153. Michael Lieder and Jake Page, *Wild Justice* (New York: Random House, 1997).

154. Indian Self-determination Act (1975).

155. Harvey Arden, "Who Owns Our Past?" *National Geographic*, March 1989, pp. 383, 388, 393.

156. According to the Indian Gaming Regulatory Act (1988), tribes can establish casinos if their reservation lies in a state that allows virtually any gambling, including charitable "Las Vegas nights."

157. Kathleen Schmidt, "Gambling a Bonanza for Indians," *Lincoln Journal Star* (Medill News Service), March 23, 1998.

158. Felicity Barringer, "Ethnic Pride Confounds the Census," *New York Times*, May 9, 1993, p. E3.

159. W. John Moore, "Tribal Imperatives," *National Journal*, June 9, 1990, p. 1396.

160. Ruth B. Ginsburg, *Constitutional Aspects of Sex-Based Discrimination* (St. Paul, Minn.: West Publishing Co. 1974), p. 2.

161. Karen DeCrow, *Sexist Justice* (New York: Vintage, 1975), p. 72.

162. Nadine Taub and Elizabeth M. Schneider, "Women's Subordination and the Role of Law," in David Kairys, ed., *The Politics of Law: A Progressive Critique*, revised ed. (New York: Pantheon, 1990), pp. 160–162.

163. *Bradwell v. Illinois*, 16 Wall. 130 (1873).

164. From an amicus curiae (friend of the court) brief by 281 historians filed in the Supreme Court case, *Webster v. Reproductive Health Services*, 106 L.Ed.2d 410 (1989).

165. Donna M. Moore, "Editor's Introduction" in Moore, *Battered Women* (Beverly Hills: Sage, 1979), p. 8.

166. Barbara Sinclair Deckard, *The Women's Movement*, 2d ed. (New York: Harper & Row, 1979), p. 303.

167. Reprinted in "Regrets, We Have a Few," *Time*, Special Issue: 75 Years of Time, 1998, p. 192.

168. DeCrow, *Sexist Justice*, p. 119.

169. Thus, Betty Friedan later felt compelled to write a book espousing the concept of motherhood. *The Second Stage* (New York: Summit, 1981).

170. For a discussion of these points, see Jane Mansbridge, *Why We Lost the ERA* (Chicago: University of Chicago Press, 1986); Mary Frances Berry, *Why ERA Failed* (Bloomington: Indiana University Press, 1986); Janet Boles, "Building Support for the ERA: A Case of 'Too Much, Too Late,' " *PS* 15 (Fall 1982): pp. 575–592.

171. Shenkman, *I Love Paul Revere*, pp. 136–137.

172. *Reed v. Reed*, 404 U.S. 71 (1971).

173. *Hoyt v. Florida*, 368 U.S. 57 (1961).

174. *Taylor v. Louisiana*, 419 U.S. 522 (1975).

175. *Stanton v. Stanton*, 421 U.S. 7 (1975).

176. "White Men Still First," *Lincoln Journal-Star*, April 1, 1995.

177. U.S. Department of Commerce, *Statistical Abstract of the United States, 1997* (Washington, D.C.: U.S. Government Printing Office, 1997), Table 645.

178. Ibid.

179. Naomi Wolf, "Stirring the Women's Movement from Its Dormant Decade," *Washington Post National Weekly Edition*, October 21–27, 1991, p. 23.

180. Ibid.

181. Susan Benesch, "The Birth of a Nation," *Washington Post National Weekly Edition*, August 4, 1986, p. 12.

182. The act also requires employers to continue health insurance coverage during the leave and to give the employee the same job or a comparable one upon her or his return.

183. Lisa Genasci, "Many Workers Resist Family Benefit Offers," *Lincoln Journal* (AP), June 28, 1995.

184. *Time*, June 28, 1993, pp. 55–56.

185. From a personal conversation with a business professor in attendance at a conference.

186. Joyce Gelb and Marian Lief Palley, *Women and Public Policies* (Princeton, N.J.: Princeton University Press, 1982), p. 102.

187. Steve Wulf, "A Level Playing Field for Women," *Time*, May 5, 1997, p. 80.

188. Jeremy L. Milk, "Women's Soccer on a Roll," *Chronicle of Higher Education* (November 3, 1993), p. A39.

189. Mary Duffy, quoted in E. J. Dionne, Jr., "Nothing Wacky about Title IX," *Washington Post National Weekly Edition*, May 19, 1997, p. 26.

190. *Mississippi University for Women v. Hogan*, 458 U.S. 718 (1982).

191. *Orr v. Orr*, 440 U.S. 268 (1979).

192. *Michael M. v. Sonoma County*, 450 U.S. 464 (1981).

193. *Rostker v. Goldberg*, 453 U.S. 57 (1981).

194. A simplified version of this scenario was used by President Johnson in support of affirmative action.

195. Early decisions include *University of California Regents v. Bakke*, 438 U.S. 265 (1978); *United Steelworkers v. Weber*, 443 U.S. 193 (1979); *Fullilove v. Klutznick*, 448 U.S. 448 (1980). For an examination of the *Bakke* ruling and its impact, see Susan Welch and John Gruhl, *Affirmative Action and Minority Enrollments in Medical and Law Schools* (Ann Arbor: University of Michigan, 1998).

196. *United Steelworkers v. Weber; Sheet Metal Workers v. EEOC*, 92 L.Ed.2d 344 (1986); *Firefighters v. Cleveland*, 92 L.Ed.2d 405 (1986); *United States v. Paradise Local Union*, 94 L.Ed.2d 203 (1987).

197. *Firefighters v. Stotts*, 467 U.S. 561 (1985); *Wygant v. Jackson Board of Education*, 90 L.Ed.2d 260 (1986).

198. *Richmond v. Croson*, 102 L.Ed.2d 854 (1989); *Adarand Constructors v. Pena*, 132 L.Ed.2d 158 (1995). The perception that minorities are taking over is also reflected in a peculiar poll finding: The average American estimates that 32% of the U.S. population is black and 21% is Hispanic (rather than just 12% and 9%). Richard Nadeau, Richard G. Niemi, and Jeffrey Levine, "Innumeracy about Minority Populations," *Public Opinion Quarterly* 57 (1993) pp. 332–347.

199. Robert J. Samuelson, "End Affirmative Action," *Washington Post National Weekly Edition*, March 6–12, 1995, p. 5.

200. Alison M. Konrad and Frank Linnehan, "Formalized HRM Structures: Coordinating Equal Employment Opportunity or Concealing Organizational Practices?" *Academy of Management Journal* 38 (June 1995), p. 787.

201. James E. Jones, "The Genesis and Present Status of Affirmative Action in Employment" paper presented at the American Political Science Association Annual Meeting, 1984: Robert Pear, *New York Times*, June 19, 1983; Nelson C. Dometrius and Lee Sigelman, "Assessing Progress Toward Affirmative Action Goals in State and Local Government," *Public Administration Review* 44 (May/June 1984) pp. 241–247; Peter Eisinger, *Black Employment in City Government* (Washington, D.C.: Joint Center for Political Studies, 1983); Milton Coleman, "Uncle Sam Has Stopped Running Interference for Blacks," *Washington Post National Weekly Edition*, December 19, 1983.

202. Gertrude Ezorsky, *Racism and Justice: The Case for Affirmative Action* (Ithaca, N.Y.: Cornell University Press, 1991), pp. 48–49, 63–65.

203. Wilson, *The Truly Disadvantaged*.

204. Donald Kaul, "Privilege in Workplace Invisible to White Men Who Enjoy It," *Lincoln Journal-Star*, April 9, 1995; Richard Morin and Lynne Duke, "A Look at the Bigger Picture," *Washington Post National Weekly Edition*, March 16–22, 1992, p. 9.

205. Eisinger, *Black Employment in City Government*.

206. Thomas J. Kane, "Racial and Ethnic Preference in College Admissions," paper presented at Ohio State University College of Law Conference, "Twenty Years after *Bakke*," April 1998.

207. Kluger, *Simple Justice*, p. 90.

208. Neal R. Peirce, "It's Later in the Day for a Nation Fashioned by European Immigrants," *Lincoln Sunday Journal-Star*, May 19, 1991.

209. Dick Kirschten, "Not Black-and-White," *National Journal*, March 2, 1991, pp. 496–500.

210. Mills, *This Little Light*, p. 132.

211. Ibid., p. 114, citing Lyndon Johnson, *The Vantage Point* (New York: Holt, Rinehart & Winston, 1971), p. 101.

212. Mills, *This Little Light*, p. xiii.

APPENDIX A

THE DECLARATION OF INDEPENDENCE*

In Congress, July 4, 1776.

A Declaration by the Representatives of the United States of America, in General Congress assembled.

When in the Course of human Events, it becomes necessary for one People to dissolve the Political Bonds which have connected them with another, and to assume among the Powers of the Earth, the separate and equal Station to which the Laws of Nature and of Nature's God entitle them, a decent Respect to the Opinions of Mankind requires that they should declare the causes which impel them to the Separation.

We hold these Truths to be self-evident, that all Men are created equal, that they are endowed by their Creator with certain unalienable Rights, that among these are Life, Liberty, and the Pursuit of Happiness—That to secure these Rights, Governments are instituted among Men, deriving their just Powers from the Consent of the Governed, that whenever any Form of Government becomes destructive of these Ends, it is the Right of the People to alter or to abolish it, and to institute new Government, laying its Foundation on such Principles, and organizing its Powers in such Forms, as to them shall seem most likely to effect their Safety and Happiness. Prudence, indeed, will dictate that Governments long established should not be changed for light and transient Causes; and accordingly all Experience hath shewn, that Mankind are more disposed to suffer, while Evils are sufferable, than to right themselves by abolishing the Forms to which they are accustomed. But when a long Train of Abuses and Usurpations, pursuing invariably the same Object, evinces a Design to reduce them under absolute Despotism, it is their Right, it is their Duty, to throw off such Government, and to provide new Guards for their future Security. Such has been the patient Sufferance of these Colonies; and such is now the Necessity which constrains them to alter their former Systems of Government. The History of the present King of Great Britain is a History of repeated Injuries and Usurpations, all having in direct Object the Establishment of an absolute Tyranny over these States. To prove this, let facts be submitted to a candid World.

He has refused his Assent to Laws, the most wholesome and necessary for the public Good.

He has forbidden his Governors to pass Laws of immediate and pressing Importance, unless suspended in their Operation till his Assent should be obtained; and when so suspended, he has utterly neglected to attend to them.

He has refused to pass other Laws for the Accommodation of large Districts of People, unless those People would relinquish the Right of Representation in the Legislature, a Right inestimable to them, and formidable to Tyrants only.

He has called together Legislative Bodies at Places unusual, uncomfortable, and distant from the Depository of their Public Records, for the sole Purpose of fatiguing them into Compliance with his Measures.

He has dissolved Representative Houses repeatedly, for opposing with manly Firmness his Invasions on the Rights of the People.

He has refused for a long Time, after such Dissolutions, to cause others to be elected; whereby the Legislative Powers, incapable of Annihilation, have returned to the People at large for their exercise; the State remaining in the mean time exposed to all the Dangers of Invasion from without, and Convulsions within.

He has endeavoured to prevent the Population of these States; for that Purpose obstructing the Laws for Naturalization of Foreigners; refusing to pass others to encourage their Migration hither, and raising the Conditions of new Appropriations of Lands.

He has obstructed the Administration of Justice, by refusing his Assent to Laws for establishing Judiciary Powers.

He has made Judges dependent on his Will alone, for the Tenure of their offices, and the Amount and payments of their Salaries.

He has erected a Multitude of new Offices, and sent hither Swarms of Officers to harass our People, and eat out their Substance.

He has kept among us, in times of Peace, Standing Armies, without the consent of our Legislatures.

He has affected to render the Military independent of, and superior to the Civil Power.

He has combined with others to subject us to a Jurisdiction foreign to our Constitution, and unacknowledged by our Laws; giving his Assent to their Acts of pretended Legislation:

For quartering large Bodies of Armed Troops among us:

For protecting them, by a mock Trial, from Punishment for any Murders which they should commit on the Inhabitants of these States:

*The spelling, capitalization, and punctuation of the original have been retained here.

For cutting off our Trade with all Parts of the World:

For imposing Taxes on us without our Consent:

For depriving us, in many cases, of the Benefits of Trial by Jury:

For transporting us beyond Seas to be tried for pretended Offences:

For abolishing the free System of English Laws in a neighbouring Province, establishing therein an arbitrary Government, and enlarging its Boundaries, so as to render it at once an Example and fit Instrument for introducing the same absolute Rule into these Colonies:

For taking away our Charters, abolishing our most valuable Laws, and altering fundamentally the Forms of our Governments:

For suspending our own Legislatures, and declaring themselves invested with Power to legislate for us in all Cases whatsoever.

He has abdicated Government here, by declaring us out of his Protection and waging War against us.

He has plundered our Seas, ravaged our Coasts, burnt our towns, and destroyed the Lives of our People.

He is, at this Time, transporting large Armies of foreign Mercenaries to compleat the works of Death, Desolation, and Tyranny, already begun with circumstances of Cruelty and Perfidy, scarcely paralleled in the most barbarous Ages, and totally unworthy the Head of a civilized Nation.

He has constrained our fellow Citizens taken Captive on the high Seas to bear Arms against their Country, to become the Executioners of their Friends and Brethren, or to fall themselves by their Hands.

He has excited domestic Insurrections amongst us, and has endeavoured to bring on the Inhabitants of our Frontiers, the merciless Indian Savages, whose known Rule of Warfare is an undistinguished Destruction, of all Ages, Sexes and Conditions.

In every state of these Oppressions we have Petitioned for Redress in the most humble Terms: Our repeated Petitions have been answered only by repeated Injury. A Prince, whose Character is thus marked by every act which may define a Tyrant, is unfit to be the Ruler of a free People.

Nor have we been wanting in Attentions to our British Brethren. We have warned them from Time to Time of Attempts by their Legislature to extend an unwarrantable Jurisdiction over us. We have reminded them of the Circumstances of our Emigration and Settlement here. We have appealed to their native Justice and Magnanimity, and we have conjured them by the Ties of our common Kindred to disavow these Usurpations, which would inevitably interrupt our Connections and Correspondence. They too have been deaf to the Voice of Justice and of Consanguinity. We must, therefore, acquiesce in the Necessity, which denounces our Separation, and hold them, as we hold the rest of Mankind, Enemies in War, in Peace, Friends.

We, therefore, the Representatives of the UNITED STATES OF AMERICA, in General Congress Assembled, appealing to the Supreme Judge of the World for the Rectitude of our Intentions, do, in the Name, and by Authority of the good People of these Colonies, solemnly Publish and Declare, That these United Colonies are, and of Right ought to be, Free and Independent States; that they are absolved from all Allegiance to the British Crown, and that all political Connection between them and the State of Great Britain, is and ought to be totally dissolved; and that as Free and Independent States, they have full Power to levy War, conclude Peace, contract Alliances, establish Commerce, and to do all other Acts and Things which Independent States may of right do. And for the support of this declaration, with a firm Reliance on the Protection of divine Providence, we mutually pledge to each other our Lives, our Fortunes, and our sacred Honor.

APPENDIX B

CONSTITUTION OF THE UNITED STATES OF AMERICA*

We the people of the United States, in Order to form a more perfect Union, establish Justice, insure domestic Tranquility, provide for the common defence, promote the general Welfare, and secure the Blessings of Liberty to ourselves and our posterity, do ordain and establish this Constitution for the United States of America.

ARTICLE I

SECTION 1. All legislative Powers herein granted shall be vested in a Congress of the United States, which shall consist of a Senate and House of Representatives.

SECTION 2. The House of Representatives shall be composed of Members chosen every second Year by the People of the several States, and the Electors in each State shall have the Qualifications requisite for Electors of the most numerous Branch of the State Legislature.

No person shall be a Representative who shall not have attained to the Age of twenty-five Years, and been seven Years a Citizen of the United States, and who shall not, when elected, be an Inhabitant of that State in which he shall be chosen.

Representatives and direct [Taxes][1] shall be apportioned among the several States which may be included within this Union, according to their respective Numbers [which shall be determined by adding to the whole Number of free Persons, including those bound to Service for a Term of Years, and excluding Indians not taxed, three fifths of all other Persons].[2] The actual Enumeration shall be made within three Years after the first Meeting of the Congress of the United States, and within every subsequent Term of ten Years, in such Manner as they shall by Law direct. The Number of Representatives shall not exceed one for every thirty Thousand, but each State shall have at Least one Representative; and until such enumeration shall be made, the State of New Hampshire shall be entitled to chuse three, Massachusetts eight, Rhode Island and Providence Plantations one, Connecticut five, New-York six, New Jersy four, Pennsylvania eight, Delaware one, Maryland six, Virginia ten, North Carolina five, South Carolina five, and Georgia three.

When vacancies happen in the Representation from any State, the Executive Authority thereof shall issue Writs of Election to fill such Vacancies.

The House of Representatives shall chuse their Speaker and other Officers; and shall have the sole Power of Impeachment.

SECTION 3. The Senate of the United States shall be composed of two Senators from each State [chosen by the Legislature thereof],[3] for six Years; and each Senator shall have one Vote.

Immediately after they shall be assembled in Consequence of the first Election, they shall be divided as equally as may be into three Classes. The Seats of the Senators of the first Class shall be vacated at the Expiration of the second year, of the second Class at the Expiration of the fourth Year, and of the third Class at the Expiration of the sixth Year, so that one third may be chosen every second Year [and if Vacancies happen by Resignation, or otherwise, during the Recess of the Legislature of any State, the Executive thereof may make temporary Appointments until the next Meeting of the Legislature, which shall then fill such Vacancies.][4]

No Person shall be a Senator who shall not have attained to the Age of thirty Years, and been nine Years a Citizen of the United States, and who shall not, when elected, be an Inhabitant of that State for which he shall be chosen.

The Vice President of the United States shall be President of the Senate, but shall have no Vote, unless they be equally divided.

The Senate shall chuse their other Officers, and also a President pro tempore, in the Absence of the Vice President, or when he shall exercise the Office of President of the United States.

The Senate shall have the sole Power to try all Impeachments. When sitting for that Purpose, they shall be on Oath or Affirmation. When the President of the United States is tried, the Chief Justice shall preside: And no Person shall be convicted without the Concurrence of two thirds of the Members present.

Judgment in Cases of Impeachment shall not extend further than to removal from Office, and disqualification to hold and enjoy any Office of honor, Trust or Profit under the United States; but the Party convicted shall nevertheless be liable and subject to Indictment, Trial, Judgment and Punishment, according to Law.

*The spelling, capitalization, and punctuation of the original have been retained here. Brackets indicate passages that have been altered by amendments to the Constitution.
1. Modified by the Sixteenth Amendment.
2. Modified by the Fourteenth Amendment.
3. Repealed by the Seventeenth Amendment.
4. Modified by the Seventeenth Amendment.

SECTION 4. The Times, Places and Manner of holding Elections for Senators and Representatives, shall be prescribed in each State by the Legislature thereof; but the Congress may at any time by Law make or alter such Regulations, except as to the Places of chusing Senators.

[The Congress shall assemble at least once in every Year, and such Meeting shall be on the first Monday in December, unless they shall by Law appoint a different Day.][5]

SECTION 5. Each House shall be the Judge of the Elections, Returns and Qualifications of its own Members, and a Majority of each shall constitute a Quorum to do Business; but a smaller Number may adjourn from day to day, and may be authorized to compel the Attendance of absent Members, in such Manner, and under such Penalties as each House may provide.

Each House may determine the Rules of its Proceedings, punish its Members for disorderly Behaviour, and, with the Concurrence of two thirds, expel a Member.

Each House shall keep a Journal of its Proceedings, and from time to time publish the same, excepting such Parts as may in their Judgment require Secrecy; and the Yeas and Nays of the Members of either House on any question shall, at the Desire of one fifth of those present, be entered on the Journal.

Neither House, during the Session of Congress, shall, without the Consent of the other, adjourn for more than three days, nor to any other Place than that in which the two Houses shall be sitting.

SECTION 6. The Senators and Representatives shall receive a Compensation for their Services, to be ascertained by Law, and paid out of the Treasury of the United States. They shall in all Cases, except Treason, Felony and Breach of the Peace, be privileged from Arrest during their Attendance at the Session of their respective Houses, and in going to and returning from the same; and for any Speech or Debate in either House, they shall not be questioned in any other Place.

No Senator or Representative shall, during the Time for which he was elected, be appointed to any civil Office under the Authority of the United States, which shall have been created, or the Emoluments whereof shall have been encreased during such time; and no Person holding any Office under the United States, shall be a Member of either House during his Continuance in Office.

SECTION 7. All Bills for raising Revenue shall originate in the House of Representatives; but the Senate may propose or concur with Amendments as on other Bills.

5. Changed by the Twentieth Amendment.

Every Bill which shall have passed the House of Representatives and the Senate, shall, before it become a Law, be presented to the President of the United States; If he approves he shall sign it, but if not he shall return it, with his objections to that House in which it shall have originated, who shall enter the Objections at large on their Journal, and proceed to reconsider it. If after such Reconsideration two thirds of that House shall agree to pass the Bill, it shall be sent, together with the Objections, to the other House, by which it shall likewise be reconsidered, and if approved by two thirds of that House, it shall become a Law. But in all such Cases the Votes of both Houses shall be determined by yeas and Nays, and the Names of the Persons voting for and against the Bill shall be entered on the Journal of each House respectively. If any Bill shall not be returned by the President within ten Days (Sundays excepted) after it shall have been presented to him, the Same shall be a Law, in like Manner as if he had signed it, unless the Congress by their Adjournment prevent its Return, in which Case it shall not be a Law.

Every Order, Resolution, or Vote to which the Concurrence of the Senate and House of Representatives may be necessary (except on a question of Adjournment) shall be presented to the President of the United States; and before the Same shall take Effect, shall be approved by him, or being disapproved by him, shall be repassed by two thirds of the Senate and House of Representatives, according to the Rules and Limitations prescribed in the Case of a Bill.

SECTION 8. The Congress shall have Power To lay and collect Taxes, Duties, Imposts and Excises, to pay the Debts and provide for the common Defence and general Welfare of the United States; but all Duties, Imposts and Excises shall be uniform throughout the United States;

To borrow Money on the credit of the United States;

To regulate Commerce with foreign Nations, and among the several States, and with the Indian Tribes;

To establish a uniform Rule of Naturalization, and uniform Laws on the subject of Bankruptcies throughout the United States;

To coin Money, regulate the Value thereof, and of foreign Coin, and fix the Standard of Weights and Measures;

To provide for the Punishment of counterfeiting the Securities and current Coin of the United States.

To establish Post Offices and post Roads;

To promote the Progress of Science and useful Arts, by securing for limited Times to Authors and Inventors the exclusive Right to their respective Writings and Discoveries;

To constitute Tribunals inferior to the supreme Court;

To define and punish Piracies and Felonies committed on the high Seas, and Offences against the Law of Nations;

To declare War, grant Letters of Marque and Reprisal, and make Rules concerning Captures on Land and Water;

To raise and support Armies, but no Appropriation of Money to that Use shall be for a longer Term than two Years;

To provide and maintain a Navy;

To make Rules for the Government and Regulation of the land and naval Forces;

To provide for calling forth the Militia to execute the Laws of the Union, suppress Insurrections and repel Invasions;

To provide for organizing, arming, and disciplining the Militia, and for governing such Part of them as may be employed in the Service of the United States, reserving to the States respectively, the Appointment of the Officers, and the Authority of training the Militia according to the discipline prescribed by Congress;

To exercise exclusive Legislation in all Cases whatsoever, over such District (not exceeding ten Miles square) as may, by Cession of particular States, and the Acceptance of Congress, become the Seat of the Government of the United States, and to exercise like Authority over all Places purchased by the Consent of the Legislature of the State in which the Same shall be, for the Erection of forts, Magazines, Arsenals, dockYards, and other needful Buildings;—And

To make all Laws which shall be necessary and proper for carrying into Execution the foregoing Powers, and all other Powers vested by this Constitution in the Government of the United States, or in any Department or Officer thereof.

SECTION 9. The Migration or Importation of such Persons as any of the States now existing shall think proper to admit, shall not be prohibited by the Congress prior to the Year one thousand eight hundred and eight, but a Tax or duty may be imposed on such Importation, not exceeding ten dollars for each Person.

The Privilege of the Writ of Habeas Corpus shall not be suspended, unless when in Cases of Rebellion or Invasion the public Safety may require it.

No Bill of Attainder or ex post facto Law shall be passed.

[No Capitation, or other direct, Tax shall be laid, unless in Proportion to the Census or Enumeration herein before directed to be taken.][6]

No Tax or Duty shall be laid on Articles exported from any State.

No Preference shall be given by any Regulation of Commerce or Revenue to the Ports of one State over those of another; nor shall Vessels bound to, or from, one State, be obliged to enter, clear, or pay Duties in another.

No Money shall be drawn from the Treasury, but in Consequence of Appropriations made by Law; and a regular Statement and Account of the Receipts and Expenditures of all public Money shall be published from time to time.

No Title of Nobility shall be granted by the United States; and no Person holding any Office or Profit or Trust under them, shall, without the Consent of the Congress, accept of any present, Emolument, Office, or Title, of any kind whatever, from any King, Prince, or foreign State.

SECTION 10. No state shall enter into any Treaty, Alliance, or Confederation; grant Letters of Marque and Reprisal; coin Money; emit Bills of Credit; make any Thing but gold and silver Coin a Tender in Payment of Debts; pass any Bill of Attainder, ex post facto Law, or Law impairing the Obligation of Contracts, or grant any Title of Nobility.

No State shall, without the Consent of the Congress, lay any Imposts or Duties on Imports or Exports, except what may be absolutely necessary for executing its inspection Laws; and the net Produce of all Duties and Imposts, laid by any State on Imports or Exports, shall be for the Use of the Treasury of the United States; and all such Laws shall be subject to the Revision and Controul of the Congress.

No State shall, without the Consent of Congress, lay any duty of Tonnage, keep Troops, or Ships of War in time of Peace, enter into any Agreement or Compact with another State, or with a foreign Power or engage in War, unless actually invaded, or in such imminent Danger as will not admit of delay.

ARTICLE II

SECTION 1. The executive Power shall be vested in a President of the United States of America. He shall hold his Office during the Term of four Years, and, together with the Vice President, chosen for the Same Term, be elected, as follows.

Each State shall appoint, in such Manner as the Legislature thereof may direct, a Number of Electors, equal to the whole Number of Senators and Representatives to which the State may be entitled in the Congress; but no Senator or Representative, or Person holding an Office of Trust or Profit under the United States, shall be appointed an Elector.

[The Electors shall meet in their respective States, and vote by Ballot for two Persons of whom one at least shall not be an Inhabitant of the same State with themselves. And they shall make a List of all the Persons voted for, and of the Number of Votes for each; which List they shall sign and certify, and

6. Modified by the Sixteenth Amendment.

transmit sealed to the Seat of the Government of the United States, directed to the President of the Senate. The President of the Senate shall, in the Presence of the Senate and House of Representatives, open all the Certificates, and the Votes shall then be counted. The Person having the greatest Number of Votes shall be the President, if such Number be a Majority of the whole Number of Electors appointed; and if there be more than one who have such Majority, and have an equal Number of Votes, then the House of Representatives shall immediately chuse by Ballot one of them for President; and if no Person have a Majority, then from the five highest on the List the said House shall in like Manner chuse the President. But in chusing the President, the Votes shall be taken by States, the Representation from each State having one Vote; A quorum for this Purpose shall consist of a Member or Members from two thirds of the States, and a Majority of all the states shall be necessary to a Choice. In every Case, after the Choice of the President, the Person having the greatest Number of Votes of the Electors shall be the Vice President. But if there should remain two or more who have equal Votes, the Senate shall chuse from them by Ballot the Vice President.][7]

The Congress may determine the Time of chusing the Electors, and the Day on which they shall give their Votes; which Day shall be the same throughout the United States.

No person except a natural born Citizen, or a Citizen of the United States, at the time of the Adoption of this Constitution, shall be eligible to the Office of President; neither shall any Person be eligible to that Office who shall not have attained to the Age of thirty five Years, and been fourteen Years a Resident within the United States.

[In Case of the Removal of the President from Office, or of his Death, Resignation, or Inability to discharge the Powers and Duties of the said Office, the same shall devolve on the Vice President, and the Congress may by Law provide for the Case of Removal, Death, Resignation or Inability, both of the President and Vice President, declaring what Officer shall then act as President, and such Officer shall act accordingly, until the Disability be removed, or a President shall be elected.][8]

The President shall, at stated Times, receive for his Services, a Compensation, which shall neither be encreased nor diminished during the Period for which he shall have been elected, and he shall not receive within that Period any other Emolument from the United States, or any of them.

7. Changed by the Twelfth Amendment.
8. Modified by the Twenty-fifth Amendment.

Before he enter on the Execution of his Office, he shall take the following Oath or Affirmation:—"I do solemnly swear (or affirm) that I will faithfully execute the Office of President of the United States, and will to the best of my Ability, preserve, protect and defend the constitution of the United States."

SECTION 2. The President shall be Commander in Chief of the Army and Navy of the United States, and of the Militia of the several States, when called into the actual Service of the United States; he may require the Opinion, in writing, of the principal Officer in each of the executive Departments, upon any Subject relating to the Duties of their respective Offices, and he shall have Power to grant Reprieves and Pardons for Offences against the United States, except in Cases of Impeachment.

He shall have Power, by and with the Advice and Consent of the Senate, to make Treaties, provided two thirds of the Senators present concur; and he shall nominate, and by and with the Advice and Consent of the Senate, shall appoint Ambassadors, other public Ministers and Consuls, Judges of the supreme Court, and all other Officers of the United States, whose Appointments are not herein otherwise provided for, and which shall be established by Law; but the Congress may by Law vest the Appointment of such inferior Officers, as they think proper, in the President alone, in the Courts of Law, or in the Heads of Departments.

The President shall have Power to fill up all Vacancies that may happen during the Recess of the Senate, by granting Commissions which shall expire at the end of their next Session.

SECTION 3. He shall from time to time give to the Congress Information of the State of the Union, and recommend to their Consideration such Measures as he shall judge necessary and expedient; he may, on extraordinary Occasions, convene both Houses, or either of them, and in Case of Disagreement between them, with Respect to the Time of Adjournment, he may adjourn them to such Time as he shall think proper; he shall receive Ambassadors and other public Ministers; he shall take Care that the Laws be faithfully executed, and shall Commission all the Officers of the United States.

SECTION 4. The President, Vice President and all civil Officers of the United States, shall be removed from Office on Impeachment for, and Conviction of, Treason, Bribery, or other high Crimes and Misdemeanors.

ARTICLE III

SECTION 1. The judicial Power of the United States, shall be vested in one supreme Court, and in such inferior Courts as the Congress may from time to time ordain and establish. The Judges, both of the supreme and inferior Courts, shall hold their Offices during good Behaviour, and shall, at stated Times, receive for their Services, a Compensation, which shall not be diminished during their Continuance in Office.

SECTION 2. The judicial Power shall extend to all Cases, in Law and Equity, arising under this Constitution, the Laws of the United States, and Treaties made, or which shall be made, under their Authority;—to all Cases affecting Ambassadors, other public Ministers and Consuls;—to all Cases of admiralty and maritime Jurisdiction;—to Controversies to which the United States shall be a Party;—to Controversies between two or more States;—[between a State and Citizens of another State;][9]—between Citizens of different States,—between Citizens of the same State claiming Lands under Grants of different States, [and between a state, or the Citizens thereof, and foreign States, Citizens or Subjects.][10]

In all cases affecting Ambassadors, other public Ministers and Consuls, and those in which a State shall be Party, the supreme Court shall have original Jurisdiction. In all the other Cases before mentioned, the supreme Court shall have appellate Jurisdiction, both as to Law and Fact, with such Exceptions, and under such Regulations as the Congress shall make.

The Trial of all Crimes, except in Cases of Impeachment, shall be by Jury; and such Trial shall be held in the State where the said Crimes shall have been committed; but when not committed within any State, the Trial shall be at such Place or Places as the Congress may by Law have directed.

SECTION 3. Treason against the United States, shall consist only in levying War against them, or in adhering to their Enemies, giving them Aid and Comfort. No Person shall be convicted of Treason unless on the Testimony of two Witnesses to the same overt Act, or on Confession in open Court.

The Congress shall have Power to declare the Punishment of Treason, but no Attainder of Treason shall work Corruption of Blood, or Forfeiture except during the Life of the Person attainted.

ARTICLE IV

SECTION 1. Full Faith and Credit shall be given in each State to the public Acts, Records, and judicial Proceedings of every other State. And the Congress may by general Laws prescribe the Manner in which such Acts, Records and Proceedings shall be proved, and the Effect thereof.

SECTION 2. The Citizens of each State shall be entitled to all Privileges and Immunities of Citizens in the several States.

A Person charged in any State with Treason, Felony, or other Crime, who shall flee from Justice, and be found in another State, shall on Demand of the executive Authority of the State from which he fled, be delivered up, to be removed to the State having Jurisdiction of the Crime.

[No Person held to Service or Labour in one State under the Laws thereof, escaping into another, shall, in Consequence of any Law or Regulation therein, be discharged from such Service or Labour, but shall be delivered up on Claim of the Party to whom such Service or Labour may be due.][11]

SECTION 3. New States may be admitted by the Congress into this Union; but no new State shall be formed or erected within the Jurisdiction of any other State; nor any State be formed by the Junction of two or more States, or Parts of States, without the Consent of the Legislatures of the States concerned as well as of the Congress.

The Congress shall have Power to dispose of and make all needful Rules and Regulations respecting the Territory or other Property belonging to the United States; and nothing in this Constitution shall be so construed as to Prejudice any Claimes of the United States, or of any particular State.

SECTION 4. The United States shall guarantee to every State in this Union a Republican Form of Government, and shall protect each of them against Invasion, and on Application of the Legislature, or of the Executive (when the Legislature cannot be convened) against domestic Violence.

ARTICLE V

The Congress, whenever two thirds of both Houses shall deem it necessary, shall propose Amendments to this Constitution, or on the Application of the Legislatures of two thirds of the several States, shall call a Convention for proposing Amendments, which, in either Case, shall be valid to all Intents and Purposes, as Part of this Constitution, when ratified by the Legislatures of three fourths of the several States, or by Conventions in three fourths thereof, as the one or the other Mode of Ratification may be proposed by the Congress; Provided that no Amendment which may be made prior to the Year One thousand eight hundred and eight shall in any Manner affect the first and fourth Clauses in the Ninth Section of the first Article;

9. Modified by the Eleventh Amendment.
10. Modified by the Eleventh Amendment.
11. Repealed by the Thirteenth Amendment.

and that no State, without its Consent, shall be deprived of its equal Suffrage in the Senate.

ARTICLE VI

All Debts contracted and Engagements entered into, before the Adoption of this Constitution, shall be as valid against the United States under this Constitution, as under the Confederation.

This Constitution, and the laws of the United States which shall be made in Pursuance thereof; and all Treaties made, or which shall be made, under the Authority of the United States, shall be the supreme Law of the Land; and the Judges in every State shall be bound thereby, any Thing in the Constitution or Laws of any State to the Contrary notwithstanding.

The Senators and Representatives before mentioned, and the Members of the several State Legislatures, and all executive and judicial Officers, both of the United States and of the several States, shall be bound by Oath or Affirmation, to support this Constitution; but no religious Text shall ever be required as a Qualification to any Office or public Trust under the United States.

ARTICLE VII

The Ratification of the Conventions of nine States, shall be sufficient for the Establishment of this constitution between the States so ratifying the Same.

Done in Convention by the Unanimous Consent of the States present the Seventeenth Day of September in the Year of our Lord one thousand seven hundred and Eighty seven and of the Independence of the United States of America the Twelfth. IN WITNESS whereof we have hereunto subscribed our Names.

Go. WASHINGTON
Presid't. and deputy from Virginia

Attest
William Jackson
Secretary

Delaware
Geo. Read
Gunning Bedford jun
John Dickinson
Richard Basset
Jaco. Broon

Massachusetts
Nathaniel Gorham
Rufus King

Connecticut
Wm. Saml. Johnson
Roger Sherman

New York
Alexander Hamilton

New Jersey
Wh. Livingston
David Brearley
Wm. Paterson
Jona. Dayton

Pennsylvania
B. Franklin
Thomas Mifflin
Robt. Morris
Geo. Clymer
Thos. FitzSimons
Jared Ingersoll
James Wilson
Gouv. Morris

Viriginia
John Blair
James Madison Jr.

North Carolina
Wm. Blount
Richd. Dobbs Spaight
Hu. Williamson

South Carolina
J. Rutledge
Charles Cotesworth Pinckney
Charles Pinckney
Pierce Butler

Georgia
William Few
Abr. Baldwin

New Hampshire
John Langdon
Nicholas Gilman

Maryland
James McHenry
Dan of St. Thos. Jenifer
Danl. Carroll

AMENDMENT I[12]

Congress shall make no law respecting an establishment of religion, or prohibiting the free exercise thereof; or abridging the freedom of speech, or of the press; or the right of the people peaceably to assemble, and to petition the Government for a redress of grievances.

AMENDMENT II

A well regulated militia, being necessary to the security of a free State, the right of the people to keep and bear arms, shall not be infringed.

AMENDMENT III

No Soldier shall, in time of peace be quartered in any house, without the consent of the owner, nor in time of war, but in a manner to be prescribed by law.

AMENDMENT IV

The right of the people to be secure in their persons, houses, papers, and effects, against unreasonable searches and seizures, shall not be violated, and no warrants shall issue, but upon probable cause, supported by oath or affirmation, and particularly describing the place to be searched, and the persons or things to be seized.

AMENDMENT V

No person shall be held to answer for a capital, or otherwise infamous crime, unless on a presentment or indictment of a Grand Jury, except in cases arising in the land or naval forces, or in the militia, when in actual service in time of war or public danger; nor shall any person be subject for the same offence to be twice put in jeopardy of life or limb; nor shall be compelled in

12. The first ten amendments were passed by Congress on September 25, 1789, and were ratified on December 15, 1791.

any criminal case to be a witness against himself, nor be deprived of life, liberty, or property, without due process of law; nor shall private property be taken for public use, without just compensation.

AMENDMENT VI

In all criminal prosecutions, the accused shall enjoy the right to a speedy and public trial, by an impartial jury of the State and district wherein the crime shall have been committed, which district shall have been previously ascertained by law, and to be informed of the nature and cause of the accusation; to be confronted with the witnesses against him; to have compulsory process for obtaining witnesses in his favor, and to have the assistance of counsel for his defence.

AMENDMENT VII

In Suits at common law, where the value in controversy shall exceed twenty dollars, the right of trial by jury shall be preserved, and no fact tried by a jury, shall be otherwise reexamined in any Court of the United States, than according to the rules of the common law.

AMENDMENT VIII

Excessive bail shall not be required, nor excessive fines imposed, nor cruel and unusual punishments inflicted.

AMENDMENT IX

The enumeration in the Constitution, of certain rights, shall not be construed to deny or disparage others retained by the people.

AMENDMENT X

The powers not delegated to the United States by the Constitution, nor prohibited by it to the States, are reserved to the States respectively, or to the people.

AMENDMENT XI (RATIFIED FEBRUARY 7, 1795)

The Judicial power of the United States shall not be construed to extend to any suit in law or equity, commenced or prosecuted against one of the United States by Citizens of another State, or by Citizens or Subjects of any Foreign State.

AMENDMENT XII (RATIFIED JUNE 15, 1804)

The Electors shall meet in their respective states, and vote by ballot for President and Vice-President, one of whom, at least, shall not be an inhabitant of the same state with themselves; they shall name in their ballots the person voted for as President, and in distinct ballots the person voted for as Vice President, and they shall make distinct lists of all persons voted for as President, and of all persons voted for as Vice-President, and of the number of votes for each, which lists they shall sign and certify, and transmit sealed to the seat of the government of the United States, directed to the President of the Senate;—The President of the Senate shall, in the presence of the Senate and House of Representatives, open all the certificates and the votes shall then be counted;—The person having the greatest number of votes for President, shall be the President, if such number be a majority of the whole number of Electors appointed; and if no person have such majority, then from the persons having the highest numbers not exceeding three on the list of those voted for as President, the House of Representatives shall choose immediately, by ballot, the President. But in choosing the President, the votes shall be taken by states, the representation from each state having one vote; a quorum for this purpose shall consist of a member or members from two-thirds of the states, and a majority of all the states shall be necessary to a choice. [And if the House of Representatives shall not choose a President whenever the right of choice shall devolve upon them, before the fourth day of March next following, then the Vice-President shall act as President, as in the case of the death or other constitutional disability of the President.][13]—The person having the greatest number of votes as Vice-President, shall be the Vice-President, if such number be a majority of the whole number of Electors appointed, and if no person have a majority, then from the two highest numbers on the list, the Senate shall choose the Vice-President; a quorum for the purpose shall consist of two-thirds of the whole number of Senators, and a majority of the whole number shall be necessary to a choice. But no person constitutionally ineligible to the office of President shall be eligible to that of Vice-President of the United States.

AMENDMENT XIII (RATIFIED ON DECEMBER 6, 1865)

SECTION 1. Neither slavery nor involuntary servitude, except as a punishment for crime whereof the party shall have been duly convicted, shall exist within the United States, or any place subject to their jurisdiction.

SECTION 2. Congress shall have power to enforce this article by appropriate legislation.

AMENDMENT XIV (RATIFIED ON JULY 9, 1868)

All persons born or naturalized in the United States, and subject to the jurisdiction thereof, are citizens of the United States and of the State wherein they reside. No State shall make or enforce any law which shall abridge the privileges or immunities of citizens of the United States; nor shall any State deprive any

13. Changed by the Twentieth Amendment.

person of life, liberty, or property, without due process of law; nor deny to any person within its jurisdiction the equal protection of the laws.

SECTION 2. Representatives shall be apportioned among the several States according to their respective numbers, counting the whole number of persons in each State, excluding Indians not taxed. But when the right to vote at any election for the choice of electors for President and Vice President of the United States, Representatives in Congress, the Executive and Judicial officers of a State, or the members of the Legislature thereof, is denied to any of the male inhabitants of such State, being [twenty-one][14] years of age, and citizens of the United States, or in any way abridged, except for participation in rebellion, or other crime, the basis of representation therein shall be reduced in the proportion which the number of such male citizens shall bear to the whole number of male citizens twenty-one years of age in such State.

SECTION 3. No person shall be a Senator or Representative in Congress, or elector of President and Vice President, or hold any office, civil or military, under the United States, or under any State, who having previously taken an oath, as a member of Congress, or as an officer of the United States, or as a member of any State legislature, or as an executive or judicial officer of any State, to support the Constitution of the United States, shall have engaged in insurrection or rebellion against the same, or given aid or comfort to the enemies thereof. But Congress may by a vote of two-thirds of each House, remove such disability.

SECTION 4. The validity of the public debt of the United States, authorized by law, including debts incurred for payment of pensions and bounties for services in suppressing insurrection or rebellion, shall not be questioned. But neither the United States nor any State shall assume or pay any debt or obligation incurred in aid of insurrection or rebellion against the United States, or any claim for the loss or emancipation of any slave, but all such debts, obligations and claims shall be held illegal and void.

SECTION 5. The Congress shall have power to enforce, by appropriate legislation, the provisions of this article.

AMENDMENT XV (RATIFIED ON FEBRUARY 3, 1870)

SECTION 1. The right of citizens of the United States to vote shall not be denied or abridged by the United States or by any State on account of race, color, or previous condition of servitude.

SECTION 2. The Congress shall have power to enforce this article by appropriate legislation.

AMENDMENT XVI (RATIFIED ON FEBRUARY 3, 1913)

The Congress shall have power to lay and collect taxes on incomes, from whatever source derived, without apportionment among the several States, and without regard to any census or enumeration.

AMENDMENT XVII (RATIFIED ON APRIL 8, 1913)

The Senate of the United States shall be composed of two Senators from each State, elected by the people thereof, for six years; and each Senator shall have one vote. The electors in each State shall have the qualifications requisite for electors of the most numerous branch of the State legislatures.

When vacancies happen in the representation of any State in the Senate, the executive authority of such State shall issue writs of election to fill such vacancies: *Provided,* That the legislature of any State may empower the executive thereof to make temporary appointments until the people fill the vacancies by election as the legislature may direct.

This amendment shall not be so construed as to affect the election or term of any Senator chosen before it becomes valid as part of the Constitution.

AMENDMENT XVIII (RATIFIED ON JANUARY 16, 1919)

SECTION 1. After one year from the ratification of this article the manufacture, sale, or transportation of intoxicating liquors within, the importation thereof into, or the exportation thereof from the United States and all territory subject to the jurisdiction thereof for beverage purposes is hereby prohibited.

SECTION 2. The Congress and the several States shall have concurrent power to enforce this article by appropriate legislation.

SECTION 3. This article shall be inoperative unless it shall have been ratified as an amendment to the Constitution by the legislatures of the several States, as provided in the Constitution, within seven years from the date of the submission hereof to the States by the Congress.[15]

AMENDMENT XIX (RATIFIED ON AUGUST 18, 1920)

The right of citizens of the United States to vote shall not be denied or abridged by the United States or by any State on account of sex.

14. Changed by the Twenty-sixth Amendment.

15. The Eighteenth Amendment was repealed by the Twenty-first Amendment.

Congress shall have power to enforce this article by appropriate legislation.

AMENDMENT XX (RATIFIED ON JANUARY 23, 1933)

SECTION 1. The terms of the President and Vice President shall end at noon on the 20th day of January, and the terms of Senators and Representatives at noon on the 3rd day of January, of the years in which such terms would have ended if this article had not been ratified, and the terms of their successors shall then begin.

SECTION 2. The Congress shall assemble at least once in every year, and such meeting shall begin at noon on the 3rd day of January, unless they shall by law appoint a different day.

SECTION 3. If, at the time fixed for the beginning of the term of the President, the President elect shall have died, the Vice President elect shall become President. If a President shall not have been chosen before the time fixed for the beginning of his term, or if the President elect shall have failed to qualify, then the Vice President elect shall act as President until a President shall have qualified; and the Congress may by law provide for the case wherein neither a President elect nor a Vice President elect shall have qualified, declaring who shall then act as President, or the manner in which one who is to act shall be selected, and such person shall act accordingly until a President or Vice President shall have qualified.

SECTION 4. The Congress may by law provide for the case of the death of any of the persons from whom the House of Representatives may choose a President whenever the rights of choice shall have devolved upon them, and for the case of the death of any of the persons from whom the Senate may choose a Vice President whenever the right of choice shall have devolved upon them.

SECTION 5. Sections 1 and 2 shall take effect on the 15th day of October following the ratification of this article.

SECTION 6. This article shall be inoperative unless it shall have been ratified as an amendment to the Constitution by the legislatures of three-fourths of the several States within seven years from the date of its submission.

AMENDMENT XXI (RATIFIED ON DECEMBER 5, 1933)

SECTION 1. The eighteenth article of amendment to the Constitution of the United States is hereby repealed.

SECTION 2. The transportation or importation into any State, Territory, or possession of the United States for delivery or use therein of intoxicating liquors, in violation of the laws thereof, is hereby prohibited.

SECTION 3. This article shall be inoperative unless it shall have been ratified as an amendment to the Constitution by conventions in the several States, as provided in the Constitution, within seven years from the date of the submission hereof to the States by the Congress.

AMENDMENT XXII (RATIFIED ON FEBRUARY 27, 1951)

No person shall be elected to the office of the President more than twice, and no person who has held the office of President, or acted as President, for more than two years of a term to which some other person was elected President shall be elected to the office of the President more than once. But this Article shall not apply to any person holding the office of President when this Article was proposed by the Congress, and shall not prevent any person who may be holding the office of President, or acting as President, during the term within which this Article becomes operative from holding the office of President or acting as President during the remainder of such term.

AMENDMENT XXIII (RATIFIED ON MARCH 29, 1961)

SECTION 1. The District constituting the seat of Government of the United States shall appoint in such manner as the Congress may direct:

A number of electors of President and Vice President equal to the whole number of Senators and Representatives in Congress to which the District would be entitled if it were a State, but in no event more than the least populous State; they shall be in addition to those appointed by the States, but they shall be considered, for the purposes of the election of President and Vice President, to be electors appointed by a State; and they shall meet in the District and perform such duties as provided by the twelfth article of amendment.

SECTION 2. The Congress shall have power to enforce this article by appropriate legislation.

AMENDMENT XXIV (RATIFIED ON JANUARY 23, 1964)

SECTION 1. The right of citizens of the United States to vote in any primary or other election for President or Vice President, for electors for President or Vice President, or for Senator or Representative in Congress, shall not be denied or abridged by the United States or any State by reason of failure to pay any poll tax or other tax.

SECTION 2. The Congress shall have power to enforce this article by appropriate legislation.

AMENDMENT XXV (RATIFIED ON FEBRUARY 10, 1967)

SECTION 1. In case of the removal of the President from office or of his death or resignation, the Vice President shall become President.

SECTION 2. Whenever there is a vacancy in the office of the Vice President, the President shall nominate a Vice President who shall take office upon confirmation by a majority vote of both Houses of Congress.

SECTION 3. Whenever the President transmits to the President pro tempore of the Senate and the Speaker of the House of Representatives his written declaration that he is unable to discharge the powers and duties of his office, and until he transmits to them a written declaration to the contrary, such powers and duties shall be discharged by the Vice President as Acting President.

SECTION 4. Whenever the Vice President and a majority of either the principal officers of the executive departments or of such other body as Congress may by law provide, transmit to the President pro tempore of the Senate and the Speaker of the House of Representatives their written declaration that the President is unable to discharge the powers and duties of his office, the Vice President shall immediately assume the powers and duties of the offices as Acting President.

Thereafter, when the President transmits to the President pro tempore of the Senate and the Speaker of the House of Representatives his written declaration that no inability exists, he shall resume the powers and duties of his office unless the Vice President and a majority of either the principal officers of the executive department or of such other body as Congress may by law provide, transmit within four days to the President pro tempore of the Senate and the Speaker of the House of Representatives their written declaration that the President is unable to discharge the powers and duties of his office. Thereupon Congress shall decide the issue, assembling within forty-eight hours for that purpose if not in session. If the Congress, within twenty-one days after receipt of the latter written declaration, or, if Congress is not in session, within twenty-one days after Congress is required to assemble, determines by two-thirds vote of both Houses that the President is unable to discharge the powers and duties of his office, the Vice President shall continue to discharge the same as Acting President; otherwise; the President shall resume the powers and duties of his office.

AMENDMENT XXVI (RATIFIED ON JULY 1, 1971)

SECTION 1. The right of citizens of the United States, who are eighteen years of age or older, to vote shall not be denied or abridged by the United States or by any State on account of age.

SECTION 2. The Congress shall have the power to enforce this article by appropriate legislation.

AMENDMENT XXVII (RATIFIED ON MAY 7, 1992)

No law, varying the compensation for the services of the Senators and Representatives, shall take effect, until an election of Representatives shall have intervened.

APPENDIX C

FEDERALIST PAPER #10

Among the numerous advantages promised by a well-constructed Union, none deserves to be more accurately developed than its tendency to break and control the violence of faction. The friend of popular governments never finds himself so much alarmed for their character and fate as when he contemplates their propensity to this dangerous vice. He will not fail, therefore, to set a due value on any plan which, without violating the principles to which he is attached, provides a proper cure for it. The instability, injustice, and confusion introduced into the public councils have, in truth, been the mortal diseases under which popular governments have everywhere perished, as they continue to be the favorite and fruitful topics from which the adversaries to liberty derive their most specious declamations. The valuable improvements made by the American constitutions on the popular models, both ancient and modern, cannot certainly be too much admired; but it would be an unwarrantable partiality to contend that they have as effectually obviated the danger on this side, as was wished and expected. Complaints are everywhere heard from our most considerate and virtuous citizens, equally the friends of public and private faith and of public and personal liberty, that our governments are too unstable, that the public good is disregarded in the conflicts of rival parties, and that measures are too often decided, not according to the rules of justice and the rights of the minor party, but by the superior force of an interested and overbearing majority. However anxiously we may wish that these complaints had no foundation, the evidence of known facts will not permit us to deny that they are in some degree true. It will be found, indeed, on a candid review of our situation, that some of the distresses under which we labor have been erroneously charged on the operation of our governments; but it will be found, at the same time, that other causes will not alone account for many of our heaviest misfortunes; and, particularly, for that prevailing and increasing distrust of public engagements and alarm for private rights which are echoed from one end of the continent to the other. These must be chiefly, if not wholly, effects of the unsteadiness and injustice with which a factious spirit has tainted our public administration.

By a faction I understand a number of citizens, whether amounting to a majority or minority of the whole, who are united and actuated by some common impulse of passion, or of interest, adverse to the rights of other citizens, or the permanent and aggregate interests of the community.

There are two methods of curing the mischiefs of faction: the one, by removing its causes; the other, by controlling its effects.

There are again two methods of removing the causes of faction: the one, by destroying the liberty which is essential to its existence; the other, by giving to every citizen the same opinions, the same passions, and the same interests.

It could never be more truly said than of the first remedy that it was worse than the disease. Liberty is to faction what air is to fire, an aliment without which it instantly expires. But it could not be a less folly to abolish liberty, which is essential to political life, because it nourishes faction than it would be to wish the annihilation of air, which is essential to animal life, because it imparts to fire its destructive agency.

The second expedient is as impracticable as the first would be unwise. As long as the reason of man continues fallible, and his is at liberty to exercise it, different opinions will be formed. As long as the connection subsists between his reason and his self-love, his opinions and his passions will have a reciprocal influence on each other; and the former will be objects to which the latter will attach themselves. The diversity in the faculties of men, from which the rights of property originate, is not less an insuperable obstacle to a uniformity of interests. The protection of these faculties is the first object of government. From the protection of different and unequal faculties of acquiring property, the possession of different degrees and kinds of property immediately results; and from the influence of these on the sentiments and views of the respective proprietors ensues a division of the society into different interests and parties.

The latent causes of faction are thus sown in the nature of man; and we see them everywhere brought into different degrees of activity, according to the different circumstances of civil society. A zeal for different opinions concerning religion, concerning government, and many other points, as well of speculation as of practice; an attachment to different leaders ambitiously contending for pre-eminence and power; or to persons of other descriptions whose fortunes have been interesting to the human passions, have, in turn, divided mankind into parties, inflamed them with mutual animosity, and rendered them much more disposed to vex and oppress each other than to cooperate for their common good. So strong is this propensity of mankind to fall into mutual animosities that where no substantial occasion presents itself the most frivolous and fanciful distinctions have been sufficient to kindle their unfriendly passions and excite their most violent conflicts. But the most common and durable source of factions has been the various and unequal distribution of property. Those who hold and those who are without property have ever formed distinct interests in society. Those who are creditors, and those who are debtors, fall under a like discrimination. A landed interest, a manufacturing interest, a mercantile interest, a moneyed interest, with many lesser interests, grow up of necessity in civilized nations, and divide them into different classes, actuated by different sentiments and views. The regulation of these various and interfering interests forms the principal task of modern legislation and involves the spirit of party and faction in the necessary and ordinary operations of government.

No man is allowed to be a judge in his own cause, because his interest would certainly bias his judgment, and, not improbably, corrupt his integrity. With equal, nay with greater reason, a body of men are unfit to be both judges and parties at the same time; yet what are many of the most important acts of legislation but so many judicial determinations, not indeed concerning the rights of single persons, but concerning the rights of large bodies of citizens? And what are the different classes of legislators but advocates and parties to the causes which they determine? Is a law proposed concerning private debts? It is a question to which the creditors are parties on one side and the debtors on the other. Justice ought to hold the balance between them. Yet the parties are, and must be, themselves the judges; and the most numerous party, or in other words, the most powerful faction must be expected to prevail. Shall domestic manufacturers be encouraged, and in what degree, by restrictions on foreign manufacturers? are questions which would be differently decided by the landed and the manufacturing classes, and probably by neither with a sole regard to justice and the public good. The apportionment of taxes on the various descriptions of property is an act which seems to require the most exact impartiality; yet there is, perhaps, no legislative act in which greater opportunity and temptation are given to a predominant party to trample on the rules of justice. Every shilling with which they overburden the inferior number is a shilling saved to their own pockets.

It is in vain to say that enlightened statesmen will be able to adjust these clashing interests and render them all subservient to the public good. Enlightened statesmen will not always be at the helm. Nor, in many cases, can such an adjustment be made at all without taking into view indirect and remote considerations, which will rarely prevail over the immediate interest which one party may find in disregarding the rights of another or the good of the whole.

The inference to which we are brought is that the *causes* of faction cannot be removed and that relief is only to be sought in the means of controlling its *effects*.

If a faction consists of less than a majority, relief is supplied by the republican principle, which enables the majority to defeat its sinister views by regular vote. It may clog the administration, it may convulse the society; but it will be unable to execute and mask its violence under the forms of the Constitution. When a majority is included in a faction, the form of popular government, on the other hand, enables it to sacrifice to its ruling passion or interest both the public good and the rights of other citizens. To secure the public good and private rights against the danger of such a faction, and at the same time to preserve the spirit and the form of popular government, is then the great object to which our inquiries are directed. Let me add that it is the great desideratum by which alone this form of government can be rescued from the opprobrium under which it has so long labored and be recommended to the esteem and adoption of mankind.

By what means is this object attainable? Evidently by one of two only. Either the existence of the same passion or interest in a majority at the same time must be prevented, or the majority, having such coexistent passion or interest, must be rendered, by their number and local situtation, unable to concert and carry into effect schemes of oppression. If the impulse and the opportunity be suffered to coincide, we well know that neither moral nor religious motives can be relied on as an adequate control. They are not found to be such on the injustice and violence of individuals, and lose their efficacy in proportion to the number combined together, that is, in proportion as their efficacy becomes needful.

From this view of the subject it may be concluded that a pure democracy, by which I mean a society consisting of a small number of citizens, who assemble and administer the government in person, can admit of no cure for the mischiefs of faction. A common passion or interest will, in almost every case, be felt by a majority of the whole; a communication and concert results from the form of government itself; and there is nothing to check the inducements to sacrifice the weaker party or an obnoxious individual. Hence it is that such democracies have ever been spectacles of turbulence and contention; have ever been found incompatible with personal security or the rights of property; and have in general been as short in their lives as they have been violent in their deaths. Theoretic politicians, who have patronized this species of government, have erroneously supposed that by reducing mankind to a perfect equality in their political rights, they would at the same time be perfectly equalized and assimilated in their possessions, their opinions, and their passions.

A republic, by which I mean a government in which the scheme of representation takes place, opens a different prospect and promises the cure for which we are seeking. Let us examine the points in which it varies from pure democracy, and we shall comprehend both the nature of the cure and the efficacy which it must derive from the Union.

The two great points of difference between a democracy and a republic are: first, the delegation of the government, in the latter, to a small number of citizens elected by the rest; secondly, the greater number of citizens and greater sphere of country over which the latter may be extended.

The effect of the first difference is, on the one hand, to refine and enlarge the public views by passing them through the medium of a chosen body of citizens, whose wisdom may best discern the true interest of their country and whose patriotism and love of justice will be least likely to sacrifice it to temporary or partial considerations. Under such a regulation it may well happen that the public voice, pronounced by the representatives of the people, will be more consonant to the public good than if pronounced by the people themselves, convened for the purpose. On the other hand, the effect may be inverted. Men of factious tempers, of local prejudices, or of sinister designs, may, by intrigue, by corruption, or by other means, first obtain the suffrages, and then betray the interests of the people. The question resulting is, whether small or extensive republics are most favorable to the election of proper guardians of the public weal; and it is clearly decided in favor of the latter by two obvious considerations.

In the first place it is to be remarked that however small the republic may be the representatives must be raised to a certain number in order to guard against the cabals of a few; and that however large it may be they must be limited to a certain number in order to guard against the confusion of a multitude. Hence, the number of representatives in the two cases not being in proportion to that of the constituents, and being proportionally greatest in the small republic, it follows that if the proportion of fit characters be not less in the large than in the small republic, the former will present a greater option, and consequently a greater probability of a fit choice.

In the next place, as each representative will be chosen by a greater number of citizens in the large than in the small republic, it will be more difficult for unworthy candidates to practice with success the vicious arts by which elections are too often carried; and the suffrages of the people being more free, will be more likely to center on men who possess the most attractive merit and the most diffusive and established characters.

It must be confessed that in this, as in most other cases, there is a mean, on both sides of which inconveniencies will be found to lie. By enlarging too much the number of electors, you render the representative too little acquainted with all their local circumstances and lesser interests; as by reducing it too much, you render him unduly attached to these, and too little fit to comprehend and pursue great and national objects. The federal Constitution forms a happy combination in this respect; the great and aggregate interests being referred to the national, the local and particular to the State legislatures.

The other point of difference is the greater number of citizens and extent of territory which may be brought within the compass of republican than of democratic government; and it is this circumstance principally which renders factious combinations less to be dreaded in the former than in the latter. The smaller the society, the fewer probably will be the distinct parties and interests composing it; the fewer the distinct parties and interests, the more frequently will a majority be found of the same party; and the smaller the number of individuals composing a majority, and the smaller the compass within which they are placed, the more easily will they concert and execute their plans of oppression. Extend the sphere and you take in a greater variety of parties and interests; you make it less probable that a majority of the whole will have a common motive to invade the rights of other citizens; or if such a common motive exists, it will be more difficult for all who feel it to discover their own strength and to act in unison with each other. Besides other impediments, it may be remarked that, where there is a consciousness of unjust or dishonorable purposes, communication is always checked by distrust in proportion to the number whose concurrence is necessary.

Hence, it clearly appears that the same advantage which a republic has over a democracy in controlling the effects of faction is enjoyed by a large over a small republic—is enjoyed by the Union over the States composing it. Does this advantage consist in the substitution of representatives whose enlightened views and virtuous sentiments render them superior to local prejudices and to schemes of injustice? It will not be denied that the representation of the Union will be most likely to possess these requisite endowments. Does it consist in the greater security afforded by a greater variety of parties, against the event of any one party being able to outnumber and oppress the rest? In an equal degree does the increased variety of parties comprised within the Union increase this security. Does it, in fine, consist in the greater obstacles opposed to the concert and accomplishment of the secret wishes of an unjust and interested majority? Here again the extent of the Union gives it the most palpable advantage.

The influence of factious leaders may kindle a flame within their particular States but will be unable to spread a general conflagration through the other States. A religious sect may degenerate into a political faction in a part of the Confederacy; but the variety of sects dispersed over the entire face of it must secure the national councils against any danger from that source. A rage for paper money, for an abolition of debts, for an equal division of property, or for any other improper or wicked project, will be less apt to pervade the whole body of the Union than a particular member of it, in the same proportion as such a malady is more likely to taint a particular county or district than an entire State.

In the extent and proper structure of the Union, therefore, we behold a republican remedy for the diseases most incident to republican government. And according to the degree of pleasure and pride we feel in being republicans ought to be our zeal in cherishing the spirit and supporting the character of federalists.

APPENDIX D

FEDERALIST PAPER #51

To what expedient, then, shall we finally resort, for maintaining in practice the necessary partition of power among the several departments as laid down in the Constitution? The only answer that can be given is that as all these exterior provisions are found to be inadequate the defect must be supplied, by so contriving the interior structure of the government as that its several constituent parts may, by their mutual relations, be the means of keeping each other in their proper places. Without presuming to undertake a full development of this important idea I will hazard a few general observations which may perhaps place it in a clearer light, and enable us to form a more correct judgment of the principles and structure of the government planned by the convention.

In order to lay a due foundation for that separate and distinct exercise of the different powers of government, which to a certain extent is admitted on all hands to be essential to the preservation of liberty, it is evident that each department should have a will of its own; and consequently should be so constituted that the members of each should have as little agency as possible in the appointment of the members of the others. Were this principle rigorously adhered to, it would require that all the appointments for the supreme executive, legislative, and judiciary magistracies should be drawn from the same fountain of authority, the people, through channels having no communication whatever with one another. Perhaps such a plan of constructing the several departments would be less difficult in practice than it may in contemplation appear. Some difficulties, however, and some additional expense would attend the execution of it. Some deviations, therefore, from the principle must be admitted. In the constitution of the judiciary department in particular, it might be inexpedient to insist rigorously on the principle: first, because peculiar qualifications being essential in the members, the primary consideration ought to be to select that mode of choice which best secures these qualifications; second, because the permanent tenure by which the appointments are held in that department must soon destroy all sense of dependence on the authority conferring them.

It is equally evident that the members of each department should be as little dependent as possible on those of the others for the emoluments annexed to their offices. Were the executive magistrate, or the judges, not independent of the legislature in this particular, their independence in every other would be merely nominal.

But the great security against a gradual concentration of the several powers in the same department consists in giving to those who administer each department the necessary constitutional means and personal motives to resist encroachments of the others. The provision for defense must in this, as in all other cases, be made commensurate to the danger of attack. Ambition must be made to counteract ambition. The interest of the man must be connected with the constitutional rights of the place. It may be a reflection on human nature that such devices should be necessary to control the abuses of government. But what is government itself but the greatest of all reflections on human nature? If men were angels, no government would be necessary. If angels were to govern men, neither external nor internal controls on government would be necessary. In framing a government which is to be administered by men over men, the great difficulty lies in this: you must first enable the government to control the governed; and in the next place oblige it to control itself. A dependence on the people is, no doubt, the primary control on the government; but experience has taught mankind the necessity of auxiliary precautions.

This policy of supplying, by opposite and rival interests, the defect of better motives, might be traced through the whole system of human affairs, private as well as public. We see it particularly displayed in all the subordinate distributions of power, where the constant aim is to divide and arrange the several offices in such a manner as that each may be a check on the other—that the private interest of every individual may be a sentinel over the public rights. These inventions of prudence cannot be less requisite in the distribution of the supreme powers of the State.

But it is not possible to give to each department an equal power of self-defense. In republican government, the legislative authority necessarily predominates. The remedy for this inconveniency is to divide the legislature into different branches; and to render them, by different modes of election and different principles of action, as little connected with each other as the nature of their common functions and their common dependence on the society will admit. It may even be necessary to guard against dangerous encroachments by still further precautions. As the weight of the legislative authority requires that it should be thus divided, the weakness of the executive may require, on the other hand, that it should be fortified. An absolute negative on the legislature appears, at first view, to be the natural defense with which the executive magistrate should be armed. But perhaps it would be neither altogether safe nor alone sufficient. On ordinary occasions it might not be exerted with the requisite firmness, and on extraordinary occasions it might be perfidiously abused. May not this defect of an absolute negative be supplied by some qualified connection between this weaker department and the weaker branch of the stronger department, by which the latter may be led to support the constitutional rights of the former, without being too much detached from the rights of its own department?

If the principles on which these observations are found be just, as I persuade myself they are, and they be applied as a criterion to the several State constitutions, and the federal Constitution, it will be found that if the latter does not perfectly correspond with them, the former are infinitely less able to bear such a test.

There are, moreover, two considerations particularly applicable to the federal system of America, which place that system in a very interesting point of view.

First. In a single republic, all the power surrendered by the people is submitted to the administration of a single government; and the usurpations are guarded against by a division of the government into distinct and separate departments. In the compound republic of America, the power surrendered by the people is first divided between two distinct governments, and then the portion allotted to each subdivided among distinct and separate departments. Hence a double security arises to the rights of the people. The different governments will control each other, at the same time that each will be controlled by itself.

Second. It is of great importance in a republic not only to guard the society against the oppression of its rulers, but to guard one part of the society against the injustice of the other part. Different interests necessarily exist in different classes of citizens. If a majority be united by a common interest, the rights of the minority will be insecure. There are but two methods of providing against this evil: the one by creating a will in the community independent of the majority—that is, of the society itself; the other, by comprehending in the society so many separate descriptions of citizens as will render an unjust combination of a majority of the whole very improbable, if not impracticable. The first method prevails in all governments possessing an hereditary or self-appointed authority. This, at best, is but a precarious security; because a power independent of the society may as well espouse the unjust views of the major as the rightful interests of the minor party, and may possibly be turned against both parties. The second method will be exemplified in the federal republic of the United States. Whilst all authority in it will be derived from and dependent on the society, the society itself will be broken into so many parts, interests and classes of citizens, that the rights of individuals, or of the minority, will be in little danger from interested combinations of the majority. In a free government the security for civil rights must be the same as that for religious rights. It consists in the one case in the multiplicity of interests, and in the other in the multiplicity of sects. The degree of security in both cases will depend on the number of interests and sects; and this may be presumed to depend on the extent of country and number of people comprehended under the same government. This view of the subject must particularly recommend a proper federal system to all the sincere and considerate friends of republican government, since it shows that in exact proportion as the territory of the Union may be formed into more circumscribed Confederacies, or States, oppressive combinations of a majority will be facilitated; the best security, under the republican forms, for the rights of every class of citizen, will be diminished; and consequently the stability and independence of some member of the government, the only other security, must be proportionally increased. Justice is the end of government. It is the end of civil society. It ever has been and ever will be pursued until it be obtained, or until liberty be lost in the pursuit. In a society under the forms of which the stronger faction can readily unite and oppress the weaker, anarchy may as truly be said to reign as in a state of nature, where the weaker individual is not secured against the violence of the stronger; and as, in the latter state, even the stronger individuals are prompted, by the uncertainty of their condition, to submit to a government which may protect the weak as well as themselves; so, in the former state, will the more powerful factions or parties be gradually induced, by a like motive, to wish for a government which will protect all parties, the weaker as well as the more powerful. It can be little doubted that if the State of Rhode Island was separated from the Confederacy and left to itself, the insecurity of rights under the popular form of government within such narrow limits would be displayed by such reiterate oppressions of factious majorities that some power altogether independent of the people would soon be called for by the voice of the very factions whose misrule had proved the necessity of it. In the extended republic of the United States, and among the great variety of interests, parties, and sects which it embraces, a coalition of a majority of the whole society could seldom take place on any other principles than those of justice and the general good; whilst there being thus less danger to a minor from the will of a major party, there must be less pretext, also, to provide for the security of the former, by introducing into the government a will not dependent on the latter, or, in other words, a will independent of the society itself. It is no less certain than it is important, notwithstanding the contrary opinions which have been entertained, that the larger the society, provided it lie within a practicable sphere, the more duly capable it will be of self-government. And happily for the *republican cause*, the practicable sphere may be carried to a very great extent by a judicious modification and mixture of the *federal principle*.

GLOSSARY

Abscam
A 1981 FBI undercover operation in which six House members and one senator were convicted of taking bribes.

Activist judges
Judges who are not reluctant to overrule the other branches of government by declaring laws or actions of government officials unconstitutional.

Adversarial relationship
A relationship in which the parties are constantly in conflict with each other.

Affirmative action
A policy in job hiring or university admissions that gives special consideration to members of traditionally disadvantaged groups in an effort to compensate for the effects of past discrimination.

Agents of political socialization
Sources of information about politics; include parents, peers, schools, the media, political leaders, and the community.

Aid to Families with Dependent Children (AFDC)
A program that provides income support for the poor.

American Civil Liberties Union (ACLU)
A nonpartisan organization that seeks to protect the civil liberties of all Americans.

Amicus curiae
In Latin, "friend of the court." A third party that gives advice in a legal case to which it is not a party.

Antifederalists
Those who opposed the ratification of the U.S. Constitution.

Antitrust legislation
Laws that prohibit **monopolies.**

Appropriations
Budget legislation that specifies the amount of authorized funds that will actually be allocated for agencies and departments to spend.

Articles of Confederation
The first constitution of the United States; in effect from 1781 to 1789.

Authorizations
Budget legislation that provides agencies and departments with the legal authority to operate; may specify funding levels but do not actually provide the funding (the funding is provided by **appropriations**).

Baker v. Carr
A 1962 Supreme Court decision giving voters the right to use the courts to rectify the malapportionment of legislative districts.

Balanced budget amendment
A proposed constitutional amendment that would require balancing the federal budget.

Balanced government
Refers to the idea that the different branches of government all represent different interests, forcing the various factions to work out compromises acceptable to all.

Bandwagon effect
The tendency of voters to follow the lead of the media, which declare some candidates winners and others losers, and vote for the perceived winner. The extent of this effect is unknown.

Bay of Pigs invasion
The disastrous CIA-backed invasion of Cuba in 1961, mounted by Cuban exiles and intended to overthrow the government of Fidel Castro.

Behavioral approach
The study of politics by looking at the behavior of public officials, voters, and other participants in politics, rather than by focusing on institutions or law.

Bible Belt
A term used to describe portions of the South and Midwest that were strongly influenced by Protestant fundamentalists.

Bilingual education
Programs where students whose native language is not English receive instruction in substantive subjects such as math in their native language.

Bill of Rights
The first 10 amendments to the U.S. Constitution.

Bills of attainder
Legislative acts that pronounce specific persons guilty of crimes.

Black Codes
Laws passed by Southern states following the **Civil War** that denied most legal rights to the newly freed slaves.

Blockbusting
The practice in which realtors would frighten whites in a neighborhood where a black family had moved by telling the whites that their houses would decline in value. The whites in panic would then sell their houses to the realtors at low prices, and the realtors would resell the houses to blacks, thereby resegregating the area from white to black.

Block grants
A system of giving federal funds to states and localities under which the federal government designates the purpose for which the funds are to be used but allows the states some discretion in spending.

Boll Weevils
Conservative Democratic members of Congress, mainly from the South, who vote more often with the Republicans than with their own party.

Brownlow Committee
Appointed by Franklin Roosevelt in 1935, the committee recommended ways of improving the management of the federal bureaucracy and increasing the president's influence over it.

Brown v. Board of Education
The 1954 case in which the U.S. Supreme Court overturned the **separate-but-equal doctrine** and ruled unanimously that segregated schools violated the Fourteenth Amendment.

Bubble concept
A policy that permits flexibility in meeting pollution standards by allowing

a company to meet an emissions standard if total emissions from all smokestacks at a factory or from all factories in a given area (under an imaginary bubble) meet the standard, even though emissions from individual smokestacks or factories fail to comply.

Budget and Accounting Act of 1921
This act gives the president the power to propose a budget and led to presidential dominance in the budget process. It also created the **Bureau of the Budget,** changed to the **Office of Management and Budget** in 1970.

Bureaucratic continuity
The stability provided by career-oriented civil servants, who remain in government for many years while presidents, legislators, and political appointees come and go.

Bureau of the Budget
Established in 1921 and later changed to the **Office of Management and Budget,** the BOB was designed as the president's primary means of developing federal budget policy.

Burger Court
The U.S. Supreme Court under Chief Justice Warren Burger (1969–1986). Though not as activist as the **Warren Court,** the Burger Court maintained most of the rights expanded by its predecessor and issued important rulings on abortion and sexual discrimination.

Canadian health care plan
A single-payer system in which individuals choose their own doctors and the province pays the doctors for services performed; fees are strictly regulated.

Capitalist economy
An economic system in which prices, wages, working conditions, and profits are determined solely by the market.

Captured agencies
Refers to the theory that regulatory agencies often end up working on behalf of the interests they are supposed to regulate.

Casework
The assistance members of Congress provide to their constituents; includes answering questions and doing personal favors for those who ask for help. Also called **constituency service.**

Caucus
Today, a meeting of local residents who select delegates to attend county, state, and national conventions where the delegates nominate candidates for public office. Originally, caucuses were limited to party leaders and officeholders who selected the candidates.

Central Intelligence Agency (CIA)
Created after World War II, the CIA is a federal agency charged with coordinating overseas intelligence activities for the United States.

Checks and balances
The principle of government that holds that the powers of the various branches should overlap to avoid power becoming overly concentrated in one branch.

City-state
In ancient Greece, a self-governing state such as Athens or Sparta, consisting of an independent city and its surrounding territory.

Civil case
A case in which individuals sue others for denying their rights and causing them harm.

Civil Rights Act of 1964
Major civil rights legislation that prohibits discrimination on the basis of race, color, religion, or national origin in public accommodations.

Civil Rights Act of 1968
Civil rights legislation that prohibits discrimination in the sale or rental of housing on the basis of race, color, religion, or national origin; also prohibits **blockbusting, steering,** and **redlining.**

Civil Service Commission
An agency established by the **Pendleton Act of 1883** to curb **patronage** in the federal bureaucracy and replace it with a **merit system.**

Civil War
The war between the Union and the Confederacy (1861–1865), fought mainly over the question of whether the national or state governments were to exercise ultimate political power. Slavery was the issue that precipitated this great conflict.

Classical democracy
A system of government that emphasizes citizen participation through debating, voting, and holding office.

Closed primary
A primary election where participation is limited to those who are registered with a party or declare a preference for a party.

Cloture
A method of stopping a **filibuster** by limiting debate to only 20 more hours; requires a vote of three-fifths of the members of the Senate.

Coalition
A network of **interest groups** with similar concerns that combine forces to pursue a common goal; may be short-lived or permanent.

Coalition building
The union of **pressure groups** that share similar concerns.

Cold War
The era of hostility between the United States and the Soviet Union that existed between the end of World War II and the collapse of the Soviet Union.

Commercial bias
A slant in news coverage to please or avoid offending advertisers.

Committee of the Whole
Refers to the informal entity the House of Representatives makes itself into to debate a bill.

Commodity groups
Interest groups that represent producers of specific products, such as cattle, tobacco, or milk producers.

Comparable worth
The principle that comparable jobs should pay comparable wages.

Concurrent resolutions
Special resolutions expressing the sentiment of Congress, passed by one house with the other concurring, but not requiring the president's signature.

Confederal system
A system in which the central government has only the powers given to it by the subnational governments.

Conference committee
A committee composed of members of both houses of Congress that is formed to try to resolve the differences when the two houses pass different versions of the same bill.

Conflict of interest
The situation when government officials make decisions that directly affect their own personal livelihoods or interests.

Conscientious objectors
Persons who oppose all wars and refuse military service on the basis of religious or moral principles.

Conservative
A person who believes that the domestic role of government should be minimized and that individuals are responsible for their own well-being.

Constituencies
The persons a member of Congress represents. For a senator, all the residents of the state; for a member of the House, all the residents of the member's district.

Constituency service
The assistance members of Congress provide to residents in their districts (states, if senators); includes answering questions and doing personal favors for those who ask for help. Also called **casework.**

Constitution
The body of basic rules and principles that establish the functions, limits, and nature of a government.

Constitutional Convention
The gathering in Philadelphia in 1787 that wrote the U.S. Constitution; met initially to revise the **Articles of Confederation** but produced a new national **constitution** instead.

Containment
A policy formulated by the Truman administration that aimed to limit the spread of communism by meeting any action taken by the Soviet Union with a countermove; led U.S. decision makers to see most conflicts in terms of U.S.-Soviet rivalry.

Contras
Rebels who have fought to overthrow the Sandinista government of Nicaragua.

Cooperative federalism
The continuing cooperation among federal, state, and local officials in carrying out the business of government.

Cost-benefit analysis
The process of evaluating a **regulation** by weighing its cost against the risk of harm if it is not implemented.

Cost overruns
The amount by which the cost of a certain project exceeds the expected cost.

Cost-plus project
A project for which the contractor is reimbursed for all of its costs in addition to a set, agreed-upon profit rate.

Court-packing plan
President Franklin D. Roosevelt's attempt to expand the size of the U.S. Supreme Court in an effort to obtain a Court more likely to uphold his New Deal legislation.

Courts of appeals
Intermediate courts between trial courts (**district courts** in the federal system) and the supreme court (the U.S. Supreme Court in the federal system).

Cracking, stacking, and packing
Methods of drawing district boundaries that minimize black representation. With cracking, a large concentrated black population is divided among two or more districts so that blacks will not have a majority anywhere; with stacking, a large black population is combined with an even larger white population; with packing, a large black population is put into one district rather than two so that blacks will have a majority in only one district.

Cradle-to-grave
Regulations for dealing with hazardous wastes that require the wastes to be identified as toxic and handled in an environmentally sound manner from the time of creation until disposition.

Credentials committee
A body responsible for examining the credentials of political convention delegates.

Criminal case
A case in which a government (national or state) prosecutes a person for violating its laws.

Cruel and unusual punishment
Torture or any punishment that is grossly disproportionate to the offense; prohibited by the Eighth Amendment.

Cuban Missile Crisis
The 1962 stand-off between the United States and the Soviet Union over an offensive missile buildup in Cuba. The Soviets finally agreed to remove all the missiles from Cuban soil.

Cumulative voting
A proposed reform to increase minority representation; calls for members of Congress to be elected from at-large districts that would elect several members at once. Each voter would have as many votes as the district had seats and could apportion the votes among the candidates as he or she wished, such as giving all votes to a single candidate.

De facto segregation
Segregation that is based on residential patterns and is not imposed by law; because it cannot be eliminated by striking down a law, it is more intractable than **de jure segregation.**

Deficit
A condition in which expenditures exceed revenues.

De jure segregation
Segregation imposed by law; outlawed by ***Brown v. Board of Education*** and subsequent court cases.

Delegated legislative authority
The power to draft, as well as execute, specific policies; granted by Congress to agencies when a problem requires technical expertise.

Demagogue
A leader who obtains political power by appealing to the emotions and biases of the populace.

Democracy
A system of government in which authority resides in the people.

Departments
Executive divisions of the federal government, such as the Departments of Defense and Labor, each headed by a cabinet officer.

Depression
A period of prolonged high unemployment.

Deregulation
Ending **regulation** in a particular area.

Detente
A policy designed to deescalate **Cold War** rhetoric and promote the notion that relations with the Soviet Union could be conducted in ways other than confrontation; developed by President Richard M. Nixon and Secretary of State Henry Kissinger.

Direct democracy
A system of government in which citizens govern themselves directly and vote on most issues; e.g., a New England town meeting.

Direct lobbying
Direct personal encounters between lobbyists and the public officials they are attempting to influence.

Direct primary
An election in which voters directly choose a party's candidates for office.

Discretionary spending
Spending by the federal government where the amount is set by annual **appropriations** bills passed by Congress; includes government operating expenses and salaries of many federal employees.

District courts
The trial courts (lower-level courts) in the federal system.

Divided government
The situation when one political party controls the presidency and the other party controls one or both houses of Congress.

Dixiecrat
A member of a group of southern segregationist Democrats who formed the States' Rights Party in 1948.

Domino theory
The idea that if one country fell under communist rule, its neighbors would also fall to communism; contributed to the U.S. decision to intervene in Vietnam.

Dred Scott case
An 1857 case in which the U.S. Supreme Court held that blacks, whether slave or free, were not citizens and that Congress had no power to restrict slavery in the territories; contributed to the polarization between North and South and ultimately to the **Civil War.**

Dual federalism
The idea that the Constitution created a system in which the national government and the states have separate grants of power with each supreme in its own sphere.

Due process
The guarantee that the government will follow fair and just procedures when prosecuting a criminal defendant.

Earned income tax credit (EITC)
A negative income tax. Instead of paying tax, persons with low incomes receive a payment from the government or a credit toward their taxes.

Education Amendments of 1972
These forbid discrimination on the basis of sex in schools and colleges that receive federal aid.

Electoral College
A group of electors selected by the voters in each state and the District of Columbia; the electors officially elect the president and vice president.

Environmental impact statement
An analysis of a project's effects on the environment; required from government agencies under the National Environment Policy Act of 1970 before any new projects could be carried out.

Environmental Protection Agency (EPA)
The regulatory agency with responsibility for pollution control; created in 1970 by President Richard M. Nixon.

Equal Credit Opportunity Act
This act forbids discrimination on the basis of sex or marital status in credit transactions.

Equal Employment Opportunity Commission (EEOC)
The EEOC enforces the **Civil Rights Act of 1964,** which forbids discrimination on the basis of sex or race in hiring, promotion, and firing.

Equal Pay Act
A statute enacted by Congress in 1963 that mandates that women and men should receive equal pay for equal work.

Equal protection clause
The Fourteenth Amendment clause that is the Constitution's primary guarantee that government will treat everyone equally.

Equal Rights Amendment (ERA)
A proposed amendment to the Constitution that would prohibit government from denying equal rights on the basis of sex; passed by Congress in 1972 but failed to be ratified by a sufficient number of states.

Establishment clause
The First Amendment clause that prohibits the establishment of a church officially supported by government.

European Union (EU)
A union of European nations formed in 1957 to foster political and economic integration in Europe; formerly called the European Economic Community or Common Market.

Exclusionary rule
A rule that prevents evidence obtained in violation of the Fourth Amendment from being used in court against the defendant.

Executive leadership
The president's control over the bureaucracy in his capacity as chief executive; achieved through budgeting, appointments, administrative reform, lobbying, and mobilizing public opinion.

Executive orders
Rules or regulations issued by the president that have the force of law; issued to implement constitutional provisions or statutes.

Executive privilege
The authority of the president to withhold information from the courts and Congress.

Exit polls
Election-day poll of voters leaving the polling places, conducted mainly by television networks and major newspapers.

Ex post facto law
A statute that makes some behavior illegal that was not illegal when it was done.

Externality
A cost or benefit of production that is not reflected in the product's market price. **Regulation** attempts to eliminate negative externalities.

Faithless elector
A member of the **Electoral College** who votes on the basis of personal preference rather than the way the majority of voters in his or her state voted.

Farm subsidies
Government payments to farmers to raise the price they receive for crops to above-market prices.

Federal Communication Commission (FCC)
A regulatory agency that controls interstate and foreign communication via radio, television, telegraph, telephone, and cable. The FCC licenses radio and television stations.

Federal Election Campaign Act
A 1974 statute that regulates campaign finance; provided for public financing of presidential campaigns, limited contributions to campaigns for federal offices, and established the **Federal Election Commission,** among other things.

Federal Election Commission
Created in 1975, the commission enforces federal laws on campaign financing.

Federalism
A system in which power is constitutionally divided between a central government and subnational or local governments.

Federalist Papers
A series of essays in support of the U.S. Constitution; written for New York newspapers by Alexander Hamilton, James Madison, and John Jay during the debate over ratification.

Federalists
Originally, those who supported the U.S. Constitution and favored its ratification; in the early years of the Republic, those who advocated a strong national government.

Federal Register
A government publication describing bureaucratic actions and detailing regulations proposed by government agencies.

Federal Reserve Board
Created by Congress in 1913, the board regulates the lending practices of banks and plays a major role in determining **monetary policy.**

Felonies
Crimes considered more serious than **misdemeanors** and carrying more stringent punishment.

Feminization of poverty
The phenomenon that the majority of families living in poverty are headed by females.

Fifteenth Amendment
An amendment to the Constitution, ratified in 1870, that prohibits denying voting rights on the basis of race, color, or previous condition of servitude.

Filibuster
A mechanism for delay in the Senate in which one or more members engage in a continuous speech to prevent the Senate from taking action.

Fireside chats
Short radio addresses given by President Franklin D. Roosevelt to win support for his policies and reassure the public during the Great Depression.

Fiscal policy
Government's actions to regulate the economy through taxing and spending policies.

Fixed-cost project
A project that a contractor has agreed to undertake for a specified sum.

Flat tax
A tax structured so that all income groups pay the same rate.

Food stamp program
A poverty program that gives poor people coupons redeemable in grocery stores for food.

Franking
The privilege of members of Congress that allows them to send free mail to their constituents.

Freedom of speech
The FirstAmendment guarantee of a right of free expression.

Free exercise clause
The First Amendment clause that guarantees individuals the right to practice their religion without government intervention.

Free trade
A policy of minimum intervention by government in trade relations.

Frontrunners
Candidates whom political pros and the media have portrayed as likely winners.

Full faith and credit
A clause in the U.S. Constitution that requires the states to recognize contracts that are valid in other states.

Fundraiser
An event, such as a luncheon or cocktail party, hosted by a legislator or candidate for which participants pay an entrance fee.

Game orientation
The assumption in political reporting that politics is a game and that politicians are the players; leads to an emphasis on strategy at the expense of substance in news stories.

Gender gap
An observable pattern of modest but consistent differences in opinion between men and women on various public policy issues.

General revenue sharing
A Reagan administration policy of giving states and cities federal money to spend as they wished, subject to only a few conditions.

Gerrymander
A congressional district whose boundaries are drawn so as to maximize the political advantage of a party or racial group; often such a district has a bizarre shape.

Glasnost
Mikhail Gorbachev's policy of opening the Soviet Union to the outside world by encouraging foreign investment, allowing more Soviet citizens to emigrate, and permitting multiparty elections in eastern Europe.

Going public
The process in which Congress or its members carry an issue debate to the public via the media; e.g., televising floor debates or media appearances by individual members.

GOP
Grand Old Party or Republican Party, which formed in 1856 after the Whig Party split. The GOP was abolitionist and a supporter of the Union.

Grace Commission
A special commission established by President Ronald Reagan to recommend ways of cutting government waste.

Grandfather clause
A device used in the South to prevent blacks from voting; such clauses exempted those whose grandfathers had the right to vote before 1867 from having to fulfill various requirements that most people could not meet. Since no blacks could vote before 1867, they could not qualify for the exemption.

Grand jury
A jury of citizens who meet in private session to evaluate accusations in a given **criminal case** and to determine if there is enough evidence to warrant a trial.

Grants-in-aid
Federal money provided to state and, occasionally, local governments to establish programs to help people such as the aged poor or the unemployed; began during the New Deal.

Grassroots lobbying
The mass mobilization of members of an **interest group** to apply pressure to public officials, usually in the form of a mass mailing.

Great Compromise
The decision of the **Constitutional Convention** to have a bicameral legislature in which representation in one house would be by population and in the other house, by states; also called the Connecticut Compromise.

Habeas corpus
Latin for "have ye the body." A writ of habeas corpus is a means for criminal defendants who have exhausted appeals in state courts to appeal to a federal **district court.**

Hatch Act
A statute enacted in 1939 that limits the political activities of federal employees in partisan campaigns.

Head of state
The president's role as a national symbol of collective unity and pride.

Health maintenance organization (HMO)
A group of doctors who agree to provide full health care for a fixed monthly charge.

Home rule
The grant of considerable autonomy to a local government.

Honoraria
Legal payments made to legislators who speak before **interest groups** or other groups of citizens.

Hyperpluralism
The idea that it is difficult for government to arrive at a solution to problems because **interest groups** have become so numerous and so many groups have a "veto" on issues affecting them.

ICBM
Intercontinental ballistic missiles, or land-based missiles.

Identity politics
The practice of organizing on the basis of sex, ethnic or racial identity, or sexual orientation to compete for public resources and influence public policy.

Ideology
A highly organized and coherent set of opinions.

Impeachment and removal
A two-step process by which Congress may remove presidents, judges, and other civil officers accused of malfeasance. The House decides questions of impeachment; if a majority favors impeachment, the Senate decides whether to remove the accused from office.

Imperial presidency
A term that came into use at the end of the 1960s to describe the growing power of the presidency.

Implied powers clause
The clause in the U.S. Constitution that gives Congress the power to make all laws "**necessary and proper**" for carrying out its specific powers.

Impoundment
A refusal by the president to spend money appropriated by Congress for a specific program.

Incrementalism
A congressional spending pattern in which budgets usually increase slightly from year to year.

Independent
A voter who is not aligned with any political party.

Independent agencies
Government bureaus that are not parts of **departments.** Their heads are appointed by and responsible to the president.

Independent counsel
See **Special prosecutor.**

Independent expenditures
Campaign contributions made on behalf of issues or candidates, but not made directly to candidates or political parties.

Independent spending
Spending on political campaigns by groups not under the control of the candidates.

Indirect democracy
A system of government in which citizens elect representatives to make decisions for them.

Indirect lobbying
Attempts to influence legislators through such nontraditional means as letter-writing campaigns.

Individualistic political culture
One of three primary political cultures in the United States. One in which politics is seen as a way of getting ahead, of obtaining benefits for oneself or one's group, and in which corruption is tolerated. See also **moralistic** and **traditionalistic political cultures.**

Inflation
The situation in which prices increase but wages and salaries fail to keep pace with the prices of goods.

Influence peddling
Using one's access to powerful people to make money, as when former government officials use access to former colleagues to win high-paying jobs in the private sector.

Informal norms
Unwritten customs that help keep Congress running smoothly by attempting to diminish friction and competition among the members.

Injunction
A court order demanding that a person or group perform a specific act or refrain from performing a specific act.

Inquisition
A medieval institution of the Roman Catholic Church used to identify and punish heretics.

Institutional approach
An investigation of government that focuses on institutions, such as Congress or the civil service, and their rules and procedures.

Institutional loyalty
An **informal norm** of Congress that calls for members to avoid criticizing their colleagues and to treat each other with mutual respect; eroded in recent decades.

Interest groups
Organizations that try to achieve at least some of their goals with government assistance.

Investigative reporting
In-depth news reporting, particularly that which exposes corruption and wrongdoing on the part of government officials and big institutions.

Iroquois Confederacy
An association of Native Americans in what is now New York State that was based on the principles of **checks and balances** and **federalism,** among other things.

Isolationism
A policy of noninvolvement with other nations outside the Americas; generally followed by the United States during the nineteenth and early twentieth centuries.

Issue consistency
The extent to which individuals who identify themselves as "**liberal**" or "**conservative**" take issue positions that reflect their professed leanings.

Issue voting
Refers to citizens who vote for candidates whose stands on specific issues are consistent with their own.

Jeffersonian Republicans (Jeffersonians)
Opponents of a strong national government. They challenged the **Federalists** in the early years of the Republic.

Jim Crow laws
Laws enacted in southern states that segregated schools, public accommodations, and almost all other aspects of life.

Joint resolutions
Measures that have the force of law and must be approved by both houses of Congress and signed by the president.

Judicial review
The authority of the courts to declare laws or actions of government officials unconstitutional.

Junkets
Trips by members of Congress to desirable locations with expenses paid by lobbyists;

the trips are ostensibly made to fulfill a "speaking engagement" or conduct a "fact-finding tour."

Jurisdiction
The authority of a court to hear and decide cases.

Justices of the peace
Magistrates at the lowest level of some state court systems, responsible mainly for acting on minor offenses and committing cases to higher courts for trial.

Keating 5
Senators Alan Cranston, John McCain, Donald Riegle, John Glenn, and Dennis DeConcini, who were investigated by the Senate for ethics violations in connection with campaign contributions they received from financier/developer Charles Keating. All later intervened on his behalf with federal regulators.

Keynesian economics
The argument by John Maynard Keynes that government should stimulate the economy during periods of high unemployment by increasing spending even if it must run **deficits** to do so; the deficits would be made up by higher employment and thus higher tax revenues during periods of prosperity.

Kitchen cabinet
A group of informal advisers, usually longtime associates, who assist the president on public policy questions.

Know-Nothing Party
An extreme right-wing party in mid-nineteenth-century America that opposed Catholics and immigrants.

Lame duck
An officeholder, legislature, or administration that has lost an election but holds power until the inauguration of a successor.

Landslide
An election won by a candidate who receives an overwhelming majority of the votes, such as more than a 10-point gap.

Leaks
Disclosures of information that some government officials want kept secret.

Legislative calendar
An agenda or calendar containing the names of all bills or resolutions of a particular type to be considered by committees or either legislative chamber.

Legislative veto
A congressional **oversight** tool that allows one or both houses to block agency actions. Though the legislative veto was held unconstitutional by the Supreme Court in 1983, legislation with provisions for legislative vetoes continues to be passed, and agencies continue to honor the vetoes.

Libel
Printed or broadcast statements that are false and tarnish someone's reputation.

Liberal
A person who believes in a national government that is active in domestic policies, providing help to individuals and communities in such areas as health, education, and welfare.

Limited government
A government that is strong enough to protect the people's rights but not so strong as to threaten those rights; in the view of John Locke, such a government was established through a **social contract.**

Line-Item veto
A proposal that would give a president the power to veto one or more provisions of a bill while allowing the remainder of the bill to become law.

Literacy tests
Examinations ostensibly carried out to ensure that voters could read and write but actually a device used in the South to disqualify blacks from voting.

Litigation
Legal action.

Lobbying
The efforts of **interest groups** to influence government.

Majority leader
The member of the majority party in the House of Representatives who is second in command to the **Speaker.** Also, the leader of the Senate, who is chosen by the majority party.

Majority-minority district
A congressional district whose boundaries are drawn to give a minority group a majority in the district.

Managed competition
An aspect of the Clinton health care plan that involved joining employers and individuals into large groups or cooperatives to purchase health insurance.

Mandamus, writ of
A court order demanding government officials or a lower court to perform a specified duty.

Mandate
A term used in the media to refer to a president having clear directions from the voters to take a certain course of action; in practice, it is not always clear that a president, even one elected by a large majority, has a mandate or, if so, for what.

Mandatory spending
Spending by the federal government that is required by permanent laws; e.g., payments for **Medicare.**

Marble cake federalism
The idea that different levels of government work together in carrying out policies; governments are intermixed, as in a marble cake.

Marbury v. Madison
The 1803 case in which the U.S. Supreme Court enunciated the doctrine of **judicial review.**

Market share
The number of members of an **interest group** compared to its potential membership; having a large market share is an advantage.

Markup
The process in which a congressional subcommittee rewrites a bill after holding hearings on it.

McCarthyism
Methods of combating communism characterized by irresponsible accusations made on the basis of little or no evidence; named after Senator Joseph McCarthy of Wisconsin who used such tactics in the 1950s.

McCulloch v. Maryland
An 1819 U.S. Supreme Court decision that broadly interpreted Congress's powers under the **implied powers clause.**

McGovern-Fraser Commission
A commission formed after 1968 by the Democratic Party to consider changes making convention delegates more representative of all Democratic voters.

Means test
An eligibility requirement for poverty programs under which participants must demonstrate that they have low income and few assets.

Media event
An event, usually consisting of a speech and a photo opportunity, that is

staged for television and is intended to convey a particular impression of a politician's position on an issue.

Media malaise
A feeling of cynicism and distrust toward government and officials that is fostered by media coverage of politics.

Medicaid
A federal-state medical assistance program for the poor.

Medicare
A public health insurance program that pays many medical expenses of the elderly and the disabled; funded through **Social Security** taxes, general revenues, and premiums paid by recipients.

Merit system
A system of filling bureaucratic jobs on the basis of competence instead of **patronage.**

Minimum tax
A proposed tax that would require corporations and individuals with high incomes to pay a certain minimum amount in federal taxes.

Minority leader
The leader of the minority party in either the House of Representatives or the Senate.

Miranda rights
A means of protecting a criminal suspect's **rights against self-incrimination** during police interrogation. Before interrogation, suspects must be told that they have a right to remain silent; that anything they say can be used against them; that they have a right to an attorney; and that if they cannot afford an attorney, one will be provided for them. The rights are named after the case *Miranda v. Arizona*.

MIRV
Stands for multiple independently targeted reentry vehicles; an offensive missile system that uses a single rocket to launch a number of warheads, each of which could be aimed at a different target.

"Mischiefs of faction"
A phrase used by James Madison in the ***Federalist Papers*** to refer to the threat to the nation's stability that factions could pose.

Misdemeanors
Crimes of less seriousness than **felonies,** ordinarily punishable by fine or imprisonment in a local rather than a state institution.

Missouri Compromise of 1820
A set of laws by which Congress attempted to control slavery in the territories, maintaining the balance between slave and nonslave states.

Mixed economies
Countries that incorporate elements of both capitalist and socialist practices in the workings of their economies.

Monetary policy
Actions taken by the **Federal Reserve Board** to regulate the economy through changes in short-term interest rates and the money supply.

Monopoly
One or a few firms that control a large share of the market for certain goods and can therefore fix prices.

Monroe Doctrine
A doctrine articulated by President James Monroe in 1823 that warned European powers not already involved in Latin America to stay out of that region.

Moralistic political culture
One of three political cultures in the United States. One in which people feel obligated to take part in politics to bring about change for the better, and in which corruption is not tolerated. See also **individualistic** and **traditionalistic political cultures.**

Most favored nation (MFN)
Trade status granted to a trading partner that permits that nation to export goods to the United States under the most advantageous **tariff** arrangements that the United States allows.

Motor voter law
A statute that allows people to register to vote at public offices such as welfare offices and drivers' license bureaus.

Muckrakers
Reform-minded journalists in the early twentieth century who exposed corruption in politics and worked to break the financial link between business and politicians.

Mutual assured destruction (MAD)
The capability to absorb a nuclear attack and retaliate against the attacker with such force that it would also suffer enormous damage; believed to deter nuclear war during the **Cold War** because both sides would be so devastated that neither would risk striking first.

NAACP (National Association for the Advancement of Colored People)
An organization founded in 1909 to fight for black rights; its attorneys challenged segregation in the courts and won many important court cases, most notably, ***Brown v. Board of Education.***

Nader's Raiders
The name given to people who work in any of the "public interest" organizations founded by consumer advocate and regulatory watchdog Ralph Nader.

National chair
The head of a political **party organization,** appointed by the **national committee** of that party, usually at the direction of the party's presidential nominee.

National committee
The highest level of **party organization;** chooses the site of the national convention and the formula for determining the number of delegates from each state.

National debt
The total amount of money owed by the federal government; the sum of all budget **deficits** over the years.

National Organization for Women (NOW)
A group formed in 1966 to fight primarily for political and economic rights for women.

NATO (North Atlantic Treaty Organization)
A mutual defense pact established by the United States, Canada, and their western European allies in 1949 to protect against Soviet aggression in Europe; later expanded to include other European nations.

Natural rights
Inalienable and inherent rights such as the right to own property (in the view of John Locke).

"Necessary and proper"
A phrase in the **implied powers clause** of the U.S. Constitution that gives Congress the power to make all laws needed to carry out its specific powers.

Neutral competence
The concept that bureaucrats should be uninvolved or neutral in policymaking and should be chosen only for their

expertise—not their political affiliation.

New Deal
A program of President Franklin D. Roosevelt's administration in the 1930s aimed at stimulating economic recovery and aiding victims of the Great Depression; led to expansion of the national government's role.

New Deal coalition
The broadly based coalition of southern conservatives, northern liberals, and ethnic and religious minorities that sustained the Democratic Party for some 40 years.

New federalism
During the Nixon administration, the policy under which unrestricted or minimally restricted federal funds were provided to states and localities; during the Reagan administration, a policy of reducing federal support for the states.

News release
A printed handout given by public relations workers to members of the media, offering ideas or information for new stories.

Nineteenth Amendment
An amendment to the Constitution, ratified in 1920, guaranteeing women the vote.

Nullification
A doctrine advocated by supporters of state-centered federalism, holding that a state could nullify laws of Congress.

Obscenity
Sexual material that is patently offensive to the average person in the community and that lacks any serious literary, artistic, or scientific value.

Obstruction of justice
A deliberate attempt to impede the progress of a criminal investigation or trial.

Occupational Safety and Health Administration (OSHA)
An agency formed in 1970 and charged with ensuring safe and healthful working conditions for all American workers.

Office of Management and Budget (OMB)
A White House agency with primary responsibility for preparing the federal budget.

Open primary
A primary election that is not limited to members of a particular party; a voter may vote in either party's primary.

Overlapping membership
The term refers to the tendency of individuals to join more than one group. This tends to moderate a group's appeals, since its members also belong to other groups with different interests.

Oversight
Congress's responsibility to make sure the bureaucracy is administering federal programs in accordance with congressional intent.

Parliamentary government
A system in which voters elect only their representatives in parliament; the chief executive is chosen by parliament, as in Britain.

Party boss
The head of a **political "machine,"** a highly disciplined state or local **party organization** that controls power in its area.

Party convention
A gathering of party delegates, on the local, state, or national level, to set policy and strategy and to select candidates for elective office.

Party identification
A psychological link between individuals and a political party that leads those persons to regard themselves as members of that party.

Party in government
Those who are appointed or elected to office as members of a political party.

Party in the electorate
Those who identify with a political party.

Party organization
The "professionals" who run a political party at the national, state, and local levels.

Patronage
A system in which elected officials appoint their supporters to administrative jobs; used by **political machines** to maintain themselves in power.

Pendleton Act of 1883
This act created the **Civil Service Commission,** designed to protect civil servants from arbitrary dismissal for political reasons and to staff bureaucracies with people who have proven their competence by taking competitive examinations.

Pentagon Papers
A top-secret study, eventually made public, of how and why the United States became embroiled in the Vietnam War; the study was commissioned by Secretary of Defense Robert McNamara during the Johnson administration.

Permanent campaign
The situation in which elected officials are constantly engaged in a campaign; fund-raising for the next election begins as soon as one election is concluded.

Personal presidency
A concept proposed by Theodore Lowi that holds that presidents since the 1930s have amassed tremendous personal power directly from the people and, in return, are expected to make sure the people get what they want from government.

Platform committee
The group that drafts the policy statement of a political party's convention.

Plea bargain
An agreement between the prosecutor, defense attorney, and defendant in which the prosecutor agrees to reduce the charge or sentence in exchange for the defendant's guilty plea.

Plebiscite
A direct vote by all the people on a certain public measure. Theodore Lowi has spoken of the "Plebiscitary" presidency, whereby the president makes himself the focus of national government through use of the mass media.

Plessy v. Ferguson
The 1896 case in which the U.S. Supreme Court upheld segregation by enunciating the **separate-but-equal doctrine.**

Pluralism
The theory that American government is responsive to groups of citizens working together to promote their common interests and that enough people belong to **interest groups** to ensure that government ultimately hears everyone, even though most people do not participate actively in politics.

Pocket veto
A legislative bill dies by pocket veto if a president refuses to sign it and Congress adjourns within 10 working days.

Policy implementation
The process by which bureaucrats convert laws into rules and activities

that have an actual impact on people and things.

Political action committee (PAC)
A committee established by corporation, labor union, or **interest group** that raises money and contributes it to a political campaign.

Political bias
A preference for candidates of particular parties or for certain stands on issues that affects a journalist's reporting.

Political culture
A shared body of values and beliefs that shapes perceptions and attitudes toward politics and government and, in turn, influences political behavior.

Political equality
The principle that every citizen of a democracy has an equal opportunity to try to influence government.

Political machines
Political organizations based on **patronage** that flourished in big cities in the late nineteenth and early twentieth centuries. The machine relied on the votes of the lower classes and, in exchange, provided jobs and other services.

Political socialization
The process of learning about politics by being exposed to information from parents, peers, schools, the media, political leaders, and the community.

Political tolerance
The willingness of individuals to extend procedural rights and liberties to people with whom they disagree.

Political trust
The extent to which citizens place trust in their government, its institutions, and its officials.

Politics
A means by which individuals and **interest groups** compete, via political parties and other extragovernmental organizations, to shape government's impact on society's problems and goals.

Poll tax
A tax that must be paid before a person can vote; used in the South to prevent blacks from voting. The Twenty-fourth Amendment now prohibits poll taxes in federal elections.

Popular sovereignty
Rule by the people.

Pork barrel
Funding for special projects, buildings, and other public works in the district or state of a member of Congress. Members tend to support such projects because they provide jobs for constituents and enhance the members' reelection chances, rather than because the projects are necessarily wise.

Power to persuade
The president's informal power to gain support by dispensing favors and penalties and by using the prestige of the office.

Precedents
In law, judicial decisions that may be used subsequently as standards in similar cases.

Precinct
The basic unit of the American electoral process—in a large city perhaps only a few blocks—designed for the administration of elections. Citizens vote in precinct polling places.

Presidential immunity
Immunity of the president from lawsuits for acts that occur during his term in office and are related to his official responsibilities.

Presidential preference primary
A **direct primary** where voters select delegates to presidential nominating conventions; voters indicate a preference for a presidential candidate, delegates committed to a candidate, or both.

Presidential press conference
A meeting at which the president answers questions from reporters.

Pressure group
An organization representing specific interests that seeks some sort of government assistance or attempts to influence public policy. Also known as an **interest group.**

Pretrial hearings
Preliminary examinations of the cases of persons accused of a crime.

Prior restraint
Censorship by restraining an action before it has actually occurred; e.g., forbidding publication rather than punishing the publisher after publication has occurred.

Private interest groups
Interest groups that chiefly pursue economic interests that benefit their members; e.g., business organizations and labor unions.

Probable cause
In law, reasonable grounds for belief that a particular person has committed a particular crime.

Productivity
The ratio of total hours worked by the labor force to total goods and services produced.

Professional association
A **pressure group** that promotes the interests of a professional occupation, such as medicine, law, or teaching.

Progressive reforms
Election reforms introduced in the early twentieth century as part of the Progressive movement; included the secret ballot, primary elections, and voter registration laws.

Progressive tax
A tax structured so that those with higher incomes pay a higher percentage of their income in taxes than do those with lower incomes.

Prohibition Party
A political party founded in 1869 that seeks to ban the sale of liquor in the United States.

Protectionism
Government intervention to protect domestic producers from foreign competition; can take the form of **tariffs,** quotas on imports, or a ban on certain imports altogether.

Public forum
A public place such as a street, sidewalk, or park where people have a First Amendment right to express their views on public issues.

Public interest
A term generally denoting a policy goal, designed to serve the interests of society as a whole, or the largest number of people. Defining the public interest is the subject of intense debate on most issues.

Public interest groups
Interest groups that chiefly pursue benefits that cannot be limited or restricted to their members.

Public opinion
The collection of individual opinions toward issues or objects of general interest.

Pure speech
Speech without any conduct (besides the speech itself).

Quorum calls
Often used as a delaying tactic, quorum calls are demands that all members of a legislative body be counted to determine if a quorum exists.

Realignment
The transition from one stable party system to another, as occurred when the **New Deal coalition** was formed.

Reapportionment
The process of redistributing the 435 seats in the House of Representatives among the states based on population changes; occurs every 10 years based on the most recent census.

Recession
Two or more consecutive three-month quarters of falling production.

Reciprocity
An **informal norm** of Congress in which members agree to support each other's bills; also called logrolling.

Reconstruction
The period after the **Civil War** when black rights were ensured by a northern military presence in the South and by close monitoring of southern politics; ended in 1877.

Redistricting
The process of redrawing the boundaries of congressional districts within a state to take account of population shifts.

Redlining
The practice in which bankers and other lenders refused to lend money to persons who wanted to buy a house in a racially changing neighborhood.

"Red Scare"
Prompted by the Russian Revolution in 1917, this was a large-scale crackdown on so-called seditious activities in the United States.

Reelection constituency
Those individuals a member of Congress believes will vote for him or her. Differs from a geographical, loyalist, or personal constituency.

Regressive tax
A tax structured so that those with lower incomes pay a larger percentage of their income in tax than do those with higher incomes.

Regulation
The actions of regulatory agencies in establishing standards or guidelines conferring benefits or imposing restrictions on business conduct.

Rehnquist Court
The U.S. Supreme Court under Chief Justice William Rehnquist (1986–); a conservative Court, but still has not overturned most previous rulings.

Religious tests
Tests once used in some states to limit the right to vote or hold office to members of the "established church."

Republic
A system of government in which citizens elect representatives to make decisions for them; an **indirect democracy.**

Reregulation
The resumption of regulatory activity after a period of **deregulation.**

Responsiveness
The extent to which government conforms to the wishes of individuals, groups, or institutions.

Restrained judges
Judges who are reluctant to overrule the other branches of government by declaring laws or actions of government officials unconstitutional.

Restrictive covenants
Agreements among neighbors in white residential areas not to sell their houses to blacks.

Retrospective voting
Voting for or against incumbents on the basis of their past performance.

Right against self-incrimination
A right granted by the Fifth Amendment, providing that persons accused of a crime shall not be compelled to be witnesses against themselves.

Right to a jury trial
The Sixth Amendment's guarantee of a trial by jury in any **criminal case** that could result in more than six months' incarceration.

Right to counsel
The Sixth Amendment's guarantee of the right of a criminal defendant to have an attorney in any **felony** or **misdemeanor** case that might result in incarceration; if defendants are indigent, the court must appoint an attorney for them.

Right to privacy
A right to autonomy—to be left alone—that is not specifically mentioned in the U.S. Constitution, but has been found by the U.S. Supreme Court to be implied through several amendments.

Rules Committee
The committee in the House of Representatives that sets the terms of debate on a bill.

Sandinistas
The name of the group that overthrew Nicaraguan dictator Anastasio Somoza in 1978 and governed Nicaragua until 1990.

Scientific polls
Systematic, probability-based sampling techniques that attempt to gauge public sentiment based on the responses of a small, selected group of individuals.

Scoop
To obtain information before another reporter; also the information so obtained.

Seditious speech
Speech that encourages rebellion against the government.

Selective perception
The tendency to screen out information that contradicts one's beliefs.

Senatorial courtesy
The custom of giving senators of the president's party a virtual veto over appointments to jobs, including judicial appointments, in their states.

Senior Executive Service
The SES was created in 1978 to attract high-ranking civil servants by offering them challenging jobs and monetary rewards for exceptional achievement.

Seniority rule
The custom that the member of the majority party with the longest service on a particular congressional committee becomes its chair; applies most of the time but is occasionally violated.

Separate-but-equal doctrine
The principle, enunciated by the U.S. Supreme Court in ***Plessy v. Ferguson*** in 1896, that allowed separate facilities for blacks and whites as long as the facilities were equal.

Separation of powers
The principle of government under which the power to make, administer, and judge the laws is split among three branches—legislative, executive, and judicial.

Setting the agenda
Influencing the process by which problems are deemed important and alternative policies are proposed.

Sharecroppers
Tenant farmers who lease land and equipment from landowners, turning over a share of their crops in lieu of rent.

Shays's Rebellion
A revolt of farmers in western Massachusetts in 1786 and 1787 to protest the state legislature's refusal to grant them relief from debt; helped lead to calls for a new national **constitution.**

Shield laws
Laws that protect news reporters from having to identify their sources of information.

Single-issue groups
Interest groups that pursue a single public interest goal and are characteristically reluctant to compromise.

Social choice
An approach to political science based on the assumption that political behavior is determined by costs and benefits.

Social contract
An implied agreement between the people and their government in which the people give up part of their liberty to the government in exchange for the government protecting the remainder of their liberty.

Social insurance
A social welfare program such as **Social Security** that provides benefits only to those who have contributed to the program and their survivors.

Socialism
An economic system in which the government owns the country's productive capacity—industrial plants and farms—and controls wages and the supply of and demand for goods; in theory, the people, rather than the government, collectively own the country's productive capacity.

Social issue
An important, noneconomic issue affecting significant numbers of the populace, such as crime, racial conflict, or changing values.

Social Security
A social welfare program for the elderly and the disabled.

Soft money
Contributions to national party committees that do not have to be reported to the federal government (and sometimes not to the states) because they are used for voter registration drives, educating voters on the issues, and the like, rather than for a particular candidate; the national committees send the funds to the state parties, which operate under less stringent reporting regulations than the federal laws provide.

Sound bite
A few key words or phrase included in a speech with the intent that television editors will use the phrase in a brief clip on the news.

Speaker of the House
The leader and presiding officer of the House of Representatives; chosen by the majority party.

Special interest caucuses
Groups of members of the House of Representatives who are united by some personal interest or characteristic; e.g., the Black Caucus.

Specialization
An **informal norm** of Congress that holds that since members cannot be experts in every area, some deference should be given to those who are most knowledgeable about a given subject related to their committee work.

Special prosecutor
A prosecutor charged with investigating and prosecuting alleged violations of federal criminal laws by the president, vice president, senior government officials, members of Congress, or the judiciary.

Speech plus conduct
Speech combined with conduct that is intended to convey ideas; e.g., a sit-in (conduct) where the protesters chant slogans (speech).

Stagflation
The combination of high inflation and economic stagnation with high unemployment that troubled the United States in the 1970s.

Standing committees
Permanent congressional committees.

Standing to sue
The principle that individuals or groups must themselves have lost rights and suffered harm before they can bring a lawsuit.

Stare decisis
Latin for "stand by what has been decided." The rule that judges should follow **precedents** established in previous cases by their court or higher courts.

"Star Wars"
The popular name for former President Reagan's proposed space-based nuclear defense system, known officially as the Strategic Defense Initiative.

States' rights
The belief that the power of the federal government should not be increased at the expense of the states' power.

Statutes
Laws passed by the legislative body of a representative government.

Steering
The practice in which realtors promoted segregation by showing blacks houses in black neighborhoods and whites houses in white neighborhoods.

Straw polls
Unscientific polls.

Structural unemployment
Joblessness that results from the rapidly changing nature of the economy, which displaces, for example, auto and steel industry workers.

Subcommittee bill of rights
Measures introduced by Democrats in the House of Representatives in 1973 and 1974 that allowed members of a committee to choose subcommittee chairs and established a fixed jurisdiction and adequate budget and staff for each subcommittee.

Subgovernment
A mutually supportive group comprising a **pressure group,** an executive agency, and a congressional committee or subcommittee with common policy interests that makes public policy decisions with little interference from the president or Congress as a whole and little awareness by the public. Also known as an iron triangle.

Subpoena
A court order requiring someone to appear in court to give testimony under penalty of punishment.

Suffrage
The right to vote.

Superdelegates
Democratic delegates, one-fifth of the total sent to the national convention who are appointed by Democratic Party organizations, in order to retain some party control over the convention. Most are public officials, such as members of Congress.

Superfund
Revenue from a tax imposed on industry, along with federal funds, that is used for cleaning up hazardous waste sites.

Super Tuesday
The day when most southern states hold **presidential preference primaries** simultaneously.

Supplemental Security Income (SSI)
A program that provides supplemental income for those who are blind, elderly, or disabled and living in poverty.

Supply-side economics
The argument that tax revenues will increase if tax rates are reduced; supposedly, more money will be available for business expansion and modernization, which will stimulate employment and economic growth and result in higher tax revenues.

Supremacy clause
A clause in the U.S. Constitution stating that treaties and laws made by the national government are to be supreme over state laws in cases of conflict.

Symbiotic relationship
A relationship in which the parties use each other for mutual advantage.

Symbolic speech
The use of symbols, rather than words, to convey ideas; e.g., wearing black armbands or burning the U.S. flag to protest government policy.

Tariff
A special tax or "duty" imposed on imported or exported goods.

Tax deductions
Certain expenses or payments that may be deducted from one's taxable income.

Tax exemptions
Certain amounts deductible from one's annual income in calculating income tax.

Teapot Dome scandal
A 1921 scandal in which President Warren Harding's secretary of the interior received large contributions from corporations that were then allowed to lease oil reserves (called the Teapot Dome); led to the Federal Corrupt Practices Act of 1925, which required reporting of campaign contributions and expenditures.

Third party
A political party made up of independents or dissidents from the major parties, often advocating radical change or pushing single issues.

Three-fifths Compromise
The decision of the **Constitutional Convention** that three-fifths of a state's slave population would be counted in apportioning seats in the House of Representatives.

Ticket splitting
Voting for a member of one party for a high-level office and a member of another party for a different high-level office.

Trade association
An **interest** or **pressure group** that represents a single industry, such as builders.

Traditionalistic political culture
One of three political cultures in the United States. One in which politics is left to a small elite and is viewed as a way to maintain the status quo. See **individualistic** and **moralistic political cultures.**

Tragedy of the commons
The concept that although individuals benefit when they exploit goods that are common to all such as air and water, the community as a whole suffers from the pollution and depletion of resources that occur; a reason for **regulation.**

Treason
The betrayal of one's country by knowingly aiding its enemies.

Truth in labeling
The requirement that manufacturers, lenders, and other business entities provide certain kinds of information to consumers or employees.

Turnout
The proportion of eligible citizens who vote in an election.

Unanimous consent agreements
Procedures by which a legislative body may dispense with standard rules and limit debate and amendments.

Underdogs
Candidates for public office who are thought to have little chance of being elected.

Unfunded mandates
Federal laws that require the states to do something without providing full funding for the required activity.

Unitary system
A system in which the national government is supreme; subnational governments are created by the national government and have only the power it allocates to them.

United Nations
An international organization formed in 1945 for the purpose of promoting peace and worldwide cooperation. It is headquartered in New York.

Unreasonable searches and seizures
Searches and arrests that are conducted without a warrant or that do not fall into one of the exceptions to the warrant requirement; prohibited by the Fourth Amendment.

Unscientific polls
Unsystematic samplings of popular sentiments; also known as **straw polls.**

Vietnam syndrome
An attitude of uncertainty about U.S. foreign policy goals and our ability to achieve them by military means; engendered among the public and officials as a result of the U.S. failure in Vietnam.

Voting Rights Act (VRA)
A law passed by Congress in 1965 that made it illegal to interfere with anyone's right to vote. The act and its subsequent amendments have been the main vehicles for expanding and protecting minority voting rights.

War Powers Act
A 1973 statute enacted by Congress to limit the president's ability to commit troops to combat.

Warren Court
The U.S. Supreme Court under Chief Justice Earl Warren (1953–1969); an activist Court that expanded the rights of criminal defendants and racial and religious minorities.

Watergate scandal
The attempt to break into Democratic National Committee headquarters in 1972 that ultimately led to President Richard M. Nixon's resignation for his role in attempting to cover up the break-in and other criminal and unethical actions.

Weber, Max
German social scientist, author of pioneering studies on the nature of bureaucracies.

Whigs
Members of the Whig Party, founded in 1834 by National Republicans and several other factions who opposed Jacksonian Democrats.

Whips
Members of the House of Representatives who work to maintain party unity by keeping in contact with party members and attempting to win their support. Both the majority and the minority party have a whip and several assistant whips.

Whistleblower
An individual employee who exposes mismanagement and abuse of discretion in an agency.

White primary
A device for preventing blacks from voting in the South. Under the pretense that political parties were private clubs, blacks were barred from voting in Democratic primaries, which were the real elections because Democrats always won the general elections.

Whitewater investigation
An investigation conducted by a **special prosecutor** into the activities of President Bill Clinton and Hillary Rodham Clinton in connection with an Arkansas land deal and other alleged wrongdoings.

Wire services
News-gathering organizations such as the Associated Press and United Press International that provide news stories and other editorial features to the media organizations that are their members.

Writ of certiorari
An order issued by a higher court to a lower court to send up the record of a case for review; granting the writ is the usual means by which the U.S. Supreme Court agrees to hear a case.

Yuppies
Young upwardly mobile professionals.

SPANISH EQUIVALENTS FOR IMPORTANT POLITICAL TERMS

Acid rain: Lluvia acida
Acquisitive model: Modelo adquisitivo
Actionable: Procesable, enjuiciable
Action-Reaction syndrome: síndrome de acción y reacción
Actual malice: Malicia expresa
Administrative agency: Agencia administrativa
Advice and consent: Consejo y consentimiento
Affirm: Afirmar
Affirmative action: Acción afirmativa
Agenda setting: Agenda establecida
Aid to Families with Dependent Children (AFDC): Ayuda para Familias con Niños Dependientes
Amicus curiae brief: Tercer persona o grupo no involucrado en el caso, admitido en un juicio para hacer valer el interés público o el de un grupo social importante
Anarchy: Anarquía
Anti-Federalists: Anti-Federalistas
Appellate court: Corte de apelación
Appointment power: Poder de apuntamiento
Appropriation: Apropiación
Aristocracy: Aristocracia
Attentive public: Público atento
Australian ballot: Voto Australiano
Authority: Autoridad
Authorization: Autorización
Bad-tendency rule: Regla de tendencia-mala
"Beauty contest": Concurso de belleza
Bicameralism: Bicameralismo
Bicameral legislature: Legislatura bicameral
Bill of Rights: Declaración de Derechos
Blanket primary: Primaria comprensiva
Block grants: Concesiones de bloque
Bureaucracy: Burocracia
Busing: Transporte público
Cabinet: Gabinete, consejo de ministros
Cabinet department: Departamento del gabinete
Cadre: El núcleo de activistas de partidos políticos encargados de cumplir las funciones importantes de los partidos políticos americanos
Canvassing board: Consejo encargado con la encuesta de una violación
Capture: Captura, toma
Casework: Trabajo de caso
Categorical grants-in-aid: Concesiones categóricas de ayuda
Caucus: Reunión de dirigentes
Challenge: Reto
Checks and balances: Chequeos y equilibrio
Chief diplomat: Jefe diplomático
Chief executive: Jefe ejecutivo
Chief legislator: Jefe legislador
Chief of staff: Jefe de personal
Chief of state: Jefe de estado
Civil law: Derecho civil
Civil liberties: Libertades civiles
Civil rights: Derechos civiles
Civil service: Servicio civil
Civil Service Commission: Comisión de Servicio Civil
Class-action suit: Demanda en representación de un grupo o clase
Class politics: Política de clase
Clear and present danger test: Prueba de peligro claro y presente
Climate control: Control de clima
Closed primary: Primaria cerrada
Cloture: Cierre al voto
Coattail effect: Effecto de cola de chaqueta
Cold War: Guerra Fría
Commander in chief: Comandante en jefe
Commerce clause: Cláusula de comercio
Commercial speech: Discurso comercial
Common law: Ley común, derecho consuetudinario
Comparable worth: Valor comparable
Compliance: De acuerdo
Concurrent majority: Mayoría concurrente
Concurring opinion: Opinión concurrente
Confederal system: Sistema confederal
Confederation: Confederación
Conference committee: Comité de conferencia
Consensus: Concenso
Consent of the people: Consentimiento de la gente
Conservatism: Calidad de conservador
Conservative coalition: Coalición conservadora
Consolidation: Consolidación
Constant dollars: Dólares constantes
Constitutional initiative: Iniciativa constitucional
Constitutional power: Poder constitucional
Containment: Contenimiento
Continuing resolution: Resolución contínua
Cooley's Rule: Regla de Cooley
Cooperative federalism: Federalismo cooperativo
Corrupt Practices Acts: Leyes Contra Acciones Corruptas
Council of Economic Advisers (CEA): Consejo de Asesores Económicos
Council of Government (COG): Consejo de Gobierno
County: Condado
Credentials committee: Comité de credenciales
Criminal law: Ley criminal
De facto segregation: Segregación de hecho
De jure segregation: Segregación cotidiana
Defamation of character: Defamación de carácter
Democracy: Democracia
Democratic Party: Partido Democrático
Détente: No Spanish equivalent
Dillon's Rule: Regla de Dillon
Diplomacy: Diplomácia
Direct democracy: Democracia directa
Direct primary: Primaria directa
Direct technique: Técnica directa
Discharge petition: Petición de descargo
Dissenting opinion: Opinión disidente
Divisive opinion: Opinión divisiva
Domestic policy: Principio político doméstico
Dual citizenship: Ciudadanía dual

Dual federalism: Federalismo dual
Economic aid: Ayuda económica
Economic regulation: Regulación económica
Elastic clause, or necessary and proper clause: Cláusula flexible, o cláusula propia necesaria
Elector: Elector
Electoral College: Colegio Electoral
Electronic media: Media electronica
Elite: Elite (el selecto)
Elite theory: Teoría elitista (de lo selecto)
Emergency power: Poder de emergencia
Enumerated power: Poder enumerado
Environmental impact statement: Afirmación de impacto ambiental
Equal Employment Opportunity Commission (EEOC): Comisión de Igualdad de Oportunidad en el Empleo
Equality: Igualdad
Equalization: Igualación
Era of good feeling: Era de buen sentimiento
Era of personal politics: Era de política personal
Establishment clause: Cláusula de establecimiento
Euthanasia: Eutanasia
Exclusionary rule: Regla de exclusión
Executive agreement: Acuerdo ejecutivo
Executive budget: Presupuesto ejecutivo
Executive Office of the President (EOP): Oficina Ejecutiva del Presidente
Executive order: Orden ejecutivo
Executive privilege: Privilegio ejecutivo
Expressed power: Poder expresado
Extradite: Entregar por extradición
Faction: Facción
Fairness doctrine: Doctrina de justicia
Fall review: Revisión de otoño
Federalist: Federalista
Federal mandate: Mandato federal
Federal Open Market Committee (FOMC): Comité Federal de Libre Mercado
Federal Register: *Registro Federal*
Federal system: Sistema federal
Federalists: Federalistas
Fighting words: Palabras de provocación
Filibuster: Obstrucción de iniciativas de ley
Fireside chat: Charla de hogar
First budget resolution: Resolución primera presupuesta
First Continental Congress: Primér Congreso Continental
Fiscal policy: Político fiscal
Fiscal year (FY): Año fiscal
Fluidity: Fluidez
Food stamps: Estampillas para comida
Foreign policy: Política extranjera
Foreign policy process: Proceso de política extranjera
Franking: Franqueando
Fraternity: Fraternidad
Free exercise clause: Cláusula de ejercico libre
Full faith and credit clause: Cláusula de completa fé y crédito
Functional consolidation: Consolidación funcional
Gag order: Orden de silencio
Garbage can model: Modelo bote de basura
Gender gap: Brecha de género
General law city: Regla general urbana
General sales tax: Impuesto general de ventas
Generational effect: Efecto generacional
Gerrymandering: División arbitraria de los distritos electorales con fines políticos
Government: Gobierno
Government corporation: Corporación gubernamental
Government in the Sunshine Act: Gobierno en la Acta: Luz del Sol
Grandfather clause: Cláusula del abuelo
Grand jury: Gran jurado
Great Compromise: Grán Acuerdo de Negociación
Hatch Act (Political Activities Act): Acta Hatch (acta de actividades políticas)
Hecklers' veto: Veto de abuchamiento
Home rule city: Regla urbana
Horizontal federalism: Federalismo horizontal
Hyperpluralism: Hiperpluralismo
Ideologue: Ideólogo
Ideology: Ideología
Image building: Construcción de imágen
Impeachment: Acción penal contra un funcionario público
Inalienable rights: Derechos inalienables
Income transfer: Transferencia de ingresos
Incorporation theory: Teoría de incorporación
Independent: Independiente
Independent candidate: Candidato independiente
Independent executive agency: Agencia ejecutiva independiente
Independent regulatory agency: Agencia regulatoria independiente
Indirect technique: Técnica indirecta
Inherent power: Poder inherente
Initiative: Iniciativa
Injunction: Injunción, prohibición judicial
In-kind subsidy: Subsidio de clase
Institution: Institución
Instructed delegate: Delegado con instrucciones
Intelligence community: Comunidad de inteligencia
Intensity: Intensidad
Interest group: Grupo de interés
Interposition: Interposición
Interstate compact: Compacto interestatal
Iron Curtain: Cortina de Acero
Iron triangle: Triángulo de acero
Isolationist foreign policy: Política extranjera de aislamiento
Issue voting: Voto temático
Item veto: Artículo de veto
Jim Crow laws: No Spanish equivalent
Joint committee: Comité mancomunado
Judicial activism: Activismo judicial
Judicial implementation: Implementación judicial
Judicial restraint: Restricción judicial
Judicial review: Revisión judicial
Jurisdiction: Jurisdicción
Justiciable dispute: Disputa judiciaria
Justiciable question: Pregunta justiciable
Keynesian economics: Economía Keynesiana
Kitchen cabinet: Gabinete de cocina
Labor movement: Movimiento laboral
Latent public opinion: Opinión pública latente
Lawmaking: Hacedores de ley
Legislative history: Historia legislativa
Legislative initiative: Iniciativa de legislación
Legislative veto: Veto legislativo
Legislature: Legislatura
Legitimacy: Legitimidad
Libel: Libelo, difamación escrita
Liberalism: Liberalismo
Liberty: Libertad
Limited government: Gobierno limitado
Line organization: Organización de linea
Literacy test: Exámen de alfabetización
Litigate: Litigar
Lobbying: Cabildeo
Logrolling: Práctica legislativa que consiste en incluir en un mismo proyecto de ley temas de diversa índole
Loophole: Hueco legal, escapatoria
Madisonian model: Modelo Madisónico
Majority: Mayoría

Majority floor leader: Líder mayoritario de piso
Majority leader of The House: Líder mayoritario de la Casa
Majority opinion: Opinión mayoritaria
Majority rule: Regla de mayoría
Managed news: Noticias manipuladas
Mandatory retirement: Retiro mandatorio
Matching funds: Fondos combinados
Material incentive: Incentivo material
Media: Media
Media access: Acceso de media
Merit system: Sistema de mérito
Military-industrial complex: Complejo industriomilitar
Minority floor leader: Líder minoritario de piso
Minority leader of the House: Líder minorial de la Casa
Monetary policy: Política monetaria
Monopolistic model: Modelo monopólico
Monroe Doctrine: Doctrina Monroe
Moral idealism: Idealismo moral
Municipal home rule: Regla municipal
Narrow casting: Mensaje dirigído
National committee: Comité nacional
National convention: Convención nacional
National politics: Política nacional
National Security Council (NSC): Concilio de Seguridad Nacional
National security policy: Política de seguridad nacional
National aristocracy: Aristocracia natural
Natural rights: Derechos naturales
Necessaries: Necesidades
Negative constituents: Constituyentes negativos
New England town: Pueblo de Nueva Inglaterra
New federalism: Federalismo nuevo
Nullification: Nulidad, anulación
Office-block (Massachusetts) ballot: Cuadro-oficina (Massachusetts), voto
Office of Management and Budget (OMB): Oficina de Administración y Presupuesto
Oligarchy: Oligarquía
Ombudsman: Funcionario que representa al ciudadano ante el gobierno
Open primary: Primaria abierta
Opinion: Opinión
Opinion leader: Líder de opinión
Opinion poll: Encuesta, conjunto de opinión
Oral arguments: Argumentos orales
Oversight: Inadvertencia, omisión
Paid-for political announcement: Anuncios políticos pagados
Pardon: Perdón
Party-column (Indiana) ballot: Partido-columna (Indiana) voto
Party identification: Identificación de partido
Party identifier: Identificador de partido
Party-in-electorate: Partido electoral
Party-in-government: Partido en gobierno
Party organization: Organización de partido
Party platform: Plataforma de partido
Patronage: Patrocinio
Peer group: Grupo de contemporáneos
Pendleton Act (Civil Service Reform Act): Acta Pendleton (Acta de Reforma al Servicio Civil)
Personal attack rule: Regla de ataque personal
Petit jury: Jurado ordinario
Pluralism: Pluralismo
Plurality: Pluralidad
Pocket veto: Veto de bolsillo
Police power: Poder policiaco
Policy trade-offs: Intercambio de políticas
Political Action Committee (PAC): Comité de acción política
Political consultant: Consultante político
Political culture: Cultura política
Political party: Partido político
Political question: Pregunta política
Political realism: Realismo político
Political socialization: Socialización política
Political tolerance: Tolerancia política
Political trust: Confianza política
Politico: Político
Politics: Política
Poll tax: Impuesto sobre el sufrágio
Poll watcher: Observador de encuesta
Popular sovereignty: Soberanía popular
Power: Poder
Precedent: Precedente
Preferred-position test: Prueba de posición preferida
Presidential primary: Primaria presidencial
President pro tempore: Presidente provisoriamente
Press secretary: Secretaría de prensa
Prior restraint: Restricción anterior
Privileges and immunities: Privilégios e imunidades
Privatization, or contracting out: Privatización
Property: Propiedad
Property tax: Impuesto de propiedad
Public agenda: Agenda pública
Public debt financing: Financiamiento de deuda pública
Public debt, or national debt: Deuda pública o nacional
Public interest: Interés público
Public opinion: Opinión pública
Purposive incentive: Incentivo de propósito
Ratification: Ratificación
Rational ignorance effect: Efecto de ignorancia racional
Reapportionment: Redistribución
Recall: Suspender
Recognition power: Poder de reconocimiento
Recycling: Reciclaje
Redistricting: Redistrictificación
Referendum: Referéndum
Registration: Registración
Regressive tax: Impuestos regresivos
Relevance: Pertinencia
Remand: Reenviar
Representation: Representación
Representative assembly: Asamblea representativa
Representative democracy: Democracia representativa
Reprieve: Tregua, suspensión
Republic: República
Republican party: Partido Republicano
Resulting powers: Poderes resultados
Reverse: Cambiarse a lo contrario
Reverse discrimination: Discriminación reversiva
Rule of four: Regla de cuatro
Rules committee: Comité regulador
Run-off primary: Primaria residual
Safe seat: Asiento seguro
Sampling error: Error de encuesta
Secession: Secesión
Second budget resolution: Resolución segunda presupuestal
Second Continental Congress: Segundo Congreso Continental
Sectional politics: Política seccional
Segregation: Segregación
Select committee: Comité selecto
Selectperson: Persona selecta
Senatorial courtesy: Cortesía senatorial
Seniority system: Sistema señiorial
Separate-but-equal doctrine: Separados pero iguales
Separation of powers: Separación de poderes
Service sector: Sector de servicio
Sex discrimination: Discriminación sexual
Sexual harassment: Acosamiento sexual
Slander: Difamación oral, calumnia
Sliding-scale test: Prueba escalonada
Social movement: Movimiento social
Social Security: Seguridad Social

Socioeconomic status: Estado socioeconómico
Solidary incentive: Incentivo de solidaridad
Solid South: Súr Sólido
Sound bite: Mordida de sonido
Soviet bloc: Bloque Soviético
Speaker of the House: Vocero de la Casa
Spin: Girar/giro
Spin doctor: Doctor en giro
Spin-off party: Partido estático
Spoils system: Sistema de despojos
Spring review: Revisión de primavera
Stability: Estabilidad
Standing committee: Comité de sostenimiento
Stare decisis: El principio característico del ley común por el cual los precedentes jurisprudenciales tienen fuerza obligatoria, no sólo entre las partes, sino también para casos sucesivos análogos
State: Estado
State central committee: Comité central del estado
State of the Union message: Mensaje sobre el Estado de la Unión
Statutory power: Poder estatorial
Strategic Arms Limitation Treaty (SALT I): Tratado de Limitación de Armas Estratégicas
Subpoena: Orden de testificación
Subsidy: Subsidio
Suffrage: Sufrágio
Sunset legislation: Legislación sunset
Superdelegate: Líder de partido u oficial elegido quien tiene el derecho de votar
Supplemental Security Income (SSI): Ingresos de Seguridad Suplementaria
Supremacy clause: Cláusula de supremacia
Supremacy doctrine: Doctrina de supremacia
Symbolic speech: Discurso simbólico
Technical assistance: Asistencia técnica
Third party: Tercer partido
Third-party candidate: Candidato de tercer partido
Ticket splitting: División de boletos
Totalitarian regime: Régimen totalitario
Town manager system: Sistema de administrador municipal
Town meeting: Junta municipal
Township: Municipio
Tracking poll: Seguimiento de encuesta
Trial court: Tribunal de primera
Truman Doctrine: Doctrina Truman
Trustee: Depositario
Twelfth Amendment: Doceava Enmienda
Twenty-fifth Amendment: Veinticincoava Enmienda
Two-party system: Sistema de dos partidos
Unanimous opinion: Opinión unánime
Underground economy: Economía subterráea
Unicameral legislature: Legislatura unicameral
Unincorporated area: Area no incorporada
Unitary system: Sistema unitario
Unit rule: Regla de unidad
Universal suffrage: Sufrágio universal
U.S. Treasury bond: Bono de la Tesoreria de E.U.A.
Veto message: Comunicado de veto
Voter turnout: Renaimiento de votantes
War Powers Act: Acta de Poderes de Guerra
Washington community: Comunidad de Washington
Weberian model: Modelo Weberiano
Whip: Látigo
Whistleblower: Privatización o contratista
White House Office: Oficina de la Casa Blanca
White House press corps: Cuerpo de prensa de la Casa Blanca
White primary: Sufrágio en elección primaria/blancos solamente
Writ of certiorari: Prueba de certeza; orden emitida por el tribunal de apelaciones para que el tribunal inferior dé lugar a la apelación
Writ of habeas corpus: Prueba de evidencia concreta
Writ of mandamus: Un mandato por la corte para que un acto se lleve a cabo
Yellow journalism: Amarillismo periodístico

NAME INDEX

Y

Z

SUBJECT INDEX

C

D

E

O

P

T

Presidents, Elections, and Congresses, 1789–1998

Year	President	Vice President	Party of President	Election Year	Election Opponent with Most Votes*
1789–1797	George Washington	John Adams	None	(1789)	None
				(1793)	None
1797–1801	John Adams	Thomas Jefferson	Fed	(1797)	Thomas Jefferson
1801–1809	Thomas Jefferson	Aaron Burr (to 1805)	Dem-R	(1801)	John Adams
		George Clinton (to 1809)		(1805)	Charles C. Pinckney
1809–1817	James Madison	George Clinton (to 1813)	Dem-R	(1809)	Charles C. Pinckney
		Elbridge Gerry (to 1817)		(1813)	DeWitt Clinton
1817–1825	James Monroe	Daniel D. Tompkins	Dem-R	(1817)	Rufus King
				(1821)	John Q. Adams
1825–1829	John Quincy Adams	John C. Calhoun	Nat R	(1824)	Andrew Jackson
1829–1837	Andrew Jackson	John C. Calhoun (to 1833)	Dem	(1828)	John Q. Adams
		Martin Van Buren (to 1837)		(1832)	Henry Clay
1837–1841	Martin Van Buren	Richard M. Johnson	Dem	(1836)	William H. Harrison
1841	William H. Harrison	John Tyler	Whig	(1840)	Martin Van Buren
1841–1845	John Tyler	(No VP)	Whig	(1840)	Took office upon death of Harrison
(1845–1849)	James K. Polk	George M. Dallas	Dem	(1844)	Henry Clay
1849–1850	Zachary Taylor	Millard Fillmore	Whig	(1848)	Lewis Cass
1850–1853	Millard Fillmore	(No VP)	Whig		Took office upon death of Taylor
1853–1857	Franklin Pierce	William R. King	Dem	(1852)	Winfield Scott
1857–1861	James Buchanan	John C. Breckinridge	Dem	(1856)	John C. Fremont
1861–1865	Abraham Lincoln	Hannibal Hamlin (to 1865)	Rep	(1860)	Stephen Douglas
		Andrew Johnson (1865)		(1864)	George B. McClellan
1865–1869	Andrew Johnson	(No VP)	Rep		Took office upon death of Lincoln
1869–1877	Ulysses S. Grant	Schuyler Colfax (to 1873)	Rep	(1868)	Horatio Seymour
		Henry Wilson (to 1877)		(1872)	Horace Greeley
1877–1881	Rutherford B. Hayes	William A. Wheeler	Rep	(1876)	Samuel Tilden
1881	James A. Garfield	Chester A. Arthur	Rep	(1880)	Winfield S. Hancock
1881–1885	Chester A. Arthur	(No VP)	Rep		Took office upon death of Garfield
1885–1889	Grover Cleveland	Thomas A. Hendricks	Dem	(1884)	James G. Blaine

* In some cases more than one opponent received Electoral College votes. In these cases only the opponent with the most votes is listed.

** Electoral College system before the Twelfth Amendment (1804). The original Constitutional provisions called for the person with the second highest total Electoral College vote to be the Vice President.

† During the administration of George Washington, Congress was not organized by formal parties; the figures are of supporters and opponents of the administration.

†† Party balance as of beginning of Congress. Only members of the two major parties in Congress are shown.

††† Received fewer popular votes than an opponent.

HR: Election decided in House of Representatives.

residents, Elections, and Congresses, 1789–1998 (cont.)

ar	President	Vice President	Party of President	Election Year	Election Opponent with Most Votes*
89–1893	Benjamin Harrison	Levi P. Morton	Rep	(1888)	Grover Cleveland
93–1897	Grover Cleveland	Adlai E. Stevenson	Dem	(1892)	Benjamin Harrison
97–1901	William McKinley	Garret A. Hobart (to 1901)	Rep	(1896)	William Jennings Bryan
		Theodore Roosevelt (1901)		(1900)	William Jennings Bryan
01–1909	Theodore Roosevelt	(No VP, 1901–1905)	Rep		Took office upon death of McKinley
		Charles W. Fairbanks (1905–1909)		(1904)	Alton B. Parker
09–1913	William Howard Taft	James S. Sherman	Rep	(1908)	William Jennings Bryan
13–1921	Woodrow Wilson	Thomas R. Marshall	Dem	(1912)	Theodore Roosevelt
				(1916)	Charles Evans Hughes
21–1923	Warren G. Harding	Calvin Coolidge	Rep	(1920)	James Cox
23–1929	Calvin Coolidge	(No VP, 1923–1925) Charles G. Dawes (1925–1929)	Rep	 (1924)	Took office upon death of Harding John Davis
29–1933	Herbert Hoover	Charles Curtis	Rep	(1928)	Alfred E. Smith
33–1945	Franklin D. Roosevelt	John N. Garner (1933–1941)	Dem	(1932)	Herbert Hoover
		Henry A. Wallace (1941–1945)		(1936)	Alfred Landon
		Harry S. Truman (1945)		(1940)	Wendell Willkie
				(1944)	Thomas Dewey
45–1953	Harry S. Truman	(No VP, 1945–1949) Alban W. Barkley	Dem		Took office upon death of Roosevelt
				(1948)	Thomas Dewey
53–1961	Dwight D. Eisenhower	Richard M. Nixon	Rep	(1952)	Adlai Stevenson
				(1956)	Adlai Stevenson
61–1963	John F. Kennedy	Lyndon B. Johnson	Dem	(1960)	Richard M. Nixon
63–1969	Lyndon B. Johnson	(No VP, 1963–1965) Hubert H. Humphrey (1965–1969)	Dem	 (1964)	Took office upon death of Kennedy Barry Goldwater
69–1974	Richard M. Nixon	Spiro T. Agnew	Rep	(1968)	Hubert H. Humphrey
		Gerald R. Ford (appointed)		(1972)	George McGovern
74–1977	Gerald R. Ford	Nelson A. Rockefeller (appointed)	Rep		Took office upon Nixon's resignation
77–1981	Jimmy Carter	Walter Mondale	Dem	(1976)	Gerald R. Ford
81–1989	Ronald Reagan	George Bush	Rep	(1980)	Jimmy Carter
				(1984)	Walter F. Mondale
89–1993	George Bush	J. Danforth Quayle	Rep	(1988)	Michael Dukakis
93–	William J. Clinton	Albert Gore	Dem	(1992)	George Bush
				(1996)	Robert Dole

			House		Senate	
Winner's Electoral College Vote %	**Winner's Popular Vote %**	**Congress**	**Majority Party**	**Minority Party**	**Majority Party**	**Minority Party**
58.1	47.8 †††	51st	166 Rep	159 Dem	39 Rep	37 Dem
		52nd	235 Dem	88 Rep	47 Rep	39 Dem
62.3	46.0	53rd	218 Dem	127 Rep	44 Dem	38 Rep
		54th	244 Rep	105 Dem	43 Rep	39 Dem
60.6	51.0	55th	204 Rep	113 Dem	47 Rep	34 Dem
		56th	185 Rep	163 Dem	53 Rep	26 Dem
64.7	51.7					
–	–	57th	197 Rep	151 Dem	55 Rep	31 Dem
		58th	208 Rep	178 Dem	57 Rep	33 Dem
70.6	56.4	59th	250 Rep	136 Dem	57 Rep	33 Dem
		60th	222 Rep	164 Dem	61 Rep	31 Dem
66.4	51.6	61st	219 Rep	172 Dem	61 Rep	32 Dem
		62nd	228 Dem	161 Rep	51 Rep	41 Dem
81.9	41.9	63rd	291 Dem	127 Rep	51 Dem	44 Rep
		64th	230 Dem	196 Rep	56 Dem	40 Rep
52.2	49.3	65th	216 Dem	210 Rep	53 Dem	42 Rep
		66th	240 Rep	190 Dem	49 Rep	47 Dem
76.1	60.3	67th	301 Rep	131 Dem	59 Rep	37 Dem
–	–	68th	225 Rep	205 Dem	51 Rep	43 Dem
71.9	54.0	69th	247 Rep	183 Dem	56 Rep	39 Dem
		70th	237 Rep	195 Dem	49 Rep	46 Dem
83.6	58.2	71st	267 Rep	167 Dem	56 Rep	39 Dem
		72nd	220 Dem	214 Rep	48 Rep	47 Dem
88.9	57.4	73rd	310 Dem	117 Rep	60 Dem	35 Rep
		74th	319 Dem	103 Rep	69 Dem	25 Rep
98.5	60.8	75th	331 Dem	89 Rep	76 Dem	16 Rep
		76th	261 Dem	164 Rep	69 Dem	23 Rep
84.6	54.7	77th	268 Dem	162 Rep	66 Dem	28 Rep
		78th	218 Dem	208 Rep	58 Dem	37 Rep
81.4	53.4					
–	–	79th	242 Dem	190 Rep	56 Dem	38 Rep
		80th	245 Rep	188 Dem	51 Rep	45 Dem
57.1	49.5	81st	263 Dem	171 Rep	54 Dem	42 Rep
		82nd	234 Dem	199 Rep	49 Dem	47 Rep
83.2	55.1	83rd	221 Rep	211 Dem	48 Rep	47 Dem
		84th	232 Dem	203 Rep	48 Dem	47 Rep
86.1	57.4	85th	233 Dem	200 Rep	49 Dem	47 Rep
		86th	283 Dem	153 Rep	64 Dem	34 Rep
58.0	49.7	87th	263 Dem	174 Rep	65 Dem	35 Rep
–	–	88th	258 Dem	177 Rep	67 Dem	33 Rep
90.3	61.6	89th	295 Dem	140 Rep	68 Dem	32 Rep
		90th	247 Dem	187 Rep	64 Dem	36 Rep
55.9	43.4	91st	243 Dem	192 Rep	57 Dem	43 Rep
		92nd	254 Dem	180 Rep	54 Dem	44 Rep
96.7	60.7					
–	–	93rd	239 Dem	192 Rep	56 Dem	42 Rep
		94th	291 Dem	144 Rep	60 Dem	37 Rep
55.2	50.1	95th	292 Dem	143 Rep	61 Dem	38 Rep
		96th	280 Dem	155 Rep	58 Dem	41 Rep
90.9	50.7	97th	243 Dem	192 Rep	53 Rep	47 Dem
		98th	269 Dem	166 Rep	54 Rep	46 Dem
97.4	59.8	99th	253 Dem	182 Rep	53 Rep	47 Dem
		100th	258 Dem	177 Rep	55 Dem	45 Rep
79.0	53.4	101st	260 Dem	175 Rep	55 Dem	45 Rep
		102nd	267 Dem	167 Rep	56 Dem	44 Rep
68.8	43.2	103rd	259 Dem	175 Rep	57 Dem	43 Rep
		104th	230 Rep	204 Dem	53 Rep	47 Dem
70.4	49.9	105th	227 Rep	208 Dem	55 Rep	45 Dem
		106th	222 Rep	213 Dem	55 Rep	45 Dem

Winner's Electoral College Vote %	Winner's Popular Vote %	Congress	House		Senate	
			Majority Party	Minority Party	Majority Party	Minority Party
**	No popular vote	1st	38 Admin †	26 Opp	17 Admin	9 Opp
		2nd	37 Fed ††	33 Dem-R	16 Fed	13 Dem-R
**	No popular vote	3rd	57 Dem-R	48 Fed	17 Fed	13 Dem-R
		4th	54 Fed	52 Dem-R	19 Fed	13 Dem-R
**	No popular vote	5th	58 Fed	48 Dem-R	20 Fed	12 Dem-R
		6th	64 Fed	42 Dem-R	19 Fed	13 Dem-R
HR**	No popular vote	7th	69 Dem-R	36 Fed	18 Dem-R	13 Fed
		8th	402 Dem-R	39 Fed	25 Dem-R	9 Fed
92.0	No popular vote	9th	116 Dem-R	25 Fed	27 Dem-R	7 Fed
		10th	118 Dem-R	24 Fed	28 Dem-R	6 Fed
69.7	No popular vote	11th	94 Dem-R	48 Fed	28 Dem-R	6 Fed
		12th	108 Dem-R	36 Fed	30 Dem-R	6 Fed
59.0	No popular vote	13th	112 Dem-R	68 Fed	27 Dem-R	9 Fed
		14th	117 Dem-R	65 Fed	25 Dem-R	11 Fed
84.3	No popular vote	15th	141 Dem-R	42 Fed	34 Dem-R	10 Fed
		16th	156 Dem-R	27 Fed	35 Dem-R	7 Fed
99.5	No popular vote	17th	158 Dem-R	25 Fed	44 Dem-R	4 Fed
		18th	187 Dem-R	26 Fed	44 Dem-R	4 Fed
HR	39.1 †††	19th	105 Admin	97 Dem-J	26 Admin	20 Dem-J
		20th	119 Dem-J	94 Admin	28 Dem-J	20 Admin
68.2	56.0	21st	139 Dem	74 Nat R	26 Dem	22 Nat R
		22nd	141 Dem	58 Nat R	25 Dem	21 Nat R
76.6	54.5	23rd	147 Dem	53 AntiMas	20 Dem	20 Nat R
		24th	145 Dem	98 Whig	27 Dem	25 Whig
57.8	50.9	25th	108 Dem	107 Whig	30 Dem	18 Whig
		26th	124 Dem	118 Whig	28 Dem	22 Whig
79.6	52.9					
–	52.9	27th	133 Whig	102 Dem	28 Whig	22 Dem
		28th	142 Dem	79 Whig	28 Whig	25 Dem
61.8	49.6	29th	143 Dem	77 Whig	31 Dem	25 Whig
		30th	115 Whig	108 Dem	36 Dem	21 Whig
56.2	47.3	31st	112 Dem	109 Whig	35 Dem	25 Whig
–	–	32nd	140 Dem	88 Whig	35 Dem	24 Whig
85.8	50.9	33rd	159 Dem	71 Whig	38 Dem	22 Whig
		34th	108 Rep	83 Dem	40 Dem	15 Rep
58.8	45.6	35th	118 Dem	92 Rep	36 Dem	20 Rep
		36th	114 Rep	92 Dem	36 Dem	26 Rep
59.4	39.8	37th	105 Rep	43 Dem	31 Rep	10 Dem
		38th	102 Rep	75 Dem	36 Rep	9 Dem
91.0	55.2					
–	–	39th	149 Union	42 Dem	42 Union	10 Dem
		40th	143 Rep	49 Dem	42 Rep	11 Dem
72.8	52.7	41st	149 Rep	63 Dem	56 Rep	11 Dem
		42nd	134 Rep	104 Dem	52 Rep	17 Dem
81.9	55.6	43rd	194 Rep	92 Dem	49 Rep	19 Dem
		44th	169 Rep	109 Dem	45 Rep	29 Dem
50.1	47.9 †††	45th	153 Dem	140 Rep	39 Rep	36 Dem
		46th	149 Dem	130 Rep	42 Dem	33 Rep
58.0	48.3	47th	147 Rep	135 Dem	37 Rep	37 Dem
–	–	48th	197 Dem	118 Rep	38 Rep	36 Dem
54.6	48.5	49th	183 Dem	140 Rep	43 Rep	34 Dem
		50th	169 Dem	152 Rep	39 Rep	37 Dem

Source for election data: Svend Peterson, *A Statistical History of American Presidential Elections*. New York: Frederick Ungar Publishing, 1963. Updates: Richard Scammon, *America Votes* 19. Washington D.C.: Congressional Quarterly, 1991; *Congressional Quarterly Weekly Report*, Nov. 7, 1992, p. 3552.

Abbreviations:

Admin = Administration supporters
AntiMas = Anti-Masonic
Dem = Democratic
Dem-R = Democratic-Republican
Fed = Federalist
Dem-J = Jacksonian Democrats
Nat R = National Republican
Opp = Opponents of administration
Rep = Republican
Union = Unionist